THE HANDBOOK OF CLINICAL PSYCHOLOGY
Theory, Research, and Practice
Volume II

VOLUME II

The Handbook of Clinical Psychology:

Theory, Research, and Practice

Edited by:

C. Eugene Walker, Ph.D.
*University of Oklahoma
Medical School*

Consulting Editors:

Frederick Kanfer, Ph.D.
University of Illinois

Alan Kazdin, Ph.D.
*Western Psychiatric Institute,
Pittsburgh*

Joseph Matarazzo, Ph.D.
*University of Oregon
Health Sciences Center*

Eliot Rodnick, Ph.D.
*University of California,
Los Angeles*

Julian Rotter, Ph.D.
University of Connecticut

DORSEY
PROFESSIONAL
SERIES

DOW JONES-IRWIN
Homewood, Illinois 60430

© DOW JONES-IRWIN, 1983

ISBN 0-87094-411-8

Library of Congress Catalog Card No. 82–73409

Printed in the United States of America

1 2 3 4 5 6 7 8 9 0 MP 0 9 8 7 6 5 4 3

Preface

Clinical psychology today represents one of the most stimulating and rapidly developing areas of professional and scientific endeavor. The swift pace of developments in the field and the staggering weight of literature produced each year make compendia and handbooks essential tools for the student, the researcher, and the practitioner.

This handbook attempts to strike a balance between scholarly review of current research literature and enlightened suggestions toward the best clinical practice. The chapters have all been prepared by highly competent individuals in the area under consideration. Sincere appreciation is expressed to the Consulting Editors who assisted in selecting topics to be covered, suggesting qualified authors, and, when called upon, editorial advice. The authors and editor owe a great debt of gratitude to Leanne Ware, research assistant, who assisted in every stage of the development of the present project, giving dedicated personal attention and much time beyond the hours for which she was paid in order for the manuscript to be completed. Special appreciation is also due Donna Hill who worked long hours typing and coordinating the preparation of the manuscript. Needless to say, however, any remaining flaws in the volume are the responsibility of the editor and the chapter authors. We hope that this handbook will prove a rewarding and useful reference.

C. Eugene Walker

Contributing authors

David Ametrano
University of Michigan
Ann Arbor, Michigan

Irene Mass Ametrano
Eastern Michigan University
Ypsilanti, Michigan

Anne Anastasi
Fordham University
Bronx, New York

Frank Andrasik
State University of New York, Albany
Albany, New York

John W. Baker II
Private Practice
New Windsor, New York

Rodney R. Baker
Veterans' Administration Medical Center
San Antonio, Texas

Alan Barclay
Wright State University
Dayton, Ohio

E. Edward Beckham
University of Oklahoma Medical School
Oklahoma City, Oklahoma

Allen E. Bergin
Brigham Young University
Provo, Utah

Stephen N. Berk
Temple University
Philadelphia, Pennsylvania

Edward B. Blanchard
State University of New York, Albany
Albany, New York

Jenny Boyer
University of Oklahoma Medical School
Oklahoma City, Oklahoma

Paul W. Clement
Fuller Theological Seminary
Pasadena, California

Nicholas A. Cummings
Biodyne Institute
San Francisco, California and
Honolulu, Hawaii

Lynnda M. Dahlquist
West Virginia University
Morgantown, West Virginia

Douglas R. Denney
University of Kansas
Lawrence, Kansas

Robert E. Doan
University of Oklahoma
Norman, Oklahoma

Jay S. Efran
Temple University
Philadelphia, Pennsylvania

Charles H. Elliott
University of Oklahoma Medical School
Oklahoma City, Oklahoma

Ian M. Evans
State University of New York,
Binghamton
Binghamton, New York

Ian R. H. Falloon
Mental Health Clinical Research Center
for the Study of Schizophrenia;
Rehabilitation Research and
Training Center for Mental Illness
Los Angeles, California

John W. Fantuzzo
Fuller Theological Seminary
Pasadena, California

Douglas S. Faust
Eastern Virginia Medical School
Norfolk, Virginia

Anitra S. Fay
Psychological Consultants
Fort Smith, Arkansas

Stephen Flanagan
Mental Health Clinical Research Center
for the Study of Schizophrenia;
Rehabilitation Research and
Training Center for Mental Illness
Los Angeles, California

David Foy
Mental Health Clinical Research Center
for the Study of Schizophrenia;
Rehabilitation Research and
Training Center for Mental Illness
Los Angeles, California

Lawrence Glanz
University of Pittsburgh
School of Medicine
Pittsburgh, Pennsylvania

Daniel C. Goldberg
Jefferson Medical College
Philadelphia, Pennsylvania

Solomon C. Goldberg
Medical College of Virginia
Richmond, Virginia

Leslie S. Greenberg
ηiversity of British Columbia
ιcouver, British Columbia

Robert M. Hamer
Medical College of Virginia
Richmond, Virginia

Sandra L. Harris
Rutgers, The State University
New Brunswick, New Jersey

Don M. Hartsough
Purdue University
West Lafayette, Indiana

Stanley D. Imber
University of Pittsburgh School of Medicine
Pittsburgh, Pennsylvania

Phillip C. Kendall
University of Minnesota
Minneapolis, Minnesota

Irving Kirsch
University of Connecticut, Storrs
Storrs, Connecticut

Walter G. Klopfer
Portland State University
Portland, Oregon

Sheldon J. Korchin
University of California, Berkeley
Berkeley, California

Margaret R. Kriss
University of Minnesota
Minneapolis, Minnesota

Michael J. Lambert
Brigham Young University
Provo, Utah

Craig W. LeCroy
University of Wisconsin—Madison
Madison, Wisconsin

Mark H. Lewin
Upstate Psychological Service Center, P.C.
Rochester, New York

Robert Paul Liberman
Mental Health Clinical Research Center
for the Study of Schizophrenia;

Rehabilitation Research and
Training Center for Mental Illness
Los Angeles, California

David Lukoff
Mental Health Clinical Research Center
for the Study of Schizophrenia;
Rehabilitation Research and
Training Center for Mental Illness
Los Angeles, California

Stephen Marder
Mental Health Clinical Research Center
for the Study of Schizophrenia;
Rehabilitation Research and
Training Center for Mental Illness
Los Angeles, California

William P. Milberg
Veterans' Administration Hospital
Boston, Massachusetts

Brendan A. Maher
Harvard University
Cambridge, Massachusetts

Peter E. Nathan
Rutgers, The State University
New Brunswick, New Jersey

Ted D. Nirenberg
Veterans' Administration Medical Center
and Brown University
Providence, Rhode Island

Roberta A. Olson
University of Oklahoma Medical School
Oklahoma City, Oklahoma

Steven C. Parkison
Walter Reed Army Medical Center
Washington, D.C.

Paul A. Pilkonis
University of Pittsburgh School of Medicine
Pittsburgh, Pennsylvania

Benjamin Pope
The Sheppard and Enoch Pratt Hospital
Towson, Maryland

Julian Rappaport
University of Illinois
Urbana-Champaign, Illinois

Sheldon D. Rose
University of Wisconsin—Madison
Madison, Wisconsin

Joseph R. Sanders
American Board of Professional Psychology
Washington, D.C.

Susan H. Sands
University of California, Berkeley
Berkeley, California

Lee Sechrest
University of Michigan
Ann Arbor, Michigan

Edward Seidman
University of Illinois
Urbana-Champaign, Illinois

Aaron Smith
University of Michigan
Ann Arbor, Michigan

Clifford H. Swensen
Purdue University
West Lafayette, Indiana

Fernando Tapia
University of Oklahoma Medical School
Oklahoma City, Oklahoma

Gary R. VandenBos
American Psychological Association
Washington, D.C.

Helen H. Watkins
University of Montana
Missoula, Montana

John G. Watkins
University of Montana
Missoula, Montana

John T. Watkins
University of Oklahoma Medical School
Oklahoma City, Oklahoma

R. Douglas Whitman
Wayne State University
Detroit, Michigan

Christine Winter
Counseling Associates
Mystic, Connecticut

Byron Wittlin
Mental Health Clinical Research Center
for the Study of Schizophrenia;

Rehabilitation Research and
Training Center for Mental Illness
Los Angeles, California

Robert Henley Woody
University of Nebraska at Omaha
Omaha, Nebraska

Contents

Volume I

within treatment variability. Multiple covariates. Heterogeneous regressions. Large treatment differences on covariate. Comparison of change in intact groups. Measurement of change. Cross-over designs. Analysis of dropouts. Multiple regression and correlation: *Pitfalls in using multiple correlation and regression. Cross validation instead of significance. Interaction terms as predictors. The art of predictor selection.* Factor analysis. Multidimensional scaling. Single-case analysis.

PART II: PSYCHOTHERAPY RESEARCH

chronic disease and with geriatric patients. The effects of psychological care on medical utilization. Negative effects of psychotherapy. Relationship between process and outcome: *Difficulty of predicting outcome from pretreatment measures. Lack of comparative outcome effects. Similarities and differences between naturally occurring, helpful relationships and formal psychotherapy.*

What is psychotherapy? Essential ingredients of psychotherapy: *The therapeutic climate. The therapeutic alliance. The therapeutic climate: A brief overview. Specific therapeutic processes. A brief recapitulation.* The movement toward rapprochement among theories of psychotherapy. To avert some misunderstanding.

PART III: DIAGNOSIS AND ASSESSMENT

History. The manuals: *DSM-III* and its predecessors: *Multiaxial diagnosis. Operational criteria. Consultation/liaison and field trials. The Diagnostic Manual.* The syndromes: *Disorders usually first evident in infancy, childhood, or adolescence. The disorders. Overall. Organic Mental Disorders. Substance Use Disorders. Schizophrenic Disorders. Paranoid Disorders. Psychotic disorders not elsewhere classified. Affective Disorders. Anxiety Disorders. Somatoform Disorders. Dissociative Disorders. Psychosexual Disorders. Factitious Disorders. Disorders of impulse control not elsewhere classified. Adjustment Disorder. Psychological factors affecting physical condition. Personality Disorders. V codes.* The present and the future.

Introduction. Communication in the interview: *Verbal content. Control and direction of verbal content. Verbal style in interview communication. Expressive aspects of interview communication. Sequence effects in the interview.*

Purposes of behavioral assessment: *Screening and needs assessment. Problem identification and goal definition. Hypothesis testing and the functional analysis. Network analysis for design or choice of therapy. Monitoring key outcomes. Evaluating general outcomes.* Measurement procedures: *Self-ratings. Direct behavioral observation in contrived settings. Naturalistic behavioral observation. Measures of psychological and psychophysiological functioning.* New developments in clinical assessment: *Assessing the physical environment. Assessing social interactions. Assessing behavioral interrelationships. Differentiation of skill and motivation.* Conclusions and future directions.

Intelligence in context: *Population changes in intelligence test performance. Interpreting present performance against antecedent background. Predicting competence in specified environments.* Comprehensive assessment of the handicapped: *Physical handicaps. Mental retardation. Learning disabilities.* Diagnostic interpretations of test performance: *Intelligence tests. Projective techniques.* Self-report personality inventories: Evolving methodology: *Empirical item selection. Construct validation. Traits and situations. Traits and states.* Health-related inventories: *Jenkins Activity Survey. Millon Behavioral Health Inventory. Health status measures.*

Diagnostic considerations: *The "brain-damaged" patient.* The evolution of current psychological and neuropsychological testing techniques. Current tests of organicity in clinical psychological assessments: The Wechsler scales: *Do V-PIQ differences provide reliable lateralizing indices? Hierarchy of cerebral functions and the Wechsler subtests. The Bender-Gestalt test. Other individual psychological tests and neuropsychological test batteries.* "Appraising the literature correctly": The rationale in selection and construction of tests and batteries for neuropsychological assessment: *The Halstead-Reitan battery (HRB). Luria's theories and the Luria-Nebraska battery (L-N). Quo Vadis?* Comparisons of functional psychiatric versus organic patients. Suggested contexts and guidelines for evaluating neuropsychological tests: *The concept of brain damage as a unitary disorder in a single psychological test function. General versus specific defects.* Suggested guidelines for evaluation of Wechsler subtest performances. Brief supplemental screening tests: *The Symbol Digit Modalities Test (SDMT). Single and Double Simultaneous Stimulation (Face-Hand) Test (SDSS). Purdue Pegboard Tests of Manual Dexterity. Benton Visual Retention Test. Other memory tests.* Sex and brain damage. Appendix: Guidelines for evaluation of individual measures of the Michigan Neuropsychological Test Battery: *1. Human Figure Drawing. 2. WAIS or WISC. 3. VOT, RCPM, and VRT. 4. Purdue Pegboard. 5. Symbol-Digit Written and Oral Substitutions. 6. Single and Double Simultaneous Stimulations. 7. Memory for Unrelated Sentences.* General principles and implications.

Introduction. How influential is the psychological report? Barriers to communication and their resolution. Importance of specifying level of behavior. How to write a psychological report. Feedback: False and true: *False feedback. True feedback.* Illustrative reports.

Volume II

PART IV: RECENT DEVELOPMENTS IN TREATMENT MODALITIES

History of hypnosis. Theories of hypnosis. Hypnotic phenomena. Hypnotic susceptibility. Techniques of hypnotic induction: *Deepening procedures.* Hypno-suggestive therapy: *Hypnosis in surgery, anesthesiology, and the control of pain. Hypnosis in internal medicine and general practice. Specialized problems in hypnotherapy. Dental hypnosis. Forensic hypnosis. Precautions, dangers, and contraindications.* Hypnoanalytic insight therapy: *The psychodynamics of hypnotic induction.* Hypnodiagnostic procedures: *Abreactions. Dream and fantasy manipulation through hypnosis. Dissociative procedures.* Hypnoanalytic ego-state therapy: *Hypnoanalytic problems of transference and countertransference.* Hypnosis research.

Reframing the questions. Central themes prominent in the social/community perspective. Domains of expansion: *Conceptions of individual behavior. Conceptions of society. Style of service delivery. Levels of analysis. The agent of transmission. Goals of intervention.* Application of the social and community perspective to problems of serious emotional disturbance.

Biofeedback defined. Response systems in biofeedback: *Blood pressure. Blood volume. Electromyography. Electroencephalography. Electrocardiology. Other.* Biofeedback instrumentation. Procedural concerns in administering biofeedback: *The therapeutic context. Evaluation for biofeedback. Biofeedback training.* A selective review and evaluation of the biofeedback-treatment literature: *Widely available applications of biofeedback. Specialized applications of biofeedback.*

Psychopharmacology. Antipsychotics: *Phenothiazines. Thioxanthenes. Butyrophenones. Clinical aspects of antipsychotics.* Antidepressants: *Monoamine oxidase inhibitors. Tricyclic anti-depressants. Stimulants. Antidepressant/anxiolytic combinations.* Sedatives: *Benzodiazepines.* Lithium. Organic treatments: *Electroconvulsive therapy.* Insulin coma treatment. The amytal interview. Psychosurgery.

Basic steps to effective behavioral treatment with children: *General review of the problem and contracting. Behavioral assessement. Systematic intervention. Follow-up.* Illustrations using the more common referral problems: *Attention deficit disorders. Conduct disorders. Anxiety disorders. Developmental reading and arithmetic disorders.* The major behavioral treatments: *Setting events. Cues, prods, and models. Primary behaviors. Consequences and feedback.* Promoting generalization. Efficient ways to identify treatments for a given problem and problems for a given treatment.

PART V: THE PRACTICE OF PSYCHOLOGY

PART VI: FORENSIC PSYCHOLOGY

PART IV

Recent developments in treatment modalities

Recent
developments
in treatment
modalities

16

Some recent developments in the treatment of neurosis

Stephen N. Berk *
and
Jay S. Efran *

The essence of neurosis is the tendency to avoid—rather than cope with—stress. If a recent estimate is correct, this neurotic avoidance of stress is the central preoccupation of approximately 20 million Americans (Coleman, Butcher, & Carson, 1980). It should be noted that the new diagnostic manual (*DSM-III*, 1980) no longer uses the term *neurosis*. Patterns which were formerly catalogued under this term have been redistributed and, in some cases, relabeled. The motive for eliminating the concept of neurosis was that it carried the surplus meaning, derived from dynamic theory, of unconscious or internal conflict. This meaning was incompatible with the thinking of a growing number of individuals who prefer learning theory to psychodynamic formulations. Thus, the new classificatory scheme aims at theoretical neutrality, focusing on observable behaviors instead of presumed dynamics or etiologies.

For this chapter, the present authors have chosen to highlight only three of the symptom patterns which were previously classified as neurotic: the phobias (including agoraphobia), the obsessive-compulsive disorders, and neurotic depression. These three syndromes were selected for discussion primarily because various new treatment strategies have been developed and evaluated in connection with them. If these were the days of Breuer and Freud, this discussion might well have centered around conversion hysteria, the disorder that first gave the field an opportunity to "cut its teeth." However, these days the condition (now a somatoform disorder) is less frequently encountered and hasn't attracted much research attention.

* Temple University, Philadelphia.

The authors wish to acknowledge the contributions of Alan M. Brody, Dennis H. Sandrock, Diane Amato, John C. Livio, Elsa R. Efran, and Karen G. Berk to the preparation of this chapter.

There are some other prominent omissions that should be mentioned. There are the dissociative disorders, such as multiple personality and the fugue states. There is a growing suspicion that many cases of multiple personality are at least partly iatrogenic: i.e., they are elaborated during psychotherapy, particularly when communication proceeds through the modality of hypnosis (Bandler & Grinder, 1979). Other than this observation, there is little to report concerning new treatments for these rare but interesting conditions.

Then there are the anxiety states. These are more common, but the present authors will include much of what needs to be said about them in the discussions of agoraphobia and the obsessional patterns. Finally, hypochondriasis (also a somatoform disorder) will not be given separate attention in this chapter. Hypochondriacal concerns are often found in and among other client complaints in both medical and psychological settings. These excessive worries about one's health will be combined with the consideration of other phobic patterns.

The central aim in writing this chapter is to provide information that will be useful to the practitioner who wants to update his or her treatment procedures in the light of recent research findings. The patterns to be described here can be "tried on," refined, and validated in the crucible of one's day-to-day clinical experience. The practitioner will recognize, of course, that further updates in practice invariably become necessary as additional collective experience accumulates and demands examination and testing. Because the focus is practical, the authors will not present an exhaustive literature review nor extended discussions of research design. For the latter, the reader is referred to works such as those by Garfield and Bergin (1978), Rachman and Wilson (1980) and Smith, Glass, and Miller (1980). Basic content references will be indicated within each subsection.

This review is organized in terms of the three forms of neurosis. However, some therapies (notably the family and systems-oriented approaches) tend to eschew these individually oriented diagnostic categories. For the sake of convenience, these approaches will be discussed in the section on depression, although it would have been just as appropriate to include discussion of them with either of the other two sections.

The present authors have not approached the recent literature as advocates of a particular therapy school: psychodynamic, behavioral, Gestalt, transactional analysis, existential, cognitive, family systems, etc. Instead, we have permitted ourselves the luxury of becoming interested in what Bateson (1979) calls the "pattern which connects." We have attempted to strip findings down to their basics to see what so-called neurotics do to get themselves called neurotic and why some modes of interaction with them are preferable to others.

In doing this work the present authors were hampered by certain conceptual and linguistic conventions manifest in the literature. For example, there is a tendency to nominalize—to turn verbs and adverbs into nouns, and to allow descriptions to masquerade as explanations. Thus, behaving aggressively is all too readily transformed into a trait name, "aggression," which is then seen as *caused* by either "aggressive drives" or "aggressive instincts." As practitioners, we end up with no more than was started with, except that we have deluded ourselves into thinking we have an explanation (Hineline, 1980).

Anxiety, which for some is the central concept of the neuroses, has fallen prey to just this sort of conceptual mischief. Sarbin (1968) has written about the history of this term and reminds us that it was originally a metaphor for distress derived from the Middle English word *anguish*. However, the metaphorical quality of the term has long since been lost, and the concept has been reified. "Thingish" usages abound. Anxiety is now talked about as a thing or quantity to be counterconditioned, extinguished, or otherwise reduced or eliminated. This "thing" is also said to be susceptible to physiological measurement as well as to measurement in various other modalities. The term makes an appearance in various theories with the status of drive, secondary drive, motive, danger signal, or evidence of disorganization (Rotter, 1954). Although it was originally a synonym for distress or suffering, the irony is that clients now claim to be suffering *from* anxiety, and many therapists agree with them! Individuals having trouble with, for instance, spiders, come to the clinic asking for relaxation therapy to get rid of their anxiety. One would think they would be more interested in getting rid of the spiders or at least figuring out how to have a better relationship with them.

It is a mistake to force *anxiety* to do work for which the term was not intended and isn't well equipped. Therefore, it is simply noted (Rotter, 1954) that most individuals use the term to inform others that they are disturbed or aroused, probably in connection with a perceived threat to their integrity.

There are some other problems. In discussing anxiety—and almost anything else, for that matter—there are theorists who insist on using the metaphysical trichotomy of cognition, affection, and conation (thought, feeling and action). But, as George Kelly points out (Maher, 1969), the cleavage of psychological processes into these classical components just "confuses everything and clarifies nothing" (p. 91). Part of the problem is that, once having split the person into these subparts, one is more or less obligated to figure out the relationship among the parts and to take separate measurements of each. This can be seen as the motivation for the current multimodal measurement craze. This also sets the stage for a debate about which part is the most important. Do thoughts determine feelings? Do feelings determine thoughts? Do actions supersede and control both of the other two? Should treatment be directed primarily, perhaps even exclusively, toward the thought processes? Should the person just be set in motion, letting nature do the rest? What if the measurements or readings taken from the various subsystems don't coincide?

The present authors' perspective is that an organism acts, acts as a whole, and receives the consequences of that action. We assume that people pose questions to the world through their actions and that they do so with their entire selves, although different kinds of questions involve different levels of risk and commitment (Kelly, 1955). Contemplating buying a car may be a lower-risk action than putting down the deposit. If the car crashes, further actions will be required, although now the high level of risk involved will probably have everyone talking the language of feelings. But it isn't necessary to reify our linguistic distinctions (thoughts versus feelings versus behaviors). There is no need to get stuck trying to put back together what we took apart in the first place.

We have created other problems for ourselves by "languaging up" our treatment or helping strategies. Interventions are almost always framed in the language of objectivity: the clients or subjects have things "done" to them and their "responses" are noted. For example, if we persuade an individual to become better acquainted with a snake he or she has been avoiding, we say that they have "received systematic desensitization" or have been "given in vivo flooding," or had a certain number of "engaged-exposure" trials (deSilva & Rachman, 1980). This terminology, which emphasizes what is done to a passive client or subject (talked about as a kind of object), hardly ever permits a clear view of what the subject is doing to us or for himself or herself. It is an especially clumsy frame in which to discuss the "reciprocal determinism" now favored by Bandura (1977) or other nonlinear patterns of influence and interaction.

Similarities among useful operations have been hidden because of the different names used by different professional subgroups. In addition, we have sometimes been led to hold on to ineffective modes of working because of the impressive titles and impeccable lineages with which they come to us. In this chapter, the authors will have occasion to point to some of the confusion created by the use of these linguistic customs.

Meanwhile, it is time to get on with the task of surveying recent treatment developments.

PHOBIAS

General characteristics

The *DSM-III* (1980) defines *phobia* as a "persistent and irrational fear of a specific object, activity, or situation that results in a compelling desire to avoid . . . the phobic stimulus" (p. 225). The person may recognize that the fear is disproportionate to any actual danger, but the avoidance reaction persists.

In a study carried out in Vermont, 76.9 per 1,000 citizens were reported to have phobic fears of one sort or another, for which about 2.2 per 1,000 sought treatment (Agras, Sylvester, & Oliveau, 1969). Those seeking treatment usually complain of fears which interrupt patterns of work, household tasks, or other daily activities.

While it may be accurate to assume that neurotic conditions, in general, have a high rate of spontaneous remission, perhaps as high as two thirds within two years of onset (Rachman & Wilson, 1980; Eysenck, 1960), the same cannot be said of phobias. They are among the most stable and persistent of mental problems (Mavissakalian & Barlow, 1981). For example, of 30 untreated phobic individuals who were followed for a period of 5 years, 20 percent remained unchanged and 33 percent actually deteriorated (Agras, Chapin, & Oliveau, 1972).

The largest single group who seek help (60 percent) is classified as agoraphobic. These individuals fear going out, mingling with the public, being in crowds, riding public transportation, sitting in theaters, being in open places, walking by themselves, and being left home alone. Agoraphobia apparently differs from the more specific phobias in that there is usually no precipitating event. Also, there is more often a history of childhood separation anxiety and a pattern of strong, continuing ties with the family of origin (Zitrin, Klein, & Woerner, 1978). Agoraphobic problems typically begin in late childhood or early adolescence. The pattern is found more commonly in women, and the course tends to be chronic but variable. There can be periods of complete remission followed by renewed flare-ups. Most agoraphobic individuals complain of spontaneous panic attacks, episodes of depersonalization, and general feelings of anxiety, helplessness, and discouragement (Goldstein, 1978).

While more of these patients will readily talk of external sources of fear, many clinicians now feel that the central fear of the agoraphobic is the fear of losing control. As Weekes (1976) puts it, the agoraphobic suffers primarily from a "fear of fear."

This diagnostic category (agoraphobia) has been very popular lately among mental health professionals, and it is likely that many of the individuals that used to be diagnosed as anxiety neurotics are now being considered agoraphobic. After all, the pattern is the familiar one of generalized anxiety bordering on panic and fears that relate to broad aspects of the environment rather than to specific, discrete stimuli. Some diagnostic confusion is generated because the agoraphobic's sense of discouragement and helplessness, as well as his or her pattern of restricted activity, tempts some diagnosticians to think in terms of a depressive illness. But the agoraphobic has not lost interest in life the same way that many depressed individuals have. In fact, the agoraphobic's symptomatology tends to be strikingly situational. While at home, or when accompanied by a trusted companion, the agoraphobic person can be quite active and productive. It is only when there is a threat to security that his or her behavior deteriorates, and frustration becomes evident. On the other hand, when agoraphobics begin to seek repeated reassurance from others and devise extensive strategies to avoid losing control, they resemble the obsessive individual. This is why thinking in terms of discrete diagnostic categories can be so difficult and so potentially limiting. Here we have two individuals, doing roughly the same thing for the same reason, and yet, since we tend to classify persons rather than actions, these individuals end up in different diagnostic categories.

To complicate the diagnostic picture further, the depersonalization aspects of the agoraphobic pattern can sometimes result in the person being seen as having a primary depersonalization disorder or even a psychosis.

The second major category of phobias is composed of the simple phobias. These are more specific fears and are generally easier to identify. They appear to cluster around three themes with slightly different patterns. The themes are: animals and other discrete stimuli, blood and injury, and social fears (Mayer-Gross, Slater, & Roth, 1969). Unlike agoraphobia, these specific fears usually begin in childhood and have a more even, chronic course without notable periods of remission. Additionally, the fears are almost always generated by confrontation (or anticipated confrontation) with the feared objects or situations. There is an absence of general anxiety, panic attacks, and depersonalization. The fear of blood and injury, unlike the others, tends to fade and disappear in early adulthood. These blood-and-injury folks also display a unique physiological response to the feared stimulus: on occasion, they faint (Mavissakalian & Barlow, 1981).

Those who fear social situations share much in common with agoraphobic individuals. For example, there is the central fear of embarrassing oneself. However, the fears of the social phobic are much more closely tied to specific situations or interactions, such as speaking in public or meeting someone of the opposite sex.

Interventions

The initial success of behavior therapy was felt in the treatment of the phobias. However, the current excitement in the field appears to be due not only to the fact that we can now better treat these conditions, but also because a clearer picture is emerging as to why some approaches work better than others. Today's therapist has a variety of methods from which to choose and some relatively solid research evidence on which to base these choices. Listed below are some of the conclusions reached in the present survey of this literature. Obviously, not everyone will agree with the present authors' interpretations of the data, and, in fact, some of these conclusions were not the ones expected when this work was initiated. Nevertheless, the intention is to state them flatly and allow them to stand as a focus for debate. The meaning of some of the statements will need to be "fleshed out" in the sections to follow:

1. So-called in vivo treatments work better than imagery-based treatments and should be used for the treatment of phobias wherever applicable (Marks, 1978).

2. Brief treatment exposures are not usually as effective as longer exposures (e.g., Stern & Marks, 1973).

3. There is no necessary relationship between client arousal level during treatment and outcome (e.g., Hafner & Marks, 1976; Marks, 1978).

4. Behavioral treatments are more effective with phobias than are either psychodynamic or pharmacological interventions (Rachman & Wilson, 1980).

5. Behavioral interventions for phobias appear capable of producing broad-based improvements that extend beyond the target symptom or presenting complaint.

6. Approaches which incorporate action are more generally successful than those construed solely in terms of cognitive manipulation or discussion methods (e.g., Ellis, 1977).

7. Many technical aspects of the behavioral treatments which once seemed crucial have not been shown to affect outcome. This is true of the relaxation training and the precise arrangement of the fear hierarchy in systematic desensitization (e.g., Rachman, 1968; Cooke, 1968). In implosion therapy, exaggerated (horror) imagery and high levels of arousal no longer seem to carry any advantage and may even prove harmful (e.g., Foa, Blau, Prout, & Latimer, 1977).

8. Self-pacing is probably as useful as therapist-guided pacing, and there is therefore no need for the client to be unduly pushed (Efran, Ascher, Webb, & Moore, 1977; Emmelkemp & Kraanen, 1977).

9. The style of the phobic individual is perennially avoidant (Andrews, 1966), and all the successful treatments seem to sabotage the individual's preference for avoidance. They provide effective opportunities to reevaluate the previously avoided object or situation for oneself.

10. Many treatment strategies can be carried out by clients themselves or by paraprofessionals without any demonstrable loss of effectiveness. Group formats can sometimes be used to provide the same level of service with increased efficiency (Rachman & Wilson, 1980).

11. Medication does not cure agoraphobia, although some believe it is useful in diminishing the intensity of panic attacks. There may be problems if the individual construes a successful confrontation with the phobic object as due to the drug effects rather than to his or her own abilities (Chambless & Goldstein, 1981; Zitrin, 1981).

Behavior therapies. Systematic desensitization (Wolpe, 1958) might be considered the great granddaddy of behavior therapies. Although to some it must now appear dated, it has aged gracefully, retaining much of its original effectiveness and continuing to attract clinical and research attention. It provides a relatively comfortable and gradual approach for the phobic individual. It can no longer be considered the most powerful technique in the behavioral armamentarium, and it seems distinctly ineffective with most agoraphobic people (Goldstein & Chambless, 1978). In its usual form, patients are first taught relaxation, with care being taken not to provoke undue anxiety at any step along the way. Initially, a fuss was made about the need to train the client in relaxation and imagery. It was also considered important to have the hierarchy properly arranged. However, none of these matters has been shown to clearly affect outcome, and the reciprocal-inhibition theory on which the procedure was originally based has been much criticized (Leitenberg, 1976). Despite these reservations, hardly anyone doubts that the method is useful, especially where the more direct, in vivo methods are impractical or would not be well-tolerated by the client.

In contrast with desensitization, implosive therapy (Stampfl & Levis, 1967) and its younger brother, imaginal flooding (Rachman, 1969), encourage more vigorous and immediate confrontations with the phobic images. Here there is little concern about the amount of anxiety aroused, and, in fact, imploders may go to great lengths to escalate anxiety level in order to speed the extinction process. Exaggerated and unrealistic imagery is suggested to the client, including references to symbolic material drawn from Freudian theory. The fantasies used in imaginal flooding are of a more ordinary sort. As indicated earlier, there is now some concern that the horror imagery of implosion is sometimes detrimental and—in the absence of evidence that it is particularly advantageous—almost all workers have adopted the flooding format.

The newest kids on the block, the in vivo methods, eschew imagery-based techniques altogether. In vivo flooding, participant modeling (Ritter, 1969), and reinforced practice (Leitenberg & Callahan, 1973) all stress actual contact with the phobic object or situation. In vivo flooding asks the person to approach the phobic stimulus as quickly as possible and remain in contact with it for a relatively prolonged period. Reinforced practice, which is based on the Skinnerian notion of shaping, encourages more graduated contact and emphasizes social reinforcement for each step taken. Participant modeling is similar to reinforced practice in that gradual exposure is encouraged; but in this method, the therapist takes some pains to model or demonstrate nonphobic behavior and situational competence at each level.

It might be noted that these methods are more similar in practice than their separate names imply. For example, most therapists—implicitly or explicitly—become models for their clients and provide many relevant cues for competent behavior, whether or not they call themselves participant modelers. Most therapists provide a good deal of encouragement and reinforcement along the way. Further, even the harshest sounding exposure procedures tend to become more pliable when applied to a live person being asked to face a feared circumstance.

What seems crucial in all these methods (and others to be discussed) is that the client undertakes a reappraisal in connection with a previously avoided object or situation. Arousal level, per se, doesn't seem to have a lot to do with it. After all, anxiety isn't the problem—it is only an indication that the problem is near.

The in vivo methods appear to be the most powerful, and this seems appropriate. As John Dewey suggested long ago, we learn best by doing. As in all education, the teacher (here called *therapist*) does not directly educate but sets up a situation in which people can educate themselves—a laboratory is provided with the proper tools, and permission to experiment is given. Within this educational model, questions such as "How long should the client be exposed to the phobic stimulus?" tend to take on a somewhat different form. To recommend standard exposure times makes as little sense in this context as it would to tell college students how fast they must read a given textbook passage or how many revisions of a term paper will be necessary to achieve an acceptable product. The literature points to the notion that self-pacing is at least as effective as anything else, and that a diminution in arousal level can serve as a rough guideline for when to end an exposure trial (Emmelkamp, 1977). This means that arousal level provides a clue to when the client's assimilatory/accommodatory sequence has run its course. However, rather than relying solely on measures of arousal, we might also just ask people to indicate when they have finished their "investigation."

Behavior therapists, as a group, do not seem to be closely attuned to issues of context. They are perhaps overly focused on individuals and symptoms. Yet, it is becoming clear that phobias occur in a social frame and that the meaning of the complaint is shaped by the patient's social system. In some systems, the avoidant style of the phobic will not be construed as a mental health issue, and in others, at certain times, it will precipitate a crisis of major proportions. Despite the fact that the language of individual psychiatry and psychology does not make it easy to focus on contextual elements or reciprocal patterns of influence (Bandura, 1977), some investigators have now begun to take more note of contextual characteristics. Milton and Hafner (1979) reported that the marital status of their agoraphobic patients related significantly to the outcome of their in vivo-exposure treatment. Those with marriages which were rated beforehand as unsatisfactory improved less during treatment and were also more likely to relapse. In an even more recent study (Barlow, Mavissakalian, & Hay, 1981), two patterns emerged: for some couples, as the phobia of the spouse cleared up, the marriage also improved; yet for others, as the phobia cleared up, the marriage deteriorated.

In these authors' experience, clients who do not respond readily to treatment at the level of symptom can often be aided if attention is redirected to the larger frame in which the symptom was generated.

Cognitive behavioral therapies.   The reader is probably aware of the controversy between the behavior therapists and those who prefer cognitive-behavioral approaches. One group takes the phrase, a *science of behavior,* rather literally, sometimes asserting that if it isn't behavior, it isn't science. The other group wants to mount a head-on assault on faulty thinking patterns, using techniques borrowed from the field of rhetoric, if necessary. The flavor of this debate can be gleaned from this sample of phrases from the titles of recent articles on the subject: "Cognitive behavior modification: A step in the wrong direction?" (Ledwidge, 1978); "Cognitive behavior modification: Misconceptions and premature evacuation" (Mahoney & Kazdin, 1979); "Cognitive behavior modification: The need for a fairer assessment" (Meichenbaum, 1979); "Cognitive behavior modification or new ways to change minds: Reply to Mahoney and Kazdin" (Ledwidge, 1979). Clearly, this debate is going to be with us for awhile, and nothing we can say here is going to stop it. However, we have already argued that splitting psychological processes in this way and reifying the splits is unproductive. In addition, when you get beyond the rhetoric and look at what is being done in treatment, the distinctions being fought over do not seem very large. All the cognitive behavioral procedures give real-life (action) assignments (Ellis, 1977), and all the behavior therapies involve discussion, anticipation, planning, and explanation (Klein, Dittman, Parloff, & Gill, 1969). The basic formula for the treatment of agoraphobia, for example, has been set down by Claire Weekes (1976) in terms of four straightforward principles: "Face—do not run away; accept—do not fight; float—do not tense; let time pass— do not be impatient with time" (p. 23). All the successful programs seem to embody these principles. This includes the behavioral, the cognitive-behavioral (e.g., Coleman, 1981), and even a recent version of transactional analysis practiced by the Gouldings (1979). In other words, you have to get clients into the situation and let them experience whatever there is to experience.

One of the cognitive behavioral methods that does look a little different is Meichenbaum's Self-Statement Training (1977), where patients are taught to be aware of their negative self-statements and to replace them with more positive and adaptive statements. They are also instructed in coping more effectively with environmental stressors. This includes breaking down situations into more recognizable and manageable units. There have been some positive findings for this approach, particularly with mild fears and test anxiety (Meichenbaum, 1972). However, there isn't evidence at this point to suggest that this procedure has any advantage over other cognitive behavioral approaches nor that it is fully applicable to more typical clinical problems. In fact, a research project by Emmel-kamp, Kuipers, and Eggeraat (1978) pitted cognitive restructuring with a self-instructional training component against prolonged-exposure treat-ments. The exposure treatments were significantly more effective. At pres-ent, these authors tend to agree with Meichenbaum's (1972) view that self-statement training be considered a supplement to other treatment modalities rather than a competitor or replacement for them.

Psychodynamic therapies. Unlike the behavioral and cognitive-behavioral therapists, analysts have focused away from the immediate symptom to broader issues of motive and origin. They have provided an extensive, but primarily descriptive, literature about the origin, course, and treatment of phobias. Unfortunately, there is little satisfactory outcome data, and what there is, isn't promising. For example, only 1 of 19 phobics who received insight-oriented psychotherapy could be regarded as com-pletely recovered, according to the results of a 23-year follow-up study. Twelve of the 19 did not appear to have improved at all (Errara & Cole-man, 1963). In another study, only 23 percent of a group of 38 agorapho-bic inpatients were considered recovered, despite the fact that they had received psychotherapy and medication (Roberts, 1964). The follow-up period for this study was 18 months to 16 years. Malan (1976) was only able to demonstrate a 50 percent improvement rate for a sample of 10 phobic patients.

Of course, it is brash to indict insight-oriented therapies by lumping together adequate and inadequate research, good and poor therapists, and psychodynamic positions of every stripe and color (the myth of unifor-mity). Bergin (1971) has argued that the results of psychotherapy are really quite variable, and when they are averaged together, the outcome is almost always a slightly positive figure. Nevertheless, the weight of available evidence with regard to phobias is that the traditional insight-oriented approaches are just not keeping pace (in terms of either results or costs) with the more direct, action-oriented modes. In contradistinction to these preconceptions, there is even evidence that the action modes are resulting in improved general adjustment and not just circumscribed symptom relief (Rachman & Wilson, 1980; Marks, 1978).

There has been a trend in psychodynamic treatments of phobia to emphasize ego functioning and develop shorter, crisper treatment formats. Sifneos (1979) has researched a technique under the acronym STAPP—short-term, anxiety-producing psychotherapy. It is designed for patients who meet certain admissions criteria: a circumscribed complaint; evidence of having established at least one meaningful relationship; the ability to interact flexibly; above-average intelligence; psychological sophistication; and motivation for change. (With all that going for you, why would you need STAPP?)

The data for his sample of neurotic patients shows a 74 percent rate of improvement. It is difficult to use this outcome statistic for purposes of comparisons with other approaches, given the unusually stringent selection criteria and the lack of breakdown by presenting complaint. However, there is a "too little, too late" quality to Sifneos' valiant attempt to provide more cost-efficient psychodynamic services.

Perhaps this is the place to remind the reader of the following, oft-quoted statement: "One can hardly ever master a phobia if one waits till the patient lets the analysis influence him to give it up. . . . One succeeds only when one can induce them . . . to go about alone and to struggle with their anxiety while they make the attempt" (1919/1959, pp. 399–400). The statement is Freud's. In the same vein, Goldfried (1980) brings to our attention Fenichel's statement that "When a person is afraid but experiences a situation in which what was feared occurs without any harm resulting, he will not immediately trust the outcome of his new experience; however, the second time he will have a little less fear, the third time still less" (1941, p. 83). Goldfried also cites the conclusion from the Menninger Foundation Psychotherapy Research Project: "Corrective experiences, provided to patients within the context of supportive therapy, resulted in as much long-lasting therapeutic change as did more traditional psychoanalytic psychotherapy (p. 944)."

Other therapies.   Two other psychological approaches to phobias shall be mentioned which will not fall readily into the previous categories. The first is redecision therapy (Goulding & Goulding, 1979), which is a modernized version of transactional analysis (Berne, 1964), and the second is Bandler and Grinder's Neuro-Linguistic Programming (1975, 1979).

In common with other TA therapists, the Gouldings rely on the central theory of ego states (child, adult, parent), and they emphasize the continuing effect that various parental injunctions (as interpreted by the child) have on the individual's life plan. Their therapy incorporates some Gestalt techniques to vitalize the work. There is, perhaps, less emphasis on identifying games and analyzing life scripts than in other TA approaches, but there is more emphasis on establishing a therapeutic contract within which an individual can redecide what to permit him/herself to do and be. While no formal outcome statistics are provided, the Gouldings make the following statements about their handling of phobias: "For some problems, redecision is all that is necessary. This is particularly true of phobias. When a person gives up being afraid and tests herself successfully in a reality situation, she will remain unafraid. . . . For some problems, the client will need practice after making a redecision" (p. 283). At another point, they claim: "We can cure most height phobias in 10 minutes and water phobias in less than half an hour. . . . Other problems may take longer, but people do make changes that seem very quick to therapists who believe therapy is a complicated, long-term process" (p. 8).

As previously indicated, the method used by the Gouldings is quite similar to the methods of action-oriented therapists; a commitment is made by the client, who then faces the previously avoided circumstance. Perhaps all the rest is window dressing.

Bandler and Grinder do not claim to have come up with a new theory of therapy. Instead, they see themselves as professional communicators and modelers. They have translated the work of therapists such as Milton Erickson and Virginia Satir, using the language of psycholinguistics and transformational grammar. They stress the importance of communicating with clients in their own language, and they suggest techniques for moving toward complete (well-formed) communicative statements. They have made much of the distinctions between left brain (verbal, logical) and right brain (nonverbal, wholistic) processing, and they have also emphasized individual preferences for using the visual, kinesthetic, and auditory modes (Bandler & Grinder, 1979). Most relevant for the current discussion is their view of phobia: "A phobia can be thought of as nothing more than one-trial learning that was never updated" (1979, p. 112). They suggest a brief conditioning treatment, where people recreate phobic experiences for themselves, with their eyes closed, and then visualize resources which they wish they had had in the original situation. These two experiences (the phobic sense and the resources) are brought together by cues (anchors) which the therapist uses. There isn't any formal data on the effectiveness of the model. Given that it appears to be a brief imagery procedure, it is doubtful that it works as well as the in vivo methods previously discussed. On the other hand, Bandler and Grinder might very well argue that the weak outcomes of other imagery procedures are due to the failure of therapists to take into account individual differences in processing modes, and to their inattention to the details of communication with the client.

Pharmacotherapy. In researching the literature, the closest finding to a clear use for medication with the phobic conditions was the suggestion that imipramine, and perhaps the MAO inhibitors, might be of some use in agoraphobia to limit or reduce the intensity of panic attacks (Zitrin, 1981). There is debate about this, with some workers (e.g., Coleman, 1981; Chambless & Goldstein, 1981) being less than impressed with the clinical effectiveness of these drugs. It is possible that they are useful only with depressed agoraphobic individuals. No one is claiming that the pharmacological effects eliminate agoraphobia—only that the drug may occasionally be useful in restoring motivation in a depressed person or in decreasing the discomfort of a panic attack. The avoidance pattern remains. There is even the possible danger that medication can limit the effectiveness of approaches to the phobic situation. This might occur if, for example, the clients attributed their having survived the phobic confrontation to drug effects rather than to their own abilities.

With simple phobias, there is rarely a need for the use of medication.

OBSESSIVE-COMPULSIVE DISORDERS

General characteristics

Obsessions are repetitive, intrusive, and unwanted thoughts which the individual generally experiences as senseless or abhorrent. The thoughts are almost invariably about the following topics: dirt/contamination, meticulousnesss/order, violence, sex, or religion (Akhtar, Wig, Varma, Pershad, & Verma, 1975).

Compulsions are repetitive and stereotyped behaviors which often go along with obsessions. The individual typically recognizes them as excessive attempts to avoid something but feels an urge to engage in the behavior anyway. The acts are sometimes resisted (especially in the beginning), but the individual may experience relief when he or she gives in to the impulse and performs the ritual (*DSM-III,* 1980). People with obsessive-compulsive patterns appear to be struggling with problems of diminished control over their behavior, but the loss of control is more apparent than real: the ritual behaviors can almost always be voluntarily postponed without very much difficulty, and it has been noted that interrupting them does not necessarily cause an increase in tension (Roper, Rachman, & Hodgson, 1973). (These facts have particular relevance to the response-prevention methods in the subsequent discussion.) It is rare that an unacceptable idea (such as "I must strangle my child") is enacted in reality, and the suicide risk for this diagnostic group is estimated to be low (Rachman & Hodgson, 1980).

Obsessive-compulsive disorders are statistically rare (about 3 percent of the neurotic population), but the chronicity, disruptiveness, and resistance to change—which characterize the pattern—give it great individual and clinical significance. There is about an equal distribution between men and women (Black, 1974; Hare, Price, & Slater, 1972).

Onset typically occurs sometime between childhood and early adulthood, with common life precipitants being sexual or marital difficulties, pregnancy, or the illness or death of a relative. There can be chronic and progressively deteriorating symptom patterns, or episodic, fluctuating patterns with periods of remission (especially in the early stages).

It was once commonly believed that, when obsessive-compulsive individuals deteriorated, they became schizophrenic or showed other psychotic patterns. This does not appear to be the case (Kringlen, 1970; Templer, 1972). There does, however, appear to be a relationship between obsessive-compulsive disturbance and depression. The nature of the relationship remains clouded, but clinicians are not surprised to hear depressive complaints along with obsessional ideation.

Interventions

Until very recently, the outlook for the treatment of obsessive-compulsive disorders was gloomy. As late as 1974, Black concluded that, with the possible exception of leucotomy, no treatment for these problems could be said to have long-term beneficial effects. The early behavioral workers did not have the same immediate success with obsessions and compulsions that they had experienced with the phobic conditions. Attempts to use systematic desensitization were basically unsuccessful (e.g., Cooper, Gelder, & Marks, 1965; Furst & Cooper, 1970), and aversion therapy did not prove very helpful either. "Thought stopping" yielded only weak and inconsistent results (Hackmann & McLean, 1975; Sookman & Solyom, 1977; Stern, Lipsedge, & Marks, 1973). In fact, none of the fantasy- or imagery-based treatments proved effective.

Behavior therapies. The outlook for successful treatment has recently brightened considerably. The reason for this new optimism relates most directly to the new emphasis on the in vivo methods presaged in the section on the phobias. In particular, the combination of in vivo exposure and response prevention seems to have led to something of a breakthrough. Participant modeling has also been used in this context to encourage the client to confront the phobic situation. The advance was first evident in a paper by Meyer (1966), who successfully treated two previously intractable, chronic obsessive-compulsive individuals. Meyer's technique stressed constant staff supervision to insure that the patients' compulsive rituals were not enacted during the treatment program. These patients maintained their improvement over a 14-month follow-up period. Levy and Meyer (1971) then treated eight chronic patients, using essentially the same method, and tracked their progress for one to six years. In every case, there was a marked decrease in compulsive behavior as well as evidence of improvement in ratings of anxiety and depression.

Perhaps the most comprehensive evaluations of this new methodology are contained in a series of studies by Rachman and his colleagues (Rachman, Hodgson, & Marks, 1971; Rachman, Marks, & Hodgson, 1973). These reports detail rather robust positive results, including: changes in clinical ratings; behavioral avoidance tests; discomfort and/or fear ratings; attitude measurements; and social-activity assessments. It is noteworthy that Rachman et al. achieved good results without using the extensive staff-supervision procedure that Meyer employed. Instead, they simply instructed their patients to refrain from performing their compulsive rituals. Exposure to the threatening stimuli was accomplished as quickly as possible, using therapist modeling to encourage the confrontation.

Continuing support for the exposure/response-prevention model has been produced by Meyer, Levy, and Schnurer (1974). Emmelkamp and Kraanen (1977) obtained a 74 percent reduction in the frequency of major compulsions, and Foa and Goldstein (1978) were able to eliminate symptoms altogether in two thirds of their patients. Significantly, these improvements appear to have spread beyond the target symptoms to include positive changes in work adjustment, social life, sexual functioning, and family relationships.

The effectiveness of these procedures does not appear to depend on the professional status of the therapist; a similar program administered by nurse therapists produced equally impressive results (Marks, Hallam, Connolly, & Philpott, 1976). It is also nice to know that this kind of treatment program, despite its harsh sound, seems to have a high rate of patient acceptability.

The rule of thumb seems to be to use participant modeling or whatever else will get the patient to confront the avoided (but objectively harmless) consequence, and to be sure that the ritual, if there is one, isn't being performed during the confrontation. Only this last twist differentiates these procedures from those recommended for the phobias. It reminds one of the well-known joke about the person who observed a friend snapping his fingers. He asked his friend, "Why are you snapping your fingers?" "To keep the elephants away," was the reply. "But there aren't any elephants around here," he noted. "Yes, I know—effective, isn't it?" With hindsight, it is possible to see that the obsessional individual has been snapping his fingers, and unless he stops (response prevention) and takes a look around at the same time (exposure), he isn't going to learn much of value about elephants.

While the news on the obsessive-compulsive front has been good lately, the battle isn't over. It is clear that there still are some patients who do not respond favorably to the exposure/response-prevention format. Foa (1979) notes that these difficult cases often tend to be depressed and that some also seem especially wedded to their obsessive pattern. Rabavilas and Boulougouris (1979) similarly note histories of mood swings with individuals who show poor overall response to behavioral treatment. It has been suggested that these patients may profit from the use of antidepressant medication in addition to the behavioral treatment regime (Marks, Stern, Mawson, Cobb, & McDonald, 1980). However, these authors make it clear that pharmacological treatment alone is insufficient to produce lasting improvements.

One wonders whether, in some of these cases, the attachment of the person to his or her pattern relates to the fact that the rest of the person's life is so bleak. It may be better to have an obsession or two than to have nothing at all!

Psychodynamic therapies.   Again, insight-oriented treatment approaches have not fared well in comparison with the behavioral strategies. The comfort they produce may not be worth the cost. There are currently attempts to make psychodynamic treatment for obsession-compulsion more direct and confrontative, with increased focus on the here and now. Most importantly, it is being suggested that the therapist insist on a commitment to action (Salzman & Thaler, 1981). The irony is that, if these suggestions are heeded, we will be right back to behavior-therapy procedures, but under a different name.

A number of authors have noted that traditional analytic approaches may unwittingly exacerbate obsessions. Noonan (1971) reported that intensive treatment may strengthen the obsessive's propensity for introspective rumination. In any event, as Salzman (1980) has stated directly, insight therapy alone rarely is enough to treat the obsessive-compulsive.

Redecision therapy. The redecision therapy approach for handling obsessive-compulsive disorders involves a number of suggested principles, of which the most basic is this: "The first contract is that the client stop performing compulsive acts, no matter how difficult this may seem. Without this contract, therapist and client support the magic that the client 'can't' control his behavior and therefore 'can't' get well" (Goulding & Goulding, 1979, p. 256). In other words, stop snapping! They propose a number of other clinical hints; for example, that the client substitute a sexual fantasy for the obsession. This derives from their expectation that many obsessive individuals are attempting to ward off sexuality, about which there have been strong, parental injunctions. They also recommend group therapy where possible, since these clients are often relatively friendless and need a social-support system.

In terms of the "pattern which connects," it is interesting that the Gouldings, coming from a rather different theoretical orientation, have essentially devised procedures similar to those of the other action-oriented therapists. The exposure/response-prevention types would probably be unhappy with their vocabulary, but not with their basic recommendations.

Surgical and pharmacological therapies. There is a point of view that obsessive-compulsive disorders are caused by a dominant frontal-lobe dysfunction. Damage in this area would result in a loss of the normal inhibitory mechanisms, which would, in turn, account for repetitive patterning. Proponents of this view cite dramatic improvement following drug therapy and/or psychosurgery as evidence for their point of view (thus committing the logical error of affirming the consequent).

Sternberg (1974) notes that a wide variety of drugs have been used to treat this disorder. It is unclear how many are actually helpful, and some may even be harmful. Because of the close association of depression with the obsessive-compulsive disorders, it is not surprising that a number of investigators have focused on the use of antidepressants. Chlorimipramine has received most of the attention and support. For a while, it was believed that this drug had specific anti-obsessional properties, but this has not turned out to be the case (Marks et al., 1980). It seems to operate only on the depressive element in the obsessive-compulsive picture.

For the majority of patients, psychological approaches remain the treatment of choice, with medication for anxiety and depression serving more limited, adjunctive roles.

Salzman and Thaler (1981) report about 60 percent improvement following the surgical cutting of tracts from the cortex to the thalamus. However, it would seem difficult to justify radical procedures like leucotomy in the current climate of increased optimism about psychological treatments.

Conclusions

Presented here are a list of conclusions for the obsessive-compulsive disorders to parallel the list presented in connection with the phobias.[1]

1.   The most powerful treatment for obsessive-compulsive disorders at this time is the combination of in vivo exposure and response prevention.

2.   Participant modeling may be useful, as an adjunct to this treatment, to encourage clients to confront the feared circumstance.

3.   Traditional psychotherapy isn't very helpful, and some say that it may exacerbate and support obsessive rumination.

4.   In all these approaches, including redecision therapy, the most critical element seems to be blocking the ritual. Fortunately, obsessive-compulsive individuals are able to voluntarily refrain from carrying out their rituals when necessary.

5.   Drug therapy may be a useful adjunct, particularly in connection with associated depression, but it doesn't provide a cure, and the avoidant pattern remains.

6.   Surgical interventions cannot be recommended at this time, given level of effectiveness of the behavioral techniques.

DEPRESSION

General characteristics

About 8 out of every 100 people will develop a severe depression at some time in their lives. Many more will experience milder depressive episodes, ranging from short-lived cases of the "blues," to extended periods when the meaningfulness of life seems to have escaped them. The neurotic depressions (now called *dysthymic disorders*) that will be considered in this chapter are basically reactive disorders uncomplicated by psychotic processes, organic brain syndromes, or general medical illness. Unlike normal depression (if there is such a thing), neurotic depression is relatively chronic (it requires a period of two years for an adult to fit the diagnostic criteria), although there may be periods of remission lasting a few days or a few weeks. A major liability for individuals in this category is the potential for suicide, which is high (*DSM-III*, 1980).

---

[1] References applicable to these conclusions have already been cited in the main discussion sections and will not be repeated here.

Phenomenologically, the individual reports feelings of sadness and helplessness, loss of interest in life, inability to experience pleasure, fatigue, sleep disturbance, social withdrawal, indecisiveness, and recurrent suicidal ideation. Individuals tend to see the world, themselves, and the future in negative terms (Beck's "cognitive triad," in Beck, Rush, Shaw, & Emery, 1979).

The complaints of the neurotically depressed usually surface early in adult life and often appear without being associated with a clear precipitant. However, careful interviewing often reveals some environmental event which had been a blow to the individual's equilibrium.

Interventions

It is with depression that the cognitive-behavioral theorists appear to have come into their own. Although it is not based on ideas that are unique or new, the "packaging" of Aaron Beck's group at the University of Pennsylvania has attracted the most clinical attention (Beck et al., 1979).

Cognitive-behavioral therapies. Beck's work was preceded and influenced by the development of rational-emotive therapy (Ellis, 1980). Both investigators believe that thoughts or cognitions, and not response consequences per se, shape and determine behavior and affect. Ellis' famous *ABC* formulation puts the matter this way: *A* (the activating event) leads to *B* (the intervening belief), which, in turn, has *C* (emotional consequences). The explicit goal of these approaches, then, is to call attention to and modify the *B*s (or faulty beliefs and assumptions). Beck has broken down faulty thinking into the following kinds of categories: arbitrary inference, selective abstraction, overgeneralization, magnification and minimization, personalization, and absolutistic/dichotomous thinking. In the therapy, systematic attempts are made to correct these thinking patterns. The client becomes a co-investigator, planning mini-experiments, collecting counterevidence, and challenging his or her own automatic thoughts and assumptions. Beck's approach is "active, directive, time-limited, and structured" (Beck et al., 1979, p. 3). He uses direct challenges, debates, and role-playing, and the clients are given homework. They may be asked to count negative thoughts with a wrist counter, to record reactions and plans, to complete graded tasks. In some cases, hour-by-hour scheduling of more positive activities is encouraged or required. As in Ellis' approach, there is a strong emphasis on reexamining the client's "should" statements—what Ellis has called *mustabatory* behavior (1980).

An important spate of studies evaluating Beck's approach has begun to appear (Beck et al., 1979; Kovacs, Rush, Beck, & Hollon, 1981; Rush, Beck, Kovacs, & Hollon, 1977; Rush, Khatami, & Beck, 1975; Shaw, 1977). This work, taken together, suggests that cognitive-behavioral therapy is at least as effective as, and perhaps superior to, antidepressant-medication therapy, therapy modeled after Lewinsohn's extinction approach (1974; 1976), and nondirective counseling. Two of the most recent of these studies (Kovacs et al., 1981; Rush et al., 1977) were especially well-controlled, large-scale studies, using multiple therapists with diverse initial biases. It is also notable that the drug effects were reported to be about the same as those in other studies. In other words, it was the cognitive-behavioral effects that were strong. It is not that the drug effects were weak. Some have suggested that lithium carbonate should have been used in some cases instead of imipramine, and there has also been criticisms of dosage levels, etc. However, the basic findings of these studies seem solid and augur well for the use of psychological treatments with reactive depression.

Another important factor was that the dropout rate for the groups receiving drug therapy was considerably higher than for those receiving cognitive-behavioral treatment. This is consistent with reports from other studies (e.g., McLean & Hakstian, 1979). Patients often find the side effects of the drugs disagreeable.

Beck's approach to depression appears quite promising; but replications in other settings and by other investigators will be required. Such efforts are now underway. As we all know, the dramatic impact of promising new procedures often wilts as time passes or when the procedures are tried by individuals further removed from the originator of the technique. Beck himself reminds us that this treatment has, thus far, only been shown effective for a limited group of depressives (unipolar, nonpsychotic outpatients). Antidepressant medication still has the best track record for the treatment of severe depression (Beck et al., 1979).

Behavioral approaches.   Two other approaches have recently been developed: Lewinsohn's (1974, 1976) extinction hypothesis, and Seligman's learned helplessness model (Abramson, Seligman, & Teasdale, 1978).

The essence of Lewinsohn's view is that depression results from a low rate of response-contingent reinforcement. "The depression amounts to the emission of no behavior, whereas not being depressed means emitting behavior. Getting reinforced for not responding leads to not emitting behavior and therefore to depression" (Friedman & Katz, 1974, p. 123). This is an appealing hypothesis—it is simple, straight-forward, and has immediate treatment implications. It has led to attempts to modify the activity level (emission rate) of depressives. Clients are asked to list and enact more positive (i.e., reinforcing) activities. Unfortunately, while there may be a correlation between being depressed and engaging in fewer pleasant activities, clinical treatment trials have been disappointing. The approach has proven less successful than Beck's approach (Shaw, 1977) and no more successful than client-centered therapy (Padfield, 1976). It should be noted, however, that Beck's package does contain an activity planning element that isn't very dissimilar to the kind of thing Lewinsohn is recommending.

In one study, where several therapies (including one based on Lewinsohn's hypothesis) were compared, all produced about equal results (Zeiss, Lewinsohn, & Munoz, 1979). Unfortunately, the measure most closely related to Lewinsohn's theory did not show the expected results. It isn't clear, at this time, whether the relatively weak showing of Lewinsohn's methods in clinical situations is due to a failure of theory or to difficulties in translating the theory into clinical operations. In any event, an exclusive focus on activity level cannot be recommended at the present time.

Seligman's model was initially based on experimental research with animals. His major contention is that some forms of depression are related to perceived loss of control over the consequences of one's behavior. An indication of the amount of attention this model has generated was the publication of a special issue of the *Journal of Abnormal Psychology* (1978, 87, No. 1), devoted to reviews of and additions to this work. Treatment for those who have learned to be helpless consists of mastery and success experiences. Some research has shown that exposure to successful experiences can lead to improvements in mild forms of depression (Klein & Seligman, 1976). However, Marks (1978) contends that it has yet to be demonstrated that mastery experiences provide anything more than temporary improvements. Seligman seems to agree, saying that "studies of learned helplessness in clinical populations have only just begun" (1978, p. 177).

As a footnote to this discussion of learned helplessness, a recent study by Alloy and Abramson (1979) showed that depressed students were more accurate in their perceptions of how much control they possessed (on an experimental task) than were nondepressed students. In other words, those who were in a better mood were operating on an illusion of greater control. The title of their article, "Judgment of contingency in depressed and nondepressed students; sadder but wiser?" is a reminder that those whom we see as more pathological are not necessarily deficient in cognitive processing skills or other abilities. They may, in fact, be dealing with aspects of the world about which the rest of us would just as soon not be bothered.

Psychodynamic therapies. Despite the lack of supportive evidence, some clinicians continue to hold that psychotherapy is the treatment of choice for the mild to moderate depressions (Chessick, 1976). Chessick notes that depression is usually only a secondary phenomenon. Once it has been dealt with, the therapist must be ready and willing to deal with the more basic, underlying themes. But, insight-oriented or supportive psychotherapies seem to have little demonstrable impact on depressive symptoms. Further, the rationale of employing insight-oriented approaches with neurotic depression must be reconsidered simply because the treatment process is often seen to last longer than the depressive episode itself (Seligman, Klein, & Miller, 1976).

Pharmacotherapy. The use of antidepressant medication in the treatment of depression has been well established. In general, the studies have reported that antidepressant drugs are more effective than placebo treatments and psychotherapeutic interventions, with the exceptions already cited. Although the evidence suggests that antidepressant drugs are the treatment of choice for severe depression, many clinicians have been concerned with potential side effects, a high patient-attrition rate, and a high relapse rate following the termination of therapy. New research trends have emphasized the combination of antidepressant medication and cognitive-behavioral psychotherapy, in an attempt to combat these problems (Weissman, Klerman, Prusoff, Sholomskas, & Padian, 1981).

Three classes of drugs have been studied: tricyclics, monoamine oxidase inhibitors (MOA), and lithium carbonate. Most of the data favors imipramine as the most effective of the tricyclic preparations (Beck, 1973; Schuyler, 1976).

MOA inhibitors also tend to be effective, but not necessarily more effective than imipramine. It might be advisable, therefore, to select the tricyclic drug when possible, since the side effects are generally less problematic.

The efficacy of lithium carbonate for the treatment of depression (in the absence of cyclothymic features) is less well established. In general, it appears wise to conclude that this drug, which requires close supervision, is not indicated for the management of mild to moderate depressions.

Family and systems therapies. Some contemporary approaches depart from the individual frame of psychopathology. Instead, they diagnose and intervene at the level of the family or natural group. Included here are many forms of family and systems-oriented therapies. While these theorists may talk about the symptoms of the identified patient, their basic interest is in the rough edges between the interacting parts of a system, the reciprocal roles in the dance, or performance of the group. They have traded the language of individual deficiency for the language of cybernetics and ecology. With some exceptions, there is not yet much systematic data on the effectiveness of these approaches, but it would be remiss to conclude this survey without briefly describing a sampling of these views. As indicated earlier, there is no particular rationale (other than convenience) for including these positions in this discussion of depression. The authors of these approaches would (most likely) consider them applicable across all of the neurotic categories covered in this chapter.

Two family-oriented positions will be compared and contrasted: Bowen's family-systems therapy (1978) and Minuchin's structured-family therapy (Minuchin, 1974; Minuchin & Fishman, 1981; Minuchin, Rosman, & Baker, 1978). Both place importance on issues of boundaries and differentiation, although they use somewhat different vocabularies and different treatment strategies. Minuchin is concerned with the structure of the nuclear family in terms of the adequacy and appropriateness of boundaries, especially between and among subsystems (e.g., the siblings versus the parents). Boundaries can be said to be clear, diffuse, or overly rigid. The nuclear family is usually seen together in the therapy room so that patterns of interaction can be observed. Minuchin joins the family as their leader and works with them—by rearranging seating patterns; blocking or encouraging the participation of certain members; assigning tasks; preventing typical patterns of problem solving; and politically siding with first one member or coalition and then another. This is an active approach concerned with structure rather than content and with the present pattern rather than historical roots or causes. Rules, such as not allowing someone to speak for someone else who is present, help break family enmeshments and support necessary individuation.

Minuchin has not yet reported systematic data for separate neurotic disorders. However, he has reported on a long series (53 cases) of families with an anorectic child. (Anorexia nervosa is now considered an eating disorder, but it had been considered a form of conversion neurosis by many.) In this area, previously characterized by pessimistic prognoses, he reports full recovery in 86 percent of the families treated—and with relatively long follow-up data at that. Although Minuchin's focus is on the family, he does use explicit behavioral techniques with the anorectic individual (such as allowing more activity only when caloric intake warrants), which justifies classifying him as an action-oriented rather than insight-oriented therapist.

Bowen (1978) takes the role of coach to a family member who is trying to differentiate himself or herself in relation to the family of origin. Most of the work in this approach is undertaken by the individual outside the consulting room. In the latest versions of the method, no attempt is made to convene the group as a whole. Unlike conventional therapy, there is no need for weekly meetings. The client sees the coach when there is something to report, when an impasse in the work has developed, or when the next phase of the project requires planning. This method is thus economical of professional time. The coach remains outside the family system (on the sidelines, so to speak), and the individual undertakes the project "for self," although with the belief that the entire system will eventually profit (become more differentiated) as the process proceeds. Frequent strategies include having the individual develop face-to-face, personal relationships with each member of his or her family. Sometimes relatives that have been cut off from the mainstream of family interaction are contacted, and ways are found for these cut-offs to be dissolved. The basic building block of relationships is thought to be the triangle. Dyads are considered unstable units which, when under tension, will "triangle in" a third person or object. The goal for the individual is to be able to stay in personal contact without becoming emotionally fused.

In a marital problem, the emphasis is on each spouse working with his or her own family of origin, rather than trying to communicate better with each other. There is an emphasis on intergenerational patterns, with clients inquiring into their roots by talking with older family members and doing family research. Bowen's approach was one of the first and most influential theoretical positions in the family-therapy movement. Unfortunately, outcome data is still mainly anecdotal and impressionistic.

Brief therapy is still another systems-oriented approach (Watzlawick, Weakland, & Fisch, 1974; Weakland, Fisch, Watzlawick, & Bodin, 1974). It is more problem-focused and, in some ways, less ambitious in its goals than the two approaches just discussed. Brief therapy is sometimes restricted to a maximum of 10 sessions and focuses on operationalizing and handling the initial complaint. It is a strategic, pragmatic approach. As the authors state, "We differ . . . with those family therapists who consider the dysfunction involved to be necessarily a fundamental aspect of the system's organization and requiring correspondingly fundamental changes in the system. Instead, we now believe that apparently minor changes in overt behavior or its verbal labeling often are sufficient to initiate progressive developments" (Weakland et al., 1974, p. 145).

These communication specialists believe that the usual sorts of solutions to problems have already been tried by the time the individual or family arrives for help, and, in fact, that these ordinary solutions mainly serve to perpetuate rather than solve the problem. (The more things change, the more they stay the same.) Therefore, they specialize in direct and indirect paradoxical injunctions, often "prescribing the symptom" rather than asking the person to eliminate it. Reframing, relabeling, recontextualizing—these are the heart of this strategic form of therapy. Of 97 cases seen in a 10-session format, the authors have reported clear success in 40 percent of the cases, significant (but not total) improvement in an additional 32 percent, and failure to reach the stated goal in 28 percent. Given the short length of time devoted to each case, one might be tempted to regard these outcome statistics as good. However, it is important to bear in mind that, although the time was short, the goals were quite specific and delimited. For these reasons, it is probably premature to embrace this methodology as a significant improvement over other approaches, but probably also unwise to reject the system as unworkable.

Conclusions

In sum, the following conclusions can be drawn regarding the treatment of neurotic depression. This list, in concert with the earlier two lists, completes this survey of recent treatment trends for neurotic conditions.[2]

---

[2] References cited earlier will not be repeated in this list.

1. Currently, Beck's cognitive-behavioral approach appears to be the most explicitly formulated and thoroughly validated approach to the treatment of neurotic depression. However, we cannot agree with his metaphysics, which holds that thoughts determine feelings and actions. (In our lexicon, thoughts *are* actions.) We consider the action sequences and assignments that he uses central to the success of his approach.

2. Lewinsohn's formulation of depression as an extinction phenomenon is theoretically interesting and appealing, but it has yet to yield a clinically viable treatment strategy.

3. Much the same can be said for Seligman's learned-helplessness model. The current revision includes more complex attribution-theory components; but despite the research attention, a competitive treatment strategy for the typical sorts of neurotic depressive complaints has yet to emerge.

4. Antidepressant medication (especially imipramine) remains the treatment of choice for severe depression. For neurotic depression, the picture is far less clear. Cognitive-behavior treatment often seems sufficient, and there isn't much evidence as yet that a combination of medication and cognitive-behavior treatment is more powerful than either used alone. With neurotic depression, the medication appears to affect overall activation level, which, in turn, may influence life circumstances.

5. The family- and systems-oriented approaches have not yet produced firm outcome data applicable to the neuroses. If the kind of evidence Minuchin presents for his treatment of anorectic families can be replicated and extended to other domains, this strategy will need to be given very serious consideration. From our point of view, his effectiveness may relate to the no-nonsense, action-oriented stance he assumes and to the degree of control over important consequences he is able to gain by working with the system as a whole.

SUMMARY

This chapter has surveyed evidence for the clinical efficacy of a variety of treatments for phobias (including agoraphobia), obsessive-compulsive disorders, and reactive depression. Our search has been for commonalities both within and across treatment domains. Since we emphasized recent empirical findings rather than anecdotal reports, we anticipated that there might be a bias in favor of the behavioral approaches—after all, workers in this group have made a point of encouraging systematic research and have developed many new journals in which to present their findings. Nevertheless, we were surprised to discover just how weak the empirics for traditional, psychodynamic approaches were, even as presented by advocates. We were also somewhat unprepared for the force of another, partly related, conclusion: effectiveness in treating all three syndromes seemed tied to the degree to which treatments encouraged real-life action, with a no-nonsense focus on facing the immediate and obvious feared situation. The direct approaches apparently had better outcomes, not just for target symptoms, but often in terms of more general assessments of relationships and life satisfactions. By contrast, the symbolic, indirect, and/or imagery-based methods repeatedly proved less effective.

In the area of depression, for example, Beck's direct and vigorous assaults on beliefs and his promptings to take appropriate action proved more effective than the somewhat more timid and less aggressively focused strategies. In treating compulsive disorders, the determined blocking of rituals (i.e., response prevention) in the context of renewed exposure to the feared stimulus (with participant modeling, if necessary) seemed to do the trick for many clients with whom just about every other treatment strategy (including surgery) had been tried and found wanting.

In dealing with fears (and the "fear of fears" which categorizes agoraphobia), a direct undercutting of the client's avoidant coping style proved most useful. Combinations of encouragement, demonstration, direction, and persuasion bring the client into rather prolonged contact with the feared situation until his or her system is forced to accommodate and assimilate. Pharmaceuticals, when used, appear most helpful as an adjunctive aid to this goal.

Some of the newer family and strategic approaches, as well as neurolinguistic programming and redecision therapy, can also be thought of as using potent direct-therapist interventions to produce concrete, positive action.

These, then, are the basic trends as we see them. We came away from this literature review with a definite sense of forward momentum and considerable optimism regarding forthcoming clarifications and innovations.

REFERENCES

Abramson, L. Y., Seligman, M. E. P., Teasdale, J. D. Learned helplessness in humans: Critique and reformulation. *Journal of Abnormal Psychology*, 1978, *87*, 49–74.

Agras, W. S., Chapin, H. N., & Oliveau, D. C. The natural history of phobia: Course and prognosis. *Archives of General Psychiatry*, 1972, *26*, 315–317.

Agras, W. S., Sylvester, D., & Oliveau, D. C. The epidemiology of common fears and phobia. *Comprehensive Psychiatry*, 1969, *10*, 151–156.

Akhtar, S., Wig, N. N., Varma, V. K., Pershad, D., & Verma, S. K. A phenomenological analysis of symptoms in obsessive-compulsive neurosis. *British Journal of Psychiatry*, 1975, *127*, 342–348.

Alloy, L. B., & Abramson, L. Y. Judgment of contingency in depressed and nondepressed students: Sadder but wiser? *Journal of Experimental Psychology: General.* 1979, *108*, 441–485.

Andrews, J. D. W. Psychotherapy of phobias. *Psychological Bulletin*, 1966, *66*, 455–480.

Bandler, R. & Grinder, J. *The structure of magic I.* Palo Alto, Calif.: Science & Behavior Books, 1975.

Bandler, R., & Grinder J. *Frogs into princes: Neuro-linguistic programming.* Moab, Utah: Real People Press, 1979.

Bandura, A. *Social learning theory.* Englewood Cliffs, N.J.: Prentice-Hall, 1977.

Barlow, D. H., Mavissakalian, M., & Hay, L. R. Couples treatment of agoraphobia: Changes in marital satisfaction. *Behavior Research and Therapy,* 1981, *19,* 245–255.

Bateson, G. *Mind and nature: A necessary unity.* New York: E. P. Dutton, 1979.

Beck, A. T. *The diagnosis and management of depression.* Philadelphia: University of Pennsylvania Press, 1973.

Beck, A. T., Rush, A. J., Shaw, B. F., & Emery, G. *Cognitive therapy of depression.* New York: Guilford Press, 1979.

Bergin, A. The evaluation of therapeutic outcomes. In A. Bergin & S. Garfield (Eds.), *Handbook of psychotherapy and behavior change.* New York: John Wiley & Sons, 1971.

Berne, E. *Games people play: The psychology of human relationships.* New York: Grove Press, 1964.

Black, A. The natural history of obsessional neurosis. In H. R. Beech (Ed.), *Obsessional states.* London: Methuen, 1974.

Bowen, M. *Family therapy in clinical practice.* New York: Jason Aronson, 1978.

Chambless, D. L., & Goldstein, A. J. Clinical treatment of agoraphobia. In M. Mavissakalian & D. H. Barlow (Eds.), *Phobia: Psychological and pharmacological treatment.* New York: Guilford Press, 1981.

Chessick, R. D. The treatment of neuroses and borderline cases. In B. B. Wolman (Ed.), *The therapist's handbook.* New York: Van Nostrand Reinhold, 1976.

Coleman, J. C., Butcher, J. N., & Carson, R. C. *Abnormal psychology and modern life* (6th ed.). Glenview, Ill.: Scott, Foresman, 1980.

Coleman, R. E. Cognitive-behavioral treatment of agoraphobia. In G. Emery, S. D. Hollon, & R. C. Bedrosian (Eds.), *New directions in cognitive therapy.* New York: Guilford Press, 1981.

Cooke, G. Evaluation of the efficacy of the components of reciprocal inhibition psychotherapy. *Journal of Abnormal Psychology,* 1968, *73,* 464–467.

Cooper, J. E., Gelder, M. G., & Marks, I. M. Results of behavior therapy in 77 psychiatric patients. *British Medical Journal,* 1965, *1,* 1222–1225.

deSilva, P., & Rachman, S. J. Is exposure a necessary condition for fear reduction? *Behavior Research and Therapy,* 1980, *19,* 227–232.

Efran, J. S., Ascher, L. M., Webb, R. E., & Moore, D. J. Should fearful individuals be instructed to proceed quickly or cautiously? *Journal of Clinical Psychology,* 1977, *33,* 535–539.

Ellis, A. Rational-emotive therapy: Research data that supports the clinical and personality hypotheses of RET and other modes of cognitive-behavior therapy. *The Counseling Psychologist,* 1977, *7,* 2–42.

Ellis, A. Rational-emotive therapy and cognitive-behavior therapy: Similarities and differences. *Cognitive Therapy and Research,* 1980, *4,* 325–340.

Emmelkamp, P. M. G. Phobias: Theoretical and behavioral treatment considerations. In J. C. Boulougouris & A. Rabavilas (Eds.), *Phobic and obsessive-compulsive disorders.* Elmsford, N.Y.: Pergamon Press, 1977.

Emmelkamp, P. M. G., & Kraanen, J. Therapist-controlled exposure in vivo versus self-controlled exposure in vivo: A comparison with obsessive-compulsive patients. *Behavior Research and Therapy,* 1977, *15,* 491–495.

Emmelkamp, P. M. G., Kuipers, A. C. M., & Eggeraat, J. B. Cognitive modification versus prolonged exposure in vivo: A comparison with agoraphobics as subjects. *Behavior Research and Therapy,* 1978, *16,* 33–42.

Errara, P., & Coleman, J. V. A long-term follow-up study of neurotic phobic patients in a psychiatric clinic. *Journal of Nervous and Mental Disease,* 1963, *136,* 267–271.

Eysenck, H. J. (Ed.). *Behavior therapy and the neuroses.* Elmsford, N.Y.: Pergamon Press, 1960.

Fenichel, O. *Problems of psychoanalytic technique.* Albany, N.Y.: Psychoanalytic Quarterly, 1941.

Foa, E. B. Failures in treating obsessive-compulsives. *Behavior Research and Therapy,* 1979, *17,* 169–176.

Foa, E. B., Blau, J. S., Prout, M., & Latimer, P. Is horror a necessary component of flooding (implosion)? *Behavior Research and Therapy,* 1977, *15,* 397–402.

Foa, E. B., & Goldstein, A. J. Continuous exposure and complete response prevention in the treatment of obsessive-compulsive neurosis. *Behavior Therapy,* 1978, *9,* 821–829.

Freud, S. (1919) Turnings in the ways of psychoanalytic therapy. In *Collected Papers* (Vol. 2, 1st American ed.). New York: Basic Books, 1959.

Friedman, R. J., & Katz, M. M. (Eds.). *The psychology of depression: Contemporary theory and research.* Washington, D.C.: Winston/Wiley, 1974.

Furst, J. B., & Cooper, A. Failure of systematic desensitization in two cases of obsessive-compulsive neurosis marked by fears of insecticide. *Behavior Research and Therapy,* 1970, *8,* 203–206.

Garfield, S. L., & Bergin, A. E. *Handbook of psychotherapy and behavior change: An empirical analysis* (2d ed.). New York: John Wiley & Sons, 1978.

Goldfried, M. R. Toward the delineation of therapeutic-change principles. *American Psychologist,* 1980, *35,* 991–999.

Goldstein, A. J. Case conference: The treatment of a case of agoraphobia by a multifaceted treatment program. *Journal of Behavior Therapy and Experimental Psychiatry.* 1978, *9,* 45–51.

Goldstein, A. J., & Chambless, D. L. A reanalysis of agoraphobia. *Behavior Therapy,* 1978, *9,* 47–59.

Goulding, M. M. & Goulding, R. L. *Changing lives through redecision therapy.* New York: Bruner & Mazel, 1979.

Hackmann, A., & McLean, C. A comparison of flooding and thought stopping in the treatment of obsessional neurosis. *Behavior Research and Therapy,* 1975, *13,* 263–269.

Hafner, J., & Marks, I. M. Exposure in vivo of agoraphobics: Contributions of diazepam, group exposure, and anxiety evocation. *Psychological Medicine,* 1976, *6,* 71–88.

Hare, E. H., Price, J. S., & Slater, E. T. Fertility in obsessional neurosis. *British Journal of Psychiatry,* 1972, *121,* 197–205.

Hineline, P. N. The language of behavior analysis: Its community, its functions, and its limitations. *Behaviorism,* 1980, *8,* 67–85.

Kelly, G. A. *The psychology of personal constructs* (2 vols.). New York: W. W. Norton, 1955.

Klein, M. H., Dittman, A. T., Parloff, M. B., & Gill, M. M. Behavior therapy: Observations and reflections. *Journal of Consulting and Clinical Psychology,* 1969, *33,* 259–266.

Klein, D. C. & Seligman, M. E. P. Reversal of performance deficits and perceptual deficits in learned helplessness and depression. *Journal of Abnormal Psychology,* 1976, *85,* 11–26.

Kovacs, M., Rush, A. J., Beck, A. T., & Hollon, S. D. Depressed outpatients treated with cognitive therapy or pharmacotherapy: A one-year follow-up. *Archives of General Psychiatry,* 1981, *38,* 33–39.

Kringlen, E. Natural history of obsessional neurosis. *Seminars in Psychiatry,* 1970, *2,* 403–419.

Ledwidge, B. Cognitive behavior modification: A step in the wrong direction? *Psychological Bulletin,* 1978, *85,* 353–375.

Ledwidge, B. Cognitive behavior modification or new ways to change minds: Reply to Mahoney and Kazdin. *Psychological Bulletin,* 1979, *86,* 1050–1053.

Leitenberg, H. (Ed.). *Handbook of behavior modification and behavior therapy.* Englewood Cliffs, N.J.: Prentice-Hall, 1976.

Leitenberg, H., & Callahan, E. J. Reinforced practice and reduction of different kinds of fears in adults and children. *Behavior Research and Therapy,* 1973, *11,* 19–30.

Levy, R., & Meyer, V. Ritual prevention in obsessional patients. *Proceedings of The Royal Society of Medicine,* 1971, *64,* 1115–1118.

Lewinsohn, P. M. A behavioral approach to depression. In R. J. Friedman & M. M. Katz (Eds.), *The psychology of depression: Contemporary theory and research.* Washington, D.C.: Winston, 1974.

Lewinsohn, P. M. Activity schedules in the treatment of depression. In J. D. Krumboltz & C. E. Thoresen (Eds.), *Counseling methods.* New York: Holt, Rinehart & Winston, 1976.

Mahoney, M. J. & Kazdin, A. E. Cognitive behavior modification: Misconceptions and premature evacuation. *Psychological Bulletin,* 1979, *86,* 1044–1049.

Maher, B. (Ed.). *Clinical psychology and personality: The selected papers of George Kelly.* New York: John Wiley & Sons, 1969.

Malan, D. H. *The frontier of brief psychotherapy.* New York: Plenum Press, 1976.

Marks, I. M. Behavioral psychotherapy of adult neurosis. In S. L. Garfield & A. E. Bergin (Eds.), *Handbook of psychotherapy and behavior change* (2nd ed.). New York: John Wiley & Sons, 1978.

Marks, I. M., Hallam, R. J., Connolly, J., & Philpott, R. *Nursing in behavioral psychotherapy.* London: Royal College of Nursing, 1976.

Marks, I. M., Stern, R. S., Mawson, D., Cobb, J., & McDonald, R. Clomipramine and exposure for obsessive-compulsive rituals. *British Journal of Psychiatry,* 1980, *136,* 1–25.

Mavissakalian, M., & Barlow, D. H. *Phobia: Psychological and pharmacological treatment.* New York: Guilford Press, 1981.

Mayer-Gross, W., Slater, E., & Roth, M. *Clinical psychiatry* (3d ed.). Baltimore: Williams & Wilkins, 1969.

McLean, P. D., & Hakstian, A. R. Clinical depression: Comparative efficacy of outpatient treatments. *Journal of Consulting and Clinical Psychology,* 1979, *47,* 818–836.

Meichenbaum, D. Cognitive modification of test-anxious college students. *Journal of Consulting and Clinical Psychology,* 1972, *39,* 370–380.

Meichenbaum, D. (Ed.). *Cognitive behavior modification: An integrative approach.* New York: Plenum Press, 1977.

Meichenbaum, D. Cognitive behavior modification: The need for a fairer assessment. *Cognitive Therapy and Research,* 1979, *3,* 127–132.

Meyer, V. Modification of expectation in cases with obsessional rituals. *Behavior Research and Therapy,* 1966, *4,* 273–280.

Meyer, V., Levy, R., & Schnurer, A. The behavioral treatment of obsessive-compulsive disorders. In H. R. Beech (Ed.), *Obsessional states.* London: Methuen, 1974.

Milton, F., & Hafner, J. The outcome of behavior therapy for agoraphobia in relation to marital adjustment. *Archives of General Psychiatry,* 1979, *36,* 807–811.

Minuchin, S. *Families and family therapy.* Cambridge, Mass.: Harvard University Press, 1974.

Minuchin, S., & Fishman, H. C. *Family therapy techniques.* Cambridge, Mass.: Harvard University Press, 1981.

Minuchin, S., Rosman, B. L., & Baker, L. *Psychosomatic families: Anorexia nervosa in context.* Cambridge, Mass.: Harvard University Press, 1978.

Noonan, J. R. An obsessive-compulsive reaction treated by induced anxiety. *American Journal of Psychotherapy,* 1971, *25,* 293–299.

Padfield, M. The comparative effects of two counseling approaches on the intensity of depression among rural women of low socioeconomic status. *Journal of Counseling Psychology,* 1976, *23,* 209–214.

Rabavilas, A. D., & Boulougouris, J. C. Mood changes and flooding outcome in obsessive-compulsive patients: Report of a two-year follow-up. *Journal of Nervous Mental Disease,* 1979, *167,* 495–496.

Rachman, S. J. The role of muscular relaxation in desensitization therapy. *Behavior Research and Therapy,* 1968, *6,* 159–166.

Rachman, S. J. Treatment by prolonged exposure to high intensity stimulation. *Behavior Research and Therapy,* 1969, *7,* 299–302.

Rachman, S. J., & Hodgson, R. J. *Obsessions and compulsions.* Englewood Cliffs, N.J.: Prentice-Hall, 1980.

Rachman, S. J., Hodgson, R. J., & Marks, I. M. The treatment of chronic obsessive-compulsive neurosis. *Behavior Research and Therapy,* 1971, *9,* 237–247.

Rachman, S. J., Marks, I. M., & Hodgson, R. J. The treatment of obsessive-compulsive neurotics by modeling and flooding in vivo. *Behavior Research and Therapy,* 1973, *11,* 463–471.

Rachman, S. J., & Wilson, G. T. *The effects of psychological therapy.* Elmsford, N.Y.: Pergamon Press, 1980.

Ritter, B. The use of contact desensitization, demonstration plus participation, and demonstration alone in the treatment of acrophobia. *Behavior Research and Therapy,* 1969, *7,* 157–164.

Roberts, A. H. Housebound housewives: A follow-up study of a phobic anxiety state. *British Journal of Psychiatry,* 1964, *110,* 191–197.

Roper, G., Rachman, S. J., & Hodgson, R. J. An experiment on obsessional checking. *Behavior Research and Therapy,* 1973, *11,* 271–277.

Rotter, J. B. *Social learning and clinical psychology.* Englewood Cliffs, N.J.: Prentice-Hall, 1954.

Rush, A. J., Beck, A. T., Kovacs, M., & Hollon, S. Comparative efficacy of cognitive therapy and imipramine in the treatment of depressed outpatients. *Cognitive Therapy and Research,* 1977, *1,* 17–37.

Rush, A. J., Khatami, M., & Beck, A. T. Cognitive and behavioral therapy in chronic depression. *Behavior Therapy,* 1975, *6,* 398–404.

Salzman, L. *Psychotherapy of the obsessive personality.* New York: Jason Aronson, 1980.

Salzman, L., & Thaler, F. H. Obsessive-compulsive disorders: A review of the literature. *American Journal of Psychiatry,* 1981, *138,* 286–296.

Sarbin, T. R. Ontology recapitulates philology: The mythic nature of anxiety. *American Psychologist,* 1968, *23,* 411–418.

Schulyer, D. Treatment of depressive disorders. In B. B. Wolman (Ed.), *The therapist's handbook.* New York: Van Nostrand Reinhold, 1976.

Seligman, M. E. P. Comment and integration. *Journal of Abnormal Psychology,* 1978, *87,* 165–179.

Seligman, M. E. P., Klein, D. C., & Miller, W. R. Depression. In H. Leitenberg (Ed.), *Handbook of behavior modification and behavior therapy.* Englewood Cliffs, N.J.: Prentice-Hall, 1976.

Shaw, B. F. Comparison of cognitive therapy and behavior therapy in the treatment of depression. *Journal of Consulting and Clinical Psychology,* 1977, *45,* 543–551.

Sifneos, P. E. *Short-term dynamic psychotherapy.* New York: Plenum Press, 1979.

Smith, M. L., Glass, G. V., & Miller, T. I. *The benefits of psychotherapy.* Baltimore: Johns Hopkins University Press, 1980.

Sookman, D., & Solyom, L. The effectiveness of four behavior therapies in the treatment of obsessive neurosis. In J. C. Boulougouris & A. D. Rabavilas (Eds.), *The treatment of phobic and obsessive-compulsive disorders.* Elmsford, N.Y.: Pergamon Press, 1977.

Stampfl, T. G., & Levis, D. J. Essentials of implosive therapy: A learning-theory-based psychodynamic behavioral therapy. *Journal of Abnormal Psychology,* 1967, *6,* 496–503.

Stern, R. S., Lipsedge, M. S., & Marks, I. M. Obsessive ruminations: A controlled trial of thought-stopping technique. *Behavior Research and Therapy,* 1973, *11,* 659–662.

Stern, R. S., & Marks, I. M. A comparison of brief and prolonged flooding in agoraphobics. *Archives of General Psychiatry,* 1973, *28,* 210.

Sternberg, M. Physical treatments in obsessional disorders. In H. R. Beech (Ed.), *Obsessional states.* London: Methuen, 1974.

Templer, D. I. The obsessive-compulsive neurosis: Review of research findings. *Comprehensive Psychiatry,* 1972, *13,* 375–383.

Watzlawick, P., Weakland, J. H., & Fisch, R. *Change: Principles of problem formation and problem resolution.* New York: W. W. Norton, 1974.

Weakland, J. H., Fisch, R., Watzlawick, P., & Bodin, A. M. Brief therapy: Focused problem resolution. *Family Process,* 1974, *13,* 141–168.

Weekes, C. *Simple effective treatment of agoraphobia.* New York: Bantam Books, 1976.

Weissman, M. M., Klerman, G. L., Prusoff, B. A., Scholomskas, D., & Padian, N. Depressed outpatients: Results one year after treatment with drugs and/or interpersonal psychotherapy. *Archives of General Psychiatry,* 1981, *1,* 51–55.

Wolpe, J. *Psychotherapy by reciprocal inhibition.* Stanford, Calif.: Stanford University Press, 1958.

Zeiss, A. M., Lewinsohn, P. M., & Munoz, R. F. Nonspecific improvement effects in depression using interpersonal-skills training, pleasant-activity schedules, or cognitive training. *Journal of Consulting and Clinical Psychology,* 1979, *47,* 427–439.

Zitrin, C. M. Combined pharmacological and psychological treatment of phobias. In M. Mavissakalian & D. H. Barlow (Eds.), *Phobia: Psychological and pharmacological treatment.* New York: Guilford Press, 1981.

Zitrin, C. M., Klein, D. F., & Woerner, M. G. Behavior therapy, supportive psychotherapy, imipramine, and phobia. *Archives of General Psychiatry,* 1978, *35,* 307–316.

17

Treatment of schizophrenia

Ian R. H. Falloon
Stephen Flanagan
David Foy
Robert Paul Liberman

David Lukoff
Stephen Marder
Byron Wittlin

Schizophrenia, one of the most prevalent and disabling of the mental illnesses, intrudes upon almost every area of human functioning in those whom it afflicts. The signs of acute episodes are characteristic symptoms of bizarre, religious, persecutory, and grandiose delusions; auditory hallucinations; incoherence; and belief that one's thoughts and actions are being controlled by outside forces or persons. Chronic impairments of apathy, social withdrawal, poverty of speech, and empty or flat affect mark the residual stage of the illness. Thoughts that are irrational, slowed cognitive processing, perceptual distortions, emotional blunting or lability, loss of problem-solving skills, social retraction, loss of instrumental role functioning, and impairments in self-care skills comprise the clinical syndrome of schizophrenia.

Treatment of schizophrenia is a major challenge to the mental health professions, since the disorder appears to occur universally in about 1 percent of the population. Within the United States, each year 100,000 to 200,000 people are afflicted by this disorder. It has been estimated that the total direct and indirect cost of schizophrenia in the United States is upward of $19 billion—close to 2 percent of the gross national product (Gunderson & Mosher, 1975).

A stress-diathesis model for understanding factors that influence the onset and course of schizophrenia helps to point clinicians in directions that may be therapeutically fruitful. The appearance or increase in characteristic schizophrenia symptoms may occur in a susceptible individual when:

1. The underlying biological diathesis or vulnerability increases.

All authors affiliated with Mental Health Clinical Research Center for the Study of Schizophrenia; Rehabilitation Research and Training Center for Mental Illness, Los Angeles.

2. Stressful life events intervene that overwhelm the individual's coping skills in social and instrumental roles.
3. The individual's social-support network weakens or diminishes.
4. Social problem-solving skills, that the individual previously had in his/her repertoire, wither as a result of:
    a. Disuse or institutionalism.
    b. Reinforcement of the sick role.
    c. Loss of motivation, interest, and pleasure in socializing.

From this conceptual framework, biological, environmental, and behavioral factors play interacting parts in the genesis, exacerbation, and remission of schizophrenic symptoms. An increase or reappearance of symptoms in a person biologically vulnerable to schizophrenia is an outcome of the balance between the amount of threat of life stressors on the one hand, and the problem-solving capacities of the individual and his/her social support network on the other. Either too much environmental change, or stressors, or too little coping skills and social support can lead to symptomatic flare-ups. The significance of this bi-directional model of symptom formation lies in the emphasis given to the active role of the patient's coping skills and support network in reducing vulnerability to schizophrenia.

Therefore, treatment of schizophrenia can logically proceed from several points of departure. The clinician can prescribe neuroleptic medication to reduce the underlying biological diathesis. From another angle, environmental modification can be employed to reduce the level of stressors impinging on the vulnerable individual—this accounts for some of the value of hospitalization, in which the patient is removed, temporarily, from stressors which may be occurring in the family or community settings. Alternatively, treatment can emphasize strengthening the patient's social-support network, as is the case in using family and group therapies. Finally, increasing the patient's resilience through training of social and problem-solving skills can also reduce likelihood of relapse. Because schizophrenia is such an elusive and severely pathological disorder, it is often necessary and desirable to employ all of the above treatment strategies concurrently in efforts to help an afflicted person. This chapter will contain brief descriptions of currently available treatment methods for use in schizophrenia.

PSYCHOPHARMACOTHERAPY

In 1952, chlorpromazine was first administered to schizophrenic and manic patients in two Paris hospitals. Clinicians quickly appreciated the importance of this new agent and, within a year, mental hospitals throughout the city had been dramatically altered. Straitjackets, seclusion, and the smell of human excrement became uncommon. Patients who previously might have spent years in the hospital could be discharged to their families.

The use of chlorpromazine spread rapidly, reaching the western hemisphere in 1954. Although some individuals may have been aided by psychotherapy, electroconvulsive treatment, or insulin coma, these treatments never reached the majority of institutionalized patients, probably because they are expensive and of questionable effectiveness. Drugs were inexpensive and did not require major changes in mental hospitals. They, therefore, could be administered to vast numbers of patients who had never been exposed to an active treatment. The effects of chlorpromazine were dramatic and led to a revolution in psychiatric treatment. Primarily as a result of drug treatment, large numbers of schizophrenic patients could be discharged from mental hospitals to live in the community. This led to a dramatic decrease in the number of inpatients in state hospitals.

In the years since chlorpromazine first became available, dozens of other drugs with similar chemical structures and therapeutic effects have come into clinical use. The term *neuroleptics* has gained acceptance as perhaps the most reasonable term for classifying all of these agents, since it recognizes that all of these drugs affect behavior and also have direct effects on the nervous system. The widely used term *major tranquilizer* seems inappropriate as some of these drugs are not at all sedating. Other commonly used terms (which are interchangeable with neuroleptic) are *antipsychotic* and *antischizophrenic*. Neuroleptics are classified according to chemical structure (See Table 1), with phenothiazine, butyrophenones, and thioxanthines being the most common. Although new neuroleptic classes are likely to become available in the future, as yet these new types have not been demonstrated to be superior to currently available compounds.

Effects of neuroleptics on acutely ill patients

Chlorpromazine is among the most sedating of the many neuroleptics available. This may explain the common impression that neuroleptics attenuate psychosis by merely calming the patient. In fact, an extensive amount of evidence suggests that these drugs are specifically antipsychotic.

The first well-executed trial of neuroleptics was performed by an NIMH Collaborative Study Group in the early 60s (Cole, 1964) and still serves as a model for clinical psychopharmacology research. Schizophrenic patients admitted to six different hospitals were randomly assigned either to neuroleptics or to a placebo. Patients on drugs improved to a much greater extent than did patients on placebo. The neuroleptics attenuated nearly all symptoms or behaviors which comprise the schizophrenic spectrum. Drugs calmed patients whose psychosis was manifested by excitement and overactivity, but they also stimulated patients who were with-

Table 1

Some characteristics of selected neuroleptics

Family name	Generic name	Brand name	Usual dose range (mg/day)	Sedative	EPS	Hypotensive
Phenothiazines	Chlorpromazine	Thorazine	300–800	+++	++	IM +++ Oral ++
	Mesoridazine	Serentil	75–300	+++	+	++
	Thioridazine	Mellaril	200–600	+++	+	++
	Fluphenozine	Prolixin	Oral 2.5–20; Decanoate 6–50 mg; IM every 7–28 days	+	+++	+
	Trifluoperazine	Stelazine	6–20	+	+++	+
Butyrophenones	Haloperidol	Haldol	6–20	+	+++	+
Thioxanthines	Thothixene	Navane	6–30	+ or ++	++	++
	Loxapine	Loxitane	60–100	+	++	+
	Molindone	Moban	50–225	++	+	0

Side effects

Source: Adapted from Baldessarini, 1980.

drawn and apathetic. At the close of six weeks of treatment, drug-treated patients had greater improvement than placebo-treated patients in common schizophrenic symptoms, such as auditory hallucinations, delusions of persecution, and incoherent speech. Drug-treated patients participated more actively in their social milieu and were less indifferent to their environment.

The NIMH findings, along with subsequent data from many other controlled studies, suggest a basis for treating acutely psychotic schizophrenic patients. All available neuroleptics are approximately equally effective, although their side effects or route of administration may differ. Positive symptoms (such as hallucinations or delusions) are relieved or eliminated in most patients; while negative deficits (such as poor judgment, social withdrawal, personality deterioration, and emotional blunting) are less responsive to drugs.

Schizophrenic patients differ markedly in their responses to neuroleptics. Although some patients improve within hours of receiving their first dose, many patients require several weeks of treatment before improvements become obvious. Patients may also show remarkable differences in the dose of medication required, with some needing as much as 20 times the amount adequate for another individual.

Drug treatment for prevention of relapse

Following recovery from an acute psychotic episode, the clinician is confronted with the problem of whether or not to continue patients on drug treatment. Substantial evidence justifies maintaining patients on neuroleptics, even if the individual is psychosis-free. Davis (1975) reviewed 24 double-blind studies of maintenance neuroleptic therapy with over 3,000 patients and found that, in all studies, many more patients relapsed on placebo than on drugs. When the results were pooled, 65 percent of patients on placebo relapsed, in contrast to only 30 percent of patients on drugs.

The demonstration of maintenance of pharmacotherapy's effectiveness in groups of patients does not mean that this mode of treatment prevents relapse in all patients or that all patients should receive it. A certain proportion of patients—3 to 49 percent in the studies reviewed by Davis— relapsed despite continuation on drugs. Schizophrenic patients are notoriously poor at complying with aftercare-treatment plans, and a substantial number—63 percent in one study—do not take their medication as prescribed. Perhaps most seriously, continuous neuroleptic use predisposes patients to tardive dyskinesia, a long-term neurological side effect consisting of involuntary muscle spasms, which is frequently irreversible.

The above problems have led to a recent reevaluation of maintenance treatment. For many schizophrenic patients—probably more than half— the risks and discomforts of long-term neuroleptic therapy are clearly outweighed by the substantial benefits of drug. In many of these individuals, psychotic relapse can be extremely costly in terms of lost jobs, diminished self-esteem, and unfulfilled family responsibilities. In other patients, long-term neuroleptic use may be more difficult to justify, and drug discontinuation should be considered. All patients should be treated on the lowest drug dose which maintains the remission.

Side effects

Extrapyramidal side effects (EPS) are the most common and the most troublesome neuroleptic side effects. Akathisia, the most common category of EPS, is a subjective feeling of motor restlessness which may be manifest in an urge to pace and an inability to sit still. The Parkinsonian syndrome consists of various motor behaviors, including: tremor at rest, a shuffling gait, slowness of movement, masklike facial expression, and rigidity. Neuroleptic-treated patients, when overmedicated, appear similar to patients with Parkinson's disease. The third type of EPS, dyskinesias, consists of involuntary, stereotyped movements of the mouth, face, limbs, or trunk. Dystonias may appear as severe spasms of the tongue, neck, or limbs. All forms of EPS are treatable by adding antiparkinson drugs (e.g., benztropine or trihexphenidyl), changing the patient to a neuroleptic with less EPS (See Table 1), or by lower drug dose. Since these reactions may be extremely uncomfortable, they should be treated as soon as possible.

Tardive dyskinesia is a form of EPS which usually appears after years of treatment with neuroleptics. It is characterized by a number of abnormal movements, any single one or combination of which may be seen. Common are abnormal mouth and tongue movements (such as lip smacking or puckering), facial grimacing, and irregular movements of the limbs, trunk, and fingers. Tardive dyskinesias are of great concern because, in many cases, they remain even after drugs are discontinued. Although they are mild in most afflicted individuals, a small percentage of patients have symptoms which affect walking, breathing, eating, and talking. At present, we are without acceptable treatments for this condition, except for dosage reduction or discontinuing of the offending drug, both of which may be impossible. In any case, the existence of tardive dyskinesia makes it important that clinicians consider carefully the possible dangers of unnecessary or overly prolonged neuroleptic use.

Neuroleptics cause a variety of side effects related to their effects on the autonomic nervous system. In particular, drowsiness, dizziness, dry mouth, urinary hesitancy, and blurred vision are common complaints. In most cases, these problems pass after several days of the drug treatment although drowsiness may restrict the use of certain drugs. Other important side effects include abnormal lactation and menstrual irregularities in some women, erectile and ejaculatory difficulties in some men, as well as uncommon skin and eye effects.

Interaction of pharmacotherapy and psychotherapy

Early prejudices against the use of drugs in schizophrenia led some individuals to assert that neuroleptic drugs interfere with the psychotherapy of schizophrenic patients. There is little or no evidence to support this viewpoint. In fact, considerable research supports the very opposite point of view: namely, that the ability of schizophrenic patients to engage in psychotherapy and other psychosocial treatments is enhanced by drug treatment.

The first systematic study of the interaction of drugs and psychotherapy was done by May and his associates with state-hospital patients. Individuals were randomly assigned to: (1) individual psychotherapy , (2) trifluoperazine, (3) the two treatments combined, or (4) neither treatment. Patients receiving psychotherapy alone did about the same as patients receiving neither treatment; while patients receiving psychotherapy plus drug did only slightly better than patients receiving drug alone. Although this study often has been criticized with regard to the experience of the psychotherapists—therapists had between six months and six years of experience—it probably reflects reasonably well a comparison of treatments as they are actually administered at most facilities. May's results provide strong support for drugs as the primary treatment modality for the acutely ill, hospitalized patient (May, 1968).

Other studies suggest that psychotherapy may actually be enhanced when patients are treated with drugs. Grinspoon, Ewalt, and Shader (1972), for example, found that schizophrenic patients were more responsive to psychotherapy when they were also treated with a drug. The weight of research evidence strongly discourages treating severely psychotic schizophrenic patients without drugs and with psychotherapy alone.

Considerable evidence suggests that drug-treated patients discharged to the community may be helped by psychotherapy. Hogarty and his co-workers at the NIMH (1974) conducted a large collaborative study in which stabilized outpatients were assigned to one of four groups— placebo, placebo plus major role sociotherapy, drug, and drug plus sociotherapy. Major role sociotherapy is a reality-oriented, supportive, problem-solving approach administered by an experienced psychiatric social worker. Drugs reduced relapse rates to a substantial degree, as one would expect. Sociotherapy alone did not have a substantial effect in preventing relapse. However, sociotherapy did have a positive effect on the patients who remained in remission and did not require rehospitalization. These individuals demonstrated better social functioning than those who did not receive major role therapy. Optimal outpatient care of schizophrenics usually requires a combination of neuroleptic drugs and some form of psychosocial treatment, including behavior modification, social-skills training, or family therapy—all of which are described in subsequent sections.

Psychopharmacotherapy: Summary

The use of neuroleptics for treating schizophrenic patients has revolutionized psychiatric treatment. Largely as a result of drug treatment, a large proportion of severely ill patients can be managed in the community rather than in mental hospitals. As with many medical treatments, the risks and costs of psychotic relapse need to be weighed against the risks of long-term drug effects, such as tardive dyskinesia. This requires individualizing the treatment of each patient. Certain individuals, especially those with reasonable insight, may benefit from interrupted drug treatment with neuroleptics reinstituted at the first sign of psychotic deterioration. In all cases, patients should be treated with the lowest dose of drug which provides adequate protection.

MILIEU THERAPY

If we consider the psychiatric milieu as the general therapeutic background upon which specific treatment interventions for psychiatric patients are superimposed, we can classify milieu according to their residential versus nonresidential nature, duration, purpose, and theoretical approach (Liberman, 1981). Some therapy settings are time limited, transitional, supportive, and temporary, with the goal of speedy return of the patients to their natural living environments. Examples are short-term psychiatric units in general and psychiatric hospitals, community mental health centers, or half-way houses. Others, such as board and care homes, custodial units at state mental hospitals, and domiciliaries at Veterans Administration hospitals, provide indefinite, long-term life and social support. Still others combine elements of short- and long-term programs, such as day hospitals, and psychosocial rehabilitation programs like Fountain House.

Positive milieu characteristics

Some structural and functional elements of inpatient settings appear related to therapeutic outcome; for example, the size of a treatment unit correlates inversely with various outcome measures (Ullmann, 1967). Short-duration inpatient stays may be as effective as longer stays; partial hospitalization (day treatment) may be as effective as inpatient care (Herz, 1977). Heterogeneity of a patient population in such characteristics as chronicity, social participation, and instrumental role skills appears to favor good outcome. Possibly secondary to modeling, interpersonal stimulation, and staff reinforcement, a mixture of 2/3 high-functioning and 1/3 low-functioning patients may produce optimal outcome for all (Fairweather, Sanders, Cressler, & Maynard, 1969). High levels of staff/patient interaction have been shown to be beneficial to post-hospital adjustment and on-ward behavioral improvement. Improvements in patient behavior occur when staff focuses on adaptive behavior rather than on symptomatic, maladaptive behavior or upon interpretations of psychopathology (VanPutten & May, 1976). The behavior therapy literature indicates that staff attention and interaction with patients can improve or worsen patients' behavior, depending on how, when, and on what the attention is focused (Liberman, McCann, & Wallace, 1976).

The optimal characteristics for an inpatient milieu are somewhat different for acute schizophrenics than for chronic patients. The recovery of acute patients is promoted by highly staffed, accepting, supportive, stimulus-decreasing, relatively long-stay environments where psychosocial interventions are viewed positively (Mosher & Keith, 1979). Four specific-milieu characteristics have been found to result in better post-hospital psychosocial adjustment for these patients: (1) small size, (2) positive staff expectations, (3) line staff who are actively involved in treatment planning and actual treatment [associated with increased staff investment and increased morale], and (4) a practical, down-to-earth, problem-solving orientation.

Treatment outcome comparisons

Paul and Lentz's study of milieu therapy (therapeutic community) versus a social-learning program (token economy) remains the premier study of inpatient milieus for chronic patients (Paul & Lentz, 1977). Milieu therapy is characterized by group activities, increased social interactions, and group pressure directed toward normal function. It promotes treating patients as responsible individuals capable of making independent decisions and utilizing greater freedom of movement. Social-learning therapy utilizes response-contingent reinforcement rather than group pressure to promote change. This is a logical extension of experimental behavioral-learning principles.

Paul and Lentz concluded that chronic patients respond best to a highly structured and organized, high-expectation milieu based on the social-learning approach, oriented toward specific behavioral change. Operational, step-wise, and time-limited goals are important in this approach. Long- and short-term goals and procedures for bringing them about are clearly and specifically defined. Feedback on patients' progress, publicly displayed in easy-to-understand language or graphics, facilitates clinical improvement.

Post-hospital adjustment of chronic patients is related to four factors:

(1) how well they learn adaptive behaviors and skills; (2) how well their bizarre, symptomatic, and maladaptive behaviors are suppressed; (3) whether continuation of therapeutic intervention is available in the community; and (4) whether social-support systems are available to the patient indefinitely (Liberman et al., 1976; Paul & Lentz, 1977). With a social-learning approach, continued aftercare, and adequate community-residential resources, as much as a 90 percent improvement and discharge rate for very chronic patients can be achieved with less than a 5 percent rehospitalization rate over 2 years (Paul & Lentz, 1977).

Milieu therapy: Summary

The findings of recent milieu studies show consistency and clinical relevance applicable to many existing hospital and aftercare programs. In particular, the shift to shorter hospital stays and the development of programs based on behavior therapy models can contribute to improved deinstitutionalization of the schizophrenic patient. Inpatient treatment for chronic patients must be integrated with community-based, psychosocial rehabilitation efforts aimed at maintaining and increasing the functional independence of patients in the community—ability to work, levels of social and interpersonal skills, life skills, and quality of living conditions. The rate of recidivism or rehospitalization may have only a modest relationship to social adjustment for schizophrenics (Mosher & Keith, 1979).

SOCIAL-SKILLS TRAINING

The advent of neuroleptic drugs in the treatment of schizophrenia allowed for deinstitutionalization of hundreds of thousands of chronic mental patients in the 1960s and 1970s. Initially, it was assumed that the patients' quality of life would improve as they were reintegrated into local community, residential, and social networks. However, it is now apparent that the neuroleptic regimen is a necessary (but not sufficient) treatment component for most chronic schizophrenics. For improvement to occur in the interpersonal quality of life, psychosocial interventions are necessary. Drug control of cognitive aberrations and psychotic symptoms, per se, does not promote the acquisition of essential instrumental and social behaviors which many chronic patients require for survival in the community.

Social-skills definition

Applying behavior-analysis principles to identify and remediate deficits in social behaviors, clinicians have developed a treatment package termed *social-skills training* that has proved effective with schizophrenics (Liberman, King, DeRisi, & McCann, 1975; Bellack & Hersen, 1979; Wallace, Nelson, Liberman, Aitchison, Lukoff, Elder, & Ferris, 1980; Liberman et al., 1980). Although specific definitions of social skills may vary across researchers or clinicians, the common, general concept refers to those interpersonal behaviors which an individual uses (1) to accomplish instrumental goals, and (2) to establish and maintain social relationships. Affective, cognitive, and motoric behavioral domains are included, as well as verbal and nonverbal modalities of communication. For example, Hersen and Bellack (1977) describe social skills as the ability to

> express both positive and negative feelings in the interpersonal context without suffering consequent loss of social reinforcement. Such skill is demonstrated in a large variety of interpersonal contexts and involves the coordinated delivery of appropriate verbal and nonverbal responses. In addition, the socially skilled individual is attuned to the realities of the situation and is aware when he is likely to be reinforced for his efforts. (p. 512)

Wallace and his colleagues place socially skilled behaviors into "receiving," "processing," and "sending" categories. Receiving skills are those cognitive behaviors necessary for accurate reception of interpersonal stimuli; processing skills are cognitive behaviors associated with evaluating response options and selecting an appropriate one; and sending skills are the verbal and nonverbal motor behaviors necessary to present the selected option in the interpersonal context (Wallace et al., 1980).

Social-skills training methods

In virtually all published reports of social-skills training, *role-playing* is the vehicle used both to assess patients' pre-treatment social competence and to train targeted behavioral excesses or deficits during treatment. Training scenes are selected either on the basis of the *individual's* past difficulties or from problem situations which have been found to apply to most of the psychiatric *population* to which the patient belongs. Reported training sessions vary in length from 15 to 90 minutes and are offered in individual or group formats. Individual training allows more intensive focus on a single patient's behavior and opportunity for more practice within sessions; while the group format provides vicarious learning opportunities from observation of other patients' behaviors. Advantages and disadvantages of the two formats have been outlined in manuals for clinicians (Liberman et al., 1975; Trower, Bryant, & Argyle, 1978).

Participants in the role-playing include the patient(s), a respondent, and the trainer (therapist). In most reports, focused instructions, modeling, feedback, and social reinforcement are applied as a package to remediate target behaviors. Modeling and feedback are accomplished in vivo or through videotape playback. Target behaviors selected for change usually include both *process* behaviors (e.g., eye contact, voice loudness or intonation, response latency, smiles, or other affective behaviors) and *content* behaviors (e.g., requests for change, compliance, hostile comments, irrelevant remarks). The sine qua non of social-skills training is the specificity of the behaviors which are targeted for change.

Related literature

Since 1971, when Serber and Nelson published one of the earliest applications of social-skills training with schizophrenic patients, approximately 35 other published studies have appeared. Many of the studies used single-case designs which inherently limit the generality of the findings. The few published group-design studies are also limited in external validity, because they failed to adequately define the patient population and control for medication effects (Wallace et al., 1980). However, there is convergence across studies with respect to several findings. First, schizophrenic patients can be trained to improve social skills in specific situations in a treatment setting. Second, moderate generalization of acquired skills to similar situations can be expected in the treatment setting. Third, participants in the training consistently report decreases in social anxiety after training.

There are also findings that limit the applicability of social-skills training. Generalization of content-based, complex conversational skills is less likely than for other, more discrete nonverbal process/content. Since complex behaviors are more critical for generating social support in the community, methods are under development to improve the learning of and durability of conversational skills (Wallace, 1981). Another limitation of social-skills training is the lack of evidence that generalization of skills occurs in the natural environment in the absence of therapist prompting.

That newly acquired social skills are presently bound to the treatment setting may not be an insurmountable problem. It is possible to employ methods that help to bridge the gap between training and utilization of skills in the real world. Future efforts can focus on training *in the natural environment* either as an adjunct to training in the treatment facility or as the exclusive training site. In addition, training can be tailored to include the patient's actual significant others (e.g., spouse, parent, friends, or employer) instead of surrogate, role-playing respondents. Patient-therapist contact can be continued over a longer period of time to provide for repeated practice, overlearning, and extensive booster treatments (including problem-solving assistance and prompting) as well as additional social-skills training. Finally, generalization can be spurred by designing treatment methods and goals that address the specific psychological deficits and community stressors experienced by schizophrenics (Liberman, Wallace, & Nuechterlein, 1981).

Social-skills training: Summary

In summary, current studies demonstrate that social-skills training improves schizophrenics' social competence and self-reported social anxiety when assessed in the treatment setting. Generalization of trained skills to situations occurring in the natural environment is the major limitation of existing approaches. Providing treatment in the natural environment over a longer period of time within a continuing therapeutic relationship is suggested as a viable future direction for clinical and research efforts.

BEHAVIOR THERAPY

The clinical and research literature on behavior therapy with schizophrenic patients is dominated by two primary treatment modalities: structured inpatient-treatment programs organized around token economies (Kazdin, 1977; Paul & Lentz, 1977), and social-skills training (Hersen & Bellack, 1976; Wallace et al., 1980). This research has demonstrated that schizophrenic patients can be helped to establish or reestablish self-help and independent-living skills, work patterns, and social and recreational participation, as well as to improve their interpersonal skills, comfort, and effectiveness. To maximize the efficacy of a treatment program, however, the clinician will want to tailor interventions to the specific behavioral excesses and deficits of the individual. Especially in cases of extreme behavioral excesses (such as delusions, hallucinations, and aggression), it is often necessary to supplement wardwide programs with intensive, individualized training and contingency-management programs. Such an individual focus may also be necessary to prepare a patient for subsequent participation in structured group programming, for example, when delusional talk interferes with social-skills training or when severe aggression limits a patient's ability to participate in a token-economy program.

Treatment programs will be reviewed which are aimed at amelioration of three major problem areas of schizophrenic patients: delusions, hallucinations, and aggression. It should be noted that decelerating or eliminating maladaptive behavior is rarely sufficient, in itself, to promote adaptive functioning. In the context of positive programming to shape or reestablish functional skills, however, deceleration techniques are appropriate and often necessary (Flanagan & Liberman, 1982).

Delusions

Delusions are beliefs which are at variance with reality, or operationally, "unrealistic verbal statements made when the patient is talking to another person" (Davis, Wallace, Liberman, & Finch, 1976). Ayllon and Haughton (1964) first demonstrated that delusional behavior is under the control of contingencies of reinforcement. Efforts to reduce or eliminate delusional talk have often employed differential reinforcement, in which delusions are extinguished by ignoring, and rational talk is concurrently reinforced with attention, praise, or material or activity incentives (Rickard, Dignam, & Horner, 1960; Rickard & Dinoff, 1962; Wincze, Leitenberg, & Agras, 1972).

Time-out from reinforcement has been applied contingent on delusions. Time-out consists of a reduction in the opportunity to engage in reinforcing activities and is effected by interrupting ongoing activities, or removing the patient to another area where reinforcement is unavailable. Davis et al., (1976) controlled delusions with brief time-out in a quiet area for each delusional response emitted and observed an increase in rational talk from 42 percent of observations in baseline to 92 percent in treatment. Cayner and Kiland (1974) also employed brief periods of time-out for delusions. Delusions brought under control in one situation may continue to occur in other situations (Liberman, Teigen, Patterson, & Baker, 1973; Wincze et al., 1972). Explicit programming for generalization and maintenance, and treatment in the patient's natural environment may facilitate generalization (Liberman, Wallace, Tergen, & Davis, 1974).

Controversy exists over potential adverse effects of eliminating delusional talk; the behavioral intervention may not eliminate the delusion but only suppress the patient's talking about the symptom (Gomez-Schwartz, 1979; Stahl & Leitenberg, 1976). Anecdotally, Schaefer and Martin (1975) reported that after token fines eliminated delusions for a period of time, a patient who was given the opportunity to verbalize her delusions showed a changed and weakened delusional system. They comment, ". . . while suppressing verbal references may not eliminate delusions per se, these references are nevertheless strong maintainers of a delusion. Deprived of verbal self-descriptive support, delusions seem to slowly die away" (p. 162). If the total treatment program is focused on establishing and maintaining a wide range of skills and adaptive behavior, the chances of other reinforced behaviors supplanting delusions in the patients' repertoire are increased.

Hallucinations

Hallucinations, as traditionally defined, present a problem for behavior analysis: if the hallucination is an auditory or visual perception with no appropriate external stimulus, then it is observable only by the patient. Strategies for behavioral assessment have included self-reports; defining the hallucination in terms of observable motor behavior, such as gestures and speech not directed to a listener; or observing disruptions in ongoing behavior as an index of hallucinatory behavior (Wallace, 1976; Alevizos & Callahan, 1977).

Bucher and Fabricatore (1970) employed self-administered shock to reduce the frequency of self-reported hallucinations. In a group study, Weingaertner (1971) found equivalent reductions in self-reported hallucinations for groups giving self-administered shocks, placebo ("subliminal shock"), and a control group. However, only the shock and placebo groups improved on symptom ratings. Therapist-administered shock, with patient cooperation, reduced hallucinatory behavior in two studies (Anderson & Alpert, 1974; Alford & Turner, 1976).

Liberman et al. (1974) investigated massed practice techniques in reducing self-reports and motoric behavior associated with hallucinations. In daily sessions, patients verbalized hallucinations or listened to recordings of hallucinatory content for 30 minutes. It was hypothesized that the response repetition would classically condition the hallucinatory content to the aversive conditions of boredom, satiation, and fatigue. Results were promising, although the authors noted the tentativeness of conclusions which could be drawn from a case study without a reversal condition.

Assaultive and disruptive behaviors

Wallace (1976) noted that, despite their importance, verbal and physical abusive behaviors have received limited attention in studies of behavior therapy with psychotic patients. Given the restrictiveness and aversiveness of emergency interventions employed with aggression in inpatient settings (such as restraint, seclusion, and sedative drugs), research to identify and evaluate effective treatments should be a high priority for the behavioral clinician. Promising alternatives include time-out and overcorrection.

Time-out. Case studies including the application of time-out for assaultive and disruptive behavior were reported by Liberman et al. (1974). For one patient, 15 minutes of time-out for each instance of banging doors reduced the frequency from 60 times per week to zero; for another patient, 15 minutes of time-out led to a 90 percent reduction of assaults and threats (from 21 incidents per week to 2 per week). These case studies provide excellent examples of how several interventions, including token economy, differential reinforcement, social-skills training, and aversive or restrictive interventions, can be integrated for maximum effectiveness. Paul and Lentz (1977) combined time-out and token fines for intolerable behaviors including aggression, severe disruption, and AWOL. Noteworthy in their study was the observation that chronic patients with severe assaultive behavior could be controlled with long durations of time-out when shorter durations were ineffective. A natural reversal-precipitated by new state policies limiting time-out durations—demonstrated the strong control over assaults exerted by the procedures and highlighted the disruptiveness to patients' progress effected by high rates of uncontrolled aggression in the inpatient setting.

Overcorrection. Developed initially with the mentally retarded (Foxx & Azrin, 1972), overcorrection combines elements of response-contingent punishment and skills and training. A person is required to make restitution, restoring the environment to a better condition than it was prior to the maladaptive behavior (restitutional overcorrection); and to practice appropriate responses repeatedly (positive-practice overcorrection), immediately after the occurrence of a maladaptive behavior. Klinge,

Thrasher, and Myers (1975) required chronic schizophrenics to lie on a bed contingent on disruptive behavior, with dramatic successes. Sumner, Mueser, Hsu, and Morales (1974) required four female patients to formulate an apology and promise to refrain from the behavior contingent on assault, property destruction, and verbal abuse. In a series of studies on overcorrection, Matson (1980) successfully applied overcorrection with behaviors such as throwing objects at other people, stereotypic behaviors, self-injury, and encopresis in chronic schizophrenics.

Behavior therapy: Summary

Schizophrenic patients exhibit a number of behavioral excesses and deficits for which individualized behavioral interventions are appropriate. Individual programs are most needed for bizarre behavior, including delusions and hallucinations, and for aggressive and disruptive behavior. These problems are often too little affected by token economy and social-skills training programs. A number of the interventions reviewed here are intrusive and potentially controversial—response-contingent electric shock, long time-out, overcorrection—and should only be considered when positive-reinforcement procedures, and less-restrictive or aversive alternatives have been considered, tried, or ruled out. Attention to ethical issues is necessary, such as maximizing the patient's participation in treatment planning, obtaining consent for interventions, and carefully evaluating the goals of treatment to be sure they are for the patient's benefit and not for institutional or staff convenience.

PSYCHOTHERAPY

Starting in the 1930's, Adolf Meyer, Harry Stack Sullivan, and Frieda Fromm-Reichmann modified classical psychoanalytic psychotherapy to fit the needs of schizophrenics. The underlying assumption of the analytic approach is that schizophrenia is the outcome of disturbed interpersonal experiences which result in distortions in perception, meaning, and logic. Through the patient-therapist relationship, interpretations, and corrective emotional experiences, these disturbances can be ameliorated and the patient can function more independently. There is a large literature of case studies and theoretical formulations focusing on the treatment of schizophrenia from the psychoanalytic perspective (Strauss, Bowers, Downey, Fleck, Jackson, & Levine, 1980), which highlights successful outcomes in selected patients.

Well-controlled experimental studies should provide information on the relative effectiveness of psychotherapeutic interventions. Unfortunately, such research has produced an array of findings allowing advocates and skeptics alike to maintain their positions. The patterns which can be extracted from the multitude of studies permit latitude for different interpretations.

Individual psychotherapy with inpatients

Most of the controlled research on psychotherapy pits neuroleptic medication against psychotherapy without medication. With few exceptions, the drug condition was superior in reducing symptoms, hospital stay, and relapse (May, 1968; Grinspoon et al., 1972). These studies had a large influence in the field and resulted in a strong affirmation of the value of medication in contrast with psychotherapy.

Two other studies, however, reported positive findings for individual psychotherapy with hospitalized schizophrenics. Karon and VandenBos (1972) found significant advantages for both (a) ego-analytic psychotherapy with medication, or (b) direct-interpretive psychotherapy without medication over usual hospital treatment with medication. In terms of total days hospitalized, an overall clinical rating, and a measure of schizophrenic thought disturbance, the psychotherapy conditions appeared superior. Rogers, Gendlin, Kiesler, and Truax (1967) also reported positive findings on a number of in-hospital measures for patients treated with individual psychotherapy versus those given the usual hospital treatment. However, medication was not controlled in their study.

May (1976) rated the controlled studies of psychotherapy with schizophrenia on a "design-relevance scale," assessing the weight of evidence for different treatments. Taking into account the soundness of the design and the direction of the findings, points were assigned to each study, with the conclusion that inpatients treated with individual psychotherapy did not improve more than a control group. Psychotherapy has not yet been shown to add significant benefit to inpatients who were treated with drugs and milieu therapy alone. However, the relative paucity of controlled research, thorny design problems in the research, and equivocal findings limit any firm conclusions about the value of individual psychotherapy for inpatient schizophrenics.

Individual psychotherapy with outpatients

The findings regarding outpatient psychotherapy for schizophrenics coalesce into a clearer pattern. In a recent study, major-role therapy (MRT) was used to help recently discharged schizophrenics resume and maintain their roles the community. The treatment was conducted by experienced social workers, who did whatever they felt was necessary to enable their clients to adjust and survive outside the hospital. When this treatment was compared to a minimal, social casework condition, with medication also controlled independently, MRT was found to have a significant positive effect on patients *who did not relapse within the first 6 months.* Between 7 and 24 months, 44 percent of the MRT patients relapsed versus 58 percent of the non-MRT patients. The social adjustment of patients receiving MRT plus drugs was significantly better than the other conditions at 18 and 24 months (Hogarty, Goldberg, Schooler, Ulrich & the Collaborative Group, 1974).

Another study compared patients who were randomly assigned to a private psychiatrist versus those assigned to a specialized aftercare clinic (Seeman, 1978). The aftercare clinic patients were assigned two therapists, a resident psychiatrist, and a nurse or occupational therapist, who all worked to provide the patient with vocational, residential, and educational opportunities as well as medical and pharmacological treatment, individual, family, and group therapy, and crisis intervention if necessary. At the end of six months, the clinic patients had spent significantly less time in hospital readmissions and significantly more were employed or in school than the private patients.

Positive results with outpatient schizophrenics occurred when treatment focused on social and occupational rehabilitation, on problem solving, and cooperation with pharmacotherapy. Therapy succeeds better when it is oriented toward support and rehabilitation rather than toward formal attempts to provide insight and deeper psychologic understanding. The more-successful psychological treatments appear to be those which focus on specific behaviors rather than on general changes in the patient's personality.

Group psychotherapy with inpatients

Of six studies comparing group therapy with usual hospital treatment, four failed to reveal any unique or impressive contribution assignable to group psychotherapy, while two studies showed positive results on social adjustment during the hospitalization.

Five studies have tested group therapy alone versus group therapy in combination with another treatment approach including videotape feedback, ward activity, dyadic social interaction, and drugs. In four of these studies, the combined treatments were superior to group treatment alone.

As with outpatient individual therapy, the theme emerges that group therapy is effective when it focuses on a specific goal. The weight of evidence is against standard group therapy, where results indicated that patients did not improve more than the control group. By contrast, however, inpatient group therapy that centered around reality or a group activity (rather than psychologic understanding) was more effective than both usual hospital or standard group therapy (May, 1976).

Group psychotherapy with outpatients

Research has suggested that more benefits may accrue to patients treated with group therapy than with individual therapy. Purvis and Miskimins (1970) found group-therapy patients had significantly lower relapse rates (35 percent) than individual-therapy patients (56 percent) and control patients (54 percent). Donlon, Rada, and Knight (1973) found that group-treated patients kept their appointments more often, socialized more, and their treatment cost less than individually treated patients. However, three other studies reported no significant difference between group- and individual-therapy groups.

Comparisons of outpatients treated with group therapy versus no group therapy also showed some advantages for group therapy. In one study, group-treated patients had fewer readmissions and a greater number of discharges from the hospital than the control group (Shattan, DeCamp, Fujii, Fross, & Wolff, 1966). Group-treated patients in another study showed greater and quicker symptomatic improvement than patients treated by chlorpromazine alone (Borowski & Tolwinski, 1969).

Other psychotherapeutic approaches

In Soteria House, a residential, community-based treatment facility where young schizophrenics are treated for periods up to six months, a psychotherapeutic approach has been developed that helps the patient to integrate the psychotic experience into a gradual reconstitution process, avoiding the use of neuroleptic drugs as much as possible. Therapists are nonprofessionals selected for their personal qualities and ability to sit with floridly psychotic patients and calm them. Patients treated in this milieu were better adjusted in the community than a matched sample given standard, brief treatment in a community mental health center (Mosher & Menn, 1978). However, it is possible to evaluate the respective contributions to treatment outcome made by the type of psychotherapeutic working-through and by living in a cohesive, supportive, "extended family" home. Another residential facility where patients are encouraged to exploit their psychosis as an opportunity to reorganize the self is Diabysis, a treatment program based upon Jungian psychology (Perry, 1976).

Psychotherapy: Summary

While the research on psychotherapy of schizophrenia is rich in clinical lore and full of intriguing leads, conclusions from it are hampered by the lack of comparability among studies. Few studies describe in an operational fashion the therapy methods used. The patients participating in studies vary greatly, both in terms of diagnostic categories and social status. The durations and intensities of therapy differ greatly across studies, as does the duration of follow-up evaluation. Research should be designed to answer the question: "What kinds of changes are produced by what kinds of interventions, applied to what kinds of patients, by what kinds of therapists, under what kinds of conditions" (Parloff, 1980, p. 291).

Despite these limitations, some general guideposts can be found from the past 30 years of experience in the psychotherapy of schizophrenics:

1. Psychotherapy is not an alternative to pharmacotherapy. Psychotherapeutic treatment should be given in conjunction with neuroleptic drugs for most patients. Drugs, psychotherapy, and psychosocial methods should play supplemental rather than competing roles.
2. Psychotherapy focused solely on insight and understanding is not effective in the treatment of schizophrenia. Attempts to alter the patient's personality have not resulted in significant improvements in symptomatic status, recidivism, vocational or social adjustment.
3. Psychotherapy should focus on the practical affairs of everyday living, such as independent living skills, social and vocational adjustment.
4. Psychotherapy can be effective in bringing about changes in schizophrenics if it is goal oriented and specifically targeted on discrete outcomes.

FAMILY THERAPY

Family therapy developed from observational research on the communication patterns of families with schizophrenic members. The early thrust of family interventions was to attempt to restructure the deviant communication hypothesized as having etiological significance. The therapy setting consisted of the identified patient and one or more family members meeting together to discuss family problems. This presented a structure for a wide variety of interventions:

Education about schizophrenia

Informing a patient and his/her family about a chronic mental disorder is an important therapist responsibility. However, controversy about the nature and causes of schizophrenia contributed to a lack of communication between therapists and patients. Improved diagnostic specificity and effective drug therapy have increased the knowledge and understanding of schizophrenia, enabling clinicians to better educate patients and their families about schizophrenia. Currently, it is perhaps best described as a complex disorder with biological- and environmental-stress components. Helping patients and their families learn about the complexity of schizophrenia through an education process serves as an important component of recently developed family interventions (Anderson, Hogarty, & Reiss, 1980; Goldstein, Rodnick, Evans, May, & Steinberg, 1978; Falloon, Boyd, McGill, Strang, & Moss, 1981).

Enhancing coping skills

Family interventions that aim to enhance the family's ability to reduce environmental stress through effective problem solving have been frequently employed. Langley developed a crisis-oriented family therapy that assisted the family at times of major stress. Laing advocated an empathic, nonintrusive approach to the family crisis to reduce the fear, helplessness, and confusion experienced by the family when the patient displayed florid symptoms (Laing & Esterson, 1964). Goldstein and his colleagues emphasized effective coping behavior in the prevention of relapses. They taught families to identify pass stressors and to develop coping strategies. Structured problem solving that utilizes a brain-storming approach has been employed in behavioral family therapy to enhance coping with present and future stressors (Boyd et al., 1981).

The problem of overdependent relationships has been specifically addressed by efforts to promote separation of the patient from his family. In some cases, complete physical separation has been instigated (Stein & Test, 1980). However, emotional separation would appear to be the major aim in reducing family tension; and this may not be realistically achieved by simply reducing physical contact. Besides, family support is a vital resource in the long-term management of a chronic illness. Another way of achieving separation may be to expand the extrafamilial activities of *all* family members, as well as providing additional support for the patient and family. Social-network therapy (Speck & Attneave, 1973), multiple-family groups (Laqueur, LaBart, & Morony, 1964), and community-support groups (Lamb, Hoffman, & Oliphant, 1976) assist in providing a supportive nonprofessional network.

Improving family communications

Distortions in family communication noted in studies of schizophrenia have been the focus of most family interventions. Specific techniques to clarify communication have included listening empathically to unclear verbal statements until the sole meaning is understood by all family members (Mosher, 1969); therapist modeling of effective communication styles and role rehearsal with feedback on family interaction (Ferber & Beels, 1969). Other interventions may be directed toward the impaired cognitive processes of the patient and, often, other family members. Families may be taught to simplify communication, reduce distraction, repeat instructions, and check that messages have been accurately received (Falloon, 1981).

Emotional expression involves not merely the ability to give and receive messages, but also includes the reciprocity of emotional transactions. This sharing of emotional and material resources has been the base for therapeutic strategies such as de-emphasizing the "sick" role, reducing "scape-goating," correcting transgenerational role taking, writing "contracts" for reciprocal task sharing, and nonverbal "sculpting" of family-transactional patterns.

Evaluation of family therapy outcome

Scientific validation for the effectiveness of family therapy with schizo-phrenia is limited. Langsley and his colleagues treated 150 randomly selected cases of acute psychiatric illness with a crisis-oriented approach aimed at preventing hospital admission. The average duration of treatment was three weeks and involved a wide variety of supportive techniques, depending on each family's needs. It is not clear how long-term follow-up care was managed, but the family crisis unit continued to assist through-out a two-year period. An 18-month assessment indicated that the family interventions may have reduced hospital care when compared to routine management of a randomly chosen control group (Langsley, Machotka, & Flomenhaft, 1971). The family-treated group showed no advantage in social adjustment and personal functioning. A subgroup of 25 families of schizophrenic patients who participated in the family treatment was compared with 25 schizophrenics who received control treatment. The families who received family therapy experienced fewer crises and man-aged to cope with them better than the controls (Langsley, Pittman, & Swank, 1969). The design of this study prevents a clear assessment of the effect of this short-term family intervention. Goldstein and his col-leagues (1978) studied 96 recently discharged schizophrenic patients for six months after treatment with (a) family therapy plus standard-dose fluphenazine ehanthate injections; (b) family therapy plus low dose of fluphenazine; (c) routine aftercare plus high dose of fluphenazine; or (d) routine aftercare plus low dose of fluphenazine. Weekly sessions of family therapy were conducted over the first six weeks post-discharge, while drug therapy was maintained throughout the six months. The ther-apy was directed toward enhancing the family's understanding of schizo-phrenia and increasing the coping potential to deal with anticipated stressors that were expected to precipitate relapses.

After six weeks of treatment, rehospitalization and symptom ratings favored family therapy. At six months, 48 percent of the routine aftercare plus low-dose medication group had relapsed while not one of the family therapy plus standard-dose group relapsed. The two remaining groups showed intermediate results. There was no difference between the groups on the symptom ratings. This study suggests that family participation in the community aftercare of patients with schizophrenia is helpful in pre-venting future hospital admission, at least when combined with adequate medication. In a study of family therapy in the treatment of acute episodes of schizophrenia, Gould and Glick (1977) concluded that the *participation* of family members during inpatient treatment was associated with improved post-hospital adjustment; however, brief family therapy did not add any benefits to unstructured contact with relatives.

Family therapy: Summary

The paucity of adequately controlled outcome studies contrasts with the richness of reports of treatment strategies and process of family therapy in schizophrenia. The published studies have tended to focus on short-term crisis-intervention issues related to hospital admission and discharge. The results are very promising and suggest that even minimal participation of families in the community management of a patient following a florid episode of schizophrenia may prevent an early return to hospital. However, there is inconclusive evidence that the specific nature of the interventions employed were responsible for the benefits noted or that positive changes in psychopathology or social functioning were associated with family therapy. Further research is needed to provide answers to these basic questions and many others, before family therapy can be considered an important contribution to the management of schizophrenia.

SUMMARY

Multiple approaches to the treatment of schizophrenia enrich the therapist's repertoire in helping patients and family members cope with this devastating disorder. While the description of treatment modalities has been presented in an isolated, sequential manner, ideal mental health services for most persons suffering with schizophrenic symptoms involve a combination of medication, family therapy, social-skills training, milieu therapy, behavior therapy, and psychotherapy. Given the ideological polarization of many professional therapists, an eclectic approach that harnesses all that is valuable in treatment is rarely accessible to consumers of services. Nonetheless, broad-spectrum and multifaceted approaches to treatment are gaining in popularity and can be expected to prevail in the coming decade.

Use of medication in schizophrenia rests upon increasing indications that an underlying genetic-biological vulnerability may contribute largely to the formation of the characteristic symptoms of this disorder. These symptoms, in most cases, can be controlled with medication; thereby permitting the individual to benefit from other therapies that require his/her attention and interpersonal participation. Rehabilitative therapies—such as social-skills training and milieu therapy—focus on repair of functional limitations, not on cure of symptoms. Attention is given to fostering improved adaptive capacity and on enabling the patient to live optimally with residual defects and impairments. Psychotherapy emphasizes developmental growth, that the schizophrenic process is a struggle to overcome impediments, and that the patient needs to understand and be helped through the schizophrenic experience. A comprehensive approach to schizophrenia needs to take into account the ways in which it is, at the same time, a disease, adaptive defects and impairments, stunted development, and insufficient social support. When multifaced treatment methods emerge from all of these avenues, the schizophrenic patient has the best chance for living a functional and quality life that is relatively free of symptoms.

REFERENCES

Alevizos, P. N., & Callahan, E. J. Assessment of psychotic behavior. In A. R. Ciminero, K. S. Calhoun, & H. E. Adams (Eds.), *Handbook of behavioral assessment*. New York: John Wiley & Sons, 1977.

Alford, G. S., & Turner, S. M. Stimulus interference and conditioned inhibition of auditory hallucinations. *Journal of Behavior Therapy and Experimental Psychiatry*, 1976, *7*, 155–160.

Anderson, C. M., Hogarty, G. E., & Reiss, D. J. Family treatment of adult schizophrenic patients: A psychoeducational approach. *Schizophrenia Bulletin*, 1980, *6*, 490–505.

Anderson, L. T., & Alpert, M. Operant analysis of hallucination frequency in a hospitalized schizophrenic. *Journal of Behavior Therapy and Experimental Psychiatry*, 1974, *5*, 13–18.

Ayllon, T., & Haughton, E. Modification of symptomatic verbal behavior of mental patients. *Behavior Research and Therapy*, 1964, *2*, 323–334.

Baldessarini, R. J. Drugs and the treatment of psychiatric disorders. In A. G. Gillman, L. F. Goodman, and A. Gillman (Eds.), *The pharmacological basis of therapeutics*. New York: Macmillan, 1980.

Bellack, A. S., & Hersen, M. *Introduction to clinical psychology*. New York: Oxford University Press, 1979.

Borowski, T., & Tolwinski, T. Treatment of paranoid schizophrenics with chlorpromazine and group therapy. *Diseases of the Nervous System*, 1969, *30*, 201–202.

Boyd, J. L., McGill, C. W., & Falloon, I. R. H. Family participation in the continuing rehabilitation of schizophrenia. *Hospital and Community Psychiatry*, 1981.

Bucher, B., & Fabricatore, J. Use of patient-administered shock to suppress hallucinations. *Behavior Therapy*, 1970, *1*, 382–385.

Cayner, J. J., & Kiland, J. R. Use of brief time-out with three schizophrenic patients. *Journal of Behavior Therapy and Experimental Psychiatry*, 1974, *5*, 141–145.

Cole (Chairman), NIMH, Psychopharmacology Service Center Collaborative Study Group, "Phenothiazine treatment in acute schizophrenia: Effectiveness." *Archives of General Psychiatry*. 1964, *10*, 246–261.

David, J. M. Overview: Maintenance therapy in psychiatry: I. Schizophrenia. *American Journal of Psychiatry*, 1975, *132*, 1237–1245.

Davis, J. R., Wallace, C. J., Liberman, R. P., & Finch, B. E. The use of brief isolation to suppress delusional and hallucinatory speech. *Journal of Behavior Therapy and Experimental Psychiatry*, 1976, *7*, 269–275.

Donlon, P. T., Rada, R. T., & Knight, S. W. A therapeutic aftercare setting for refractory chronic-schizophrenic patients. *American Journal of Psychiatry,* 1973, *130,* 682–684.

Fairweather, G. W., Sanders, D. H., Cressler, D. C., & Maynard, H. *Community life for the mentally ill: An alternative to institutional care.* Hawthorne, N.Y.: Aldine Publishing, 1969.

Falloon, I. R. H. Communication and problem-solving skills training with relapsing schizophrenics and their families. In M. R. Lansky (Ed.), *Family therapy and major psychopathology.* New York: Grune & Stratton, 1981.

Falloon, I. R. H., Boyd, J. L., McGill, C. W., Strang, J. S., & Moss, H. B. Family-management training in the community care of schizophrenia. In M. J. Goldstein (Ed.), *Family treatment for schizophrenia.* San Francisco: Jossey-Bass, 1981.

Ferber, A., & Beels, C. Changing family-behavior programs. *International Psychiatry Clinics.* 1970, *7,* 27–55.

Flanagan, S. G., & Liberman, R. P. Ethical issues in the practice of behavior therapy. In M. Rosenbaum (Ed.), *Ethics and values in psychotherapy.* New York: Free Press, 1982.

Foxx, R. M., & Azrin, N. H. Restitution: A method of eliminating aggressive-disruptive behavior of retarded and brain-damaged patients. *Behavior Research and Therapy,* 1972, *10,* 15–27.

Goldstein, M. J., Rodnick, R. H., Evans, J. R., May, P. R. A., & Steinberg, M. Drug and family therapy in the aftercare treatment of acute schizophrenia. *Archives of General Psychiatry,* 1978, *35,* 1169–1177.

Gomez-Schwartz, B. The modification of schizophrenic behavior. *Behavior Modification,* 1979, *3,* 439–468.

Gould, E., & Glick, I. D. The effects of family presence and brief family intervention on global outcome for hospitalized schizophrenic patients. *Family Process,* 1977, *4,* 503–510.

Grinspoon, L., Ewalt, J. R., & Shader, R. I. *Schizophrenia: Pharmacotherapy and psychotherapy.* Baltimore: Williams & Wilkins, 1972.

Gunderson, J. G., & Mosher, L. R. The cost of schizophrenia. *American Journal of Psychiatry,* 1975, *132,* 901–905.

Hersen, M., & Bellack, A. S. Social-skills training for chronic psychiatric patients: Rationale, research findings, and future directions. *Comprehensive Psychiatry,* 1976, *17,* 559–580.

Hersen, M., & Bellack, A. S. Assessment of social skills. In A. R. Ciminero, R. S. Calhoun, & H. E. Adams (Eds.), *Handbook of behavioral assessment.* New York: John Wiley & Sons, 1977.

Herz, M. I., Endicott, J., & Spitzer, R. L. Brief hospitalization: A two-year follow-up. *American Journal of Psychiatry,* 1977, *134,* 502.

Hogarty, G. E., Goldberg, S. C., Schooler, N. R., Ulrich, R. F., & The Collaborative Study Group. Drug and sociotherapy in the aftercare of schizophrenic patients. II: Two-year relapse rates. *Archives of General Psychiatry,* 1974, *31,* 603–608.

Karon, B. P., & VandenBos, G. R. The consequences of psychotherapy for schizophrenic patients. *Psychotherapy: Theory, Research, and Practice,* 1972, *9,* 111–119.

Kazdin, A. E. *The token economy.* New York: Plenum Press, 1977.

Klinge, V., Thrasher, P., & Myers, S. Use of bedrest overcorrection in a chronic schizophrenic. *Journal of Behavior Therapy and Experimental Psychiatry,* 1975, *6,* 69–73.

Laing, R. D., & Esterson, A. *Sanity, madness, and the family.* London: Tavistock, 1964.

Lamb, H. R., Hoffman, A., & Oliphant, E. No place for schizophrenics: The unwelcome consumer speaks out. *Psychiatric Annals,* 1976, *6,* 688–692.

Langsley, D., Machotka, R., & Flomenhaft, K. Avoiding mental hospital admission: A follow-up study. *American Journal of Psychiatry,* 1971, *127,* 1391–1394.

Langsley, D. G., Pittman, F. S., & Swank, G. E. Family crises in schizophrenia and other mental patients. *Journal of Nervous and Mental Disease,* 1969, *149,* 270–276.

Laqueur, M. P., LaBart, H. A., & Morony, E. Multiple-family therapy. *Current Psychiatric Therapy,* 1964, *4,* 150–154.

Liberman, R. P. Research on the psychiatric milieu. In J. Gunderson, L. Mosher, & C. Will (Eds.), *Principle and practice of milieu therapy.* New York: Jason Aronson, 1981.

Liberman, R. P., King, L. W., DeRisi, W. J., & McCann, M. *Personal effectiveness.* Champaign, Ill.: Research Press, 1975.

Liberman, R. P., McCann, M., & Wallace, C. J. Generalization of behavior therapy with psychotics. *British Journal of Psychiatry,* 1976, *129,* 490–496.

Liberman, R. P., Teigen, J., Patterson, R., & Baker, V. Reducing delusional speech in chronic paranoid schizophrenics. *Journal of Applied Behavior Analysis,* 1973, *6,* 57–64.

Liberman, R. P., Wallace, C. J., & Nuechterlein, K. The nature of schizophrenia and social-skills training. In J. Curran & P. Monte (Eds.), *Social skills in clinical practice.* New York: Guilford Press, 1981.

Liberman, R. P., Wallace, C. J., Teigen, J., & Davis, J. Interventions with psychotic behaviors. In K. S. Calhoun, H. E. Adams, & K. M. Mitchell (Eds.), *Innovative treatment methods in psychopathology.* New York: John Wiley & Sons, 1974.

Liberman, R. P., Wallace, C. J., Vaughn, C. E., Snyder, K. S., and Rust, C. Social and family factors in the course of schizophrenia. In J. S. Strauss, M. Bowers, T. W. Downey, S. Sleck, S. Jackson, & I. Levine (Eds.). *Psychotherapy of Schizophrenia.* New York: Plenum Press, 1980.

Matson, J. L. Behavior-modification procedures for training chronically institutionalized schizophrenics. In M. Hersen, R. M. Eisler, & P. M. Miller (Eds.), *Progress in behavior modification* (Vol. 9). New York: Academic Press, 1980.

May, P. R. A. *Treatment of schizophrenia.* New York: Science House, 1968.

May, P. R. A. When, what, and why?: Psychopharmacology and other treatments in schizophrenia. *Comprehensive Psychiatry,* 1976, *17,* 683–693.

Mosher, L. R. Schizophrenogenic communication and family therapy. *Family Process,* 1969, *8,* 43–63.

Mosher, L. R., & Keith, S. J. Research on the psychosocial treatment of schizophrenia: A summary report. *American Journal of Psychiatry,* 1979, *136,* 623–631.

Mosher, L. R., & Menn, A. Z. Community residential treatment for schizophrenia: Two-year follow-up. *Hospital and Community Psychiatry,* 1978, *29,* 715–723.

Parloff, M. B. Discussion: New directions. In J. S. Straus, M. Bowers, T. W. Downey, S. Fleck, S. Jackson, & I. Levine (Eds.), *The psychotherapy of schizophrenia.* New York: Plenum Press, 1980.

Paul, G. L., & Lentz, R. J. *Psychosocial treatment of chronic mental patients: Milieu versus social-learning programs.* Cambridge, Mass.: Harvard University Press, 1977.

Perry, J. *Roots of renewal in myth and madness.* San Francisco: Jossey-Bass, 1976.

Purvis, S. A., & Miskimins, R. W. Effects of community follow-ups on post-hospital adjustments of psychiatric patients. *Community Mental Health Journal,* 1970, *6,* 371–382.

Rickard, H. C., Dignam, P. J., & Horner, R. F. Verbal manipulation in a psychotherapeutic relationship. *Journal of Clinical Psychology,* 1960, *16,* 364–367.

Rickard, H. C., & Dinoff, M. A follow-up note on "Verbal manipulation in a psychotherapeutic relationship." *Psychological Reports,* 1962, *11,* 506.

Rogers, C. R., Gendlin, E. G., Kiesler, D. J., & Truax, C. B. *The therapeutic relationship and its impact.* Madison: University of Wisconsin Press, 1967.

Schaefer, H. H., & Martin, P. L. *Behavioral therapy.* New York: McGraw-Hill, 1975.

Seeman, M. V. Clinic versus private treatment for psychosis. *Journal of Clinical Psychiatry,* 1978, *39,* 213–216.

Serber, M., & Nelson, P. The ineffectiveness of systematic desensitization and assertive training in hospitalized schizophrenics. Journal of Behavior Therapy and Experimental Psychiatry, 1971, *2,* 107–109.

Shattan, S. P., DeCamp, L., Fujii, E., Fross, G. G., & Wolff, R. J. Group treatments of conditionally discharged patients in a mental health clinic. *American Journal of Psychiatry,* 1966, *122,* 798–805.

Speck, R., & Attneave, C. *Family networks.* New York: Random House, 1973.

Stahl, J. R., & Leitenberg, H. Behavioral treatment of the chronic mental hospital patient. In H. Leitenberg (Ed.), *Handbook of behavior modification and behavior therapy.* Englewood Cliffs, N.J.: Prentice-Hall, 1976.

Stein, L. I., & Test, M. A. An alternative to mental hospital treatment. I: Conceptual model, treatment program, and clinical evaluation. *Archives of General Psychiatry,* 1980, *37,* 329–399.

Strauss, J. S., Bowers, M., Downey, T. W., Fleck, S., Jackson, S., & Levine, I. *The psychotherapy of schizophrenia.* New York: Plenum Press, 1980.

Sumner, J. H., Mueser, S. T., Hsu, L., & Morales, R. G. Overcorrection treatment for radical reduction of aggressive-disruptive behavior in institutionalized mental patients. *Psychological Reports,* 1974, *35,* 655–662.

Trower, P., Bryant, B., & Argyle, M. *Social skills and mental health.* Pittsburgh: University of Pittsburgh Press, 1978.

Ullmann, L. P. *Institution and outcome: A comparative study of psychiatric hospitals.* Elmsford, N.Y.: Pergamon Press, 1967.

VanPutten, T., & May, P. R. A. Milieu therapy of the schizophrenias. In L. J. West & D. E. Flinn (Eds.), *Treatment of schizophrenia.* New York: Grune & Stratton, 1976.

Wallace, C. J. Assessment of psychotic behavior. In M. Hersen & A. S. Bellack (Eds.), *Behavioral assessment: A practical handbook.* Elmsford, N.Y.: Pergamon Press, 1976.

Wallace, C. J. Assessment of psychotic behavior. In M. Hersen & A. S. Bellack (Eds.), *Behavioral assessment: A practical handbook* (2nd ed.). Elmsford, N.Y.: Pergamon Press, 1981.

Wallace, C. J., Nelson, C. J., Liberman, R. P., Aitchison, R. A., Lukoff, D., Elder, J. P., & Ferris, C. A review and critique of social-skills training with schizophrenic patients. *Schizophrenia Bulletin,* 1980, *6,* 42–63.

Weingaertner, A. H. Self-administered aversive stimulation with hallucinating hospitalized schizophrenics. *Journal of Consulting and Clinical Psychology,* 1971, *36,* 422–429.

Wincze, J. P., Leitenberg, H., & Agras, W. S. The effects of token reinforcement and feedback on the delusional verbal behavior of chronic paranoid schizophrenics. *Journal of Applied Behavior Analysis,* 1972, *5,* 247–262.

18

Treatment of disorders of impulse control

John T. Watkins, Ph.D. *

INTRODUCTION

Persons unable to control their urges may be viewed as yielding to irresistible impulses and acting on the spur of the moment, without forethought. They are controlled by a compulsion and may be victims of unconscious processes and the eruption of impulses which drive them to the acts they commit. The *Diagnostic and Statistical Manual of Mental Disorders* (*DSM-III*) of the American Psychiatric Association (1980) defines the essential features of Disorders of Impulse Control as the following: (1) failure to resist an impulse, drive, or temptation to perform some act that is harmful to the individual or to others. There may or may not be conscious resistance to the impulse. The act may or may not be premeditated or planned; (2) an increasing sense of tension before committing the act; (3) an experience of either pleasure, gratification, or release at the time of committing the act. The act is ego-syntonic in that it is consonant with the immediate conscious wish of the individual. Immediately following the act there may or may not be genuine regret, self-reproach, or guilt. (APA,1980).

Important criteria that stand out in regard to impulse-control disorders are the compulsiveness, repetitiveness, and/or social deviancy of the behavior. Persons seemingly are driven to perform the acts which get them into trouble. There is a repetition of the act in spite of past detection, apprehension, public exposure, or other negative consequences. There also may be a quality of bizarreness in the sense that the behavior does not generate rewards which would seem to justify the risks (e.g., kleptomania) or the behavior is considered strange and deviant by society (e.g., indecent exposure.)

The conditions classified under Disorders of Impulse Control are the

---

* University of Oklahoma Health Sciences Center, Oklahoma City.

590

following: pathological gambling, kleptomania, pyromania, explosive disorder (intermittent or isolated), and the paraphilias such as pedophilia, exhibitionism, and voyeurism. Substance-use disorders are also considered to be disorders of impulse control but will not be considered here, since they are addressed elsewhere in this text. All of the above types of disorders are usually viewed as antisocial, and frequently persons with these disorders experience legal difficulties.

THEORETICAL PERSPECTIVES AND ETIOLOGY

Sociological factors in antisocial behavior and deviancy

Factors such as poverty, broken homes, parental rejection, strong mother and weak father, ghetto conditons, cultural deprivation, developmental lag, poor schools, pornography, and the media's highlighting of crime and aggression have been offered as important factors in antisocial behavior. Those who grow up impoverished, disadvantaged, and deprived are viewed as high risk for developing deviant behaviors. The crime rate is in fact often higher in ghetto areas, and young males living in these innercity areas are more likely than any other subgroup in society to have prison records. There are, however, several major problems with attributing behavioral dyscontrol to sociological factors. First, even in the most unfavorable environments, only a minority of persons are aggressive, deviant, or criminal. Second, persons react to the same environment differently. Poverty, adversity, and deprivation may be found in the backgrounds of many persons whose behaviors are highly regarded and valued by society. And, conversely, upper-class families with all the advantages may have their black sheep. Thus, if sociological factors cause deviance or a deficit in the development of impulse control, why does this occur in only a few persons rather than most or all afflicted persons? Third, the same or similar patterns of family and sociological variables are often advanced to explain the alcoholic personality, schizophrenia, and other psychiatric disorders. The above factors seem at best to raise the probability of a person so subjected to be at higher risk for the development of some type of deviancy, but are of questionable value in understanding the antecedents of behavioral dyscontrol and predicting specific types of deviancy.

Another sociological view of deviancy has been that deviant behavior is a matter of cultural relativism. In all social groups, there are deviant behaviors, i.e., behaviors that distinguish the individual by virture of his being labeled different by the reference group. What may be a departure from the normative standards in one culture may not be unusual behavior in the next culture. Erikson (1962, p. 308) proposed that "deviance is not a property inherent in certain forms of behavior: it is a property conferred upon these forms by the audiences which directly or indirectly witness them." Becker (1963, p. 9) contended that "deviance is not a quality of the act the person commits, but rather a consequence of the application by others of rules and sanctions to the 'offender.' The deviant is one to whom that label has successfully been applied; deviant behavior is behavior that people so label." Scheff (1963) has argued that, once a person has become labeled by society, friends, and family as being deviant, it is very difficult for the labeled deviant to change the pattern of behavior that has contributed to his being so labeled. Scheff speculated that "labeling may create a social type, a pattern of 'symptomatic' behavior in conformity with the stereotyped expectations of others" (p. 451). Once labeled as deviants, persons may retain their deviant behavior, because they are rewarded for playing the stereotyped deviant role and are punished when they attempt to return to conventional roles. Thio (1978, p. 9) stated, "deviant behavior is no longer to be an absolutely unchanging part of the person. Instead, it is simply . . . a norm-violating act . . . deviance and the deviant person are now defined relative to a given norm, time, or society." This sociological view is also reflected in the psychological explanation of abnormal behavior by Ullmann and Krasner (1969), who proposed that psychopathology is more "in the eye of the beholder" than an inherent part of the person. Durkheim (1938) went so far as to suggest that, were we to rid ourselves of present offensive behaviors in society, the social order would only identify, define, and create replacements. Durkheim said, "Imagine a society of saints, a perfect cloister of exemplary individuals. Crimes, properly so-called, will there be unknown; but faults which appear venial to the layman will create there the same scandal that the ordinary offense does in the ordinary consciousness" (pp. 68–69). Not all sociologists agree that deviant behavior is primarily in the eye of the beholder. Akers (1968, p. 463) asserted that, "People can and do commit deviant acts because of the particular contingencies and circumstances in their lives, quite apart from or in combination with the labels others apply to them." Gibbs (1972) contended that the deviant label is imposed on a person's behavior because the behavior is deviant, rather than the reverse.

Biological bases of impulse-control disorders

Most biological studies of impulsive individuals have focused on the sociopath and the sexual deviant. This review will consider those studies, in that the disorders of impulse control do have antisocial features, although it is recognized that not all impulsive persons are sociopathic or sexually deviant.

Mark and Ervin (1970) reported that assaultive persons evidenced more abnormal electroencephalograms than the general population. There have been other reports of psychopaths showing an unusually high incidence of abnormal markings. However, when comparisons were later made with the frequency of abnormal markings in samples of normal individuals, it was found that the normal subjects' EEGs had about the same proportion of abnormalities (Ullmann & Krasner, 1969). Bandura (1973, pp. 30–31) pointed out that, "Cerebral disorder can accompany aggression either as cause, as effect, or as a joint product of other conditions. It is conceivable that deviant EEG patterns may, in many cases, be merely accompaniments of aggression and not its cause." For instance, assaultive people are frequently involved in altercations, accidents, and forcible arrests which might result in head injuries (Bach-y-Rita, Lion, Climent, & Ervin, 1971).

The genetic anomaly, trisomy-23, in which the male possesses an extra Y-chromosome (XYY), has been advanced to account for violent behavior. These males are reported to be taller and bigger than the average male. Jacobs, Brunton, and Melville (1965) reported 2.9 percent of the criminal population they studied to have the extra Y-chromosome, compared to only 2 percent in the general population. However, most of the XYY prisoners have been convicted for offenses against property rather than person. Price and Whatmore (1967) also found XYY criminals to have a lower incidence of physical and sexual assault than matched XY prisoners. The suggested relationship between the XYY chromosomal anomaly and violence has been challenged on several bases. Appropriate control groups have not been studied. The genetic difference has been confounded with height, in that the XYY prisoners have not been compared with individuals in the normal population of about the same height. The XYY karyotype is also confounded with other variables such as physical statute and social conditions. Comparisons should include control for factors such as social status, education, and environmental factors conducive to violence. It is not clear what role, if any, an extra Y-chromosome plays in behavioral dyscontrol. The XYY criminal may be less-inclined to anger outbursts and loss of control than his XY counterpart.

Eysenck (1970) has suggested that a dysfunction in the autonomic nervous system may account for the psychopath having difficulty forming strong, conditioned responses of fear and anxiety. Hare (1970) found a number of differences in autonomic responsivity in the psychopath in terms of stimuli that typically evoked fear and anxiety in the normal person. Lykken (1957) reported that sociopaths were clearly defective as compared to normals in their ability to develop anxiety. He found them defective as measured in three areas: (1) they indicated experiencing less anxiety in social and life situations which typically are reported to be embarrassing or frightening by the general public; (2) they did poorer than normals in an avoidance-learning situation in which incorrect responses were shocked; and (3) they showed less GSR reactivity and conditionability in a classical-conditioning paradigm.

Snyder (1980), in his review of the biological aspects of mental disorder, cited no biological bases for the paraphilias, kleptomania, and pyromania. Snyder further suggested that patterns of sexual behavior often treated as deviations probably do not represent genuine mental disorders.

The biological and physiological studies on sociopathic, assaultive, and impulsive individuals are inconclusive. Furthermore, all problems of impulse control clearly do not fall under antisocial personality disorder, although these may be overlapping classifications. Moran (1975) stated that a common misconception concerning gamblers who are in difficulty is that they are all psychopaths. Moran found that in only one fourth of his sample could the label *psychopath* be justifiably applied. It is difficult to ignore the literature on sociopathic individuals, and yet, one must recognize that there may be little generalization to persons with circumscribed problems in impulse control.

Psychoanalytic theories

Freud equated gambling with vice; and the ultimate vice was masturbation. The passion for play (gaming) was an equivalent of the old compulsion to masturbate. Freud (1950, p. 222) stated, ''The irresistible nature of the temptation, the solemn resolutions which are nevertheless invariably broken, the stupefying pleasure, and the bad conscience which tell the subject that he is ruining himself (committing suicide), all these elements remain unaltered in the process of substitution.''

Kleptomania refers to the morbid impulse to steal which is rooted in childhood sexuality, e.g., as a mode of reclaiming affection which has been withheld or as symbolic of a definite wish often associated with penis envy (Hinsie & Campbell, 1960).

Pyromania has been suggested to provide a form of sexual expression and release. The pyromaniac is arrested in psychosexual development and experiences a sense of power and exhilaration through setting and watching fires. The redness, heat, and unleashed force are symbolic of passion and sexual climax. This symbolism is reflected in popular music, such as José Feliciano's ''Light My Fire.'' Some fire setters have reported that they experienced sexual orgasm while watching the fire.

There has been considerable interest in the sexual perversions, which are related in one way or another to the Oepidus complex, the unconscious, and repression. The sexual deviations are considered to be merely the conscious part of a much larger unconscious system. In addition to the expression of sexual impulses, the perversions have the defensive function of protecting the person from castration anxiety emanating from unresolved Oedipal conflicts. According to Rosen (1964), deviant symptoms serve both sexual and nonsexual functions. The latter defend against anxiety, depression, and object loss, acting mainly as self-esteem regulators.

Gillespie (1956), in discussing the structure and etiology of sexual perversion, has suggested that there is a splitting of the ego as a defensive process. Strong castration anxiety leads to a partial regression to pre-genital levels. According to Gillespie, "A successful perversion evades psychosis by means of a split in the ego, which leaves a relatively normal part capable of coping with external reality, while allowing the regressed part to behave in the limited sexual sphere in a psychotic manner" (pp. 36–37). Thus, perversion cannot be understood as simply an uncontained impulse from the id, in that the ego is centrally involved. By accepting the perversion and allowing a circumscribed outlet to sexuality, "the ego is then able to ward off the other elements of the Oedipus complex . . . [albeit] at the price of the permanent split in itself and partial denial of reality" (p. 39).

Rooth (1975) described the development of exhibitionism as being associated with a seductive relationship with the mother and severe castration anxiety arising from the child's incestuous yearnings. "The act of exposure compactly enables the exhibitionist to express his revolt against his mother, find an outlet for his frustrated incestual aims, and also assert his individuality and masculinity. It has the further functions of inviting the victim to expose herself and prove that she is not castrated, while her initial reaction reassures the exhibitionist of his continuing potency" (p. 219).

The exhibitionist shows others that he is not castrated and may be retaliating against females who have made him feel so inadequate. Fenichel (1945) saw exhibiting as giving the individual reassurance and reducing castration anxiety through the confirmation by an audience that he does indeed have a penis. Exhibitionism, for Fenichel, represents a denial of castration with over-cathexis of a partial instinct. Many have noted that the exhibitionist often is dominated by his mother or wife and have speculated that the act is a protest and demonstration of the exhibitionist's virility and manly independence (e.g., Rickles, 1942). Bromberg (1965) said that the exhibitionist wishes to sexually arouse females in order to reassure himself of his own masculinity and, at the same time, express contempt for women. Other psychic determinants have included "organ inferiority" (Adler, 1917) and "narcissism and infantile regression" (Stekel, 1920).

The psychodynamics of the voyeur are similar, in that he too is suffering from castration anxiety. Some writers speculate that the voyeur was traumatized by viewing the primal scene and allays castration anxiety by reexperiencing the frightening scenes viewed as a child. Obendorf (1939) contended that the voyeur is seeking to see the fantasied phallus of the female in order to reassure himself that it exists.

The obscene telephone caller has also been described as harboring anger toward women stemming from the relationship with an over-protective and domineering mother. The fear of castration anxiety and female rejection leads to a less anxiety-provoking approach. There is also the wishful hope that females will be excited as he, the telephone caller, is. The telephone provides the safety of anonymity and physical distance and allows the caller to ensure that he does not get too emotionally involved. Nadler (1968) suggested that the telephone protects the obscene caller from the danger of acting out his rage and murderous fantasies.

Psychoanalysts have not given the attention to pedophilia that they have to other sexual deviations. The descriptions of pedophiles from some studies are similar to the personality patterns observed in other deviations, and one might assume that the psychodynamics are similar. Kurland (1960), in his review of clinical studies, found that pedophiles were reported to have suffered from infantile deprivation, fear of maternal separation, and an inability to directly express aggression. As adults they were passive, immature persons. Gebhard, Gagnon, Pomeroy, and Christenson (1965) described pedophiles as moral, conservative, and sexually restrained with their wives. They were not usually violent men and seldom attempted intercourse with the child. Pedophilia may also occur within one's family, in which case, it is regarded as incest. Although Gebhard et al. speculated that the most frequent type of incest occurs between brothers and sisters, father-daughter incest is the form that generates the most concern and legal sanctions. Incest on the part of fathers may occur with daughters of all ages, from infancy up. Martin (1960), in studying men incarcerated for incest with daughters (pedophilia and incest with pubescent daughters), found that, on the Blacky Test, they differed from other prisoners by being more orally dependent and showing higher castration anxiety and unresolved Oedipal conflicts.

Lester (1975) stated that the sexual deviant expresses directly those impulses which the neurotic represses and brings to expression only in symbolic form. Psychoanalysts view the basic mechanism in perversions to be the Oedipal castration anxiety aroused in the child by a phallic mother. The outlet taken is illustrated by Lester (1975, p. 211) as follows:

> The child obtains reassurance by either wishing to be the mother (transvestism); by displacing the imagined penis onto a symbolized object, thereby simultaneously affirming and denying its existence (fetishism); by reaffirming its presence and power through the reactions of others (exhibitionism); or by seeking visual images to displace the threatening mother image (voyeurism).

In summary, all sexual deviants have poor ego strength and control over impulses. For the psychoanalyst, these are signs of severe personality disturbance which need to be treated if the person is to resolve Oedipal conflicts and progress beyond pre-genital functioning. The impulses are to be understood as the result of unconscious conflicts, drives, and compromises by the ego.

Behavioral theories

The social-learning formulation of Ullmann and Krasner (1969) accounts for impulsive behavior as an insufficiency of "effective reinforcing stimuli" to maintain appropriate behavior. That is, pro-social or acceptable behaviors undergo extinction, and the person seeks new sources of stimulation. Anger outbursts, embezzlement, telling the boss off, not reporting for work, or dropping a love relationship may be perceived as impulsive by observers but are, in actuality, under stimulus and reinforcement control. In the case of the sociopath, Ullmann and Krasner further postulated that the person has had the "wrong things reinforced," including behaviors which have led to avoidance of blame and punishment rather than learning to differentiate right from wrong. The sociopath is also said to have experienced an early environment in which, unlike most individuals, he has not developed his own and other peoples' behavior as "secondary reinforcements" (pp. 454–457).

Sexual deviance has been viewed by Ullman and Krasner (1969) as behavior under control of an inappropriate "discriminative stimulus" (pp. 478–481). They speculated that the pairing of sexual release with a deviant response (e.g., exhibiting) leads to various situations in which the deviant behavior comes by itself to have strong stimulus control. Support for their contention can be found in anecdotal reports in which: voyeuristic behavior was evidently conditioned in a boy whose mother was physically and verbally seductive while appearing nude before him (Litin, Giffin, & Johnson, 1956); exhibitionism was conditioned in a boy whose mother enjoyed exhibiting herself to him and looking at her son's nude body (Giffin, Johnson, & Litin, 1954); and fetishism was conditioned in a boy whose mother responded affectionately whenever he stroked her dress (Johnson, 1953). A study by Rachman (1966), in which a mild fetish was created under laboratory conditions, has further supported the notion that previously neutral stimuli may come to have sexually arousing properties. A photograph of women's boots was presented prior to slides of sexually stimulating nude females. Changes in penile tumescence indicated that male subjects exhibited sexual arousal to subsequent presentations of the boots alone and showed a similar response to other types of shoes. Other behavioral therapists have also emphasized the classical-conditioning basis for much sexual deviancy, stating that any stimulus associated with sexual excitement and orgasm tends to become conditioned in a classical way and leads to arousal in the future.

Another conditioning sequence has been advanced by McGuire, Carlisle, and Young (1965), who suggested that deviant sexual acts result from masturbatory conditioning. The person has or sees a sexual experience which stimulates fantasy, which itself may not be deviant initially. Later, during masturbation, the person recalls the fantasy, reinforces the fantasy through orgasm, varies the fantasy during subsequent masturbation, and seeks out new stimulus situations to provide further fantasies for later masturbation. The initial deviant act is engaged in to supply new fantasy material to be used during masturbation. Then, the strength of the deviant act is increased with each pairing of deviant fantasy and masturbatory orgasm. Some indirect support for the McGuire et al. hypothesis was found in a study by Evans (1968), who administered identical quantities of aversive treatment to a number of exhibitionists. Subsequent to treatment, Evans compared two groups of subjects, 10 who reported exhibiting themselves and 10 who had not exhibited during the six-month follow-up. Histories revealed that clients who did not exhibit themselves after treatment had not used deviant masturbatory fantasies prior to treatment, while those who exhibited after treatment had used deviant fantasies prior to treatment (p < .05). An inverse relationship between deviant fantasy and treatment outcome has been reported by other investigators as well (Rooth & Marks, 1974). Cox and Daitzman (1979, p. 69) concluded that "exhibitionism appears to be a learned response strengthened and maintained by covert masturbatory fantasies and overt exhibitionistic behaviors."

Cognitive and phenomenological theories

The cognitive-phenomenological view is that the person with an impulse control disorder acts as if he has no control and is at the mercy of his impulses, when in fact, he actively and consciously chooses to do what he does. Far from being beyond control, his actions—when analyzed—reveal premeditation, i.e., prior reflection upon whether or not to give in to the urge, mental rehearsal, and often, careful selection of situations in which desires may most safely be yielded to.

The impulsive individual acts and talks as if his urges were external to him in the sense of happening to him. This may, in part, be because of a dim awareness of his own thought processes but mainly is an abdication of responsibility for acting on his urges. The cognitive-phenomenological view is that the individual's experiencing of himself in the world (e.g., "I can't help [control] myself.") is a function of the way in which he perceives, fantasizes, and thinks. This approach does not find it necessary to either endorse or reject the possible influences of biology, early childhood experiences, unconscious dynamic processes, social learning, classical conditioning, etc. However, the primary etiological factor is seen to be the person's present way of construing his experience; past influences, actual or conjectural, are excuses for continuing to act on impulses in the present.

The central factor in the loss of control is the person himself. Matza (1969) has pointed out that, "the subject has mediated the whole experience. There was no process of becoming (deviant) without him . . . *he* made an object of himself. *He* intuited the idea . . . *he* gave birth to, or created an act" (pp. 122–123). In talking about becoming deviant (becoming a marijuana user), Matza observed the following:

What is found in the world is not unwitting or unintentional; it is merely a consciousness and intentionality that did not bother announcing itself or making itself explicit because it was too engrossed *doing* the thing. It did not describe itself bringing something into being. But, nonetheless, in doing the thing . . . persons in the world *used* consciousness and *assumed* intention. Being human, they could do no other . . . it becomes apparent that anyone can become a marijuana user and that *no one* has to. (p. 100)

Watkins (1977) reported that impulse disorders act *as if* their desires were organismic needs which had to be met. The impulsive individual develops little tolerance for delay in gratification or for settling for substitute satisfactions. The person in the process of losing control thinks he has to have what he wants, when he wants it, and thus, his desires take on an urgency that easily propels him into acting upon his impulse. With such low tolerance for discomfort or temptation, the individual comes to believe (and wants to believe) that his urges are irresistible and compelling. Watkins described several case studies of individuals who brought about and perpetuated their being out of control via experiencing their impulses *as if* they had to act upon them and cognitively and consciously choosing to do so.

TREATMENT APPROACHES

Medical treatments

Biological therapies of impulse control disorders have included the oral administration of lithium carbonate, intramuscular injections of medroxyprogesterone acetate, oral administration of cyproterone acetate (unavailable in the United States), and surgical castration.

1. Lithium carbonate. Moskowitz (1980) described the treatment with lithium carbonate of 3 compulsive gamblers. The similarity of the thrill response associated with experiences at gambling to that observed in manic-depressive disorder suggested that lithium carbonate might be an effective treatment. Moskowitz treated three patients with lithium carbonate, six hundred mg., three times a day. Gambling was eliminated or markedly reduced. Two patients reported that "the thrill was gone." From his description of the three successfully treated cases, one would question whether his patients may have been manic-depressive disorders. There was a distinct periodicity associated with the gambling engaged in by two of the patients. They experienced heightened enthusiasm, optimism, grandiosity, and poor judgement. One patient's moods cycled between a superconfident gambling, sexually active phase to a depressed, apologetic phase, in a frequency of about once every three or four months. The second patient took risks, not only in his gambling, but by driving recklessly, sometimes even when he was exhausted from having stayed up all night. Moskowitz concluded that compulsive gamblers may include many diagnostic types, including manic-depressive patients.

Sheard, Marini, Bridges, and Wagner (1976) conducted a double-blind, placebo-controlled study of the effect of lithium on agressive behavior with prisoners in a medium-security institution. The 66 subjects ranged in age from 16 to 24 years, were physically healthy and nonpsychotic, and had histories of chronic impulsive-aggressive behavior. The five-month experimental protocol began with one medication-free month that served as a control. Subjects then received lithium or placebo medication daily for three months. The fifth month was again drug-free. There was a significant reduction in aggressive behavior in the lithium group, as measured by a decrease in infractions involving violence. In the lithium group, infractions declined progressively month by month to zero by the fourth month. The number of infractions started to rise again in the fifth month, which was drug-free. The authors concluded that lithium can have a clinically useful effect upon impulsive-aggressive behavior.

2. Anti-androgens.   Laschet and Laschet (1975) and Cooper, Ismail, Phanjoo, and Love (1972) have reported on cyproterone acetate, a synthetic progesterone derivative which has potent anti-androgen properties. Cyproterone acetate has received considerable attention in Europe but is unavailable in this country. However, in the United States, there have been several studies reported in which medroxyprogesterone acetate (MPA; Depo-Provera, Upjohn) has been used. Medroxyprogesterone acetate is a synthetic, steroidlike progesterone which inhibits testosterone biosynthesis and is effective in lowering plasma-testosterone levels. Intramuscular injection of 300 mgs. of MPA every 7 to 10 days has been a typical treatment regimen for paraphilic behavior, while lower dosages have been used for treatment of aggressive behavior. The measurable drop in the plasma-testosterone level indicates that MPA shuts off testicular production of the male sex hormone, most probably by breaking the cycle of feedback between gonadotropin release from the pituitary and testosterone release from the testicle. Money (1970) observed that it is still an open question as to whether the therapeutic benefit to behavior is by reason of the functional castration effect alone. He stated that "an additional possibility is that medroxyprogesterone acetate has a direct effect, at the cellular level, on brain cells in the hypothalamic- and limbic-system nuclei that are directly contributory to the governance of sexual and erotic functioning" (p. 172).

Money (1970) reported on the behavioral response in eight male sex offenders treated with medroxyprogesterone acetate. The response was good in three cases, one of which showed a remission of paraphiliac behavior and urges for 3½ years. In a case study presented in detail, the author concluded that "there has been a psychic realignment so that bizarre eroticism, once expressed, is now negatively coded in the mind and brain and its expression vetoed" (p. 171). The results were not as impressive with several other patients, who either dropped out of treatment and/or resumed their former paraphiliac behavior.

Several investigators have reported on the effectiveness of MPA in treating a variety of sexual and aggressive disorders, including aggressive homosexuality, transvestism, homosexual pedophilia, homosexual incest, rape, sodomy, and exhibitionism (Money, 1972; Blumer & Migeon, 1975; Barry & Ciccone, 1975). Blumer and Migeon (1975) treated 6 patients with sexual deviations, 11 temporal-lobe epileptics characterized by episodic irritability and rage reactions, and 5 other patients with severe anger-aggressive behavior disorder. Sexual deviants were typically treated with 300 mgs. of Depo-Provera every 10 days, while the temporal-lobe epileptics were given 100 mgs. every 7 to 10 days. The findings with sexual deviants are difficult to interpret. On the one hand, they all seemingly reported a decrease in sexual arousal. However, some dropped out of treatment, and others were discontinued without explanation provided. While there was a lack of recurrance of deviant behavior on the part of some reported cases, long-term follow-up of all cases was not reported. Of the 11 temporal-lobe epileptics, 7 patients showed good-to-excellent results (2 patients had unsatisfactory results, 2 patients discontinued treatment), while all patients (6 of 9) with episodic violence showed a very significant improvement.

Barry and Ciccone (1975) reported on the use of Depo-Provera in the treatment of three aggressive sexual offenders, who had been arrested for impulsive, assaultive sexual conduct, including sodomy and rape. They were treated with medroxyprogesterone acetate, 300 mgs., IM every 10 days following which they reported relief from the impulse to misbehave sexually. The two married subjects were able to continue sexual relations with their spouses to a satisfactory degree. The third patient, an adolescent, was able to socialize comfortably with girls rather than being assaultive. Long-term follow-ups were not available, in that the first two cases were sentenced to prison in spite of their responding to the medication, while the third case had been maintained on MPA for only eight months at the time of the authors' report.

Money, Wiedeking, Walker, Migeon, Meyer, and Borgaonkar (1975) treated antisocial and/or sex-offending males with anti-androgen therapy plus counseling. Thirteen males with the 47,XYY genotype and 10 who were 46,XY were given MPA in combination with a counseling program. Those with the XY genotype were all sex offenders, and those with the XYY genotype were antisocial offenders (primarily robbery and destructiveness) with or without sexual offenses. The combined treatment program was beneficial in helping sex offenders to regulate their behavior, and in five instances (3 XY and 2 XYY) there was a remission of paraphiliac symptoms. However, measured effects of Depo-Provera on assaultive behavior against persons and destructive behavior against things failed to demonstrate a suppressive effect on aggressiveness. The authors concluded that their study did not justify the assumption of an androgen-aggression relationship in the XYY antisocial offenders. The findings did not indicate an unequivocal change in the XYY men with the so-called aggressive types of behavior, whereas MPA proved to have a very direct effect on sexual behavior in both the 47,XYY and 46,XY genotypes.

Pinta (1978) treated a homosexual pedophile with psychotherapy and medroxyprogesterone acetate. Administered for a two-month period, MPA caused a prompt and drastic reduction in obsessive fantasies and in the anxiety and depression generated by them. MPA was observed to have psychological benefits that outlived its physiologic activity. During the four months following treatment, there were periodic recurrences of homosexual fantasies toward young boys; however, they were not as intense as previously and were unaccompanied by obsessive concern and depression. The author observed that the use of MPA may have resulted in the patient developing an optimism toward the future and a sense of mastery over his impulses that continued even after drug treatment was discontinued, implying that the psychological benefits of MPA may outlive its biological response.

Spodak, Falck, and Rappeport (1978) reported a favorable outcome in three of six sexual-deviant treatment cases treated with medroxyprogesterone acetate, 400 mgs. IM per week. Their patients included four pedophiles, one sadist, and one exhibitionist. Two of the pedophiles were rearrested for the same behavior, although they had previously reported a reduction in the frequency of paraphilic behavior during treatment. The exhibitionist reported no change in his paraphilic behavior during treatment and terminated therapy on his own.

Berlin and Meinecke (1981) reported on 20 men with recurrent paraphiliac behavior who were placed on medroxyprogesterone acetate. Only 3 of the 20 patients showed recurrences of sexually deviant behavior, while taking medication. However, of the 11 patients who discontinued MPA against medical advice, 10 relapsed. The authors' impression was that the men appeared to do well in response to anti-androgenic medication as long as they continued taking it and as long as their problems were rather clearly confined to unconventional sexual cravings. They concluded that the prognosis may depend not only on the effects of medication on the deviant thoughts and cravings comprising the syndrome, but also on other features of the person manifesting the syndrome, such as his attitude about treatment and commitment to it. When MPA is discontinued, allowing the sexual appetite to heighten or return, behaviors engaged in to satisfy that appetite are also likely to be reinstated. Walker (1977), who has observed problems in patient compliance with long-term MPA use, has also indicated that patients return to previous sexual patterns when medication is discontinued.

Gagné (1981) has reported just the opposite effect, in that none of the 40 improved patients he treated returned to pre-treatment sexual behavior as the testosterone levels returned to normal. Gagné treated 48 male patients with long-standing histories of deviant sexual behavior with MPA and milieu therapy for up to 12 months. Forty subjects responded positively, all within three weeks, with diminished frequency of sexual fantasies and arousal, decreased desire for deviant sexual behavior, increased control over sexual urges, and improvement in psychosocial functioning. The patients' reports of disappearance of deviant sexual behavior were at times confirmed by members of their immediate milieu. Improvement in psychosocial functioning was apparent after two or three months. Seven patients who had never been interested in women reported feeling attracted to them and were able to have sexual intercourse. After termination of hormonal therapy, patients were contacted by a staff member for a period of three years. None of the 40 improved patients returned to his pre-treatment sexual behavior, even though the testosterone levels returned to normal.

3. Surgical castration. Studies of surgical castration have indicated a sharp drop in libido and sexual activities following castration, and the recidivism rate among castrates is considerably lower than among those who have refused the surgical procedure. Langelüddeke (1963) and Cornu (1973) reported that 20 percent and 28 percent, respectively, of castrates stated that the operation had positively influenced their lifestyle in that they felt happier and more balanced. However, depression, feelings of inadequacy, isolation, and passivity were frequent complaints by almost one third of the subjects studied.

In a review and critique of the most important empirical studies conducted in the field of surgical castration in Germany, Switzerland, Norway, and Denmark, Heim and Hursch (1979) concluded that there is no scientific or ethical basis for castration in the treatment of sex offenders. While it would at first appear that the risk of committing a subsequent sexual crime is reduced for sexual offenders after they have been castrated and released, the real percentage for recidivism may be higher, in that castrated sex offenders with a low risk of recidivism (mainly first offenders) should have been eliminated from the total of the sample population studied. This was not done in any of the four European studies surveyed. Another problem in evaluating the effects is that the decision to be castrated was voluntary in one sample, and those who asked for it may have been very different from those who rejected it. Heim and Hursch also pointed out that one of the most persistent myths about sex offenders is that such crimes are rooted in an abnormally strong sexual drive. Findings reported by Rada, Laws and Kellner (1976), indicating that plasma-testosterone levels in rapists and child molesters are not significantly different from those in normals, have reemphasized that there is no physiological or hormonal reason—and therefore, no medico-scientific legitimacy—for practicing castration. Inferences drawn from animal investigation would seem not to justify castration in humans. Beach (1970) discovered that male dogs continue to copulate for years after castration. Rogers (1976) concluded that, in many animals, castration after puberty had little effect on sexual performance. Eibl (1978) demonstrated that the sexual responsiveness of castrated males is much more varied than had been supposed. Of 38 castrated sex offenders whose erections were measured while viewing a sex movie, 50 percent exhibited full erections, although time since castration ranged from three to five years. Heim (1981) reported that sexual manifestations caused by castration varied considerably, and castration effects on male sexuality are not predictable with certainty. While frequency of coitus, masturbation, and sexual thoughts were found to be strongly reduced after castration, it was shown that male sexual capacity was not extinguished. Once the central excitatory mechanism has been sensitized by androgen, this neuromechanism may remain in an excitable state (Beach, 1944), and the effects of castration may depend mainly upon the subject's psychological attitude toward castration (Ford & Beach, 1951).

Psychoanalytic treatment

Rosen (1968, p. 795) has described the psychoanalytic treatment of sexual deviation as follows:

> In psychotherapy, the therapist helps to undo the repressions and other ego mechanisms, so that the unconscious infantile instinctual wishes, past traumatic experiences, and painful anxieties can be brought to consciousness and faced by the patient with the mature adult portion of his ego. In severe cases, phobic, obsessional, and character defences are often present, making treatment increasingly difficult. Several cases referred for psychotherapy after they had failed with behaviour therapy were of this type. Their ego defences were increased by the behaviour therapy, and they had suffered intensely in behaviour therapy due to the intensified instinctual repression. In one case, paranoid manifestations became overt. When behaviour therapists claimed that no symptom substitutes have taken place, their overlooking of inner dynamics really precludes proper assessment.

Rosen (1968) indicated that the aim of psychotherapy is twofold: (1) to assist the patient in giving up his preferred but deviant form of sexual pleasure which also contains suffering elements, and (2) to remove the barriers to normal heterosexual intercourse. Resistances and underlying fantasies must be explored and the accompanying affect released. Due to the castration-and-separation anxiety, attachment to an object is extremely threatening for the patient. In the psychotherapeutic situation, the patient transfers onto the therapist the actual details of previous fixations and reality reinforcements, which can then be dealt with. Treatment cannot be hurried, because of the need for working through. In addition, the severe depression many patients must transcend in the transference before they are capable of proper object relationships is painful and repetitive, and it needs skill and time for its consumption.

Rosen (1964, p. 293) reported good results with psychotherapy in a series of exhibitionists. However, Rosen (1968) concluded that there is a great need for further case studies, as well as individual studies, in this field and that, while there are many people practicing analytic psychotherapy of sexual deviation, little of their work is reported to others, at least not systematically. This situation has not changed in recent years. Berlin and Meinecke (1981, p. 602) came to an identical conclusion, stating, "To our knowledge, there have been no well-controlled clinical trials to demonstrate that any of the individual or group psychodynamic methods result in sustained behavioral change in these conditions."

Behavioral therapies

Behavioral therapies to alter impulsive behaviors have included altering social contingencies, removal of positive reinforcement, stimulus satiation, flooding, orgasmic reconditioning, sensate focusing, social-skills training, and several types of aversive counterconditioning, including electrical aversion therapy, covert sensitization, and shame-aversion therapy.

1. Altering social contingencies. Kraft (1970) treated a case of compulsive shoplifting by altering the social consequences. The client was instructed as follows: "Whenever you steal an article from a shop, you must send the correct amount of money to the shop using a plain envelope. Later you must return to the shop and make sure that you do *not* steal on the next occasion." Success was reported in three months, during which time she stole only three articles, each of which she subsequently paid for. Change in the client's behavior pattern was attributed to three factors: the act of stealing being transformed into a purchase, although payment was delayed; a modification of expectations via the patient being trained to reenter the shop on a subsequent occasion *without* stealing; the client's awareness that she was now purchasing unnecessary articles for which she had little use.

In an institutional setting, Wetzel (1966) treated a boy who had exhibited compulsive stealing for several years duration by first enhancing an available, positive reinforcer and then making the removal of this positive reinforcer contingent upon the stealing behavior. The boy was treated successfully over a 90-day period. Wetzel speculated that, during the final stage of treatment, there may have been the onset of new social reinforcers for the nonstealing behavior in the form of favorable responses by peers and staff.

2. Stimulus satiation. Peck and Ashcroft (1970) treated five patients with a stimulus-satiation technique for pathological gambling. The subjects were bombarded throughout the day with gambling-associated materials. The results were mixed, in that one client refrained from gambling for over a year, one person showed no treatment effects at all, and three participants relapsed after varying periods of abstinence. Jones (1981) reported having treated over 20 children, ages 7 to 12, for firesetting by a satiation or flooding technique. He had each child light fires in the presence of the therapist and parents. The children dropped burning sticks, paper, etc., into a water pail. Treatment was conducted twice per week initially and later once per week, with the parents carrying out the procedure at home between office visits. The children were also seen in individual, group therapy, or activity-play therapy. After one year of treatment, none was ever reported to have tried to start a fire alone. Marshall (1979) treated two heterosexual pedophiles with satiation therapy by pairing prolonged masturbation of one-hour duration with the verbalization by the patient of his deviant sexual fantasies. A decreased penile arousal was reported at 6- and 10-month followups.

3. Reconditioning. Jackson (1969) described a voyeur who, after the act of peeping sporadically, would masturbate (reinforcing his voyeurism on an intermittant schedule). Treatment consisted of having the client masturbate in the privacy of his bedroom to the most exciting pornographic picture he had. He was to focus on the picture at the time of orgasm, not on voyeuristic fantasies. This was done for two weeks, by the end of which the subject reported no desire to look into windows. The next step involved pairing his orgasm with a nude picture, upon which he was to concentrate at the point of ejaculation. Further progress was rapid, and the client reported no urges to peep and actually experienced two satisfactory heterosexual relations. Treatment was terminated after eight sessions. The subject stated at the nine-month follow-up that his desire for voyeurism had dissipated, and his sexual energies were directed along more socially acceptable lines. Jackson concluded that, by associating orgasm with sexual stimuli of decreasing similarity and arousal potential from voyeuristic fantasy, the client developed a positive attraction to more acceptable objects.

Kremsdorf, Holmen, and Laws (1980) treated a heterosexual pedophile for eight weeks with orgasmic reconditioning. The subject masturbated to fantasies (spoken aloud) of adult females without deviant fantasies being employed at all. That is, it was not necessary for the subject to use deviant fantasies initially to become aroused. The results were an increased response to slides of female adults and a decreased response to female children. These gains were maintained at a two-month follow-up.

4. Aversive conditioning. Barker and Miller (1966) reported three cases of pathological gambling to have been successfully treated by the use of electric-aversion therapy. The procedure involved shocking the subjects while playing a "one-armed bandit." However, a one- to two-year follow-up revealed that the maintenance of behavioral change was quite mixed. There had been no relapses for one person 2 years following treatment, but the other two cases relapsed after 1 and 1.5 years, respectively. Goorney (1968) treated a compulsive horse-race gambler. Three activities associated with horse-race gambling were selected for aversive conditioning. A 35-volt electric shock was delivered 15 times each 10-minute session, five sessions per day, over nine days of treatment, for a total of 45 sessions and 675 electric shocks. A 12-month follow-up revealed the subject to still be in remission. Seager (1970) treated 14 gamblers by using slides of gambling activities or newspapers in which one out of four pages was a racing sheet. Shock was delivered upon the Ss turning to the racing page. Seager's conclusion was that the "results do not arouse enthusiasm," in that only five persons remained free of the problem for periods of one to three years following treatment.

Using a different, physically aversive approach, Keutzer (1972) treated a person for kleptomania by having her hold her breath until "mildly painful" every time the impulse to steal was experienced, both in stores and whenever imagining stealing during the day. The client kept a log during a baseline week plus six weeks of treatment, recording the frequency, days, number of stores, dollar value of items stolen, and list of items. The treatment sessions were once a week, with the client self-administering treatment between sessions. Impulses to steal increased upon initiation of breath holding to a high of 47 on the third day but diminished by week 4 to 10-12 conditioning trials per day. There was no stealing during week 6, which became the last treatment week. A follow-up 10 weeks later revealed that the person was not currently stealing, but she reported having relapsed on two occasions during week 7.

Rosenthal (1973) used aversive shock with a heterosexual pedophile in two different ways. First, fixed-punishment pairing, in which the intensity and duration were held constant, produced no increase in latencies of imagining deviant behavior and also no decrease in temptations toward children. Second, the shock duration was varied as a function of S's response latencies, i.e., increased latencies led to decreased duration. Also, any large drops in latency from prior, longer latencies were punished by lengthy shock durations. This response-contingent shaping was successful in lengthening latencies to the point of S having difficulty obtaining the image. Urges were lost, and there were no further acts. There was no recurrence during the 32-month follow-up. Kohlenberg (1974) found aversive conditioning not to be effective in reducing the number of thoughts or number of prowling incidents by a homosexual pedophile. Sensate focus à la Masters and Johnson with a cooperative adult male was successful in developing sexual arousal to him, and generalization to other adult males later. The number of pedophilic incidents decreased sharply subsequent to the second treatment.

Marshall (1971) used a combined-treatment approach, in which a pedophile was first treated with aversive therapy for 30 sessions over a period of three weeks. Second, desensitization of heterosexual anxiety was begun in conjunction with training in social skills. Social-skills training involved imitation of the therapist, role-playing, and reversal of roles, and was directed specifically at situations involving females. The second aspect of treatment required 15 45-minute sessions over a period of two months. The S reported significant changes in masturbatory fantasy after aversive therapy, in that fantasy which had previously been to pedophilic material was now exclusively to adult female images. A combination of treatments has been used in other studies as well. Marshall and McKnight (1975) treated "dangerous sexual offenders" from a penitentiary, including one heterosexual and two homosexual pedophiles. Treatment consisted of aversion, social-skills training, and a ward-based program. Dependent measures included a sexual attitude scale, ratings of slides, and penile tumescence, all of which changed in a positive direction. The post-treatment results were that one relapsed after release, one desisted from contact with young boys but failed to develop adult sexual relationships, and one remained incarcerated (which meant that treatment results went untested).

Rhodes and Levinson (1977) treated a child molester with 3 months of aversive conditioning and 10 months of psychotherapy. S was shocked on female child pictures, but not on female adult pictures. Treatment consisted of 26 sessions of 45 minutes' duration over a three-month period. The ratings of young girls (pictures) went from attractive to unattractive. S reported no further attraction to young girls, and his behavior and impulses stopped. The same findings were obtained 3, 6, and 12 months later. It was not clear how the second treatment contributed to the cessation of molesting behavior or maintenance of behavioral change.

Evans (1968) reported on 10 exhibitionists who received aversion therapy involving variable-intensity shock following exposure to 20 deviant image-provoking phrases projected on a screen. The Ss required different lengths of treatment to achieve the criteria of no exhibitionistic urges or acts, depending upon whether or not they engaged in deviant-masturbatory fantasies. The five subjects with nondeviant fantasies required a median of 4 weeks of aversion therapy, while the five subjects who fantasized exposing themselves during masturbation required a median of 24 weeks of treatment. Two subjects in the deviant fantasy group were still acting on their urges at the six-month follow-up. Fookes (1969) treated seven exhibitionists with electric shock, six of whom lost their desire for their perversion. Treatment consisted of electric shock, while the client imagined himself exposing, and while actually exposing himself during the session. There were up to 500 shocks administered during an hourly session, and treatment lasted from 7 to 10 months. The mean follow-up period was 39.5 months. Raymond (1969) treated six exhibitionists with aversion therapy, reporting that all showed an apparent change in attitude. While one client relapsed after 5 months, the other five remained free of their exhibitionism 6 to 24 months later. MacCulloch, Williams, and Birtles (1971) reported on a 12-year-old boy, who was treated for his proclivity to exhibit to specific types of older females. Treatment consisted of 18 20-minute sessions in which shock was delivered upon the presentation of slides of older females. Slides of age-appropriate girls signaled shock termination. Masturbation fantasies were still deviant at the conclusion of treatment but were exclusively age-appropriate six weeks later. Urges to exhibit were also absent, and these gains were found at a five-month follow-up.

Miller and Haney (1976) combined aversion, aversion relief, social- and sexual-skills training, support, and insight-oriented therapy in their treatment of a pedophiliac exhibitionist. The client was improved after three months of treatment as follows: (1) positive rating of pictures of immature females decreased, (2) high frequency of deviant fantasies decreased markedly, and (3) he developed a mature sexual relationship. Rooth and Marks (1974) evaluated aversive conditioning versus stimulus-control procedures, using a cross-over design with 12 exhibitionists. Shock was applied when the patient imagined exposing himself or described exposing in front of a mirror. The stimulus-control procedure involved the client disrupting the chain of events which led to exposure. Relaxation training was a third treatment. Each patient received eight sessions of each treatment. A significant treatment effect was found when the first two treatments were compared to the third, and there was a positive sequence effect in which aversive shock was most effective when administered first, and the stimulus-control procedures were most effective when preceded by aversive trials.

Treatment of multiple urges in the same study has been reported by Feldman, MacCulloch, and MacCulloch (1968). "Anticipatory-avoidance learning" was used with two tranvestites, one compulsive masturbator, one sadist with pedophilia, and one fetishist. The subjects were exposed to sexual stimuli on slides and could avoid electric shock most of the time by making a response to remove the sexual stimuli from view. Only two of the persons responded to treatment. Bancroft and Marks (1968) reported initial improvement ranging from 72 percent to 100 percent among the several sexual deviations they treated. One year following treatment, the improvement rate dropped to 57 percent, and there was a complete absence of deviation in only 6 of 40 cases (15 percent). Hallam and Rachman (1972) treated seven patients with different deviant sexual behaviors with electrical-aversion therapy. Four made discernable progress, and three failed to respond. The successful cases showed a significant increase in the time required to imagine deviant sexual material, which the authors saw as providing some support for the conditioning theory of aversion therapy. Marshall (1973) treated a mixed group of deviants by modifying sexual fantasies ($n = 12$). Treatment consisted of aversive shock to the fantasies and orgasmic reconditioning via shifting to appropriate heterosexual stimuli and thoughts just prior to masturbatory orgasm. In 11 of 12 Ss, there was a reduction in rated attractiveness of deviant fantasies and an increase in attractiveness of appropriate fantasies. These ratings were matched by changes in penile volume. There was a disappearance of the behavior and a change in attitude immediately following treatment. Ten of the 11 successful cases were followed for a period of 3 to 16 months, during which time 2 Ss relapsed.

5. Covert sensitization. Covert sensitization (aversive imagery) is a procedure in which extremely noxious scenes are paired with scenes of the undesired behavior. Barlow, Leitenberg, and Agras (1969) treated deviant sexual urges with this procedure. Their design consisted of a baseline period, and acquisition phase (during which sexually arousing scenes were paired with nauseous scenes), an extinction phase (during which sexually arousing scenes were presented alone), and reacquisition. The two subjects exposed to the experimental condition of sensitization (acquisition phase) reported a drop in frequency of sexual urges, and the arousal value of stimuli—as measured by GSR—diminished. During the extinction phase, the arousal increased upon exposure to sexually arousing scenes. During the reacquisition phase, covert sensitization again led to a reduction in arousal and the frequency of sexual urges. These results suggested that pairing noxious scenes with sexually arousing scenes is a crucial procedure in covert sensitization.

Harbert, Barlow, Hersen, and Austin (1974) used a type of covert sensitization in which the subject visualized molesting his daughter followed by scenes of embarrassment upon being discovered by his wife and priest. There were 150 pairings over 15 days of inpatient treatment. Booster sessions occurred at two weeks and at one, two, three, and six months. The dependent measures included penile volume percent of change and a card sort of 10 scenes with the daughter into five classifications ranging from "no desire" to "very much desire." Interest and arousal were eliminated, with the exception of some renewed interest in the form of deviant fantasies at three months.

Levin, Barry, and Gambaro (1977) treated a pedophile sequentially with regular, covert sensitization and two variations. In one variation, psychologically aversive imagery (guilt, shame) was used, and in the other variation, physically aversive imagery (vomiting) was supplemented by an odiferous chemical, valeric acid. Dependent measures included penile erection and subjective ratings of slides and imagined scenes of girls and women. Treatment produced a significant decrease in sexual response to girls, with most of the change occurring during the second and third phases of covert sensitization, during which psychological imagery and chemically supplemented physical imagery were employed. Sexual responsivity to women also increased. Improvements were stable when measured at four evaluations over a 10-month follow-up period.

Maletzky (1974) treated 10 successive-exhibitionistic patients with "assisted" covert sensitization in which a vial of valeric acid was placed under the client's nose at critical points during scene presentations. There were 11 to 19 sessions with the therapist, plus in vivo sessions conducted by the client with the use of valeric acid. Not only was overt exposing behavior eliminated, but exhibitionistic fantasies, urges, and dreams ceased as well. Evaluations carried out at 3-, 6-, and 12-month intervals revealed no return of the behavior. A temptation test was employed, whereby the author hired a female to place herself in situations that had a high probability of eliciting exposing behavior. The temptation tests were conducted at post-treatment and one year later. One person failed the test at post-treatment but not at follow-up. All other subjects passed the test. Also, no patients were apprehended for indecent exposure during the course of treatment or the follow-up period.

Brownell and Barlow (1976) used a multiple-baseline design in their treatment of a person for exhibitionism and molestation. The patient was given covert sensitization for exhibitionism every other day for the first six weeks of treatment, while on an inpatient unit. The client was then administered covert sensitization twice per week for 10 weeks, for both urges to exhibit and urges for sexual contact with his stepdaughter. The aversive scene, paired with the deviant scene, consisted of being discovered by his wife or children. The dependent measures included ratings of scenes on a five-point scale of arousal and number of urges to expose and have sexual contact with the daughter. The treatment effect was specific to the target problem treated. Exhibitionistic urges and ratings dropped during the first treatment phase, while ratings and urges to molest remained unchanged. However, both types of urges and stimuli ratings decreased to zero during the second phase of treatment. These changes persisted during an 11-week follow-up period.

Brownell, Hayes, and Barlow (1977), using a single-subject experimental methodology, evaluated the relationship between distinct patterns of deviant sexual arousal and heterosexual arousal. Five subjects, each exhibiting two patterns of deviant arousal, were treated with covert sensitization. A multiple-baseline design allowed simultaneous measurement of two patterns of deviant arousal for each subject. Each form of deviant arousal did not decline until sequentially treated. Physiological and self-report measures of arousal further revealed that heterosexual arousal did not increase as deviant arousal declined, and conversely, deviant arousal did not decline when heterosexual arousal was first increased. There was a lack of generalization, in that each pattern of deviant arousal failed to decline until it was specifically treated with covert sensitization. That is, reduction of one pattern of deviant arousal had no effect upon other arousal patterns.

6. Shame aversion. Shame-aversion therapy, as described by Serber (1970), requires the exhibitionist to expose himself repeatedly to a mixed-sex audience who show no apprehension or particular interest in his penis. The client is instructed to describe past and present thoughts, feelings, and acts of exposure. The audience asks questions to promote greater disclosure. The procedure may lead to an extinction of the client's gratification from and expectation of either a stunned, shocked, or interested response from the victim. The procedure, furthermore, may be highly noxious and anxiety-provoking, so as to produce an aversive conditioning of the various aspects of exhibiting. Reitz and Keil (1971) described an exhibitionist who participated in 20 shame-aversion sessions during six months of treatment. Exposures were to four nurses, who remained impassive. The subject reported extreme embarrassment and eventually stopped exposing himself during the sessions. Over a year later, he reported no incidents of public exposure and a reduction in urges.

Stevenson and Jones (1972) had an exhibitionist go through 12 sessions of the above procedure. The client's behavior was discussed and related to his current feelings of anxiety, which were maintained at a high level by the intimacy of questioning and by the proximity of the audience. The treatment also included visualization of himself in a full-length mirror and videotape recording and playback. The frequency of exhibiting decreased from five exposures per month, eight years duration, to no exposures during a one-year follow-up. Although the subject was apprehensive and anxious about the sessions, the authors minimized the role of shame in this treatment case. They attributed the results to three other sources: negative practice, implosive therapy (flooding), and symptom scheduling.

Jones and Frei (1977) used provoked anxiety in the treatment of 15 subjects, who had been exhibiting for a mean duration of seven years, ranging in frequency from 8 to 12 exposures per month. The treatment consisted of undressing before a mixed audience, just as in the shame-aversion therapy described above. Videotaping and video playback were introduced after the fourth session. Subjects reported feelings of heightened tension and sweating. The authors claimed that shame and disgust played only a minor part in the treatment. They stated that the treatment could be understood as "aversive conditioning, though not only to the behavioural components of the act, but also to the particular cognitive accompaniments which seem necessary to sustain the behaviour." Follow-up of the 15 subjects ranged from nine months to five years. Exhibiting and related behavior were eliminated in 10 of the 15 subjects. Of the five showing further symptoms, three relapsed, and two masturbated (while remaining out of sight of the women being viewed). The five received further treatment with positive results.

Cognitive Therapies

Mahoney and Arnkoff (1978) grouped contemporary cognitive therapies under either cognitive-restructuring therapies, cognitive-skills therapies, or problem-solving therapies. While all psychotherapies may be attempts to assess and therapeutically alter clients' perceptions of themselves and their world, Mahoney declared that "the distinguishing feature of cognitive-learning therapies is their simultaneous endorsement of the importance of cognitive *processes* and the functional promise of experimentally developed *procedures*" (p. 703).

Meichenbaum and Novaco (1978, pp. 318–319) have stated that certain common treatment components seem to underlie the many different cognitive-behavioral treatment approaches, depending upon the particular treatment package employed:

1. Didactic presentation (often in the form of Socratic dialogue) and guided self-discovery of the role of cognitions in contributing to the client's subjective distress and performance inadequacies.
2. Training in the systematic observation and discrimination of self-statements and images, and self-monitoring of maladaptive behaviors.
3. Training in the fundamentals of problem solving (e.g., problem definition, anticipation of consequences, etc.).
4. Modeling, rehearsal, and encouragement of positive self-evaluation, coping, and attentional-focusing skills.
5. Graduated in vivo performance assignments.
6. The use of various behavior therapy procedures, such as relaxation training, coping-imagery training, and behavioral rehearsal.

Little attention has been given to impulse control by cognitive therapists, compared to the attention paid to anxiety, depression, and other types of disorders. Novaco's (1975) cognitive therapy for anger control and Watkins' (1977) cognitive restructuring and coping-skills training for a variety of impulse disorders will be considered. Novaco's treatment of anger utilizes a stress-inoculation procedure similar to that developed by Meichenbaum and Cameron (1972) for stress and phobic disorders. The stress-inoculation approach is a coping-skills therapy which involves three basic steps: cognitive preparation, skill acquisition and rehearsal, and application practice.

1. Stress inoculation for anger control. The central cognitive devices for anger regulation are a task orientation to provocation and coping self-statements. A task orientation involves attending to desired outcomes and implementing a behavioral strategy directed at producing these outcomes (Novaco, 1977a). Self-instructions are used to modify the appraisal of provocation and to guide coping behavior. The self-instructions are designed to apply to various stages of a provocation sequence: (a) preparing for provocation, (b) impact and confrontation, (c) coping with arousal, and (d) subsequent reflection in which the conflict is either resolved or unresolved. The following examples illustrate the kind of self-statements employed (Meichenbaum & Novaco, 1978, pp. 324–325):

1. *Preparing for a provocation:* "This could be a rough situation, but I know how to deal with it. Remember, stick to the issues and don't take it personally."
2. *Impact and confrontation:* "As long as I keep my cool, I'm in control of the situation. You don't need to prove yourself. Don't make more out of this than you have to."
3. *Coping with arousal:* "Relax and slow things down. Time to take a deep breath. My anger is a signal that it's time for problem solving."
4. *Subsequent reflection, conflict unresolved:* "Forget about the aggravation. Thinking about it only makes you upset. Try to shake it off."
5. *Subsequent reflection, conflict resolved:* "I handled that one pretty well. That's doing a good job! I could have gotten more upset than it was worth."

In addition to the cognitive aspects, Novaco's stress-inoculation procedure includes somatic (e.g., relaxation training) and behavioral aspects (e.g., assertion, role-playing, problem-solving action). Novaco's approach appears to be both a cognitive, coping-skills therapy and a task-oriented, problem-solving therapy. Novaco has not only used his approach with clients presenting with anger dyscontrol but also with police officers, in order to teach them to better manage their anger in the face of provocations from citizens (Novaco, 1977b).

Meichenbaum and Novaco (1978) have advocated "that the skills training conveys to participants a sense of control. This sense of control in turn influences participants' internal dialogue, which in turn influences ability to cope, and so on. The goal is to reverse the maladaptive, vicious cycle that leads to a sense of learned helplessness and to implement an adaptive, virtuous cycle that leads to a sense of learned resourcefulness" (p. 326). They also emphasize that the cognitive, skills-training procedure has generalization built into the package and that these techniques could be applied to other populations, such as child abusers, hypertensives, etc.

2. Cognitive restructuring and coping skills. Watkins (1973, 1977) has described the cognitive determinants and treatment of persons presenting with impulse-control problems (such as gambling, shoplifting, fire setting, impulse buying, obscene phone calls, window peeking, exhibiting, and molestation). Persons with impulse dyscontrol are *not* acting on the spur of the moment, although many would have us believe that their urges are sudden, compelling, and irresistible, and their behavior is unplanned. Some clients contend that they did not fully know what they were doing when committing impulsive acts. They frequently claim to have had no awareness of their thought processes prior to or at the moment of acting out and often externalize the blame by saying, "*It* (the urge) made me do it; I could not help myself."

The impulsive individual uses his feelings to justify the way he is. He pretends or may believe that he cannot help himself. He may come into therapy wondering aloud as to why he is the way he is. Some impulsive individuals appear to be quite psychologically minded, seeking to uncover the root causes of their impulses. It is easy for the therapist to get seduced into an archeological expedition into the causes and precursors of those feelings. Occasionally, a client can recall an early experience which may have led to his current behavior, e.g., a voyeur recalls peering into a window years ago and having masturbated afterwards. However, usually no original cause is found, the causes remain elusive, or insight arrived at is purely conjectual.

Perhaps some clients have a need to know and are struggling to make some sense out of their behavior, but answering "why" questions does not mean that one discovers "how to," that is, how to curb the impulse and change one's behavior. It is far more advisable to work on changing the thinking, rather than chasing down causes. Once the thinking changes, so will the feelings and behavior change. After weeks of monitoring his thinking, questioning the necessity of acting upon impulses which heretofore have propelled him into action, and substituting new thought patterns, the client reports a reduction in his acting out. He may also no longer experience the impulses with the previous frequency or urgency, or the client may report that the occasional, intense impulses experienced can be handled by stopping to consider his thoughts prior to acting upon urges and engaging in the new problem-solving, cognitive strategies.

Responsibility and eventual behavior change are fostered by increasing the client's awareness of his role in acting on his impulses, delving into the actual thoughts preceding and accompanying the urge, pointing out that the client himself has not always acted upon each urge experienced but rather has selected when to maintain control and when to relinquish control, and confronting his insistence on immediate gratification.

The treatment strategies in this approach include cognitive restructuring, self-instructional training, cognitive rehearsal, generation of alternatives, and homework assignments which are illustrated as follows:

1. *Cognitive restructuring.* Clients are asked to describe, in considerable detail, the stimulus situations in which their urges occur. They are to recall the exact instant they became aware of their urges and what thoughts were occurring at the moment. Should they recall no thoughts or images, the therapist can suggest that from their behavior and description of the stimulus situation they must have been thinking something like, "I want this, she looks too good to pass up, (etc.)." The first homework assignment may be to keep a notebook in which they record all future urges, descriptions of the situation, and stream of thoughts occurring at the time. Detection of thoughts may be facili-

tated by the therapist prompting the client to make "I" statements which express desires, e.g., "I want to (take this, set this on fire, show myself to her, etc.)." A further set of self-statements entailing demands are identified, e.g., "I've got to do this now, I have to look in the window, I can't stand the tension," etc. Clients are next confronted on how they have equated desires with demands. Repeated questioning by the therapist and by the clients themselves produces a discrimination that "While I may want to do this, I do not need to." Clients may learn, for the first time, that it is not really necessary to act upon these impulses, even though they wish to and experience temporary discomfort when foregoing the pleasure of the moment.

2. *Self-instructional training.* In addition to cognitive restructuring, clients are taught how to substitute new, coping self-statements, such as, "I can handle it. Remember to think. I don't *have to* do this, just because I want to. Put it out of your mind. Keep on going." Self-instructional training can be assigned to clients (both within and between sessions) for practice.

3. *Cognitive rehearsal.* Guided imagery and role-playing are used during treatment sessions in order to practice how past situations in which control was lost could have been handled successfully and to prepare for future situations in which temptations are anticipated.

4. *Generation of alternatives.* Coping with emotional arousal is further assisted by training clients to develop alternate responses. For example, clients with sexual urges are taught to plan ahead as to what other sexual releases are available to them. At the onset of an impulse, they are to tell themselves, "I'll wait and have sex with my wife, I can always masturbate and the tension will go away," etc.

5. *Homework assignments.* Recording urges and associated thoughts between treatment sessions is important in the training of clients to systematically monitor their cognitive processes and for involving clients in taking responsibility for their own treatment and behavioral change. Another self-help assignment involves clients approaching, in a graduated fashion, stimulus situations in which they have previously lost control, for the purposes of rehearsing their newly developed cognitive skills and developing confidence that they can control.

Certain treatment issues and client features are recurrent in cognitive therapy of impulsive clients. These are "development of control," "absolutistic thinking," the role of "deciding to change," "development of self-esteem," and "defenses and resistance."

Being out of control. The person with impulse-control problems acts as if he has no control and is at the mercy of his impulses; when in fact, he actually chooses to do what he does. He perceives, reflects upon, and evaluates the situation in determining whether he will act.

When first discussing his behavior, the client may be genuinely unaware of his thought processes and role in deciding upon his actions. Careful examination of the situation in which the client has acted out will reveal that he has had thoughts of how attractive the prospective act is to him and, furthermore, that he has evaluated the risks involved. For example, the kleptomaniac (who is beset by a sudden urge to steal an item of small value), may come to acknowledge that, upon seeing the object, he was attracted to it. As he reached for the item, he quickly glanced around to see if anyone was observing, and then he pocketed the item. The act of shoplifting may have occurred in less than five seconds. However, the client has mentally processed that he would like to have the item and that there is a low probability of being apprehended at the moment. These cognitive processes occur rapidly, are unobservable by others, and the suddenness of the act may give the appearance that it is beyond the person's conscious control.

In a group treatment program, a client was discussing how attractive he found a girl in short shorts standing in line in front of him at a bank teller's window. She possessed many of the stimulus features which had been sexually arousing to him when he had exposed himself. When asked how he could possibly control himself from exhibiting to her, he explained that, as many times as he had exhibited, he had never had the compulsion to do so in a bank. After all, he observed, he might be on camera, and there is a bank guard who might apprehend him. He and other members of the group laughed about the image of someone exhibiting in a bank. Each member described stimulus situations in which he would never act on his respective urge (exhibiting, shoplifting, etc.). The clients recognized that their dyscontrol was not attributable to some urge external to themselves over which they had no control. Quite to the contrary, they acknowledged that they chose when they would act on their impulses. Controlling themselves in some situations suggested that they might learn to control themselves in those situations in which they had acted out.

Absolutistic thinking. The impulsive person may engage in all-or-none thinking. That is, he believes that he has absolutely no control over his urges. They happen to him, and he has to act upon them as if he were being victimized. Focusing, during cognitive therapy, on the thoughts accompanying the acts reveals that the client is in the role of decision maker. Monitoring and recording his thoughts provide additional evidence that there are times during which he thinks about satisfying his desires, yet refrains from doing so for external ("people are watching") or internal ("not now") reasons. These variations in his behavior are important, for it can be pointed out to the client that he does not always yield to his impulses and therefore has already demonstrated, even prior to beginning treatment, that control is possible.

The impulsive individual may become discouraged if, after initial success in cognitive therapy, he again has an anger outburst, shoplifts, etc. He is like the depressed client reported by Beck, Rush, Shaw, and Emery (1979), who, during a period of dieting, became more depressed when she "slipped" and indulged herself in an ice cream cone. She, too, engaged in absolutistic thinking. In spite of having successfully lost several pounds, she believed that all was lost because she had failed to control her diet on this one occasion and that, furthermore, this proved that she was a failure as a person which she had believed all along. The impulsive client can be encouraged to recognize that relinquishing control in a situation does not mean that all is lost. Loss of control once does not mean that full or fuller control cannot be developed.

Deciding to change.   Many presenting persons are under duress. Their family or the court has given them an ultimatum that they must do something about their behavior, or else. Some come to treatment feeling guilty and remorseful and declare that they have wanted to stop all along. Others may be going through the motions, in order to get someone to take the heat off. Sometimes it is not until after the impulsive client has been working in cognitive therapy toward increasing his awareness of cognitions and countering with new thought patterns that he comes to a point of actually choosing to be different. Clients have stated that they are not all that persuaded as to the potential benefits of what they are doing. Some actively resist and argue that changing their self-statements is mechanical, artificial, or just a "head trip." For those treated in a group context, the decision to change may be facilitated by the opportunity for observing the changes being made by other persons further along in treatment and reflecting upon their own condition. One client remarked toward the end of his six months of treatment, "When I first came into group, I heard what you were saying and tried what you told me to practice. In spite of my success the first couple of months in not exhibiting, I hadn't decided to stop. Along about the third month, I realized that I could stop, and it was then that I decided I would stop."

In cognitive therapy, there may be many ways of arriving at the same endpoint. The above-mentioned client illustrates that cognitive rehearsal and behavioral homework assignments may have initially been mechanically performed, but perhaps led to an increased skill in handling urges, a reappraisal of his problem-solving ability, a reduction in feelings of helplessness and hopelessness, an increased sense of self-efficacy, a reappraisal of his possibilities, and, finally, a decision to change.

Developing self-esteem.   Most impulsive persons suffer from poor self-esteem and a negative view of self. Following their acts, they are often ashamed of their behavior and may be contrite for a while.

Learning to gain control over one's behavior leads to an increase in confidence and self-esteem. The person who has been acting on impulse comes to appreciate that he can alter his behavior. He may have believed that his behavior was beyond his control and despaired over the possibility of ever being able to stop what he was doing. Learning that his behavior is not inevitable and that he need not act on his feelings of the moment puts him back in charge. He may derive a sense of accomplishment and competency from his newly experienced control. No longer need he act on a whim of the moment. Now he knows what to do. He has become aware of the thoughts that occur with the impulses. He can begin to weigh the necessity of acting upon the urge. As one client expressed it, "I am so much more confident in myself now. I am talking much more freely about my feelings and problems with my wife, now that I know there is something I can do about it (molestation). Also, I am more competent in my work; even when I don't know what to do, I figure that maybe I can figure it out."

Defenses and resistance. Persons presenting for treatment are often already utilizing one or more strategies for coping with their impulses. Having referred themselves for treatment, or having been referred by the court, the person may have resolved not to repeat the act. One often sees clients utilizing one of the following three A's: Avoidance, Aversiveness, Activity. The client protects himself from acting on his urges by avoiding temptation. He stays away from stimulus situations in which he has previously acted out, or he may enter those critical situations only with a companion in tow. One shoplifter avoided department stores for months after her arrest. An exhibitionist would not go driving in his car without a family member with him. An obscene telephone caller was exceedingly uncomfortable when home alone and would avoid looking at the telephone. Avoidance is a useful strategy for openers.

Clients who have had families threaten to ostracize them for their behavior or who have been arrested, jailed, and publicly exposed often experience embarrassment, guilt, and revulsion. They speak of the aversiveness of their recent experience and enumerate the negative consequences for self and family. These negative consequences are uppermost in their mind in the first few weeks following their ordeal. Early in treatment, the client may frequently review these consequences and assure the therapist that he has learned his lesson. The aversiveness of his recent experience is thought by him to be enough to deter him from further acting on his urges.

The client may also throw himself into high-pitched activity. He gets a new job, a second job, works on physical fitness, enrolls in night school, reads the Bible, etc. He is sure that, with his new commitment to a life full of busyness and substitute activities, he will not only not act on his impulses but will also be much too occupied to experience or even think about them.

The strategies of avoidance, recall of aversiveness, and heightened activity may serve the client well. They get him through a period of vulnerability to both the onslaught of further impulses and his anxiety about the consequences of further losses of control. The risk of repeating the acts during the first few weeks following apprehension is reduced. In this sense, his defenses protect him. However, there is a negative, illusory aspect also involved, in that the client may be deceiving himself into thinking that these are sufficient conditions for deterrence. For instance, it is not feasible for persons living a normal life to permanently avoid the marketplace, telephones, the opposite sex, or children. The aversive aspects of recent experiences diminish with time and may be suddenly overshadowed by the resurgence of the impulse. One can stay only so busy, and even highly structured activities are no guarantee against further impulses and opportunities for acting on them. For instance, one client announced, in the second treatment session, that he had solved his problem by having started a new job and enrolling in courses during the evenings. The very next session, he reported that he had again exhibited during a 30-minute period between getting off work and arriving at his next destination.

Two other defenses occasionally recognized in the person with impulse control disorder are denial and abdication of responsibility. Some clients will deny past, present, or future impulses. They may describe the incident or incidents for which they have been apprehended as having been characterized by no feelings or affective arousal. The kleptomaniac may contend that he has no personal interest in or attraction to the object stolen. The pedophile may disclaim any sexual interest or arousal and claim that he was merely touching the child in a fatherly way. Further exploration usually reveals his denial to be deliberate distortion or perceptual inattention to what he was feeling and experiencing at the time of the act. Second, the client may admit to having experienced urges in the past, but he now claims that that is all behind him, that there have been no recent urges, and that there will be no future recurrence. This stance may be prompted by his reluctance to take on the role of a client in therapy who has a real problem which he has been unsuccessful in handling alone. Some clients rigidly adhere to this position and are not accessible to exploring their thoughts, images, and feelings.

Abdication of responsibility takes many forms. The stand of some clients is, "There is nothing I can do. I can't stop myself when I get the compulsion to . . ." Some clients may genuinely believe in their powerlessness, in that thus far, they have been so unsuccessful in stopping their problem behavior. Another type of abdication involves the espousal of religious beliefs in such a way as to place the course of events before a higher power. One client exclaimed, "I have prayed about this quite a bit. I have put my trust in the Lord. I have taken this to Him, and I know that He will see me through this. My faith is that He will take care of this." Such patients can wrap themselves in the sanctity of their professed faith and thwart attempts to engage them in the process of discovering how their behavior occurs and ways in which they can actively develop self-control.

Denial and abdication of responsibility are not useful defenses. They do not provide protection but only a false safety. They are ways of "washing one's hands" of past misdeeds and refusing to face reality squarely. They promote false optimism and hinder or preempt the reeducative process of how to control one's urges.

CONCLUSIONS AND RECOMMENDATIONS FOR PRACTICE

The medical and behavioral therapies have demonstrated that clients may change when treated with any one of the several biological or behavioral procedures reviewed in this chapter. All of the studies could be critiqued on one or more bases. Many are case-study reports on only one or a few individuals. Most produced mixed results and had too brief a follow-up period to assess the lasting effects of respective treatments. Even when the same treatment approach was used, therapists often varied widely in what they did procedurally with research subjects. Treatment outcome was sometimes confounded, in that patients may have received multiple interventions concomitantly, such as medroxyprogesterone acetate plus milieu therapy or aversive conditioning plus social-skills training. In spite of the methodological shortcomings, the medical and behavioral therapies probably produced beneficial effects with certain clients under specific conditions. Of all of the approaches, the behavioral therapies of impulse control have no equal in regard to the empirical studies generated.

The apparent effectiveness of lithium carbonate, anti-androgens, and surgical castration as treatments for problems of aggressiveness or sexual deviancy may be attributable to biological and/or psychological changes produced. For instance, there may be a similar genetic basis in manic-depressive disorder and certain other impulse-control disorders which accounts for the positive response to lithium carbonate. While the elimination or control of sexual deviancy through functional or surgical castration has been demonstrated, the etiological factors are poorly understood (Berlin & Meinecke, 1981). The reduction in testosterone levels may produce only a temporary suppressant effect, which dissipates post-treatment (Berlin & Meinecke, 1981) or leads to marked improvement in psychosocial functioning and, subsequently, an absence of a return to pre-treatment sexual behavior (Gagné, 1981). The relative roles of biological and psychological changes are, at this time, unknown.

Recent cognitive therapies have specified their procedures and have begun to treat problems of impulse control. It should be possible to evaluate the efficacy of cognitive treatments, although assessing the effects of alterations in cognitions alone may be difficult, in that most cognitive therapies are actually "cognitive-behavioral packages" in which there is a simultaneous focusing on feelings, actions, role-playing, cognitive rehearsal of future behavioral sequences, homework assignments, etc. Thus, isolating the cognitive variable to measure its effect may be elusive and illusory.

The behavioral therapies seem to have ignored personality and cognitive variables, except in passing. For example, Feldman (1966) reported markedly different results of aversion-relief therapy in the treatment of homosexual urges, depending upon the interest of the clients in changing. Evans (1970) showed that clients engaging in deviant masturbatory fantasies had a slower and poorer response to aversion therapy. Levin, Barry, and Gambaro (1977) observed that shame and guilt may have been overlooked as individual differences which may portend for a better treatment outcome. Jones and Frei (1977) did not consider their provoked-anxiety approach to have been successful simply as a function of aversive conditioning. They viewed the high level of anxiety as facilitating reexamination of habitually held attitudes and the revised assessment of the deviant behavior. Jones and Frei concluded, "These cognitive and confrontational aspects of treatment in the high-anxiety setting are not accounted for by the conditioned-avoidance model." Human- and animal-learning research has frequently found that cognitive factors can either greatly facilitate or greatly diminish conditioning effects, and Bandura (1973) has observed that advanced information-processing capacities render human behavior more subject to social and cognitive control.

Behavioral therapies have been predicated upon the belief that conditioning trials are necessary for changes in behavior and emotions to occur, and that then changes in attitude may follow. Hallam, Rachman, and Falkowski (1972) discovered serendipitously that these changes do not occur in one direction only. They treated alcoholic subjects with electrical aversion, on an inpatient unit. A control group of alcoholic patients who attended group meetings, AA talks, etc. was also examined. The successful cases, regardless of whether they were in the treatment or in the control condition, showed a significant heart-rate sensitivity to alcoholic stimuli and attitudinal effects. There were also strong suggestions from the data that, if patients do not report subjective or attitudinal shifts post-treatment, their clinical prognosis is poor. The authors found the most interesting outcome of their investigation to be in the control group. The successful cases in the control condition shared with the aversion-therapy successes the only two clinically significant variables of change, viz., persisting heart-rate sensitivity and the same attitudinal shifts on the evaluative and anxiety factors. The persisting heart-rate responsivity of the control group was not expected, which led the authors to conclude that, if a general therapeutic improvement takes place, then the patient becomes physiologically sensitive to alcoholic stimuli. Hallam et al. (1972, p. 13) stated that, their findings "provide another example of 'mediation' from attitude change to physiological change and 'mediation' may not work in one direction only." Although their findings appeared to favor a cognitive explanation of aversion-therapy effects, they cited earlier arguments by Rachman and Teasdale (1969) to the effect that "a purely cognitive explanation is as unsatisfactory as a purely noncognitive explanation" (p. 117).

With the development of recent cognitive therapies, there may be a movement toward a more-holistic and integrated view of human behavior. Thoughts, images, and fantasies alter the emotional state of the person, yet do not operate in a vacuum. Bandura (1973) described behavior as regulated by stimuli, reinforcement, and cognitions, none of which operate independently, but rather, actions are controlled by two or more of these influences. Bandura offered the following examples:

> In order to establish and to maintain effective stimulus control, the same actions must produce different consequences, depending on the cues that are present. Stimulus and cognitive influences, in turn, can alter the impact of prevailing conditions of reinforcement. Cognitive events, however, do not function as autonomous causes of behavior. Their nature, their emotion-arousing properties, and their occurrence are under stimulus and reinforcement control (pp. 52–53).

Changes produced by the behavior therapies or medical treatments may also be found eventually to be attributable to a chain of events. For example, aggressive behavior or sexual deviation may be brought under external control via manipulation of social contingencies, aversive-conditioning trials, lithium carbonate, medroxyprogesterone acetate, etc. With the alteration in stimulus and reinforcement conditions, the client observes that he is responding differently physiologically and behaviorally to stimuli which heretofore were associated with loss of control. His behavioral success may lead to a lessening of feelings of helplessness and greater optimism about the possibility of change. There may be a growing awareness that, "I don't have to do that any more," followed by an increased sense of self-control. Throughout this process, there may be a shift from external control to internal control, whereby the client attributes the maintenance of behavioral change to his own conscious and active decisions that he does not have to, and is not going to, engage in the old behavior. The external control initially provided by drugs or electric shock may have faded, while internal controls developed and maintained the behavioral change.

Bandura (1977) has suggested that the apparent divergence of theory and practice can be reconciled by postulating that cognitive processes mediate change but that cognitive events are induced and altered most readily by the experience of mastery arising from effective performance. His theory of *self-efficacy* is based on the principal assumption that psychological procedures, whatever their form, serve as means of creating and strengthening expectations of personal efficacy. It is hypothesized that expectations of personal efficacy determine whether coping behavior will be initiated, how much effort will be expended, and how long it will be sustained in the face of obstacles and aversive experiences. Mastery expectations influence performance and are, in turn, altered by the cumulative effects of one's efforts.

A similar formulation has been advanced by Scheff (1963), in his discussion of the sociocultural dynamics of mental disorder. In discussing the role of self-image, Scheff observed the following:

> For the person who sees himself as endowed with the trait of self-control, self-control is facilitated, since he can imagine himself enduring stress during his imaginative rehearsal, and also while under actual stress. For a person who has acquired an image of himself as lacking the ability to control his own actions, the process of self-control is likely to break down under stress. Such a person may feel that he has reached his "breaking point" under circumstances which would be endured by a person with a "normal" self-conception. This is to say, a greater lack of self-control than can be explained by stress tends to appear in those roles for which the culture transmits imagery which emphasizes lack of self-control. In American society, such imagery is transmitted for the roles of the very young and very old, drunkards and drug addicts, gamblers, and the mentally ill (p. 420).

A holistic view would be that any of the treatment approaches which produce a positive result are likely to be characterized by cognitive, affective, behavioral, and physiological changes. A difference between cognitive and other therapies may be that cognitive therapies intentionally focus upon cognitive components, in the belief that internal control is more likely to result. The advantages of cognitive therapy or a combined, integrative approach would seem to be that one is teaching the client a set of coping skills and a problem-solving approach, which will lead to greater personal resourcefulness and ability to generalize to new or unexpected situations. Laws (1980, p. 211) has stated that it is "essential that clients become their own agents of change . . . Clients, after all, think and presumably they think about the goals of therapy [and] strategies of the behaviour change."

Attributing control to oneself may be a critical factor in behavioral change and in promoting generalization. Davison and Valins (1969) and Davison, Tsujimoto, and Glaros (1973) reported a greater persistance in treatment gains when clients attributed the gains to their own self-control, rather than to some external agent. Kopel and Arkowitz (1975) also found that behavioral procedures which maximized self-attributions of behavioral change facilitated maintenance. Bandura (1977) reported that enhanced self-efficacy, once established, tends to generalize to other situations in which performance was self-debilitated.

While all of the treatment procedures described in this chapter merit serious scientific consideration, they raise social and ethical questions. One could elect shame-aversion therapy as the treatment seeming to produce the most-immediate results with exhibitionists, but shaming the client may be repugnant to some therapists. Electrical-aversion therapy may be more acceptable but, due to its anticipated painfulness, is refused by a significant number of clients, which suggests that those submitting themselves to treatment may be doing so because of legal coercion. The medical ethics involved in treating sexual deviants have been examined by Halleck (1981) who has stated,

> The current work with anti-androgens will inspire demands for an escalated use of biological treatments by those who desire more social control. It is certain to elicit a powerful cry of alarm from civil libertarians. Psychiatrists will once again be in the center of controversy. This controversy is too important to justify our taking a passive stance . . . that we are just practicing medicine. We need to develop ethical guidelines for the use of anti-androgen drugs right now (p. 643).

The treatments in this chapter could be ordered on a continuum (from drastic to benign) as follows: surgical castration, electrical-aversion therapy, shame aversion, anti-androgen injections, lithium carbonate, covert sensitization, stimulus satiation or flooding, altering social contingencies, reconditioning, social-skills training, cognitive therapy. At the more drastic end of the continuum are those therapies which are the most intrusive, painful, irreversible, or potentially damaging. Which type of client, with which impulse-control disorder, of what magnitude or severity, should each of the above treatment procedures be prescribed or warranted? There are, at present, no empirical answers to the above question; but in the face of increasing public demand for social control and the questionable genuineness of the consent of subjects who participate in our experiments, it may behoove us to lean toward the most humanistic and benign treatments, lest we develop cures worse than the diseases. Ethical questions surely will be raised if the more radical procedures are used prior to more benign ones having been attempted.

SUMMARY

Persons with disorders of impulse control are characterized by a failure to resist an impulse, often an increasing sense of tension before committing the act, and either pleasure or a reduction in tension at the time of committing the act. Sociological, biological, and several different psychological perspectives of these disorders were reviewed. Sociological factors associated with deviant behavior were not found to be markers specific to disorders of impulse control versus other behavioral or psychiatric disorders. The biological and physiological studies on impulsive individuals were found to be inconclusive. The review of the biological aspects of mental disorders revealed that generally there were no demonstrated biological bases for the paraphilias, kleptomania, and pyromania. The psychoanalytic approach is long on theory and exceedingly short on demonstrated treatment effectiveness. The Oedipus complex and castration anxiety or penis envy were posited as the central factors in nearly all disorders of impulse control, from gambling to the paraphilias. Other psychological theories reviewed included the behavioral and cognitive theories. The behavioral approach has emphasized the classical-conditioning basis for much sexual deviancy, postulating that any stimulus associated with sexual excitement and orgasm tends to become conditioned in a classical way and leads to arousal in the future. The cognitive approach emphasizes the centrality of the person himself in the loss of control. The subject is seen as mediating the whole experience and only acting *as if* the impulses were irresistable.

The most-promising approaches in the treatment of disorders of impulse control appear to be the behavioral, medical, and cognitive approaches, while most of the outcome studies have been conducted in either the behavioral or biological treatments of these disorders. Overall, the studies suggest that specific subgroups of impulse-control disorders are benefitted by certain behavioral or medical treatments. However, a few of the methodological shortcomings are that there are mixed results within studies, the outcomes are not consistent across studies, there is often too little follow-up, there may be high rates of relapse, and there is often a confounding of the specific treatment with other concomitant interventions. The change mechanisms are poorly understood, even in the studies producing the most-impressive outcome and maintenance.

A chain-of-events theory was proposed by the author, which views behavioral change as being initiated from any one of several approaches. For example, cognitive therapy may lead to an increased awareness of and skill in handling urges, a reappraisal of one's problem-solving ability, a reduction in feelings of helplessness, an increased sense of self-control, a reappraisal of one's possibilities, a decision to change, increased abstention, gradual extinction or diminution of the urge, substitution of prosocial behaviors, etc. In contrast, the aversive and anti-androgen therapies may first produce a marked change in drive state, which may then be followed by the client's responding to his behavioral abstention with a lessening of feelings of helplessness, a greater optimism about the possibility of change, an increased sense of self-control, etc., such that a similar endpoint is reached. A holistic model, in which physiological, behavioral, or cognitive changes may result in subsequent changes in the other respective systems, was offered. Such a model was viewed as consistent with Bandura's (1977) theory of self-efficacy. Cognitive therapy or a combined, integrated approach—in which external controls are faded while internal controls are developed—were viewed as important to the issues of maintenance of behavioral change and generalization of control to new stimulus situations.

REFERENCES

Adler, A. Organ inferiority. In *The neurotic constitution: Outlines of a comparative individualistic psychology and psychotherapy.* (B. Glueck & J. E. Lind, trans.). New York: Moffat & Yard, 1917.

Akers, R. L. Problems in the sociology of deviance: Social definition and behavior. *Social Forces,* 1968, *46,* 463.

American Psychiatric Association. *Diagnostic and statistical manual of mental disorders* (3rd ed.). Washington, D.C.: Author, 1980.

Bach-y-Rita, G., Lion, J. R., Climent, C. E., & Ervin, F. R. Episodic dyscontrol: A study of 130 violent patients. *American Journal of Psychiatry,* 1971, *127,* 1473–1478.

Bancroft, J., & Marks, I. Electric-aversion therapy of sexual deviations. *Proceedings of the Royal Society of Medicine,* 1968, *61,* 796–799.

Bandura, A. *Aggression: A social-learning analysis.* Englewood Cliffs, N.J.: Prentice-Hall, 1973.

Bandura, A. Self-efficacy: Toward a unifying theory of behavioral change. *Psychological Review,* 1977, *84,* 191–215.

Barker, J. C., & Miller, M. Aversion therapy for compulsive gambling. *British Medical Journal,* 1966, *2,* 115.

Barlow, D. H., Leitenberg, H., & Agras, W. S. Experimental control of sexual deviation through manipulation of the noxious scene in covert sensitization. *Journal of Abnormal Psychology,* 1969, *74,* 597–601.

Barry, D. J., & Ciccone, J. R. Use of Depo-Provera in the treatment of aggressive sexual offenders: Preliminary report of three cases. *Bulletin of the American Academy of Psychiatry Law.* 1975, *3,* 179–184.

Beach, F. A. Experimental studies of sexual behavior in male mammals. *Journal of Clinical Endocrinology,* 1944, *4,* 126–134.

Beach, F. A. Hormonal effects on sociosexual behavior in dogs. In E. J. Plotz & H. Gibian (Eds.), *Mammalian reproduction.* New York: Springer, 1970.

Beck, A. T., Rush, A. J., Shaw, B. F., & Emery, G. *Cognitive therapy of depression.* New York: Guilford Press, 1979.

Becker, H. S. *Outsiders.* New York: Free Press, 1963.

Berlin, F. S., & Meinecke, C. F. Treatment of sex offenders with anti-androgenic medication: Conceptualization, review of treatment modalities, and preliminary findings. *American Journal of Psychiatry,* 1981, *138,* 601–607.

Blumer, D., & Migeon, C. Hormone and hormonal agents in the treatment of aggression. *Journal of Nervous and Mental Disease,* 1975, *160,* 127–137.

Bromberg, W. Sex offense as a disguise. *Correctional Psychiatry,* 1965, *11,* 293–298.

Brownell, K. D., & Barlow, D. H. Measure and treatment of two sexual deviations in one person. *Journal of Behavior Therapy and Experimental Psychiatry,* 1976, *7,* 349–354.

Brownell, K. D., Hayes, S. C., & Barlow, D. H. Patterns of appropriate and deviant sexual arousal: The behavioral treatment of multiple sexual deviations. *Journal of Consulting and Clinical Psychology,* 1977, *45,* 1144–1155.

Cooper, A. J., Ismail, A. A., Phanjoo, A. L., & Love, D. L. Anti-androgen (cyproterone acetate) therapy in deviant hypersexuality. *British Journal of Psychiatry,* 1972, *120,* 58–64.

Cornu, F. *Catamnestic studies on castrated sex delinquents from a forensic-psychiatric viewpoint.* Basel, Germany: Karger, 1973.

Cox, D. J., & Daitzman, R. J. Behavioral theory, research, and treatment of male exhibition-ism. In M. Hersen, R. M. Eisler, & P. M. Miller (Eds.), *Progress in behavior modification* (Vol. 7). New York: Academic Press, 1979.

Davison, G. C., Tsujimoto, T. N., & Glaros, A. G. Attribution and the maintenance of behavior change in falling asleep. *Journal of Abnormal Psychology*, 1973, *82*, 124–133.

Davison, G. C., & Valins, S. Maintenance of self-attributed and drug-attributed behavior change. *Journal of Personality and Social Psychology*, 1969, *11*, 25–33.

Durkheim, E. *The rules of sociological method*. New York: Free Press, 1938.

Eibl, E. Treatment and aftercare of 300 sex offenders, especially with regard to penile plethysmography. In Justizministerium Baden-Württemberg (Ed.), *Proceedings of the German conference of treatment possibilities for sex offenders in Eppingen, 1977*. Stuttgart: 1978.

Erickson, K. T. Notes on the sociology of deviants. *Social Problems*, 1962, *9*, 308.

Evans, D. R. Masturbatory fantasy and sexual deviation. *Behaviour Research and Therapy*, 1968, *6*, 17–19.

Evans, D. R. Subjective variables and treatment effects in aversion therapy. *Behaviour Research and Therapy*, 1970, *8*, 147–152.

Eysenck, H. J. *Crime and personality*. London: Paladin, 1970.

Feldman, M. P. Aversion therapy for sexual deviation: A critical review. *Psychological Bulletin*, 1966, *65*, 65–79.

Feldman, M. P., MacCulloch, M. J., & MacCulloch, M. L. The aversion-therapy treatment of a heterogenous group of five cases of sexual deviation. *Acta Psychiatrica Scandinavia*, 1968, *44*, 113–123.

Fenichel, O. Denial of castration with over-cathexis of a partial instinct. *The psychoanalytic theory of neurosis*. New York: W. W. Norton, 1945.

Fookes, B. H. Some experiences in the use of aversion therapy in male homosexuality, exhibitionism, and fetishism-transvestism. *British Journal of Psychiatry*, 1969, *115*, 339–341.

Ford, C., & Beach, F. A. *Patterns of sexual behavior*. New York: Harper & Row, 1951.

Freud, S. Dostoievsky and parricide. In *Collected papers* (Vol. 5). Hogarth Press: 1950; and in *The complete psychological works* (Vol. 21). London: Hogarth Press, 1961.

Gagné, P. Treatment of sex offenders with medroxyprogesterone acetate. *American Journal of Psychiatry*, 1981, *138*, 644–646.

Gebhard, P., Gagnon, J., Pomeroy, W., & Christenson, C. *Sex offenders*. New York: Harper & Row, 1965.

Gibbs, J. P. Issues in the defining of deviant behavior. In R. A. Scott & J. D. Douglas (Eds.), *Theoretical perspectives on deviance*. New York: Basic Books, 1972.

Giffin, M. W., Johnson, A. M., & Litin, E. M. Antisocial acting out, II: Specific factors determining antisocial acting out. *American Journal of Orthopsychiatry*, 1954, *24*, 668–684.

Gillespie, W. H. The structure and etiology of sexual perversion. In S. Lorand & M. Balint (Eds.), *Perversions: Psychodynamics and therapy*. New York: Gramercy, 1956.

Goorney, A. B. Treatment of a compulsive horse-race gambler by aversion therapy. *British Journal of Psychiatry*, 1968, *114*, 329–333.

Hallam, R.S., & Rachman, S. Some effects of aversion therapy on patients with sexual disorders. *Behaviour Research and Therapy*, 1972, *10*, 171–180.

Hallam, R. S., Rachman, S., & Falkowski, W. Subjective, attitudinal, and physiological effects of electrical-aversion therapy. *Behaviour Research and Therapy*, 1972, *10*, 1–13.

Halleck, S. L. The ethics of anti-androgen therapy (editorial). *American Journal of Psychiatry*, 1981, *138*, 642–643.

Harbert, T. L., Barlow, D. H., Hersen, M., & Austin, J. B. Measurement and modification of incestuous behavior: A case study. *Psychological Reports*, 1974, *34*, 79–86.

Hare, R. D. *Psychopathology: Theory and research.* New York: John Wiley & Sons, 1970.

Heim, N. Sexual behavior of castrated sex offenders. *Archives of Sexual Behavior*, 1981, *10*, 11–19.

Heim, N., & Hursch, C. J. Castration for sex offenders—Treatment or punishment: A review and critique of recent European literature. *Archives of Sexual Behavior*, 1979, *8*, 281–304.

Hinsie, L. E., & Campbell, R. J. *Psychiatric Dictionary.* New York: Oxford University Press, 1960.

Jackson, B. T. A case of voyeurism treated by counterconditioning. *Behaviour Research and Therapy*, 1969, *7*, 133–134.

Jacobs, P. A., Brunton, M., & Melville, M. M. Aggressive behavior, mental subnormality, and the XYY male. *Nature*, 1965, *208*, 1351–1352.

Johnson, A. M. Factors in the etiology of fixations and symptom choice. *Psychoanalytic Quarterly*, 1953, *22*, 475–496.

Jones, F. D. Therapy for firesetters (letter). *American Journal of Psychiatry*, 1981, *138*, 261–262.

Jones, I. H., & Frei, D. Provoked anxiety as a treatment of exhibitionism. *British Journal of Psychiatry*, 1977, *131*, 295–300.

Keutzer, C. S. Kleptomania: A direct approach to treatment. *British Journal of Medical Psychology*, 1972, *45*, 159–163.

Kohlenberg, R. J. Treatment of a homosexual pedophiliac using in vivo desensitization: A case study. *Journal of Abnormal Psychology*, 1974, *83*, 192–195.

Kopel, S. A., & Arkowitz, H. The role of attribution and self-perception in behavior change: Implications for behavior therapy. *Genetic Psychology Monographs*, 1975, *92*, 175–212.

Kraft, T. Treatment of compulsive shoplifting by altering social contingencies. *Behaviour Research and Therapy*, 1970, *8*, 393–394.

Kremsdorf, R. B., Holmen, M. L., & Laws, D. R. Orgasmic reconditioning without deviant imagery: A case report with a pedophile. *Behaviour Research and Therapy*, 1980, *18*, 203–207.

Kurland, M. Pedophilia erotics. *Journal of Nervous and Mental Diseases*, 1960, *131*, 394–403.

Langelüddeke, A. *Castration of sexual criminals.* Berlin: de Gruyter, 1963.

Laschet, U., & Laschet, L. Anti-androgens in the treatment of sexual deviations of men. *Journal of Steroid Biochemistry*, 1975, *6*, 821.

Laws, D. R. Treatment of bisexual pedophilia by a biofeedback-assisted self-control procedure. *Behaviour Research and Therapy*, 1980, *18*, 207–211.

Lester, D. *Unusual sexual behavior: The standard deviations.* Springfield, Ill.: Charles C Thomas, 1975.

Levin, S. M., Barry, S. M., & Gambaro, S. Variations of covert sensitization in the treatment of pedophilic behavior: A case study. *Journal of Consulting and Clinical Psychology,* 1977, *45,* 896–907.

Litin, E. M., Giffin, M. E., & Johnson, A. M. Parental influence in unusual sexual behavior in children. *Psychoanalytic Quarterly,* 1956, *25,* 37–55.

Lykken, D. F. A study of anxiety in the sociopathic personality. *Journal of Abnormal and Social Psychology,* 1957, *55,* 6–10.

MacCulloch, M. J., Williams, C., & Birtles, C. J. The successful application of aversive therapy to an adolescent exhibitionist. *Journal of Behavior and Experimental Psychiatry,* 1971, *2,* 61–66.

Mahoney, M. J., & Arnkoff, D. B. Cognitive and self-control therapies. In S. L. Garfield & A. E. Bergin (Eds.), *Handbook of psychotherapy and behavior change: An empirical analysis* (2d ed.). New York: John Wiley & Sons, 1978.

Maletzky, B. M. "Assisted" covert sensitization in the treatment of exhibitionism. *Journal of Consulting and Clinical Psychology,* 1974, *42,* 34–40.

Mark, V. H., & Ervin, F. R. *Violence and the brain.* New York: Harper & Row. 1970.

Marshall, W. L. A combined-treatment method for certain sexual deviations. *Behaviour Research and Therapy,* 1971, *9,* 293–294.

Marshall, W. L. The modification of sexual fantasies: A combined-treatment approach to the reduction of deviant sexual behavior. *Behaviour Research and Therapy,* 1973, *11,* 557–564.

Marshall, W. L. Satiation therapy: A procedure for reducing deviant sexual arousal. *Journal of Applied Behavior Analysis,* 1979, *12,* 377–389.

Marshall, W. L., & McKnight, R. D. An integrated-treatment program for sexual offenders. *Canadian Psychiatric Association Journal,* 1975, *20,* 133–138.

Martin, J. O. A psychological investigation of convicted incest offenders by means of projective techniques. *Dissertation Abstracts International,* 1960, *21,* 241.

Matza, D. *Becoming deviant.* Englewood Cliffs, N.J.: Prentice-Hall, 1969.

McGuire, R. M., Carlisle, J. M., & Young, B. G. Sexual deviations as conditioned behaviour: A hypothesis. *Behaviour Research and Therapy,* 1965, *2,* 185–190.

Meichenbaum, D., & Cameron, R. *Stress innoculation: A skills-training approach to anxiety management.* Unpublished manuscript, University of Waterloo, 1972.

Meichenbaum, D., & Novaco, R. Stress innoculation: A preventative approach. In C. Speilberger & I. Sarason (Eds.), *Stress and anxiety (Vol. 5).* New York: John Wiley & Sons, 1978.

Miller, H. L., & Haney, J. R. Behavior and traditional therapy applied to pedophiliac exhibitionism: A case study. *Psychological Reports,* 1976, *39,* 1119–1124.

Money, J. Use of an androgen-depleting hormone in the treatment of male sex offenders. *The Journal of Sex Research,* 1970, *6,* 165–172.

Money, J. The therapeutic use of androgen-depleting hormones. In Resnick & Wolfgang (Eds.), *Treatment of the sex offender,* International Psychiatry Clinics series, Vol. 8, No. 4, Boston: Little, Brown, 1972.

Money, J., Wiedeking, C., Walker, P., Migeon, C., Meyer, W., & Borgaonkar, D. 47,XYY and 46,XY males with antisocial and/or sex-offending behavior: Anti-androgen therapy plus counseling. *Psychoneuroendocrinology,* 1975, *1,* 165–178.

Moran, E. Pathological gambling. *British Journal of Psychiatry,* 1975, *9,* 416–428.

Moskowitz, J. A. Lithium and lady luck: Use of lithium carbonate in compulsive gambling. *New York State Journal of Medicine*, 1980, *80*, 785–788.

Nadler, R. P. Approach to the psychology of obscene telephone calls. *New York State Journal of Medicine*, 1968, *68*, 521–526.

Novaco, R. W. *Anger control: The development and evaluation of an experimental treatment.* Lexington, Mass.: D. C. Heath, 1975.

Novaco, R. W. Stress innoculation: A cognitive therapy for anger and its application to a case of depression. *Journal of Consulting and Clinical Psychology*, 1977, *45*, 600–608. (a)

Novaco, R. W. A stress-innoculation approach to anger management in the training of law enforcement officers. *American Journal of Community Psychology*, 1977, *5*, 327–346. (b)

Obendorf, C. P. Voyeurism as a crime. *Journal of Criminal Psychopathology*, 1939, *1*, 103–111.

Peck, D. F., & Ashcroft, J. B. Untitled paper. Presented to second Conference on Behaviour Modification, Kilkenny, Ireland, 1970.

Pinta, E. R. Treatment of obsessive homosexual pedophilic fantasies with medroxyprogesterone acetate. *Biological Psychiatry*, 1978, *13*, 369–373.

Price, W. H., & Whatmore, P. B. Behaviour disorders and pattern of crime among XYY males identified at a maximum security hospital. *British Medical Journal*, 1967, *1*, 533–536.

Rachman, S. Sexual fetishism: An experimental analog. *Psychological Record*, 1966, *16*, 293–296.

Rachman, S., & Teasdale, J. *Aversion therapy and behaviour disorders: An analysis.* London: Routledge & Kegan Paul, 1969.

Rada, R., Laws, D., & Kellner, R. Plasma-testosterone levels in the rapist. *Psychosom. Med.*, 1976, *28*, 257–268.

Raymond, M. J. Aversion therapy for sexual deviations. *British Journal of Psychiatry*, 1969, *115*, 979–980.

Reitz, W. E., & Keil, W. E. Behavioral treatment of an exhibitionist. *Journal of Behavior Therapy and Experimental Psychiatry*, 1971, *2*, 67–69.

Rhodes, R. J., & Levinson, M. Sexual deviancy treatment: A case study of a child molester. *Journal of the Kansas Medical Society*, 1977, *78*, 122–124.

Rickles, N. K. Exhibitionism. *Journal of Nervous and Mental Diseases*, 1942, *95*, 11–17.

Rogers, L. Male hormones and behavior. In B. Lloyd & J. Archer (Eds.), *Exploring sex differences.* New York: Academic Press, 1976.

Rooth, F. G. Indecent exposure and exhibitionism. *British Journal of Psychiatry*, 1975, *9*, 212–222.

Rooth, F. G., & Marks, I. M. Persistent exhibitionism: Short-term response to aversion, self-regulation, and relaxation treatments. *Archives of Sexual Behavior*, 1974, *3*, 227–248.

Rosen, I. *The pathology and treatment of sexual deviation.* New York: Oxford University Press, 1964.

Rosen, I. The basis of psychotherapeutic treatment of sexual deviation. *Proceedings of the Royal Society of Medicine*, 1968, *61*, 793–796.

Rosenthal, T. L. A case study. *Journal of Nervous and Mental Disorders,* 1973, *156,* 440–443.

Scheff, T. J. The role of the mentally ill and the dynamics of mental disorder. *Sociometry,* 1963, *26,* 436–453. Reprinted in T. Millon (Ed.), *Theories of psychopathology and personality* (2d ed.). Philadelphia: W. B. Saunders, 1973.

Seager, C. P. Treatment of compulsive gamblers by electrical aversion. *British Journal of Psychiatry,* 1970, *117,* 545–553.

Serber, M. Shame-aversion therapy. *Journal of Behavior Therapy and Experimental Psychiatry,* 1970, *1,* 213–215.

Sheard, M. H., Marini, J. L., Bridges, C. I., & Wagner, E. The effect of Lithium on impulsive-aggressive behavior in man. *American Journal of Psychiatry,* 1976, *133,* 1409–1413.

Snyder, S. H. *Biological Aspects of Mental Disorder.* New York: Oxford University Press, 1980.

Spodak, M. K., Falck, Z. A., & Rappeport, J. R. The hormonal treatment of paraphiliacs with Depo-Provera. *Criminal Justice and Behavior,* 1978, *5,* 304–313.

Stekel, W. Narcissism and infantile regression. *Zeitschrift fur Sexualwissenschaft und Sexualpolitik,* 1920, *7,* 241.

Stevenson, J., & Jones, I. H. Behavior-therapy techniques for exhibitionism. A preliminary report. *Archives of General Psychiatry,* 1972, *27,* 839–841.

Thio, A. *Deviant behavior.* Boston: Houghton Mifflin, 1978.

Ullmann, L. P., & Krasner, L. *A psychological approach to abnormal behavior.* Englewood Cliffs, N. J.: Prentice-Hall, 1969.

Walker, P. A. *MPA as an anti-androgen for the rehabilitation of sex offenders.* Paper presented at the Association of Sex Therapists and Counselors, Charleston, S.C., April 1977.

Watkins, J. T. Rational-emotive therapy and the treatment of behavioral excesses. *Rational Living,* 1973, *8,* 29–31.

Watkins, J. T. The rational-emotive dynamics of impulsive disorders. In A. Ellis & R. Grieger (Eds.), *Handbook of rational-emotive therapy.* New York: Springer, 1977.

Wetzel, R. Use of behavioral techniques in a case of compulsive stealing. *Journal of Consulting Psychology,* 1966, *30,* 367–374.

19

Treatment of substance abuse

Ted D. Nirenberg, Ph.D.*

The physical and psychological effects of substance abuse are serious and pervasive problems for the abuser and for society. Treatment of substance abuse has focused on alcohol abuse, obesity, cigarette smoking, and drug abuse.

The present chapter focuses primarily on alcohol abuse for three reasons. First, the space limitation of the chapter precludes a thorough review of each of the addictive behaviors. A cursory review of each of the substances would be too limited in depth. Second, research focusing on the treatment of alcohol abuse has frequently been the forerunner and impetus for investigations regarding the other addictive behaviors. Third, there is evidence that the understanding and treatment of the various substance abuses are similar (Miller, 1980). For instance, the misuse of the various substances tends to result in similar health risks, which increase in severity when the substances are combined. The use or misuse of one substance also appears to trigger the use or misuse of another substance, and there appears to be a positive correlation between addictions. As Miller (1980) pointed out, addictive behaviors may be viewed as part of a more general behavior pattern, involving a person's belief about personal health and safety. The abuses of the different substances also share similar assessment strategies (i.e., self-reports, direct-behavioral observations, and physiological monitoring), involve physical and/or psychological dependence, have been assumed to share similar etiological bases (e.g., arousal theory, external responsiveness, and learning theory) and respond to similar treatment strategies (e.g., relaxation, physical exercise, self-management, and contingency management).

---

* Veterans Administration Medical Center, Providence, Rhode Island, and Brown University.

ASSESSMENT

While the traditional view of alcohol abuse assumes many commonalities among alcohol abusers, empirical evidence suggests that alcohol abuse represents a complex, multidimensional problem, which frequently varies in intensity and etiology. Therefore, a detailed assessment of alcohol use and of the variables that maintain alcohol abuse is essential in order to enable the clinician to formulate the most effective treatment plan. The technology of assessment of alcohol abuse has improved at a rapid rate during the past decade.

Understanding alcohol abuse requires assessment of the antecedents and the consequences of alcohol use as well as the alcohol drinking itself. The present review of assessment strategies will focus primarily on assessment of the actual drinking response (i.e., the rate and the amount of alcohol consumption). It should be stressed, however, that a functional analysis of alcohol abuse would also include evaluation of a complex assortment of possible antecedent and consequential variables including, for example, marital, vocational, assertiveness and social skills, irrational thoughts, financial problems, and physical health (Sobell, Sobell, & Nirenberg, 1981). A review of the assessment procedures for many of these areas is presented elsewhere in the present volume and, therefore, will not be addressed here. The assessment of the drinking response has included: (1) standardized drinking scales; (2) analogue drinking measures; (3) self-monitoring; (4) breath tests; and (5) biochemical indicants of drinking. While each of these methods contributes to the overall assessment of alcohol abuse, no single method has been found to be totally adequate.

The standardized drinking scales (which are usually easy to administer) essentially attempt to differentiate alcoholics from nonalcoholics. These scales have been designed to assess alcoholism by either indirect or direct questioning about alcohol use. For example, the MacAndrew Scale (AMac; MacAndrew, 1965), an indirect approach, derived a typical response profile of alcoholics from 49 items abstracted from the Minnesota Multiphasic Personality Inventory (MMPI). Typically, alcoholics reported themselves to have physical effects of excessive alcohol intake; religious beliefs; history of school problems; few problems with concentration, sex, or self-image; and to be outgoing and social. The Michigan Alcohol Screening Test (MAST; Selzer, 1971), a more direct approach, contains 25 items which address drinking habits. While these scales may be useful as initial screening devices to identify the alcohol abuser, they are not very useful in subsequent treatment.

Client self-reports of drinking have clearly been the most frequently used evaluation tool. While traditionally the validity of alcoholics' self-reports has been assumed to be rather poor, recent investigations have found that, under certain conditions, the alcoholics' self-reports are quite accurate (Sobell & Sobell, 1975; Sobell & Sobell, 1978; Polich, Armor, & Braiker, 1980; Sobell, Sobell, & VanderSpek, 1979). Significant information may be obtained from clients during the initial interview. This should include information regarding: (1) specific quantities of alcohol normally consumed via available quantity-frequency scales or time-line procedures (Maisto, Sobell, Cooper, & Sobell, 1981; Sobell, Cellucci, Nirenberg, & Sobell, 1981); (2) location and contexts of drinking; (3) drinking patterns; (4) the situational determinants of drinking (e.g., angry, depressed, negative self-statements, bored, and lonely); (5) presence and history of alcohol-withdrawal symptoms; (6) indicants of tolerance (i.e., highest blood-alcohol level recorded, most alcohol consumed in one day); and (7) health history. Asking clients to maintain self-monitoring (drinking-awareness) forms prior to and during treatment is also helpful. On self-monitoring forms, clients can provide information regarding the date and time of drinking, type and amount of alcohol consumed, and the situational determinants of drinking (Sobell & Sobell, 1973a; Nirenberg, Sobell, Ersner-Hershfield, 1981). Additionally, reports by client collaterals (e.g., friends, family, employers) provide a reliability check of client self-report as well as a source of unique information.

Analogue drinking measures, in which clients are given access to alcoholic beverages, provide an assessment of the rate, style, and amount of drinking. In one very popular analogue measure, the taste-rating task (Marlatt, Demming, & Reid, 1973; Miller & Hersen, 1972), a subject is presented with a few glasses containing either alcoholic or nonalcoholic beverages and then asked to rate each beverage on several dimensions. Supposedly unaware that consumption is being measured, the subject is then asked to taste each drink as much as needed to make their ratings. While one study indicated that a subject's consumption during the taste test was predictive of the subject's response to treatment (Miller, Hersen, Eisler, & Elkin, 1974), the extent that drinking in such contrived situations conducted in laboratory settings is representative of a client's regular drinking patterns needs further investigation. In an attempt to observe clients drinking in a more natural environment, several investigators have monitored client drinking in a simulated bar (Sobell, Schaefer, & Mills, 1972) or in a living room setting (Miller, Becker, Foy, & Wooten, 1976).

The use of breath tests to determine blood-alcohol levels (BALs) of clients provides a reliable and valid measure of a subject's level of alcohol intoxication. Breath testing is useful during assessment, treatment, and as an outcome measure. For instance, alcohol intoxication during assessment, even in small amounts, can jeopardize the accuracy of a patient's self-report (Sobell & Sobell, 1978). Routine breath tests can screen out intoxicated patients, who then can be rescheduled for their assessment interview. While a therapist may feel capable in determining the level of intoxication of patients, the phenomenon of acquired tolerance to alcohol allows some patients to appear sober, even though they have a high blood-alcohol level (Maisto, Henry, Sobell, & Sobell, 1978; Sobell, Sobell, & VanderSpek, 1979). Inexpensive, portable breath-alcohol testers make it possible for clients to accurately determine their own BAL. For instance, a subject who is about to operate a motor vehicle can use a breath tester to determine whether he is legally under the influence of alcohol (Sobell, VanderSpek, & Saltman, 1980). Additionally, as an outcome measure, random breath tests provide a means to validate subject self-report of recent alcohol use.

There have been several recent investigations examining the utility of biochemical markers as an assessment of drinking behavior (e.g., Ryback, Eckardt, & Pautler, 1980; Reyes & Miller, 1980; Rosalki & Rau, 1972). It appears that gamma-glutamyl transpeptidase (GGT) and serum glutamic oxalacetic transaminase (SGOT), enzymes normally found in low levels in the blood serum, are reactive to abusive alcohol consumption (e.g., Reyes & Miller, 1980; Davis, 1980; Ryback et al., 1980; Rosalki & Rau, 1972). Compared to nonalcohol-abuser controls, GGT & SGOT levels are significantly higher in alcoholics and problem drinkers (e.g., Rollason, Pincherle, & Robinson, 1972; Burrows, Feldman, & McBridge, 1975; Reyes & Miller, 1980). These enzyme levels also appear to be reactive to periods of sustained abstinence from alcohol—among problem drinkers with elevated enzyme levels after a three- to four-week period of abstinence, enzyme levels significantly reduce (Pomerleau & Adkins, 1980). Although enzyme levels cannot precisely assess drinking behavior that has occurred over long periods of time, they can provide an objective measure of recent changes in abusive drinking patterns. The use of GGT and SGOT levels alone to assess alcohol abuse should be tempered, however, since conditions other than alcohol might produce abnormal elevations—diabetes, heart failure, liver or pancreatic disorders, or use of barbituates, opiates, or dilantin (e.g., Rollason et al., 1972; Westwood, Cohen, & McNamara, 1978; Goldberg & Martin, 1975; Spencer-Peet, Wood, & Glatt, 1973). However, when used in conjunction with a screening for physical variables related to elevated enzyme levels, periodic monitoring of enzyme levels provides an excellent source of additional outcome data.

TREATMENT GOALS

Treatment goals should be developed based upon the comprehensive assessment of the client's life functioning. Since clients enter treatment with differing past experiences, abilities, strengths, and dysfunctions, these factors should be carefully considered and incorporated into the treatment plan.

As noted earlier, since drinking is seldom an alcohol abuser's only problem, and since alcohol misuse damages many aspects of a person's life, treatment should focus on several components of life functioning;

therefore, several treatment goals should be developed. When problems are identified, treatment goals first must be prioritized, so that the most acute problem will be addressed at the onset. For example, a chronic alcoholic initially should be detoxed and have access to adequate room and board. Unless these fundamental yet critical objectives are met, addressing more complex problems (e.g., marital conflict, unemployment, or interpersonal-skills deficits) may be extremely difficult and probably fruitless. It is therefore necessary to set short- and long-term goals in a prioritized fashion. Whereas long-term goals represent the aim and ultimate purpose of therapy, short-term goals are usually incremental, proximal objectives that relate in a stepwise progression to a long-term goal. Short-term goals provide a mechanism to shape the client toward a long-term goal, thereby providing numerous opportunities to reinforce the client's initial behavior change.

When developing treatment goals and choosing the strategies to accomplish these goals, one must be cognizant that different treatment goals and strategies require different costs for clients. A therapist should strive to develop, not simply the most effective treatment, but rather a treatment that is effective and minimally restrictive. For example, the most effective treatment for an alcohol abuser who drinks abusively in response to peer pressure simply would be to restrict him to an environment which contains no peer pressure to drink. This strategy would, however, be quite restrictive and costly to the client, since he may be forced to avoid friends who drink, find a new job in which few fellow employees drink, and avoid drinking situations (e.g., restaurants, bars, and parties). On the other hand, an effective but less restrictive strategy would involve assertiveness training, in which the client learns to handle peer pressure.

The most controversial issue regarding the treatment of alcohol abuse has been the drinking goal itself—abstinence versus moderate (nonproblem) drinking. The traditional disease model, supported by Alcoholics Anonymous, assumes that alcoholism is governed by an irreversible disease entity; therefore, the only viable treatment goal is abstinence. While a goal of abstinence appears very useful for many alcohol abusers, there has been substantial and growing evidence of successful nonabstinent treatment outcomes (Armor, Polich, & Stambul, 1976; Sobell & Sobell, 1976; Vogler, Compton, & Weissbach, 1975). A few correlational studies suggest that clients most likely to succeed in a nonabstinence-oriented program are those who reported a shorter history of drinking problems and less pre-treatment alcohol-consumption and alcohol-withdrawal symptomatology. Also, when selecting a drinking goal, one should consider client choice and physical contraindications of further drinking (e.g., cirrhosis, pancreatitis, or diabetes).

Once selecting a drinking goal, the therapist and client should not feel compelled to restrict themselves to the specific, chosen goal. Treatment planning frequently requires updating and revision. For example,

if a client is unable to maintain a moderate drinking goal following intensive treatment efforts, this information is critical and may suggest that
abstinence is more appropriate.

Abstinence and nonabstinence goals also are not mutually exclusive
and can be used quite effectively at different times with the same client.
A recent case of the present author serves as a good example. The
client, a 21-year-old college student, reported a three-year history of alcohol abuse. A functional analysis of the client's drinking behavior revealed
that his abusive drinking was related to: (1) inadequate interpersonal
skills; (2) a lack of adequate problem-solving skills; and (3) inadequate
life-planning skills (i.e., poor self-direction). The client requested training
on how to drink in a nonproblem fashion. A three-phase treatment program included: (a) drug-enforced abstinence (client self-administered disulfiram for two months); (b) self-enforced abstinence—client abstained
from drinking without disulfiram for one month; (c) nonproblem drinking—client engaged in nonproblem drinking. The drug-enforced abstinence was intended to provide: (1) the therapist an opportunity to observe
and evaluate the client's behavior without the interference of alcohol;
(2) the therapist an opportunity to train social skills and problem-solving
skills, while the client was deprived of his most salient coping behavior—
drinking; and (3) the client an opportunity to practice these skills, without
the interference of alcohol. The self-enforced abstinence served to extend
the abstinence period and demonstrate to the client that he could abstain
from alcohol on his own. The final phase of nonproblem drinking provided
an opportunity for the client to self-monitor his drinking behavior, practice
nonproblem-drinking skills, and receive therapeutic feedback and support. A one-year follow-up evaluation (including three interviews and
monthly telephone contacts with the client) revealed that the client was
functioning well and engaging in occasional, nonproblem drinking. Similarly, the utilization of pre-programmed moderate drinking with clients
who ultimately strive for abstinence may be useful. For example, a client
who initially may be unable to abruptly abstain from alcohol may benefit
by being reinforced for reducing alcohol consumption gradually.

TREATMENT TECHNIQUES

Behavioral treatment of alcohol abuse, although still viewed by many
professionals as limited to aversive therapy and the modification of response contingencies, has (over the past decade) evolved into a multidimensional treatment strategy. Behavioral techniques have been used to
modify behaviors which precipitate problem drinking, to develop alternative adaptive behaviors, to modify the actual drinking response, as well
as to change response contingencies which reinforce abusive drinking.

Social-skills training

Several studies have suggested that problem drinkers, as compared to nonproblem drinkers, are more likely to drink excessively in situations which commonly elicit specific interpersonal behaviors. For example, Miller, Hersen, Eisler, and Hilsman (1974) found that alcoholics exposed to a stressful, interpersonal role-playing conflict subsequently drank significantly more alcohol than after participating in a nonstressful role-playing situation. Miller and Eisler (1977) found that, although inpatient alcoholics reported themselves as generally more assertive than nonalcoholic psychiatric inpatients, a behavioral test indicated that the alcoholics were only more assertive in expressing positive feelings and were equally assertive in expressing negative feelings. Additionally, they noted that the least assertive alcoholics drank more than the most assertive. Higgins and Marlatt (1975) found that male college students, who anticipated being socially evaluated by a female, significantly increased their alcohol consumption. Male and female subjects, provoked to anger and not given the opportunity to retaliate, also consumed more alcohol in a taste-rating task than did those who were allowed to retaliate after provocation (Marlatt, Kosturn, & Lang, 1975). In a review of the literature on interpersonal competence in alcoholics, O'Leary, O'Leary, and Donovan (1976) concluded that "prealcoholic" teenagers exhibited more social-skills deficits than did their moderate-drinking and abstinent peers.

Few investigations have examined the effects of alcohol consumption on subsequent interpersonal behavior. While some experimental studies have reported that alcoholics exhibit increased socializing after consuming alcoholic beverages (Griffiths, Bigelow, & Liebson, 1974; 1975; Tamerin & Mendelson, 1969), it is not known whether these findings generalize to nonlaboratory settings.

Marlatt and Rohsenow (1980) have reviewed a number of studies which highlight the importance of mediating cognitive factors on subsequent alcohol effects. For instance, Lang, Goeckner, Adesso, and Marlatt (1975) found that males who believed they had consumed an alcoholic beverage (blood-alcohol concentration of .10 percent) exhibited significantly more aggression when provoked than did subjects who believed they had consumed only tonic water. Surprisingly, the actual amount of alcohol consumed, although it led to increased reaction time, did not influence subsequent aggression.

Overall, it appears that alcohol abusers: (1) have inadequate social skills and, consequently, may not receive appropriate social reinforcement; (2) drink abusively in response to interpersonal situations with which they cannot adequately cope; and then (3) alter their interpersonal behavior, either as a result of alcohol consumption or by simply believing that they have consumed alcohol. Similar findings have been suggested for other substance abusers.

Investigations evaluating the efficacy of social-skills training with substance abusers have focused primarily on assertiveness training. Assertiveness training is designed to teach people to communicate personal rights and feelings to others so as to derive maximum reinforcement. Training typically consists of therapeutic instruction, modeling, role-playing, and feedback. Hirsch, von Rosenberg, Phelan, and Dudley (1978) examined the utility of assertiveness training with inpatient alcoholics. In addition to routine inpatient care, 102 subjects were randomly assigned to: (1) an assertiveness-training group involving 10 hours of assertiveness training; (2) a minimal assertiveness-training group, including 2 hours of open-ended discussion on why group members behave unassertively and how to distinguish assertive and unassertive behaviors; or (3) a no-treatment control group. Comparison of pre- and post-scores on the Rathus Assertiveness Scale, Behavioral Assertiveness Test, and Assertive Behavior Index indicated that subjects in the 10-hour assertiveness-training group exhibited significantly more assertiveness than either other group. However, the influence of training on alcohol consumption was not addressed.

Eisler, Miller, Hersen, and Alford (1974) used assertiveness training with a 52-year-old outpatient alcoholic reporting a six-year history of alcohol abuse. Excessive drinking was precipitated by the patient's inability to respond effectively with marital disagreements, usually involving the discipline of his daughter, amount of time he spent with his wife, and his wife's disapproval of even his moderate drinking. He reported that he would remain passive and allow his wife to predominate. Training focused on four areas of assertive behavior, including: (1) duration of looking, (2) duration of speech, (3) requests made of his wife, and (4) latency of response. Pre- and post-training videotaped observation of the couple's interaction showed improvement for all assertion areas. Both husband and wife indicated a large decline in the subject's alcohol consumption. Also, weekly breath-alcohol levels declined, from a mean of .08 percent prior to training, to .02 percent after training.

Freedberg and Johnston (1978; 1979) examined the effects of assertiveness training as a component of a comprehensive treatment program with employed alcoholics. According to one-year follow-up results, the abstinence rate among subjects who received assertiveness training was higher (36 percent) than that among subjects who had not received the training (24 percent). Subjects receiving assertiveness training also tended to have a higher improvement rate (72 percent as compared to 57 percent in the control group), and more improved self-reports of assertiveness, employment status, work productivity, and psychological functioning. In an earlier study, in an attempt to examine the utility of videotape feedback in assertiveness training, Scherer and Freedberg (1976) also found that employed alcoholics exposed to six sessions of assertiveness training exhibited more improvement on a self-report assertion scale. In addition, they found that assertiveness training with or without videotape feedback was equally effective. Videotape equipment, therefore, may only increase the cost of training.

Faced with the familiar temptations, "Have a beer," or "Aren't you going to drink?" many problem and nonproblem drinkers report that they have difficulty refusing. Reports of relapse among problem drinkers frequently revolve around the inability of the person to refuse social pressure to drink (Marlatt, 1978). Foy, Miller, Eisler, and O'Toole (1976) used assertiveness training to teach drink-refusal skills to two chronic alcoholics who had difficulty in resisting social pressure to drink. Drink-refusal skills included: (1) requesting that the pusher refrain from offering drinks; (2) offering an alternative to the pusher (e.g., "Let's have a cup of coffee instead"); (3) changing the drinking conversation to a different topic; (4) duration of direct eye contact and affect when communicating with the pusher. At a three-month follow-up assessment, subjects exhibited improvement on drink-refusal skills, and they reported better control over their drinking.

In an interesting study, Hamilton and Maisto (1979) found that alcoholics and nonalcoholics did not differ in regard to assertive behavior but, rather, showed significant differences on the amount of self-reported discomfort felt when performing assertive behavior. It may therefore be useful to focus not only on assertive-behavior training but also on ways to reduce the amount of psychological discomfort felt by alcoholics in assertion-required situations.

Problem-solving skills

The inability of many alcoholics to effectively deal with problem situations prompted several investigators to incorporate problem-solving training into treatment programs. Problem-solving training, as outlined by D'Zurilla and Goldfried (1971), consists of a general orientation, problem definition and formulation, generation of alternatives, decision making, and verification.

Intagliata (1978) used problem-solving training with inpatient alcoholics. Although the authors indicated that subjects receiving problem-solving training did better on a behavioral problem-solving task at a predischarge assessment than subjects not exposed to problem-solving training, at a one-month follow-up, only 14 of the 22 contacted subjects reported that they had utilized the problem-solving skills. The authors also noted that, at follow-up, subjects seemed to have forgotten significant portions of the training materials. As the authors noted, the use of follow-up refresher sessions may improve treatment maintenance.

Chaney, O'Leary, and Marlatt (1978) evaluated the effectiveness of problem solving with assertiveness training. Forty inpatient alcoholics were randomly assigned to either the skills-training, discussion, or control groups. The skills-training group consisted of eight semiweekly, 90-minute sessions focusing on problem-solving and assertiveness skills. Through the use of instruction, modeling, feedback, and role-playing, subjects were trained to deal with a variety of problem situations. Subjects in the discussion group discussed the same problem situations as were used in the skills group, but in a nondirective manner. The control group was exposed to only routine treatment activities. At a one-year follow-up, subjects in the skills-training group, as compared to the discussion and control groups, reported fewer total number of days drunk, fewer total number of drinks consumed, and a shorter average drinking-period length.

Vocational skills

In our society, since a person's worth is frequently based upon his/her work productivity and success, employment status undoubtedly has an enormous effect on an individual's behavior. While alcohol abuse among workers has received much attention as an economic problem to industry, the influence of employee vocational skills on alcohol abuse has received little attention (USDHEW, 1981). In a case study by Foy, Massey, Dyer, Ross, and Wooten (1979), three male alcoholics received assertiveness training to help them deal effectively with "on-the-job" situations which require assertive responding (e.g., You have had a very busy day at work and are tired. Your boss comes up to you and asks you to stay late for the third time this week.). While the authors reported improvement on assertiveness ratings at a six-month follow-up, the influence of training on drinking behavior was not reported.

Miller, Stanford, and Hemphill (1974) included vocational counseling in a comprehensive treatment program for alcoholics. The program entailed eight weeks of inpatient care, followed by one year of outpatient care. In addition to vocational counseling, the program included a functional analysis of alcohol-related behaviors, a token-economy ward system, covert sensitization, and training in social skills, self-management skills, relaxation, and recreational activities. Vocational counseling, which was considered one of the most important aspects of the program, entailed training on preparing a job resume, interviewing for jobs, and on effectively responding to difficult interactions with an employer or co-worker. In addition, a contract was negotiated between subjects and their employers, regarding the subject's use of disulfiram. Follow-up evaluations, conducted from 8 to 24 months, indicated that 62 percent of the subjects who had completed the program were either abstinent or were drinking in a more improved manner. However, since subjects received all components of the treatment program, it is not possible to delineate the utility of the vocational component.

Disulfiram

When a person taking disulfiram (Antabuse) ingests even a small amount of alcohol, a very unpleasant reaction occurs characterized by nausea, flushing, increased skin temperature, and hypotension. While the disulfiram-alcohol reaction has been well documented (Kitson, 1977; Sauter, Boss, & von Wartburg, 1977), the efficacy of disulfiram treatment on alcohol abuse has been equivocal (Fuller & Roth, 1979; Kwentus & Major, 1979; Mottin, 1973). When taken once per day as prescribed, disulfiram is an effective deterrent to drinking for up to two or three days. This serves well for motivated, abstinent clients who have sudden urges to drink but who, nonetheless, continue taking disulfiram on a daily basis.

Compliance with disulfiram treatment, however, is usually quite poor (Paulson, Krause, & Iber, 1977; Gerrein, Rosenberg, & Manohar, 1973; Blackwell, 1973), with reports that as few as 1 percent of disulfiram users maintained their prescribed dosage after one year (Lubetkin, Rivers, & Rosenberg, 1971). In an attempt to improve compliance in an outpatient treatment program, Bigelow, Strickler, Liebson, and Griffiths (1976) utilized refundable deposits as an incentive for consistent administration of disulfiram. Twenty male outpatient alcohol abusers posted a monetary deposit, which was refunded contingent upon their taking disulfiram daily for three months. Failure to take their disulfiram (as agreed upon in a contract signed by the subject and the therapist) resulted in only partial refunds. While subjects reported longer periods of abstinence following the program than during the preceding three years, since a control group was not used, the actual utility of the refundable deposits is unclear. Also, in an attempt to reduce the poor compliance of oral disulfiram administration, disulfiram which is fat soluble has been subcutaneously implanted in alcohol abusers (Wilson, 1975; Obholzer, 1974). Although this procedure eliminates the need for daily administration of disulfiram, disulfiram implants have been reported to produce variable blood levels of disulfiram (Wilson, 1975) and sporadic and variable intensity disulfiram-alcohol reactions (Malcolm, Madden, & Williams, 1974; Kline & Kingstone, 1977).

Traditionally, the efficacy of disulfiram was based upon an aversion or fear model. Patients were given a loading dose of disulfiram, followed by a dose of alcohol, so they could experience the negative reaction and were then simply told to maintain a daily dosage of disulfiram. Theoretically (and quite understandably), the patient learned to fear consuming alcohol when taking disulfiram. However, the simple fear model has been found to be insufficient, as documented by a high relapse rate among disulfiram users. An alternative approach utilizes disulfiram as a time-limited component of a multifaceted treatment program. Disulfiram is first presented as providing a time-out from the pressures of making decisions about drinking. During this time-out period, the client acquires a new behavior repertoire that will substitute for problem drinking. When the client reaches a predetermined behavioral goal, disulfiram administration is interrupted, to allow for testing the strength of the new skills. The outcome of this trial determines the advisability of reinstating or discontinuing disulfiram.

Aversive conditioning

While early reports of aversive conditioning seemed promising, recent studies have questioned the efficacy of these methods. Aversive conditioning involves the pairing of a noxious stimulus (i.e., electric shock, nausea, or apnea-inducing substances, or covert aversive events) with the sight, smell, and/or taste of alcohol. Theoretically, through Pavlovian conditioning, drinking, or alcohol-related cues, following repeated association with the noxious stimulus, comes to elicit an aversive reaction similar to that elicited by the noxious stimulus. As a consequence, subsequent alcohol consumption is extinguished.

Electrical-aversion conditioning pairs faradic shock with the sight, smell, or taste of alcohol (this method should be distinguished from electroconvulsive therapy (ECT), in which electric current is passed through the brain). Electrical-aversion procedures have varied widely across studies, regarding the site of shock delivery (i.e., fingers, legs, and feet), the intensity and duration of shock, and the conditioning paradigm employed. While electrical aversion has been the most commonly used aversion method, several reviews have concluded that electrical aversion is relatively ineffective with alcoholics (Nathan & Briddell, 1977; Wilson, 1978).

Chemical-aversion conditioning involves the use of substances (such as emetine and anectine, which produce nausea and vomiting and respiratory paralysis, respectively). While chemical aversion appears more effective than electrical aversion, it is more difficult to administer since: (1) the therapist has less-precise control over the onset, intensity, and duration of the chemical reaction; (2) it is limited to only one conditioning trial per session; (3) it requires close medical supervision; (4) averse drug reactions are possible; and (5) the generally debilitating nature of the treatment may result in both patient and staff resistance.

Several early-treatment outcome studies at Shadel Hospital (Seattle, Washington) on the efficacy of chemical aversion reported abstinence rates between 60–70 percent at one-year follow-ups (Lemere & Voegtlin, 1950; Voegtlin & Broz, 1949; Voegtlin, 1940; Voegtlin, Lemere, Broz, & O'Hollaren, 1942). However, because these studies exposed subjects to several additional treatment procedures (i.e., family and vocational counseling and disulfiram), it is not possible to delineate the utility of the aversion component. Since these early studies, reports on the efficacy of chemical aversion have been equivocal: with abstinence rates at 6- to 12-month follow-ups ranging from a mere 4 percent to as high as 63 percent (e.g., Wiens, Montague, Manaugh, & English, 1976; Neubuerger, Matarazzo, Schmidt, & Pratt, 1980; Miller, Dvorak, & Turner, 1960; Wallerstein, 1956). In a review of several of these studies, Miller and Hester (1980) concluded that chemical aversion was somewhat effective with highly motivated patients with intact jobs and marriages and middle to high socioeconomic status, but less effective with other patient populations.

The relative success of chemical as compared to electrical aversion has been explained in terms of the biological appropriateness of the two aversive stimuli (Revusky, 1973; Wilson & Davison, 1969). This hypothesis is based upon experimental research with animals, which has shown that taste aversions are more easily conditioned when the noxious, unconditioned stimulus is sickness (elicited by poison or x rays), rather than electric shock. Therefore, the use of nausea, rather than shock, as the unconditioned stimulus should more effectively produce taste aversion to alcohol.

In covert sensitization, typically subjects are first verbally guided in detailed imagery depicting a scene in which the subject usually drinks alcohol. When they imagine that they are about to drink alcohol, they are instructed to immediately imagine intense feelings of nausea and general malaise. Similar to electrical- and chemical-aversive conditioning, the pairing of the imaginal aversion and the thought of drinking are believed to produce a conditioned aversion to alcohol. Covert sensitization may be the most promising of the aversive techniques, since it is based upon nausea (a biologically appropriate aversion) but, at the same time, has fewer of the practical disadvantages of chemical aversion. Despite early encouraging reports on the clinical efficacy of covert sensitization (Anant, 1967; Cautela, 1966; Ashem & Donner, 1968), the recent use of covert sensitization with other treatment components and inadequate post-treatment follow-up make it difficult to delineate its effectiveness (Little & Curran, 1978; Elkins & Murdock, 1977). In one of the few controlled studies, Hedberg and Campbell (1974) compared covert sensitization, electrical aversion, systematic desensitization, and behavioral family therapy. Subjects were male outpatients, who chose either an abstinence or controlled-drinking treatment goal. While subjects in the covert-sensitization group reported much lower rates of goal attainment (40 percent) than either the behavioral family therapy (74 percent) or the systematic-desensitization groups (67 percent), the electrical-aversion group (in which 66 percent dropped out) showed only negligible changes (0 percent).

Nonproblem-drinking skills

With the introduction of nonproblem drinking as an optional goal for treatment, came greater interest in the development of techniques to train clients how to drink appropriately. As a prerequisite, came investigations aimed at studying specific situational determinants of drinking. Although it was common knowledge that problem drinkers drank more than social drinkers, information regarding the particular drinking characteristics and patterns of the problem drinker was scant. A comparison of alcoholics with nonproblem drinking community volunteers revealed that alcoholic subjects not only drank more but gulped their drinks more, drank faster, and sipped their drink less often than nonproblem drinkers (Schaefer, Sobell, & Mills, 1971; Sobell, Schaefer, & Mills, 1972). Alcoholics also more often ordered straight drinks, while nonproblem drinkers usually ordered mixed drinks; and nonproblem drinkers were able to name significantly more mixed drinks ($M = 10.3$) than alcoholics ($M = 3.9$) (Sobell, Sobell, & Schaefer, 1971; Williams & Brown, 1974).

Setting variables were found to influence alcohol consumption. Rosenbluth, Nathan, and Lawson (1978), observing men and women patrons (ages 18–22) of a university-sponsored beer parlor, found that: (1) subjects in groups drank more than those in dyads; (2) mixed-sex dyads drank faster than same-sex dyads; and (3) males drank more and faster than females. Caudill and Marlatt (1975) investigated the influence of another person, who modeled either high- or low-drinking rates, on a subject's total wine consumption in a wine-tasting task. Subjects exposed to high-drinking models drank significantly more wine and took more sips than subjects in the low-model group or no-model control. Garlington and DeRicco (1977) also found that subjects changed their drinking rates in the direction of either a high- or low-drinking model.

Based upon the preliminary evidence of problem-drinking response style and setting influences, a few investigators have attempted to modify the drinking behavior of problem drinkers. Mills, Sobell, and Schaefer (1971) utilized negative contingencies to change the drinking style of 13 inpatient alcoholics. Subjects were given the opportunity to order, at most, five standard alcoholic beverages. Strong electrical shocks (not harmful but described as quite annoying by subjects) were delivered when subjects ordered or consumed more than three drinks or gulped a straight drink. Mild shocks were delivered when subjects ordered and gulped a mixed drink or ordered and sipped a straight drink. Subjects were not punished when they ordered or sipped three or less mixed drinks or ordered nonalcoholic drinks. Although the investigators reported that subjects exhibited favorable within-session changes (including a greater tendency to order mixed versus straight drinks, a decrease in the frequency of gulping, and a reduction in consumption to three or less drinks per session), no post-treatment follow-up of these subjects was reported.

Miller, Becker, Foy, and Wooten (1976), using a multiple-baseline design, evaluated the influence of verbal instruction on the drinking style of three chronic alcoholic subjects. While subjects complied with instructions to change one of the drinking-style components in the direction of moderation (reduce sip amount, increase intersip interval, or decrease alcohol content of their mixed drink), it led to an undesirable concomitant change in the other components (to a more abusive drinking style). These results suggest that, unless training procedures focus on all drinking-style components simultaneously, a subject's overall alcohol consumption may not change.

Strickler, Bradlyn, and Maxwell (1981), attempting to teach moderate drinking behaviors to 32 young male adults (ages 19–24), examined the efficacy of four procedures: (1) instructions and feedback; (2) instructions, feedback, and self-monitoring; (3) instructions, feedback, self-monitoring, and moderation practice; and (4) no-treatment. The instruction component consisted of a videotape presentation, which provided a rationale for and information on drinking in a moderate style. All treatment subjects were given specific feedback regarding their sip frequency, mean intersip interval, mean sip amount, mean drink duration, and interdrink intervals. Subjects in the self-monitoring groups were asked to maintain drinking record forms, on which they recorded the start and finish times for each drink consumed and the time for each sip. The moderation practice consisted of first viewing a videotape of a model drinking in a moderate style and then practice in moderate drinking. Treatment consisted of two 50-minute sessions, during which subjects were exposed to their respective training procedures and were given access to beer. Assessment included a 50-minute ad lib drinking session conducted at pre- training and at post-training. Subjects exposed to moderation practice (in addition to instructions, feedback, and self-monitoring) exhibited the most significant, post-training changes. However, the influence of training on drinking at follow-up and in extra-treatment settings was not addressed.

Blood-alcohol level (BAL) discrimination training has also been used to teach moderate drinking. Typically, in BAL discrimination training, subjects consume a beverage with varying amounts of alcohol (the actual amount of which the subject may or may not be told) and then are asked to estimate their BAL. Feedback on the accuracy of their BAL estimations is then provided, typically, via a breath-alcohol analyzer. Subjects are asked to attend to interoceptive (physical sensations) and/or exteroceptive cues (instructions and verbal feedback), so they would be able to identify different BALs. Several investigations have shown that alcoholics and nonproblem drinkers can, with practice, learn to accurately estimate their BAL (e.g., Lovibond & Caddy, 1970; Caddy & Lovibond, 1976; Silverstein, Nathan, & Taylor, 1974). BAL discrimination training has also occasionally been combined with discriminated, conditioned aversion to high BALs (Caddy & Lovibond, 1976; Vogler, Weissbach, Compton, & Martin, 1977). In this procedure, after reaching a specified BAL, subjects received painful electric shocks if they consumed additional drinks. While several investigators have incorporated BAL discrimination training into multifaceted behavioral treatment programs, the contribution of the BAL component has not been ascertained.

Relaxation

Relaxation training has received much attention in the treatment of substance abuse. While the common belief that "people drink to relieve stress" is not without its debacles, several investigations have suggested that relaxation training may be a very important treatment component with alcohol abusers and also in the prevention of alcohol abuse. In a comparison of three different relaxation procedures, Marlatt and Marques (1977), using 41 nonalcoholic college students as subjects, compared the effects of: (1) meditation involving subvocal repetition of the word "one," passive attitude, and relaxed muscles (based upon Beary & Benson, 1974); (2) progressive muscle relaxation (based upon Jacobson, 1938); (3) instructions to read enjoyable, relaxing materials (attention-placebo control); and (4) no-treatment. During the six weeks of treatment, subjects in the treatment groups were instructed to practice their respective relaxation procedure twice daily and then record their subjective level of relaxation experienced and the amount of time spent practicing relaxation. Daily self-monitoring revealed that the meditation, relaxation, and attention-placebo groups all had similar reductions in their daily alcohol consumption which were significantly more positive than the no-treatment control group. Furthermore, on an analogue drinking test, known as the Taste-Rating Task (Marlatt, et al., 1973), the no-treatment control group significantly increased their alcohol consumption from pre-treatment to post-treatment, whereas the three relaxation groups showed no change. At follow-up, the mean daily alcohol consumption of each of the three relaxation groups tended to increase from the post-treatment level but were below pre-treatment levels. This general increase may have resulted from the rather poor subject participation in relaxation practice during follow-up. In addition, since the meditation group practiced relaxation more often than the other two relaxation groups at follow-up, the benefits of the meditation procedure may have longer maintenance.

Strickler, Tomaszewski, Maxwell, and Suib (1979) compared the influence of a muscle-relaxation audiotape, sensitization audiotape (a person with public-speaking anxiety described a few aversive public-speaking experiences), and an audiotape on neutral material (the history of an island in Chesapeake Bay) on the drinking behavior of 24 college students supposedly about to perform a public-speaking task. Prior to treatment and then again following exposure to one of the three treatment procedures, subjects had access to four 12-ounce beers, which were available during a 50-minute session. During the post-treatment assessment, subjects in the relaxation group drank significantly less than did subjects in the sensitization or neutral groups. In addition, at post-treatment, subjects in the relaxation group had a significantly lower sip rate (less-abusive style) than the sensitization group.

In a study with 30 inpatient alcoholics, Parker, Gilbert, and Thoreson (1978) compared the efficacy of progressive muscle-relaxation training, meditation training (Beary & Benson, 1974) and quiet-rest relaxation (attention-placebo control group). All groups exhibited reductions in state anxiety. However, on the blood pressure measure, while the progressive relaxation and meditation groups showed decreased diastolic blood pressures and stable systolic levels, the attention-placebo group had increased systolic and diastolic readings. The significantly higher blood pressures of the control subjects came as they neared their imminent discharge from the hospital. Apparently, the relaxation and meditation groups were better able to handle the increasing stress associated with the problems of reentry into the community. While preliminary evidence regarding the efficacy of relaxation and meditation training appears promising, further investigation is needed on the maintenance and generalization of its effects.

Self-management

Self-management refers to training individuals to mediate their own treatment—teach them to analyze their behavior, set behavioral goals, rearrange situational determinants, and then manipulate response contingencies. In self-management, the person becomes, as noted by Goldfried and Merbaum (1973), "the principal agent in guiding, directing, and regulating those features of his own behavior that might eventually lead to desired positive consequences" (p. 11). Self-management programs with alcohol abusers generally include: (1) self-monitoring of alcohol consumption and/or alcohol-related behaviors; (2) functional analysis of problem, as well as nonproblem, drinking behavior; and (3) manipulation of antecedent and consequential determinants of problem drinking.

Self-monitoring, an important component of self-management, is a process by which individuals maintain a record of their drinking and/or specified situational determinants of their drinking (e.g., cravings, feelings of depression, anxiety, or anger). Self-monitoring not only provides an assessment of alcohol consumption but also provides essential information regarding antecedents and consequences of drinking. Following the identification of the situational determinants of problem drinking, the alcohol abuser is instructed on how to alter them so as to reduce future abusive drinking.

The author treated a 42-year-old factory worker, who reported a seven-year history of alcohol abuse. A functional analysis of his drinking behavior—based on therapeutic interviews and self-monitoring—revealed that his problem drinking occured primarily when: (1) he was paid at work; (2) he socialized with heavy drinkers; (3) he had arguments with his wife over "spending a lot of his paycheck for beer for his drinking buddies"; and (4) he became bored at home. In an effort to minimize problem drinking, the client agreed to and received instruction on the following self-control strategies:

1. To arrange for his boss to deposit his paycheck directly into his bank account.
2. Set up a family budget with his wife.
3. Decrease the frequency of socializing with heavy drinkers.
4. Set up specific activities to do at home when he became bored (e.g., play with children, read, yardwork, sports, and exercise).
5. Keep alcoholic-beverage supply at home to a minimum.
6. Utilize drink-refusal skills when confronted by "alcohol pushers."
7. When he feels as though he is beginning to drink too much or he "craves" a drink, he will refer to a predeveloped list of aversive consequences that may occur if he drinks too much (e.g., high blood pressure, arguments with wife, loss of employment, loss of respect of his children) and positive consequences that may occur if he abstains from drinking or moderates his drinking (e.g., good health, good relationship with wife, employment and respect from children).

At a six-month follow-up, the client and his wife reported that his alcohol consumption had decreased significantly (a maximum of three standard drinks on any one day), and his employment and family life were very satisfying.

Murray and Hobbs (1977) reported a case study which utilized self-administered punishment with a married couple. In a multiple-baseline design, the husband and wife were asked to administer self-imposed time-out when they: (1) mixed a drink with more than one ounce of alcohol; (2) consumed any alcoholic beverage in less than 30 minutes; or (3) consumed more than four alcoholic beverages in one day. Self-reports of both subjects indicated that their alcohol consumption was significantly less during treatment and follow-up than at baseline. In another study examining self-administered punishment, Wilson, Leaf, and Nathan (1975) found that self-administered punishment (shock) was as effective as experimenter-administered punishment at reducing the alcohol consumption of eight chronic alcoholics. Additionally, self-imposed contingencies as opposed to therapist-administered contingencies may be more useful in establishing long-term maintenance of treatment gains, since contingencies could continue to be delivered in the extratreatment environment. In one of the few controlled-outcome studies on self-management, W. R. Miller (1978) compared: (1) self-control training; (2) self-control training plus BAL discrimination training, including aversive countercon-ditioning and avoidance conditioning; and (3) aversive counterconditioning. Thirty-two male and 14 female problem drinkers were randomly assigned to one of the treatment groups, each of which met for 10 30-minute sessions. The self-control strategies consisted of identification and alteration of antecedents of drinking, reduction of drinking rate, and practice of alternative behaviors to be used in situations where alcohol typically was abused. All three treatment groups exhibited a significant reduction in alcohol consumption at the end of treatment and at a three-month follow-up. While the aversive-counterconditioning group showed the least improvement at treatment end and at a 3-month follow-up, a 12-month follow-up indicated equal improvement for all groups. The improvement of the subjects in the aversive-counterconditioning group at the 12-month follow-up may have resulted from their use of a self-help manual (designed to teach self-control procedures), which was distributed to a random sample of subjects at the end of treatment and to all subjects at their 3-month follow-up interview.

Miller, Gribskov, and Mortell (1981) compared two different forms of self-control training: a bibliotherapy group versus a therapist-adminis-tered group. The bibliotherapy group received a self-help manual, which explained self-monitoring procedures, self-control strategies, and alterna-tives to the use of alcohol. The therapist-administered group members met with a therapist during 10 weekly meetings, which focused on meth-ods of self-control in addition to the self-help manual. Self-monitoring data and reports of significant collaterals at a three-month follow-up re-vealed that both treatment groups exhibited a significant reduction in alcohol consumption. The addition of therapist meetings did not signifi-cantly effect subject functioning.

In a related study, Miller and Taylor (1980) examined the relative effectiveness of four forms of self-control training: (1) self-control training-bibliotherapy, subjects received a self-help manual and minimal therapist contact; (2) self-control training-individual therapy, subjects received a self-help manual and 10 individual sessions with a therapist, focusing on the manual materials; (3) self-control training plus relaxation-individual therapy, subjects received a self-help manual, 10 group sessions with a therapist, focusing on the manual materials and relaxation training. Sub-jects were 41 problem-drinker community volunteers. Similar to W. R. Miller's earlier studies, no significant differences were found among the four treatment groups. Overall, improvement rates at 3-month and 12-month follow-ups were 84 percent and 69 percent, respectively. Consis-tent with the earlier studies, the bibliotherapy-alone procedure was the most cost-effective method.

Contingency management

Contingency management approaches attempt to rearrange consequences of drinking, so that problem drinking is punished and nonproblem drinking is reinforced. Several investigations have shown that environmental contingencies are quite effective in modifying the alcoholic's
drinking behavior. For example, in two studies conducted at Baltimore
City Hospital, alcoholics were given access to alcoholic beverages. If
they consumed more than five ounces of alcohol per day, they were
restricted to an "impoverished" environment. While these contingencies
were in effect, subjects reduced their alcohol consumption, as compared
to baseline periods (Cohen, Liebson, & Faillace, 1971; 1972; Cohen,
Liebson, Faillace, & Allen, 1971). The contingent use of social isolation
also appears useful. Alcoholics, who were submitted to a 10- to 15-minute
time-out from social contact immediately after they ordered and received
an alcoholic beverage, significantly reduced their alcohol consumption
(Bigelow, Liebson, & Griffiths, 1974; Griffiths, Bigelow, & Liebson, 1977).

Liebson, Tommasello, and Bigelow (1978) used methadone to reinforce
alcohol abstinence among 25 male methadone patients. Subjects were
randomly assigned to one of two 6-month treatment groups: (1) reinforced-
disulfiram group, in which patients received methadone only if they took
disulfiram (250 mg); and (2) nonreinforced-disulfiram group, in which
patients were given methadone noncontingently but were advised to
take disulfiram regularly. The reinforced-disulfiram group drank on significantly less days during treatment (2 percent) than did the nonreinforced
group (21 percent). As compared to the noncontingent group, the reinforced-disulfiram group also spent less time using illicit drugs, had fewer
arrests, and spent more time employed. In a related study, Bigelow et
al. (1976) found that subjects who were required to post a monetary
deposit, which was refunded contingent upon taking disulfiram, reported
longer periods of abstinence than they did during the preceding three
years.

In one of the few controlled studies with "skid-row" alcoholics, Miller
(1975)—with the cooperation of several community social service agencies (e.g., Salvation Army and Missions)—examined the utility of contingent reinforcement. Twenty alcoholics, with a history of frequent public-
intoxication arrests and infrequent employment, participated. For subjects
in the contingent-reinforcement group, the community agencies provided
their reinforcements (e.g., food, clothing, shelter, cigarettes) only when
subjects had a blood-alcohol level of less than .10 percent (assessed
by random breath tests). Abusive drinking (BAL greater than .10 percent)
resulted in a five-day suspension of goods and services. The noncontingent (control) group received goods and services irrespective of their
sobriety. Assessment (conducted at two months after the procedures began) indicated that contingent reinforcement led to a reduction of alcohol

consumption, a decline of public drunkenness arrests, and an increase in time employed. Interestingly, community services are usually not only made noncontingent on prosocial behavior but are frequently made contingent upon negative behaviors. Typically, community services direct the most assistance to individuals who behave in the most negative manner—the more a person drinks, the more assistance he receives.

Contingency contracting also seems to be useful in treating problem drinkers. Contracting involves establishing the therapist's and client's treatment responsibilities and the consequences of performing or not performing these responsibilities. Ersner-Hershfield and Sobell (1979) compared the effectiveness of four different forms of contracting: (1) verbal contract–verbal agreement; (2) verbal contract–written agreement; (3) written contract–verbal agreement; (4) written contract–written agreement; and (5) no contract. All contracts referred to the guidelines of attendance and treatment termination. Subjects were 50 court-referred alcohol abusers, whose termination from treatment would result in their referral back to court. The authors found that the contracts were most effective at reducing unexcused absences when the method of presentation and agreement were the same. All contracts were effective at reducing the incidence of referral back to court for poor attendance.

COMPREHENSIVE TREATMENT PROGRAMS

Many treatment programs have incorporated several different treatment techniques to form so-called broad spectrum, multimodal, or comprehensive programs. Based on the realization that alcohol abuse represents a complex, multidimensional problem, the use of multiple-treatment techniques may indeed improve treatment efficacy. For example, although nonproblem drinking-skills training may improve the manner in which a nonassertive client drinks, unless he/she also is trained to be more assertive, his/her abusive drinking style may continue.

In one of the earliest published comprehensive treatment programs, Sobell and Sobell (1973b) evaluated the effectiveness of Individualized Behavior Therapy (IBT) which included: (1) a functional analysis of each subject's drinking behavior to assess situational determinants; (2) videotape self-confrontation of drunken behavior; (3) problem-solving training; (4) assertiveness training; (5) aversive contingencies for abusive drinking behavior; and (6) practice in nonproblem drinking (not presented to IBT subjects in the abstinence-treatment-goal group). Seventy inpatient chronic alcoholics were preselected for a treatment goal of abstinence or nonproblem drinking. Patients preselected for the abstinence treatment goal ($n = 30$) were randomly assigned to the IBT program with a goal of abstinence or to a conventional abstinence-oriented program. Patients preselected for the nonproblem drinking goal ($n = 40$) were randomly assigned to the IBT program with a goal of nonproblem drinking or to the conventional abstinence-oriented program. An elaborate one-, two-, and three-year follow-up evaluation revealed that patients in both IBT groups were functioning better than their respective, conventional treatment control groups (Sobell & Sobell, 1973b; Sobell & Sobell, 1976; Caddy, Addington, & Perkins, 1978).

Vogler et al. (1975) compared two comprehensive programs presented to 42 inpatient chronic alcoholics. Program 1 consisted of: (1) videotaped self-confrontation of drinking behavior; (2) BAL discrimination training, with contingent shock for high BALs; (3) discriminated-avoidance practice; (4) alcohol education; (5) behavioral counseling (i.e., alternative and incompatible response training, contingency contracting, problem solving, assertion training, role-modeling communication skills, and relaxation training). Program 2 received alcohol education and behavioral counseling. In addition, all patients had access to regular hospital programs, including group therapy sessions, Alcoholics Anonymous meetings, hydrotherapy, vocational rehabilitation, and art and music therapy. Twelve- and 18-month follow-up evaluations revealed that, while subjects in both programs exhibited a significant decrease in alcohol consumption, those in the more comprehensive group (program 1) exhibited the most improvement (Vogler et al., 1975; Vogler et al., 1977).

In a recent evaluation of a multifaceted treatment program with middle-income problem drinkers, Pomerleau, Pertschuk, Adkins, and Brady (1978) compared a behavioral and a traditional psychotherapy program. The traditional program (which stressed an abstinence goal) consisted of psychotherapy focusing on tension, nonassertiveness, and depression; confrontation of denial of drinking problem; and social support for non-drinking. The behavioral program (emphasizing a nonproblem-drinking goal) included: (1) a functional analysis of drinking; (2) contingency management; (3) training alternatives to drinking; (4) behavior therapy, focusing on problems associated with problem drinking; and (5) maintenance of behavior change. Subjects in the behavioral group were also required to deposit $300—which was refundable contingent upon attendance, record keeping, BAL at sessions, and involvement in nondrinking activities. At a 12-month follow-up, patients' reports revealed that 72 percent of the behavioral treatment subjects were abstinent (6 percent) or had reduced their alcohol consumption below pre-treatment levels (66 percent); whereas 50 percent of the traditional group subjects were either abstinent (14 percent) or had reduced their alcohol consumption (36 percent).

While it appears that multifaceted treatment programs are warranted to meet the needs of problem drinkers, the indiscriminate inclusion of multiple components may not significantly contribute to the effectiveness of a program and may even reduce potential treatment gains. Miller (1978), for example, found that including BAL discrimination training, discriminated-aversive counterconditioning, and avoidance conditioning with self-control training did not contribute to the success rate. In fact, the addition of certain procedures (i.e., intense interpersonal confrontation or aversive conditioning) seems to increase the frequency of patient attrition from therapy (e.g., Pomerleau & Adkins, 1980). Future evaluation of different combinations of treatment techniques must be conducted to identify the most cost-effective programs.

THE ATTRITION PROBLEM

The client-dropout rate in alcohol-treatment programs is quite high, with reports that from 28 to 80 percent of all clients discontinue treatment after attending between one and four treatment sessions (Baekeland, Lundwall, & Shanahan, 1973; Chafetz, Blane, Abram, Gotner, Lacy, McCourt, Clark, & Meyers, 1962; Gertler, Raynes, & Harris, 1973). It is quite evident that the effectiveness of treatment efforts is reduced if clients are not compliant. As noted earlier, contingency contracting and the use of refundable deposits made contingent upon client responsibilities have been effective in improving attendance and compliance. Nirenberg, Sobell, and Sobell (1980), in a series of three investigations, examined the effectiveness of several follow-through procedures designed to increase the return rate of clients who prematurely dropped out of treatment. They found that follow-through letters and telephone contacts with dropouts significantly increased clients' returns to treatment. The follow-through procedures were also found to be relatively inexpensive and effective in obtaining important follow-up information from clients who did not return to treatment. While alcohol-treatment programs are usually low on staff, inundated with clients, and probably find immediate relief from the high dropout rate, such attempts to encourage dropouts who are in need of further treatment to return to treatment may, in the long run, reduce the number of clients who hit the proverbial "bottom" and return to treatment centers in need of even more intensive help.

MAINTENANCE

For clients who do complete a treatment program, an issue of continuing concern is the long-term maintenance of treatment gains. It is all too common for abstinent or nonproblem-drinking clients to "slip" and begin to drink in a problem fashion (a process referred to as *relapse*).

In a preliminary analysis of possible antecedents to relapse, Chaney et al. (1978) found that usually relapse was preceded by negative interpersonal situations involving criticism or social pressure to drink, or negative feelings including anger, anxiety, boredom, and depression. Litman, Eiser, Rawson, and Oppenheim (1979), in a comparison of relapsers and survivors (subjects who remained abstinent for at least six months), stressed the importance of coping behaviors. Relapsers not only reported that they used coping behaviors less often, but they utilized fewer types of effective coping strategies.

In an attempt to reduce the incidence of relapse, Chaney et al. (1978) presented coping skills training to inpatient alcoholics. Patients were instructed on ways to cope with several potentially high-risk situations. At a one-year follow-up, patients who received coping skills instruction reported shorter and less-severe relapse episodes, as compared to two control groups.

Post-treatment contacts with clients also appear helpful in maintaining treatment effects. Booster sessions, conducted at intervals of one to three months following treatment, can be used to review treatment strategies, discuss current crises, or simply reinforce success. Interestingly, frequent and continuing follow-up interviews intended to simply gather outcome data have serendipitously led to improved outcome (Ersner-Hershfield, Sobell, Sobell, & Maisto, 1979). Integrating client-treatment improvements into their natural environment (e.g., community-reinforcement program, Hunt & Azrin, 1973) and the use of post-treatment manuals to review treatment strategies (e.g., Miller, 1978) have also been helpful in maintaining treatment gains.

Marlatt (1978) has hypothesized an interesting cognitive model of relapse—"abstinence-violation effect." He postulated that when substance abusers are committed to voluntary abstinence and then violate that commitment by drinking, the individual may continue to drink because of a combined cognitive-dissonance and personal-attribution effect. The cognitive dissonance, created by drinking but also having a strong commitment not to drink, produces a conflict state resulting in "guilt for having given in to temptation." Personal attribution of failure produces feelings of personal weakness and, subsequently, a decline in self-control. To reduce the negative influence of the abstinence-violation effect, Marlatt has suggested the use of "programmed relapse," whereby the individual experiences the effects of a drink under the therapist's supervision and is then given instruction on ways to cope with the potentially negative situation.

NEW DIRECTIONS AND FUTURE TRENDS

Over the past decade, interest and research regarding the treatment of addictive behaviors have generated many therapeutic techniques. While the efficacy of many of these techniques has received empirical support, other techniques need further evaluation. The realization that addictive behaviors represent a multidimensional problem has resulted in the combination of several treatment techniques to form comprehensive treatment programs. While multiple treatment techniques are essential for adequate treatment, it is necessary to delineate the essential treatment components of these comprehensive programs in an effort to determine the least restrictive as well as the most cost-effective treatment program.

While the quality of treatment outcome evaluation has improved in recent years, several methodological problems are still present. For instance, Sobell and Sobell (1979) have noted a need for: (1) more reliable and valid outcome measures; (2) planned versus retrospective assessments; (3) the use of multiple outcome measures to assess convergent validity; (4) evaluation of pre-treatment behavior; (5) detailed descriptions of subject populations and treatment components; and (6) greater length and frequency of assessment intervals.

Finally, the continually rapid increase in the incidence of problems related to the addictions clearly justifies the need for primary and secondary prevention programs. It is quite apparent that treatment programs alone are not sufficient. While the evaluation of the effectiveness of prevention programs has been inadequate (Miller, Nirenberg, & McClure, 1983; Nirenberg, Miller, & McClure, 1981), recent federal initiatives in the area of prevention may stimulate further research.

SUMMARY

Substance abuses, including alcohol abuse, obesity, cigarette smoking, and drug abuse, present a significant health problem. The present chapter focuses specifically on the assessment and treatment of alcohol abuse, in a manner so as to serve as a model for the other addictive behaviors.

During the past decade, the realization that alcohol abuse represents a complex, multidimensional problem has clearly demonstrated a need for a detailed assessment. The understanding of alcohol abuse requires not only the measurement of alcohol drinking itself, but also the assessment of the antecedents and consequences of alcohol use. Based upon the comprehensive assessment of the substance abuser's life functioning, treatment goals are developed. These goals should be individualized to fit the needs of each client.

Treatment techniques have focused upon the modification of behaviors which precipitate problem drinking and the contingencies which reinforce abusive drinking, modification of the actual drinking behavior, and the development of alternative adaptive behaviors. While the efficacy of many of these treatment techniques has received empirical support, other techniques are in need of further evaluation. Several utilization and application issues are discussed, including the use of comprehensive-treatment programs, attrition from alcohol treatment programs, and maintenance of treatment gains.

REFERENCES

American Psychiatric Association. *Diagnostic and Statistical Manual* (*DSM-III*) (3rd ed.). Washington, D.C.: Author, 1980.

Anant, S. S. A note on the treatment of alcoholics by a verbal aversion technique. *Canadian Journal of Psychology,* 1967, *8,* 19–22.

Armor, D. J., Polich, J. M., & Stambul, H. B. Alcoholism and treatment. Report R–1739– NIAAA. Santa Monica, Calif.: Rand Corporation, 1976.

Ashem, B., & Donner, L. Covert sensitization with alcoholics: A controlled replication. *Behaviour Research and Therapy,* 1968, *6,* 7–12.

Baekeland, F., Lundwall, L., & Shanahan, I. J. Correlates of patient attrition in the outpatient treatment of alcoholism. *Journal of Nervous and Mental Disease,* 1973, *157,* 99–107.

Beary, J. F., & Benson, H. A simple psychophysiologic technique which elicits the hypometabolic changes of the relaxation response. *Psychosomatic Medicine,* 1974, *36,* 115–120.

Bigelow, G., Liebson, I., & Griffiths, R. Alcoholic drinking: Suppression by a brief time-out procedure. *Behaviour Research and Therapy,* 1974, *12,* 107–115.

Bigelow, G., Strickler, D., Liebson, I., & Griffiths, R. Maintaining disulfiram ingestion among outpatient alcoholics: A security-deposit contingency-contracting procedure. *Behavior Research and Therapy,* 1976, *14,* 378–381.

Blackwell, B. Drug therapy: Patient compliance. *New England Journal of Medicine,* 1973, *289,* 249–252.

Burrows, S., Feldman, W., & McBridge, F. Serum gamma-glutamyl transpeptidase. *American Journal of Clinical Pathology,* 1975, *64,* 311–314.

Caddy, G. R., Addington, H. J., & Perkins, D. Individualized behavior therapy for alcoholics. A third-year independent double-blind follow-up. *Behavior Research and Therapy,* 1978, *16,* 345–362.

Caddy, G. R., & Lovibond, S. H. Self-regulation and discriminated aversive conditioning in the modification of alcoholics' drinking behavior. *Behavior Therapy,* 1976, *7,* 223–230.

Caudill, B. D., & Marlatt, G. A. Modeling influences in social drinking: An experimental analogue. *Journal of Consulting and Clinical Psychology,* 1975, *43,* 405–415.

Cautela, J. R. Treatment of compulsive behavior by covert sensitization. *Psychological Record,* 1966, *16,* 33–41.

Chafetz, M. E., Blane, H. T., Abram, H. S., Gotner, J., Lacy, E., McCourt, W. F., Clark, E., & Meyers, E. Establishing treatment relations with alcoholics. *Journal of Nervous and Mental Disease,* 1962, *134,* 395–409.

Chaney, E. F., O'Leary, M. R., & Marlatt, G. A. Skill training with alcoholics. *Journal of Consulting and Clinical Psychology,* 1978, *46,* 1092–1104.

Cohen, M., Liebson, I., & Faillace, L. A. The role of reinforcement contingencies in chronic alcoholism: An experimental analysis of one case. *Behaviour Research and Therapy,* 1971, *9,* 375–379.

Cohen, M., Liebson, I., & Faillace, L. A technique for establishing controlled drinking in chronic alcoholics. *Diseases of the Nervous System,* 1972, *33,* 46–49.

Cohen, M., Liebson, I. A., Faillace, L. A., & Allen, R. P. Moderate drinking by chronic alcoholics. *Journal of Nervous and Mental Disease,* 1971, *153,* 434–444.

Davis, M. Alcoholic liver disease: What the practicing clinician needs to know. *British Journal of Addiction,* 1980, *75,* 19–26.

D'Zurilla, T. J., & Goldfried, M. R. Problem solving and behavior modification. *Journal of Abnormal Psychology,* 1971, *78,* 107–126.

Eisler, R. M., Miller, P. M., Hersen, M., & Alford, H. Effects of assertive training on marital interaction. *Archives of General Psychiatry,* 1974, *30,* 643–649.

Elkins, R. L., & Murdock, R. P. The contribution of successful conditioning to abstinence maintenance following covert-sensitization (verbal-aversion) treatment of alcoholism. *IRCS Medical Science: Psychology & Psychiatry; Social & Occupational Medicine,* 1977, *5,* 167.

Ersner-Hershfield, S. M., & Sobell, L. C. *Behavioral contracts with clients court-referred for alcohol treatment.* Paper presented at the annual meeting of the Association for the Advancement of Behavior Therapy, San Francisco, 1979.

Ersner-Hershfield, S. M., Sobell, L. D., Sobell, M. B., & Maisto, S. A. *The therapeutic value of follow-up interviews for alcohol abusers: An empirical evaluation.* Paper presented at the annual meeting of the American Psychological Association, New York, September 1979.

Foy, D. W., Massey, F. H., Dyer, J. D., Ross, J. M., & Wooten, L. S. Social-skills training to improve alcoholics' vocational interpersonal competency. *Journal of Counseling Psychology,* 1979, *26,* 128–132.

Foy, D. W., Miller, P. M., Eisler, R. M., & O'Toole, D. H. Social-skills training to teach alcoholics to refuse drinks effectively. *Journal of Studies on Alcohol,* 1976, *37,* 1340–1345.

Freedberg, E. J., & Johnston, W. E. The effects of assertion training within the context of a multimodal alcoholism-treatment program for employed alcoholics. Substudy No. 976. Toronto: Addiction Research Foundation, 1978.

Freedberg, E. J., & Johnston, W. E. Changes in drinking behaviour, employment status, and other life areas for employed alcoholics 3, 6, and 12 months after treatment. *Journal of Drug Issues,* 1979, *4,* 523–534.

Fuller, R. K., & Roth, H. P. Disulfiram for the treatment of alcoholism: An evaluation in 128 men. *Annals of Internal Medicine,* 1979, *90,* 901–904.

Garlington, W. K., & DeRicco, D. A. The effect of modeling on drinking rate. *Journal of Applied Behavior Analysis,* 1977, *10,* 207–212.

Gerrein, J. R., Rosenberg, C. M., & Manohar, V. Disulfiram maintenance in outpatient treatment of alcoholism. *Archives of General Psychiatry,* 1973, *28,* 798–802.

Gertler, R., Raynes, A. E., & Harris, N. Assessment of attendance and outcome at an outpatient alcoholism clinic. *Quarterly Journal on Studies of Alcohol,* 1973, *34,* 955–959.

Goldberg, D. M., & Martin, J. V. Role of gamma-glutamyl transpeptidase activity in the diagnosis of hepatobiliary disease. *Digestion,* 1975, *12,* 132–146.

Goldfried, M. R., & Merbaum, M. (Eds.) *Behavior change through self-control.* New York: Holt, Rinehart, & Winston, 1973.

Griffiths, R. R., Bigelow, G. E., & Liebson, I. A. Suppression of ethanol self-administration in alcoholics by contingent time-out from social interactions. *Behavior Research and Therapy,* 1974, *12,* 327–334.

Griffiths, R. R., Bigelow, G. E., & Liebson, I. A. Effect of ethanol self-administration on choice behavior—money versus socializing. *Pharmacology, Biology, and Behavior,* 1975, *3,* 443–446.

Griffiths, R. R., Bigelow, G. E., & Liebson, I. A. Comparison of social time-out and activity time-out procedures in suppressing ethanol self-administration in alcoholics. *Behavior Research and Therapy,* 1977, *15,* 329–336.

Hamilton, F., & Maisto, S. A. Assertive behavior and perceived discomfort of alcoholics in assertion-required situations. *Journal of Consulting and Clinical Psychology,* 1979, *47,* 196–197.

Hedberg, A. G., & Campbell, L. A comparison of four behavioral treatments of alcoholism. *Journal of Behavior Therapy and Experimental Psychiatry,* 1974, *5,* 251–256.

Higgins, R. L., & Marlatt, G. A. Fear of interpersonal evaluation is a determinant of alcohol consumption in male social drinkers. *Journal of Abnormal Psychology,* 1975, *84,* 644–651.

Hirsch, S. M., von Rosenberg, R., Phelan, C., & Dudley, H. K. Effectiveness of assertiveness training with alcoholics. *Journal of Studies on Alcohol,* 1978, *39,* 89–97.

Hunt, G. M., & Azrin, N. J. A community-reinforcement approach to alcoholism. *Behaviour Research and Therapy,* 1973, *11,* 91–104.

Intagliata, J. C. Increasing the interpersonal problem-solving skills of an alcoholic population. *Journal of Consulting and Clinical Psychology,* 1978, *46,* 489–498.

Jacobson, E. *Progressive relaxation.* Chicago: University of Chicago Press, 1938.

Kitson, T. M. The disulfiram-ethanol reaction: A review. *Journal of Studies on Alcohol,* 1977, *38,* 96–113.

Kline, S. A., & Kingstone, E. Disulfiram implants: The right treatment but the wrong drug? *Canadian Medical Association Journal,* 1977, *116,* 1382–1383.

Kwentus, J., & Major, L. F. Disulfiram in the treatment of alcoholism. *Journal of Studies on Alcohol,* 1979, *40,* 428–446.

Lang, A. R., Goeckner, D. J., Adesso, V. J., & Marlatt, G. A. Effects of alcohol aggression in male social drinkers. *Journal of Abnormal Psychology,* 1975, *84,* 508–518.

Lemere, F., & Voegtlin, W. L. An evaluation of the aversion treatment of alcoholism. *Quarterly Journal of Studies on Alcohol,* 1950, *11,* 199–204.

Liebson, I. A., Tommasello, A., & Bigelow, G. E. A behavioral treatment of alcohol methadone patients. *Annals of Internal Medicine,* 1978, *89,* 342–344.

Litman, G. K., Eiser, J. R., Rawson, N. S., & Oppenheim, A. N. Differences in relapse precipitants and coping behavior between alcohol relapsers and survivors. *Behaviour Research and Therapy,* 1979, *17,* 89–94.

Little, L. M., & Curran, J. P. Covert sensitization: A clinical procedure in need of some explanations. *Psychological Bulletin,* 1978, *85,* 513–531.

Lovibond, S. H., & Caddy, G. R. Discriminated-aversive control in the moderation of alcoholics' drinking behavior. *Behavior Therapy,* 1970, *1,* 437–444.

Lubetkin, B. S., Rivers, P. C., Rosenberg, C. M. Difficulties of disulfiram therapy with alcoholics. *Quarterly Journal of Studies on Alcohol,* 1971, *32,* 168–171.

MacAndrew, C. The differentiation of male alcoholic outpatients from nonalcoholic outpatients by means of the MMPI. *Quarterly Journal of Studies on Alcohol,* 1965, *26,* 238–246.

Maisto, S. A., Henry, R. R., Sobell, M. B., & Sobell, L. C. Implications of acquired changes in tolerance for the treatment of alcohol problems. *Addictive Behaviors,* 1978, *3,* 51–55.

Maisto, S. A., Sobell, L. C., Cooper, A. M., & Sobell, M. B. Comparison of two techniques to obtain retrospective reports of drinking behavior from alcohol abusers. *Addictive Behaviors,* 1982, *7,* 33–38.

Malcolm, M. T., Madden, J. S., & Williams, A. E. Disulfiram implantation critically evaluated. *British Journal of Psychiatry,* 1974, *125,* 485–489.

Marlatt, G. A. Craving for alcohol, loss of control, and relapse: A cognitive-behavioral analysis. In P. E. Nathan, G. A. Marlatt, & T. Loberg (Eds.), *Alcoholism: New directions in behavioral research and treatment.* New York: Plenum Press, 1978.

Marlatt, G. A., Demming, B., & Reid, J. B. Loss-of-control drinking in alcoholics: An experimental analogue. *Journal of Abnormal Psychology,* 1973, *81,* 233–241.

Marlatt, G. A., Kosturn, C. F., & Lang, A. R. Provocation to anger and opportunity for retaliation as determinants of alcohol consumption in social drinkers. *Journal of Abnormal Psychology,* 1975, *84,* 652–659.

Marlatt, G. A., & Marques, J. K. Meditation, self-control, and alcohol use. In R. B. Stuart (Ed.)., *Behavioral self-management: Strategies, techniques, and outcome.* New York: Brunner & Mazel, 1977.

Marlatt, G. A., & Rohsenow, D. J. Cognitive processes in alcohol use: Expectancy and the balanced-placebo design. In N. K. Mello (Ed.), *Advances in substance abuse: Behavioral and biological research.* Greenwich, Ct.: JAI Press, 1980.

Miller, E. C., Dvorak, A., & Turner, D. W. A method of creating aversion to alcohol by reflex conditioning in a group setting. *Quarterly Journal of Studies on Alcohol,* 1960, *21,* 424–431.

Miller, P. M. A behavioral-intervention program for chronic public-drunkenness offenders. *Archives of General Psychiatry,* 1975, *32,* 915–922.

Miller, P. M. Theoretical and practical issues in substance-abuse assessment and treatment. In W. R. Miller (Ed.), *The addictive behaviors: Treatment of alcoholism, drug abuse, smoking, and obesity.* Elmsford, N.Y.: Pergamon Press, 1980.

Miller, P. M., Becker, J. V., Foy, D. W., & Wooten, L. S. Instructional control of the components of alcoholic drinking behavior. *Behavior Therapy,* 1976, *7,* 472–480.

Miller, P. M., & Eisler, R. M. Assertive behavior of alcoholics: A descriptive analysis. *Behavior Therapy,* 1977, *8,* 146–149.

Miller, P. M., & Hersen, M. Quantitative changes in alcohol consumption as a function of electrical-aversive conditioning. *Journal of Clinical Psychology,* 1972, *28,* 590–593.

Miller, P. M., Hersen, M., Eisler, R. M., & Elkin, T. E. A retrospective analysis of alcohol consumption on laboratory tasks as related to therapeutic outcome. *Behaviour Research and Therapy,* 1974, *12,* 73–76.

Miller, P. M., Hersen, M., Eisler, R. M., & Hilsman, G. Effects of social stress on operant drinking of alcoholics and social drinkers. *Behaviour Research and Therapy,* 1974, *12,* 67–72.

Miller, P. M., Nirenberg, T. D., & McClure, G. Prevention of alcohol abuse. In B. Tabakoff, P. Sutker, & C. Randall (Eds.). *Medical and psychosocial aspects of alcohol abuse.* New York: Plenum Press, 1983.

Miller, P. M., Stanford, A. G., & Hemphill, D. P. A social-learning approach to alcoholism treatment. *Social Casework,* 1974, *55,* 279–284.

Miller, W. R. Behavioral treatment of problem drinkers? A comparative outcome study of three controlled-drinking therapies. *Journal of Consulting and Clinical Psychology,* 1978, *46,* 74–86.

Miller, W. R., Gribskov, C. J., & Mortell, R. L. Effectiveness of a self-control manual for problem drinkers with and without therapist contact. *International Journal of the Addictions,* 1981, *16,* 1247–1254.

Miller, W. R., & Hester, R. K. Treating the problem drinker: Modern approaches. In W. R. Miller (Ed.), *The addictive behaviors: Treatment of alcoholism, drug abuse, smoking, and obesity.* Elmsford, N.Y.: Pergamon Press, 1980.

Miller, W. R., & Taylor, C. A. Relative effectiveness of bibliotherapy, individual and group self-control training in the treatment of problem drinkers. *Addictive Behaviors,* 1980, *5,* 13–24.

Mills, K. C., Sobell, M. B., & Schaefer, H. H. Training social drinking as an alternative to abstinence for alcoholics. *Behavior Therapy,* 1971, *2,* 18–27.

Mottin, J. L. Drug-induced attenuation of alcohol consumption: A review and evaluation of claimed, potential, or current therapies. *Journal of Studies on Alcohol,* 1973, *34,* 444–472.

Murray, R. G., & Hobbs, S. A. The use of self-imposed time-out procedure in the modification of excessive alcohol consumption. *Journal of Behavior Therapy and Experimental Psychiatry,* 1977, *8,* 377–380.

Nathan, P. E., & Briddell, D. W. Behavioral assessment and treatment of alcoholism. In B. Kissin & H. Begleiter (Eds.), *The biology of alcoholism* (Vol. 5): *Treatment and rehabilitation of the chronic alcoholic.* New York: Plenum Press, 1977.

Neubuerger, O. W., Matarazzo, J. D., Schmidt, R. E., & Pratt, H. H. One-year follow-up of total abstinence in chronic alcoholic patients following emetic counterconditioning. *Alcoholism: Clinical and Experimental Research,* 1980, *4,* 306–312.

Nirenberg, T. D., Miller, P. M., & McClure, G. Comparative efficacy of alcohol abuse-prevention strategies. Research in progress at Georgia Southern College, 1981.

Nirenberg, T. D., Sobell, L. C., & Ersner-Hershfield, S. *Self-monitoring of drinking consumption and alcohol-related thoughts.* Unpublished manuscript, 1981.

Nirenberg, T. D., Sobell, L. C., & Sobell, M. B. Effective and inexpensive procedures for decreasing client attrition in an outpatient alcohol treatment program. *American Journal of Drug and Alcohol Abuse,* 1980, *7(1),* 73–82.

Obholzer, A. M. A follow-up study of nineteen alcoholic patients treated by means of tetra-ethyl-thiuram disulfide (Antabuse) implants. *British Journal of Addiction,* 1974, *69,* 19–23.

O'Leary, D. E., O'Leary, M. R., & Donovan, D. M. Social-skill acquisition and psychosocial development of alcoholics: A review. *Addictive Behaviors,* 1976, *1,* 111–120.

Parker, J. C., Gilbert, G. S., & Thoreson, R. Anxiety management in alcoholics: A study of generalized effects of relaxation techniques. *Addictive Behaviors,* 1978, *3,* 123–127.

Paulson, S. M., Krause, S., & Iber, F. L. Development and evaluation of a compliance test for patients taking disulfiram. *Johns Hopkins Medical Journal,* 1977, *141,* 119–125.

Polich, J. M., Armor, D. J., & Braiker, H. B. Patterns of alcoholism over four years. Santa Monica, Calif.: Rand Corporation, 1980.

Pomerleau, O. F., & Adkins, D. Evaluating behavioral and traditional treatment for problem drinkers. In L. C. Sobell, M. B. Sobell, & E. Ward (Eds.), *Evaluating alcohol- and drug-abuse treatment effectiveness: Recent advances.* Elmsford, N.Y.: Pergamon Press, 1980.

Pomerleau, O. F., Pertschuk, M., Adkins, D., & Brady, J. P. A comparison of behavioral and traditional treatment for middle-income problem drinkers. *Journal of Behavioral Medicine,* 1978, *1,* 187–200.

Revusky, S. H. Some laboratory paradigms for chemical-aversion treatment of alcoholism. *Journal of Behavior Therapy and Experimental Psychiatry,* 1973, *4,* 15–17.

Reyes, E., & Miller, W. R. Serum gamma-glutamyl transpepticase as a diagnostic aid in problem drinkers. *Addictive Behaviors,* 1980, *5,* 59–65.

Rollason, J. G., Pincherle, G., & Robinson, D. Serum gamma-glutamyl transpeptidase in relation to alcohol consumption. *Clinica Chemica Acta,* 1972, *39,* 75–80.

Rosalki, S. B., & Rau, D. Serum gamma-glutamyl transpeptidase activity in alcoholism. *Clinica Chemica Acta,* 1972, *39,* 41–47.

Rosenbluth, J., Nathan, P. E., & Lawson, D. M. Environmental influences on drinking by college students in a college pub: Behavioral observation in the natural environment. *Addictive Behaviors,* 1978, *3,* 117–121.

Ryback, R. S., Eckardt, M. J., & Pautler, C. P. Biochemical and hematological correlates of alcoholism. *Research Communications in Chemical Pathology and Pharmacology,* 1980, *27,* 533–550.

Sauter, A. M., Boss, D., & von Wartburg, J. P. Reevaluation of the disulfiram-alcohol reaction in man. *Journal of Studies on Alcohol,* 1977, *38,* 1680–1695.

Schaefer, H. H., Sobell, M. B., & Mills, K. C. Baseline-drinking behavior in alcoholics and social drinkers: Kind of drinks and sip magnitude. *Behaviour Research and Therapy,* 1971, *9,* 23–27.

Scherer, S. E., & Freedberg, E. J. Effects of group-videotape feedback on development of assertiveness skills in alcoholics: A follow-up study. *Psychological Reports,* 1976, *39,* 983–992.

Selzer, M. L. The Michigan Alcoholism Screening Test: The quest for a new diagnostic instrument. *American Journal of Psychiatry,* 1971, *127,* 1653–1658.

Silverstein, S. J., Nathan, P. E., & Taylor, H. A. Blood-alcohol level estimation and controlled drinking by chronic alcoholics. *Behavior Therapy,* 1974, *5,* 1–15.

Sobell, L. C., Cellucci, A., Nirenberg, T. D., & Sobell, M. B. Do quantity-frequency data underestimate drinking-related health risks? *American Journal of Public Health,* 1982, *72,* 823–828.

Sobell, L. C., & Sobell, M. B. A self-feedback technique to monitor drinking behavior in alcoholics. *Behaviour Research and Therapy,* 1973, *11,* 237–238. (a)

Sobell, L. C., & Sobell, M. B. Outpatient alcoholics give valid self-reports. *Journal of Nervous and Mental Disease,* 1975, *161,* 32–42.

Sobell, L. C., & Sobell, M. B. Validity of self-reports in three populations of alcoholics. *Journal of Consulting and Clinical Psychology,* 1978, *46,* 901–907.

Sobell, L. C., & Sobell, M. B. *Outcome criteria and the assessment of alcohol-treatment efficacy.* Paper presented at the conference on Evaluation of the Alcoholic: Implications for Research, Theory and Treatment, Hartford, Connecticut, October 1979.

Sobell, L. C., Sobell, M. B., & Nirenberg, T. D. Development of differential-treatment profiles. In E. M. Pattison & E. Kaufman (Eds.), *The American handbook of alcoholism.* New York: Gardner Press, 1981.

Sobell, L. C., Sobell, M. B., & Schaefer, H. H. Alcoholics name fewer mixed drinks than social drinkers. *Psychological Reports,* 1971, *28,* 493–494.

Sobell, L. C., VanderSpek, R., & Saltman, P. Utility of portable breath-alcohol testers for drunken-driver offenders. *Journal of Studies on Alcohol,* 1980, *9,* 930–934.

Sobell, M. B., Schaefer, H. H., & Mills, K. C. Differences in baseline-drinking behaviors between alcoholics and normal drinkers. *Behaviour Research and Therapy,* 1972, *10,* 257–268.

Sobell, M. B., & Sobell, L. C. Individualized behavior therapy for alcoholics. *Behavior Therapy,* 1973b, *4,* 49–72.

Sobell, M. B., & Sobell, L. C. Second-year treatment outcome of alcoholics treated by individualized behavior therapy: Results. *Behavior Research and Therapy*, 1976, *14*, 195–215.

Sobell, M. B., Sobell, L. C., & VanderSpek, R. Relationship between clinical judgment, self-report, and breath-analysis measures of intoxication in alcoholics. *Journal of Consulting and Clinical Psychology*, 1979, *47*, 204–206.

Spencer-Peet, J., Wood, D. C. F., & Glatt, M. M. Screening test for alcoholism. *The Lancet*, 1973, *ii*, 1089–1090.

Strickler, D. P., Bradlyn, A. S., & Maxwell, W. A. Teaching moderate-drinking behaviors to young-adult heavy drinkers: The effects of three training procedures. *Addictive Behaviors*, 1981, *6*, 345–354.

Strickler, D. P., Tomaszewski, R., Maxwell, W. A., & Suib, M. The effects of relaxation instructions on drinking behavior in the presence of stress. *Behaviour Research and Therapy*, 1979, *17*, 45–51.

Tamerin, J. S., & Mendelson, J. H. The psychodynamics of chronic inebriation: Observations of alcoholics during the process of drinking in an experimental-group setting. *American Journal of Psychiatry*, 1969, *125*, 886–899.

U.S. Department of Health, Education, and Welfare (USDHEW). *Fourth Special Report to the U.S. Congress on Alcohol and Health.* (DHEW Publication No. (ADM) 79–832). Washington, D.C.: U.S. Government Printing Office, 1978.

Voegtlin, W. L. The treatment of alcoholism by establishing a conditioned reflex. *American Journal of the Medical Sciences*, 1940, *199*, 802–810.

Voegtlin, W. L., & Broz, W. R. The conditioned-reflex treatment of chronic alcoholism: X. An analysis of 3,125 admissions over a period of 10.5 years. *Annals of Internal Medicine*, 1949, *30*, 580–597.

Voegtlin, W. L., Lemere, F., Broz, W. R., & O'Hollaren, P. Conditioned-reflex therapy of alcoholic addiction: V. Follow-up report of 1,042 cases. *American Journal of the Medical Sciences*, 1942, *203*, 525–528.

Vogler, R. E., Compton, J. V., & Weissbach, T. A. Integrated behavior-change techniques for alcoholics. *Journal of Consulting and Clinical Psychology*, 1975, *43*, 233–243.

Vogler, R. E., Weissbach, T. A., Compton, J. B., & Martin, G. T. Integrated behavior-change techniques for problem drinkers in the community. *Journal of Consulting and Clinical Psychology*, 1977, *45*, 267–279.

Wallerstein, R. S. Comparative study of treatment methods for chronic alcoholism: The alcoholism research at Winter V. A. Hospital. *American Journal of Psychiatry*, 1956, *113*, 228–233.

Westwood, M., Cohen, M. I., & McNamara, H. Serum gamma-glutamyl transpeptidase activity: A chemical determinant of alcohol consumption during adolescence. *Pediatrics*, 1978, *62*, 560–562.

Wiens, A. N., Montague, J. R., Manaugh, T. S., & English, C. J. Pharmacological aversive counterconditioning to alcohol in a private hospital: One-year follow-up. *Journal of Studies on Alcohol*, 1976, *37*, 1320–1324.

Williams, R. J., & Brown, R. A. Differences in baseline-drinking behavior between New Zealand alcoholics and normal drinkers. *Behavior Research and Therapy*, 1974, *12*, 287–294.

Wilson, A. Disulfiram implantation in alcoholism treatment: A review. *Journal of Studies on Alcohol*, 1975, *36*, 555–565.

Wilson, G. T. Alcoholism and aversion therapy: Issues, ethics, and evidence. In G. A. Marlatt, & P. E. Nathan (Eds.), *Behavioral approaches to alcoholism.* New Brunswick, N. J.: Rutgers Center of Alcohol Studies, 1978.

Wilson, G. T., & Davison, G. C. Aversion techniques in behavior therapy: Some theoretical and meta-theoretical considerations. *Journal of Consulting and Clinical Psychology,* 1969, *33,* 327–329.

Wilson, G. T., Leaf, R. C., & Nathan, P. E. The aversive control of excessive alcohol consumption by chronic alcoholics in the laboratory setting. *Journal of Applied Behavior Analysis,* 1975, *8,* 13–26.

20

The treatment of sexual dysfunctions

Daniel C. Goldberg, Ph.D. *

OVERVIEW: A CONCEPTUAL CONTROVERSY

During the 20th century, an expanding body of literature has attempted to explain the nature of sexual dysfunctions in human interaction. However, investigators of human sexuality have been unable to reach consensus on an issue central to the treatment of sexual dysfunctions. The question that lacks resolution is whether clinicians can, or should, help people distressed over sexual matters by *directly* focusing on the presenting sexual problem itself.

On the one hand, sexual dysfunctions can be seen as behaviorally manifested symptoms of intrapsychic conflict which rest at the central core of the person (Fenichel, 1945; Freud, 1905). Therefore, sexual problems should not be the direct focus of treatment. Rather, reconstruction of the self through insight into the lasting impact of critical, early childhood experiences is the more salient task at hand. Resolution of inner conflicts in this way will, in turn, lead to a reduction or elimination of behavioral symptoms. In fact, focusing treatment directly on the sexual symptom may even be counterproductive and a form of collusion with the client, since this treatment approach legitimizes the defensive structure of the client (Sullivan, 1953). By contrast, others think that it is not necessary to give such important consideration to the retrospective, etiological roots of sexual difficulties in order to effect treatment gains. Sexual dysfunctions can be seen as learned behavior patterns, which can operate and be treated as a unique aspect of the individual's life. Even with a high degree of marital adjustment and satisfaction, people can indeed experience difficulties in their sexual interactions (Frank, Anderson, & Rubenstein, 1978; Kaplan, 1974). Therefore, it is not a necessary precondition of

---

* Jefferson Medical College, Philadelphia.

successful sex therapy to encompass the more remote or deeper elements of the individual's psychic life. A significant improvement in the person's well-being can be achieved through concentrating directly on the sexual dysfunction.

A historical perspective helps to highlight how this controversy has unfolded and how the treatment of sexual dysfunctions has developed. Freud's theoretical views on human sexualtiy gave scientific credence to the social mores that characterized the Victorian era and surrounded Freud when he was constructing his ideas. Freud implied that the libido (or sexual instinct) was a dangerous, raging urge that, if not channeled into proper aims, could lead to disasterous consequences throughout adult life. The emphasis on the bridling of sexual forces supported an air of distrust and fear, which characterized the beliefs of his contemporaneous society: in effect, one should have only certain sexual thoughts and behaviors if one is to be mature.

Kinsey and his associates (1948, 1953) lessened the mystery and danger implied by the psychoanalytic approach to sexuality by attempting to describe what people were actually doing, regardless of the dictates associated with social imperatives. The primary effect of publishing data underscoring the pervasiveness of many sexual behaviors was to normalize various sexual acts. For example, clitoral stimulation played an important role in sexual responsiveness for over 75 percent of women surveyed, and the majority of women masturbated at least once, sometime in their life. Approximately 11 percent of the women had never experienced an orgasm. Many of the findings were quite revealing about male sexuality as well. Seventy-five percent of men ejaculated within two minutes of penetration. Over one third of all men had at least one homosexual experience which included attainment of orgasm. Extramarital affairs would take place for 50 percent of the men at some point in their marital lives. Overall, the efforts of Kinsey and his co-workers made a significant impact on the norms associated with sexual behavior. Exposing typical sexual practices gave a stimulus to more open sexual communication. These findings helped many people diminish their fears and negative attributions about such matters as masturbation and clitoral stimulation.

While Kinsey et al. did much to de-mystify the sexual instinct, their work was not without negative effects. The process of normalization decreased tolerance for variations in sexual behavior, even while it increased acceptance in other instances. By quantifying sexual behaviors, a standard for a healthy relationship was established. If two to three orgasms per week were not experienced by the male, some underlying problem was assumed to exist in the relationship and/or in the psychological growth of the individual. New pressures to perform were thus an outgrowth of "bringing sex out of the closet" (May, 1969).

Overall, the work of Kinsey et al. did much to foster a challenge to Freud's generally narrow outlook on sex. They implied that various forms of sexual behaviors should not be seen as manifestations of psychopathology and immaturity. Because sexual behaviors such as situational inorgasmia and ejaculation soon after entry were quite typical, intrapsychic conflicts need not be at their roots.

Masters and Johnson (1970) described a treatment approach which extended the de-mystification of sexual functioning initiated by Kinsey et al.'s findings. Because of the years of faulty learning and the mysteries surrounding sex, it was quite normal for relationships that were otherwise satisfying to be confronted with sexual dysfunctions. They even estimated that 50 percent of all marriages have sexual problems (Lehrman, 1970). Couples simply need to relearn (or perhaps, even learn for the first time) how to experience sexual pleasure and deal with the anxiety that had developed vis-à-vis the sexual episode. Performance anxiety was the central feature of sexual dysfunctions, and Masters and Johnson attempted to desensitize people to this destructive, goal-oriented perspective toward sexual interactions. Alleviating the sexual symptom was the primary purpose of Masters and Johnson's direct-treatment approach.

Since Masters and Johnson's original writings, a fourth phase has taken place in the evolution of treating sexual dysfunctions. This development could be described as a shift away from conceiving sexual problems as a highly distinct entity based primarily on faulty or insufficient learning. Instead, sexual concerns are seen as pertaining to the totality of a person's interpersonal experience. Quantification of sexual behavior has given way to a concentration on the subjective quality of sexual interactions. As opposed to behavioral dysfunctions (such as erectile failure), more and more clients have begun to present difficulties in the area of sexual desire. Masters and Johnson's approach presumed that "they would if they could, but they can't." Their techniques are not as effective for clients who "could if they would, but they won't." Treatment of cases such as low sexual desire need a more comprehensive treatment focus (Kaplan, 1979).

In addition, some clinicians sense that new types of clients have presented themselves to sex therapy clinics (Dickes, 1980). Clients seem to be more passive, more defensive, and less able to bring about rapid symptom relief with the direct-treatment methods, when compared with those clients screened by Masters and Johnson for their therapy. One could speculate that, since the early 1970s, a number of self-help books for both men and women have significantly aided many individuals who could benefit from a direct-behavioral approach (Barbach, 1975; Heiman, LoPiccolo, & LoPiccolo, 1976; Kline-Graber & Graber, 1975; Zilbergeld, 1978). The availability of these books has provided many potential clients with an alternative to therapy. Women's and men's consciousness-raising groups have paid some attention to how socialization has led to sexual inhibitions, and these programs may also have provided important sources of support. Those clients that do still choose to seek help for

sexual dysfunctions by means of sex therapy may have presenting problems that are more resistent to change for a wide variety of reasons.

One could describe these historical shifts in the treatment of sexual
dysfunctions as the field's maturing process. The euphoria that surrounded
the initial claims of significant, lasting treatment effectiveness (Masters
& Johnson, 1970) have given way to a more modest and scientific approach to understanding the value of the direct-treatment approach popularized by Masters and Johnson (Goldberg, 1981a; Levine, 1980). Sexual
interactions represent a complex of forces that must include the interface
of physiological, psychological, and sociological events. Given this complexity, the conceptual controversy that has surrounded the treatment
of sexual dysfunctions may be giving way to a new appreciation of the
common elements inherent in different psychological perspectives (Dollard & Miller, 1950; Wachtel, 1977). Therapists may be missing some
important agents to the change process by strictly adhering to one treatment approach (Sollod & Kaplan, 1976). Rather, the presenting problems
and characteristics of individuals may require that a wide variety of techniques need to be used, depending on how the individual(s) experiences
the therapeutic endeavor (Kaplan, 1979).

THEORETICAL FOUNDATIONS FOR TREATING SEXUAL DYSFUNCTIONS

Psychoanalytic approach

Psychoanalytic theory maintains that failure to successfully manage
psychosexual development is the primary etiological factor promoting
adult sexual dysfunctions (Fenichel, 1945; Rosen, 1977). A set of sexual
forces called the *Oedipal* or *Electra* complex emerges from the mother-
father-child triangle, due to the competition between the child and father
for the mother's affection and love. For boys, the child becomes angry
at his father's presence and even turns to rage, in that he would like to
"extinguish" his father so that he could have the mother all to himself.
The child senses that his yearnings are forbidden, and the consequence
of his wish to take primary possession of his mother fosters the experience
of castration anxiety. The child resolves this fear by repudiating his competition with the father and his sexual interest in his mother. Instead, he
identifies with the father and parental injunctions. Because of fears of
punishment, the boy renounces his sexual wishes for his mother and
uses mechanisms such as sublimation to gratify his sexual instinct. As
he approaches adolescence, the sexual instincts are typically channeled
into different, more appropriate aims.

Girls have a somewhat similar task to accomplish (Kaplan, 1974). Like
boys, their initial, primary attachment is with the mother, but shifts to
the father when the girl discovers that the father possesses greater physical

attributes than the mother—a penis. The girl discovers that she has a major inadequacy, and penis envy typically develops. Resentment of men and anger toward the mother is promoted by this envy. These sexual wishes toward her father become a source of anxiety and, because of them, the girl fears the loss of her mother's love. Under optimal circumstances, the girl suppresses these wishes, then renounces her desires, and susequently identifies once again with her mother.

The seeds of sexual dysfunctions can be found in the failure to successfully cope with these early instinctual wishes. The inability to differentiate adult object choices from one's parent can promote a number of sexual problems, in that early sexual traumas are reexperienced. For example, low sexual desire can be the consequence of anxiety, if the wish for a partner is equated with the wish for one's opposite-sex parent. Erectile dysfunction could result from castration anxieties, if the individual does, in fact, have sex with a woman whom he identifies with his mother. Female inorgasmic problems can be seen as a continuing inability to renounce penis envy and experience vaginal excitement.

Other psychoanalytic investigators have placed a greater emphasis on the development of the ego as the primary etiological source of sexual dysfunctions. Levay and Kagle (1977) developed a diagnostic system based on ego dysfunctions (Keiser, 1959). They indicated that sexual dysfunctions are the result of poor ego functioning in three critical areas— pleasure, intimacy, and cooperation. Development of autonomy is also an important quality of the ego which can influence the development of sexual dysfunctions. Lovers need to accept their essential separateness as individuals (Kuten, 1976). The symbiotic unity that was once experienced in childhood with one's opposite-gender parent cannot be regained. Acknowledgement of this loss of primal love or the acceptance of its lack through the expression of anger fosters self-acceptance and the ability to feel sexual longing for one's mate. The hypothesis seems to follow that accepting both love and hate toward one's partner builds honesty and subsequently allows for the flow of sexual energy.

Despite the theoretical elaboration provided by many investigators, reviews of the literature have failed to confirm the value of psychoanalysis for treating sexual dysfunctions (Hogan, 1978; Reynolds, 1977; Wright, Perreault, & Mathieu, 1977). O'Connor and Stern (1972) found little treatment success using psychodynamic therapy. One would also expect to find more psychopathology among those distressed by sexual problems than among those who are sexually functional. Research has failed to support this hypothesis as well. For example, Cooper (1965) found that schizophrenic females were more sexually responsive than a sample of neurotics. Fisher (1973) could not explain the etiology of inorgasmia by differentiating orgasmic and inorgasmic women on the basis of overall psychopathology.

Behavioral approach

Behaviorists underscore the value of overt, observable phenomena in explicating the dynamics associated with sexual dysfunctions. The most basic paradigm is that of social reinforcement: people respond in predictable ways when they are confronted by particular stimuli. In effect, people have learned to exhibit patterns of behavior in order to attain certain goals.

Applying this generic principle to sexual interactions, sexual dysfunctions can be considered conditioned anxiety reactions to stimuli that are perceived as sexual in nature. The central purpose to therapy is to desensitize the person to the anxiety-producing situation. This lessening of anxiety is achieved by utilizing a graduated hierarchy of sexual stimuli and thereby teaching the person to tolerate and enjoy sexual encounters. A number of different methods have been used to produce desensitization. Sexual scenes can be presented and experienced through imagination or *in vivo,* while forbidding the goal of orgasm or erection (Lazarus, 1963, 1977; Wolpe, 1958). Relaxation training (Jacobson, 1938) can be used as an adjunct in helping people concentrate and visualize the sexual stimuli.

Masters and Johnson's direct-treatment approach (1970) extended the principle of progressive desensitization to working with the couple as the behaving unit. Banning intercourse and having the couple focus on nongenital forms of touching are examples of their program, which is designed to eliminate sources of anxiety. The positive reinforcement gained from the touching assignments or sensate focus would estinguish the sexual dysfunctions.

A number of clinicians have attempted to integrate a cognitive component into the behavioral approach. The fact that not all people respond in the same way to sexual stimuli indicates that cognitive events may be significant modifiers in predicting sexual dysfunctions. Restructuring attitudes has been a critical component of sex therapy (Annon, 1974; Ellis, 1975; LoPiccolo, 1977). Irrational beliefs may be at the heart of sexual dysfunctions and, culturally, these beliefs can be fostered by cultural stereotypes. Zilbergeld (1978) highlights 10 myths that are particularly relevant for men:

Myth 1. Men shouldn't express certain feelings.

Myth 2. Sex is a performance.

Myth 3. A man must orchestrate sex.

Myth 4. A man always wants and is always ready to have sex.

Myth 5. All physical contact must lead to sex.

Myth 6. Sex equals intercourse.

Myth 7. Sex requires an erection.

Myth 8.   Good sex is increasing excitement, terminated only by orgasm.

Myth 9.   Sex should be natural and spontaneous.

Myth 10.   In this enlightened age, the preceding myths no longer have any influence on us.

Sexual interactions need to conform to these standards in order to attain satisfaction. The problem is twofold: these beliefs are nearly impossible to consistently realize, and the performance anxiety which they generate can lead to sexual dysfunctions. Also, the myths are self-maintained. Men do not have to be bound by these prescriptions if they choose to restructure their sexual expectations and adopt a more flexible and exploratory perspective on sex. It should be noted that many women are guided by these same myths; therefore, female partners can have an impact on a male's efforts to alter his sexual script.

Some investigators have explored the relationship between cognitive events and psychophysiology in order to find an explanation for the development of sexual dysfunctions (Heiman, 1977). Individuals often report little if any subjective excitement, even though they are demonstrating signs of physiological arousal in response to sexual stimuli. Women seem to be less able than men to experience a subjective sense of excitement when objective signs of genital arousal are present. The inability to cognitively label one's sexual excitement may be an alternative explanation for the development of sexual dysfunctions. By helping people focus on and heighten their awareness of bodily sensations, an individual may benefit from cognitive (as opposed to behavioral) skills in order to function effectively. Schachter (1964) provides some theoretical basis for these laboratory findings. Two factors seem to be critical in maximizing a person's arousal. First, there must be recognizable autonomic activation. By implication, all excitable emotions such as fear, anxiety, joy, and elation begin with this nonspecific, physiological stimulation. Second, situational cues perceived by the person suggest an emotional label for the general activation. People make an attribution to their activation (e.g., that it is *sexual* in nature). Therefore, sexual dysphoria may represent an inability to label one's bodily activity as pleasurable. As Schacter suggests, the social context in which one has a sexual encounter can significantly shape how aroused the person becomes.

As with the psychoanalytic approach, studies that attempt to assess the effectiveness of behavioral methods have been plagued with research problems such as lack of a control group, different samples, and poor and/or nonspecific outcome criteria (Hogan, 1978; Reynolds, 1977). Masters and Johnson claim to have achieved success with approximately 80 percent of the cases they have treated. Others have not been as successful (Ansari, 1975; Cooper, 1970). Mathews, Bancroft, Whitehead, Hackman, Julier, Bancroft, Gath, & Shaw (1976) found support for the value of incorporating behavioral assignments in a counseling program for sexual problems. Recent evidence (LoPiccolo, 1981) seems to confirm their conclusion that a dual-team sex-therapy format offers no beneficial features beyond those provided by one therapist. Goldberg (1981a) points out that after achieving post-therapy gains, clients with most sexual dysfunctions have returned to pre-therapy levels, when using self-report behavioral indices. However, on nonbehavioral measures, such as overall satisfaction, clients have sustained changes that they made post-therapy. These data suggest that planned follow-up visits may be a necessary part of a behavioral-treatment program, if sexual dysfunctions are to remain extinguished.

In one review of outcome studies, consistent positive results from sex therapy were found (Kinder & Blakeney, 1977). Situational orgasmic dysfunction was more resistant to change than were other sexual difficulties. Premature ejaculation and primary orgasmic problems were most amenable to change. These authors claim that symptom substitution has not occurred, as a psychoanalytic formulation may prodict. As do other reviewers, Kinder and Blakeney sound a note of caution in the confidence of their conclusions, due to the need to have more-precise reporting of diagnoses, process variables, and treatment goals enunciated in research reports.

Integrative frameworks

A number of efforts have begun, which attempt to integrate various theoretical perspectives, thereby providing expanded conceptual sophistication to understanding sexual interactions. A common element among many of the newer theories is the emphasis on cognitive factors. Thus, the field of sex therapy seems to be moving away from a behavioral model—which has been stereotypically ascribed to sex therapy since its inception (Reynolds, 1977).

Byrne (1977) utilizes a social-psychological framework in developing a model of sexual behavior. The model is responsive, in that it implies that people primarily react to sexual stimuli. This outlook can be compared with a proactive schema, which sees people as seeking out various sexual situations. Certain relationships are proposed in the model, as illustrated by different kinds of arrows in Figure 1. The arrows with solid lines suggest a hypothesized antecedent-consequence relationship, while the dotted lines indicate ancillary connections between the different constructs (located in the boxes). The arrows with dot-dash lines illustrate feedback loops and the potential effects that rewards and punishments will have on the person.

Byrne's model suggests that cognitive processes (like fantasies) can promote or inhibit sexual arousal and behavior. Other significant events which precede sexual behaviors include expectations and internal judgements (i.e., evaluative responses), which have the potential to inhibit will-

Figure 1

Byrne's sexual-behavior sequence

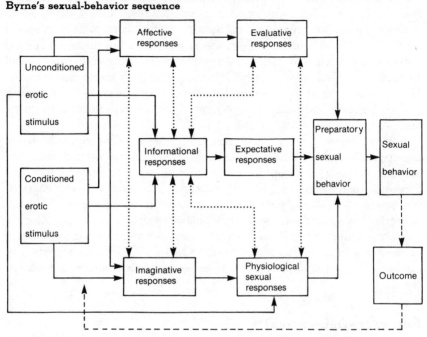

This figure is reprinted from Don Byrne, Social psychology and the study of sexual behavior, *Personality and Social Psychology Bulletin,* Winter 1977, *3*(1), Copyright 1977 by the Society for Personality and Social Psychology, Inc., with permission of Sage Publications, Inc.

ingness to engage in sexual behaviors despite having the affective inclination to do so. In effect, Byrne has attempted to account for sexual dysfunctions by developing an expanded learning paradigm. He has attempted to provide a schema for the "black box" that lies between stimuli and responses, processes that are not addressed by classic learning theory.

Apfelbaum (1976) synthesizes physiological factors with immediate and remote psychological variables, in accounting for the etiology of sexual dysfunctions. Apfelbaum raises questions about the value of lists describing etiological factors that promote sexual dysfunctions, such as those provided by L. LoPiccolo (1980). These lists do not offer adequate guidelines for separating sexually functional individuals from those with dysfunctions. For some individuals, performance anxiety and spectatoring may serve as arousal triggers, while for others, these feelings have an inhibiting effect. Some functional individuals utilize defense mechanisms such as denial in order to perform sexually. Repetitive, mechanistic behaviors (such as the male always being on the top during intercourse) may be a manifestation of how these defense mechanisms operate.

Apfelbaum's model attempts to explain how the use of similar defense mechanisms and other psychological processes could characterize sexually dysfunctional individuals *and* functional individuals. His major premise is that factors involved in the development of sexual dysfunctions can be grouped into two levels of analysis. The "first-order cause of sexual dysfunction" is a somatic vulnerability to stress and anxiety. This notion is an expansion on Kaplan's (1974) earlier notions regarding a constitutional, innate predisposition to somatic reactivity. While she was not able to indicate what anatomical structures and processes are responsible for this physiological sensitivity, she indicates that this relatively may provide an explanation for certain unexpected behavior patterns. For example, a very *low* level of this sensitivity to stress and anxiety may explain some couples' ability to have passionate sexual interactions, despite the presence of much marital tension.

If people do *not* suffer from somatic reactivity (that is, are *not* vulnerable to stressful events), a number of defense mechanisms are then available in order to function effectively. Automatic functioning aided by defense mechanisms allows them to behave in a sexually satisfying manner, even with low levels of arousal. They may need spontaneity, which allows them to focus in on their bodily sensations and thus block out all else (including potential negative feelings, such as anger toward one's partner).

In Apfelbaum's two-stage model (Figure 2) this first-order physiological sensitivity is a necessary precondition to the onset of sexual dysfunction. However, a second psychological precondition is required in the etiology of sexual problems, even if this somatic reactivity is present. People need to be concerned about their sexual performance. Once these two conditions are met, then a wide assortment of factors come into play. Individual differences will determine which factor becomes paramount. These influences emerge from psychoanalytic, behavioral, sociological, physiological, and systems theories.

Mosher (1980) offers yet another theoretical explanation for the presence of sexual dysfunctions. He implies that current theories do not ac-

Figure 2

Apfelbaum's stage model

| Somatic vulnerability | + | Performance anxiety | + | Early and late traumas
Religious orthodoxy
Character restrictions
Relationship problems
Inability to communicate
Unaroused or dysfunctional partner
Depression
Fears of loss of control and of intimacy | Sexual dysfunctions |

count for the generalized sexual malaise that people can experience without necessarily exhibiting any behavioral deficits. Feelings of disconnectedness and low sexual desire may be the outgrowth of an inability to become involved in a *sexual-contact episode*. People typically experience their *depth of involvement*, be it shallow or deep, along three dimensions. (See Figure 3) *Involvement in sexual role enactment* means that people may be focused on how they behave in a sexual way. Specific characteristics of the sexual-contact episode (such as lighting, time of day, and initiating events) can be particularly important. An individual's sexual script can be quite defined (Gagnon & Simon, 1973) and, in effect, become a requirement, if deep involvement is to take place.

A second dimension of depth of involvement is *involvement in sexual trance*. Mosher likens this type of involvement to that which is achieved in a hypnotic state. People can become highly engrossed in the bodily sensations during sex and this ability to "let go" can be described in two ways. People become so involved in the momentary feelings of excitement that there is a fading of a *generalized reality orientation* (GRO). In addition, people seem to construct a *special sexual orientation* (SSO), which is a perceptual stance that allows observed stimuli to take on sexual meaning (e.g., heavy breathing becomes a pleasurable sound).

Depth of involvement can also vary according to a third dimension, *involvement with one's sexual partner*. The *latitude of partner acceptance* can be quite wide, in that people have a low level of selectivity and investment in terms of with whom they choose to become sexual. For another person, the latitude can be quite limited, in that only very few individuals can satisfy the person's requirements regarding whom the person chooses to engage in sexual interactions. The person may also need to experience a significant bond with the person (i.e., a *strong depth of engagement*) for them to feel much involvement in the sexual encounter.

Figure 3

Mosher's three dimensions of depth of involvement in human sexual response

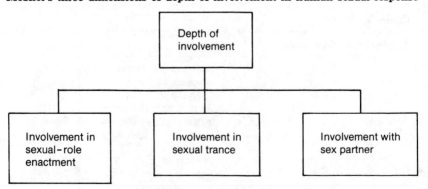

People's sexual script will determine which dimension they prefer, if their depth of involvement is to be high. They may like one of the three dimensions much more than the other two, and Mosher describes this phenomenon as the *preferred-dimension structure*. Some couples may experience much distress if their preferred dimensions either lack congruence or if they as individuals lack flexibility in being able to experience sex by shifting through all three dimensions in a particular sexual-contact episode.

One of the problems with the previous theoretical frameworks is that they are basically monadic models. Typically, the unit of analysis is the individual, not the couple. Seeing sexual behavior from a dyadic unit of analysis has been rare (Verhulst & Heiman, 1979). The sexual well-being of individuals is a function of their individual characteristics as well as of how they perceive their social environment, such as how responsive they consider their partner to be.

Lewin's field theory (1935) can be used as the basis of a dyadic theoretical network that attempts to integrate many different constructs—including those presented in the previously described theories—into a dynamic whole. Figure 4 is an illustration of how this holistic framework might operate with two hypothetical individuals.

Before applying the model, an explication of its basic components is in order. Lewin considered human experience to be a phenomenological enterprise. All psychic events can be described by developing a mental map called the *life space*, which is the psychological representation of the person's social environment. The life space is divided into different *regions*, which are cognitive pictures of different aspects to the person's life. These regions have both positive and negative features which Lewin describes as the specific *valances* within a region. In Figure 4,[1] work is a highly valued component of person B's life. Sex is not an important aspect of the life space and, in fact, is to be avoided, since sex is associated with a predominance of negative valences.

The *persona* is the psychological representation of the person and contains the idiosyncratic traits of the person. Some traits are somewhat peripheral, while others represent central needs for the persona. The *motoric perceptual boundary* is a boundary surrounding the persona and serves as a filtering mechanism to how the persona views the life space. Ellis' (1962) irrational beliefs are similar in function to the motoric perceptual boundary. Particular needs are activated by the momentary state of the life space, as well as by the contemporaneous external situation

---

[1] Figure 4 represents a model that is adapted from Lewin's field theory. It attempts to represent two people, without reference to gender. While the regions of one person's life space do not have to be in another person's life space, any labels used to indicate certain constructs could be used in both halves of the model. For example, physiological elements influence both people. The figure was drawn in such a manner as to maximize simplicity.

Figure 4

Application of Lewin's field theory to develop a holistic model of sexual interaction

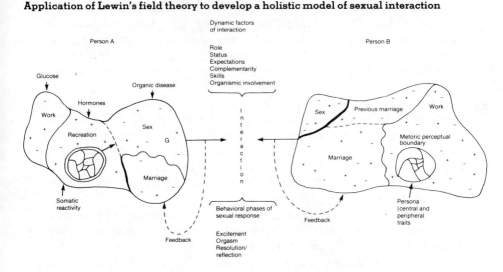

in which the person is behaving. The persona recognizes a goal region by deciding which region is most positively charged at a particular point in time. If a region is more highly valued than the one where the persona presently rests, then the persona finds a *path* through the life space and *locomotes* to this goal region.

Locomotion (i.e., thinking about or being motivated to behave in a particular way) is not a simple, unidirectional process, because the persona will encounter *barriers* surrounding each region when it tries to reach a particualr goal region. The barriers have special characteristics, depending on the nature of the region. Porous boundaries allow easy locomotion, but may result in one region "leaking" into another region; thus, poor differentiation of the life space results. By contrast, boundaries can be quite rigid, thereby inhibiting the persona from entering them. Elastic boundaries promote the expansion of one region into another region. Therefore, one region can "take over" the life space; thus, perseverating on one particular life area happens. Elastic boundaries restrict locomotion, but offer much less resistance than do rigid boundaries.

Certain components of the model illustrated in Figure 4 go beyond the basic elements of Lewin's field theory. *Feedback* from the sexual interaction loops back into the life space and may effect the nature of certain regions. For example, if the person's partner plays different types of roles than did his first wife, the boundary between his previous marriage and his present marriage may become less porous. *Behavioral phases of sexual response* are similar to those described by Masters and Johnson (1966), except for the addition of a "reflection" phase (Goldberg, 1981b).

This phase incorporates post-orgasm aspects of a sexual interaction such as caressing, eye contact, and other behaviors characterizing the termination of a sexual episode. *Dynamic aspects of the interaction* are those described by Sarbin and Allen (1968) and are among the constructs of role theory. Role, status, expectations (held by the other person about the role taker's behavior), complementarity (how well the roles fit together), skills, and organismic involvement (the effort which a person gives to enacting a role) all will impact on sexual interactions.

Physiological and biochemical elements are included in the model, since they can also make an important contribution on the psychological readiness of the persona to desire sexual interactions. Glucose, hormones, various organic diseases (such as vascular insufficiency and diabetes), and somatic reactivity to stress can function as modifiers of psychological valences. They can promote a certain predisposition to experiencing one's psychological world in a particular manner.

Figure 4 represents an application of the model for two particular individuals. The persona on the left is locomoting toward the goal region of sex and, thus, is experiencing much sexual desire. Person A (for the purposes of this application, a woman) is currently thinking about physical exercise. Aided by a need for play, sex and recreation have a porous boundary between them so that there is a functional linkage between the two, in that person A often can turn her attention to sexual interactions when thinking about recreational activities. Sex may indeed have a playful meaning to the persona. The person has some negative, albeit ambivalent, feelings about her marriage (i.e., both positive and negative valences), and thinking about it directly is avoided by its partially rigid boundary. Note that the boundary around sex is elastic. Therefore, when sex is imagined (and perhaps even performed), it "takes over" the marital region. This equation between sex and marriage (aided by the elastic boundary) can help promote satisfaction about her marriage. In essence, when sex is good, the marriage is on solid ground. Overall, one might not predict the development of sexual dysfunctions for person A.

Person B presents a very different picture. His persona is currently situated in the work region; and since work is so highly valued relative to the other regions, the persona will most likely stay there. A need for achievement may be activated at the present moment. Given this situation in the life space, work predominates the person's cognitive activity. Thoughts about sex are highly unlikely, given the rigid boundary around sex as well as the predominance of negative valences in the region. He is highly ambivalent about his marriage (i.e., equal number of positive and negative valences), which may be fostered by many negative feelings left over from a previous marriage which are "leaking" into the region representing his current marriage. Due to his motoric perceptual boundary, he may even be filtering his perceptions of the marriage in catastrophic terms (such as "I'll always be a failure in relationships"). Person

B may be prone to develop such sexual dysfunctions as low sexual desire and situational erectile failure.

Not all constructs in the model were used in this case example, since the purpose of the application is to illustrate how the model can be utilized in a practical manner. The model can serve as a guiding framework for analyzing sexual interactions between two people, thereby helping to determine the major etiological factors operating for any particular person(s). Regardless of which theoretical framework is most useful to the clinician or researcher, theory can serve an important role in understanding the reasons for sexual dysfunctions. Appreciating the etiology as well as the dynamics associated with maintaining a dysfunctional sexual pattern can help in planning for the assessment and treatment of sexual dysfunctions.

ASSESSMENT

There are at least three critical goals in conducting a comprehensive assessment of sexual dysfunctions. The first is to understand the current nature and historical parameters of the sexual difficulty. Second, it is important to assess the degree to which physiological factors are operating to promote the sexual problem. Third, it is necessary to determine how sex fits dynamically into other areas of the person's life space. For example, some individuals may use the sexual dysfunction as a defense (or barrier in Lewin's field theory) against becoming aware of underlying, unconscious conflict (Kaplan & Kohl, 1972). In order to accomplish these three goals and capture the complexity of sexual behavior, a number of evaluation procedures are necessary. Because no single perspective provides a total picture of the person (and couple), assessment is aided by developing an interdisciplinary approach. Psychological and medical personnel need to bring together their skills to conduct the assessment as well as to jointly discuss the findings, so that an appropriate treatment plan can be created.

The need for a thorough assessment has become even more paramount as the field develops more expertise and sophistication in detecting organic factors in the etiology of sexual dysfunctions (Leiblum & Pervin, 1980). It was once commonly assumed that only 10 percent of erectile dysfunction cases were primarily due to organic deficits (Hastings, 1963; Masters & Johnson, 1970). This proportion is being revised by most clinicians; some are estimating that in only 42 percent of clients can organic problems be completely ruled out, and a purely psychogenic explanation for the dysfunction be given (Jacobs, Fishkin, Goldman, & Cohen, 1981). In one study, nearly three quarters of men with erectile dysfunctions had at least some organic disease (Schumacher & Lloyd, 1981). Unfortunately, advances have not been as swift in understanding the physiology of female sexual response as they have been in studying male sexual behavior.

General issues in approaching assessment

Discussing sexual behavior is a form of interaction that can be filled with anxiety for many individuals, and this anxiety can be amplified when the interaction takes place with a stranger. However, it needs to be pointed out that these feelings may not be the sole province of the client but can also be experienced by the assessor, regardless of whether this person is a psychologist, nurse, or physician. In short, transference and counter-transference are operating throughout the course of the assessment. This dynamic implies that the quality of the information can be shaped by how the assessor handles these thoughts and feelings. An inner experience of comfort and acceptance are critical components during as interview, and being aware of one's own sexual attitudes is an essential aspect of developing a positive atmosphere in the assessment. Some workshops, such as *Sexual Attitude Restructuring* (SARs), initially developed by the National Sex Forum, have been designed to help clinicians and educators become more aware of their own negative attitudes toward sex and of how these internal programs might influence their behavior.

These attitudes can be skillfully masked by clinicians. Their denial can seem quite reasonable, if an assessment of sexual concerns is not directly related to the reasons for the client's visit, as is the case in family-medicine clinics. Health professionals might claim that asking questions about sexual matters is both inappropriate and irrelevant as a source of clinical information. However, in one study, a sexual assessment was found to be useful. A group of physicians in a general medical group practice received training in how to perform a sex-history interview. Sex history taking was then incorporated into the assessment of 232 of their patients, 91 percent of whom reported that it was appropriate for their doctors to ask questions about sex. Moreover, physicians thought that, in 50 percent of the patients interviewed, information garnered from sex histories influenced their treatment plan in some way (Glasgow & Ende, 1981).

A second issue in assessment is that the level of knowledge concerning sexual functioning still remains low among health and mental health care practitioners, despite recent advances. The field has yet to develop a protocol for assessing the organic components of female sexual dysfunctions. In male dysfunctions, evaluating potential physiological contributors to sexual problems is done by excluding the possible effects of various factors. Failure to find organic disease however, does not necessarily mean that the dysfunction must have a psychogenic origin. It may be a reasonable conclusion, but the *total* picture of the physiological basis for sexual dysfunction is simply not well enough comprehended at this date.

Overall, five systems seem to be of primary importance in conducting a sexual assessment: vascular, urological (or gynecological), neurological, endocrinological, and psychological. However, it is possible for one system to be responsible for the *etiology* of the problem, while a different system is operating to help *maintain* the dysfunction. For example, a hormonal imbalance may be promoting painful intercourse for a woman. However, her partner's negative reactions and her guilt may exacerbate the problem. Treating the physical aspect of the dysfunction alone may be too limited, since the psychological system is operating as well. However, it is useful to have a clear picture of the major sexual dysfunction being diagnosed, before specific procedures for assessing these systems' contributions are introduced.

Diagnosis: Major sexual dysfunctions

There are a wide variety of specific sexual dysfunctions that may be experienced by clients. It must be kept in mind that the couple, as a dynamic entity, is the behaving unit that needs to be understood, even though sexual dysfunctions are typically described in a manner which implies that the dysfunction is associated with one person alone. Partners can be symptom-free in an overt, behavioral sense, but clearly be making a significant impact on their partner's dysfunction (Cole, Blakeney, Chan, Chesney, & Creson, 1979; Derogatis & Meyer, 1979). For example, a man may be deeply troubled by intermittent erectile difficulties and see these failures as a sign of the aging process, a situation which terrifies him. His female partner may respond with comments such as "I don't care if you're performing fine each time. It's stupid to worry about it. Just forget it and it will go away by itself." This reaction may inhibit discussions concerning the basis of his feelings, thereby reinforcing his performance anxiety. The dysfunction could therefore be maintained by the partner, despite her full capabilities of functioning sexually.

The four phases of sexual response can be used as a paradigm for classifying various major sexual dysfunctions. Masters and Johnson (1966) indicated that there were four phases—*excitement, plateau, orgasm,* and *resolution.* Others have begun to add more of a cognitive flavor to determination of the stages of sexual response, by indicating that a sexual encounter begins with some level of desire. Thus, *sexual desire* was coined as a distinct phase of the sexual-response cycle (Kaplan, 1979). Others have attempted to include post-orgasm events in the characterization of human sexual response, and Levine (1980) described this as a *satisfaction* phase. Goldberg (1981b) used the phrase *reflection* to indicate that both behavioral (eg., eye contact) and cognitive (eg., feeling of need satisfaction) elements should be included in this last phase. A synthesis of cognitive-behavioral representations of the four phases of human sexual response is in Figure 5.

Certain dysfunctions may not be clearly understood just by reading the label, and some explanation is, therefore, useful. *Sexual aversion* is a severe form of low sexual desire and should not be thought of as a distinct dysfunction. It represents one end of the desire continuum, with

Figure 5

Major sexual dysfunctions in phases of human sexual response

1. *Desire phase dysfunction*
   Male and female: Low sexual desire
                          and aversion

2. *Arousal phase dysfunction*
   Male: Erectile dysfunction
   Female: Excitement phase dysfunction or general sexual dysfunction.

3. *Orgasm phase dysfunction*
   Male: Premature ejaculation
                 Inhibited or retarded ejaculation
                 Retrograde ejaculation
                 Anhedonic orgasm
   Female: Inorgasmia

4. *Reflection/satisfaction phase dysfunction*
   Male and female: (No common labels)

5. *Other*
   Male and female: Dyspareunia
   Female: Vaginismus

hyperactive sexual desire at the other end. Sexual aversion means that the individual has clearly negative feelings regarding sexual interactions. Emotions of extreme dislike such as disgust distinguish aversion from low sexual desire. However, low sexual desire is not as clear a dysfunction as it may appear on the surface. One could argue that it has a behavioral component, such as frequency of sexual activity of no more than once every two weeks. Amount of nonpartner sexual activity might also be relevent, such as masturbatory behavior. Some might contend that thoughts or fantasies are also important indicators of individual sexual-desire levels. The primary point is that there is no uniform, operational definition of low sexual desire. Perhaps the single most important feature of the dysfunction is that the level of desire is distressing to the client(s) involved.

Erectile dysfunction (or impotence) can be divided into two categories: the ability to achieve an erection and the ability to maintain an erection following tumescence. *Excitement phase dysfunction* (or general sexual dysfunction) is used less and less by clinicians as a distinctly female dysfunction. Nevertheless, Kaplan (1974) describes it as a substitute for ''frigidity'' and uses the label to mean an absence of erotic enjoyment from sexual stimuli and/or touching. As a subjective experience, this problem is quite similar to low sexual desire and may have little heuristic value, given the addition of low sexual desire as a category for sexual dysfunctions.

Premature ejaculation has been a troublesome behavior to label and define, since it requires an operational definition that may merely reflect the value system of the clinician. For example, Masters and Johnson (1970) apply this dysfunction in cases where the male ejaculates any time before the female reaches orgasm in at least 50 percent of their sexual interactions. However, this pattern may represent the chosen script of many couples. Others have tried to avoid this approach by relying simply on the length of time between the point of vaginal penetration and male ejaculation (Schover, Friedman, Weiler, Heiman, & LoPiccolo, 1981). However, the specification of time categories (e.g., one to three minutes, four to seven minutes, etc.) also may imply an unintentional value system for how long men should be able to maintain themselves before ejaculation occurs. Kaplan (1974) offers a third approach by pointing to the role of voluntary control over when ejaculation occurs. When this control is lacking, the diagnosis of premature ejaculation is then applied. Most clinicians seem to follow Kaplan's definition in determining the presence of premature ejaculation.

Inhibited ejaculation means that a male is not able to ejaculate during sexual activities. In some cases, he is unable to ejaculate at all; while in others, much effort and use of techniques can eventually lead to an ejaculatory response. Typically, males who are troubled by this behavior can ejaculate with few problems during masturbation. It is interaction with another individual that promotes this behavioral deficit.

Retrograde ejaculation occurs when there is the experience of orgasm with no apparent ejaculate, because the fluid is emitted into the bladder. *Anhedonic orgasm* takes place when there is no feeling of pleasure associated with ejaculation. Sometimes, no full ejaculation occurs and only seepage of semen accompanies the experience of orgasm.

The inability to experience an orgasm is described by the term *inorgasmia*. A variety of labels have been used to describe this dysfunction (such as *preorgasmia* and *anorgasmia*), but they are all referring to the same behavior. People have debated the wisdom of using particular labels. For example, preorgasmia sounds more hopeful and less clinically final than inorgasmia. However, preorgasmia may raise false hopes for some women; thus, the label of inorgasmia is preferred for some clients.

The final two dysfunctions do not clearly fall within one of the phases of sexual response and are, therefore, classified separately. *Dyspareunia* is the experience of pain during sex. Typically, females as opposed to males present this dysfunction, but it is possible for a male to complain of pain in his genital area during sex. *Vaginismus* can be described as the involuntary closure of the vaginal opening, due to spasms in the pubococcygeal muscles surrounding the vagina. Penile penetration is not possible and, if intercourse is attempted, much pain can be experienced by the female.

In all of these dysfunctions, qualifiers should be used to specify the time and conditions under which the dysfunction becomes operable. In terms of time, *lifelong* versus *not lifelong* can be used to describe when the problem began. Lifelong should be applied when the problem has existed throughout the person's entire adult life. Some clinicians use the terms *primary* and *secondary* as synonymous with lifelong and not lifelong. Another important qualifier pertains to the circumstances surrounding the exhibition of the problem. The dysfunction is *global* if the sexual problem surfaces in all situations, such as masturbation, with various partners, and at all times of the year. When the sexual dysfunction is experienced only during certain circumstances, the problem is described as *situational* in nature. For example, the diagnosis of inorgasmia should include the qualifiers not lifelong and situational, if a woman has recently lost her ability to be orgasmic with her partner during intercourse, but still can have orgasm through her own stimulation.

Despite the use of these qualifiers, diagnostic classifications for sexual dysfunctions usually suffer from a number of problems (Schover et al., 1981). Imprecision of behavioral meaning, conflicting operational definitions, prejoritive language (through labels such as "impotence" to describe erectile dysfunction), and seeing sexual dysfunction from a unidimensional point of view are some of the problems associated with most existing classification schemas. Schover et al. (1981) describe a multiaxial descriptive system in use at the Sex Therapy Center at SUNY-Stony Brook. This diagnostic model includes six axes, and an individual can receive a diagnosis from each axis. There are over 50 different, specific behaviors that make up a total picture of the individual's functional difficulties. For example, a person can have both low sexual desire and difficulties maintaining erections in this diagnostic system. This multiaxial approach seems to fit more closely with clinical realities than trying to determine one definitive diagnosis for a person.

Protocol for assessing sexual dysfunctions

A protocol for evaluating sexual dysfunctions is given in Figure 6 as an example of a comprehensive, interdisciplinary assessment plan. It represents an outline for the steps that are utilized at the Sexual Function Center of Jefferson Medical College. It can easily be modified, depending on the purposes and perspectives of other clinical settings.

The medical evaluation is particularly geared to assessing those dysfunctions which are presented by males. The protocol should be expanded and altered when the assessment focuses on the female's functioning. However, given the lack of certainty about how physiological

Figure 6

Protocol for sexual dysfunctions

I. Intake
  A. Instruments for evaluation
    1. Sexual Interaction Inventory (LoPiccolo & Steger, 1974)
    2. Derogatis Sexual Functioning Inventory (Derogatis & Melisaratos, 1979)
    3. Sexual History Form (Stony Brook, 1981)
    4. Four Phases of Sexual Functioning (Goldberg, 1981)
    5. Marital Adjustment Test (Locke & Wallace, 1959)
    6. Dyadic Adjustment Scale (Spanier, 1979)
    7. Medical Screening Form (Weiler, 1979)
  B. Interview
    1. Presenting complaints
    2. History of problem
    3. Current and previous relationship history
    4. Personal history and defense mechanisms
    5. Medical-systems review
    6. Mental-status review

II. Evaluation of vascular, neurological, urological, and endocrinological systems
  A. Physician examination (urologist, neurologist, gynecologist, endocrinologist, and/or internist where appropriate)
  B. Blood laboratory studies
    1. CBC
    2. SMA-12
    3. Serum testosterone and free testosterone
    4. FSH
    5. LH
    6. Prolactin
    7. Estrogen
    8. T3 and T4
    9. Glucose tolerance test (if warranted)
  C. Special studies
    1. Penile blood pressure by Doppler Ultrasound method
    2. Pudendal nerve latency
    3. Sleep laboratory for nocturnal penile tumescence (NPT) monitoring
    4. Other diagnostic work-ups such as arteriogram

III. Differential diagnosis
  A. Review findings with couple/client
  B. Counseling sessions, as needed, to understand implications of diagnosis and options

IV. Treatment
  A. Sex therapy
  B. Marital therapy
  C. Individual or group therapy
  D. Penile prosthesis
  E. Revascularization
  F. Exogenous hormonal treatment
  G. Other medical interventions

Source: adapted from Jacobs, J., Fishkin, R., Goldman, A., & Cohen, S. *A multidisciplinary approach to the evaluation and management of male sexual dysfunction.* Paper presented at the annual meeting of the American Urology Association, Greenbrier, Virginia, 1981.

elements affect female sexuality, the medical evaluation part of the protocol is limited to male sexual dysfunctions. This lack of understanding is becoming particularly apparent in light of recent research suggesting that women have the capacity to emit a fluid from the urethra at the point of orgasm which is homologous to male semen (Perry & Whipple, 1981; Belzer, 1981). A female equivalent to the prostate gland (called the Grafenberg Spot) is being hypothesized as a possible anatomical structure associated with this sexual response. Further research is currently underway to determine how much confidence can be placed in these initial reports.

Certain points need to be emphasized which are not specified in the outline of the protocol. Under optimal conditions, intake should include utilization of some written instruments. What people reveal on paper and what they discuss in the intake interview may be dissimilar. For example, a man may be willing to identify transvestism as an arousal mechanism on a questionnaire, even though the topic is too laden with conflict to be discussed in the interview. In addition, discrepancies between partners' responses can be noticed through examination of the written data. Differences in partners' perceptions then need to be addressed in the intake interview. In addition, validated instruments can serve as a data base for outcome research. Assessment instruments should cover both sexual and relationship issues, and the protocol lists some of the instruments which clinicians could use. A thorough listing and review of various instruments was completed by Schiavi (1979).

The intake interview itself allows the therapist to develop a clinical impression of the couple. It is a rich opportunity to directly observe the couple in terms of who talks the most, who is the initiator, what their body language looks like, and how they look at one another. These observations can help to identify central themes that may be of importance for the couple, such as power struggles and unresolved sources of resentment. Some sexual dysfunctions may be closely related to the qualities in the relationship (McGovern, Stewart, & LoPiccolo, 1975), and some clinicians consider sex therapy to be unwise if the marital distress is too severe (Sager, 1976). While couples with sexual dysfunctions might interact relatively well in other nonsexual matters (Hartman, 1980), one needs to see that the couple's total relationship can be observed in how they manage and cope with sexual difficulties (Greene, Lustig, & Lee, 1976). Thus, the actual process of the intake interview contains a valuable reservoir of information concerning the individual(s) and their dynamic interaction.

The protocol indentifies six major areas to examine during the intake interview. Gathering data about presenting complaints should include a review of all four of the phases of sexual functioning noted previously. Inquiry into specific sexual behaviors (whether or not the discussion is initiated by the clients) may help to put the presenting complaint in a context. For example, sexual intercourse may last for two minutes, with five minutes of foreplay that includes little direct clitoral stimulation. This may indicate that premature ejaculation is an underlying difficulty quite central to the presenting complaint of inorgasmia. For many reasons, it may be more threatening to this particular couple to deal with the male's premature ejaculation than to work on the female's inorgasmia.

Exploring the history of the problem helps to develop notions about events surrounding the onset of the difficulty. There may have been traumatic events in the person's adult life (such as the death of a spouse) which triggered the development of a sexual dysfunction. When assessing the interpersonal dynamics for the clients, both current and previous relationships should be discussed. A similar pattern of behavior may be detected in previous relationships, or the sexual dysfunction may represent a quite different set of events than has ever been experienced before. For some individuals, sexual problems may develop only when relationships become more intimate.

While the couple is the behaving unit for treatment, attention needs to be paid to the personal history of each individual. Their own characterological structure may inhibit the treatment process, and potential idiosyncratic resistances should be identified.

A review of medical systems should be conducted during the intake interview, as well as during parts of the medical evaluation. A number of medications can produce side effects which impact on sexual functioning (Kaplan, 1979). Other medical concerns have a direct influence on sexual behavior, such as diabetes, hypertension, spinal cord injuries, myocardial infarctions, pelvic pathology, and bladder disorders. LoPiccolo and LoPiccolo (1978) and Kolodny, Masters, & Johnson, (1979) discuss in detail many medical problems and their specific roles in sexual dysfunctions. General daily habits should also be explored with the clients. Eating and sleeping difficulties can signal possible signs of depression. Tobacco and alcohol consumption may have a negative impact on vasocongestion during sexual excitement.

The medical evaluation typically follows the intake interview. The blood work-up is a key component to this assessment. However, it needs to be noted that our understanding of the hormonal and biochemical bases of sexual behavior remains incomplete. This unclarity is, in part, associated with the faulty methodology used in many research projects, such as treating blood samples from different subjects as comparable, even though they were drawn at different times in the day (Schiavi & White, 1976). Schwatz, Kolodny, & Masters (1980) found no difference in the plasma-testosterone levels of sexually dysfunctional men, when compared to sexually functional men. Furthermore, testosterone levels were not related to therapy outcome. Benkert, Witt, Adam, & Leitz (1978) indicated that administration of exogenous testosterone to men with no abnormal levels of plasma testosterone had little effect on erectile capacities of male subjects beyond placebo. The prevailing hypothesis seems to be that, if people have hormone levels that are within the normal range, additional amounts of hormones will have little impact on their sexual behavior. However, there may be limitations in only assessing the total level of circulating hormones. For example, some investigators are suggesting that only a certain portion of total plasma testosterone is available to the person (Davidson, 1977), and this is the amount that is free or unbounded (that is, not attached to protein). There may also be interactions among the different hormones, so that the combined effect of particular hormones (such as testosterone and estrogen or testosterone and prolactin) may be more significant than evaluating each hormone as a separate entity (Jacobs, Fishkin, Goldman, & Cohen, 1981).

Special physiological studies can also provide important data in the assessment of male sexual dysfunctions. Sexual arousal involves vasocongestion; therefore, vascular insufficiency needs to be ruled out. Penile blood pressure can be measured through the Doppler technique, which records a pressure of the four arteries in the penis. Organic deficiencies can be suspected if the ratio between the penile blood pressure and the brachial pressure is less than .80 (Abelson, 1975; Gaskell, 1971). Some investigators are suggesting that an abnormal Doppler reading can be a sign of vascular constriction brought about by smoking cigarettes, and cessation of smoking will bring back vascular capabilities (Forsberg, Gustavii, Hojerback, & Olsson, 1979; Forsberg & Olsson, 1980). However, the data contain too few cases to be confident about this relationship at the present time.

The detection of organic deficits in male sexual dysfunction can be aided by using a sleep laboratory to assess nocturnal penile tumescence (NPT). Natural body rhythms will effect erections during 80-to-95 percent of REM sleep in normal males (Fisher, Gross, & Zuch, 1965). Men with an organic basis to their sexual dysfunctions failed to show these sleep erections (Karacan, 1970); Karacan, Williams, Thornby, & Sallis, 1975). However, problems with solely relying on NPT monitoring for the purposes of differential diagnosis have been noted, since some clients with a primarily psychogenic origin may do poorly in the sleep lab for many reasons, such as anxiety in that setting (Fisher, Schiavi, & Lear, 1975). Still others have pointed out that one could have much nocturnal expansion (NPT) without the rigidity that is required for intercourse, and thus rigidity estimates must be part of the NPT monitoring (Godec & Cass, 1981; Wein, Fishkin, Carpiniello, & Malby, 1981). If NPT proves to be abnormal, sleep disorders like sleep apnea and narcolepsy need to be ruled out, since some evidence exists for an association between sexual dysfunction and sleep problems (Schmidt & Wise, 1981). Treating the sleep disorder may restore erectile functioning. Thus, NPT needs to be seen as one component in the assessment of male sexual dysfunction, not the definitive feature in estimating the degree of organic impairment.

Another special test is the pudendal nerve latency. Response to this laboratory procedure helps to uncover the existence of neuropathy in an area central to sexual functioning.

This complex of psychological and medical information will lead to the diagnosis and the recommendation for treatment options most beneficial for the person. A full discussion and, possibly, counseling sessions with the clients need to be conducted, since the findings may have a tremendous impact on the persons involved. Too often, clinicians and physicians tend to ignore the psychological significance of the assessment findings for the clients. Most particularly, as evaluation supporting the large prevalence of organic factors may lead to fears of abandonment, threatened self-esteem, or marital distress. Denial may take place, in an effort to bind the anxiety that is activated by what the client(s) perceive as the assessment's implications. The assessment may promote a grief reaction, since a deathlike situation has taken place, in that the couple's sexual script seems no longer possible.

Many treatment options are available to the person after the assessment is completed. A predominantly organic etiology does not mean that a medical intervention should be immediately recommended. Sex therapy has proved to be quite useful in cases of hyperprolactinemia (Schwartz, 1981), diabetes (Zilbergeld, 1980), and other various medical disorders, such as heart disease (Schumacher & Lloyd, 1981). Even where behavioral changes may not be a treatment outcome or even a possibility, sex therapy could be helpful in restructuring the couple's sexual interactions, so that sexual satisfaction is indeed possible.

If a psychological form of intervention is chosen by clients and/or recommended by the therapist, clinicians may differ regarding the implications of severe marital distress. Until research is conducted, systematically comparing the relative effectiveness of marital therapy to sex therapy, clinical judgements and bias will determine the treatment of choice. One resolution to this dilemma has been suggested by Leiblum, Rosen, & Pierce (1976), who proposed the use of the Locke-Wallace Marital Adjustment Test (1959) as a useful screening device to estimate the amount of marital dissatisfaction. Two standard deviations below the mean would signal that sex therapy would be contraindicated.

DIRECT INTERVENTION APPROACHES

Principles in direct treatment

There are a number of generic principles that form the basis for direct-treatment approaches to modifying sexual dysfunctions (LoPiccolo, 1977). Specific activities enacted during sex therapy can be tied to at least one of the following principles:

Mutual responsibility. Couples may enter therapy with the notion that the sexual dysfunction belongs to one person. However, sex therapy is founded on the fact that amelioration of sexual difficulties requires the participation of both partners, by realizing that each has a part to play in generating sexual satisfaction. This principle is not just a philosophical stance, but represents a recognition of the couple as a dynamic system. A change in one member of the couple will impact on the sexual functioning of the other. Change can be blocked by the partner, since a homeostatic security can be threatened if one's partner changes. Participation of both members of the couple begins when each person takes responsibility for his or her own sexuality. Taking responsibility is often blocked by an atmosphere of blame in the couple's perceptions of the causes for the sexual problem. Altering this perspective is a major, initial task in therapy.

Information and education. Adequate knowledge of sexual behavior is a critical component to fostering satisfying sexual interactions. Some couples may lack information about such matters as anatomy and the sexual response cycle. Overall, ignorance seems to be less of an issue as time passes, since books, movies, television, and other information sources about sex become more easily available and accepted. However, faulty assumptions about sexual development can still influence how people perceive themselves and their bodies at various points in their life cycle. For example, people still tend to distort the influence of the aging process and deny themselves the opportunity for a fulfilling sex life.

Attitude change. People are programmed from early childhood to hold negative images of sex. Learning to distrust sexuality is promoted by faulty sexual metaphors, closed doors, and lack of parent-child sex education. Examining these attitudes and how they potentiate inhibitions about sexual interactions needs to be incorporated into treatment.

Eliminating performance anxiety. People often rely on a goal-oriented sexual script, where intercourse frequency, erectile-latency time, and "no-hands" orgasms become the hallmarks of sexual skills. Sex therapy attempts to modify this concentration by substituting a process orientation, which emphasizes pleasure and emotional intimacy for this achievement orientation. Typically, performance aspects of sexual functioning have been thought of as the province of men. However, as women have taken a more active role in sexual interactions, many women are falling prey to anxieties associated with adequacy in sexual performance.

Increasing communication and effectiveness of sexual technique. This fifth principle is accomplished by having the person gain extensive self-knowledge about his or her body in such areas as awareness of preferences and dislikes, arousal triggers, and sources of inhibition. If one is to communicate with another, then awareness of one's self is a necessary pre-condition. Many individuals tend to rely on "mind reading" to accomplish effective communication, perhaps even attributing noncaring feelings to their partner if they themselves have to reveal to their partner specific desires related to sexual interactions. "I shouldn't have to tell her" is the form of resistance often expressed. Therapy aims to help people directly reveal their needs and preferences through both verbal and nonverbal communication. In addition, sex therapy focuses on building a skill repertoire that helps to deal with and possibly extinguish the dysfunction. This does not mean, however, that becoming a sexual gymnast is the goal of sex therapy. Rather, skill building in sexual technique involves helping the person develop and perceive new options, such as a slower pace to noncoital activities, so that they widen the range of available sexual behaviors and achieve a heightened level of emotional involvement.

Changing destructive lifestyles and sex roles.   Clients are often blind to the ways in which they have set up their lives in an extremely destructive manner. Clients have difficulties finding an opportunity to have sex. Resistant to dealing with the purpose behind their lifestyle, clients often flee into helplessness by pointing to the "reality" of such influences as children, job pressures, family demands, and physical exhaustion. Little time is left for themselves, let alone for sexual interactions. Therapists need to be quite active in helping clients learn negotiating and problem-solving skills, in order to rearrange their lives and create environments which *they* control, not ones which control *them*. Some of the stresses that are engendered by these lifestyles may be associated with sex-role expectations and behavior. The couple may do household tasks in a prescribed manner without joint participation of the other. Furthermore, one person may be invested in maintaining a dominant position in the relationship and disapprove of efforts toward autonomy by the other (e.g., getting a job). This role rigidity may segregate the couple and disallow opportunities for cooperative effort. Moreover, sex-role behaviors can foster resentment, and sexual dysfunctions may be an associated phenomenon. Socialized patterns can be noticed in the sexual arena as well. For example, social norms foster the belief that men typically are the more sexual creatures and should always be prepared to have sex at a moment's call. A more flexible approach to sexual interactions may be promoted by having men recognize and verbalize when they do *not* feel like having sex. In short, the initiator's role can be mutually shared by both men and women.

Prescribing changes in behavior.   Sex therapy relies on what takes place outside of the treatment setting as a major, if not central, agent of change. Therapists utilize a set of behavioral assignments that are given to the clients each week. The focus of therapy sessions is often related to the individuals' experiences when they perform these assignments. While some of these assignments concentrate on each person as an entity, apart form the relationship, others can zero in on marital dynamics. Then the assignments center around the sexual relationship of the couple, they are designed to help the individuals learn to concentrate on the pleasure of the encounter, not the goal orientation which intercourse can imply. At the onset of treatment, banning intercourse and the touching of genitals often helps to relieve the couple of the pressure to perform and the cycle of failure which may have built up over time.

However, clients will not always do the assignments and will find reasons for their inability or unwillingness to give the necessary time to the change effort. Kaplan (1979) describes this resistance as an expected event in therapy, and it often needs to be confronted by the client if significant progress is to be made. She points out that this approach may require more time than the 15-session format often used as a guideline by sex therapists. Compliance is approached in alternative ways by other therapists. Direct observation of clients as they do sexual activities has been described as one option available to therapists (Hartman & Fithian, 1974), but this approach has little popular support from most clinicians in the field. Another controversial approach is to institute a security-deposit system where clients deposit half of their total treatment fee with the therapist. For each occurrence of noncompliance (e.g., not showing up for therapy or not doing the assignments), clients agree at the outset of therapy to forfeit one quarter of their deposit (Lobitz & LoPiccolo, 1972). In essence, clients need to be presented with consequences for the choices they make and, thus, become responsible for their resistance.

Application of sex therapy principles in treatment

In the actual conduct of therapy, any one or more of these principles could be operating at a given time. For some clients, treatment will emphasize particular principles; while for others, new targets for change will need to be devised. In short, treatment needs to be individualized, by taking into account the psychological, cultural, and relational context of the individuals concerned.

Nevertheless, some treatment strategies may have generalized usefulness regardless of the presenting sexual dysfunction. Outcome research in sex therapy has not attempted to specify which aspects of the treatment are most effective, for which particular clients, with which specific dysfunctions, and at what point in the treatment. While precise rationales for effecting change may be lacking, clinicians often utilize a common set of experiences designed to achieve the six purposes cited above. Therefore, any one therapeutic technique may accomplish multiple goals.

Figure 7 outlines some of the treatment techniques that therapists might employ in helping people with their sexual dysfunction(s). It should be noted that it does identify an association between the particular strategies and the phase of treatment (i.e., beginning, middle, or end). This subdivision is based on the author's own experience, as well as on what is traditionally done in sex therapy. The implied sequence is not based on clinical research. Most important, the listing does not represent an exhaustive list of tools available to the therapist. It has been constructed as an illustration of the types of assignments that serve as a major aspect of the change process in the direct-treatment approach to sexual dysfunctions.

The development of charts such as those presented here runs the risk of promoting a simplistic, "cookbook" approach to the treatment of sexual dysfunctions. The chart should only serve as an illustration for depicting some of the activities that therapist may utilize in sex therapy. It would be a misunderstanding to view the chart as a prescription for what should be done with all clients. Nevertheless, this author's selection of what should be included in the listing implies the existence of some important guidelines for conducting effective sex therapy:

1. Affective, cognitive, and behavioral dimensions of the individuals need to be addressed through the use of at-home assignments and therapy sessions.
2. Sex therapy needs to extend beyond a focus on the couple and include an analysis of the psychological significance associated with sexual interactions for each individual.
3. Incorporation of other treatment modalities (such as marital, Gestalt, and systems therapy) may be a helpful adjunct to the therapy. By having multifaceted targets of change, the lasting effectiveness of sex therapy might be improved.

While certain home assignments could be used with nearly any client, each sexual dysfunction represents a special set of circumstances that requires particular treatment strategies. Some of the major elements to treating each dysfunction are listed below.

Low sexual desire. Among all the dysfunctions, low sexual desire seem to be the most resistant to treatment. This assessment may be due to the possibility that more psychopathology is found among these clients than is noticed in people with genitally oriented sexual dysfunctions, like premature ejaculation.

When helping couples with low sexual desire, Kaplan (1979) indicates that sex therapy may need to be extended for a longer period of time than is usually done. Psychodynamic interpretations (and maybe even individual therapy) may be required to move through the defensive structures of certain clients. Beyond sensate focus I and II, Kaplan proposes that the following may be useful:

Self-stimulation without the pressure of the partner's presence.

Developing arousal triggers through sharing erotic fantasies and materials with one's partner.

A slow pace to lovemaking with no expectations for intercourse unless each member of the couple genuinely is open to having coitus.

Extensive communication about what each is feeling at the moment before sex begins.

Repressed anger may be a critical etiological characteristic of low sexual desire for many clients (Kaplan, 1979; LoPiccolo, 1980). Therefore, the proximal psychological effects of distal events should be explored with the couple, in the hope of working through the feelings which are inhibiting sexual motivation. Treatment could also include desensitizing the couple to the experience of anger, so that clients become more comfortable with and knowledgable about acknowledging anger as it is experienced at any given moment.

Despite these suggestions for treatment, the field lacks a treatment approach which is empirically supported through research. While many clinicians have no definitive answer for how to successfully intervene with low-sexual-desire clients, approaches used to treat other sexual dysfunctions do not seem to have sufficient impact with low-sexual-desire clients. Thus, clinicians need to rely on their own judgment and experience when deciding what might be most fruitful in helping these individuals.

Erectile dysfunction. The psychological significance of erectile dysfunction can be quite dramatic. While promoting a pejorative outlook on the dysfunction, describing the behavior as "impotence" may, in fact, accurately capture the affective experience for many men when they are having trouble attaining or maintaining an erection. When erection difficulties are coupled with negative attributions to the aging process, death and erectile dysfunction may become linked. While these perceptions may be a distortion or irrational way of filtering the meaning of erectile dysfunction (Ellis, 1980), they are examples of the symbolic importance which this sexual problem can have.

The initial stage of treatment needs to directly deal with attitudes and reactions to the dysfunction. Clients should be told that they cannot "will" an erection, so their intense efforts to "work on" erectile capacity are probably futile. They should be reassured that erections represent a natural reflex that will occur when appropriate psychic and physical stimula-

Figure 7

Sample of general strategies for sex therapy with couples

Stage of treatment	General strategy	Particulars
Beginning	Sex history	Three sessions: one for each person and one to discuss implications of sex history with couple.
	Autobiography	Story of self and/or story of relationship using "chapter headings" to label shifts in one's life.
	Mirror exercise	Observe self with no clothes and without judgments.
	Self-exam	Identify body parts on own, then with partner.
	Readings	Read erotic materials or various books.
	Movies	See movies that may be arousing.
	Sensate focus I	Alternate between giver and receiver role.
		Explore each other's bodies, not touching genitals and breasts.
		No intercourse.
		Communicate preferences and experience.
Middle	Initiation	Initiate being sexual for 1–2 minutes in a variety of situations with partner without advancing to other forms of sexual behavior.
	Negotiation training	Learn to become assertive without being demanding.
		Initiation and refusal strategies for sex.
		Learn and practice empathy and incorporation techniques.
	Communication training	"I feel . . ." and "I fear . . ." statements.
		Improve listening skills.
		Efforts at self-disclosure.
	Function to dysfunction	Write reasons for needing to remain (or have partner remain) dysfunctional.
	Sensate focus II	Same general procedure as I, but add genital and breast areas as other options.

Caring days	List 25–30 behaviors that are considered caring.
	Each one must be behaviorally specific, fairly easy to do, and phrased in positive manner.
	Clients check off items on list when they do a caring behavior.
	After a while, each checks off items when he/she notices the other person doing items on list.
Arousal triggers	Identify what promotes arousal and what inhibits arousal, in terms of self-statements, environment, and behavior of the other.
Going on date	Each initiates asking other for a date.
	Ask out other in novel way.
Script expansion	Build a joint fantasy or playful game around sex.
Mechanisms of change	Review changes and lack of changes in self and in partner.
	Identify future goals.
	Describe maintenance plan.
Termination	
Booster session	Follow-up session at three months and one year after termination.

tion take place. The paradox is that when people place less importance on the need to have erections for enjoyable sex, the natural vasocongestive responses of the penis will take place. Various intrapsychic issues can surface when reorienting the couple toward pleasure and away from goal attainment. For example, the female partner may be expressing much hostility toward her partner, with the threat of divorce stated as a consequence if more satisfying sexual interactions are not forthcoming. Underneath this tough veneer may be fears of her own inadequacies and that she has lost her attractiveness as a woman. As for men, many hold the belief that they must be in control of the sexual episode. After encountering episodes of erectile dysfunction, they begin to shy away from initiating sex so that the experience of incompetence is avoided. At any time during treatment, the male or female may be unwilling to confront these attitudes and underlying feelings. When this occurs, more direct confrontation of the sabotaging behavior needs to happen. In short, there may be many reasons for the performance anxiety that is typically associated with erectile failure, and uncovering the basis of this anxiety is a major first step in therapy.

Assignments typically include the first two sensate-focus exercises, which attempt to lessen the concentration of genitally focused sexual interactions. Two additional techniques can also be used during sensate focus II. The female should stop touching the male's penis when he achieves an erection and should once again explore other parts of her partner's body. When the penis becomes flaccid, touching the genital area can recommence. Masters and Johnson (1970) describe this procedure as the "teasing technique." Believing that erections can fluctuate and that they are not lost forever can be an important part of the treatment. Annon (1974) suggests that the use of paradoxical intention can also be quite useful. Men are instructed not to have an erection during the touching exercise, and they should try to remain soft. If they get an erection, this means that goal orientation still dominates, not pleasure orientation.

Once erections begin to occur and anxiety is lessened, the couple can approach intercourse. The first step can be described as "stuffing," where an erect penis is not a requirement for intercourse. The woman inserts the penis into her vagina, with no thrusting to follow (the "quiet vagina," as it is sometimes called). Next, slow thrusting with no ejaculation can begin, with full thrusting and ejaculation to follow in later exercises.

At any point in the treatment sequence, clinicians often incorporate various axtivities where the female can be stimulated and reach orgasm through noncoital activities. Attending to the female partner's concerns can have an important purpose beyond the direct physical and emotional fulfillment of her own needs. This purpose is the realization that satisfying sex does not *require* an erection. Achieving this perspective can aid in decreasing performance anxiety and dependence.

Premature ejaculation. The goal of treating the inability to ejaculate when desired is to increase ejaculatory latency (i.e., the time between intromission and ejaculation). The amount of intravaginal containment which is subjectively satisfying can vary, and clinicians need to be aware of their own value systems (as well as the client's) when treating this dysfunction. Increasing ejaculatory latency is accomplished by raising the threshold for how much stimulation is required for ejaculation to occur. Men suffering from premature ejaculation need very little stimulation and thus have a low threshold. Another way of viewing premature ejaculation is that these men are not able to distinguish between high levels of arousal and the point of ejaculatory inevitability (i.e., they no longer have voluntary control over their orgasmic response and, thus, ejaculation must occur). Therefore, stimulus generalization has occured in this blending of arousal and the point of ejaculatory inevitability.

Two major techniques have been prescribed for treating men with premature ejaculation. Semans (1956) was the first to describe the *pause technique*. It involves having the female manually stimulate the male until some level of arousal is achieved. This amount needs to be less than is required to reach the point of ejaculatory inevitability. When arousal is heightened, the male gives a signal to stop stimulation and the couple turns to other forms of caressing until the level of excitement decreases. This start-stop sequence should be repeated four or five times, after which, ejaculation can be allowed. The male should next try to have his arousal increase before he gives the signal to stop stimulation. In essence, he is trying to approximate the point of ejaculatory inevitability and thus build up his threshold. The next step is to add a lubricant so that a sensation approximating vaginal containment is simulated. The same progressive start-stop sessions are held, so that increasing amounts of arousal are recognized and tolerated by the male. Following these activities, the same procedure is used during intercourse. When arousal is increasing, the male withdraws, allowing his excitement to lessen, and repenitration follows. Fewer withdrawals should be required as greater voluntary control over the ejaculatory response develops.

The second procedure is outlined by Masters and Johnson (1970) and is known as the *squeeze technique*. The same sequence as was indicated for the start-stop approach could be used, but instead of simply pausing to lessen arousal, the female squeezes the male's penis. Pressure is exerted just below the frenulum of the penis when the male feels that ejaculation is soon to take place. The urge to ejaculate should decrease. The couple should be advised to avoid squeezing when the point of ejaculatory inevitability has been reached. Attempting to prevent ejaculation by squeezing at this point might create future physiological problems, which result in retrograde ejaculation (i.e., ejaculation into the bladder).

No research has compared the relative effectiveness of each procedure. However, they both seem to be effective, and clinicians could select either, depending on the couple's choice. An additional phase of the treatment could involve the male doing self-stimulation on his own, before adding the partner to the process. Concentrating and learning to discriminate among sensations during sexual excitement may be aided by eliminating performance anxiety, which is felt when the partner is present. Also, by understanding his own body responses, the male might be able to communicate more accurately when he is with his partner, during either the pause or squeeze methods (Lobitz & LoPiccolo, 1972).

Inhibited ejaculation.   Delayed ejaculation, as well as the absence of ejaculatory abilities, have been grouped under this dysfunction. Similar to the case of low sexual desire and aversion, retarded ejaculation and absent ejaculation can be seen as a continuum for how difficult it is for the male to achieve intravaginal orgasms. It is quite common to see this problem being situational to vaginal penetration; thus, the goal of the treatment is to have ejaculation take place during intercourse.

This dysfunction can often go untreated and even unnoticed. Some males may fake an orgasm in order to avoid its detection. Satisfaction of the female is typically achieved, since erectile capacity is long-lasting, thereby aiding the orgasmic capacity of the female. Moreover, the male may be too embarrased to reveal his difficulty. Culturally based fantasies of "lasting forever" may even make inhibited ejaculation be perceived as a skill, as opposed to anything approaching a distressful situation. Factors such as these make this dysfunction relatively rare in occurrence (Masters & Johnson, 1970).

The treatment program involves the planning of successive steps which lead to ejaculation during intercourse. One such program might begin with the male masturbating to orgasm, with his partner in the next room. Then, his partner can be present in the room during the masturbatory exercise. Next, she gets closer and closer to him during future self-stimulation assignments, as his penis becomes progressively nearer to her vagina. Following these self-stimulation sessions, intercourse is followed by the female touching her partner until orgasm is attained. Intravaginal ejaculation takes place by using the "bridge" technique, where the male inserts his penis when the point of ejaculatory inevitability is reached. The female stimulates the base of her partner's penis during thrusting. Earlier insertion can eventually promote a fading of this manual stimulation, so that ejaculation can take place through vaginal stimulation alone. Clearly, the treatment approach needs to be tailored to the individual needs of the clients.

Inorgasmia.   For organizational purposes, both global- and situational-orgasmic dysfunctions have been included in this section. However, it needs to be recognized that these two conditions describe very different circumstances. Clearly, it is not pathological (and perhaps even typical) for women not to have an orgasm during intercourse (Hite, 1976; Kinsey et al., 1953). In fact, more intense orgasms seem to be fostered through masturbation, as opposed to intercourse and partner stimulation (Masters & Johnson, 1966). The inability to have an orgasm through intercourse may simply be a matter of inadequate time devoted to foreplay or clitoral stimulation during intercourse. Gebhard (1966) indicated that, if couples regularly spend at least 21 minutes engaging in foreplay, only 8 percent of the women surveyed failed to attain an orgasm. Given all this, a serious question exists regarding whether situational inorgasmia should be considered a dysfunction and, thus, whether clients should be accepted for therapy. Most clinicians appear to resolve this dilemma by relying on the distress of the clients as the final determinant regarding the advisibility of treatment.

Additionally, the field of human sexuality has yet to reach consensus regarding what is the nature of a female orgasm and the larger issues of the components of female sexual response. Despite Masters and Johnson's (1966) evidence that there is only one type of orgasm and that it is clitoral in nature, other researchers remain convinced that there is more than one type of orgasm (Sherfey, 1966). Singer (1973) describes two types of orgasms: one is vulval (i.e., clitoral), while the other is uterine. The latter type is deeper and involves greater trust and security in the relationship. There may be an anatomical basis for this dual-orgasm theory. Recent research has investigated whether women have a structure called the Grafenberg Spot on the anterior wall of the vagina. Stimulation of this area may trigger these deeper orgasms and, for some women, may be related to the ability to ejaculate a fluid at the point of orgasmic release (Perry & Whipple, 1981). Additional research in needed in order to further assess these preliminary findings. The central point is that there are significant gaps in our understanding of the phenomena associated with female orgasm.

For women with global inorgasmia, Lobitz and LoPiccolo (1972) lay out a nine-step series of assignments, which rely on masturbatory experiences. Step 1 involves self-exploration of the woman's genitals by using a mirror and diagrams. In addition, the woman begins a daily program of Kegel exercises (Kegal, 1952). These exercises, initially developed to aid women with urinary-stress incontinance, involve the contraction and release of the vaginal musculature. While some research questions the utility of these exercises (Sutan, Chambless, Stern, Williams, Lifshitz, Hazzard, & Kelly, 1980), evidence seems to be growing to substantiate a relationship between vaginal muscle strength and female sexual responsiveness (Graber & Kline-Graber, 1979; Messe, 1981). In the next two steps, the woman explores her genitals using both tactile and visual stimulation, with the goal of locating pleasurable areas of the vaginal area. Steps 4 and 5 involve intense physical and psychic stimulation, while using fantasy, lubricants, and erotic materials as aids to arousal. If orgasm has yet to occur, step 6 incorporates the use of a vibrator. Role-playing the experience of letting go during orgasm can also be useful here (Hilliard, 1960). In fact, exaggerating and having fun with this role-play can be included in the couple's assignments later in the nine-step program (Lobitz & LoPiccolo, 1972). The male partner becomes involved at step 7, and increasing his skills is an important aspect of the program. At first, he is present when the woman reaches orgasm as she shows him her arousal triggers, which she has discovered on her own. During step 8, he implements what she has taught him by stimulating her to orgasm. Coitus is achieved at step 9, while the male partner concurrently uses manual and vibrator stimulation.

Another aspect to the treatment of inorgasmia involves the use of orgasm triggers (Heiman et al., 1976). These strategies seem to provide the little bit extra that may be needed when excitement is quite high, and orgasm is near. These triggers may include such behaviors as deep breathing, Kegel exercises, hanging one's head over the edge of the bed, and using erotic language.

In general, the cognitive component to orgasmic difficulties plays a key role in the disinhibition of sexual arousal (Rook & Hammon, 1977). In fact, treatment may only change subjective measures of arousal, such as attitudes and general satisfaction, and not objective indices, such as vaginal-pulse amplitude and orgasmic frequency (Wincze, Hoon, & Hoon, 1978). While the nine-step program appears to form the basis for treating women with global inorgasmia, it can be modified to help women with situational-orgasmic problems. However, when inorgasmia takes place only in the presence of one's partner, clinicians should suspect that relationship issues may be the primary difficulty that needs attention (Snyder, LoPiccolo, & LoPiccolo, 1975).

Vaginismus. Desensitization is again the hallmark for treating women who exhibit a spasm of the muscles surrounding the vaginal opening (the pubococcygeal muscle). These spasms prevent intercourse, but may not necessarily take place under all circumstances. For example, the woman may tolerate a pelvic examination at a doctor's office. Therapy attempts to effect gradual dilation of the vagina. The nine-step program described for inorgasmia can be used as the foundation for helping women with vaginismus. Many of the treatment goals for these two dysfunctions can overlap, such as decreasing anxiety and increasing self-knowledge.

Graduated dilation can be initiated by utilizing graduated dilators, which are plastic, penis-like objects inserted into the vagina on a daily basis. A lubricant can often prove helpful. An alternative is to use the woman's own fingers, where she progresses to inserting three fingers at one time. Once anxiety is reduced on her own, the woman's partner is included in the treatment, and the same series of exercises are completed. The last step is to begin intercourse with no thrusting. Starting with the woman in the superior position can often provide a measure of control and comfort. In some instances, the transition to including the partner is aided by having the woman hold and guide her partner's hand during the process of insertion. Intercourse, with slow thrusting, can begin later at the initiation of the woman.

Moreover, sex therapists need to pay more systematic attention to those people who do not do so well in treatment. Researchers have reported such optimisitc success rates to substantiate a direct-treatment approach that an aura of a guaranteed cure has come to be associated with sex therapy. However, these glowing expectations may make it quite difficult for people to deal with the outcome of therapy, if the treatment program is usually so successful with most people. The pressure from this level of aspiration may promote resistence in treatment and may even deter people from seeking out therapy. A more thorough analysis of treatment failures may help to determine whether the field has promoted a set of expectations about treatment success, which are counterproductive to a number of people.

Summary of treatment approaches

The six generic principles for the direct treatment of sexual dysfunctions can be seen operating in the specific techniques just described. Regardless of the outcome of sex therapy, clients are asked to make a significant effort in altering their sexual-behavior patterns. Since change often involves the unknown, and thus can be quite frightening, clients will usually do something during therapy to resist the process of change, such as become bored or cancel appointments because they are too "busy." Pointing this out even at the start of therapy can help to make this resistance predictable and thus give clients the permission to struggle with and work through their inner experience.

However, various individuals are raising some important questions about sex therapy (Sobel, 1981) and are urging the field—as it is constituted currently—to review where it is going. Indeed, the field may have ignored an important contradiction when treatment programs were first developed. Most treatment plans in sex therapy are designed to lead toward intercourse, as the ultimate expression of sexual intimacy. Typically, intercourse is the last step in helping couples. This progression, however, may be fostering an unintended mixed message: couples are supposed to be pleasure- and process-oriented, so that they will be better able to attain the goal of sex—intercourse. This mixed message may be one of the key reasons for the inability of clients to sustain the behavioral changes which they exhibited immediately after therapy ended (Goldberg, 1981a). In essence, couples may not really know where to focus their attention: should they focus on the process of having pleasure or should they attempt to find ways in which they can complete their sexual experience? It seems that the field of sex therapy needs to review this apparent contradiction and modify its basic treatment approach, so that it does not promote the very performance anxiety that it is intending to reduce. Building sexual intimacy might be a more appropriate goal than building sexual performance.

FUTURE CHALLENGES

Treatment for people without partners

Sex therapy—as it is typically practiced—is a couple-centered treatment approach. However, there are a number of individuals who have sexual dysfunctions but do not have available sexual partners. For some, divorce or the death of a spouse may be the primary reason for this situation. For others, their celebate social status may be for more functional reasons, such as lack of social skills, or difficulty developing a close relationship with another person. In some cases, a partner may exist but be unwilling to be associated with treatment (Zilbergeld, 1980). Techniques used during a group-treatment approach are based on some of the strategies designed for couples, but so as not to require a partner (Heinrich & Price, 1977; Price et al., 1981; Zilbergeld, 1975). Research suggests that inclusion of social-skills training (such as role-playing, with a female therapist, how to ask a woman out on a date) may be a critical element in dealing with male sexual dysfunction (Lobitz & Baker, 1979). Improvements in sexual functioning may not necessarily be reported by clients when utilizing behavioral indices as the outcome measure, but might be detected when evaluating general sexual satisfaction and enjoyment (Price el al., 1981). The use of groups for the treatment of inorgasmia has been employed for a number of years (Barbach, 1975).

As the assessment of sexual dysfunctions grows in its sophistication, more and more people need to face the meaning of an organic component to their dysfunction. Couples groups for these people may be a useful future direction to explore. Talking with other couples may help them to manage the impact of this new information.

Diagnoses emphasizing an organic etiology

When erectile dysfunction is due primarily to organic factors, surgical interventions are a treatment option. In some instances, physicians attempt to increase bloodflow in the penis by revascularization of the corpus cavernosa, but only about 33 percent of men opting for this surgery attain sufficient rigidity for intercourse (Zorgniotti, Rossi, Padula, & Makovsky, 1980). Inserting a penile prosthesis is the surgery most often recommended by physicians. This procedure was initially explored by a number of investigators in developing a rigid, rodlike device which effects a permanent erection (Scott et al. 1973; Small et al., 1975). A second type of prosthesis is one that is inflatable, allowing for tumescence and detumescence to be simulated. Evaluation of the effectiveness of both procedures has been quite positive (Malloy, Wein, & Carpiniello, 1980; Sotile, 1979). In approximately 90 percent of the cases, satisfactory results were achieved, meaning that intercourse could take place. There seems to be more overall failure in the rodlike device, with more post-operative complications in the inflatable prosthesis. Nevertheless, there are a number of limitations to the evaluations conducted thus far. No research has explored subjective satisfaction in an in-depth manner with *both* the male and female. Research questions have been vague and focused solely on the ability to achieve intercourse. Also, existing literature lacks information on screening guidelines, in terms of who would *not* be good candidates for penile prosthesis. Marital distress, pseudo-cooperative complementarity between partners (Ravitch & Wyden, 1974), and psychopathology are examples of areas needing careful assessment, if a penile prosthesis is to be recommended to a client. Physicians may be colluding with the clients' wish to bind their anxiety after hearing the organic diagnosis. Physicians may be contributing to the wish to "fix things up fast," if protheses are quickly recommended with no thorough screening and counseling.

Sexual dysfunctions and medical illness

The mind-body controversy is starting to quiet, as people begin to recognize the enormous interface between psychological and medical issues. Psychological concerns can promote systemic reactions, while biologically based problems can indeed influence the psychic life of the individual. This generalization can be applied to sexual dysfunction. Many medical disorders can create concerns for people about how their sexual interactions will be affected. Myocardial infarctions leave many men fantasizing about impending death if they allow themselves to be aroused. Spinal cord injuries do not prevent a satisfying sex life, but many people suffering from this disability need to learn the many options that still remain. Menopause and hysterectomies can create many physiological and psychological changes in how a woman experiences her body. These are just some of the many medical problems that can cause or be associated with sexual dysfunctions.

Sexual counseling and therapy is beginning to be integrated into medical settings in order to help in the management and treatment of medical illness. Nevertheless, more needs to be done to expand these consultative efforts. For example, medical personnel need to see sexual matters as an intergral part of intakes, physical exams, and follow-up procedures. Too often the assumption is made that there is no sexual difficulty, if the client does not mention its existence.

Values in the treatment of sexual dysfunctions

Treatment of sexual dysfunctions explores the phenomenology of sexual feelings and behavior. The act of physically bonding with another can be a source of intense pleasure and a means of experiencing intimacy with one's partner. Clearly, there are a number of values which could be found in this statement. Indeed, this should be the case, since human sexuality is shaped by the existence both personal and cultural values. Clinicians cannot treat people without bringing their own values to the therapeutic endeavor. Sex therapists need to avoid becoming overly reactive to criticisms suggesting that sex therapy simply involves the dogmatic espousal of hedonistic values with clients. Therapists need to be cognizant of any attempts they might make to avoid the influence of these values on the course of treatment by hiding behind the "scientific" basis of recommendations made during treatment (Szasz, 1981). In fact, values can become manifest and be explored in therapy sessions. By discussing values openly, clients will increase their awareness and, subsequently, take more responsibility for the values which contribute to as well as compromise their own sexual satisfaction.

SUMMARY

This chapter presents the reader with an overview of many controversial issues surrounding the treatment of sexual dysfunctions. Theoretical approaches are viewed from the standpoint of treatment for sexual dysfunctions, with an emphasis on the integrative frameworks. General issues in assessment are addressed, in light of the increasing need to detect possible organic factors in the etiology.

The diagnosis of sexual dysfunctions are grouped into four phases: desire, excitement/arousal, orgasm, and reflection/satisfaction, for both males and females. A protocol for evaluating sexual dysfunctions is provided for the reader, with suggested modifications for specific clients.

Direct treatment during sex therapy is linked to at least one generic principle listed in the chapter, with emphasis on personalizing the therapy for the client's needs. Several strategies for specific dysfunctions are presented by this author, with final attention to future challenges in the area of sexual-dysfunction therapy.

REFERENCES

Abelson, D. Diagnostic value of the penile pulse and blood pressure: A Doppler study of impotence in diabetes. *Journal of Urology*, 1975, *113*, 636.

Annon, J. S. *The behavioral treatment of sexual problems.* Honolulu: Kapiolani Health Services, 1974.

Ansari, J. M. A. A study of 65 impotent males. *British Journal of Psychiatry*, 1975, *127*, 337–341.

Apfelbaum, B. *On the etiology of sexual dysfunction.* Paper presented at the second annual meeting of the Eastern Association for Sex Therapy (now the Society of Sex Therapists and Researchers), Philadelphia, 1976.

Barbach, L. G. *For yourself: The fulfillment of female sexuality.* Garden City, N.Y.: Anchor Books, 1975.

Belzer, E. G. Orgasmic expulsions of women: A review and heuristic inquiry. *The Journal of Sex Research*, 1981, *17*, 1–2.

Benkert, O., Witt, W., Adam, W., & Leitz, A. Effects of testosterone decanoate on sexual potency and the hypothalmic-pituitary-gonaldalaxis of impotent males. *Archives of Sexual Behavior*, 1978, *8*, 471–479.

Byrne, D. Social psychology and the study of sexual behavior. *Personality and Social Psychology Bulletin*, 1977, *3*, 3–30.

Caird, W., & Wincze, J. P. *Sex therapy: A behavioral approach,* New York: Harper & Row, 1977.

Cole, C. M., Blakeney, P. E., Chan, F. H., Chesney, A. P., & Creson, D. L. The myth of symptomatic versus asymptomatic partners in the conjoint treatment of sexual dysfunction. *Journal of Sex and Marital Therapy*, 1979, *5*, 79–89.

Cooper, A. The prevalence of menstrual disorders in psychiatric patients. *British Journal of Psychiatry*, 1965, *111*, 155–167.

Cooper, H. J. Frigidity, treatment, and short-term prognosis. *Journal of Psychosomatic Research*, 1970, *14*, 133–147.

Davidson, J. M. Neurohormonal bases of male sexual behavior. *International review of physiology: Reproductive physiology II.* (Vol. 13). Baltimore: University Park Press, 1977.

Derogatis, L. R. & Melisaratos, N. The DSFI: A multidimensional measure of sexual functioning. *Journal of Sex and Marital Therapy*, 1979, *5*, 244–281.

Derogatis, L. R. & Meyer, J. K. The invested partner in sexual disorders: A profile. *American Journal of Psychiatry*, 1979, *136*, 1545–1549.

Dickes, R. *Psychoanalysis and brief sex therapy.* Paper presented at the annual convention of the Society of Sex Therapists and Researchers, Boston, 1980.

Dollard, J., & Miller, N. E. *Personality and psychotherapy: An analysis in terms of learning, thinking, and culture.* New York: McGraw-Hill, 1950.

Ellis, A. *Reason and emotion in psychotherapy.* Seacaucus, N.J.: Lyle Stuart, 1962.

Ellis, A. The rational-emotive approach to sex therapy. *The Counseling Psychologist*, 1975, *5*, 14–22.

Ellis, A. Treatment of erectile dysfunction. In S. Lieblum & L. Pervin (Eds.), *Principles and practice of sex therapy.* New York: Guilford Press, 1980.

Fenichel, O. *The psychoanalytic theory of neurosis.* New York: W. W. Norton, 1945.

Fisher, C., Gross, J., & Zuch, J. Cycle of penile erection on synchronous with dreaming (REM) sleep: Preliminary report. *Archives of General Psychiatry*, 1965, *12*, 29.

Fisher, C., Schiavi, R., & Lear, H. The assessment of nocturnal REM erection in a differential diagnosis of sexual impotence. *Journal of Sex and Marital Therapy*, 1975, *1*, 277.

Fisher, S. *The female orgasm.* New York: Basic Books, 1973.

Forsberg, L., Gustavii, B., Hojerback, T., & Olsson, A. M. Impotence, smoking, and B-blocking drugs. *Fertility and Sterility,* 1979, *31,* 589–591.

Forsberg, L., & Olsson, A. M. Vascular constriction and smoking. Presented at Second International Conference on Vasculogenic Impotence, Monaco, 1980.

Frank, E., Anderson, C., & Rubenstein, D. Frequency of sexual dysfunction in "normal" couples. *New England Journal of Medicine,* 1978, *299,* 111–115.

Freud, S., (1905) My views on the part played by sexuality in the etiology of the neuroses. In E. Jones, Ed. *Collected papers* (Vol. 1). New York: Basic Books, 1959.

Gagnon, J., & Simon, W. *Sexual conduct.* Hawthorne, N.Y.: Aldine Publishing, 1973.

Gaskell, P. The importance of penile blood pressure in case of impotence. *Canadian Medical Association Journal.* 1971, *105,* 1047–1052.

Gebhard, P. H. Factors in marital orgasm. *The Journal of Social Issues,* 1966, *22,* 58–95.

Glasgow, M. & Ende, J. *Sexual problems of patients seen in a general-medicine group practice: Implications for physician training.* Paper presented at the annual meeting of the Society for the Scientific Study of Sex, New York, 1981.

Godec, C. J., & Cass, A. S. Quantifications of erection. *The Journal of Urology,* 1981, *126,* 345–347.

Goldberg, D. *Factors related to the lasting effectiveness of sex therapy.* Paper presented at the 89th annual convention of the American Psychological Association, Los Angeles, 1981. (a)

Goldberg, D., *Four phases of the sexual-response cycle.* Unpublished manuscript, Jefferson Medical College, 1981. (b)

Graber, B., & Kline-Graber, J. Female orgasm: Role of pubococcygeus muscle. *Journal of Clinical Psychiatry,* 1979, *40,* 348–351.

Greene, B., Lustig, N., & Lee, R. Clinical observation of sex as a reverberation of the total relationship. *Journal of Sex and Marital Therapy,* 1976, *2,* 284–288.

Hartman, L. M. The interface between sexual dysfunction and marital discord. *American Journal of Psychiatry,* 1980, *137,* 576–579.

Hartman, W. E., & Fithian, M. A. *Treatment of sexual dysfunction,* New York: Jason Aronson, 1974.

Hastings, D. W. *Impotence and frigidity.* London: Churchill, 1963.

Heiman, J. R. A psychophysiological exploration of sexual-arousal patterns in females and males. *Psychophysiology,* 1977, *14,* 266–274.

Heiman J., LoPiccolo, L., & LoPiccolo, J. *Becoming orgasmic: A sexual-growth program for women,* Englewood Cliffs, N.J.: Prentice-Hall, 1976.

Heinrich, A., & Price, S. *Group treatment of men and women without partners.* Paper presented at the 85th annual convention of the American Psychological Association, San Francisco, 1977.

Hilliard, M. *A woman doctor looks at love and life.* New York: Permabook, 1960.

Hite, S. *The Hite report.* New York: Macmillan, 1976.

Hogan, D. R. The effectiveness of sex therapy: A review of the literature. In J. LoPiccolo & L. LoPiccolo (Eds.), *Handbook of sex therapy.* New York: Plenum Press, 1978.

Jacobs, J., Fishkin, R., Goldman, A., & Cohen, S. *A multidisciplinary approach to the evaluation and management of sexual dysfunction.* Paper presented at the annual meeting of the American Urology Association, Greenbrier, Va., 1981.

Jacobson, E. *Progressive relaxation.* Chicago: Chicago University Press, 1938.

Kaplan, H. S. *The new sex therapy.* New York: Brunner & Mazel, 1974.

Kaplan, H. S. *Disorders of sexual desire.* New York: Brunner & Mazel, 1979.

Kaplan, H. S., & Kohl, K. Adverse reactions to rapid treatment of sexual problems. *Psychosomatics,* 1972, *13,* 3–5.

Karacan, I. Clinical value of nocturnal erection in the prognosis and diagnosis of impotence. *Medical Aspects of Human Sexuality,* 1970, *4,* 27–34.

Karacan, I., Williams, R. I., Thornby, J. I., & Salis, M. A. Sleep-related tumescence as a function of age. *American Journal of Psychiatry,* 1975, *132,* 932–937.

Kegel, A. H., Sexual functions of the pubococcygeus muscle. *Western Journal of Obstetrics and Gynecology,* 1952, *60,* 521–524.

Keiser, S. Body ego during orgasm. *Psychoanalytic Quarterly,* 1952, *21,* 153–166.

Kinder, B. N., & Blakeney, P. Treatment of sexual dysfunction: A review of outcome studies. *Journal of Clinical Psychology,* 1977, *33,* 523–530.

Kinsey, A. C., Pomeroy, W. B., & Martin, C. E. *Sexual behavior in the human male.* Philadelphia: W. B. Saunders, 1948.

Kinsey, A. C., Pomeroy, W. B., Martin, C. E., & Gebhard, P H. *Sexual behavior in the human female.* Philadelphia: W. B. Saunders, 1953.

Kline-Graber, G., & Graber, B. *Woman's orgasm—A guide to sexual satisfaction.* Indianapolis, Ind.: Bobbs-Merrill, 1975.

Kolodny, R., Masters, W., & Johnson, V. *Textbook of sexual medicine.* Boston: Little, Brown, 1979.

Kuten, J. Anger, sexuality, and the growth of the ego. *Journal of Sex and Marital Therapy,* 1976, *2,* 289–296.

Lazarus, A. The treatment of chronic frigidity by systematic desensitization. *Journal of Nervous and Mental Disorders,* 1963, *136,* 272–278.

Lazarus, A. *In the mind's eye: The power of imagery for personal enrichment.* New York: Rawson Associates, 1977.

Lehrman, N. *Masters and Johnson explained.* Chicago: Playboy Press, 1970.

Leiblum, S. R., & Pervin, L. A. (Eds.). *Principles and practice of sex therapy.* New York: Guilford Press, 1980.

Leiblum, S. R., Rosen, R. C., & Pierce, D. Group-treatment format: Mixed sexual dysfunction. *Archives of Sexual Behavior,* 1976, *5,* 313–322.

Levay, A. N., & Kagle, A. Ego deficiencies in the areas of pleasure, intimacy, and cooperation: Guidelines in the diagnosis and treatment of sexual dysfunctions. *Journal of Sex and Marital Therapy,* 1977, *3,* 10–18.

Levine, S. Conceptual suggestion for outcome research in sex therapy. *Journal of Sex and Marital Therapy,* 1980, *6,* 102–108.

Lewin, J. *A dynamic theory of personality.* New York: McGraw-Hill, 1935.

Lobitz, W. C., & Baker, E. L. Group treatment of single males with erectile dysfunction. *Archives of Sexual Behavior,* 1979, *8,* 127–138.

Lobitz, W. C., & Lobitz, G. K. Clinical assessment in the treatment of sexual dysfunction. In J. LoPiccolo & L. LoPiccolo (Eds.), *Handbook of sex therapy,* New York: Plenum Press, 1978.

Lobitz, W. C., & LoPiccolo, J. New methods in the behavioral treatment of sexual dysfunction. *Journal of Behavior Therapy and Experimental Psychiatry,* 1972, *3,* 265–271.

Locke, H. J., & Wallace, K. Short marital-adjustment and prediction tests: Their reliability and prediction. *Marriage and Family Living,* 1959, *21,* 251–255.

LoPiccolo, J. Direct treatment of sexual dysfunction in the couple. In J. Money & H. Musaph (Eds.), *Handbook of sexology.* New York: Elsevier/North-Holland Biomedical Press, 1977.

LoPiccolo, J. *Research advances in sex therapy.* Paper presented at the 89th annual convention of the American Psychological Association, Los Angeles, 1981.

LoPiccolo, J., & LoPiccolo, L. (Eds.). *Handbook of sex therapy.* New York: Plenum Press, 1978.

LoPiccolo, J., & Steger, J. C. The sexual interaction inventory: A new instrument for assessment of sexual dysfunction. *Archives of Sexual Behavior,* 1974, *3,* 585–595.

LoPiccolo, L. Low sexual desire. In S. Leiblum & L. Pervin (Eds.), *Principles and practices of sex therapy.* New York: Guilford Press, 1980.

Malloy, T. R., Wein, A. J., & Carpiniello, V. L. Comparison of the inflatable penile and the Small-carrion prosthesis in the surgical treatment of erectile impotence. *The Journal of Urology,* 1980, *123,* 678–679.

Masters, W. H., & Johnson, V. E. *Human sexual response.* Boston: Little, Brown, 1966.

Masters, W. H., & Johnson, V. E. *Human sexual inadequacy.* Boston: Little, Brown, 1970.

Mathews, A., Bancroft, J., Whitehead, A., Hackman, A., Julier, B., Bancroft, J., Gath, D., & Shaw, P. The behavioral treatment of sexual inadequacy: A comparative study. *Behavior Research and Therapy,* 1976, *14,* 427–436.

May, R. *Love and will.* New York: W. W. Norton, 1969.

McGovern, K. B., Stewart, R. C., & LoPiccolo, J. Secondary orgasmic dysfunction, I: Analysis and strategies for treatment. *Archives of Sexual Behavior,* 1975, *4,* 265–276.

Messe, M. *Vaginal musculative contraction as an enhancer of sexual arousal.* Paper presented at the Annual Meeting of the Society for the Scientific Study of Sex, New York, 1981.

Mosher, D. L. Three dimensions of depth of involvement in human sexual response. *The Journal of Sex Research,* 1980, *16,* 1–42.

O'Connor, J. F., & Stern, L. O. Results of treatment in functional sex disorders. *New York State Journal of Medicine,* 1972, *72,* 1927–1934.

Perry, J. D., & Whipple, B. Pelvic muscle strength of female ejaculators: Evidence in support of a new theory of orgasm. *The Journal of Sex Research,* 1981, *17,* 22–39.

Price, S. C., Reynolds, B. S., Cohen, B. D., Anderson, A. J., Schochet, B. V. Group treatment of erectile dysfunction for men without partners: A controlled evaluation. *Archives of Sexual Behavior,* 1981, *10,* 253–267.

Ravich, R. H., & Wyden, B. *Predictable pairing.* New York: Peter H. Wyden, 1974.

Reynolds, B. S. Psychological treatment models and outcome results for erectile dysfunction: A critical review. *Psychological Bulletin,* 1977, *84,* 1218–1238.

Rook, K. S., & Hammon, C. L. A cognitive perspective on the experience of sexual arousal. *Journal of Social Issues,* 1977, *33,* 7–29.

Rosen, I. The psychoanalytic approach to individual therapy. In J. Money & H. Musaph (Eds.), *Handbook of sexology.* New York: Elsevier/North-Holland Biomedical Press, 1977.

Sager, C. J. The role of sex therapy in marital therapy. *American Journal of Psychiatry,* 1976, *133,* 555–558.

Sarbin, T. & Allen, V. Role theory. In G. Lindsey & E. Aronson (Eds.), *The handbook of social psychology.* Reading, Mass.: Addison-Wesley Publishing, 1968.

Schachter, S. The interaction of cognitive and physiological determinants of emotional state. In L. Berkowitz (Ed.), *Advances in experimental social psychology.* New York: Academic Press, 1964.

Schiavi, R. (Ed.). The assessment of sexual and marital function. *Journal of Sex and Marital Therapy,* 1979, *5.*

Schiavi, R. C., & White, D. Androgens and male sexual function: A review of human studies. *Journal of Sex and Marital Studies,* 1976, *2,* 214–228.

Schmidt, H. S., & Wise, H. A. Significance of impaired penile tumescence and associated polysomnographic abnormalities in the impotent patient. *The Journal of Urology,* 1981, *126,* 348–352.

Schover, L. R., Friedman, J., Weiler, S. J., Heiman, J. R., & LoPiccolo, J. The multiarial descriptive system for the sexual dysfunctions: An alternative to *DMS-III. Archives of General Psychiatry,* 1981.

Schumacher, S. & Lloyd, C. W. Physiological and psychological factors in impotence. *The Journal of Sex Research,* 1981, *17,* 40–53.

Schwartz, M. *Sex therapy and hyperprolactinemia.* Paper presented at the annual conference of the Society of Sex Therapists and Researchers, New York, 1981.

Schwartz, M. F., Kolodny, R. C., & Masters, W. H. Plasma-testosterone levels of sexuality functional and dysfunctional men. *Archives of Sexual Behavior,* 1980, *9,* 355–360

Scott, F. B.; Bradley, W. E.; and Timm, G. W. Management of erectile impotence: Use of implantable inflatable prosthesis. *Urology.,* 1973, *2,* 80–87.

Semans, J. H. Premature ejaculation: A new approach. *Southern Medical Journal,* 1956, *49,* 353–357.

Sherfey, J. J. The evolution of female sexuality in relation to psychoanalytic theory. *Journal of the American Psychoanalytic Association,* 1966, *14,* 28–128.

Singer, I. *The goals of human sexuality.* New York: Schochen, 1973.

Small, H. P., Carrion, H. M., and Gordon, J. A. *Small-Carrion penile prosthesis: New implant for management of impotence.* Urology, 1975, *5,* 479–486.

Snyder, A., LoPiccolo, L., & LoPiccolo, J. Secondary orgasmic dysfunction, II: Case study. *Archives of Sexual Behavior,* 1975, *4,* 277–284.

Sobel, D. Sex therapy: As popularity grows, critics question whether it works. *New York Times,* November 4, 1981.

Sollod, R. N., & Kaplan, H. S. The new sex therapy: An integration of behavioral, psychodynamic, and interpersonal approaches. In J. Clayhorn (Ed.), *Successful Psychotherapy.* New York: Brunner & Mazel, 1976.

Sotile, W. M. The penile prosthesis: A review. *Journal of Sex & Marital Therapy,* 1979, *5,* 90–102.

Spanier, G. B. The measurement of marital quality. *Journal of Sex and Marital Therapy,* 1979, *5,* 288–300.

Staff of Sex Therapy Center. *Sexual History Form.* Stony Brook, N.Y.: 1981.

Sullivan, H. S. *The interpersonal theory of psychiatry.* New York: W. W. Norton, 1953.

Sultan, F. E., Chambless, D. L., Stern, T., Williams, A., Lifshitz, J. L., Hazzard, M., & Kelly,

L. *The relationship of pubococcygeal condition to female sexual responsiveness in a normal population.* Paper presented at the Association of the Advancement of Behavior Therapy, New York, 1980.

Szasz, T. *Sex by prescription.* New York: Penguin Books, 1981.

Verhulst, J., & Heiman, J. R. An international apporach to sexual dsyfunctions. *American Journal of Family Therapy,* 1979, *7,* 19–36.

Wachtel, P. *Psychoanalysis and behavior therapy.* New York: Basic Books, 1977.

Weiler, S. Medical Screening Form. Unpublished instrument, Sex Therapy Center at SUNY-Story Brook, 1981.

Wein, A., Fishkin, R., Carpiniello, V., & Malby, T. Expansion without significant rigidity during nocturnal penile-tumescence testing: A potential source of misinterpretation. *The Journal of Urology,* 1981, *126,* 343–344.

Wincze, J. P., Hoon, E. F., & Hoon, P. W. Multiple-measure analysis of women experiencing low sexual arousal. *Behavior Research and Therapy,* 1978, *16,* 43–49.

Winoker, G., Guze, S. B., & Pfeiffer, E. Developmental and sexual factors in women: A comparison between control, neurotic, and psychotic groups. *American Journal of Psychiatry,* 1958, *115,* 1097–1100.

Wolpe, J. *Psychotherapy by reciprocal inhibition.* Palo Alto, Calif.: Stanford University Press, 1958.

Wright, S., Perreault, R., Mathieu, M. Treatment of sexual dysfunction: A review. *Archives of General Psychiatry,* 1977, *34,* 881–890.

Zilbergeld, B. Group treatment of sexual dysfunction in men without partners. *Journal of Sex and Marital Therapy,* 1975, *1,* 204–214.

Zilbergeld, B. *Male sexuality.* New York: Banton, 1978.

Zilbergeld, B. Alternatives to couples counseling for sex problems: Group and individual therapy. *Journal of Sex and Marital Therapy,* 1980, *6,* 3–18.

Zorgniotti, A., Rossi, G., Padula, G., & Makovsky, R. Diagnosis and therapy of vasculogenic impotence. *The Journal of Urology,* 1980, *123,* 674–677.

21

Crisis intervention and brief psychotherapy

Clifford H. Swensen*
and
Don M. Hartsough*

Although crisis intervention and brief psychotherapy are seen, these days, as new developments, a more accurate view is that recent endeavors to develop crisis-intervention services and short-term psychotherapy are really an attempt to get back to the basics in psychological treatment.

In one sense, all psychotherapy represents some kind of crisis intervention. Patients typically request psychotherapy when something has happened in their lives that indicates that things are out of control and when action needs to be taken to get them back under control. And, as a general rule, innovations in psychological treatment start as short-term methods of treatment.

Jones (1955, pp. 31–32, 79–80) describes analyses Freud conducted that consisted of four hours of treatment in one instance, three weeks in a second instance, and three or four evenings plus two sessions a week for three weeks in a third instance. Rogers (1951, p. 10) notes that when client-centered therapy first began, the typical duration of therapy was five or six interviews. Part of the basis for recommending the use of more recent innovations in psychotherapy, such as rational-emotive therapy (Ellis, 1962), behavior therapy (Ullman & Krasner, 1965), and cognitive therapy (Beck, 1976), is that they take less time than standard psychotherapy.

In a sense, the history of short-term therapy is the history of attempts to shorten a process that has shown a rather persistent tendency to lengthen. Although psychoanalysis was originally, in some instances at least, a relatively short-term method of treatment, by the 1920s, it had become a long-term treatment, prompting efforts to develop shorter meth-

---

* Purdue University, Lafayette, Indiana.

ods (Balint, 1972, chap. 2; Butcher & Koss, 1978; Marmor, 1979; Small, 1979, chap. 1). The massive number of traumatic disorders produced by World War II (Grinker & Speigel, 1945), combined with a shortage of personnel to administer psychotherapy, provided a powerful stimulus to the development of short-term methods, a trend which continued after the war (Alexander & French, 1946; Menninger, 1958). This trend has been augmented by the development of nonpsychoanalytically derived psychotherapies since the 1950s.

Although the history of attempts to develop useful methods of short-term psychotherapy would seem to suggest that this is an unusually ardu-ous task, the fact is that most psychotherapy is short term, and short-term therapy is what most patients expect to get. Reviews of studies reveal that the median length of psychotherapy is six sessions (Garfield, 1978), and that even among private practitioners, the median length of treatment is only eight sessions (Koss, 1979). Further, 70 percent of patients expect therapy to last for 10 sessions or less (Garfield & Wolpin, 1963).

It is fortunate that most therapy is, in fact, short term because of the growing pressure of social necessity. The point has been made (e.g., Marmor, 1979; Small, 1979) that there is not only pressure to provide psychological services for a larger number of people but specifically to provide psychological services for previously underserved populations, such as the blue-collar class, minorities, and people with comparatively lower levels of education. For those who have been relatively little reached by standard psychotherapeutic methods, short-term methods—with their emphasis upon patient preparation for therapy, activity and directiveness on the part of the therapist, and a limited duration of treatment—provide an approach to psychological treatment that is more nearly in harmony with the patients' expectations, and more likely to produce positive results. The increase in third-party payments for psychotherapy and the increased concern with the cost-effectiveness of various forms of tax-supported treat-ment have added the pressure to reduce the cost of treatment. Obviously brief therapy, if it is effective, is considerably less expensive than time-unlimited psychotherapy.

When, to these pressures, is added the fact that brief-therapy methods seem to be just about as effective as time-unlimited therapy (e.g., Butcher & Koss, 1978; Small, 1979, p. 324; Sifneos, 1972, chap. 8), it would appear that short-term psychotherapy is destined to be the therapy of choice for most patients.

Crisis intervention is the generic name for a helping orientation that focuses on intensive, immediate work with people in the throes of an unsettling life circumstance. Programs offering some form of crisis inter-vention include telephone hot lines and walk-in centers (Rosenbaum & Calhoun, 1977), emergency rooms and psychiatric units of general hospi-tals (Getz, Fujita, & Allen, 1975; Greenhill, 1979), suicide-prevention centers (Motto, 1979), rape-crisis centers (Hoff & Williams, 1975), family-counseling services (Jaffe, Thompson, & Paquin, 1978), disaster-relief centers (Cohen & Ahearn, 1980), and the emergency services of mental health clinics (Rusk & Gerner, 1972). An in-depth examination of crisis intervention in such diverse settings would certainly reveal varied treatment methods, types of helping personnel, and even interpretations of what is meant by crisis intervention. Even more disquieting is the fact that there are no commonly accepted standards or ethical guidelines for the practice of crisis intervention (Lee, 1977), although some have been offered (Motto, Brooks, Ross & Allen, 1974).

The crisis-intervention movement has been at the leading edge of community mental health and human services for the last decade or more. It has been largely a grass-roots effort, however, with affiliation to several professional disciplines (and ownership by none) and only sporadic national leadership. Such diversity within the movement has provided broad support and tremendous energy, but also a lack of cohesiveness and direction. A major source of this diffusion is the heterogeneous origin of crisis intervention.

There appear to be several antecedents of present-day crisis intervention. A form of brief therapy and environmental management was developed, as has been mentioned, during World War II with combat personnel suffering from traumatic neuroses. The condition was viewed as transient and situational (i.e., combat related), although, in keeping with psychiatric thinking at the time, it was designated as a pathological disorder (Kardiner, 1941). The two major sources of crisis intervention, as practiced currently, are represented by the Lindemann-Caplan-Harvard community mental health program—based on work done during World War II and continued through the early 1960s—and the suicide-prevention movement that began in Los Angeles in 1958. The first has contributed a configuration of crisis intervention analogous to public health, in that populations at-risk for psychological harm are targeted for professional services, and emphasis is placed on early case detection and prevention (Caplan, 1964).

The contribution of the Shneidman-Farberow-Litman group in California provides a different but overlapping configuration. Accessibility to the target population is gained individually, at the instigation of the distressed person or family, by means of a 24-hour telephone or walk-in service. Most important, the intervention is typically performed by paraprofessionals, selected and trained specifically for that task (Farberow, Shneidman, Litman, Wold, Heilig, & Kramer, 1966). The influence of the two sources is consistent with other recent innovations in community mental health concerning the location and recipients of services, the helpers, and the helping methods (Golann, 1970).

A final influence came during the decade of the counterculture, roughly, 1966–1976, a time of experimentation in human relationships and distrust of social institutions, including mental health. To reach the disaffected, many of whom were young and in crisis, communities started hundreds of peer-help counseling services purposely identified as non-traditional. Although many of these programs have folded for lack of stable direction or external support, there remains among many crisis-intervention workers a humanistic spirit and a democratic organizational philosophy. The surge of energy infused into crisis work by the tens of thousands of volunteer paraprofessionals represents a broadening of mental health care that merits professional attention.

Because crisis intervention is the most urgent kind of situation for psychotherapeutic intervention, we should perhaps discuss it before turning to the topic of short-term psychotherapy in general.

CRISIS INTERVENTION

Program models for crisis intervention

The two lineages of crisis intervention described earlier have resulted in two somewhat different philosophies of how to aid persons in crisis. The approaches give rise to operational models that are not mutually exclusive and, in fact, can be combined effectively. Some explication of the models, however, may reduce the confusion that occurs when one sees differing versions of crisis intervention. The first is a *public-health model,* in that timely assistance is brought to members of a population exposed to some sort of hazard with presumed psychological risk. Intervention is thought to be both prophylactic and restorative. Examples of the public-health model include programs for mothers of premature or stillborn infants, widows, divorcees, surgery patients, and disaster victims. Services are often delivered at the site of the hazard or where targeted persons have gathered for other activities, for example, hospital emergency rooms, disaster-relief centers, juvenile court, morgues, and the like. The reader is referred to Parad, Resnik and Parad (1976) as a sourcebook of such programs. Caplan and his colleagues at Harvard and in Israel fostered the development of many programs casting crisis intervention in the public-health mold, and more recently, he has supplemented this model with a social-support model for the long-term adjustments caused by crisis (Caplan, 1974).

The second approach derives from the suicide-prevention centers started in the Los Angeles area over two decades ago. Its shape and character were most influenced by the originators of the Los Angeles Suicide Prevention Center (Farberow & Shneidman, 1965). This is the *crisis-center model,* generally considered to represent a radical innovation in mental health, because of the prime reliance on paraprofessionals, who are given major counseling responsibilities for callers, and because of the 24-hour availability of services, often by telephone. (The model includes services with a centralized answering point, rather than a central facility for workers.) The objective of the crisis-center model is to minimize the barriers between need and resource, in operational terms, to make immediately available, at no fee, a trained helper for any person who requests assistance for any type of personal problem. Although the early centers were designed for suicidal callers, it became apparent that the model had applicability for many human problems, and later programs were planned as general purpose centers.

Many crisis-intervention programs, of course, are creative variations of the two models. Stelmachers, Lund, and Meade (1972) describe a crisis center located adjacent to the emergency room of a general hospital (public-health model) and staffed by both volunteers and mental health professionals, who run a 24-hour crisis hot line (crisis-center model). With the advent of mandated emergency services for comprehensive community mental health centers, a third model of crisis intervention has emerged. Following Butcher and Maudal (1976), it may be labeled the *crisis-therapy model.* Crisis therapy provides formal treatment, usually by a mental health professional, and involves careful assessment of both precipitating factors and the client's personality problems. In this model of intervention, several interviews may be planned, although the therapist is cautioned to make each interview self-contained, as if it "will be the last contact with the patient" (Butcher & Maudal, 1976, p. 614). Crisis therapy is a reversion toward traditional methods of intervention, especially when it is designed to help the patient gain insight into why a particular set of events precipitated a crisis for that particular person. Although it is, perhaps, too early to forecast what effect the crisis-therapy model will have on the crisis-intervention movement, it seems clear that crisis intervention has now become part of the conventional mental health system in many communities, and thus may be in some danger of losing its unique character (Brockopp, 1976).

Values and crisis intervention

The practitioner who anticipates using crisis intervention should be aware of the values it represents. For any treatment orientation, it is instructive to know "what you get for what you give up." The following are five value statements concerning both community and individual participation in crisis intervention. They refer mostly to the public-health and crisis-center models described earlier, rather than to crisis therapy.

Provision of an immediate helping response. People in psychological distress are seen as having the right to expect some form of personal helping response promptly upon a clear request for aid, although responding does not imply that the distress will end or that a solution will be forthcoming. Consequently, communities have an obligation to provide easily accessible services for families and individuals in crisis and/or psychiatric emergency.

Bridge to the mental health establishment. Many potential recipients resist entering the professional mental health establishment. Therefore, communities should bridge the gap between the "natural" and "contrived" or establishment mental health systems (Levy, 1973) with visible, organized outreach programs.

Avoidance of the patient role. A counterpart to the bridging value is the value placed on avoiding the patient role for people whose personal problems can be managed largely through their own resources. To many, the label *patient* conveys sickness, passivity, and helplessness, and it is thus counterproductive to effective crisis coping. A crisis-intervention program should filter through to traditional mental health only those persons (a) who request referral, or (b) for whom crisis intervention is inappropriate, or (c) who are deteriorating psychologically, or (d) for whom a prolonged-stress situation warrants professional care.

Relief of distress as a legitimate goal. Symptom relief per se is a reasonable focus for people in crisis, as it may permit a more-adaptive coping with stressful situations (Butcher & Maudal, 1976). Although the helper may deem crisis a propitious opportunity to explore extensively into the recipient's life and personality for antecedents of the current crisis, the helper should first be assured that this is a goal of the person being helped and that, if further therapy is contemplated, both its costs and benefits are well understood. Horowitz (1976) provides an excellent model showing a therapeutic choice that must be made between proceeding with stress-event work or diverting to character and/or conflict analysis (p. 268). He also notes that work on a core neurotic conflict may be taken up after the stress-event work is completed.

Inherent helping qualities as necessary and (almost) sufficient. A high value for the crisis-intervention worker is placed on the basic human qualities of perceptiveness, empathy, warmth, respect for others, ability to assess people and situations, good judgement, and an allegiance to the truth, even though upsetting. Crisis intervention demands a goodly share of such attributes, whether the helper is a professional or an unpaid volunteer. Following "Litman's Law" (Heilig, 1970), such qualities are *more* salient as the loss is more profound and sudden; or, by contrast, professional training is required of a helper for disturbances that are unrelated to a current situation. A quality crisis-intervention program contains not only workers with natural talent but also provides for their selection, pre-service training, in-service training, and supervision— processes to which experienced paraprofessionals can also contribute.

There are other values embedded in a community-oriented movement such as crisis intervention and, to some extent, each program defines a unique value position in its own community. Indeed, an asset of the diffusion noted earlier in crisis intervention is an ability to shape programs according to unique community values.

Definition of a crisis

The following is offered as a working definition of crisis. A crisis is a time during which events experienced by an individual or family produce a rupture in the usual patterns of affect, behavior, or images of self, such that some modification of these patterns must be accomplished in order to assimilate the new experience.

Theoretical formulations of crisis have been more precise than the operational definitions that emerge from the field. Rosenbaum and Calhoun (1977) comment that, "In practice, centers rarely apply definitions in determining whether a crisis actually exists, but rather use the working definition that a person is in crisis if he perceives himself to be so" (p. 327). The authors see three concepts as common to most crisis theories: (a) a precipitating situation that is (b) time-limited, with the limits yet to be defined, and (c) that causes disruption in the individual's problem-solving abilities (Rosenbaum & Calhoun, 1977). This is a workable definition for the practitioner and leads naturally toward assessment. Other defining characteristics of crisis frequently mentioned in the literature include: (a) less defensiveness (Halpern, 1973) and a sometimes dramatically increased openness to being helped, which Dixon and Burns (1974) see as forming the basis for crisis intervention; (b) the potential for positive change, first mentioned by Thomas (1909), a social scientist who saw crisis as a cause of social change; (c) slow resolution (a few days to a month) of the disequilibrium precipitated by the situation (Bloom, 1963); (d) the relative absence of pre-crisis psychopathology (Baldwin, 1979); (e) the possible presence of a single disorienting percept (Taplin, 1971) that carries symbolic meaning of the crisis for the individual; and (f) changes in self-concept, work efficiency, and interpersonal relationships (Hansell, 1976).

By definition, crisis refers to a person-situation interaction, and most workers find it useful to differentiate between the *crisis situation*, which produces the precipitating event and subsequently may exaggerate or diminish its effects, and the *crisis state*, which describes the distressed individual. As clinicians, we sometimes choose to concentrate treatment on the client's coping abilities (reduce the crisis state), but as crisis interveners, a whole second front is opened to us. Rape, for example, is a precipitating event that may generate loving support or emotional distance from lovers, spouses, parents, and friends, and their reaction becomes part of the social surround attached to the crisis. While the precipitating event cannot be undone, astute environmental management may change the character of what follows for the victim. Erikson (1976) describes a classic example of how crises may build upon themselves needlessly. Victims of the 1972 Buffalo Creek flood, whose homes up and down the valley were destroyed, were assigned to trailer villages according to bureaucratic convenience, rather than by pre-disaster geography or kinship. This artificial hodgepodge compounded tensions in a population already in crisis from losing loved ones, property, and community, and antisocial behavior reputedly increased to a significant degree. Disaster workers have subsequently learned to be more sensitive to interpersonal and social characteristics of the victim population.

The person-situation distinction is an important one for applied research; as patterns of response to various crisis situations become more thoroughly understood, the worker will be able to anticipate individual needs more precisely and be more directive in the resolution of a particular crisis.

Dynamics of a crisis

A crisis is not a static situation, but a fluid, dynamic experience, a process of living wherein events, relationships, and feelings often "loom larger than life" for the people involved. Yet, the crisis experience, in its broadest outlines, is fairly predictable. It consists of three major processes, often appearing as sequential but overlapping phases that the person in crisis goes through. The timing, oscillation, and eventual completion of all three phases are factors less predictable than their mere presence. The three processes may be labeled *shock, realization,* and *integration.* The whole process may take several days to more than a year and, in the latter case, probably entail subprocesses, as parts of the total crisis are individually confronted and worked through.

Shock refers to the inability of a person's cognitive system to integrate highly discrepant or discordant information and the tendency to "shut down" psychologically for a period of time (Taplin, 1971). While shock following crisis is sometimes given the semiperjorative label of *denial,* it should be appreciated as a necessary, even healthy, means of adapting to severe, unanticipated situations. The dysfunctional aspect of denial in this context is not its presence, but its continuation after the work of confronting the crisis situation should have started. A shock phase allows the person in crisis to delay a full recognition of the crisis and its potential impact; in the meantime, internal resources may be quietly summoned up, and significant others may gather to provide support and initiate the realization process. Periodic displays of strong emotion at this time are common. For example, Horowitz (1976) describes an "almost-reflexive emotional expression" upon first impact of the crisis that he aptly labels *outcry* (p. 261). Gradually, the distressed individual abandons an attitude of disbelief and begins searching for a coping strategy. Self-statements during this search may signal important aspects of the process to follow, for example, "I'm a survivor, I can do it," *versus* "When you're old and alone, living is hardly bearable."

The term *realization* is used, following Parkes (1970), to connote the work that is ahead in a second process of crisis: that of making the events and their consequences *real* to the individual. It is during this time that emotionality, instability, and feelings of being vulnerable and helpless are strongest—in other words, the crisis is at its peak. In situations of severe loss, the realization process may take many months and may be marked by periodic retreats to a denial pattern, as well as by episodes of great anguish, which diminish over time. Reminders of the crisis event are often painful but have the valuable function of advancing the process of realization. Productive realization probably requires moderation—over-control of emotions in order to blot out memories of the crisis is harmful, but so is obsessive rumination and preoccupation with it. Thus, the intervener who provides periodic opportunities to ventilate feelings and experiment with new perspectives of the crisis is performing a most valuable service.

Integration occurs as the individual assimilates the total crisis experience. Emotional integration typically requires more time than intellectual understanding, and both are considered necessary for successful integration. From a successful working-through process, people gain self-confidence and strength of character. An important characteristic of successful assimilation is the assignment of meaning to the precipitating event, a meaning that may be altered by the individual to comply with significant personal themes. For example, an adolescent may become more mature and independent following parental divorce, even though, at the time, the experience involved mostly pain and uncertainty. The work of integration thus affords an opportunity to modify the very events that initially were such powerful intrusions, although the modifying must be done psychologically and retrospectively.

Facilitating realization and problem solving

Successful crisis resolution begins with psychological acceptance of the precipitating event, a process described here as realization. Regarding the crisis of grief, for example, Parkes (1970) says, "It is a process of realization, of making psychologically real an external event which is not desired and for which coping plans do not exist" (p. 465). The first goal of crisis intervention is to promote realization. This is done by providing a safe environment for the recognition and expression of painful feelings, by confronting the event in a calm and objective manner, by showing a warm regard for the person in distress, and by supplying new information and perspectives on the event in order to widen the person's view of it. It is only when some measure of realization has taken place that problem solving can begin. A common mistake of crisis workers-in-training is to begin problem solving too early (Knowles, 1979), a tendency easily corrected in training (Hartsough, 1976).

To be effective, crisis intervention must be keyed to the phase or process of crisis exhibited by the person to be helped. A person in psychological shock needs physical comfort, the presence of supportive significant others, reassurance, and an ample opportunity to talk, often repetitively, about the precipitating event. Those who decline to talk may be encouraged to do so, as others disclose their own reactions, but should not be forced. Uncovering types of interviews are not appropriate for individuals in psychological shock.

The typical crisis contact is with someone already in the realization phase, because emotionality and distress are strongest at this time. Several stage models of intervention have been suggested in the literature (Echterling, Hartsough, & Zarle, 1980; Litman, Farberow, Shneidman, Heilig, & Kramer, 1965; McCarthy & Berman, 1971; Schlenker, 1970) and bear close similarity to one another. The worker must first establish rapport and set a positive climate for helping; assessment of the crisis can then begin, as well as working through the attendant feelings; finally, problem-solving or follow-up action planning is appropriate. Research has provided a partial validation for this model of intervention, although the concept of stages was found to be too rigid. Echterling et al. observed 59 calls to a crisis telephone service and demonstrated that intervener behavior varied with the progress of the call: (a) rapport building was high initially and at the end of the call (a "hello-goodbye" effect); (b) assessment was higher in the first two portions than in the last third; and (c) problem solving increased significantly toward the end of the call (Echterling et al., 1980). Further, the differential patterns were found to be related to successful outcomes. Using the same data, Echterling and Hartsough (1981) showed that a low level of initial problem solving, followed by high levels at the end of the call, produced successful calls, as judged by independent raters using both affective and cognitive criteria. Unsuccessful calls showed the reverse pattern.

An earlier study of crisis interviews in a psychiatric emergency room by Rusk and Gerner (1972) reached conclusions similar to those of the Echterling and Hartsough study. The authors found that therapists who talked less in the first third of the interview, and more during the last third, were associated with patients who showed the greatest decreases in anxiety and depression from pre- to post-treatment. Results of these two studies could be the basis for advice offered by Butcher and Maudal (1976), "Especially in crisis therapy one should guard against the inclination to do or say too much too soon. Astute listening and observation are absolutely necessary to formulating the problem adequately" (p. 619).

Research on intervener effectiveness indicates that most facilitative behaviors involve giving clear and accurate information, being supportive and reassuring, and providing new perspectives on the situation (Slaikeu & Willis, 1978). The surprising result of one study was that clichéd responses, such as, "Take it one day at a time," or "Every cloud has its silver lining," were seen as helpful by callers in crisis (Delfin, 1978). The importance of providing useful, accurate, and up-dated information to callers is generally overlooked in crisis telephone services, with the result that this task is frequently mishandled (Apsler & Hodas, 1976). A study by Delfin and Hartsough (1979) illustrated the use of programmed materials by trainees of a crisis telephone service to overcome this deficit.

Realization and problem solving can be facilitated by several tactics, in addition to those mentioned above. One is to help the person distinguish between solvable and unsolvable situations, for example, to see that a significant other's behavior may not be changeable. A second tactic is to break down the crisis situation into manageable pieces and to select the most important and workable problem for immediate attack (Golan, 1978). Contracting with the recipient of intervention regarding action steps to be taken is also an effective means of directing post-interview behavior. Third, the helper may label feelings and clarify communication between the recipient and significant others. Finally, there may be a need to help the individual maintain control of the situation by pacing his or her efforts, for example, to give permission for recreational time-outs from the work of crisis resolution, and to allow denial when it appears.

Horowitz (1976) sees the oscillation between denial and intrusion patterns as the most important feature of extended therapy with people in crisis. He notes that the patient, by establishing therapeutic contact, may reduce emotional pressures to the point of reinstituting ideational denial and emotional numbing. Because the patient is less pressured by feelings, fewer feelings are disclosed, and the patient may appear as boring or unmotivated by the therapist. Lack of enthusiasm on the part of the therapist may result in premature termination or relentless digging for the proper material or emotions. Instead, the author suggests adapting to the patient's pace and waiting for a return of the intrusive mode, when the emotional impact of the crisis recurs.

While a formulation of the therapist role by Horowitz sounds substantially like that for conventional therapy, Butcher and Maudal (1976) portray an active, directive therapist, who assesses quickly, intervenes decisively, and takes command of major aspects of the problem-solving process. Thus, the authors state, "The role of the therapist here is viewed in an entirely different light than in the therapeutic teachings of a few years ago. Psychologists have relinquished some of their cherished ideals such as, 'The therapist is a mirror,' or 'A therapist never initiates contact with the patient.' It is likely that the benefits of these ideals have always existed more in the mind of the therapist than the patient anyway"

(p. 637). France (1975) occupies a middle position regarding the helper role and includes empathic listening, accurate referral, and being a "technique-equipped behavior changer."

Two helper roles have been demonstrated as essential for effective crisis intervention: (a) giving clear and accurate information and (b) being a warm and supportive human being who is willing to become involved—within limits—in another's distress (Carothers & Inslee, 1974; Slaikeu & Willis, 1978; Speer & Schultz, 1975). Crisis intervention highlights the latter role because of the tenuous nature of many contacts.

Paraprofessional selection, training, and supervision

Paraprofessionals carry much of the responsibility for crisis intervention, especially in services using the crisis-center model. The worker is often an unpaid volunteer, selected for qualities of judgement, verbal ability, motivation, and maturity, but, nevertheless, working independently of immediate professional supervision. The psychologist, who is mindful of quality-control issues in all helping relationships, will also be concerned about the selection, training, and supervision of crisis workers.

Standard practice dictates the use of a formal selection procedure. In addition, most centers encourage rigorous self-assessment by the prospective volunteer, so that selection may become a growth-enhancing experience (Hartsough, 1976). Performance in training is the major basis for making selection decisions, but it may be replaced or augmented by staff-screening interviews (McCord & Packwood, 1973). Earlier efforts to select workers through personality tests (Heilig, Farberow, Litman & Shneidman, 1968) or special-assessment devices (Fowler & McGee, 1973; McGee, Knickerbocker, Fowler, Jennings, Ansel, Zelenka, & Marcus, 1972) have not been widely accepted. On the whole, the selection systems for screening paraprofessional crisis workers seem effective, although they are also time consuming and somewhat inefficient.

The training of crisis paraprofessionals has been criticized as being atheoretical and unsystematic (Dixon & Burns, 1974, 1975). Training programs have developed locally and without benefit of formal national guidelines. However, the informal network among crisis services has encouraged the widespread sharing of training lore, including training formats, techniques, and materials. The result is a striking consistency in the structure and content of crisis-training programs. Most are intensive, that is, completed within six weeks, and require 25–50 hours of participation. The principle of participatory learning through call-simulated role-playing is widely used. A critical feature of the role-playing technique is the feedback conveyed to the learner on both positive and negative aspects of his or her performance. To enhance the feedback process, trainers attempt to create a positive learning environment.

A peer-training model is often employed by the extensive use of experienced volunteers (Hartsough, 1976). One advantage of the peer model is the additional in-service training given to seasoned workers. Experience shows that most crisis-intervention programs have, in fact, devoted considerable energy toward developing a rationale and structure for their own training programs, which typically are not disseminated in the professional literature, but instead used internally for administrative purposes.

Supervision is probably the weakest area of most crisis-intervention programs. Doyle, Foreman, and Wales (1977) cite surveys to show that slightly less than one fourth of the centers provided immediate supervision for paraprofessional counselors, whereas nearly one-half gave no supervision after pretraining. Approximately one third offered delayed supervision to the worker (e.g., the following day or later in the week). The study by Doyle and his colleagues revealed that immediate supervision was necessary to sustain the types of helping patterns learned in pretraining. Further, without close supervision, the worker is prone toward less intrusiveness and activity in the vital problem-solving phase of intervention (Doyle et al., 1977). While logistics make the 24-hour availability of immediate supervision virtually impossible, both volunteers and staff should be aware of its critical importance for maintaining a quality service.

Professional versus paraprofessional crisis intervention: Who owns the territory?

Durlak (1979) conducted a comprehensive review of the comparative effectiveness of paraprofessional and professional helpers of all types. In 95 percent of the 42 studies reviewed, paraprofessionals were either equal to or significantly favored over their professional counterparts. For crisis work specifically, paraprofessionals have shown equal or superior levels of warmth, empathy, and caring (Knickerbocker & McGee, 1973; O'Donnell & George, 1977). In two other studies (DeVol, 1976; Getz, Fujita, & Allen, 1975), neither group was significantly more effective.

Four levels of crisis intervention were identified by Jacobson and his colleagues (Jacobson, Strickler, & Morley, 1968; Morley, 1970), with the clear implication that the highest level belonged only to mental health professionals. This seems a reasonable conclusion, as the fourth level involves an individually created approach that considers not only the individual's current crisis situation, but also the relationship of present to past crises, and the whole personality. The other three levels are environmental manipulation, a general-support approach restricted to active listening, and a generic approach involving standard tactics for well-known crises. Paraprofessionals are considered well equipped by the authors for the first three levels, but not sufficiently trained in abnormal psychology, psychodynamics, or personality theory for the fourth.

One difficulty with the Jacobson et al. formulation is that most crisis-intervention training programs involving paraprofessionals also encourage an individual approach, rather than a packaged or general support notion. That is, the helper is taught to respond to the caller as a person who has a unique perspective, yet who may need confrontation from a caring and assertive other. No restrictions are put on exploring what the crisis means emotionally to the individual. With the possible exception of longer-term crisis therapy, it is doubtful that a formal knowledge of psychodynamics is essential to the intervention process, or at least, this necessity needs to be demonstrated. One might hypothesize that there is more overlap between professional and paraprofessional workers than envisioned by Jacobson, and that major differences in therapeutic effectiveness reside in personal qualities of the helper, such as age and life experience.

Reviews of the effectiveness of crisis-intervention programs generally are positive, although methodological problems plague the area (Auerback & Kilmann, 1977; Rosenbaum & Calhoun, 1977). Individual studies, representing a wide range of settings and evaluation techniques, reflect not only the diversity of the field, but also the need for standard evaluation approaches (Bagley, 1968; Bleach & Claiborn, 1974; Getz, Fujita, & Allen, 1975; Jaffe, Thompson, & Paquin, 1978; Maris & Connor, 1973; O'Donnell & George,1977; Slaikeu, Lester, & Tulkin, 1973; Slaikeu, Tulkin, & Speer, 1975; Slaikeu & Willis, 1978; Slem & Cotler, 1973; Stelmachers et al., 1972; Williams, Lee, & Polak, 1976). These evaluations suggest a number of roles for the professional in crisis intervention. The most obvious one is the clinical back-up and consultant for the frontline crisis worker. O'Donnell and George (1977), for example, found that in a crisis center located in a professional setting, 28 percent of the total calls handled went on to the mental health center professional staff, and 7 percent required hospitalization. A second role is to assist in training and supervision of volunteer paraprofessionals (Doyle et al., 1977; Dixon & Burns, 1974, 1975; France, 1975). Finally, there is a great need for the psychologist and other professionals in research and theory development.

The next section, discussing short-term psychotherapy, more properly addresses the therapeutic function of the professional, functioning at the fourth level described by Jacobson et al. (1968).

SHORT-TERM PSYCHOTHERAPY

Short-term psychotherapies derive from a variety of psychotherapeutic traditions (Burke, White, & Havens, 1979; Grayson, 1979; Small, 1979). The most common source of what has been officially labeled *short-term* therapy is the psychoanalytic tradition (Balint, 1972; Malan, 1963, 1976; Mann, 1973; Marmor, 1979; Sifneos, 1972), but behavior-therapy methods are usually utilized in therapy that is limited in time (Burke et al., 1979; Lazarus, 1972), and other therapeutic approaches have contributions to make to the strategy and tactics of short-term therapy (Bandler & Grinder, 1975, 1976, 1979; Haley, 1963, 1973; Kendall & Hollon, 1979).

Most practicing therapists use a variety of methods derived from different therapeutic traditions (Small, 1979, p. 19), a practice that is recommended as making good therapeutic sense (Burke et al., 1979; Lazarus, 1972), and which serves to stimulate the development of some kind of meta-theory which will serve as a basis for integrating the various theories and techniques of psychotherapy. The area of greatest integrative activity is in the growing rapprochement between behavioral and cognitive therapies (Kendall & Hollon, 1979). Kendall and Hollon suggest an *S-O-R* paradigm as the basis of integration, in which both classical and operant conditioning are integrated within a paradigm that includes cognitive components. Other bases that have been suggested for the integration of analytic, cognitive, behavioral, and existential therapies are Erikson's developmental stages (Burke et al., 1979) and Loevinger's stages of ego development (Swensen, 1980). The pressure of external forces that promises to continue to stimulate the development of effective, short-term methods of psychotherapy should provide an additional stimulus to the continued development of a single, integrated paradigm for psychotherapy.

Regardless of the source of the therapy, all short-term methods have certain features in common (Butcher & Koss, 1978; Small, 1979). The first characteristic is that the therapy is time limited. Generally, this means that the course of therapy is less than 25 sessions—in some cases, as few as one or two sessions (Haley, 1963, 1973). Because the time is limited, it is necessary to determine rapidly the nature of the problem, make an explicit initial assessment of the problem, and plan specific treatment which focuses upon the core problem or problems of the patient. Accurate, rapid assessment requires a therapist who is experienced, able to come to a valid conclusion about a case, and determine a method of treatment that is likely to be successful. Further, the necessity for dealing rapidly with a variety of different kinds of cases requires a therapist who is flexible in approach, a trait generally expected to be found more frequently in an experienced therapist than in a relative beginner. In this regard, short-term therapy is different from crisis intervention, in that the crisis-intervention worker is frequently a paraprofessional with relatively little experience, who turns the client over to a professional if the problem is beyond the paraprofessional's experience, or if the contact extends beyond the immediate crisis period. But it should be pointed out that experience is also a factor in crisis intervention, in that the experienced paraprofessional intervener can develop a more individualized, flexible approach than can those paraprofessionals with little experience. Thus, most approaches to short-term therapy assume that the therapist will be experienced.

Because the therapy must move rapidly, it is necessary for the therapist to be active and directive in the treatment, regardless of which techniques are used. Techniques that are commonly used include preparatory instructions to the patient to prepare the patient for the kinds of things that will be done in psychotherapy, and to induce an expectancy of improvement in the patient. Most therapies encourage the patient to ventilate feelings about the crisis that prompted psychotherapy.

All methods agree that the relationship between the therapist and the patient is an important factor in the treatment, whether the treatment is dynamic (Malan, 1963, 1976) or behavioral (Lazarus, 1972).

In reviewing the research on short-term psychotherapy, Butcher and Koss (1978) concluded that the important elements in short-term therapy are:

1. A positive relationship between the therapist and the patient.
2. Directive interpretations by the therapist.
3. Pre-therapy preparation of the patient, especially to encourage the patient to expect improvement.

Types of problems and patients

In view of the fact that most psychotherapy is short-term (e.g. Garfield, 1978), the question of which kinds of problems and which kinds of patients are especially amenable to short-term treatment would appear to be academic. However, there have been criteria applied to the selection of patients for short-term psychotherapy. These criteria have generally been applied to candidates for dynamic short-term therapy. Sifneos (1972) lists the following criteria as being important for the selection of patients: (1) above-average intelligence; (2) must have had at least one meaningful relationship with another person during previous life (a meaningful relationship is one in which something has been given up for the other person); (3) must express some emotion appropriately during the initial interview, and show some degree of flexibility; (4) must be able to voice a chief complaint; and (5) must be motivated for change. The criteria for motivation are: the ability to recognize that the symptoms are psychological, a tendency to be introspective, a willingness to participate actively in treatment, curiosity about oneself, a willingness to understand oneself, a willingness to experiment and change, expect to make sacrifices for therapy, and expect therapy to bring about a positive change. In Sifneos' view, a patient who meets four or fewer of these critria may be considered to lack necessary motivation.

The criteria listed by Sifneos would seem to restrict the applicability of short-term therapy. However, indications are that, as was indicated earlier in the chapter, short-term therapy is applicable to a wide range of patients with a wide variety of complaints (e.g., Small, 1979) and, particularly, to patients for whom standard psychotherapy has not appeared to be particularly applicable. Butcher and Koss (1978) summarize the literature by concluding that short-term therapy seems to be generally viewed as particularly applicable to patients who: (1) have a problem with an acute onset, (2) have had a previous, good adjustment, (3) have the ability to form good relationships with other people, and (4) have high motivation.

Ursano and Dressler (1974) found that there was no difference in age, sex, occupation, education, or marital status between patients referred for standard therapy and those referred for short-term therapy. Those referred for short-term therapy did differ from those referred for standard therapy in length of the disturbance, previous adjustment, ability to relate to the therapist, and in suffering less discomfort. Those referred for brief therapy appeared to be suffering from situational kinds of disorders.

The kinds of situational disorders most commonly suffered (Dressler, Donovan, & Geller, 1976) are interpersonal conflicts resulting in insult, arguments, or rejection. The most common emotions reported are sadness, guilt, anger, and anxiety.

The discussion above does not produce any definitive conclusions to the question of which kinds of patients, with which kinds of problems, are best served by short-term therapy. The current, conventional wisdom suggests that those best served by short-term therapy are people whose general functioning in life has been successful, but who have been temporarily derailed by some environmental stress that exceeded their coping capacity. This conclusion is provisional, pending extensive further research, which will surely broaden and sharpen the applicability of short-term therapy. Clinical experience (e.g., Small, 1979) indicates that short-term treatment is useful to a broader range of patients than those suffering temporary, situational upset.

The therapist

There is general agreement (e.g., Butcher & Koss, 1978; Small, 1979) that the short-term psychotherapist should be highly experienced. It is necessary for the therapist to formulate the problem rapidly and outline a treatment procedure. The therapist must be active and directive in order to keep the therapy focused upon the central problem and moving toward a resolution of that problem. It is also necessary for the therapist to rapidly establish a good, therapeutic relationship with the patient. All of these demands of short-term therapy appear to require a therapist who is experienced and able to move surely and quickly down the abbreviated path to therapeutic success.

But how to develop such a therapist? The general recommendations (e.g., Small, 1979) are that the therapist should be experienced in general psychotherapy before attempting short-term psychotherapy. There is wisdom to this recommendation. It is certainly true that, after extensive experience, most therapists find that, with many patients, it is possible to significantly reduce the length of therapy by cutting quickly to what past therapeutic experience has taught is the essence of the problem.

However, the statistics cited at the beginning of this chapter suggest that short-term psychotherapy is not a special brand of therapy but, rather, that short-term therapy is *the* standard brand of therapy. This would suggest that budding therapists should be taught short-term methods in their basic training. At least one survey (Clarkin, Frances, Taintor, & Warburg, 1980) indicates that most training programs provide such experience.

Therapy preparation

Ordinarily, the first step in psychotherapy is an initial interview, in which the patient's case history is taken. However, research (Nash, Hoehn-Saric, Battle, Stone, Imber, & Frank, 1965; Frank, 1974; Heitler, 1976; Butcher & Koss, 1978) indicates that patients are more likely to improve in therapy, become more involved in therapy, and are more satisfied with therapy if they have received some preliminary preparation for therapy. This therapy preparation appears to be especially effective with relatively uneducated and unsophisticated patients who are unfamiliar with psychotherapy. In this respect, short-term therapy differs from crisis intervention, in which there is no time for preparation.

This preparation is designed to, in effect, give the prospective patient an explanation of what will happen in psychotherapy, what the therapist does, what the patient is expected to do, and what kinds of things the patient is likely to experience in therapy. This therapy preparation produces, of course, certain expectancies in the patient, and it is hoped that training will produce an expectancy of being helped by therapy. Small (1979) concludes that, "any interaction which heightens expectation of help will lead to symptom decrease and mood improvement" (p. 49).

Assessment and planning therapy

Perhaps there is no single element of short-term psychotherapy more important than the assessment process. The success of psychotherapy conducted within a time limit necessarily depends upon a rapid and useful assessment of the nature of the problem, and the selection of a course of treatment that has a high probability of solving the problem.

The one common element in assessment for all kinds of psychotherapy is the interview, in which a case history is obtained which provides the basic information from which a case formulation can be constructed and treatment planned. However, the kind of information obtained and the use made of that information varies considerably from one therapist to another, depending upon the theoretical proclivities of the therapist. In view of the fact that, as we shall eventually discover in this chapter, approximately 70 percent of patients improve regardless of the brand of therapy used, it would appear that the important thing is not so much what kind of case formulation is produced, but rather that it be produced and that both the therapist and the patient have faith in it. There is more than one way to skin a cat.

Dynamic psychotherapies concentrate upon formulating a conception of the patients's personality dynamics and focusing upon a specific, key conflict. The essence of the assessment process depends upon focusing upon the most significant conflict and devoting the therapy to the solution of that conflict (Balint et al., 1972; Malan, 1963, 1976). Some (Sifneos, 1972) choose, in collaboration with the patient, the conflict which will be the focus of the therapeutic effort.

Others, however, work from a somewhat more narrow focus. Mann (1973) sees the root of the problem as lying within the universal conflicts of human existence. The central and recurring crisis in life is that of separation versus individuation. Other universal conflicts are dependency versus independency, activity versus passivity, and self-esteem versus loss of self-esteem. The problem is found in the failure to resolve one of these crises, and the solution is found in the resolution of this crisis.

Milton Erickson (Haley 1963, 1973), who was noted for producing remarkable cures in incredibly short periods of time, tended to approach assessment from the point of view of developmental crises. Each stage of human existence produces a crisis to be resolved, and the problems presented by patients typically center around a failure to resolve the crisis of a particular stage. The stages Erickson used were based upon the family life cycle. These stages include: courtship, marriage, childbirth and dealing with young children, middle marriage, separation of parents from children, and retirement and old age. Within each of these stages, a variety of developmental tasks may present themselves.

Behavior therapy (e.g., Dengrove, 1972) concentrates upon determining the maladaptive behaviors that are to be extinguished, the reinforcements that are maintaining those behaviors, and the development of alternative, adaptive behaviors that are to be learned and reinforced in the place of the maladaptive behaviors.

In practice, it is quite common to combine a variety of these assessment views (e.g., Lazarus, 1972). For example, a patient who complains of being unable to establish satisfactory relationships with members of the opposite sex may not have learned effective social skills (a behavioral assessment), may have an unresolved fear of being dominated by members of the opposite sex (a psychodynamic assessment), and may have failed to resolve the developmental crisis of isolation versus intimacy (a developmental assessment). All of these assessments are, in their own way, true, and all suggest courses of treatment that are not necessarily mutually exclusive, and might with some profit and relatively little ineffi-

ciency be pursued more or less simultaneously. Certainly, the development and the exercise of adaptive social skills with the opposite sex
should contribute toward resolving the developmental crisis and also
increase the patient's self-esteem relative to the opposite sex, so that fears
of domination begin to be perceived as inappropriate.

An integral part of the process of assessment and treatment planning
is setting goals for therapy. Ordinarily these goals will be limited (Butcher
& Koss, 1978) and focused upon the specific symptoms which the patient
brought into psychotherapy. The goals may be the acquisition of, or
extinction of, specific behaviors, or the resolution of some intrapsychic
conflict. However, the resolution of an intrapsychic conflict is presumably
manifested by a change in the patient's behavior or feelings, and behavior
and feelings are quite specific. The goals may be chosen by the therapist
(Haley, 1973) or by the patient in consultation with the therapist (Sifneos,
1972). As a matter of practical fact, any successful therapy necessarily
requires a minimum amount of cooperation and agreement between the
patient and the therapist, so that whatever goal or goals are chosen for
therapy, the likelihood of the success of the endeavor is enhanced by
patient-therapist agreement.

Since research (Ursano & Dressler, 1974) suggests that the chief difference between time-limited psychotherapy and unlimited psychotherapy
is in the number of problems upon which the therapy focuses, it would
appear that, if the therapy is to be brief, it must necessarily focus upon
one or two specific problems upon which the therapist and the patient
agree.

The scheduling of sessions plays an important part in therapy planning.
It is generally recommended (Butcher & Koss, 1978; Small, 1979) that
the first session be scheduled as soon as feasible after the patient requests
an appointment, in order to prevent the symptoms from becoming chronic.
As a general rule, sessions are scheduled for approximately one hour,
once per week. The frequency of sessions may be increased to more
than once per week in order to provide more support for the patient.
The length of the sessions may be shortened to less than an hour in
order to decrease the patient's dependency. The intensification of emotional expression may be produced by marathon sessions that last for
several hours, or even for more than a day. Research suggests (Bierenbaum, Nichols, & Schwartz, 1976) that the most satisfactory, all-purpose,
time scheduling is for one hour, once per week. This scheduling produces
the most emotional catharsis, the most change in behavior, and seems
to be most satisfactory to patients.

Therapy relationship

There is a general consensus that a positive relationship between the
therapist and the patient is essential to successful brief psychotherapy

(Butcher & Koss, 1978; Small, 1979). Research (e.g., Frank, 1974; Strupp, 1980a, 1980b, 1980c, 1980d) suggests that the relationship between the therapist and the client is the single most important element in determining the success or failure of the psychotherapy. Strupp (1980a), writing from a dynamic point of view, concludes that, "whether they openly acknowledge it or not, individuals approaching a psychotherapist are seeking a 'good' human relationship and a satisfying relatedness" (p. 603). Lazarus (1972), writing from a behavioral point of view, makes a similar point in stating that, "all patients who recover in treatment make a strong attachment to their therapist" (p. 21).

Having established the fact that the relationship between the therapist and the patient is important does not answer the question of how a good relationship is to be established. Research would suggest that it is important for the therapist to genuinely care about the patient (Swensen, 1971) and that the therapist like the patient (Sloane, Staples, Cristol, Yorkston, & Whipple, 1975). The vast literature on interpersonal relationships (e.g., Swensen, 1973) would seem to be applicable to this problem. One powerful factor in the inducement of liking is reward of one person by another. Milton Erickson's (Haley, 1963, 1973) method of emphasizing the positive aspects of the patient would seem to be one way of rewarding the patient and, thus, promoting the development of a positive relationship. Emphasizing the positive consists of taking the "half-full, rather than half-empty" approach to the patient's life. If, for example, the patient describes a series of failed enterprises, the therapist can compliment the patient for persisting to try in spite of failure.

Therapy techniques

This section is divided into those techniques that are used by most approaches to brief therapy, those techniques that are particularly identified with the psychodynamic therapies, techniques that are essentially behavioral, and techniques that are not readily classified into the usual categories of therapeutic endeavor.

General techniques. Most approaches to brief therapy (Butcher & Koss, 1978; Small, 1979) stress the importance of quick intervention in order to prevent the symptoms from becoming chronic, and to provide immediate relief if the patient is, as is often the case, in an emotional crisis. This ordinarily means scheduling the first appointment within 24 to 48 hours after the first contact with the patient. In cases of extreme emergency, such as potential suicide, the importance of making immediate and continuous telephone contact available to the patient has been stressed (Small, 1979).

Because the course of therapy is short, it is necessary for the therapist to be active in the therapeutic process (Butcher & Koss, 1978; Sifneos,

1972; Small, 1979) and flexible in the choice of techniques and the application of those techniques.

Environmental manipulation is frequently used, particularly if it is evident that the patient is living or working in an undesirable situation it is feasible to change. Examples are: moving out of an undesirable living situation, avoiding a person who is a source of unnecessary tension or conflict, or, in the case of a student, dropping a course that demands work beyond that which the patient is currently able to meet.

Catharsis and the ventilation of strong emotion are almost inevitably a part of any kind of psychotherapy, but especially of short-term therapy. Often, the discussion of an emotionally loaded situation and the expression of the emotion connected with that situation, in themselves provide substantial relief for the patient.

Support, reassurance, and encouragement are also commonly used by short-term therapists of various persuasions. Support assures the patient that help is possible and available. Support consists of paying attention to the patient, indicating to the patient that the problem, which seems overwhelming, is solvable, and indicating ways in which the problem might be solved. Reassurance is part of the same general package. Often, the fear, depression, and anxiety the patient feels are more a function of the fact that the patient has a problem than a function of the problem itself. That is, the patient is frightened and anxious because of the unfamiliar feelings of fear and anxiety produced by the basic problem, and this secondary fear and anxiety are greater than the primary fear and anxiety produced by the original problem. When the patient is reassured that the problem, and the feelings produced by the problem, are not unusual and not a sign that psychological disaster is imminent, the subsequent relief removes a significant portion of the emotional upset. People often get more upset because they are upset than they do over the unavoidably distressing vicissitudes of life. Encouragement is especially stressed by Erickson (Haley 1963, 1973), who points out to the patient the positive aspects of the patient's response. For example, the patient who expresses hopelessness must have some hope, otherwise the time, energy, and expense of psychotherapy would not have been attempted in the first place. The passive patient has, nonetheless, endured, and the patient who has failed repeatedly has, at least, continued to try. There is a danger with uncritical encouragement, however. The emphasis upon the positive must be a positive that the patient cannot deny. Otherwise, the therapist's encouragement merely tells the patient that the therapist does not understand the situation, and this perceived failure to understand has the unfortunate effect of confirming the patient's fears, rather than allaying them.

Most therapies use suggestion in some form. These may be quite explicit, as are the directions used in behavior therapy. The problem is to make suggestions that the patient will follow. All patients have a tendency to resist the suggestions of the therapist. This resistance may be rooted in some dynamic reason (as analytic theory would suggest) or be rooted in ordinary habit and behavioral inertia. Therefore, it is important that suggestions be made in such a way that the patient will follow them. Erickson (Haley, 1963, 1973) developed the technique of discussing the patient's problem, leading up to a suggested solution, but then diverging on a tangent in the discussion, leaving the patient hanging on the edge of a suggested action. The tension of teetering on the edge of a suggested action makes the patient much more likely to accept the suggestion, when it finally comes, if only to break the tension of anticipation. Erickson stresses the importance of getting the patient to *do* something. Once the pattern of behavior has changed, even slightly, the patient has begun to move away from a maladaptive pattern of behavior and toward a more adaptive pattern of behavior. In making suggestions and encouraging the patient, it is important that the suggestions fit within the pattern of the patient's thinking and behaving, and that these suggestions lead to an action that is different, however slightly, from the previous, unsuccessful behavior.

Dynamic techniques. Dynamic approaches to short-term psychotherapy (Balint et al., 1972; Binder & Smokler, 1980; Haley, 1973; Malan, 1963, 1976; Mann, 1973; Marmor, 1979; Sifneos, 1972) stress focusing upon a key conflict, and interpreting and working through that conflict. Ursano and Dressler (1974) suggest, in fact, that the chief distinction between short-term therapy and unlimited psychotherapy is that brief therapy focuses upon a single conflict, while ordinary therapy is either unfocused or focused upon many conflicts.

The nature of the focus may be on the therapist-patient relationship (Balint et al., 1972), the basic separation-individuation conflict (Mann, 1973), the developmental stage of the patient (Haley, 1973; Burke et al., 1979), a nuclear childhood experience (Binder & Smokler, 1980), or some other, unspecified type of conflict. In any case, the basic technique of the therapist is to quickly identify the single most important conflict, keep the therapy focused on this conflict, and keep the patient working on this conflict. If the conflict on which the therapy is to be focused is chosen jointly by the therapist and the patient (Sifneos, 1972), the agreement becomes a kind of contract to which the therapist and the patient commit themselves.

Behavioral techniques. Behavioral techniques also emphasize focusing therapy, but the focus is upon specific maladaptive behaviors rather than upon underlying psychological conflict (Butcher & Koss, 1978; Lazarus, 1972; Rathus & Nevid, 1977; Sloane et al., 1975). The most commonly used behavioral techniques are relaxation, systematic desensitization, modeling, rehearsal, and guided practice. Reviewing the research literature, Marks (1978) concludes that the single most important and effective behavioral technique is to systematically expose the patient to the feared and avoided stimulus, extinguishing the maladaptive response. Generally, the most successful applications of behavioral techniques combine a variety of techniques. Commonly used combinations are systematic desensitization, modeling, rehearsal, and guided practice, with feedback of the change in behavior to the patient.

Other techniques.   A wide variety of other techniques have been proposed for use in short-term psychotherapy. Perhaps the most intriguing of these techniques are those developed by Milton Erickson (Bandler & Grinder, 1975, 1976, 1979; Haley, 1963, 1973). Haley (1963) summarizes these methods by concluding that, "the basic rule of brief psychotherapy would seem to be to encourage the symptom in such a way that the patient cannot continue to utilize it" (p. 55). This is accomplished by, in effect, asking the patient to continue to do whatever the patient is already doing. This undercuts the patient's resistance because, by instructing the patient to continue the current behavior, the patient is now doing what the therapist suggests. Thus, having established the pattern of the patient following the therapist's instructions, the therapist then subtly suggests that the patient vary the behavior slightly in the direction of more-adaptive behavior. The technique might be likened to falling in step with another person with whom you are walking and then, having established the pattern, altering your own step slightly and thus inducing your companion also to alter pace in order to continue to remain in step. This technique requires a high degree of sensitivity to the patient's feelings and behavior.

Bandler and Grinder (1979) suggest finding out, in detail, the steps of feeling, thought, and behavior that lead to the undesired behavior. The undesired behavior can then be altered by instructing the patient to change the order in which the steps occur, deleting a step, inserting additional steps, or in other inventive ways disrupting the maladaptive pattern, and inserting in its place a more adaptive pattern.

Other suggested techniques include confrontation (Sifneos, 1972), marathon encounter (Small, 1979), guided fantasy (Bandler & Grinder, 1979), eidetics (Ahsen & Lazarus, 1972) and description of early memories (Binder & Smokler, 1980). There are, of course, many other techniques that have been proposed and used. Of the invention of new therapeutic techniques, there is no end.

Termination of therapy

There is no general agreement on the termination of therapy. It is generally agreed that some specific time limit should be stated at the beginning of therapy, but relatively few insist upon adhering to the stated limit (e.g., Mann, 1973). Probably the most common method is to taper off the frequency of sessions and finally terminate when the patient expresses satisfaction with the results achieved. Most therapists tell the patient that additional sessions may be scheduled in the future, if the patient feels the need. Although Mann stresses the importance of the reality of the time limit to therapy, in view of the fact that most patients remain in therapy for only six sessions or so, it probably would be more in keeping with reality if the therapist began with the assumption that the patient is going to allow six sessions or so for the therapy to get to where it is going, so the therapist had best be about the business of therapy so that it can be completed in the time the patient allots for it.

Hazards of short-term therapy

There has been developing an increased awareness that therapy can harm as well as help (e.g., Bergin & Lambert, 1978). Severely disturbed patients appear to be particularly at risk. Small (1979, chap. 22) stresses the dangers in oversimplification, failure to carefully diagnose so that the problem is not fully understood, and plunging into therapy without a careful and accurate assessment of the problem. Overlooking the transference relationships, particularly with seriously disturbed patients, may also lead to serious difficulty. It is important for the therapist to be open and flexible, so that deterioration in the patient's condition can be quickly recognized, the case reassessed, and the therapeutic technique revised.

Reviews (e.g., Butcher & Koss, 1978; Small, 1979) of studies of brief psychotherapy indicate that brief psychotherapy is about as effective as unlimited psychotherapy. Most studies report improvement in about 70 percent of the cases. The differences between treated and untreated groups appear to be maximum at the conclusion of therapy, but the differences tend to disappear over time, leading Butcher and Koss (1978) to conclude that therapy serves chiefly to speed up the process of change, thus reducing the duration and total amount of suffering. In comparing various approaches to brief therapy, they also conclude that, "there is little support for a statement of significant superiority for any of the diverse approaches to brief psychotherapy examined to date" (1978, p. 756).

SUMMARY

Although brief psychotherapy is generally seen as a relatively new innovation, in actuality most psychotherapy is relatively brief. Further, the pressure of large numbers of people needing therapy combined with the pressure to develop relatively economical forms of therapy indicate that brief psychotherapy will be the form of treatment received by most patients in the future. Crisis intervention is a special case of brief psychotherapy, in which a traumatic incident has caused the need for rapid intervention.

Present-day crisis intervention is characterized by a diversity of approaches, techniques, and helpers. Programs generally fall into one of two models, or a combination of them: namely, the public-health model or the crisis-center model. The former employs an outreach philosophy, and the latter is distinguished by 24-hour availability of services. A third model, crisis therapy, is emerging as a means of providing brief professional psychotherapy for patients in mental health settings.

A crisis involves the confrontation and assimilation of an unwanted environmental event through an emotional and intellectual process called realization. This process is facilitated by a variety of therapeutic tactics and the involvement of a warm and supportive helper.

Helpers in crisis intervention include both paraprofessionals and professionals, and the latter can also occupy roles as clinical backups, trainers, supervisors, researchers, and theory builders.

Brief psychotherapy derives from a variety of psychotherapeutic traditions. These traditions have produced a variety of techniques. Most therapists, regardless of the tradition from which they stem, use a variety of techniques. This rampant eclecticism reveals a need for, and is stimulating the development of, a meta-theory which will integrate the various approaches to psychotherapy.

All brief forms of psychotherapy have certain characteristics in common. They stress quick diagnosis and treatment planning, pre-therapy preparation of the patient, activity and flexibility on the part of the therapist, the importance of a positive relationship between the patient and the therapist, and focusing therapy on a limited (but crucial) area of the patient's behavior.

There is some disagreement concerning the selection of patients for brief psychotherapy, with the consensus seeming to be that brief methods are especially suited to patients who have had a previous good adjustment, and whose distress derives primarily from a stressful environmental situation.

Brief psychotherapy has its dangers, particularly with seriously disturbed patients.

Research indicates that brief psychotherapy is about as effective as time-unlimited therapy. There does not appear to be any difference in effectiveness among the various methods of brief psychotherapy.

REFERENCES

Ahsen, A. & Lazarus, A. A. Eidetics: An internal behavior approach. In Lazarus, A. A. (Ed.) *Clinical Behavior Therapy.* New York: Brunner/Mazel, 1972, pp. 87–99.

Alexander, F., & French, T. M. *Psychoanalytic therapy.* New York: Ronald Press, 1946.

Apsler, R., & Hodas, M. B. Evaluating hotlines with simulated calls. *Crisis Intervention,* 1976, *7,* 111–121.

Auerback, S. M., & Kilmann, P. R. Crisis intervention: A review of outcome research. *Psychological Bulletin,* 1977, *84,* 1189–1217.

Bagley, C. The evaluation of a suicide prevention scheme by an ecological method. *Social Science and Medicine,* 1968, *2,* 1–14.

Baldwin, B. A. Crisis intervention: An overview of theory and practice. *Counseling Psychologist,* 1979, *8,* 43–52.

Balint, M., Ornstein, P. H., & Balint, E. *Focal psychotherapy: An example of applied psychoanalysis.* Philadelphia: J. B. Lippincott, 1972.

Bandler, R., & Grinder, J. *The structure of magic* (2 vols.). Palo Alto, Calif.: Science and Behavior Books, 1975, 1976.

Bandler, R., & Grinder, J. *Frogs into princes: Neurolinguistic programming.* Moab, Utah: Real People Press, 1979.

Beck, A. T. *Cognitive therapy and the emotional disorders.* New York: New American Library, 1976.

Bellack, L. The therapeutic relationship in brief psychotherapy. *American Journal of Psychotherapy,* 1979, *33,* 564–571.

Bergin, A. E., & Lambert, M. J. The evaluation of therapeutic outcomes. In S. L. Garfield & A. E. Bergin (Eds.), *Handbook of psychotherapy and behavior change.* New York: John Wiley & Sons, 1978.

Bierenbaum, H., Nichols, M. P., & Schwartz, A. J. Effects of varying session length and frequency in brief psychotherapy. *Journal of Consulting and Clinical Psychology,* 1976, *44,* 790–798.

Binder, J. L., & Smokler, I. Early memories: A technical aid to focus in time-limited psychotherapy. *Psychotherapy: Theory, Research, and Practice,* 1980, *17,* 52–62.

Bleach, G., & Claiborn, W. L. Initial evaluation of hotline telephone crisis centers. *Community Mental Health Journal,* 1974, *10,* 387–394.

Bloom, B. Definitional aspects of the crisis concept. *Journal of Consulting Psychology,* 1963, *27,* 498–502.

Brockopp, G. W. Hanging loose at a suicide prevention and crisis service: Or a design for the future. *Crisis Intervention,* 1976, *7,* 111–121.

Burke, J. D., White, H.S., & Havens, L. L. Which short-term therapy? *Archives of General Psychiatry,* 1979, *36,* 177–186.

Butcher, J. N., & Koss, M. P. Research on brief and crisis-oriented therapies. In S. L. Garfield & A. E. Bergin (Eds.), *Handbook of psychotherapy and behavior change.* New York: John Wiley & Sons, 1978.

Butcher, J. N., & Maudal, G. R. Crisis intervention. In I. B. Weiner (Ed.), *Clinical methods in psychology.* New York: John Wiley & Sons, 1976.

Caplan, G. *Principles of preventive psychiatry.* New York: Basic Books, 1964.

Caplan, G. *Support systems and community mental health.* New York: Behavioral Publications, 1974.

Carothers, J. E., & Inslee, L. J. Level of empathic understanding offered by volunteer telephone services. *Journal of Counseling Psychology,* 1974, *21,* 274–276.

Clarkin, J. F., Frances, A., Taintor, Z., & Warburg, M. Training in brief therapy: A survey of psychiatric residency programs. *American Journal of Psychiatry*, 1980, *137*, 978–979.

Cohen, R. E., & Ahearn, F. L. *Handbook for mental health care of disaster victims.* Baltimore: Johns Hopkins University Press, 1980.

Delfin, P. E. Components of effective telephone intervention: A critical-incidents analysis. *Crisis Intervention*, 1978, *9*, 50–68.

Delfin, P. E., & Hartsough, D. M. Increasing informational competence in crisis workers through programmed instruction. *American Journal of Community Psychology*, 1979, *7*, 111–115.

Dengrove, E. Practical behavioral diagnosis. In A. A. Lazarus (Ed.), *Clinical behavior therapy.* New York: Brunner & Mazel, 1972.

DeVol, T. E. Does level of professional training make a difference in crisis-intervention counseling? *Journal of Community Health*, 1976, *2*, 31–35.

Dixon, M. C., & Burns, J. L. Crisis theory, active learning, and the training of telephone-crisis volunteers. *Journal of Community Psychology*, 1974, *2*, 120–125.

Dixon, M. C., & Burns, J. L. The training of telephone crisis-intervention volunteers. *American Journal of Community Psychology*, 1975, *3*, 145–150.

Doyle, W. W., Foreman, M. E., & Wales, E. Effects of supervision in the training of nonprofessional crisis-intervention counselors. *Journal of Counseling Psychology*, 1977, *24*, 72–78.

Dressler, D. M., Donovan, J. M., & Geller, R. A. Life stress and emotional crises: The idiosyncratic interpretation of life events. *Comprehensive Psychiatry*, 1976, *7*, 549–558.

Durlak, J. A. Comparative effectiveness of paraprofessional and professional helpers. *Psychological Bulletin*, 1979, *86*, 80–92.

Echterling, L. G. & Hartsough, D. M. Relationship of telephone crisis intervention process to successful crisis resolution. Paper read at Eleventh International Congress for Suicide Prevention and Crisis Intervention, Paris, 1981.

Echterling, L. G., Hartsough, D. M., & Zarle, T. H. Testing a model for the process of telephone crisis intervention. *American Journal of Community Psychology*, 1980, *8*, 715–725.

Ellis, A. *Reason and emotion in psychotherapy.* Secaucus, N.J.: Lyle Stuart, 1962.

Erikson, K. T. *Everything in its path: Destruction of community in the Buffalo Creek flood.* New York: Simon & Schuster, 1976.

Farberow, N. L., & Shneidman, E. S. (Eds.). *The cry for help.* New York: McGraw-Hill, 1965.

Farberow, N. L., Shneidman, E. S., Litman, R. E., Wold, C. I., Heilig, S. M., & Kramer, J. Suicide prevention around the clock. *American Journal of Orthopsychiatry*, 1966, *36*, 551–558.

Fowler, D. E., & McGee, R. K. Assessing the performance of telephone crisis workers: The development of a technical effectiveness scale. In D. Lester & G. Brockopp (Eds.), *Crisis intervention and counseling by telephone.* Springfield, Ill.: Charles C Thomas, 1973.

France, K. Evaluation of lay volunteer crisis telephone workers. *American Journal of Community Psychology*, 1975, *3*, 145–150.

Frank, J. D. Therapeutic components of psychotherapy: A 25-year progress report of research. *Journal of Nervous and Mental Disease*, 1974, *159*, 325–542.

Garfield, S. L. Research on client variables in psychotherapy. In S. L. Garfield & A. E. Bergin (Eds.), *Handbook of psychotherapy and behavior change.* New York: John Wiley & Sons, 1978.

Garfield, S. L., & Wolpin, M. Expectations regarding psychotherapy. *Journal of Nervous and Mental Disease,* 1963, *137,* 353–362.

Getz, W. L., Fujita, B. N., & Allen, D. The use of paraprofessionals in crisis intervention: Evaluation of an innovative program. *American Journal of Community Psychology,* 1975, *3,* 135–144.

Golan, N. *Treatment in crisis situations.* New York: Free Press, 1978.

Golann, S. E. Community psychology and mental health: An analysis of strategies and a survey of training. In I. Iscoe & C. D. Speilberger (Eds.), *Community psychology: Perspectives in training and research.* New York: Appleton-Century-Crofts, 1970.

Grayson, H. *Short-term approaches to psychotherapy. New York: Human Sciences Press, 1979.*

Greenhill, M. H. Psychiatric units in general hospitals: 1979. *Hospital and Community Psychiatry,* 1979, *30,* 169–182.

Grinker, R. R., & Speigel, J. P. *War neuroses.* Philadelphia: Blakiston, 1945.

Haley, J. *Strategies of psychotherapy.* New York: Grune & Stratton, 1963.

Haley, J. *Uncommon therapy: The psychiatric techniques of Milton H. Erickson, M. D.* New York: W. W. Norton, 1973.

Halpern, H. A. Crisis theory: A definitional study. *Community Mental Health Journal,* 1973, *9,* 342–349.

Hansell, N. *The person-in-distress.* New York: Human Sciences Press, 1976.

Hartsough, D. M. *Lafayette Crisis Center Volunteer Training Program.* Program report read at Southeastern Psychological Association, New Orleans, 1976.

Heilig, S. M. Training in suicide prevention. *Bulletin of Suicidology,* 1970, *6,* 41–44.

Heilig, S. M., Farberow, N. L., Litman, R. E., & Shneidman, E. S. The role of nonprofessional volunteers in a suicide-prevention center. *Community Mental Health Journal,* 1968, *4,* 287–295.

Heitler, J. B. Preparatory techniques in initiating psychotherapy with lower-class, unsophisticated patients. *Psychological Bulletin,* 1976, *83,* 339–352.

Hoff, L. A., & Williams, T. Counseling the rape victim and her family. *Crisis Intervention,* 1975, *6,* 2–13.

Horowitz, M. J. Diagnosis and treatment of stress-response syndromes: General principles. In H. J. Parad, H. L. P. Resnik & L. G. Parad (Eds.), *Emergency and disaster management: A mental health sourcebook.* Bowie, Md.: Charles Press, 1976.

Jacobson, G. F., Strickler, M., & Morley, W. E. Generic and individual approaches to crisis intervention. *American Journal of Public Health,* 1968, *58,* 338–343.

Jaffe, P. G., Thompson, J. K., & Paquin, M. J. Immediate family-crisis intervention as preventive mental health: The family-consultant service. *Professional Psychology,* 1978, *9,* 551–560.

Jones, E. *The life and work of Sigmund Freud* (Vol. 2). New York: Basic Books, 1955.

Kardiner, A. *The traumatic neuroses of war.* New York: Hoeber, 1941.

Kendall, P. C., & Hollon, S. D. *Cognitive-behavioral interventions.* New-York: Academic Press, 1979.

Knickerbocker, D. A. & McGee, R. K. Clinical effectiveness of nonprofessional and professional telephone workers in a crisis intervention center. In D. Lester and G. W. Brockopp (Eds.), *Crisis intervention and counseling by telephone.* Springfield, IL: Charles C. Thomas, 1973.

Knowles, D. On the tendency of volunteer helpers to give advice. *Journal of Counseling Psychology,* 1979, *26,* 352–354.

Koss, M. P. Length of psychotherapy for clients seen in private practice. *Journal of Consulting and Clinical Psychology,* 1979, *47,* 210–212.

Lazarus, A. A. *Clinical behavior therapy.* New York: Brunner & Mazel, 1972.

Lee, W. G. Situational ethical issues in crisis-intervention counseling. *Crisis Intervention,* 1977, *8,* 19–24.

Levy, L. The role of a natural mental health service delivery system in dealing with basic human problems. In G. A. Specter, & W. L. Claiborn (Eds.), *Crisis Intervention.* New York: Behavioral Publications, 1973.

Litman, R. E., Shneidman, E. S., Heilig, S. M., & Kramer, J. A. Suicide prevention telephone service. *Journal of American Medical Association,* 1965, *192,* 21–25.

Lorion, R. P. Patient and therapist variables in the treatment of low-income patients. *Psychological Bulletin,* 1974, *81,* 334–354.

Malan, D. H. *A study of brief psychotherapy.* London: Tavistock Publications, 1963.

Malan, D. H. *The frontier of brief psychotherapy: An example of the convergence of research and clinical practice.* New York: Plenum Press, 1976.

Mann, J. *Time-limited psychotherapy.* Cambridge, Mass.: Harvard University Press, 1973.

Maris, R., & Connor, H. E. Do crisis services work? A follow-up of a psychiatric-outpatient sample. *Journal of Health and Social Behavior,* 1973, *14,* 311–322.

Marks, I. Behavioral psychotherapy of adult neuroses. In S. L. Garfield & A. E. Bergin (Eds.), *Handbook of psychotherapy and behavior change.* New York: John Wiley & Sons, 1978.

Marmar, J. Short-term dynamic psychotherapy. *American Journal of Psychiatry,* 1979, *136,* 149–155.

McCarthy, B. W. & Berman, A. L. The development of a student operated crisis center. *Personnel and Guidance Journal,* 1971, *49,* 523–528.

McCord, J. B., & Packwood, W. T. Crisis centers and hotlines: A survey. *Personnel and Guidance Journal,* 1973, *51,* 723–728.

McGee, R. K., Knickerbocker, D. A., Fowler, D. E., Jennings, B., Ansel, E. L., Zelenka, M. H., & Marcus, S. Evaluation of crisis-intervention programs and personnel: A summary and critique. *Life-Threatening Behavior,* 1972, *2,* 168–182.

Menninger, K. *Theory of psychoanalytic technique.* New York: Basic Books, 1958.

Morley, W. E. Theory of crisis intervention. *Pastoral Psychology,* 1970, *21,* 14–20.

Motto, J. A. New approaches to crisis intervention. *Suicide and Life-Threatening Behavior,* 1979, *9,* 173–184.

Motto, J. A., Brooks, R. M., Ross, C. P., & Allen, N. H. *Standards for suicide and crisis centers.* New York: Behavioral Publications, 1974.

Nash, E. H., Hoehn-Saric, R., Battle, C. C., Stone, A. R., Imber, S. D., & Frank, J. D. Systematic preparation of patients for short-term psychotherapy: II. Relation to characteristics of patient, therapist, and the psychotherapeutic process. *Journal of Nervous and Mental Disease,* 1965, *140,* 374–383.

O'Donnell, J. M., & George, K. The use of volunteers in a community mental health center emergency and reception service: A comparative study of professional and lay telephone counseling. *Community Mental Health Journal,* 1977, *13,* 3–12.

Parad, H. J., Resnik, H. L. P., & Parad, L. G. (Eds.). *Emergency and disaster management: A mental health sourcebook.* Bowie, Md.: Charles Press, 1976.

Parkes, C. M. The first year of bereavement. *Psychiatry,* 1970, *33,* 444–466.

Rathus, S. A., & Nevid, J. S. *Behavior therapy: Strategies for solving problems in living.* New York: New American Library, 1977.

Rogers, C. R. *Client-centered therapy.* Boston: Houghton-Mifflin, 1951.

Rosenbaum, A., & Calhoun, J. F. The use of the telephone hotline in crisis intervention: A review. *Journal of Community Psychology,* 1977, *5,* 325–339.

Rusk, T. N., & Gerner, R. H. A study of the process of emergency psychotherapy. *American Journal of Psychiatry,* 1972, *128,* 882–885.

Schlenker, M. The telephone therapy program: Problems and prospects. *Crisis Intervention,* 1970, *2,* 11–16.

Sifneos, P. E. *Short-term psychotherapy and emotional crises.* Cambridge, Mass.: Harvard University Press, 1972.

Slaikeu, K. A., Lester, D., & Tulkin, S. R. Show versus no-show: A comparison of referral calls to a suicide-prevention and crisis service. *Journal of Consulting and Clinical Psychology,* 1973, *40,* 481–486.

Slaikeu, K. A., Tulkin, S. R., & Speer, D. C. Process and outcome in the evaluation of telephone-counseling referrals. *Journal of Consulting and Clinical Psychology,* 1975, *43,* 700–707.

Slaikeu, K. A., & Willis, M. A. Caller feedback on counselor performance in telephone crisis intervention: A follow-up study. *Crisis Intervention,* 1978, *9,* 42–49.

Slem, C. M., & Cotler, S. Crisis phone services: Evaluation of a hotline program. *American Journal of Community Psychology,* 1973, *1,* 219–227.

Sloane, R. B., Staples, F. R., Cristol, A. H., Yorkston, N. J., & Whipple, K. Short-term analytically oriented psychotherapy versus behavior therapy. *American Journal of Psychiatry,* 1975, *132,* 373–374.

Small, L. *The briefer psychotherapies* (2d ed.). New York: Brunner & Mazel, 1979.

Speer, D. C., & Schultz, M. An instrument for assessing caller-reported benefits of calls to a telephone crisis center. *Journal of Consulting and Clinical Psychology,* 1975, *43,* 102.

Stelmachers, Z. T., Lund, S. H., & Meade, C. J. Hennepin County Crisis Intervention Center: Evaluation of its effectiveness. *Evaluation,* 1972, 61–65.

Strupp, H. H. Success and failure in time-limited psychotherapy: A systematic comparison of two cases: Comparison I. *Archives of General Psychiatry,* 1980, *37,* 595–603. (a)

Strupp, H. H. Success and failure in time-limited psychotherapy: A systematic comparison of two cases: Comparison 2. *Archives of General Psychiatry,* 1980, *37,* 708–716. (b)

Strupp, H. H. Success and failure in time-limited psychotherapy: With special reference to a lay counselor. *Archives of General Psychiatry,* 1980, *37,* 831–841. (c)

Strupp, H. H. Success and failure in time-limited psychotherapy: Further evidence: Comparison 4. *Archives of General Psychiatry,* 1980, *37,* 947–954. (d)

Swensen, C. H. Commitment and the personality of the successful psychotherapist. *Psychotherapy: Theory, Research, and Practice,* 1971, *8,* 31–36.

Swensen, C. H. *Introduction to interpersonal relations.* Glenview, Ill.: Scott, Foresman, 1973.

Swensen, C. H. Ego development and a general model for counseling and psychotherapy. *The Personnel and Guidance Journal,* 1980, *58,* 382–388.

Taplin, J. Crisis theory: Critique and reformulation. *Community Mental Health Journal,* 1971, *7,* 12–23.

Thomas, W. I. *Source book of social origins.* Chicago: University of Chicago Press, 1909.

Ullman, L. P., & Krasner, L. *Case studies in behavior modification.* New York: Holt, Rinehart, & Winston, 1965.

Ursano, R. H., & Dressler, D. M. Brief versus long-term therapy: A treatment decision. *Journal of Nervous and Mental Disease,* 1974, *159,* 164–171.

Williams, W. V., Lee, J., & Polak, P. R. Crisis intervention: Effects of crisis intervention on family survivors of sudden-death situations. *Community Mental Health Journal,* 1976, *12,* 128–136.

22

Principles of consultation-liaison psychology

Douglas S. Faust, Ph.D. *

The practice of consultation-liaison psychology, briefly defined as the provision of psychological services within the general medical setting, represents a significant extension of the work of the traditional clinical psychologist. It is the intent of this chapter to describe the scope of involvement of psychologists in acute care medical settings and the unique contributions of the consultation-liaison psychologist, as distinguished from the more general area of behavioral medicine and the more specific tasks of the consultation-liaison psychiatrist. A brief introduction to the training and background required and an outline for the provision of consultation-liaison services will also be provided.

Increasing numbers of psychologists have become involved in the general medical sector, whether viewed primarily as teachers (Authier, 1979; Sladen, 1979), consultants (Bibace & Walsh, 1979; Bloom, 1979; Schroeder, 1979), or as members of the medical-treatment team (Drotar, 1977; Keith, 1979; Lewis, 1978; Linton, 1981; Stabler, 1979). One recent survey of health-service providers indicates that 30 percent of the reporting psychologists provide some direct service to hospital inpatients (Dorken & Webb, 1979a, 1979b), and an increasing number of medical schools offer full medical-staff membership to psychologists (Copeland, 1980; Matarazzo, Lubin, & Nathan, 1978). Whether in or out of the hospital setting, psychologists find themselves working with increasing numbers of patients whose psychological problems anticipate or are associated with physical health problems and their treatment or consequences. Some of these medical problems will be obvious, but most will not; as a consequence, it is becoming increasingly important for the clinical psychologist to be highly skilled in the recognition of the medical factors which may precipitate, mimic, or present as disturbances of behavior, emotion, or

* Assistant Professor, Department of Psychiatry and Behavioral Sciences, Department of Pediatrics, Eastern Virginia Medical School, Norfolk, Virginia.

cognition (Hall, 1980; Hall, Gardner, Popkin, LeCann, & Stickney, 1981; Hall, Popkin, Devaul, Faillace, & Stickney, 1978; Strain & Grossman, 1975). The majority of the mental health problems present in the general population—the most recent estimate indicates that 15 percent of the U.S. population is affected—are not addressed in traditional mental health care settings; current NIMH figures estimate that three fifths of these individuals are initially identified and treated in the general medical (primary care) setting (Reiger, Goldberg, & Taube, 1978). Conversely, it has been observed that psychologically disturbed individuals demonstrate an overall higher morbidity for physical disease far in excess of that found in the general population (Hall, 1980; Koranyi, 1979).

Recognition of the existence of this common patient population reflects curiously on an article by Jastrow (1929), written 50 years ago, when he noted the overlapping concerns of psychology and medicine and called for a return to a "sympathetic kinship," a point echoed by others of that age (Abrahams, 1935). Behavioral medicine, an area reviewed at length in another chapter of this volume, is the modern manifestation of this kinship. The emergence of behavioral medicine as an "interdisciplinary field" (Schwartz & Weiss, 1978a, 1978b) has broadened the scope for all psychologists working in the biomedical area. Consultation-liaison psychology represents a significant clinical portion of that area.

Although many of the basic skills used in traditional service-delivery modes (assessment, individual, family- and group-therapy techniques) are applicable in work with persons in the medical setting, the approach, range of problems, and scope of the problems addressed differ significantly.

Traditionally, the provision of mental health services in the nonpsychiatric medical setting has been the responsibility of the psychiatrist. Trained as physicians, consultation-liaison psychiatrists have relied heavily upon an organic approach to the treatment of mental disturbance, use of psychotropic medications, and competence in recognizing the psychological manifestations of physical illness. Consultations to general medical units have historically been limited to work with patients who manifest acute or chronic symptoms of psychological disturbance, or who display somatic symptoms which seem to be closely related to psychological factors, as in psychosomatic disease considered in the narrow sense (Iwasaki, 1979). In the former instance, the consultant's role was to assist the referring physician in the management of the patient through the use of psychotropic medications or by the transfer of the patient to a specialized psychiatric-treatment unit. In cases involving psychosomatic illness, the patient would be transferred to the consultant for psychotherapeutic follow-up and then returned to the family physician following treatment.

While these types of consultation requests still constitute a significant portion of the referrals to both psychologists and psychiatrists in consultation to medical units, other areas of involvement have emerged. These include increased attention to those psychological factors which have been demonstrated to affect a patient's response to illness, its treatment, and its consequences; less directly, they involve providing liaison (teaching) services to staff in special-care units, intensive care, cardiac-care units, renal dialysis, burn treatment, and hospice units, and consultation regarding the relationships between staff and physicians and the patient and their families. Recent innovative, applied research in the hospital has resulted in clinically relevant changes in the management of clinic areas, patient compliance, and patient education. Strain (1977) notes that the standard psychiatric-training program does not adequately prepare the resident with sufficient skills to adequately address these latter kinds of problems, a concern shared by others in the area (Houpt, Orleans, George, & Brodie, 1980; Iwasaki, 1979; Lipowski, 1975, 1977, 1979; Lloyd, 1980; McKegney, 1972; Orleans, Houpt, & Trent, 1979; Pasnau, 1975). By contrast, the clinical psychologist has many of the key skills (consultation, applied research, systematic behavioral analysis—at the individual, family, and systems levels—and familiarity with brief-intervention techniques) necessary to address these areas. It is this which constitutes the major contribution of the behavioral scientist in the medical setting.

DEFINITION

Consultation psychology may be defined as the services provided by psychologists outside of specialized behavioral- or psychiatric-treatment units: (1) to assist the nonpsychiatric physician in the diagnosis of patients on whose behalf psychological intervention appears indicated and (2) to provide appropriate treatment to those patients, either directly or in cooperation with other members of the medical team. In addition, consultation psychology provides a basis for research in the behavioral aspects of medical illness.

Although the terms *consultation* and *liaison* are often used interchangably, liaison is a somewhat different aspect of a consultant's work. *Liaison psychology* refers to the services provided primarily to the physician and staff, tying together the treatment of the patient and family, using educational conferences, psychosocial-teaching rounds, and specialized meetings intended to integrate psychosocial theory and practice (Krakowski, 1977; Wellisch & Pasnau, 1979).

Psychological-consultation services to medical patients are, by the nature of the setting and the relatively few professional staff involved in the provision of the services, short-term and diagnostic in nature. As a consequence, consultative services focus on the identification of psychological disturbance, the relief of primary symptoms, and the provision of management suggestions (whether inpatient or outpatient), rather than on the long-term resolution of the problem (Drotar, 1979; Frank, Heller, & Kornfeld, 1979; Grey, Genel, & Tamborlane, 1980; Kahana, 1972;

Lewis, 1978). Problems requiring more extensive intervention are then referred to an appropriate resource.

The complex etiology of psychological problems, as they may present in the medical setting, requires an approach to the patient which is significantly different from that used in the traditional medical consultation. In the medical model, the house officer, resident, or attending physician calls in a specialist to offer advice on a specific diagnosis or treatment issue. The consultant reads the medical record, examines the patient, performs or orders the indicated tests, and renders an opinion, usually to the primary care physician. In cases involving psychological or emotional problems, the etiology and formulation of treatment are much more idiosyncratic, and resolution is dependent upon the development of a cooperative relationship with the patient (Koocher, Sourkes, & Keane, 1979), a process which may extend well beyond the period of the inpatient hospital care.

Relatively little has been published regarding the use of psychologists in a consultation-liaison capacity in the general medical setting, despite extensive development of the concepts of traditional consultation-liaison psychiatry (Fink, 1977; Kimball, 1979b; Kimball & Krakowski, 1979; Krakowski, 1973; Lipowski, 1967a, 1967b, 1968, 1974; Pasnau, 1975; Schwab, 1968; Strain & Grossman, 1975). Lipowski's (1974) observation that only the medically trained psychiatrist can fill the widening gap between the "overspecialized physician" and the "psychosocially oriented but medically naive behavioral scientist" is characteristic of many writers in the area and reflects traditional professional and economic concerns. By contrast, preliminary research on the utilization of the psychologist-consultant in the medical setting indicates widespread acceptance by practicing physicians.

Results of a questionnaire administered to the physicians of the general medical and neurological services of a large Veterans Administrative Medical Center served by a psychological consultation-liaison service indicated overall acceptance of psychologists in this role (Schenkenberg, Peterson, Wood, & DaBell, 1981). Seventy-five percent of those responding felt that the psychologist's lack of formal medical training did not significantly impair his/her effectiveness, and 86 percent felt that the fact that psychologists cannot prescribe medication did not represent an important issue in the context of a medical/neurological unit. Ready availability and close contact with the medical team were viewed as critically important variables in this sample.

Billowitz and Friedson (1979) compared the percentage of consultant recommendations followed as a function of professional training (psychology versus psychiatry) and type of recommendation. No significant differences were found between consultants on recommendations involving disposition, fitness for surgery, management following discharge, medication (including, but not limited to, antipsychotics), other services to assist the patient, ward management, and their needs to obtain further information for diagnosis (Gabinet & Friedson, 1980).

Consultation-liaison psychology thus addresses the acute, short-term, applied aspects of the practice of behavioral science in the nonpsychiatric medical setting—the secondary and tertiary aspects of care, as they have been characterized by Caplan (1964, 1970). Potentially free of the organic biases inherent in traditional consultation-liaison psychiatry, and less tightly bound to the medical or disease model of illness, the consultation-liaison psychologist directs his or her primary attention to "observables"—patient behaviors, the effect of the medical environment, the patient's reaction to disease or illness, and the complex interactions of the medical treatment team.

TRAINING

With increasing numbers of psychologists interested in working in health care settings, greater numbers of programs have become available to offer formal training and supervision. By and large, these have been developed in association with established clinical training programs, with all or a significant portion of the training received in the context of a medical center, university hospital, or general medical-surgical hospital (Belar, 1980; Burnstein, Barnes, & Quesada, 1976; Cohen, Lubin, & Nathan, 1979; Olbrisch & Sechrest, 1979). As with any new subspecialty training area, there exists no single program intended to train clinical psychologists in consultation-liaison work. However, training is available at both the internship and post-doctoral level (Faust, Ulissi, & Thurber, 1980; Wellisch & Pasnau, 1979).

The psychologist interested in consultation-liaison practice should be thoroughly trained in the basic clinical skills, with a strong orientation toward the brief psychotherapies and crisis-intervention and rapid-assessment techniques. While not expected to demonstrate the degree of sophistication in medical matters evidenced in the resident or house officer, certain basic skills are essential in order to provide effective consultation. A basic familiarity with general medical/hospital jargon (abbreviations, style, and format of medical charts and record keeping) are important; the beginner is referred to any good medical dictionary (e.g., Dorland's, 1974). Second, the medical psychologist should have a general familiarity with the basic structure and function of the human body and the organ systems, with emphasis on the impact of changes in bodily function on cognitive function (e.g., changes in liver or metabolic function which may present as an acute organic brain syndrome and the normal, short-term distortions of thought which may follow major heart surgery). The consultant should be familiar with the disease model of illness and its implications for care and treatment within the traditional medical setting. Finally, the consultation-liaison psychologist should have formulated a model, based upon an understanding of the principles of human behavior and learning, to account for the patient's response to the illness situation (Haynes, Taylor, & Sackett, 1979; Magrab, 1978; Pomerleau & Brady, 1979; Schwartz & Weiss, 1978a).

An important aspect of training in consultation-liaison psychology is an awareness of the behavior-medicine interface. This may be broadly broken down into four general areas in which expertise should be sought.

First, the consultation-liaison psychologist should have a thorough grounding in the impact of commonly used psychotropic medications as they may be used to supplement routine medical care (e.g., for use as hypnotic sedatives, tranquilizers, or analgesics) (Strain, 1975). Recent research has shown that 9 to 12 percent of all patients seen in general-medicine clinics will have psychotropic medication prescribed for them by the nonpsychiatric physician (Davidson, Raft, Lewis, & Gebhardt, 1975; Regier et al., 1978). Prescriptive practices vary with the numerous categories of psychotropic agents used, with only limited consultation sought regarding their use (Popkin, Mackenzie, Hall, & Callies, 1980; Popkin, Mackenzie, Hall, & Garrard, 1979). A number of recent articles in this area are available for review by the clinician (Perl, Hall, & Gardner, 1980; Shader, DiMascio, & Appleton, 1970; Strain, 1975).

Second, the clinician should develop a working familiarity with the behavioral side effects of commonly used medications (e.g., antihyperten-rives, autonomic nervous system blockers—MAOs, cardiac glycosides, anticonvulsants, hormonal supplements, and many of the chemotherapeutic agents) and their potentially toxic reactions. Many of these are reviewed in detail in handbooks, such as the *Physician's Desk Reference*, and specialty publications (Hall, 1980; Hall, Stickney, & Gardner, 1980).

Third, the consulting psychologist should have an explicit understanding that certain diseases may initially present with behavioral abnormalities (pancreatic cancer presenting premorbidly as depression), that changes in behavior may represent a complication of a disease or treatment (steroid psychosis), and be aware of the unique psychosocial-adjustment problems associated with specific disease populations. The *Merck Manual* is a handy guide to the presenting characteristics and primary treatment offered in many major diseases, and more specific references on consultation regarding psychological-behavioral problems associated with individual specialty areas are available. These include: infectious disease (Schwab, 1980), endocrine dysfunction (Grey et al., 1980; Moore, 1978; Popkin & Mackenzie, 1980; Waring, Weisz, Heilbrunn, Lefcoe, & Green, 1980), cardiovascular disease (Cassem & Hackett, 1971; Frank et al., 1979; Guynn, 1980; Hackett, Froese, & Vasquez, 1973), pulmonary disorders (Petrich & Holmes, 1980), gastrointestinal and genitourinary (Leukensmeyer, 1980; Mills & Stunkard, 1976; Schuster, 1980), malignancies and hematologic disorders (Agle & Mattsson, 1979; Koocher et al., 1979; Lewis, 1978; O'Malley & Koocher, 1977; Popkin, 1980), seizures and other neurological disturbances (Kirkpatrick & Hall, 1980; Lipowski, 1975), and orthopedic problems (Linton, 1981).

Finally, as in the traditional nonmedical setting, behavior may be interpreted as the person's response to a stressful, otherwise unresolved, situation. Thus, behavior may represent the somatic presentation of an emotional problem (conversion hysteria) or be a learned response to stressful, nonmedically related stimuli (chronic pain).

ESTABLISHING THE CONSULTEE-CONSULTANT RELATIONSHIP

The process of establishing a psychological consultation-liaison service will necessarily involve educating potential consultees on the form and range of services available and the format by which they may be obtained. It will also involve recognition of the common obstacles to effective consultation; these stem from failure to recognize the process of the generation of a consultation, from the divergent expectations of the parties involved, and from the differences between the process of psychological consultation and the medical model (Abram, 1971; Billowitz & Friedson, 1979; Gabinet & Friedson, 1980; Guggenheim, 1978; Hull, 1979; Krakowski, 1973; O'Malley & Koocher, 1977; Sasser & Kinzie, 1979). On the whole, psychological consultation is requested too frequently by a few physicians and too infrequently by many. The quality of the referral is often poor, and as a consequence, the experience is not very rewarding to the referring physician, the patient, the consultant (Altrocchi, 1981).

The two basic kinds of consultations typically used have been the patient-centered model and the consultee-oriented model (Schwab, 1968). The patient-centered (or case-centered) model follows the form of the traditional medical consultation—emphasizing diagnosis, evaluation of existing problem, and recommendation for treatment or appropriate disposition for the patient. As such, it is the most commonly sought form of consultation in the medical setting. In its most rigid form, the consultant deals primarily with the patient and addresses only the explicit questions raised by the referring physician. Typically, the referral question is found to be more complex than initially indicated. This is expecially true in the case of psychological consults, where environmental and interpersonal issues will play a significant role in the patient's reaction in the medical situation, resulting in a broadening of the consultation.

The consultee-oriented (or learning-centered) referral involves working with the physician or other referral source in structuring the problem and in identifying or providing the necessary service. Schiff and Pilot (1959) have identified four situations for which the consultee-oriented approach seems particularly appropriate: (1) where there has been a breakdown in the physician-patient relationship; (2) where a lack of consensus has developed between the patient and the medical staff about the severity of an illness, resulting in the patient leaving the hospital against medical advice; (3) where there appears to be a mismanagement of coexisting medical and psychological problems; and (4) where discord among the staff stemming from divergent points of view regarding patient management may potentially impair the quality of patient care. Whichever model is employed, the special character of the psychological consultation (reflecting patient fears and fantasies about being seen by a psychologist, e.g., "Does my doctor think I'm crazy?") makes the establishment of a close working relationship between the physician and the consulting psychologist particularly crucial.

It is possible to distinguish among four groups of patients for whom consultation-liaison services play an important role in the nonpsychiatric medical setting. These are: (1) patients who demonstrate marked changes in emotional, behavioral, or cognitive function as a consequence of planned or anticipated medical care and treatment; (2) patients who may be expected to require counseling, evaluation, or therapy as a consequence of major or anticipated changes in their physical condition (e.g., terminal illness, major surgery, amputation or other disfigurement, chronic illness); (3) patients whose psychological disturbance is first detected while seeking treatment in the medical setting; and (4) patients with known psychological problems who are receiving required medical care.

CONDUCTING THE CONSULTATION

The request for consultative services always carries with it both explicit and implicit components. Recognition of both is crucial to the effective provision of services to the hospitalized patient.

The explicit request for consultation may take many forms. They may be vaguely stated (please evaluate; please see Mr. Jones and tell me what you think; check on the patient in room 512). More-specific questions are typically asked, requesting assistance in evaluating lethality, presence or absence of psychiatric disturbance, or a specific behavioral-management question.

Recognition of the covert reasons for referral will contribute significantly to the relative success or failure of the consultation. An example will be helpful in clarifying this point.

> A referral was received from a medical subspecialist, requesting a psychological evaluation of a chronically ill child. Ostensibly, the request was explained to the parents as an academically oriented, psychometric evaluation; however, in discussion with the physician, it became apparent that he desired a surreptitious evaluation of what he felt might be significant psychosomatic components to the symptoms reported by the family, for which he could not account medically. Working with the physician and the family together, the latter evaluation was undertaken.
>
> The results were presented with attention to the child's relative strengths,

essentially normal psychological status, and a gentle caution regarding the potential adverse effects on psychological development which are a function of chronic physical disease. As the child's medical condition worsened, the psychologist continued to work with both the family and the physician, until the youngster's death, many months later.

Consideration should be given to staff (nursing, as well as medical) concerns about the patient, their difficulties with the patient, and their personal attitudes or dilemmas which would affect their attitudes toward both the consultant or psychological problems in general.

Consultation requests may be made by telephone, in a personal meeting between the referring physician and the consultant, or by a written note. Obviously, the direct and personal contact provides the consultant with the most information about the reasons for the referral and the particular concerns of the physician. Whatever the nature of the request, the consultant should ask the referring physician to complete a written-consultation form. In addition to helping the physician structure the request for services, it provides the consultant with identifying information critical to record keeping and ensures that the intended patient receives the desired services (see Figure 1). Finally, agreement should be reached, at the time consultation services are requested, whether or not the results of the psychological evaluation should be discussed with the patient.

Problem-oriented medical record

A key skill in providing consultation-liaison service in the medical setting is the capacity to effectively utilize the extant medical record, both

Figure 1

INPATIENT CONSULTATION REQUEST—PEDIATRIC PSYCHOLOGY

Children's Hospital of the King's Daughters
Norfolk, Virginia

Patient name:	Chart no.:
Home address:	DOB:
Parent/guardian:	Age:
Phone:	Room:
Medical diagnosis and problems:	Anticipated D/C:
Reason for referral:	
Referring physician:	

current and past. The most frequently used format—the problem-oriented medical record (POMR)—was devised by Weed (1968, 1969). The Weed system and its derivatives (Dickie & Bass, 1980; Ruth, Rigden, & Brunworth, 1979) have been used in a variety of settings and have been adapted for use in psychiatric treatment (Allen, Webb, & Gold, 1980; Grant & Maletzky, 1972; Reese, 1980). The POMR emphasizes evaluation and management of the patient's medical problems by objective. The basic model is outlined in Figure 2. While this is offered as a guide to the typical hospital chart, the same format can be (and often is) utilized in the routine medical record of the family or specialist physician.

Figure 2

Problem-Oriented Medical Record

  I. Data base (admission note)
      Chief complaints, patient profile, related social data, present illness, past history, review of systems (ROS), physical examination, results of laboratory tests.
  II. Problem list
      A numbered list of problems which enumerates all problems past and present of consequence for treatment.
  III. Initial plan
      A list of diagnostic and therapeutic plans for each of the numbered problems.
  IV. Progress notes
      A. Narrative notes
          1. Subjective data (symptomatic, patient reported data)
          2. Objective data (results of brief evaluation patient, laboratory tests, or other studies)
          3. Assessment and clinical impression
          4. Planned treatment
      B. Flow sheets (vital signs, results of laboratory tests)
      C. Discharge summary

The *data base* is prepared at the time that treatment is initiated, and it includes a summary note, by the attending physician, which provides detailed background information on the reasons for admission, relevant social history, current and past medical history, results of a physical examination completed at the time of admission, and the results of any laboratory tests which may have been administered at the time of admission.

The *problem list* consists of an enumeration of all medical problems, both past and present, which are of consequence to the proposed course of treatment; the numbered list can be added to as new problems arise. In recent years, these lists have incorporated relevant psychological and behavioral problems (e.g., depression, enuresis, anxiety), reflecting increased recognition of the impact these problems have on the management of the patient.

The admission note concludes with the statement of an *initial plan,* both diagnostic and therapeutic, for each of the numbered problems identified on the original problem list. Intentions to request consultation from medical and psychological specialists are first noted here and then transferred to the medical order sheet. As with the initial problem list, the treatment plan is expanded to incorporate new findings and revisions beyond the initial diagnosis.

The results of each contact between the patient and his or her primary physician, consultants, or other allied health services are recorded in the *progress notes.* Narrative notes should be dated, with the name of the service or division providing consultation (e.g., pediatrics, psychology, surgery, internal medicine) clearly stated. Each narrative note should be related to the initial list of problems and numbered accordingly. A frequently used approach to daily assessment of patient progress (best known by its acronym, SOAP) involves a four-step analysis by problem area. *Subjective* (patient-reported) or symptomatic findings are recorded. These are followed by a list of *objective* findings, consisting of the results of an examination by the physician or consultant, laboratory tests, or other data. An *assessment* or impression based upon these findings is formulated, and a *plan* of treatment is outlined. *Flow sheets* are used to expedite the recording of such standardized data as vital signs, laboratory values, or serial evaluations. At the conclusion of treatment, a *discharge summary* is prepared by the primary health-care provider, which reviews efforts to treat each of the problems identified in the initial problem list, their current status, and outlines plans for further evaluation and treatment, if indicated.

Nurse's notes are, typically, a separate part of the medical chart and provide the consulting psychologist with a running record of changes in the physical status of the patient, behaviors and responses to various stimuli (e.g., visitors, medications, compliance, appetite, mental status, degree of cooperation), and the involvement of other allied health personnel (occupational therapy, physical therapy, dietary specialists, respiratory therapy, or other related areas).

Review of the medical record

Following receipt of the consultation request, and prior to seeing the patient, the consultant should review the recent medical record and, where necessary or indicated, the complete medical record. Whereas the latter may not be practical or even fruitful in the case of adult consultation requests, when providing consultant services for children it is usually helpful to become familiar with the general outlines of the medical history (including problems associated with pregnancy and delivery, developmental milestones, childhood diseases, immunizations, previous medical care and treatment, and the child's reactions to these). More generally, the consultant reviewing the medical record would be interested in the following:

1. Is the medical history complete; does it provide the consultant with additional information with which to make an informed assessment?
2. What was the admitting diagnosis, and what were the significant problems (medical, social, psychological) which were noted at that time? To what degree have these significantly changed since the time of admission? What does the patient or family know about the diagnosis, prognosis, and proposed treatment?
3. Has the medical work-up been completed? Is consultation sought only because all physical findings and laboratory tests were within normal limits?
4. What additional information may be obtained from reviewing either the medical or nursing-staff progress notes? Have any unusual or distinctive behaviors or emotional reactions been observed, and if so, in what context (with certain visitors, during certain periods of the day, or in association with procedures being performed, other planned activities)? Are the staff's views on the patient in agreement with those of the referring physician?
5. What medications have been or are currently being given or withdrawn? Could they contribute to presenting psychopathology (for example, withdrawal of steroids resulting in an acute brain syndrome)? How are medications being given (intravenous, intramuscular, intrathecal) and under what circumstances (every 4 hours, every 12 hours, when needed)?

Although not always noted in the medical record, it is necessary to know how and in what context the patient and his family have been told to expect the psychological consultation and the reasons they have been given for requesting the services of the consultant. Although the stigma attached to talking with psychologists and psychiatrists in the professional context has diminished, many patients and their families regard a "psychological consult" as an implication that their physician regards them as "crazy" or malingerers or may feel that they have been abandoned and are no longer able to be helped by standard medical techniques. The response of the unprepared patient varies and may range from decompensation and withdrawal to active anger and denial. Pragmatically, parents of children not notified in advance of a request for a psychological consult by the primary care physician may refuse to pay the bill for that service.

Basic medical work-up

Although few consulting psychologists have the background and preparation to critically review or interpret the results of the many medical/

laboratory tests used in the medical setting, a brief review of the range of procedures utilized will quickly alert the psychologist to the possible alternative treatments or diagnoses which have been considered in the evaluation of the patient, the absolute number of tests undertaken, and the degree of invasiveness which the patient has already endured or failed to endure.

Depending on the familiarity of the consultation-liaison psychologist with medical tests, such a review may be helpful in structuring the psychological evaluation, suggesting a potential need for other tests to rule out additional factors not considered by the referring physician (e.g., heavy-metal intoxication) or recent changes in the patient's condition which may account for newly noted disturbance (e.g., dementia, delusions, hallucinations, or acute ataxia), which may warrant additional medical evaluation.

The setting

The traditional hospital setting, which is well equipped to facilitate the medical examinations and evaluations of patients by the physician, is not especially well suited for the evaluation of psychological disturbance or status. When seeing inpatients, the psychological consultant may have difficulty in obtaining privacy. This author has conducted interviews at various times in hospital playrooms, in treatment rooms with patients receiving hydrotherapy for extensive burns, in emergency rooms, in hallways, in waiting rooms during chemotherapy treatments, at bedside with terminally ill patients, in intensive-care units, and in most hospital specialty units. If the patient is ambulatory, every effort should be made to find a suitable, private location in which to conduct the interview—an empty patient room, a conference area, a ''quiet'' or ''family'' room, a private office, or a medical examining room. On those occasions when the patient cannot be moved, or when a private interview area cannot be obtained, bedside consultations with curtains drawn are necessary. While this setting may not be comfortable to the beginning consultant, the typical patient is familiar with this quasi-private format for most medical examinations and can respond appropriately.

Scheduling of the consultation

There is a tendency, especially among inexperienced consultants and reinforced by the traditional medical setting, to regard the psychological consult as having a lower priority than not only scheduled medical tests, but also any other activity already scheduled for the patient (occupational therapy, physical therapy, recreational or respiratory therapy). The consequences of being willing to provide services ''only when convenient'' are a denigration of the importance of the consultation which is offered, with implications for lowered self-esteem and the reinforcement of poor medical attitudes toward the role of the psychological consult, decreased likelihood of being able to provide the patient or physician with timely recommendations, and increased likelihood of noncompliance with these recommendations—as the patient may perceive the psychologist as "less than a doctor." In order to avoid these complications, the consulting psychologist should plan—with the referring physician at the time of the initial consultation or chart review—a scheduled time for the evaluation of the patient in a way which demonstrates a reasonable amount of flexibility.

A frequent problem in the inpatient setting is the request by a physician that a patient be seen prior to discharge, which is scheduled "within the hour." Unless sufficient time is available to provide an adequate and thorough response to such requests within the stated parameters (taking into consideration the referring problem, its chronicity, and any other factors which may have elicited the consultation request at that time), it is usually in the patient's best interest to either schedule an outpatient follow-up visit or to request that the patient be held until the consultation request can be adequately addressed.

Conversely, sensitivity must be maintained to the truly urgent or emergency consultation. Suspicions of suicidal behavior, the threat of suicide, frank psychosis, or drug overdose are perhaps the most frequent causes of emergency consultation, and they should be honored on a priority basis (Bristol & Docherty, 1981; Gerson & Bassuk, 1980; Lipowski, 1977).

Interview of the patient

It is in the contact with the patient that the traditional skills of the clinical psychologist are applied. Its purpose is to describe and assess in detail the basis for significant differences in emotion, cognition, and behavior as they apply to the referral question and to make recommendations regarding treatment. A straightforward introduction and statement of role and purpose for seeing the patient ("Hello, I'm Dr. Faust. I'm a psychologist. Your physician, Dr. Jones, told you I would be coming by to talk with you about . . .") are helpful in orienting the patient and provide a context from which a brief mental-status exam may be undertaken (see Figure 3), if indicated.

The first task is to make at least an approximate diagnosis regarding the presence or absence of a psychosis, especially delirium. In cases involving physical illness, the consultant should not aim at determining whether the disease is organic or not, but rather at discerning the influences of both intrinsic and extrinsic factors. Similarly, when pain is involved in the patient's complaint, the consultant must consider the existence of depression, schizophrenia, hysteria, "compensation neurosis,"

Figure 3

Mental Status Exam

I. General information
  A. Level of consciousness (alert, lethargic, stuporous, stable, fluctuating)
  B. Cooperation
  C. Reliability of information provided
  D. Motor status/posture
  E. Affect
  F. Language
  G. Patterns of thought

II. Specific information
  A. Orientation (person, place, time)
  B. Insight
  C. Remote memory (storage and retrieval)
    1. Previously learned material
    2. Naming visual stimuli
    3. General fund of information
  D. Recent memory
    1. General information
    2. Immediate recall
    3. Delayed recall
  E. Calculation
  F. Abstract thinking
  G. Judgment

---

hypochondriasis, or malingering. None but the last-mentioned diagnosis negates the coexistence of organic illness (Krakowski, 1977).

The task of differential diagnosis should include an assessment of personality, environmental, and social variables which may influence response to treatment. Formal psychometric assessment may be postponed if urgency is required in assessing the specific problem responsible for the consultation. A brief interview with the family may be helpful in delineating interpersonal strengths and problems and in identifying support available for the patient outside of the medical setting. Additional factors which would be relevant include educational and cultural levels, previous adjustment to medical disability, and the patient's own understanding of his illness or disease. A careful assessment of patient behaviors (observed directly and as recorded in nursing notes or other patient records) will be helpful.

Recommendations and treatment

As previously indicated, it may be necessary to expand and reformulate the referral question on the basis of the patient interview/assessment.

The consulting psychologist should independently clarify what are the relevant issues which account for the referral problem. The possibility of organic factors, psychosis, and alternative diagnoses should be considered, and important factors should be summarized in the preparation of a brief report. A copy of the final report, complete with recommendations, should be sent to the referring physician and should be discussed with him or her (either by phone or in person) at the earliest opportunity. As noted previously, the decision whether or not the results of the psychological evaluation should be discussed with the patient should have been made at the time of the initial consultation request. While professionally and ethically obligated to review the results of our work with the patient, in the consultation context the primary relationship is between the referral source (the consultee) and the consultant. The referring physician may or may not wish for the consultant to discuss the findings with the patient or may elect to not follow the recommendations of the consultant (Engelhardt & McCullough, 1979; Kimball, 1979a; Murray, 1979).

Formal reports should avoid unnecessary psychological jargon, be explicit, and include practical recommendations for immediate and long-term management of the patient. Where possible and appropriate, the consultant should participate in the implementation of the recommendations, while making clear to both the referring physician and the patient that such actions occur only with the consent and agreement of the primary physician.

LIAISON

Implementation of treatment recommendations, where permitted, will typically involve the cooperation and support of other members of the health care team (nurses, residents, interns) in addition to the attending physician. Effective cooperation emerges, not on the basis of the individual consultation, but on the basis of a well-established, working relationship with all of these individuals, based on trust, openness, and availability. As previously mentioned, staff concerns regarding management of a patient should be solicited at the onset of the evaluation. Their cooperation is sought in obtaining information about the patient—behavioral observations, social history, and brief medical history. Finally, their suggestions may be helpful in formulating realistic treatment goals and strategies for the individual patient. As a consequence of this process, the consultant becomes perceived by the staff as available, interested, concerned, respecting their personal skills and abilities in both the medical and behavioral areas.

Toward that end, the hospital-based consulting psychologist should seek to be visible and available to staff at all levels for routine consultation and teaching. The fundamental point is the need to talk directly with "front-line" patient care staff regarding the psychological problems they encounter and the sort of consultation that would be of greatest value. The goal of this liaison process is to increase the psychological sophistication of all staff, so that they are better able to anticipate needs for consultative services (rather than after the fact of a psychological crisis) and better able to differentiate between those for whom indirect consultation will suffice (Koocher, Sourkes, & Keane, 1979).

It is important to recognize that the comprehensive provision of hospital-based consultation-liaison services includes more than work with patients and their families. Physicians and staff may want and require support in working in the naturally stressful hospital environment. Their concerns will typically be twofold: (1) the way they should act which would maximally, psychologically benefit the patients in their care, and (2) the opportunity to ventilate their own responses to the pain, disease, disability, and death with which they work. While the former can be addressed in group in-services and workshops, the latter is more frequently undertaken on a one-to-one basis. Whether accomplished at the nursing station, the conference room or office, or over a cup of coffee, these brief, supportive consultations require the same degree of professionalism and confidentiality given to regular patient contacts.

It is important to note briefly in this context that, from time to time, individual staff members may solicit professional consultation or may be identified (by their co-workers, supervisors, or other sources) as demonstrating unusual signs of psychological distress. In many instances, the consulting psychologist—as an available, concerned, representative member of the profession—may be asked to provide initial evaluation or screening of the individuals involved. Typically, it will be better to refer these individuals to other professionals in the community, should intensive or lengthy evaluation and treatment appear indicated; however, each psychological consultant should develop his/her own guidelines in this regard.

PROBLEMS AND POTENTIAL PITFALLS

Lipowski (1974) has observed that relatively few individuals remain in consultation-liaison work for more than a few years. Reasons for this unusual mobility need to be examined and overcome.

Economic factors would seem to play a major role. While an increasing need for consultation-liaison services has been demonstrated, it is not possible under prevailing conditions to maintain an income comparable to that of the private practice psychologist. Much of the work, especially in liaison areas, is time-consuming and not renumerated. Funds have to come from the departments that are the recipients of the consultant's liaison services; the best solution would appear to be a salary for a block of time—which could be spent in consulting, in supervising trainees, and in other teaching duties (Lipowski, 1974).

The nature of relations with colleagues in both psychology and medicine are often discouraging. Associates in the mental health areas may speculate on why the psychologist is not working with "the truly mentally ill." At the same time, the psychologist may be encountering much indifference, ambivalence, and hostility from his potential consultees in the medical areas. A pioneering spirit, a rugged sense of one's skills and orientation, and a healthy respect for the complex arena in which services are to be provided are required in the development of a consultation-liaison service.

The effective consultation-liaison psychologist in the medical context learns to function in both medical and psychological worlds. Typically, the bulk of the referrals for which services are requested will come from the primary care medical community, with specific requests emerging from the various specialties and subspecialties. As a consequence, it is helpful to develop and maintain good professional and social relationships within the referral community. Attendance at teaching clinics, grand rounds presentations, and participation in teaching programs at all levels allow the psychologist to remain visible and to demonstrate his own unique skills and abilities.

Consultation-liaison psychology is time-consuming, challenging, and demanding; it requires highly refined clinical skills and abilities, fluency in the principles of disease and its treatment as practiced in the medical setting, and sensitivity to the skills and abilities of others in medicine and the allied health areas. It is highly important, therefore, to establish limits on the types and scope of services available.

There is a tendency to adopt what has been characterized as a "super-helper syndrome": the consultant is available all the time and assumes responsibility for "curing" the patient, relieving fears, reducing aberrant behaviors, and resolving the situation. Obviously, not all referral problems can be resolved. The sheer magnitude of the psychosocial factors which can adversely effect the behaviors of patients simply cannot be adequately addressed by the efforts of one (or even a dozen) highly effective consultants. To attempt to do so undermines the credibility of the consultant in those areas where he can be effective. It is essential to establish—at the time of referral—the limited scope of the services to be provided and, for some patients, the unlikelihood that anything can be done to alter the existing situation.

A second potential pitfall in the provision of consultation-liaison services is the assumption that a given group of similar behaviors represents the same underlying process, hence requiring the same intervention. As was outlined previously, a given behavior may represent a premorbid symptom, a complication of a disease or its treatment, an emotional reaction to organic disease or its treatment, the somatic presentation of underlying emotional problems, or a learned-behavior pattern unrelated to the medical problem or setting. Each distinct etiology would require a distinct approach, if relief is to be obtained.

The consultation-liaison psychologist is frequently asked to provide a specific intervention—e.g., "we need an intelligence test on this kid," "hypnotize this patient so he will be more compliant," "arrange for a transfer to a psychiatric unit." While it is true that the most helpful consultation request is that which specifies the problem to be addressed, such overspecific requests fail to acknowledge the potential involvement of those factors which the psychologist is best equipped to evaluate. It is the responsibility of the consultation-liaison psychologist to determine the requisite intervention, on the basis of his evaluation of the patient's condition and clinical situation.

A related problem is the automatic acceptance or assumption that a patient's problem is psychiatric in origin without adequate supporting data. In a recently published, remarkably sensitive and humorous account of life inside a general medical hospital, Shem (1978) portrays psychiatry or psychology services as the ultimate dumping ground for the patient without obvious physical disorder or whose behavior exceeds traditionally appropriate behavior for the medical setting. The assumption of psychological disturbance without supporting evidence may result in a premature discontinuation of medical evaluation and treatment because "it's only a psychiatric problem." As noted in the beginning of this chapter, such assumptions fail to recognize the potential for the presentation of psychological problems as a premorbid indicator of physical disease. In a review of work with both adult and child patients referred for psychological evaluation of hysteric conversion, Dubowitz and Herser (1976) reported that 33 to 46 percent of those cases were found—on discharge or later follow-up—to have an organic basis for their presenting symptom. Those percentages compare favorably with other clinical populations evaluated by this author. A brief case study will illuminate this point:

> An adolescent female received an extensive work-up for multiple pain complaints. On medical exam, she was found to have a low-grade hematologic disorder, for which she received treatment. No basis for the pains were found. Following work-up for hysterical personality (conversion type, secondary to physical disease), she was discharged from the hospital on placebo "pain" medication, which was later withdrawn in a graduated fashion. Two months later, she was readmitted with multisite pain; a bone scan performed at that time showed serious metastic bone cancer, unrelated to the earlier medical problem.

Finally, it should be clear that the task of the consultation-liaison psychologist is to facilitate the work of the medical team and the primary care physician, not to assume responsibility for the patient.

Differential diagnosis, collaborative care, teaching, and research describe the primary functions of the consultation-liaison psychologist. Very rarely are the distinctions between those areas clear-cut, as the management of the psychosocial factors which influence the nature and quality of the experience of the person in the medical setting have their origin in institutional (hospital), service (medical and psychology staff), and personal (patient and family) spheres. Knowledge of the medical setting, of the general principles of disease and its treatment, of potential conflict between the patient and caregivers, and flexibility in approach are all key components in the effective practice of consultation-liaison psychology.

SUMMARY

Differential diagnosis, collaborative care, teaching, and research describe the primary functions of the consultation-liaison psychologist. Knowledge of the medical setting, of the general principles of disease and its management, of sources of potential conflict between the patient and caregivers, and flexibility in approach are all key components in the effective provision of consultation-liaison services.

This chapter briefly reviews the origins and function of the consultation-liaison role for the clinical psychologist in the nonpsychiatric medical setting. Following an introduction to the medical setting and record keeping, the consultation process is described—from its initiation by the primary care provider or specialist through the provision of a completed report. The importance of liaison services for staff and professionals is underlined, as are potential problem areas and pitfalls.

REFERENCES

Abrahams, A. Physical aspects of psychological disease. *The Lancet,* 1935, *228,* 473–476.

Abram, H. Interpersonal aspects of psychiatric consultations in a general hospital. *Psychiatry in Medicine,* 1971, *2,* 321–326.

Agle, D., & Mattsson, A. Psychological complications of hemophilia. In M. Hilgartner (Ed.), *Hemophilia in children.* Littleton, Mass.: PSG Publishing, 1979.

Allen, R., Webb, L., & Gold, R. Validity of problem-oriented record system for evaluating treatment outcome. *Psychological Reports,* 1980, *47,* 303–306.

Altrocchi, J. Personal communication, May 1981.

Authier, J. The family life-cycle seminars: An innovative health care psychology program. *Professional Psychology,* 1979, *10,* 451–457.

Belar, C. Training the clinical psychology student in behavioral medicine. *Professional Psychology,* 1980, *11,* 620–627.

Bibace, R., & Walsh, M. Clinical developmental psychologists in family-practice settings. *Professional Psychology,* 1979, *10,* 441–450.

Billowitz, A., & Friedson, W. Are psychiatric consultants' recommendations followed? *International Journal of Psychiatry in Medicine*, 1979, *9*, 179–189.

Bloom, L. Psychology and cardiology: Collaboration in coronary treatment and prevention. *Professional Psychology*, 1979, *10*, 485–490.

Bristol, J., & Docherty, J. Trends in emergency psychiatry in the last two decades. *American Journal of Psychiatry*, 1981, *138*, 623–628.

Burstein, A., Barnes, R., & Quesada, G. Training clinical psychologists in medical settings: Ideological and practical considerations. *Professional Psychology*, 1976, *32*, 396–402.

Caplan, G. *Principles of preventive psychiatry*. New York: Basic Books, 1964.

Caplan, G. *The theory and practice of mental health consultation*. New York: Basic Books, 1970.

Cassem, N., & Hackett, T. Psychiatric consultation in a coronary care unit. *Annals of Internal Medicine*, 1971, *75*, 9–14.

Cohen, L., Lubin, B., & Nathan, R. Graduate-degree training in psychology in medical centers. *Professional Psychology*, 1979, *10*, 110–114.

Copeland, B. Hospital privileges and staff membership for psychologists. *Professional Psychology*, 1980, *11*, 676–683.

Davidson, J., Raft, D., Lewis, B., & Gebhardt, M. Psychotropic drugs in general medical and surgical wards of a teaching hospital. *Archives of General Psychiatry*, 1975, *32*, 507–511.

Dickie, G., & Bass, M. Improving problem-oriented medical records through self-audit. *Journal of Family Practice*, 1980, *10*, 487–490.

Dorken, H., & Webb, J. The hospital practice of psychology: An interstate comparison. *Professional Psychology*, 1979, *10*, 619–630. (a)

Dorken, H., & Webb, J. Licensed psychologists in health care: A survey of their practices. In C. Kiesler, N. Cummings, & G. VandenBos (Eds.), *Psychology and national health insurance: A resource book*. Washington, D.C.: American Psychological Association, 1979. (b)

Dorland's illustrated medical dictionary. Twenty-fifth edition. Philadelphia: W. B. Saunders, 1974.

Drotar, D. Clinical psychological practice in a pediatric hospital. *Professional Psychology*, 1977, *8*, 72–80.

Dubowitz, V., & Herser, L. Management of children with nonorganic (hysterical) disorders of motor function. *Developmental Medicine and Child Neurology*, 1976, *18*, 358–368.

Engelhardt, H., & McCullough, L. Confidentiality in the consultation-liaison process. *Psychiatric Clinics of North America*, 1979, *2*, 403–413.

Faust, D., Ulissi, S., & Thurber, S. Post-doctoral training opportunities in pediatric psychology: A review. *Journal of Pediatric Psychology*, 1980, *5*, 277–286.

Fink, P. The relationship of psychiatry to primary care. *American Journal of Psychiatry*, 1977, *134*, 126–129.

Frank, K., Heller, S., & Kornfeld, D. Psychological intervention in coronary heart disease: A review. *General Hospital Psychiatry*, 1979, *1*, 18–23.

Gabinet, L., & Friedson, W. The psychologist as frontline mental health consultant in a general hospital. *Professional Psychology*, 1980, *11*, 939–945.

Gerson, S., & Bassuk, E. Psychiatric emergencies: An overview. *American Journal of Psychiatry*, 1980, *137*, 1–11.

Grant, R., & Maletzky, B. Application of the Weed system to psychiatric records. *Psychiatry in Medicine*, 1972, *3*, 119–129.

Grey, M., Genel, M., & Tamborlane, W. Psychosocial adjustment of latency-aged diabetics: Determinants and relationship to control. *Pediatrics*, 1980, *65*, 69–73.

Guggenheim, F. A market-place model of consultation psychiatry in the general hospital. *American Journal of Psychiatry*, 1978, *135*, 1380–1383.

Guynn, R. Psychiatric presentation of cardiovascular disease. In R. Hall (Ed.), *Psychiatric presentations of medical illness*. New York: Spectrum, 1980.

Hackett, T., Froese, A., & Vasquez, E. Psychological management of the CCU patient. *Psychiatry in Medicine*, 1973, *4*, 89–105.

Hall, R. (Ed.). *Psychiatric presentations of medical illness: Somatopsychic disorders*. New York: Spectrum, 1980.

Hall, R., Gardner, E., Popkin, M., LeCann, A., & Stickney, S. Unrecognized physical illness prompting psychiatric admission: A prospective study. *American Journal of Psychiatry*, 1981, *138*, 629–635.

Hall, R., Popkin, M., Devaul, R., Faillace, L., & Stickney, S. Physical illness presenting as psychiatric disease. *Archives of General Psychiatry*, 1978, *35*, 1315–1320.

Hall, R., Stickney, S., & Gardner, E. Behavioral toxicity of nonpsychiatric drugs. In R. Hall (Ed.), *Psychiatric presentations of medical illness*. New York: Spectrum, 1980.

Haynes, R., Taylor, D., & Sackett, D. (Eds.). *Compliance in health care*. Baltimore: Johns Hopkins University Press, 1979.

Houpt, J., Orleans, C., George, L. & Brodie, H. The role of psychiatric and behavioral factors in the practice of medicine. *American Journal of Psychiatry*, 1980, *137*, 37–47.

Hull, J. Psychiatric referrals in general practice. *Archives of General Psychiatry*, 1979, *36*, 406–408.

Iwasaki, T. Teaching liaison psychiatry and clinical practice of psychomatic medicine in the general hospital. *Bibliotheca Psychiatrica*, 1979, *159*, 32–38.

Jastrow, J. Relation of medicine to psychology. *Journal of the American Medical Association*, 1929, *92*, 720–723.

Kahana, R. J. Studies in medical psychology: A brief survey. *Psychiatry in Medicine*, 1972, *3*, 1–22.

Keith, K. *The behavioral/pediatric interface: Evolution of a relationship in practice*. Paper presented at the annual convention of the Association for Advancement of Behavior Therapy, San Francisco, 1979.

Kimball, C. The issue of confidentiality in the consultation-liaison process. *Bibliotheca Psychiatrica*, 1979, 159, 82–89. (a)

Kimball, C. Reactions to illness—An acute phase: The interplay of environmental factors in intensive-care units. *Psychiatric Clinics of North America*, 1979, *2*, 307–319. (b)

Kimball, C., & Krakowski, A. (Eds.). The teaching of psychosomatic medicine and consultation-liaison psychiatry: Reactions to illness. *Bibliotheca Psychiatrica*, 1979, *159*.

Kirkpatrick, B., & Hall, R. Seizure disorders. In R. Hall (Ed.), *Psychiatric presentations of medical illness*. New York: Spectrum, 1980.

Koocher, G., Sourkes, B., & Keane, W. Pediatric oncology consultations: A generalizable model for medical settings. *Professional Psychology,* 1979, *9,* 467–474.

Koranyi, E. Morbidity and rate of undiagnosed physical illnesses in a psychiatric clinic population. *Archives of General Psychiatry,* 1979, *36,* 414–419.

Krakowski, A. Liaison Psychiatry: Factors influencing the consultation process. *Psychiatry in Medicine,* 1973, *4,* 439–446.

Krakowski, A. The process of consultation. In E. Wittkower & H. Warnes (Eds.), *Psychosomatic medicine: Its clinical applications.* New York: Harper & Row, 1977.

Leukensmeyer, W. Psychiatric Presentations of Selected Genitourinary Disorders. In R. C. W. Hall (Ed) *Psychiatric Presentations of Medical Illness.* New York: Spectrum, 1980, 209–221.

Lewis, S. Considerations in setting up psychological consultations to a pediatric hematology-oncology team. *Journal of Clinical Child Psychology,* 1978, *7,* 21–22.

Linton, J. The psychologist on a spinal cord injury team in a community medical center. *Professional Psychology,* 1981, *12,* 229–236.

Lipowski, A. Consultation-liaison psychiatry: Past, present, and future. In R. Pasnau (Ed.), *Consultation-liaison psychiatry.* New York: Grune & Stratton, 1975.

Lipowski, Z. J. Review of consultation psychiatry and psychosomatic medicine. I: General principles. *Psychosomatic Medicine,* 1967, *29,* 153–171. (a)

Lipowski, Z. J. Review of consultation psychiatry and psychosomatic medicine. II: Clinical aspects. *Psychosomatic Medicine,* 1967, *29,* 201–224. (b)

Lipowski, Z. J. Review of consultation psychiatry and psychosomatic medicine. III: Theoretical issues. *Psychosomatic Medicine,* 1968, *30,* 395–422.

Lipowski, Z. J. Consultation-liaison psychiatry: An overview. *American Journal of Psychiatry,* 1974, *131,* 623–630.

Lipowski, Z. J. Psychosomatic medicine in the seventies: An overview. *American Journal of Psychiatry,* 1977, *134,* 233–244.

Lipowski, Z. J. Consultation-liaison psychiatry: Past failures and new opportunities. *General Hospital Psychiatry,* 1979, *1,* 3–10.

Lloyd, G. Liaison psychiatry from a British perspective. *General Hospital Psychiatry,* 1980, *2,* 46–51.

Lukensmeyer, W. Psychiatric presentations of selected genitourinary disorders. In R. Hall (Ed.), *Psychiatric presentations of medical illness.* New York: Spectrum, 1980.

Magrab, P. (Ed.). *Psychological management of pediatric problems.* Baltimore: University Park Press, 1978.

Matarazzo, J., Lubin, B., & Nathan, R. Psychologists membership on the medical staffs of university teaching hospitals. *American Psychology,* 1978, *39,* 23–29.

McKegney, F. P. Consultation-liaison teaching of psychosomatic medicine and opportunities and obstacles. *Journal of Nervous and Mental Disorders,* 1972, *154,* 198–205.

Mills, M., & Stunkard, A. Behavioral changes following surgery for obesity. *American Journal of Psychiatry,* 1976, *133,* 527–531.

Moore, G. The adult psychiatrist in the medical environment. *American Journal of Psychiatry,* 1978, *135,* 413–419.

Murray, G. Ethical problems in liaison psychiatry. *Psychiatric Annals,* 1979, *9,* 75–79.

Olbrisch, M., & Sechrest, L. Educating health psychologists in traditional graduate training programs. *Professional Psychology,* 1979, *10,* 589–595.

O'Malley, J., & Koocher, G. Psychological consultation to a pediatric oncology unit: Obstacles to effective intervention. *Journal of Pediatric Psychology,* 1977, *2,* 54–57.

Orleans, C., Houpt, J., & Trent, P. Models for evaluating teaching in consultation-liaison psychiatry. III: Conclusion-oriented research. *General Hospital Psychiatry,* 1979, *1,* 322–329.

Pasnau, R. O. *Consultation-liaison psychiatry.* New York: Grune & Stratton, 1975.

Perl, M., Hall, R., & Gardner, E. Behavioral toxicity of psychiatric drugs. In R. Hall (Ed.), *Psychiatric presentations of medical illness.* New York: Spectrum, 1980.

Petrich, J., & Holmes, T. Psychiatric presentations of pulmonary disorders. In R. Hall (Ed.), *Psychiatric presentations of medical illness.* New York: Spectrum, 1980.

Pomerleau, O., & Brady, J. (Eds.). *Behavioral medicine: Theory and practice.* Baltimore: Williams & Wilkins, 1979.

Popkin, M. Psychiatric presentation of hematologic disorders. In R. Hall (Ed.), *Psychiatric presentations of medical illness.* New York: Spectrum, 1980.

Popkin, M., & Mackenzie, T. Psychiatric presentations of endocrine dysfunction. In R. Hall (Ed.), *Psychiatric presentations of medical illness.* New York: Spectrum, 1980.

Popkin, M., Mackenzie, T., Hall, R., & Callies, A. Consultees' concordance with consultants' psychotropic drug recommendations: Related variables. *Archives of General Psychiatry,* 1980, *37,* 1017–1021.

Popkin, M., Mackenzie, T., Hall, R., & Garrard, J. Physician's concordance with consultants' recommendations for psychotropic medications. *Archives of General Psychiatry,* 1979, *36,* 386–398.

Reese, W. Psychiatric treatment and record organized by objectives. *Journal of Clinical Psychiatry,* 1980, *41,* 405–411.

Reiger, D., Goldberg, I., & Taube, C. The de facto U.S. mental health services system. *Archives of General Psychiatry,* 1978, *35,* 685–693.

Ruth, D. H., Rigden, S., & Brunworth, D. An integrated family-oriented problem-oriented medical record. *Journal of Family Practice,* 1979, 8, 1179–1184.

Sasser, M., & Kinzie, J. Evaluation of medical-psychiatric consultation. *International Journal of Psychiatry in Medicine,* 1979, *9,* 123–134.

Schenkenberg, T., Peterson, L., Wood, D., & DaBell, R. Psychological consultation/liaison in medical and neurological settings: Physician's appraisal. *Professional Psychology,* 1981, *12,* 309–317.

Schiff, S., & Pilot, M. An approach to psychiatric consultation in the general hospital. *Archives of General Psychiatry,* 1959, *1,* 349–357.

Schroeder, C. Psychology in a private pediatric practice. *Journal of Pediatric Psychology,* 1979, *4,* 5–18.

Schuster, M. Psychiatric manifestations of gastrointestinal disorders. In R. Hall (Ed.), *Psychiatric presentations of medical illness.* New York: Spectrum, 1980.

Schwab, J. *Handbook of psychiatric consultation.* New York: Appleton-Century-Crofts, 1968.

Schwab, J. Psychiatric manifestations of infectious disease. In R. Hall (Ed.), *Psychiatric presentations of medical illness.* New York: Spectrum, 1980.

Schwartz, G., & Weiss, S. Behavioral medicine revisited: An amended definition. *Journal of Behavioral Medicine,* 1978, *1,* 249–252. (a)

Schwartz, G., & Weiss, S. Yale Conference on Behavioral Medicine: A proposed definition and statement of goals. *Journal of Behavioral Medicine,* 1978, *1,* 3–12. (b)

Shader, R., DiMascio, I., & Appleton, W. *Psychotropic drug side effects: Clinical and theoretical perspectives.* Baltimore: Williams & Wilkins, 1970.

Shem, S. *The house of God.* New York: Dell Publishing, 1978.

Sladen, B. Health care psychology and graduate education. *Professional Psychology,* 1979, *10,* 841–851.

Stabler, B. Emerging models of psychologist-pediatrician liaison. *Journal of Pediatric Psychology,* 1979, *4,* 307–313.

Strain, J. Psychopharmacological treatment of the medically ill. In J. Strain & S. Grossman (Eds.), *Psychological care of the medically ill: A primer in liaison psychiatry.* New York: Appleton-Century-Crofts, 1975.

Strain, J. The medical setting: Is it beyond the psychiatrist. *American Journal of Psychiatry,* 1977, *134,* 253–256.

Strain, J., & Grossman, S. (Eds.), *Psychological care of the medically ill: A primer in consultation-liaison psychiatry.* New York: Appleton-Century-Crofts, 1975.

Waring, E., Weisz, G., Heilbrunn, C., Lefcoe, D., & Green, R. A pilot evaluation of liaison psychiatry in a diabetic outpatient clinic. *Psychiatric Journal of the University of Ottawa,* 1980, *5,* 53–57.

Weed, L. Medical records that guide and teach. *New England Journal of Medicine,* 1968, *278,* 593–600.

Weed, L. *Medical records, medical education, and patient care.* Cleveland: Case Western Reserve, 1969.

Wellisch, D., & Pasnau, R. Psychological interns on a consultation-liaison service. *General Hospital Psychiatry,* 1979, *1,* 287–292.

23

Cognitive-behavioral interventions*

Philip C. Kendall†
and
Margaret R. Kriss†

> The meaning [of thought] is further limited to beliefs that rest upon some kind of evidence or testimony . . . In some cases, a belief is accepted with slight or almost no attempt to state the grounds that support it. In other cases, the ground or basis for a belief is deliberately sought and its adequacy to support the belief examined. This process is called reflective thought; it alone is truly educative in value. . . . (Dewey, 1910, pp. 1–2)

Remarkably, these opening statements from Dewey's *How We Think* (1910) capture important facets of the current practice of cognitive-behavioral interventions. For instance, several cognitive-behavioral strategies have identified the centrality of either or both: (a) personal beliefs, and (b) careful and systematic verification of the basis for such beliefs.[1] Although the field does not rest on a single, unitary principle, cognitive-behavioral therapists do endorse the educational value of testing and clarifying beliefs or, "reflective thought," in Dewey's terms.

Cognitive-behavioral interventions have been developed for the treatment of various forms of psychopathology. In general, the interventions combine both behavioral strategies and cognitive processes, in the effort to achieve behavioral and cognitive change. According to Mahoney

---

* Portions of this article were prepared while the first author was a Fellow at the Center for Advanced Study in the Behavioral Sciences, Stanford, California. He is grateful for financial support provided by the National Institute of Mental Health (5-T32-MH14581-05) and the John D. and Catherine T. MacArthur Foundation. He is also grateful to the University of Minnesota Graduate School Grant Program for their support of his research over the years and to Jane Gendron and Marcia Smith for their assistance.

† University of Minnesota, Minneapolis.

[1] Beliefs are referred to here in a general sense, intending to refer to a wide range of cognitive constructs.

(1977), cognitive-behavioral approaches developed out of a dissatisfaction with the narrow definitions and limitations of insight-oriented and behavioral therapies. In addition to recognizing the limitations of each school, therapists began to adopt a more interactionist view (i.e., between organismic and environmental influences) of the processes of adjustment and behavioral change. Cognitive-behavioral approaches to treatment can be seen as a bidirectional integration of therapeutic perspectives. Examples of this bidirectionality of movement (Kendall & Hollon, 1979) are evident in the orientations of several present-day cognitive-behavioral therapists. Ellis and Beck, founders of rational-emotive therapy and cognitive therapy for depression, respectively, came from psychoanalytically oriented backgrounds, and their cognitively oriented therapies now include behavioral strategies. Goldfried, Meichenbaum, and Mahoney, forerunners in the development of current cognitive-behavioral therapies, were originally associated with behavior-modification orientations.

Definitions of cognitive-behavioral interventions are difficult to construct. When definitions are proposed, most are intentionally broad, so as to avoid prematurely restricting or stagnating the development of new approaches (see Mahoney, 1977). For instance, Kendall and Hollon (1979) offered the following:

> It is not yet another new, exotic therapy. Rather, it is a purposeful attempt to preserve the demonstrated efficiencies of behavior modification within a less doctrinaire context and to incorporate the cognitive activities of the client in the efforts to produce therapeutic change. (p. 1)

We have chosen to maintain a broad definition of cognitive-behavioral interventions to guide us in preparing the present work. Our plan is to present the reader with an understanding of the basic tenets of various cognitive-behavioral interventions, including a description of the "how to" of the procedures and a select review of the outcome literature.

To accomplish these goals, we have chosen to organize the various cognitive-behavioral interventions by the type of disorder that is treated. We discuss the major interventions for anxiety, depression, and childhood behavior problems; and we include a section on other applications to illustrate the broad range of disorders that have been treated with cognitive-behavioral interventions. We conclude with a discussion of important issues that face both researcher and therapist.

A word about our title: The once-predicted incompatibility of the cohabitation of "cognitive" and "behavioral" treatment approaches has been put to rest. The phrase *cognitive-behavioral* is no longer an oxymoron. Indeed, this hyphenated label has come to stand for systematic and integrated psychological treatments. We prefer "interventions" to "therapy," since *intervention* is an umbrella term that includes therapeutic (remedial), preventative, and enhancement practices.

ANXIETY DISORDERS

The past two decades have witnessed somewhat of a dramatic shift in the treatment of anxiety disorders, with the introduction of cognitive-behavioral interventions. Our conceptualizations of the anxiety disorders have been modified, and our treatment strategies have been adjusted to include a direct, therapeutic focus on the client's cognitive processing of situational information.

Although there are currently a variety of cognitive-behavioral interventions in use for the treatment of anxiety, only a few will be described in detail. While the major premises of these interventions for anxiety are similar, there are differences in the specific methods employed to effect cognitive change. Our exploration of cognitive-behavioral treatments for anxiety includes discussions of rational-emotive therapy (RET), cognitive restructuring, and stress inoculation. Although these interventions are most frequently applied to the treatment of anxiety disorders, they have also been applied to a variety of other psychological problems. Such applications will be discussed in a later section.

Rational-emotive therapy

Background.   The questions of whether or not RET is aptly categorized as a cognitive-behavioral therapy remains a topic of discussion (Ellis, 1973, 1980; Zettle & Hayes, 1980). Since Ellis' RET (1962) was one of the first therapies to conceptualize faulty thinking patterns as a potential focus of intervention, and since the intervention relies on behavioral procedures and cognitive strategies, we chose to classify RET as a cognitive-behavioral intervention. More specifically, Ellis claims that psychological disorders result from *irrational* thought patterns. Although this is consistent with the cognitive-behavioral perspective, the various cognitive-behavioral interventions differ in regard to how the concept of "faulty" thinking is operationalized.

Ellis defines irrational thoughts as either being empirically false (e.g., "It will never be sunny again") or as thoughts that cannot be empirically verified (e.g., "I have no self-worth"). With regard to the latter example, Ellis is quite insistent that personal worth is not ratable. He suggests that irrational thoughts serve no useful function to individuals and only lead to self-defeating or self-destructive consequences.

Irrational thought patterns are said to arise from *assumptions* that constitute the individual's basic belief system. The most common beliefs that are seen in clinical cases are that one must be loved and approved by others at all times; that one must always be thorough, competent, and achieving, in order to have any self-worth; and the tendency to view an event as a failure or catastrophe when something goes wrong. Ellis and Greiger (1977) provided a very complete list of the irrational beliefs that clients may hold. While these beliefs reflect the general nature of the pathology, they are difficult for clients to identify by self-report and to recognize as behavior. Typically, it is more promising to work at the level of more specific thoughts and to gradually confront beliefs at a later instance.

A major premise of RET is that what clients say to themselves (their thoughts) has a major impact on the way they feel and behave. It is assumed that clients who self-verbalize many irrational thoughts will experience more distress than clients with fewer irrational self-statements. The goal of RET, then, is to help clients modify their self-statements, their underlying beliefs and, untimately, their life philosophy.

The essence of RET can be summarized by a discussion of Ellis' *ABC* model (see also Ellis, 1977). *A* (the activating experience) refers to the situation or event that the client is exposed to, while *C* (the consequences) is the emotion or behavior that the client reports resulted from *A*. The client is frequently unaware, however, that *B* (the mediating belief) is essentially a series of thoughts or self-statements that follow the situation (*A*) and cause the experience of psychological distress (*C*). The model can be extended to include treatment. *D* refers to the process whereby the therapist and/or client dispute and modify the irrational beliefs, and *E* stands for the effect of confronting the irrational beliefs. This last stage should result, for the client, in some relief from psychological distress. This basic *ABC* model, with modifications, has been adopted by many cognitive-behavioral therapists, but the specifics of the *B* stage differ for the various treatment procedures.

The techniques of RET. While the rationale for RET has been explicitly formulated by Ellis, the specific techniques designed to carry out the goals of RET have not been as systematically outlined. Goldfried, Decenteceo, and Weinberg (1974) responded to this undesired state of affairs by developing very specific guidelines to effect change in irrational beliefs. By introducing some very specific guidelines, Goldfried et al. actually created a treatment approach that differed in significant ways from RET; hence, the approach will be examined in a later section. It may be helpful, however, for the RET therapist in search of some structure to review Goldfried et al.'s suggestions. What follows is a general description of methods used by an RET therapist.

The first task of the therapist is to determine the external events that precipitate clients' anxieties. This is typically done through standard interviewing techniques (see also Sutton-Simon, 1981). Next, the therapist listens for and points out to clients the irrational thoughts and beliefs that clients self-verbalize. A helpful homework assignment at this stage may be for clients to read Ellis and Harper's (1973) *A Guide to Rational Living*, which offers a clear introduction to commonly held irrational beliefs and how they play a role in emotions. The therapist will then assist the client in altering his or her beliefs and thought patterns. This can be done by having the client examine, in a scientifically critical manner, the validity of his/her self-statements. The therapist helps the client make critical discriminations between those statements that are objectively true and those that are irrational.

For example, a client who has a phobia of driving a car may have the following self-statements: "I won't be able to start the car"; "The neighbors will laugh at me"; "My anxiety may be so bad that I will faint"; and "I am a helpless, worthless, and stupid person." The therapist would then help the client examine the logical relationship of his/her self-statements and point out that the chain is not logically consistent. While it may be possible that the client *will* have trouble starting the car, the neighbors *may* laugh, and the client *might* even faint, it is not a logial step to conclude that he or she is worthless. By eliminating the irrational thinking, the client is likely to experience less anxiety.

At first, the therapist may prompt the client to make appropriate reevaluations of thoughts. As the client becomes more adept at rational reevaluation, however, the prompts fade out. Other techniques used to help clients rationally reevaluate their thoughts include cognitive exercises, rational role reversal, rational-emotive imagery, and in vivo desensitization. Homework exercises are generally assignments in which the client examines his or her irrational self-statements or beliefs and then practices disputing them. Rational role reversal is a process by which client and therapist switch roles, and the client leads the therapist through a problem using the *ABC* model. In rational-emotive imagery, clients are instructed (both in and between therapy sessions) first to imagine anxiety-provoking situations, then to determine the thoughts that mediate distress, and finally to modify them. The technique of in vivo desensitization instructs clients to engage in behaviors that are extremely frightening to the client and/ or occasion panic attacks. This procedure is intended to demonstrate that a client can cope more effectively if the client alters his/her self-statements or, if anxiety is experienced, to help convince the client that it was not a catastrophe.

Sample studies. One of the first well-controlled studies of the RET approach was conducted by Meichenbaum, Gilmore, and Fedoravicius (1971), who compared an RET-like intervention, systematic desensitization, and a combined desensitization-and-RET approach to the treatment of speech-anxious college students. The RET approach utilized was somewhat different than the typical RET approach, in that most of the therapy time was spent helping clients gain insight into how irrational thoughts mediate their anxiety. Relatively little time was devoted to practicing rational reevaluation. Nevertheless, the results indicated that the rational-emotive and desensitization treatments were equally effective in reducing speech-anxiety levels and were significantly better than the control groups, as assessed by behavioral, cognitive, and self-report measures. Post hoc analyses revealed an interesting treatment by client interaction, in which desensitization appeared more effective for clients with a circumscribed speech-anxiety problem, while RET was most effective for clients with a more generalized, social anxiety.

Trexler and Karst (1972) compared the efficacy of RET to an attention placebo (relaxation training) and a waiting-list control in the treatment of speech-anxious college students. Results provided support for the superiority of RET over the waiting-list control. The superiority of RET as compared to the attention placebo did not receive as strong support in this study as found in Meichenbaum et al.'s study, as the behavioral indicators of anxiety during a speech failed to show improvement.

A recent study by Lipsky, Kassinove, and Miller (1980) is especially noteworthy, as it is one of the only studies to compare the effectiveness of RET with a clinical sample (as opposed to analogue studies where college students are treated). In general, the clients were described as either "neurotic" or "adjustment reaction of adulthood." Furthermore, this study evaluated several of the components of RET by comparing RET treatments with or without rational role reversal or rational-emotive imagery.

Lipsky et al. (1980) reported that "on each dependent variable used, RET, either alone or in combination with rational role reversal or rational-emotive imagery, was superior to both no-contact and a realistic alternate treatment condition" (p. 371). They further noted that both rational role reversal and rational-emotive imagery were useful adjuncts to RET, with large proportions of the dependent variables evidencing superior results for the "RET-plus" conditions. One limitation of this study, however, is that only verbal self-report measures were included as indices of treatment outcome.

While these studies provide support for RET in the treatment of anxiety disorders, many writers who are involved with cognitive-behavioral therapy (Meichenbaum, 1977b; Mahoney, 1977) and RET (DiGuiseppe, Miller, & Trexler, 1977; Zettle & Hayes, 1980) point out that RET is not a totally proven therapy. In fact, both the present and earlier reviewers recognize the limited nature of the data in support of the utility of RET. A major criticism of the RET outcome literature is the scarcity of controlled studies of RET with clinical samples. Perhaps the work of Lipsky et al. will encourage other researchers to accept this challange.

Another question requiring attention is whether there are regional differences in the degree to which clients will accept or be comfortable with the confrontive quality of RET (Kendall, 1982). One might hypothesize that there would be differences, since urban communities (e.g. New York City) are seen by many as having a higher tolerance than rural communities (e.g. Willow Springs, Missouri) for interpersonal confrontation. In conclusion, while practitioners are encouraged to consider adopting the *ABC* model and to implement some of the RET techniques in the treatment of anxiety, researchers are cautioned to the need for clinical evaluations of the efficacy of RET.

Cognitive restructuring

Background.   The phrase "cognitive restructuring" means different things to different people! At the most general extreme, it is synonymous with "cognitive therapy" and can be said to refer to any treatment that seeks to modify behavior by altering the client's pattern of thought. At the most specific extreme, cognitive restructuring refers to a technique, developed by Goldfried et al. (1974), called systematic rational restructuring. Unlike the more delimited meaning associated with labels such as RET, cognitive therapy for depression, and self-instructional training, cognitive restructuring appears to be used as a descriptive term referring to interventions that employ "RET-like, Meichenbaumish, and Goldfriedian" strategies. To avoid contributing to this confusion of terminology, we discuss systematic rational restructuring as the cognitive-restructuring technique.

Systematic rational restructuring developed from Goldfried's search for a more coping-skills-oriented approach. In coping-skills training, a variety of techniques are taught to clients, in order to provide an active skill that they use on their own in coping with a variety of anxiety-eliciting situations. Coping-skills training helps the client identify cues of anxiety and execute behaviors that will reduce or eliminate tension. Unlike mastery interventions, where it might be assumed that clients will not experience anxiety once treatment is completed, coping-skills training expects future incidents of anxiety and teaches clients to deal with anxiety when it is experienced. The ultimate goal, then, is to provide clients with resources to cope independently with their life stresses (e.g., self-control desensitization, Goldfried, 1971).

The goal of self-control desensitization was to modify systematic desensitization (Wolpe, 1958), in order to "construe systematic desensitization as more of an active process, directed toward learning of a general anxiety-reducing skill, rather than the passive desensitization to specific aversive stimuli" (p.228). Self-control desensitization exemplifies how the self-control and coping traditions have effected behavioral and cognitive-behavioral strategies. In developing systematic rational restructuring, RET was interpreted in a self-control framework. While relaxation was the self-control technique in self-control desensitization, cognitive change was to be developed as the self-control skill in systematic rational restructuring.

The techniques of systematic rational restructuring.   Goldfried et al. (1974) outlined four distinct stages of systematic rational restructuring: presentation of rationale, overview of irrational assumptions, analysis of client's problems in cognitive terms, and teaching the individual to modify his/her internal sentences (see also Goldfried, 1979).

Presentation of rationale.   In the first stage, the basic premises of rational restructuring are explained to clients. The therapist's main goal is to help clients accept that beliefs, assumptions, and self-statements mediate emotional arousal. It is important for clients to be made aware of the automatic quality of their thoughts and to realize that they do not deliberately tell themselves certain things prior to or during stressful situations. Since the rationale underlying this therapy may be very new to clients, therapists are encouraged to devote plenty of time to this phase. It may be more frequent than desired that a therapist discovers, in the middle stages of therapy, that the client really does not grasp or accept the basic premises of the therapy. To avoid this, the therapist provides many examples to demonstrate the connection between thoughts and emotions. It is also helpful to have the client explain the rationale/philosophy back to the therapist and to have each client generate his or her own examples of the relationship between thoughts and feelings.

Overview of irrational assumptions.   Before examining the nature of client's assumptions, it is important to have clients acknowledge the unreasonableness or unrealistic nature of certain beliefs to which individuals often adhere. Rather than arguing with clients and trying to convince them of the irrationality of certain beliefs (the more common practice when Ellis employs RET), an attempt is made to have clients arrive at this viewpoint by offering their own arguments regarding the unreasonableness of certain beliefs. To promote this attitude change, the therapist usually plays the devil's advocate and, hence, gives clients the task of convincing the "irrational" therapist that his or her views are, in fact, unreasonable or unrealistic. The goal is not only to help clients recognize that certain beliefs are irrational but also to guide them in generating specific reasons (which may later be used as coping statements) for the unreasonableness of their assumptions.

Analysis of client's problems in cognitive terms.   The goal of this phase is to explore with clients the specific situations in which they become anxious and then to guide them, in a Socratic-like fashion, to come to the realization that their irrational beliefs and self-statements play a role in their anxiety. The analysis of how the client's self-statements affect their feelings should be approached at two levels: (*a*) whether the client is correctly interpreting the situation and (*b*) the implications or meaning of the way in which the client has interpreted the situation.

Teaching the individual to modify internal sentences.   The goal of this phase is to have clients learn to modify their irrational self-statements in situations in which anxiety is experienced. When clients experience anxiety, they are instructed to attend to what they are thinking about in the situation. In this way, anxiety becomes a cue for clients to stop and attend to their thoughts. Furthermore, the cue serves to break up the automatic quality of self-statements and allows clients the opportunity to more realistically reevaluate their beliefs.

In order to provide clients with practice in rational reevaluation, behavioral rehearsal is utilized either through role-playing or through the use of imagery. Clients are helped to create a hierarchy of anxiety-provoking situations and are then encouraged to practice coping behavior. Since rational reevaluation is designed to serve as a coping skill, clients are told to "stay" in the situation until they have been successful in reducing their upset. After the procedure is described to clients, the therapist serves as a model and demonstrates out loud the process of rational reevaluation in the face of an anxiety-provoking situation. Clients are then presented with the first situation in the hierarchy, and they are instructed to think out loud their thoughts and feelings. The therapist's role, at this point, is to prompt clients to help them reevaluate their beliefs. As clients become more skilled at reevaluating their beliefs, the therapist offers fewer prompts. In addition to practice during therapy sessions, clients are encouraged to use this procedure in situ whenever they experience emotional upset. A transcript from Goldfried and Davison (1976) illustrates some of these techniques (see Figure 1).

Figure 1

Transcript of cognitive-behavioral treatment of anxiety

> **Therapist:** I'm going to ask you to imagine yourself in a given situation, and to tell me how nervous you may feel. I'd then like you to think aloud about what you might be telling yourself that is creating this anxiety, and then go about trying to put your expectations into a more realistic perspective. From time to time, I will make certain comments, and I'd like you to treat these comments as if they were your own thoughts. OK?
>
> **Client:** All right.
>
> **Therapist:** I'd like you to close your eyes now and imagine yourself in the following situation: You are sitting on stage in the auditorium, together with the other school board members. It's a few minutes before you have to get up and give your report to the people in the audience. Between 0 and 100 percent tension, tell me how nervous you feel.
>
> **Client:** About 50.
>
> **Therapist:** (Now to get into his head.) So I'm feeling fairly tense. Let me think. What might I be telling myself that's making me upset?
>
> **Client:** I'm nervous about reading my report in front of all these people.
>
> **Therapist:** But why does that bother me?
>
> **Client:** Well, I don't know if I'm going to come across all right. . . .
>
> **Therapist:** (He seems to be having trouble. More prompting on my part may be needed than I originally anticipated.) But why should that upset me? That upsets me because. . . .
>
> **Client:** . . . because I want to make a good impression.

Figure 1 (*concluded*)

Therapist: And if I don't. . . .

Client: . . . well, I don't know. I don't want people to think that I'm incompetent. I guess I'm afraid that I'll lose the respect of the people who thought I knew what I was doing.

Therapist: (He seems to be getting closer.) But why should that make me so upset?

Client: I don't know. I guess it shouldn't. Maybe I'm being overly concerned about other people's reactions to me.

Therapist: How might I be overly concerned?

Client: I think this may be one of those situations where I have to please everybody, and there are an awful lot of people in the audience. Chances are I'm not going to get everybody's approval, and maybe that's upsetting me. I want everyone to think I'm doing a good job.

Therapist: Now let me think for a moment to see how rational that is.

Client: To begin with, I don't think it really is likely that I'm going to completely blow it. After all, I have prepared in advance and have thought through what I want to say fairly clearly. I think I may be reacting as if I already have failed, even though it's very unlikely that I will.

Therapist: And even if I did mess up, how bad would that be?

Client: Well I guess that really wouldn't be so terrible after all.

Therapist: (I don't believe him for one moment. There is a definite hollow ring to his voice. He arrived at that conclusion much too quickly and presents it without much conviction.) I say I don't think it'll upset me, but I don't really believe that.

Client: That's true. I would be upset if I failed. But actually, I really shouldn't be looking at this situation as being a failure.

Therapist: What would be a better way for me to look at the situation?

Client: Well, it's certainly not a do-or-die kind of thing. It's only a ridiculous committee report. A lot of people in the audience know who I am and what I'm capable of doing. And even if I don't give a sterling performance, I don't think they're going to change their opinion of me on the basis of a five-minute presentation.

Therapist: But what if some of them do?

Client: Even if some of them do think differently of me, that doesn't mean that I would be different. I would still be me no matter what they thought. It's ridiculous of me to base my self-worth on what other people think.

Therapist: (I think he's come around as much as he can. We can terminate this scene now.) With this new attitude toward the situation, how do you feel in percentage of anxiety?

Client: Oh, about 25 percent.

Therapist: OK, let's talk a little about some of the thoughts you had during that situation before trying it again.

Source: From *Clinical Behavior Therapy* by Marvin R. Goldfried and Gerald D. Davison, Copyright 1976 by Holt, Reinhart & Winston. Reprinted by permission of Holt, Rinehart & Winston.

Sample studies.   In a controlled study of systematic rational restructuring, Goldfried, Linehan, and Smith (1978) compared this procedure
to a prolonged-exposure group and a waiting-list control group in the
treatment of test-anxious adults. This comparison was conducted to determine whether it was merely the prolonged exposure to a hierarchy of
anxiety-engendering items that would result in successful reduction of
test anxiety, or whether the actual reevaluation of cognition was necessary.
The results indicated that systematic rational restructuring was superior
to the other treatments on self-report measures of test anxiety and generalization of anxiety reduction in social-evaluative situations. The exposure-
alone treatment also produced significant anxiety reduction but was not
as effective as systematic rational restructuring.

The efficacy of systematic rational restructuring in the treatment of
social anxiety was evaluated in a study by Kanter and Goldfried (1979).
This treatment was compared with self-control desensitization, a combination of the two procedures, and a waiting-list control. The results indicated
that all three treatment conditions led to significant decreases in anxiety
at posttreatment, and these results were either maintained or improved
upon at follow-up. A further evaluation of the overall pattern of results
led Kanter and Goldfried to conclude that rational restructuring was more
effective than desensitization in reducing anxiety and irrational beliefs,
and that it produced more within-group improvements than desensitization. The authors point out, however, that the treatment conditions did
not differ on behavioral and physiological measures. The question of
whether modification of cognitions has a greater effect on subjective feelings and less of an effect on behavior needs to be explored further.

While the majority of attention in this section has been devoted to
Goldfried and his colleagues' variant of cognitive restructuring, there
are several different cognitive restructuring approaches that have recently
been studied. The various cognitive restructuring procedures differ mostly
with regard to the amount of emphasis placed on a rational reevaluation
of irrational beliefs ("evaluation") versus emphasis placed on substituting
positive self-statements for negative self-statements ("substitution"). This
latter approach in itself varies, with differential emphasis by therapists
placed on using positive self-statements (e.g., "It may not be so bad if
someone rejects me") versus coping self-statements (e.g., "Okay, now
take a deep breath and try the task slowly"). The approach taken by
Goldfried and his colleagues has clearly been with emphasis on evaluation, while treatment procedures used by other researchers (e.g., Fremouw
& Zitter, 1978; Woodward & Jones, 1980) placed more emphasis on
substitution.

Recognizing that cognitive-restructuring procedures differ on the number of and emphasis on various treatment components, Glogower, Fremouw, and McCroskey (1978) conducted a study to determine the relative
effectiveness of various treatment components, including "insight into

negative self-statements" and "knowledge and rehearsal of coping statements." Their results suggested that, to maximize the effectiveness of cognitive restructuring in the treatment of communication anxiety, coping self-statements should be emphasized, and the identification and insight into negative self-statements should also be included. Note, however, that this study did not compare systematic rational restructuring against more substitution-type therapies, since systematic rational restructuring does a lot more than merely have subjects gain insight into and monitor their negative self-statements. Additional inquiries with clinical cases will advance our knowledge of these promising procedures.

Stress-inoculation training

Background. Stress-inoculation training was developed by Meichenbaum and Cameron (1973a) to provide clients with methods of coping with stressful situations. Since its introduction in 1973, these procedures have been applied to the treatment of a variety of problems, including: multiphobias (Meichenbaum & Cameron, 1973a), test anxiety (Hussian & Lawrence, 1978; Holroyd, 1976), stress of psychiatric hospitalization (Holcomb, 1979), and invasive medical procedures (Kendall, Williams, Pechacek, Graham, Shisslak, & Herzoff, 1979).

The rationale underlying this intervention is to teach clients that they need *not* feel helpless and overwhelmed when experiencing stress. Instead, they are helped to learn ways of dealing with stress in small doses, in order to prevent the stress from increasing to uncontrollable levels. Clients are, hence, "inoculated" against uncontrollable levels of stress by being exposed to and helped to cope with mild levels of stress.

Techniques of stress inoculation. Three stages have been outlined by Meichenbaum and Cameron for stress-inoculation training: education, skills training, and application training. While most researchers using this intervention strategy have adopted use of this tri-stage model, there are, nonetheless, notable fluctuations across studies in the manner in which each of the stages are carred out. Jaremko (1979) has provided a very helpful review of the variations in procedures used by different researchers.

Education phase. Meichenbaum and Turk (1976) have outlined two major components that should take place in this stage: presentation of rationale and division of stress into stages. Meichenbaum and his colleagues teach clients that stress leads to physical arousal, which then ultimately leads to negative self-statements. Jaremko (1979) suggests using a three-component rationale, in which stress creates physical arousal, which then leads to an appraisal of the situation (e.g., "I feel shaky so, therefore, I must be anxious"), and finally leads to negative self-statements.

The second component of this phase is to teach clients that a stress reaction takes place in stages. Meichenbaum and Turk suggest four stages: preparing for a stressor, confronting a stressor, being overwhelmed by a stressor, and self-reinforcement for having coped. The importance of this phase is for clients to learn that stress reactions are not as automatic as previously thought and that they can intervene in the middle of the reaction with various learned techniques. One note of caution: Jaremko stated that "a stringent test of the contribution of the educational rationale of stress inoculation has yet to be undertaken" (p. 37).

Skills training. In this phase, the client is taught the coping skills that are used to deal with stress. Typically, the therapist teaches the client a variety of techniques, with the goal to enable the client to choose the ones that are most helpful in specific situations. Some researchers have attempted to assess their client's coping styles in order to more carefully tailor a "coping menu" for them (Kendall et al., 1979). For example, if a client suggests that, in the past, he has coped best by *avoiding* stressful situations, it may be helpful to teach him or her distraction techniques.

Jaremko (1979) discusses three types of techniques that are taught to the client: physical means of coping, cognitive restructuring or self-instructions, and generalized cognitive strategies. Physical-coping strategies include muscle relaxation and deep-breathing methods. Cognitive-restructuring techniques include both replacement self-statements (identification and modification of negative self-statements) and coping self-statements. Generalized cognitive strategies, according to Jaremko, "may be referred to as a specified way of perceiving or dealing with a stressor" (p. 41). Such strategies are typically presented "cafeteria style" and may include: distraction, somatization, in vivo emotive imagery, and attention focusing.

The skill-training phase was distinguished by Jaremko as that which was considered most important by a number of researchers (Novaco, 1976; Horan, Hackett, Buchanan, Stone, & Demchik-Stone, 1977; Hussian & Lawrence, 1978). What is less clear, however, is whether certain skills are differentially effective for the anxiety disorders. Furthermore, it is unclear whether certain combinations of techniques are more or less effective than alone.

Application training. This final stage involves the patient's actual application and practice of the newly acquired skills in stressful situations. It is essential that the client have the opportunity to actually engage, either imaginally or in vivo, in the use of coping skills. The stressful experiences can be hierarchically arranged, thus increasing the likelihood that the patient will experience successful coping. Several researchers (Turk 1975; Jaremko, 1979; Novaco, 1976) have successfully utilized a "coping-imagery" procedure, in which the client is first instructed to imagine failing but is then guided in regaining control and eventually coping successfully. This procedure is different from "mastery imagery," in which clients imagine always being in control. Kazdin (1974), Meichenbaum (1971), and Sarason (1975) have shown that a coping model produced better treatment effects than did a mastery model. Other procedures used in this stage include: therapist modeling "coping" behavior, having clients role-play giving advice on how to cope with stress, or using clients teaching skills to other clients (Fremouw & Harmatz, 1975). There are clearly differences in the way this phase of treatment is implemented, and more studies are needed to determine the relative contribution of the various treatment components to treatment outcome. It is advised that therapist and client work together in deciding which methods of application training best promote the learning process.

Sample studies. A number of studies have demonstrated the utility of stress-inoculation training (e.g., Holcomb, 1979; Holroyd, 1976; Hussian & Lawrence, 1978; Meichenbaum & Cameron, 1973a; Kendall et al., 1979; Turk, 1975). In the Meichenbaum and Cameron study, the authors compared a modified form of stress-inoculation training (education and skill-training phases only) to a systematic-desensitization group and a waiting-list control group for treating multiphobic clients. In order to test the degree of treatment generalization, one half of the clients were directly helped to deal with their fear of snakes, while the other half were treated for fear of rats. The results indicated that stress inoculation was the most effective treatment in reducing avoidance behavior and in promoting treatment generalization. The systematic desensitization treatment was not effective in transferring treatment effects to the nontargeted phobia.

More recently, Holcomb (1979) evaluated stress-inoculation procedures for patients hospitalized for severe stress reactions. The stress reactions covered a wide range of disorders (e.g., depressive neurosis, anxiety neurosis). The stress-inoculation training included autogenic training as a relaxation-coping skill, cognitive restructuring as a cognitive-change procedure, and rehearsal and modeling as performance-oriented behavioral procedures. Stress inoculation was compared to chemotherapy and to a combination of stress inoculation and chemotherapy.

The results showed a decrease in subjective distress (seven measures of distress were combined via multivariate methods to produce this dependent variable) for all three treatment groups over the first pretreatment week; but the group that received only stress inoculation was significantly superior to a chemotherapy-only group in reducing subjective distress over the course of treatment. While these data are preliminary and one would like to see long-term follow-up, they do suggest the utility of stress-inoculation training with clinical patients suffering severe stress. Moreover, Holcomb's data suggest that stress-inoculation procedures were more effective than chemotherapy in reducing subjective distress. Given the heterogeneity of these clinical patients, these data are most encouraging; but additional research is essential to address the likelihood of change occurring on measures of improvement other than patient self-report.

Kendall et al. (1979) compared the effectiveness of a cognitive-behavioral, stress-inoculation-like treatment and a patient-education treatment in reducing the stress of patients undergoing cardiac catheterization. To control the effects of the increased attention given to treated patients, an attention-placebo control group was employed. A final control group completed the assessment measures but received only the typical, current hospital experiences (i.e., current-conditions control). The results of the Kendall et al. (1979) study indicated that patients' self-reported anxiety was significantly lower after the intervention for the cognitive-behavioral, patient education, and attention-placebo groups than for the current-hospital-conditions controls. However, self-reported anxiety levels *during* the catheterization were significantly lower only for the cognitive-behavioral and patient-education groups. Physicians and technicians independently rated the patients' behavior during catheterization, and these ratings indicated that the patients receiving the cognitive-behavioral treatment were best adjusted (e.g., least tense, least anxious, most comfortable). The patient-education group was rated as better adjusted than the two control groups but significantly less well adjusted than the cognitive-behavioral group.

As is generally true for the cognitive-behavioral interventions for anxiety, stress-inoculation training has been shown to be an effective anxiety-reduction procedure. Moreover, stress inoculation has been applied to other disorders, such as pain and anger. Nevertheless, additional inquiries are necessary to further delineate the most effective intervention strategy and to demonstrate efficacy with additional clinical samples.

DEPRESSION

The cognitive therapy outlined by Beck (1976) and colleagues (Beck, Rush, Shaw, & Emery, 1979) has generally received accepting gestures from psychiatry and psychology, and from cognitively and behaviorally oriented psychotherapists. In our coverage of the treatment of depression, we will devote most of the attention to the Beck approach, describing its theory, procedures, and empirical support. However, we will also briefly review several other cognitive-behavioral interventions that have been applied to the treatment of depression.

Cognitive therapy for depression

Background. Cognitive therapy grew out of Beck's cognitive theory of depression (Beck, 1963, 1976): a theory of depression which states that an individual's emotions and behavior are determined by the way he or she construes the world. It is assumed that depressed individuals have a distorted and unrealistic view of their world. Depressed persons are said to exhibit what Beck (1967) calls a "negative cognitive triad," in that they tend to view *themselves,* their *world,* and the *future* in negative ways. Such negative and distorted modes of information processing are seen in the thought and beliefs that depressed patients hold. Hollon and Beck (1979) have described several different forms of cognitive distortion that are frequently exhibited by depressed clients. They include: selective abstraction (drawing a conclusion based on one of many factors), arbitrary influence (drawing a conclusion in the absence of sufficient evidence), overgeneralization (drawing a sweeping conclusion on the basis of a single instance), magnification and minimization (errors in evaluating performance—emphasizing weakness and ignoring strengths), and all-or-none thinking (black or white, no gray!). (See also Krantz & Hammen, 1979; Lefebvre, 1981). Underlying and mediating these negative cognitive processes are deeply held assumptions and beliefs that are said to effect both depressed mood and behavioral passivity.

Growing directly and logically out of this theory, the aim of cognitive therapy is, therefore, to identify, rationally test, and modify the dysfunctional and maladaptive cognitions that underlie depression. Although the therapy is labeled *cognitive,* it incorporates both behavioral and cognitive principles and, therefore, is considered a cognitive-behavioral intervention by most experts.[2] Beck et al.'s motivation for labeling the therapy as such is probably due to their desire to place emphasis on cognitive change as being the key factor in the treatment. Nevertheless, behavioral techniques occupy a significant position within the therapy sessions. The rationale underlying their use, however, is primarily cognitive, as behaviors provide the evidence necessary to help the depressed person realize that alternative perceptions of him or herself, the world, and the future are possible.

The majority of time in therapy is devoted to labeling beliefs and expectations as *hypotheses,* and then scientifically examining the validity of such beliefs (Hollon & Beck, 1979). A major assumption of this therapy is that, by modifying the depressive's cognitions, there will be a resulting improvement in the cognitive, behavioral, biochemical, and affective components of syndrome depression. It is important for the reader to note that this assumption does not imply that only cognitive factors play a role in the etiology of depression.

---

[2] Beck's approach has been labeled *cognitive therapy of depression.* However, because the approach relies on cognitive and behavioral treatment procedures and seeks to change cognitions and behavior, it is most reasonable to refer to the approach as cognitive-behavioral. Regarding Beck's procedures for the treatment of depression, we use cognitive therapy and cognitive-behavioral therapy interchangeably.

Techniques of cognitive therapy

Although we will provide a summary of the major techniques, a thorough description (along with a week-by-week treatment plan) is available in Beck et al.'s (1979) *Cognitive Therapy of Depression*. The therapy is a time-limited intervention that typically takes place in 20 sessions.

Behavioral techniques play a major role in Beck's cognitive therapy, especially in the early stages of treatment. Such techniques are necessary to animate the severely depressed client, who is likely to be withdrawn and, perhaps, suicidal. Furthermore, data gathered by behavioral self-monitoring can later be used for hypothesis testing when the focus of therapy shifts to a more cognitive emphasis.

Cognitive techniques are used to help clients monitor maladaptive thoughts and rationally reevaluate them. Also, as is true in cognitive-behavioral therapy in general, it is very important that the client learn the cognitive rationale. That is, the therapist must assure that clients understand the relationship between their cognitions and feelings and the role of mediational beliefs (as in the *ABC* model). Last, clients must come to realize the automatic quality of their thoughts.

Therapeutic collaboration.   The basic relationship between therapist and client is one of team work (or collaborative empiricism), in that both participants work together in identifying problem areas and in designing experiments to test beliefs (Hollon & Beck, 1979). The term *collaborative empiricism* implies that data jointly generated by experiments are used to challenge the clients strongly held beliefs (see Figure 2). Therapist persuasion or credibility are not the major tools used to produce change. Another aspect of this therapeutic relationship is that both therapist and client decide together what homework will be most beneficial to the client. Furthermore, it is extremely important to fully explain to the client the rationale behind the various steps within treatment, including the purpose of homework assignments. This procedure de-mystifies the therapeutic process, puts the client on more of an "equal" level with the therapist, and maximizes the client's motivation to work in and out of therapy.

Self-monitoring.   An important skill to teach clients very early in therapy (typically, starting in the first session) is to self-monitor various phenomena such as mood, energy level, and ongoing activities, including pleasure and mastery experiences. Such phenomena are typically rated on an hour-to-hour basis. Mood and energy level are most easily rated on a 0-to-100 scale. Such ratings are extremely useful, both as assessment material and as data to test out hypotheses. These data may "prove," for example, that a client does have some good times when mood is lifted or that a client does get more work done than previously believed.

Figure 2

Two illustrations of how the therapist guides the client in "testing out" certain assumptions

---

Illustration 1

Therapist: Other than your subjective opinion, what evidence do you have that you are ugly?

Patient: Well, my sister always said I was ugly.

Therapist: Was she always right in these matters?

Patient: No. Actually, she had her own reasons for telling me this. But the *real reason* I know I'm ugly is that men don't ask me out. If I weren't ugly, I'd be dating now.

Therapist: That is a possible reason why you're not dating. But there's an alternative explanation. You told me that you work in an office by yourself all day and spend your nights alone at home. It doesn't seem like you're giving yourself opportunities to meet men.

Patient: I can see what you're saying, but still, if I weren't ugly, men would ask me out.

Therapist: I suggest we run an experiment: that is, for you to become more socially active, stop turning down invitations to parties and social events and see what happens. (p. 253)

Illustration 2

Patient: My son doesn't like to go to the theater or to the movies with me anymore.

Therapist: How do you know that he doesn't want to go with you?

Patient: Teenagers don't actually like to do things with their parents.

Therapist: Have you actually asked him to go with you?

Patient: No, as a matter of fact, he did ask me a few times if I wanted him to take me . . . but I didn't think he really wanted to go.

Therapist: How about testing it out by asking him to give you a straight answer?

Patient: I guess so.

Therapist: The important thing is not whether or not he goes with you but whether you are deciding for him what he thinks instead of letting him tell you.

Patient: I guess you are right but he does seem to be inconsiderate. For example, he is always late for dinner.

Therapist: How often has that happened?

Patient: Oh, once or twice . . . I guess that's really not all that often.

Therapist: Is he coming late to dinner due to his being inconsiderate?

Patient: Well, come to think of it, he did say he had been working late those two nights. Also, he has been considerate in a lot of other ways. (pp. 155–156)

Source: From Beck, A. T., Rush, A. J., Shaw, B.F., and Emery, G. D., *Cognitive therapy of depression*, New York: Guilford Press, 1979, pp. 155–156 and 253.

Furthermore, such monitoring may help clients recognize connections between certain mood states and activities. For example, a client previously believing that work was responsible for his or her depressed mood may discover that work is, in fact, associated with improved mood. Monitoring of pleasure and mastery experiences may help the therapist assess whether the client is actually incapable of having pleasure (skill deficit) or whether it is due to cognitive discounting of the experiences (see Beck et al., 1979).

The Beck Depression Inventory (BDI) (Beck, Ward, Mendelson, Mock, & Erbaugh, 1961) and the Automatic Thoughts Questionnaire (ATQ) (Hollon & Kendall, 1980) are also useful therapeutic aids. Both of these instruments can be administered before the beginning of each session. In addition to giving therapist and client a quick measure of the severity of the client's depression, the assessments are also helpful in providing data to the client when he or she questions whether any progress has been made. The ATQ contains a list of thoughts that discriminate depressives from nondepressives. These can serve as an assurance to clients that their ruminations are not unique, and it can serve also as a quick way of eliciting some of the thoughts that are troublesome to the patient.

Activity scheduling.   Many depressed clients withdraw from the activities they once found reinforcing, believing that any attempt would either result in failure or would not be enjoyable. For many depressed clients, anticipatory ruminations prevent them from getting started on an activity. The purpose, then, of activity scheduling is to make the getting-started component simpler. Client and therapist schedule, on an hour-by-hour basis, the client's entire day. Since activity can frequently interrupt rumination, activity scheduling provides the opportunity to demonstrate to clients that improvement is, at least, a possibility.

Graded-task assignments.   Many depressed persons have difficulty engaging in projects, as they ruminate about the size of the job and the possibility of many obstacles. Graded-task assignments divide the task into smaller subtasks and order the tasks from least to most difficult. The client is encouraged to reinforce himself or herself after completion of each subtask, in order to give oneself a sense of competence.

The Dysfunctional Thoughts Record (DTR).   The DTR (see Beck et al., 1979) can be used to facilitate the identification and evaluation of dysfunctional thoughts that mediate emotional upset. Several sessions may be devoted strictly to filling in the first three columns of the record (i.e., the situation, thoughts, and feelings). After the client has become proficient in this process, both in and out of therapy, the client is then helped to rationally reevaluate the thoughts by collecting data relevant to a certain belief. Hollon and Beck (1979) suggest three questions as responses to an automatic thought:

1. What's my evidence?
2. Is there another way of looking at that?
3. Even if it is true, is it as bad as it seems? (p. 190).

The last two columns of the record provide the opportunity to record such reevaluations and the resulting change in feelings.

As the client becomes skillful at identifying and modifying these thoughts, the focus of therapy shifts to identification of the underlying assumptions that appear to organize the automatic thoughts. The identification and analysis of such assumptions follows a similar process of collaborative empirical investigation.

Termination.   Issues of termination need to be discussed at all stages of therapy. It is crucial for clients to treat termination not as the "end of their troubles" but as a time to independently apply the learned-coping techniques whenever they experience emotional upset. One specific technique that may be useful is "planned relapse" (see also Marlatt, 1979). The client is asked to generate the "worst possible event" that might result in the return of depressive feelings. The client is first instructed to imagine this stressful situation, with the accompanying depressive thoughts and feelings, and second, to use the skills learned in therapy, thus demonstrating that future problems can be handled in adaptive ways.

Sample studies of Beck's procedures.   Several studies have been conducted to assess the effectiveness of Beck's therapy. For example, Rush, Beck, Kovacs, and Hollon (1977) compared cognitive therapy to pharmacotherapy in the treatment of unipolar depression. Their results indicated that both interventions demonstrated statistically significant decreases in depressive symptomatology. Furthermore, cognitive therapy proved superior to pharmacotherapy on all of the measures. A striking finding was that 78.9 percent of the patients in cognitive therapy showed marked clinical improvement or remission of symptoms, as compared to 22.7 percent of the pharmacotherapy patients. In addition, the dropout rate was significantly higher for patients receiving pharmacotherapy. Follow-up—at three months, six months, and one year (Kovacs, Rush, Beck, & Hollon, 1981)—demonstrated maintenance of the effects and continued differences between the groups. This study was one of the first to demonstrate that a psychosocial intervention was superior to pharmacotherapy in the treatment of depression.

Group-therapy procedures were examined by Shaw (1977). In Shaw's study, depressed counseling center clients were assigned to either behavioral therapy, cognitive therapy (modeled after Beck), nondirective therapy, or a waiting-list control. Using self-reported depression and blind clinician ratings, Shaw reported that subjects receiving the cognitive therapy evidenced greater improvement on both measures than did subjects in all of the other conditions. However, a recent study of group-cognitive therapy and group-behavioral therapy for the treatment of depressed Puerto Rican women (Comas-Diaz, 1981) suggested that cultural factors may be important. While these results indicated that both treatments were superior to a waiting-list control group, there were no significant differences between the two experimental interventions at post-treatment. The behavioral intervention was shown, however, to be slightly superior in maintenance of treatment effects at follow-up.

The interested reader is referred to several additional studies that have provided support for Beck's cognitive therapy in the treatment of depression (e.g., Dunn 1979; Rush & Watkins, 1981; Shaw & Hollon, 1978). Individual research currently in progress (e.g., Hollon, Wiemer, & Tuason, 1979) and the eventual report of the outcome of the NIMH collaborative study of the treatment of depression will provide additional information pertinent to the efficacy of psychological treatments for depression.

Other cognitive-behavioral interventions for depression.

Several other interventions employing cognitive and behavioral strategies have been developed for the treatment of depression. Before reviewing several different approaches, a note of caution is warranted. A "semantic dilemma" (Kendall, 1982) exists in the designation of interventions for depression. Therapies labeled strictly *cognitive* or *behavioral* may, in actuality, employ both cognitive and behavioral components. Likewise, therapies labeled *cognitive-behavioral* may, in fact, employ almost exclusively cognitive or exclusively behavioral components. In still other cases, what has been labeled *cognitive therapy* by title has, in only limited fashion, any resemblance to Beck's cognitive therapy. Clearly, the evaluation of cognitive-behavioral procedures for the treatment of depression will not be capable of cumulative examination until this "semantic dilemma" is clarified.

Zeiss, Lewinsohn, and Munōz (1979) evaluated the efficacy of cognitive therapy in comparison to interpersonal-skills training and pleasant-events scheduling. The cognitive-therapy treatment was designed to change the way patients think about reality. Kelly's (1955) fixed-role therapy was adapted such that each client was instructed to take on a role (or characterization), as prepared by the therapist. Patients received a rationale, stressing the importance of thoughts, and were taught to identify, categorize, and count certain thoughts. Self-monitoring of thoughts occurred each day. In addition, thought stopping, insertion of positive thoughts, self-instructional training, and rational-emotive procedures were included.

This form of cognitive therapy is different from Beck's cognitive therapy.

The results of this study indicated that, although all treatment modalities significantly alleviated depression, there were no significant differences between the various treatments on self-reports, behavioral observations, or ratings by others. Thus, while this form of cognitive therapy received support, it was not proven to be superior to other psychosocial interventions in the treatment of depression.

Encouraging results for a cognitive-behavioral intervention came from McLean and Hakstian's (1979) major outcome study, in which four modes of treatment for clinically depressed patients were compared. The four conditions were: short-term psychotherapy (insight-oriented), relaxation therapy, behavioral therapy, and drug therapy. The behavior therapy incorporated some cognitive rationale and methods (in addition to the behavioral principles) and, therefore, might be considered a cognitive-behavioral intervention. The clients receiving this therapy condition were informed that their depression was the result of ineffective coping techniques, and the treatment emphasized teaching effective ways to cope with stress. The task of therapy was to help clients to avoid their negative cognitive habits by engaging their environments. Clients were exposed to models, graduated-practice exercises, and the monitoring of achievements.

Results of this study indicated that the behavioral (cognitive-behavioral) treatment was clearly superior to the other treatments on self-report measures at post-treatment and marginally superior at three-month follow-up. The short-term psychotherapy fared most poorly, and there were no significant differences between relaxation and drug treatments. Unfortunately, the outcome indices were based solely on self-report.

Although this study leans more on the behavioral strategies that exist within cognitive-behavioral therapy, it can be said to share some common emphasis with cognitive-behavioral procedures. As a result, while it clearly provides supportive evidence for behavioral therapy of depression, it may also be suggestive of the merits of the cognitive-behavioral perspective. Furthermore, this is again one of the few studies to report superior effects from a psychological (rather than a pharmacological) treatment, with cognitive-behavioral therapy being the victor in both cases.

Several other studies have provided support for cognitive-behavioral interventions in the treatment of depression (Fuchs & Rehm, 1977; Shipley & Fazio, 1973; Taylor & Marshall, 1977). In each of these studies, the cognitive-behavioral interventions differ on the degree of emphasis placed on cognitive versus behavioral components, and on the exact means of effecting cognitive change (e.g., rational emotive versus empirical hypothesis-testing techniques).

It appears that some literature has provided support for cognitive-behavioral treatments of depression. Several recent reviews of the literature on the treatment of depression have similarly concluded that a combination of behavioral and cognitive intervention strategies appear most promising in the treatment of depression (see individual contributions in Rehm, 1981; Whitehead, 1979).

INTERVENTIONS FOR CHILDREN

While a great deal of emphasis has been placed on *modification* of dysfunctional cognitions in the adult client, the emphasis of the cognitive-behavioral interventions as applied to children has been different. The child client has been most frequently characterized not as suffering from dysfunctional cognitions but rather as *lacking* cognitions in situations in which such thinking behavior would be very useful. The focus of cognitive-behavioral interventions for children has been to train these clients to use thinking processes in order to modify their behavior problems (Kendall, 1981b).

Several different cognitive-behavioral approaches have been taken in the treatment of childhood disorders. We have chosen to discuss three of the most widely studied approaches: self-instructional training, social perspective-taking training, and social-cognitive problem-solving training. The latter two interventions have focused mainly on changing social behavior, while the former approach has been applied to nonsocial academic as well as interpersonal behavior.

Self-instructional training

Self-instructional training (Meichenbaum, 1975; 1977a) has been the most widely studied cognitive-behavioral intervention for children, with the target disorders typically being impulsivity/hyperactivity, nonself-control, and aggression. These target problems are typical, since theoretical guidelines suggest that these types of problems are associated with deficits in internal, mediational processing (Camp, 1977; Kendall, 1977). Of late, however, the applications of self-instructional procedures have broadened beyond impulsivity/hyperactivity to include reading (Malamuth, 1979) and math difficulties (Genshaft & Hirt, 1980), and attention problems (Burgio, Whitman, & Johnson, 1980). Self-instructional procedures have also expanded to adult disorders, with some researchers using self-instructions to treat test anxiety (Meichenbaum, 1972), assertiveness problems (Craighead, 1979), dating-skills deficits (Glass, Gottman, & Schmurak, 1976), and schizophrenia (Meichenbaum & Cameron, 1973b). Our attention in this section, however, will be focused on the application of self-instructional training in the treatment of impulsive/hyperactive, nonself-controlled, and aggressive children.

The development of a self-instructional intervention for children was launched by Meichenbaum and Goodman (1971). These researchers based their therapy on the theoretical models developed by Luria (1961) and Vygotsky (1962). Luria had studied the manner in which language acquires a self-regulatory function over overt behavior in young children. Vygotsky discussed the central role that internalized language seems to play in the development of abstract and symbolic thought and emphasized the continuing importance of internalized language or private speech in the self-regulation of behavior through childhood and into the adult years. The approach used by Meichenbaum and Goodman involves training children in the explicit use of appropriate strategies of self-verbalization, in order to regulate their behavior.

Basic self-instructional training approach. The initial self-instructional training procedure developed by Meichenbaum and Goodman was designed to teach impulsive children how to develop self-control and engage in problem-solving behavior. These children were identified as performing very poorly on problem-oriented tasks, as they tended to respond quickly without thorough deliberation.

The actual training centered around more effective means to solve problems. Various training tasks were used, ranging from simple sensorimotor tasks such as copying line patterns, to more complex problem-solving tasks such as performing the Raven Progressive Matrices (Raven, 1938). The therapist instructed the children to verbalize various task-relevant instructions out loud, while problem solving. The self-statements used included: defining *what* the nature and demands of the task are, planning *how* to go about meeting the demands, monitoring *how well* the problem solving is going (including coping with errors), and self-reinforcement for appropriate behavior.

In order to teach the child the verbal self-instructions, the therapist modeled a fading procedure. The five steps involved in this process were: first, the therapist modeled appropriate self-verbalizations out loud, while working on the task; second, the child performed the same task, while the therapist instructed the child out loud; third, the child was instructed to perform the task, while self-verbalizing out loud; fourth, the child performed the task, while whispering the self-instructions; and finally, the child performed the task, using covert self-verbalizations.

An example taken from Meichenbaum and Goodman (1971) nicely illustrates the sequence of self-instructions that a therapist might model to a child:

> Okay, what is it I have to do? You want me to copy the picture with the different lines. I have to go slowly and be careful. Okay, draw the line down, down, good; then to the right, that's it; now down some more to the left. Good, I'm doing fine so far. Remember, go slow. Now back up again. No, I was supposed to go down. That's okay. Just erase the line carefully. . . . Good. Even if I make an error I can go slowly and carefully. Okay, I have to go down now. Finished. I did it. (p. 117)

Sample studies.   The question of the efficacy of a self-instructional
approach in treating various childhood disorders has been addressed
by many researchers. Typically, the self-instructional training is modeled
after Meichenbaum and Goodman's approach, although researchers vary
in the degree to which they modify the basic approach. We will review
some of the major studies in the literature and, when necessary, point
out how the various self-instructional programs might differ.

Meichenbaum and Goodman's (1971) initial two studies assessed the
effectiveness of self-instructional training in modifying the behavior of
"impulsive" school children. Their results demonstrated the effectiveness
of self-instructions in producing a more cognitively reflective approach
in the trained subjects over control children, leading to improved scores
on a series of nonsocial-problem tasks (e.g., Porteus Maze Test, Porteus,
1955; Matching Familiar Figures (MFF) test, Kagan, 1966). A follow-up
assessment, one month later, indicated that the improvement in the trained
versus untrained groups had been maintained. However, no generalization of training effects was apparent on classroom observations of inappropriate (off-task) behavior or on teacher ratings.

In their second study, Meichenbaum and Goodman (1971) tested
whether cognitive modeling (without behavioral rehearsal of self-instructions) was sufficient to teach self-control to impulsive children. In order
to test this notion, self-instructional training was compared to modeling
and control groups. The results indicated that the self-instructional training
and modeling both resulted in a significant increase in response latencies,
but that only the self-instructional procedures resulted in a decrease in
errors. Meichenbaum and Goodman concluded that "the experimenter's
cognitive modeling was a necessary but not sufficient condition for engen-
dering self-control in impulsive children" (Meichenbaum, 1977a, p. 33).
Although the data are not overwhelming, these studies served a seminal
role in the advancment of cognitive-behavioral interventions with children.

In a more recent study, Douglas, Parry, Marton, and Garson (1976)
evaluated the effectiveness of a self-instructional approach in teaching
hyperactive boys to use more-effective and less-impulsive strategies for
approaching cognitive tasks, academic problems, and social situations.
Douglas et al. expanded upon the modeling component of Meichenbaum
and Goodman's approach by occasionally giving children direct instruction in specific search, focusing, and attention-deployment strategies. Another interesting component of their approach was training children together in pairs in the later sessions. The rationale given for this procedure
was to attempt to make the training environment more similar to the classroom and to provide children with an opportunity for peer-interaction
training. Overall, the findings provided some supportive evidence for
the effectiveness of self-instructional training procedures with children.
More specifically, though some measures did not evidence desired
changes, changes in both latency and error measures on the MFF, im-

provement on measures of reading ability, and beneficial changes on the Porteus Maze Test were evident following training. However, the evidence for generalization to classroom behavior and to situations outside of the training situation was not strong.

Similar findings were reported by Parrish and Erickson (1981)—that is, changes were found on academic task performance but not on ratings of classroom behavior. Furthermore, their study contrasted several different cognitive strategies to modify impulsivity: (a) scanning-strategy instructions, (b) verbal self-instructions, (c) scanning-strategy instructions plus verbal self-instructions, and (d) attention control. These comparisons suggested that the verbal self-instructions and scanning-strategy instructions were sufficient to modify impulsive-task performance. Contrary to expectations, the combined treatment was not superior.

While the training focus of the two previous intervention programs was primarily geared to the modification of nonsocial, academic-type problems, Camp, Blom, Hebert, and van Doorninck (1977) applied self-instructional methods directly to the training of interpersonal problem-solving skills in aggressive boys. The selection of aggressive subjects was based on prior research, which suggested that young, aggressive boys, despite verbal-intellectual skills, show a verbal-mediational deficiency. That is, aggressive boys showed more immature private speech than nonaggressive boys and less-adequate private speech for self-regulation on a variety of cognitive and motor tasks (e.g., Camp, 1977; Camp, van Doorninck, Zimet, & Dahlem, 1977). Problem-solving training content included cognitive impersonal problems (after Meichenbaum & Goodman, 1971) as well as interpersonal problem-solving games as developed by Spivack and Shure (1974). The specifics of the content of Spivack and Shure's training procedure will be described in a later section.

Camp et al.'s self-instructional training was based on developing answers to four basic questions: What is my problem? What is my plan? Am I using my plan? How did I do? To initially engage the children in the process of rehearsing the self-instructions, a copycat game was used, in which the children repeated self-statements modeled by the experimenter. The copycat procedure was gradually phased out, and the child was encouraged to verbalize his or her own strategy and eventually to bring the problem analysis and strategy planning to a covert level.

Results showed that both trained and nontrained aggressive children improved on teacher ratings of aggressive behavior. Teachers did rate the experimental group, however, as showing a significant improvement on prosocial behaviors as compared to aggressive controls. On cognitive measures, the treated group showed improvement over aggressive controls on some measures, but not on others. A promising finding was that at post-test, cognitive test scores for the treated group were similar to the scores of a normal reference group and different from the scores of aggressive controls.

As the authors pointed out, one factor that might have limited program effectiveness was the high level of verbal output and silliness shown by the aggressive boys (handled mainly by ignoring it). In this context, Kendall (1977; 1981b) has argued for the inclusion of systematically applied behavioral contingencies to enhance the effectiveness of cognitive training programs.

Self-instructions within combined cognitive and behavioral interventions. The cognitive-behavioral intervention employed by Kendall and his colleagues differs from the programs discussed previously in that, in addition to self-instructions, these interventions place a special emphasis on modeling and the employment of behavioral contingencies. The modeling procedure differs, in that the therapist models all stages of the self-verbalization process from speaking out loud, to a whisper, and finally, to covert verbalization. Therapists also model self-instructional problem solving in relation to their own tasks. For instance, locating the training materials for each session often requires searching through a briefcase of materials. The therapist talks out loud to him/herself, while searching for the relevant material. Children were also given a visual aid in the form of a cue card that stated in pictures and words, "stop, listen, look, and think" (after Palkes, Stewart, & Kahana, 1968).

For the behavioral contingencies, children were given tokens (at the start of each session) that could be exchanged (at the end of the session) for material rewards. Children lost chips, however, for mistakes made either in failing to follow procedures of self-instructional training, hurrying, or in giving the wrong answer to a problem. In addition, social reward and praise were given for appropriate behavior.

Sample studies. Kendall and his colleagues have conducted several outcome studies that provide some support for the utility of their cognitive-behavioral self-control treatment—a treatment designed to reduce impulsivity in social situations and on task performance. In their first controlled, group-treatment study, Kendall and Finch (1978) applied their procedures to the training of various cognitive/attentional tasks in impulsive, emotionally disturbed children. A control group received exposure to the training tasks and received noncontingent rewards at the end of sessions; but this group did not receive modeling or verbal self-instructions, nor was response-cost contingent upon errors.

Results indicated that treated children performed significantly less impulsively on the latency and errors scores from an impulsivity measure (MFF test). In addition, the treated children were rated by teachers as significantly less-impulsive in the classroom. These treatment effects remained evident at follow-up. Several self-report measures of impulsivity did not show treatment effects.

Additional analyses of data from the Kendall and Finch outcome study have focused on the effects of the treatment on the verbal behavior of the children (Kendall & Finch, 1979b). For example, the MFF test performance of the impulsive children (treated and controlled) was tape-recorded and examined, along with performances by children classified as reflective. Coding of the verbal behavior indicated that, while nonsignificant effects were found for several specific codes, the impulsive children that had received treatment evidenced a significant increase in total on-task verbal behavior at post-treatment. Furthermore, it was found that the treated impulsive children asked more task-related questions than did the reflective children and that the off-task verbal behavior of the treated impulsives at follow-up was consistently identical to the low rate of the reflectives. These findings add support to the notion that the treated children were verbalizing differently as a result of the treatment.

Kendall and Wilcox (1980) addressed the question of how the *type* of self-instructions taught to children effects treatment outcome. Should children be instructed to use self-guiding speech that is *specific* to each task that they work on, or should the emphasis be on the use of general, *conceptual* self-instructions? Kendall and Wilcox hypothesized that the use of conceptual self-instructions would be more effective in producing treatment generalization. In this study, nonself-controlled, teacher-referred, classroom-problem children were randomly assigned to concrete training, conceptual training, or an attention/placebo control group. Training covered interpersonal-problem areas as well as academic-impersonal tasks. Engaging in role-play was a required part of the treatment.

Blind teacher ratings of self-control and hyperactivity evidenced therapeutic generalization to the classroom setting at post-treatment and at a one-month follow-up. The treatment effects were stronger for the conceptually trained children. Normative comparisons indicated that the teachers' ratings of self-control and hyperactivity for the conceptually treated children were within normal limits, as defined in Kendall and Wilcox.

A one-year follow-up of the children in this study (Kendall, 1981c) provided some, although limited, support for the long-term effectiveness of the treatment. It was found that conceptually trained children showed significantly better recall of the material they had learned than did either concrete-training or control children, and they were rated by new classroom teachers as not sufficiently lacking in self-control to warrant referral. Numerous improvements were found for all subjects in all groups, and these effects were attributed to increased age.

In a later study, Kendall and Zupan (1981) addressed whether group treatment would produce greater generalization than would individual training. Since group treatment provides training in a therapeutic context that is similar to the setting in which generalization is desired, and since the group situation would provide multiple peer models, group training was thought to facilitate generalization. Recall that this procedure was used in the Douglas et al. (1976) study, but the addition of the group-treatment component was not systematically evaluated in that study. Kendall and Zupan's (1981) cognitive-behavioral procedures, while including training in cognitive tasks, had primary focus on the training of interpersonal problem solving. The results indicated that there were some improvements for all treatment conditions, yet only the individual and group cognitive-behavioral treatments evidenced improvements on teachers' blind ratings of self-control at post-treatment and on the children's performance on a measure of perspective-taking at follow-up. In relation to normative data, the individual and group treatments placed children within nondeviant limits on ratings of self-control. Apparently, although the group-treatment condition had a more interpersonal context than the individual condition, both treatments led to comparable improvements.

A one-year follow-up of this study (Kendall, 1982) provided further support. Pre-treatment to one-year follow-up improvements were found for children across treatment conditions, but only the children receiving group treatment were *not* significantly different from nonproblem children on ratings of self-control; and only the children receiving individual treatment were not significantly different from nonproblem children on hyperactivity ratings. Structured interviews indicated that individually treated children showed significantly better recall of the ideas they had learned and produced significantly more illustrations of use of the ideas than either the group-treatment or the nonspecific-treatment conditions.

The evidence produced by the studies of Kendall and his colleagues supports a *combined cognitive-and-behavioral therapy.* In the studies where some evidence of generalization was provided, the treatment combined cognitive self-instructional training with behavioral contingencies, role-playing, and modeling. Some other recent studies have also provided support for a combined treatment (Cameron & Robinson, 1980; Varni & Henker, 1979) and have suggested the superiority of the combined approach over cognitive or behavioral strategies alone (Barabash, 1978; Kendall & Braswell, 1982c; Neilans & Israel, 1981). While the treatment procedures require further exploration with clinical cases, and further study of the most efficacious manner of producing generalization is required, the research provides cautious optimism for the continued development of cognitive-behavioral self-control training for children.

Clinical and research suggestions. Several suggestions have been proposed by Meichenbaum (1977a) and elaborated elsewhere (e.g., Kendall, 1977; Kendall & Finch, 1979a) as important considerations to facilitate the implementation of self-instructional training. These suggestions include: (*a*) using the child's own medium of play to initiate and model self-talk, (*b*) using tasks that require sequential cognitive strategies, (*c*) using peer teaching by having children cognitively model while performing for another child, (*d*) guarding against the child using the self-statements in a rote, noninvolved fashion, (*e*) supplementing the self-instructional training with behavioral contingencies, (*f*) training the problem-solving self-instructions under conditions of low emotional arousal but, subsequently, requiring the child to engage in self-instructions under high emotional arousal, and (*g*) involving the parents and the schools, in order to increase the breadth of the context of training.

Social perspective-taking training

Background. Perspective-taking training has been derived from research into the development of a child's cognitive ability to take the perspective (or role) of another person in a social interaction. Mead (1934) stressed the importance of the role-taking process for social development, and Piagetian theory later provided the basis for a series of pioneering studies (Feffer & Gourevich, 1960; Flapan, 1968; Flavell, Botkin, Fry, Wright, & Jarvis, 1968). The basic idea is that children, as they develop, emerge from a relative state of egocentrism, in which they are unable to accurately differentiate their own internal emotional states, thoughts, and perceptions, from those of other persons.

Social perspective-taking training has been applied both to normal and deviant samples of children. When applied to normal samples, the rationale is generally to help children more effectively apply their relativistic or perspectivistic cognitive styles to interpersonal problem solving. With deviant populations, however, there is an assumption of a delay in the acquisition of various perspective-taking skills that is hypothesized to be causally related to acquisition of various forms of social deviancy. The goal with deviant populations, then, is to train children with the cognitive skills necessary to acquire prosocial styles of behavior.

Procedures and sample studies. One of the most frequently cited series of perspective-taking training studies with deviant populations are those of Chandler and his associates (Chandler, 1973; Chandler, Greenspan, & Barenboim, 1974). In the first Chandler study, treatment was applied to chronically delinquent boys, with the goal being to teach role-taking skills and decrease the rate of delinquency. Training involved having the children write and videotape role-play skits of events involving persons of their own age. Each skit was replayed until each participant had occupied each different role of the characters in the skit, and videotapes were reviewed at the end of each set. The rationale for this procedure was to help children step outside of their egocentric views and assume roles or perspectives different from their own. The outcome of this study revealed that, relative to no-treatment controls and to an attention-control group who watched animated and documentary films, the experimental children improved significantly on a measure of social-cognitive role-taking skill. Perhaps the most exciting and clinically significant

finding of this study was that the experimental group showed significantly
lower recidivism rates at an 18-month follow-up.   •

In a second study, Chandler et al. (1974) compared two different
types of perspective taking: role-taking training and referential-communication training (based on procedures of Botkin, 1966; Shantz & Wilson,
1972). Referential-communication training involves improving a child's
accuracy of verbal communication, that is, his or her ability to take a
listener's informational needs into account when communicating a verbal
message. A series of referential-communication games (see Greenspan,
Zlotlow, Burka, & Barenboim, 1973) were used in which children were
frequently interrupted from play to engage in discussion of how successful
players were in verbally cooperating with each other. When it was determined that failure of communication had occurred, children were asked
to play back (all conversations were tape-recorded) their discussion in
order to determine the reason for failure. Both experimental groups improved significantly on role-taking measures, while only children in the
referential-communication group showed significant improvement on referential-communication measures. Comparisons on ratings of behavioral
improvement (12 months after training) showed only a trend toward
greater improvement in the two treatment groups, as compared to no-
treatment controls. However, significant correlations were obtained between the degree of behavioral improvement and the degree of improvement on the social-cognitive tasks. Several other perspective-taking studies
(e.g., Elardo & Caldwell, 1976; Iannotti, 1978) also have provided evidence suggestive of treatment effectiveness (see also Urbain & Kendall,
1980).

Problem-solving training

Background.   Briefly, problem-solving training aims at teaching children modes of dealing with problematical social situations (e.g., two children having to share one toy) in ways that will facilitate prosocial behavior.
Training emphasis takes place at the level of cognitive thinking processes,
in contrast to interventions that teach more discrete behaviors.

For several years, Spivack, Shure, Platt, and their colleagues have
been working on the assessment and training of interpersonal cognitive
problem-solving (ICPS) skills in children (Shure & Spivack, 1978; Spivack,
Platt, & Shure, 1976; Spivack & Shure, 1974). They describe several
ICPS abilities, which they suggest are related to successful interpersonal
problem solving. Three abilities have received the greatest attention and
have shown some relationships to measures of social adjustment in
children: (a) alternative thinking, the ability to generate multiple, potential-
alternative solutions to a given interpersonal-problem situation; (b) conse-

quential thinking, the ability to foresee the immediate and more long-range consequences of a particular alternative and to use this information in the decision-making process; and (c) means-ends thinking: the ability to elaborate or plan a series of specific actions (a means) to attain a given goal, to recognize potential obstacles to reaching the goal, and to use a realistic time framework in implementing a means to the goal.

Procedures and sample studies.   The problem-solving training programs developed by Spivack and Shure and associates are presented in the form of specific training scripts, consisting of structured daily activities and discussion to teach component ICPS skills. The training script for preschoolers (Spivack & Shure, 1974) consists of a sequence of 46 short (20 to 30 minutes) daily lessons, activities, and games conducted by the preschool teacher. The program first involves teaching a number of skills felt (though not demonstrated) to be prerequisite for problem solving—namely, linguistic concepts such as same-different and if-then and the ability to identify basic emotions (happy, angry, sad). The remainder of the program is devoted to a series of hypothetical and actual interpersonal-problem situations and is divided sequentially into three parts: (a) enumerating solutions only, (b) enumerating consequences only and (c) pairing specific solutions with specific consequences. Teacher demonstration and puppet play are used to illustrate the training concepts, and whenever possible, the problem-solving methods are applied to actual problems that arise among the children in school (see also D'Zurilla & Nezu, 1982, for a discussion of social problem-solving procedures with adults).

The results of the program indicated that the trained children improved, relative to no-treatment controls, on measures of alternative and consequential thinking as well as on a measure of overt behavioral adjustment derived from the Devereux Child Behavior Rating Scale (Spivack & Spotts, 1966). Although the teachers were not blind to the experimental conditions when they rated the children at posttest, improvement was maintained at follow-up one year later, when children were rated by new teachers who were unaware of the experimental conditions. However, the absence of some type of control-group procedure other than a no-treatment group makes it impossible to examine to what extent the problem-solving training itself was responsible for the outcomes, as opposed to factors that were not specific to the training, such as special attention and expectancy for change. It is also difficult to determine which of the component skills taught might have been most responsible for the observed improvements. Note, however, that recent data have provided only slight support for the ecological validity of the ICPS measures (Kendall & Fischler, 1981) and have failed to support the effectiveness of the training (Rickel, Eshelman, & Loigman, 1981). The addition of communications training and behavioral strategies and working with each child's family may be necessary to achieve changes with difficult populations (e.g., Alexander & Parsons, 1973; Klein, Alexander, & Parsons, 1977).

Cognitive-behavioral interventions for children: General strategies

Despite the diversity of cognitive-behavioral interventions for children, the training programs, as they are put into practice, have several similarities. Although they differ in specific-training content, the studies usually involve one or more of the following instructional methods (Urbain & Kendall, 1980): (a) direct verbal instruction to the child, (b) modeling, (c) environmental reinforcement (material rewards, social praise, response cost), (d) role-play and behavior rehearsal, (e) self-instructional training, (f) self-reinforcement, and (g) feedback and group discussion. We encourage the application of the combination of these methods, particularly self-instructions, modeling, role-playing, and behavioral contingencies. There also appears to be considerable overlap of training content across the different training approaches, including emotional, academic, interpersonal, and cognitive tasks. Quality applications include all of these content areas.

OTHER APPLICATIONS

Up to now, we have restricted our discussion to the cognitive-behavioral interventions that have most frequently been applied to the treatment of anxiety, depression, and childhood behavior disorders. Such a strict categorization of treatments by disorder, however, does not exist in clinical practice. In recent years, various cognitive-behavioral interventions have been applied to a multitude of psychological disorders. Our goal in this next section is to provide an overview of the "expanded terrain" to which cognitive-behavioral interventions have been applied. We have chosen to organize this section by treating each disorder separately.

Assertion problems

Self-instructional training has been applied to clients with assertion problems. Craighead (1979) demonstrated that a self-instructional training program was significantly superior to no-treatment or placebo controls on behavioral tests, self-reported behavior, and self-reported thoughts related to assertiveness. Craighead's treatment included discussion of irrational beliefs regarding assertion, individual's personal rights, and the consequences of assertive behaviors. The therapist worked to help the client identify irrational self-statements and served as a model who generated self-statements that would counter the irrational ones.

Cognitive-restructuring interventions have received a great deal of attention in the treatment of assertiveness (e.g., Alden, Safran, & Weideman, 1978; Carmody, 1978; Hammen, Jacobs, Mayol, & Cochran, 1980; Linehan, Goldfried, & Goldfried, 1979; Safran, Alden, & Davidson, 1980). In these studies, cognitive restructuring techniques were compared to behavioral skills-training interventions, and the results have generally shown both interventions to be effective on behavioral and self-report measures. A frequently researched question with this population is whether level of anxiety interacts with type of treatment provided. Since the results are equivocal, application of cognitive restructuring appears useful across levels of client anxiety.

A third cognitive-behavioral intervention aimed at the treatment of assertiveness is covert modeling (Cautela, 1971). Covert modeling is a procedure whereby a client imagines models engaging in desired behaviors. In two controlled studies, Kazdin (1979, 1980) provided strong support for this treatment of assertion problems. Furthermore, Kazdin presented evidence that both covert and overt rehearsal strategies were equally effective and that a client's tendency to elaborate on imagery instructions should be encouraged.

Eating disorders

Cognitive-restructuring techniques have been suggested as useful in the treatment of obesity (Mahoney & Mahoney, 1976) and anorexia nervosa (Leon, 1979). Mahoney and Mahoney's weight-reduction program combines self-monitoring, environmental programming, and cognitive-restructuring techniques, in order to teach clients self-controlled eating behavior. Their cognitive-restructuring component includes monitoring food-related thoughts, evaluating whether such thoughts are appropriate or realistic to the situation, and training in modifying such maladaptive thoughts.

Leon (1979) has suggested that cognitive-restructuring procedures be applied to the treatment of the distorted body image associated with anorexia and to clients' irrational beliefs about the necessity for total self-control. In a recent paper, Garner and Bemis (1982) have suggested a cognitive-behavioral treatment for anorexia that is based on Beck's cognitive therapy. Clearly, interest in the application of cognitive-behavioral interventions to the treatment of eating disorders is quite recent, and controlled outcome studies are needed before any conclusions can be drawn.

Covert-conditioning interventions have also been applied to the treatment of eating disorders. Covert-conditioning interventions differ from other cognitive-behavioral treatments, in that the former are more imagery-based, whereas the latter are more verbal- or language-based (Mahoney & Arnkoff, 1978). Two covert-conditioning procedures that have received the most attention are coverant control (Homme, 1965) and covert sensitization (Cautela, 1966). Coverant-control procedures instruct clients to first rehearse a negative coverant (i.e., an abbreviation for covert operant; e.g., "overeating is disgusting"); second, to follow it by a positive coverant (e.g., "I'll feel better when I eat less"); and finally, to have the client reinforce him/herself with a pleasant activity. Studies evaluating this strategy for the treatment of obesity have found unimpressive results, as they have been unable to demonstrate the treatment as more effective than attention-control groups (Horan & Johnson, 1971; Tyler & Straughan, 1970).

In covert sensitization, clients are instructed to imaginally associate the undesired behavior with an extremely aversive consequence. Studies evaluating this intervention have also demonstrated minimal treatment influence (Diament & Wilson, 1975; Elliott & Denney, 1975; Foreyt, & Hagen, 1973; also see discussions in Leon, 1979; and Mahoney & Arnkoff, 1978).

Anger control

The stress-inoculation model has been extended to the treatment of anger (Novaco, 1979). The three treatment phases (i.e., cognitive preparation, skill acquisition, and application training) remain generally intact, and modifications of the procedures relate most directly to the target problem—anger. Previously reported evidence supports the effectiveness of the cognitive-behavioral control of anger (Novaco, 1975, 1977), and recent evidence adds further corroboration. Stress inoculation has also been applied with success to clients (two families) whose lack of control of anger had resulted in child abuse (Denicola & Sandler, 1980).

Systematic rational restructuring for anger control was conducted by Hamberger and Lohr (1980). Their results suggested that the cognitive-behavioral intervention was effective in modification of irrational beliefs and intense levels of emotional distress.

Pain

Cognitive-behavioral procedures for the regulation of pain have received support (see discussion by Turk & Genest, 1979). Holroyd, Andrasik, and Westbrook (1977) compared a stress-coping training procedure that included techniques from Beck, Goldfried, and Meichenbaum's therapy procedures to biofeedback training in the treatment of tension headaches. Results demonstrated that only the cognitive-behavioral intervention showed substantial improvement of daily recordings of headaches. An important aspect of this stress-coping procedure was that the treatment was not tailored specifically to tension headaches. Rather, the treatment focused on providing general skills for coping with stress, as it was assumed that maladaptive cognitions and the resulting emotional disturbances precipitate tension headaches (see also Holroyd & Andrasik,

1982). Positive results were also found by Mitchell and White (1977), who employed a broad-based cognitive-behavioral intervention in the treatment of migraine headaches (see also Hackett & Horan, 1980; Horan, Hackett, Buchanan, Stone, & Demchik-Stone, 1977; Klepac, Hauge, Dowling, & McDonald, 1981).

Obsessive-compulsive disorders

McFall and Wollersheim (1979) presented a cognitive-behavioral formulation and approach to treating obsessive-compulsive disorders. These authors suggested that clients first be trained in identifying and discriminating a wide range of emotional states and, second, learn cognitive-restructuring techniques. Emphasis within the cognitive-restructuring component is given to helping clients realize that they overevaluate the dangerousness of events and underestimate their abilities to cope with threat. Empirical investigation has not yet been conducted.

An evaluation of the effectiveness of a self-instructional intervention for the treatment of obsessive-compulsive problems has been conducted by Emmelkamp, van der Helm, van Zanten, and Plochg (1980). Patients were randomly assigned to either exposure in vivo or to self-instructions and exposure in vivo. The results indicated significant improvements for all subjects, with no enhancing effects for self-instructional training. Kendall (1982) argued that these nonenhancing results question whether the nature of the pathology of obsessive-compulsive neurosis is too similar to the self-instructional intervention strategy. Obsessive-compulsive clients are already engaging in excessive self-talk, rumination, and self-doubting; and a treatment that feeds into this pathological system, without systematic altering of the existing thought pattern, may not be desired. Cognitive-restructuring techniques, on the other hand, may be more appropriate for this clinical population.

Academic achievement

In addition to treating clinical disorders, cognitive-behavioral interventions have been applied to individuals with test anxiety and poor academic achievement. Self-instructional training has helped seventh-grade females who received low math-achievement scores (Genshaft & Hirt, 1980) and test-anxious college students (Meichenbaum, 1972). The differential effectiveness of rational restructuring was compared to self-instructional training in the treatment of test anxiety (Cooley & Spiegler, 1980) and for helping college students adapt to their academic major department and improve their academic performance (Kim, 1980). The results of these studies suggested that both types of cognitive-behavioral interventions have some merit in improving academic performance (see Kendall & Braswell, 1982a, for a discussion of assessments for cognitive-behavioral interventions in the schools). Holroyd (1976) demonstrated the superiority of a cognitive-behavioral intervention that included training in rational reevaluation and learning task relevant coping self-statements to systematic desensitization in the treatment of test anxiety.

Test anxiety has also been treated with covert modeling (Harris & Johnson, 1980). In this study, subjects were randomly assigned to covert modeling combined with study-skills training, self-control desensitization combined with study-skills training, or study-skills training alone. The results favored the covert-modeling group, since it was the only treatment to show improvement on academic performance measured during an academic quarter subsequent to treatment.

Childhood behavior problems

Although self-instructional and other problem-solving therapies have been most frequently applied to children, several researchers have recently suggested adapting cognitive-restructuring procedures to children and adolescents (see discussions by Bedrosian, 1981; DiGuiseppe, 1981). Forman (1980) reported on an application of cognitive restructuring to aggressive elementary school children. The cognitive-restructuring intervention consisted of describing aggression-provoking situations, stating what each person was likely thinking in the situation, developing a script of thoughts that would not have led them to get angry, and having the children close their eyes and imagine the aggression-inducing situation while thinking the nonaggressive thoughts. Both cognitive restructuring and a response-cost program were significantly more effective than a placebo-control in reducing aggressive behavior.

Miscellaneous

Among the diverse areas receiving attention are athletic performance (see Mahoney, 1979; Mahoney & Arnkoff, 1978), problem drinking (see Marlatt, 1979), sexual problems (Steger, 1978), and smoking cessation (see Pechacek & Danaher, 1979).

ISSUES

In reviewing the research and clinical descriptions of the various cognitive-behavioral interventions described in this chapter, we recognized several topics of concern that deserve explanation and further consideration. First and foremost is the "semantic dilemma" that exists within the cognitive-behavioral literature.[3] Names given to various treatment inter-

---

[3] The semantic dilema readily translates into a methodological and evaluative concern when one attempts to cumulatively review the outcome literature. The problem exists both for studies that claim to employ the same procedures (but, in fact, operationalize the treatment differentially) and studies that operationalize the treatment similarly (but employ different labels).

ventions are inconsistent. For example, the term *rational restructuring* has been used interchangeably with the terms *cognitive therapy* and *cognitive-behavior therapy* and has included under its rubric such therapies as RET, self-instructional training, systematic rational restructuring, Beck's cognitive therapy for depression, and stress-inoculation training. These therapies differ in important ways and may be effective for very different reasons. We hope that the terminological turmoil will terminate.

To better understand the differences between the various adult cognitive-behavioral interventions, we have outlined some of the distinctions between rational-emotive therapy, systematic rational restructuring, stress-inoculation training, and Beck's cognitive therapy for depression. Five dimensions are used for comparison: (a) theoretical orientation of the therapy, and its associated target of change, (b) nature of the therapeutic relationship, (c) principle cognitive change agent, (d) source of evidence on which reappraisals are based, and (e) degree of emphasis on self-control. As seen in Figure 3, each therapy has a different profile based on these five dimensions. When comparing the different interventions in this way, it appears that systematic rational restructuring and stress inoculation (and systematic rational restructuring and cognitive therapy of depression) are quite similar to each other, as they differ on only one dimension. In contrast, RET and cognitive therapy are quite dissimilar from each other, as they differ on four out of five dimensions.

Figure 3

Cognitive-behavioral interventions for adults: Suggested distinctions

Therapy	Theoretical orientation/ target of change	Nature of therapeutic relationship	Principal cognitive change agent	Source of evidence on which to base reappraisal	Emphasis on self-control
Rational-emotive therapy	Insight-oriented/philosophical	Didactic and confrontive	Rational reevaluation	Rational	Low
Systematic rational restructuring	Cognitive and behavioral	Collaborative	Rational reevaluation	Rational*	High
Stress-inoculation training	Cognitive and behavioral	Collaborative	Some rational reevaluation—more emphasis on training task-relevant self-statements	Rational*	High
Cognitive therapy of depression	Cognitive and behavioral	Collaborative	Rational reevaluation	Empirical	High

* These procedures also rely on performance-based strategies to facilitate client reevaluation and, thereby, rely to some degree on empirical evidence.

At present, we cannot determine the importance of each dimension in affecting therapeutic change. It is likely that there may be interaction effects, since different dimensions may play a greater role in therapeutic change, depending on the type of client, therapist, or client problem. Furthermore, some of these dimensions may not be relevant to differential-treatment outcome, and there may be other, more relevant dimensions that have not been mentioned. However, once researchers and clinicians have available a more systematic and universal language to use in talking about different therapies, we will then be able to determine more precisely the elements of therapy that have the desired treatment effects.

A second major problem within the cognitive-behavioral literature pertains to the lack of cognitive assessments. In regard to treatment, cognitive assessments are necessary (a) to confirm the effects of treatment procedures on cognitions and (b) to identify the mechanisms of change (Kendall, 1981a; Kendall & Korgeski, 1979). The confirmation of treatment effects is crucial, since one must demonstrate that cognitive-behavioral interventions do, indeed, alter subjects' internal dialogue or self-statements, and one must also examine whether subjects in noncognitive interventions show similar cognitive change. Cognitive-assessment procedures are also necessary when comparing several different treatments. Such measures allow researchers to determine the qualitative and quantitative differences (i.e., the change in frequency and content of cognition) across different types of treatment procedures (see also Glass & Arnkoff, 1982; Kendall & Braswell, 1982a, 1982b; Kendall & Hollon, 1981; Merluzzi, Glass, & Genest, 1981).

Specification of the *mechanism of change* in therapy has emerged as a hot issue in treatment-outcome studies. Many researchers and clinicians have adopted Bandura's model of self-efficacy (Bandura, 1977, 1978; Bandura, Adams, & Beyer, 1977) in explaining the effectiveness of their interventions. That is, the client improvements are the results of performance-based procedures, but the mechanism of change is an increase in the client's sense of perceived self-efficacy. While the concept of self-efficacy has theoretical and practical value, it has too frequently been applied indiscriminantly as the mechanism of change, when self-efficacy has not been assessed and/or when several different interventions are shown to be equivalent in outcome. The invoking of self-efficacy appears as a platitude, unless systematic attempts are made to measure self-efficacy. Fortunately, several researchers have taken this challenge in assessing self-reported self-efficacy (Bandura, Adams, Hardy, & Howells, 1980; Hammen et al., 1980; Kazdin, 1980; Zeiss et al., 1979), and have provided support for an increase in self-efficacy as a function of treatment. Additional research is necessary to further our understanding of the mechanism underlying behavior change. Along this line of inquiry, Hollon (1981) has generated ratings of therapy process, identified factors within these ratings, and examined their relationship to outcome. Additional examination of process data (following demonstrated outcome) will likely be valuable in understanding the mechanisms of behavior change (Kendall, 1982).

While the initial task of psychotherapy researchers was to determine whether or not psychotherapy was effective, the task took on a new direction when Kiesler (1966), Paul (1969), Strupp and Bergin (1969), and others called for the study of which therapy, provided by which therapist, works best for which client, with which client problem? Fortunately, current clinical researchers are addressing this multipronged question. However, portions of the question are receiving attention, while other aspects of it have been somewhat ignored. Specifically, it is typical for researchers to vary and examine the type of therapy and type of client problem, while therapist variables are rarely examined. This state of affairs is troublesome, since an understanding of therapist variables is essential for maximizing therapist-client matching, and since therapists not only differ on therapist characteristics (age, sex, personality) but also, in their expertness in providing the treatment. Clinical research examining the effects of variations in the *quality* of treatment is sorely needed. This is not to suggest that some clients be given "poor" treatment, but rather that we must examine the relationship between independent judgements of the quality of therapy and the observed outcome.

A question that readers may ask when critiquing treatment-outcome studies is whether or not the statistically significant changes are clinically significant. That is, do the treated clients return to within-normal limits on outcome measures or do they remain significantly different (though statistically, significantly improved) than their adjusted counterparts. We suggest that future researchers include normative comparisons (see Kendall & Norton-Ford, 1982) in their research reports in order to allow the reader the opportunity to address this question (e.g., Kendall & Zupan, 1981; Meichenbaum, 1971; Patterson, 1974).

A potential problem facing the cognitive-behavioral clinician is the client's reluctance to complete assignments, such as homework. It may be useful for clinicians to apply behavioral contingency-management procedures, such as reward and response-cost, to increase the likelihood that clients follow through on homework. Behavioral contingencies have been successfully integrated with cognitive training in children (Kendall, 1977; Kendall & Finch, 1979a, 1979b), and researchers and clinicians might consider implementing these behavioral techniques with adults. The intent would be to increase client compliance, especially with severely ill clients and/or clients at the beginning phases of treatment. In addition to the use of behavioral contingencies, Beck et al. (1979) provides several useful tips for dealing with client reluctance as well as a variety of other problems (see chap. 14 of Beck et al., 1979).

While we have made an attempt to provide the reader with guidelines for implementing the various treatment approaches, we strongly recommend that the interested reader consult the treatment manuals and primary sources for a more complete description of the treatment procedure.

SUMMARY

Cognitive-behavioral methods of intervention, as they apply to the treatment of psychological disorders, are discussed. In the areas of anxiety, depression, and childhood behavior disorders, an overview of various specific interventions is presented. Discussion is directed to the background, techniques, and sample studies of many cognitive-behavioral interventions.

Expanded applications of many cognitive-behavioral intervention strategies are currently being applied to a multitude of psychological disorders. These disorders are discussed in terms of the interventions. In concluding, the authors present important issues—for both the clinician and researcher—in the area of cognitive-behavioral interventions.

REFERENCES

Alden, L., Safran, J., & Weideman, R. A comparison of cognitive- and skills-training strategies in the treatment of unassertive clients. *Behavior Therapy*, 1978, *9*, 843–846.

Alexander, J. F., & Parsons, B. V. Short-term behavioral intervention with delinquent families. *Journal of Abnormal Psychology*, 1973, *81*, 219–225.

Bandura, A. Self-efficacy: Toward a unifying theory of behavioral change. *Psychological Review*, 1977, *84*, 191–215.

Bandura, A. Reflections on self-efficacy. *Advances in Behavioral Research and Therapy*, 1978, *1*, 237–269.

Bandura, A., Adams, N. E., & Beyer, J. Cognitive processes mediating behavioral change. *Journal of Personality and Social Psychology*, 1977, *35*, 125–139.

Bandura, A., Adams, N. E., Hardy, A. B., & Howells, G. N. Tests of the generality of self-efficacy theory. *Cognitive Therapy and Research*, 1980, *4*, 39–66.

Barabash, C. *A comparison of self-instruction training, token-fading procedures, and a combined self-instruction/token-fading treatment in modifying children's impulsive behavior.* Unpublished doctoral dissertation, New York University, 1978.

Beck, A. T. Thinking and depression. I: Idiosyncratic content and cognitive distortions. *Archives of General Psychiatry*, 1963, *9*, 324–333.

Beck, A. T. *Depression: Clinical, experimental, and theoretical aspects*. New York: Harper & Row, 1967.

Beck, A. T. *Cognitive therapy and the emotional disorders*. New York: International Universities Press, 1976.

Beck, A. T., Rush, A. J., Shaw, B. F., & Emery, G. *Cognitive therapy of depression*. New York: Guilford Press, 1979.

Beck, A. T., Ward, C. H., Mendelson, M., Mock, J. E., & Erbaugh, J. K. An inventory for measuring depression. *Archives of General Psychiatry*, 1961, *4*, 561–571.

Bedrosian, R. C. The application of cognitive therapy techniques with adolescents. In G. Emery, S. D. Hollon, & R. C. Bedrosian (Eds.), *New directions in cognitive therapy.* New York: Guilford Press, 1981.

Botkin, P. T. *Improving communication skills in sixth graders through training in role-taking.* Unpublished doctoral dissertation, University of Rochester, 1966.

Burgio, L. D., Whitman, T. L., & Johnson, M. R. A self-instructional package for increasing attending behavior in educable mentally retarded children. *Journal of Applied Behavior Analysis,* 1980, *13,* 443–460.

Cameron, M. I., & Robinson, V. M. J. Effects of cognitive training on academic and on-task behavior of hyperactive children. *Journal of Abnormal Child Psychology,* 1980, *8,* 405–419.

Camp, B. W. Verbal mediation in young aggressive boys. *Journal of Abnormal Psychology,* 1977, *86,* 145–153.

Camp, B. W., Blom, G. E., Hebert, F., & van Doorninck, W. J. "Think aloud": A program for developing self-control in young aggressive boys. *Journal of Abnormal Child Psychology,* 1977, *5,* 157–169.

Camp, B. W., van Doorninck, W. J., Zimet, S. G., & Dahlem, N. W. Verbal abilities in young aggressive boys. *Journal of Educational Psychology,* 1977, *69,* 129–135.

Carmody, T. P. Rational-emotive, self-instructional, and behavioral assertion training facilitating maintenance. *Cognitive Therapy and Research,* 1978, *2,* 241–253.

Cautela, J. R. Treatment of compulsive behavior by covert sensitization. *Psychological Record,* 1966, *16,* 33–41.

Cautela, J. R. Covert conditioning. In A. Jacobs & L. B. Sacks (Eds.), *The psychology of private events: Perspectives on covert-response systems.* New York: Academic Press, 1971.

Chandler, M. J. Egocentricism and antisocial behavior: The assessment and training of social perspective-taking skills. *Developmental Psychology,* 1973, *9,* 326–332.

Chandler, M. J., Greenspan, S., & Barenboim, C. Assessment and training of role-taking and referential-communication skills in institutionalized emotionally disturbed children. *Developmental Psychology,* 1974, *10,* 546–553.

Comas-Diaz, L. Effects of cognitive and behavioral group treatment on the depressive symptomatology of Puerto Rican women. *Journal of Consulting and Clinical Psychology,* 1981, *49,* 627–632.

Cooley, E. J., & Spiegler, M. D. Cognitive versus emotional coping resources as alternatives to test anxiety. *Cognitive Therapy and Research,* 1980, *4,* 159–166.

Craighead, L. W. Self-instructional training for assertion-refusal behavior. *Behavior Therapy,* 1979, *10,* 529–542.

Denicola, J., & Sandler, J. Training abusive parents in child management and self-control skills. *Behavior Therapy,* 1980, *11,* 263–270.

Dewey, J. *How we think.* Lexington, Mass.: D. C. Heath, 1910.

Diament, C., & Wilson, G. T. An experimental investigation of the effects of covert sensitization in an analogue eating situation. *Behavior Therapy,* 1975, *6,* 499–509.

DiGiuseppe, R. A. Cognitive therapy with children. In G. Emory, S. D. Hollon, & R. C. Bedrosian (Eds.), *New directions in cognitive therapy.* New York: Guilford Press, 1981.

DiGiuseppe, R. A., Miller, N. J., & Trexler, L. D. A review of rational-emotive psychotherapy outcome studies. *Counseling Psychologist,* 1977, *1,* 64–72.

Douglas, V. I., Parry, P., Marston, P., & Garson, C. Assessment of a cognitive-training program for hyperactive children. *Journal of Abnormal Child Psychology,* 1976, *4,* 389–410.

Dunn, R. J. Cognitive modification with depression-prone psychiatric patients. *Cognitive Therapy and Research,* 1979, *3,* 307–317.

D'Zurilla, T. J., & Nezu, A. Social problem solving in adults. In P. C. Kendall (Ed.), *Advances in cognitive-behavioral research and therapy* (Vol. 1). New York: Academic Press, 1982.

Elardo, P. T. & Caldwell, B. M. *The effects of an experimental social development program on children in the middle childhood period.* Unpublished manuscript, University of Arkansas at Little Rock, 1976.

Elardo, P. T., & Cooper, M. *Project AWARE: A handbook for teachers.* Reading, Mass.: Addison-Wesley Publishing, 1977.

Elliott, C. H., & Denney, D. R. Weight-control through covert sensitization and false feedback. *Journal of Consulting and Clinical Psychology,* 1975, *43,* 842–850.

Ellis, A. *Reason and emotion in psychotherapy.* Secaucus, N.J.: Lyle Stuart, 1962.

Ellis, A. Are cognitive-behavior therapy and rational therapy synonymous? *Rational Living,* 1973, *8,* 8–11.

Ellis, A. The basic clinical theory of rational-emotive. In A. Ellis & R. Grieger (Eds.), *Handbook of rational-emotive therapy.* New York: Springer, 1977.

Ellis, A. Rational-emotive therapy and cognitive-behavior therapy: Similarities and differences. *Cognitive Therapy and Research,* 1980, *4,* 325–340.

Ellis, A., & Greiger, R. (Eds.). *Handbook of rational-emotive therapy,* New York: Springer, 1977.

Ellis, A., & Harper, R. A. *A guide to rational living.* Hollywood, Calif.: Wilshire, 1973.

Emmelkamp, P. M. G., van der Helm, M., van Zanten, B. L., & Plochg, I. Treatment of obsessive-compulsive patients: The contribution of self-instructional training to the effectiveness of exposure. *Behavior Research and Therapy,* 1980, *18,* 61–66.

Feffer, M. H., & Gourevich, V. Cognitive aspects of role-taking in children. *Journal of Personality,* 1960, *28,* 383–396.

Flapan, D. *Children's understanding of social interaction.* New York: Columbia University Teachers College Press, 1968.

Flavell, J. H., Botkin, P. T., Fry, C. L., Wright, J. W., & Jarvis, P. E. *The development of role-taking and communication skills in children.* New York: John Wiley & Sons, 1968.

Foreyt, J. P., & Hagen, R. L. Covert sensitization: Conditioning or suggestion? *Journal of Abnormal Psychology,* 1973, *82,* 17–23.

Forman, S. A comparison of cognitive-training and response-cost procedures in modifying aggressive behavior of elementary school children. *Behavior Therapy,* 1980, *11,* 594–600.

Fremouw, W. J., & Harmatz, M. G. A helper model for behavioral treatment of speech anxiety. *Journal of Consulting and Clinical Psychology,* 1975, *43,* 652–660.

Fremouw, W. J., & Zitter, R. E. A comparison of skills training and cognitive restructuring-relaxation for the treatment of speech anxiety. *Behavior Therapy,* 1978, *9,* 248–259.

Fuchs, C. Z., & Rehm, L. P. A self-control behavior-therapy program for depression. *Journal of Consulting and Clinical Psychology,* 1977, *45,* 206–215.

Garner, D. M., & Bemis, K. M. A cognitive-behavioral approach to anorexia nervosa. *Cognitive Therapy and Research,* 1982, *6,* 123–150.

Genshaft, J. L., & Hirt, M. L. The effectiveness of self-instructional training to enhance math achievement in women. *Cognitive Therapy and Research,* 1980, *4,* 91–97.

Glass, C. R., & Arnkoff, D. B. Think cognitively: Selected issues in cognitive assessment and therapy. In P. C. Kendall (Ed.), *Advances in cognitive-behavioral research and therapy* (Vol. 1). New York: Academic Press, 1982.

Glass, C., Gottman, J., & Shmurak, S. Response-acquisition and cognitive self-statements modification approaches to dating-skill training. *Journal of Counseling Psychology,* 1976, *23,* 520–526.

Glogower, F. D., Fremouw, W. J., & McCroskey, J. C. A component analysis of cognitive restructuring. *Cognitive Therapy and Research,* 1978, *2,* 209–223.

Goldfried, M. R. Systematic desensitization as training in self-control. *Journal of Consulting and Clinical Psychology,* 1971, *37,* 228–234.

Goldfried, M. R. Anxiety reduction through cognitive-behavioral intervention. In P. C. Kendall & S. D. Hollon (Eds.), *Cognitive-behavioral interventions: Theory, research, and procedures.* New York: Academic Press, 1979.

Goldfried, M. R. Toward the delineation of therapeutic-change principles. *American Psychologist,* 1980, *35,* 991–999.

Goldfried, M. R., & Davison, G. C. *Clinical behavior therapy.* New York: Holt, Rinehart & Winston, 1976.

Goldfried, M. R., Decenteceo, E. T., & Weinberg, L. Systematic rational restructuring as a self-control technique. *Behavior Therapy,* 1974, *5,* 247–254.

Goldfried, M. R., Linehan, M. M., & Smith, J. L. Reduction of test anxiety through cognitive restructuring. *Journal of Consulting and Clinical Psychology,* 1978, *46,* 32–39.

Greenspan, S., Zlotlow, S., Burka, A., & Barenboim, C. *A manual of referential-communication games.* Unpublished manuscript, University of Rochester, 1973.

Hackett, G., & Horan, J. Stress inoculation for pain: What's really going on? *Journal of Counseling Psychology,* 1980, *27,* 107–116.

Hamberger, K., & Lohr, J. M. Rational restructuring for anger control: A quasi-experimental case study. *Cognitive Therapy and Research,* 1980, *4,* 99–102.

Hammen, C. L., Jacobs, M., Mayol, A., & Cochran, S. D. Dysfunctional cognitions and the effectiveness of skills and cognitive-behavioral assertion training. *Journal of Consulting and Clinical Psychology,* 1980, *48,* 685–695.

Harris, G., & Johnson, S. B. Comparison of individualized covert modeling, self-control desensitization, and study-skills training for alleviation of test anxiety. *Journal of Consulting and Clinical Psychology,* 1980, *48,* 186–194.

Holcomb, W. *Coping with severe stress: A clinical application of stress-inoculation therapy.* Unpublished doctoral dissertation, University of Missouri-Columbia, 1979.

Hollon, S. D. *Toward a theory of therapy for depression: Concepts and operations.* Paper presented at the American Psychological Association, Los Angeles, California, August 25, 1981.

Hollon, S. D., & Beck, A. T. Cognitive therapy of depression. In P. C. Kendall & S. D. Hollon (Eds.), *Cognitive-behavioral interventions: Theory, research, and procedures.* New York: Academic Press, 1979.

Hollon, S. D., & Kendall, P. C. Cognitive self-statements in depression: Development of an automatic-thoughts questionnaire. *Cognitive Therapy and Research*, 1980, *4*, 383–395.

Hollon, S. D., Wiemer, M. J., & Tuason, V. B. *Cognitive therapy in relation to drugs in depression.* Unpublished grant prospectus, University of Minnesota and St. Paul-Ramsey Medical Center, 1979.

Holroyd, K. A. Cognition and desensitization in the group treatment of test anxiety. *Journal of Consulting and Clinical Psychology*, 1976, *44*, 991–1001.

Holroyd, K. A., & Andrasik, F. A cognitive-behavioral approach to recurrent tension and migraine headache. In P. C. Kendall (Ed.), *Advances in cognitive-behavioral research and therapy* (Vol. 1). New York: Academic Press, 1982.

Holroyd, K. A., Andrasik, F., & Westbrook, T. Cognitive control of tension headache. *Cognitive Therapy and Research*, 1977, *1*, 121–133.

Homme, L. E., Perspectives in psychology. XXIV: Control of coverants, the operants of the mind. *Psychological Record*, 1965, *15*, 501–511.

Horan, J., Hackett, G., Buchanan, J., Stone, C., & Demchik-Stone, D. Coping with pain: A component analysis. *Cognitive Therapy and Research*, 1977, *1*, 211–221.

Horan, J. J., & Johnson, R. G. Coverant conditioning through a self-management application of the Premack principle: Its effect on weight reduction. *Journal of Behavior Therapy and Experimental Psychiatry*, 1971, *2*, 243–249.

Hussian, R. A., & Lawrence, P. S. The reduction of test, state, and trait anxiety by test-specific and generalized stress-inoculation training. *Cognitive Therapy and Research*, 1978, *2*, 25–38.

Iannotti, R. J. Effect of role-taking experiences on role-taking, altruism, empathy, and aggression. *Developmental Psychology*, 1978, *14*, 119–124.

Jaremko, M. E. A component analysis of stress inoculation: Review and prospectives. *Cognitive Therapy and Research*, 1979, *3*, 35–48.

Kagan, J. Reflection-impulsivity: The generality and dynamics of conceptual tempo. *Journal of Abnormal Psychology*, 1966, *71*, 17–24.

Kanter, N. J., & Goldfried, M. R. Relative effectiveness of rational restructuring and self-control desensitization in the reduction of interpersonal anxiety. *Behavior Therapy*, 1979, *10*, 472–490.

Kazdin, A. E. Covert modeling, model similarity, and reduction of avoidance behavior. *Behavior Therapy*, 1974, *5*, 325–340.

Kazdin, A. E. Imagery elaboration and self-efficacy in the covert-modeling treatment of unassertive behavior. *Journal of Consulting and Clinical Psychology*, 1979, *47*, 725–733.

Kazdin, A. E. Covert and overt rehearsal and elaboration during treatment in the development of assertive behavior. *Behavior Research and Therapy*, 1980, *18*, 191–201.

Kelly, G. A. *The psychology of personal constructs* (2 vols.). New York: W. W. Norton, 1955.

Kendall, P. C. On the efficacious use of self-instructional procedures with children. *Cognitive Therapy and Research*, 1977, *1*, 331–341.

Kendall, P. C. Assessment and cognitive-behavioral interventions: Purposes, proposals, and problems. In P. C. Kendall & S. D. Hollon (Eds.), *Assessment strategies for cognitive-behavioral interventions.* New York: Academic Press, 1981. (a)

Kendall, P. C. Cognitive-behavioral interventions with children. In B. B. Lahey & A. E. Kazdin (Eds.), *Advances in clinical child psychology* (Vol. 4). New York: Plenum Press, 1981. (b)

Kendall, P. C. One-year follow-up of concrete versus conceptual cognitive-behavioral self-control training. *Journal of Consulting and Clinical Psychology*, 1981, *49*, 748–749. (c)

Kendall, P. C. Individual versus group cognitive-behavioral self-control training: One-year follow-up. *Behavior Therapy*, 1982, *13*, 241–247.

Kendall, P. C. Cognitive processes and procedures in behavior therapy. In C. M. Franks, G. T. Wilson, P. C. Kendall, & K. Brownell (Eds.), *Annual review of behavior therapy: Theory and practice*. (Vol. 8). New York: Guilford Press, 1982.

Kendall, P. C., & Braswell, L. Assessment for cognitive-behavioral interventions in the schools. *School Psychology Review*, 1982, *11*, 21–31. (a)

Kendall, P. C., & Braswell, L. On cognitive-behavioral assessment: Model, method, and madness. In D. C. Spielberger & J. N. Butcher (Eds.), *Advances in personality assessment* (Vol. 1). Hillsdale, N.J.: Lawrence Erlbaum Associates, 1982. (b)

Kendall, P. C. & Braswell, L. Cognitive-behavioral self-control therapy for children: A components analysis. *Journal of Consulting and Clinical Psychology*, 1982, *50*, 672–689. (c)

Kendall, P. C., & Finch, A. J., Jr. A cognitive-behavioral treatment for impulsivity: A group-comparison study. *Journal of Consulting and Clinical Psychology*, 1978, *46*, 110–118.

Kendall, P. C., & Finch, A. J., Jr. Analyses of changes in verbal behavior following a cognitive-behavioral treatment for impulsivity. *Journal of Abnormal Child Psychology*, 1979, *7*, 455–464. (a)

Kendall, P. C., & Finch, A. J., Jr. Developing nonimpulsive behavior in children: Cognitive-behavioral strategies for self-control. In P. C. Kendall & S. D. Hollon (Eds.), *Cognitive-behavioral interventions: Theory, research, and procedures*. New York: Academic Press, 1979. (b)

Kendall, P. C., & Fischler, G. L. *Behavioral and adjustment correlates of problem-solving: Validational analyses of interpersonal cognitive problem-solving measures.* Manuscript submitted for publication, University of Minnesota, 1982.

Kendall, P. C., & Hollon, S. D. (Eds.), *Cognitive-behavioral interventions: Theory, research, and procedures.* New York: Academic Press, 1979.

Kendall, P. C., & Hollon, S. D. (Eds.) *Assessment strategies for cognitive-behavioral interventions.* New York: Academic Press, 1981.

Kendall, P. C., & Korgeski, G. P. Assessment and cognitive-behavioral interventions. *Cognitive Therapy and Research*, 1979, *3*, 1–21.

Kendall, P. C., & Norton-Ford, J. D. Therapy-outcome research methods. In P. C. Kendall & J. N. Butcher (Eds.), *Handbook of research methods in clinical psychology*. New York: John Wiley & Sons, 1982.

Kendall, P. C., & Wilcox, L. E. A cognitive-behavioral treatment for impulsivity: Concrete versus conceptual training in nonself-controlled problem children. *Journal of Consulting and Clinical Psychology*, 1980, *48*, 80–91.

Kendall, P. C., Williams, L., Pechacek, T. F., Graham, L., Shisslak, C., & Herzoff, N. Cognitive-behavioral and patient-education interventions in cardiac catheterization procedures: The Palo Alto medical psychology project. *Journal of Consulting and Clinical Psychology*, 1979, *47*, 49–58.

Kendall, P. C., & Zupan, B. A. Individual versus group application of cognitive-behavioral self-control procedures with children. *Behavior Therapy*, 1981, *12*, 344–359.

Kiesler, D. J. Some myths of psychotherapy research and the search for a paradigm. *Psychological Bulletin*, 1966, *65*, 110–136.

Kim, N. S. Cognitive-behavioral treatment for students' adaptation to academic major departments and improvement of academic performance. *Behavior Therapy*, 1980, *11*, 256–262.

Klein, N. C., Alexander, J. F., & Parsons, B. V. Impact of family systems intervention on recidivism and sibling delinquency: A model of primary prevention and program evaluation. *Journal of Consulting and Clinical Psychology*, 1977, *45*, 469–474.

Klepac, R. K., Hauge, G., Dowling, J., & McDonald, M. Direct and generalized effects of three components of stress inoculation for increased pain tolerance. *Behavior Therapy*, 1981, *12*, 417–424.

Kovacs, M., Rush, J., Beck, A. T., Hollon, S. D. Depressed outpatients treated with cognitive therapy or pharmacotherapy. *Archives of General Psychiatry*, 1981, *38*, 33–39.

Krantz, S., & Hammen, C. Assessment of cognitive bias in depression. *Journal of Abnormal Psychology*, 1979, *88*, 611–619.

Lefebvre, M. F. Cognitive distortion and cognitive errors in depressed psychiatric and low back pain patients. *Journal of Consulting and Clinical Psychology*, 1981, *49*, 517–525.

Leon, G. R. Cognitive-behavior therapy for eating disturbances. In P. C. Kendall & S. D. Hollon (Eds.), *Cognitive-behavioral interventions: Theory, research, and procedures*. New York: Academic Press, 1979.

Linehan, M. M., Goldfried, M. R., & Goldfried, A. Assertion therapy: Skill training or cognitive restructuring. *Behavior Therapy*, 1979, *10*, 372–388.

Lipsky, M. J., Kassinove, H., & Miller, N. J. Effects of rational-emotive therapy, rational role reversal, and rational-emotive imagery on the emotional adjustment of community mental health center patients. *Journal of Consulting and Clinical Psychology*, 1980, *48*, 366–374.

Luria, A. R. *The role of speech in the regulation of normal and abnormal behavior*. New York: Liveright, 1961.

Mahoney, M. J. Reflections on the cognitive-learning trend in psychotherapy. *American Psychologist*, 1977, *32*, 5–13.

Mahoney, M. J. Cognitive skills and athletic performance. In P. C. Kendall & S. D. Hollon (Eds.), *Cognitive-behavioral interventions: Theory, research, and procedures*. New York: Academic Press, 1979.

Mahoney, M. J., & Arnkoff, D. B. Cognitive and self-control therapies. In S. L. Garfield & A. E. Bergin (Eds.), *Handbook of psychotherapy and behavior change* (2d ed.). New York: John Wiley & Sons, 1978.

Mahoney, M. J., & Mahoney, K. *Permanent weight control: A total solution to the dieter's dilemma*. New York: W. W. Norton, 1976.

Malamuth, Z. N. Self-management training for children with reading problems: Effects on reading performance and sustained attention. *Cognitive Therapy and Research*, 1979, *3*, 279–289.

Marlatt, G. A. Alcohol use and problem drinking: A cognitive-behavioral analysis. In P. C. Kendall & S. D. Hollon (Eds.), *Cognitive-behavioral interventions: Theory, research, and procedures*. New York: Academic Press, 1979.

McFall, M. E., & Wollersheim, J. P. Obsessive-compulsive neurosis: A cognitive-behavioral formulation and approach to treatment. *Cognitive Therapy and Research,* 1979, *3,* 333–348.

McLean, P. D., & Hakstian, A. R. Clinical depression: Comparative efficacy of outpatient treatments. *Journal of Consulting and Clinical Psychology,* 1979, *47,* 818–836.

Mead, G. *Mind, self, and society.* Chicago: University of Chicago Press, 1934.

Meichenbaum, D. H. Examination of model characteristics in reducing avoidance behavior. *Journal of Personality and Social Psychology,* 1971, *17,* 298–307.

Meichenbaum, D. H. Cognitive modification of test-anxious college students. *Journal of Consulting and Clinical Psychology,* 1972, *39,* 370–380.

Meichenbaum, D. H. Self-instructional methods. In F. Kanfer & A. Goldstein (Eds.), *Helping people change.* Elmsford, N.Y.: Pergamon Press, 1975.

Meichenbaum, D. H. *Cognitive-behavior modification: An integrative approach.* New York: Plenum Press, 1977. (a)

Meichenbaum, D. H. Dr. Ellis, please stand up. *Counseling Psychologist,* 1977, *7,* 43–44. (b)

Meichenbaum, D. H., & Cameron, R. *Stress inoculation: A skills-training approach to anxiety management.* Unpublished manuscript, University of Minnesota, 1973. (a)

Meichenbaum, D. H., & Cameron, R. Training schizophrenics to talk to themselves: A means of developing attentional controls. *Behavior Therapy,* 1973, *4,* 515–534. (b)

Meichenbaum, D. H., Gilmore, J. B., & Fedoravicius, A. Group insight versus group desensitization in treating speech anxiety. *Journal of Consulting and Clinical Psychology,* 1971, *36,* 410–421.

Meichenbaum, D. H., & Goodman, J. Training impulsive children to talk to themselves: A means of developing self-control. *Journal of Abnormal Psychology,* 1971, *77,* 115–126.

Meichenbaum, D. H., & Turk, D. The cognitive-behavioral management of anxiety, anger, and pain. In P. Davidson (Ed.), *Behavioral management of anxiety, depression, and pain.* New York: Bruner/Mazel, 1976.

Merluzzi, T. V., Glass, C. R., & Genest, M. (Eds.). *Cognitive assessment.* New York: Guilford Press, 1981.

Mitchell, K. R., & White, R. G. Behavioral self-management: An application to the problem of migraine headaches. *Behavior Therapy,* 1977, *8,* 213–222.

Neilans, T. H., & Isreal, A. C. Toward maintenance and generalization of behavior change: Teaching children self-regulation and self-instructional skills. *Cognitive Therapy and Research,* 1981, *5,* 189–197.

Novaco, R. W. *Anger control: The development and evaluation of an experimental treatment.* Lexington, Mass.: D. C. Heath, 1975.

Novaco, R. W. Treatment of chronic anger through cognitive and relaxation controls. *Journal of Consulting and Clinical Psychology,* 1976, *44,* 681.

Novaco, R. W. A stress-inoculation approach to anger management in the training of law enforcement officers. *American Journal of Community Psychology,* 1977, *5,* 327–346.

Novaco, R. W. The cognitive regulation of anger and stress. In P. C. Kendall & S. D. Hollon (Eds.), *Cognitive-behavioral interventions: Theory, research, and procedures.* New York: Academic Press, 1979.

Palkes, H., Stewart, M., & Kahana, B. Porteus Maze performance of hyperactive boys after training in self-directed verbal commands. *Child Development,* 1968, *39,* 817–826.

Parrish, J. M., & Erickson, M. T. A comparison of cognitive strategies in modifying the cognitive style of impulsive third grade children. *Cognitive Therapy and Research,* 1981, *5,* 71–84.

Patterson, G. R. Interventions for boys with conduct problems: Multiple settings, treatments, and criteria. *Journal of Consulting and Clinical Psychology,* 1974, *42,* 471–481.

Paul, G. I. Behavior-modification research: Design and tactics. In C. M. Franks (Ed.), *Behavior therapy: Appraisal and status.* New York: McGraw-Hill, 1969.

Pechacek, T. F., & Danaher, B. G. How and why people quit smoking. In P. C. Kendall & S. D. Hollon (Eds.), *Cognitive-behavioral interventions: Theory, research, and procedures.* New York: Academic Press, 1979.

Porteus, S. D. *The Maze test: Recent advances.* Palo Alto, Calif.: Pacific Books, 1955.

Raven, J. C. *Progressive matrices: A perceptual test of intelligence, individual form.* London: H. K. Lewis, 1938.

Rehm, L. P. (Ed.). *Behavior therapy for depression.* New York: Academic Press, 1981.

Rickel, A. U., Eshelman, A. K., & Loigman, G. A. *A longitudinal study of social problem solving training: Cognitive and behavioral effects.* Manuscript submitted for publication, Wayne State University, 1981.

Rush, A. J., Beck, A. T., Kovacs, M., & Hollon, S. D. Comparative efficacy of cognitive therapy and pharmacotherapy in the treatment of depressed outpatients. *Cognitive Therapy and Research,* 1977, *1,* 17–38.

Rush, A. J., & Watkins, J. T. Group versus individual cognitive therapy: A pilot study. *Cognitive Therapy and Research,* 1981, *5,* 95–103.

Safran, J. D., Alden, L. E., & Davidson, P. O. Client anxiety level as a moderator variable in assertion training. *Cognitive Therapy and Research,* 1980, *4,* 189–200.

Sarason, I. G. Test anxiety and the self-disclosing coping model. *Journal of Consulting and Clinical Psychology,* 1975, *43,* 148–153.

Shantz, C. U., & Wilson, K. E. Training communication skills in young children. *Child Development,* 1972, *43,* 693–698.

Shaw, B. F. Comparison of cognitive therapy and behavior therapy in the treatment of depression. *Journal of Consulting and Clinical Psychology,* 1977, *45,* 543–551.

Shaw, B. F., & Hollon, S. D. *Cognitive therapy in a group format with depressed outpatients.* Unpublished manuscript, University of Western Ontario, London, Ontario, 1978.

Shipley, C. R., & Fazio, A. F. Pilot study of a treatment for psychological depression. *Journal of Abnormal Psychology,* 1973, *82,* 372–376.

Shure, M. B., & Spivack, G. *Problem-solving techniques in childrearing.* San Francisco: Jossey-Bass, 1978.

Spivack, G., Platt, J. J., & Shure, M. B. *The problem-solving approach to adjustment.* San Francisco: Jossey-Bass, 1976.

Spivack, G., & Shure, M. B. *Social adjustment of young children: A cognitive approach to solving real-life problems.* San Francisco: Jossey-Bass, 1974.

Spivack, G., & Spotts, J. *The Devereux child behavior rating scale manual.* DeDan, Pa.: Devereux Foundation, 1966.

Steger, J. C. Cognitive-behavioral strategies in the treatment of sexual problems. In J. P.

Foreyt & D. P. Rathjen (Eds.), *Cognitive behavior therapy: Research and application.* New York: Plenum Press, 1978.

Strupp, H., & Bergin, A. Some empirical and conceptual bases for coordinated research in psychotherapy: A critical review of issues, trends, and evidence. *International Journal of Psychiatry,* 1969, *7,* 18–90.

Sutton-Simon, K. Assessing belief systems: Concepts and strategies. In P. C. Kendall & S. D. Hollon (Eds.), *Assessment strategies for cognitive-behavioral interventions.* New York: Academic Press, 1981.

Taylor, F. G., & Marshall, W. L. Experimental analysis of a cognitive-behavioral therapy for depression. *Cognitive Therapy and Research,* 1977, *1,* 59–72.

Trexler, L. D., & Karst, J. O. Rational-emotive therapy, placebo, and no-treatment effects on public-speaking anxiety. *Journal of Abnormal Psychology,* 1972, *79,* 60–67.

Turk, D. *Cognitive control of pain: A skills-training approach.* Unpublished manuscript, University of Waterloo, 1975.

Turk, D. C., & Genest, M. Regulation of pain: The application of cognitive and behavioral techniques for prevention and remediation. In P. C. Kendall & S. D. Hollon (Eds.), *Cognitive-behavioral interventions: Theory, research, and procedures.* New York: Academic Press, 1979.

Tyler, V. O., & Straughan, J. H. Coverant control and breath holding as techniques for the treatment of obesity. *Psychological Record,* 1970, *20,* 473–478.

Urbain, E. S., & Kendall, P. C. Review of social-cognitive problem-solving interventions with children. *Psychological Bulletin,* 1980, *88,* 109–143.

Varni, J. W., & Henker, B. A self-regulatory approach to the treatment of three hyperactive boys. *Child Behavior Therapy,* 1979, *1,* 171–192.

Vygotsky, L. S. *Thought and language.* Cambridge, Mass.: MIT Press, 1962.

Whitehead, A. Psychological treatment of depression: A review. *Behavior Research and Therapy,* 1979, *17,* 495–509.

Wolpe, J. *Psychotherapy by reciprocal inhibition.* Stanford: Stanford University Press, 1958.

Woodward, R., & Jones, R. B. Cognitive-restructuring treatment: A controlled trial with anxious patients. *Behavior Research and Therapy,* 1980, *18,* 401–407.

Zettle, R. D., & Hayes, S. C. Conceptual and empirical status of rational-emotive therapy. In M. Hersen, R. M. Eisler, & P. M. Miller (Eds.), *Progress in behavior modification* (Vol. 9). New York: Academic Press, 1980.

Zeiss, A. M., Lewinsohn, P. M., & Munöz, R. F. Nonspecific improvement effects in depression using interpersonal-skills training, pleasant-activity schedules, and cognitive training. *Journal of Consulting and Clinical Psychology,* 1979, *47,* 427–439.

24

Behavioral medicine: Background and implications

*Charles H. Elliott**

The last five years have witnessed both the emergence and the substantial growth of a new field known as behavioral medicine. Blanchard (1977) noted that one of the first uses of the term appeared to have been in the title of a book published only 10 years ago (Birk, 1973). Since then, the term has been used with increasing frequency, but often with contradictory meanings. The first formal attempt to define the field was made by the Yale Conference on Behavioral Medicine in 1977, which was sponsored both by the Yale University Departments of Psychology and Psychiatry and by the National Heart, Lung, and Blood Institute. At the conference, the following definition of behavioral medicine emerged:

> Behavioral medicine is the field concerned with the development of behavioral science knowledge and the techniques relevant to the understandings of physical health and illness, and the application of this knowledge and these techniques to prevention, diagnosis, treatment and rehabilitation. Psychoses, neuroses, and substance abuse are included only in so far as they contribute to physical disorders as an endpoint. (Schwartz & Weiss, 1978b, p. 7)

By contrast, Asken (1979) narrowly defined behavioral medicine as a subset of medical psychology and, more specifically, as "The study of psychological *reactions* that occur secondarily or as a result of physical illness and its treatment" (emphasis added). Subsequently, Masur (1979) presented a schematic representation (see Figure 1) of behavioral medicine which is consistent with the revised definition of behavioral medicine formulated by the behavioral biomedical scientists at the National Academy of Sciences (Schwartz & Weiss, 1978a). This revised definition puts a greater emphasis on the interdisciplinary nature of the field as well

---

* University of Oklahoma Health Sciences Center, Oklahoma City.

Figure 1

A schematic representation of behavioral medicine

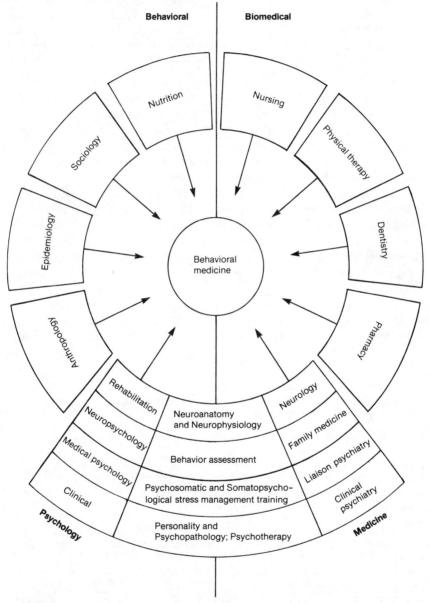

Source: Masur, F. T., An update on medical psychology and behavioral medicine. *Professional Psychology,* 1979, *10,* 259–264. Copyright 1979 by the American Psychological Association. Reprinted by permission of the author.

as on the integration of behavioral and biomedical factors. Futhermore, this revised definition has been gaining increasing acceptance and status:

> Behavioral medicine is the *interdisciplinary* field concerned with the development and *integration* of behavioral *and* biomedical science knowledge and techniques relevant to health and illness and the application of this knowledge and these techniques to prevention, diagnosis, treatment, and rehabilitation. (Schwartz & Weiss, 1978a, p. 250)

Figure 2 depicts a conceptual matrix, which Schwartz and Weiss (1978a) suggest can serve to organize some of the types of problems with which the field of behavioral medicine is likely to be concerned.

This conceptual matrix, as well as the latest revised definition of behavioral medicine, avoids any reference to a particular theoretical viewpoint, as well as to any problems that can emanate from an implied "mind/body dualism." However, a number of prominent writers have suggested that the principles of behavior therapy and behavior modification were or should be synonymous with at least the subdomain of behavioral medicine concerned with intervention strategies (e.g., Blanchard, 1977; Brady, 1977; Pomerleau & Brady, 1979). The term *behavioral,* although easily associated with behavior therapy and behavior modification, apparently was intended to refer to behavioral in a generic sense, such as in behavioral science (Masur, 1979).

The use of the term *behavioral* in a generic sense and the emphasis on the interdisciplinary nature of the field may represent the clearest strength (but also possibly the most substantial drawback) to this newly

Figure 2

A conceptual matrix that serves to organize the kinds of problems with which behavioral medicine is expected to be concerned.

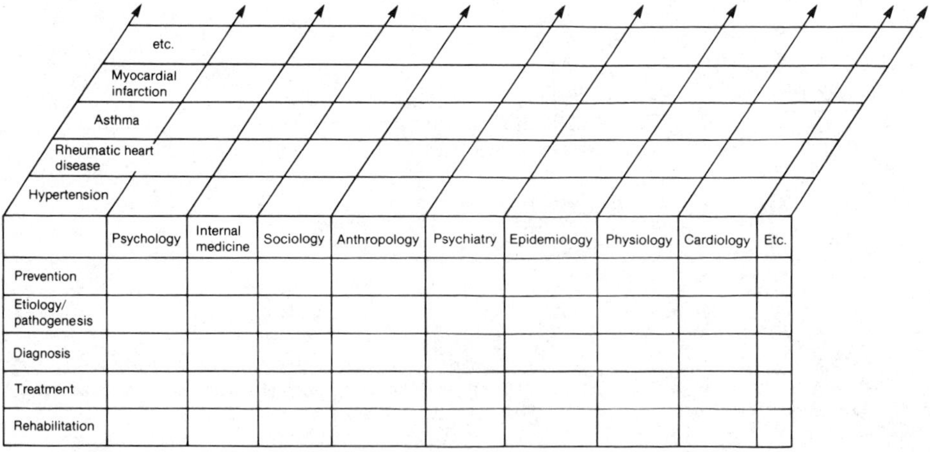

Source: After Schwartz and Weiss, 1978a.

emerging field. The strength is readily apparent in a number of investigative areas, such as psychoneuroimmunology, which involve such complex, interconnected systems that no one discipline could readily combine the expertise from the divergent areas required for its development (Holden, 1980). One potential drawback was pointed out by Masur (1979), who stated, "As any movement becomes overly inclusive in its scope, it runs the risk of becoming overextended to the point where it loses internal consistency and eventually weakens itself for lack of theoretical clarity or practical applicability" (p. 260).

Pomerleau and Brady (1979) suggested that a further drawback of the Yale Conference definition of behavioral medicine lies in its failure to give sufficient credit to the experimental analysis of behavior for the development and source of a substantial amount of the activity currently underway in the field. Thus, they proposed a compromise definition of behavioral medicine as follows:

> The clinical use of techniques derived from the experimental analysis of behavior therapy and behavior modification—for the evaluation, prevention, management, or treatment of physical disease or physiological dysfunction; and (b) the conduct of research contributing to the functional analysis and understanding of behavior associated with medical disorders and problems in health care. (Pomerleau & Brady, 1979, p. XIII)

A drawback in this definition may be that it fails to emphasize the previously noted integration of behavioral and biomedical science. In any case, Pomerleau and Brady (1979) correctly noted that a field is ultimately defined by what it does. Recent research reviewed in this chapter would suggest that a definition incorporating the broader focus of interdisciplinary integration, as suggested by Schwartz and Weiss (1978a), will ultimately prevail. At the same time, it is clear that the experimental analysis of behavior and behavior therapy have been the dominant sources of clinical techniques in the areas of behavioral medicine concerned with prevention, treatment, and rehabilitation. However, the field will probably profit most by avoiding a dogmatic adherence to a single theoretical viewpoint. Rather, it will be more important to maintain an allegiance to sound, scientific principles and methodologies (as is, indeed, exemplified by behavior therapies). This point was underscored by Hersen (1981), who made a plea to his behaviorally oriented colleagues to consider including empirical findings that are derived from sources other than the behavioral camp. Hersen further made the point that a variety of findings and concepts from the areas of alcoholism, schizophrenia, and depression may have considerable value even though, at times, they are couched in psychoanalytic jargon. The issue, therefore, would not seem to be the theoretical origin of a particular concept or technique, but rather its scientific basis.

To some investigators, it has appeared that the field of behavioral medicine overlaps other disciplines (such as psychosomatic medicine, holistic medicine, health psychology, and behavioral health) to such an extent that little distinguishes them. Some clarification of these related areas would thus seem appropriate. Psychosomatic medicine was, in many ways, a direct precursor of behavioral medicine, but it has failed to achieve many of its initial objectives. Psychosomatic medicine has been especially hampered by: (1) an overemphasis on certain research issues which have been relatively unproductive, such as the search for particular, ill-defined personality patterns associated with particular "medical" diseases; (2) a relative failure to develop specific strategies for treating, controlling, or preventing physical symptoms; (3) a preoccupation with factors associated with disease *onset* and the neglect of other critical factors, such as those associated with exacerbations of disease; (4) a failure to eliminate problems associated with Cartesian mind/body dualism (e.g., misconceptions of causality and unnecessary concern with "functional" versus "organic" disease) from work within the field inself; and (5) a relative overemphasis of psychodynamic theory and the neglect of empirical work in the behavioral sciences in areas such as learning theory and psychophysiology (Engel, 1977; Graham, 1979; Holden, 1980; Schwartz & Weiss, 1977; Shapiro, 1979; Sifneos, 1979). In a recent presidential address to the American Psychosomatic Society, Graham (1979) lamented that difficulties such as these have substantially reduced the potential impact of psychosomatic medicine on the field of medicine in general.

Merely coining a new term such as *behavioral medicine* will obviously not ameliorate the difficulties that have plagued psychosomatic medicine to date, but the change appears to be more than semantic. This contention is particularly clear in the heavy emphasis within behavioral medicine on empirical research, truly reflecting an integration of biological and behavioral knowledge (Holden, 1980).

Holistic medicine is a concept which was apparently developed in response to some of the same concerns that led to the establishment of behavioral medicine. Holistic (or wholistic, as it sometimes appears) health care has been defined by Ardell (1977) as:

> viewing a person and his/her wellness from every possible perspective, taking into account every available concept and skill for the person's growth toward harmony and balance. It means treating the person, not the disease. It means using mild, natural methods whenever possible. For the person, it means engaging in a healthier lifestyle to enjoy a higher level of wellness. The wholistic approach promotes the interrelationship and unity of body, mind, and spirit. It encourages healthy, enjoyable activity on all of these levels of existence. (p. 5)

The primary difference between holistic medicine and behavioral medicine seemingly lies in much greater emphasis on established, *scientific* principles within the field of behavioral medicine (Shapiro, 1979).

The term *health psychology* was recently proposed as a discipline-specific term in a presidential address to the American Psychological Association's Division of Health Psychology (Matarazzo, 1980).[1] Matarazzo suggested that the term is ideal for encompassing the role of psychology as a science and a profession in the domains of both health and psychology. Although some writers have used the term *health psychology* as synonymous with behavioral medicine, it has already been noted that the trend is in the direction of reserving the term *behavioral medicine* to refer to a broader, interdisciplinary field. However, health psychology has certainly been a major, if not dominant, force within the field of behavioral medicine. Weiss, in fact, made the bold claim that the center stage belongs to psychology, largely because of its primary role as a *science* of behavior (Armstrong, 1981). Furthermore, as early as 1975, Asken correctly observed that one of the unique contributions psychology has to offer to this field (which has often relied too heavily on uncontrolled clinical case studies) is in the area of research methodology. Matarazzo (1980) recently presented an initial definition of health psychology as follows:

> Health psychology is the aggregate of the specific educational, scientific, and professional contributions of the discipline of psychology to the promotion and maintenance of health, the prevention and treatment of illness, and the identification of etiologic and diagnostic correlates of health, illness, and related dysfunctions. (p. 815)

Subsequently, the Division of Health Psychology of the American Psychological Association approved a slightly amended definition, reported by Matarazzo (1982) as:

> Health psychology is the aggregate of the specific educational, scientific, and professional contributions of the discipline of psychology to the promotion and the maintenance of health, the prevention and treatment of illness, the identification of etiologic and diagnostic correlates of health, illness, and related dysfunction, and to the analysis and improvement of health care systems and health policy formation. (p. 4)

Matarazzo (1980) further proposed that a new specialty area within behavioral medicine be given recognition, in order to accelerate recent developments in the area of prevention. He proposed that this subspecialty be called *behavioral health* and offered the following definition:

> Behavioral health is an interdisciplinary field dedicated to promoting a philosophy of health. It stresses *individual responsibility* in the application of behavioral and biomedical science knowledge and techniques to the *maintenance* of health and the *prevention* of illness and dysfunction by a variety of self-initiated, individual or shared activities. (p. 813)

---

[1] The term *health psychology* has gained increasing acceptance, as opposed to *medical psychology*, largely because the former encompasses a broader range of activities and interests than the latter (Matarazzo, 1980).

SIGNS OF GROWTH: BEHAVIORAL MEDICINE
AND HEALTH PSYCHOLOGY

The growth of behavioral medicine and its related subdomain, health psychology, has been phenomenal; and numerous indicants of this growth exist. It was noted that the initial attempt at defining the field occurred in 1977 (Schwartz & Weiss, 1978b) and was reformulated the following year (Schwartz & Weiss, 1978a). The *Journal of Behavioral Medicine* was first published in March 1978. The Behavioral Medicine Special Interest Group (of the Association for the Advancement of Behavior Therapy) was begun in December 1977. The Academy of Behavioral Medicine Research was formed under the auspices of the National Academy of Science in April 1978, with David Hamburg, Stephen Weiss, and Neal Miller cited as particularly active in the formation of the Academy (Holden, 1980). The major impetus for the development of the Society of Behavioral Medicine came from the Association for the Advancement of Behavior Therapy's Special Interest Group on Behavioral Medicine. From that group, an Organizing Committee for the Society of Behavioral Medicine was composed of Michael F. Cataldo, Alan R. Gruber, David A. Clayman, and David Mostofsky (Woodward, 1982).

The Society of Behavioral Medicine held its first annual convention in December 1979 and also began the society publication of *Behavioral Medicine Update* in 1979. The Society of Behavioral Medicine began publication of the *Behavioral Abstracts* (on a quarterly basis, in 1980) to aid in keeping up with the burgeoning literature in the field. Approximately 250 abstracts, from a wide range of journals and topics, are included in each issue. The multidisciplinary nature of these organizations and publications is clear. For example, the Society of Behavioral Medicine solicits members from diverse groups—such as epidemiologists, psychologists, physiologists, physicians, nurses, dentists, sociologists, and health educators, among others. Membership in that group stood at 608 in August 1979 and had grown to about 1,000 in January 1982.

The field has gone from its very inception only a few years ago to the establishment of numerous clinics, laboratories, and programs across the country, under the rubric of behavioral medicine. Textbooks in the area have also been proliferating at an amazing rate and have included (but are not necessarily limited to!) the following: *Behavioral Medicine: Changing Health Lifestyles* (Davidson & Davidson (Eds.), 1980); *Behavioral Medicine, Assessment and Treatment Strategies* (Doleys, Meredith, & Ciminero (Eds.), 1982); *The Comprehensive Handbook of Behavioral Medicine* (Ferguson & Taylor, 1980, 1981); *Behavioral Approaches to Medicine: Application and Analysis* (McNamara (Ed.), 1979); *Behavioral Medicine: Practical Applications in Health Care* (Melamed & Siegal, 1980); *Biofeedback: Clinical Applications in Behavioral Medicine* (Olton

& Noonberg, 1980); *Medical Psychology: Contributions to Behavioral Medicine* (Prokop & Brady (Eds.), 1981); *Health Psychology* (Stone, Cohen, & Adler (Eds.), 1979); *Behavioral Approaches to Medical Treatment* (Williams & Gentry, 1977); and *Behavioral Science in Medicine* (Winefield & Peay, 1980).

Similar growth has occurred in the discipline-specific area of health psychology discussed by Matarazzo (1980). Thus, the American Psychological Association's Division 38—Health Psychology—was formed in 1978. Almost 10 years prior to that development, Schofield (1969) had urged a greater role for psychologists in the area of health-related research. Subsequent to Schofield's suggestion, the APA's task force on health research (1976) noted the substantial contributions of psychological research in the area of mental health, while pointing out the tremendous potential for such research to increase the understanding of illness and health. Masur (1979) recently reviewed some of the new organizations, newsletters, and interest groups that reflect a rapidly increasing interest in health-related areas among psychologists. Previous to the establishment of many of these organizations and groups, Asken (1975) reviewed evidence which demonstrated that this increased interest in medical-health psychology was becoming discernible by the early 1970s.

This increased interest as well as the recent trends toward collaborative-integrative research efforts are undoubtedly due, in part, to the employment of psychologists in medical settings, which began to show signs of growth as early as the mid-1950s. Prior to 1950, less than one third of the medical schools surveyed employed a full-time psychologist (Witkin, Mensh, & Cates, 1972). From 1955 to 1964, a 187 percent increase in employment of psychologists at medical schools was reported. A later survey (Wagner & Stegeman, 1964) demonstrated a slower, 31 percent growth rate from 1964 to 1967–1969 (Witken et al., 1972). Although the increase has slowed since the 1955–1964 period, a survey conducted in 1976 indicated that a steady growth of about 11 percent per year has continued since 1964 (Lubin, Nathan, & Matarazzo, 1978). McNett (1981b) recently reported that similar growth has apparently continued from 1976 to 1981. This trend has substantially outstripped other growth rates (such as number of medical schools, number of medical students, and American Psychological Association membership) which might otherwise be invoked to account for the increased employment of psychologists at medical schools (Matarazzo, Lubin, & Nathan, 1978). This same survey noted that, as of 1976, 113 out of 115 accredited medical schools employed psychologists, with the mean number of psychologists being 20. In fact, today approximately 5 percent of the American Psychological Association's 50,000 members are on the faculty of a medical school on either a full- or part-time basis (Matarazzo, 1980). Witken et al. (1972) noted that psychology's growth in medical schools has followed rather uniquely individualized patterns and has been dependent upon factors such as the attitude of the chairperson of psychiatry toward psychologists, the interests of other departmental chairs in recruiting psychologists into their departments, and qualities of psychologists already at the school, among others. Regardless of the specific reasons, psychologists are obviously in demand at medical schools; and their increased numbers clearly allow the contact with medical colleagues that is a prerequisite to the interdisciplinary-collaborative emphasis within the field of behavioral medicine.

Collaborative research efforts, using an integrated model of disease and health, have received support from a number of governmental funding agencies as well. For example, the behavioral-medicine branch was formed within the National Heart, Lung, and Blood Institute (NHLBI) shortly following the initial Yale Conference on Behavioral Medicine. The NHLBI has been one of the most active divisions of the National Institutes of Health (NIH) in promoting research and research-training programs that focus on an integration of behavioral and biological components. Matarazzo (1980) has recently reviewed the substantial growth of support from the NHLBI as well as a number of developments within NIH that have occurred in response to increasing numbers of grant applications involving a variety of behavioral-medicine issues. In particular, the NIH formed an ad hoc behavioral-medicine study section to review grants made to the division of research grants at NIH. The section's major concern was recently outlined as follows:

> The behavioral medicine study section reviews the applications involving both biomedical and behavioral science, theory, and methods in the investigation of problems relating to health/illness in humans. These proposals may range from explorations of basic "brain-body" mechanisms to psychological studies on the modification of behavior and health-enhancing directions. Although applications referred to this study section may come from investigators representing a variety of disciplines (e.g., medicine, psychology, anthropology, physiology, biology, sociology), the common element involves the prevention, diagnosis, or treatment of illness by behavioral means. (Weiss & Shields 1979, p. 337)

The rapid growth in both interest and support for behavioral medicine and the subdomain of health psychology obviously has not emerged from thin air, but rather has been presaged by numerous developments and trends, particularly in the fields of psychology and medicine. Matarazzo (1980), Asken (1975), Brady (1977), Engel (1977), Knowles (1977), McMahon and Hastrup (1980), and Schofield (1976a,b) are among those who have traced some of these developments. Note will be made of only a few general factors which appear to have provided a particularly strong impetus to the emergence and growth of the field.

MAJOR FACTORS RESPONSIBLE FOR GROWTH OF THE FIELD

The first of these factors has been the emergence of data strongly suggesting that environmental and lifestyle factors have become the primary cause of morbidity and mortality, at least in developed countries (Brady, 1977). Along this vein, Sexton (1979) observed, "a review of present knowledge suggests a behavioral component associated with at least nine of the leading causes of death" (p. 3). These include: diseases of the heart; malignant neoplasms; cerebrovascular disease; accidents; influenza; pulmonary diseases, such as bronchitis, emphysema, and asthma; and certain diseases of early childhood. A similar list in 1900 indicated that acute, infectious diseases accounted for a greater percentage of morbidity and mortality than today. As Sexton noted, considerable progress has been made in the treatment of acute, infectious diseases. The shift to chronic and lifestyle-related disorders has created a new set of problems, which will likely require an increased responsibility of the individual for his/her own health.

A second factor creating an impetus for the growth of behavioral medicine is related to the first factor. This is reflected in a growing realization that improvements in overall health and mortality have not followed directly from significant advances in medical knowledge and availability over the last several decades. For example, a Canadian-government working document, "A New Perspective on the Health of Canadians" (Lalonde, 1974), determined that mortality rates changed very little for the nation following the introduction of extensive, cost-free health services to all Canadians. Shapiro (1979) further noted that mortality rates actually *declined* following two different periods of reduced medical care (which resulted from a malpractice crisis and a residents' strike). Shapiro aptly noted that such data need to be interpreted cautiously but still should be taken seriously.

We are clearly reaching an asymptote in the benefits derived from current health expenditures. Burns (1979) recently noted that health care costs in the United States rose from 4.6 percent of the gross national product in 1950 to 8.3 percent in 1975. More recently, estimates have placed current health care costs in excess of 10 percent of the gross national product (Matarazzo, 1982), representing a serious impact upon the economy. Finally, Burns (1979) reported that only 2 to 2.5 percent of health-care expenditures are directed toward disease prevention and control, and that only about .5 percent is spent on health, education, and the improvement of health-service delivery. At least one investigator suggested that doubling current health spending would result in little effect on mortality rates, given that spending continued with the same priorities and criteria that exist today (Abelson, 1976). By contrast, it has been suggested that simply an aggressive, nationwide program to identify and treat hypertensives could save $3 billion annually, reduce death, and increase productivity (Kristein, Arnold, & Wynden, 1977). Epstein and Martin (1977) recently reviewed a wide variety of behavioral-medicine strategies, which ultimately may prove to be cost-effective approaches to disease prevention. Pomerleau and Brady (1979) and Matarazzo (1980) made note of a number of studies which, although preliminary in nature, already have begun to demonstrate the cost effectiveness of behavioral-medicine strategies for: (1) reducing overutilization of unnecessary laboratory tests, (2) increasing patient adherence, (3) promoting a more healthy lifestyle, and (4) improving treatment outcomes for certain medically related problems.

Furthermore, Rosen and Weins (1979) reviewed two studies—and presented data of their own—which consistently demonstrated that referral for psychological services can substantially reduce subsequent utilization of medical services. In their study, even a three- to five-hour psychological evaluation led to significantly reduced use of medical services over the following year. The authors noted that this finding may have been partially a result of the *physician* reducing the initiation of clinic visits because of a better understanding of the problem and diagnosis following the psychological evaluation. Unfortunately, Rosen and Weins (1979) did not appear to have statistically controlled for moderately large differences in the base rate of medical-service use among the groups in their study. A more comprehensive review was provided by Jones and Vischi (1979), who found that 12 of 13 studies demonstrated reduced utilization of medical services following mental-health interventions. The authors noted that methodological problems existed in all of these studies, but they inferred that the consistency of these findings strongly suggested that utilization of medical services is generally reduced following outpatient psychotherapy, especially in organized health-care settings, such as HMO's. However, it should be pointed out that the methodological problems in these studies were generally quite substantial. In addition, the authors failed to consider numerous alternative causes for the reduction in medical utilization.

The importance of such findings clearly suggests the need for replication with sound methodology. If these encouraging results continue to be replicated, the reduced medical utilization following psychological services may be due, in part, to the fact that "all illnesses are, to some degree, stressful" (Schofield, 1976b, p. 7). Furthermore, these stresses may significantly affect the patient's response to medical regimens in self-defeating ways. One survey, by Noren, Frazier, Altman, and DeLozier (1980), noted that family practitioners, on the average, spent about 13 minutes with each patient—a situation which (even if unavoidable) is obviously too short in duration to effectively reduce illness-related stress and might even exacerbate it.

The effects of such stresses are also related to a third impetus to the growth of behavioral medicine. This impetus comes from research which has clearly demonstrated relationships between so-called psychological and biochemical-physiological response systems that were more complex than previously realized. In fact, some researchers are now talking about a new paradigm—based upon systems theory—involving feedback loops instead of simple cause-and-effect chains (Holden, 1980). McMahon and Hastrup (1980), Engel (1977), Pomerleau and Brady (1979), Stein, Schiavi, and Camerino (1976), and Riley (1981) are among those who have recently reviewed some of the research on these highly complex interactions. For example, Ader and Cohen (1975) presented data demonstrating that suppression of the antibody response could be classically conditioned. In that report, immunosuppression was conditioned to occur in response to the neutral stimulus of saccharin, after repeated pairing with an immunosuppressant, cyclophosphamide. Pomerleau and Brady (1979) declare that this kind of data "indicate the power of conditioning procedures, and they *support strongly the notion that whenever one can specify a neurally mediated response which is pathognomonic, there is a strong possibility that this response can be brought under stimulus control*" (p. XXII, emphasis added).

The complexity of clearly defining such neurally mediated, pathognomonic responses is substantial, however. For example, although stress has been shown to lead to immunosuppression, some studies have shown a potentiation of the immune response following exposure to some stresses under certain circumstances (e.g., Monjan & Collector, 1977; Stein et al., 1976). Studies by Stein et al. (1976) and Riley (1981) indicate that a wide variety of mediating factors are probably responsible for these effects—including various hormones, each of which have differential effects on the immune system. In addition, the type, duration, intensity, and frequency of the stressors, as well as the organism's stage of biological development at the time of stress administration, need to be considered in such investigations.

The fourth impetus to the growth of behavioral medicine can be found in the suggestion by a number of practitioners that behaviorally based intervention for medical conditions may not only at times be more effective but also entail fewer negative side effects than standard medical strategies (e.g., Pomerleau & Brady, 1979; Shapiro, 1979; Epstein, Eisler, & Miller, 1979). Later in Chapter 25 a number of the medical conditions for which behavioral-medicine intervention strategies have been shown to hold some promise are reviewed. While it is true that iatrogenic effects from such applications appear to be rare, they can and do occur. For example, Hock, Rogers, Reddi, and Kennard (1978) found that, when using assertiveness training without the use of conmitant relaxation training, asthmatic symptomology actually worsened. Furthermore, programs designed to increase patient adherence to medical-treatment regimens may require more frequent monitoring of the patient. Take the example of an asthmatic who only takes about one half of his/her prescribed doses of Theopholine. The patient could easily develop toxic blood levels of the drug, if his or her compliance was suddenly increased to 100 percent, in the absence of regular checks on blood Theopholine levels.

DANGERS OF OVERSELL AND UNDERSELL

Clearly, the forces creating the current enthusiasm for behavioral medicine have been substantial. At the same time, most responsible investigators in the field (e.g., Pomerleau & Brady, 1979; Agras, 1975) have noted that this zeal can create a problem with oversell. The review in Chapter 25 will hopefully make it clear that behavioral medicine has shown definite potential for improving prevention, diagnosis, treatment, and rehabilitation of a variety of medically related problems. However, relatively few well-controlled studies substantiating the efficacy of these approaches are available. Thus, the *potential* and *promise* of the field must not be confused with actual *claims* of established efficacy. Fortunately, one of the major tenets, apparently embedded within the field, is the necessity for rigorous scientific methodology.

Parenthetically, it should be noted that another potential problem for this field is actually a possibility of undersell. On the one hand, it is critical to require that claims of efficacy be backed by substantial, rigorously derived data; on the other hand, many investigators do not seem to require the same criteria for negative results. For example, Hagen (1981) noted that it has "become fashionable to knock behavioral treatments of obesity" (p. 89). And yet, in his review, he demonstrates that, although initial hopes have not been realized, a great deal has been learned about obesity; also, some behavioral packages have shown at least moderate effectiveness in well-controlled studies. It will be quite important for behavioral-medicine researchers not to abandon a particular problem area or intervention strategy before considering a number of important issues, such as: (1) the characteristics of treatment "failures," (2) the adequacy of the treatment intervention in terms of length, completeness, conceptualization, etc., (3) therapist characteristics and skills, and (4) various "predictors" of the successful cases that are found. It is interesting how frequently almost obviously inadequate applications of a therapy technique result in the conclusion that the strategy failed.

This kind of conclusion is easily reached by investigators and practitioners who have not received sufficient training in the use of a particular psychological strategy. This problem further emphasizes the advantage of collaborative efforts. Obviously, no matter how thoroughly and adequately a given treatment strategy is applied, behavioral medicine will not provide the ultimate cure for all problems. The goal will be to determine the strategies which are effective for particular problems and patient groups under specified conditions. As the field develops, it is likely that the answers will often involve some combination of medical and psychological strategies.

Along this line of dealing with seemingly negative results is the issue of placebos. Frequently, so-called placebo groups are included in research investigating both psychological- and medical-treatment strategies. Originally, such comparison groups were used out of the need to ensure that drugs exerted effects that were more substantial than the frequently large, nonspecific effects obtained from presumably inert placebos. Indeed, numerous investigators have substantiated that placebos are not only quite potent in some circumstances but can also exert effects over a prolonged period of time (e.g., Rachman & Phillips, 1975). With behavioral-medicine interventions, it is also important to isolate the causative factors responsible for treatment effects, including those derived from "placebo effects." However, it may be at least as profitable to understand the nature of the placebo effect as well as to enhance it, rather than to simply dismiss it as "only placebo." For example, it appears clear that placebos, expectancies, perceived control, and other related, cognitive variables can influence important biochemical reactions in addition to psychological-behavioral ones (e.g., Peterson, 1982). The reader may wish to take note of the fact that, at the beginning of the chapter on behavioral-medicine intervention techniques, a review is made of the various phases of study required for the thorough investigation of behavioral-medicine interventions. Unfortunately, some problem areas will require an enormous investigative effort before all these phases of study can be completed.

IMPLICATIONS FOR TRAINING OF PROFESSIONAL GROUPS

By definition, behavioral medicine is a multidisciplinary field that places an emphasis on integrative-collaborative research and treatment. Yet, relatively few professionals have received more than brief formal training outside their own discipline. For example, Asken (1975), described the training of most psychologists as "medicophobic" in nature. Concurrent with the growth of the field has been an increasing awareness of the desirability of broadening the training base for professionals who have an active interest in the field.

For example, the division of health psychology of the American Psychological Association is currently planning to hold a training conference to deal with a variety of issues related to the training models and curricula that would be most appropriate for programs in health psychology. Asken (1975) noted that a proposal to establish a professional degree program in health-care psychology was made as early as 1974 (Wirt, 1974). In 1975, the first health-psychology program was reported to have been established at the University of California at San Francisco (Armstrong, 1981). Belar recently organized a roster of training programs for the division of health psychology within the American Psychological Association (Armstrong, 1981).

A current debate surrounding the development of these programs is whether they will lead to the development of a distinctly separate subspecialty within psychology or will simply be subsumed under a variety of currently existing specialty areas. Matarazzo (1980) and the APA Task Force on Health Research (1976) have both noted that almost every discipline within psychology has the potential for making unique and significant contributions to the field of behavioral medicine, at least in the area of research. In fact, Matarazzo (1980) recently observed, "I believe that the opportunities today for graduate training in almost all facets of psychology are unparalleled and require only that faculties in psychology approach this challenge no less vigorously than they did the challenge and opportunities made available for research and training in mental health beginning in 1945" (p. 811). Olbrisch and Sechrest (1979) and Schofield (1976a) have also recently made note of the need for developing specialized training in health psychology and have provided general suggestions for the development of these training programs. Some have recently suggested that clinical training is a prerequisite to such programs. Thorough training in clinical or counseling psychology is undoubtedly a necessity for health psychologists who provide direct service. However, such a background is probably not essential for the experimental psychologist in the field, although some exposure to service and treatment methods would possibly add to the relevance and clinical significance of research efforts in this area.

Swan, Piccione, and Anderson (1980) have made one of the first attempts, to date, to delineate specific suggestions for the training of health psychologists working in the field of behavioral medicine. These suggestions included the following: (1) thorough training in an applied doctorate program in psychology, with substantial knowledge of behavioral assessment and treatment interventions as well as of the general scientific principles of human behavior, (2) epidemiology, (3) anatomy, physiology, and psychophysiology, (4) pharmacology, particularly in areas of pain and stress management, (5) medical/surgical intervention in terms of current recommendations for various disorders, (6) instrumentation in the area of psychophysiological recording and assessment techniques, (7) specialized treatments such as biofeedback and hypnosis, among others, (8) general clinical issues regarding medical patients, and (9) neuropsychology. The authors noted that the internship has the potential to provide much more of the required knowledge for the health psychologist than has typically been the case. It should be equally clear that the internship year is not likely to be a sufficient period of time for thorough training in all of the areas they listed. Whether additional training is best accomplished through changes in graduate training or in the development of postdoctoral programs is a point that will likely lead to great debate. An additional factor which may aid in the delivery of training in health psychology is the simple issue of labeling psychology interns as *residents* as a means of giving these students greater parity with medical and psychiatry residents (McNett, 1981). Such residencies may quite profitably be developed into advanced programs of two, three, or more years for some specialty areas. One drawback to such prolonged residencies may be a reluctance on the part of psychology students to engage in years of extra training, when they will typically receive *at best* 75 percent of the salary of their psychiatry colleagues (and often, even less opportunity to supplement these salaries) upon graduation and subsequent employment (McNett, 1981b).

Just as psychologists have typically lacked substantial training in the biomedical sciences, Brady (1973) has been a leader in noting that medical-training programs have typically included only very limited exposure to the areas of learning theory and the principles of applied behavioral analysis. This survey indicated that, as of nine years ago, only 4 percent of medical school education programs required courses on these topics, with a mean of three class hours devoted to behavior therapy. Clinical electives in junior and senior years were more common and revealed a mean of 20 class hours devoted to these areas. He noted that most psychiatry chairpersons surveyed felt that a greater exposure was highly desirable for medical students but had not occurred, due primarily to "limited faculty interest" and/or "limited faculty with sufficient knowledge, training, or experience in behavior therapy" (p. 22).

Wexler (1976) observed that the behavioral sciences have often failed in their mission of training medical students because of a relative lack of information that can be readily "converted" into specific clinical skills that would be useful in solving the practitioner's specific clinical problems. McClelland, Staples, Weisberg, and Bergin (1973) and McDermott (1979) have also urged that medical education provide a greater exposure to mental-health techniques. For example, McClelland et al. (1973) reviewed studies showing that pediatricians spend about 25 percent of their time discussing issues such as infant feeding, prophylaxis of disease, child safety, and child-rearing advice. A greater amount of training in mental health (and especially, behavioral analysis and other topics with "applied value") would undoubtedly be of substantial assistance in such work. This value is increased even further, when one considers the application of this knowledge to some of the other areas in the following chapter. Wexler (1976) suggested that material with high "application value" would include learning theory, psychological aspects of pain, communication theory, and psychopharmacology, among others. A survey of medical-education training and behavioral analysis, more recent than Brady's (1973) report, would be highly desirable. It is likely that training opportunities have increased, and if this increase is found to be large, it will likely add even greater impetus to the behavioral-medicine movement.

Behavioral medicine, and related developments, have also led some to suggest revisions in psychiatry-training programs. Brady (1973) also conducted a survey of residency programs in psychiatry. The results of this survey revealed that 59 percent of such programs had required courses in behavior therapy, with a mean of 10 class hours. However, only 11 percent of the programs surveyed had required practicum experiences in behavior therapy. The practicums that did exist ranged from a few hours to a year, with a median of two months. Residency directors agreed with the desirability of increasing training in this area, although they noted that this development was limited by the same factors that had limited increased training in medical-education programs (i.e., limited faculty interest and/or expertise).

An additional trend in regard to psychiatric training lies in the area of increasing the emphasis on medicine per se. Rappaport (1975) noted that psychiatrists often make relatively little use of their medical training and recommended an increase in the psychiatrists' focus and training in medicine. Certainly, psychiatry's contribution to behavioral medicine would be enhanced if changes were made in the frequent tendency of many psychiatrists to virtually forget their medical training.

The current author recently conducted an informal survey of a number of nurses who have been especially active in the area of behavioral medicine. There was a virtually unanimous agreement that current nursing education rarely provides exposure to the techniques of behavioral assessments and interventions, except occasionally in "small doses" in the specialized area of psychiatric nursing. Barnard (1980), Dunbar (1982), and O'Neal (1982) all recently noted the desirability of such training and observed that much of it is likely to occur at the master's degree level. According to Barnard (1980), there will likely be even more advanced training in research and behavioral technologies at the Ph.D. level in nursing. Dunbar (1982) recently suggested that there is a need for defining the roles and responsibilities of nurses with various levels of training (which range from unlicensed aids, to LPNs, to various educational levels of RNs, master's degrees, and now a growing number of Ph.D.s). It will be interesting to see if nursing delineates these roles and responsibilities more successfully than psychology has, with regard to the master's level versus doctorate level and the resulting problems that continue to plague the field.

Social work is another professional group that has begun an expansion of training in the area of "medical social work." The majority of these professionals hold master's degrees, but there is a clear trend toward an increasing number of such practitioners to hold a doctoral degree (Kindy, 1981). Traditionally, training in this area has not emphasized behavioral technologies. However, Kindy (1981) recently underscored the need for medical social workers to acquire skills in the implementation of research and evaluation studies (for which behavioral-analysis strategies would be particularly appropriate). Furthermore, Kindy (1981) and Wilson (1982) both observed the desirability of greater training for social workers in the area of administration of health care delivery systems.

The recommendations regarding training and education of psychologists, physicians, nurses, psychiatrists, social workers, and other, related professional groups are not meant to imply that each of these groups will lose their identity in some sort of ambiguous amalgam. Rather, it is likely that various educational programs will retain much of their current emphases. The advent of behavioral medicine has simply led to the revelation that much can be gained by greater exposure to the clinical and scientific methods within various disciplines, as a means of increasing the quality and frequency of collaborative efforts in research, service, and teaching.

IMPLICATIONS FOR ROLE FUNCTIONS OF PROFESSIONAL GROUPS

However, it is possible (and probably desirable) that increased opportunities for interdisciplinary training will also lead to role functions for some professionals that depart somewhat from what has been practiced traditionally. For example, McClelland et al. (1973), among others, have noted that pediatricians not only can, but for practical reasons should, be equipped to provide their patients at least brief counseling. This model of practice has come to be known as "behavioral pediatrics." A physician appropriately trained in behavioral pediatrics would not only be able to provide brief parent and child counseling for common problems but would likely also be able to have increased success with other clinical problems (such as medical adherence, "unhealthy" lifestyles, emotional reactions to physical illness, enuresis and encopresis, and so on). In addition, such a physician would likely be more effective in both referring to and utilizing consultation from other mental-health professionals. A physician practicing "behavioral pediatrics" would not be attempting to take over the role of psychologists, psychiatrists, etc., but rather would be increasing his/her effectiveness through greater familiarity of the interface between behavioral and medical disciplines.

The role of nurses in general health care began to expand in the 1960s, with the introduction of the concept "nurse practitioner" (Barnard, 1980). In particular, the nurse practitioner role led to a much greater emphasis on the nurses's responsibilities and functions within the areas of assessment of the patient and his/her family and the identification and management of patient problems within the medical intervention process. Barnard (1980) recently noted that there is a great need for systematic research to evaluate the impact of such expanded nursing interventions. She further noted that behavioral-analysis techniques provide great potential for both increasing the effectiveness of these interventions as well as for evaluating their outcome.

Dunbar (1982) reported, in a personal communication, that behavioral medicine is providing nurses with substantial opportunities for expanded functions in at least the following areas: (1) inpatient medical wards (particularly with the emergence of behavioral-medicine units at some hospitals); (2) occupational-health nursing in industry, with an emphasis on prevention; (3) community-public health, with an emphasis on chronic-disease management; and (4) private physician's offices, especially in regard to aiding patient compliance, prevention, and education. In many of these areas, a much greater degree of autonomy seems to be evolving for nurses with the appropriate level of training. Once again, *collaboration* is a key ingredient. For example, Barnard (1980) noted that, in some of the above areas, nursing techniques have been applied successfully for years, and behavioral analysis is needed to validate both the efficacy of the techniques as well as the new role functions of nurses.

With regard to medical social work, Kindy (1981) discussed the fact that social workers have traditionally provided *ancillary* services. However, with the increased emphasis on the doctorate degree and increased training in areas such as health-care systems and research, the potential exists for medical social workers to become more involved in health-care planning and administration. Kindy (1981) further noted that "social workers have begun to influence health-care plans for individual patients by *collaborating* as *independent practitioners* with physicians, nurses, and other health professionals in a team approach to comprehensive health care" (p. 17) and urged that this shift toward professional autonomy continue. Wilson (1982) noted that such independence may not be possible in many current medical settings. However, he also observed that medical social workers have the potential to expand their role functions, especially in the areas of patient advocacy, program evaluation, epidemiology, and health-care delivery systems.

With respect to the role of psychiatrists, it was previously noted that there is a trend toward a greater emphasis on so-called medical psychiatry (Rappaport, 1975). In general, this includes not only a greater emphasis upon consultation-liaison-type activities but may also lead to a much more sophisticated use of knowledge which is evolving in the field of brain-behavior relationships and, even more specifically, brain-biochemical processes. Some have even suggested that this trend may lead to psychiatry becoming a subspeciality of the field of neurology.

The role of the health psychologist also is departing from traditional lines. Over a decade ago, Schofield (1969) observed, "the opportunities for psychologists to play a much expanded and valuable role among all the health-related disciplines are so many and so varied as to defy cataloging" (p. 574). Wright (1967), over 15 years ago, proposed an initial definition of one such role area which he termed *pediatric psychology*. Further, Rachman and Phillips (1975) suggested that so-called trouble-shooting psychologists may be called into a wide variety of hospital areas whenever a behavioral or emotional factor is an obstacle to effective treatment administration or prevention plans. Wiggins (1976) made the observation that psychologists have a substantial role to play in health-maintenance organizations in various ways that may contribute to their cost effectiveness. Schneider (1980) further made the point that the psychologist's role tends to broaden and increase in effectiveness, simply through repeated exposure to patients with the same medical diagnosis, which allows the psychologist to increase his/her understanding of the issues and needs of that particular patient group. McNett (1981b) noted that a partial list of activities of psychologists in medical schools would include: family medicine, neurology, rehabilitation, pain and sleep clinics, pediatrics, and cardiology, among others. Some have even suggested that the psychologist's role in these areas may ultimately lead to limited prescription-writing authority, in a manner analogous to dentistry (assuming, of course, that training programs continue in their current direction of greater exposure to the biological sciences).

An important caveat was issued by Knapp and Vandecreek (1981), who reviewed the potential for expanded malpractice and other legal risks concomitant with the increased involvement of psychologists in the management of physical diseases. The authors described the range of these risks and made a number of cogent suggestions which should be observed by psychologists engaged in active practice within the field of behavioral medicine.

Unfortunately, a number of psychologists have cited an additional pragmatic issue as responsible for inhibiting the growth of psychologists' roles and contributions within the field of behavioral medicine. This issue involves the fact that much of the service and research within the field of behavioral medicine occurs in hospitals and medical schools. Psychologists are frequently excluded from functioning as autonomous professionals, in the sense that they do not enjoy recognized status on medical staffs or voting privileges (e.g., Brandsma, 1980; Matarazzo et al., 1978; Schneider, 1980; Witken et al., 1972). Witkin et al. (1972) noted that often the consequence of lacking autonomy is having the role of psychology determined by another profession, usually psychiatry.

Matarazzo et al. (1978) reported that relatively few medical schools allow psychologists full voting-membership privileges, which is a situation that deteriorated further after the Joint Commission on Accreditation of Hospitals (JCAH) completed a number of reaccreditation site visits. However, the authors also noted that JCAH policies actually allow for more discretion on this issue than is readily apparent, and six hospitals recently revised their bylaws to include psychologists as full voting members.

Schneider (1980) made the point that, in many medical hospitals, psychologists function largely as consultants to physicians, much as many medical specialists, which makes the question of *admissions privileges* relatively less important in those settings. Furthermore, James Webb, from the Division of Health Psychology within the American Psychological Association, stated recently that admission and discharge privileges "are probably the least important of what psychologists are after" in medical settings (McNett, 1981b). (Although, in psychiatric and mental health settings, these issues tend to become more important.) However, voting privileges and staff membership are important for psychology to make its full contribution to behavioral-medicine areas. Otherwise, psychologists may: (1) not have free access to patient populations and problem areas of interests, (2) not have an imput to quality control, (3) have little imput to decisions and policies, and (4) sometimes be unable to even attend medical staff meetings (McNett, 1981b).[2] The Hospital Privileges Survey of 1979 revealed that a full 32 percent of psychologists may not even attend medical staff meetings, and an additional 37 percent can attend but not vote (McNett, 1981b). Matarazzo reported that only nine medical schools/teaching hospitals give psychologists full membership status on their medical staffs (McNett, 1981b). It was also recently noted that many psychologists confuse the "right to practice" within hospital settings with the basic medical staff-membership issue (McNett, 1981b). Further, Matarazzo stated that voting membership does *not* automatically lead to autonomy over such other vital issues as hiring, promotion, compensation, etc.

Numerous actions by the American Psychological Association and its political-action group, the Association for the Advancement of Psychology, have been designed to address the problem of staff membership and related issues. In addition, in Ohio, the attorney general's office has an antitrust suit against the Joint Commission on the Accreditation of Hospitals because of their restrictive policies. Furthermore, the New Jersey Psychological Association has recently established a task force to determine steps to be taken regarding the question of hospital privileges (McNett, 1981b).

The "second-class citizenship" and loss of status that can result from restrictive hospital staff-membership policies may partly account for the relative underrepresentation of psychologists in medical settings outside of medical schools. For example, McNett (1981b) compiled data that revealed that psychologists are employed at general hospitals at a rate roughly equal to 1 percent of their employment rate at medical schools. Thus, out of approximately 7,000 acute-care general hospitals, McNett's

---

[2] The current author's experience is somewhat of an anomaly in this respect. He is the director of a consultation-liaison division of a mental-health service within this country's largest children's medical hospital. This position (rarely held by psychologists) has certainly facilitated an access to patient populations. Strangely though, he has no voting privileges and is a member only of the affiliate medical staff.

survey was only able to identify approximately 700 full-time psychologists employed in them. Bamgbose, Smith, Jesse, and Groth-Marnat (1980) surveyed 36 general hospital administrators. Data from that survey indicated a substantial interest in increasing the number of psychologists employed, but resistance from psychiatrists (as well as indirectly from physicians, who invariably consult psychiatrists first) has slowed their plans. In contrast, Gabinet and Friedson (1980) have presented anecdotal evidence that some psychologists can perform consultation and liaison work in acute-care general hospitals very effectively and with a *high* degree of acceptance, *when given the opportunity to do so.* Matarazzo has suggested that separate departments of medical-health psychology may be the most effective means of insuring such autonomy, access, and acceptance for the profession, although others have felt that reasonable and functional autonomy can be achieved through informal means (McNett, 1981b).

Resolving the issue of psychologists' autonomy can have substantial benefit to the field of behavioral medicine. When offered free access to patient populations, psychologists have shown the ability to devise extremely creative approaches to a variety of medical problems, and some of these approaches are reviewed in the following chapter. Furthermore, with regard to the field of psychiatry, Witkin et al. (1972) aptly stated,

> Relationships between psychiatry and psychology should be complimentary in research, teaching, and practice areas. The maturity of both disciplines should provide this. In the practice area, competition exists between psychiatry and clinical psychology because of an overlap of therapeutic ambitions. This competition complicates the separation discussed above.

Most practitioners and researchers within the field of behavioral medicine eschew competition over territoriality issues and, instead, focus on efforts to enhance collaborative research and service. Only time will determine whether these efforts will overcome the struggles over status, turf, and resources. The movement of psychology into areas other than traditional mental-health arenas simultaneously provides opportunities for a veritable explosion of the role, function, and employment of psychologists, as well as for the danger for severe battles over these same areas. Hopefully, the trends and philosophies within behavioral medicine will help to avert that danger.

SUMMARY

In this chapter, various definitions of behavioral medicine have been reviewed, as well as their relative strengths and weaknesses. In addition, numerous signs of the extremely rapid growth in this field were noted. Essentially, four major factors were reviewed which were considered to be responsible for much of this growth. These included: (1) evidence that environmental and lifestyle factors have become the primary causes of morbidity and mortality, (2) we have reached an asymptote in the benefits being derived from health expenditures, and behavioral medicine may ultimately provide strategies for increasing cost effectiveness of our health-care system, (3) the results of recent research indicating complex feedback loops between so-called psychological factors and biochemical-physiological factors, and (4) the fact that, in many cases, behavioral-medicine strategies may entail fewer negative side effects than certain medical-treatment approaches. The dangers of oversell were certainly noted; but, in addition, the significant potential for undersell was also suggested.

This new, emerging field has substantial implications for the training of various health professional groups. These implications were reviewed, and suggestions were made. In addition, changing training models are likely to lead to somewhat new role functions for various professional groups. Some of these possibilities were also reviewed. Finally, with regard to role functions, the desirability of various health professional groups operating in a more collaborative fashion was noted. In some cases, this collaboration is likely to be enhanced by a somewhat greater degree of autonomy for various professional groups than currently exists in the health-care system.

REFERENCES

Abelson, P. H. Cost-effective health care. *Science,* 1976, *192,* 619.

Ader, R., & Cohen, N. Behaviorally conditioned immunosuppression. *Psychosomatic Medicine,* 1975, *37,* 333–340.

Agras, S. Forward. In R. C. Katz & S. Zlutnick (Eds.), *Behavior therapy and health care.* Elmsford, N.Y.: Pergamon Press, 1975.

APA Task Force on Health Research. Contributions of psychology to health research. *American Psychologist,* 1976, *31,* 263–274.

Ardell, D. *High level wellness: An alternative to doctors, drugs, and disease.* Emmaus, Pa.: Rodale Press, 1977.

Armstrong, B. Health psychology: A growing field as training programs abound. *APA Monitor,* 1981, *12,* 14 & 34.

Asken, M. J. Medical psychology: Psychology's neglected child. *Professional Psychology,* 1975, *6,* 155–160.

Asken, M. J. Medical psychology: Toward definition, clarification, and organization. *Professional Psychology,* 1979, *10,* 66–73.

Barnard, M. Behavioral approaches to nursing. *The Behavior Therapist,* 1980, *3,* 11–12.

Bamgbose, O., Smith, G. T., Jesse, R. C., & Groth-Marnat, G. A survey of the current and future directions of professional psychology in acute general hospitals. *Clinical Psychology,* 1980, *33,* 24–25.

Birk, L. (Ed.). *Biofeedback: Behavioral medicine.* New York: Grune & Stratton, 1973.

Blanchard, E. B. Behavioral medicine: A perspective. In R. B. Williams, Jr. & W. D. Gentry (Eds.), *Behavioral approaches to medical treatment.* Cambridge, Mass.: Ballinger Publishing, 1977.

Brady, J. P. Place of behavior therapy in medical student and psychiatric resident training. *Journal of Nervous and Mental Disease,* 1973, *157,* 21.

Brady, J. P. Concluding remarks. In R. B. Williams & W. D. Gentry (Eds.), *Behavioral approaches to medical treatment.* Cambridge, Mass.: Ballinger Publishing, 1977.

Brandsma, J. M. One month in the life of a medical center psychologist. *The Clinical Psychologist,* 1980, *34,* 13–14.

Burns, K. Social learning and behavioral health care. *Psychotherapy and Psychosomatics,* 1979, *32,* 6–15.

Davidson, P. O., & Davidson, S. M. (Eds.). *Behavioral medicine: Changing health lifestyles.* New York: Brunner & Mazel, 1980.

Doleys, D. M., Meredith, R. L., & Ciminero, A. R. (Eds.). *Behavioral medicine: Assessment and treatment strategies.* New York: Plenum Press, 1982.

Dunbar, B. Personal communication to author, 1982.

Engel, G. Need for a new medical model: Challenge for biomedicine. *Science,* 1977, *196,* 129–136.

Epstein, L., Eisler, R. M., & Miller, P. M. Behavioral medicine. *Association for Advancement of Behavior Therapy Newsletter,* 1979, *4,* 5–6.

Epstein, L. H., & Martin, J. E. Behavioral medicine I: Prevention. *Association for Advancement of Behavior Therapy Newsletter,* 1977, *4,* 5–6.

Ferguson, J. M., & Taylor, C. B. (Eds.). *The comprehensive handbook of behavioral medicine (vol. 1): Systems intervention.* New York: Spectrum, 1980.

Ferguson, J. M. & Taylor, C. B., (Eds.). *The comprehensive handbook of behavioral medicine (vol. 2): Syndromes and special areas.* New York: Spectrum, 1981.

Ferguson, J. M. & Taylor, C. B., (Eds.). *The comprehensive handbook of behavioral medicine (vol. 3): Extended applications and issues.* New York: Spectrum, 1980.

Gabinet, L., & Friedson, W. The psychologist as frontline mental health consultant in a general hospital. *Professional Psychology,* 1980, *11,* 939–945.

Graham, D. T. What place in medicine for psychosomatic medicine? *Psychosomatic Medicine,* 1979, *41,* 357–367.

Hagen, R. L. Behavioral treatment of obesity: Progress but not panacea. In J. M. Ferguson & C. B. Taylor (Eds.), *The comprehensive handbook of behavioral medicine (Vol. 2): Syndromes and special areas.* New York: Spectrum, 1981.

Hersen, M. Complex problems require complex solutions. *Behavior Therapy,* 1981, *12,* 15–29.

Hock, R. A., Rodgers, C. H., Reddi, C., & Kennard, D. W. Medicopsychological interventions in male asthmatic children: An evaluation of physiological change. *Psychosomatic Medicine,* 1978, *40,* 210–215.

Holden, C. Behavioral medicine: An emergent field. *Science,* 1980, *209,* 479–481.

Jones, K. R. & Vischi, T. Impact of alcohol, drug abuse, and mental health treatment on medical care utilization. *Medical Care,* 1979, *17,* 29–61.

Kindy, P. Focus . . . On medical social work. *Behavioral Medicine Update: Society of Behavioral Medicine,* 1981, *3,* 6–8.

Knapp, S., & Vandecreek, L. Behavioral medicine: Its malpractice risks for psychologists. *Professional Psychology,* 1981, *12,* 677–683.

Knowles, J. H. The responsibility of the individual. In J. H. Knowles (Ed.), *Doing better and feeling worse: Health in the United States.* New York: W. W. Norton, 1977.

Krakowski, A. J. Liaison psychiatry: A service for averting dehumanization of medicine. *Psychotherapy and Psychosomatics,* 1979, *32,* 164–169.

Kristein, M. M., Arnold, C. B., & Wynden, R. L. Health economics and preventive care. *Science,* 1977, *195,* 457–462.

Lalonde, M. *A new perspective on the health of Canadians: A working document.* Ottawa, Canada: Ministry of Health and Welfare, 1974.

Lubin, B., Nathan, R. G., & Matarazzo, J. D. Psychologists in medical education. *American Psychologist,* 1978, *33,* 339–343.

Masur, F. T. An update on medical psychology and behavioral medicine. *Professional Psychology,* 1979, *10,* 259–264.

Matarazzo, J. D. Behavioral health and behavioral medicine: Frontiers for a new health psychology. *American Psychologist,* 1980, *35,* 807–817.

Matarazzo, J. D. Behavioral health's challenge to academic, scientific, and professional psychology. *American Psychologist,* 1982, *37,* 1–14.

Matarazzo, J. D., Lubin, B., & Nathan, R. G. Psychologist's membership on the medical staffs of university teaching hospitals. *American Psychologist,* 1978, *33,* 23–29.

McClelland, C. Q., Staples, M. D., Weisberg, I., & Bergin, M. E. Practitioner's role in behavioral pediatrics. *Journal of Pediatrics,* 1973, *82,* 325–331.

McDermott, J. Mental health training for primary care physicians. *Clinical Psychologist,* 1979, *32,* 25.

McMahon, C. E., & Hastrup, J. L. The role of imagination in the disease process: Post-Cartesian history. *Journal of Behavioral Medicine,* 1980, *3,* 205–217.

McNamara, J. R. (Ed.). *Behavioral approaches to medicine: Application and analysis.* New York: Plenum Press, 1979.

McNett, I. Psychologists in medical settings: The academic scene. *APA Monitor,* 1961, *12,* 12–13, 66–68(a).

McNett, I. Psychologists in medical settings: General hospitals. *APA Monitor,* 1981, *12,* 144(b).

Melamed, B. J., & Siegal, L. J. *Behavioral medicine: Practical applications in health care.* New York: Springer, 1980.

Monjan, A. A., & Collector, M. I. Stress-induced modulation of the immune response. *Science,* 1977, *196,* 307–308.

Noren, J., Frazier, T., Altman, I., & DeLozier, J. Ambulatory medical care: A comparison of internists and family practitioners. *New England Journal of Medicine,* 1980, *302,* 11–16.

Olbrisch, M., & Sechrest, L. Educating health psychology in traditional graduate-training programs. *Professional Psychology,* 1979, *10,* 589–595.

Olton, D. S., & Noonberg, A. R. *Biofeedback: Clinical applications in behavioral medicine.* Englewood Cliffs, N.J.: Prentice-Hall, 1980.

O'Neal, S. Personal communication to author, 1982.

Peterson, C. Learned helplessness and health psychology. *Health Psychology,* 1982, *1,* 153–168.

Pomerleau, O. F., & Brady, J. P. *Behavioral medicine: Theory and practice.* Baltimore: Williams & Wilkins, 1979.

Prokop, C. K., & Brady, J. P. (Eds.). *Medical psychology: Contributions to behavioral medicine.* New York: Academic Press, 1981.

Rachman, S. J., & Phillips, C. Placebo power: Self-control of bodily functions. *Psychology and medicine.* London: Temple Smith, 1975.

Rappaport, M. Medicine-orientated psychiatry. *Hospital and Community Psychiatry,* 1975, *26,* 12.

Riley, V. Psychoneuroendocrine influences on immunocompetence and neoplasia. *Science,* 1981, *212,* 1100–1109.

Rosen, J., & Weins, A. Changes in medical problems and the use of medical services following psychological intervention. *American Psychologist,* 1979, *34,* 420–431.

Schneider, A. Psychologists in comprehensive health care settings. *The Clinical Psychologist,* 1980, *33,* 8–9.

Schofield, W. The role of psychology in the delivery of health services. *American Psychologist,* 1969, *24,* 565–584.

Schofield, W. The psychologists as a health professional. *Professional Psychology,* 1976, *31,* 263–274.(a)

Schofield, W. Psychology as a health profession. *Professional Psychology,* 1976, *7,* 5–7.(b)

Schwartz, G. E., & Weiss, S. M. What is behavioral medicine? *Psychosomatic Medicine,* 1977, *39,* 377–381.

Schwartz, G. E., & Weiss, S. M. Behavioral medicine revisited: An amended definition. *Journal of Behavioral Medicine,* 1978, *1,* 249–251.(a)

Schwartz, G. E., & Weiss, S. M. Yale Conference on Behavioral Medicine: A proposed definition and statement of goals. *Journal of Behavioral Medicine,* 1978, *1,* 3–12.(b)

Sexton, M. M. Behavioral epidemiology. In O. F. Pomerleau & J. P. Brady (Eds.), *Behavioral medicine: Theory and practice.* Baltimore: Williams & Wilkins, 1979.

Shapiro, D. Biofeedback and behavioral medicine in perspective. *Biofeedback and Self-Regulation,* 1979, *4,* 371.

Sifneos, P. E. The difficulties in teaching "psychosomatic medicine." *Psychotherapy and Psychosomatics,* 1979, *32,* 218–222.

Stone, G. C., Cohen, F., & Adler, N. E. (Eds.), *Health Psychology—A Handbook: Theories, Applications, & Challenges of a Psychological Approach to the Health Care System.* San Francisco: Jossey-Bass, 1979.

Stein, M., Schiavi, R. C., & Camerino, M. Influence of brain and behavior on the immune system. *Science,* 1976, *191,* 435–440.

Swan, G. E., Piccione, A., & Anderson, D. C. Internship training in behavioral medicine: Program description, issues, and guidelines. *Professional Psychology,* 1980, *11,* 339–346.

Wagner, N. N., & Stegeman, K. L. Psychologist in medical education: 1964. *American Psychologist,* 1964, *19,* 689–690.

Weiss, S. M., & Shields, J. L. The National Institute of Health and Behavioral Medicine. *Professional Psychology,* 1979, *10,* 30–33.

Wexler, Murray. The behavioral sciences in medical education: A view from psychology. *American Psychologist,* 1976, *31,* 275–283.

Wiggins, J. Psychology as a health program in the health maintenance organization. *Professional Psychology,* 1976, *31,* 9–13.

Williams, R. B., & Gentry, W. D. *Behavioral approaches to medical treatment.* Cambridge, Mass.: Ballinger Publishing, 1977.

Wilson, W. Personal communications to author, 1982.

Winefield, H. R., & Peay, M. Y. *Behavioral science in medicine.* Baltimore: University Park Press, 1980.

Wirt, R. *Proposals for professional degree programs leading to the master of science and doctor of psychology in health care psychology.* Unpublished proposal submitted by the faculty of the Division of Health Care Psychology, Health Sciences Center, University of Minnesota, January 1974.

Witkin, H. A., Mensh, I. N., & Cates, J. Psychologists in medical schools. *American Psychologist,* 1972, *27,* 434–440.

Woodward, J. Personal communication, January 1982.

Wright, L. The pediatric psychologist: A role model. *American Psychologist,* 1967, *22,* 323–325.

25

Behavioral medicine: Assessment, patient management, and treatment interventions

Roberta A. Olson*
and
Charles H. Elliott*

The current chapter is organized according to some of the major intervention areas currently receiving substantial attention within the field of behavioral medicine. These areas include: assessment, general patient-management issues, and treatments for medical disorders. The section on treatments for medical disorders has been organized in a manner similar to that used by Epstein, Katz, and Zlutnick (1979)—that is, according to some of the major bodily organ systems for which at least a moderate body of behavioral medicine literature currently exists. The area of health care delivery systems is not included; a review of this area has recently been compiled by Epstein and Ossip (1979). The emerging subdivision known as behavioral dentistry has also been excluded. The interested reader is referred to the September 1981 issue of the *Journal of Behavioral Medicine,* which was devoted to a review of this growing specialty. Finally, the voluminous area of pain management will be covered only as it relates directly to patient-management issues and to specific disorders (such as tension and migraine headaches). More-comprehensive coverage of pain may be found in Sanders (1979), Weisenberg (1977), Zlutnick and Taylor (1982), and Jay and Elliott (in press).

Since the range of topics reviewed is quite broad, the intent is obviously not to provide an extensive review of each area. Rather, recent reviews will be noted when they exist, and only some of the most salient issues

* University of Oklahoma, Health Sciences Center, Oklahoma City.

and directions that are currently evolving within each topic area will be discussed.

ASSESSMENT

Elliot (see Chapter 24) noted that the field of psychosomatic medicine has been plagued by an overemphasis on the assessment of global personality constructs as they may relate to the development of specific disease entities, which has produced relatively little of substantial importance. In addition, there has been a traditional emphasis on assessing differences between so-called functional and organic disorders, such as outlined in the *DSM-III.*—e.g., somatoform disorders (conversion disorder, psychogenic pain disorder, and hypochondriasis), factitious disorders, malingering, and psychological factors contributing to the exacerbation of a "medical disorder." While distinguishing among these categories is, at times, useful and interesting, such an understanding does not always lead to an increased ability to develop treatment-intervention strategies. Furthermore, an overconcern with distinctions between so-called functional and organic disorders tends to ignore the important interactive-feedback loops that often have been observed between presumably psychological and physiological variables.

A number of potentially more fruitful areas of assessment strategies have begun to emerge. For example, Melamed and Siegel (1980) recently provided a thorough review of standard behavioral-assessment strategies as they can be applied to behavioral medicine in ways that may lead more directly to treatment-intervention planning. They demonstrated the value of a thorough "functional analysis" of behavior across multiple response systems, including self-report, overt behavior, and physiological responses. In regard to the physiological-response system, greater sophistication is developing rapidly and now frequently includes assessment of biochemical reactions in addition to the more common assessment of specific nervous system responses. Broad-based behavioral assessments have much to offer this emerging field; even the private physician could probably profit from the use of simple, self-monitoring record forms for patients with headaches, asthma, seizures, etc. Such records could lead to the rapid assessment of important antecedent-consequent relationships which, in many cases, could aid both diagnostic and treatment processes.

Another area of particular promise is the assessment of various levels and types of cognitions. For example, Meichenbaum and Butler (1979) have noted that specific self-statements, current concerns, cognitive styles, imagery, expectations, appraisals, and meaning systems may have a significant impact on an individual's affective (as well as physiological) states and can be assessed in a variety of interesting ways. Kendall and Korgeski (1979) also recently reviewed a wide variety of approaches for the multidimensional assessment of these various levels of cognition. Unfortunately, to date there has been relatively little direct application of these assessment strategies to behavioral-medicine problems. However, perusal of these recent reviews requires very little imagination for suggesting a wide variety of applications of these assessment strategies to behavioral-medicine problems.

Cognitive variables that currently appear to have relevance to a variety of behavioral-medicine problems and which *have* received some research in this area include the following: (a) a cluster of cognitive traits, called alexithymia, which—according to Singer (1977)—represents a group of patients especially refractory to traditional psychological therapies, (b) a variety of cognitive styles, such as engagement-involvement (e.g., Singer, 1977); helplessness-hopelessness (e.g., Singer, 1977); the somewhat similar and related styles of repression-sensitization, minimization-vigilant focusing, and monitor-distractor (briefly reviewed by Willis, Elliott, & Jay, 1982); and internal-external locus of control. Strickland (1978) reviewed a wide body of research with respect to the relationship of locus-of-control expectancy to health attitudes and behaviors. In regard to the latter construct, Willis et al. (1982) noted that an individual's responses on general measures of locus of control may be less useful than more specific measures such as "health locus of control" (e.g., Parcel & Meyer, 1978), or even locus-of-control measures designed for specific population groups, such as perhaps a "diabetic locus-of-control scale," an "asthmatic locus-of-control scale," etc.

Mash and Terdal (1981) recently emphasized this point and noted that behavioral assessment has tended to focus on general principles of assessment, without taking into account specific characteristics of the target population. Therefore, they stress the considerable need for developing "population-specific" assessment techniques. A number of these were reviewed with respect to specific behavioral-medicine disorders, in the areas of asthma, juvenile diabetes, childhood obesity, seizure disorders, sleep disturbances, and elimination problems. Additionally, more population-specific assessment scales and techniques relevant to behavioral medicine have been recently reviewed by Barlow (1981), Doleys, Meredith, and Ciminero (1982), McNamara (1979), and Russo, Bird, and Masek (1980).

With respect to compliance, the variable known as the health-belief model has shown some potential for increasing the understanding of the determinants of health-related behavior (e.g., Becker, Maiman, Kirscht, Halfner, & Drachman, 1977). This issue is briefly discussed in the following chapter.

In various sections throughout the rest of this chapter, the reader will note that substantial interest is currently being generated by the interactions between various cognitive individual-difference variables (such as those reviewed above) and various situational-contextual variables. Finally, it will be noted that substantial interest also exists in regard to increasing the understanding of physiological subtypes, particularly as they interact with such situational and individual-difference variables.

This is not to imply that traditional assessments (such as the MMPI, Rorschach, etc.) are of no value with respect to behavioral medicine. For example, the MMPI has shown considerable promise with respect to the area of chronic pain (e.g., Strassberg, Reimherr, Ward, Russell, & Cole, 1981). Rather, the suggestion is simply that more-refined analysis of *specific* individual-difference variables (as they interact with situational and physiological variables) within the context of specific, target populations may be of greater value. Furthermore, such analyses may increase the ability to identify the types of subjects that will be most responsive to particular kinds of treatments and under what conditions. As Hersen (1981) recently noted, behavioral-intervention techniques often have a deceptive appearance of simplicity. The illusory nature of this becomes clear as one begins to review the intricacies of a wide range of assessment strategies.

Shapiro, Schwartz, Ferguson, Redmon, and Weiss (1977) noted that three phases of study are generally required for new drugs to be incorporated into *standard* practice and that behavioral techniques will likely have to undergo a similar sequence prior to achieving wide acceptance. Taylor (1980a) reviewed the major issues that require study within each of these phases, as applied to the problem of hypertension. Below is a list of these phases, including the areas in each which may require study for a wide variety of behavioral interventions for medical disorders:

Phase 1

1. *Basic physiological effects:* In many cases, relaxation, cognitive techniques, assertion training, and even operant conditioning are likely to have physiological effects. These effects are especially important to understand with respect to the treatment of some medical disorders. The areas of hypertension, pain, asthma, seizure disorders, and circulatory disorders, among a long list of others, are areas through which improved treatments might evolve from an increased understanding of the effects of behavioral strategies on phenomenons such as biogenic amines, endorphines, a wide variety of hormones, metabolism, and other biochemical and physiological responses. For example, Taylor (1980a) recently provided a review of the intricate physiological, psychological, and environmental variables which interact in the regulation of blood pressure, often through feedback loops.

2. *Dose-effect relations:* With respect to behavioral-medicine strategies, this issue is particularly relevant to the study of the length of treatments and the amount of practice actually engaged in, as they affect the system of interest across various populations.

3. *Side effects:* Although serious side effects are unusual with behavioral interventions, it has been noted that they can and do occur and should be studied.

4. *Generalization:* As noted by Denney (see Chapter 27), many studies have been concerned only with so-called phasic effects that are measured in a laboratory or clinic, while the subject is being administered a technique such as relaxation. Tonic effects are those which are sustained, accrued through practice, and generalized outside of the clinic setting. Relatively few studies of such generalization have been conducted for many of the medical disorders reviewed.

Phase 2

1. This phase involves comparisons between so-called active agents and placebos. The current authors agree with Taylor's (1980a) suggestion that this type of research is needed. However, it must also be recognized that placebos have their own dose-effect relation, that they undoubtedly exert their effects through cognitive-mediational processes, and that these require systematic study. Simply labeling a technique a placebo is inadequate; rather, the method of placebo induction, as well as its specific effects on various cognitive processes, are important to understand. Even the possibility that placebo-induced cognitive changes may be put into active practice by some subjects is another issue that has largely been ignored in the literature to date. It is possible that, with behavioral interventions, the very concept of placebos may ultimately be replaced by a number of concepts reflecting various cognitive subcomponents of the concept placebo.
2. This phase also involves studies on the interaction between various subtypes within a given medical disorder and treatment. Frequently, behavioral-medicine interventions to date have regarded a given medical disorder as homogeneous in nature. However, physiological subgroups exist for many of these and are important to consider.

Phase 3

This phase involves broad clinical trials in large subject samples. Taylor (1980a) has noted the danger of conducting such trials prematurely due to current enthusiasm within the field. Clearly, the efficacy of these trials can be enhanced through the knowledge gained through studies of the phase 1-and phase 2-type.

Finally, prior to the review of current treatments for medical disorders, a note should be made of several cogent observations recently offered by Hersen (1981). He noted that much of our behavioral-research efforts and conclusions, to date, have been diluted through inappropriate grouping of cases and the frequent failure to realize that one disorder can have different etiologies and treatments. Furthermore, Hersen declared that, in the area of alcoholism, "most treatment programs only have dealt with a small portion of the problem" (p. 23). This statement is equally applicable to many of the other areas with which behavioral medicine is concerned. Finally, Hersen observes that, in many areas, the synergistic effects of combining behavioral and pharmacological strategies is quite exciting. Unfortunately, relatively few studies of such combinations have been conducted to date.

However, the various phases of study reviewed above, as well as comparisons of treatments and their possible combinations, can easily involve an enormous research undertaking. For example, the study of pharmacological agents is quite complicated in and of itself, but the study of behavioral interventions can often involve even greater complexity. Furthermore, with respect to some behavioral-medicine intervention strategies for particular medical disorders, the relative rarity of the disorder will, at times, preclude systematic group-outcome studies. In these cases, limited-N designs, as recently reviewed by Hayes (1981) and Hersen and Barlow (1976), may be particularly appropriate. This approach would also be an appropriate starting point for the behavioral treatment of medical disorders currently lacking highly effective treatments or when these treatments are plagued by serious side effects.

PATIENT MANAGEMENT

COMPLIANCE-ADHERENCE

Patient adherence to medications and medical regimes is often the major factor in obtaining a successful outcome from therapy. Nonadherence to medical regimes can include failure to: (1) enter into or continue a treatment program, (2) keep follow-up or referral appointments, (3) take prescribed medication, and (4) restrict or change one's activities, including smoking, diet, and exercise (Kasl, 1975). Medication noncompliance has received more attention than the other areas of nonadherence, both in assessment and treatment. Blackwell (1976) and Dunbar and Agras (1980) have extensively reviewed the problem of treatment adherence. Estimates of noncompliance or errors in medication in general medical practice for adults range from 33 percent (Becker & Maiman, 1975) to 85 percent (Stewart & Cluff, 1972), and noncompliance with medication for children has been estimated to range from 20 to 80 percent (Cuskey & Litt, 1980).

Haynes and Sackett (1976) reviewed 185 compliance studies. Less than half of the studies were judged to have minimally acceptable methodological designs. Only 15 percent of these studies had employed a randomized design. A major problem identified in these studies was lack of a clear definition of compliance and of accurate methods of assessment.

Assessment

Assessment of patient's compliance with medications is particularly difficult. The least-reliable method is self-report (Park & Lipman, 1964;

Rickles & Briscoe, 1970). Patients tend to overestimate their compliance (Gordis, 1976). Counting pills is slightly more accurate than patient reports but still not reliable (Roth, Caron, & Hsi, 1970). Biochemical measures to assess blood or urine levels of a drug or tracer element can be more accurate. Yet, patients may take medications prior to testing and remain noncompliant at other times. Most biochemical measures do not provide information on the degree of adherence over time, nor do they provide any clues to patterns of patient's compliance and noncompliance. Individual differences in absorption and metabolic rates also limit the reliability of such tests. Laboratory tests are often expensive and do not allow immediate feedback to patients or physician, and therapeutic levels may be difficult to specify (Soutter & Kennedy, 1974).

The use of physiological outcomes as a basis for assessment and compliance has also been found to be unreliable. For example, Haynes, Sackett, Gibson, Taylor, Hackett, Roberts, and Johnson (1976) found 57 of the 100 hypertensive patients were compliant with medications. Only 35 patients had acceptable blood pressure measures, 12 of these patients were *poor compliers,* while 34 *good compliers* had failed to achieve acceptable blood pressure measures. Obviously, compliance is only one factor in obtaining a positive outcome.

Interestingly, patients *admitting* to noncompliance are almost always accurate (Feinstein, Wood, Epstein, Taranta, Simpson, & Tursky, 1959) and are more likely to improve with compliance intervention than patients denying noncompliance (Haynes et al., 1976; Johnson, Taylor, Sackett, Dunnett, & Shimizu, 1977). In summary, no one method of assessing compliance is adequate, although the use of two or more measures is generally considered to be preferable (Dunbar & Agras, 1980).

Almost 200 factors have been suggested to be related to compliance behavior (Haynes & Sackett, 1976). Four general factors which consistently appear to affect compliance are: (1) the patient and his/her family understanding the medical regime and believing in the efficacy of the therapy, (2) the duration and complexity of the medical regime, (3) the professional's interactions with the patient, and (4) the organization of the health care setting. Each factor affecting compliance will be briefly reviewed, and relevant treatment strategies will be discussed.

The patient.   Common sense would suggest that motivated patients will comply with medical regimes, while nonmotivated patients would not be expected to comply. Yet, motivational level per se does not appear to be a major factor in patient compliance (Davis, 1968). Equally surprising is the report that no specific, personality variables or socioeconomic factors have been consistently associated with compliance (Marston, 1970). Severity of illnesses and intellectual ability have also been predictive of compliance (Epstein & Masek, 1978).

On the other hand, the patient's perception of the *nature of the illness* and beliefs concerning treatment may contribute to the patient's compliance or noncompliance. Kirscht and Rosenstock's (1979) review of the literature suggests that patients will comply with preventative behaviors (innoculations, diet, exercise) or medical interventions (chemotherapy), if they define the potential or existing illness as a real and personal threat and believe treatment is likely to be beneficial.

Dunbar and Agras (1980) identify the patient's lack of knowledge about the medical regime, *not* the disease, as a major factor in compliance. Patients often do not accurately recall medical information or instruction (Boyd, Covington, Stanaszck, Coussons, 1974; Ley, Bradshaw, Eaves & Walker, 1973). The patient's recall of medical instructions has been related to the amount of information given at each visit. Small amounts of information—given at each visit (Joyce, Capla, Mason, Reynolds, & Matthews, 1969) and organized according to specific categories (Ley et al., 1973)—have significantly increased patient's recall. Visual aids (Boyd et al., 1974), written instructions accompanied by the physician's discussion of these medication regimes (Dickey, Mattar, & Chudzek, 1975), and other methods of reducing complexity have significantly increased medication compliance, especially for patients with *acute* illnesses (Cole & Emmanuel, 1971; Sharpe & Mikeal, 1974).

Modifications or additional instructional components for *chronic* patients requiring long-term medication have generally *not* been effective in increasing compliance (Sackett, Gibson, Taylor, Haynes, Hackett, Roberts, & Johnson, 1975). For example, education for hypertensive patients (concerning their disease, treatment, and problems in compliance) had no effect on the patient's compliance (Caplan, Robinson, French, Caldwell, & Shinn, 1976). Instructional strategies appear to affect the patient's ability to recall and understand the required regime. While this is an important factor in increasing compliance in *acute* care patients, Melamed and Siegel (1980) suggest that *stability* of chronic symptoms may actually reinforce noncompliance. Compliance in acute illnesses is generally accompanied by relief from symptoms, while compliance for prophylactic purposes or chronic illnesses only keep the symptoms stable. Even in acute illnesses, patients discontinue medications (such as antibiotics) when the symptoms or infection have disappeared (Cuskey & Litt, 1980; Twaddle & Sweet, 1970). Chronic care patients initially need well-designed instructional regimes. But, perceptions of the illness, reinforcement for medication compliance, and short-term rewards for compliance need to be considered to enhance the continued compliance of long-term, chronic care patients.

Medication regime.   The medication regime has been considered the single most important determinant of compliance (Dunbar & Agras, 1980). The *complexity, duration,* and *side effects* of medication regimes have each been found to impact on compliance. The more complex the medication regime, the higher the probability of noncompliance (Blackwell, 1973). Combination drugs, used to simplify medication regimes, have been found to be moderately effective in increasing compliance with hypertensive patients (Clark & Troop, 1972; David, Welborn, & Pierce, 1975).

With long-term or chronic patients, *involvement of the patient* in the treatment strategy has shown promising results. Behavioral strategies to increase medication compliance in patients recently experiencing a myocardial infarction included patient-initiated activity hierarchy, self-monitoring of biobehavioral data, and weekly review sessions with the therapist. All seven previously noncompliant patients showed significant increases in medication compliance, when patients were allowed control and involvement in their own treatment (Baile, Bernard, & Engel, 1978).

Blackwell (1973) reports that alarming or unexpected side effects are frequently cited by *patients* as a reason for terminating medications. Yet, studies have shown that patient-reported side effects account for only a small proportion of all noncompliant patients (e.g., Weintraub, Au, & Lasagna, 1973). Educating or forewarning the patient about potential side effects have also not been found to affect the incidence of patients reporting side effects nor of the patients complying with medications.

The professional.   The clinician's style or interaction with the patient can dramatically affect the patient's compliance (Baekland & Lundwall, 1975). Clinicians' behaviors—including warmth and empathy (Charney, 1972; Francis, Korsch, & Morris, 1969), providing individualized instructions and feedback, as well as providing a brief time for general socialization (Korsch & Negrete, 1972)—positively affect patient compliance. Ongoing contact between clinician and patient allows for the emergence of a trusting relationship. Compliance has been consistently found to be improved when the patient sees the same clinician at each visit (Alpert, 1964; Becker, 1976; Becker, Drachman, & Kirscht, 1972).

The health care setting and organization.   The setting for health care has been found to be an important aspect of compliance. Clinic staff providing a warm and personalized approach to patients encourages a positive identification with the clinic, and it has been associated with good patient compliance (Caldwell, Cobb, Dowling & deTonga, 1970; Finnerty, 1974; Glogaw, 1970; and Shamerak, 1971). A short waiting time (Hieb & Waug, 1974) and an appointment with a specific physician were found to decrease a patient's missed appointments (Rockart & Hofmann, 1969). Patients given extra counseling concerning medication side effects and problems associated with taking medication had a 90 percent clinic attendance, while the clinic "as usual" group had a 60 percent attendance (Rehder, McCoy, Blackwell, Whitehead, & Robinson, 1977).

Overall, behavioral-medicine approaches to compliance are also at a relatively embryonic stage. Controlled-outcome studies are few and far between, individual cognitive-difference variables have rarely been considered, and relatively little imagination has been devoted to the development of reinforcement techniques for good compliance. In part, the problem can be attributed to the inherent measurement difficulties in this area, but it is likely that far more can be accomplished than has been to date.

PREPARATION FOR MEDICAL/DENTAL PROCEDURES AND SURGERY

A number of factors may increase stress and significantly contribute to a patient's adverse emotional reactions, perceptions of pain, and rate of recovery from surgery. These can include an unfamiliar setting, prehospitalization personality, previous hospitalizations, type of illness, and treatment required. Factors specific to children include separation from parents, level of cognitive development, and parental reactions to the child's illness and treatment (Vernon, Foley, Sipowicz, & Schalman, 1965; Willis et al., 1982). Unfortunately, most studies investigating preparation of patients for surgery or medical procedures have failed to control for these essential variables known to be major determinants of psychological distress (Melamed & Siegel, 1975; Vernon et al., 1965).

An additional, glaring methodological deficiency has been in the assessment of anxiety. Frequently, only global ratings by the patients, staff, or parents concerning reactions to treatments have been used as outcome measures. Melamed and Siegel (1975) were among the first to use sophisticated behavioral observations as one measure of anxiety in hospitalized children. Scales of pain or distress are bahavioral measures which may be of value (e.g., Burish & Lyles, 1981; Jay & Elliott, in press; Katz, Kellerman, & Siegel, 1980; Wernick, Jaremko, & Taylor, 1981; Wilson, 1981). In addition, some self-report measures of anxiety, distress, and pain have been shown to be reasonably reliable and valid (e.g., Burish & Lyles, 1981; Jay & Elliott, in press; Wernick, et al., 1981).

Finally, although rather rarely collected, physiological measurements of various kinds would be an important refinement in studies of patients' reactions to various medical and dental procedures. Some of the physiological measures which have been found to discriminate between good copers and poor copers at various times have included blood pressure and pulse rates (e.g., Burish & Lyles, 1981), assays of epinephrine (e.g., Wilson, 1981), and palmar sweat index (Melamed & Siegel, 1975). The measurement of endorphine levels do not appear to have been assessed in any such studies to date, probably because of the extreme complexity of the assay methods that are required.

Surgical preparation for adults

Methods for helping to prepare adults for surgery—with the intent of reducing their distress and improving their recovery—have included: (a) relaxation strategies, (b) basic information concerning the procedures to be conducted, (c) sensory information concerning the bodily sensations that the patient can expect to feel at various points prior to and following surgery, and (d) cognitive-coping skills. Wilson (1981) reviewed a variety of studies which indicated that relaxation training (to date) has demonstrated only moderate success as a prepatory technique for adults. However, he also noted that the techniques used have been quite brief and provided only during pre-operative periods. Therefore, he conducted a study in which the relaxation training was somewhat more intensive and available on cassette tape for patients to use as often as they wished, after their surgery. In the best controlled study of the preparation of adults for surgery to date, Wilson compared the following groups: (1) a control group receiving usual hospital procedures, (2) a sensory-information group which received information concerning both procedures and sensations that they would be experiencing during abdominal surgery, (3) a relaxation-training group which had constant access to a cassette for relaxation whenever they desired, and (4) a relaxation-plus-information group. In general, Wilson's results demonstrated that the relaxation technique was far more effective than the other strategies on a variety of behavioral, self-report, and physiological variables. The sensory-information strategy appeared to have relatively little effect on any of the dependent variables, except for hospital stay which, as in the relaxation-training group, was reduced. Wilson's sample consisted of 70 patients undergoing either cholecystectomy or total abdominal hysterectomies. He noted that, even if the relaxation and information procedures don't generalize to other surgical procedures, over 1 million Americans undergo one of those surgeries each year (Haupt, 1980). Thus, reduction in hospital stay for this type of patient alone could be of substantial value.

There have been a few comparisons between the treatment techniques of "basic information concerning procedures" and "information concerning bodily sensations." These studies have generally shown that, while basic information concerning procedures is, at times, somewhat helpful (e.g., Vernon & Bigelowe, 1974), sensory information seems to be somewhat more effective (e.g., Johnson, 1975; Johnson, Rice, Fuller, & Endress, 1978). At least one comparative group-outcome study with adult surgical patients demonstrated that "cognitive coping skills" were more effective than pre-operative information, a contact-control treatment, and even a combination of cognitive-coping skills and pre-operative information (Langer, Janis, Wolfer, 1975). The cognitive-coping skills included reappraisal of anxiety-arousing events, calming self-talk, and cognitive control through selective attention. The approach significantly reduced both pre-and post-operative stress, as well as requests for pain medication and sedatives.

Preparation of adults for painful medical procedures

For many medical procedures, it is generally not recommended that patients be fully anesthetized, thus making reactions to the procedures more difficult to control. Strategies similar to those used in preparing adults for surgery have been used in preparing adults for medical procedures. A series of relatively well-controlled, group treatment-outcome studies have shown that various cognitive coping-skill strategies have substantial effectiveness in reducing stress and anxiety, as measured across multiple-response systems for both the medical procedure of cardiac catheterization (Kendall, Williams, Pachacek, Graham, Shisslak, & Herzoff, 1979) and highly painful, medical treatments for burn injuries (Wernick et al., 1981). Furthermore, Burish and Lyles (1981) recently reported that relaxation was quite helpful in reducing a variety of adverse side effects demonstrated by adult patients in response to cancer chemotherapy. However, no differences were found between the conditions in terms of frequency of vomiting. By contrast, Redd, Andresen, and Nainagawa (1982) successfully controlled anticipatory emesis in adult patients who were receiving cancer chemotherapy. In this study, hypnosis was utilized within a staggered-baseline design in combination with a reversal design across six subjects. Emesis was successfully suppressed in all patients by the hypnotic procedures. Unfortunately, concomitant measures of anxiety, distress, and discomfort and physiological measures of arousal were not assessed. Finally, providing sensory information has been found to be helpful in reducing distress of patients compared to control groups for patients undergoing endoscopic examinations (e.g., Johnson & Leventhal, 1974).

In summary, it appears that a number of strategies have shown a high degree of promise for alleviating the stress in adults undergoing uncomfortable and/or painful medical treatment. To date, these strategies have not been systematically compared with each other, there have been no systematic attempts to ascertain the specific cognitive mechanisms underlying the success of these procedures, and the behavioral-observation scales utilized have generally been rather crude. Furthermore, it would be valuable to compare these strategies to medications and to assess the possible synergistic effects of combining medications with behavioral strategies.

Preparation of children for surgery

With respect to preparing children for surgery per se, two studies stand out as the best controlled and methodologically sophisticated to date. The first was reported by Melamed and Siegel (1975), who demonstrated that the use of filmed coping model effectively reduced children's emotional reactions during the hospital stay and facilitated emotional adjustment during the post-hospital period. Children who viewed the modeling film were significantly less anxious pre-operatively and had fewer behavioral problems post-operatively.

The second study was more recently reported by Peterson and Shigetomi (1981). In this study, 66 children undergoing tonsillectomies were compared in the following groups: (a) information only, (b) coping, (c) filmed modeling, and (d) coping plus filmed modeling. The coping procedures consisted of relaxation training, distracting mental imagery, and comforting self-talk. The information procedure was delivered in the context of the "Big Bird Puppet Party," in which the experimenter told the children a story of the Big Bird Puppet going to the hospital to get its tonsils out and explained the various procedures that he would undergo, while the puppet pantomimed those activities. In the combined treatment, the children first received the puppet information, then the coping strategies, and finally observed a coping model using the film "Ethan has an Operation," which was utilized by Melamed and Siegel (1975). Several measures indicated that coping procedures were somewhat more effective than modeling-only procedures. However, the largest differences were found between the children receiving the combined coping-and-modeling treatment and those in the other groups. These results were obtained across a fairly wide variety of self-report, observer reports, and behavioral observations. Many of these results however, were of marginal statistical significance. It may be that the inclusion of children as young as two-and-one-half years of age in the sample group and the lack of a no-treatment condition attenuated the differences among the groups.

Preparation of children for dental procedures

With respect to reducing children's fears concerning dental treatment, modeling has been consistently found to be an effective treatment (Johnson & Machen, 1973; Machen & Johnson, 1974; Melamed, Hawes, Heivy, & Glick, 1975; Melamed, Weinstein, Hawes, & Katin-Borland, 1975; White, Akers, Green, & Yates, 1974). In addition, however, a package of cognitive-coping skills (consisting of positive self-statements, relaxation, and distracting imagery) and a strategy using sensory information concerning a description of the sights, sounds, and bodily sensations to be experienced, were both found to be approximately equal in effectiveness for helping children during dental procedures. Children receiving both of these strategies displayed fewer disruptive behaviors, were rated as less anxious, more cooperative, and had lower post-treatment pulse rates than the contact-control group (Siegel & Peterson, 1980).

Preparation of children for highly painful medical procedures

The literature currently lacks almost any systematic investigation into strategies for helping children endure painful medical procedures (such as, treatment for burn injuries, lumbar punctures, and bone marrow aspirations). Quite frequently, children react to these procedures with such high levels of screaming, crying, flailing, and other indicants of distress that physical restraint is essential—yet difficult—to employ. At times, this distress has been so great that needed procedures could not even be performed (Humphrey, 1982).

After substantial clinical efforts in these areas, several controlled, limited-N design studies have recently been completed at Oklahoma Children's Memorial Hospital. In the first, Elliott and Olson (1982) demonstrated that a cognitive-behavioral treatment package (including relaxation, imagery, cognitive-coping statements, and tangible reinforcers for the child) effectively reduced behavioral distress, as measured by a sophisticated observational scale similar to that recently reported by Katz, et al., (1980). This study reported results obtained with eight children, ages 5 to 12, who had shown signs of extreme behavioral distress. The first four children were given no treatment and demonstrated increased distress throughout the observational periods. Three of four children treated with the cognitive-behavioral treatment package showed dramatic and highly significant reductions in observed distress. The final child was given treatment, yet showed relatively little response to it. Of the four treated children, the three "successes" showed little generalization of coping skills on the days that the children were not coached in the use of the procedures.

Therefore, the design essentially consisted of a staggered-baseline design, in conjunction with a reversal design. This study suggests that it may be essential to not only present the children with the cognitive-behavioral treatment package but also to coach them in those strategies during the actual painful medical procedure. Clinical impressions previous to the initiation of this study indicated that the role of reinforcement also seemed to be highly significant. When children could be strongly reinforced for coping attempts, it appeared as though they became dominated by the "current concerns" of obtaining their reinforcements; whereas, when no reinforcers had been made available, it appeared as though children were dominated by "current concerns" of obtaining sympathy, nurturance, and/or avoidance.

A similar study has recently been completed by Jay, Elliott, Olson, and Ozolins (1982), in which a staggered-baseline design was utilized to demonstrate the effectiveness of cognitive-coping strategies (in the form of a brief relaxation-breathing technique, emotive imagery, attention-distraction, and reinforcement) to treat children with cancer who were undergoing the highly painful diagnostic procedures of lumbar punctures and bone marrow aspirations. In vivo practice and modeling with a doll were also utilized as part of this treatment package. Initial data from this study have been highly encouraging as well. These same authors have recently completed a videotape for modeling the use of these coping strategies, which may aid in delivery of the treatment to a larger number of children and simplify its delivery by trained paraprofessionals. Current research in progress includes comparisons of the cognitive-treatment package to medications and an attention-control group.

Individual-difference variables

Individual coping styles or characteristic manners of dealing with stress have been suggested as important intervening variables which may account for the success or failure of various preparation strategies for some subjects. In fact, a number of investigators (e.g., Janis, 1958) have suggested that behavioral preparations for surgery may potentially be *harmful* to patients who use certain coping strategies (such as denial). At this point, findings of more-recent and better-controlled studies have suggested that these individual-difference variables do not result in subjects being harmed by the presentation of coping strategies or preparatory information, but rather that subjects with certain coping styles (such as repression and/or denial) may not benefit as much by such treatments (Wilson, 1981). It may be that different treatment strategies will be more effective for individuals with certain types of coping styles, but this remains relatively uninvestigated at this point. Part of the problem, in this regard, lies in clearly defining the individual-difference variable of interest. For example, Wilson's (1981) use of the term *denial* does not seem to be quite the same as that utilized by other investigators studying similar phenomenon.

Overall, the assessment of pre-hospital cognitive-coping styles has shown only limited predictive value concerning anxiety, pain tolerance, or post-surgical adjustment. It may be that assessment techniques focusing on "current concerns" and the patient's "perceived control" of the situation will be particularly useful to examine, especially as they may elucidate interactions with different types of treatment strategies.

BEHAVIORAL TREATMENTS FOR MEDICAL DISORDERS

CARDIOVASCULAR SYSTEM

Hypertension

Hypertension is a highly significant health problem that has possibly received as much attention in the behavioral-medicine literature as any other medical problem. This attention has been due, in part, to the extremely high incidence of the disorder. Early estimates have suggested that approximately 23 million Americans are afflicted with hypertension, the vast majority of whom are of the "essential hypertension" type (U.S. Public Health Service, 1973), which is diagnosed when demonstrable physical causes are apparently absent (Blanchard, 1979). This disorder has been clearly associated with increased risks from life-threatening conditions, such as coronary artery disease, atherosclerosis, and nephrosclerosis (e.g., Kannel, Gordon, & Schwartz, 1971). The significance and prevalence of hypertension was highlighted further by information presented more recently at a joint U.S./U.S.S.R. symposium sponsored by the National Heart, Lung, and Blood Institute. Those data indicated that increased morbidity and mortality from hypertension results from diastolic pressures as low as 70mm HG (Miller, 1981). Furthermore, even occasional large increases in an individual's resting pulse and blood pressure level have been implicated as potential predictors of a shortened life span (Merrill, 1966).

The excitement over the application of behavioral-medicine strategies to this problem was fueled by early reports of the control of blood pressure in normotensive subjects (Shapiro, Tursky, Gershon, & Stern, 1969), as well as by data indicating that relatively small (10mm HG) reductions in diastolic pressures of a hypertensive population reduced their mortality over a five-year span (Miller, 1981). In addition, current drug therapies have been widely cited as frequently resulting in noncompliance, as well as in highly undesirable side effects, such as headaches, dizziness, impotence, and gastrointestinal difficulties, among others (Moser, 1977).

Unfortunately, some of the early optimism regarding the behavioral managment of hypertension has been dampened by subsequent complications. For example, confusion exists over basic terms such as *borderline, early,* and *labile* hypertension (Kolata, 1979). Subgroups apparently exist even within the category of borderline hypertension, including differences in cardiac output and peripherial resistence in arterioles (Harrell, 1980). Harrell has provided a thorough review of physiological subtypes within the essential-hypertension population.

In addition, treatment-outcome studies have almost universally been confounded by methodological difficulties, such as measurement techniques (Taylor, 1980a), failure to control for habituation to the research or clinic setting, inadequate baselines (Seer & Raeburn, 1980), failure to include measurements collected from the natural environment (Bair & Levenberg, 1979), failure to clearly define the population subgroup, and failure to include control groups and follow-ups (Taylor, 1980a). Excellent reviews of these methodological issues, as well as of treatment outcome data, have been compiled recently (Blair & Levenburg, 1979; Blanchard, 1979; Kolata, 1979; Lynch, Long, Thomas, Malinow, & Katcher, 1981; Stratton, 1978; Seer & Raeburn, 1980; Taylor, 1980a).

The situation with regard to treatment-outcome studies borders on chaos, although a few initial conclusions seem to be emerging from recent reviews. The major treatment modalities to date have included: relaxation methods (generally of the "passive" type—see Denney, Chapter 27; biofeedback directly on blood pressure, as well as of other response systems presumably designed to reduce blood pressure by lowering sympathetic arousal or muscle tension; and combination treatments. Some of the conclusions that are *tentatively* suggested by recent extensive reviews include: (1) various relaxation and meditation techniques have generally demonstrated small, but significant, reductions in blood pressure for hypertensive subjects. However, only a very few studies have used no-treatment controls or follow-ups of a significant length (Seer & Raeburn, 1980; Taylor, 1980a). Furthermore, the physiological mechanisms of these relaxation strategies are not well understood. (2) Most biofeedback procedures involving direct feedback on blood pressure have reported modest phasic and short-term effects, but follow-up data were almost totally absent. Some of the better-controlled studies have failed to replicate initial positive outcomes. Some evidence exists to suggest that intermittent (rather than beat-by-beat) feedback may be slightly more efficacious (Blanchard, 1979). (3) Combination treatments (involving biofeedback and various other types of relaxation and meditation) have demonstrated the largest reductions in blood pressure.

Kallman and Gilmore (1981) reviewed a number of studies which utilized a combination of biofeedback, relaxation, and meditation. Generally, the biofeedback in these studies was of either the EMG or thermal type. Several of these studies utilized control groups as well as follow-ups of six months or more (e.g., Love, Montgomery, & Moeller, 1974; Patel, 1975; Patel & North, 1975). It should be noted that most of these studies utilized more than the usual number of treatment sessions for treatment-outcome studies (ranging from 12 to 36 sessions) and, furthermore, generally placed substantial emphasis upon practice at home. Unfortunately, systematic data concerning such home practice have not been collected in these studies. Collection of such data and further replications are clearly called for in studies of such combination treatments. Their efficacy may be due to the home practice, the possibility of subjects being able to choose the particular aspects of treatment which they individually find most useful, or some unique aspect of the synergestic effects of the various components. At-home practice, along with self-monitoring of blood pressures, could also lead some subjects to an awareness of the situational cues which may be responsible for exacerbations of their hypertension. With this information, subjects could learn to avoid such situations or reduce the stress associated with them.

Denney (see Chapter 27) noted that Jorgensen, Houston, and Zurawski (1981) recently completed a controlled study of anxiety-management training which, compared to a nontreatment control, resulted in significant differences in blood pressure readings between groups during nonstressful periods, but readings taken during exposure to a laboratory stressor were less clear. It may be that demonstrating efficacy in response to a laboratory stressor will prove to be an essential outcome measure in such research. This possibility is increased by evidence from a 25-year longitudinal study which showed that the best predictors of subsequent heart disease were: (*a*) resting systolic blood pressure, (*b*) serum cholesterol level, and (*c*) the best predictor of all—*diastolic blood pressure increases in response to a laboratory cold pressor test* (Keys, Taylor, Blackburn, Brozek, Anderson, & Simonson, 1971). Further support for this assumption was provided recently by Light (1981), who reported that a group of young *healthy* males could be differentiated on the basis of increased heart rates and systolic pressures during a variety of stressors, but *not* when relaxed. The group demonstrating this heightened cardiovascular reactivity also had a greater incidence of parents with hypertension than the group without significant cardiovascular responsiveness.

With respect to individual differences, a number of variables have recently been cited as potentially important when developing treatment strategies for the management of hypertension. These include: locus of control, availability of coping responses, type *A* coronary-prone behavior, anger, anxiety, and sex (e.g., Whitehead, Blackwell, DeSilva, & Robinson, 1977), which have all been shown to interact with the development of hypertension. However, this interaction generally *depends upon the particular physiological subtype of hypertension* and/or various situational-contextual variables. For example, Esler, Julius, Zweifler, Randall, Harburg, Gardiner, and Dequattro (1977) have recently presented evidence suggesting that patients with mild essential hypertension (along with elevated levels of plasma renin, higher heart rates, and elevated plasma norepinephrine concentrations) could be differentiated from patients with essential hypertension, with normal renin levels. The elevated-renin group were guilt prone, controlled, and had a high level of unexpressed anger. Those authors speculated that the high blood pressure of that group was sustained by overactivity of the sympathetic nervous system. Shapiro (1979) speculated about the role of conditioning in the development of excessive sympathetic tone, as well as the possibility that different subgroups of patients would respond differentially to behavioral or pharmacological treatments.

Locus of control is another individual-difference variable which has been shown to interact with stressors and blood pressure elevations. For example, DeGood (1975) found that subjects with an internal locus of control showed higher elevations in blood pressure in laboratory situations in which they had no control over shock exposure. On the other hand, subjects with an external locus of control showed greater increases in blood pressure when they were allowed to control the timing of shock intervals. Harrell (1980) further reviewed evidence concernig the relationship between type *A* coronary-prone behavior (discussed in detail in the next chapter) to blood pressure. Currently, evidence for this relationship is somewhat tentative but suggestive of a relationship between high blood pressure and certain type-*A* individuals, who are particularly prone to become self-involved in environmental events.

The availabiltiy of coping responses is another individually and situationally determined variable that appears to have importance in this line of research. For example, Manuck, Harvey, Lechleiter, and Neal (1978) determined that available coping responses can lead to increases in systolic blood pressure, but only when these coping responses were difficult to use. A recent report by Lynch et al. (1981) has revealed a relationship between the more basic coping response of talking and blood pressure in both normotensive and hypertensive subjects. In this study, increases in blood pressure in response to talking were substantially higher for hypertensives with the highest resting arterial pressures in comparison to normotensives.

Furthermore, Linden and Feuerstein (1981) reviewed evidence suggesting that at least a significant subgroup of hypertensives are likely to display deficits in social skills. Thus, these authors noted that, depending upon the particular group of hypertensives and the nature of any assertiveness deficits found, cognitive restructuring, anxiety reduction, skills training or some combination thereof, may be useful strategies for reducing blood pressure, especially in response to specific social stressors. Shapiro (1979) has also speculated that assertion training in combination with biofeedback and relaxation may be of particular value for the subclass of patients with hypertension in conjunction with unexpressed anger or submissiveness. Bair and Levenberg (1979) have provided what appears to be the only report to date of the treatment of essential hypertension through a multimodal-behavioral approach. They reported on a highly successful response in an "N of 1" study, in which the treatment consisted of relaxation training, positive-covert imagery, role rehearsal of positive and negative feelings, rational disputation of irrational fears and needs, and sensory-awareness exercises. At least for certain subgroups of hypertensives, this sort of multimodel approach would appear to have substantial merit. However, no systematic group-outcome studies of this type have been reported to date.

In summary, Harrell (1980) has suggested that much is to be gained by assessments of between-subject physiological and psychological differences. Physiologically, renin levels and cardiac autonomic balance appear promising, while psychological variables (such as, suppressed hostility, locus of control, and actual use and availability of coping responses during stress) have particular promise, especially as they interact with the aforementioned, physiological variables. Further, Harrell noted that the use of specific blockade drugs during stress administration will aid in determining the physiological pathways that result in blood pressure elevations.

Another promising line of investigation in this area would be a detailed analysis of subjects who respond versus those who fail to respond to treatments with both drugs and behavioral interventions. Apparently, the only study to date that has made such a comparison was reported by

Seer and Raeburn (1980). *Responders* (as contrasted with nonrespond-ers) to meditation training were characterized by the following: a signifi-cantly longer hypertension history, higher pre-test diastolic blood pres-sures (suggesting the possible role of the law of initial values), reports of feeling more relaxed at the pre-test, and evaluation of the techniques as easier to use. Finally, subjects who rated their health more negatively tended to be nonresponders more often than those that rated their health as very good. This comparison of responders and nonresponders was not especially comprehensive, but the authors can be commended for making an initial effort in this regard.

Seer and Raeburn (1980) found greater reductions in the subjects' diastolic pressures. This finding contradicts a variety of data reviewed by Shapiro and Surwit (1976), which suggested that diastolic pressure is more difficult to reduce. Shapiro and Surwit further noted that diastolic pressure has been frequently cited as more critical than systolic pressure from a medical standpoint, especially during later stages of hypertension. However, resting systolic pressures have been found to be predictive of the development of coronary heart disease. Therefore, Shapiro and Surwit suggested that treatments may be most efficacious if work is con-ducted on those who are in the early stages of developing hypertension, concentrating on reductions in systolic blood pressure levels. This hypoth-esis remains untested at this point, however.

Another point noted by some investigators (e.g., Shapiro & Surwit, 1976; Stratton, 1978) is the degree to which the treatment induces a state of confidence or belief in a patient that he is indeed able to exert some degree of control over his blood pressure. Such a perception may be quite critical in determining whether patients will engage in the at-home practice which may be predictive of treatment outcome.

Weiss has recently further pointed out the need for studies combining drugs and various relaxation strategies, with the ultimate goal of "wean-ing" subjects off the drugs (Holden, 1980). He stated that drug and relaxation methods seem to potentiate each other and that people may be more motivated to use relaxation to escape the negative side effects of the drugs. However, it will likely be important for patients to demonstrate the ability to sustain decreased blood pressure levels in response to a variety of stressors prior to total elimination of drug therapies. Furthermore, continued long-term home monitoring of blood pressure would seem to be an obvious necessity for such patients to ensure that relapses have not occurred.

Finally, a recent review by Lieberman (1980) indicated that children's blood pressures are correlated with those of their parents; and, in some cases, it is possible to begin tracking elevated blood pressures at an age as young as three. The potential for behavioral interventions may be even greater if—and when—patterns of hypertension can be identified at such earlier stages.

Migraine headaches

As Denney (Chapter 27) noted, considerably fewer treatment-outcome studies have been conducted on migraine headaches. Many of the intervention strategies that have been attempted can be classified according to his recommended, "active-passive" dimension. In general, migraine headaches involve a vascular condition characterized by severe episodic pain, often preceded by various prodromal symptoms (Cinciripini, Williamson, & Epstein, 1981). Numerous subtypes of this disorder have been described and have been reviewed by Cinciripini et al. (1981). Unfortunately, the majority of treatment-outcome studies to date have failed to adequately describe their subject samples in these terms.

In a recent, excellent review of this area, Adams, Feuerstein, and Fowler (1980) noted that as many as 12 million persons in the United States may suffer from some form of migraine headaches. They observed that, from a biological perspective, variables of greatest interest have included the roles of vascular activity, heredity, and seratonins. Frequently implicated, psychological variables have included unexpressed anger (cf. Harrison, 1975) as well as the role of Trait × Situation interactions. Currently, the specific role and possible interaction of these hypothesized, etiological factors have not been established.

In the area of treatment, Adams et al. (1980) have noted that medications have not been shown to be adequately efficacious to date. Reviews of behavioral interventions have begun to *consistently* demonstrate that a wide variety of methods are significantly more effective than medical placebos, including temperature feedback alone, various relaxation strategies, and temperature feedback in combination with autogenic training (e.g., Adams et al., 1980; Andrasik & Blanchard, Chapter 32 in the present work; Blanchard, Andrasik, Ahles, Teders, & O'Keefe, 1980; Kallman & Gilmore, 1981). These results have generally led to the conclusion that relaxation and/or cognitive variables (such as, perceived control) may be responsible for the results that are being obtained (cf. Blanchard et al., 1980; Cohen, McArthur, & Rickles, 1980).

Blanchard et al. (1980) noted that further comparisons of relaxation and biofeedback strategies may be of little value at this time. However, other psychological strategies (such as cognitive-coping skills, assertion training, desensitization, and combinations thereof) may be worthwhile. Several studies by Mitchell and his colleagues (e.g., Mitchell, 1971; Mitchell & Mitchell, 1971; Mitchell & White, 1977) have provided suggestive evidence that a package of techniques (including thought stopping, time-out, assertion training, cognitive restructuring, and relaxation, among others) was more effective than limited treatments. However, methodological problems included suspect data-collection methods, a small *N*, and a lack of physiological data. Further, indirect support for therapeutic approaches that include active anxiety-management techniques have been provided by Price and Blackwell (1980), who found slightly higher trait-anxiety scores among migraine sufferers than in a normal-control group. Additional support for the rationale of including assertion training in treatments for this group was provided by their finding that migraine sufferers tended to inhibit their feelings much more than a normal-control group, following the observation of a stressful film.

At this point, the research literature in the area of migraine headaches would seem to point to the following recommendations for future research: (1) comparison of medications with behavioral intervention as well as combinations of medications and behavioral intervention, as suggested by Blanchard et al. (1980); (2) greater study of Trait × Situational variables as well as Trait × Situational × Physiological subtypes; (3) assessment of antecedent and consequent events for migraine headache sufferers, as suggested by Cinciripini et al. (1981), may lead to more-refined treatment intervention; (4) the study of potential predictors of treatment success (cf. Blanchard et al., 1980); (5) further controlled investigations into cognitive-coping skills in conjunction with relaxation techniques; and (6) perhaps most important of all—systematic post-treatment assessment of subjects, to determine what they actually did during and after treatment. For example, Andrasik and Holroyd (1980) recently found that subjects in various types of biofeedback training for (tension) headaches enumerated 11 strategies following treatment that they used to control their headaches. Seven of these strategies are often employed in cognitive coping-skills programs.

In conclusion, various behavioral and relaxation strategies have begun to consistently demonstrate relatively better results from behavioral interventions than medical placebos. The underlying mechanisms are poorly understood, but Andrasik and Holroyd (1980) offered the highly appealing suggestion that the critical variable may be for subjects to "learn to monitor the insidious onset of headache symptoms and engage in some sort of coping response incompatable with the further exacerbations of symptoms" (p. 584). Finally, the patient's motivation or "subject-expected utility" of change must not be ignored in this area. Although migraine headaches can be highly debilitating, consequent events to the headaches have the potential to override any of the patient's motivation to actually use coping responses (cf. Fordyce, Fowler, & DeLateur, 1968).

Cardiac arrhythmias

The reader is referred to several recent, comprehensive reviews of the behavioral control and tratment of cardiac arrhythmias (e.g., Blanchard, 1979; Engle, 1977; Feuerstein & Ward, 1980; Kallman & Gilmore, 1981). Blanchard (1979) noted that it is somewhat paradoxical that biofeedback research has been substantial in the area of cardiac rate, but that relatively little clinical application has been made of this research. This lack of application may be due, in part, to the relative infrequency of the disorders in contrast to hypertension and headaches, as well as to the extreme medical seriousness of the problem, which often leads to reliance upon established, pharmacological treatments. For example, Shapiro and Surwit (1976) noted that one of the major types of cardiac arrhythmias—known as premature ventricular contractions (PVC)—has been associated with diminished coronary artery (as well as cerebral) blood flow, in addition to a significantly increased possibility of sudden death. Feuerstein and Ward (1980) reviewed substantial evidence suggesting that psychological factors have been shown to affect both the rhythmicity and conduction within healthy and diseased hearts. They noted that it has also been shown that PVCs can be classically conditioned, even in subjects who have had no history of heart disease (Perez-Cruet, 1962). Such conditioning leads to the obvious implication that cardiac arrhythmias could even be conditioned to various environmental stimuli (Fuerstein & Ward, 1980).

Engel (1977) noted the high potential for findings such as these to increase both the understanding and the control of cardiac arrhythmias. In spite of this potential, Engel observed that cardiologists currently virtually ignore the potential role of psychosocial and behavioral factors within heart disease, as evidenced by less than 10 pages out of a total of over 4,000 pages in recent American textbooks on cardiology devoted to emotional or psychological-behavioral variables.

Premature ventricular contractions. With respect to premature ventricular contractions (PVCs), a number of studies employing heart rate biofeedback have been conducted by Engel and his associates (e.g., Engel & Bleecker, 1974; Engel & Melmon, 1968; Weiss & Engel, 1971). They have rather convincingly demonstrated that such training can lead to a substantial reduction in the frequency of PVCs, for at least some patients. In fact, Feuerstein and Ward (1980), in their review of these studies (as well as other replications), suggested that approximately 50 percent of these patients can eliminate or reduce the frequency of PVCs with heart rate-biofeedback training. It should be noted that several aspects of this training seem to be particularly helpful. The first is the use of binary feedback, in both a visual and an auditory form. The second has been that, with most of these studies, subjects are taught to both increase and decrease their heart rates, as well as to maintain the heart rate within a given range. The third is that these training sessions have generally been far more extensive and lengthy than most behavioral interventions; and the fourth is that they are usually followed by graduated weaning. Shapiro and Surwit, (1976) have noted that as many as 50 to 60 sessions, utilizing different types of contingencies, have been conducted in some cases. Currently, the role of these four factors is quite unclear, in that there has not yet been a single controlled *group-outcome* study for the behavioral intervention of PVCs.

Sinus tachycardia.   Abnormally high cardiac rate is the other type of cardiac arrhythmia, and it has received moderate attention in the research to date. Once again, the total number of cases has been small, and no controlled group-outcome studies have been conducted. Yet, a variety of studies reported in previously noted reviews have indicated that heart rate biofeedback also may be efficacious for the treatment of such arrhythmias. Shapiro and Surwit (1976) speculated that such effects may be due, in part, to the specific, circumscribed nature of the disorder.

It should also be noted that an even smaller number of studies have indicated that relaxation training of various types (as well as hypnosis) may improve the management of at least certain types of cardiac arrhythmias, possibly through the reduction of arousal levels (Feuerstein & Ward, 1980). Feuerstein and Ward suggested that, although we do not know the type of patient who will respond best to relaxation procedures, such skills are more easily learned than regulation of heart rate. Thus, they recommended initial relaxation training, followed by biofeedback training only if relaxation training fails to ameliorate the arrhythmias.

Future research in the area of cardiac arrhythmias is needed to answer a number of important questions. First, Engel (1977) noted that the use of various autonomic drugs with differential effects on heart functioning (during both feedback and nonfeedback phases) may help elucidate some of the underlying physiological mechanisms. A second area of substantial importance is the further investigation of environmental stimuli that have been clearly associated with cardiac arrhythmias in some cases. For this group of patients, it may be possible to determine which stressors are related to the patient's arrhythmias and, through some combination of relaxation and/or biofeedback, reduce the arrhythmia in response to the specific stressors (Feuerstein & Ward, 1980). Finally, there once again has been a general failure to inquire as to what subjects are actually doing to raise and lower their heart rates. One would expect that some of these strategies are rather idiosyncratic and involve various kinds of imagery, self-statements, etc. A thorough analysis of subject strategies, however, may lead to ways of improving the efficacy and provide information about which subjects would benefit the most, from which kind of strategy.

Raynaud's disease

A painful, functional disorder, Raynaud's disease involves episodes of vasoconstriction, generally in the hands and feet. The disorder is frequently elicited either by cold stimulation and/or emotional stress (Spittell,

1972). Shapiro and Surwit (1976) have noted that medical-pharmacological approaches to this disorder have not been especially effective (e.g., Fairburn, Juergens, & Spittell, 1972). Initial efforts to ameliorate this disorder from a behavioral standpoint focused primarily upon training subjects to increase the skin temperature in their hands by providing direct biofeedback of skin temperature. Most of these initial efforts involved a single patient or small groups and were largely uncontrolled. However, they provided suggestive evidence that such training could be effective in ameliorating the disorder. Feedback on blood volume per se has been utilized in a smaller number of studies and has shown some potential as well (e.g., Schwartz, 1972).

A substantial advance in understanding the treatment of Raynaud's disease has been made by two recent, well-controlled studies (Surwit, Pilon, & Fenton, 1978; Keefe, Surwit, & Pilon, 1980). These studies, in combination, have provided data supporting the following: (1) autogenic training by itself, progressive-relaxation training by itself, or a combination of skin temperature biofeedback with autogenic training all demonstrated significant and substantial improvements in symptoms associated with Raynaud's disease; (2) there were no differences between these three behavioral-treatment strategies; (3) these strategies showed significantly greater improvement than a no-treatment group; (4) the treatments uniformly demonstrated that they could increase the patient's ability to maintain digital temperatures during a laboratory cold-stress test; (5) the effect of the treatment strategies appeared to be a rather general one, since vasomotor control was accompanied by decreases in heart rates within the sessions; (6) the patients demonstrated progressive improvements in their ability to deal with the laboratory cold-stress test over the training, which is the opposite of what usually occurs in untrained patients; and (7) in the second study, the symptom improvement was maintained by all of the patients, nine weeks after the start of training. Finally, Keefe et al. (1980) suggested that these relatively simple and economical relaxation strategies may be of substantial value to patients in the management of other disorders, such as vasospastic symptoms of scleroderma and other collagen vascular diseases. Further work is clearly needed in two areas: (1) an improved understanding of the underlying physiological mechanisms that are responsible for the improvements and (2) controlled studies which employ longer follow-up periods.

Chronic arterial occlusive disease

The possibility of relaxation therapy and/or biofeedback for the improvement of peripheral blood flow in patients with chronic arterial occlusive disease and intermittent claudication was also recently demonstrated in a report by Greenspan, Lawrence, Esposito, & Vorhees (1980). Eleven patients with this disorder were selected on the basis of: having participated in an exercise program, but with relatively little improvement in symptoms; having a maximum treadmill-walking time of less than five minutes; and demonstrating an ankle blood pressure of less than 60 HG, following exercise. The authors noted that, due to the risks involved with surgery as well as the relative failure of vasodilators to ameliorate the condition, biofeedback and relaxation therapy would present a particularly appealing approach. Experimental-group patients received combined EMG and temperature biofeedback, along with progressive muscle-relaxation training, over a 13-week period. Results were compared to a waiting-list control group. All of the patients in the group receiving the behavioral-treatment package improved their maximal treadmill-walking time, as well as their exercise ankle blood pressure. The waiting-list group showed minimal improvements, but also improved after being administered the same behavioral package three months following the administration of the strategies to the first group. The relative role of the biofeedback and relaxation, of course, could not be separated in this study. However, indications from research in the areas of Raynaud's disease, migraine headaches, and hypertension, would suggest that a relaxation response alone might account for the results obtained.

RESPIRATORY SYSTEM

Asthma

Bronchial asthma is an intermittent, variable, and reversible airway obstruction (Chai, 1975), characterized by episodes of breathlessness, and caused by constriction of the smooth muscles of the bronchiole tubes, edema of the cell walls, or hypersecretion of mucus (either separately or in combination). Air exchange is thereby decreased and can be completely obstructed. Triggers associated with asthma attacks include atopy (allergies), infection, physical exertion, and stress. The significance of the type of physiological changes and the nature of the particular triggering stimulation may vary from patient to patient and from episode to episode in the same patient (Hock, Rodgers, Reddi Kennard, 1978). Reduction or disappearance of symptoms is influenced by severity, age of onset, sex, other atopic manifestations, nasal polyps, seasonal changes, and infections.

A major difficulty in the investigation of asthma is a failure to agree upon a definition of asthma with clear criteria (Alexander & Solanch, 1981). Traditionally, asthmatics have been subclassified as intrinsic (due to infections of unknown causes), extrinsic (due to allergens), and mixed. Others have created more-complex classification systems (cf. Read & Townley, 1978). Alexander and Solanch (1981) have argued that the subgroup classifications of intrinsic versus extrinsic asthma are overly simplistic and potentially harmful definitions to both the patient and his/

her family and stated, "Since its cause (intrinsic asthma) is unknown, it is the kind of asthma that is often claimed to be 'all in the head,' leading to confused and inconsistent treatment strategies as well as much embarrassment, guilt, and frustration for both patient and family" (p. 6). In all probability, few (if any) cases of asthma could be considered 100 percent extrinsic or intrinsic. For example, both conditioning and stress have some potential to effect pulmonary functioning, even with asthmatics usually considered to be highly extrinsic in nature.

Recent reviews have generally concluded that no single asthmatic or pre-asthmatic personality has been clearly established. For example, Creer (1979) summarized the findings by stating, "The degree to which patients with asthma differ from supposedly normal people is generally a function of the instrument or technique used to assess the groups' subjects. In essence, the greater the proven reliability and validity of the instrument, the less the likelihood that significant differences will be found" (p. 2).

There is no single, authoritative source for the estimate of the incidence of asthma. The American Lung Association (1975) estimates about 1 percent of the population suffers from asthma and between 5 and 15 percent of all children under 16 years of age are afflicted with this disorder. Male-to-female ratio is approximately 2 to 1. Estimates have been made that from 12 to 68 percent of all asthmatic children will become asymptomatic (Siegel, Katz, & Rachelefsky, 1978). Mortality due to asthma has been estimated to be between 2,000 (Segal, 1976) and 4,000 (Davis, 1972) per year.

Assessment: Dependent measures of asthma.   Dependent measures of asthma include physiological, symptomatic, and behavioral measures. Pulmonary-function tests are essential in the objective physiological assessment of asthma. The spirometer and peak flow meter are the most frequently used instruments in the diagnosis and management of asthma. The *spirometer* assesses several pulmonary functions: (1) Forced expiratory volume (FEV_1) is the amount of air exhaled in the first second. This test is the most widely used in the diagnosis and management of all chronic lung diseases (Huber, 1975) and reflects decreases in the patient's large airway passages; (2) Maximum midexpiratory flow rate (MMFR) measures the average rate of air flow during the middle half of the forced expiration and indicates changes in both large and small airways (Chai, 1975); and (3) Forced vital capacity (FVC) is the maximum volume of air that can be expelled subsequent to a maximum inspiration and is a measure of total lung capacity, which is decreased during an asthma attack (Snider, 1976).

The *peak flow meter* measures the peak expiratory flow rate (PEFR), which is the amount of expiratory air blown in the initial 0.1 seconds following maximum inspiration. An advantage of the PEFR is that it is available in a small, handheld version, and it may be used by the patient at home, so that daily respiratory functions can be measured (Renne, Nau, Dietiker, & Lyon, 1976). Knapp and Wells (1978) have identified three major problems associated with the above measures of pulmonary functioning: (1) the measures are effort-dependent in nature (Alexander, Miklich, & Hershkoff, 1972); (2) the excessive exertion on repeated trials may be harmful to the patient (Danker, Miklich, Pratt, & Creer, 1975); and (3) the measurements require extensive cooperation by the patient (Knapp & Wells, 1978). Recently, more-complex measures of pulmonary functions which do not have the drawbacks of the spirometer and peak flow meter have been made available. The body plethysmograph and the forced-oscillation technique provide a measurement of the total respiratory resistance (TRR). The measurement of TRR is not dependent upon effort and requires minimal patient cooperation. Additionally, some methods of measuring TRR can provide auditory or visual feedback (for a review of TRR, see Feldman, 1976).

Symptomatic measures of asthma include the frequency, duration, severity, and periodicity of asthma attacks (Creer, 1979). Frequency and duration of hospital visits and ER visits have been considered to be both symptomatic and behavioral measures of asthma. Additional behavioral measures include: number of missed days of school (King, 1980), activity restrictions, frequency of bronkometer usage (Sirota & Mahoney, 1974), amount of medication (King, 1980), and compliance with medication. Creer (1979) and Purcell and Weiss (1970) have noted that symptomatic changes in asthma are desirable, but often these changes are accompanied by only marginal changes in pulmonary functions. In any well-controlled study of asthma, it is necessary to assess multiple dependent measures to determine the effects of behavioral interventions. It is important to note that many treatment-outcome studies reporting changes in pulmonary functions only report *statistically* significant levels of improvement. Statistical significance has been obtained by as little as a mean increase of 4 percent in pulmonary functions (Alexander & Solanch, 1981). Specialists in pulmonary functions report that *clinically* significant changes require *at least* a 10 to 15 percent change in general pulmonary functions (Reyes, 1982). By contrast, *during an asthma attack,* improvements of 25 to 100 percent would be required for clinical significance (Alexander & Solanch, 1981). A further cautionary note is that a patient's self-report and clinical symptoms (such as wheezing) do not always correlate with physiological findings (Engstrom, 1964; Chai, Purcell, Brady, & Falliers, 1968). McFadden, Kiser, and deGroot (1973) reported that many subjects recovering from an asthma attack became overtly symptom-free; yet, airway conductance was 50 percent below the patient's predicted normal airflow value.

Intervention objectives. Alexander and Solanch (1981) suggest the purpose of behavioral-intervention procedures with asthmatics may have one of three discreet and separate objectives. The first objective has been to alter general pulmonary functions and/or asthma symptoms *directly* (i.e., episodes of coughing, wheezing, etc.). The second goal has been to either: (*a*) reduce negative or maladaptive emotions resulting from having asthma and/or (*b*) reduce negative emotions which may elicit or exacerbate asthmatic episodes. Changes in general lung functions per se would not be considered as a *primary* goal in this respect. The third goal in the treatment of asthma has the objective of altering maladaptive, manipulative, or disruptive behaviors which are asthma-related. Target behaviors (such as, malingering or manipulative and attention-seeking behaviors) are reduced through behavioral-modification techniques. In the discussion of treatment modalities, it is important to assess both the type of treatment used as well as the investigator's expected-outcome goal.

Biofeedback training. A variety of biofeedback techniques have been used in the attempt to increase patients' respiratory functioning and reduce clinical symptoms of asthma (such as, wheezing, asthma episodes, and emergency room visits). Unfortunately, the outcome of these procedures has generally been relatively unimpressive. The initial studies (e.g., Danker et al., 1975; Kahn, Staerk, & Bonk, 1974) focused on biofeedback utilizing peak expiratory flow rate (PEFR). Slight changes with this technique have been noted during treatment sessions, but little improvements on asthma severity have generalized to the asthmatic's home situation, with the use of this technique. In part, this failure may be due to the previously noted inadequacy of the peak expiratory flow rate measure.

Two studies have more recently utilized what may be a more appropriate biofeedback technique in terms of total respiratory resistance (TRR). This is a *noneffort-dependent* measure of respiratory function which can be delivered on a breath-by-breath basis. In the first study by Feldman (1976), significant reductions were found in total respiratory resistance, as well as several other measures of pulmonary function, during the biofeedback training. These improvements were comparable to moderate, clinically significant changes produced by one isoproterenol-inhalation therapy. However, assessment of symptomatic changes, generalization, and follow-up data were not included in this study.

Vachon and Rich (1976) also utilized the total respiratory resistance (TRR) biofeedback method with a digital-feedback system in a series of studies. In these studies, biofeedback on TRR—in conjunction with contingent reinforcement—effectively reduced respiratory resistance and produced improvements in pulmonary functioning equivalent to one inhalation of isoproterenol. Unfortunately, the improved TRR demonstrated by that group was not maintained during five-minute intertrial rest periods, and no follow-up data was gathered. Biofeedback technology in the area of asthma is not especially advanced at this point in time (Alexander & Solanch, 1981), and it is possible that, as further advances are made in technology, subjects will be able to demonstrate more substantial improvements over a longer period of time.

Biofeedback training has also been used in *combination* with various relaxation-training strategies for asthmatic children (Davis, Saunders, Creer, & Chai, 1973; Katses, Glans, Crawford, Edwards, & Scherr, 1976; Scherr, Crawford, Sergent, & Scherr, 1975). Biofeedback training, in most of these cases, was of the EMG type designed to assist relaxation. To date, results of this strategy also have not been overly impressive. However, it should be noted that Davis et al. (1973) demonstrated that milder asthmatics showed the largest improvements with biofeedback-assisted relaxation. Unfortunately, brief baselines and limited follow-up data did not allow for examination of possible symptomatic improvement or continued improvement of pulmonary functions. Furthermore, it has been noted by a number of recent reviewers (Andrasik & Blanchard, Chapter 32; Denney, Chapter 27; Walker, 1979) that biofeedback has rarely shown consistent advantages over relaxation techniques, when the goal is simple-tension reduction. Of course, it is possible that the combination of the two strategies allow some subjects to utilize the technique most appropriate for them, leading to somewhat better results.

Relaxation.   A series of studies by Alexander and his colleagues (Alexander, Cropp, & Chai, 1979; Alexander, White, & Wallace, 1977; Alexander et al., 1972) have consistently demonstrated that progressive-muscle relaxation can lead to *statistically* significant improvements in pulmonary functions in controlled studies. Unfortunately, the clinical significance of these improvements have not been overly impressive. In addition, generalization of therapeutic gains to the natural environment has generally not been assessed. Furthermore, it should be noted that these studies were performed on *severe,* inpatient asthmatics.

A particularly exciting application of relaxation training to asthma was reported by Devine and Hock (1980), who used the combination of relaxation training and parent training with 22 children in a counterbalanced design, in an attempt to increase pulmonary functions and reduce the frequency of asthmatic attacks at home. Relaxation training was found to increase general pulmonary functioning by 13 percent (a moderately clinically significant finding), while parent training increased pulmonary functions by approximately 4 percent (a clinically nonsignificant finding). However, parent training reduced the *number* of asthma attacks in the home by 70 percent, while relaxation alone reduced asthma attacks in the home by 40 percent. This was one of the first studies to combine systematic parent training with relaxation training, in order to alter the asthmatic child's environment. However, these strategies were used on outpatients, who likely had somewhat milder cases of asthma.

It should also be noted that a recent review on relaxation therapy in the treatment of asthma (Erskine-Miliss & Schonell, 1981) suggested that mental-relaxation techniques (such as transcendental meditation and autogenic training) may be more effective than muscle relaxation. This conclusion, of course, contradicts almost every other review of the effects of relaxation on other types of problems. However, it appears that the authors failed to take into account the potentially significant variable of subject age. In fact, several of the studies cited to support their contention were conducted with adult asthmatics. It may very well be that adult asthmatics and children with only mild to moderate severity of asthma symptomology will demonstrate clinically significant findings with relaxation training much more readily than the severe cases of inpatient children, many of whom are cortisteroid dependent.

Systematic desensitization. Systematic desensitization, first described by Wolpe (1958), allows the subject to practice *imaginary* scenes of graded anxiety-provoking situations, while in a relaxed state. Tal and Miklich (1976) found asthmatic children's pulmonary functions were adversely affected by imagining scenes of anger or fear, while relaxation exercises produced an improvement in airway resistance. The relatively ᶠew comparisons between relaxation and systematic desensitization have shown a slight tendency for the latter treatment to be more effective (e.g., Moore, 1965; Yorkston, McHugh, Brady, Serber, & Sergeant, 1974; Erskine-Milliss & Schonell, 1981).

However, another study utilizing systematic desensitization (but not in comparison with relaxation training) produced only modest results. Miklich, Renne, Creer, Alexander, Chai, Davis, Hoffman, and Danker-Brown (1977) compared systematic desensitization for 19 moderate to severe asthmatic children, with no treatment for 7 children. At post-treatment, there was a significant difference between the treatment and control groups' forced expiratory volume$_1$ (FEV$_1$). The treatment group at follow-up had reduced maintenance medications and appeared to have somewhat more-stable symptomotology. However, on other measures—including hospitalizations and subjective reports—there were no differences between the two groups.

Deconditioning of asthma. A majority of asthmatic children develop bronchospasms after a moderate amount of exercise. Kahn and Olson (1977) suggested exercise could be considered as a conditioned stimulus for asthmatic episodes. They hypothesized that exercise-induced asthma attacks may be a result of faulty conditioning of the bronchial airways, in which exercise (conditioned stimulus) has been paired with allergens or infection (unconditioned stimulus), which have resulted in an asthma attack (unconditioned response). Fifty asthmatic chldren (ages 8 to 15 years old) were classified as reactors or nonreactors, based on a standardized treadmill-exercise test. The reactors were randomly assigned to a control or treatment group. A classical-extinction paradigm was designed in which, for seven days, the conditioned stimulus (exercise) was now presented without the conditioned response (asthma attack). To prevent an asthma episode, the treatment-group children inhaled isoproterenol through an intermittent, positive-pressure breathing (IPPB) apparatus immediately before each exercise period. The reactor-control group inhaled room air, while the nonreactors did not receive any treatment. The experimental group showed a significant reduction of FEV_1 after the extinction trials, and a majority of these children maintained these gains in a six-month follow-up period. These results are exciting and further investigation of this approach is clearly warranted.

Use of a similar strategy with asthmatics who have other precipitants to their attacks represented an interesting extension of this idea and was recently reported by Kahn (1977). In this study, 40 children in an experimental group were trained to decrease airway resistance by the delivery of biofeedback training on the child's FEV_1 (forced expiratory volume). After this initial training, the subjects were then taught to utilize their skill in response to mild episodes of bronchospasm—which were elicited in the treatment setting through a variety of different methods. Compared to a no-treatment control group, subjects who had received the biofeedback training demonstrated fewer and shorter asthma atttacks over a one-year follow-up. The biofeedback and application-training procedure utilized in this report is quite similar to the stress-inoculation procedures reviewed by Denney in Chapter 27. This approach could represent one of the more promising treatments for the behavioral control of asthmatic episodes. However, much more research will be needed to determine the possible role played by variables such as placebos, expectancies, individual differences, and "dose-response curves," before definitive conclusions can be reached.

Assertiveness training.   Hock et al. (1978) suggested that asthmatic children, as a group, may be deficient in assertiveness skills and relatively unable to express feelings of anger or frustration. Therefore, they compared eight-week treatment programs which included: (1) relaxation training, (2) assertiveness training, and (3) relaxation combined with assertiveness training. In addition, two control groups were used, including: (1) a medical-management group and (2) a leaderless, peer discussion plus medical management group. Results at the end of eight weeks of treatment indicated no changes in the two control groups in terms of pulmonary functions or asthmatic episodes. Relaxation training with or without assertiveness training was effctive in reducing the *number* of asthmatic attacks and increasing FEV_1 levels to those comparable to nonasthmatic children. Although not statistically significant, the relaxation training alone was superior to the relaxation-and-assertiveness group. Four weeks after treatment termination, FEV_1 increases were maintained, but unaccountably, the subjects' number of asthmatic attacks had returned to pre-treatment levels. The assertiveness-training group demonstrated significantly less improvement than the other groups, which Hock suggested may be due to the fact that assertiveness training *increased* stress in those children, who did not receive relaxation training.

Operant conditioning. In all cases reported below, behavioral treatments were successfully employed to affect asthma-related behaviors. In only one case was the treatment expected to change the patient's pulmonary functions. In all other studies, as expected, changes in the subject's target behavior did not result in changes in lung functions or medication requirements. For example, Renne and Creer (1976) reported positive reinforcement and shaping have been used to train asthmatic children in the proper use of inhalation therapy.

Satiation was used in a case in which a child frequently requested a brief hospitalization to escape stressful events at school (Creer, 1978). Each time the child requested admission, he was hospitalized for three days—whereas before, each admission had been for only one day. Eight months prior to treatment, the child had 33 separate admissions. Eight months after treatment, the child had been hospitalized 12 times.

Extinction has been used to reduce or eliminate coughing episodes used as an attention-getting device. In this account, a rapid decrease in bedtime coughing was achieved by making parental attention contingent upon noncoughing periods (Neisworth & Moore, 1972).

Time-out from positive reinforcement was used successfully to treat malingering in asthmatic children hospitalized at the National Asthma Center (Creer, 1970; Creer, Weinberg, & Molk, 1974). Finally, response cost was successfully employed in the treatment of two asthmatics who, through chronic school absenteeism, had failed to learn how to attend to classroom materials and instruction.

Tracheostomy dependency

It has been estimated that approximately 20 percent of tracheostomized children become dependent on cannula breathing and will fail to gain spontaneously natural respiration functions with the occlusion of the cannula or the closure of the tracheal incision (Wright, Schaefer, & Solomons, 1979). Symptoms associated with tracheostomy addiction include gasping and wheezing, followed by labored breathing, with deep substernal retractions and cyanosis leading to unconsciousness and eventual death, if the tracheostomy tube or cannula is not reintroduced (Wright et al., 1979). The potential gravity of the condition can be gauged by the findings of Venebals (1959), who reported that of 12 patients "addicted" to tracheostomized respiration, 4 died following decannulation.

The etiology of this condition remains an intriguing empirical question. The primary psychological hypothesis presently assumes that, during the time the child is tracheostomized, the normal muscular breathing pattern is eroded through disuse while, at the same time, breathing responses which are incompatible with normal breathing are strengthened and reinforced (Wright, Nunnery, Eichel, & Scott, 1969). Before 1970, the accepted treatment for tracheostomy addiction was to allow the cannula to remain in place until the child was older; then, hopefully, the trachea would be stronger or larger in circumference and allow breathing without a cannula (Crooks, 1954). Potential problems included continued erosion of the normal breathing reflex as well as possible retardation of the child's intellectual and emotional growth, higher susceptibility to infection, and the need for regular medical attention to the cannula itself.

Wright and his colleagues have developed a successful method for restoring normal breathing in children dependent on cannula breathing. This method presumably combines respondent and operant conditioning, in order to systematically reinforce normal breathing, while weakening the incompatible breathing that occurs through a cannula.

The actual procedures involved in this method include occlusion of the cannula for progressively longer time intervals, throughout a standard 22-day period. During the occlusion intervals, maximal pleasurable stimulation (usually in the form of social attention) is delivered to the child by nurses and family members; while during nonocclusion intervals, sensory stimulation is minimized by darkening the room, draping the crib, and eliminating all but the essential adult contacts. The initial occlusion intervals are brief (three to six minutes) for the first few days of the procedure and are lengthened as the child experiences successful breathing responses. This technique has been shown to be virtually 100 percent effective (Wright, et al., 1979).

Although the procedures developed by Wright and his colleagues have been quite effective, several drawbacks are evident, including lengthy hospitalization and the extended isolations between occlusions, which parents and nursing staff alike find highly stressful.

Elliott and Olson (1982) reported the successful decannulation of four children, using a variation of the Wright method. In this study, more frequent occlusion trials (up to eight per day) were employed, instead of the standard three trials per day. Because of the increased practice, the length of each occlusion was increased more rapidly. The average length of time required for successful decannulation in this study was 14 days, or approximately a 38 percent decrease as compared to the Wright method.

Social isolation in the study by Elliott and Olson was far from complete with two of the four children. Therefore, the role actually played by social isolation becomes difficult to determine without further study. However, radical and sudden departures from the use of isolation procedures would not seem wise because of the potential for life-threatening complications, and previous reports of failure to decannulate when using the seemingly similar procedures of graduated occlusion without conditioning (Groves & Mares, 1963) or graduated occlusion within a simple operant-conditioning paradigm (Berry, 1972).

Elliott and Olson (1982) suggested that the role of positive social reinforcement and/or distraction might be quite important. On numerous occasions, breathing was observed to become less labored when the child was being effectively reinforced and distracted through various kinds of play and interaction. Further systematic observation of this phenomenon will be necessary to substantiate the role played by these variables.

CENTRAL NERVOUS SYSTEM

Seizure disorders

The terms *seizure disorder* and *epilepsy* are most often used virtually synonymously. Clinically, four subdivisions of this disorder frequently have been recognized, including: (1) grand mal epilepsy (major and haut mal), along with various subgroups; (2) petite mal (Pykno epilepsy); (3) psychomotor epilepsy (temporal lobe epilepsy, psychic or psychic equivalent or variant), along with various subgroups; and (4) autonomic epilepsy (diencephalic). More recently, Mostofsky (1981) noted that the more complete table of international classifications of epileptic seizures has gained greater acceptance. The major categories of seizures listed in that table include: (1) three major categories of partial seizures, which all have a local onset; (2) eight types of generalized seizures, without local onset; (3) unilateral seizures; and (4) unclassified epileptic seizures. Unfortunately, Mostofsky notes that there is little in this taxonomic system which aids in determining whether one particular subgroup is more related to anxiety and stress than any other, whether various subgroups are more disabling than others, and perhaps more importantly, whether certain subgroups will be more responsive to behavioral-intervention strategies than others. In the absence of a complete neurological diagnostic system, Mostofsky suggested that behaviorally oriented researchers develop an independent taxonomic system with relevant diagnostic indices.

Seizure disorders generally have in common sudden paroxysmal bursts of neuronal activity which can affect motor, sensory, and cognitive functions in various ways. These effects may be relatively minor, as would often be the case with petite mal attacks, or they may be quite major, in the form of convulsive attacks which include the loss of consciousness, as would generally be the case with grand mal seizures. Seizure disorders consist of a wide variety of symptom complexes and are not a specific disease. There is no single cause for seizures; and numerous factors have been cited as responsible for the development of predispositions for these paroxysmal discharges, such as brain lesions, peri-natal injuries, metabolic disorders, and infections (Schmidt & Wilder, 1968); while a large number of other cases are of unknown etiology and are termed *idiopathic* in nature (Epstein, Katz, & Zlutnick, 1979).

Regardless of etiology, once a predisposition for these paroxysmal discharges has been developed, a variety of emotional stresses and environmental events have clearly shown the potential to trigger the neuronal bursts, in some cases. In fact, Schafer, Millman, and Levine (1979) have suggested that seizures can be thought of as a final link in a chain of behavioral events. Janowsky, Laxer, and Rushmer (1980) further provided convincing evidence that rats could be classically conditioned to show paroxysmal spike activity in response to an auditory stimulus, thus suggesting the possibility that at least some reflex epilepsy in humans may come about from the pairing of external events with abnormal paroxysmal activity in the brain.

In the area of treatment, medications for seizure disorders have shown a substantial degree of effectiveness. However, a significant proportion of patients remain refractory to medication approaches, and estimates are that at least 25 to 50 percent of children have not received complete control of seizure activity, in spite of chemical interventions (Epstein et al., 1979; Schaefer et al., 1979). The estimates on the prevalence of this disorder have ranged from 1 to 2 percent of the population, which would suggest that at least several million individuals in the United States alone suffer from the disorder (Wright et. al., 1979). Given this high prevalence and the substantial number of patients refractory to medical interventions, the use of behavioral strategies to control seizures would seem highly desirable. Promising reviews of such behavioral applications have been compiled recently by Mostofsky and Balaschak (1977), Epstein, Katz, and Zlutnick (1979), Mostofsky (1978, 1981), and Blanchard (1979).

Unfortunately, there has been a relative unawareness of these strategies among the medical profession; and, indeed, the prevalent attitude has been that disorders with demonstrable organic causes rule out psychological interventions, even though lip service is often given to interactive approaches (Mostofsky, 1981). Furthermore, Gannt (1970) argued that consequences are not likely to reduce seizures, due to the fact that seizures themselves (especially of the grand mal variety) are so aversive in and of themselves that operant reinforcers would be unlikely to control them. In response, Mostofsky (1981) noted that considerable evidence already exists suggesting that consequences can indeed alter seizure activity. The same argument could also be applied to the phenomenon of self-injurious behavior, which is also quite aversive but has, nonetheless, been shown to be controlled by operant reinforcers.

The reviews of behavioral-intervention approaches to the control of seizure activity could be grouped according to the following four classifications; (1) operant conditioning (e.g., time-out, aversion strategies, competing responses, interrupting-response chains); (2) classical conditioning (e.g., systematic desensitization, extinction, and fading procedures); (3) self-control strategies (e.g., cue-controlled relaxation and thought stopping); and (4) cortical biofeedback. Mostofsky (1981) suggested that, although little is currently known about how to decide which treatment will be most efficacious for which problem, some factors certainly can aid in this decision. These include whether or not handicaps are present, the presence or absence of prodromal auras, and whether the intervention is presented in an outpatient or inpatient setting. The reader is referred to the previously noted reviews in this area for details concerning these various behavioral-intervention strategies. It should be noted however, that the vast majority of reports have been uncontrolled case studies and have failed to include systematic follow-up data.

Several notable exceptions to this trend should be mentioned. For example, Cataldo, Russo, and Freeman (1979) utilized a multiple baseline-reversal design, which demonstrated that contingent reinforcers could significantly affect seizure rate. The patient previously had been exhibiting both myoclonic and grand mal seizures at a high rate, in spite of the use of most major anticonvulsive drugs (including dilantin, phenobarbitol, tegretol, mysolin, and clonazepam). The addition of corroborative physiological EEG data to the observational data enhanced the strength of the authors' conclusion. Furthermore, a 16-week follow-up indicated continued, reduced seizure activity.

A second well-controlled study was recently reported by Wells, Turner, Bellack, and Hersen (1978). In this study, a variant of an *A-B-C-B* design was utilized, to demonstrate the reduction of seizures in a 22-year-old female who had had a seizure disorder for 19 years at the rate of two to eight seizures per day, in spite of receiving several anticonvulsant medications. Results of this study, which employed cue-controlled relaxation, showed significantly reduced frequency of psychomotor seizures which was maintained over a three-month follow-up. Similarly, Cinciripini, Epstein, and Kotanchik (1980) recently reported that a behavioral-treatment package substantially reduced seizure activity in a seven-year-old white male, while introducing and removing anticonvulsant medications did not affect these changes. Furthermore, the reduction in seizure activity was maintained at an eight-month follow-up.

Additional conclusions are possible from the recent reviews of the literature in this area. First, there currently exists *well over 60 studies* in which different behavioral strategies have produced seizure reductions in patients who have otherwise been refractory to medications (Mostofsky & Balaschak, 1977). Second, it would appear that, for the phenomenon known as reflex epilepsy, procedures involving classical conditioning of extinction and fading probably show the greatest promise, although the procedures can require a rather long treatment-intervention process (Mostofsky & Balaschak, 1977; Forster, 1972). Third, research on cortical biofeedback, although promising, is poorly understood. Much of the original work in this area was performed by Sterman, Howe, and MacDonald (1970), who extrapolated from studies on cats (Lubar, 1975), indicating that cats could be trained to emit a sensory-motor rhythm (SMR) which seemed to suppress movement and create substantial resistance to drug-induced seizures. However, it has become less clear whether there is a clearly definable sensory-motor rhythm response in human beings which will have a similar effect. Furthermore, Blanchard (1979), as well as Andrasik and Blanchard (see Chapter 32), noted that Sterman and others have begun to focus less on SMR-biofeedback training and more on a refined analysis of the irregularities of the total EEG, followed by subsequent corrections. Thus, the attempt is to normalize the energy distribution of the frequency band. This work has exciting potential, but has not yet revealed the underlying mechanisms to explain the results of cortical-biofeedback research.

Overall, a number of important suggestions for methodological improvements have been advanced by Mostofsky and Balaschak (1977) and should be reviewed by the serious investigator. There is a substantial need for controlled group-outcome studies in this area; it is quite surprising that none of these have appeared in the literature to date; and further investigation into the comparison and/or combination of behavioral interventions with medications would seem warranted.

Movement disorders (choreas and tics)

The disorders of choreas and tics could be included within the section on the musculoskeletal system. However, as Mostofsky (1981) noted, they share certain commonalities with epilepsy, such as a proxysmal quality; onset preceeded by an aura; and frequently, an unspecified organic basis. However, these disorders are not characterized by abnormal EEG readings or loss of consciousness. Medical treatments are most commonly in the forms of drugs (Valium, Haldol, and L-Dopa). Disorders of the musculoskeletal system which are results of damage to the central nervous system (e.g., sequelae to a stroke) and which may have the potential for behavioral intervention through neuromuscular reeducation have been reviewed by Andrasik and Blanchard (see Chapter 32).

Choreas. There are wide varieties of subtypes of choreas which, in general, tend to involve ceaseless occurrence of rapid, highly complex, jerking movements that can appear to be well coordinated but are actually performed involuntarily. Very little in the form of behavioral interventions has been reported in the literature for these disorders. Mostofsky (1981) did recently report on a single case, in which choreic movements were substantially reduced through contingent reward. He also noted that reports by Bird and Cataldo (1978), as well as by Cleeland (1973), suggest that biofeedback techniques may hold some promise for the treatment of these disorders. It is likely that this type of intervention could be primarily adjunctive to medical interventions.

Tics. This disorder has received considerably more attention in the behavioral literature. Essentially, tics can be defined as a sudden, brisk, intermittent, but frequently recurring, muscle spasm that has no apparent purpose. Once again, there are a wide variety of tics, with perhaps the most dramatic being the Gilles de la Tourette syndrome. The Tourette syndrome consists of a number of features, including: a typical onset below the age of 16; multiple motor tics; and various vocal utterances, often of an obscene nature (Mostofsky, 1981).

Mostofsky further noted that the medical community has been quite resistant to the suggestion that Tourette syndrome may be treatable through any kind of behavioral-intervention means. Birk (1978) is one physician who stands apart from that general viewpoint.

The more common, *specific form* of tics has been treated by a variety of methods, with some of the most encouraging results coming from an initial study by Azrin and Nunn (1973), who used a broad-based, multiple-component strategy called *habit reversal*. The strategy included: increasing the patient's awareness of the occurrence of the habit; strengthening antagonistic behavior; and rearranging reinforcement contingencies that might be maintaining the habit. Research such as this initial study has lead to the growing tendency to consider tics as learned responses that can be counterconditioned (Schaefer et al., 1979). Studies have since indicated that reinforcement by the mother (Schulman, 1974), massed practice (Rafi, 1962), time-out (Lahey, McNees, & McNees, 1973), and self-monitoring (Hutzel, Platzek, & Logue, 1974) all show some promise in the treatment of specific tic disorders. These have typically been single-case studies, with the exception of that by Azrin and Nunn (1973). This study consisted of a series of *A-B* designs precluding an assessment of the specific variable which may have been responsible for the change.

A more recent report, by Azrin, Nunn, and Frantz (1980), demonstrated a direct comparison between their habit-reversal strategy and negative practice. The habit-reversal group showed almost total elimination of various tics over an 18-month follow-up, while the negative-practice group (essentially, massed practice) was still exhibiting tics at a rate of about 70 percent of baseline levels at the end of treatment and at a 4-month follow-up. Thus, habit-reversal strategies appear to hold considerable promise for the elimination of specific tics.

Treatment of Gilles de la Tourette syndrome

Haldol has frequently been found to be at least moderately effective; and, indeed, many consider the disorder to exclusively involve the basal ganglia or the lack of necessary inhibitory mechanisms within the central nervous system. In fact, Shapiro, Shapiro, Brunn, and Sweet (1978) recently suggested that further investigation into the possible use of psychological interventions in the treatment of Tourette syndrome is useless. Nonetheless, Mostofsky has reviewed substantial evidence suggesting that learning quite likely plays a significant role in the development of

Tourette syndrome, and that furthermore, learning approaches may have the potential to increase the arousal of critical cortical-inhibition areas or even to develop new interrelationships between the thalamus cortex and basal ganglia.

Evidence for such plasticity within the central nervous system has been thoroughly reviewed by Rosenweig and Bennett (1980), who noted that the potential for plasticity in the adult nervous system has now been sufficiently demonstrated in the following areas; (a) functional changes at existing synapses, (b) changes between active and quiescent states of neurons or parts of neurons, (c) anatomical changes in axon terminals, dendrites, dendritic spines, and synapses, and (d) proliferation of "glial cells " (p. 183). These points are also relevant with regard to the previous section on seizure disorders. As Mostofsky (1981) commented, it is quite conceivable that conditioning principles are applicable to cells and their aggregates.

Currently, an interesting variety of behavioral interventions has been attempted for the control of Tourette syndrome, with varying degrees of success. At this point, the following conclusions regarding the behavioral treatment of Tourette syndrome can be made. First, a number of strategies—such as, positive and negative reinforcement in conjunction with time-out and massed practice (Miller, 1970); self-monitoring combined with reciprocal inhibition (Thomas, Abrams & Johnson, 1971); self-monitoring combined with role-playing (Hutzell et al., 1974); reinforcement of incompatable behaviors and the adjunctive use of community members as reinforcing agents (Doleys & Kurtz, 1974); relaxation training (Mostofsky, 1981); relaxation in conjunction with positive imagery (Friedman, 1980), among others—have led to substantial symptom reductions for *some* patients. However, very similar strategies have sometimes failed to ameliorate symptoms (e.g., Canavan & Powell, 1981). Second, these have generally been single-case studies. However, several of them have employed multiple-baseline and/or reversal signs, which would strongly suggest that the treatments indeed were responsible for the changes in the frequency of the occurrence of the symptoms, although the underlying mechanisms involved could not be ascertained. Third, it is interesting to note that several of the above studies included assertion training or social-skills training within their package. The rationale for this may be partly based on the fact that stress and/or social situations sometimes are known to elicit Tourette-associated tics. This often causes these children to withdraw from social situations and may even lead to subsequnt deficits in social skills. Thus, such training may not only improve these skills but may also reduce anxiety and the potential for those situations to precipitate tic behavior.

At this point, further recommendations for research in this area include the following; (a) More effort in identifying particular precipitants, at least in some patients, would be useful and may lead to the successful application of strategies such as cue-controlled relaxation. (*b*) It is interesting to note that massed practice has been one of the primary aversive strategies utilized even though, in many of these cases, it has been necessary to use it over an extremely long period of time. It may be that an investigation into other techniques—such as, habit reversal or more-potent, less time-consuming, aversive procedures—would be indicated. (*c*) The study of a recent suggestion by Thompson, O'Quinn, and Logue (1979), who stated,

> It is possible that meaningful subgroups could be identified within Tourette syndrome on the basis of type, location, and extent of dysfunction interacting with psychological stress factors. These subgroups may be differentially responsible to pharmacological and behavior therapies. Interdisciplinary case studies that utilize neuropsychological data may prove to be a good vehicle for subgroup identification. (p. 385)

Along this line, an interesting area of investigation would be comparisons of medical and behavioral interventions (as well as their combinations) as they interact with identified subgroups.

MUSCULOSKELETAL SYSTEM

Neuromuscular rehabilitation

Biofeedback has been the only behavioral intervention used to any extent in the treatment of neuromuscular rehabilitation. The reader is thus directed to Andrasik and Blanchard's review of the literature (Chapter 32) in this area. Those authors concluded that biofeedback has had success in treating large extremity dysfunction, primarily: foot drop as a result of a cardiovascular accident; upper extremity dysfunctions; and spasmodic torticollis and dystonia. Definitive, controlled-outcome studies have yet to be carried out in this area, although results to date have been highly promising.

Adolescent idiopathic scoliosis

Although systematic, controlled-outcome data are lacking, Dworkin (1982) recently reported on encouraging preliminary data indicating the value of operant-conditioning procedures for the treatment of idiopathic scoliosis. Dworkin reviewed data indicating that the incidence of this disorder is approximately 1 percent of the population and that it occurs at the onset of puberty, most commonly in females. If left untreated, the end result of the disease process is a deformation of the spinal column. Typical orthopedic treatment for this disorder has consisted of having the adolescent wear a rather clumsy device—known as the Milwaukee brace—which must be worn for approximately 23 hours a day, for several years. As an alternative, Dworkin attempted the use of a posture-training device, which would deliver a signal (in the form of a tone) whenever posture was incorrect. Varying types of tones and schedules for their delivery upon incorrect posture were attempted prior to establishing a set protocol. Initial data on the first 12 patients with this device demonstrated it to be at least as effective as the Milwaukee brace, if not more so. Dworkin also reviewed a number of studies in progress that are designed to provide more adequately controlled assessments of the efficacy of the posture-training device. If subsequent data continue to be equally promising, it is likely that this strategy will come to largely replace the more cumbersome treatment approaches with braces.

Tension headaches

Pain from headaches is one of the most commonly reported physical complaints. Surveys (e.g., Ogden, 1952) indicate that up to 65 percent of the nonclinical population report periodic headaches. Most headaches can be classified as either migraine, tension, or a combination of the two (ad hoc Committee on Classification of Headaches, 1962). Tension headaches account for approximately 80 percent of all headaches recorded (Appenzeller, 1969). The most prevalent pharmacological treatment has been aspirin, although centrally acting tranquilizers and muscle relaxers have frequently been prescribed (e.g., Friedman, 1964). Medical management has been moderately-to-greatly effective, for a large number of patients. However, long-term use of medication can create unwanted psychological and physical side effects; furthermore, a significant number of subjects fail to be aided by these agents.

Traditionally, tension headaches have been thought to be the result of sustained contractions of the shoulder, neck, scalp, or facial muscles. Treatments based on this model assume that pain is a direct function of the level of muscular activity in these areas, and reduction of tonic muscle contraction would be directly associated with reduction in headache pain. The majority of researchers have assumed a linear relationship between physiological changes and cognitive reports of pain, independent of environmental factors (e.g., Norton & Neilson, 1977). However, data has failed to demonstrate consistent relationships between EMG levels and reports of headache pain, whether at rest or during the actual headaches (e.g., Epstein & Able, 1977; Epstein, Able, Collins, Parker, & Cinciripini, 1981; Haynes, Griffin, Mooney, & Parise, 1975). Therefore, at least in terms of making differential diagnoses among various headache types, frequently one has to rely substantially upon subjective reports of the type of pain. In the case of tension headaches, pain tends to be symmetrical in distribution—whether bandlike, bitemporal, or occipital—and characterized by a steady ache (Williams, 1977). Williams made the further important point that, even though clear and specific organic causes of headaches are of relatively low incidence, it is quite important to conduct a meticulous search for such signs and symptoms by a thorough neurological assessment, to rule out the possibility of various intracranial processes.

Given the failure of data to demonstrate clear relationships between EMG levels and headache pain, other theories have been noted to account for the development of these headaches. These have been reviewed by Epstein and Cinciripini (1981) and include the following: (a) Possibly, patients with a very short history of tension headaches obtain their headaches from actual, increased muscle tension. However, as the symptoms continue for a long period of time, it may be that environmental contingencies come to control the headaches, independent of EMG activity. This suggestion is, of course, consistent with ideas advanced by Fordyce (1976). Furthermore, the suggestion leads to a clear, testable prediction which is: "The degree of relationship between the EMG activity and headache report may be negatively correlated with duration of symptoms" (Epstein & Cinciripini, 1981, p. 235). To date, this hypothesis has not been empirically tested. (b) It is possible that tension-headache patients are hypersensitive to very small changes in EMG activity. (c) It may be that vasoconstriction of the arteries—which supply the muscles presumably producing the headaches—is largely responsible for them. These latter two possibilities are basically untested to date as well.

Treatment.　As in all areas of psychological intervention, adequate assessment is essential. The assessment of tension headaches should include baseline measurements, sufficient population sizes and descriptions, sensitive diagnostic criteria, and a follow-up on maintenance effects. One of the more difficult aspects of assessment in tension headaches has been the search for sensitive criteria for diagnosis and changes in duration, intensity, and frequency of the occurrence of tension-headache pain.

Basically, three approaches have been attempted for the modification of tension headache pain. These include various biofeedback strategies, relaxation techniques, and cognitive stress-management procedures. Biofeedback and relaxation techniques were originally based on the assumptions that long-term muscle tension results in headache pain, and the reduction of muscle activity would reduce or eliminate this pain. Relatively few researchers have examined treatments which focus on the prevention of environmental events which lead to sustained muscular tension or on the modification of reinforcers which maintain and increase the severity or frequency of headache-pain episodes (Epstein & Cinciripini, 1981).

Blanchard et al. (1980), using meta-analysis procedures, examined over 50 studies using EMG biofedback and/or relaxation. Overall results indicated that EMG biofeedback, relaxation alone, or the two together lead to essentially equivalent treatment outcomes. The mean decrease in subjectively reported headache pain was approximately 60 percent, with these treatment strategies. Placebo treatments, whether medical, psy-

chological, or simple headache monitoring, were significantly less effective and averaged approximately 35 percent improvement. A high degree of similarity of outcomes using EMG biofeedback or relaxation
appeared to support Silver and Blanchard's (1978) suggestion that the
final, common pathway for successful treatment of tension headaches is
relaxation or lowered arousal—whether achieved through EMG biofeedback or various relaxation techniques.

One recent report (Cram, 1980) made the interesting suggestion that
training subjects in the ability to *maintain* their EMG levels within a narrow
basal range of activity may be more effective than training subjects to
simply reduce EMG activity. Indeed, his six-month follow-up data suggested that EMG-stability training resulted in the greatest improvement
in reduced headache activity as compared to EMG-relaxation training,
which failed to maintain gains. However, it is quite important to point
out that this conclusion is, at best, quite tentative. At follow-up, the sample
consisted of only 22 subjects across four groups. In addition, the group
with the seemingly best results (EMG-stability training) had lost three subjects, because they had undergone psychotherapy during the intervening
time. It is quite possible that those subjects were cases of substantial
failure and thus may have been led to seek other therapy, rendering
Cram's conclusion regarding the follow-up data somewhat suspect.

The third approach to the management of tension headaches is through
cognitive stress-management procedures. Three recent reports involving
controlled treatment-outcome studies of cognitive stress management of
tension headaches have indicated that cognitive stress management appears quite promising and may even be superior to EMG-biofeedback
strategies (Holroyd & Andrasik, 1978; Holroyd, Andrasik, & Westbrook,
1977; Kremsdorf, 1978). Furthermore, Holroyd and Andrasik (1980) recently reported on a two-year follow-up, which demonstrated that cognitive therapy continued to demonstrate better outcomes for tension headache than biofeedback.

A number of directions would seem to be indicated for future research
in this area. As Blanchard et al. (1980) stated, it will probably not be
productive to continue to compare various relaxation-training strategies
and biofeedback with each other. However, one variable which would
appear to be of significant importance is a greater analysis of individual-
difference variables. Williams (1977) recently made the suggestion that
the variable of "need to control" may be quite important, with respect
to a certain percentage of tension-headache patients. Furthermore, Cram
(1980) reported on an especially interesting individual-difference variable. In this report, Cram noted that subjects who demonstrated very small
responsiveness to EMG activity during mild stress tended to show much
more consistent reductions in their reports of headache activity following
treatment, as compared to subjects who demonstrated high EMG responsivity during mild stress. This finding was apparently regardless of the

treatment group to which the subjects were assigned. These data, of course, contradict the assumption that subjects who are particularly responsive to mild stress (in the form of increased EMG activity) would be the ideal candidates for such biofeedback. Cram, in fact, noted the possibility that such high-EMG "responders" may be particularly good candidates for additional treatment, in the form of cognitive stress-management procedures. It would also be interesting to determine whether high- and low-EMG responders could be differentiated on the basis of the duration of their headache symptomology.

A second potentially valuable area of investigation would be the evaluation of the relative efficacy of various psychological and pharmacological agents separately and in combination with subsequent "weaning" from drug therapy.

A third area for future research on tension headaches would be investigation of active versus passive stress-management approaches, as reviewed by Denney (see Chapter 27). In fact, a report by Holroyd, Andrasik, and Noble (1980) reviewed a number of studies which could suggest that one of the differences between the efficacy of biofeedback and relaxation training—as opposed to placebo treatments—may be due to differences in the degree to which subjects are led to actively employ what they have learned upon the onset of their symptoms. For example, in their study, subjects who received EMG biofeedback demonstrated significantly greater improvements in their headache activity as compared to a pseudotherapy procedure, which had an equivalent credibility. However, the pseudogroup was given a rationale which actually *discouraged* them from utilizing their techniques during actual headache-eliciting stresses, while the opposite was true for the biofeedback group.

A fourth area of investigation which has been suggested concerns analyzing subjects who fail to improve with initial treatments and attempting additional treatments with them. This may eventually lead to useful information concerning treatments which may be most efficacious for particular subjects (Blanchard et al., 1980).

A fifth area of interest would be consideration of the role of operant reinforcers in the modification of headache behaviors and the patient's coping efforts. To date, Fowler (1975) has been one of the few to investigate the potential of social reinforcement on headache behavior. However, his report was simply a case study; and the actual role played by operant reinforcers with respect to headaches remains simply an intriguing suggestion at this time.

DERMATOLOGICAL SYSTEM

The skin is subject to many disease processes which may have an emotional component. Disorders of the skin have traditionally been classified as organic, functional, or a combination of the two. However, attempts to differentiate organic and functional types of dermatitis through psychological tests have generally proven unsuccessful.

The exact incidence and prevalence of neurodermatitis (inflammations of the skin) as well as other skin disorders considered to have emotional components (e.g. urticaria "hives," atopic dermatitis, and eczema) is not known (Risch & Ferguson, 1981). Estimates from 70 percent (Ingram, 1948) to 100 percent (Lynch, Hinckley & Cowan, 1945) of patients in various settings, have been found to have a psychogenic component to skin disorders (Brown, 1967; Brown, 1959).

In the past 40 years, the search for specific personality traits or for personality disorders associated with dermatologic patients has generated various and discrepant findings. Specific emotional factors which have been suggested to predispose or precipitate dermatological problems range from depression (Musaph, 1968) to sadomasochistic and exhibitionistic tendencies (Miller, 1948). Currently, general emotional stress is the only widely accepted and frequently cited factor associated with neurodermatitis (Risch & Ferguson, 1981).

Scratching

In the initial assessment of dermatologic problems, it is necessary to have a thorough medical evluation to determine (*as best as is possible*) the role of specific, clearly defined organic factors and the provision of appropriate medications when needed. Yet, the secondary effects of maladaptive behaviors (such as scratching) can clearly exacerbate lesions, irregardless of their specific, original etiology. Risch and Ferguson (1981) suggested that behaviorally exacerbated lesions can first be maintained by negative reinforcement and second by positive reinforcement. Scratching, quickly but only temporarily, relieves an aversive stimulus (such as itching or burning). Additionally, as lesions remain or worsen, scratching may be maintained and positively reinforced by the attention of others. From this model, it is assumed that response prevention for scratching and reinforcement of nonscratching behaviors will eventually eliminate the maladaptive behaviors and allow the lesions to heal.

There have been approximately nine case studies reporting such use of behavioral interventions in the treatment of compulsive scratching, all of a case-study nature. In most cases, the patient had suffered from neurodermatitis or another skin disorder for years, and psychopharmacologic or psychotherapeutic treatments had been unsuccessful. Treatment periods ranged from 3 to 13 sessions. Most studies reported total remission at the end of treatment and maintenance of effects from three months to four years after treatment.

Techniques have included: removal of positive reinforcement; initiation of incompatable responses; aversive conditioning, accompanied by relaxation or systematic desensitization; and assertiveness training (e.g., Dobes,

1977; Allen & Harris, 1966; Bar & Kaypers, 1973; Cataldo, Varni, Russo, & Estes, 1980; Watson, Tharp, & Knisberg, 1972; Ratliff & Stein, 1968). The lack of controlled, outcome studies in this area is discouraging and yet, the success with previously refractory problems and maintenance of therapeutic gains suggest that behavioral treatments (especially for the problem of scratching) have a high degree of promise.

Hives, hyperhidrosis, and eczema

Very little in the way of any systematic, behavioral intervention has been attempted with this particular subset of dermatological problems. However, one study (Daniels, 1973) utilized relaxation, systematic desensitization, and thought stopping to treat a patient with hives who had been unresponsive to allergy injections or antihistamines. Both anxiety and difficulty expressing anger had been noted. Within 12 weeks of treatment, the hives were eliminated, and they had not recurred over a 23-month follow-up period. In a second case (Bar & Kaypers, 1973), systematic desensitization paired with assertiveness training was effective in treating a case of severe palmar hyperhidrosis (excessive sweating of the hands). The therapist hypothesized that palmar hyperhidrosis was reinforcing, in that it gave the shy patient a reason for withdrawing from work and social situations. Within several weeks, the sweat-gland activity had markedly decreased; and at a one-year follow-up, the patient was found to be asymptomatic and socially active. Finally, in the study by Miller, Coger, & Dymonal (1974), two patients with dyshydrotic eczema were successfully treated with biofeedback. The patients were taught to control their skin conductance through analogue-tone biofeedback. They were further instructed to practice daily for 30 minutes. Within four weeks, the eczematous lesions were absent, although the hyperhidrosis remained unchanged in these particular cases.

At this time, it appears clear that behavioral interventions have a high potential for eliminating the problem of scratching (which can exacerbate a wide variety of dermatological problems). However, no controlled, outcome studies have been conducted for dermatological problems which may either be directly caused or exacerbated by stress.

Icthyosis

Barber (1978) recently reported on several case studies, in which hypnosis had been used to significantly improve the symptomology of several patients with severe cases of icthyosis (fish skin disease). This is an extremely debilitating disease and is also extremely refractory to medical treatments. Barber made the suggestion that the effects of hypnosis may have been due to learned control over blood flow, which aided in the alleviation of the symptomology. Once again, further investigations of a controlled nature in this area would seem both warranted and interesting.

Dermatitis

Barber (1978) also reported on the results of a study, in which 13 subjects highly susceptible to dermatitis (when exposed to plants similar to poison ivy) were subjected to various experimental manipulations (Ikemi and Nakagawa, 1962). Conclusions from that study included:

> (a) at least some aspects of the dermatitis can be produced by a harmless substance when the individual is led to believe it is the dermatitis-producing substance, (b) the dermatitis generally can be inhibited when the individual is led to believe that the poisonous leaves are harmless leaves, (c) formal hypnotic-induction procedures are not necessary or especially useful in producing these effects, and (d) it appears that the critical variable in producing the phenomena is the subjects' belief that a harmless substance is actually a dermatitis-producing substance and, vice versa, that a dermatitis-producing substance is actually a harmless substance. (p. 2)

Obviously, suggestion and similar cognitive variables have an exciting potential to alter skin responses.

ENDOCRINE SYSTEM

Behavioral-medicine research on the endocrine system is at an embryonic stage. A new term of this subspecialty has been designated *psychoneuroendocrinology*. Three excellent reviews have recently appeared in the literature which were concerned with at least significant portions of this field (Woods & Burchfield, 1980; Tarnow & Silverman, 1981–82; and Sklar & Anisman, 1981). Taken together, these reviews—along with several other recent studies—suggest that this area of investigation has exciting potential, although direct-treatment intervention resulting from this research has been quite limited up to now.

Woods and Burchfield have discussed the fact that, in many ways, the endocrine system is similar to—and may actually be considered a branch of—the nervous system. They support this contention by findings that include the fact that many cells which secrete hormones have electrical properties as well as action potentials that are analogous to those observed in neurons in the brain. Furthermore, most hormones are either directly secreted by neurons or influenced by them (directly through neural projections to the secretory cells or indirectly through the hypothalamo-hypophyseal axis). The fact that hormones are either directly or indirectly secreted by neural projections increases the probability that conditioning of hormonal responses would be possible. One of the greatest drawbacks to research in this area, unfortunately, is in the area of technology. Many of the assays of hormones are so complex and time consuming that it would be difficult to imagine methods by which they could be conditioned. Conceivably, these technologies will develop to the degree that conditioning will become more feasible. Woods and

Burchfield (1980) noted that, in some research, changes of hormone levels has simply been inferred from observed changes in physiological parameters assumed to be associated with them. However in others, direct measures of the hormones themselves have been made.

Another suggestion recently made by Woods and Burchfield has exciting implications as well. They reported on evidence reviewed by Leshner (1975) indicating that, "endocrinological imprinting occurs during the development of animals and dictates the responses of their endocrine systems later in life" (Woods and Burchfield, 1980, p. 247). The obvious difficulty of generalizing these findings to humans was noted. However, it is interesting to speculate upon the possible existence of critical periods and the impact of stressful events during such periods for subsequent endocrinological responsiveness in humans. For example, Seligman (1975) reviewed a variety of reports suggesting that both animals and humans who experience severe losses and/or periods of uncontrollable stress became far more susceptable to depressions in later life. Along this line, Maas (1975) noted that a variety of subgroups of depressed patients may demonstrate various biochemical abnormalities (including such hormonal alterations as abnormal norepinepherine metabolism and/ or abnormal seratonin metabolism). It is interesting to speculate about the existence of a subgroup of depressed patients (as well as of patients predisposed to certain "physical" illnesses), who may have experienced an early loss or other trauma and, thus, may become predisposed to hormonal imbalances through a classically conditioned overgeneralization to other kinds of stimuli.

Diabetes

Woods and Burchfield (1980) also reviewed a wide variety of evidence which indicated that the cephalic phase of insulin secretion can be readily classically conditioned to certain discriminative stimuli, including the taste of saccharin and the smell and sight of a meal. The authors noted that an insulin response has also been elicited under hyponosis, when subjects were told they were eating a desirable meal. Furthermore, an excellent review by Tarnow and Silverman (1981–82) noted a variety of diabetogenic hormones which are counterregulatory in the sense of having insulin-opposing effects. Many of these hormones have been found to show increases under stress in both normal children and diabetics. Tarnow and Silverman further noted that a group of particularly labile diabetics under stress showed unusually increased concentrations of ketones, free fatty acids, and glucose.

Johnson (1980) also reviewed the role of stress in diabetes and concluded the following: (1) evidence exists that stress induced during family interviews leads to increased arousal and free fatty acid production that does not cease immediately upon termination of the interview, at least for some subgroups of children with diabetes and (2) family therapy with some of these children has reportedly shown good results (Baker, Minuchin, Milman, Leibman, & Todd, 1977; Minuchin, Rosman, & Baker, 1978), but control groups have not been included within these studies.

Fowler, Budzynski, and Vandenbergh (1976) were the first to report on the use of EMG-biofeedback relaxation training with a diabetic patient, in order to decrease the necessary level of insulin and the number of episodes of ketoacidosis. This attempt was based on previously noted research, indicating that levels of blood glucose can be altered by emotional stresses. A portable, EMG-feedback unit—along with a cassette-tape series—were given to the patient to practice twice daily for 30 to 40 minutes each time, for over a two-month period. During the six-week baseline, daily insulin needs averaged 85 units. During the final six weeks of the training phase, 59 units were required. Furthermore, at the very end of training, the requirement had been reduced to 43 units. A six-month follow-up indicated a daily, average insulin requirement of 52 units. In addition, the patient reported decreased incidence of emotionality and diabetic fluctuations. Obviously, during any such training, extremely regular checks (either through urine or glucose analysis) would be required, to insure that insulin dosages were correct through the training period. This was simply an N-of-one study; but, in conjunction with the previously noted, family-therapy approaches as well as the clearly demonstrated relationships of stresses to insulin requirements, it is surprising that further controlled studies have not been conducted.

Tarnow and Silverman (1981–82) made several additional, cogent comments concerning the treatment of diabetics, given this type of data. These included: the importance of careful education of the patient and his or her parents (as opposed to the tendency of some physicians to stress the catastrophic consequences of failure to follow treatment to such an extent that stress levels are undoubtably increased for both parents and patients); the need to be aware that children often hear fictitious myths about diabetes which disturb them, and the need to dispel these as judiciously as possible; and finally, that antianxiety drugs may be helpful on occasion, for some of these patients, to reduce central nervous system reactivity to stress. In addition, cognitive stress management may have some potential for diabetics who might tend to overly catastrophize about their illness or about particular stresses in their environment.

Cancer

Both Riley (1981) and Sklar and Anisman (1981) have reviewed considerable data on the complex interactions between stress and hormonal, neurochemical, and immunological functioning. Sklar and Anisman further noted that evidence exists (in both animals and humans) that stress associated with surgery and/or with bereavement has been found to be associated with depressed lymphocyte function. Furthermore, current evidence suggests that metastases (release of tumor cells into the circulatory system) is sometimes associated with surgical procedures, but it is also quite possible, according to recent research, that the *stress* associated with such surgery may account for at least a portion of these metastases (e.g., Lundey, Lovett, Wolinski, & Conran, 1981). This research could lead to the speculation that some of the procedures designed to prepare patients for coping with (and reducing stress in response to) surgery may even have beneficial effects upon subsequent metastases (see section on patient management).

Obesity

In the area of obesity, Schachter (1971) and Schachter and Rodin (1974) have suggested that obese individuals are far more responsive to external stimuli associated with eating. Woods and Burchfield (1980) speculated that some of these individuals have such conditioned oversecretions of insulin that it could lead to an exacerbation of their obesity. Unfortunately, Elliott and Denney (1975) and Hagen (1981) have noted that techniques (such as covert sensitization) designed simply to reduce responsiveness to external food-related cues have been relatively ineffective in and of themselves. Current reviews suggest that more-comprehensive programs are necessary for the treatment of obese individuals, although it is possible that a subgroup of obese individuals who are particularly responsive to external cues or to specific, problem foods could be aided by such procedures.

GASTROINTESTINAL SYSTEM

Behavioral-medicine research in the area of gastrointestinal disorders (e.g., vomiting, the irritable-bowel syndrome, diarrhea, ulcers, food refusal, and anorexia) has shown significant promise but perhaps even fewer instances of controlled, outcome studies than almost any of the other areas reviewed in this chapter. Therefore, this section will make note of the current "state of the art" in this area as well as offer suggestions for future research endeavors.

Vomiting

Chronic ruminative vomiting in infants is an especially serious disorder, as highlighted by Taylor (1980b), who reviewed reports of mortality rates ranging from approximately 12 percent to as high as 21 percent from causes such as dehydration, malnutrition, and increased susceptibility to disease. A variety of medical approaches to the problem have been attempted (including surgery, antiemetic drugs, and dietary changes) but have had varying degrees of success. Success by medical means has generally been least effective in those cases where no organic etiology can be determined (Epstein et al., 1979). Obviously, thorough medical evaluation to reveal the presence or absence of specific organic factors (such as duodenal ulcers or hyperacidity) is essential. The presence of such factors would not rule out behavioral interventions but would be likely to change the nature of such treatment.

Because of the severity and life-threatening nature of the disorder, behavioral-intervention strategies have focused on techniques designed to bring about the most rapid elimination of the symptoms as is possible. Lang and Melamed (1969) were one of the first to demonstrate the efficacy of electric shock for the rapid elimination of persistent vomiting and rumination in a nine-month-old baby. Subsequently, a variety of reports have substantiated that electric shock can eliminate chronic vomiting quite rapidly in infants (for some of whom, medical procedures had proved ineffective) and maintain the removal of systems over prolonged follow-ups (Cunningham & Linscheid, 1976; Toister, Condron, & Arthur, 1975; Wright & Thalassinos, 1973).

Obviously, the use of electric shock with infants is not only controversial but frequently objectionable to parents and medical staff alike. Of course, one answer to this objection could be found in the life-threatening nature of the disorder. Nevertheless, less-aversive procedures would be desirable and have, at times, been shown to be successful. One such alternative with a six-month-old boy was the successful use of the combination of a thickened-cereal diet (making regurgitation more difficult), contingent use of affection and time-out, and contingent use of highly seasoned tabasco sauce on the tongue upon observing preemetic behavior. After only three days, vomiting behavior had completely ceased (Murray & Keefe, 1976). A more recent study utilized what essentially amounted to extinction procedures in successfully eliminating chronic, ruminative vomiting in a nine-month-old girl (Wright, Brown, & Andrews, 1978). However, this procedure required a total of 68 days for complete elimination of the symptoms. Another relatively attractive alternative to the use of electric shock has been the use of unsweetened lemon juice contingent upon prevomiting behavior (e.g., Sajwaj, Libet, & Agras, 1974; O'Neal, White, King, & Carek, 1979). These initial reports have been encouraging, although Ruprecht, Hanson, Pocrnich, and Murphy (1980) noted that potential risks could include irritation of the infant's mouth, aspiration of the juice, and erosion of tooth enamel. These authors made recommendations which would substantially reduce these possible complications. Still, the exploration of other aversive-tasting substances (but with a PH value above 3.5), which could be placed on the tongue in a few drops, might be an attractive alternative to lemon juice.

Krajewski (1980) recently reported that psychogenic regurgitation is distinguishable from psychogenic vomiting, in that regurgitation is presumed to be due to a weakened gastroesophageal sphincter, which allows stomach contents to flow back readily. For such cases, he recommends an esophageal-exercise program to improve the competency of the gastro-esophageal sphincter and reports on the successful use of this strategy with one case.

Chronic vomiting also can occur in adults and is not always traceable to organic pathology or bulimia. At times, it appears to result from conditioned aversions and/or fears associated with gastrointestinal surgery (e.g., Redd, 1980) and chemotherapy for cancer (e.g. Burish & Lyles, 1981; Redd, Andresen & Nainagawa, 1982). In other cases, stress and/or depression have been implicated as the primary precipitants (Swanson, Swenson, Huizenga, Melson, 1976). Regardless of the specific cause (assuming the lack of a clear, organic pathology), the use of other, less-aversive conditioning procedures has been found to be effective in eliminating chronic vomiting in adults. These strategies have included extinction (Alford, Blanchard, & Buckley, 1972); restitutional overcorrection (Duker & Seys, 1977); shaping and time-out (Ingersoll & Curry, 1977); forced-vomiting practice (Spergel, 1975); counterconditioning with sips of ginger ale to induce forward peristalsis, which is incompatible with vomiting (Morgan & O'Brien, 1972); emotive imagery, as an incompatible response, combined with in vivo desensitization (Tasto & Chesney, 1974); in vivo desensitization (Redd, 1980); and hypnosis (Redd et al., 1982). With the exception of the study by Redd et at. (1982), these have been uncontrolled, case studies. However, their relatively large number, the inclusion of follow-up data indicating sustained symptom relief, and the fact that strategies such as antiemetics had often been tried first without success attest to the substantial potential of these various behavioral interventions.

Irritable-bowel syndrome, diarrhea, Crohn's disease

These various disorders can have different causes but generally are associated with increased gastric motility. It is particularly interesting to note that the irritable-bowel syndrome has been considered to be the most frequent problem encountered by gastroenterologists, with estimates that it is present in 50 to 70 percent of their patients (Davis, 1978). The effects of stress on gastric motility have been quite well documented (e.g., Schaefer, et al., 1979); and, in addition, Taylor (1980b) reviewed data indicating that the relationship of stress to gastric motility has been clearly documented in the literature as far back as the late 1940s. Of additional interest to behavioral researchers is the fact that Taylor (1980b) noted over 400 papers—reviewing the effects of 18 anticholinergic drugs—failed to demonstrate one instance in which a controlled study demonstrated clinically significant physiological effects of these drugs on colonic motility, as long as they were given orally. In spite of this overwhelming evidence, anticholinergic medicines remain a frequent recommendation for this disorder.

Given the rather dismal picture from a pharmacological standpoint and the well-known association between stress and these disorders, it is surprising that very little in the way of behavioral-intervention research has been conducted to date. Two different approaches to this problem have appeared in the literature. The first of these involved a variety of stress-management techniques which demonstrated successful treatment of severe and chronic diarrhea (Cohen & Reed, 1968; Hedberg, 1973). The three patients in these two studies had chronic diarrhea for a prolonged period of time, but the studies were basically uncontrolled, case-study reports. The second approach to these disorders has been the use of biofeedback. Furman (1973) employed such feedback of five female patients, who suffered from disorders of the lower gastrointestinal tract in the absence of organic pathology. The biofeedback that Furman utilized consisted of amplifying bowel sounds (through an electronic stethoscope played through a loud speaker) so that the patient could hear her intestinal sounds (which would presumably be reflective of peristaltic activity). Furman reported significant improvements in all five patients, some of whom had been virtually toilet-bound for life. However, quantified data was not reported, nor were control groups included. The final approach to the use of biofeedback with these disorders was recently reported by Bueno-Miranda, Cerulli, and Schuster (1976). In this case, the biofeedback was somewhat different and involved feedback of the rectosigmoid distention of patients with irritable-bowel syndrome. The technique consisted of inserting three balloons rectally in such a way that feedback could be given on increasing and decreasing the distention in rectosigmoid space. Fourteen of 21 patients were successful at learning to increase and decrease this distention; but, unfortunately, the specific effects of this training on their functional-bowel syndrome was not clear.

Finally, a brief note will be made of a recent report concerning the psychological aspects of Crohn's disease (Gerbert, 1980). Crohn's disease (regional ileitis) involves a chronic condition of unknown etiology and is frequently characterized by scarring and thickening of the bowel, diarrhea, pain, loss of weight, and anemia. Additionally, fistulas, intestinal obstructions, and perianal abscesses are common complications. Gerbert (1980) reviewed substantial evidence suggesting that stressful events seem to be related at least to the exacerbation and possibly to the onset of disease symptomology for a significant percentage of patients. Gerbert aptly noted that most of the studies in this area have been flawed with major methodological problems. Thus at present, the relationship among stressors, psychopathology, personality factors, and Crohn's disease is entirely unclear. Such factors may exacerbate, cause, or even result from the disease itself. However, the author did note that the association between stress, personality factors, and Crohn's disease is sufficiently strong that further research in this area, both in terms of specific underlying mechanisms and the exploration of adjunctive psychological-treatment strategies, certainly would seem warranted.

Peptic ulcers and ulcertive colitis

Peptic ulcers can involve an ulceration of the mucus membrane of the stomach, duodenum, or the esophagus and are generally most directly caused by peptic activity (acidic gastric juices). However, numerous other factors have been implicated in the development of ulcers. The role of psychosocial factors in the production of gastric acid secretions and the exacerbation of ulcerative diseases have been well known for some time and have been reviewed and further substantiated by two recent studies (Wolcott, Wellisch, Robertson, & Arthur, 1981; Ackerman, Manaker, & Cohen, 1981). There is a paucity of behavioral-treatment research in this area as well. Taylor (1980b) reviewed two studies, in which biofeedback was utilized to give subjects direct feedback on gastric acid secretions. These studies were interesting, but the techniques were somewhat cumbersome and only moderately effective.

A somewhat different approach to the treatment of a peptic duodenal ulcer was reported by Brooks and Richards (1980), which represents the only controlled, outcome study in the area that the current authors were able to locate. Eleven patients were given anxiety-management training (as described in Chapter 27 by Denney). In addition to anxiety-management training, these patients were given assertiveness training—which included restructuring of erroneous beliefs concerning assertive behavior and the rehearsal of effective, behavioral responses in situations relevant to their home environments. This package was termed *emotional-skills training* and was compared to a so-called attention-placebo group. At a 60-day follow-up, those who had received the emotional-skills package reported reduced ulcer symptomology, less comsumption of antacid medication, and reduced days of pain. Of even greater significance was the fact that a three-and-one-half-year follow-up demonstrated that the emotional-skills group showed a far lower rate of ulcer recurrence. However, it should be pointed out that their attention-placebo group might better have been termed a *minimal-treatment-control group.* Upon inspection, it would not appear to have been an equally credible treatment, in that placebo patients apparently only received a handbook concerning the general relationship between anxiety and ulcers and charts for recording ulcer pain.

It is not clear why the area of ulcers has received such little attention in the behavioral literature, given the well-known effects of stress (at least in the exacerbation of the disease). It may be, in part, due to the fact that ulcers tend to respond quite well to medications, even though they do recur quite frequently. In fact, one of the primary differences between groups in the study reported by Brooks and Richards (1980) was reduced recurrence of ulcers in the anxiety-management group, at the three-one-half-year follow-up.

General food-refusal disorders

Food refusal (which may be either a complete refusal or refusal to consume adequate nutrition) is another problem which frequently occurs in children, without being sufficiently advanced as to categorize it as anorexia. However, in many of these cases, the long-term effects of failure to consume sufficiently nutritious diets or to consume a sufficient number of calories due to a medical condition can create a substantial problem. Once again, a variety of studies (largely of a case-study nature) have demonstrated the potential for contingencies to influence this behavior (e.g., White, 1959; Palmer, Thompson, & Linscheid, 1975; Thompson, Palmer, & Linscheid, 1977; Wright, 1971; Hatcher, 1979). Although controlled studies are clearly needed, the variety of studies demonstrating effective long-term results and the extremely refractory nature of many of the problems with which the techniques have been utilized suggest that behavioral approaches have considerable promise for this kind of problem.

Anorexia nervosa

Anorexia nervosa is an extremely serious and frequently life-threatening disorder, characterized by self-imposed restrictions on food intake and subsequent weight loss and severe malnutrition. Mortality rates from this disorder are significant and have been estimated generally in the range of 5 to 15 percent, although the prevalence of this disorder is not extremely high—estimates of its incidence range from about 1 per 100,000 to as high a 5 to 75 per 100,000 (Wright et al., 1979). However, the incidence appears to be rising.

A number of authors have noted the importance of a thorough medical evaluation, prior to making the diagnosis of anorexia nervosa, to rule out a variety of specific organic pathologies, some of which (such as certain hypothalamic tumors) can be quite difficult to diagnose (e.g., Heron & Johnston, 1976; White, Kelly & Dorman, 1977). Even when specific, clearly defined, organic factors have been ruled out, some controversy still exists concerning the possible etiological role played by subtle malfunctions of the hypothalamus or other endocrine systems. None of these possible malfunctions have been firmly established as causative factors, and most authors speculate that they are more likely a *result* of severe malnutrition rather than a cause of it (e.g., Agras & Werne, 1981).

A wide variety of psychological factors have also been suggested as possible causative agents, some of which have been reviewed by Agras and Werne (1981). Once again, no firm evidence exists for any specific psychological factors as direct, causative agents in the development of this disorder. Although cause and effect has not been established, a distortion of body image (in the sense of feeling fat, even when actually emaciated) has received substantial attention in the literature. In fact, in the recently revised *Diagnostic and Statistical Manual* (*DSM-III*) of mental disorders of the American Psychological Association, disturbed body image is included as part of the criteria for the diagnosis of anorexia nervosa. At least one recent report indicated that the *degree* of overestimation of body size was a significant predictor for treatment outcome (Casper, Halmi, Goldberg, Eckert, & Davis, 1979).

Research on this problem has generally been quite unsystematic and has suffered numerous methodological problems, such as: (*a*) diagnostic variability (in this respect, *DSM-III* may be of value in regard to standardization), (*b*) failure to evaluate the prevalence of other, "psychiatric" disturbances in the subject sample, (*c*) variable criteria for reporting results, (*d*) failure to adequately describe the subject sample, (*e*) the general emphasis on case reports and anecdotal data, and (*f*) a tendency to mix combinations of treatments in unsystematic ways that make specific effects indeterminable (e.g., Agras & Werne, 1981; Van Buskirk, 1977; Kellerman, 1977).

Van Buskirk (1977) noted that, in terms of evaluating treatment-outcome studies, it may be best to consider results in the form of a two-phase perspective. The first is the short-term perspective, which refers to fast weight gains which are often needed to avert a medical catastrophe. Second is the long-term perspective, which emphasizes maintenance of weight gains and/or psychological adjustment. The importance of long-term maintenance and follow-ups was underscored by Van Buskirk (1977), who noted that the only deaths reported in the studies reviewed occurred when outpatient follow-up therapy was not utilized.

Purely medical approaches to the problem have predominantly been conducted on an inpatient basis and include the following: tube feedings, major tranquilizers, minor tranquilizers, antidepressants, insulin, electroconvulsive therapy, hyperalimentation, and cyproheptadine (periactin) (e.g., Goldberg, Halmi, Eckert, Casper, & Davis, 1979; Maloney & Farrell, 1980; Bhanji, 1979). The relative efficacy of these approaches has never been compared. However, Maloney and Farrell (1980) recently noted that hyperalimentation may be the *only* option for a very small subgroup of extremely refractory patients. They reported on four such patients, who demonstrated a surprising degree of acceptance of hyperalimentation after having been extremely resistant to numerous other therapies. Furthermore, the hyperalimentation and subsequent weight gain were associated with improved affect, sociability, and receptivity to psychotherapy, possibly due, in part, to a return of electrolyte balance and general improvements resulting from decreased malnutrition.

Psychological-treatment interventions for anorexia nervosa have generally consisted of: (a) some form of general psychotherapy, such as psychoanalysis, (b) a variety of behavior therapies, (c) family therapy, or (d) some combination of these. Comparisons of these approaches on either the short- or long-range perspective is almost impossible at this time, due to the previously noted methodological problems with outcome research in this area.

Nevertheless, Bruch (1977) has been a particularly outspoken proponent of analytically based psychotherapies for anorexia and has sharply criticized behavior-modification approaches. In fact, she has stated, "serious depression, psychotic disorganization, and suicidal attempts follow so often that this approach (behavior modification) must be considered dangerous. It seems to undermine the last vestiges of self-esteem and to destroy the crucial hope of ever achieving autonomy and self-determination" (p. 105). The current authors frankly consider this statement to be irresponsible and totally unsubstantiated by recent data. In fact, Kellerman (1977) replied to these charges with a review of behavioral-treatment strategies that demonstrated follow-up data on 13 patients treated by behavioral strategies. Sixty-nine percent of them had maintained their *full* weight gain, and the rest had maintained partial gains. Most of these cases also reported improved social functioning and increased self-esteem. Indeed, *one* patient had committed suicide, but this appeared totally unrelated to her behavioral treatment. In addition, deaths and/ or suicides have been reported in the follow-up data by Bruch and others, using psychoanalytic therapy. Kellerman (1977) further made the allegation that Bruch's conception of "behavior modification" appears to be incomplete, at best. Finally, Wolpe (1975) observed that: (a) much of Bruch's own work is similar to behavioral treatments, and (b) there is a great difference between condemning a therapeutic approach that fails when used improperly and condemning a therapeutic approach that fails when used appropriately.

Agras and Werne (1981) have made a more recent review of behavioral treatment (which has generally been conducted on an inpatient basis) of anorexia nervosa. In the first part of this review, they noted that evidence from controlled studies currently supports the following: (a) the existence of a functional relationship between contingencies (negative and positive reinforcement) and eating behavior, (b) informational feedback (on the number of calories consumed, weight, and number of mouthfuls eaten at each meal) adds to the effect of positive reinforcement, (c) the *size* of a meal is positively correlated with the amount anorexics consume, and (d) reinforcement for one-half-pound daily weight gain results in faster gains than "routine hospital care," as demonstrated in one multiple-baseline study of seven subjects (Perschuk, Edwards, & Pomerleau, 1978).

Agras and Werne (1981) also reviewed a particularly thorough, behavior-management approach (used at Stanford University Hospital) which has shown promising initial data; but it is too early to determine its overall impact. Their survey of other behavioral-therapy approaches (compared with a potpourri of other, nonbehavioral approaches) could only *tentatively* conclude that the major advantage of behavioral approaches (in both long- and short-term results) appears, at this time, to be in terms of greater *consistency* in outcome, possibly due to a greater degree of precision with which such treatment programs tend to be specified. As Agras noted, this improved consistency is no small advantage. This conclusion must be considered tentative, given that even the term, *behavior therapy*, can be used to refer to a wide variety of treatment strategies (e.g., operant reinforcement, systematic desensitization, assertiveness training, and cognitive restructuring, among others) and that the populations in the different studies may not be comparable. Both Kellerman (1977) and Stunkard (1972) noted the advantage of designing behavior programs with individualized reinforcers and a thorough, behavior analysis of the *total* context of the problem. Few behavioral programs to date have truly implemented these recommendations rigorously.

The most comprehensive and impressive behavioral-treatment program described in the literature to date was reported by Poole and Sanson (1978). Their intervention consisted of contingency reinforcement for weight gains (measured *three* times per day), feedback on progress, lower "response cost" for eating (by placing a refrigerator in the patient's room loaded with a variety of foods and high calorie beverages), *collaborative* contracting with patients, and finally, concomitant family therapy. Although the sample size reported in this initial study was only five, the weight gains in the hospital were the largest reported to date (average of over 8.5 pounds per week). Furthermore, this gain was sustained over follow-up periods averaging six months, although the value of even longer follow-ups can not be overemphasized in this area.

Family therapy has been recommended more and more frequently in the literature, over the past 5 to 10 years, quite often as an adjunct to behavioral intervention (Poole & Sanson, 1978). The rationale for family therapy is generally based upon the common clinical observations that either certain eating behaviors of the anorexic patient are directly reinforcing because of the advantages given to the patient over family members or because attention to a marital conflict (which might be highly threatening to the patient) can be deflected more innocuously onto the anorexic patient (e.g., Rosen, 1980; Liebman, Minuchin, & Baker, 1974; Minuchin, Baker, Rosman, Liebman, Milman, & Todd, 1975). Unfortunately, systematic data demonstrating the efficacy of this promising and interesting approach is currently lacking.

The only controlled, group-outcome studies on anorexia that the current authors have found was reported by Eckert, Goldberg, Halmi, Casper, and Davis (1979) and Goldberg et al. (1979). In these studies, over three hospitals, 81 female anorexics were compared in the conditions of (a) drug (cypropheptadine) versus placebo, (b) behavior therapy versus no behavior therapy, and (c) the three hospitals themselves. However, no combinations of drug and behavior therapy were included in the comparison. Preliminary conclusions from these ongoing studies to date are that: (1) cypropheptadine (periacton) was found to be more effective than placebos (in a double-blind study) only for a subgroup of most severe anorexics and (2) the behavior-therapy group gained almost 25 percent more during the hospital stay than the nonbehavior-therapy group, but variability in the data precluded statistical significance of this finding, *except* for a subset of patients with no prior outpatient treatments. Unfortunately, no follow-up data were presented, and the behavior-therapy procedures did not appear to follow usual recommendations (e.g., individualized reinforcers were not used, and the schedule of reinforcers was over five days rather than shorter periods).

Finally, a note will be made of several interesting suggestions for enhancing outpatient maintenance of weight gains made by anorexics in the hospital. These include the use of: (1) *randomly* scheduled, follow-up therapy sessions in conjunction with contracted hospitalization, if weight goals are not adhered to (Poole & Sanson, 1978), (2) the use of regular telephone contact (McGlynn, 1980), and (3) dealing on an outpatient basis with the idiosyncratic eating habits that anorexics often demonstrate (Rosen, 1980). These habits often include, among others, hiding or hoarding food, and eating when family members are out of sight. Rosen reported data on 12 such patients, who had initially gained adequate weight through operant-conditioning procedures, but had developed highly idiosyncratic, disturbing eating patterns at home (which he speculated might eventually have led to weight relapses). Normal eating was established in these patients by prescribing that their *entire* eating behavior had to be conducted in their secret clandestine fashion, until they totally rejected their inappropriate eating habits. Within three days, all 12 patients resumed normal eating and sustained this pattern for one to six years. The author noted several possible explanations for his results, including an "escape paradigm" and/or the removal of the advantages the previous behaviors had given to patients over other family members. Due to the careful way that the author explained the procedures to the patients, none perceived them as punitive in nature.

Bulimia

Considerable debate currently exists as to whether bulimia (recurrent episodes of binge eating, followed by self-induced vomiting) represents a disorder that is a subtype or separate disorder from anorexia nervosa. According to the *DSM-III* of the American Psychiatric Association, bulimia rarely occurs in those with anorexia nervosa or vice versa. However,

Casper, Eckert, Halmi, Goldberg, and Davis (1980) reported that a high percentage of anorexic patients in their sample (approximately 47 percent) resorted to bulimia, at least periodically, to maintain their extremely low body weight.

An almost complete lack of treatment literature exists for this particular problem. Rosen and Leitenberg (1982) reported on the use of an exposure-plus-prevention procedure within a multiple-baseline design, across three food classes. Thus, the patient was required to binge eat at a public restaurant without being allowed to experience the anxiety relief associated with going to the restroom to vomit. Under these conditions, the patient was uncomfortable, but did not vomit. As the procedure was sequentially applied (for six sessions) to each food class, vomiting, discomfort, and binging substantially decreased. With additional post-treatment instructions, the patient's vomiting decreased to zero within 44 days. Over a 10-month follow-up, only one relapse occurred. The authors made the further observation that both their data and treatment procedures were quite similar to those of Foa and Goldstein (1978), who reported successful treatment of obsessions and compulsions. These results led the authors to speculate that "vomiting in bulimia nervosa is an escape-avoidance response reinforced by anxiety reduction" (p. 117) and that "binging" may actually be more of a *consequence* to vomiting than the other way around.

One other recent report of a bulimic college student utilized a variety of behavioral procedures, to successfully eliminate the maladaptive symptoms and concomitantly improve her social-emotional functioning over a six-month follow-up (Linden, 1980). It is interesting to note that one of the major treatment components in that study was the use of "response delay" and "stimulus control" (having the patient delay vomiting and allowing it only in certain situations), which were quite similar to the "response prevention" used by Rosen and Leitenberg (1982). Clearly, more systematic investigations need to be conducted in this area.

GENITOURINARY SYSTEM

Enuresis

Enuresis is possibly the most common problem with which behavioral medicine is concerned. Encopresis is included in this section because both can be considered elimination disorders. Sexual dysfunctions are thoroughly reviewed by Goldberg in Chapter 20 and will not be discussed.

Enuresis is typically divided into two categories: primary and secondary. The primary enuretic has never achieved continance, while the secondary enuretic has demonstrated continual continance for at least six months in the past. Approximately 15 to 20 percent of all five year olds are enuretic (Lovibond & Coote, 1970). The incidence of enuresis in boys is about 1.5 times as great as in girls.

In the past, enuresis was thought to be due to an emotional disorder. Later large-scale studies failed to confirm this hypothesis (Cullen, 1966). Enuresis is now thought to be due to an organic disorder (in a small percentage of cases) or more often due to faulty learning (Walker, 1978). Both Walker (1978) and Doleys (1978) suggest that treatment for enuresis may begin as early as five or six years of age.

Assessment of enuresis generally entails three components: (1) medical screening, to rule out specific neurologic or urologic pathology; (2) clinical interview, to assess occurrence (day/night), history of enuresis, past treatment, medical history of family members, behavioral problems, and home and family environment (Doleys, 1978); (3) behavioral recordings of the frequency of enuresis. The most frequently used modes of treatment for enuresis will be reviewed. The reader is directed to an in-depth review of the topic by Walker (1978).

Pharmacological treatments using tricyclic antidepressants (imipramine and amitrityline) have reported 30 percent total remission. Yet, only 5 to 40 percent of these children *remain* continent when the drug is withdrawn (Blackwell, 1973; Shaffer, 1977). Mahoney, Laferte, and Mahoney (1973) and Meadow (1974) suggest pharmacologic treatment is useful in bringing about rapid, temporary relief and would be most effective when used as an adjunct to other behavioral therapies which have demonstrated more-permanent effects.

The bladder capacity of enuretics has generally been found to be lower than nonenuretics (Zaleski, Gerrard, & Shokier, 1973; Starfield & Mellits, 1968). Therefore, bladder-expansion and -retention exercises have been used to increase the functional bladder capacity of enuretics. The child is usually given extra fluids during the day and rewarded for retaining the urine for increasing intervals of time. Unfortunately, results from the use of this technique have been mixed, at best (Kimmel & Kimmel, 1970; Starfield & Mellits, 1967). By contrast, Walker (1978) has *combined* bladder-retention exercises with sphincter-control exercises. Once the child is able to retain urine for 20 or 30 minutes, he or she then practices starting and stopping the flow of urine. On a clinical basis, Walker has reported approximately an 80 percent effectiveness rate with this combined-exercise method (Walker, 1982).

The most thoroughly researched treatment for nocturnal enuresis is the pad and bell. This apparatus is assumed to be based either on a classical-conditioning model (Mowrer & Mowrer, 1938) or on an aversive-conditioning model (Lovibond, 1964). A review of all studies using the pad and bell between 1960 and 1975 (Doleys, Ciminera, Tollison, Williams, & Wells, 1977) reported that there was a 75 percent rate of remission but a 41 percent relapse rate. Parental noncompliance has been the most frequently reported cause of treatment failures (Doleys et al.,

1977). The pad and bell have been found to be superior to nighttime awakening (Catalina, 1976), imipramine (McConaghy, 1969), and retention-training exercises (Allen, 1976). Intermittent scheduling of the alarm (Finley, Besserman, Bennett, Clapp, & Finley, 1973) and overlearning (Young & Morgan, 1972) have been used to reduce the rate of relapse. Using an intermittent schedule, there was a significant reduction in relapse rates when compared to the traditional pad-and-bell method. Overlearning was also used to test the child's control after achieving dryness with the urine alarm. Overlearning requires the child to drink 10 to 32 ounces of fluid before bedtime. This method achieved a lower relapse rate (13 percent) as compared to the bell and pad without overlearning (35 percent) (Morgan, 1978).

Azrin, Sneed, and Foxx (1973, 1974) have employed a multimethod approach to nocturnal enuresis. This method includes positive practice, positive reinforcement, bladder-retention exercises, nighttime awakening, negative reinforcement, and cleanliness training. Azrin reports all of the children achieved two consecutive weeks of dry nights, although seven children required reinitiation of post-training supervision. Doleys et al. (1977) attempted to replicate this study and found only 8 of the 13 children achieved two consecutive weeks of dry nights, and 38 percent of these children relapsed.

Encopresis

Encopresis is defined as "involuntary fecal soiling by the child in his clothing beyond the age at which toilet training should have occurred, and in the absence of organic pathology" (Walker, 1978, p. 164). Incidence rates for encopresis range from 1.5 percent (Bellman, 1966) to 5.7 percent (Olatawura, 1973), with males outnumbering females 5 to 1 (Levine, 1975). Encopresis, like enuresis, has been described as either primary (continuous) or secondary (discontinuous). Unfortunately, authors have used a variety of definitions or have simply included all encopretics in many studies, making comparisons of data across studies more difficult.

Walker (1978), in a comprehensive review of the literature, suggests three general categories for encopresis: manipulative soiling, chronic diarrhea (Davidson, 1973), and chronic constipation resulting in impaction and psychogenic mega colon (Ravitch, 1958). In each case, a medical exam is essential, to determine the presence of any specific organic pathology, prior to the initiation of psychologically based treatment. Yates (1970) and Wright (1973) reported that relatively few children use soiling as a manipulation or avoidance tactic. When this appears to be the case, family counseling and behavioral treatment involving reinforcement for nonsoiling are suggested.

Fitzgerald (1975) and Levine (1975) estimated 80 percent to 94 percent of the cases of encopresis are a result of chronic constipation resulting in psychogenic mega colon. Wright (1973) has employed a treatment regime combining cathartics, immediate rewards for appropriate toileting, rewards for clean clothing at the end of the day, and a mild punishment for fecal incontinence. Occasional stool softeners or dietary manipulations, such as adding fiber or bulk to the diet and decreasing dairy products, have been used as an adjunct to this program. Fourteen subjects were treated using this method, and all stopped soiling. The average treatment was 16.93 weeks, for completion of the program. Only one child relapsed and, when placed on the program again, soiling ceased. This program has continued to be used for several years at the Mental Health Consultation-Liaison Service of Oklahoma Children's Memorial Hospital, with excellent results.

Young (1973) used a combination of senokot (a medication to reduce colonic inertia and aid in the initiation of gastroileal reflex) and social reinforcement for appropriate toileting. Successful outcomes within one year were reported in 19 of the 24 cases, and three more children achieved fecal continence in more than one year. Symptoms recurred for four of the children during a six-month to six-year follow-up. Case studies of operant techniques for the treatment of encopresis include positive reinforcement (Neale, 1963), positive and negative reinforcement (Edelman, 1971), token economies for children (Nilsson, 1976) and token economics for adult, institutionalized, retardates (Giles & Wolf, 1966). Foxx and Azrin's (1973) "Full Cleanliness Training" was successfully adapted for an encopretic (Doleys & Arnold, 1975). Finally, occasional case histories have reported successful outcomes using self-hypnosis with children (Olness, 1976; Baer, 1961; Goldsmith, 1962) for the control of encopresis.

SUMMARY

A number of issues currently receiving attention in the behavior-medicine literature are reviewed in this chapter, in the areas of assessment, patient management, and behavior treatments for medical disorders. In the area of assessment, it is noted that, in addition to traditional techniques, the development of population-specific assessment techniques holds considerable promise. Furthermore, much is likely to be gained by a refined analysis of certain individual-difference variables, particularly as they interact with situational variables and physiological subtypes.

In the area of patient management, some of the major factors likely responsible for problems of noncompliance to medical regimens are reviewed. In addition, reviews are presented on interventions designed to aid in the preparation of patients (both children and adults) for medical, dental, and surgical procedures.

The review of behavioral treatments for medical disorders is organized according to some of the major bodily organ systems which have received at least moderate attention in the literature to date. Major systems reviewed included the cardiovascular system (in particular, hypertension, migraine headaches, cardiac arrhythmia, Raynaud's disease, and chronic arterial occlusive disease), the respiratory system (asthma and tracheostomy dependency), the nervous system (seizure disorders and movement disorders), the musculoskeletal system (ideopathic scoliosis and tension headaches), the dermatological system (scratching, hives, hyperhidrosis, ichthyosis, eczemia, and dermatitis), the endocrine system (basic issues and treatment implications for the disorders of diabetes, cancer, and obesity), the gastrointestinal system (vomiting, general food disorders, anorexia nervosa and bulimia), and the genitourinary system (enuresis and encopresis).

Overall, the literature reviewed in this chapter demonstrates an exciting potential to improve the treatment outcome for a variety of medical disorders. In some cases, this improved outcome can be obtained through a purely behavioral intervention; while in many other cases, the behavioral intervention will likely be in the form of adjunctive techniques or involve a synergistic combination with various medical interventions. Unfortunately, a sufficient body of data from controlled, outcome studies to allow for *definitive* conclusions regarding the efficacy of behavior-medicine interventions has not yet been accumulated, for most of the areas reviewed. The authors have attempted to make note of the types of studies which will be required in order to make such conclusions.

REFERENCES

Ackerman, S. H., Manaker, S., & Cohen, M. I. Recent separation and the onset of peptic ulcer disease in older children and adolescents. *Psychosomatics Medicine*, 1981, *43*, 305–310.

Adams, H. D., Feuerstein, M., & Fowler, J. L. The migraine headache: A review of parameters, theories, and interventions. *Psychological Bulletin*, 1980, *87*, 217–237.

Ad hoc Committee on Classification of Headaches. *Journal of American Medical Association*, 1962, *179*, 717–718.

Agras, S., & Werne, J. Disorders of eating. In S. M. Turner, K. S. Calhoun, & H. F. Adams (Eds.), *Handbook of clinical behavior therapy.* New York: John Wiley & Sons, 1981.

Alexander, A. B., Cropp, G. J. A., & Chai, H. Effects of relaxation training on pulmonary mechanics in children with asthma. *Journal of Applied Behavior Analysis*, 1979, *12*, 27–35.

Alexander, A. B., Miklich, D. R., & Hershkoff, H. The immediate effects of systematic relaxation on peak expiratory flow rates in asthmatic children. *Psychosomatic Medicine*, 1972, *34*, 388–394.

Alexander, A. B., & Solanch, L. S. Psychological aspects in the understanding and treatment of bronchial asthma. In J. M. Ferguson & C. B. Taylor (Eds.), *The comprehensive handbook of behavioral medicine* (Vol. 2). New York: Spectrum, 1981.

Alexander, A. B., White, P. D., & Wallace, H. M. Training and transfer of training effects in EMG biofeedback-assisted muscular relaxation. *Psychophysiology,* 1977, *14,* 551–559.

Alford, G. S., Blanchard, E. B., & Buckley, T. M. Treatment of hysterical vomiting by modification of social contingencies: A case study. *Journal of Behavioral Therapy and Experimental Psychiatry,* 1972, *3,* 209–212.

Allen, K. E., & Harris, F. R. Elimination of a child's excessive scratching by training the mother in reinforcement procedures. *Behavior Research and Therapy,* 1966, *4,* 79–84.

Allen, R. B. *Bladder capacity and awakening behavior in the treatment of enuresis.* Unpublished doctoral dissertation, University of Vermont, 1976.

Alpert, J. J. Broken appointments. *Pediatrics,* 1964, *53,* 127–132.

American Lung Association, *Introduction to lung diseases* (6th ed.). 1975.

Andrasik, F., & Holroyd, K. A. A test of specific and nonspecific effects in the biofeedback treatment of tension headache. *Journal of Consulting and Clinical Psychology,* 1980, *48,* 575–586.

Appenzeller, O. Vasomotor function in migraine. *Headache,* 1969, *9,* 147–155.

Azrin, N. H., & Nunn, R. G., Habit reversal: A method of eliminating nervous habits and tics. *Behavior Research and Therapy,* 1973, *11,* 619–628.

Azrin, N. H., Nunn, R. G., & Frantz S. E. Habit reversal versus negative-practice treatment of tics. *Behavior Therapy,* 1980, *11,* 169–178.

Azrin, N. H., Sneed, T. J., & Foxx, R. M. Dry bed: A rapid method of eliminating bedwetting (enuresis) of the retarded. *Behavior Research and Therapy,* 1973, *11,* 427–434.

Azrin, N. H., Sneed, T. J., & Foxx, R. M. Dry bed: A rapid elimination of childhood enuresis. *Behavior Research and Therapy,* 1974, *12,* 427–434.

Baekland, F., & Lundwall, L. Dropping out of treatment: A critical review. *Psychological Bulletin,* 1975, *82,* 738–783.

Baer, R. F. Hypnosis applied to bowel and bladder control in multiple sclerosis, syringomyelia, and traumatic transverse myelitis. *American Journal of Clinical Hypnosis,* 1961, *4,* 22–23.

Baile, W., Bernard, T., & Engel, B. T. Behavioral strategy for promoting treatment compliance following myocardial infarction. *Psychosomatic Medicine,* 1978, *40,* 413–419.

Bair, S. L., & Levenberg, S. B. Multimodal behavioral approach to the treatment and management of essential hypertension. *Psychotherapy: Theory, Research, and Practice,* 1979, *16,* 310–315.

Baker, L., Minuchin, S., Milman, L., Leibman, R., & Todd, T. Psychosomatic aspects of juvenile diabetes mellitus: A progress report. In Z. Lavon, (Ed.), *Diabetes in juveniles: Medical and rehabilitation aspects. Modern problems in pediatrics* (Vol.12). New York: Karger, 1977.

Bar, H. J., & Kaypers, B. R. M. Behavior therapy in dermatological practice. *British Journal of Dermatological,* 1973, *88,* 591–598.

Barber, T. X. Hypnosis, suggestions, and psychosomatic phenomena: A new look from the standpoint of recent experimental studies. In J. L. Fosshage & P. Olsen (Eds.), *Healing: Implications for psychotherapy. New York: Human Sciences Press, 1978.*

Barlow, D. H. (Ed.). *Behavioral assessment of adult disorders.* New York: Guilford Press, 1981.

Becker, M. H. Sociobehavioral determinant of compliance. In D. L. Sackett & R. B. Haynes (Eds.), *Compliance with therapeutic regimens.* Baltimore: Johns Hopkins University Press, 1976.

Becker, M. H., Drachman, R. H., & Kirscht, J. P. Predicting mothers' compliance with pediatric regimens. *Journal of Pediatrics,* 1972, *81,* 843–845.

Becker, M. H., & Maiman, L. A. Sociobehavioral determinants of compliance with health and medical care recommendations. *Medical Care,* 1975, *13,* 10–24.

Becker, M. H., Maiman, L. A., Kirscht, J. P., Halfner, D. P., & Drachman, R. H. The health-belief model and dietary compliance: A field experiment. *Journal of Health and Social Behavior,* 1977, *18,* 348–366.

Bellman, M. Studies on encopresis. *Acta Paediatrica Scandinavica,* 1966, *170,* 1–137.

Berry, K. K. An apparent failure of conditioning to alter tracheostomy addiction. *Nebraska Medical Journal,* 1972, *57,* 435–438.

Bhanji, S. Anorexia nervosa: Physician's and psychiatrist's opinions and practice. *Journal of Psychosomatic Research,* 1979, *23,* 7–11.

Bird, B. L., & Cataldo, M. F. Experimental analysis of EMG feedback in treating dystonia. *Annals of Neurology,* 1978, *3,* 310–315.

Birk, L. Behavior therapy and behavioral psychotherapy. In A. M. Nicholi (Ed.), *The Harvard guide to modern psychiatry.* Cambridge: Harvard University Press, 1978.

Blackwell, B. Drug therapy: Patient compliance. *New England Journal of Medicine,* 1973, *289,* 249–252.

Blackwell, B. Treatment adherence. *British Journal of Psychiatry,* 1976, *129,* 513–531.

Blanchard, E. B. Biofeedback and the modification of cardiovascular dysfunction. In H. J. Gatchel & K. P. Price (Eds.), *Clinical applications of biofeedback: Appraisal and status.* Elmsford, N.Y.: Pergamon Press, 1979.

Blanchard, E. B., Andrasik, F., Ahles, T. A., Teders, S. J., & O'Keefe, D. Migraine and tension headache: A meta-analytic review. *Behavior Therapy,* 1980, *11,* 613–631.

Boyd, J. R., Covington, T. R., Stanaszck, W. F., & Coussons, R. T. Drug defaulting—Part 1: Determinants of compliance. *American Journal of Hospital Pharmacy,* 1974, *31,* 362–364.

Brooks, G. R., & Richards, F. C. Emotional-skills training: Treatment program for a duodenal ulcer. *Behavior Therapist,* 1980, *11,* 198–207.

Brown, D. G. Psychosomatic correlates in contact dermatitis: A pilot study. *Journal of Psychosomatic Research,* 1959, *4,* 132–139.

Brown, D. G. Emotional disturbance in eczema: A study of symptom-reporting behavior. *Journal of Psychosomatic Research,* 1967, *11,* 27–40.

Bruch, H. Psychotherapy in eating disorders. *Canadian Psychiatric Association Journal,* 1977, *22,* 102–107.

Bueno-Miranda, F., Cerulli, M., & Schuster, M. M. Operant conditioning of colonic motility in irritable bowel syndrome (IBS). *Gastroenterology,* 1976, *70,* 867.

Burish, T. G., & Lyles, J. N. Effectiveness of relaxation training in reducing adverse reactions to cancer chemotherapy. *Journal of Behavioral Medicine,* 1981, *4,* 65–78.

Caldwell, J. R., Cobb, S., Dowling, M. D., & deTonga, D. The dropout problem in antihypertensive treatment. *Journal of Chronic Disease,* 1970, *22,* 579–592.

Canavan, A. G. M., & Powell, G. E. The efficacy of several treatments of Gilles de la

Tourette syndrome as assessed in a single case. *Behavior Research and Therapy,* 1981, *19,* 549–556.

Caplan, R. D., Robinson, E. A. R., French, J. R. P., Caldwell, J. R. & Shinn, M. *Adhering to medical regimens: Pilot experiments in patient education and social support.* Ann Arbor: University of Michigan, 1976.

Casper, R. C., Eckert, E. D., Halmi, K. A., Goldberg, S. C., & Davis, J. M. Bulimia. *Archives of General Psychiatry,* 1980, *37,* 1030–1035.

Casper, R. C., Halmi, K. A., Goldberg, S. C., Eckert, E. D., & Davis, J. M. Disturbances in body-image estimation as related to other characteristics and outcome in anorexia nervosa. *British Journal of Psychiatry,* 1979, *134,* 60–66.

Cataldo, M. F., Russo, D. C., & Freeman, J. M. A behavior-analysis approach to high-rate myoclonic seizures. *Journal of Autism and Developmental Disorders,* 1979, *9,* 413–427.

Cataldo, M. F., Varni, J. W., Russo, D. C., & Estes, S. A. Behavior-therapy techniques in treatment of exfoliative dermatitis. *Archives of Dermatology,* 1980, *116,* 919–922.

Catalina, D. A. Enuresis: The effects of parent-contingent wake-up. *Dissertation Abstracts International,* 1976, *37,* 28.

Chai, H. Management of severe, chronic perennial asthma in children. *Advances in Asthma and Allergy,* 1975, *2,* 1–12.

Chai, H., Purcell, L., Brady, K., & Falliers, C. J. Therapeutic and investigational evaluation of asthmatic children. *Journal of Allergy,* 1968, *41,* 23–36.

Charney, E. Patient-doctor communication: Implications for the clinician, *Pediatric Clinics of North America,* 1972, *19,* 263–279.

Cinciripini, P. M., Epstein, L. H., & Kotanchik, N. L. Behavioral intervention for a self-stimulatory, attending, and seizure behavior in a cerebral palsied child. *Journal of Behavioral Therapy and Experimental Psychiatry,* 1980, *11,* 313–316.

Cinciripini, P. M., Williamson, D. A., & Epstein, L. H. Behavioral treatment for migraine headaches. In J. M. Ferguson & C. B. Taylor (Eds.), *The comprehensive handbook of behavioral medicine: Syndromes and special areas* (Vol.2). New York: Spectrum, 1981.

Clark, G. M., & Troop, R. One tablet combination-drug therapy in the treatment of hypertension. *Journal of Chronic Disease,* 1972, *25,* 57–64.

Cleeland, C. S. Behavior techniques in modification of spasmodic torticollis. *Nuerology,* 1973, *23,* 1241–1247.

Cohen, M. J., McArthur, D. L., & Rickles, W. H. Comparison of four biofeedback treatments for migraine headache: Physiological and headache variables. *Psychosomatic Medicine,* 1980, *42,* 463–480.

Cohen, S. I., & Reed, J. The treatment of nervous diarrhea and other conditioned autonomic disorders by desensitization. *British Journal of Psychiatry,* 1968, *114,* 1275–1280.

Cole, P., & Emmanuel, S. R. Drug consultation: Its significance to the discharged hospital patient. *American Journal of Hospital Pharmacy,* 1971, *28,* 954–960.

Cram, J. R. EMG biofeedback and the treatment of tension headaches: A systematic analysis of treatment components. *Behavior Therapy,* 1980, *11,* 699–710.

Creer, T. L. The use of a time-out from positive-reinforcement procedure with asthmatic children. *Journal of Psychosomatic Research,* 1970, *14,* 117–120.

Creer, T. L. Psychologic aspects and management. In E. Middleton, Jr., C. E. Reed, & E. F. Ellis (Eds.), *Allergy: Principles and practice.* St. Louis: C. V. Mosby, 1978.

Creer, T. L. *Asthma therapy: A behavioral health care system for respiratory disorders.* New York: Springer, 1979.

Creer, T. L., Weinberg, E., & Molk, L. Managing a hospital-behavior problem: Malingering. *Journal of Behavioral Therapy and Experimental Psychiatry,* 1974, *5,* 259–262.

Crooks, J. Noninflammatory laryngeal stridor in infants. *Archives of Disease in Childhood,* 1954, *29,* 12–17.

Cullen, K. S. Clinical observations concerning behavior disorders in children. *Medical Journal of Australia,* 1966, *1,* 712–715.

Cunningham C. E., & Linscheid, T. R. Elimination of chronic infant rumination by electric shock. *Behavior Therapy,* 1976, *7,* 231–234.

Cuskey, W. R., & Litt, I. F. Compliance with pediatric-medication regimens. In S. J. Yaffe (Ed.), *Pediatric pharmacology.* New York: Grune & Stratton, 1980.

Daniels, L. K. Treatment of urticaria and severe headache by behavioral therapy. *Psychosomatics,* 1973, *14,* 347–351.

Danker, P. S., Miklich, D. R., Pratt, C., & Creer, T. L. An unsuccessful attempt to instrumentally condition peak expiratory flow rates in asthmatic children. *Journal of Psychosomatic Research,* 1975, *19,* 209–213.

David, N. A., Welborn, W. S., & Pierce, H. I. Comparison of multiple- and combination-tablet drug therapy in hypertension. *Current Therapy Research,* 1975, *18,* 741–754.

Davidson, M. Chronic nonspecific diarrhea syndrome: Irritable colon of childhood. In S. S. Gellis & B. M. Kagan (Eds.), *Current pediatric therapy.* Philadelphia: W. B. Saunders, 1973.

Davis, D. J. NIAID initiatives in allergy research. *The Journal of Allergy and Clinical Immunology,* 1972, *49,* 323–328.

Davis, M. H., Saunders, D. R., Creer, T. L., & Chai, H. Relaxation training facilitated by biofeedback apparatus as a supplemental treatment in bronchial asthma. *Journal of Psychosomatic Research,* 1973, *17,* 121–128.

Davis, M. S. Physiologic, psychological, and demographic factors in patient's compliance with doctor's orders. *Medical Care,* 1968, *6,* 115–122.

Davis, W. D. The irritable-bowel syndrome—How to recognize and manage it. *Modern Medicine,* 1978, *16,* 62–65.

DeGood, D. E. Cognitive-control factors in vascular-stress response. *Psychophysiology,* 1975, *12,* 399–401.

Devine, J. E. & Hock, R. A. *Relaxation and parent training in the treatment of bronchial asthma.* Paper presented at the meeting of the American Psychological Association, Montreal, September 1980.

Dickey, F. F., Mattar, M. E., & Chudzek, G. M. Pharmacist counseling increases drug-regimen compliance. *Hospitals,* 1975, *49,* 85–88.

Dobes, R. W. Amelioration of psychosomatic dermatosis by reinforced inhibition of scratching. *Journal of Behavior Therapy and Experimental Psychiatry,* 1977, *8,* 185–187.

Doleys, D. M. Assessment and treatment of childhood enuresis. In A. J. Finch & P. C. Kendal (Eds.), *Treatment and research in child psychopathology.* New York: Spectrum, 1978.

Doleys, D. M., & Arnold, S. Treatment of childhood encopresis: Full-cleanliness training. *Mental Retardation*, 1975, *13*, 14–16.

Doleys, D. M., Ciminera, A. R., Tollison, J. W., Williams, C. L., & Wells, K. C. Dry-bed training and retention-control training: A comparison. *Behavior Therapy*, 1977, *8*, 541–548.

Doleys, D. M. & Kurtz, P. S. A behavioral treatment program for the Gilles de la Tourette's syndrome. *Psychological Reports*, 1974, *35*, 43–48.

Doleys, D. M., Meredith, R. S., & Ciminero, A. R. (Eds.). *Behavioral psychology in medicine: Assessment and treatment strategies*. New York: Plenum Press, 1982.

Duker, P. C., & Seys, D. M. Elimination of vomiting in a retarded female using restitutional correction. *Behavior Therapy*, 1977, *8*, 255–257.

Dunbar, J. M., & Agras, S. Compliance with medical instructions. In J. M. Ferguson & C. B. Taylor (Eds.), *The comprehensive handbook of behavioral medicine: Extended applications and issues* (vol. 3). New York: Spectrum, 1980.

Dworkin, B. R. Instrumental learning for the treatment of disease. *Health Psychology*, 1982, *1*, 45–61.

Eckert, E. D., Goldberg, S. C., Halmi, K. A., Casper, R. C., & Davis, J. M. Behavior therapy in anorexia nervosa. *British Journal of Psychiatry*, 1979, *134*, 55–59.

Edelman, R. I. Operant-conditioning treatment of encopresis. *Journal of Behavior Therapy and Experimental Psychiatry*, 1971, *2*, 71–73.

Elling, R., Whittemore, R., & Green, M. Patient participation in a pediatric program. *Journal of Health and Human Behavior*, 1960, *1, 183*.

Elliott, C. H., & Denny, D. Weight control through covert desensitization and false feedback. *Journal of Consulting and Clinical Psychology*, 1975, *43*(6), 842–850.

Elliott, C. H., & Olson, R. A. *The management of children's behavioral distress in response to painful medical treatment for burn injuries*. Unpublished manuscript, Oklahoma Health Sciences Center, 1982.

Elliott, C. H., & Olson, R. A. Variations in conditioning procedures for the decannulation of tracheostomy-dependent children: Clinical and theoretical implications. *Health Psychology*, 1982, *1*, 389–397.

Engel, B. T. Cardiac arrhythmias. In R. B. Williams & W. D. Gentry (Eds.), *Behavioral approaches to medical treatment*. Cambridge, Mass.: Ballinger Publishing, 1977.

Engel, B. T., & Bleecker, E. R. Application of operant-conditioning techniques to the control of cardiac arrhythmias. In P. A. Obrist, A. H. Black, J. Brener, & L. V. DiCara (Eds.), *Cardiovascular psychophysiology*. Hawthorne, N.Y.: Aldine Publishing, 1974.

Engel, B. T., & Melmon, L. Operant conditioning of heart rate in patients with cardiac arrhythmias. *Conditional Reflex*, 1968, *3*, 130.

Engstrom, I. Respiratory studies in children. XI: Mechanics of breathing, lung volumes, and ventilatory capacity in asthmatic children from attack to system-free status. *Acta Paediatrica Scandinavica*, 1964, *155*, 1–60.

Epstein, L. H., & Able, G. G. An analysis of biofeedback-training effects for tension-headache patients. *Behavior Therapy*, 1977, *8*, 37–47.

Epstein, L. H., Able, G. G., Collins, F., Parker, L., & Cinciripini, P. M. The relationship between frontalis muscle activity and self-reports of headache pain. *Behavior Research and Therapy*, 1978, *16*, 153–160.

Epstein, L. H., & Cinciripini, P. M. Behavioral control of tension headaches. In J. M. Ferguson

& C. B. Taylor (Eds.), *The comprehensive handbook of behavioral medicine: Syndromes and special areas* (Vol. 2). New York: Spectrum, 1981.

Epstein, L. H., Katz, R. C., & Zlutnick, S. Behavioral medicine. In M. Hersen, R. M. Eisler, & P. M. Miller (Eds.), *Progress in behavior modification*. New York: Academic Press, 1979.

Epstein, L. H., & Masek, B. J. Behavioral control of medical compliance. *Journal of Applied Behavioral Analysis,* 1978, *11*, 1–9.

Epstein, L. H., & Ossip, D. Health-care delivery. In J. R. McNamara (Ed.), *Behavioral approaches to medicine: Application and analysis*. New York: Plenum Press, 1979.

Erskine-Milliss, J., & Schonell, M. Relaxation therapy in asthma: A critical review. *Psychosomatic Medicine,* 1981, *43*, 365–372.

Esler, M. Julius, S., Zweifler, A., Randall, O., Harburg, E., Gardiner, H., & Dequahro, V. Mild high renin? essential hypertension and neurogenic human hypertension. *New England Journal of Medicine,* 1977, *296* (8), 405–411.

Fairburn, J. F., Juergens, J. L., & Spittell, J. A., Jr. (Eds.). *Allen, Barker, & Hines: Peripheral vascular diseases*. Philadelphia: W. B. Saunders, 1972.

Feinstein, A., Wood, H., Epstein, J., Taranta, A., Simpson, R., & Tursky, E. A controlled study of the three methods of prophylaxis against streptococcal infection in a population of rheumatic children. *New England Journal of Medicine,* 1959, *260*, 697.

Feldman, G. M. The effect of biofeedback training on respiratory resistance of asthmatic children. *Psychosomatic Medicine,* 1976, *38*, 27–34.

Feuerstein, M., & Ward, M. M. Psychological treatment of cardiac arrhythmias. In J. M. Ferguson, & C. B. Taylor (Eds.), *The comprehensive handbook of behavioral medicine: Systems interventions* (Vol. 1). New York: Spectrum, 1980.

Finley, W. W., Besserman, R. L., Bennett, L. F., Clapp, R. K., & Finley, P. M. The effect of continuous, intermittent, and "placebo" reinforcement on the effectiveness of the conditioning treatment for enuresis nocturna. *Behavior Research and Therapy,* 1973, *11*, 289–297.

Finnerty, F., Jr. New techniques for improving patient compliance. *The hypertension handbook*. West Point, Pa.: Merck, Sharp & Dohme, 1974.

Fitzgerald, J. F. Encopresis, soiling, constipation: What's to be done? *Pediatrics,* 1975, *56*, 348–349.

Foa, E. B., & Goldstein, A. Continuous exposure and complete-response prevention in the treatment of obsessive-compulsive neurosis. *Behavior Therapy,* 1978, *9*, 821–829.

Fordyce, W. F. *Behavioral methods for chronic pain and illness*. St. Louis: C. V. Mosby, 1976.

Fordyce, W. F., Fowler, R. S., & Delateur, B. An application of behavior-modification techniques to a problem of chronic pain. *Behavior Research and Therapy,* 1968, *6*, 105–107.

Forster, F. M. The classification and conditioning treatment of the reflex epilepsies. *International Journal of Neurology,* 1972, *9*, 73–86.

Fowler, J., Budzynski, T., & Vandenbergh, R. Effects of an EMG-biofeedback relaxation program on the control of diabetes: A case study. *Biofeedback and Self-Regulation,* 1976, *1*, 105–112.

Fowler, R. Operant therapy for headache. *Headache,* 1975, *15*, 63–68.

Foxx, R. M., & Azrin, N. H. Dry pants: A rapid method of toilet training children. *Behavior Research and Therapy,* 1973, *11,* 435–442.

Francis, V., Korsch, B. M., & Morris, M. J. Gaps in doctor-patient communication: Patients' responses to medical advice. *New England Journal of Medicine,* 1969, *280,* 535–540.

French, T. M., & Alexander, F. Psychogenic factors in bronchial asthma. *Psychosomatic Medicine Monographs,* 1941, *4.*

Friedman, A. Reflection on the problem of headache. *Journal of the American Medical Association,* 1964, *190,* 121–123.

Friedman, S. Self-control in the treatment of Gilles de la Tourette syndrome: Case study with 18-month follow-up. *Journal of Consulting and Clinical Psychology,* 1980, *48,* 400–402.

Furman, S. Intestinal biofeedback in functional diarrhea: A preliminary report. *Journal of Behavior Therapy and Experimental Psychiatry,* 1973, *4,* 317–321.

Gannt, W. H., & B. F. Skinner and his contingencies. *Conditional Reflex,* 1970, *5,* 63–74.

Gerbert, B. Psychological aspects of Crohn's disease. *Journal of Behavioral Medicine,* 1980, *3,* 41–58.

Giles, D. K., & Wolf, M. M. Toilet training institutionalized severe retardates. *American Journal of Mental Deficiency,* 1966, *70,* 766–780.

Glogaw, E. Effects of health-education methods on appointment breaking. *Public Health Reports,* 1970, *85,* 441–450.

Goldberg, S. C., Halmi, K. A., Eckert, E. D., Casper, R. C., & Davis, J. M. Cyproheptadine in anorexia nervosa. *British Journal of Psychiatry,* 1979, *134,* 67–70.

Goldsmith, H. Chronic loss of bowel control in a nine-year-old child. *American Journal of Clinical Hypnosis,* 1962, *4,* 191–192.

Gordis, L. Methodologic issues in the measurement of patient compliance. In D. L. Sackett & R. B. Haynes (Eds.), *Compliance with therapeutic regimens.* Baltimore: Johns Hopkins University Press, 1976.

Greenspan, K., Lawrence, D. F., Esposito, D. B., & Vorhees, A. B. The role of biofeedback and relaxation therapy in arterial occulsive disease. *Journal of Surgical Research,* 1980, *29,* 387–394.

Groves, J. W., & Mares, A. A means of effecting decannulation after tracheostomy. *Archives of Laryngology and Otology,* 1963, *77,* 937–942.

Hagen, R. L. Behavioral treatment of obesity: Progress but not panacea. In J. M. Ferguson & C. B. Taylor (Eds.), *The comprehensive handbook of behavioral medicine: Syndromes and special areas* (Vol. 2). New York: Spectrum, 1980.

Harrell, J. P. Psychological factors and hypertension: A status report. *Psychological Bulletin,* 1980, *87,* 482–501.

Harrison, R. Psychological testing in headache: A review. *Headache,* 1975, *15,* 177–185.

Hatcher, R. P. Treatment of food refusal in a two-year-old child. *Journal of Behavior Therapy and Experimental Psychiatry,* 1979, *10,* 363–367.

Haupt, B. J. *Utilization of short-stay hospitals: Annual summary for the United States, 1978* (DHEW Publication No. 80–1797). Washington, D.C.: U.S. Government Printing Office, 1980.

Hayes, S. C. Single-case experimental design and empirical clinical practice. *Journal of Consulting and Clinical Psychology,* 1981, *49,* 193–211.

Haynes, R. B., & Sackett, D. L. An annotated bibliography on the compliance of patients with therapeutic regimens. In D. L. Sackett and R. B. Haynes (Eds.), *Compliance with therapeutic regimens: Appendix I.* Baltimore: Johns Hopkins University Press, 1976.

Haynes, R. B., Sackett, D. L., Gibson, E. S., Taylor, D. W., Hackett, B. C., Roberts, R. S., & Johnson, A. L. Improvement of medication compliance in uncontrolled hypertension. *Lancet,* 1976, *1,* 1265–1268.

Haynes, S., Griffin, P., Mooney, D., & Parise, M. Electromyographic biofeedback and relaxation instruction in the treatment of muscle-contraction headaches. *Behavior Therapy,* 1975, *6,* 672–678.

Hedberg, A. G. The treatment of chronic diarrhea by systematic desensitization: A case report. *Journal of Behavior Therapy and Experimental Psychiatry,* 1973, *4,* 67–68.

Heron, G. B., & Johnston, D. A. Hypothalmic tumor presenting as anorexia nervosa. *American Journal of Psychiatry,* 1976, *133,* 580–582.

Hersen, M. Complex problems require complex solutions. *Behavior Therapy,* 1981, *12,* 15–29.

Hersen, M., & Barlow, D. *Single-case experimental designs: Strategies for studying behavior change.* Elmsford, N.Y.: Pergamon Press, 1976.

Hieb, E., & Wang, R. I. H. Compliance: The patient's role in drug therapy. *Wisconsin Medical Journal,* 1974, *73,* 152–153.

Hock, R. A., Rodgers, C. H., Reddi, C. L., & Kennard, D. W. Mediopsychological interventions in male asthmatic children: An evaluation of physiological change. *Psychosomatic Medicine,* 1978, *40,* 210–215.

Holden, C. Behavioral medicine: An emergent field. *Science,* 1980, *209,* 479–481.

Holroyd, K. A., & Andrasik, F. Coping and the self-control of chronic tension headache. *Journal of Consulting and Clinical Psychology,* 1978, *46,* 1036–1045.

Holroyd, K. A., & Andrasik, F. *Do the effects of cognitive therapy endure? A two-year follow-up of tension-headache sufferers treated with cognitive therapy or biofeedback.* Paper presented at the American Association of Behavior Therapy annual convention, New York, 1980.

Holroyd, K. A., Andrasik, F., & Noble, J. A comparison of EMG biofeedback and a credible pseudotherapy in treating tension headache. *Journal of Behavioral Medicine,* 1980, *3,* 29–39.

Holroyd, K. A., Andrasik, F., & Westbrook, T. Cognitive control of tension headache. *Cognitive Therapy and Research,* 1977, *1,* 121–133.

Huber, G. L. Indications for pulmonary functions tests and blood gast studies in asthma. In T. L. Petty (Ed.), *The asthmatic patient in trouble.* Greenwich, Conn.: Upjohn, 1975.

Humphrey, G. B. Personal communication, 1982.

Hutzell, R. R., Platzek, D., & Logue, P. E. Control of symptoms of Gilles de la Tourette syndrome by self-monitoring. *Journal of Behavioral Therapy and Experimental Psychiatry,* 1974, *5,* 71–76.

Ikemi, Y., & Nakagawa, S. A psychosomatic study of contagious dermatitis. *Kyushu Journal of Medical Science,* 1962, *13,* 335–350.

Ingersoll, B. F., & Curry, F. Rapid treatment of persistence, vomiting in a 14-year-old female by shaping and time-out. *Journal of Behavior Therapy and Experimental Psychiatry,* 1977, *8,* 305–307.

Ingram, J. T. Some aspects of the treatment of skin diseases. *British Medical Journal,* 1948, *1,* 187–191.

Janis, I. L. *Psychological stress.* New York: John Wiley & Sons, 1958.

Janowsky, J. S., Laxer, K. D., & Rushmer, D. S. Classical conditioning of kindled seizures. *Epilepsia,* 1980, *21,* 393–398.

Jay, S. M., & Elliott, C. Assessment and management of pain in pediatric cancer patients. In G. B. Hemphrey, L. P. Dehner, G. B. Grindey, & R. T. Acton (Eds.), *Pediatric oncology* (Vol. 3). Boston: Martinus Nishoff, in press.

Jay, S. M., Elliott, C., Olson, R., & Ozolins, M. *Reduction of distress in pediatric cancer patients undergoing painful medical procedures using behavior-therapy techniques.* Unpublished manuscript, Oklahoma University, 1982.

Johnson, A. L., Taylor, D. W., Sackett, D. L., Dunnett, C. W., & Shimizu, A. G. Self-blood-pressure-recording: An aid to blood pressure control? *Annals of the Royal College of Physicians and Surgeons of Canada,* 1977, *10,* 32–36.

Johnson, J. E. Stress reduction through sensation information. In I. G. Sarason & C. C. Spielberger (Eds.), *Stress and anxiety* (Vol. 2). New York: Hemisphere, 1975.

Johnson, J. E., & Leventhal, H. Effects of accurate expectations and behavioral instructions on reactions during a noxious medical examination. *Journal of Personality and Social Psychology,* 1974, *29,* 710–718.

Johnson, J. E., Rice, V. H., Fuller, S. S., & Endress, P. Sensory information, instruction in a coping strategy, and recovery from surgery. *Registered Nursing Health,* 1978, *1,* 4–17.

Johnson, R., & Machen, J. B. Behavior-modification techniques and maternal anxiety. *Journal of Dentistry for Children,* 1973, *40,* 272–276.

Johnson, S. B. Psychosocial factors in juvenile diabetes: A review. *Journal of Behavioral Medicine,* 1980, *3,* 95–113.

Jorgensen, R. S., Houston, B. K., & Zurawski, R. M. Anxiety-management training in the treatment of essential hypertension. *Behavior Research and Therapy,* 1981, *19,* 467–474.

Joyce, C. R. B., Capla, G., Mason, M., Reynolds, E., & Matthews, J. A. Quantitative study of doctor-patient communication. *Quarterly Journal of Medicine,* 1969, *38,* 183–194.

Kallman, W. M., & Gilmore, J. D. Vascular disorders. In S. M. Turner, K. S. Calhoun, & H. E. Adams (Eds.), *Handbook of clinical behavior therapy.* New York: John Wiley & Sons, 1981.

Kahn, A. U., & Olson, D. L. Deconditioning of exercise-induced asthma. *Psychosomatic Medicine,* 1977, *39,* 382–392.

Kahn, A., Staerk, M., & Bonk, C. Role of counterconditioning in the treatment of asthma. *Journal of Psychosomatic Research,* 1974, *18,* 89–92.

Kannel, W. B., Gordon, T., & Schwartz, M. J. Systolic versus diastolic blood pressure and risk of coronary heart disease. *American Journal of Cardiology,* 1971, *27,* 335–343.

Kasl, S. V. Issues in patient adherence to health-care regimens. *Journal of Human Stress,* 1975, *1,* 5–17.

Katses, H., Glans, K. D., Crawford, P. L., Edwards, J. E., & Scherr, M. S. Operant reduction of frontalis EMG activity in the treatment of asthma in children. *Journal of Psychosomatic Research,* 1976, *20,* 453–459.

Katz, E. R., Kellerman, J., & Siegel, S. E. Behavioral distress in children with cancer undergoing medical procedures: Developmental considerations. *Journal of Consulting and Clinical Psychology,* 1980, *48,* 356–365.

Keefe, F. J., Surwit, F. S., & Pilon, R. N. Biofeedback autogenic training, and progressive relaxation in the treatment of Raynaud's disease: A comparative study. *Journal of Applied Behavioral Analysis,* 1980, *13,* 3–11.

Kellerman, J. Anorexia nervosa: The efficacy of behavior therapy. *Journal of Behavior Therapy and Experimental Psychiatry,* 1977, *8,* 387–390.

Kendall, P., & Korgeski, G. Assessment and cognitive-behavioral interventions. *Cognitive Therapy and Research,* 1979, *3,* 1–22.

Kendall, P. C., Williams, L., Pachacek, T. F., Graham, L. E., Shisslak, C., & Herzoff, N. Cognitive-behavioral and patient-education interventions in cardiac catherization procedures: The Palo Alto medical psychology project. *Journal of Consulting and Clinical Psychology,* 1979, *47,* 49–58.

Keys, A., Taylor, H. L., Blackburn, H., Brozek, J., Anderson, J. T., & Simonson, E. Mortality and coronary heart disease among men studied for 23 years. *Archives of Internal Medicine,* 1971, *128,* 201–214.

Kimmel, H. D., & Kimmel, E. An instrumental-conditioning method for the treatment of enuresis. *Journal of Behavior Therapy and Experimental Psychiatry,* 1970, *1,* 121–123.

King, N. J. The behavioral management of asthma and asthma-related problems in children: A critical review of the literature. *Journal of Behavioral Medicine,* 1980, *3,* 169–189.

Kirscht, J. P., & Rosenstock, I. M. Patient's problems in following the recommendations of health experts. In G. C. Stone, F. Cohen, & N. E. Adler (Eds.), *Health psychology.* San Francisco: Jossey-Bass, 1979.

Knapp, T. J., & Wells, L. A. Behavior therapy for asthma: A review. *Behavior Research and Therapy,* 1978, *16,* 103–115.

Kolata, G. B. Is labile hypertension a myth? *Science,* 1979, *204,* 489.

Korsch, B. M., & Negrete, V. F. Doctor-patient communication. *Scientific American,* 1972, *227,* 66–74.

Krajewski, T. F. Psychogenic regurgitation: A specific entity and suggested treatment. *Journal of Behavior Therapy and Experimental Psychiatry,* 1980, *11,* 263–266.

Kremsdorf, R. B. *Biofeedback and cognitive-skills training: An evaluation of their relative efficacy.* Paper presented at the Biofeedback Society of America, 1978.

Lahey, B., McNees, P., & McNees, M. Control of an obscene "verbal tic" through time-out in an elementary school classroom. *Journal of Applied Behavior Analysis,* 1973, *6,* 101–104.

Lang, P. J., & Melamed, D. G. Case report: Avoidance-conditioning therapy of an infant with chronic ruminative vomiting. *Journal of Abnormal Psychology,* 1969, *74,* 1–9.

Langer, E. J., Janis, I. L., & Wolfer, J. A. Reduction of psychological stress in surgical patients. *Journal of Experimental Social Psychology,* 1975, *11,* 155–165.

Leshner, A. I. A model of hormones and agonistic behavior. *Physiological Behavior,* 1975, *15,* 225–235.

Levine, M. D. Children with encopresis: A descriptive analysis. *Pediatrics,* 1975, *56,* 412–416.

Ley, P., Bradshaw, P. W., Eaves, D., & Walker, C. M. A method for increasing patients' recall of information presented by doctors. *Psychological Medicine,* 1973, *3,* 217–220.

Lieberman, E. Pediatric hypertension. In *Hypertension update: Mechanisms, epidemiology, evaluation, management.* Bloomfield, N.J.: Health Learning Systems, 1980.

Liebman, R., Minuchin, S., & Baker, L. The role of the family in the treatment. *Journal of the American Academy of Child Psychiatry,* 1974, *13,* 264–274.

Light, K. C. Cardiovascular responses to effortful active coping: Implications for the role of stress in hypertension development. *Psychophysiology,* 1981, *18,* (3), 216–225.

Linden, W. Multi-component behavior in a case of compulsive binge-eating followed by vomiting. *Behavior Therapy and Experience Psychiatry,* 1980, *11,* 297–300.

Linden, W., & Feuerstein, M. Essential hypertension and social-coping behavior. *Journal of Human Stress,* 1981, *7,* 28–34.

Love, U. A., Montgomery, D. C., & Moeller, T. A. (Working Paper 1). Thesis, Nova University Hospital, Ft. Lauderdale, 1974.

Lovibond, S. H. *Conditioning and enuresis.* New York: Macmillan, 1964.

Lovibond, S. H., & Coote, M. A. Enuresis. In C. G. Costello (Ed.), *Symptoms of psychopathology: A handbook.* New York: John Wiley & Sons, 1970.

Lubar, J. F. Behavioral management of epilepsy through sensorimotor rhythm: EEG-biofeedback conditioning. *National Spokesman,* 1975, *June,* 6–7.

Lundey, J., Lovett, E. J., Wolinski, S. M., & Conran, P. Immune impairment and metastic tumor growth. *Psychological Bulletin,* 1981, *89,* 369–406.

Lynch, F. W., Hinckley, R. G., & Cowan, D. W. Psychosomatic studies in dermatology: B. Psychobiologic studies of patients with atopic eczema (disseminated neuridermatitis). *Archives of Dermatology and Syphiology,* 1945, *51,* 251–260.

Lynch, J. J., Long, J. M., Thomas, S. A., Malinow, K. L., & Katcher, A. H. The effects of talking on the blood pressure of hypertensive and normotensive individuals. *Psychosomatic Medicine,* 1981, *43,* 25–33.

Maas, J. W. Biogenicamines and depression: Biochemical and pharmacological separation of two types of depression. *Archives of General Psychology,* 1975, *32,* 1357–1361.

Machen, J. B., & Johnson, R. Desensitization, model learning, and the dental behavior of children. *Journal of Dental Research,* 1974, *53,* 83–87.

Mahoney, D. T., Laferte, R. O., & Mahoney, S. E. Observation on sphincter-augmenting effect of imipramine in children with urinary incontinence. *Urology,* 1973, *1,* 317–323.

Maloney, M. J., & Farrell, M. K. Treatment of severe weight loss in anorexia nervosa with hyperalimentation and psychotherapy. *American Journal of Psychiatry,* 1980, *137,* 310–314.

Mann, R. A. The behavior-therapeutic use of contingency contracting to control an adult-behavior problem: Weight control. *Journal of Applied Behavioral Analysis,* 1972, *5,* 99–109.

Manuck, S. B., Harvey, A. H., Lechleiter, S. L., & Neal, K. S. Effects of coping on blood pressure responses to threat of aversive stimulation. *Psychophysiology,* 1978, *15,* 544–549.

Marston, M. Compliance with medical regimens: A review of the literature. *Nursing Research,* 1970, *19,* 312–323.

Mash, E. J. & Terdal, L. G. Behavioral assessment of childhood disturbance. In E. J. Mash

& L. G. Terdal (Eds.), *Behavioral assessment of childhood disorders.* New York: Guilford Press, 1981.

McConaghy, N. A controlled trial of imipramine, amphetamine, pad-and-bell conditioning, and random awakening in the treatment of nocturnal enuresis. *Medical Journal of Australia,* 1969, *2,* 237–239.

McFadden, E. R., Jr., Kiser, R., & deGroot, W. J. Acute bronchial asthma: Relations between clinical and physiological manifestations. *New England Journal of Medicine,* 1973, *288,* 221–225.

McGlynn, F. D. Successful treatment of anorexia nervosa with self-monitoring and long distance praise. *Journal of Behavior Therapy and Experimental Psychiatry,* 1980, *11,* 283–286.

McNamara, J. R. (Ed.). *Behavioral approaches to medicine application and analysis.* New York: Plenum Press, 1979.

Meadow, R. Drugs for bed-wetting. *Archives of Disease in Childhood,* 1974, *49,* 257.

Meichenbaum, D., & Butler, L. Cognitive ethology: Assessing the streams of cognition and emotion. In K. Blankstein, P. Pliner, & J. Polivy (Eds.), *Advances in the study of communication and affect: Assessment and modification of emotional behavior* (Vol. 6). New York: Plenum Press, 1979.

Melamed, B. G., Hawes, R., Heivy, E., & Glick, J. The use of filmed modeling to reduce uncooperative behavior in children during dental treatment. *Journal of Dental Research,* 1975, *54,* 797–801.

Melamed, B. G., & Siegel, L. J. Reduction of anxiety in children facing hospitalization and surgery by use of filmed modeling. *Journal of Consulting and Clinical Psychology,* 1975, *43,* 511–521.

Melamed, B. G., & Siegel, L. J. Designing, implementing, and evaluating a behavioral-intervention program. *Behavioral medicine: Practical applications in health care.* New York: Springer, 1980.

Melamed, B. G., Weinstein, D., Hawes, R., & Katin-Borland, M. Reduction of fear-related dental-management problems using filmed modeling. *Journal of American Dental Association,* 1975, *90,* 822–826.

Merrill, J. P. Hypertensive vascular disease. In J. V. Harrison, R. D. Adams, T. L. Bennett, W. H. Resnik, G. W. Thorn, & M. M. Wintrobe (Eds.), *Principles of internal medicine.* New York: McGraw-Hill, 1966.

Miklich, D. R., Renne, C. M., Creer, T. L., Alexander, A. B., Chai, H., Davis, M. H., Hoffman, A., & Danker-Brown, P. The clinical utility of behavior therapy as an adjunctive treatment for asthma. *The Journal of Allergy and Clinical Immunology,* 1977, *60,* 285–294.

Miller, A. L. Treatment of a child with Gilles de la Tourettes syndrome using behavior-modification techniques. *Journal of Behavioral Therapy and Experimental Psychiatry,* 1970, *1,* 319–321.

Miller, M. L. Psychodynamic mechanisms in a case of neurodermatitis. *Psychosomatic Medicine,* 1948, *10,* 309–316.

Miller, N. E. President's column. *The Health Psychologist,* 1981, *3,* 1.

Miller, R. M., Coger, R. W., & Dymonal, A. M. Biofeedback skin-conductance conditioning in dyshydrotic eczema. *Archives of Dermatology,* 1974, *109,* 737–738.

Minuchin, S., Baker, L., Rosman, B., Liebman, R., Milman, L., & Todd, T. A. Conceptual model of psychosomatic illness in children. *Archives of General Psychology,* 1975, *32,* 1031–1038.

Minuchin, S., Rosman, B., & Baker, L. *Psychosomatic families.* Cambridge, Mass.: Harvard University Press, 1978.

Mitchell, K. R. A note on the treatment of migraine using behavior-therapy techniques. *Psychological Reports,* 1971, *28,* 172–191.

Mitchell, K. R., & Mitchell, D. M. Migraine: An exploratory-treatment application of programmed behavior-therapy techniques. *Journal of Psychosomatic Research,* 1971, *15,* 137–157.

Mitchell, K. R., & White, R. G. Behavioral self-management: An application to the problem of migraine headaches. *Behavior Therapy,* 1977, *8,* 213–221.

Moore, N. Behavior therapy in bronchial asthma: A controlled study. *Journal of Psychosomatic Research,* 1965, *9,* 257–276.

Morgan, J., & O'Brien, J. S. The counterconditioning of a vomiting habit by sips of ginger ale. *Journal of Behavior Therapy and Experimental Psychiatry,* 1972, *3,* 135–137.

Morgan, L. Relapse and therapeutic response in the conditioning treatment of enuresis: A review of recent findings on intermittent reinforcement, overlearning, and stimulus intensity. *Behavior Research and Therapy,* 1978, *16,* 273–279.

Moser, M. Report of the Joint National Committee on Detection, Evaluation, and Treatment of High Blood Pressure: A cooperative study. *Journal of the American Medical Association,* 1977, *237,* 255–261.

Mostofsky, D. I. Epilepsy: Returning the ghost to psychology. *Professional Psychology,* 1978, *9,* 87–92.

Mostofsky, D. I. Recurrent paroxysmal disorders of central nervous system. In S. M. Turner, K. S. Calhoun, & H. E. Adams (Eds.), *Handbook of clinical behavior therapy.* New York: John Wiley & Sons, 1981.

Mostofsky, D. I., & Balaschak, B. A. Psychobiological control of seizures. *Psychological Bulletin,* 1977, *84,* 723–750.

Mowrer, O. H., & Mowrer, W. M. Enuresis—A method for its study and treatment. *American Journal of Orthopsychiatry,* 1938, *8,* 436–459.

Murray, M. E., & Keefe, D. K. Behavioral treatment of ruminations. *Clinical Pediatrics,* 1976, *15,* 591–596.

Musaph, H. Psychodynamics in itching states. *International Journal of Psychoanalysis,* 1968, *49,* 336–340.

Neale, D. H. Behavior therapy and encopresis in children. *Behavior Research Therapy,* 1963, *1,* 139–149.

Neisworth, J. T., & Moore, F. Operant treatment of asthmatic responding with the parent as therapist. *Behavior Therapy,* 1972, *3,* 95–99.

Nilsson, D. E. Treatment of encopresis: A token economy. *Journal of Pediatric Psychology,* 1976, *4,* 42–46.

Norton, R. G., & Neilson, W. R. Headaches: The importance of consequent events. *Behavior Therapy,* 1977, *8,* 504–506.

Ogden, H. D. Headache studies: Statistical data. *Journal of Allergy,* 1952, *23,* 58–75.

Olatawura, M. O. Encopresis: A review of 32 cases. *Acta Paediatrica Scandinavica,* 1973, *62,* 358–364.

Olness, K. Autohypnosis in functional megacolon in children. *American Journal of Clinical Hypnosis,* 1976, *19,* 28–32.

O'Neal, P. M., White, J. L., King, C. R., & Carek, D. J. Controlling childhood rumination through differential reinforcement of other behavior. *Behavior Modification,* 1979, *3,* 355–372.

Palmer, S., Thompson, R. J., & Linscheid, T. R. Applied behavior analysis in the treatment of childhood feeding problems. *Developmental Medicine and Child Neurology,* 1975, *17,* 333–339.

Parcel, G. S., & Meyer, M. P. Development of an instrument to measure children's health locus of control. *Health Education Monitor,* 1978, *6,* 149–159.

Park, L. C., & Lipman, R. S. A comparison of patient dosage-deviation reports with pill counts. *Psychopharmacologic,* 1964, *6,* 299–302.

Patel, C. 12-month follow-up of yoga and biofeedback in the management of hypertension. *Lancet,* 1975, *1,* 62–64.

Patel, C., & North, W. R. Randomized controlled trial of yoga and biofeedback in management of hypertension. *Lancet,* 1975, *2,* 93–95.

Perez-Cruet, J. Conditioning of extraseptoles in humans, with respiratory maneuvers as unconditioned stimuli. *Science,* 1962, *137,* 160–161.

Perschuk, M. J., Edwards, M., & Pomerleau, O. F. *A multiple-baseline approach to behavioral intervention in anorexia nervosa.* Unpublished manuscript, 1978.

Peterson, L., & Shigetomi, C. The use of coping techniques to minimize anxiety in hospitalized children. *Behavior Therapy,* 1981, *12,* 1–14.

Poole, D., & Sanson, R. W. A behavioral program for the management of anorexia nervosa. *Australian and New Zealand Journal of Psychiatry,* 1978, *12,* 49–53.

Price, K., & Blackwell, S. Trait levels of anxiety and psychological response to stress in migraineurs and normal controls. *Journal of Clinical Psychology,* 1980, *36,* 658–660.

Purcell, K., & Weiss, J. H. Asthma. In C. C. Costello (Ed.), *Symptoms of psychopathology.* New York: John Wiley & Sons, 1970.

Rafi, A. A. Learning theory and the treatment of tics. *Journal of Psychosomatics Research,* 1962, *6,* 71–76.

Ratliff, R. G., & Stein, N. H. Treatment of neurodermatitis by behavior therapy: A case study. *Behavior Research and Therapy,* 1968, *6,* 397–399.

Ravitch, M. M. Pseudo Hirschsprung's disease. *Annals of Surgery,* 1958, *147,* 781–795.

Read, C. E., & Townley, R. Asthma: Classification and pathogenesis. In F. Middleton, C. E. Reed, & E. F. Ellis (Eds.), *Allergy: Principles and practice* (Vol. 2). St. Louis: C. V. Mosby, 1978.

Redd, W. H. In vivo desensitization in the treatment of chronic emesis following gastrointestinal surgery. *Behavior Therapy,* 1980, *11,* 421–427.

Redd, W. H., Andresen, G. V., & Nainagawa, R. Y. Hypnotic control by anticipatory emesis in patients receiving cancer chemotherapy. *Journal of Consulting and Clinical Psychology,* 1982, *50,* 14–19.

Rehder, T. L., McCoy, L. K., Blackwell, B., Whitehead, W., & Robinson, A. *Improving compliance by counseling and pill container.* Unpublished manuscript, 1977.

Renne, C. M., & Creer, T. L. The effects of training on the use of inhalation-therapy equipment by children with asthma. *Journal of Applied Behavior Analysis,* 1976, *9,* 1–11.

Renne, C. M., Nau, E., Dietiker, K. E., & Lyon, R. *Latency in seeking asthma treatment as a function of achieving successively higher flow-rate criteria.* Paper presented at the tenth annual convention of the Association for the Advancement of Behavior Therapy, New York, December 1976.

Reyes, S. Personal communication, 1982.

Rickles, K., & Briscoe, E. Assessment of dosage deviation in outpatient drug research. *Journal of Clinical Pharmacology*, 1970, *10*, 153–160.

Riley, V. Psychoneuroendocrine influences on immunocompetence and neoplasia. *Science*, 1981, *212*, 1100–1109.

Risch, E., & Ferguson, J. M. Behavioral treatment of skin disorders. In J. M. Ferguson & C. B. Taylor (Eds.), *The comprehensive handbook of behavioral medicine: Syndromes and special areas* (Vol. 2). New York: Spectrum, 1981.

Rockart, J. F., & Hofmann, P. B. Physician and patient behavior under different scheduling systems in a hospital-outpatient department. *Medical Care*, 1969, *7*, 463–470.

Rosen, J. L., & Leitenberg, H. Bulimia nervosa: Treatment with exposure and response prevention. *Behavior Therapy*, 1982, *13*, 117–124.

Rosen, L. W. Modification of secretive or ritualized eating behavior in anorexia nervosa. *Behavior Therapy and Experimental Psychiatry*, 1980, *11*, 101–104.

Rosenweig, M. R., & Bennett, E. L. How plastic is the nervous system? In J. M. Ferguson & C. B. Taylor (Eds.), *The comprehensive handbook of behavioral medicine: Systems interventions* (Vol. 1). New York: Spectrum, 1980.

Roth, H. P., Caron, H. S., & Hsi, B. P. Measuring intakes of a prescribed medication: A bottle count and tracer technique compared. *Clinical Pharmacology and Therapy*, 1970, *11*, 228–237.

Ruprecht, M. J., Hanson, R. H., Pocrnich, M. A., & Murphy, R. J. Some suggested precautions when using lemon juice (citric acid) in behavior-modification programs. *The Behavior Therapist*, 1980, *3*, 12.

Russo, D. C., Bird, B. L., & Masek, B. J. Assessment issues in behavioral medicine. *Behavioral Assessment*, 1980, *2*, 1–18.

Sackett, D. L., Gibson, E. J., Taylor, D. W., Haynes, R. B., Hackett, B. C., Roberts, R. K., & Johnson, A. L. Randomized clinical trial of strategies for improving medication compliance in primary hypertension. *Lancet*, 1975, *1*, 1205–1207.

Sajwaj, T., Libet, J., & Agras, S. Lemon-juice therapy: The control of life-threatening rumination in a six-month-old infant. *Journal of Applied Behavioral Analysis*, 1974, *7*, 557–563.

Sanders, S. H. Behavioral assessment and treatment of clinical pain: Appraisal of current status. *Progress in Behavior Modification*, 1979, *8*, 249–291.

Schachter, S. Some extraordinary facts about obese humans and rats. *American Psychologist*, 1971, *26*, 129–144.

Schachter, S., & Rodin, J. *Obese humans and rats.* Hillsdale, N.J.: Lawrence Erlbaum Associates, 1974.

Schaefer, C. E., Millman, H. L., & Levine, G. F. *Therapies for psychosomatic disorders in children.* San Francisco: Jossey-Bass, 1979.

Scherr, M. S., Crawford, P. L., Sergent, C. B., & Scherr, C. A. Effects of biofeedback techniques on chronic asthma in a summer-camp environment. *Annals of Allergy*, 1975, *35*, 289–295.

Schmidt, R., & Wilder, B. *Epilepsy.* Philadelphia: F. A. Davis, 1968.

Schulman, M. Control of tics by maternal reinforcement. *Journal of Behavior Therapy and Experimental Psychiatry,* 1974, *5,* 95–96.

Schwartz, G. E. Biofeedback as therapy: Some theoretical and practical issues. *American Psychologist,* 1972, *28,* 666–673.

Seer, P., & Raeburn, J. M. Meditation training and essential hypertension: A methodological study. *Journal of Behavioral Medicine,* 1980, *3,* 59–71.

Segal, M. S. Death in bronchial asthma. In E. B. Weiss & M. S. Segal (Eds.), *Bronchial asthma: Mechanisms and therapeutics.* Boston: Little, Brown, 1976.

Seligman, M. E. *Helplessness: On depression, development, and death.* San Francisco: W. H. Freeman, 1975.

Shaffer, D. Enuresis. In M. Rutter & L. Herson (Eds.), *Child psychiatry: Modern approaches.* Philadelphia: Blackwell Scientific Publications, 1977.

Shamerak, K. L. Reduce your broken-appointment rate: How one children-and-youth project reduced its broken-appointment rate. *American Journal of Public Health,* 1971, *61,* 2400–2404.

Shapiro, A. K., Shapiro, E. S., Brunn, R. D., & Sweet, R. D. *Gilles de la Tourette syndrome.* New York: Raven Press, 1978.

Shapiro, D. Biofeedback and behavioral medicine in perspective. *Biofeedback and Self-Regulation,* 1979, *4,* 371–378.

Shapiro, D., Schwartz, G. E., Ferguson, C. E., Redmon, D. P., & Weiss, S. M. Behavioral methods in the treatment of hypertension. *Annals of Internal Medicine,* 1977, *86,* 626–636.

Shapiro, D., & Surwit, R. S. Learned control of physiological function and disease. In H. Leitenberg (Ed.), *Handbook of behavior modification and behavior therapy.* Englewood Cliffs, N.J.: Prentice-Hall, 1976.

Shapiro, D., Tursky, B., Gershon, E., & Stern, M. Effects of feedback and reinforcement on the control of human systolic blood pressure. *Science,* 1969, *163,* 588–590.

Sharpe, T. R., & Mikeal, R. Patient compliance with antibiotic regimens. *American Journal of Hospital Pharmacy,* 1974, *31,* 479–484.

Shipley, R. H., Butt, J. H., & Horowitz, B. A. Preparation to reexperience a stressful medical examination: Effect of repetitious videotape exposure and coping style. *Journal of Consulting and Clinical Psychology,* 1979, *47,* 485–492.

Siegel, L. J., & Peterson, L. Stress reduction in young dental patients through coping skills and sensory information. *Journal of Consulting and Clinical Psychology,* 1980, *48,* 785–787.

Siegel, S. C., Katz, R., & Rachelefsky, G. S. Asthma in infancy and childhood. In E. Middleton, Jr., C. E. Reed, & E. F. Ellis (Eds.), *Allergy: Principles and practice.* St. Louis: C. V. Mosby, 1978.

Silver, B. V., & Blanchard, E. B. Biofeedback and relaxation training in the treatment of psychophysiologic disorders: Or, are the machines really necessary? *Journal of Behavioral Medicine,* 1978, *1,* 217–239.

Singer, M. T. Psychological dimensions in psychosomatic patients. *Psychotherapy and Psychosomatics,* 1977, *23,* 13–27.

Sirota, A. D. & Mahoney, M. J. Relaxing on cue: The self-regulation of asthma. *Journal of Behavior Therapy and Experimental Psychiatry,* 1974, *5,* 65–66.

Sklar, L. S., & Anisman, H. Stress and cancer. *Psychological Bulletin,* 1981, *89,* 369–406.

Snider, G. L. The interrelationships of asthma, chronic bronchitis, and emphysema. In E. B. Weiss & M. S. Segal (Eds.), *Bronchial asthma: Mechanism and therapeutics.* Boston: Little, Brown, 1976.

Soutter, B. R. & Kennedy, M. B. Patient compliance assessment in drug trials: Usage and methods. *Australian and New Zealand Journal of Medicine,* 1974, *4,* 360–364.

Spergel, S. M. Induced-vomiting treatment of acute compulsive vomiting. *Journal of Behavior Therapy and Experimental Psychiatry,* 1975, *6,* 85–86.

Spittell, J. A., Jr. Raynaud's phenomenon and allied vasospastic conditions. In J. F. Fairburn, J. L. Juergens, & J. A. Spittell, Jr. (Eds.), *Allen, Barker, & Hines: Peripheral vascular diseases.* Philadelphia: W. B. Saunders, 1972.

Starfield, B. Functional bladder capacity in enuretic and nonenuretic children. *Journal of Pediatrics,* 1967, *70,* 777–782.

Starfield, B., & Mellits, E. D. Increase in functional bladder capacity and improvements in enuresis. *Journal of Pediatrics,* 1968, *72,* 483–487.

Sterman, M. B., Howe, R. C., & MacDonald, L. R. Facilitation of spindle-burst sleep by conditioning of electroencephalographic activity while awake. *Science,* 1970, *167,* 1146–1148.

Stewart, R. B., & Cluff, L. E. Commentary: A review of medication errors and compliance in ambulant patients. *Clinical Pharmacology and Therapy,* 1972, *13,* 463–468.

Strassberg, D. S., Reimherr, F., Ward, M., Russell, S., & Cole, A. The MMPI and chronic pain. *Journal of Consulting and Clinical Psychology,* 1981, *49,* 220–226.

Stratton, R. Behavior therapy in treatment of hypertension: State of the art. *Biological Psychology Bulletin,* 1978, *5,* 104–112.

Strickland, B. R. Internal-external expectancies and health-related behaviors. *Journal of Consulting and Clinical Psychology,* 1978, *46,* 1192–1211.

Stunkard, A. New therapies for the eating disorders: Behavior modification of obesity and anorexia nervosa. *Archives of General Psychiatry,* 1972, *26,* 391–398.

Surwit, R. S., Pilon, R., & Fenton, C. H. Behavioral treatment of Raynaud's disease. *Journal of Behavioral Medicine,* 1978, *1,* 323–335.

Swanson, D. W., Swenson, W. M., Huizenga, K. A., & Melson, S. J. Persistent nausea without organic cause. *Mayo Clinic Proceedings,* 1976, *51,* 257–262.

Tal, A., & Miklich, D. R. Emotionally induced decreases in pulmonary flow rates in asthmatic children. *Psychosomatic Medicine,* 1976, *38,* 190–200.

Tarnow, J. D., & Silverman, S. W. The psychophysiological aspects of stress in juvenile diabetes mellitus. *International Journal of Psychiatry in Medicine,* 1981–82, *11,* 25–44.

Tasto, D. L., & Chesney, M. Muscle-relaxation treatment for primary dysmenorrhea. *Behavior Therapy,* 1974, *5,* 668–672.

Taylor, C. B. Behavioral approaches to hypertension. In R. M. Ferguson & C. B. Taylor (Eds.), *The comprehensive handbook of behavioral medicine: Systems intervention* (Vol.1). New York: Spectrum, 1980.(a)

Taylor, C. B. The gastrointestinal system: Practices and promises of behavioral approaches. In J. M. Ferguson & C. B. Taylor (Eds.), *The comprehensive handbook of behavioral medicine: Syndromes and special areas* (Vol. 2). New York: Spectrum, 1980.(b)

Thomas, E. J., Abrams, K. S., & Johnson, J. B. Self-monitoring and reciprocal inhibition in the modification of multiple tics of Gilles de la Tourette syndrome. *Journal of Behavioral Therapy and Experimental Psychiatry,* 1971, *2,* 159–171.

Thompson, R. J., O'Quinn, A. N., & Logue, P. E. Gilles de la Tourette syndrome: A review and neuropsychological aspects of four cases. *Journal of Pediatric Psychology,* 1979, *4,* 371–388.

Thompson, R. J., Palmer, S., & Linscheid, T. R. Single-subject design and interaction analysis in the behavioral treatment of a child with a feeding problem. *Child Psychiatry and Human Development,* 1977, *8,* 43–53.

Toister, R. P., Condron, L. W., & Arthur, D. Faradic therapy of chronic vomiting in infancy: A case study. *Journal of Behavior Therapy and Experimental Psychiatry,* 1975, *6,* 55–59.

Twaddle, A. C., & Sweet, R. H. Factors leading to preventable hospital admissions. *Medical Care,* 1970, *8,* 200.

U.S. Public Health Service. National conference on high blood pressure education: Report of proceedings. Washington, D.C.: U.S. Government Printing Office, 1973.

Vachon, L., & Rich, E. S. Visceral learning in asthma. *Psychosomatic Medicine,* 1976, *38,* 122–130.

Van Buskirk, J. S. A two-phase perspective on the treatment of anorexia nervosa. *Psychological Bulletin,* 1977, *84,* 529–538.

Venebals, A. W. Tracheostomy in childhood. *Medical Journal of Australia,* 1959, *17,* 141–143.

Vernon, D. T., & Bigelowe, D. Effect of information about a potentially stressful situation on response to stress impact. *Journal of Personality and Social Psychology,* 1974, *29,* 50–59.

Vernon, D. T., Foley, F. M., Sipowicz, R. R., & Schalman, J. L. *The psychological responses of children to hospitalization and illness.* Springfield, Ill.: Charles C Thomas, 1965.

Walker, C. E. Enuresis and encopresis. In P. Magrab (Ed.), *Psychological management of pediatric problems.* Baltimore: University Park Press, 1978.

Walker, C. E. Treatment of children's disorders by relaxation training: The poor man's biofeedback. *Journal of Clinical Child Psychology,* 1979, *Spring,* 22–25.

Walker, C. E. Personal communication, 1982.

Watson, P. L., Tharp, R. G. & Knisberg, J. Case study in self-modification: Suppression of inflammatory scratching while awake and asleep. *Journal of Behavior Therapy and Experimental Psychiatry,* 1972, *3,* 213–215.

Weintraub, M., Au., W. Y. W., & Lasagna, L. Compliance as a determinant of serum digoxin concentration. *Journal of the American Medical Association,* 1973, *224,* 481–485.

Weisenberg, M. Pain and pain control. *Psychological Bulletin,* 1977, *84,* 1008–1044.

Weiss, T., & Engel, B. T. Operant conditioning of heart rate in patients with premature ventricular contractions. *Psychosomatic Medicine,* 1971, *33,* 301–312.

Wells, K. C., Turner, S. M., Bellack, A. S., & Hersen, M. Effects of cue-controlled relaxation on psychomotor seizures: An experimental analysis. *Behavior Research and Therapy,* 1978, *16,* 51–53.

Wernick, R. L., Jaremko, M. E., & Taylor, P. W. Pain management in severely burned adults: A test of stress innoculation. *Journal of Behavioral Medicine,* 1981, *4,* 103–109.

White, I. H., Kelly, P., & Dorman, K. Clinical picture of atypical anorexia nervosa associated with hypothalmic tumor. *American Journal of Psychiatry,* 1977, *134,* 323–325.

White, J. G. The use of learning theory in the psychological treatment of children. *Journal of Clinical Psychology,* 1959, *15,* 227–229.

White, W., Akers, J., Green, J., & Yates, D. Use of imitation in the treatment of dental phobias in early childhood: A preliminary report. *Journal of Dentistry for Children,* 1974, *26,* 106.

Whitehead, W. E., Blackwell, B., DeSilva, H., & Robinson, A. Anxiety and anger in hypertension. *Journal of Psychosomatic Research,* 1977, *21,* 383–389.

Williams, R. B. Headache. In R. B. Williams & W. D. Gentry (Eds.). *Behavioral approaches to medicine.* Cambridge, Mass.: Ballinger Publishing, 1977.

Willis, D. J., Elliott, C. H., & Jay, S. Psychological effects of physical illness and its concomitants. In J. M. Tuma (Ed.), *Handbook for the practice of pediatric psychology.* New York: John Wiley & Sons, 1982.

Wilson, J. F. Behavioral preparation for surgery: Benefit or harm. *Journal of Behavioral Medicine,* 1981, *4,* 79–102.

Wolcott, D. L., Wellisch, D. K., Robertson, C. R. & Arthur, R. J. Serum gastrin and the family environment in duodenal ulcer cases. *Psychosomatic Medicine,* 1981, *43,* 501–507.

Wolpe, J. *Psychotherapy by reciprocal inhibition.* Stanford: Stanford University Press, 1958.

Wolpe, J. Behavior therapy in anorexia nervosa and in general. *Journal of the American Medical Association,* 1975, 233.

Woods, S. C., & Burchfield, S. R. Conditioned endocrine responses. In J. M. Ferguson & C. B. Taylor (Eds.), *The comprehensive handbook of behavioral medicine: Systems interventions* (Vol. 1). New York: Spectrum, 1980.

Wright, D. F., Brown, R. A., & Andrews, M. E. Remission of chronic ruminative vomiting through a reversal of social contingencies. *Behavior Research and Therapy.* 1978, *16,* 134–135.

Wright, L. Conditioning of consumatory responses in young children. *Journal of Clinical Psychology,* 1971, *27,* 416–420.

Wright, L. Handling the encopretic child. *Professional Psychology,* 1973, *4,* 137–144.

Wright, L., Nunnery, A., Eichel, B., & Scott, R. Behavioral tactics for reinstating natural breathing in tracheostomy-addicted infants. *Pediatric Research,* 1969, *3,* 275–278.

Wright, L., Schaefer, A., & Solomons, G. *Encyclopedia of pediatric psychology.* Baltimore: University Park Press, 1979.

Wright, L., & Thalassinos, P. Success with electroshock in habitual vomiting. *Clinical Pediatrics,* 1973, *12,* 594–597.

Yates, A. J. *Behavior therapy.* New York: John Wiley & Sons, 1970.

Yorkston, N. J., McHugh, R. B., Brady, R., Serber, M., & Sergeant, H. G. S. Verbal desensitization in bronchial asthma. *Journal of Psychosomatic Research,* 1974, *18,* 371–376.

Young, G. C. The treatment of childhood encopresis by conditioned gastroileal-reflex training. *Behavior Research and Therapy,* 1973, *11,* 499–503.

Young, G. C., & Morgan, R. T. T. Overlearning in the conditioning treatment of enuresis. *Behavior Research and Therapy,* 1972, *10,* 419–420.

Zaleski, A., Gerrard, J. W., & Shokier, M. H. K. Nocturnal enuresis: The importance of a small bladder capacity. In I. Kolvin, R. C. MacKeith, & S. R. Meadow (Eds.), *Bladder control and enuresis.* Philadelphia: W. B. Saunders, 1973.

Zlutnick, S., & Taylor, C. B. Chronic pain. In D. M. Doleys, R. L. Meridith, & Anthony R. Ciminero (Eds.), *Behavioral medicine: Assessment and treatment strategies.* New York: Plenum Press, 1982.

26

Behavioral medicine: Lifestyle and prevention

Charles H. Elliott*
Robert E. Doan*
Roberta A. Olson*
and
E. Edward Beckham*

Prevention of illness and disease and the promotion of healthy lifestyles represent a particularly promising area of behavioral medicine. Some major areas in which behavioral change can improve the health of Americans include: (*a*) changing lifestyles involving maladaptive consumption, such as smoking, alcohol, and obesity; (*b*) altering behavior patterns associated with increased risks to health, such as type *A* coronary behavior and risk taking; (*c*) promoting healthy lifestyles, such as exercise, nutritious diets, relaxation for stress management, and adequate outlets for play and recreation; and (*d*) examining the problems of compliance and maintenance of changing lifestyles. A review will be made of some of the highlights of major research efforts in these areas and of several projects which have been aimed at communitywide efforts to promote healthy lifestyles.

CHANGING MALADAPTIVE-CONSUMPTION HABITS

Research investigations aimed at changing various maladaptive-consumption habits are quite extensive; however, the majority of these treatment investigations have been seriously flawed by methodological and/ or conceptual problems. In addition, the vast majority of these intervention efforts seem to have been designed with one or more of the following

---

* University of Oklahoma Health Sciences Center, Oklahoma City.

unwarranted and/or *unsubstantiated* assumptions: (1) It is often assumed that subjects coming in for help have reached the decision to change. Bellack and Schwartz (1976) put this point quite succinctly, "all patients *voluntarily* coming for treatment can be presumed to *desire* change. This *desire* is not sufficient to generate change and is *not* predictive when considered in "isolation" (p. 126, emphasis added). Thus, desiring to change can be readily distinguished from reaching an actual *decision* to change. Bellack and Schwartz further reviewed a number of motivational variables which may lead to such decisions. One of the most interesting of these is what Mitchell and Biglan (1971) and Mausner (1973) have termed *subjective expected utility for change*. This construct incorporates both the subjects' expectancies of outcome in response to changing, and/or *not* changing, as well as his or her subjective value of the outcome in each case. Upon inspection of most treatment programs, it is estimated that over 90 percent of the investigator's efforts have been devoted to the simple delivery of treatment techniques aimed at the "behavior change induction" phase rather than decision making and/or maintenance. (2) Another common assumption is that patients will automatically practice and apply psychological techniques, no matter how complex or how quickly they are thrown at them. (3) Once behavioral change has occurred, further work on maintenance is often seemingly considered unnecessary. This issue is considered to be of such importance that a separate section is devoted to examining the factors which contribute to the maintenance of healthy lifestyles. (4) Often, studies deal with subjects as though the same treatment techniques will work in about the same way, for almost everyone with the same problem. (5) Many treatments seem to have been designed on the assumption that aversive techniques are relatively better at suppressing consumption habits than techniques designed at developing positive alternatives to them. (6) When stress-reduction strategies are a primary part of a program, it is often assumed that they will be utilized automatically and generalized and that there is relatively little need to concomitantly restructure the meaning patients attach to stress-arousing stimuli. (7) The assumption is often made that negative affective states (e.g.,depression and/or anxiety) that may be contributing to or exacerbating the maladaptive-consumption habits can be basically ignored (it should be noted that the presence of such negative affective states may occur as a *consequence* of attempting behavioral change and may hinder progress, even if they were not present *prior* to treatment).(8) Finally, it often appears that the investigator assumes that the physiological effects of a particular substance consumed can be ignored. A number of researchers have noted the prevalence of these problems, but relatively few treatment strategies have thoroughly taken them into account up to now. As treatments become more sophisticated in these respects, one might predict that improved outcomes will result.

Alcohol

Numerous myths about alcohol abuse have existed, but they have been generally dispelled in recent literature. The first of these concerns the notion of so-called alcoholism as a medical disease. Current conceptualizations of alcoholism tend to consider it more in the following terms: "the acquisition of particular drinking behaviors is considered to be a discriminated operant response; that is, a behavior which only occurs in the presence of certain antecedent stimuli (including internal physiological factors, cognitions, and enviromental factors), and which is acquired and maintained because of these consequences" (Sobell & Sobell, 1981, p. 217). Additional assumptions which had been prevalent in the early literature include some of the following: the fact that alcoholics metabolize alcohol in ways that are different from nonalcoholics, that all alcoholics lose control after one drink, that so-called reformed or dry alcoholics are the best therapists for alcoholics, and that all alcoholics drink simply to reduce tension or anxiety. Nathan and Lansky (1978) have reviewed a substantial body of data indicating the invalidity of most of these earlier myths. However, Zeiner (1981) recently reviewed a variety of evidence that provided some preliminary indications that there may indeed be differences in biological sensitivity to alcohol in some individuals and certain racial groups. Zeiner speculated that these differences in sensitivity may effect the probability of developing alcoholism for certain people. However, numerous, alternative variables for the results reviewed will need to be ruled out by subsequent research, prior to the full acceptance of this hypothesis.

Large numbers of treatment-outcome studies have been conducted on alcohol abuse and have been reviewed in detail by Nirenberg in Chapter 19. As he noted, most of these have been plagued by substantial methodological problems. However, a few tentative indications have begun to emerge from the literature. Because these indications may have implications for other areas of lifestyle change, they will be briefly reviewed. The first of these indications is that multimodal, broad-based treatment strategies have often been found to be at least somewhat more effective than more-limited treatment approaches (Miller & Foy, 1981; Nathan, 1980; Rimm & Masters, 1979; Smith, 1980; Vogler, Compton, & Weissbach, 1975). Such broad-spectrum approaches may be more effective due to the fact that: (a) they address a broader range of the overall problem, as noted by Hersen (1981); (b) they allow individuals to select the components of the treatment which may be most relevant to their particular needs; (c) alcoholism is a multiply determined problem and, therefore, may require more than a single-treatment strategy, and (d) such treatments may simply involve a greater degree of demand effect and intensity level. It is important to point out, however, that current reviews have not demonstrated multimodal, broad-based strategies to be vastly superior to other treatment programs. In fact, some studies have failed to demonstrate significantly greater treatment efficacy for these broad-based programs (e.g., Miller, Taylor, & West, 1980). The second indication suggested by current literature is the importance of taking therapist variables into account. For example, Miller et al. (1980) found that two thirds of the success of their subjects was accounted for by the degree of the therapist's accurate empathy. The third factor concerns the issue of treatment complexity (Wilson, 1980). Wilson suggested that, if a treatment package is overly complex, client adherence may be reduced. Therefore, it may be quite important for behavioral packages to avoid overwhelming clients with too many strategies, delivered over too short a time. The fourth factor, which appears to be of substantial importance, is taking into account individual-difference variables. Some of these may be rather general variables, such as the essential-reactive distinction noted in the previous chapter. Another general, individual-difference variable (almost totally neglected in the literature to date) is that of negative affective states, such as depression and/or anxiety. And yet, Pottenger, McKernon, Patrie, Weissman, Ruben, and Newberry (1968) found that approximately 60 percent of the alcoholics in their study were depressed, both at the beginning of treatment and at a one-year follow-up. In addition, this study indicated that far more of the patients who were depressed at follow-up were still drinking than were those who were not depressed at follow-up. Wehl and Turner (1982) suggested that, whether depression leads to the abuse of alcohol or is a consequence of alcoholism, treatment of it may still be an essential ingredient in an intervention program. In fact, these investigators found that six, 1½-hour, individualized sessions of cognitive therapy (in addition to a standard, six-week, inpatient program) for depression resulted in significantly greater reductions in depression, compared to a standard-treatment group and to a standard-treatment group which also received a *group* cognitive-behavior therapy. In addition, the individualized cognitive-behavior therapy substantially reduced dropout rate during treatment. As yet, their study lacks corroborative data regarding whether or not this effect on depression will lead to continued, long-term effects on drinking consumption, but it is, nevertheless, quite exciting in terms of its potential and implications.

Other individual-difference variables may be more subtle and involve a careful analysis of a given person's environment, reinforcement history, attitude, etc. Therefore, one of the greatest tasks which will face researchers in the area of alcohol and drug abuse will be the development of effective predictors for determining which individuals will profit the most from which kind of treatment. One particularly important predictor variable would be in regard to which individuals will profit the most from programs designed to achieve total abstinence versus controlled drinking. This issue is elaborated by Miller (1982), in a review of some 20 studies that evaluate various methods of training moderation (as opposed to total abstinence). When the stated goal was moderation, the total average success rate was 70 percent. Success was judged by abstinent, controlled, or improved drinking rates, at one-year follow-ups. Miller further stated that several of these studies have produced abstinence rates comparable to studies with total abstinence as a goal, in addition to producing large numbers of subjects who were successful in controlling their drinking.

Obesity

Obesity is one of the most serious and prevalent health problems in the United States, with as many as 80 million Americans being estimated as dangerously overweight (Hagen, 1981). The condition can create a substantial risk factor for a variety of illnesses, including cardiovascular disease, diabetes mellitus, gall bladder disease, and some musculoskeletal disorders involving weightbearing joints (Henderson & Enelow, 1976; Van Itallie, 1979; Wiley & Camacho, 1980).

Behavioral approaches to obesity have also involved a wide variety of procedures, including: social-support engineering (e.g., Matson, 1977), aversion therapies (Meyer & Crisp, 1964; Wijesinghe, 1973), covert sensitization (Elliott & Denney, 1975), cognitive restructuring (Steffen & Myszak, 1978), self-reinforcement and monitoring (Romanczyk, 1974), exercise prescriptions (Ferguson, 1975; Stuart, 1971), and stimulus control (Abrams & Allen, 1974). Once again, it has been extremely difficult to establish the efficacy of these various treatment strategies, due to a number of common methodological problems. These have included small sample sizes, short treatment periods—which generally range from only 2 to 12 sessions (Stuart, 1980)—use of mildly overweight subjects, inadequate follow-ups, overconcern with ascertaining the effectiveness of relatively minor differences in technique, and failure to assess therapist qualities (Hall, Hall, Hanson, & Borden, 1974; Jeffrey, Wing, & Stunkard, 1978; Rimm & Masters, 1979; Stunkard, 1981).

In spite of the substantial methodological weaknesses in most studies, as well as the wide range and combinations of treatments which have been utilized, a few tentative trends seem to be emerging from the literature. These include the following: (1) there is a large variability of weight change during treatment and an even greater variability afterward; (2) the skill of the therapist has, at times, emerged as an important variable in treatment outcome, although it has rarely been assessed (Rimm & Masters, 1979); (3) treatment-outcome predictors have been relatively hard to isolate; but recently, several have been determined to be at least moderate predictors of treatment success, including the amount of weight loss early in the program (Jeffrey et al., 1978), the percentage of initial overweightness, amount of internal or external control of the individual (Carrol, Yates, & Gray, 1980), and an equation incorporating measurement of fat cell number, basal metabolism, and cephalic insulin stimulation (Sullivan, Bjuro, Garrellick, Krotiewski, & Perrson, in press). Stunkard and

Mahoney (1976) further suggested that some people may have a biological predisposition for becoming obese and will require a semistarvation program in order to maintain ideal weight, according to standard charts. Physiological assessments may allow identification of these individuals and a reevaluation of their appropriate weight goals (Stunkard, 1979); (4) some progress has been made in reducing the number of dropouts from such programs (Stunkard, 1979); and (5) only in a few studies have clinically significant weight losses been maintained for a majority of the subjects (cf. Abramson, 1977; Jeffrey et al., 1978; Rimm & Masters, 1979; Stunkard, 1981).

The literature seems to indicate that, while the results of behavioral treatment of obesity have been somewhat disappointing—in terms of providing a specific solution to the problem—positive strides have been made, upon which future research and programs can be built. Stuart (1980), in particular, has isolated a number of sources which may be responsible for many of the failures in the behavioral treatment-outcome literature. These include the following: (1) an overemphasis on the selection of targets for change that are negatively oriented. This problem is exacerbated by the fact that aversive techniques are unlikely to be carried out by subjects in their home environments. Stuart pointed out that this emphasis has failed to develop what may be a more successful approach of devising constructive means for increasing pleasurable alternatives to eating; (2) incomplete planning—for example, he states that very few programs have even specified prescriptions for food intake and/or energy-expenditure suggestions; (3) an overemphasis on techniques designed simply to control eating, rather than changing the factors that maintain the urge to eat; (4) the area of service delivery or, as he noted, the importance of selecting therapists with the best possible characteristics, in addition to creating the optimal environment for the delivery of behavioral treatments (frequently, this may even be within the context of self-help settings); and (5) a failure to evaluate the extent to which subjects actually comply with instructions for behavioral change. By instituting such assessments, one would assume that the quality of treatments could be greatly enhanced by the knowledge gained.

In addition, it is quite possible that weight loss (and changes in other maladaptive-consumption habits) involves at least a two-stage process. The first is a decision-making one, and the second involves coping with the decision. Most behaviorally oriented, weight-control strategies fail to pay sufficient attention to the decision-making process and concentrate solely on techniques designed to aid clients in the coping phase. A recent study by Borrie and Suedfeld (1980) lends some indirect support to this hypothesis. They found that a program involving 24 hours of restricted-environmental stimulation, in combination with a series of self-management messages and a simple diet manual, resulted in significantly greater weight losses than three other treatments, at a six-month follow-up period. The average weight loss at that point in time was not profound (approximately 6 kg.), but it was statistically significant; and the study utilized better-than-average methodology. A review of their procedures would suggest that one of the most parsimonious explanations for the results is that the 24-hour period of restricted-environmental stimulation, along with the dieting manual, aided the subjects in reaching or completing the decision-making phase regarding weight loss. The dieting manual included a variety of individual instructions in behavioral self-control, relaxation, exercises, and dieting information. These strategies may have aided in the actual coping phase through the six months following the initial treatment session.

Additional recommendations for improved treatment strategies can also be made. The first of these is the possibility of combining behavioral interventions with specific kinds of diets. Second would be the possibility of combining behavioral interventions with judicious use of pharmaceutical aids aimed at appetite suppression (cf, Bray, 1974). Third, broader assessments of the relevant individual-cognitive issues may be worthwhile. Fourth, at least with some subgroups of patients, the inclusion of intervention strategies aimed at concomitant (and possibly contributory) negative affective states may improve outcomes. A study that illustrates this point was conducted by Pitta, Alpert, and Perelle (1980), who presented indirect evidence that a program including a substantial component of therapy for depression may aid in the weight-loss attempts of subjects who are most depressed prior to trying to lose weight. The study lacked control groups, however, and definitive conclusions are, therefore unwarranted. And, fifth, including spouses and/or significant others in weight-loss programs may enhance treatment efficacy (Abramson, 1977; Jeffrey et al., 1978; Rimm & Masters, 1979; Stunkard, 1981; Weisz & Bucher, 1980). Stuart (1980) reviewed a variety of studies that were reasonably consistent in suggesting that including a spouse in the treatment program can add to the effectiveness of the weight loss obtained. Yet, a more recent study by Pearce, LeBow, and Orchard (1981) suggested that the involvement of the spouse in a treatment program *may function largely to prevent the spouse from sabotaging their partner's weight-loss efforts.* In this study, they found that a group in which husbands were simply asked *not* to participate and/or sabotage yielded weight losses which were just as great as a group in which husbands were solicited as therapeutic aids at 2-, 3-, 6-, and 12-month follow-ups. Futhermore, both the groups (in which husbands were given specific instructions) resulted in significantly greater weight losses than an insight-control group and a no-treatment control group (neither of which involved husbands).

Smoking

Smoking has been implicated as contributory to a wide variety of diseases, including: coronary heart disease, lung cancer, and emphysema.

Some of the early attempts at the treatment of smoking fell into the catego-ries of simple medical advice, hypnosis, and various types of group ther-apy, all of which were generally found to be relatively ineffective. A number of excellent reviews have recently been made of behavioral approaches to the treatment and prevention of smoking behavior (e.g., Pechacek & McAlister, 1980; Pomerleau, 1980; Rimm & Masters, 1979). Elliott and Denney (1978) reviewed a wide variety of behavioral tech-niques that have been utilized for smoking, which included: systematic desensitization (Pyke, Agnew, & Kopperud, 1966), rapid smoking (Lando, 1975, 1976; Lichtenstein, Harris, Birchler, Wall, & Schmahl, 1973; Schmahl, Lichtenstein, & Harris, 1972; Sutherland, Amit, Golden, & Ro-senberger, 1975), covert sensitization (Sachs, Bean, & Morrow, 1970), aversive conditioning (Berecz, 1972), stimulus control (Bernard & Efran, 1972), contingency contracting (Lawson & May, 1970), and behavior rehearsal (Steffy, Meichenbaum, & Best, 1970). Furthermore, McFall (1978) presented a comprehensive review of the methodological prob-lems commonly associated with treatment-outcome research on smoking. Although many of the studies in this area have been plagued by these difficulties, a number of studies employing relatively good methodology do exist. Pechacek and McAlister (1980) reviewed extensive data indicat-ing that almost all strategies produced dramatic reductions in smoking behavior at the end of treatment; but results have been quite discouraging, in terms of follow-up periods 3 to 12 months later. In fact, seldom more than 13 percent of subjects in treatment programs are still abstinent three to six months after treatment. Pechacek and McAlister (1980) and Elliott and Denney (1978) have both concluded that multiple-component, broad-based treatment packages have generally shown the most encouraging results. However, some treatments with seemingly similar components have not shown equivalent effectiveness. Identifying the components and the subject samples especially responsive to them will be an important research task.

From the current authors' review of recent smoking literature, a number of recommendations for future investigation are possible. The first of these is a need to correlate reductions in smoking with a variety of other possible health changes. These may include positive changes (such as reduced risk of developing lung cancer and reductions in blood pressure) which could serve to further motivate subjects or negative changes (such as weight increases) which could discourage subjects from their efforts to reduce smoking rates. Weight change is one concern frequently cited by many people who are attempting to reduce their smoking. Apparently, no study has involved a systematic, controlled evaluation of the correlation between reductions in smoking and these other health factors.

The second recommendation would, once again, be a more-thorough evaluation of individual cognitive issues. In particular, the cognitive issues leading to the decision to quit smoking may be quite important and somewhat separate from issues involved with attempting to cope with that decision. Another cognitive variable that seems to have substantial importance has been highlighted recently by Condiotte and Lichtenstein (1981). In their study, the variable of self-efficacy, as described by Bandura (1977), was predictive of subjects who would ultimately relapse. Thus, subjects who had the greatest sense of self-efficacy at the end of treatment were least likely to relapse later.

A third area of future research that may be of value is the investigation of attempts to teach some smokers strategies for learning to continue to smoke at a *controlled,* medically safer level. This is quite similar to the arguments in regard to controlled drinking versus total abstinence, in the area of alcohol abuse. For example, Fox, Brown, and Katz (1981) found that a nicotine-fading plus self-monitoring group was more successful at reducing smoking and lowering tar-nicotine levels than subjects in a self-monitoring group alone, or subjects in a slighlty modified, American Cancer Society smoking-reduction program. The overall n of the study (38) at the $2\frac{1}{2}$-year follow-up was not overly impressive. However, the fact that the nicotine-fading plus self-monitoring group was demonstrating 40 percent abstinence and, in addition, that *all* of the nonabstainers were smoking cigarettes substantially lower in nicotine and tar than their baseline brand was quite interesting. In fact, the nonabstainers had reduced their tar and nicotine levels by 60 to 70 percent from their baseline levels. The differences between the groups were quite substantial and statistically significant. Nicotine fading, in general, in the literature has not been demonstrated to result in significantly greater improvements than any other strategy. However, Fox et al. (1981) combined self-monitoring with inclusion of goals which involved nonabstinence, but with lower tar-nicotine levels. The fact that, two-and-one-half years later, the group of nonabstainers was still successful in reducing their tar-nicotine levels lends substantial support for the possibility that this may be a far more practical goal for many subjects.

The fourth recommendation that needs further investigation in this area is the issue of booster sessions. Although a number of investigators have failed to find substantially increased efficacy from the use of booster sessions, the Los Angeles Kaiser-Permante group (1979) found a highly substantial effect from the use of 14 maintenance sessions, over a 12-month period. It is quite possible that the use of booster sessions will be of far greater value if they are maintained for a longer time than has typically been the case in most smoking studies to date. (Futher discussion of this issue is found in the maintenance section of this chapter.)

A fifth area of research which seems warranted would be a review of the package studies that have been shown to be effective to date. Ultimately, conducting factor-analytic studies of the package programs to determine the factors most responsible for their efficacy will be needed.

Once this determination is made, those factors can, perhaps, be enhanced.

A sixth area is in regard to prevention. It may be that much greater success will be obtained from developing strategies designed to prevent youths from beginning to smoke, as opposed to waiting until they are adults and helping them to quit smoking. In fact, Hurd, Johnson, Pechacek, Bast, Jacobs, and Luepker (1980) recently reported on an eight-month, school-based, smoking-prevention program conducted with 1,526 seventh-grade students. This program demonstrated substantial reductions in smoking incidents in the target group of students, relative to a control population. Along the same line, a recent study by Glasgow, McCaul, Freeborn, and O'Neill (1981) suggested that information presented to adolescents concerning the immediate health effects of smoking may be much more effective than information presented to them in terms of long-range health consequences of smoking. In their studies, they found that presenting information regarding the *immediate* health consequences of smoking resulted in changes in the adolescents' beliefs about smoking and their future intentions to smoke. The authors speculated that this might be due, in part, to the fact that this information was new to the adolescents and, therefore, was remembered more readily than the frequently heard warnings concerning long-term deleterious effects of smoking.

A seventh area of investigation that seems worthy of further study is the effects of nicotine. Gilbert (1979) for example, reviewed a number of studies indicating the paradoxical effects of nicotine on the system. Physiologically, nicotine serves to arouse a variety of bodily systems and yet, paradoxically, seems to result in self-report and behavioral indicants of reduced emotional arousal for many subjects. This effect needs further investigation, especially as it may interact with smoking behavior.

CHANGING MALADAPTIVE LIFESTYLES

Type A coronary-prone behavior

Type A behavior, a concept which was pioneered by Friedman and Rosenman (1959), has lead to a substantial body of research. Some of the most common characteristics which seem to be assessed by various measures of Type A behavior include the following: a sense of time urgency, working at maximum capacity regardless of the presence or absence of time deadlines, aggressiveness, competitiveness, and hurried restlessness. At the same time, Type As also tend to be characterized as confident, ambitious, goal directed, and extroverted, which are traits generally viewed as somewhat positive in our society.

Research in this area has been escalating at a rapid rate, in part due to a landmark study, which was conducted on a longitudinal basis, known as the Western Collaborative Group Study (Rosenman, Friedman, Straus, Wurm, Kositchek, Haan, & Werthessen, 1964), in which 3,500 males from the ages of 35 to 59 were followed for a period of 8½ years. The results of that study indicated that Type A men were between two and six times more likely to have coronary heart disease (CHD) than were Type B males, with the higher figure associated with the men in the 39- to 49-year-old age group. These results have continued to be substantiated in subsequent research (Rosenman, Brand, Jenkins, Friedman, Straus, & Wurm, 1975; Williams, Haney, Lee, Kong, Blumenthal, & Whalen, 1980). Interest in researching the nature of this phenomenon has been fueled, in part, by the fact that CHD is, by far, the leading cause of death in the United States, and that 26 percent of those dying are under the age of 65 (Suinn, 1980). Two excellent reviews of this phenomenon have recently appeared in the literature. The first was by Suinn (1980), and the second was by the Review Panel on Coronary-Prone Behavior and Coronary Heart Disease (1981). The second review concluded that evidence currently suggests that the risks imposed by Type A behavior are above and beyond the risks associated with age, hypertension, serum cholesterol, and smoking. Furthermore, the relative magnitude of this risk is similar to that associated with the latter three of those variables.

As stated above, research has linked Type A behavior with coronary heart disease, but this correlation has yet to be isolated as a direct causative factor. This point was emphasized by the review panel (1981) in their overview of several possible models. The first model assumes that Type A behavior directly causes coronary disease via physiologic mechanisms. This suggests that modifying Type A behavior would also cause a change in the pathophysiological factors which lead to heart disease. The second model views Type A behavior and coronary disease as parallel but independent outcomes of a central aggressive trait that exhibits itself both psychophysiologically (Type A) and somatically (coronary disease). This model suggests that stress-related psychophysiological changes may or may not have importance in coronary disease and contains the possibility that altering Type A behavior would have little or no effect on heart disease incidence. The constitutional, aggressive trait suggested in this second model could arise from genetic predisposition or early experiential learning. Depending upon which of these models (if either) proves accurate, the implications for successful intervention could be drastically different.

To date, there have been two major approaches to the assessment of Type A behavior. These are: (1) the structured-interview technique (Rosenman et al., 1964), and (2) a variety of self-administered questionnaires. The structured-interview technique (SI) uses interview recordings which are rated by trained judges, both in terms of how the actual questions are answered and the behavioral responses of those being rated while doing so. Unfortunately, as the Review Panel on Coronary-Prone Behavior (1981) noted, the structured interview has changed in format over the years, and this makes comparisons with current and past data more difficult. Furthermore, it was noted that the most recent form of the SI can classify approximately 75 percent of all subjects as Type A. In addition to this problem, the Jenkins Activity Scale (JAS), a self-administered questionnaire (Jenkins, Rosenman, & Friedman, 1967), can be scored on an ordinal basis, but it is often used on a dichotomous basis. The structured interview also has generally been used as a two-point dichotomized scale. Therefore, the review panel appropriately suggested that scores for both the structured interview and various self-administered questionnaires (such as the Jenkins Activity Scale) be transformed into continuous scales with ordinal properties, in order to determine "dose-response curves." The JAS scale is the most commonly used, self-administered questionnaire and has been shown to have a 72 percent correlation with the structured-interview technique (Zyzanski & Jenkins, 1970).

Two other self-administered questionnaires were designed to tap similar information as the structured interview. The Bortner scale (Bortner, 1969) and the Framingham Type *A* (Haynes, Levine, Scotch, Feinleib, & Kannel, 1978) scale have been shown to significantly correlate with the structured interview and have also been associated with coronary heart disease (Adler & Galeazzi, 1977; Haynes, Feinleib, and Kannel, 1980). A variety of other self-administered questionnaires designed to measure some form of Type A behavior have been developed and will not be reviewed in detail here. However, it should be pointed out that a recent study by Chesney, Black, Chadwick, and Rosenman (1981) indicated that the association between the structured interview and some of the other self-administered questionnaires was rather weak and that caution should be exercised in making firm conclusions about the Type *A* behavior pattern from these instruments. Obviously, these various instruments are measuring somewhat overlapping yet different, constructs. It will be important to determine which aspects of Type A behavior are responsible for the relationship to coronary heart disease. This point was aptly stated by Roskies (1980), "Not all Type A behavior is necessarily coronary-prone behavior, and the distinction between what is and what is not is crucial if we hope to develop effective and efficient intervention programs" (p. 308).

Presently, very little emphasis has been placed upon defining characteristics of Type B behavior. One exception to this trend is a recent study by Herman, Blumenthal, Black, and Chesney (1981), who found that Type B subjects endorsed items—such as calm, quiet, cautious, mild, peaceable, easy-going, slow, and silent—as applying to themselves to a far greater extent than Type A subjects.

An additional area of investigation which has received little attention up to this point is the potential relationship between Type A behavior and other illnesses and accidents. The review panel once again noted that some preliminary data suggests Type A subjects may be a greater risk for accidents, suicide, and homicide. However, these findings have not always been replicated (Review Panel, 1981). There is also a paucity of studies relating Type A behavior to other diseases, such as peptic ulcers or other so-called psychosomatic disorders.

Another area of investigation which has generated a significant amount of attention has been the attempt to determine the physiological mechanisms that presumably underlie the increased vulnerability to coronary heart disease in Type A individuals. These mechanisms are poorly understood; however, those postulated have included hypertension, elevated plasma cholesterol, triglycerides (Friedman, 1979), and the role of catecholamines (Review Panel, 1981). A recent report in *Medical News* (1981) suggested that a "supercharging with norepenephrine" may be responsible for much of the effect of Type A behavior, *especially when those individuals fail to maintain control over their environments*. The suggestion of norepenephrine being an underlying mechanism is interesting, in the sense that hostility and anger have also been related to Type A behavior, and earlier research in that area has indicated that those who are prone to anger also are prone to the overproduction of norepenephrine (e.g., Ax, 1953; Schachter, 1957; Williams et al., 1980). The role of coping skills and the perception of one's ability to control various situations and tasks have been implicated as potentially significant mediators in the influence of Type A behavior on the physiological reactions of these individuals (Gastorf, 1981; Jennings & Choi, 1981; McCranie, Simpson, & Stevens, 1981; Vickers, Herirg, Rahe, & Rosenman, 1981).

Finally, it should be noted that the review panel suggested that depression may mask Type A characteristics on some of the various measurement techniques currently in use. Given that depression is a risk factor for a variety of illnesses, it is quite possible that, when Type A subjects feel that they are no longer in control and are lacking adequate coping skills, they may be more susceptable to the physiological sequelae to their behavior than other Type A individuals. In fact, research by Glass (1977a, 1977b) supported the notion that Type A individuals are even more prone to feelings of helplessness when they are in situations that are beyond their control. Thus, over all, the *depressed* Type A person may not only be more difficult to assess as a Type A individual but may also be at far greater and more eminent risk from the consequences of their personality predisposition. In general, this suggests that far more research on the interactions of personality predispositions × situational challenges × coping repertoire may be quite productive.

Interventions to date in this area have been relatively few, and the current state of the art is such that large-scale intervention trials may not be justified at this time. However, it has been suggested that limited-intervention strategies be designed in the attempt to reveal distinctive subgroups of Type A individuals which are more responsive to particular-intervention strategies and/or which may show differential physiological mechanisms underlying their behavior (Review Panel, 1981). The major intervention research thus far has been conducted by Suinn (1975) and Suinn and Bloom (1978), who sought to allay the stress aspects of this syndrome through a form of anxiety-management training (see Denney, Chapter 27), which utilizes imagery to arouse anxiety and relaxation strategies to cope with it. Additional interventions have been conducted by Roskies (1978) and Roskies, Spevack, Surkis, Cohen, and Gilman (1978), in which in vivo practice of relaxation techniques were stressed. Rosenman and Friedman (1977) used group psychotherapy with behavioral techniques of relaxation training and environmental self-management. Roskies (1980) also suggested that these approaches be supplemented by cognitive and social tension-reducing techniques a la Bower and Bower (1976) and Meichenbaum (1977).

More recently, Blumenthal, Williams, Williams, and Wallace (1980) conducted a study, in which a 10-week, supervised-exercise program was successful in reducing physiological, cardiovascular-risk factors as well as Jenkins Activity Scale scores. It was concluded that exercise programs can be successful in modifying both the physiological and psychological variables associated with increased coronary risks in a nonclinical sample of healthy adults.

Suinn (1980) has made several suggestions for interventions, based on his experience with Type A individuals, including the following: (1) intervention should be brief, due to the nature of Type A people, (2) that it have a tangible element of impact, in terms of relaxation or diminished stress due to coping, (3) that it include self-management programs that stress the absence of the therapist, (4) that it help Type A people accept that losing their Type A behavior won't necessarily lead to failure, and (5) that early interventions stress *salient* behavior changes. The difficulty in working with this kind of population was underscored in a recent study by Herman et al. (1981), in which they found that Type A individuals were able to identify and endorse characteristics of themselves which generally are seen as positive traits, but were unable to recognize and/or endorse items which (although they apply to them) are generally seen in more negative terms. Therefore, these individuals do not tend not to be prime candidates for requesting help in changing their behavior.

Janis and Rodin (1979) noted, in regard to the target behavior of smoking, that cognitive confrontations, emotional role-playing, and emotional confrontations may be particularly advantageous strategies for overcoming resistance to change. It would seem that similar strategies might be useful to induce Type A individuals to engage in behavior-change strategies, as well. However, any intervention strategy for such individuals should also focus heavily upon the training of adaptive-coping responses in the face of stress, since Type A individuals may be particularly susceptible in situations in which they have perceived themselves to not be in control. As noted previously, large-scale interventions, at this time, are probably premature, as suggested by the review panel. However, it has been pointed out that, as further information and knowledge are gained, it may ultimately be possible for physicians to rather readily pick out Type A individuals during medical-history examinations (Review Panel, 1981). This information, in conjunction with simple, additional screening instruments—such as a Beck Depression Inventory (or other similar instruments)—may allow the identification of especially high-risk individuals, who could be referred for appropriate intervention.

Future research has been recommended in several areas. First, cross-cultural studies were suggested by the Review Panel on Coronary-Prone Behavior. One such study, by Kornitzer, Kittel, DeBacker, and Dramaix (1981)—with a population sample of over 19,000 male subjects between the ages of 40 and 59 years in Belgium (in conjunction with other studies which they reviewed)—tended to "verify the fact that subjects with this behavior pattern are prone to coronary heart disease without regard to social class or cultural background" (p. 144). Second, the variable of sex has been relatively understudied at this point. Most studies have focused on men, given that they tend to be at higher risk for coronary heart disease. However, further studies on the relationship of sex to Type A behavior would be warranted. Finally, it has been recommended that further research on Type A behavior be conducted with children. One such study recently presented evidence that Type A behavior can be measured in children as early as kindergarten (Matthews & Angulo, 1980). However, a more recent study—by Lawler, Allen, Critcher, and Standard (1981)—raised the question as to what age and for which sex physiological concomitants of Type A behavior are manifested. Type A behavior patterns have also recently been studied in adolescents (e.g., Siegel & Leitch, 1981; Siegel, Matthews, & Leitch, 1981), but these studies, to date, have failed to examine the relationship of physiological concomitants and/or reactivity to stress or environmental conditions.

In summary, an extensive body of research exists on Type A behavior and its relationship to coronary heart disease. The potential of this research is exciting; although, at the present time, merely the existence of Type A behavior in a particular individual is not sufficient to warrant referral to an intensive-intervention program. Much more needs to be learned about postulated physiological mechanisms, the specific subcomponents of Type A behavior that maximally predict coronary heart disease, and finally, greater analysis of the role played by coping responses under various types of situational challenges.

Risk taking

One potential target area, although it hasn't yet been addressed in large-population groups, is risk taking. Risk-taking behaviors which lead to accidents are a major cause of mortality and morbidity in our society. Accidents are the leading cause of death in children who are past the infant period (National Center for Health Statistics, 1978) and occur more in males than in females (Manheimer, Dewey, Mellinger, & Corsa, 1966; Mechanic & Cleary, 1980) This risk taking can cover a wide range of behaviors (riding motorcycles, failure to fasten seat belts, daredevil stunts, etc.), and attempts have been made to identify the characteristics of this population subgroup. Manheimer and Mellinger (1967) identified such factors as extroversion, aggression, impulsivity, carelessness, and lack of discipline as being statistically related to an increased risk of an accident. A more recent study—by Matheny (1980)—suggests a cognitive element may be related to the incidence of accidents from an early age. Children scoring the most errors on the Elkind and Weiss (1967) Visual-Perceptual Exploration Test at age six also had the most accidents between ages six and nine. These children may have a different manner of employing attention, relative to their enviroment, which may play a part in creating a greater at-risk situation for them.

There seems to be a paucity of well-controlled research in terms of treatment-intervention outcomes, and it would appear that this would be a most fruitful area for further exploration. One example of a specific-intervention effort is the recent study by Christopherson and Gyulay (1981), who successfully increased the use of car seats among eight mothers by 62 percent at a six-month follow-up and 37 percent at a 12-month follow-up. State governments are also becoming involved in attempts to curb various risk-taking behaviors, including stiffer fines and sentences for drunk driving and mandatory use of motorcycle helmets and infant car seats; but data are lacking in regard to the efficacy of these efforts. Futher research in the area could be profitable.

PROMOTING HEALTHY LIFESTYLES

The behavioral interventions discussed previously in this chapter have emphasized the elimination or reduction of certain maladaptive or unhealthy lifestyle ingredients, rather than the acquisition of healthy ones. While it is apparent that there is ample opportunity and need within Western society for helping those who have already acquired maladaptive lifestyles, it is equally apparent that the need for this type of intervention could be drastically reduced by programs that promote styles of living that tend to yield health as an outcome.

The implication seems clear: the health of a nation cannot be improved by only treating and spending greater sums of money on the negative outcomes of unhealthy lifestyles; but conversely, it would be improved by emphasizing the antecedents to these outcomes and developing means of education and intervention at that level. This point was stated very succinctly by Knowles (1977):

. . . over 99 percent of us are born healthy and made sick as a result of personal misbehavior and environmental conditions. The solution to the problems of ill health in modern American society involves individual responsibility, in the first instance, and social responsibility through public legislation and private voluntary efforts, in the second instance. (p. 58)

Matarazzo (1982) points out that it is, perhaps, time the field of psychology paid as much attention to the physical health of the nation as it has to the mental health thereof, and this challenge of behavioral health is open to almost every area of psychology to have opportunity for input and service *with people who are currently healthy.* The remainder of this chapter will discuss those positive lifestyle ingredients which tend to not only make one more healthy but also less prone to engage in the maladaptive lifestyles which have been discussed earlier.

Exercise

Although exercise has long been viewed as an important ingredient in a healthy lifestyle, it has largely been overlooked by the literature (Epstein & Wing, 1980). This is true, despite the indication that exercise seems to lend itself quite well to the behavioral principles of stimulus and reinforcement control and is ideally suited for measurement techniques (Chiroco & Stunkard, 1960). This neglect is even more surprising when one considers the available literature which suggests that exercise has the direct effect of influencing body weight (e.g., Gwinup, 1975), cardiovascular efficiency (e.g., Cooper, Pollack, Martin, White, Linnerud, & Jackson, 1976; Fox, Naughton, & Haskell, 1971), and one's general attitude of well-being (e.g., Folkins, 1976; Ismail & Trachtman, 1973), as well as indirectly modifying other behaviors—such as, the consumption of excessive amounts of alcohol, cigarettes, and food—which are generally considered to be negative influences upon one's health (Keir & Lauzon, 1980). Exercise may even have the potential to become a positive addiction, which could aid in overcoming the more negative habits noted above (Keir & Lauzon, 1980). This speculation is supported by (a) Taggert, Parkinson, and Carruthers (1972), who suggest that exercise leads to enjoyment via triggered adrenal secretions, which stimulate the pleasure center in the hypothalamus, and (b) the finding that prolonged exercise may cause the release of pain-killing endorphins within the body, which act on the nervous system to soothe one's mood and create a feeling of euphoria (Bortz, Angwin, Mefford, Boarder, Noyce, & Barchas, 1981).

The same problems exist with exercise—in regard to maintenance and compliance—as in the other areas we have discussed. Dropout rates have generally been quite similar, varying from 30 to 65 percent (Carmody, Senner, Malinow, & Matarazzo, 1980; Gwinup. 1975; Mann, Garrett, Farhi, Murray, & Billings, 1969). Two approaches to exercise seem reasonable. The first is for those who have a high need to engage in exercise (due to substantial health needs) and would involve comprehensive, broad-based programs, as previously suggested in the areas of smoking, alcoholism, and obesity. These programs would likely require as much emphasis on maintenance and decision making as do treatment interventions in those other areas. The second approach to increased exercise has been suggested by Mahoney and Mahoney (1976), who stated that, for some subjects, it may be a more-appropriate goal to incorporate exercise within their lifestyle in minor, small-step ways—such as, taking the stairs up one or two flights instead of the elevator or parking the car two blocks from work instead of immediately adjacent. However, no systematic studies have been carried out on different strategies for increasing compliance with exercise, in terms of broad-based versus more-limited approaches.

Nutrition-diet

There are literally hundreds of texts, articles, and self-help books on nutrition and diet available at any given time. It is an area that seems to be of concern to a large portion of the population of the United States, and the picture that emerges is one of general confusion and lack of accurate information on the part of many. This point was succinctly stated by Edleman (1980):

> Nutrition is the most politically charged area of science that I've ever seen. People go around, armed with very little evidence, wanting to sweep away dogmas and replace them with another group of myths just as bad. We've got to remain humble and admit we don't know very much about nutrition right now. (p. 1)

The concern manifested by the general population is, in part, fueled by the number of people who suffer from obesity in our society, as well as by the mounting evidence correlating nutrition and diet to the incidence of certain prevalent diseases in our society. Yet, as a nation, we seem to be moving in the direction of fast foods and between-meal snacking, as opposed to three, well-balanced meals per day (Navia, 1977). Most of these changes seem to be influenced by the mass-advertising media, with television, in particular, being highly influential. Masover and Stamler (1977) conducted research dealing directly with this concern in Chicago and found that, on four selected television stations, 70 percent of the paid-advertising time was taken to promote foods generally high in fat, unsaturated fat, cholesterol, sugar, and/or salt, while only 3 percent of the advertising time was devoted to fresh fruit and juices. The implications of saturation advertising are readily seen, when considered in relationship to the general public's poor nutritional-knowledge base, and provide ''more than'' adequate reason for concern.

This concern becomes even greater, when the evidence linking diet to various types of common diseases is considered. In a comprehensive effort, conducted by the American Society for Clinical Nutrition (1979), a number of the high diet-disease links were studied, which included: carbohydrates and dental caries, alcohol and liver disease, salt and hypertension, and cholesterol and/or fat with heart disease.

There are some guidelines which have emerged for a diet conducive to good health. In a recent report by the Food and Nutrition Board (1980), these are outlined and can be summarized in terms of the following ingredients: (1) a wide variety of foods should be included in the diet, as opposed to relying on any one source for the essential elements of nutrition; (2) total fat intake should be reduced to comprise approximately 35 percent of the diet, and the fats used should be primarily the unsaturated variety; (3) the use of refined sugar should be reduced and replaced by intake of complex carbohydrates—such as cereals, fruits, potatoes, beans, and nuts; (4) in many instances, a reduction in the consumption of alcohol would be beneficial, especially as a means of controlling caloric intake; (5) the consumption of sodium should be reduced; and (6) one of the most beneficial changes that could be made in general-nutritional practices would be a maintenance of an ideal body weight, as opposed to obesity. Finally, according to the Food and Nutrition Board (1980), fiber is an important ingredient in a balanced diet, although it is not yet possible to recommend a specific level of daily intake. Due to the possible risk of lowered mineral absorption, it is not recommended that one drastically increase fiber intake; rather, a balanced consumption of vegetables, fruits, and whole-grain cereal products is both desirable and adequate. The board suggests that the above recommendations can be accomplished without extreme dietary changes and can be easily implemented within the U.S. food supply.

There seems to be little or no research investigating the promotion of good diet and nutrition, other than some community-intervention efforts (which will be discussed later in this chapter). Most studies in this area have concentrated on interventions which deal with the results of dysfunctional diets (obesity) rather than the promotion of healthy ones. Clearly, there is a need for research in this area, in terms, of attempting to isolate the most effective means of influencing the largest number of people. Some suggestions in this regard are made by Jeffrey and Lemnitzer (1981) and include: (1) establishment of dietary goals, in order that public awareness might be increased regarding guidelines on nutritional information, the kinds of food processes, and the types of foods advertised; (2) improvement of nutritional education to the public in general; (3) investigation of the role of food labeling and consumption; (4) research into the role of vending machines in the consumption habits of the public; (5) investigation of the role of advertising, in regard to effects on eating habits and consumption; and (6) examination of which crops are being supported by tax and agriculture subsidy, in relation to good nutritional concepts.

Relaxation and stress management

No discussion of lifestyle (as related to health) would be complete ~without the mention of the potential effects of stress and anxiety upon the physiological and psychological systems of humans. Healthy lifestyle promotion in this area focuses upon the development of good coping responses and recognizes that some stress and anxiety is unavoidable in today's world. One of the most significant of the coping responses that can be acquired is relaxation, both formal and informal.

Formal relaxation refers basically to the acquiring of a skill (via structured practice) that is reflected in physiological changes in the parasympathetic nervous system (Hess, 1954) and that can be measured by lowered oxygen consumption, lowered respiratory rate, lowered heart rate and alpha-wave brain activity, reduced blood pressure, reduced muscle tones, and lowered galvanic skin conduction (Benson, 1975). There has been extensive research in this area, and a review of this subject is provided by Denney in Chapter 27. The addition of some form of formal relaxation would probably be beneficial to most people, and the chance for negative outcomes in this area is relatively small.

Leisure time (play and recreation)

Relaxation, either as a formal or an informal strategy, can produce the desired results of decreased tension or stress. The wise use of leisure time has many implications in this area and is almost certainly a necessary ingredient in a healthy lifestyle. Unfortunately, Western society has seemingly sponsored an attitude that play and recreation are only suitable for children. According to Walker (1975), the work-oriented person is not happy unless engaged in something related to work and can never get enough to satisfy the need. Leisure time and vacations become real agony for this type of individual, as they spend the majority of the time thinking about work, worrying about work, and wishing they were back at work. In short, they are obsessed with the work ethic and have many of the same type of problems to which alcoholics are subject; but instead of drinking, they work. No time is left for developing a healthy lifestyle.

Walker (1975) and Sheehan (1978) both point out that the inevitable result of this sort of one-sided lifestyle will be boredom and a lifestyle that contains no fun or spontaneity, which can very possibly lead to the withdrawal and retreat characteristic of most emotional disturbance. Sheehan calls it playing defense all of the time without ever stopping to engage in the creative aspects of offense. They both suggest that the remedy of this potential problem can be found in play and recreation. This point is partially supported by recent research into the beneficial effects of physical activity on depression (e.g., Blue, 1979; Holmes, 1972). (However, as pointed out by Browman (1981) in a recent review, there is yet to be a complete substantiation of this position.) It is also interesting to note that the results of a leisure-time questionnaire, administered to over 400 patients in the psychiatric ward and care unit at St. Anthony's hospital in Oklahoma City, indicated that the vast majority of them had very inadequate leisure-time interests (Doan, 1982). It seems that, as suggested by Walker (1975), a "tactical retreat" from the stresses of life can be very conducive toward maintaining good health, both physically and mentally.

In order for the retreat to be an effective one, there are several ingredients—suggested by Sheehan (1978)—necessary to insure that a different cognitive set is maintained in this area of life. It is suggested that, if one carries the same Type A time-consciousness and workaholic attitudes into the leisure aspect of life, then little will have been accomplished, other than to add fuel to an already roaring fire. Play must be approached differently in order to be effective. It leaves society and its work ethic far behind and transports one into an existence where only the present exists and where the past and future are forgotten. It is a real and healthy tactical retreat. It speaks for putting balance back into the nation's lifestyle and hints that increased health would be the outcome.

Psychology in general (and specifically, behavioral medicine) would seem to be in an ideal position to intervene in this aspect of lifestyle. Unfortunately, the field seems to have been just as susceptible to the syndrome discussed above as any other; thus, little has been accomplished in this regard. The behavior of Western society—in relation to leisure time, play, and recreation—could certainly be improved; and it would seem that the point of first attack could perhaps best be in the area of habitual cognitions and attitudes about play itself. There would seem to be a wealth of opportunity for research and service in this area.[1]

COMPLIANCE AND MAINTENANCE

Compliance with suggested, healthy lifestyles and disease-prevention behaviors and maintenance of these new behaviors are considered major problems for all areas discussed in this chapter. The preceding sections of this chapter have reviewed behavioral interventions currently being used in attempts to change common, maladaptive-consumption habits and lifestyles and methods to promote healthy lifestyles and management of stress. One clear conclusion from research is that maintenance of new behaviors is rarely achieved with a high percentage of patients, over prolonged follow-up periods. Successful intervention strategies must initially obtain the individual's compliance and then must demonstrate main-

---

[1] Unfortunately, it could be questioned whether the typical, highly productive researchers (and chapter writers!) are in a position to conduct such research, given that many of these individuals tend to have personal lives somewhat antithetical to the lifestyles noted above.

tenance of these changes. Marlatt (1978) suggested that the maintenance factor may well be the most important criteria by which the success or nonsuccess of an intervention program should be judged. Three major factors have been identified as essential components in obtaining initial compliance and long-term maintenance of behavior change and healthy lifestyles. These include the individual's perception of behavior change, continued following of the patient's maintenance of new behaviors, and the use of contingency contracting to increase maintenance.

The individual

Two constructs relevant to the individual's compliance and maintenance of behavior change are the health-belief model (Becker & Green, 1975) and the attributional model (Kopel & Arkowitz, 1975). The health-belief model states, "behavior is predicted from the value of an outcome to an individual, and from the individual's expectations that a given action will result in that outcome" (Becker & Green, 1975, p. 175). The health-belief model includes the individual's perception of potential susceptibility, severity, and the benefits—as opposed to barriers—of seeking and complying with the suggested behavior change. The previously noted concept of "subjecting expected utility of change" suggests hypotheses that are quite similar to those advanced by the health-belief model.

Attribution theory has also provided a rich source of ideas, with regard to the factors responsible for maintenance of behavior change. For example, Kopel and Arkowitz (1975) suggested that behavioral changes are maintained more easily when they are attributed to the self, as opposed to external sources. Marlatt (1978) substantially elaborated upon the role of attributional tendencies and related cognitive variables in the determination of maintenance of behavioral changes, Marlatt's theory originally was designed to provide an explanation of variables critical to relapse in subjects who have been treated for alcoholism, although he further suggested that these same factors are likely applicable to other maladaptive-consumption habits, as well. The theory essentially consists of the following points: once a subject has achieved an initial abstinence, it is quite likely that he/she will confront a variety of high-risk situations that will necessitate a decision on the part of the subject. If the subject has an effective-coping response in his/her repertoire, it is quite likely that he/she will employ it. Such a use of this coping response will allow the subject to withstand the temptation and possibly even increase his/her perception of control. If, on the other hand, the subject does not have a coping response in his/her repertoire, relapse will be much more likely. Marlatt termed this concept the *abstinence-violation effect* and stated that it consists of two cognitive issues. The first of these elements is cognitive dissonance, in the sense that the subject finds himself/herself engaging in a behavior of consumption, in spite of a prior perception of being in total control. Marlatt termed the second cognitive variable the *personal-attribution effect,* which refers to the tendency of the person to attribute the consumptive behavior to a personal weakness, rather than simply the lack of an available coping response. These cognitive elements of cognitive dissonance and personal attribution which make up the abstinence-violation effect lead to a decreased sense of self-efficacy (Bandura, 1977) in the person, which vastly increases the likelihood of further over-consumptive behavior.

The validity of this model has been partially supported in a study by Condiotte and Lichtenstein (1981). In this study, it was found that smoking patients who relapsed exhibited severe guilt reactions and tended to make very personal attributions, followed by dramatic declines in their feelings of self-efficacy. The first relapse was usually followed by complete relapse into their former smoking behavior. The few subjects who did not completely relapse, however, did not show this affective/cognitive tendency, demonstrated an increase in their self-efficacy, and were able to continue to control their smoking. An additional aspect of the data from this study was quite interesting, in that it demonstrated that the group most likely not to completely relapse after only one initial relapse consisted of the subjects with the highest post-treatment self-efficacy ratings. This finding contradicts a suggestion made by Marlatt and Gordon (1980), but it is quite possible that this result may be explained by interactions between the individual's goal of total versus partial control and his/her sense of self-efficacy.

Marlatt's model of relapse and maintenance leads to the obvious conclusion that behavior-change strategies should also devote attention to potentially high-risk situations. Marlatt further reported upon data with alcoholics, indicating that high-risk areas can be basically grouped as follows: (1) coping with negative intrapersonal states; (2) personal conflict with another; and (3) social pressure. It is interesting to note that Marlatt found that only 10 percent of the relapses in this study were caused by physiological cravings. In attempting to combat the above-mentioned high-risk situations, Marlatt proposes interventions that include skills training (via direct instruction, modeling, coaching, assertiveness training, and stress management), lifestyle interventions (e.g., jogging, meditation, and relaxation training), relapse rehearsal (e.g., situational imagery and programmed rehearsal), and controlled-use skills (e.g., cognitive restructuring).

Reminders and follow-up sessions

Compliance with keeping follow-up appointments has been increased through the use of reminders (Nazarian, Michalier, Charney, & Coulter, 1974), letters, and/or telephone calls (Gates & Colborn, 1976). Shipley (1981) found the use of follow-up letters to subjects significantly improved smoking-maintenance rates but interacted with individual-difference variables to a large degree. Colletti and Kopel (1979), Dubren (1977), and Jeffrey and Wing (1979) all found that the use of telephone calls following treatment intervention helped prevent relapses and improved maintenance rates on the problems of smoking and obesity. Letter or phone call reminders have particular promise, in the sense that they are quite cost efficient.

Additional methods for improving maintenance and reducing relapses have also been suggested by various investigators. One of the most common of these is the use of booster sessions, at regular intervals, after the initial therapy has terminated. Although the data on the use of booster sessions has been somewhat variable, there is at least some support in the literature for this approach (Brightwell, 1976; Kingsley & Wilson, 1977). However, this quite likely depends on the type and frequency of such booster sessions and, as Hall and Hall (1981) suggested, such sessions should "make follow-up as much like the treatment as possible" (p. 159).

Contingency contracting

Contingency contracting has been used with varying degrees of success to alter: maintenance of medication for hypertensive patients; (Steckel & Swain, 1977), weight loss for obese patients (Mann, 1972); control of drug abuse (Boudin, 1972); and smoking (Neisworth, 1972). In addition, a home-based, contingency-management program was reported to significantly increase children's compliance with dental hygiene (Claerhout & Lutzker, 1981). The use of written instructions and a contingent point system increased compliance for diet, urine testing, and foot care to nearly 100 percent in juvenile diabetics (Lowe & Lutzker, 1979). Wing, Epstein, Marcus, & Shapira (1981) found that the use of strong monetary contingencies—in the form of returnable deposits, which were dependent upon weight loss and session attendance—were successful in producing improved results in a weight-control program. This suggests that strong monetary contracts, which give subjects their own money back over a prolonged period of time, may be a very powerful way of promoting maintenance of behavior change.

The factors of compliance and maintenance of healthy lifestyles are now being recognized as vital components of any intervention program. There have been few, well-controlled outcome studies. Investigation and use of individual cognitive differences and the development of potent reinforcement techniques for the maintenance of healthy lifestyles are needed.

PROGRAMS AIMED AT LARGE POPULATIONS

The California Three Community Study—by the Stanford University group—aimed at changing diet, exercise, and smoking behaviors in a single, communitywide, prevention program (Stanford Heart Disease Prevention Program, 1977; Meyer, Nash, McAllister, McCoby, & Farquhar, 1980). A control community was compared with two treatments: (1) a media campaign, and (2) a media campaign combined with face-to-face, intensive instruction. Smoking treatment consisted of a variety of techniques to disrupt smoking cues and to substitute incompatible behavior for smoking. Of subjects in the intensive-treatment condition, 50 percent were not smoking at the end of three years. However, this figure could be reduced to as low as 32 percent, if all treatment dropouts were still smoking. Dietary-modification procedures were multifaceted and involved self-monitoring, modeling, and practice of alternative-shopping and food-preparation behaviors. Overweight individuals in the intensive-treatment group lost an average of 8.5 pounds during the program but regained an average of 5.3 pounds during the subsequent year. The final target of intervention was physical activity. The intensive treatment used behavior prescriptions (advice), modeling, and reinforcement to increase activity. No change in behavior in this area was found, however.

The overall results showed that the intensive-media campaign combined with face-to-face instruction had greater impact than the media campaign alone. A multiple-factor equation for risk of heart disease showed a 28 percent reduction in risk for persons in the combination treatment. Media-only subjects achieved more modest gains. No face-to-face group without media was included, which would have provided information on whether the media campaign enhanced the one-to-one treatment.

A somewhat similar project to the Stanford Heart Disease Prevention program was a public health intervention entitled The North Karelia Project, which was conducted in Finland (Koskela, Puska, & Tuomilehto, 1976; Puska, 1979; Puska, Koskela, Pakarinen, Puumalainen, Soininen, & Tuomilheto, 1976). These kinds of programs have been severely criticized by two different investigators (i.e., Kasl, 1980; Leventhal, Safer, Cleary, & Gutmann, 1980). Included in these criticisms is the fact that these kinds of intervention strategies are extremely expensive in time, dollars, and effort. In addition, these critiques have noted that these intervention strategies may not generalize to communities of different types. Finally, Leventhal suggested that these studies were undertaken prior to having an adequate knowledge of the intervention strategies that will be maximally effective on a communitywide basis.

Another intervention strategy that may have particular promise is the emergence of company projects designed to influence the health habits of employees. These include the Johnson & Johnson Live for Life Program (Wilbur, 1980–1981) and the Control Data Corporation Stay Well Program (Naditch, 1980–1981). At this point, it is too early to determine whether these programs are going to be substantially effective in changing health habits of their employees. However, it should be noted that companies possess a particularly advantageous position, in the sense that they have the potential to apply a number of very desirable reinforcement contingencies as an integral part of their programs. The contingencies that companies control could be potentially cost effective and implemented more easily than communitywide efforts. Presumably, a company's cost and time would be more than compensated by reduced absenteeism on the part of workers and, perhaps, increased productivity as well.

SUMMARY

The focus of this chapter is on behavioral medicine research and intervention in the areas of prevention and lifestyles. It is noted that changes in maladaptive lifestyles and behaviors, in addition to the promotion of *healthy* lifestyles, may hold some of the greatest promise for improving the health of the nation as a whole.

A review is presented of the burgeoning literature on attempts aimed at changing maladaptive-consumption habits, such as alcoholism, smoking, and obesity. Common methodological problems and inadequacies in treatment design are reviewed, along with suggestions for future research which may lead to improved outcomes. To date, outcomes in these areas have been relatively disappointing. A review is also made of more general, maladaptive lifestyles and behaviors, such as Type *A* coronary-prone behavior and risks-taking behavior. Research in the area of Type *A* behavior has generated substantial interest, although significant gaps remain in the understanding of the specific nature of the relationship between this behavior pattern and the development of heart disease. It is noted that risk-taking behaviors are major causes of mortality and morbidity in our society, although relatively little research has been conducted in this area.

Finally, a review is presented on the promotion of healthy lifestyles. Specific areas discussed included exercise, diet-nutrition, relaxation, and recreation-play. Once again, relatively little has been conducted in the way of well-controlled studies in these areas, although such efforts would be quite valuable. Once general changes in lifestyles have been effected, the considerable difficulties in *maintaining* these changes were noted.

Finally, a brief review is made of intervention approaches aimed at large population groups. Some of these have been at the community level and others within large business organizations. These approaches are quite new, but may hold considerable promise for significant improvements in the health of large numbers of people.

REFERENCES

Abrams, J. L., & Allen, G. J. Comparative effectiveness of situational programing, financial payoffs, and group pressure in weight reductions. *Behavior Therapy*, 1974, *5*, 391–400.

Abramson, E. E. Behavioral approaches to weight control. *Behavior Research and Therapy*, 1977, *15*, 355–363.

Adler, R. H., Galeazzi, R. L. Persönlichkeitszüge (typ A) Bei Patienten Claudicudio Intermitins. I. Ergebnisse Des Bortner-Tests. *Schweizerische* Wochenschr, 1977, *107*, 1833–1835.

American Society for Clinical Nutrition. Symposium report of the task force on the evidence relating six dietary factors to the nation's health. *The American Journal of Clinical Nutrition*, 1979, *32*, 2621–2748. (Supplement)

Ax, A. F. Physiological differentiation between fear and anger in humans. *Psychosomatic Medicine*, 1953, *15*, 433.

Bandura, A. Self-efficacy: Toward a unifying theory of behavioral change. *Psychological Review*, 1977, *84*, 191–215.

Becker, M. H., & Green, L. W. A family approach to compliance with medical treatment: A selective review of the literature. *International Journal of Health Education*, 1975, *18*, 2–11.

Bellack, A. S., & Schwartz, J. S. Assessment for self-control programs. In M. Hersen & A. S. Bellack (Eds.), *Behavioral assessment: A practical handbook*. Elmsford, N.Y.: Pergamon Press, 1976.

Benson, H. *The relaxation response*. New York: Avon Books, 1975.

Berecz, J. Modification of smoking behavior through self-administered punishment of imagined behavior: A new approach to aversion therapy. *Journal of Consulting and Clinical Psychology*, 1972, *38*, 244–250.

Bernard, H. S., & Efran, J. S. Eliminating versus reducing smoking using pocket timers. *Behavior Research and Therapy*, 1972, *10*, 399–401.

Blue, F. R. Aerobic running as a treatment for moderate depression. *Perceptual Motor Skills*, 1979, *48*, 228.

Blumenthal, J. A., Williams, R. S., Williams, R. B., & Wallace, A. G. Effects of exercise on the Type *A* (coronary-prone) behavioral pattern. *Psychosomatic Medicine*, 1980, *42*(2), 289–296.

Borrie, R. A., & Suedfeld, P. Restricted environmental-stimulation therapy in a weight-reduction program. *Journal of Behavioral Medicine*, 1980, *3*(2), 147–161.

Bortner, R. W. A short rating scale as a potential measure of pattern *A* behavior. *Journal of Chronic Disease*, 1969, *22*, 87–91.

Bortz, W. M., Angwin, P., Mefford, I. N., Boarder, M. R., Noyce, N., & Barchas, J. D. Catecholamines, dopamine, and endrophin levels during extreme exercise. *New England Journal of Medicine*, 1981, *305*, 466–467.

Boudin, H. M. Contingency contracting as a therapeutic tool in deceleration of amphetamine use. *Behavior Therapy*, 1972, *3*, 604.

Bower, S. A., & Bower, G. H. *Asserting yourself*. Reading, Mass.: Addison-Wesley Publishing, 1976.

Bray, G. A. Pharmacological approach to the treatment of obesity. In G. A. Bray & J. E. Bethune (Eds.), *Treatment and management of obesity*. New York: Harper & Row, 1974.

Brightwell, D. R. One-year follow-up of obese subjects treated with behavior therapy. *Diseases of the Nervous System*, 1976, *37*, 593–594.

Browman, C. P. Physical activity as a therapy for psychopathology: A reappraisal. *Journal of Sports Medicine*, 1981, *21*, 192–197.

Carmody, T. P., Senner, J. W., Malinow, M. R., & Matarazzo, J. D. Physical-exercise rehabilitation: Long-term dropout rate in cardiac patients. *Journal of Behavioral Medicine,* 1980, *3*(2), 163–168.

Carroll, L. J., Yates, B. T., & Gray, J. J. Predicting obesity reduction in behavior and nonbehavior therapy from client characteristics: The self-evaluation measure. *Behavior Therapy,* 1980, *11,* 189–197.

Chesney, M. A., Black, G. W., Chadwick, J. H., & Rosenman, R. H. Psychological correlates of the Type *A* behavior pattern. *Journal of Behavioral Medicine,* 1981, *4*(2), 217–230.

Chiroco, A. M., & Stunkard, A. J. Physical Activity and human obesity. *New England Journal of Medicine,* 1960, *263,* 935–940.

Christopherson, E. R., & Gyulay, J. E. Parental compliance with car-seat usage: A positive approach with long-term follow-up. *Journal of Pediatric Psychology,* 1981, *6*(3), 301–312.

Claerhout, S., & Lutzker, J. R. Increasing children's self-initiated compliance to dental regimens. *Behavior Therapy,* 1981, *12,* 165–176.

Colletti, G., & Kopel, S. A. Maintaining behavior change: An investigation of three maintenance strategies and the relationship of self-attribution to the long-term reduction of cigarette smoking. *Journal of Consulting and Clinical Psychology,* 1979, *47*(3), 614–617.

Condiotte, M. M., & Lichtenstein, E. Self-efficacy and relapse in smoking-cessation programs. *Journal of Consulting and Clinical Psychology,* 1981, *49,* 648–658.

Cooper, K. H., Pollock, M. L., Martin, R. P., White, S. R., Linnerud, A. L., & Jackson, A. Physical-fitness levels versus selected coronary-risks factors. *Journal of American Medical Association,* 1976, *236*(2), 166–169.

Doan, M. J. Personal communication, 1982.

Dubren, R. Self-reinforcement by recorded telephone messages to maintain nonsmoking behavior. *Journal of Consulting and Clinical Psychology,* 1977, *45,* 358–360.

Edleman, R. ASCN task force rates various diet and disease relationships. *Nutrition Notes,* 1980, *81,* 1.

Elkind, D., & Weiss, J. Studies in perceptual development III: Perceptual exploration. *Child Development,* 1967, *38,* 1153–1161.

Elliott, C. H., & Denny, D. R. Weight control through covert sensitization and false feedback. *Journal of Consulting and Clinical Psychology,* 1975, *43,* 842–850.

Elliott, C. H., & Denny, D. R. A multiple-component treatment approach in smoking reduction. *Journal of Consulting and Clinical Psychology,* 1978, *46,* 1330–1339.

Epstein, L. H., & Wing, R. R. Behavioral approaches to exercise habits and athletic performance. In J. M. Ferguson & C. B. Taylor (Eds.), *The comprehensive handbook of behavioral medicine: Systems intervention,* (Vol. 1). New York: Spectrum, 1980

Ferguson, J. M. A clinical program for the behavioral control of obesity. In B. J. Williams, S. Martin, & J. P. Foreyt (Eds.), *Obesity: Behavioral approaches to dietary management.* New York: Brunner/Mazel, 1975.

Folkins, C. H. Effects of physical training on mood. *Journal of Clinical Psychology.* 1976, *32*(2), 385–388.

Food and Nutrition Board. *Recommended dietary allowances.* Washington, D.C.: National Academy of Sciences, 1980.

Fox, S. M., Naughton, J. P., & Haskell, W. L. Physical activity and the prevention of coronary heart disease. *Annals of Clinical Research,* 1971, *3,* 404–432.

Fox, R. M., Brown, R. A., & Katz, I. Nicotine fading and self-monitoring for cigarette abstinence or controlled smoking: A two-and-one-half-year follow-up. *The Behavior Therapist,* 1981, *4*(2), 21–23.

Friedman, M. The modification of Type *A* behavior in post-infarction patients. *American Heart Journal,* 1979, *97,* 551–560.

Friedman, M., & Rosenman, R. H. Association of specific, overt-behavior patterns with blood and cardiovascular findings. *Journal of the American Medical Association,* 1959, *169,* 1286–1295.

Gastorf, J. W. Physiologic reaction of Type *A*s to objective and subjective challenge. *Journal of Human Stress,* 1981, *7,* 16–20.

Gates, S. J., & Colborn, D. K. Lowering appointment failures in a neighorhood health center. *Medical Care,* 1976, *14,* 263–267.

Gilbert, D. G. Paradoxical-tranquilizing and emotion-reducing effects of nicotine. *Psychological Bulletin,* 1979, *36,* 643–661.

Glasgow, R. E., McCaul, K. D., Freeborn, V. B., & O'Neill, H. K. Immediate and long-term health consequences of information in the prevention of adolescent smoking. *The Behavior Therapist,* 1981, *4*(5), 15–16.

Glass, D. C. *Behavior patterns, stress, and coronary heart disease.* New York: John Wiley & Sons, 1977. (a)

Glass, D. C. Stress, behavior patterns, and coronary disease. *American Scientist,* 1977, *65,* 177–187. (b)

Gwinup, G. Effect of excercise alone on the weight of obese women. *Archives of Internal Medicine,* 1975, *135,* 676–680.

Hagen, R. L. Behavioral treatment of obesity: Progress but not panacea. In J. M. Ferguson & C. B. Taylor (Eds.), *The comprehensive handbook of behavioral medicine: Syndromes and special areas* (Vol. 2). New York: Spectrum, 1981.

Hall, S. M., & Hall, R. G. Maintaining change. In J. M. Ferguson, & C. B. Taylor (Eds.), *The comprehensive handbook of behavioral medicine: Extended applications and issues* (Vol. 3). New York: Spectrum, 1981.

Hall, S. M., Hall, R. G., Hanson, R. W., & Borden, B. L. Permanence of two self-managed treatments of overweight in university and community populations. *Journal of Consulting and Clinical Psychology,* 1974, *42,* 781–786.

Haynes, S. G., Feinleib, M., & Kannel, W. B. The relationship of psychological factors to coronary heart disease in the Framingham study III: Eight-year incidence of coronary heart disease. *American Journal of Epidemiology,* 1980, *3,* 37–58.

Haynes, S. G., Levine, S., Scotch, N. A., Feinleib M., & Kannel, W. B. The relationship of psychosocial factors to coronary heart disease in the Framingham study I: Methods and risk factors. *American Journal of Epidemiology,* 1978, *107,* 362–383.

Henderson, J. B., & Enelow, A. J. The coronary risk-factor problem: A behavioral perspective. *Preventive Medicine,* 1976, *5,* 128–148.

Herman, S., Blumenthal, J., Black, G. M., & Chesney, M. A. Self-ratings of Type *A* (coronary-prone) adults: Do Type *A*'s know they are Type *A*'s? *Psychosomatic Medicine,* 1981, *43*(5), 405–413.

Hersen, M. Complex problems require complex solutions. *Behavior Therapy,* 1981, *12,* 15–29.

Hess, W. R. *Diencephalon: Autonomic and extrapyramidal functions.* New York: Grune & Stratton, 1954.

Holmes, D. J. *Psychotherapy.* Boston: Little, Brown, 1972.

Hurd, P. D., Johnson, C. A., Pechacek, T., Bast, L. P., Jacobs, D. R., & Luepker, R. V. Prevention of smoking in seventh-grade students. *Journal of Behavioral Medicine,* 1980, *3*(1), 15–28.

Ismail, A. H., & Trachtman, L. E. Jogging the imagination. *Psychology Today,* 1973, *6,* 78–82.

Janis, I. L., & Rodin, J. Attribution, control, and decision making: Social psychology and health care. In G. C. Stone, F. Cohen, & N. E. Adler (Eds.), *Health psychology.* San Francisco: Jossey-Bass, 1979.

Jeffrey, D. B., & Lemnitzer, N. Diet, exercise, obesity, and related health problems: A macroenvironmental analysis. In J. M. Ferguson & C. B. Taylor (Eds.), *The comprehensive handbook of behavioral medicine: Syndromes and special areas* (Vol. 2). New York: Spectrum 1981.

Jeffrey, R. W., & Wing, R. R. Frequency of therapist contact in th treatment of obesity. *Behavior Therapy,* 1979, *10,* 186–192.

Jeffrey, R. W., Wing, R. R., & Stunkard, A. J. Behavioral treatment of obesity: The state of the art, 1976. *Behavior Therapy,* 1978, *9,* 189–199.

Jenkins, C. D., Rosenman, R. H., & Friedman, M. Development of an objective psychological test for the determination of the coronary-prone behavior pattern in employed men. *Journal of Chronic Disease,* 1967, *20,* 371–379.

Jennings, J. R., & Choi, S. Type *A* components and psychological responses to an attention-demanding performance task. *Psychosomatic Medicine,* 1981, *43*(6), 475–487.

Kasl, S. V. Cardiovascular-risk reduction in a community setting: Some comments. *Journal of Consulting and Clinical Psychology,* 1980, *48*(2), 143–149.

Keir, S., & Lauzon, R. Physical activity in a healthy lifestyle. In P. O. Davidson & S. M. Davidson (Eds.), *Behavioral medicine: Changing health lifestyles.* New York: Brunner/Mazel, 1980.

Kingsley, R. C., & Wilson, G. T. Behavior therapy for obesity: A comparative investigation of long-term efficacy. *Journal of Consulting and Clinical Psychology,* 1977, *45,* 288–298.

Knowles, J. H. *Doing better and feeling worse: Health in the United States.* New York: W. W. Norton, 1977.

Kopel, S., & Arkowitz, H. The role of attribution and self-perception in behavior change: Implications for behavior therapy. *Genetic Psychological Monographs,* 1975, *95,* 175–212.

Kornitzer, M., Kittel, F., DeBacker, G., & Dramaix, M. The Belgian heart disease prevention project: Type *A* behavior pattern and the prevalence of coronary heart disease. *Psychosomatic Medicine,* 1981, *43*(2), 133–145.

Koskela, K., Puska, P., & Tuomilehto, J. The North Karelia project: A first evaluation. *International Journal of Health Education,* 1976, *19,* 59–66.

Lando, H. A. A comparison of excessive and rapid smoking in the modification of chronic smoking behavior. *Journal of Consulting and Clinical Psychology,* 1975, *43,* 350–355.

Lando, H. A. Aversive conditioning and contingency management in the treatment of smoking. *Journal of Consulting and Clinical Psychology,* 1976, *44,* 312.

Lawler, K. A., Allen, M. T., Critcher, E. C., & Standard, B. A. The relationship of physiological responses to the coronary-prone behavior pattern in children. *Journal of Behavioral Medicine,* 1981, *4*(2), 203–216.

Lawson, D. M., & May, R. B. Three procedures for the extinction of smoking behavior. *Psychological Record,* 1970, *20,* 151–157.

Levanthal, H., Safer, M. A., Cleary, P. D., & Gutmann, M. Cardiovascular-risk modification by community-based programs for lifestyle changes: Comments on the Stanford study. *Journal of Consulting and Clinical Psychology,* 1980, *48,* 150–158.

Lichtenstein, E., Harris, D. E., Birchler, G. R., Wahl, J. M., & Schmahl, D. P. A comparison of rapid smoking, warm, smoky air, and attention placebo in the modification of smoking behavior. *Journal of Consulting and Clinical Psychology,* 1973, *40,* 92–98.

Los Angeles Kaiser-Permante Medical Care Program. Control program: Its purpose and implications for an HMO. *Professional Psychology,* 1979, *34,* 409–417.

Lowe, K., & Luztker, J. R. Increasing compliance to medical regimens with the juvenile diabetic. *Behavior Therapy,* 1979, *10,* 57–64.

Mahoney, M. J., & Mahoney, K. Treatment of obesity: A clinical exploration. In B. J. Williams, S. Martin, & J. P. Foreyt (Eds.), *Obesity: Behavioral approaches to dietary management.* New York: Brunner/Mazel, 1976.

Manheimer, D., Dewey, J., Mellinger, G., & Corsa, L. 50,000 child-years of accidental injuries. *Public Health Reports,* 1966, *81,* 519–533.

Manheimer, D. I., & Mellinger, G. D. Personality characteristics of the child accident repeater. *Child Development,* 1967, *38,* 491–513.

Mann, G. V., Garrett, H. L., Farhi, A., Murray, H., & Billings, F. T. Exercise to prevent coronary heart disease: An experimental study of the effects of training on risk factors for coronary disease in men. *American Journal Medicine,* 1969, *46,* 12–27.

Mann, R. A. The behavior-therapeutic use of contingency contracting to control an adult-behavior problem: Weight control. *Journal of Applied Behavioral Analysis,* 1972, *5,* 99–109.

Marlatt, G. A. *Addictions: A cognitive behavioral-treatment approach.* BMA Audio Cassettes. New York: Guilford Press, 1978.

Marlatt, G. A., & Gordon, J. R. Determinant of relapse: Implications for the maintenance of behavior change. In P. O. Davidson & S. M. Davidson (Eds.), *Behavioral medicine: Changing health lifestyles.* New York: Brunner/Mazel, 1980.

Masover, L., & Stamler, J. Address to the convention of the American Public Health Association, 1976. In U.S. Senate Select Committee on Nutrition and Human Needs (Ed.), *Dietary goals for the United States.* Washington, D.C.: U.S. Government Printing Office, 1977.

Matarazzo, J. D. Behavioral health's challenge to academic, scientific, and professional psychology. *American Psychologist,* 1982, *37*(1), 1–14.

Matheny, A. P. Visual-perceptual exploration and accident liability in children. *Journal of Pediatric Psychology,* 1980, *5*(4), 343–351.

Matson, J. L. Social reinforcement by the spouse weight control: A case study. *Journal of Behavior Therapy and Experimental Psychiatry,* 1977, *8,* 327–328.

Matthews, K. A., & Angulo, J. Measurement of the Type *A* behavior pattern in children. *Journal of Pediatric Psychology,* 1980, *51,* 466–475.

Mausner, B. An ecological view of cigarette smoking. *Journal of Abnormal Psychology,* 1973, *81,* 115–126.

McCranie, E. W., Simpson, M. E., & Stevens, J. S. Type A behavior, field dependence, and serum lipids. *Psychosomatic Medicine,* 1981, *43,* 107–116.

McFall, R. M. Smoking-cessation research. *Journal of Consulting and Clinical Psychology,* 1978, *46*(4) 703–712.

Mechanic, D., & Cleary, P. D. Factors associated with the maintenance of positive health behavior. *Preventive Medicine,* 1980, *9,* 805–814.

Medical News report. CHD stress reactions seems unrelated to Type A, Type B. *Medical News,* May 25, 1981.

Meichenbaum, D. *Cognitive behavior modification: An integrative approach.* New York: Plenum Press, 1977.

Meyer, A. J., Nash, J. D., McAllister, A. L., Maccoby, N., & Farquhar, J. W. Skills training in a cardiovascular health-education campaign. *Journal of Consulting and Clinical Psychology,* 1980, *48,* 129–142.

Meyer, V., & Crisp, A. H. Aversion therapy in two cases of obesity. *Behavior research and Therapy,* 1964, *2,* 143–147.

Miller, P. M., & Foy, D. W. Substance abuse. In S. M. Turner, K. S. Calhoun, & H. E. Adams (Eds.), *Handbook of clinical behavior therapy.* New York: John Wiley & Sons, 1981.

Miller, W. R. Treating problem drinkers: What works? *The Behavior Therapist,* 1982, *5*(1), 15–18.

Miller, W. R., Taylor, C. A., & West, J. C. Focused versus broad-spectrum behavior therapy for problem drinkers. *Journal of Consulting and Clinical Psychology,* 1980, *48*(5), 590–601.

Mitchell, T. R., & Biglan, A. Instrumentality theories: Current uses in psychology. *Psychological Bulletin,* 1971, *76,* 432–454.

Naditch, M. P. The Control Data Corporation Stay Well program. *Behavioral Medicine Update,* 1980–1981, *2*(4), 9–10.

Nathan, P. Ideal mental health services for alcoholics. In P. O. Davidson & S. M. Davidson (Eds.), *Behavioral medicine: Changing health lifestyles.* New York: Brunner/Mazel, 1980.

Nathan, P., & Lansky, D. Problems in research on the addictions. *Journal of Consulting and Clinical Psychology,* 1978, *46*(4), 713–726.

National Center for Health Statistics, Division of Vital Statistics. *U.S. national health survey.* Washington, D.C.: U.S. Government Printing Office, 1978.

Navia, J. TV advertising of food to children. In U.S. Senate Select Committee on Nutrition and Human Needs (Ed.), *Dietary goals for the United States.* Washington, D.C.: U.S. Government Printing Office, 1977.

Nazarian, L. F., Michalier, J., Charney, E., & Coulter, M. P. Effect of a mailed appointment reminder on appointment keeping. *Pediatrics,* 1974, *53,* 349–352.

Neisworth, J. T. Elimination of cigarette smoking through gradual phase out of stimulus controls. *Behaviorally Speaking,* 1972.

Pearce, J. W., LeBow, M. D., & Orchard, J. Role of spouse involvement in the behavioral treatment of overweight women. *Journal of Consulting and Clinical Psychology,* 1981, *49*(2), 236–244.

Pechacek, T. F., & McAlister, A. L. Strategies for the modification of smoking behavior: Treatment and prevention. In J. M. Ferguson & C. B. Taylor (Eds.), *The comprehensive handbook of behavior therapy: Extended applications and issues* (Vol. 3). New York: Spectrum, 1980.

Pitta, P., Alpert, M., & Perelle, I. Cognitive stimulus-control program for obesity with emphasis on anxiety and depression reduction. *International Journal of Obesity,* 1980, *4,* 227–233.

Pomerleau, O. F. Why people smoke: Current psychological models. In J. M. Ferguson & C. B. Taylor (Eds.), *The comprehensive handbook of behavioral medicine: Extended application and issues* (Vol. 3). New York: Spectrum, 1980.

Pottenger, M., McKernon, J., Patrie, L. E., Weissman, M. M., Ruben, H. L., & Newberry, P. The frequency and persistence of depressive symptoms in the alcohol cluster. *Journal of Nervous and Mental Disease,* 1968, *166,* 562–570.

Puska, P. The North Karelia project: An example of health promotion in action. In J. L. Swhartz (Ed.), *Progress in smoking cessation: Proceedings of the International Conference of Smoking Cessation,* 1978. New York: American Cancer Society, 1979.

Puska, P., Koskela. K., Parkarinen, H., Puumalainen, P., Soininen, V., & Tuomilehto, J. The North Karelia project: A program for community control of cardiovascular diseases. *Scandinavian Journal of Social Medicine,* 1976, *4,* 57–60.

Pyke, S., Agnew, N. M., & Kopperud, J. Modification of air-overlearned maladaptive response through a relearning program: A pilot study on smoking. *Behavioral Research and Therapy,* 1966, *4,* 197–203.

Review Panel on Coronary-Prone Behavior and Coronary Heart Disease. Coronary-prone behavior and coronary heart disease: A critical review. *Circulation,* 1981, *63*(6), 1199–1215.

Rimm, D. C., & Masters, J. C. *Behavior therapy: Techniques and empirical findings.* New York: Academic Press, 1979.

Romancyzk, R. G. Self-monitoring in the treatment of obesity: Parameters of reactivity. *Behavior Therapy,* 1974, *5,* 531–540.

Rosenman, R. H., Brand, R. J., Jenkins, C. D., Friedman, M., Straus, R., & Wurm, M. Coronary Heart disease in the Western Collaborative Group study: Final follow-up experience of 8½ years. *Journal of the American Medical Association,* 1975, *233,* 872–877.

Rosenman, R. H., & Friedman, M. Modifying Type A behavior pattern. *Journal of Psychosomatic Research,* 1977, *21,* 323–333.

Rosenman, R. H., Friedman, M., Straus, R., Wurm, M., Kositchek, R., Haan, W., & Werthessen, N. T. A predictive study of coronary heart disease. *Journal of the American Medical Association,* 1964, *189,* 15–22.

Roskies, E. Changing the Type *A* behavior pattern in a nonclinical population. Research proposal submitted to Health and Welfare, Canada, January 1978.

Roskies, E. Considerations in developing a treatment program for the coronary-prone (Type A) behavior pattern. In P. O. Davidson & S. M. Davidson (Eds.), *Behavioral medicine: Changing health lifestyles.* New York: Brunner/Mazel, 1980.

Roskies, E., Spevack, M., Surkis, A., Cohen, C., & Gilman, S. Changing the coronary-prone (Type *A*) behavior pattern in a nonclinical population. *Journal of Behavioral Medicine,* 1978, *1,* 201–217.

Sachs, L. B., Bean, H., & Morrow, I. J. Comparison of smoking treatments. *Behavior Therapy,* 1970, *1,* 465–472.

Schachter, J. Pain, fear, and anger in hypertensives and normotensives. *Psychomatic Medicine*, 1957, *19*, 17.

Schmahl, D. P., Lichtenstein, E., & Harris, D. E. Successful treatment of habitual smokers with warm, smoky air and rapid smoking. *Journal of Consulting and Clinical Psychology*, 1972, *38*, 105–111.

Sheehan, G. *Running and being*. New York: Grune & Stratton, 1978.

Shipley, R. H. Maintenance of smoking cessation: Effect of follow-up letters, smoking motivation, muscle tension, and health locus of control. *Journal of Consulting and Clinical Psychology*, 1981, *49*(6), 982–984.

Siegel, J. M., & Leitch, C. J. Behavioral factors and blood pressure in adolescents: The Tacoma study. *American Journal of Epidemiology*, 1981, *113*, 171–181.

Siegel, J. M., Matthews, K. A., & Leitch, C. J. Validation of the Type A interview assessment of adolescents: A multidimensional approach. *Psychosomatic Medicine*, 1981, *43*(4) 311–321.

Smith, J. W. Abstinence-oriented alcoholism-treatment approaches. In J. M. Ferguson & C. B. Taylor (Eds.), *The comprehensive handbook of behavioral medicine: Extended application and issues* (Vol. 3). New York: Spectrum, 1980.

Sobell, M. B., & Sobell, L. Nonproblem drinking as a goal in the treatment of problem drinkers. In J. M. Ferguson & C. B. Taylor (Eds.), *The comprehensive handbook of behavioral medicine: Extended applications and issues* (Vol. 3). New York: Spectrum, 1981.

Stanford Heart Disease Prevention Program. Community education for cardiovascular health, *Lancet*, 1977, *1*, 1192–1195.

Steckel, S. B., & Swain, M. A. *Written contracts to improve adherence in hypertensive patients*. Paper presented at the National Conference on High Blood Pressure Control, Washington, D.C., 1977.

Steffen, J. J., & Myszak, K. A. Influence of pre-therapy induction upon the outcome of a self-control weight-reduction program. *Behavior Therapy*, 1978, *9*, 404–409.

Steffy, R. A., Meichenbaum, D., & Best, J. S. Aversion and cognitive factors in the modification of smoking behavior. *Behavior Research and Therapy*, 1970, *8*, 115–125.

Stuart, R. B. A three-dimensional program for the treatment of obesity. *Behavior Research and Therapy*, 1971, *9*, 177–186.

Stuart, R. B. Weight loss and beyond: Are they taking it off and keeping it off? In P. O. Davidson & S. M. Davidson (Eds.), *Behavioral medicine: Changing health lifestyles*. New York: Brunner/Mazel, 1980.

Stunkard, A. J. Behavioral medicine and beyond: The example of obesity. In O. F. Pomerleau & J. P. Brady (Eds.), *Behavioral medicine, theory, and practice*. Baltimore: Williams & Wilkins, 1979.

Stunkard, A. J. Obesity. In S. Arieti & H. K. H. Brodie (Eds.), *American handbook of psychiatry: Advances and new directions* (2d ed., Vol. 7). New York: Basic Books, 1981.

Stunkard, A. J., & Mahoney, M. J. Behavioral treatment of the eating disorders. In H. Leitenberg (Ed.), *Handbook of behavior modification and behavior therapy*. Englewood Cliffs, N.J.: Prentice-Hall, 1976.

Suinn, R. M. The cardiac stress-management program for Type A patients. *Cardiac Rehabilitation*, 1975, *5*(4), 13–15.

Suinn, R. M. Pattern A behaviors and heart disease: Intervention approaches. In J. M. Ferguson & C. B. Taylor, (Eds.), *The comprehensive handbook of behavioral medicine: Systems intervention* (Vol. 1). New York: Spectrum, 1980.

Suinn, R. M., & Bloom, L. J. Anxiety-management training for Type A persons. *Journal of Behavioral Medicine,* 1978, *1,* 25–35.

Sullivan, L., Bjuro, R., Garrellick, G., Krotiewski, M., & Perrson, G. The predictive value of adipose tissue cellularity, basal metabolism rate, and cephalic insulin stimulation in the treatment of obesity. *International Journal of Obesity,* in press.

Sutherland, A., Amit, Z., Golden, M., & Rosenberger, Z. Comparison of three behavioral techniques in the modification of smoking behavior. *Journal of Consulting and Clinical Psychology,* 1975, *43,* 443–447.

Taggert, P., Parkinson, T., & Carruthers, M. Cardiac response to thermal, physical, and emotional stress. *British Medical Journal,* 1972, *4,* 71–76.

Van Itallie, T. B. Obesity: Adverse effects on health and longevity. *American Journal of Clinical Nutrition,* 1979, *32,* 2723–2733.

Vickers, R. R., Herirg, L. K., Rahe, R. H., & Rosenman, R. H. Type A behavior pattern and coping and defense. *Psychosomatic Medicine,* 1981, *43*(5), 381–396.

Vogler, R. E., Compton, J. V., & Weissbach, T. A. Integrated-behavior change for alcoholics. *Journal of Consulting and Clinical Psychology,* 1975, *43*(2), 233–243.

Walker, C. E. *Learn to relax.* Englewood Cliffs, N.J.: Prentice-Hall, 1975.

Wehl, C. K. & Turner, R. W. *Group versus individual cognitive-behavioral therapy for depressed alcoholics.* Paper to be presented at American Psychological Association convention, Washington, D.C., 1982.

Weisz, G., & Bucher, B. Involving husbands in treatment of obesity—Effects on weight loss, depression, and marital satisfaction. *Behavior Therapy,* 1980, *11*(5), 643–650.

Wijesinghe, B. Massed electrical-aversion treatment of compulsive eating. *Journal of Behavioral Therapy and Experimental Psychiatry,* 1973, *4,* 133–135.

Wilbur, C. S. The Johnson & Johnson Live for Life program. *Behavioral Medicine Update,* 1980–1981, *2*(4), 7–8.

Wiley, J. A., & Comacho, T. L. Lifestyle and future health: Evidence from the Alameda County study. *Preventive Medicine,* 1980, *9,* 1–21.

Williams, R. B., Haney, T. L., Lee, K. L., Kong, V., Blumenthal, J. A., & Whalen, R. E. Type A behavior, hostility, and coronary atherosclerosis. *Psychosomatic Medicine,* 1980, *42,* 539–549.

Wilson, G. T. Cognitive factors in lifestyle changes: A social-learning perspective. In P. O. Davidson & S. M. Davidson (Eds.), *Behavioral medicine: Changing health lifestyles.* New York: Brunner/Mazel, 1980.

Wing, R. R., Epstein, L. H., Marcus, M., & Shapira, B. Strong monetary contingencies for weight loss during treatment and maintenance. *Behavior Therapy,* 1981, *12,* 702–710.

Zeiner, A. R. Are differences in the disulfiram-alcohol reaction the basis of racial differences in biological sensitivity to ethanol? In A. J. Schelter (Ed.), *Drug dependence and alcoholism* (Vol. 1). New York: Plenum Press, 1981.

Zyzanski, S. J., & Jenkins, C. D. Basic dimensions of the coronary-prone behavior pattern. *Journal of Chronic Disease,* 1970, *22,* 781–795.

27

Relaxation and stress management training

*Douglas R. Denney**

The focus of this chapter is the management of stress-related disorders through the use of relaxation. A review of this topic is no small undertaking. A substantial portion of the research in the field of behavior therapy bears on this topic and, as Barlow (1980) has noted recently, the progress achieved here effectively represents "in a microcosm, the success story of behavior therapy" (p. 320).

This progress is all the more noteworthy in light of the problems that continue to plague pharmacological treatments for stress-related disorders, such as beta-adrenergic blockers and benzodiazepines. Several investigators (e.g., Ramsay, Greer, & Bagley, 1973; Tyler & Lader, 1973) have indicated that the therapeutic effects of beta-adrenergic blockers are confined to autonomic symptoms and have cautioned against equating these circumscribed effects with clinical improvement in anxiety. The benzodiazepines appear to have a more diffuse impact upon stress-related disorders, but they also possess harmful side effects and have been implicated in a significant pattern of abuse.

One of the important advantages of behavioral as opposed to pharmacological treatments for stress-related disorders is illustrated in a study by Davison, Tsujimoto, and Glaros (1973). Insomniacs were administered a treatment package consisting of a hypnotic drug, a relaxation procedure, and instructions for establishing a regular bedtime routine. Subjects reported substantial reductions in their sleep onset latencies during a 7-day period when the treatment package was in force. They were then divided into two groups. Half were told they had received an optimal dosage of the drug, shown to be maximally effective for inducing sleep. The other half were told they had received a minimal dosage of the drug, shown to be ineffective for inducing sleep. The drug was now discontinued while subjects practiced their relaxation and bedtime rou-

---

* University of Kansas, Lawrence.

tines and monitored their sleep behaviors for another four days. Subjects in the minimal-dosage group, who had been led to attribute their improved sleep behavior to their own self-initiated procedures, maintained their improvement throughout this period. Those in the maximal-dosage group, who had been led to attribute their improved sleep behavior to the drug, now returned to their pre-treatment levels of insomnia.

An inherent advantage may accrue to the types of behavioral procedures reviewed in the present chapter, one involving clients' causal attributions concerning the success achieved in treating their stress-related disorders. Gains that clients attribute to external sources (such as drugs) are unlikely to persist once the drug is withdrawn. Indeed, such external attributions may underlie the very phenomenon of psychological drug dependence. On the other hand, clients seem to personally embrace the gains they are able to attribute to stress management procedures, probably because of their active involvement in implementing these procedures. In a sense, the procedures and the salutary effects that result are "owned" by the client, rather than being attributed to some impersonal external source.

HISTORICAL ANTECEDENTS

Relaxation has been a little-recognized component of various "traditional" systems of therapy (e.g., psychoanalysis, hypnotherapy) and of age-old systems of meditation (e.g., Hatha yoga, Zen meditation). However, there exist two explicit historical antecedents to the use of relaxation as a treatment for stress-related disorders. These antecedents evolved at roughly the same time—in the early decades of this century—and shared a number of similarities, but their eventual divergence within the field of behavior therapy serves as a backdrop for one of the principal distinctions drawn among stress management procedures.

In 1929, Jacobson introduced a technique known as progressive relaxation aimed at bringing about a state of muscle relaxation, in order to diminish stress and to promote the restoration of psychological and physical well-being to his clients. Jacobson adhered to an extreme peripheralist view of emotion, aligning with the James-Lange theory of the day and emphasizing the importance of afferent feedback from tensed muscles as a necessary component of emotional experience. Based on this view, the generation of emotions such as anxiety is impossible when the musculature is relaxed, and it is for this reason one finds so much emphasis devoted to muscle exercises in progressive relaxation. Clients were instructed to recline and to follow a fixed sequence of exercises, alternately tensing and then relaxing major muscle groups throughout their body. As training continued, the tensing instructions were eliminated, and the procedure consisted of simply relaxing the muscle groups in an orderly sequence, all the while attending to the feelings of relaxation brought about in each group. Progression to each successive muscle group was contingent upon the attainment of relaxation in the preceding group, and this progression was noted to occur more rapidly as the client accumulated experience with the technique. It was not uncommon for Jacobson (1938) to prescribe as many as 200 sessions of progressive relaxation for some of his clients.

At about the same time, the German neuropsychiatrist, Shultz (1932), was introducing a technique known as autogenic training aimed at bringing about "a psychophysiological shift from a normal state to the autogenic state, which facilitates and mobilizes the otherwise inhibited activity of recuperative and self-normalizing brain mechanisms" (p. 1). Here again, the emphasis lay upon regular practice in attaining a specialized state of relaxation in order to diminish stress. Shultz, however, was not burdened with the same peripheralist views of emotion as was Jacobson and was, therefore, more comfortable incorporating elements of meditation and hypnotic suggestion into his autogenic technique. Clients reclined with their eyes closed in a quiet, comfortable setting and focused their attention on a sequence of six standard autogenic formulae—pertaining to feelings of heaviness and warmth in their limbs, regularity of their heartbeats and respiration, warmth and comfort in their abdomens, and cooling on the surface of their foreheads. The emphasis in these exercises, as in most meditation exercises, was upon passive concentration: "any goal-directed effort, active interest, or apprehensiveness must be avoided" (Luthe, 1963, p. 176).

Thus, while both progressive relaxation and autogenic training encouraged clients to attend to somatic experiences, the latter procedure contained more of a passive, meditative quality. This distinction became considerably greater in the latter half of the century under the catalyzing influence of behavior therapy. Progressive relaxation was adopted by Wolpe (1958) as a technique for evoking a potent reciprocal inhibitor of anxiety during systematic desensitization, and thereafter, the development of progressive relaxation was inextricably tied to that of desensitization. Autogenic training remained generally beyond the pale of behavior therapy for another decade, eventually being assimilated with other meditative techniques, and often as an adjunct to biofeedback training for the management of stress-related disorders. As a result, autogenic training retained its passive, meditative qualities, and today it constitutes perhaps the most appropriate historical antecedent to the techniques referred to in this chapter as "passive stress management." In contrast, progressive relaxation continued to evolve, along with desensitization, toward more active forms of self-control, eventually coming to serve as the nucleus of a second set of techniques referred to here as "active stress management." This subsequent development can be attributed largely to a seminal paper by Goldfried (1971).

Wolpe viewed relaxation as a response inherently incompatible with anxiety. By contiguously pairing this response with anxiety-arousing stimuli, the bond between these stimuli and the conditioned fear response they currently elicited would be weakened. This was the counterconditioning model first illustrated by Jones (1924) upon which systematic desensitization was formulated. Goldfried suggested a reinterpretation of desensitization as training in self-control. To him, it seemed more appropriate

> to construe systematic desensitization as more of an active process, directed toward learning of a general anxiety-reducing skill, rather than the passive desensitization of specific aversive stimuli. . . . During the process of systematic desensitization, the client is taught to become sensitive to his proprioceptive cues for tension and to react to these cues with his newly acquired skill in muscular relaxation. . . . According to this view, then, what the client learns is a means of actively coping with anxiety, rather than an immediate replacement for it. (pp. 228–229)

Goldfried suggested a number of modifications in systematic desensitization to further exploit its potential as a method for training self-control. These modifications involved both the treatment rationale and the desensitization procedure itself. Clients were to be told they were learning relaxation as a coping skill they could use to diminish anxiety arising in any setting. The purpose of the treatment sessions was, thus, to train clients in methods of relaxation, to help them to recognize tension cues as signals to initiate relaxation, and to allow them to practice relaxing away anxiety arising from a set of imaginary scenes presented by the therapist. Having demonstrated to themselves that they could diminish anxiety with relaxation, clients were to begin actively applying their relaxation skills in real-life settings. As for procedural modifications, Goldfried recommended greater attention be paid to relaxation training, not only to assist clients to achieve voluntary control over their relaxation response, but also to help them learn to discriminate proprioceptive cues of tension and relaxation. Hierarchies no longer needed to be constructed around a common theme but, instead, could include scenes from a diversity of events, all of which elicited anxiety. Clients were not to be allowed to terminate a scene whenever they signaled a disruption in their state of relaxation. Instead, they were to continue imagining the scene, while attempting to relax away the accompanying feelings of anxiety, signaling a second time when they had succeeded in regaining a state of deep relaxation. Only then were they to be allowed to terminate the scene. Finally, clients were to be given explicit instructions in the use of relaxation to diminish anxiety in real-life settings, and time was to be set aside during the later treatment sessions to allow for discussion of these attempted applications.

Despite Goldfried's crucial paper, one could argue that active stress management techniques were educed by clients before they were discovered by behavior therapists. Several investigators (e.g., Paul & Shannon, 1966) noted that although relaxation was introduced to clients as a reciprocal inhibitor within the framework of counterconditioning, desensitization clients tended to construe relaxation as a coping strategy for actively reducing stress in their lives and proceeded to use relaxation in this way. For example, such clients often reported spontaneously applying their newly acquired relaxation skills to reduce insomnia (Sherman, 1972). One of the byproducts of Goldfried's reformulation was a renewed interest in the possibility of using variations of desensitization to treat a greater variety of stress-related disorders other than circumscribed phobias. The principal focus of the present chapter is the treatment of pervasive or general anxiety, although an attempt is also made to illustrate the range of disorders that have been treated through various stress management procedures during the last decade.

Following the publication of Goldfried's paper, there was a rapid expansion in active stress management techniques, in which the principal goal was to teach clients a relaxation-based coping strategy that could be effectively applied to stressful situations encountered beyond the treatment setting. In contrast, the principal goal of passive stress management techniques remained one of teaching clients a method for evoking a specialized state of deep relaxation and of insuring that clients evoked this state on a regular basis each day in a quiet, comfortable setting. Passive stress management techniques sought to capitalize on real or purported benefits accruing from the regular practice of relaxation in a tranquil environment. Active stress management techniques attempted to make use of relaxation as a coping strategy to be applied to stressful environments. This distinction is of fundamental importance in organizing the treatment literature pertaining to relaxation-based therapies.

VARIATIONS OF ACTIVE AND PASSIVE STRESS MANAGEMENT TRAINING

Before proceeding with a review of the research concerning active and passive stress management training, it will be useful to consider in somewhat closer detail the specific techniques that compose these two categories. In the case of passive stress management training, the only potentially important source of variation between techniques involves the induction method used to evoke the client's relaxation response. Most investigators, such as Benson (1975), have tended to view relaxation as a unified, integrated state. Benson has described four basic elements that combine to elicit a unique hypometabolic state termed *the relaxation response*. The four elements are (*a*) a quiet environment, (*b*) a comfortable position permitting a marked reduction in muscle tonus, (*c*) an attitude of passive, nongoal-oriented detachment, and (*d*) a mental device or constant stimulus upon which to fix one's attention, such as a mantra, an autogenic formula, or simply one's own breathing. The response elicited by these elements was characterized as "an integrated hypothalamic response which results in generalized decreased sympathetic nervous system activity and perhaps also increased parasympathetic activity" (Benson, Beary, & Carol, 1974, p. 34).

In contrast to this integrated view, Davidson and Schwartz (1976; Davidson, 1978) have argued that there may be several forms of relaxation, characterized by different patterns of psychological and physiological changes and evoked by different relaxation procedures. In their most ambitious scheme, these writers suggested that cognitive, somatic, and attentional modes of relaxation should be distinguished and that each of these might be further subdivided according to left- versus right-hemispheric meditation. However, in garnering evidence for their view, Davidson and Schwartz generally limited their discussion to the distinction between cognitive and somatic forms of relaxation. Much of Davidson and Schwartz's argument is based upon Lang's (1969) contentions regarding the multimodal nature of anxiety and upon item analytic studies (e.g., Barratt, 1972; Buss, 1962; Corah, 1964; Hamilton, 1959) of common anxiety scales showing that items typically cluster around cognitive and somatic symptoms of anxiety. They reason that, if different forms of anxiety exist, then perhaps there are complementary forms of relaxation to dampen cognitive and somatic anxiety, and various methods for inducing relaxation should be contrasted in terms of their efficacy in bringing about these different forms of relaxation.

Conflict between integrated and multimodal positions regarding relaxation has prompted much basic research into the changes resulting from various relaxation methods. It is beyond the scope of the present chapter to review this research. Many of the studies are reviewed by Borkovec and Sides (1979), with respect to progressive relaxation and by Woolfolk (1975), with respect to meditation. It is useful, however, to consider the distinction between phasic and tonic effects of relaxation that emerges from such a review. Phasic effects are those that occur during the induction of relaxation and, thus, are studied while subjects are engaging in whatever relaxation method is of interest to the investigator. Tonic effects are more sustained, extending beyond the induction period and accruing to subjects through the regular practice of the technique. The vast majority of studies pertaining to relaxation effects has been focused upon phasic changes. However, the more relevant questions with respect to passive stress management techniques concern tonic effects. Indeed, the therapeutic benefits derived from passive stress management techniques can be thought of as some of the tonic effects of relaxation. It is, therefore, unfortunate that so little attention has been paid to tonic, as compared to phasic, changes in the basic research concerning the effects of relaxation.

The distinction between phasic and tonic effects is relevant to the controversy between integrated and multimodal views of relaxation. Davidson and Schwartz derived much of the empirical support for their multimodal view from studies in which two or more relaxation methods were directly compared. Their review of these studies happens to be rather selective. They devoted considerable attention to research by Paul (1969b) and Langen (1969) in which differences between various relaxation methods are found, but ignored other research (e.g., Paul & Trimble, 1970; Walrath & Hamilton, 1975) in which no such differences appeared. Nevertheless, even if these comparative studies lent consistent support to Davidson and Schwartz's thesis, one should note that, without exception, these studies focus on phasic effects. The relevance of these findings with respect to the therapeutic impact of relaxation within passive stress management training is obscure.

There is a related issue concerning the clinical significance of whatever disparities exist in the comparative studies cited by Davidson and Schwartz. These writers are extrapolating far beyond such disparities, claiming that independent *patterns* can be discerned and suggesting that lawful relationships exist between these patterns and various relaxation-induction methods. In general, these extrapolations have not been confirmed, and Davidson and Schwartz themselves seem to be modifying their position regarding Benson's relaxation response (e.g., Schwartz, Davidson, & Goleman, 1978).

In conclusion, when considering relaxation within the context of passive stress management training, one is reasonably justified in treating relaxation as an integrated concept. There exist a host of methods (e.g., progressive relaxation, autogenic training, meditation, hypnotic inductions, biofeedback techniques) for inducing relaxation, and thus far research has failed to establish that their resultant effects differ in any lawful or clinically significant way according to the type of induction employed.

In contrast to the general homogeneity that one finds among passive stress management techniques, the techniques that comprise active stress management training are more diverse and can be subdivided into two groups: applied relaxation techniques and self-control rehearsal techniques. These techniques are arrayed along a continuum, as illustrated in Figure 1.

At the far left of the continuum is the component common to all stress management procedures (both passive and active): training in the induction of relaxation using any of the various methods already described. In applied relaxation techniques, this induction training is supplemented by a self-control rationale (Goldfried, 1971) and explicit instructions in the in vivo application of relaxation. The two principal applied relaxation techniques discussed in the literature are cue-controlled relaxation training and applied relaxation training. These are positioned along the continuum in Figure 1 according to the extent to which each emphasizes the application of relaxation in stressful situations.

Figure 1

A continuum of active stress management techniques

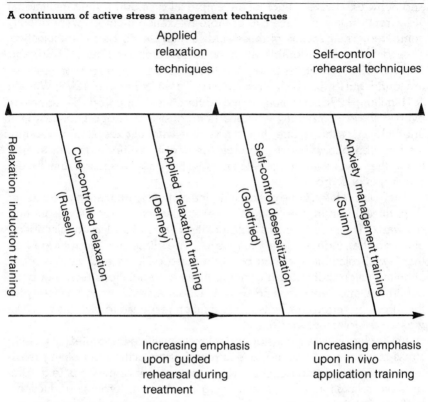

Source: Adapted from Denney, 1980.

Cue-controlled relaxation was first suggested by Cautela (1966) as a means of establishing a verbal cue for eliciting relaxation. The procedure consisted of first training clients in progressive relaxation and then instructing them to concentrate on their breathing and to subvocalize a verbal cue (such as the word *calm*) with each exhalation, so that the verbal cue might come to be paired with the state of relaxation. Since clients were supposed to self-produce this cue whenever they felt themselves becoming anxious outside the consultation setting, the procedure qualifies as an applied relaxation technique. However, little emphasis has ever actually been placed upon application training in cue-controlled relaxation.

A number of case studies illustrate the use of cue-controlled relaxation training with various kinds of specific fears, including test anxiety (Russell, Miller, & June, 1974; Russell & Sipich, 1973, 1974), speech anxiety (Gurman, 1973), dental anxiety (Beck, Kaul, & Russell, 1978), fear of snakes (Russell & Matthews, 1975), fear of driving (Russell, Lent, & Sipich, 1977), and fear of flying (Reeves & Mealiea, 1975). Comparative studies have shown cue-controlled relaxation to be as effective as systematic desensitization in reducing test anxiety (Russell, Miller, & June, 1975; Russell, Wise, & Stratoudakis, 1976) and speech anxiety (Russell & Wise, 1976). Counts, Hollandsworth, and Alcorn (1978) found cue-controlled relaxation to be significantly more effective than a placebo condition, whereas two studies by McGlynn and his colleagues (Marchetti, McGlynn, & Patterson, 1977; McGlynn, Kinjo, & Doherty, 1978) indicated no differences between cue-controlled relaxation and placebo conditions. None of the studies that attempted to assess generalization (Counts et al., 1978; Marchetti et al., 1977; McGlynn et al., 1978; Russell et al., 1975; Russell et al., 1976; Russell & Wise, 1976) found cue-controlled relaxation training to result in reduction in fears not specifically targeted for treatment. Perhaps generalization would improve if greater emphasis were placed on application of this technique as a coping strategy.

Applied relaxation training combines instruction in relaxation with a self-control rationale and assistance in helping clients apply their relaxation skills in real-life settings. Compared to cue-controlled relaxation training, applied relaxation training usually encompasses a more heterogeneous set of relaxation induction methods and more explicit instructions regarding the application of relaxation skills. While progressive relaxation remains the most common method for inducing relaxation, some investigators (e.g., Hutchings, Denney, Basgall, & Houston, 1980) have supplemented this method with a variety of other induction exercises to deepen relaxation, shorten the time necessary for its induction, and improve its applicability to real-life settings. When a variety of induction methods are introduced, clients are encouraged to fashion individualized relaxation programs appropriate to their particular needs.

It is unfortunate that so little attention has been paid to application training in active stress management techniques. Typically, clients are merely instructed to begin applying their relaxation skills outside of treatment and are given time to discuss successes and failures in these attempts. However, in some instances of applied relaxation training (Hutchings et al., 1980), four additional recommendations are incorporated within application training. First, this phase of treatment is delayed until clients have attained considerable proficiency at inducing relaxation in nonstressful settings. Second, whenever possible, clients' initial applications are structured so that the settings in which these occur are graduated in difficulty. Third, clients are helped to formulate adaptations of their relaxation programs to fit the particular settings in which application will occur. Finally, clients are informed of the possibility that their level of success in initial attempts may be something less than total and that the result may not be complete absence of distress but, instead, an enhanced sense of control over the distress and an ability to prevent it from interfering with effective performance.

As in the case of cue-controlled relaxation, most outcome studies pertaining to applied relaxation training have focused upon specific fears such as interview anxiety (Zeisset, 1968), speech anxiety (Goldfried & Trier, 1974), test anxiety (Chang-Liang & Denney, 1976), and dental anxiety (Miller, Murphy, & Miller, 1978). These studies have shown applied relaxation training to be as effective as systematic desensitization (Chang-Liang & Denney, 1976; Zeisset, 1968) and more effective than placebo conditions (Chang-Liang & Denney, 1976; Goldfried & Trier, 1974). Furthermore, Chang-Liang and Denney found that the effects of applied relaxation training generalized to two measures of general anxiety, whereas those of systematic desensitization were confined to the measures of test anxiety specifically targeted for treatment.

The second subcategory of active stress management training shown in Figure 1 involves self-control rehearsal techniques. These techniques include the same self-control rationale and application training components of applied relaxation techniques, plus an additional component known as "guided rehearsal." This component is usually interposed between relaxation induction training and application training. During guided rehearsal, the client is confronted with some representative stressful situations within the consultation setting, usually either through imagery or role-playing. When clients begin to experience distress in response to the situation, they are told to concentrate on this experience, noting the early signs of distress and the manner in which these are manifested. Clients then rehearse the use of their coping skills to reduce the distress, continuing until they have completely regained a state of relaxation. Thus, the guided rehearsal component that distinguishes self-control rehearsal techniques has two objectives: training in the early discrimination of stress cues and practice in the use of relaxation to reduce stress arising within the relatively safe confines of the treatment setting.

The two principal self-control rehearsal techniques featured in the literature are self-control desensitization and anxiety management training. These are presented along the continuum in Figure 1 according to the extent to which each technique emphasizes the guided rehearsal component.

Self-control desensitization encompasses the rationale and procedural modifications that Goldfried (1971) recommended for systematic desensitization. These were described in an earlier section of this chapter. Because of the theoretical thrust of Goldfried's paper, several investigators undertook to compare self-control and systematic desensitization. Almost all of these studies have focused upon test anxiety (Deffenbacher & Parks, 1979; Denney & Rupert, 1977; Lent & Russell, 1978; Spiegler, Cooley, Marshall, et al., 1976; Zemore, 1975); the only exception was a study by

Jacks (1972) dealing with acrophobia. These studies have consistently shown self-control desensitization to be at least as effective as systematic desensitization, with both treatments resulting in greater fear reduction than untreated controls. Denney and Rupert (1977) also included a placebo condition and reported several outcome measures on which subjects in the self-control desensitization condition evidenced greater improvement than those in either the systematic desensitization condition or the placebo condition.

Studies by Zemore (1975) and by Goldfried and Goldfried (1977) have addressed the question of whether the hierarchy in self-control desensitization must contain scenes that are related to subjects' specific fears or whether irrelevant scenes that are, nevertheless, able to elicit anxiety might be used during guided rehearsal. In these studies, self-control desensitization was found to be more effective than untreated (Zemore, 1975) or placebo (Goldfried & Goldfried, 1977) conditions and resulted in significant reductions in the targeted fear regardless of whether relevant or irrelevant scenes were used in the hierarchy. This point bears on the other self-control rehearsal technique to be discussed—anxiety management training.

The greatest emphasis on guided rehearsal is found within anxiety management training (Suinn, 1975a, 1976, 1977), and for this reason, it is located furthest to the right in Figure 1 among self-control rehearsal techniques. In contrast to self-control desensitization, hierarchical arrangements of fear-provoking scenes are not used, and there is a more purposeful attempt to provoke anxiety by whatever means are most effective. The stimuli introduced during guided rehearsal need bear no relation to stressful situations in the client's life, and, therefore, a greater latitude is permitted in these stimuli. Clients have been asked to recall anxiety-provoking memories from their pasts, to focus attention on physiological arousal, to concentrate on frightening passages from literature or electronic "mood music," or to contemplate receiving a painful electric shock.

Several comparative studies have shown anxiety management training to be as effective as systematic desensitization in treating math anxiety (Richardson & Suinn, 1973; Suinn & Richardson, 1971) and test anxiety (Deffenbacher & Shelton, 1978; Richardson & Suinn, 1974). In addition, Deffenbacher, Michaels, Michaels, and Daley (1980) found anxiety management training to be as effective as self-control desensitization in reducing test anxiety and in generalizing to a variety of nontargeted fears. However, the most important outcome research concerning anxiety management training has centered on its effectiveness in the treatment of general anxiety. These studies will be described in a later section.

One conclusion is clear from this survey of the techniques composing active and passive stress management training. Passive stress management techniques are far more homogeneous than active stress management techniques. This is probably due to the inherently less complicated goal of passive stress management training. Proponents seem to assume that the tonic effects of relaxation will accrue to clients automatically, provided the relaxation methods are practiced with faithful regularity. Once this assumption is accepted, the only potentially important source of variation among passive stress management techniques involves the methods used to induce the relaxation response. Thus far, the evidence for different tonic effects stemming from different induction methods is not at all compelling. On the other hand, the issue of how best to teach clients a relaxation-based coping strategy to actively apply in stressful situations is inherently more complicated and, accordingly, has spawned a more varied array of techniques. The continuum present in Figure 1 is an attempt to impose some organization on this array by highlighting distinctions thought to be both empirically and clinically meaningful.

STRESS MANAGEMENT TRAINING AND PSYCHOPHYSIOLOGICAL DISORDERS

Over the last decade, stress management procedures have been used to treat a variety of psychophysiological disorders. In the cases of essential hypertension, tension headache, migraine headache, and asthma, both active and passive stress management techniques have been investigated. These disorders are, therefore, featured in the present section.

Before proceeding with this review, a comment regarding biofeedback is in order. Many of the studies mentioned in this section involve some form of biofeedback training. There are two principal ways in which biofeedback has been applied to the treatment of psychophysiological disorders. One is relevant to the topic of this chapter; the other is not. The irrelevant use of biofeedback entails direct monitoring of the pathophysiology underlying a particular disorder. The goal here is to provide clients with veridical feedback concerning this pathophysiological process so that they can attain a degree of voluntary control over the process and thereby attenuate their symptoms. For example, clients with sinus tachycardia (Scott, Blanchard, Edmundson, & Young, 1973) and premature ventricular contractions (Weiss & Engel, 1971) have been treated with heart rate biofeedback to help them learn to regulate their heart rate in a direct, voluntary fashion. The other use of biofeedback, as a general aid in learning to relax, is definitely relevant to the focus of this chapter. The most common form of biofeedback encountered in these latter instances is EMG feedback from the frontalis muscle. Other forms include EEG alpha feedback, hand temperature feedback, and skin conductance (GSR) feedback.

It would appear that, while the first use of biofeedback—applied to specific pathophysiological processes—may still hold promise, the second use—as an aid to learning general relaxation—offers little advantage over verbal induction methods. Some studies involving normal subjects (e.g., Coursey, 1975; Haynes, Moseley, & McGowan, 1975; Reinking & Kohl, 1975) report advantages for biofeedback-assisted relaxation training, whereas others (e.g., Mohr, 1975; Sheridan, Boehm, Ward, & Justesen, 1976; Staples & Coursey, 1975) do not. However, in the case of research with clients, the majority of studies (e.g., Cox, Freundlich, & Meyer, 1975; Haynes, Griffin, Mooney, & Parise, 1975) have found no differences between biofeedback-assisted relaxation and verbal induction methods. Even when advantages are found (e.g., Hutchings & Reinking, 1976), they are slight and probably insufficient to justify the added expense of providing biofeedback to clients. Furthermore, Alexander (1975) has raised doubts about the extent to which voluntary reduction of frontalis muscle activity through EMG biofeedback generalizes to other muscles and thus evokes an overall state of relaxation. Similar concerns have been voiced by Plotkin (1976, 1977; Plotkin & Cohen, 1976) with respect to EEG alpha biofeedback. Finally, Glueck and Stroebel (1975) have questioned whether biofeedback-assisted relaxation is as effective as other induction methods when it comes to extending relaxation beyond the consultation setting.

Biofeedback training is thus included in the present chapter when it is used as a general aid to relaxation within either active or passive stress management training. However, as the preceding research indicates, its effectiveness in this capacity is probably no different than any other induction method.

Essential hypertension

The majority of studies pertaining to the treatment of hypertension involve passive stress management techniques, usually some form of meditation (Benson, Rosner, Marzetta, & Klemchuk, 1974a, 1974b; Blackwell, Bloomfield, Gartside, et al., 1976; Datey, Deshmukh, Dalvi, & Vinekar, 1969; Pollack, Weber, Case, & Laragh, 1977; Seer & Raeburn, 1980; Stone & DeLeo, 1976). Other passive stress management techniques that have been examined include frontalis EMG biofeedback combined with autogenic exercises (Love, Montgomery, & Moeller, 1974; Moeller, 1973; Moeller & Love, 1974), progressive relaxation (Shoemaker & Tasto, 1975), and metronome-conditioned relaxation (Brady, Luborsky, & Kron, 1974). Most of these studies have lacked independent control groups. However, Stone and DeLeo (1976) compared meditation training with an untreated control and found significant reductions in treated subjects' systolic and diastolic blood pressures. Love et al. (1974) reported similar results in their controlled investigation of a treatment combining frontalis EMG biofeedback and autogenic relaxation.

Only two studies involving passive stress management training (Blanchard, Miller, Abel, et al., 1979; Seer & Raeburn, 1980) have included a placebo condition to control for nonspecific treatment factors, such as demand and expectancy. In neither instance were significant differences found between treatment and placebo conditions.

Three studies (Blanchard et al., 1979; Shoemaker & Tasto, 1975; Surwit, Shapiro, & Good, 1978) have compared passive stress management training with blood pressure biofeedback, a treatment that is tied directly to the pathophysiology of hypertension. In two of these studies (Blanchard et al., 1979; Surwit et al., 1978), neither treatment was found to be superior to the other. Shoemaker and Tasto (1975) claimed greater reductions in blood pressure following progressive relaxation as compared with biofeedback. However, their study was conducted over only a brief period, and their biofeedback procedure did not provide subjects with continuous readings of blood pressure.

With respect to active stress management, both applied relaxation techniques (Beiman, Graham, & Ciminero, 1978; Frankel, Patel, Horwitz, et al., 1978; Patel, 1973, 1975a, 1975b; Patel & North, 1975; Taylor Farquhar, Nelson, & Agras, 1977) and self-control rehearsal techniques (Bloom & Cantrell, 1978; Jorgensen, Houston, & Zurawski, 1981) have been evaluated. Patel's procedure was the first active stress management technique to appear in the literature. Subjects received a host of relaxation induction methods, including EMG and GSR biofeedback training, progressive relaxation, and meditation exercises, and were then encouraged to apply relaxation to stressful situations during the course of their day. The procedure, therefore, qualifies as an applied relaxation technique, although it appears that application training received little emphasis. Patel reported substantial reductions in blood pressure following applied relaxation training, compared with a placebo condition in which subjects were simply instructed to take daily rests (Patel, 1975b; Patel & North, 1975). Using a similar applied relaxation technique, Taylor et al. (1977) replicated Patel's findings with respect to systolic blood pressure, but found no differences between this technique and either a placebo or an untreated control condition in terms of diastolic blood pressure. Moreover, a recent study by Frankel et al. (1978) indicated no differences between applied relaxation training, placebo, or untreated control conditions in either systolic or diastolic blood pressure.

Studies involving self-control rehearsal techniques have only recently appeared in the hypertension literature, beginning with Bloom and Cantrell's (1978) discussion of the use of anxiety management training with a single client. Jorgensen et al. (1981) have recently completed a controlled investigation of anxiety management training, comparing this procedure with an untreated control. These investigators found significant differences between groups in blood pressure readings collected during nonstressful periods, but no differences on readings collected during exposure to a laboratory stressor.

Tension headache

Studies dealing with the treatment of tension headaches are often difficult to categorize as instances of active or passive stress management training. Often it appears that investigators intended subjects to apply relaxation skills in the manner of an active stress management technique, but either failed to signal this intention to subjects or neglected to communicate this to readers when describing the methodology of the study (e.g., Fichtler & Zimmerman, 1973; Philips, 1977; Wickramasekera, 1972, 1973). Several of these studies included instructions for daily home practice of relaxation. However, it appears that this practice was to be conducted in a tranquil setting, rather than in one involving situational stresses or symptoms of approaching headaches. These studies were, therefore, classified as examples of passive stress management training.

To complicate matters further, as in the case of systematic desensitization, subjects occasionally seemed to have spontaneously converted their relaxation training into an actively applied technique. Despite the fact that their frontalis EMG biofeedback procedure was conducted as passive stress management training, Budzynski, Stoyva, and Adler (1970) described one of the later stages in the course of subjects' mastery of relaxation in which the subjects became capable of spontaneously reducing or aborting headaches by evoking relaxation. Similarly, Epstein and Abel (1977) noted that subjects who showed the most substantial improvement in response to their passive stress management procedure were those who spontaneously began applying their relaxation skills to reduce headache symptoms.

In all, the research pertaining to tension headache is about equally divided between studies of passive stress management (Budzynski et al., 1970; Budzynski, Stoyva, Adler, & Mullaney, 1973; Epstein & Abel, 1977; Fichtler & Zimmerman, 1973; Kondo & Canter, 1977; McKenzie, Ehrishman, Montgomery, & Barnes, 1974; Philips, 1977; Wickramasekera, 1972, 1973) and studies of applied relaxation techniques within active stress management (Chesney & Shelton, 1976; Cox et al., 1975; Epstein, Hersen, & Hemphill, 1974; Haynes et al., 1975; Hutchings & Reinking, 1976; Mitchell & White, 1976; Tasto & Hinkle, 1973). Frontalis EMG biofeedback is by far the most common method for inducing relaxation, regardless of whether the study entails passive or active stress management (Budzynski et al., 1970; Budzynski et al., 1973; Epstein & Abel, 1977; Epstein et al., 1974; Kondo & Canter, 1977; Philips, 1977; Wickramasekera, 1972, 1973). Verbal induction methods, usually involving progressive relaxation exercises, are encountered less frequently (Fichtler & Zimmerman, 1973; McKenzie et al., 1974; Mitchell & White, 1976; Tasto & Hinkle, 1973). Four of the studies categorized as active stress management (Chesney & Shelton, 1976; Cox et al., 1975; Haynes et al., 1975; Hutchings & Reinking, 1976) featured comparisons between

frontalis EMG biofeedback and progressive relaxation. These studies indicated the two induction methods were equally effective at reducing headache activity when used within the context of applied relaxation training.
Regardless of the induction method used, applied relaxation training has
been shown to result in significant reductions in tension headaches relative to placebo (Cox et al., 1975; Haynes et al., 1975) or untreated control
conditions (Chesney & Shelton, 1976).

Migraine headache

A considerably smaller number of studies have been directed toward
the treatment of migraine headaches. However, those that have been
reported are again divided equally into passive stress management training (Andreychuk & Skriver, 1975; Benson, Klemchuk, & Graham, 1974;
Blanchard, Theobald, Williamson, et al., 1978) and active stress management training (Mitchell & Mitchell, 1971; Mitchell & White, 1977). The
passive stress management techniques examined in the first set of studies
include meditation (Benson et al., 1974), progressive relaxation (Blanchard et al., 1978), EEG alpha biofeedback training (Andreychuk & Skriver, 1975), and a treatment combining hand temperature biofeedback
with autogenic exercises (Andreychuk & Skriver, 1975; Blanchard et al.,
1978). In the only study employing an independent control group, Blanchard et al. (1978) found progressive relaxation to be slightly more effective than their treatment combining temperature biofeedback and autogenic exercises. However, both conditions resulted in less headache
activity than untreated controls.

The active stress management techniques examined in the second set
of studies included both applied relaxation training (Mitchell & Mitchell,
1971; Mitchell & White, 1977) and self-control desensitization (Mitchell
& Mitchell, 1971). Mitchell has also strongly advocated using assertion
training as a supplement to active stress management techniques when
treating migraine clients.

Asthma

Passive stress management techniques in the treatment of asthma include meditation (Wilson, Honsberger, Chiu, & Novey, 1975), progressive relaxation alone and in combination with assertion training (Hock,
Rodgers, Reddi, & Kennard, 1978), and progressive relaxation in combination with frontalis EMG biofeedback (Scherr, Crawford, Sergent, &
Scherr, 1975). The two studies employing independent control groups
(Hock et al., 1978; Scherr et al., 1975) have shown the combined procedures featuring progressive relaxation to be particularly effective at reducing asthmatic symptoms.

Physicians have long advised asthma patients to try relaxing during asthma attacks in order to reduce the severity of these attacks. This recommendation, consistent with active stress management training, has prompted a number of studies concerning the phasic effects of relaxation on various measures of pulmonary function. Most of these studies report reliable increases in peak expiratory flow rate or forced expiratory volume following progressive relaxation (Alexander, 1972; Alexander, Miklich, & Hershkoff, 1972; Tal & Miklich, 1976) or frontalis EMG biofeedback training (Kotses, Glaus, Crawford, et al., 1976; Kotses, Glaus, Bricel, et al., 1978), although such changes are typically small in magnitude (Alexander, Cropp, & Chai, 1979) and may be limited to less severe cases of asthma (Davis, Saunders, Creer, & Chai, 1973). Since these studies are only concerned with phasic changes, they are not considered treatment outcome studies. Their function, however, is to establish an empirical foundation for the use of relaxation as an active stress management technique applied to the symptoms of asthma.

The only outcome study exemplifying active stress management in the treatment of asthma was conducted by Khan, Staerk, and Bonk (1973). The treatment involved a self-control rehearsal technique in which subjects were first trained in progressive relaxation and were then given an opportunity to practice their coping skills with mild asthmatic symptoms elicited in the treatment setting. Respiratory feedback was provided during this guided rehearsal phase to indicate subjects' progress at coping with the symptoms. The technique resulted in significant reductions in the frequency of asthma attacks, medication levels, and emergency hospital visits, compared with untreated controls. These reductions persisted for 12 months following treatment.

Stress management training procedures have been examined in conjunction with a host of other psychophysiological disorders beyond those featured above. In particular, passive stress management techniques have been used to treat cardiac arrhythmias (Benson, Alexander, & Feldman, 1975; Lown, Temte, Reich, et al., 1976), Raynaud's disease (Jacobson, Hackett, Surman, et al., 1973; Jacobson, Manschreck, & Silverberg, 1979; Stephenson, 1976), and phantom limb pain (McKechnie, 1975; Sherman, 1976; Sherman, Gall, & Gormly, 1979). On the other hand, active stress management techniques have been applied to the treatment of ulcers (Beaty, 1976; Brooks & Richardson, 1980), colitis (Harrell & Beiman, 1978; Mitchell, 1978), myofascial pain (Stenn, Motherskill, & Brooke, 1979), dysmenorrhea (Chesney & Tasto, 1975; Quillen & Denney, 1982), and type-A coronary-prone behavior pattern (Jenni & Wollersheim, 1979; Suinn, 1974, 1975b; Suinn, Brock & Edie, 1975). The four disorders reviewed in this section are only those conditions that have garnered attention from investigators of both active and passive stress management training. This is also true in the case of general anxiety, the problem focused upon in the remainder of this chapter.

PASSIVE STRESS MANAGEMENT AND
GENERAL ANXIETY

One of the tonic effects of relaxation that has been claimed with great consistency is the reduction of somatic and psychological symptoms of anxiety (e.g., Stoyva & Budzynski, 1973). Suggestive evidence to support this claim can be found in post hoc studies of experienced meditators compared with nonmeditating controls. Several studies have indicated lower scores on common self-report measures of general anxiety (Davidson, Goleman, & Schwartz, 1976; Hjelle, 1974) and more rapid recovery following stressful stimulation (Goleman & Schwartz, 1976; Orme-Johnson, 1973; Williams & West, 1975) among meditators. Such studies, however, are confounded by a number of factors involving subject selection. Long-term meditators have usually embraced a much broader spiritual and philosophical system beyond merely the faithful practice of relaxation, and the extent to which results based on such individuals can be generalized to the population at large or to persons suffering from various stress-related disorders remains questionable (Smith, 1975, 1978).

Other investigators have conducted longitudinal studies of subjects who had already made an independent decision to learn meditation, but were available for baseline assessment before receiving their training. These studies reveal significant declines in self-report measures of general anxiety (Ballou, 1973; Ferguson & Gowan, 1973; Orme-Johnson, Arthur, Franklin, et al., 1973) and in spontaneous skin conductance responses (Orme-Johnson, Kiehlbauch, Moore, & Bristol, 1973) when self-selected subjects practice meditation over a 4–10-week period. Although all of these studies included a group of nonmeditating controls, subjects were not randomly assigned to the two conditions, and there was no assurance that the samples were, therefore, comparable. Self-selected meditators—by their very decision to seek training in meditation—may, for example, be more motivated to change and more likely to display improvements, regardless of what training they receive.

Less favorable results are, in fact, reported when subjects are randomly assigned to meditation and control conditions. Goldman, Domitor, and Murray (1979) assigned normal college students to three conditions: meditation, antimeditation, and untreated control. The antimeditation condition served as a control for nonspecific factors and involved a bogus technique purportedly exercising the nondominant cerebral hemisphere. Although all three groups reported significant reductions on self-report measures of general anxiety, there were no differences between the groups. Likewise, Boswell and Murray (1979) assigned normal college students to a transcendental meditation condition, an antimeditation condition in which subjects were instructed to concentrate on their daily problems while taking leisurely walks, a progressive relaxation condition, and an untreated control condition. Again, self-report measures of general anxiety declined significantly over the course of treatment, but there were no differences between any of the groups. In a study conducted with alcoholics, Parker, Gilbert, and Thoreson (1978) compared meditation and progressive relaxation with a control condition in which subjects were simply told to rest quietly on their own for 15 minutes twice daily. Subjects in all three groups showed significant declines in heart rate and self-reported general anxiety after three weeks of treatment, but again, no differences between groups were found.

The treatment periods in these studies were exceedingly brief, ranging from five days in the first study to three weeks in the third. It is possible that the beneficial tonic effects of relaxation would not appear in so short a time. Zuroff and Schwartz (1978) examined changes in normal college students randomly assigned to transcendental meditation, progressive relaxation, and untreated control conditions, over a 9-week period. This study included a host of outcome measures pertaining to general anxiety, locus of control, social desirability, maladjustment levels, drug usage, and arousal during a social role-playing task. The only significant difference between groups occurred on one of the two self-report measures of general anxiety, with meditation subjects showing a greater decline than subjects in the other two conditions.

These four studies that feature random assignment of subjects are methodologically sound, although the treatment periods were usually brief and the subjects were not seeking treatment for general anxiety. Therefore, one might question the extent to which these results can be generalized to the issue of passive stress management training as a treatment for general anxiety. Unfortunately, most of the treatment outcome studies directly addressed to this issue lack the methodological sophistication of these former studies.

Multiple-case studies have illustrated the use of passive stress management techniques to treat anxiety neurotic clients. Girodo (1974) discussed the use of transcendental meditation with nine such clients whose symptoms had persisted from 5 to 71 months prior to treatment. Mathew, Ho, Kralik, and Claghorn (1979) treated 11 anxiety neurotic clients using progressive relaxation training supplemented by daily home practice. Raskin, Johnson, and Rondesveldt (1973) reported on the use of frontalis EMG biofeedback with 10 anxiety neurotic clients whose symptoms had persisted for at least three years and who had received individual therapy for the last two years. In general, clinically important improvements were noted in approximately half of the clients in these studies. Raskin et al. also observed generalization of treatment effects to five of six subjects who suffered from insomnia and to all four subjects who suffered from tension headaches.

As a follow-up on Raskin et al.'s study, Canter, Kondo and Knott (1975) randomly assigned 28 anxiety neurotic subjects to frontalis EMG biofeedback or progressive relaxation training, administered over 10 to 25 sessions. Frontalis muscle activity declined for all subjects over the course of treatment, with biofeedback subjects achieving lower levels than progressive relaxation subjects at termination. Global ratings of anxiety symptoms made by therapists and by the subjects themselves indicated improvement in 86 percent of the biofeedback subjects and in 50 percent of the progressive relaxation subjects.

Townsend, House, and Addario (1975) compared the effectiveness of relaxation therapy and conventional group therapy in treating 30 psychiatric inpatients selected on the basis of general anxiety. Subjects in relaxation therapy received nine sessions of frontalis EMG biofeedback training and practiced relaxing to taped progressive relaxation instructions each day for a period of four weeks. Those in group therapy met for 16 sessions of group discussion concerning problems of anxiety. Significant declines in frontalis muscle activity and in two self-report measures of general anxiety occurred only for subjects in the relaxation condition. Of the ten subjects who completed relaxation therapy, four were judged to be clinically improved. Of the eight who completed group therapy, none were so designated.

Benson and his colleagues (Benson, Frankel, Apfel, et al., 1978) compared the effectiveness of relaxation training through meditation and through self-hypnosis, using a sample of 69 psychiatric patients suffering from general anxiety and anxiety-related problems. After receiving instruction in their respective techniques, subjects were told to practice relaxation two or three times daily for eight weeks. Attrition rates were very high, and post-treatment data were available for only 16 subjects in each treatment condition. On the basis of standardized symptom interviews conducted before and after treatment, 34 percent of the subjects were judged to be clinically improved, with no differences between conditions. On the basis of self-report, 63 percent of the subjects indicated substantial improvement in various anxiety symptoms, again with no differences between conditions.

Smith (1975) reported a study by Vahia and his colleagues (Vahia, Doongaji, Jeste, et al., 1973) involving 95 psychoneurotic patients who had failed to benefit from insight-oriented psychotherapy. Subjects were randomly assigned to meditation or control conditions. Those in the meditation condition received training in both yogic meditation and physical stretching exercises; those in the control condition received training in the stretching exercises alone. Blind psychiatric assessments of various neurotic symptoms indicated substantial clinical improvement in 73 percent of the meditation subjects, compared with 42 percent of the controls, after six weeks. Subjects in the meditation condition also scored significantly lower on the MMPI and on a self-report measure of general anxiety relative to controls.

Two additional controlled outcome studies were conducted by Smith (1976), involving college students who responded to campus ads offering free treatment for anxiety. In the first study, subjects were randomly assigned to transcendental meditation, a placebo condition known as "periodic somatic inactivity," or untreated control. Subjects in the meditation condition were trained in transcendental meditation and told to practice twice daily while those in the placebo condition were trained to sit quietly in a comfortable position with eyes closed for an equivalent period of time. Post-testing conducted 3.5 months later revealed significant declines in self-report measures of general anxiety, muscle tension, and autonomic arousal for both meditation and placebo conditions relative to untreated control; however, there were no differences between the former two conditions.

In the second study, Smith compared transcendental meditation with an antimeditation placebo condition. In the latter condition, subjects were taught to sit quietly and engage a sequence of positive thoughts such as a fantasy or daydream. Post-testing conducted after 11 weeks again revealed significant declines in general anxiety, muscle tension, and autonomic arousal, but no differences between the two conditions. As in previous studies, subject attrition was very high, with 59 percent and 53 percent dropping from the meditation and placebo conditions in the first study and 48 percent and 30 percent dropping from these respective conditions in the second study.

With the exception of Smith's research, the treatment-outcome studies reviewed here offer a fair amount of evidence supporting the clinical effectiveness of passive stress management in the treatment of general anxiety. Smith's results, on the other hand, are similar to those of previously cited investigations (i.e., Boswell & Murray, 1979; Goldman et al., 1979; Parker et al., 1978; Zuroff & Schwartz, 1978) involving subjects who were not clinically anxious and, therefore, not seeking treatment. Because of his use of placebo conditions controlling for the regular practice of sitting quietly, as well as for various nonspecific treatment factors, Smith's studies represent the most competently designed outcome studies bearing on passive stress management. It is disconcerting when the best methodological studies also yield the most equivocal results concerning the effectiveness of passive stress management training. However, it might be well to consider the level of general anxiety represented by Smith's subjects. Perhaps the high attrition rates in these studies reflect the fact that marginally or temporarily anxious subjects could not justify continuing to spend the effort to practice the treatments. If the subjects in Smith's studies did suffer from only moderate levels of anxiety, this might explain why the placebo conditions fared so well. Various investigators (Bernstein & Nietzel, 1977; Borkovec, 1973; Borkovec & O'Brien, 1976; Rickels & Downing, 1967) have noted that moderately anxious subjects are more susceptible to placebo effects than are highly anxious subjects.

A number of additional methodological problems plague almost all of the treatment outcome studies reviewed here. None of these studies have included systematic follow-up assessments or checks on subject's compliance with instructions to practice at home. These are curious omissions, given that the underlying basis by which passive stress management training is thought to operate is through the gradual accumulation of benefits from regular practice.

The assessment of treatment effects within these studies is generally of poor quality. Most of the studies make no attempt to document that subjects have indeed acquired the ability to evoke an adequate state of relaxation, despite the fact that a variety of phasic physiological measures are available for this purpose. Furthermore, all but one of the studies (i.e., Mathew et al., 1979) depend exclusively on self-report measures for assessing tonic effects of relaxation. Indeed, there has been a general neglect of the development of tonic indices of stress and relaxation within the area of psychophysiology. Most common psychophysiological measures reflect discrete autonomic responses and are ill suited to the task of evaluating tonic changes. However, biochemical assays of neuroendocrine factors (e.g., Jevning, Wilson, & VanderLaan, 1978) and biogenic amines (e.g., Stone & DeLeo, 1976) may begin to yield more appropriate measures for future studies of passive stress management training.

ACTIVE STRESS MANAGEMENT AND GENERAL ANXIETY

Earlier sections of this chapter have noted that clients receiving relaxation training in conjunction with passive stress management or systematic desensitization often spontaneously convert their training into an applied coping strategy. In a similar fashion, 10 of the generally anxious subjects who received frontalis EMG biofeedback as passive stress management training in Raskin et al.'s (1973) study reported having spontaneously attempted to apply relaxation in anxiety-arousing situations. Most stated that these attempts were of little value, since they had only learned to relax in a supine position with their eyes closed. However, three subjects who reported success at these attempts were among the four subjects judged to have shown the greatest improvement in this study.

Another source of evidence supporting active stress management training is available through laboratory studies in which subjects are taught a relaxation method and are then exposed to some kind of stressful stimulus. Several studies indicate substantially smaller autonomic changes when subjects employed progressive relaxation (Connor, 1974; Davidson & Hiebert, 1971; Folkins, Lawson, Opton, & Lazarus, 1968; Paul, 1969a; Paul & Trimble, 1970), cue-controlled relaxation (Ewing & Hughes, 1978), autogenic exercises (Lindemann, 1973), or meditation (Goleman & Schwartz, 1976) during the presentation of various laboratory stressors.

A study by Puente and Beiman (1980) also evaluated the effects of meditation in inhibiting physiological responses to stress, as did earlier-mentioned studies by Boswell and Murray (1979) and Goldman et al. (1979). In these studies, meditation did not appear to inhibit subjects' stress reactions. The difference here is that subjects were not explicitly told to apply their meditation exercise to the stressful situation they were about to face and were not led to expect that such application would attenuate their autonomic response to the stressor. As already noted, these are important elements within active stress management training.

Shortly after offering his reformulation, Goldfried (1973) reported the successful treatment of a generally anxious adolescent girl using self-control desensitization. A second case report, again using self-control desensitization, appeared the following year (Arkowitz, 1974). Controlled-outcome studies bearing on the use of active stress management training in treating general anxiety, however, have centered almost totally upon Suinn's technique of anxiety management training.

The first such investigation was conducted by Nicoletti (1972) and involved subjects who complained of either speech anxiety or general anxiety. Subjects were randomly assigned to anxiety management training or untreated control conditions. Speech anxious subjects who received anxiety management training declined on the single measure of speech anxiety and on one of the five measures of general anxiety. Generally anxious subjects in the anxiety management training condition declined on four of the measures of general anxiety.

Edie (1972) compared three variations of anxiety management training applied to generally anxious subjects. In one condition, anxiety arousal during guided rehearsal was accomplished by having subjects visualize imaginary scenes of anxiety-provoking stimuli. In another condition, this was accomplished by having subjects focus upon the physical experience of anxiety without the use of imaginal scenes. In the third condition, both methods for arousing anxiety were used. College students seeking help for general anxiety were randomly assigned to one of the three conditions or to an untreated control. Self-report measures indicated that all three treatment conditions resulted in lower levels of general anxiety than the untreated control. No differences were discovered between the three variations of anxiety management training.

The studies by Nicoletti (1972) and Edie (1972) omitted controls for nonspecific treatment factors. This omission was corrected in a study by Shoemaker (1976) conducted with outpatients selected on the basis of general anxiety. Shoemaker compared anxiety management training with an implosive therapy condition in which subjects were exposed to their most anxiety-provoking scenes without the benefit of relaxation training, a relaxation training condition in which subjects simply received training in progressive relaxation, a placebo condition in which subjects met to discuss common problems associated with anxiety, and an untreated control condition. Posttest and 1-month follow-up assessments indicated that the 15-session anxiety management training condition was more effective than either control condition in reducing various self-report measures of state and trait anxiety. No differences were found for either implosive therapy or relaxation training relative to the two control conditions.

A more elaborate program of research has been underway at the University of Kansas to evaluate the effectiveness of various stress management procedures in treating general anxiety. The three studies that have been completed within this program share some methodological features that set them apart from most of the preceding studies concerning active and passive stress management training. First, special care has been taken to insure that the subjects in these studies truly suffer from chronic, general anxiety. For each study, approximately 800 undergraduate students were screened using the neuroticism scale of the Eysenck Personality Inventory and the Taylor Manifest Anxiety Scale. Students scoring in the upper 15 percent of the distributions on each of these scales were readministered the scales about a week later. Only those students whose scores still exceeded the original cutoffs were retained as subjects in these studies. There is often considerable variability in respondents' self-reports on trait measures of emotionality. By retesting prospective subjects and selecting only those individuals with markedly elevated scores on both occasions, problems posed by the typical instability of these measures were diminished.

Second, each of the three studies included a placebo condition to control for nonspecific treatment effects. The actual procedure introduced to placebo subjects differed from study to study. Several writers (e.g., Kazdin & Wilcoxon, 1976; Wilkins, 1973) have suggested that measures of subjects' expectancies concerning the likelihood of benefiting from the treatment they are receiving should be collected to demonstrate that the placebo condition within a study engenders expectancies that are comparable to those of the valid treatment conditions. In each of the present studies, expectancy ratings were collected at several junctures during the course of study, and analyses of these ratings demonstrated that the placebo condition had generated expectancies as favorable as those of the valid treatments.

Third, whereas most of the previous studies involving general anxiety have depended exclusively upon self-report measures, the present studies also included performance, physiological, and cognitive assessments. In addition to the typical battery of self-report measures of trait anxiety administered before and after treatment, a laboratory stress procedure was conducted with each subject about four weeks after treatment. Subjects were required to perform a stressful task, such as repeating a series of digits backwards (Hutchings et al., 1980; Basgall, Denney, Hutchings, & Houston, 1981) or delivering an extemporaneous speech (Marquis & Denney, 1981). Performance was scored on the tasks themselves, and physiological measures (i.e., heart rate and skin conductance) were collected over the course of the stress procedure. At the end of the procedure, subjects were questioned concerning their thoughts and feelings during the stressful task. Houston (1977) has observed that, during stressful tasks, trait anxious persons fail to mobilize an organized coping strategy and become excessively preoccupied with themselves or with the threatening aspects of the present situation. Therefore, subjects' responses to the questionnaire were scored by two judges, with respect to preoccupation with self, preoccupation with threat, and lack of a coping strategy. Interjudge agreement was deemed sufficiently high (70–78 percent) to warrant analysis of yet a third type of outcome measure, reflecting subjects' cognitive activities during the stress procedure.

Finally, each of the present studies employed a lengthy follow-up evaluation of treatment effects. A battery of self-report measures of general anxiety was completed by the subjects in each study 12 months after the termination of treatment.

In the first of these studies (Hutchings et al., 1980), anxiety management training was compared with an applied relaxation training condition, a relaxation-only condition, a placebo condition, and an untreated control condition. In terms of the continuum presented in Figure 1 the study can be viewed as a systematic dismantling of anxiety management training, permitting an evaluation of the guided rehearsal, application training, relaxation training, and nonspecific treatment components of this active stress management technique. Applied relaxation training encompassed the last three components but omitted the guided rehearsal portion of the procedure. The relaxation-only condition encompassed relaxation training and nonspecific treatment components but omitted application training. The placebo condition, which involved a variation of Marcia's T-scope therapy (Marcia, Rubin, & Efran, 1969), encompassed only the nonspecific treatment factors, and the untreated control condition completed the design.

Although only one significant difference occurred between anxiety management training and applied relaxation training, more consistently significant changes across various self-report measures of anxiety were found for subjects in the former condition. This differential consistency was again noted one year later at the time of the follow-up assessment. Significant effects were largely confined to self-report measures, with one exception. The cognitive coping measure derived from subjects' interviews following the laboratory stress procedure indicated that subjects in anxiety management training had evidenced fewer maladaptive cognitions than subjects in all other conditions.

As a component analysis of anxiety management training, this study indicated that relaxation training in conjunction with nonspecific treatment factors had little impact upon general anxiety. When application training including both a self-control rationale and explicit instructions concerning the use of relaxation in real-life settings was added, the resulting applied relaxation training procedure was moderately successful at reducing some measures of general anxiety. The addition of guided rehearsal led to the most effective procedure examined in this study: anxiety management training.

The second study (Marquis & Denney, 1981) offered a comparison between anxiety management training and "stress innoculation training" (Meichenbaum, 1975; Meichenbaum & Turk, 1976). The critical difference between these two treatments involves a procedural component that has hitherto been ignored in the present review. The component is cognitive restructuring (cf. Chapter 23).

The goals of cognitive restructuring are to teach clients to recognize habitual and maladaptive ways in which they construe stressful situations in their lives and then to train clients to modify these irrational thoughts and to adopt a more rational and adaptive stance toward the situations in question. In stress innoculation training, clients are taught both relaxation and cognitive restructuring as coping strategies for dealing with problematic situations. Comparions between stress innoculation training and purely relaxational forms of stress management training have been conducted with respect to the treatment of animal fears (Meichenbaum & Cameron, 1974), test anxiety (Hahnloser, 1974; Holroyd, 1976; Lavigne, 1974; Meichenbaum, 1972; Osarchuk, 1974; Scrivner, 1974; Thompson, Giebstein, Kuhlenschmidt, 1980), speech anxiety (Meichenbaum, Gilmore, & Fedoravicious, 1971; Norman, 1975), interpersonal anxiety (Kanter & Goldfried, 1976), and anger (Novaco, 1975, 1976), and in the reduction of experimentally induced pain (Hackett & Horan, 1980). The results of these studies are mixed. However, even for those that claim some superiority for stress innoculation training, differences are confined to only a small subset of outcome measures, and direct comparisons with relaxation-based therapy conditions rarely attain significance.

Goldfried (1977) suggested that procedures employing cognitive restructuring might be especially useful in treating general anxiety, and the addition of this component to anxiety management training seemed to be the next logical step in our program of research. Generally anxious subjects were randomly assigned to stress innoculation training, anxiety management training, a placebo condition, or an untreated control condition. The procedures in the first two conditions were practically identical, except for the addition of a cognitive restructuring component in stress innoculation training. The placebo condition involved a pseudomeditation procedure patterned after the placebo condition used by Holroyd (1976) and combining body awareness exercises and passive reflection on a series of neutral scenes.

Significant differences did not emerge when stress innoculation training and anxiety management training were directly compared. However, in terms of the consistency of significant changes across various self-report measures of anxiety, the results tended to favor anxiety management training during both the posttest and the 12-month follow-up assessments. These results suggest that cognitive restructuring per se added nothing to the overall effectiveness of stress management training with generally anxious college students. Post-experimental interviews indicated that this component was somewhat difficult to comprehend and much too complicated to employ as a coping strategy within stressful settings. Whereas most subjects at follow-up could still cite instances in which they had successfully applied their relaxation skills, virtually none were using cognitive restructuring as an applied coping strategy. While not necessarily denying the possible utility of encouraging clients to restructure their beliefs regarding various sources of difficulty in their lives, one is nevertheless led to question the value of cognitive restructuring as a form of active stress management.

The last study completed in this program of research (Basgall et al., 1981) was designed to compare active and passive stress management techniques. Generally anxious college students were randomly assigned to anxiety management training, meditation training, a placebo condition, or an untreated control condition. The anxiety management training condition was identical to that of the preceding studies. Meditation training included instructions and practice in a zen meditation technique in which subjects were trained to sit quietly with their eyes closed and to count their exhalations repetitively from 1 to 10. The rationale accompanying this treatment emphasized the cumulative anxiety-reducing effects to be gained through regular practice of the procedure in a quiet environment. Time was set aside during each treatment session for subjects to discuss their experiences while practicing at home. The placebo condition was termed *self-actualization therapy* and consisted of a program of self-contemplation in relation to written passages concerning the topic of self-actualization. Subjects read a different passage at the beginning of each day, reflected on the passage as it applied to their own lives, and repeated this procedure at the end of the day. Other passages were introduced for group discussion during the treatment sessions.

As in the preceding studies, significant results were confined to self-report measures of general anxiety and did not extend to performance or physiological measures collected during the laboratory stress procedure. The self-report measures indicated a slight advantage for anxiety management training in terms of the consistency of significant reductions in general anxiety at posttest.

The follow-up assessment was especially important in this third study, since one might expect passive stress management techniques such as meditation to require a greater amount of time before their effects would accumulate sufficiently to influence the outcome measures. However, 12 months after treatment, subjects who had received anxiety management training were still showing more consistently significant reductions on report measures of general anxiety than were those in the meditation condition. This difference did not seem attributable to a different level of compliance at the time of the follow-up. About 60 percent of the subjects contacted in each condition reported practicing their respective techniques at least two times each week.

OVERVIEW

A host of studies pertaining to relaxation-based treatments for stress-related disorders have been presented in this chapter. These treatments have been segregated into active and passive stress management techniques, a distinction which seems to have been lurking about since the early history of relaxation therapies and which was brought into focus through Goldfried's reformulation of desensitization. This distinction has not been awarded appropriate recognition as an organizing principle in stress management training. One might well question why the distinction has been so commonly ignored.

A likely reason is that investigators have been perpetually sidetracked by far less important debates over the relative effectiveness of various relaxation induction methods. This issue eventually culminated in Davidson and Schwartz' (1976) elaborate scheme suggesting certain forms of relaxation induced through certain methods to ameliorate certain types of stress-related disorders. A vast number of studies have been conducted to determine the specific effects of relaxation resulting from various induction methods. As indicated in this chapter, most of these studies deal with phasic effects and are, therefore, only tangentially related to the therapeutic uses of relaxation. Tonic effects, which are more relevant, especially in connection with passive stress management training, have remained largely unexplored—except within the context of treatment outcome studies themselves. Overall, the results of these numerous studies, involving phasic and tonic effects alike, indicate far more chaos than consistency. Certainly no consistent pattern of effects has been found to characterize any particular relaxation induction method. This being the case, hopefully the debate over the relative merits of one induction method over another can finally be laid to rest.

By failing to draw an explicit distinction between active and passive stress management training, investigators have neglected to perform the kind of comparative research illustrated in the one study by Basgall et al. (1981). Thus, it is impossible to offer any conclusions regarding which form of stress management training is the more effective with which types of clients having which types of stress-related disorders. However, the question is a vital one and will hopefully capture investigators' attention now that the taxonomic distinction between active and passive stress management has been described. Until then, a few speculations with regard to this question must necessarily suffice.

With respect to client differences, it is possible that the two forms of stress management training may be differentially effective according to clients' preferred locus of control (Rotter, 1966). Active stress management training, in particular, would seem to be more consistent with an internal locus of control. Along similar lines, Rosenbaum (1980) recently published a self-control schedule that may prove a useful source of client variables which interact with active versus passive stress management training.

As for different types of stress-related disorders, it is interesting to note the types of disorders that have thus far garnered relatively greater attention from purveyors of active or passive stress management techniques. The majority of outcome studies concerning hypertension have involved passive stress management training, whereas the majority of studies concerning phobia and insomnia have involved active stress management training. Outcome studies concerning general anxiety, tension headache, and migraine are about equally divided between active and passive techniques.

This distribution may be interpreted in terms of the cues which clients must utilize in successfully applying relaxation as an active coping strategy. As the study by Edie (1972) illustrated, two sets of cues can be employed by clients in this regard. One set arises from the threatening situation. Clients may come to recognize that certain situations produce the stresses that exacerbate their disorders. Stimuli arising from these situations can signal clients to initiate their relaxation-based coping strategy. The other set of potentially available cues are embedded in the physical and psychological symptoms of the disorder itself. In this instance, the symptoms themselves come to signal clients to initiate their coping strategy.

In the case of hypertension, neither set of cues is typically available to clients. The disorder is generally asymptomatic, and the linkage between particular types of threatening situations and rises in blood pressure remains vague for most clients. While the disorder may initially be closely aligned with specific fluctuations in stresses, hypertension soon becomes a more enduring or tonic disorder with some degree of independence from particular situational stressors. Since the cues for initiating a specific coping strategy are generally not available to clients with hypertension, the preponderance of stress management techniques applied to this disorder has been passive rather than active, perhaps by default.

In the cases of insomnia and phobia, the symptoms of these disorders are readily apparent to the client and arise in situations that are highly circumscribed. With these sources of cues intact, it is not surprising that the preponderance of stress management techniques for these disorders has been active rather than passive. Indeed, in the case of both disorders, it seems that clients themselves began converting relaxation as an applied coping strategy before this alternative occurred to behavior therapists.

For general anxiety, tension headaches, and migraine headaches, the cues that might assist clients in using relaxation as an applied coping strategy are only moderately available. While the symptoms of these disorders are easily discerned, the linkage between particular stressful situations and these disorders is usually vague. These latter associations can often be clarified during the early course of treatment. It is not uncommon for clients to report a clearer perception of the relationship between their disorder and the external stresses they face over the course of their day as one of the early gains in stress management training. To the extent that such linkages can be forged, the possibility of employing active rather than passive stress management techniques to treat the client's disorder is improved.

SUMMARY

The chapter reviews relaxation-based interventions for anxiety and stress-related disorders, including phobias, general anxiety, hypertension, tension headaches, migraine headaches, and asthma. An essential distinction is drawn between passive and active stress management techniques, and both the origins and underlying objectives of these techniques are delineated.

REFERENCES

Alexander, A. B. Systematic relaxation and flow rates in asthmatic children: Relationship to emotional precipitants and anxiety. *Journal of Psychosomatic Research*, 1972, *16*, 405–410.

Alexander, A. B. An experimental test of assumptions relating to the use of electromyographic biofeedback as a general relaxation technique. *Psychophysiology*, 1975, *12*, 656–662.

Alexander, A. B., Cropp, G. J. A., & Chai, H. Effects of relaxation training on pulmonary mechanics in children with asthma. *Journal of Applied Behavior Analysis*, 1979, *12*, 27–35.

Alexander A. B., Miklich, D. R., & Hershkoff, H. The immediate effects of systematic-relaxation training on peak expiratory flow rates in asthmatic children. *Psychosomatic Medicine*, 1972, *34*, 388–394.

Andreychuck, T., & Skriver, C. Hypnosis and biofeedback in the treatment of migraine headache. *International Journal of Clinical and Experimental Hypnosis*, 1975, *23*, 172–183.

Arkowitz, H. Desensitization as a self-control procedure: A case report. *Psychotherapy: Theory, Research, and Practice*, 1974, *11*, 172–174.

Ballou, D. Transcendental-meditation research: Minnesota State Prison. In D. P. Kanellakos & P. C. Ferguson (Eds.), *The psychobiology of transcendental meditation*. Los Angeles: Maharishi International University Press, 1973. (Abstract)

Barlow, D. H. Behavior therapy: The next decade. *Behavior Therapy*, 1980, *11*, 315–328.

Barratt, E. S. Anxiety and impulsiveness: Toward a neuropsychological model. In C. D. Spielberger (Ed.), *Anxiety: Current trends in theory and research* (Vol. 1). New York: Academic Press, 1972.

Basgall, J., Denney, D. R., Hutchings, D., & Houston, B. K. *Anxiety-management training and meditation in the reduction of chronic anxiety.* Unpublished manuscript, University of Kansas, Lawrence, 1981.

Beaty, E. T. *Feedback-assisted relaxation as a treatment for gastric ulcers.* Paper presented to the seventh annual meeting of the Biofeedback Research Society, Colorado Springs, February 1976.

Beck, F. M., Kaul, T. J., & Russell, R. K. Treatment of dental anxiety by cue-controlled relaxation. *Journal of Counseling Psychology,* 1978, *25,* 591–594.

Beiman, I., Graham, L. E., & Ciminero, A. R. Self-control progressive-relaxation training as an alternative nonpharmacological treatment for essential hypertension: Therapeutic effects in the natural environment. *Behaviour Research and Therapy,* 1978, *16,* 271–375.

Benson, H. *The relaxation response.* New York: Morrow, 1975.

Benson, H., Alexander, S., & Feldman, C. L. Decreased premature ventricular contractions through the use of the relaxation response in patients with stable ischemic heart disease. *Lancet,* 1975, *2,* 380–385.

Benson, H., Beary, J. B., & Carol, M. The relaxation response. *Psychiatry,* 1974, *37,* 37–46.

Benson, H., Frankel, F. H., Apfel, R., et al. Treatment of anxiety: A comparison of the usefulness of self-hypnosis and a meditational-relaxation technique. *Psychotherapy and Psychosomatics,* 1978, *30,* 229–242.

Benson, H., Klemchuk, H. P., & Graham, J. R. The usefulness of the relaxation response in the therapy of headache. *Headache,* 1974, *14,* 49–52.

Benson, H., Rosner, B. A., Marzetta, B. R., & Klemchuk, H. P. decreased blood pressure in borderline hypertensive subjects who practiced meditation. *Journal of Chronic Diseases,* 1974, *27,* 163–169. (a)

Benson, H., Rosner, B. A., Marzetta, B. R., & Klemchuk, H. P. Decreased blood pressure in pharmacologically treated hypertensive patients who regularly elicited the relaxation response. *Lancet,* 1974, *9,* 389–391. (b)

Bernstein, D. A., & Nietzel, M. T. Demand characteristics in behavior modification: The natural history of a "nuisance." In M. Hersen, R. M. Eisler, & P. M. Miller (Eds.), *Progress in behavior modification* (Vol. 4). New York: Academic Press, 1977.

Blackwell, B., Bloomfield, S., Gartside, P., et al. Transcendental meditation in hypertension: Individual response patterns. *Lancet,* 1976, *1,* 223–226.

Blanchard, E. B., Miller, S. T., Abel, G. G., et al. Evaluation of biofeedback in the treatment of borderline essential hypertension. *Journal of Applied Behavior Analysis,* 1979, *12,* 99–109.

Blanchard, E. B., Theobald, D. E., Williamson, D. A., et al. Temperature biofeedback with treatment of migraine headache. *Archives of General Psychiatry,* 1978, *35,* 581–588.

Bloom, L. J., & Cantrell, D. Anxiety-management training for essential hypertension in pregnancy. *Behavior Therapy,* 1978, *9,* 377–382.

Borkovec, T. D. The role of expectancy and physiological feedback in fear research: A review with special reference to subject characteristics. *Behavior Therapy,* 1973, *4,* 491–505.

Borkovec, T. D., & O'Brien, G. T. Methodological and target-behavior issues in analogue therapy-outcome research. In M. Hersen, R. M. Eisler, & P. M. Miller (Eds.), *Progress in behavior modification* (Vol. 3). New York: Academic Press, 1976.

Borkovec, T. D., & Sides, J. K. Critical procedural variables related to the physiological effects of progressive relaxation: A review. *Behaviour Research and Therapy,* 1979, *17,* 119–125.

Boswell, P. C., & Murray, E. J. Effects of meditation on psychological and physiological measures of anxiety. *Journal of Consulting and Clinical Psychology,* 1979, *47,* 606–607.

Brady, J. P., Luborsky, L., & Kron, R. E. Blood pressure and reduction in patients with essential hypertension through metronome-conditioned relaxation: A preliminary report. *Behavior Therapy,* 1974, *5,* 203–209.

Brooks, G. R., & Richardson, F. C. Emotional skills training: A treatment program for duodenal ulcer. *Behavior Therapy,* 1980, *11,* 198–207.

Budzynski, T. H., Stoyva, J. M., & Adler, C. S. Feedback-induced relaxation: Application to tension headache. *Journal of Behavior Therapy and Experimental Psychiatry,* 1970, *1,* 205–211.

Budzynski, T. M., Stoyva, J. M., Adler, C. S., & Mullaney, D. T. EMG biofeedback and tension headache: A controlled outcome study. *Psychosomatic Medicine,* 1973, *35,* 384–496.

Buss, A. H. Two anxiety factors in psychiatric patients. *Journal of Abnormal and Social Psychology,* 1962, *65,* 426–427.

Canter, A., Kondo, C. Y., & Knott, J. R. A comparison of EMG feedback and progressive muscle relaxation training in anxiety neurosis. *British Journal of Psychiatry,* 1975, *127,* 470–477.

Cautela, J. R. A behavior-therapy treatment of pervasive anxiety. *Behaviour Research and Therapy,* 1966, *4,* 99–109.

Chang-Liang, R., & Denney, D. R. applied relaxation as training in self-control. *Journal of Counseling Psychology,* 1976, *23,* 183–189.

Chesney, M. A., & Shelton, J. L. A comparison of muscle-relaxation and electromyogram-biofeedback treatments for muscle-contraction headache. *Journal of Behavior Therapy and Experimental Psychiatry,* 1976, *1,* 221–225.

Chesney, M. A., & Tasto, D. L. The effectiveness of behavior modification with spasmodic and congestive dysmenorrhea. *Behaviour Research and Therapy,* 1975, *13,* 245–253.

Connor, W. H. Effect of brief relaxation training on autonomic response to anxiety-evoking stimuli. *Psychophysiology,* 1974, *11,* 591–599.

Corah, N. L. Neuroticism and extraversion in the MMPI: Empirical validation and exploration. *British Journal of Social and Clinical Psychology,* 1964, *3,* 168–174.

Counts, D. K., Hollandsworth, J. G., & Alcorn, J. D. Use of electromyographic biofeedback and cue-controlled relaxation in the treatment of test anxiety. *Journal of Consulting and Clinical Psychology,* 1978, *56,* 990–996.

Coursey, R. D. Electromyograph feedback as a relaxation technique. *Journal of Consulting and Clinical Psychology,* 1975, *43,* 825–834.

Cox, D. J., Fruendlich, A., & Meyer, R. G. Differential effectiveness of relaxation techniques and placebo with tension headaches. *Journal of Consulting and Clinical Psychology,* 1975, *43,* 892–898.

Datey, K. K., Deshmukh, S. N., Dalvi, C. P., & Vinekar, S. L. "Shavasan": A yogic exercise in the management of hypertension. *Angiology,* 1969, *20,* 325–333.

Davidson, P. O., & Hiebert, S. F. Relaxation training, relaxation instruction, and repeated exposure to a stressor film. *Journal of Abnormal Psychology,* 1971, *78,* 154–159.

Davidson, R. J. Specificity and patterning in biobehavioral systems: Implications for behavior change. *American Psychologist,* 1978, *33,* 430–436.

Davidson, R. J., Goleman, D. J., & Schwartz, G. E. Attentional and affective concomitants of meditation: A cross-sectional study. *Journal of Abnormal Psychology,* 1976, *85,* 235–238.

Davidson, R. J., & Schwartz, G. E. The psychobiology of relaxation and related states: A multiprocess theory. In D. I. Mostofsky (Ed.), *Behavioral control and modification of physiological activity.* Engelwood Cliffs, N.J.: Prentice-Hall, 1976.

Davis, M. H., Saunders, D. R., Creer, T. L., & Chai, M. Relaxation training facilitated by biofeedback apparatus as a supplemental treatment in bronchial asthma. *Journal of Psychosomatic Research,* 1973, *17,* 121–128.

Davison, G. C., Tsujimoto, R. N., & Glaros, A. G. Attribution and the maintenance of behavior change in falling asleep. *Journal of Abnormal Psychology,* 1973, *82,* 124–133.

Deffenbacher, J. L., Michaels, A. C., Michaels, T., & Daley, P. C. A comparison of anxiety-management training and self-control desensitization. *Journal of Counseling Psychology,* 1980, *27,* 232–239.

Deffenbacher, J. L., & Parks, D. H. A comparison of traditional and self-control systematic desensitization. *Journal of Counseling Psychology,* 1979, *26,* 93–97.

Deffenbacher, J. L., & Shelton, J. L. Comparison of anxiety-management training and desensitization in reducing test and other anxieties. *Journal of Counseling Psychology,* 1978, *25,* 277–282.

Denney, D. R. Self-control approaches to the treatment of test anxiety. In I. G. Sarason (Ed.), *Test anxiety: Theory, research, and applications.* Hillsdale, N.J.: Lawrence Erlbaum Associates, 1980.

Denney, D. R., & Rupert, P. A. Desensitization and self-control in the treatment of test anxiety. *Journal of Counseling Psychology,* 1977, *45,* 272–280.

Edie, C. *Uses of AMT in treating trait anxiety.* Unpublished doctoral dissertation, Colorado State University, Ft. Collins, 1972.

Epstein, L. H., & Abel, G. G. An analysis of biofeedback-training effects for tension-headache patients. *Behavior Therapy* 1977, *8,* 37–47.

Epstein, L. H., Hersen, M., & Hemphill, D. P. Music feedback in the treatment of tension headache: An experimental case study. *Journal of Behavior Therapy and Experimental Psychiatry,* 1974, *5,* 59–63.

Ewing, J. W., & Hughes, H. H. Cue-controlled relaxation: Its effect on EMG levels during aversive stimulation. *Journal of Behavior Therapy and Experimental Psychiatry,* 1978, *9,* 39–44.

Ferguson, P. C., & Gowan, J. The influence of the practice of transcendental meditation on anxiety, depression, aggression, neuroticism, and self-actualization. In D. P. Kanellakas & P. C. Ferguson (Eds.), *The psychobiology of transcendental meditation.* Los Angeles: Maharishi International University Press, 1973. (Abstract)

Fichtler, J., & Zimmerman, R. R. Changes in reported pain from tension headaches. *Perceptual and Motor Skills,* 1973, *36,* 712.

Folkins, C. H., Lawson, K. D., Opton, E. M., & Lazarus, R. S. Densensitization and the experimental reduction of threat. *Journal of Abnormal Psychology,* 1968, *73,* 100–113.

Frankel, B. L., Patel, D. J., Horwitz, D., et al. Treatment of hypertension with biofeedback and relaxation techniques. *Psychosomatic Medicine*, 1978, *40*, 276–293.

Girodo, M. Yoga meditation and flooding in the treatment of anxiety neurosis. *Journal of Behavior Therapy and Experimental Psychiatry*, 1974, *5*, 157–160.

Glueck, B. C., & Stroebel, C. F. Biofeedback and meditation in the treatment of psychiatric illnesses. *Comprehensive Psychiatry*, 1975, *16*, 303–321.

Goldfried, M. R. Systematic desensitization as training in self-control. *Journal of Consulting and Clinical Psychology*, 1971, *37*, 228–234.

Goldfried, M. R. Reduction of generalized anxiety through a variant of systematic densensitization. In M. R. Goldfried & M. Merbaum (Eds.), *Behavior change through self-control*. New York: Holt, Rinehart & Winston, 1973.

Goldfried, M. R. The use of relaxation and cognitive relabeling as coping skills. In R. B. Stuart (Ed.), *Behavioral self-management: Strategies, techniques, and outcomes*. New York: Bruner & Mazel, 1977.

Goldfried, M. R., & Goldfried, A. P. Importance of hierarchy content in self-control of anxiety. *Journal of Consulting and Clinical Psychology*, 1977, *45*, 124–134.

Goldfried, M. R., & Trier, C. S. Effectiveness of relaxation as an active coping skill. *Journal of Abnormal Psychology*, 1974, *83*, 348–355.

Goldman, B. L., Domitor, P. J., & Murray, E. J. Effects of Zen meditation on anxiety reduction and perceptual functioning. *Journal of Consulting and Clinical Psychology*, 1979, *47*, 551–556.

Goleman, D. J., & Schwartz, G. E. Meditation as an intervention in stress reactivity. *Journal of Consulting and Clinical Psychology*, 1976, *44*, 456–466.

Gurman, A. S. Treatment of a case of public-speaking anxiety by in vivo desensitization and cue-controlled relaxation. *Journal of Behavior Therapy and Experimental Psychiatry*, 1973, *4*, 51–54.

Hackett, G., & Horan, J. J. Stress innoculation for pain: What's really going on? *Journal of Counseling Psychology*, 1980, *27*, 107–116.

Hahnloser, R. M. *A comparison of cognitive restructuring and progressive relaxation in test-anxiety reduction.* Unpublished doctoral dissertation. University of Oregon. Eugene, 1974.

Hamilton, M. The assessment of anxiety states by rating. *British Journal of Medical Psychology*, 1959, *32*, 50–55.

Harrell, T. H., & Beiman, I. Cognitive-behavioral treatment of the irritable-colon syndrome. *Cognitive Therapy and Research*, 1978, *2*, 371–375.

Haynes, S. N., Griffin, P., Mooney, D., & Parise, M. Electromyographic biofeedback and relaxation instructions in the treatment of muscle-contraction headaches. *Behavior Therapy*, 1975, *6*, 672–678.

Haynes, S. N., Moseley, D., & McGowan, W. T. Relaxation training and biofeedback in the reduction of frontalis-muscle tension. *Psychophysiology*, 1975, *12*, 547–552.

Hjelle, L. A. transcendental meditation and psychological health. *Perceptual and Motor Skills*, 1974, *39*, 623–629.

Hock, R. A., Rodgers, C. H., Reddi, C., & Kennard, D. W. Medicopsychological interventions in male asthmatic children: An evaluation of physiological change. *Psychosomatic Medicine*, 1978, *40*, 210–215.

Holroyd, K. A. Cognition and desensitization in the group treatment of test anxiety. *Journal of consulting and Clinical Psychology*, 1976, *44*, 991–1001.

Houston, B. K. Dispositonal anxiety and the effectiveness of cognitive coping strategies in stressful laboratory and classroom situations. In C. D. Spielberger & I. G. Sarason (Eds.), *Stress and anxiety* (Vol. 4). Washington: Hemisphere, 1977.

Hutchings, D. F., Denney, D. R., Basgall, J., & Houston, B. K. Anxiety management and applied relaxation in reducing general anxiety. *Behaviour Research and Therapy*, 1980, *18*, 181–190.

Hutchings, D. F., & Reinking, R. H. Tension headaches: What form of therapy is most effective? *Biofeedback and Self-Regulation*, 1976, *1*, 183–190.

Jacks, R. N. *Systematic desensitization versus a self-control technique for the reduction of acrophobia.* Unpublished doctoral dissertation, Stanford University, Palo Alto, California, 1972.

Jacobson, A. M., Hackett, T. P., Surman, O., & Silverberg, E. Raynaud's phenomenon: Treatment with hypnotic and operant techniques. *Journal of the American Medical Association*, 1973, *225*, 739–740.

Jacobson, A. M., Manschreck, T. C., & Silverberg, E. Behavioral treatment of Raynaud's disease: A comparative study with long-term follow-up. *American Journal of Psychiatry*, 1979 *136*, 844–846.

Jacobson, E. *Progressive relaxation.* Chicago: University of Chicago Press, 1938.

Jenni, M. A., & Wollersheim, J. P. Cognitive therapy, stress-management training, and the Type A behavior pattern. *Cognitive Therapy and Research*, 1979, *3*, 61–73.

Jevning, R., Wilson, A. F., & VanderLaan, E. F. Plasma prolactin and growth hormone during meditation. *Psychosomatic Medicine*, 1978, *40*, 329–333.

Jones, M. C. The elimination of children's fears. *Journal of Experimental Psychology*, 1924, *7*, 382–390.

Jorgensen, R. S., Houston, B. K., & Zurawski, R. M. Anxiety management training in the treatment of essential hypertension. *Behaviour Research and Therapy*, 1981, *19*, 467–474.

Kanter, N. J., & Goldfried, M. R. *Relative effectiveness of rational restructuring and self-control desensitization for the reduction of interpersonal anxiety.* Unpublished manuscript, State University of New York at Stony Brook, 1976.

Kazdin, A. E., & Wilcoxon, L. A. Systematic desensitization and nonspecific treatment effects: A methodological evaluation. *Psychological Bulletin*, 1976, *83*, 729–758.

Khan, A. V., Staerk, M., & Bonk, C. Role of counterconditioning in the treatment of asthma. *Journal of Asthma Research*, 1973, *11*, 57–62.

Kondo, C. Y., & Canter, A. True and false electromyographic feedback: Effect on tension headache. *Journal of Abnormal Psychology*, 1977, *86*, 93–95.

Kotses, H., Glaus, K. D., Bricel, S. K., et al. Operant muscular relaxation and peak expiratory flow rate in asthmatic children. *Journal of Psychosomatic Research*, 1978, *22*, 17–23.

Kotses, H., Glaus, K. D., Crawford, P. L., et al. Operant reduction of frontalis EMG activity in the treatment of asthma in children. *Journal of Psychosomatic Research*, 1976, *20*, 453–458.

Lang, P. The mechanics of desensitization and the laboratory study of human fear. In

C. M. Franks (Ed.), *Behavior therapy: Appraisal and status.* New York: McGraw-Hill, 1969.

Langen, D. Peripheral changes in blood circulation during autogenic training and hypnosis: Results of experimental research. In L. Chertok (Ed.), *Psychophysiological mechanisms of hypnosis.* Berlin: Springer-Verlag, 1969.

Lavigne, J. V. *The relative efficacy of cognitive-behavior rehearsal and systematic desensitization on the treatment of test anxiety.* Unpublished doctoral dissertation, University of Texas, Austin, 1974.

Lent, R. W. & Russell, R. K. Treatment of test anxiety by cue-controlled desensitization and study-skills training. *Journal of Counseling Psychology,* 1978, *25,* 217–224.

Lindemann, H. *Relieve tension the autogenic way.* (K. Kellen, trans.). New York: Wyden, 1973.

Love, W. A., Montgomery, D. D., & Moeller, T. A. (Working Paper 1). Unpublished manuscript, Nova University, Ft. Lauderdale, 1974.

Lown, B., Temte, J. B., Reich, P., et al. Basis for recurring ventricular fibrillation in the absence of coronary heart disease and its management. *The New England Journal of Medicine,* 1976, *294,* 623–629.

Luthe, W. Autogenic training: Method, research, and application in medicine. *American Journal of Psychotherapy,* 1963, *17,* 174–195.

Marchetti, A., McGlynn, F. D., & Patterson, A. S. Effects of cue-controlled relaxation, a placebo treatment on changes in self-reported and psychophysiological indices of test anxiety among college students. *Behavior Modification,* 1977, *1,* 47–72.

Marcia, J. E., Rubin, B. M., & Efran, J. S. Systematic desensitization: Expectancy change or counterconditioning. *Journal of Abnormal Psychology,* 1969, *74,* 382–387.

Marquis, J. M., & Denney, D. R. *Anxiety management training and stress innoculation training in the treatment of general anxiety.* Unpublished manuscript, University of Kansas, Lawrence, 1981.

Mathew, R., Ho, B. T., Kralik, P., & Claghorn, J. L. Anxiety and serum prolactin. *American Journal of Psychiatry,* 1979, *136,* 715–717.

McGlynn, F. D., Kinjo, K., & Doherty, G. Effects of cue-controlled relaxation, a placebo treatment, and no treatment on changes in self-reported test anxiety among college students. *Journal of Clinical Psychology,* 1978, *34,* 707–714.

McKechnie, R. J. Relief from phantom-limb pain by relaxation exercises. *Journal of Behavior Therapy and Experimental Psychiatry,* 1975, *6,* 262–263.

McKenzie, R. E., Ehrisman, W. J., Montgomery, P. S., & Barnes, R. H. The treatment of headache by means of electroencephalographic biofeedback, *Headache,* 1974, *13,* 164–172.

Meichenbaum, D. H. Cognitive modification of test anxious college students. *Journal of Consulting and Clinical Psychology,* 1972, *39,* 370–380.

Meichenbaum, D. H. A self-instructional approach to stress management: A proposal for stress innoculation training. In C. D. Spielberger & I. G. Sarason (Eds.), *Stress and anxiety* (Vol. 2). New York: John Wiley & Sons, 1975.

Meichenbaum, D. H., & Cameron, R. The clinical potential of modifying what clients say to themselves. *Psychotherapy: Theory, Research, and Practice,* 1974, *11,* 103–117.

Meichenbaum, D. H., Gilmore, J. B., & Fedoravicious, A. Group insight versus group desensitization in treating speech anxiety. *Journal of Consulting and Clinical Psychology,* 1971, *36,* 410–421.

Meichenbaum, D. H., & Turk, D. The cognitive-behavioral management of anxiety, anger, and pain. In P. O. Davidson (Ed.), *The behavioral management of anxiety, depression, and pain.* New York: Bruner & Mazel, 1976.

Miller, M. P., Murphy, P. J., & Miller, T. P. Comparison of electromyographic feedback and progressive relaxation training in treating circumscribed anxiety-stress reactions. *Journal of Consulting and Clinical Psychology,* 1978, *46,* 1291–1298.

Mitchell, K. R. Self-management of spastic colitis. *Journal of Behavior Therapy and Experimental Psychiatry,* 1978, *9,* 269–272.

Mitchell, K. R., & Mitchell, D. M. Migraine: An exploratory treatment application of programmed behavior therapy techniques. *Journal of Psychosomatic Research,* 1971, *15,* 137–157.

Mitchell, K. R., & White, R. G. Self-management of tension headaches: A case study. *Journal of Behavior Therapy and Experimental Psychiatry,* 1976, *7,* 387–389.

Mitchell, K. R., & White, R. G. Behavioral self-management: An application to the problem of migraine headaches. *Behavior Therapy,* 1977, *8,* 213–221.

Moeller, T. A. *Reduction of arterial pressure through relaxation training and correlates of personality in hypertensives.* Unpublished doctoral dissertation, Nova University, Ft. Lauderdale, 1973.

Moeller, T. A., & Love, W. A. *A method to reduce arterial hypertension through muscular relaxation.* Unpublished manuscript, Nova University, Ft. Lauderdale, Fla., 1974.

Mohr, L. E. *EMG-biofeedback facilitation of progressive relaxation and autogenic training: A comparative study.* Unpublished doctoral dissertation, University of Iowa, Iowa City, 1975.

Nicoletti, J. *Anxiety-management training.* Unpublished doctoral dissertation, Colorado State University, Ft. Collins, 1972.

Norman, W. H. *The efficacy of self-instructional training in the treatment of speech anxiety.* Unpublished doctoral dissertation. Pennsylvania State University, University Park, 1975.

Novaco, R. W. *Anger control: The development and evaluation of an experimental treatment.* Lexington, Mass.: D. C. Heath, 1975.

Novaco, R. W. Treatment of chronic anger through cognitive and relaxation controls. *Journal of Consulting and Clinical Psychology,* 1976, *44,* 681.

Orme-Johnson, D. W. Autonomic stability and transcendental meditation. *Psychosomatic Medicine,* 1973, *35,* 341–349.

Orme-Johnson, D. W., Arthur, G., Franklin, L., et al. Transcendental meditation and drug-abuse counselors. In D. P. Kanellakos & P. C. Ferguson (Eds.), *The psychobiology of transcendental meditation.* Los Angeles: Maharishi International University Press, 1973. (Abstract)

Orme-Johnson, D. W., Kiehlbauch, J., Moore, R., & Bristol, J. Personality and autonomic changes in meditating prisoners. In D. P. Kanellakos & P. C. Ferguson (Eds.), *The psychobiology of transcendental meditation.* Los Angeles: Maharishi International University Press, 1973. (Abstract)

Osarchuk, M. M. *A comparison of a cognitive, a behavior therapy, and a cognitive-and-behavior therapy treatment of test-anxious college students.* Unpublished doctoral dissertation, Adelphi University, New York, 1974.

Parker, J. C., Gilbert, G. S., & Thoreson, R. V. Reduction of autonomic arousal in alcoholics: A comparison of relaxation and meditation techniques. *Journal of Consulting and Clinical Psychology,* 1978, *46,* 879–886.

Patel, C. H. Yoga and biofeedback in the management of hypertension. *Lancet*, 1973, *2*, 1053–1055.

Patel, C. H. Twelve-month follow-up of yoga and biofeedback in the management of hypertension. *Lancet*, 1975, *1*, 62–65. (a)

Patel, C. H. Yoga and biofeedback in the management of "stress" in hypertensive patients. *Clinical Science and Molecular Medicine*, 1975, *48*, 171–174. (Supplement) (b)

Patel, C. H., & North, W. R. S. Randomized controlled trial of yoga and biofeedback in management of hypertension. *Lancet*, 1975, *2*, 93–95.

Paul, G. L. Physiological effects of relaxation training and hypnotic suggestion. *Journal of Abnormal Psychology*, 1969, *74*, 425–437. (a)

Paul, G. L. Inhibition of physiological response to stressful imagery by relaxation training and hypnotically suggested relaxation. *Behaviour Research and Therapy*, 1969, *7*, 249–256. (b)

Paul, G. L., & Shannon, D. T. Treatment of anxiety through systematic desensitization in therapy groups. *Journal of Abnormal Psychology*, 1966, *71*, 124–135.

Paul, G. L., & Trimble, R. W. Recorded versus "live" relaxation training and hypnotic suggestion for reducing physiological arousal and inhibiting stress response. *Behavior Therapy*, 1970, *1*, 285–302.

Philips, C. The modification of tension-headache pain using EMG biofeedback. *Behaviour Research and Therapy*, 1977, *15*, 119–129.

Plotkin, W. B. On the self-regulation of the occipital alpha rhythm: Control strategies, states of consciousness, and the role of physiological feedback. *Journal of Experimental Psychology: General*, 1976, *105*, 66–99.

Plotkin, W. B. On the social psychology of experiential states associated with EEG-alpha biofeedback training. In J. Beatty & H. Legewie (Eds.), *Biofeedback and behavior*. New York: Plenum Press, 1977.

Plotkin, W. B., & Cohen, R. Occipital alpha and the attributes of the "alpha experience." *Psychophysiology*, 1976, *13*, 16–21.

Pollack, A. D., Weber, M. A., Case, D. B., & Laragh, J. H. Limitations of transcendental meditation in the treatment of essential hypertension. *Lancet*, 1977, *1*, 71–73.

Puente, A. E., & Beiman, I. The effect of behavior therapy, self-relaxation, and transcendental meditation on cardiovascular stress response. *Journal of Clinical Psychology*, 1980, *36*, 291–295.

Quillen, M. A., & Denney, D. R. Self-control of dysmenorrheic symptoms through pain management training. *Journal of Behavior Therapy and Experimental Psychiatry*, 1982, *13*, 123–130.

Ramsay, I., Greer, S., & Bagley, C. Propranolol in neurotic and thyrotoxic anxiety. *British Journal of Psychiatry*, 1973, *122*, 555–560.

Raskin, M., Johnson, G., & Rondestveldt, J. W. Chronic anxiety treated by feedback-induced muscle relaxation: A pilot study. *Archives of General Psychiatry*, 1973, *28*, 263–267.

Reeves, J. L., & Mealiea, W. L. Biofeedback-assisted cue-controlled relaxation for the treatment of flight phobias. *Journal of Behavior Therapy and Experimental Psychiatry*, 1975, *6*, 105–109.

Reinking, R. H., & Kohl, M. Effects of various forms of relaxation training on physiological and self-report measures of relaxation. *Journal of Consulting and Clinical Psychology*, 1975, *43*, 595–600.

Richardson, F. C., & Suinn, R. M. A comparison of traditional desensitization, accelerated mass desensitization, and anxiety-management training in the treatment of mathematics anxiety. *Behavior Therapy,* 1973, *4,* 212–218.

Richardson, F. C., & Suinn, R. Effects of two short-term desensitization methods in the treatment of test anxiety. *Journal of Counseling Psychology,* 1974, *21,* 457–458.

Rickels, K., & Downing, R. Drug- and placebo-treated neurotic outpatients. *Archives of General Psychiatry,* 1967, *16,* 369–372.

Rosenbaum, M. A schedule for assessing self-control behaviors: Preliminary findings. *Behavior Therapy,* 1980, *11,* 109–121.

Rotter, J. B. Generalized expectancies for internal versus external control of reinforcement. *Psychological Monographs,* 1966, *80*(whole No. 1).

Russell, R. K., Lent, R. W., & Sipich, J. F. Incorporating cue-controlled relaxation and systematic desensitization in reduction of anxiety. *Psychological Reports,* 1977, *40,* 635–638.

Russell, R. K., & Matthews, C. O. Cue-controlled relaxation and in vivo desensitization in the treatment of a snake phobia. *Journal of Behavior Therapy and Experimental Psychiatry,* 1975, *6,* 49–51.

Russell, R. K., Miller, D. E., & June, L. N. Group cue-controlled relaxation in the treatment of test anxiety. *Behavior Therapy,* 1974, *5,* 572–573.

Russell, R. K., Miller, D. E., & June, L. N. A comparison between group-systematic desensitization and cue-controlled relaxation in the treatment of test anxiety. *Behavior Therapy,* 1975, *6,* 172–177.

Russell, R. K., & Sipich, J. F. Cue-controlled relaxation in the treatment of test anxiety. *Journal of Behavior Therapy and Experimental Psychiatry,* 1973, *4,* 47–49. (a)

Russell, R. K., & Sipich, J. F. Treatment of test anxiety by cue-controlled relaxation. *Behavior Therapy,* 1973, *5,* 673–676. (b)

Russell, R. K., & Wise, F. Treatment of speech anxiety by cue-controlled relaxation and desensitization with professional and paraprofessional counselors. *Journal of Counseling Psychology,* 1976, *23,* 583–586.

Russell, R. K., Wise, F., & Stratoudakis, J. P. Treatment of test anxiety by cue-controlled relaxation and systematic desensitization. *Journal of Counseling Psychology,* 1976, *23,* 563–566.

Scherr, M. S., Crawford, P. L., Sergent, C. B., & Scherr, C. A. Effects of biofeedback techniques on chronic asthma in a summer-camp environment. *Annals of Allergy,* 1975, *35,* 289–295.

Schultz, J. H. *Das autogene training.* Stuttgart: Thieme Verlag, 1932.

Schwartz, G. C., Davidson, R. J., & Goleman, D. J. Patterning of cognitive and somatic processes in the self-regulation of anxiety: Effects of meditation versus exercise. *Psychosomatic Medicine,* 1978, *40,* 321–328.

Scott, R. W., Blanchard, E. B., Edmundson, E. G., & Young, L. D. A shaping procedure for heart rate control on chronic tachycardia. *Perceptual and Motor Skills,* 1973, *37,* 327–328.

Scrivner, V. W. *Systematic desensitization and cognitive modification with high emotionality and high worry subjects.* Unpublished doctoral dissertation, University of Texas, Austin, 1974.

Seer, P., & Raeburn, J. M. Meditation training and essential hypertension: A methodological study. *Journal of Behavioral Medicine,* 1980, *3,* 59–71.

Sheridan, C. L., Boehm, M. B., Ward, L. B., & Justesen, D. R. *Autogenic biofeedback, autogenic phrases, and biofeedback compared.* Paper presented to the seventh annual meeting of the Biofeedback Research Society, Colorado Springs, February 1976.

Sherman, A. R. Real-life exposure as a primary therapeutic factor in the desensitization treatment of fear. *Journal of Abnormal Psychology,* 1972, *79,* 19–28.

Sherman, R. A. *Case reports of treatment of phantom limb and stump pain with a combination of electromyographic biofeedback and verbal relaxation techniques.* Paper presented to the seventh annual meeting of the Biofeedback Research Society, Colorado Springs, February 1976.

Sherman, R. A., Gall, N., & Gormly, J. Treatment of phantom-limb pain with muscular-relaxation training to disrupt the pain-anxiety-tension cycle. *Pain,* 1979, *6,* 47–55.

Shoemaker, J. E. *Treatments for anxiety neurosis.* Unpublished doctoral dissertation, Colorado State University, Ft. Collins, 1976.

Shoemaker, J. E., & Tasto, D. L. The effects of muscle relaxation on blood pressure of essential hypertensives. *Behaviour Research and Therapy,* 1975, *13,* 29–48.

Smith, J. C. Meditation on psychotherapy: A review of the literature. *Psychological Bulletin,* 1975, *82,* 558–564.

Smith, J. C. Psychotherapeutic effects of transcendental meditation with controls for expectation of relief and daily sitting. *Journal of Consulting and Clinical Psychology,* 1976, *44,* 630–637.

Smith, J. C. Personality correlates of continuation and outcome in meditation and erect-sitting control treatments. *Journal of Consulting and Clinical Psychology,* 1978, *46,* 272–279.

Spiegler, M. C., Cooley, E. J., Marshall, G. J., et al. A self-control versus a counterconditioning paradigm for systematic desensitization: An experimental comparison. *Journal of Counseling Psychology,* 1965, *23,* 83–86.

Staples, R., & Coursey, R. D. *A comparison of EMG feedback with two other relaxation techniques.* Paper presented to the sixth annual meeting of the Biofeedback Research Society, Colorado Springs, February 1975.

Stenn, P. G., Motherskill, K. J., & Brooke, R. I. Biofeedback in a cognitive-behavioral approach to treatment of myofascial pain-dysfunction syndrome. *Behavior Therapy,* 1979, *10,* 29–36.

Stephenson, N. L. *Two cases of successful treatment of Raynaud's disease with relaxation in biofeedback training in supportive psychotherapy.* Paper presented to the seventh annual meeting of the Biofeedback Research Society, Colorado Springs, February 1976.

Stone, R. A., & DeLeo, J. Psychotherapeutic control of hypertension. *The New England Journal of Medicine,* 1976, *294,* 80–84.

Stoyva, J. M., & Budzynski, T. H. Cultivated low arousal—An antistress response? In L. V. DiCara (Ed.), *Limbic and autonomic nervous system research.* New York: Plenum Press, 1974.

Suinn, R. M. Behavior therapy for cardiac patients. *Behavior Therapy,* 1974, *5,* 569–571.

Suinn, R. M. Anxiety-management training for general anxiety. In R. M. Suinn & R. Weigel (Eds.), *The innovative psychological therapies.* New York: Harper & Row, 1975. (a)

Suinn, R. M. The cardiac stress management program for Type *A* patients. *Cardiac Rehabilitation,* 1975, *5,* 13–15. (b)

Suinn, R. M. Anxiety-management training to control general anxiety. In J. Krumboltz & C. Thorensen (Eds.), *Counseling methods.* New York: Holt, Rinehart & Winston, 1976.

Suinn, R. M. *Manual for anxiety-management training (AMT).* Unpublished manuscript, Colorado State University, Ft. Collins, 1977.

Suinn, R. M., Brock, L., & Edie, C. A. Behavior therapy for Type *A* patients. *American Journal of Cardiology,* 1975, *36,* 269.

Suinn, R. M., & Richardson, F. Anxiety-management training: A nonspecific behavior-therapy program for anxiety control. *Behavior Therapy,* 1971, *2,* 498–510.

Surwit, R. S., Shapiro, D., & Good, M. I. Comparison of cardiovascular biofeedback, neuromuscular feedback, and meditation in the treatment of borderline hypertension. *Journal of Consulting and Clinical Psychology,* 1978, *46,* 252–263.

Tal, A., & Miklich, D. R. Emotionally induced decreases in pulmonary flow rates in asthmatic children. *Psychosomatic Medicine,* 1976, *38,* 190–200.

Tasto, D. L., & Hinkle, J. E. Muscle relaxation treatment for tension headaches. *Behaviour Research and Therapy,* 1973, *11,* 347–349.

Taylor, C. B., Farquhar, J. W., Nelson, E., & Agras, S. Relaxation therapy and high blood pressure. *Archives of General Psychiatry,* 1977, *34,* 339–342.

Thompson, J. G., Griebstein, M. G., & Kuhlenschmidt, S. L. Effects of EMG biofeedback and relaxation training in the prevention of academic underachievement. *Journal of Counseling Psychology,* 1980, *27,* 97–106.

Townsend, R. E., House, J. F., & Addario, D. A comparison of biofeedback-mediated relaxation and group therapy in the treatment of chronic anxiety. *American Journal of Psychiatry,* 1975, *132,* 598–601.

Tyler, P. J., & Lader, M. H. Effects of beta adrenergic blockade with sotalol in chronic anxiety. *Clinical Pharmocology and Therapeutics,* 1973, *14,* 418–426.

Vahia, N. S., Doongaji, D. R., Jeste, D. V. et al. Further experience with the therapy based upon concepts of Patamjali in the treatment of psychiatric disorders. *Indian Journal of Psychiatry,* 1973, *15,* 32–37.

Walrath, L. C., & Hamilton, D. W. Autonomic correlates of meditation and hypnosis. *American Journal of Clinical Hypnosis,* 1975, *17,* 190–197.

Weiss, T., & Engel, B. T. Operant conditioning of heart rate in patients with premature ventricular contractions. *Psychosomatic Medicine,* 1971, *33,* 301–321.

Wickramasekera, I. Electromyographic-feedback training and tension headache: Preliminary observations. *American Journal of Clinical Hypnosis,* 1972, *15,* 83–85.

Wickramasekera, I. The application of verbal instructions and EMG-feedback training to the management of tension headache: Preliminary observations. *Headache,* 1973, *13,* 75–76.

Wilkins, W. Expectancy of therapeutic gain: An empirical and conceptual critique. *Journal of Consulting and Clinical Psychology,* 1973, *40,* 69–77.

Williams, P., & West, M. A. EEG responses to photic stimulation in persons experienced in meditation. *Electroencephalography and Clinical Neurophysiology,* 1975, *39,* 519–522.

Wilson, A. F., Honsberger, R., Chiu, J. T., & Novey, H. S. Transcendental meditation and asthma. *Respiration,* 1975, *32,* 74–80.

Wolpe, J. *Psychotherapy by reciprocal inhibition.* Stanford: Stanford University Press, 1958.

Woolfolk, R. L. Psychophysiological correlates of meditation. *Archieves of General Psychiatry,* 1975, *32,* 1326–1333.

Zeisset, R. M. Densensitization and relaxation in the modification of psychiatric patients' interview behavior. *Journal of Abnormal Psychology,* 1968, *73,* 13–24.

Zemore, R. Systematic densensitization as a method of teaching a general anxiety-reducing skill. *Journal of Consulting and Clinical Psychology,* 1975, *43,* 157–161.

Zuroff, D. C., & Schwartz, J. C. Effects of transcendental meditation and muscle relaxation on trait anxiety, maladjustment, locus of control, and drug use. *Journal of Consulting and Clinical Psychology,* 1978, *46,* 264–271.

28

Family therapy

Steven C. Parkison, *

In the last few years, family therapy has experienced a growth in popularity that is, perhaps, unsurpassed in the field of mental health. While the concepts, theories, and therapeutic strategies of treating entire families were virtually nonexistent 25 years ago, in the last 5 years, the field has progressed and grown at an explosive pace. There has been a proliferation of family therapy journals, books, workshops, institutes of training, and professional organizations. Family therapy has advanced from initially being a specific treatment used only with limited problems in families to an entire orientation to treating psychological problems. The presentation of a single family therapy is, of course, impossible, since the field consists of several distinct schools or orientations to treatment. One of these approaches is based on a learning theory or conditioning model of treatment. Since the behavioral perspective is covered elsewhere in this book, this chapter will present the models of treatment based upon systems theory.

As with most new developments in psychotherapy, the excitement and enthusiasm of discovery creates both advantages and disadvantages. The growth and attention in family therapy has been focused primarily on treatment strategies with families. Development of a sound theoretical base and accompanying research has lagged behind. Only recently have professionals in the family therapy field attempted to pull together a sound theory of family functioning. Research developments and results have been neglected in most texts on family therapy, even though a number of individuals have begun to produce systematic studies of both the process and the outcome of family therapy.

This chapter will attempt to meet four goals. Because it is believed that, to properly evaluate a school of therapy, one must consider from whence that theory has sprung, a historical perspective of family therapy will be presented. Second, an attempt will be made to present an overview of family therapy theory. Next, a clinical perspective on the actual practice

---

* Staff Psychologist, Walter Reed Army Medical Center, Washington, D.C.

of family therapy will be offered. Finally, research results will be presented and evaluated. It is hoped that this method of presentation will aid both in learning about family therapy and in developing a perspective from which to compare a family orientation to more traditional therapy orientations.

HISTORICAL PERSPECTIVE

In one form or another, the family has always been considered and included in theories of development and psychopathology. Traditionally, this has involved family influences upon personality development. The family-therapy orientation developed as a radical shift to this traditional view (Haley, 1971a, 1971b).

In the late 1940s and early 1950s, the influence of the family was reconsidered by a number of isolated groups and individuals. During this period, systems theory was rapidly developing and had an acknowledged influence on the development of family therapy. An emphasis on interactional patterns was advanced by the cybernetic model of Wiener (1947). Many investigators applied this model to family interactions and began to appreciate the interactional patterns producing problem behavior. Investigators began to shift the focus of their treatment from the individual to the family system, as it was beginning to be recognized that problems such as schizophrenia might be due to the organization of the family and, in particular, to the communicational aspects of the family. These developments required that previous thinking in individual psychopathology theory and therapy be abandoned and that the sight and focus of pathology be shifted to the family system.

In 1952, Bateson, an anthropologist interested in communication, obtained a Rockefeller Foundation grant to study unusual human communication, such as paradox. With this grant, Bateson assembled a group of individuals from diverse backgrounds. A more creative group of researchers one could not imagine. The group continued together for some 10 years and, in addition to Bateson, included Haley, Jackson, Fry, Weakland, and later, Satir. In 1956, the group published "Toward a Theory of Schizophrenia" (Bateson, Jackson, Haley, & Weakland, 1956), an article still considered a classic and debated in the literature (Weakland, 1974). The concept of the double-bind communication as a crucial factor in the development of schizophrenia was introduced in this article and, almost immediately, sparked interest in family therapy. The group, led primarily by Jackson, began to do therapy with not only the schizophrenic patients, but also with the families of these patients. While still together, the group continued to produce a wealth of information about the contribution of families to various psychological problems. The main focus of the group was on differing communication styles in families. They also proposed how these communicational styles created problems that usually involved the children in these families. The group also was heavily influenced by the therapeutic strategies utilized by Erickson and by his unique approach to dealing with family problems (Haley, 1967, 1973). Twenty-five years later, the influence of this group continues and is best typified by the interactional school of family therapy.

During this same period, Ackerman, a child psychiatrist, began to recognize the contribution of the family to psychological problems of children. He began to have sessions with the entire family and soon theorized on the development and treatment of dysfunctional families. Ackerman shifted his emphasis of treatment toward the family system and, in 1958, published the first book on diagnosis and treatment of dysfunctional families, *The Psychodynamics of Family Life.* Ackerman and Jackson joined in 1960 to found what remains today the most influential journal in the family therapy field, *Family Process.*

Another family therapy pioneer, Whitaker, began working with entire families, in the late 1940s. When in 1946 he moved to Emory University Medical School, he began working with schizophrenics and found that working with the entire family in the session was effective. Whitaker was possibly the first therapist to expand the concepts of family treatment to include the extended family. His sessions would include grandparents, aunts, uncles, and other relatives who would participate and were involved in the family. Whitaker has developed his humor and whimsical style into a therapy of the absurd that is particularly effective in the treatment of schizophrenic families (Whitaker & Keith, 1981). Whitaker continues to be an active contributor to the family therapy field.

Bowen, much like Ackerman, began working with families while he was at the Menninger Clinic. In 1954, Bowen and Wynne, another pioneer in the field, began a project at NIMH to study and treat schizophrenic patients while these patients' families lived in the hospital. Again, these clinicians developed a family orientation in virtual isolation of others working in the field. In 1956, Bowen moved to Georgetown University. He continues to be a major influence in the field, especially in the area of family system theory (Bowen, 1978).

While it is not possible to present all the early contributors to family therapy, several others deserve mention. An approach called "Multiple impact therapy" (MacGregor, 1967; Ritchie, 1971) was developed at Galveston, Texas. This approach involved a team of professionals from different backgrounds (psychology, psychiatry, social work) working intensively for a two-day period with a family. During this period, the team attempted to impact on the various subsystems of the family and on the general family funtioning. The Galveston group developed two important ideas: first, family systems are more amenable to change during times of crisis and, second, the probability of change is greater at the beginning of therapy than at later stages in therapy.

Minuchin, together with Haley and Montalvo, developed an approach at the Philadelphia Child Guidance Center referred to as structural therapy. Minuchin (1974) and his approach emphasize the subsystems and organizational hierarchy in families. This approach has been particularly effective with psychosomatic families (Minuchin, Rosman, & Baker, 1978).

In 1961, Watzlawick, an Austrian psychologist, became fascinated with the communication work of the Bateson group. He soon began to analyze tapes of family therapy sessions and, along with Jackson and Beavin, produced one of the best treatments of family communication theory (Watzlawick, Beavin, & Jackson, 1967).

The 1960s and 1970s were periods of rapid growth and development in family therapy. Previously isolated groups began to share ideas and information. While different family therapy perspectives began to melt into each other in the 1960s, the field began to diversify in the 1970s. Even though treatment strategies advanced rapidly, research and theoretical developments were slower to mature. Presently, the field continues a healthy growth as an accepted treatment modality.

THEORETICAL PERSPECTIVE

The difference between an individual and a family orientation to therapy is much more than how many people are in the treatment room. The difference between these two orientations is one of differing epistemologies. The two orientations function from different realities, involving both the treatment and etiology of human problems. Since all therapists operate from an epistemological base, and this base determines how problems are conceptualized, the understanding of one's epistemological base is critical.

Individual orientations to therapy, such as traditional psychoanalysis, adopt a Western epistemology. Dell (1980) points out that Western thinking is primarily an "Aristotelian/Cartesian/Newtonian epistemology" (p. 328). This view proposes that reality consists of objects which possess characteristics. These characteristics constitute the actual object. The form of this object is determined by the quantities of its characteristics. The behavior of objects can be predicted, once one knows the different characteristics of the objects. This epistemology underpins Newtonian physics and traditional psychopathology. Individual diagnosis and treatment are founded upon this view of reality. Individuals are viewed as possessing certain traits, characters, or personalities that determine their behavior. Diagnosis is based upon how much of differing traits of characteristics any one individual possesses. Symptoms are considered to arise from conflicts between characteristics within an individual. Keeney (1979) suggests that this is a linear theory. Pathological behavior is viewed as traceable in a linear, cause-and-effect fashion, from intrapsychic mechanisms. Commonly, this represents a medical model, with the patient suffering an illness. The treatment that follows logically from this epistemology is focused on the individual and, for successful treatment, the individual must change intrapsychic constructs or traits. It is postulated that, once the conflicts between traits are identified and understood (i.e., insight), then this conflict can be resolved, and the symptom will disappear.

A family or systems orientation represents an entirely different epistemology or reality. A systems orientation is an epistemology of pattern and is typified by the relationship between objects. It tends to ignore the objects themselves and focuses exclusively on the relationship of objects. As Dell (1980) points out,

> It is a relational reality in which the actuality of any "object" is inseparable from the pattern in which it is embedded. The pattern or context is primary; the object within it is secondary. Patterns are assessed in terms of quality rather than quantity. (p. 329)

The behavior of objects can only be understood in the context of the pattern or system in which they exist. Family therapy is postulated on this epistemology, which is more typical of Eastern thought and not based on classical physics. Symptoms then can only be understood in the context in which they occur. Keeney (1979) refers to this approach as an "ecosystemic" epistemology.

Unlike an individual orientation, family therapy contends that individuals do not have inherent traits or characters apart from their interactional pattern, but rather behave in response to patterns of relationships. It is not possible to understand an individual's behavior without understanding the pattern or environment in which that individual exists. Unlike an individual orientation, a family orientation views diagnosis as understanding the pattern of a system. Thus, diagnosis becomes understanding how a problem behavior is sensible rather than nonsensical. It follows that the treatment that derives from this epistemology involves changing the system or pattern of relationships of the patient. As the therapist actively intervenes in the system, the patterns of that system are changed, and consequently, the behavior presented as a problem is also changed.

This curvilinear epistemology can be directly applied to families. Minuchin (1974) has pointed out four important features of the family system. First, the family is an open system with various interactional patterns and, as an open system, it is in a constant state of transformation. The family system adapts its structure to both internal and external inputs, with the direction of this adaptation determined by the interactional patterns in the family. Interactional patterns can be viewed as implicit rules that determine how, when, and with whom members of the family interact. These patterns are developed over time and become an automatic function within the family. The flexibility of these patterns determines how well the family accommodates to both internal and external stresses.

Families also progress through various developmental stages to which they must adapt in order to remain functional. These stages consist of such occurrences as the birth of the second child, the first child entering school, or the last child leaving home. Each of these developmental stages can create disturbances or stresses of various intensities. As Haley (1980) noted, the time of most stress in a system or organization is when a member enters or leaves that system. When the interactional patterns of the family lack flexibility to accommodate these stresses, then one or more of the family members may develop symptomatic behavior that will restabilize the family. Family problems are most likely to develop during these developmental states and, if not resolved, will create chronic dysfunction within the family.

A third aspect of the family system is the existence of an influence hierarchy within the family. Within a family, there are differing levels of authority or power. For example, parents typically must have more authority than the children, in order to lead the family. Parents must also have rather equal authority, in order to work together on family matters. When this hierarchy becomes confused or disorganized, the family structure and functioning are also disorganized.

Last, families share with open systems the tendency to maintain themselves. This concept is very important and frequently misunderstood. A family system moves toward stability rather than instability. This does not mean that the family necessarily works toward eliminating problems, but rather that the family tends to maintain its structure and interactional patterns. Many times, the only way for a family to maintain its structure is for one of the members to develop symptomatic behavior, thus the family stabilizes around this member's problem. Families then resist changes that threaten to change the structure or organization of that family.

The following generalizations about a symptom's appearance and presence in a system have been postulated by Keeney (1979). Disruptions in a relationship system may produce symptomatic behavior in any part of the system. Symptomatic behavior may shift position in a system such that a change in one part of the system may produce problems in another part. An example of this may be found in families when one child changes his behavior, and another child becomes symptomatic. Additionally, when parents in a family are having problems in their relationship, a child in that family may become symptomatic. Another principle involves what Speck (1967) calls "ripple effects." This principle involves the idea that system change in one part radiates throughout the system and may produce change in other parts of the system. The family therapist understands symptoms as metaphoric communication about the structure and functioning of the system. For example, the therapist may understand the repeated running away from home of a young child as communicating that one of the parents wishes to run away from the marriage.

It should be apparent, from this discussion, that a family orientation is much more than simply how many people are involved in the therapy. The individual approach represents a linear analysis of behavior and individuals. The family orientation involves a curvilinear analysis of relationships, in that continuous feedback loops structure the relationships and the behavior of individuals in those relationships. These two realities are incompatible. Comprehending the difference between these two is essential, if one is to understand family therapy.

CLINICAL PERSPECTIVE

The field of family therapy has diversified into a number of different therapy models. While there is substantial theoretical agreement on the family system being the problem for therapy, there still are numerous disagreements on how to approach the therapy of families. A few of the major approaches will be presented here, with emphasis on the unique aspects of each.

The strategic approach to family therapy has been most noted for its use of paradoxical interventions. This approach is strategic, because the therapist attempts to develop a specific intervention aimed at disrupting the interactional pattern that supports the presenting problem. Strategic therapists attempt to increase their leverage in the family system, so that they may directly influence the interactional patterns in the family. Examples of this approach are Haley's (1980) strategic approach to schizophrenics, the Milan group's (Palazzoli-Selvini, Boscolo, Cecchin, & Prata, 1978) use of paradox with anorexic families, the very unique work of Erickson (Haley, 1973), and Berenson's (1976) approach to alcoholic family members.

The development of the structural approach to family therapy is best illustrated by the work of Minuchin (1974), at the Philadelphia Child Guidance Clinic. The emphasis of this approach is on the structural aspects of interactions in the family. According to this approach, psychological problems occur when the power hierarchy of the family becomes disorganized. Thus, the focus of this treatment model is to reorganize the family structure.

Another approach (commonly labeled an *interactional* view) is best typified by the Mental Research Institute group (Bodin, 1981). The focus of this group has been on how problems are perpetuated by the family solutions to these problems. Watzlawick, Weakland, and Fisch (1974) have brilliantly presented this approach.

Whitaker has developed a unique approach that he calls "symbolic-experiental" family therapy (Whitaker, 1975; Whitaker & Keith, 1981). While it is difficult to deduce if this approach developed more from theory or from Whitaker's own approach to life, it is fair to say that he has developed an effective way to help families overcome problems. Whitaker takes a tongue-in-cheek approach to problems and escalates the irrationality of symptomatic behavior to a level of absurdity. This helps the family change patterns of interactions and overcome problems. This approach has been particularly effective with problems of aggressive behavior in families. One final approach to family therapy is based upon learning theory and involves such modalities as behavioral parent training (Gordon & Davidson, 1981) and systematic-parent training (Miller, 1975). An excellent review of these behavioral approaches has been presented by Hamerlynck, Handy, and Mash (1976). The approach presented by Barton and Alexander (1981) represents an integration of systems and learning theories. This therapy model combines the theory of how family systems function with the effective behavioral interventions developed from the learning model. While the approach has not received wide attention, it is certainly a significant step in combining two highly effective schools of therapy.

While these models of treatment have distinct differences, they share several commonalities of treatment and theory. The attempt here will be to present what family therapists do in the therapy setting, by utilizing the commonalities among the different family therapy models. This presentation should be viewed as a generalization on family therapy in a clinical setting. Several recent publications (Gurman & Kniskern, 1981a; Haley, 1980; Papp,1977) present excellent and more extensive reviews of the clinical practice of family therapy.

Since family therapists view problems as interactional difficulties in the family system, therapy is not limited to any particular symptoms or problems. A few examples of the problems treated with family therapy are: *alcoholism* (Andolfi, 1980; Berenson, 1976); *stomachaches* and *vomiting* (Madanes, 1980; Stanton, 1980); *schizophrenia* (Haley, 1980; Palazzoli-Selvini et al., 1977, 1978, 1980; Weakland, Fisch, Watzlawick, & Bodin, 1974; Zuk, 1971, 1975); *behavior problems and delinquency* (Erickson, 1962; Haley, 1980; Hare-Mustin, 1976; Watzlawick et al.,1974; Weakland et al., 1974); *depression* (Hare-Mustin, 1976; Watzlawick & Coyne, 1980; Zuk, 1975); *drug abuse and addiction* (Haley, 1980; Stanton & Todd, 1979); *school problems and truancy* (Garrigan & Bambrick, 1975; Papp, 1980; Rohrbough, Tennen, Press, White, & Raskin, 1977; Watzlawick et al., 1974): and *suicidal gestures* (Papp, 1980; Whitaker, 1975).

In clinical practice, the family usually consists of mother, father, and at least one child, who is identified by the family as the patient. At most clinics, the family does not specifically request family therapy but requests help for the identified patient. Since the therapist is interested in the interactional patterns of the family, traditional tools such as personality testing and data from individual interviews are of little use. The entire family is interviewed together, and data is collected on the interactional patterns in the family.

The setting for this interview usually consists of a room with chairs situated in a manner that allows family members to freely arrange themselves. Since the structure of a family's interactional patterns are not only reflected in their communication, but also in how they seat themselves, this freedom allows the therapist to begin to detect the interactional process.

The family therapist, in many ways, represents a different type of therapist than that of some traditional approaches. Because the therapist works with an active interactional system, the therapist must be active and directive in working with the family. Since the family presents interactional patterns from which they see no escape, the therapist must be an active system changer. The passive therapist soon learns how quickly a family can paralyze themselves and the therapist. As discussed earlier, the family system tends toward stability and, therefore, works toward neutralizing the system and cause changes.

The actual process of family therapy can be divided into three stages. While these stages may overlap, they do represent three distinct phases in the therapy process.

The first of these stages spans the period from the original contact with the family to the finalization of goals for the therapy. Because family therapy is present- and problem-oriented, lengthy history taking is generally viewed as unnecessary. The focus in this initial stage is on present, ongoing interactions and on the family's current solutions to their problems. During this stage, several issues must be resolved in order for the therapy to have a high probability of success. The first issue is who will attend the first family therapy session. Since it is generally agreed that seeing the entire family is necessary for at least the first session, the goal here is to get all the family members to attend this session. This goal may be easily achieved or may develop into a monumental struggle, but it must be won by the therapist. Perhaps the single most important factor in successfully engaging the entire family in the therapy process is the conviction and determination of the therapist to have all the members of the family present for the session. The more ambivalent the therapist is about the presence of the entire family, the more difficult will be the process of convening the family for the session. Numerous ways to attract missing members to therapy have been outlined by Palazzoli-Selvini et al. (1978), Starr (1981), and Bauman (1981). Common strategies of engaging the missing member include the therapist personally telephoning the missing member or members to request their attendance, while refusing to meet with only the members that did come to the session. Or, in response to a member's refusal because he/she is not the "problem," the therapist may agree with this statement, then request his/her help with the identified patient.

Once the family is present for the session, the therapist must begin to join that family system and to establish a therapeutic system. Minuchin (1974) has defined this process as the therapist's acceptance of and blending with the organization and style of the family. It includes the therapist honoring the structure of the hierarchies in the family, speaking the family language, and accepting the communicational patterns of the family. Absence of the joining process can doom the therapy process to failure. An eloquent description of this process has been presented by Minuchin (1974).

A third issue that must be dealt with in this first stage involves the issue of responsibility and blame. Since the family usually presents a child as the identified patient, and this has been followed by the therapist's request that the entire family come in for the session, the parents may assume that they will be blamed for the problem. The issue of blame may surface in numerous ways. The parents may present a long list of solutions that they have tried and that have failed, thereby absolving the parents of any blame. Or, the parents may rather brutally attack the child for having the problem. When the issue of blame is presented in the latter fashion, one should avoid siding with the child against the parents and rather, shift the focus onto the interactions of the family unit. The therapist should expect that, until the issue of blame is resolved, members in the family will defend themselves from responsibility for the problem. If this issue is not successfully laid to rest, the probability is low that the family will continue therapy. The best approach to resolving this issue is the therapist's respectful approach to the family and the acknowledgement of the distress that the problem is causing the family as a whole. Usually, once the therapist joins with the family to solve the problem, this issue is quickly put aside, and the therapy process can begin.

The final issue to be resolved in this stage is the setting of a therapeutic goal. While the implicit goal of family therapy is to change the interactional patterns of the family, this goal may not be directly stated to the family. Rather, the therapist should negotiate with the family on a behavior to be changed. The specificity with which the goal is presented depends on one's approach to family therapy. While it may appear that goals follow directly from the presentation of the problem, such is not always the case. Frequently, members of the family will agree on the problem but disagree radically on the goals of therapy. Here, the therapist can begin the therapy process through the negotiation with the family of a therapy goal. More about goal setting may be found in Aponte (1974), and Fisch, Watzlawick, Weakland, and Bodin (1973).

The second stage of the therapy process involves the therapeutic interventions utilized in changing the interactional patterns of the family. Characteristically, family therapists take a pragmatic view to the process of change and attempt to utilize techniques that are effective in changing families. These techniques are aimed at reducing problem behaviors and aiding the family to become more functional. Since the focus of family therapy is on the interactions of the family, the techniques are designed to alter these interactional patterns. Most family therapists do not see emotional insight as necessary for change and so focus on change and away from the gaining of emotional insight by the family.

Because family interactional patterns represent a unique system, the interventions must be tailored to that particular system. Presentation of these interventions may appear quite illogical, when viewed apart from the family system. Many of these interventions also require a certain amount of creativity on the part of the therapist (Erickson, in Haley, 1973). Two of the most investigated techniques will be presented here as an illustration.

Perhaps the technique that has drawn the most attention is the paradoxical intervention. A number of writers have described this technique (Haley, 1963; Palazzoli-Selvini, 1978; Papp, 1980; Watzlawick et al., 1974). In actual practice, this technique usually involves directing the patient to continue the problem behavior, rather than requiring change. The therapist may ask that the behavior continue as it is, increase in frequency or duration, or be done in a different setting. A basic rule to the use of therapeutic paradox—as proposed by Haley (1963)—is "to encourage the symptom in such a way that the patient cannot continue to utilize it" (p. 55). For example, a child may be referred to therapy because of temper tantrums. These tantrums are reported to occur only at home and only when both parents are present. Further, the parents report that the tantrums occur most frequently when they are engaged in a discussion and the child is excluded. The parents feel that the tantrums are caused by the child's continual need for attention. The mother describes numerous attempts to stop these tantrums, usually by pleading at length with the child to stop and to act in a more adult fashion. The result of these solutions has been an increase in tantrum behavior. The parents feel it is important that the child receive as much attention as possible but are frustrated with the tantrums. The therapist may ask the child to demonstrate a tantrum in the office and then criticize certain aspects of the tantrum as needing improvement to qualify as a well-done tantrum. The therapist may then ask the parents to attend to the child differently for the next week. Specifically, the therapist asks the parents to help the child improve his tantrums by grading two practice tantrums each day. Here, the parents could be asked to discuss (between just themselves) the recommendations for improvements in the quality of the tantrum and to present these recommendations to the child after each tantrum. This solution has been "tailored" to the family, for its meets the needs of the parents to attend to the child and also to be able to discuss things between just themselves without the child's intrusion. This solution also encourages the problem behavior in a way that prevents the child from utilizing it. The choice of this paradoxical solution is based on satisfying the needs presented by the parents while decreasing the occurrence of the problem. This represents the tailoring that is required for successful paradoxical solutions.

While the mechanism of this type of intervention is still open to debate, it remains a particularly effective technique with resistant families and specific behavior problems. A word of caution is in order here. As Haley

(1980) pointed out, the use of paradoxical interventions can produce extremes in behavior and should be used with caution. The effective paradox is not as simple as it appears and should only be used with a thorough understanding of its effects or under competent supervision.

Another useful family-therapy technique is the redefining or "reframing" of problems or behaviors. The power of reframing is based upon the notion that behaviors are determined, not by reality per se, but rather by perceptions or images of reality. If perceptions of reality change, then consequently behaviors will also change. With families, the process of reframing usually involves changing the interpretation of a behavior (i.e., the motivation for that behavior) from a negative to a positive. For example, parents cannot continue to berate a child for aggressive behavior when the motivation for that behavior is reframed as a misguided attempt by the identified patient to teach the younger siblings how to deal with conflict. Here, the new frame (a helpful attempt to educate siblings) can fit all the presented facts but ascribes a different and positive motivation to the behavior. This frame blocks the feedback loop of anger begetting more anger and opens the way for new interactions by the family.

A further example to briefly illustrate the use of reframing is a family that recently presented to the author with problems of the oldest son leaving the home. The mother and oldest son of this family had always been particularly close. The son was becoming increasingly angry with what he perceived as the mother's overprotectiveness of him, especially when he attempted to rent an apartment across town. His anger would culminate in a loud argument between mother, father, and son, about the son's treatment of the mother. After these arguments, the son would feel guilty about hurting his mother's feelings and about leaving home. This cycle of behavior had been continuing, with increasing frequency, over the last year. Here, the intervention involved both reframing and symptom prescription. The son was seen alone and told that, while it appeared his mother was overprotective, in reality, she was just experimenting with ways to help her children leave home successfully. It was explained to him that the strategy she was currently using was to make the departure as difficult as possible, so as to increase the probability of his successful departure. The son was told that this was a common strategy used by old-fashioned mothers. The son readily accepted the explanation. This explanation reframed the mother's interference as a positive helpfulness.

The parents were then seen, and the mother was complimented on her willingness to sacrifice her time (i.e., time involved in the interference) in order to help her son leave home successfully. It was explained to the mother that her son was evidently having trouble deciding how and when to leave home and that her interference was just the "medicine" he needed to help him successfully depart. She was encouraged to continue the interference for as long as she felt her son needed it. The family returned two weeks later, reporting that things were going well. The son had rented an apartment across town and gotten a job all on his own. The mother stated she felt great relief that her son was finally "standing on his own two feet." Six-month follow-up showed the family doing well and the son engaged to be married. In this example, the family was not asked to do anything differently; rather, the motivations for their problem behaviors were reframed in a manner that created change.

While the technique of reframing is by no means new and, most likely, is an essential part of all successful therapy interventions, the family therapy movement has highlighted its use and developed it in creative ways. Possibly the best treatment of reframing has been presented by Watzlawick et al. (1974).

The final stage of family therapy is the disengagement of the therapist from the family. Since family therapists generally view therapy as a brief process of getting families "unstuck" from patterns of interaction, termination is accomplished as soon as positive change occurs. The aim of the termination is to extend the therapeutic influence beyond the actual therapy sessions. The rapid disengagement is seen as preventing negative effects from an interminable process of therapy.

This presentation of the family therapy process is, admittedly, brief and a gross oversimplification of a complex process. The serious student can find a wealth of clinical theory and techniques in various journals (particularly *Family Process*) and in numerous, excellent manuscripts on the process of family therapy. A few of the books that may be helpful to those wishing to develop more expertise in family therapy include: Gurman and Kniskern (1981b), Haley (1971, 1980), Minuchin (1974), Palazzoli-Selvini et al. (1978), and Watzlawick et al. (1974).

RESEARCH PERSPECTIVE

The last decade has been a period of phenomenal growth in family therapy outcome research. While the 1960s were marked by a scarcity of family therapy research, the 1970s have seen a proliferation of outcome studies. The first review of family therapy-outcome studies (Wells, Dilkes, & Trivelli, 1972) contained only 13 studies, as compared to 90 studies reviewed by Gurman and Kniskern, in 1978. Over 15 reviews of outcome research have appeared in the literature since 1972. It is beyond the scope of this chapter to present a thorough review of the outcome studies in this area. The reader interested in a more extensive review is referred to the excellent reviews by Gurman and Kniskern (1978), Masten (1979), and Patterson and Fleischman (1979). In this section, the present author will attempt the perilous task of summarizing what can be inferred about the effects of family therapy, based upon the results of existing outcome research and review of this research.

Initially, it would be helpful to know if the use of family therapy is any more beneficial than no formal treatment. Gurman and Kniskern (1981a), in an excellent review of the field, have reported an average improvement rate of 73 percent in a number of controlled outcome studies of nonbehavioral family therapy. The bulk of these studies used an untreated control group as comparison. Considering these results, family therapy does appear to be an effective treatment of psychological problems, as compared to no treatment. It should be noted here that these improvement figures are close to the two third improvement rate for individual therapy cited by Garfield and Bergin (1978).

Additionally, some studies have reported that there may be detrimental effects from family therapy (e.g., Coughlin & Wimberger, 1968; Sigal, Barrs, & Doubilet, 1976; Weakland et al., 1974). Gurman and Kniskern (1978), after reviewing the field, have estimated that the rate of deterioration from family therapy is 2.1 percent. While this deterioration rate appears constant across different schools of family therapy, a number of therapists' variables appear related to deterioration. Deterioration is more likely if the therapist is directly confrontive early in therapy (Guttman, 1973), is inactive in structuring the early stages of treatment (Shapiro & Budman, 1973), and does not support or moderate feedback in the family (Alkire & Brunse, 1972).

The research comparing family therapy to different modalities (such as individual psychotherapy) has produced some interesting results. Every study evaluated in the Gurman and Kniskern (1978) review demonstrated family therapy at least equal (and in 10 of the 14 studies, superior) to other modalities, such as individual psychotherapy (Love, Kaswan, & Bugental, 1972), inpatient programs (Hendricks, 1971), and methadone programs (Stanton & Todd, 1978). While many of these studies suffered from methodological difficulties, and the number of studies is far too low to be considered definite proof of any superiority of family therapy, the results—taken together—strongly suggest at least the equivalence of family therapy to other modalities of treatment. In addition, several studies utilizing structural family therapy (Minuchin, 1974) deserve particular note. These well-designed studies (Minuchin, Baker, Rosman, Liebman, Milman, & Todd, 1975; Minuchin et al., 1978; Rosman, Minuchin, Liebman, & Baker, 1976; Stanton & Todd, 1978) have produced some very persuasive evidence about the effectiveness of this approach with adolescent psychosomatic problems and drug addiction problems.

At this time, comparisons among the different schools of family therapy are not possible. Other than the work with the structural approach, well-designed studies comparing different approaches to family therapy have been scarce.

Two other treatment factors have received enough research attention to warrant comment. The first of these factors is the importance of the inclusion of the father in family treatment. While clinicians have continued to stress this point (e.g., Haley, 1980), only recently have studies supported this stance. It appears that the father's inclusion in therapy greatly increases the probability of the family continuing in therapy (Shapiro & Budman, 1973) and the probability of successful outcome (Love et al, 1972; Postner, Guttman, Sigal, Epstein, & Rakoff, 1971). The relationship skills of the therapist also appear related to outcome in family therapy. As an individual therapy, the ability of the therapist to form a positive relationship with the family is related to both the family continuing in therapy and positive therapy outcome (Postner et al., 1971; Shapiro, 1974; Spector, Guttman, Sigal, Rakoff, & Epstein, 1970).

The research on family therapy, at this time, appears to support several conclusions. Family therapy does appear to be an effective treatment for psychological problems at levels equal to other treatment modalities and superior to other modalities in treating some adolescent psychosomatic and drug addiction problems. Deterioration rates appear to be low, but deterioration does occur in family therapy and appears related to several therapist variables. The inclusion of the father in the therapy process appears important to both good outcome and family continuance in therapy. Finally, good relationship skills of the therapist appear related to positive outcome in family therapy.

The field of family therapy continues a rapid, healthy growth and maturation in not only treatment and theory, but also in research areas. Much of the excitement and enthusiasm that surrounded the beginnings of family therapy continue today. For the field to continue its growth, research efforts must continue to develop a solid base of knowledge. More attention is needed to developing a sound theory of how families function and how therapeutic interventions affect the family. The hope in the 1980s is that those who work with families can fulfill many of the promises and hopes that have been generated in this area.

SUMMARY

The influence of the family on individual development and growth has been of continual interest to the field of clinical psychology. Recently, that interest has grown to include working directly with entire families in a therapy setting. The development of family therapy began in the 1950s and has continued at a rapid pace. Today, the field is enjoying a healthy development and expansion. Conceptualizing the family from traditional, individual theory has been abandoned in favor of a theory of systems and patterns of family interactions.

Currently, the field of family therapy consists of many different models of therapy. The commonality here is the belief that the unit of focus in therapy should be the family system, not the individual members. Family therapy research, particularly therapy outcome research, is a rapidly growing area. Current therapy outcome research suggests that family therapy is at least as effective as other treatment modalities, on a wide variety of psychological problems. Family therapy also appears to be more effective than other modalities in the treatment of adolescent psychosomatic problems and substance abuse. Also, the research suggests that the father's involvement in the therapy is critically important to successful outcome. Finally, the relationship skills of the therapist appear strongly related to outcome. Family therapy appears to hold a great deal of potential for helping families, and thus individuals, overcome psychological problems.

REFERENCES

Ackerman, N. *The psychodynamics of family life.* New York: Basic Books, 1958.

Alkire, A., & Brunse, A. Impact and possible casualty from videotape feedback in marital therapy. *Journal of Consulting and Clinical Psychology*, 1974, *42*, 203–210.

Andolfi, M. Prescribing the families' own dysfunctional rules as a therapeutic strategy. *Journal of Marital and Family Therapy*, 1980, *6*, 29–36.

Aponte, H. Organizing treatment around the family's problems and their structural bases. *Psychiatric Quarterly*, 1974, *48*, 8–12.

Barton, C., & Alexander, J. Functional family therapy. In A. Gurman & D. Kniskern (Eds.), *Handbook of family therapy.* New York: Brunner & Mazel, 1981.

Bateson, G., Jackson, D., Haley, J., & Weakland, J. Toward a theory of schizophrenia. *Behavioral Science*, 1956, *1*, 251–264.

Bauman, M. Involving resistant family members in therapy. In A. Gurman (Ed.), *Questions and answers in the practice of family therapy.* New York: Brunner & Mazel, 1981.

Berenson, D. A family approach to alcoholism. *Psychiatric Opinion*, 1976, *13*, 33–38.

Berenson, D. The therapist's relationship with couples with an alcoholic member. In E. Kaufman & P. Kaufmann (Eds.), *An empirical analysis* (2nd ed.). New York: John Wiley & Sons, 1978.

Bodin, A. The interactional view: Family therapy approaches of the Mental Research Institute. In A. Gurman & D. Kniskern (Eds.), *Handbook of family therapy.* New York: Brunner & Mazel, 1981.

Bowen, M. *Family therapy in clinical practice.* New York: Jason Aronson, 1978.

Coughlin, F., & Wimberger, H. Group family therapy. *Family Process*, 1968, *7*, 37–50.

Dell, P. Researching the family theories of schizophrenia: An exercise in episemological confusion. *Family Process*, 1980, *19*, 321–326.

Erickson, M. The identification of a secure reality. *Family Process*, 1962, *1*, 294–303.

Fisch, R., Watzlawick, P., Weakland, J., & Bodin, A. On unbecoming family therapists. In A. Ferber, M. Mendolsohn, & A. Napier (Eds.), *The book of family therapy.* Boston: Houghton Mifflin, 1973.

Garrigan, J., & Bambrick, A. Short-term family therapy with emotionally disturbed children. *Journal of Marriage and Family Counseling*, 1975, *1*, 379–385.

Gordon, S., & Davidson, N. Behavioral parent training. In A. Gurman & D. Kniskern (Eds.), *Handbook of family therapy.* New York: Brunner & Mazel, 1981.

Gurman, A., & Kniskern, D. Research on marital and family therapy: Progress, perspective, and prospect. In S. Garfield & A. Bergin (Eds.), *Handbook of psychotherapy and behavior change: An empirical analysis* (2d ed.). New York: John Wiley & Sons, 1978.

Gurman, A., & Kniskern, D. Family therapy outcome research: Knowns and unknowns. In A. Gurman & D. Kniskern (Eds.), *Handbook of family therapy.* New York: Brunner & Mazel, 1981. (a)

Gurman, A., & Kniskern, D. (Eds.). *Handbook of family therapy.* New York: Brunner & Mazel, 1981. (b)

Guttman, H. A contraindication for family therapy: The prepsychotic or postpsychotic young adult and his parents. *Archives of General Psychiatry,* 1973, *2,* 352–355.

Haley, J. *Strategies of psychotherapy.* New York: Grune & Stratton, 1963.

Haley, J. (Ed.). *Advanced techniques of hypnosis and therapy: Selected papers of Milton H. Erickson.* New York: Grune & Stratton, 1967.

Haley, J. Family therapy: A radical change. In J. Haley (Ed.), *Changing families.* New York: Grune & Stratton, 1971. (a)

Haley, J. A review of the family therapy field. In J. Haley (Ed.), *Changing families.* New York: Grune & Stratton, 1971. (b)

Haley, J. *Uncommon therapy.* New York: W. W. Norton, 1973.

Haley, J. *Problem-solving therapy.* San Francisco: Jossey-Bass, 1976.

Haley, J. *Leaving home: The therapy of disturbed young people.* New York: McGraw-Hill, 1980.

Hamerlynck, L., Handy, L., & Mash, S. (Eds.). *Behavior modification and families.* New York: Brunner & Mazel, 1976.

Hare-Mustin, R. Paradoxical tasks in family therapy: Who can resist? *Psychotherapy: Theory, Research and Practice,* 1976, *13,* 128–130.

Hendricks, W. Use of multifamily counseling groups in treatment of male narcotic addicts. *International Journal of Group Psychotherapy.* 1971, *21,* 84–90.

Keeney, B. Ecosystemic episemology: An alternative paradigm for diagnosis. *Family Process,* 1979, *18,* 117–130.

Love, L., Kaswan, J., & Bugental, D. Differential effectiveness of three clinical interventions for different socioeconomic groupings. *Journal of Consulting and Clinical Psychology,* 1972, *39,* 347–360.

MacGregory, R. Progress in multiple impact theory. In N. Ackerman, F. Beatman, & S. Sherman (Eds.), *Expanding theory and practice in family therapy.* New York: Family Services Association of America, 1967.

Madanes, C. Protection, paradox, and pretending. *Family Process,* 1980, *19,* 73–85.

Masten, A. Family therapy as a treatment for children: A critical review of outcome research. *Family Process,* 1979, *18,* 323–336.

Miller, W. *Systematic parent training.* Champaign, Ill.: Research Press, 1975.

Minuchin, S. *Families and family therapy.* Cambridge, Mass.: Harvard University Press, 1974.

Minuchin, S., Baker, L., Rosman, B., Liebman, R., Milman, L., & Todd, T. A conceptual model of psychosomatic illness in children. *Archives of general psychiatry,* 1975, *32,* 1031–1038.

Minuchin, S., Rosman, B., & Baker, L. *Psychosomatic families: Anorexia nervosa in context.* Cambridge, Mass.: Harvard University Press, 1978.

Palazzoli-Selvini, M. *Self-starvation: From individual to family therapy in the treatment of anorexia nervosa.* New York: Jason Aronson, 1978.

Palazzoli-Selvini, M., Boscolo, L., Cecchin, G., & Prata, G. Family rituals: A powerful tool in family therapy. *Family Process,* 1977, *16,* 445–453.

Palazzoli-Selvini, M., Boscolo, L., Cecchin, G., & Prata, G. *Paradox and counterparadox: A new model in the therapy of the family in schizophrenic transaction.* New York: Jason Aronson, 1978.

Palazzoli-Selvini, M., Boscolo, L., Cecchin, G., & Prata, G. Hypothesizing-circularity-neutrality: Three guidelines for the conductor of the session. *Family Process,* 1980, *19,* 3–12.

Papp, P. (Ed.). *Family therapy full-length case studies.* New York: Gardner Press, 1977.

Papp, P. The Greek chorus and other techniques of paradoxical therapy. *Family Process,* 1980, *19,* 45–57.

Patterson, G., & Fleischman, M. Maintenance of treatment effects: Some considerations concerning family systems and follow-up data. *Behavior Therapy,* 1979, *10,* 168–173.

Postner, R., Guttman, H., Sigal, H., Epstein, N., & Rakoff, V. Process and outcome in conjoint family therapy. *Family Process,* 1971, *10,* 451–473.

Ritchie, A. Multiple impact therapy: An experiment. In J. Haley (Ed.), *Changing families.* New York: Grune & Stratton, 1971.

Rohrbaugh, M., Tennen, H., Press, S., White, L., Raskin, P., & Pickering, M. *Paradoxical strategies in psychotherapy.* Symposium presented at the meeting of the American Psychological Association, San Francisco, 1977.

Rosman, B., Minuchin, S., Liebman, R., & Baker, L. Input and outcome of family therapy in anorexia nervosa. In J. Claghorn (Ed.), *Successful psychotherapy.* New York: Brunner & Mazel, 1976.

Shapiro, R. Therapist attitudes and premature termination in family and individual therapy. *Journal of Nervous and Mental Disease,* 1974, *159,* 101–107.

Shapiro, R., & Budman, S. Defection, termination, and continuation in family and individual therapy. *Family Process,* 1973, *12,* 55–67.

Sigal, J., Barrs, C., & Doubilet, A. Problems in measuring the success of family therapy in a common clinical setting: Impasse and solutions. *Family Process,* 1976, *15,* 225–233.

Speck, R. V. Psychotherapy of the social network of a schizophrenic family. *Family Process,* 1967, *6,* 208–214.

Spector, R., Guttman, H., Sigal, J., Rakoff, V., & Epstein, N. Time sampling in family therapy sessions. *Psychotherapy,* 1970, *7,* 37–40.

Stanton, M. Family therapy: Systems approaches. In G. Sholevar, R. Benson, & B. Blinder (Eds.), *Emotional disorders in children and adolescents: Medical and psychological approaches to treatment.* Jamaica, N.Y.: S. P. Medical Books, 1980.

Stanton, M., & Todd, T. Some outcome results and aspects of structured family therapy with drug addicts. In D. Smith, S. Anderson, M. Buxton, T. Chung, N. Gottlieb, & W. Harvey (Eds.), *A multicultural view of drug abuse.* Cambridge, Mass.: Schenkman, 1978.

Stanton, M., & Todd, T. Structural family therapy with drug addicts. In E. Kaufman & P.

Kaufmann (Eds.), *The family therapy of drug and alcohol abuse.* New York: Gardner Press, 1979.

Starr, S. Dealing with common resistances to attending the first family therapy session. In A. Gurman (Ed.), *Questions and answers in the practice of family therapy.* New York: Brunner & Mazel, 1981.

Watzlawick, P., Beavin, J., & Jackson, D. *Pragmatics of human communication.* New York: W. W. Norton, 1967.

Watzlawick, P., & Coyne, J. Depression following stroke: Brief, problem-focused treatment. *Family Process,* 1980, *19,* 13–18.

Watzlawick, P., Weakland, J., & Fisch, R. *Change: Principles of problem formation and problem resolution.* New York: W. W. Norton, 1974.

Weakland, J. "The double bind theory" by self-reflexive hindsight. *Family Process,* 1974, *13,* 269–277.

Weakland, J., Fisch, R., Watzlawick, P., & Bodin, A. Brief therapy: Focused problem resolution. *Family Process,* 1974, *13,* 141–168.

Wells, R., Dilkies, T., & Trivelli, N. The results of family therapy: A critical review of the literature. *Family Process,* 1972, *II,* 189–207.

Whitaker, C. Psychotherapy of the absurd: With a special emphasis on the psychotherapy of aggression. *Family Process,* 1975, *14,* 1–16.

Whitaker, C., & Keith, D. Symbolic experiential family therapy. In A. Gurman & D. Kniskern (Eds.), *Handbook of family therapy.* New York: Brunner & Mazel, 1981.

Wiener, N. Time, communication, and the nervous system. In R. W. Miner (Ed.), *Teleological mechanisms.* Annals of the New York Academy of Sciences, 1947, *50.*

Zuk, G. *Family therapy: A triadic-based approach.* New York: Behavioral Publications, 1971.

Zuk, G. *Process and practice in family therapy.* Haverford, Pa.: Psychiatry & Behavioral Science Books, 1975.

29

Group therapy: A behavioral and cognitive perspective

*Sheldon D. Rose**
and
*Craig W. LeCroy**

Four men and three women were just completing relaxation exercises led by a group therapist, Jane. Several of the group had made themselves comfortable on the couch and chairs; others sat on the floor. When Jane indicated that the group was ready to review the activities of each member during the past week, they took out the notes and diaries which described their social achievements and their handling of problem situations.

Annie reported on a new situation which made her feel frustrated and angry, yet powerless to do anything about it. Her co-worker, Joanne, who had been on the job three months longer than she, was still, after a year, giving her advice on all aspects of her job. In the group discussion of a recent event, Annie stated that she was afraid to tell Joanne to stop because it upset her to make anyone angry. Ron asked, "What would be so terrible if someone got angry with you, Annie?" Annie claimed, "That would be horrible. I would just die!" After exploring in detail Annie's response to the situation, the members—in response to a request from Jane—gave examples of events in which they had made others angry and how it all passed without physical or psychological damage. Annie even recalled such an event. She said, "In this case, with Joanne, I think I'm ready to take my chances and say something to her." The group applauded. At Annie's request, a number of statements she might express were suggested and demonstrated by the group members. She practiced several of these, with Jane playing a calm "Joanne." Afterward, the group gave her feedback. She practiced again, with "Joanne" getting increasingly angry, and Annie adding an instruction to herself to relax. She then contracted with the group to use the statements she had practiced with Joanne the next time she

* University of Wisconsin, Madison.

gave Annie any advice. Annie pointed out how her excessive concern about people getting angry seems to prevent her from doing a lot of things that she felt needed to be done, and this was probably something for her to continue to work on in subsequent weeks.

Other members continued to tell about their experiences. With some clients, problem solving was used to help them come to a decision as to what they might do in a given situation. With others, cognitive restructuring—replacing self-defeating thoughts (e.g., Annie's concern for making people angry) with coping statements (e.g., "her *anger* is *her* problem")— was used to facilitate action. Just as with Annie, other group procedures— such as role-played demonstration (modeling), practice (rehearsal), and group feedback—were used to help them find specific words for dealing with their situations.

After all other persons explained what new problems they faced or what they had been doing about their problems during the week, the members paired off (subgrouping) to develop their weekly treatment plans. The plans state what behaviors each person intends to try out during the period prior to the next group session (e.g., Annie intended—at the first possible opportunity—to tell Joanne to stop bossing her around).

The group then suggested adjustments to each other's plans. When this was completed, Jane summarized what had happened during that meeting, what new ideas they had considered, and the plans for next week. After a few questions were answered, the members evaluated the session in writing. Then, each member made an appointment to see or call his or her partner ("buddy") during the week, At the conclusion, most helped themselves to coffee and cookies and chatted with each other before departing.

The above summary contains excerpts from a session in which behavior therapy is being carried out in a group. The focus of this therapy is on the development of social, cognitive, and active coping skills necessary to improve the quality of the clients' relationships with others and help them to cope more effectively with the myriad of stress and problematic situations with which they are confronted. Through such procedures, each client is helped to learn not only a wide variety of verbal and nonverbal behaviors and cognitive skills, but also to differentiate among those situations requiring the application of such skills. They also learn to both receive and give help to others.

OVERVIEW

Research suggests that social-skill deficits are linked to major psychiatric problems. Studies by Zigler and Phillips and their colleagues (Levine & Zigler, 1973; Phillips & Zigler, 1961, 1964; Zigler & Phillips, 1960, 1962) with psychiatric patients showed that the level of social competence (based on global measures of educational, vocational, and marital attainment) was related to the degree of psychiatric impairment. Lewinsohn has convincingly demonstrated a relationship between interpersonal deficits and such clinical phenomena as depression (Lewinsohn, Weinstein, & Alper, 1970; Libet & Lewinsohn, 1973). Argyle (1969) has pointed out how social-skill deficits can be antecedent to a variety of other clinical syndromes. For this reason, social-skill training (which includes modeling, rehearsal, coaching, and feedback) provides a key set of procedures in this approach as one means of reducing social-skill deficits.

Of course, some persons—for whom social skills may or may not be lacking—are still unable to function without high levels of anxiety or other distress. For such clients as these, it appears that certain interpersonal and intrapersonal events are accompanied by distorted cognitions, which in turn elicit anxiety and other strong emotions. Under intense anxiety, the performance of adaptive or coping behavior is limited or even inhibited. For these persons, cognitive procedures—such as stress inoculation (Meichenbaum, 1977) or cognitive restructuring (Beck, 1976)—can be combined with social-skill training procedures to enhance social functioning and reduce anxiety (Thorpe, 1975).

Thus, behavior group therapy refers to the practice of behavior and cognitive behavior therapies in groups. It combines the concreteness and technological sophistication of behavior therapy with the principles of group dynamics, in the pursuit of individual treatment goals.

Behavior group therapy, like behavior therapy, involves assessment and data collection, which form the basis for the selection of behavioral strategies. In order to evaluate the effects of the strategies, the behavior and cognition of clients is monitored. Once desired changes are obtained, the focus shifts to transfer and maintenance of these changes in preparation for termination. As in other group approaches, the group is used to give clients the opportunity to model and provide leadership for each other, to give clients responsibility for their own decisions, and to facilitate the establishment of therapeutic norms which influence the client to attend, to homework outside the group, and to self-disclose.

The major behavioral and cognitive strategies involve variants of assertion training, cognitive restructuring, modeling, and operant procedures, which are described in detail later in this chapter. The major group procedures are group goal setting, subgrouping, group contingencies, and group feedback. Group data collection is also carried out, to determine whether group problems exist which can be dealt with in the group. Let us look in more detail at how the group context impinges on therapeutic process.

THE GROUP CONTEXT

Since the context in which therapy takes place is the group, a number of assumptions about the advantages and limitations of the group guide and delimit the therapist's role. Because many problems are social-interactional in nature, the presence of other clients provides an opportunity for practicing new social-interactional skills with peers in a protected setting.

The group gives clients an opportunity to learn and practice many behaviors and cognitions, as they respond to the constantly changing group demands. The clients must learn to offer other clients feedback and advice and, as a result, develop important skills for leadership. By helping others, clients usually learn to help themselves more effectively than when they are solely the recipient of therapy.

In group interaction, powerful norms arise that serve to control the behavior of individual clients who deviate from pro-therapeutic norms. If these norms (informal agreements among members, as to preferred modes of action and interaction in the group) are introduced and effectively maintained by the therapist, they serve as efficient therapeutic tools (see Lawrence & Sundel, 1972, for examples of how such norms are used in behavior group therapy). The group pressures deviant members to conform to such norms as attending regularly, reinforcing peers who do well, and analyzing problems. Of course, antitherapeutic norms may also be generated in groups, as indicated by such behaviors as erratic attendance, noncompletion of agreed-upon assignments, and constant criticism of therapists; these norms work against the attainment of therapeutic goals.

To prevent or to deal with such problems, the therapist can call upon a modest body of experimentally derived knowledge about norms and other group phenomena, in which individual behavior both influences and is influenced by the various attributes of the group (see Cartwright & Zander, 1968, for an extensive summary). In addition to modifying the norms of the group, the therapist can facilitate the attainment of both individual and group treatment goals by such procedures as modifying the cohesiveness of the group, the status pattern, or the communication structure in the group. Much of the power of group therapy is lost if negative group attributes or group problems are not dealt with as they occur.

Another unique characteristic of therapy in groups is the opportunity for peer reinforcement. Each person is given the chance to learn or to improve his or her ability to mediate rewards for others in social-interactive situations (with spouse, family, friendship groups, work group). The therapist can structure a therapeutic situation in which each person has frequent opportunity, instructions, and even rewards for reinforcing others in the group. Reinforcement is a highly valued skill in our society; there is some research to suggest that as a person learns to reinforce others, he or she is reciprocally reinforced by others, and mutual liking also increases (Lott & Lott, 1961).

More accurate assessment is an additional benefit of group therapy. Many aspects of a problem which elude even the most sensitive therapist often become clearly spelled out during an intensive group discussion.

The group provides clients with a major source of feedback about what in their behavior is annoying to others and about what makes them attractive to others. This is helpful, especially when clients cannot pinpoint their own problems.

In addition to facilitating assessment, the group facilitates treatment by making available a variety of models, coaches, role players for behavioral rehearsal, peoplepower for monitoring, and partners for use in a buddy system or pairing off of one client with another, for work between sessions.

Since the group supplies so many of its own therapeutic needs and gives simultaneous treatment to a number of people, this type of therapy appears to be less costly than individual treatment, in terms of staff and money.

Finally, the group serves as a control on the therapist's value imposition. Clients in groups appear to be less accepting of the arbitrary values imposed by therapist action than a single client in a therapeutic dyad. A group of people can more easily disagree with the therapist than can the individual. The group therapist is constantly forced by group members to make his/her values explicit.

The group, of course, is not without major limits. Although a group contract may prevent excessive wandering to irrelevant topics, it also may serve to deter the exploration of idiosyncratic needs of any one individual. Each person needs to be allotted some time at every meeting to discuss unique problems. Therefore, no one or two persons can be permitted to dominate it. Some clients may even feel severely restricted by such a concern for involvement of all other members. For many, the group may slow their tempo of learning.

Another disadvantage of the group is the absence of an absolute guarantee of confidentiality. Although the clients contract to hold any discussion of individual problems in the group in strict confidence, they are not necessarily committed to the professional ethics of the therapist. The absence of this guarantee may also restrict the degree to which some clients are inclined to self-disclose or even limit the extent to which the therapist can urge them to self-disclose. It should be noted that in our experience actual breaches of confidentiality are rare.

For those few whose problems require more detailed and individualized examination or whose social anxiety is so great they cannot function in a group, the group may not be the preferred context of therapy. However, this does not infer that complex problems cannot be dealt with in a group. Behavior group therapy can be looked at as a continuum, from short-term training groups to intensive long-term therapy (Shoemaker, 1977). At the training end of the continuum, groups focus solely on teaching a narrow range of highly specific behaviors (for example, assertion, parenting skills, marital communication, and anxiety reduction). The tools utilized are specific social-interactive exercises and a limited range of the above-mentioned interventions, especially social-skill training. Because of the restricted number of sessions, a highly specific agenda at each meeting is used, and only limited flexibility is permitted. Most research on small group therapy has evaluated this type of program.

At the intensive end of the continuum, the above interventions are all used as needed, but individualization is much greater, and group problems and processes are dealt with as learning experiences. Moreover, the problems dealt with are usually more complex and more varied in therapy groups than those in the training groups; because of greater individualization, more attention is also given to assessment in the long-term therapy groups.

Now that we have reviewed some basic assumptions as to the advantages of the group as the context of therapy, let us examine what therapists actually do in behavior group therapy to facilitate the learning of social and cognitive skills by the clients within the constraints of the above assumptions.

THERAPIST ACTIVITIES

At least nine major categories of therapist activities generally found in behaviorally oriented group therapy can be identified. Although there is some degree of overlapping, each category is different enough to describe separately. These categories include: organizing the group, orienting the members to the group, establishing group attraction, assessing the problem and possibilities for resolving it, monitoring the behaviors determined as problematic, evaluating the progress of treatment, planning for and implementing specific change procedures, modifying group attributes, and establishing transfer and maintenance programs for behavior changes occurring in the group. Each category consists of a series of still more specific activities, some of which are described below and in Table 1.

Beginning the group

In the initial phase of group therapy, the therapist focuses on three major activities: organizing the group, orienting the clients, and building group attraction.

Organizational activities. These involve discussion and decision making about type of group, duration of group, length of meetings, number of therapists, location of meetings, nature of fees and/or deposits, and similar structural concerns. During the pre-group interview and in the first session, the group members may be involved in some of these decisions, such as when and where the group is to meet and the length of meetings. They also may help decide whether new members should

Table 1

Therapist activities in a behavior therapy group

Session	Organization	Orientation	Attraction	Assessment	Monitoring	Evaluation	Treatment	Group Process	Maintenance
Pregroup	X	X		X	X	X			
1	X	X	X	X	X	X			
2		X	X	X	X	X			
3			X	X	X	X		X	
4				X	X	X	X	X	
5				X	X	X	X	X	
6				X	X	X	X	X	X
7				X	X	X	X	X	
8			X	X	X	X	X	X	X
9				X	X	X	X	X	
10				X	X				X
Follow-up				X	X				X

X = Occurrence in a given meeting of the activity indicated above

be added. In the pre-group interview, clients decide whether the thera-pist's description of the group's focus adequately meets what they per-ceive to be their needs. Most intensive therapy groups are 14 to 18 weekly sessions in length, with several "booster" sessions at one- to six-month intervals. Short-term training groups are four to eight sessions. Some therapists have successfully used open-ended groups for intensive therapy. As clients achieve treatment goals or no longer feel the need for group support, they terminate. New members are added at that time. The more experienced member orientates the new members, which pro-vides an opportunity for leadership.

Orientation.   This refers to those activities in which the therapist in-forms the client of the group's purposes and content and of the responsibil-ities of the clients to themselves and to the others. It also involves the process of negotiating the content of the general treatment contract. In the process of orientation, the therapist is usually the major contributor, who provides information and case studies as examples. In open-ended groups or in groups with clients experienced in behavior therapy, the clients themselves will assume this role. As seen in Table 1, the major therapist activities of the pre-treatment interview and the first session are concerned with orientation.

Building group cohesion.   This activity focuses on increasing the attraction of the group members to each other, to the therapist, and to the content of the program.

Increased group cohesion has been found to be positively associated with group effectiveness (Liberman,1970). Flowers and Booraem (1980) have identified many other correlates of cohesion, such as increased problem disclosure and role flexibility during group sessions.

Research by Liberman (1970) also suggests that the group therapist can directly influence the level of group cohesion. Therapists were trained to use social reinforcement and were effective in shaping, modifying, and facilitating verbal behavior reflecting cohesiveness.

Strategies employed to increase group cohesion include: providing food at meetings, varying the content of meetings, providing audiovisual aids, providing incentives, judicious use of humor, use of group exercises, and goal-oriented interactive games. Assessment, monitoring, and evaluation are also a part of beginning the group, but because these activities continue throughout treatment and are so central to the approach of this type of therapy, these are discussed under a separate section.

Assessment, monitoring, and evaluation

Assessment. As defined earlier, assessment is the group activity concerned with determining the behavior and cognitions to be modified, situations experienced as stressful, and the characteristics of the individual and his or her environment that will facilitate or obstruct remediation of the problem.

The assessment process in group treatment cannot be overemphasized. Group therapists in treatment settings must go beyond preliminary information and initial complaints in determining treatment strategies, by careful exploration of detailed information required to decide whether the group is appropriate, the kind of group that is appropriate, the type of goals the client can aim at while in the group, and the evaluation of whether session and treatment goals are attained. Effective assessment requires pre-group interviews, which explore the stressful situations the clients are experiencing and their behavioral, cognitive, and affective responses to those situations. From these interviews and subsequent contacts, information is acquired about resources and barriers which impinge on the effectiveness of treatment. Interviews should be supplemented by role-play tests, behavioral inventories and checklists, and observations in and out of the group (as a means of zeroing in on specific target areas). Group data—such as participation, satisfaction, attendance, and assignment completion—provide a basis of evaluating whether group problems exist and whether group goals are being attained. Group members enhance each other's assessment by being maximally involved as testers and interviewers of each other, as collectors of observational data, as judges of each other's role-plays, and as providers of feedback as the basis of goal selection. Such involvement not only increases the interpersonal attraction, it mobilizes the full power of the group as the context and means for assessment (see Rose, 1981, for details on the assessment process and how specific procedures are applied in the group setting).

Although assessment begins at the pre-group interview, it is constantly refined throughout treatment. In the pre-group interview and early in treatment, members are encouraged to present the reasons they have come to the group. Clients are taught to define their problems in terms of directly observed behavior and descriptions of their inner states (affect and cognitions) as responses to the situations which they perceive as stressful or otherwise problematic. The group members are taught how to help each other to specify the environmental conditions impinging on them in each problem.

One of the most crucial steps in ongoing assessment is the analysis of situations viewed as problematic or stressful by the client. In this analysis, an attempt is made to identify a time-limited event in terms of what was happening, who was involved, and where it occurred. Additionally, the clients are asked which moment in time was the most difficult for them. At this critical moment, the clients are asked to describe their behavioral, affective, and cognitive responses. Among specific affectual responses are their satisfaction with their behavioral response and the intensity of their anxiety or anger. If the client is not at least somewhat dissatisfied with the response, the problem may not warrant working on at that time.

If the problem identified by the client is that he or she does not know how to respond in the specific situation, problem-solving and social-skill training need to be considered. If the problem is one of self-depreciation or excessive self-demand, then cognitive restructuring may be called for. If the situation is unchangeable (e.g., a client has a rigid and highly critical boss, yet he is in a high-paying job for which there are few better possibilities) coping-skill training may be useful (e.g., learning to relax when the boss criticizes and learning when and how to avoid certain kinds of stress). In the case of complex problems, all three approaches may be necessary, in order to achieve the client's goal.

Monitoring. Behaviors (and the situations in which they occur), once defined, are systematically observed and measured in some way, usually by the client and occasionally by others, prior to the application of any explicit change procedure. For example, the client will rate his or her anxiety level four times a day. The process of data collection is carried on throughout treatment and is concluded only at the follow-up interview.

The therapist uses the data, as it is collected, to evaluate the effectiveness of specific treatment procedures, the group meetings, and the course of therapy. Effectiveness is determined on the basis of whether the goals of a given technique, a given meeting, or a given therapy have, indeed, been achieved. If it is discovered that the format of a given meeting has been partially or totally unsuccessful (because of the high frequency of critical comments on the session's evaluation, low participation in the meeting, and failure of most members to complete their weekly assignments), the format can be changed. Changes, thus, are brought about by a review of data, not only by intuitive hunches. Because of the abundance of data and the regularity of feedback, change procedures can be designed and carried out as soon as a specific problem has been identified.

Evaluation. Monitoring makes it possible to evaluate the degree to which individual treatment goals are achieved. By keeping a record of ongoing progress, the therapist and others with whom the data is shared can ascertain what kind of clients can best use the procedures commonly found in various models of group therapy. Each therapist can expand the knowledge base further, if research controls are established. In behavior therapy, if all treatment steps and problems are explicated, the total treatment of each group and of each client can be viewed as an experiment, in which the client and the group are observed before, during, and after treatment. Variations of this time-series model without a control group have been suggested by a number of authors (Sidman, 1960; Campbell & Stanley, 1963; Hersen & Barlow, 1976) as a means to strengthen the conclusion of a causal connection between treatment and outcome. Such designs as the multiple baseline, the *ABAB* model, and other time-series designs (see Hersen & Barlow, 1976) are especially suited to small samples.

Therapeutic planning

Therapeutic planning in groups has two components: individualized and group planning. Group planning is preceded by an analysis of the data about individuals and the group to determine common skill deficits. On this basis, training programs are then selected, for example, problem-solving, giving and receiving feedback, relaxation, role-playing, cognitive self-analysis, and/or other skills which are required to mediate the individualized therapy.

These basic therapeutic skills are taught through group exercises and other interactive procedures, usually in a six-hour marathon session at the beginning of therapy or incorporated in each of the first six to eight sessions for 15–30 minutes.

Individualized treatment planning involves each individual in consultation with the therapist and the other clients in the group, determining which individual situations need to be worked on, whether social-skill training, problem-solving, cognitive restructuring, or other techniques might be the necessary approach to resolving that problem.

Since social-skill training, cognitive restructuring, problem-solving, and group intervention are the major intervention strategies used, let us examine each of these more closely.

Social-skill training. Combs and Slaby (1977) define social skills as, "the ability to interact with others in a given social context in specific ways that are societally acceptable or valued and, at the same time, personally beneficial, mutually beneficial, or beneficial primarily to others" (p. 162).

Social-skills training involves several critical assumptions (Bellack & Hersen, 1978). The first is that interpersonal behavior is based on a distinct set of skills which are primarily learned behaviors. Thus, how one behaves in an interpersonal situation depends on the individual's repertoire of effective social behaviors. The second aspect is that socially skilled behavior is situationally specific. It is important to recognize that cultural and situational factors determine social norms or what may be expected of an individual. Third, effective functioning (e.g., making a friend) depends on an individual's social skill and, if effective, is a powerful source of reinforcement. Social skills facilitate receiving reinforcement and avoiding problematic behavior.

Further, Bellack and Hersen (1978) describe three general categories that make up the components of social skills: conservational skills, social-perception skills, and skills necessary for special problem situations. With regard to conversational skills, Hersen and Bellack point out that every social interaction is dependent on one's ability to initiate, maintain, and terminate a conversation. With regard to social perception, that is, accurate perception of the social situation, the following skills have been identified as relevant: listening, getting clarification, maintaining relevancy, timing, and identifying emotions. Last, it is important to attend to special problem situations, which are particularly difficult because they are stressful, even though they may be infrequent. Such situations place unique demands on the individual—such as, dealing with imposition of others, job interviews, or dealing with an oppressive boss.

Research on social-skills training has revealed that no specific components are universally effective across different subject populations and different problems. Whereas McFall and Twentyman (1973) found that coaching (instructing a client how to perform in a specific situation) and rehearsal (role-played practice) were important components of assertive training and that symbolic modeling (observing others) contributed little, Eisler, Hersen, and Miller (1973) found modeling and instructions to be the most critical elements in social-skills training, with psychiatric clients. It appears that different training components are effective in producing different aspects of social skills (Edelstein & Eisler, 1976; Hersen, Eisler, Miller, Johnson & Pinkston, 1973) and that results have different effects, depending on the subject population (Eisler, Fredericksen, & Peterson, 1978). In general, it appears that a complete treatment package is important when teaching complex response patterns (Hersen et al., 1973; Rimm, Snyder, Depue, Haanstad, & Armstrong, 1976).

Prior to the initiation of social-skill training, the therapist discusses with members the rationale of the procedures and provides examples. Where possible, the therapist draws upon those members who have used the procedures to share their evaluation of these experiences with the group.

Social-skill training involves the application of those behavioral procedures already mentioned, usually in the order identified in Figure 1. Let us look at what each of these steps entail, as they are applied in a group context.

During social-skill training, the therapist enlists the group members in helping each client to determine, in a specific situation, at a specific "critical moment," what is to be achieved. The group members are asked to provide suggestions as to how that set of goals can be achieved. The group helps each client evaluate those suggestions in the areas of relative risk, appropriateness, compatibility with personal style, and probable effectiveness. Ultimately, it is the client who decides upon an overall strategy.

Usually, the therapist or a group member models the desired verbal and nonverbal behavior, in a brief, role-played demonstration. The client evaluates how realistic the modeled situation was and states what he or she finds useful in the performance of the model.

The client then practices or rehearses his or her own role in the situation, utilizing the agreed-upon behaviors. In subsequent rehearsals, the difficulty and complexity of the situation is gradually increased. Where the client has difficulty in carrying out the strategy, he or she may be coached or assisted by the therapist or another member. If coaching is used, it is usually eliminated in subsequent rehearsals. Following each rehearsal, the client receives feedback from the group, as to what was done well and what might be done differently. After several increasingly difficult rehearsals, the client assigns to him/herself a homework assignment to either: try out some of the new behaviors learned in the group, role-play, observe one's self in a new situation, and/or keep a diary. Homework is an essential part of this approach and is used as a means of increasing time spent on therapeutic endeavors and for transferring therapeutic activities to the real world.

Let us look briefly at the details of these procedures, as they were applied to Annie in the first example.

> Annie had been annoyed when her co-worker gave her advice. She did nothing about it except get upset. In the group, the members recommended a number of things she could say. The alternative she liked best was to say, in a firm tone, that she appreciated all the help she had been given, but now it was important for her (Annie) to do everything on her own. If she was in trouble, she'd ask. Otherwise, please, no help needed! Thoma demonstrated, in a role-play, how Annie might say it (modeling). When

Figure 1

Social skill training

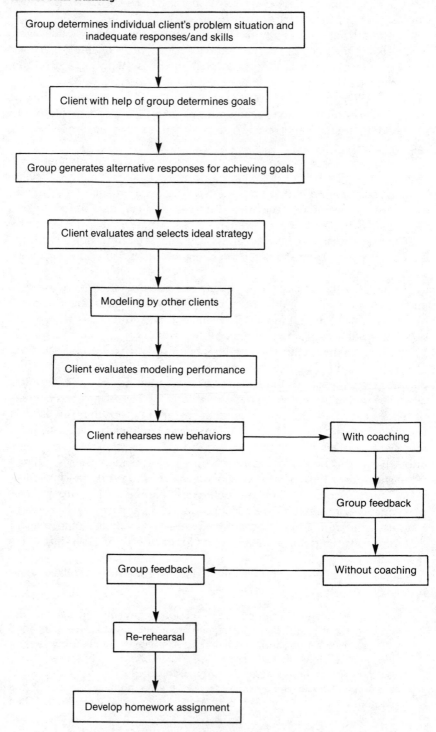

Annie was asked about risk involved in making the above statement, she thought the risk was far greater if she did nothing. Although it wasn't her style, she said, it was a style she would like to acquire. By using cognitive procedures, she has already resolved that the potential anger of Joanne would no longer be of major concern. Annie role-played the situation being herself (behavioral rehearsal), with Jane playing the role of Joanne. Most thought she was quite impressive and pointed to specific actions they thought she had done well. Glen and Jean thought she might speak a little more slowly and emphatically (group feedback). After a second rehearsal, Annie said she couldn't wait for the real Joanne to give her advice, so she could try out her new skills; but just in case, she'd practice a half-dozen more times with her buddy, Thoma, during the week (using the buddy system as homework).

Most of these same procedures (such as modeling, rehearsal, and homework) are also used in the modification of cognitions. In addition, a number of specific adaptations and uniquely cognitive procedures are applied, which we discuss in the following section.

Cognitive restructuring. In describing their cognitive responses during stress situations, clients often reveal self-defeating thoughts or severely distorted beliefs about themselves, in relation to the world about them. For example, in the initial excerpt, Annie was certain that some catastrophy would befall her if anyone became angry with her. In some cases, these cognitions seem to generate so much anxiety for an individual that the client would be unable to make use of social-skill training in developing and trying out specific alternatives for coping with stress, as it occurs in the real world. Under these conditions, some form of restructuring of cognitions may be necessary. Cognitive restructuring refers to the process of identifying and evaluating one's own cognitions, recognizing the deleterious effect of maladaptive cognitions, and replacing these cognitions with more appropriate cognitions (Beck, 1976). Much of the supporting data for cognitive restructuring has come from a series of recent studies conducted by Fremouw and associates (Fremouw & Harmatz, 1975; Fremouw & Zitter, 1978; Glogower, Fremouw, & McCroskey, 1978) and from the work of Meichenbaum (1977). Cognitive restructuring has been used effectively to help anxious clients cope with text anxiety (Goldfried, Linehan & Smith, 1978; Meichenbaum, 1972), speech anxiety (Fremouw & Harmatz, 1975; Fremouw & Zitter, 1978; Thorpe, Amatu, Blakey, & Burns, 1976), and social-interpersonal anxiety (Elder, 1978; Glass, Gottman, & Shmurak, 1976), and to treat depression (Taylor & Marshall, 1977) and pain-related stress (Langer, Janis & Wolfer, 1975; Turk, 1975). This procedure also is used in conjunction with other therapeutic strategies when the client's belief system becomes part of the change target. Although this support may seem extensive, few of these studies have controlled for placebo or expectation effects.

The major steps in cognitive restructuring, as we generally follow them, are described in Figure 2.

Just as in social-skill training, the provision of a rationale for cognitive restructuring is an imperative first step (Meichenbaum, 1977). As a part of this step, clients are provided with examples, evidence of effectiveness, and an overview of the major steps. Members are encouraged to provide to others their own examples of the relationship between cognitions, anxiety, and behavior. An example of a rationale might be the following:

> No one is free from stress. The way we view ourselves, what we say to ourselves, and what we expect from ourselves may strongly influence how stressful a given situation becomes and how anxious we may feel. One person might view seeing his car being towed away for a parking violation as a terrible tragedy, and he might brood about it for a week, with an intense headache; another person in the same situation might reflect casually that is was an expensive parking fee, pay the fine, and go off on her own business without further concern. The situation is the same; the stress experienced is dramatically different! Changing the first person's view of the situation to more realistic proportions may result in reduced anxiety, better problem solving, and, in general, more comfortable living. This is what this group is all about: helping each person to discover inefficient, harmful—or a word we'll use a lot—self-defeating thoughts and to replace them with coping thoughts and actions which work better for each of us. Does anyone else have examples of the relationship of experienced stress to the way they thought or evaluated themselves in a given situation?

The following step is to identify each client's particular self-defeating or irrational cognitions, through analysis of logical inconsistencies and long-range consequences of pervasive cognitions. This is done through the analysis of cognitive responses to stress situations brought in by the clients, who are interviewed by the other members of the group. The group provides each participant with feedback on the accuracy of their congitions.

This step is exemplified by group members helping a client, Glen, recognize his self-defeating statements:

> Glen told about a situation in which he had wanted to ask a girl in his class for a date. He failed to do so because, as he thought, "She'll just say no to a klutz like me." The group members pointed out to Glen two apparent, self-defeating cognitions. The first implied, "If she says no, I'll be devastated," and the second was stated explicitly: he considered himself a klutz—a totally inept individual. Jane had the group deal with each cognition, one at a time. The members interviewed Glen. Kerry asked for any successes at all in approaching and talking to women. Glen gave a couple of examples. Jane asked if the women in the group had experienced Glen as a klutz. "To the contrary," Annie smiled. The discussion continued, with both Glen and the group providing evidence inconsistent with Glen's self-description.

Figure 2

Steps in cognitive restructuring

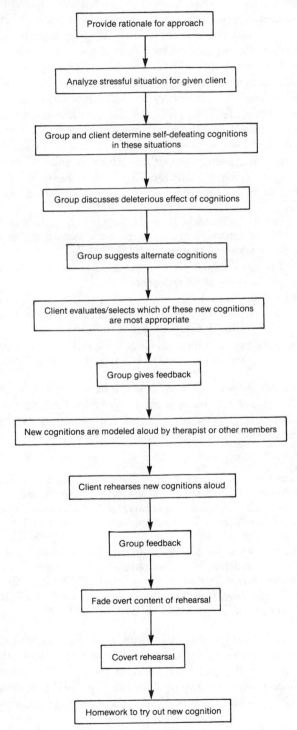

Group exercises may be first used to teach clients to differentiate be-tween self-defeating and coping statements (see Rose, 1980, exercise 26). Additional exercises are sometimes used to encourage clients to learn how to identify and analyze their own cognitions. Group participants provide each other not only with feedback, but with repeated and varied models of a cognitive analysis for each other.

Often, convinced recognition of the self-defeating cognitions is suffi-cient to warrant change (Ellis, 1962, 1979); but more often, in our experi-ence and that of Beck (1976) and Meichenbaum and Cameron (1973), further steps must be employed. Thus, the subsequent step is to solicit ideas from the client and from other group members, as to potential self-enhancing or coping cognition which facilitate problem solving or effective actions. In the following continuation of Glen's group interview:

Jane: In a similar situation, what else might Glen say to himself that would accurately portray his response, instead of, I'm such a klutz, she would never go out with me?

Jerry: I've got to admit, lots of people don't view me as a klutz, and maybe she won't either.

Thoma: Everyone's klutzy once in a while and, in the group, I'm learning how to approach people. Let's try it out now. The worst that can happen is that she'll say no.

Annie: What do you think about . . . So what if I feel klutzy, I can do something about it, like asking her for a date.

After the client decides on a set of accurate and comfortable cognitive statements, cognitive modeling is used—in which the client imagines the stressful situation, experiences the initial self-defeating statements, stops him or herself, and replaces the self-defeating with a coping statement. For example:

> Jane asked Jerry to demonstrate to Glen how Glen might handle himself in that situation. I'll help you if you get stuck (coaching). Jerry began, "OK, I imagine I see this girl in the library, OK? She seems real nice. I know her from class. There's a movie tonight at the Student Union. I'd really like to ask her to go with me. Got the picture? But I think—Oh she'd *never* go out with a klutz like me. Wait a minute! (Note the shift statement) I feel like a klutz sometimes, but other people find me attractive. (Glen seems at a loss, so Jane coaches him at this time) . . . Oh yes, and I have been working on making friends in the group so, damn it, I'll ask her for a date." Jane asked, "OK Glen, how does that sound?"

In cognitive rehearsal, the client goes through the same steps as the model but adapts his or her own style. Afterward, the client gets feedback from the group. The client may need to be coached, during the first few trials. Finally, when feeling confortable, the client practices the entire process silently (covert rehearsal). In the above example, Glen duplicated in a cognitive rehearsal much of what Jerry had said. Now Jane asks the group for feedback:

Jane: Well, what did Glen say to himself, or how did he say it, which should prove useful to him?

Thoma: He sounded like he believed it.

Annie: He was really into the situation.

Jerry: For sure, he improved on my version. I especially liked the way he switched from the self-defeating statements.

Jane: (After a pause) What might he have done differently?

Glen: I forgot to say, After all, plenty of people don't think I'm a klutz.

It should be noted that Jane focuses first on positive feedback, before asking for ways of improving. Now, after several practices, Jane shifts to a covert rehearsal.

OK, let's try again—only this time let's do it silently—all of you might practice your own situation at the same time.

Usually, after several trials in the group, an assignment to practice a number of times at home is developed with the client. Ultimately, it must be tried out in the real world.

Thus, in the final step, homework is developed at the end of one session and is monitored at a subsequent session. Assignments are usually developed in pairs and then discussed in the large group. Homework is developed at successive levels of difficulty each week. For example, it might initially focus on learning to discriminate in general between self-defeating and self-enhancing or coping cognitions. Later, the focus might be on identifying and evaluating the clients' cognitive responses to their own situations or shifting from the practice of self-defeating responses to coping skills, with the addition of self-praise for one's achievements. Homework may be carried out with buddies from the group or with a friend or family member.

Of course, in most problems, just learning to perceive or evaluate oneself in a situation differently may not be enough. Social-skill training was necessary to help Glen with the actual words he needed to talk to women; and coping skills (such as relaxation or deep breathing) may be necessary to either think or speak appropriately. One cognitive procedure which behavior therapists have found particularly useful for certain types of problems (e.g., anger control, stress, persistant pain) is stress inoculation.

Stress inoculation. This procedure is quite similar to cognitive restructuring but goes beyond it to teach physical (as well as cognitive and social) coping skills. Designed by Meichenbaum and Cameron (1973), stress inoculation is aimed at providing a client with a set of skills to deal with future stressful situations. Stress inoculation has three important facets: orienting the client to the nature of stressful reactions; cognitive and overt modeling and rehearsing of various physical and cognitive skills; and helping the client to apply these skills during exposure to highly stressful situations. This approach has been used to aid abusive clients and law enforcement personnel in anger control (Novaco, 1975, 1977) and to teach others how to manage anxiety, stress, tension, headaches, and pain (see Mahoney & Arnkoff, 1978, for a review of this research).

Since most of these procedures have already been explained, except for physical or active coping skills, let us look briefly at these.

Coping-skill training. In addition to overt interactive responses, which are usually taught through social skill-training procedures, a number of other, more general, behavioral strategies have been found effective in coping with both specific and general stress situations (Horan, Hackett, Buchanan, Stone, Demchik-Stone, 1977). These include: relaxation, deep breathing, enquiry, and (in some cases) avoidance of the stress situation (see Barrios & Shigetomi, 1979, for a review of the research on coping-skill training).

Relaxation and deep breathing are taught to the group as group exercises. The skills are demonstrated, members practice the skills in pairs, give each other feedback, and, finally, with the help of instructional tapes, they practice the skills at home. Once learned, the group discusses when and where such procedures should be used.

Teaching clients when to use enquiry (collection of information) in stress situations is taught as each person brings in a stress situation. The question is always asked: what information do you need to reduce the ambiguity of this situation? Avoidance, too, is often looked at as one alternative response, in every stress situation. However, the question must be asked, as to whether the costs or risks of avoidance are greater than utilizing a cognitive coping strategy.

One additional, cognitively based strategy in group therapy is systematic problem solving, which we consider a fundamental component of behavior group therapy.

Problem solving. Several studies have shown that emotionally distressed individuals are not very efficient problem solvers (see, for example, Spivack & Levine, 1963; Platt & Spivack, 1972a, 1972b; Platt, Scura & Hannon, 1973). Emotionally distressed individuals tend to use more impulsive and aggressive solutions to problematic situations and are less capable of means-ends thinking than their "normal" peers (Shure & Spivack, 1972). The term *problem solving* has been used by helping professionals to explain a particular systematic process between therapist and client, which leads to the resolution of problematic situations experienced by the client (see Heppner, 1978, for a review of the problem solving literature).

The use of problem solving in behavior group therapy involves teaching group members a systematic paradigm in approaching and resolving problems. The skills of problem solving consist of: (1) sensitivity to the existence of or the potential for interpersonal problems; (2) alternative thinking, i.e., generating alternative solutions to an interpersonal problem; (3) means-ends thinking, i.e., planning in detail the steps which would be needed to carry out a solution to an interpersonal problem; (4) consequential thinking, i.e., thinking what the consequence of each potential solution is likely to be, before implementation of the solutions; and (5) social-causal thinking, i.e., understanding and appreciating the complex, dynamic-reciprocal nature of human interaction.

The problem-solving process follows a series of four basic steps:

1. General orientation. The general orientation provides group members with an initial set of expectations. The group leader explains how the problem-solving method helps individuals develop skills in thinking through and handling difficult problems.
2. Problem definition and formulation. In order to use the problem-solving process effectively, it is essential to define the problem. Without a clear definition of the problem, the solution to the problem can never be clear or specific. To obtain a clear definition, D'Zurilla and Goldfried (1971) suggest that an individual:
    a. Define all aspects of the situation in "operational" terms.
    b. Formulate or classify elements of the situation appropriately so as to separate relevant from irrelevant information, identify his primary goals, and specify the major subproblems, issues, or conflicts (p. 113).
3. Generation of alternatives. Generating or brainstorming many alternative solutions is the core of problem solving. Group members take turns in suggesting as many alternatives as possible. Four guidelines are used.
    a. No criticism.
    b. Get as many ideas as possible.
    c. Be concrete—state ideas in terms of action.
    d. Accept ideas for part of the problem.
4. Decision making and implementation. In making a decision, the group member tries to anticipate all likely consequences of each suggested alternative. The other group members help the problem solver predict all possible consequences. The group members then discuss how to implement the particular solution.

Group problem-solving training is frequently an integrated addition to the social-skills training discussed earlier. The group is used to help individual members clarify their problem, brainstorm a large number of response alternatives, evaluate the response alternatives, and prepare each member to implement the treatment plan and monitor the implementation.

Frequently in behavior group therapy, problem solving is not only taught to group members as an intervention but also used to deal with current group problems (dominance of several individuals, interpersonal conflict, low productivity) which impede progress (see Rose, 1977b, pp. 132–151). In this case, it is used not to increase problem-solving skills, but to help resolve a group problem or modify group attributes.

Modifying group attributes. Group and individual procedures are often used together to modify group attributes, which include the level of group cohesion, the distribution of group participation, the agreement to certain group norms, the status of various members in the group, or the domination of a given member over others in the group (see Bavelas, Hastorf, Gross, & Kite, 1965). It is this concern for influencing group phenomena to mediate the modification of individual behavior that distinguishes group from individual therapy. We have already looked at group cohesion. Let us look at one other of these attributes in more detail.

Modification of group structure (such as the communication pattern among members) was illustrated in a group of six members, in which data revealed that two members spoke almost 60 percent of the time and one less than 5 percent of the time. After presenting the data to the group, they agreed that participation was a problem and developed a plan to implement it at that meeting. The more active members agreed to reformulate the previous speaker's position before making a point of their own (recapitulation); the less-active members agreed to write down any thoughts they had relevant to the subject, if they were disinclined to speak up. The leader agreed to call upon them to review their notes. The group practiced the complex plan for the following five minutes and decided to use it only twice a meeting, for 20 minutes, since it was somewhat disruptive. They also agreed to end it, once the distribution of participation was somewhat more even. Thus, the plan utilized problem solving, recapitulation cueing by the leader, and rehearsal.

Another group, with a similar problem, utilized primarily cognitive procedures. The members analyzed their thinking whenever they were expected to participate, and the group helped each to determine whether a given thought was self-enhancing.

Other procedures commonly used have been verbal reinforcement of inactive participants for even brief contributions and role-play practice (with a buddy, prior to a meeting) as to what might be said at the meeting. Similar procedures have been used to deal with other group attributes, such as nontherapeutic norms (see, e.g., Lawrence & Sundel, 1972).

It should be noted that changing a group attribute involves each client working on specific behaviors and cognitions needed to be employed in extragroup situations.

No discussion of behavior therapy, whether in groups or individual, is complete without a discussion of the principles of transfer (generalization) and maintenance of change.

Transfer and maintenance of behavioral change

Transfer of change or generalization involves the application of those strategies designed to facilitate the transfer of learning occurring in the treatment situation to the real world of the client. There are two major types of procedures for transfer: intragroup procedures (such as behavioral rehearsal) simulate the real world and represent a preparatory step toward performance outside the group; and extragroup procedures (such as the behavioral assignment), in which the client tries out the rehearsed behavior in the community. Other extragroup techniques include meeting in the homes of the clients and using the buddy system outside of the group.

Maintenance of change refers to strategies oriented toward maintaining the goal level or quality of behavior achieved during the course of treatment long after treatment is terminated. Several techniques are used, such as the gradual fading of the treatment procedures, thinning of the reinforcement schedules (i.e., reducing frequency and regularity of rewards), and overlearning the new behavior through frequent trials. Overlearning of simple tasks is probably not sufficient. It is also necessary to review summary rules or cognitive strategies, in order that the more complex patterns of functioning be maintained (Rosenthal & Bandura, 1978). In groups, this review is often carried out at the end of each meeting.

In preparing for termination, the attraction of other groups is increased, relative to the therapy groups. Clients are encouraged to join nontherapeutic groups, in order to practice their newly learned skills under less-controlled conditions. Greater reliance is placed on the decisions of the clients, as they increasingly perform the major leadership tasks in the group. The role of the therapist shifts from direct therapist to consultant. These activities not only serve to make termination easier on the clients, but they permit them to function independently of a therapist. This independence is necessary not only for the maintenance of changes beyond the end of the group, but in making the client more comfortable in dealing with new problems, should or when they happen. Clients are prepared for potential setbacks, unsympathetic relatives and friends, and unpredicted pressure, through role-play of situations simulating the above conditions. It should be noted that preparation for the transfer and maintenance of change is found throughout treatment. As early as the third or fourth meeting, partners are working with each other outside of the group, rehearsal is occurring within the group, and behavioral assignments are given to practice the desired behavior outside of the group.

PRELIMINARY OUTCOMES

A crucial issue of concern is whether behavior group therapy is an effective form of treatment. Because of the methdological problems of doing research with the small group as a unit of change, the number of controlled group-outcome experiments in this area is limited. A number of projects have been carried out in the context of small groups, usually without reference to the group attributes and group procedures. These, at least, have suggested that social-skill groups are indeed more effective in developing social skills than wait list or placebo control groups (see, e.g., Hedquist & Weinhold, 1970; Weinman, Gelbart, Wallace, & Post, 1972; Rimm, Hill, Brown & Stuart, 1974; MacDonald, Linquist, Kramer, McGrath & Rhyne, 1975; Wolfe & Fodor, 1977).

In the Interpersonal-Skill Training and Research Project (Rose, 1977a), we carried out three different experiments with clinical populations. In these experiments, group therapy—following the model discussed in this paper (but without cognitive restructuring)—was compared to discussion-placebo groups and/or other group methods (see Schinke & Rose, 1977; DeLange, 1976; Toseland & Rose, 1978). These projects dealt with such differing populations as "typical social agency self-referrals," women, and the elderly. Except with the elderly, the above-described approach was significantly superior to the other group approaches on a behavior role-play test. With the elderly, the behavior group therapy program was as effective as a problem-solving approach, but both were more effective than the nondirective discussion group. In general, however, these studies involved basically social-skill training, problem solving, and group modification.

Of course, cognitive restructuring alone may not work for everyone. Safran, Alden, and Davidson (1980) found that, in a comparison of the effectiveness of behavioral-skills training and cognitive restructuring, client anxiety functioned as a mediating variable on treatment effectiveness. While low-anxiety subjects benefited equally well from skills-training or cognitive restructuring procedures, high-anxiety subjects benefited more from skills training on behavioral measures and showed a nonsignificant trend to benefit more from cognitive restructuring on self-report measures.

Recent research (Schwartz & Gottman, 1976; Thorpe, 1975; Linehan, Goldfried, & Goldfried, 1979) suggests potential value in a combined cognitive behavioral approach. In particular, Linehan et al. (1979) found that a combined behavioral rehearsal/rational restructuring therapy was superior to behavioral rehearsal, systematic rational restructuring, relationship, and waiting list control groups. Such a combination appears to provide the client with an opportunity for more individualized sets of treatment procedures.

In conclusion, adequate empirical support exists for most of the components of behavior group therapy. Preliminary data suggest that these components in combination do add to the effectiveness of the program. The behavior and cognitive model of group therapy—which combines social-skill training, cognitive restructuring, coping-skill training, problem solving, and group process modification—offers a promising set of alternatives to the group treatment of clients with complex and varied problems.

Obviously, a behavioral and cognitive approach to group therapy is not the only one or even the one most commonly utilized. Although some are quite similar, most are quite different, in terms of underlying supportive theory, operating principles, use of group process, reliance on empirical support, and goals toward which therapy aims.

Some of the foremost group-therapeutic orientations are presented in this section for purposes of comparison. Since most of these alternative approaches are only touched upon here, references to more thorough presentations are provided to the interested reader.

One of the forms of group therapy most different than the one presented here is the psychoanalytic approach. The focus is similar to that of individual psychoanalytic treatment: namely, personality change through making unconscious conflicts conscious, interpreting past experiences, working through defenses, and analyzing transference feelings. Whitaker and Liberman (1965) describe what they call nuclear conflicts and group focal conflicts. The basis of these conflicts are the unconscious fears and desires of the individuals and of the group as a whole. This suggests that unconscious motives are not only relevant to one's behavior within the group, but also that the group process is influenced by the unconscious fears and desires of the group as an entity. In a similar manner, Durkin (1964) sees resistance as a very basic part of the psychodynamic group. As group members work with one another, their resistances begin to be manifested. As they show up, they are analyzed and interpreted.

Psychoanalytic group theory differs widely, with regard to how much emphasis is placed upon group dynamics. Whereas Slavson (1959) argues that even the most common group dynamics should not be permitted to operate, theorists like Bion (1961) argue that the therapist must pay close attention to forces operating in the group. For Bion, the patient becomes the group, and the group therapist's interpretations are directed to the group as a whole, rather than to any individual member. Additional sources of information on psychoanalytic groups can be found in Locke (1961), Mullan and Rosenbaum (1978), and Wolf and Schwartz (1962).

A more popular approach to group therapy, along psychoanalytic lines, is transactional analysis (TA). Originally developed by Berne (1961), TA focuses upon ego states (parent, adult, and child), "life scripts," or how people and games people play (Berne, 1964) are actions about past premises. Goulding and Goulding (1979) describe the client's role, whereby they "learn to be more aware of the ego state they are in, they learn to better handle their feelings, to better recognize their position in their life script, to be more aware that they have been, or are, game playing" (p. 26). Although without an empirical base, TA is particularly suited for groups, because the focus is on interaction between people. Further reading can be found in Berne (1964, 1966), Goulding and Goulding (1979), Harris (1967), and Steiner (1974).

Encounter groups are less theoretically oriented and more of an intensive group experience. In essence, group members learn to encounter themselves and others. In order to accomplish this, group members must strive to be honest and open with each other and to relate their perceptions and feelings. To help facilitate the encounter, therapists utilize a variety of group models (such as Gestalt or psychodrama) and a wide variety of group exercises. Encounter groups tend to be very global in purpose— from psychotherapeutic to personal growth (see Liberman, Yalum, & Miles, 1973).

The client-centered model focuses on developing relationships based on an empathetic understanding, warmth, and genuineness. Group therapy is practiced in a nondirective manner, allowing group members to develop their own potential, as they are encouraged by the group to self-disclose. The leader allows the group to develop entirely on its own— any planned procedure is to be avoided (see Rogers, 1970). Once group members begin to accept and trust one another, it is assumed they are willing to self-disclose and to begin to take action toward behavior change. Readers are directed to the major works written by Rogers on groups (1970) and individual counseling (1961, 1977).

Gestalt therapy (founded by Perls) focuses on how people must take personal responsibility for their own life in order to change. The group approach is very action-oriented and works directly with the process— the here and now. Perls (1973) refers to Gestalt therapy as an experimental therapy, whereby group members deal with their immediate experience. When the past is dealt with, it is brought into the group and acted out in the present. In Gestalt groups, leaders use specific techniques (such as making the rounds, fantasy approaches, rehearsal techniques, and dream work). Further information about Gestalt can be found in Perls (1969) and Perls, Hefferline, and Goodman (1951) and specific information about Gestalt groups in Feder and Ronall (1980). More general information about the stages of groups and the process of group therapy in the models described above can be found in Corey (1980), Gazda (1975, 1978), and Yalom (1975).

Although there is a significant overlapping in each of these approaches, with the approach presented in this chapter, there are significant differences. In behavior group therapy, clients work toward specific, concrete behavioral or cognitive change goals. In all of the above approaches, the goals are general and diffuse. In behavior group therapy, therapists draw upon as much contemporary empirical research as possible, to support their use of procedures. In all the other approaches, virtually no outcome research on procedures or programs exists (one notable exception is the work by Liberman et al., 1973).

As a part of its empirical focus, ongoing group data is utilized in this approach, to assess the state of group process in behavior group therapy. In all the other approaches, the therapist relies solely on his or her own insights.

Finally, in behavior group therapy, the meetings initially are highly focused and structured and move successively toward the assumption of leadership by the clients. In most of the other approaches, the structure is highly delimited in the beginning. Structure, if any, evolves from the group.

In this chapter, we have also omitted describing at least one other behavioral group-therapy model: the treatment of phobias through the use of group systematic desensitization (see Paul, 1966; Wolpe, 1973). This approach is quite similar in its focus on behavior change, in its reliance on empirically supported method, and in its continued monitoring and evaluation.

The model presented in this chapter, however, suggests an approach to the treatment of a wider range of behavioral and cognitive targets, utilizes a wider range of change procedures, and makes greater use of group process.

SUMMARY

In this chapter, we have presented a method of treatment in groups, which focuses on utilizing behavioral, cognitive, and group procedures, to facilitate the attainment of individual treatment goals. These goals basically involve cognitive and behavior change.

Basically, this is an empirical approach, which draws heavily on research and clinical experience for its support and the selection of treatment procedure; it makes use of continued assessment, monitoring, and evaluation, throughout the various group phases; and it makes extensive use of the group in helping individuals to achieve their specific treatment goals.

Use of the group involves modifying group cohesion, structuring the content, modifying distribution of participation, and group problem solving.

Generally, the specific techniques involved in social-skill training, cognitive restructuring, and systematic problem solving are integrated—with group procedures mentioned above—into a unified treatment technology.

REFERENCES

Argyle, M. *Social interaction.* Hawthorne, N.Y.: Aldine Publishing, 1969.

Barrios, B. A., & Shigetomi, C. C. Coping-skills training for the management of anxiety: A critical review. *Behavior Therapy,* 1979, 10, 491–522.

Bavelas, A., Hastorf, A. H., Gross, A. E., & Kite, W. R. Experiments on the alteration of group structure. *Journal of Experimental and Social Psychology,* 1965, *1,* 55–70.

Beck, A. T. *Cognitive therapy and the emotional disorders.* New York: International Universities Press, 1976.

Bellack, A. S., & Hersen, M. Chronic psychiatric patients and social-skills training. In M. Hersen & A. S. Bellack (Eds.), *Behavior therapy in the psychiatric setting.* Baltimore: Williams & Wilkins, 1978.

Berne, E. *Transactional analysis in psychotherapy.* New York: Grove Press, 1961.

Berne, E. *Games people play.* New York: Grove Press, 1964.

Berne, E. *Principles of group treatment.* New York: Oxford University Press, 1966.

Bion, W. R. *Experiences in groups and other papers.* London: Tavistock Publications, 1961.

Campbell, D. T., & Stanley, J. C. *Experimental and quasi-experimental designs for research.* Skokie, Ill.: Rand McNally, 1963.

Cartwright, D., & Zander, A. (Eds.). *Group dynamics: Research and theory.* New York: Harper & Row, 1968.

Combs, M. L., & Slaby, D. A. Social-skills training with children. In B. B. Lahley & A. E. Kazdin (Eds.), *Advances in clinical child psychology* (Vol. 1). New York: Plenum Press, 1977.

Corey, G. *Theory and practice of group counseling.* Monterey, Calif.: Brooks/Cole, Publishing, 1980.

DeLange, J. *Effectiveness of systematic desensitization and assertive training with women.* Doctoral dissertation, University of Wisconsin School of Social Work, Madison, 1976.

Durkin, H. E. *The group in depth.* New York: International Universities Press, 1964.

D'Zurilla, T. J., & Goldfried, M. R. Problem solving and behavior modification. *Journal of Abnormal Psychology,* 1971, *78,* 107–126.

Edelstein, B. A., & Eisler, R. M. Effects of modeling and modeling with instructions and feedback on the behavioral components of social skills. *Behavior Therapy,* 1976, *7,* 382–389.

Eisler, R. M., Frederiksen, L. W., & Peterson, G. L. The relationships of cognitive variables to the expression of assertiveness. *Behavior Therapy,* 1978, *9,* 419–427.

Eisler, R. M., Hersen, M., & Miller, P. M. Effects of modeling on components of assertive behavior. *Journal of Behavior Therapy and Experimental Psychiatry,* 1973, *4,* 1–6.

Elder, J. *Comparison of cognitive restructuring and response acquisition in the enhancement of social competence in college freshman.* Doctoral dissertation, West Virginia University, 1978.

Ellis, A. *Reason and emotion in Psychotherapy.* Secaucus, N.J.: Lyle Stuart, 1962.

Ellis, A. *Humanistic psychotherapy.* New York: McGraw-Hill, 1979.

Feder, B., & Ronall, R. (Eds.). *Beyond the hot seat: Gestalt approaches to group.* New York: Brunner & Mazel, 1980.

Flowers, J. V., & Booraem, C. D. Three studies toward a fuller understanding of behavioral group therapy: Cohesion, client flexibility, and outcome generalization. In D. Upper & S. M. Ross (Eds.), *Behavior group therapy.* Campaign, Ill.: Research Press, 1980.

Fremouw, W. J., & Harmatz, M. G. A helper model for behavioral treatment of speech anxiety. *Journal of Consulting and Clinical Psychology,* 1975, *43,* 652–660.

Fremouw, W. J., & Zitter, R. E. A comparison of skills training and cognitive restructuring—Relaxation for the treatment of speech anxiety. *Behavior Therapy,* 1978, *9,* 248–259.

Gazda, G. M. (Ed.). *Basic approaches to group psychotherapy and group counseling* (2d ed.). Springfield, Ill.: Charles C Thomas, 1975.

Gazda, G. M. *Group counseling: A developmental approach* (2d ed.). Boston: Allyn & Bacon, 1978.

Glass, C. R., Gottman, J. M., & Shmurak, S. H. Response acquisition and cognitive self-statement modification approaches to dating-skills training. *Journal of Counseling Psychology*, 1976, *23*, 520–525.

Glogower, F. D., Fremouw, W. J., & McCroskey, J. C. A component analysis of restructuring. *Cognitive Therapy and Research*, 1978, *2*, 209–223.

Goldfried, M. R., Linehan, M. M., & Smith, J. L. Reduction of test anxiety through cognitive restructuring. *Journal of Consulting and Clinical Psychology*, 1978, *46*, 32–39.

Goulding, M., & Goulding, R. *Changing lives through redecision therapy.* New York: Brunner & Mazel, 1979.

Harris, T. *I'm OK—you're OK.* New York: Avon Books, 1967.

Hedquist, F. J., & Weinhold, B. K. Behavioral group counseling with socially anxious and unassertive college students. *Counseling Psychologist*, 1970, *17*, 237–242.

Heppner, P. P. A review of the problem-solving literature and its relationship to the counseling process. *Journal of Counseling Psychology*, 1978, *25*, 366–375.

Hersen, M., & Barlow, D. H. *Single-case experimental designs.* Elmsford, N.Y.: Pergamon Press, 1976.

Hersen, M., Eisler, R. M., Miller, P. M., Johnson, M. B., & Pinkston, S. G. Effects of practice, instructions, and modeling on components of assertive behavior. *Behavior Research and Therapy*, 1973, *11*, 443–451.

Horan, J. J., Hackett, G., Buchanan, J. D., Stone, C. I., & Demchik-Stone, D. Coping with pain: A component analysis of stress inoculation. *Cognitive Therapy and Research*, 1977, *1*, 211–221.

Langer, E. J., Janis, I. L., & Wolfer, J. A. Reduction of psychological stress in surgical patients. *Journal of Experimental Social Psychology*, 1975, *11*, 155–165.

Lawrence, H., & Sundel, M. Behavior modification in adult groups. *Social Work*, 1972, *17*, 34–43.

Levine, V., & Zigler, E. The essential-reactive distinction in alcoholism: A developmental approach. *Journal of Abnormal Psychology*, 1973, *81*, 242–249.

Lewinsohn, P. M., Weinstein, M. S., & Alper, T. A. A behavioral approach to the group treatment of depressed persons: A methodological contribution. *Journal of Clinical Psychology*, 1970, *26*, 525–632.

Liberman, M. A., Yalom, I., & Miles, M. *Encounter groups: First facts.* New York: Basic Books, 1973.

Liberman, R. P. A behavioral approach to group dynamics. I: Reinforcement and prompting of cohesiveness in group therapy. *Behavior Therapy*, 1970, *1*, 141–175.

Libet, I., & Lewinsohn, P. M. The concept of social skill with special references to the behavior of depressed persons. *Journal of Consulting and Clinical Psychology*, 1973, *40*, 304–312.

Linehan, M. M., Goldfried, M. R., & Goldfried, A. P. Assertion therapy skill training or cognitive restructuring. *Behavior Therapy*, 1979, *10*, 372–388.

Locke, N. *Group psychoanalysis: Theory and technique.* New York: New York University Press, 1961.

Lott, A. J., & Lott, B. E. Group cohesiveness, communication level, and conformity. *Journal of Abnormal and Social Psychology*, 1961, *62*, 408–412.

MacDonald, M. L., Linquist, C. U., Kramer, J. A., McGrath, R. A., & Rhyne, L. L. Social-skills training: The effects of behavior rehearsal in groups on dating skills. *Journal of Counseling Psychology,* 1975, *22,* 224–230.

Mahoney, M. J., & Arknoff, D. Cognitive and self-control therapies. In S. L. Goldfield & A. E. Bergin (Eds.), *Handbook of Psychotherapy and behavior change.* New York: John Wiley & Sons, 1978.

McFall, R. M., & Twentyman, C. T. Four experiments on the relative contributions of rehearsal, modeling, and coaching to assertion training. *Journal of Abnormal Psychology,* 1973, *81,* 199–218.

Meichenbaum, D. Cognitive modification of test-anxious college students. *Journal of Consulting and Clinical Psychology,* 1972, *39,* 370–380.

Meichenbaum, D. *Cognitive behavior modification.* Morristown, N.J.: General Learning Press, 1974.

Meichenbaum, D. *Cognitive behavior modification.* New York: Plenum Press, 1977.

Meichenbaum, D., & Cameron, R. Training schizophrenics to talk to themselves: A means of developing attentional controls. *Behavior Therapy,* 1973, *4,* 515–534.

Mullan, H., & Rosenbaum, M. *Group psychotherapy: Theory and practice* (2d ed.). New York: Free Press, 1978.

Novaco, R. W. *Anger control: The development and evaluation of an experimental treatment.* Lexington, Mass.: D. C. Heath, 1975.

Novaco, R. W. Stress inoculation: A cognitive therapy for anger and its application to a case of depression. *Journal of Consulting and Clinical Psychology,* 1977, *45,* 600–608.

Paul, G. *Insight versus desensitization in psychotherapy.* Stanford: Stanford University Press, 1966.

Perls, F. *Gestalt therapy verbatim.* Moab, Ut.: Real People Press, 1969.

Perls, F. *The Gestalt approach and eyewitness to therapy.* New York: Bantam, 1973.

Perls, F. Hefferline, R., & Goodman, P. *Gestalt therapy: Excitement and growth in the human personality.* New York: Dell Publishing, 1951.

Phillips, L., & Zigler, E. Social competence: The action-thought parameter and vicariousness in normal and pathological behaviors. *Journal of Abnormal and Social Psychology,* 1961, *63,* 137–146.

Phillips, L., & Zigler, E. Role orientation the action-thought dimension and outcome in psychiatric dimensions. *Journal of Abnormal and Social Psychology,* 1964, *68,* 381–389.

Platt, J., Scura, W. C., & Hannon, J. R. Problem-solving thinking of youthful incarcerated heroin addicts. *Journal of Community Psychology,* 1973, *1,* 278–281.

Platt, J., & Spivack, G. Problem-solving thinking of psychiatric patients. *Journal of Consulting and Clinical Psychology,* 1972, *39,* 148–151. (a)

Platt, J., & Spivack, G. Social competence and effective problem-solving thinking in psychiatric patients. *Journal of Clinical Psychology,* 1972, *28,* 3–5. (b)

Rimm, D., Hill, G. A., Brown, N. N., & Stuart, J. E. Group assertive training in treatment of expression of inappropriate anger. *Psychological Reports,* 1974, *34,* 791–798.

Rimm, D. C., Snyder, J. J., Depue, R. A., Haanstad, M. J., & Armstrong, D. P. Assertive training versus rehearsal and the importance of making assertive response. *Behavior Research and Therapy,* 1976, *14,* 315–321.

Rogers, C. *On becoming a person.* Boston: Houghton Mifflin, 1961.

Rogers, C. *Carl Rogers on encounter groups.* New York: Harper & Row, 1970.

Rogers, C. *Carl Rogers on personal power: Inner strength and its revolutionary impact.* New York: Delacorte Press, 1977.

Rose, S. D. Assertive training in groups: Research in clinical settings. *Scandinavian Journal of Behavior Therapy,* 1977, *6,* 61–86. (a)

Rose, S. D. *Group therapy: A behavioral approach.* Englewood Cliffs, N.J.: Prentice-Hall, 1977. (b)

Rose, S. D. Group therapy: *A behavior cognitive problem-solving approach exercise manual.* Madison: University of Wisconsin, 1980.

Rose, S. D. Assessment in groups. *Social Work Research and Abstracts,* 1981, *17,* 29–37.

Rosenthal, T., & Bandura, A. Psychological modeling: Theory and practice. In S. L. Garfield & A. E. Bergin (Eds.), *Handbook of psychotherapy and behavior change* (2d ed.). New York: John Wiley & Sons, 1978.

Safran, J. D., Alden, L. E., & Davidson, P. O. Client anxiety level as a moderator variable in assertion training. *Cognitive Therapy and Research,* 1980, *4,* 189–200.

Schinke, S. P., & Rose, S. D. Interpersonal-skill training in groups. *Journal of Counseling Psychology,* 1977, *23,* 442–448.

Schwartz, R. M., & Gottman, J. M. Towards a task analysis of assertive behavior. *Journal of Consulting and Clinical Psychology,* 1976, *44,* 910–920.

Shoemaker, M. E. Developing assertiveness: Training or therapy? In R. E. Albenti (Ed.), *Assertiveness innovation, applications, issues.* San Luis Obispo, Calif.: Impact Publishers, 1977.

Shure, M. B., & Spivack, G. Means-ends thinking, adjustment, and social class among elementary school-aged children. *Journal of Consulting and Clinical Psychology,* 1972, *38,* 348–353.

Sidman, M. *Tactics of scientific research.* New York: Basic Books, 1960.

Slavson, S. R. Parallelisms in the development of group psychotherapy. *International Journal of Group Psychotherapy,* 1959, *9,* 44–51.

Spivack, G., & Levine, M. *Self-regulation in acting-out and normal adolescents* (Report No. M–4531). Washington D.C.: National Institute of Health, 1963.

Steiner, C. *Scripts people live: Transactional analysis of life scripts.* New York: Grove Press, 1974.

Taylor, F. G., & Marshall, W. L. Experimental analysis of a cognitive behavioral therapy for depression. *Cognitive Therapy and Research,* 1977, *1,* 59–72.

Thorpe, G. L. Desensitization, behavior rehearsal, self-instructional training, and placebo effects on assertive refusal behavior. *European Journal of Behavioural Analysis and Modification,* 1975, *1,* 30–44.

Thorpe, G. L., Amatu, H. I., Blakey, R. S., & Burns, L. E. Contributions of overt instructional rehearsal and "specific insight" to the effectiveness of self-instructional training: A preliminary study. *Behavior Therapy,* 1976, *7,* 504–511.

Toseland, R., & Rose, S. D. Evaluating social-skill training for older adults in groups, *Social Work Research and Abstracts,* 1978, *14,* 28–33.

Turk, D. *Cognitive control of pain: A skills-training approach for the treatment of pain.* Unpublished master's thesis, University of Waterloo, 1975.

Weinman, B., Gelbart, P., Wallace, M., & Post, M. Inducing assertive behavior in chronic schizophrenics: A comparison of socioenvironmental, desensitization, and relaxation therapies. *Journal of Consulting and Clinical Psychology,* 1972, *39,* 246–252.

Whitaker, D. S., & Lieberman, M. A. *Psychotherapy through the group process.* New York: Atherton Press, 1965.

Wolf, A., & Schwartz, E. K. *Psychoanalysis in groups.* New York: Grune & Stratton, 1962.

Wolfe, J. L., & Fodor, I. G. Modifying assertive behavior in women: A comparison of three approaches. *Behavior Therapy,* 1977, *8,* 567–574.

Wolpe, J. *The practice of behavior therapy.* Elmsford, N.Y.: Pergamon Press, 1973.

Yalom, I. *The theory and practice of group psychotherapy* (2d ed.). New York: Basic Books, 1975.

Zigler, E., & Phillips, L. Social effectiveness and symptomatic behaviors. *Journal of Abnormal and Social Psychology,* 1960, *61,* 231–238.

Zigler, E., & Phillips, L. Social competence and the process-reactive distinction in psychopathology. *Journal of Abnormal and Social Psychology,* 1962, *65,* 215–222.

30

Hypnotherapy*

John G. Watkins†
and
Helen H. Watkins†

Hypnosis is one of the most fascinating and puzzling psychological phenomena. The unusual ways in which astounding changes can be made in human perception, memory, motivation, and behavior through this modality have intrigued researchers, therapists, entertainers, and the general public for several centuries. Accordingly, it is not surprising that many attempts have been made to incorporate it into the procedures of psychotherapy, since such modifications are the goals of psychological treatment.

Hypnotherapy, however, does not mean treatment by hypnosis but rather, within hypnosis. Hypnosis is a condition, generally considered an altered state of consciousness, during which the desired changes may be induced. It is a medium within which may be practiced many widely varied approaches to treatment: psychoanalytic, humanistic, cognitive, and behavioral. Techniques from all of these areas have been incorporated into the practice of clinical hypnosis. Since hypnotherapy may include such diverse tactics as reinforcement, analysis of the transference, suggestion, dream and fantasy analysis, ventilation, abreaction, desensitization, modeling, and cognitive restructuring, it must be considered an eclectic therapy. The characteristic which distinguishes it from all of these other fields is the use of induction techniques to place the individual in an altered state, wherein these procedures may be more effective. In addition, the condition of hypnosis makes possible certain manipulations which are unique to hypnotherapy simply because it does not seem possible to accomplish them in the conscious condition.

---

* The authors of this paper have currently in press a two-volume "teaching" textbook in the field of hypnotherapy: *Clinical Hypnosis: Vol. I. Hypnotherapeutic technique; Vol. II. Hypnoanalytic technique* (New York: Irvington Press).

† University of Montana.

HISTORY OF HYPNOSIS

In the late 1700s, Franz Anton Mesmer, a Viennese physician, was introduced to the principle of the magnet by Maxmillian Hell, the royal astronomer in Vienna. If a piece of magnetized metal was held in front of the eyes of a subject, the individual became transfixed and went into a state of trance, wherein suggestions of health and well-being could eliminate symptoms of illness. Mesmer soon found that he could accomplish the same result by holding his hand before the subjects. He reasoned that a magnetic fluid emanated from living tissue, which he termed, *animal magnetism* (Mesmer, 1981).

He created quite a sensation in Paris with his clinic, which contained a baquet (or wooden tub) filled with broken glass and minerals and which was believed to transmit magnetism from its protruding rods. The sick flocked to him, and there were many reports of cures. A royal commission, appointed by King Louis XVI and headed by Benjamin Franklin, investigated his practice. It concluded that animal magnetism was only a product of imagination. Discredited, Mesmer left France and never returned. However, while the commission debunked the theory of animal magnetism, it did not account for the well-verified examples of successful treatment. Thus ended the first cycle of "boom and bust" (overenthusiasm and disillusionment), which has so characterized the history of hypnosis.

Although there was continued interest among Mesmer's followers, the number of mesmerists (or magnetists) declined during the next half century. In 1845, in Calcutta, a skilled surgeon, James Esdaile, began using hypnosis as his anesthesia. During a period of seven years, he performed over two thousand "painless" operations, including some 300 major surgeries, such as amputations, removal of scrotal tumors, etc. He also noted that surgical shock was rare in hypnotized patients (Esdaile, 1957).

In England, Elliotson (1843) and Braid (1899) promoted the practice of hypnotism. Elliotson, a distinguished physician, was president of the Royal Medical and Chirurigical Society (a position comparable to that of president of the American Medical Association). Yet, he was bitterly attacked by both the medical profession and the clergy. Here again, we find history repeating itself: the pattern being the "discovery" of hypnotic phenomena by a prominent physician or scientist, attacks on him by the medical establishment, and great efforts on his part to reestablish his scientific respectability. Braid coined the term *hypnosis* after the Greek word for sleep and was the first to recognize its psychological, rather than magnetic, nature. He probably should be credited as the true father of psychosomatic medicine.

In the United States at this time, Phineas Quimby, a lay hypnotist, practiced hypnosis; but he is more known for his student, Mary Baker Eddy, who founded a religious-psychological form of treatment, Christian Science. She denied that her teachings had anything to do with hypnosis.

In 1864, Liebeault (1866), a poor man's doctor, settled in Nancy, France. He treated the peasants' illnesses by suggestive hypnosis and wrote a book which—at that time—is reported to have sold only six copies. A distinguished neurologist, Bernheim (1964), professor in the University of Nancy Medical School, visited Liebeault's clinic, with the intention of exposing him as a charlatan. Bernheim became so intrigued with Liebeault's work that he formed a team with him and continued many experiments in hypnosis. These two and their associates came to be known as the Nancy school of hypnosis.

Another distinguished neurologist in Paris, Charcot (1890), tried to reestablish the magnetic theory; but in a contest of experiments with the Nancy school, the psychological theories of hypnosis as a form of suggestion prevailed. Charcot was the instructor of Janet (1925), who subsequently used hypnosis to investigate many cases of amnesia and multiple personality.

Freud visited Bernheim and became interested in hypnosis as a possible way of treating hysterias. From Breuer, another prominent Viennese physician, Freud learned about the technique of abreaction, wherein a patient is induced to reexperience early traumas. These two discovered that early sexual seductions seemed to be at the origin of hysterical symptoms, and these symptoms could be relieved after an emotional reliving of the trauma. It was through hypnosis that Freud discovered unconscious processes. However, he found the intensity of the hypnotic relationship too uncomfortable and abandoned it (Kline, 1958). Freud claimed that the results of hypnotic therapy were only temporary and that the presumed childhood seductions were not real but fantasies—a position which has been maintained by many of his followers in psychoanalysis ever since. In view of the present-day research and the great complexity of proven hypnoanalytic procedures, it would seem that Freud's rejection of hypnosis was premature and deprived the discipline of psychoanalysis of a very valuable tool for probing and treating unconscious processes. Freud felt more comfortable with the procedure of free association which, combined with his later discoveries of dream analysis and transference reactions, came to constitute the primary psychoanalytic techniques. Freud's argument that "hypnosis bypassed the ego" and, hence, could achieve only temporary results has not been borne out by modern practice and research.

During World War I, Hadfield in England and Simmel in Germany used hypnoanalytic procedures to treat war neuroses. Simmel had his German soldiers, under hypnosis, abreactively destroy dummies dressed in French combat uniforms. In World War II, Watkins (1949), at the Welch Convalescent Hospital in Florida, treated a wide variety of conditions by hypnosis, with procedures ranging from simple suggestion to complex hypnoanalytic techniques.

During the 1930s, Hull (1933), a prominent American psychologist, published the first book on experimental hypnosis; and Erickson began a series of papers describing ingenious and novel techniques of using hypnotic suggestion. Erickson later became the first president of the American Society of Clinical Hypnosis and editor of the *American Journal of Clinical Hypnosis*. His unique methods have been widely studied as a model of therapeutic communication (1952, 1964, 1967; see also Bandler & Grinder, 1975).

In 1949, the Society for Clinical and Experimental Hypnosis was formed. It consisted of psychiatrists and psychologists who had made substantial contributions to the literature. At about the same time, Heron in Minneapolis and Burgess at Concordia College trained many dentists in the techniques of hypnosis, for purposes of relaxation and anesthesia.

Because of a controversy as to whether the practice of hypnosis should be reserved only for highly qualified mental health specialists or broadened to include physicians who had received three-day seminars, the American Society of Clinical Hypnosis (ASCH) was formed by splitting off from the Society for Clinical and Experimental Hypnosis (SCEH). Much interprofessional strife resulted between the two competing organizations. SCEH established specialty boards designed to certify high-level practitioners: the American Board of Medical Hypnosis, the American Board of Hypnosis in Dentistry, and the American Board of Examiners in Psychological Hypnosis. The psychological board achieved official recognition from the American Psychological Association. In 1967, with a mandate from the Society for Clinical and Experimental Hypnosis, Raginsky and J. G. Watkins founded the International Society of Clinical and Experimental Hypnosis, with Raginsky serving as its first president and Watkins (who was chair of its Organizing Committee) as its first executive secretary. The goal was to bring researchers and practitioners throughout the world into one organization. Gradually, the intersociety strife declined, and in 1972, the international society was reorganized under the name of the International Society of Hypnosis, with Ernest Hilgard of Stanford University as its president.

Since 1960, there has been a flourishing of hypnosis research in many universities, and the modality has become respectable as a form of clinical practice and scientific experimentation. At the time of this writing (1981), the greatest danger seems to be a return of boom conditions, wherein everyone, from the police force to the lay person, wants to practice hypnosis.

THEORIES OF HYPNOSIS

Many different theories have been proposed to explain hypnotic phenomena, no one of which is fully adequate. It has been described as a form of sleep (Bernheim, 1964; Hull, 1933). However, electroencephalograph patterns more nearly resemble those of waking or relaxing subjects than sleeping ones. Attempts have been made to explain hypnosis on a physiological basis. Pavlov (1923) described it as a form of partial cortical inhibition, and Schneck (1953) considered it as a primitive psychophysiological state. Crasilneck and Hall (1975) held that it was a neurological response involving the hippocampus.

Perhaps the most prominent and continuing theory is the view that it is an altered state of consciousness (Braid, 1899; Liebeault, 1866; Bernheim, 1964; Weitzenhoffer, 1953). In this respect, the altered state (or trance) theory is related to the view that it is a form of dissociation, as proposed by Janet (1925), and the neodissociation theory of Hilgard (1977).

From a behavioral point of view, it has sometimes been described in ideomotor terms—one behaves in line with one's conceptions, such as moving the finger in trying to describe a spiral staircase. Barber (1969) denies that a trance or altered state of consciousness is essential to explain it but insists that hypnosis is simply a form of task motivation. Both White (1941) and Sarbin and Coe (1972) believe that it is a kind of goal-directed role-playing. Indeed, there is much about hypnosis that seems to be role-playing. However, much more than role-playing must be involved when a hypnotized patient will endure an amputation without pain.

The factor of regression seems to be prominent in hypnotic behavior. Gill and Brenman (1959), who are psychoanalysts, describe hypnosis as a form of regression in the service of the ego—just as sleep is. Meares (1961) regards hypnosis as a kind of atavistic regression, wherein the individual reverts to primitive thinking and behavior, such as characterized with the prehistoric development of the human species.

Hypnosis has also been described as an unconscious process, as a loss of ego boundaries (Kubie & Margolin, 1944), as a form of contemplative meditation (Naruse, 1962), and as a modality for the manipulation of ego or object cathexes (J. G. Watkins, 1978).

A number of attempts have been made to relate it to the phenomena of transference, as observed in psychoanalytic therapy (Ferenczi, 1926; Watkins 1963b) or even to view it as a state-relationship hence, as an altered state of consciousness which occurs in an intensive interpersonal relationship (Kline, 1955; J. G. Watkins, 1978). However, this view does not explain such conditions as highway hypnosis (where an individual driving at night on a long, straight stretch of road enters a trance by staring at the dividing line). Researchers generally prefer to retain the trance concept without the relationship aspect, since the person of the hypnotist can constitute a confounding variable.

In general, we may summarize by saying that the present theories of hypnosis are more descriptive than explanatory. Each emphasizes some aspect, while ignoring or slighting some other facet of hypnotic behavior.

It may be that only some multifactor theory (role-playing, trance, and archaic involvement, hence regression) will do adequate justice to the complex set of phenomena known as hypnosis (Shor, 1962).

HYPNOTIC PHENOMENA

The most noticeable aspect of hypnotic behavior is the increased suggestibility demonstrated by subjects and patients. Kline (1958) has pointed out the loss of criticality, which characterizes the hypnotic condition. Hypnotized subjects will carry out actions which would seem ludicrous to them in the conscious state. In so doing, they are often amnesic or unaware that the suggestions had been planted in them by the hypnotist, and they will rationalize their behavior (for example, climbing on a chair and looking out of a window, because "I heard someone outside trying to get into the house").

Visual, auditory, olfactory, tactual, and kinesthetic hallucinations can be induced as in seeing a nonexistent person or failing to perceive one standing in front of the subject. Alterations in attitude can be suggested. Behaviors can be carried out during the hypnotic state and also following return to full awareness (post-hypnotic suggestions). These latter are the most valuable therapeutically.

Suggestions may last from a few seconds up to many years, there being great individual variability, depending on the hypnotizability of the subject and the skill of the hypnotist. Dreams and fantasies can be suggested which are aimed at eliciting unconscious attitudes toward the therapy, the therapist, the present status of a treatment, and its prognosis.

Orne (see Fromm & Shor, 1979, pp. 518–565) has proposed that the condition of hypnosis is characterized by trance logic, and an individual who is only simulating hypnosis can be distinguished from a truly hypnotized one by the presence of this factor. Trance logic represents the tendency of a hypnotized subject to freely mix his perceptions derived from reality with those from his imagination. The double hallucination test has been reported as being able to distinguish between a truly hypnotized individual and a simulator. Following induction of hypnosis, the subject is told that he will see a certain person known to him sitting in an empty chair in front of him. When the subject reports seeing the individual, his attention is then directed to the real person, who has been placed behind him. Orne (1959) reported that the truly hypnotized individuals were able to see both the real person and the hallucinated image of him but did not become seriously disturbed by this inconsistency. However, other investigators (Johnson, Maher & Barber, 1972; McDonald & Smith, 1975; Blum & Graef, 1971) were unable to fully verify Orne's findings.

Another test of the reality of hypnosis said to be based on trance logic is the circle-touch test. A one-to two-inch circle is drawn on the subject's hand or arm, and he is told, under hypnosis, that this area will be completely anesthetized. He is then instructed to say yes when he is touched outside the circle and no when touched inside the circle. According to trance-logic theory, the truly hypnotized person will say no when touched inside the circle, while the simulator, recognizing the incongruity of the instruction, will refuse to respond when so touched.

Apparently, the only study to date which has attempted to validate this test is one by Eiblmayr (1981). She found that simulators and reals gave the no response with about equal frequency when touched inside the circle. However, a yes response, when touched within the circle, did differentiate moderately hypnotizable subjects (but not the highly hypnotizable ones) from simulators. The subjects who so responded indicated later that they had experienced the touch as being just outside the peripheral boundary. Hence, they reported the fact of being touched but displaced the site of the touch to outside the circle. Eiblmayr did not find that trance logic was a significant factor in the process.

From the hynoanalytic viewpoint, the ability of hypnotized subjects to mainfest hypermnesia (or superior memory) is extremely valuable. A common demonstration is to have a hypnotized subject name everybody in the first-grade class and where they sat or to recite memorized passages which have been forgotten for years. Recently, this ability has been enlisted in the interrogation of witnesses to crimes. Some subjects can be regressed to earlier periods in their life, where they apparently act out behaviors appropriate to that time (for example, reading, writing, or speaking like a six-year-old). Whether regression is true, real, and accurate has been the subject of many experimental investigations. Its status is controversial.

HYPNOTIC SUSCEPTIBILITY

The ability to be hypnotized has been the subject of much research (Hilgard, 1965). Since not all people can respond hynotically, the number of patients that can be treated with hynotherapy is restricted. Perhaps some 20 percent can enter a deep (or somnambulistic) trance—characterized by the ability to carry out bizarre suggestions under hypnosis—to walk about and talk while in that state, and, upon emerging, to be amnesic to what they said and did. Half of all subjects are able to achieve some level of trance, light or intermediate, while a quarter or more appear to be resistant to hypnotic induction. Hilgard (1965) originally viewed hypnotizability as a relatively fixed trait; some people had it and some not. As such, it was not amenable to much change. However, other practitioners believe that the personality of the hypnotist, the psychodynamics of the interaction between hypnotist and subject, and the unconscious needs of the subject are significant factors in determining whether or not the subject is hypnotized and to what degree Watkins (1963a).

A number of susceptibility tests have been devised. In one, the subject is asked to extend both arms and imagine that weights are being placed in one of them. The sinking of that hand in relation to the other would indicate susceptibility to the suggestion. In another test, the subject is told to place the hands a foot apart, with the palms facing each other, and to imagine that a strong, magnetic force is drawing the hands together.

A number of objective scales have been standardized to test hypnotic susceptibility. The original and best known (Weitzenhoffer & Hilgard, 1959) is the Stanford Hypnotic Susceptibility Scale. This measures, on a scale of 0 to 12, the degree to which subjects respond to a standardized set of suggestions, which present 12 suggested tasks (ranging from arm rigidity to perception of a hallucinated fly). Many researchers utilize this test, and it occupies a position in hypnosis experimentation like the Stanford-Binet Test did in studies of mental ability. A group form of this test is the Harvard Group Test of Hypnotic Susceptibility (Shor & Orne, 1962). The tasks are similar, but the subjects themselves report their positive or negative reactions to the suggestions.

Designed to measure different aspects or levels of hypnosis, newer forms of the Stanford scales have been published (Weitzenhoffer & Hilgard, 1967). A Children's Hypnotic Susceptibility Test has been published by London (1962). Spiegel (1972) has proposed a susceptibility test, based on the hypothesis that the highly hypnotized individual can roll his eyes back into the forehead so that only the white shows. However, this test has not received significant validation from others.

TECHNIQUES OF HYPNOTIC INDUCTION

The most widely used technique is probably some form of eye fixation. Discovered by Braid, it consists of having subjects focus their eyes on an object, either close or at a distance. The hypnotist then repetitively gives suggestions, like: "As you are staring at this pencil, your eyes are getting very tired; they are becoming heavy and want to pull down. They are coming down, down, down. They are almost closing, closing, closing." Suggestions are precisely timed to the reactions of the subject. Initial verbalization describes how the subject's eyes are getting tired. If they blink, the hypnotist immediately calls attention to this fact. The suggestions are always kept close to the reality of the subject's behavior. They follow behavior at first and lead it later. The hypnotist's voice is characterized by repetition, monotony, and firmness. The general principle is that attention is focused first on some small aspect of the subject's functioning. Gradually, this is expanded to include more and more of the behavioral, perceptual, and cognitive processes, until he/she is totally involved in the hypnotic situation. The words of the hypnotist have become the experienced reality of the subject.

Another technique widely used is that of hand levitation. The subject is told to focus attention on his hand, which is on the desk in front of him. Suggestions are given, such as: "Notice each of your fingers. Feel the pressure of the hand on the desk. You will become aware of every tiny sensation in your hand—and if you concentrate well enough, you will notice that one finger begins to feel different from the others. It may tingle or feel numb. It may feel cool or slightly warm. I wonder which finger it is that feels different from the others. It may be the index finger. Perhaps the ring finger. It could be the little finger, the middle finger, or maybe the thumb. But when you have discovered which finger it is, that finger will lift itself. It seems to be the index finger. It is now getting stiff and numb, as it lifts itself off the desk. And now the stiff numbness is spreading to the other fingers. Now the whole hand. The hand is becoming lighter and lighter, as if it wants to float up into the air. It is floating toward the face, and you realize that the closer it gets to the face, the deeper you are relaxing. When it touches the face, you will go into a very deep, deep relaxation. Touching, touching, touching."

Here, the suggestions start out with attention to minor sensations in the hand, then in one finger spreading to the others, then to the arm, as more and more of the person of the subject becomes hypnotically involved. This technique requires very careful timing.

In another approach (arm drop), the arm is held out, with the hand level with the top of the head. The subject is told to stare at one of the fingers, either with eyes open or closed. Suggestions, like the following, may then be given: "The more you concentrate on your finger, the heavier the hand will become. And as the hand and arm become heavier, the hand begins to move down. And as it moves down, you begin to move down with it into a state of relaxation, but you will not enter a deep state until the hand is all the way down." In this approach, the natural tendency for the arm to become tired and to lower is enlisted into the patter of suggestions. One suggestion is tied to another ("As your hand moves down, you will go down with it into a state of relaxation," etc.). A play is made on the word *down,* so that it means simultaneously a sinking of the arm and a sinking of the subject into a hypnotic state. Again, timing is important, in that the hypnotist's suggestions are kept close to the reality of the subject's behavior.

Although there are many techniques and many variations of each, two general attitudes seem to characterize hypnotic inductions. These have been described by Ferenczi (1926) as "father hypnosis" and "mother hypnosis." In the first, the hypnotist uses a forceful and commanding voice. Ferenczi likened this to the German father of his time, who secured obedience in the family by authority and domination. This manner of approach is frequently employed by stage hypnotists; but it is also used by some clinical hypnotherapists, especially when dealing with acute and severe pain problems.

Mother hypnosis is characterized by the gentle, persuading voice, which Ferenczi compared to the German housewife and mother of his day. She controlled by softness. For example, the crying child is soothed, by the gentle suggestions of the mother, that the injured hand "will not hurt anymore." Most clinical hypnosis, especially of the hypnoanalytic type, involves this gentler approach. At times, the subject's efforts are enlisted nondirectly, in the form of self-suggestion. ("When you wake up, you will be able to remember that part of these frightening things which you are ready to remember.") Such a suggestion might follow the discovery and reliving of an early, traumatic experience.

A dissociative (or subject-object) technique is a sophisticated approach to hypnotic induction, in which the subject is told to imagine, in his mind's eye, an individual sitting in a chair beside him who is wearing his clothes (described) and who has the face which he sees when he looks into a mirror. The hypnotist then proceeds to hypnotize the imaginary figure, while the subject watches "that person over there who looks like you" getting sleepier and sleepier. "That person" closes their eyes and relaxes in the chair. Or, "that person's" hand is rising into the air, as he/she goes deeper and deeper. As the subject views "that person" in his mind's eye, he becomes increasingly involved in the hypnotic modality. The hypnosis is indirect, since the subject is only watching "that person," who looks like himself, "over there" become hypnotized. Toward the end of the induction, the subject may be told: "That person over there is now deeply hypnotized. You see how comfortable and relaxed he/she is, and you, too, would like to enjoy such a deep state. So you get up (in the mind's eye), walk over to that chair, turn around, and sit down in it. Now your head coincides with that person's head, your arms with their arms, your body with their body. And, as you take on that person's body, you also take on his/her deep feelings of hypnotic relaxation."

In this induction, subject and object are manipulated. An image of the patient is hypnotized. When the patient rejoins the image, the patient, too, enters a state of hypnosis.

The foregoing are only representative of the many techniques for hypnotizing. It is not our province here to try to teach hypnotic induction. These can be learned from standard texts (see Cheek & LeCron, 1968; Crasilneck & Hall, 1975; Kroger, 1977; Meares, 1961; Weitzenhoffer, 1957). Because of the complexities and intricacies of hypnosis, it is better to seek courses and workshops given by the American Society of Clinical Hypnosis and the Society for Clinical and Experimental Hypnosis. Workshops are also sometimes given by Division 30 (Hypnosis) of the American Psychological Association. In addition, a number of medical schools and graduate schools of psychology offer responsible training in hypnosis.

The major hypnosis societies have taken the position that hypnotherapy should be taught only to physicians, psychologists (doctoral level), or clinical social workers. There is today much controversy as to who legitimately and ethically should practice hypnosis. However, with some exceptions, there is general agreement that only research scientists and qualified mental health professionals should be engaged in the independent practice of hypnotherapy.

Deepening procedures

Hypnosis is not an either-or. It is a matter of degree. Subjects can be more or less involved in the hypnotic modality, hence, in a lighter or deeper trance. A great deal of hypnotherapy (both suggestive therapy and analytic therapy) can be accomplished in light states. However, most practitioners would agree that, the deeper the degree of hypnotic involvement, the more likely that a hypnotic suggestion will be incorporated into a significant level of personality functioning, and the more likely that it will be carried out. Accordingly, after the practitioner has achieved a certain amount of hypnotic response, (such as is manifested by deep relaxation and eye closure), it may be desirable to employ certain deepening techniques to involve the subject even more in the modality. Hypnotic involvement is probably on a continuum. That is, suggestibility tests merge imperceptibly into induction techniques and these, in turn, into deepening procedures. The same principles apply at all levels. Unless the subject has responded by going rapidly into a very deep trance, the hypnotist will usually employ a set of suggestions designed to deepen the trance state.

For example, the subject may be asked to imagine walking down stairs with thick carpets, while the hypnotist counts steps. The subject may also be involved in fantasies, such as: "Imagine you are lying on a green, grassy slope in the hills, miles away from where anybody could disturb you. It is a warm day, and the sun is shining down. The sky is a deep, rich blue color, and a few fluffy clouds are floating overhead. It seems as if the whole world is saying to you, 'deeper, deeper, deeper.' "

Since induction and deepening techniques are only variations of the same process, the subject who has attained relaxation by the eye-fixation method might be administered the hand-levitation procedure to deepen the involvement. Listening to fantasied music, looking at imagined beautiful scenes—or even listening to an actual metronome—may be employed to deepen the trance state, preparatory to the giving of therapueutic suggestions.

HYPNO-SUGGESTIVE THERAPY

The earliest uses of hypnosis were in symptom control: removing pain, getting the anorexic patient to eat, improving the patient's attitude toward the hospital, helping to concentrate in studies, stopping smoking, controlling weight, and reducing anxiety. The same principles for implanting suggestions used during hypnotic induction apply in the implementation of therapeutic suggestions. They should be tied together. They should not directly contradict the patient's belief system or motivational structure. Preferably, they should be given when the hypnotic state has been deepened as much as possible. When the symptoms are neurotic and maintained by strong primary or secondary gains, the suggestions should not attack the entire neurotic structure at once. Rather, the changes should be wrought in bits and pieces. For example, the therapist may, during the first session, suggest to a hypnotized hysteric only that he/she will be able to sleep well tonight, rather than attempt to remove a hand paralysis at once. The building of confidence, hope, and good relationship through resonance with the needs of the patient may pay off better than dramatic attempts to reverse symptoms immediately through suggestion. However, sometimes a patient's needs for relief from pain may impel the hypnotherapist to proceed more directly.

Hypnosis in surgery, anesthesiology, and the control of pain

Pain is a universal experience, one that people seek to avoid. Since hypnosis can alter perception, it may be very useful, at times, in modifying and even eliminating the experience of pain. Two specific components of pain have been identified: *sensory pain* and *suffering.* Sensory pain warns the individual that something is wrong and often indicates the site of the disturbance. It can be essential for the person's survival. However, the suffering component is the aspect whose elimination or diminution is most welcome, and it is in this area that hypnosis is often of assistance. Both chemoanalgesia and hypnoanalgesia can knock out the suffering component of pain. In one case, the administration of morphine gave the patient relief for some three hours; suggestions of pain relief under hypnosis also relieved the patient for the same length of time.

Hilgard & Hilgard (1975) have made the most complete study, to date, of the effect of hypnotic suggestion on pain. They discovered that, even when the pain is eliminated overtly, it can still be experienced covertly by an underlying, cognitive structural system, which they called "the hidden observer." The pain is dissociated by hypnotic suggestion, but other aspects of the personality can apparently be aware of it. The Hilgards suggested analgesia in the hand of a hypnotized subject. When the anesthetized hand was placed in circulating ice water, the subject was able to hold it there for a longer period of time without evincing great discomfort and often reported that he did not feel pain, or a least that it was much lesser in intensity. However, when the hidden observer was contacted under hypnosis, it reported that the pain was still being experienced at covert levels. Hilgard concluded that some hypnotized individuals were capable of parallel processing of an experience simultaneously at overt and covert (unconscious) levels. Only some 40 percent of highly hypnotizable individuals manifested the hidden-observer phenomenon. Watkins and Watkins (1979-1980) replicated some of the Hilgard's approach to the hidden-observer phenomena and reported that the pain was being experienced by "ego states"—partial syndromes of personality, which had been previously identified in hypnoanalytic therapy, and which act like "covert multiple personalities." The area is under continuous investigation.

Hypnoanalgesia has been successfully used with such conditions as cancer, phantom limb, tic doloreux, migraine, and intractable pain. It is usually treated either by dissociating the individual from his body ("You are now sitting in that chair over there, watching that woman who looks like you having a baby on the delivery table") or by suggestions of warmness and numbness, thus letting some other sensation replace the feeling of pain. A numbness (which is suggested by imagining the hand thrust in ice water or by stroking a finger) can be transmitted to another part of the body—such as creating a numb area on the arm for a frightened child who is anticipating an injection. By anesthetizing the surface of a hand, the numbness can be transmitted through a bandage onto a burned area, thus permitting the removal of the bandage without pain.

While few operations today are conducted with only hypnoanesthesia (as did Esdaile), many surgeons and anesthesiologists are finding that, by combining hypnoanesthesia with chemoanesthesia, a smaller amount of the chemical becomes necessary. This promotes quicker post-surgical recovery and, in some cases, may make the difference as to whether surgery is possible.

Marmer (1959) suggests four major indications for the use of hypnosis in anesthesiology: to overcome anxiety and fear; to provide a more pleasant reaction from anesthesia and aid in post-operative recovery; to raise the pain threshold; and to induce anesthesia and analgesia, so as to reduce the needed amount of chemoanesthesia. The use of hypnosis to reduce pre-operative stress is alone of great value in many operations.

Some obstetricians have found it of value to teach their pregnant patients to prepare for labor and delivery by developing self-hypnosis. They learn, under a trance state, to render their hand numb by stroking. When the labor pains come, they can place the hand on their abdomen and remove the suffering, while continuing to be aware of the fact of the contraction. Through such techniques, a complete delivery may sometimes be accomplished, with a need only for local analgesia at the time of the episiotomy (see Kroger, 1977, pp. 227-241; Cheek & LeCron, 1968, pp. 123-136).

Hypnosis in internal medicine and general practice

There are many uses for hypnosis in the practice of general medicine. Doctors, who have been trained in hypnotic techniques, or psychologists may be called upon by physicians to aid in the treatment programs of their patients.

Some patients are very resistant to the insertion of diagnostic instruments in the orfices of the body, such as the bronchoscope, gastroscope, proctoscope, etc. With one patient, who gagged so much that the gastroscope could not be used, hypnosis was employed. Under a trance state, the glottis was relaxed, the gastroscope inserted, and a tentative diagnosis of duodenal ulcer was verified. Efforts to reduce blood pressure through hypnotic suggestions have not been too successful. However, hypnotic suggestions of warmth paired with relaxation have been reported of value in improving compromised coronary circulation in cases of angina pectoris. The elevation of skin temperature by suggesting that one's hands are in warm water has been found helpful in cases of Buerger's and Raynaud's diseases.

Weight control is especially useful for the obese patient who is a cardiovascular case. Suggestions are sometimes given that the patient will really enjoy eating, but that after the first few bites, he/she will feel very full ("like after a Thanksgiving Day dinner") and will not wish to eat further. The desire for quantity of food is replaced with emphasis on the quality of eating. Under hypnosis, patients may be asked to fantasize tables filled with rich and fattening foods. These are then associated with feelings of distaste. On the other hand, through hypnotic visualization, tables filled with salads and other low-calorie foods are conditioned to arouse the appetite (see ASCH, 1973; Crasilneck & Hall, 1975, 147–166).

Asthmatics often precipitate their attacks by their very fear of them. Hypnotic relaxation and suggestions of freedom from anxiety may help reduce such attacks. Kroger and Fezler (1976) have reported studies in which the combination of systematic desensitation with hypnosis was effective in reducing wheezing.

The skin is very sensitive to emotions and suggestion. Hypnosis has been used especially to treat neurodermatitis. Suggestions of a fantasied "healing lotion" will often reduce or eliminate itching. Ikemi & Nakagawa (1962) demonstrated that dermatitis, precipitated by noxious-lacquer trees, could be reversed under hypnosis. Patients, when told under hypnosis that they were not near such trees (but who were actually placed in close proximity), did not develop skin lesions. Those who were told hypnotically they were close to such trees did develop the dermatitis. There are many reports of the successful treatment of pruritus, numular eczema, neurotic excoriation, and warts by hypnosis. Not only has hypnotic suggestion been helpful but, in more-stubborn cases, hypnoanalysis has proved of value when the neurotic "meaning" of the symptom was disclosed and experiential insight achieved (see Schneck, 1963, pp. 122–142; Crasilneck & Hall, 1975, pp. 267–278).

Kline (1954) found, when suggestions under hypnosis were given to psoriasis patients, that the afflicted areas would feel warm, then cool, then light, then heavy, then larger, then smaller, then the lesions cleared. It was almost as if he was teaching them how to control their skin's behavior by altering its perceptions.

In the practice of orthopedic medicine, it is often difficult to get patients to adapt to artificial limbs, crutches, or other prosthetic devices. Under hypnosis, patients can be given feelings of familiarity to accompany the installation of such devices, so they can become accustomed to the unfamiliar sensations.

Specialized problems in hypnotherapy

With release of the surgeon general's report on the dangers of smoking, many individuals try to stop the habit. Since smoking is an addiction, this usually involves a considerable struggle, accompanied by much anxiety and tests of will power. Many approaches have been suggested to help people to stop smoking: behavioral, psychotherapeutic, chemical, etc. Hypnosis has made its contribution in this area. The simplest technique is to pair suggestions of bitterness or distaste to the smoking. Occasionally, this procedure works. However, relapses are high, and more sophisticated techniques of hypnotherapy are required. Spiegel (1970) reports 20 percent success after six months of no smoking in hard-core smokers, with a one-session approach. H. H. Watkins (1976) described a five-session approach, involving a combination of hypnosis plus imagined fantasies (such as enjoying a good day after one's lungs are free of smoke or buying a desired article with the money that would be saved). She combined a behavioral reinforcement technique with individualized motivations, under hypnosis, and reported a success rate of 67 percent in a six-month follow-up. The entire October 1970 issue of the *International Journal of Clinical and Experimental Hypnosis* is devoted to hypnotic techniques for the stopping of smoking.

There are a number of reports of hypnotherapy with alcoholics. Kroger and Fezler (1976) have indicated substantial success in combining the usual aversion treatment with hypnosis. Very limited success has been reported with drug addicts (see Kroger, 1977, pp. 308–320; Crasilneck & Hall, 1975, pp. 245–247).

Nail biting in children has been successfully treated by suggestions that the tendency to put the fingers in the mouth will be met by a countermovement of the hands away from the mouth.

Stuttering is another condition which has been treated by a variety of hypnotic techniques. Some of these use suggestions of calmness and relaxation (Meares, 1961). Others (Crasilneck & Hall, 1975) reported improvement when they asked the stutterer to speak in a whisper, either in or out of hypnosis. Most practitioners agree that stuttering is one of the more difficult disabilities to treat.

Hiccoughs have been found to respond well to hypnotic suggestion (see Dorcus & Kirkner, 1955; Kroger, 1977, pp. 306–307).

A common problem with which hypnotherapists in university centers must deal is the matter of study habits. Difficulties in concentrating can often be improved by suggestions which eliminate distractions or which are tied to specific study hours of the day. However, even a symptom of this type can be based on complex, underlying conflicts (see ASCH, 1973, pp. 106–110).

Dental hypnosis

The greatest problem reported by dentists in the use of hypnosis seems to be the time required in initial inductions and deepenings. Otherwise, this modality has substantial contributions to make to dental practice (see Moss, 1952).

Fear and anxiety keeps many patients from their dentists. Cavities are allowed to go unchecked, until only extraction is possible. Hypnotic relaxation can often reduce such dental phobias. Patients are hypnotically conditioned to relaxation in the dental chair. They learn to be involved in pleasant fantasies, while the dental work is being done. The numbness which can be induced in the finger of a good hypnotic subject (as previously described) may be transferred, by rubbing the fingers over the gum area of an afflicted tooth. Even if the analgesia is not strong enough to permit work without any novocaine or procaine, it may be sufficient to eliminate the initial pain of a needle, which some people greatly fear.

Salivation, as well as bleeding, can often be restricted hypnotically, and the use of the hypnotic modality to accustom one to the feel of new prosthetic devices can make new dentures more comfortable. Here, the hypnotherapist suggests that, when the individual runs his tongue over the new dentures, this stimulus will evoke a memory of his original teeth. The familiarity of his original teeth then fuses with the present impression, and he loses the sensation of strangeness.

Bruxism is a condition in which individuals grind their teeth, often in their sleep. Unless checked, it may result in completely wearing away the enamel and in loss of teeth. One treatment approach is to suggest, under hypnosis, that the individual will sleep with the teeth a quarter of an inch apart. Whenever the teeth touch, this will wake up the sleeper. However, when the teeth are pulled apart, sleep will immediately return. Here, a behavioral self-punishment procedure is being established by hypnotic suggestion.

Forensic hypnosis

The newest field of interest for hypnotic clinicians is the realm of law enforcement (Hibbard & Worring, 1981). Under hypnosis, memories can be stimulated, and witnesses have been able to provide identifying data to police departments, which resulted in apprehension of the guilty party. There is no doubt that hypnosis can stimulate memory. However, there are dangers inherent in its use for this purpose, as have been pointed out by Orne (1979). First, there is a possibility that the hypnotist may make suggestions which are picked up, so that the subject reports fantasies or pseudo-memories as real. Hilgard and Loftus (1979) have reported that, while individuals under hypnosis remember more facts, they also "remember" more false "facts." Accordingly, the hypnotic interview of a witness must be undertaken with the greatest care. Videotaping is most desirable, and courts are beginning to insist on a very high degree of competence in the hypnotist—even as they are increasingly permitting the use of hypnotically derived testimony. A series of recent papers on this area can be found in the October 1979 issue of the *International Journal of Clinical and Experimental Hypnosis*.

In addition to the stimulating of memories, hypnosis has proved of significance in evaluating the state of mind of a defendant when he committed a crime. While it is known that individuals can lie under hypnosis and, of course, it is likely that defendants will represent themselves in the best light possible, still there is a reduction of criticality, and, at times, the defendant may clearly demonstrate, under hypnosis, that he was at fault. Within the past few years, courts have begun to permit juries to observe videotapes of hypnotic interrogations and regressions and to make their own judgment as to validity. This entire area is controversial. The legal profession is both interested in and wary of hypnotic contributions to law enforcement (Spector & Foster, 1977).

Precautions, dangers, and contraindications

A question often asked is whether there are types of conditions in which hypnosis should not be used or patients who should not be hypnotized. The answer is not clear. It used to be considered proper to avoid hypnosis with borderline psychotics and latent homosexuals, on the premise that full-fledged psychotic or other catastrophic reactions could be induced. Since hypnosis has the ability to penetrate conscious defenses and stimulate more concrete thinking and primary-process ideation, it would seem that caution should be exercised, especially by novices in the field. It is also true that some paranoid individuals may regard hypnosis as an attempt to control their minds—such a conception thus precipitating delusions of persecution. Recent experience tends to minimize those fears. However, the question has not yet been laid to rest. Skilled practitioners have reported successfully using hypnotic techniques with schizoid reactions and borderline schizophrenics, but most hypnotherapists are careful in this area. Hypnosis has been found to be the treatment of choice when working with dissociative reactions, such as amnesias and multiple personalities.

A more controversial question lies over whether individuals can be hypnotized against their will or can be made to commit antisocial behaviors against their ethical principles.

One school of thought (Orne, 1972; Conn, 1972) holds that the human organism has built-in controls, and it will protect itself by refusing to enter hypnosis, unless it chooses to do so. They also hold that an individual would not undertake immoral or unethical actions, unless he/she already had a prediliction for such behavior.

Another group of researchers and practitioners argue that, if hypnosis is potent enough to anesthetize an arm, it can anesthetize a conscience— hence, making underlying, antisocial motivations operative (Kline, 1972; Watkins, 1972). Watkins (1947, 1951) described studies in which an individual was "forced" into a trance state, in spite of a monetary reward if she successfully resisted. Other studies apparently demonstrated the inability of a hypnotized subject to keep a secret and withhold highly confidential information. In one case, a young lieutenant was induced to attack a friend with a knife, by having him hallucinate a battlefield scene in which he was being approached by an enemy soldier with a bayonet. Of course, this did not demonstrate an act in violation of his conscience, but rather a hypnotically manipulated misperception of the situation. However, if a crime had actually been committed, the individual's only defense in court would have been that he was impelled to do it through hypnosis. The entire issue is still controversial, with prominent workers in the field lined up on both sides. Much further research will be required to settle this issue; and, because of its nature and the danger to human subjects, it is questionable that definitive studies can be done.

HYPNOANALYTIC INSIGHT THERAPY[1]

Traditionally, hypnosis has been viewed as a technique of suggestion. In fact, Freud and present-day psychoanalysts have held that its therapeutic effect comes primarily from symptom suppression. They did not consider it as a modality for the facilitation of the analytic process. Even when insights did occur under hypnosis, it was held that these had "bypassed the ego" and, thus, did not involve genuine personality reconstruction (Freud, 1946).

An alternate view is to consider a patient's state of consciousness as lying on a continuum, with wide-awake (sitting up) alertness at one end and a deep hypnotic trance at the other. In between are intermediate states, such as relaxation on the analytic couch (hypnoidal), light hypnosis, intermediate hypnosis, deep hypnosis, and (at the extreme) the profound (or plenary) trance state, which is almost a coma. As one proceeds from the first condition to the last, the ego does not suddenly abdicate. Rather, it progressively diminishes, as increasing amounts of primitive, unconscious material become manifest.

In analytic therapy, the purpose is to elicit unconscious material and then, by working through, to egotize and reintegate it into the conscious

---

[1] See especially Schneck, 1965; Watkins, J. G., 1968; and Wolberg, 1945.

personality. The unconscious material raised from repression is like raw material. The ego is the processing factory. Reintegrative insight and personality reconstruction are the end products. An important question is, at what point on this continuum can the process—of lifting repressions, making conscious previously unconscious material, and ego-tizing it— be most expeditiously accomplished. It would seem that neither the psychoanalytic position of light relaxation on the couch (large ego-integrating factory and little unconscious, raw material) or the deep hypnosis position (small ego-integrating factory and huge quantities of unconscious, raw material) would be the most efficient. Rather, some middle position, perhaps in an intermediate hypnotic state, might best combine the release of preconscious and unconscious derivatives with the greatest amount of ego. Perhaps a weaving back and forth between the hypnoidal and deeper trance positions might also be effective. Hypnoanalysts do not necessarily quarrel with the basic tenets of psychoanalytic theory. However, they would hold that the flexibility offered in varying the state of consciousness (and hence, the ego control) offers an opportunity for improving the traditional psychoanalytic techniques of free association, dream interpretation, and analysis of the transference, as practiced in the normal, couch-relaxed (hypnoidal) position. They would suggest that psychoanalysts ought to reexamine the possibilities of practicing their therapy in the hypnotic modality, rather than ignoring it simply because Freud rejected it. Other analytic and insight therapies, even including client-centered therapy (Rogers, 1951), might find hypnosis facilitating to their own procedures.

The psychodynamics of hypnotic induction[2]

The alteration of an individual's state of consciousness is a process sensitive to many factors. The words (techniques) employed by the hypnotist and also the underlying meanings which the subject ascribes to hypnosis will influence his response. Accordingly, the sophisticated hypnotherapist does not simply parrot the words used in the various hypnotic-induction procedures. He/she must be sensitive to the inner needs of the patient and must tailor the induction and deepening with consideration of the patient's inner motivational processes, as these are understood or inferred.

Some individuals may regard hypnosis as a kind of sexual seduction. Movies and television plays often condition people to such belief. If this is the case, their reaction to hypnotizing suggestions may reflect inner needs. An unconscious *fear* of seduction could be expected to promote resistance to hypnosis. An unconscious *desire* to be seduced might facilitate hypnosis.

---

[2] Watkins, J. G., 1963a.

Dependency needs may foster an increased hypnotizability, if the hypnotist employs a technique which caters to them. On the other hand, the desk-pounding executive with an ulcer, who is engaged in an inner struggle with his dependency needs, may be highly resistant to hypnosis or to an induction technique in which he views himself as losing control.

The loss of consciousness is equated by some individuals as a kind of death: a psychic death. If this is greatly feared, the hypnotherapist will do well to investigate and resolve such an attitude before undertaking hypnotic induction. All of these considerations may be significant not only for induction, but also for the degree or depth of trance that an individual is willing to accept. Fears elicited under hypnosis may, at times, impel a subject to lighten his hypnotic involvement—even to the point of emerging from trance—or conversely, to deepen it—so that the fearing ego is almost completely removed from the threatening material. Therapists are seldom aware of all these conditions in their patients, but they should be cognizant of the fact that hypnotic responses can be significantly influenced by such factors.

HYPNODIAGNOSTIC PROCEDURES

As one moves from the more hypnosuggestive therapies to the approaches which emphasize insight and personality reorganization, hypnosis offers a number of sophisticated methods for exploring the patient's past and present.

Horizontal and vertical exploration are approaches which involve interviewing the patient under hypnotic regression. The past and present living space of an individual might be conceptualized as a three-dimensional solid (such as a cube), which has been developing, over the years, in a vertical direction. The upper surface represents patterns of behavior and experience in the here and now. As the individual develops, the patterns on the surface of the present change. Older ones are buried underneath and exist only in the recollections or traces of the past. Such an analogy, of course, is greatly simplified, since we have no evidence that the past is frozen in the engrams of the brain in complete or unaltered form. However, such a conceptualization is a foundation of the analytic therapies, which seek to uncover the past and reintegrate it into the individual's present behavior and experience.

From this viewpoint, hypnotic regression means taking the person experientially back to earlier periods of his life. He/she may be told under hypnosis that, "You are forgetting about what year it is. You are becoming younger, 12 years old, 11 years old, 10, 9, 8, 7, 6. You are six years old, and you are in school. The teacher is standing in front of you. What's her name?" When sufficient facts, which one believes to be true, have been elicited to indicate a true regression to that age level, the individual is interviewed to determine adjustment to school, playmates, relationships with parents and siblings, fears, etc. In other words, that plane of the lifespace solid, characterized by the six-year-old regression, is studied. This constitutes horizontal exploration. Suppose, in the course of such an exploration, one finds that there was conflict with an older brother. It then becomes possible to trace the development of the brother relationship by regressing the patient successively to ages 3, 5, 8, 11, 14, 17, etc. Such a procedure constitutes vertical exploration.

Projective or role-playing techniques may be employed by the therapist taking the role of the patient's best friend (say, at the age of 8) and engaging in an intimate conversation regarding attitudes toward parents, school, the other sex, etc. Constructive suggestions may be implanted at regressed levels. For example, one therapist regressed a frigid woman to the age of 13 and, in the role of the patient's mother, gave her permission to enjoy sex in her marriage. The frigidity was resolved. In this way, hypnodiagnostic procedures sometimes turn into therapy.

If a patient is conditioned to go into hypnosis at the tap of a pencil and to emerge from hypnosis on hearing two taps, it is possible to conduct an interview at two different levels of consciousness. This has been termed the *in-and-out* method. Thus, a patient might consciously describe her relationship with a sister as being "fairly good" but, in hypnosis, state, "I hate her guts." This technique has uncovered either a repressed hatred or, at least, an ambivalence.

Abreactions

The release of a strong affect, such as fear or rage, can often have a dramatic effect on symptoms. Freud learned of this approach from Breuer (Freud & Breuer, 1953) but later abandoned it. The hypnotized patient is regressed back to the original, emotionalized incident and—through suggestion—induced to relive it to the fullest. This may involve shouting, screaming, cursing, etc. The reaction is continued to exhaustion, at which time, reassurance and interpretations are administered. With the release of the bound affect, the patient becomes more amenable to both suggestions and insightful interpretations. Personality reorganization is facilitated. The technique is especially powerful where a neurotic symptom is specifically related to a traumatic experience (Watkins & Watkins, 1978). Care must be taken not to precipitate a full-blown psychotic reaction in a borderline patient.

H. H. Watkins (1980) has developed a variation called "the silent abreaction," which is designed to meet the problem of an abreaction becoming too noisy in a professional office. It involves an experiential fantasy of symbolizing one's frustrations (or frustrating people) into a large stone, which then is beaten to relieve rage perceptually and experientially but not verbally or motorically, as in the traditional abreaction.

Sometimes, the specific incident or time which is affect laden is not known. A technique called "the affect bridge" (J. G. Watkins, 1971) then becomes quite useful. For example, a patient describes an irrational fear while applying for a job. It occurred while being interviewed by the personnel manager. The patient is hypnotically regressed to this experience, and the fear is built up. All aspects of the scene (time, place, personnel manager, etc.) are then ablated by suggestion ("You will forget all about where you are. The only thing you can experience is the fear— pure fear alone with no content"). The individual is next regressed back to "some place where you first experienced this same fear. Where are you?" Perhaps the patient now describes an incident where he was severely punished by his father. He is then asked to return to the interview with the personnel manager. He sees his father's face on the manager and becomes aware of how his fear of the employment situation was precipitated through transference. The affect bridge is another very powerful hypnoanalytic technique. It has often precipitated therapeutic experiences, within a session or two, which might have taken months with more traditional psychoanalytic methods.

Dream and fantasy manipulation through hypnosis

In psychoanalytic therapy, patients are asked to associate to the elements in their dreams, as a step toward interpretation of their meaning. When an individual, under hypnosis, is asked to relive a dream which had previously been reported consciously, he usually describes it with greatly increased detail. A dream initially reported in a sentence or two may require a page or more to record, if described under hypnosis. Hypnotized patients also may report dreams when, in the conscious state, they had denied dreaming that night. Accordingly, there is increased source material available to the hypnoanalyst. Suggestions can also be implanted in patients, to the effect that they will dream about the present status of the therapy, their feelings about the analyst, predictions as to their future health, etc. Such prognostications are, of course, subject to distortions, even as are memories. Sometimes they may represent wishes more than accurate predictions of the future. Still, they represent valuable data, which may aid the hypnoanalyst in planning therapeutic strategies. They cannot be accepted on face value as fact; they also cannot be lightly dismissed as untrue.

Projective techniques can be used to aid in the interpretation of dreams. Perhaps the patient has reported a dream, in which a tall man, dressed in black, approached her on the street. She felt considerable anxiety and looked the other way. Under hypnosis, she is induced to relive the dream, which she does with enhanced detail. At the moment when the tall man is approaching her, she is asked to go up to him and ask his name, or to look carefully at his face to see if she recognizes it. This is a hypnoanalytic version of the active imagination techniques used by

Jungian analysts (Adler, 1948). Through combinations of active visualization, associations, and projections, the interpretation of dreams is facilitated. Not only dreams, but also memories of incidents can be altered
projectively, perhaps to try out different behaviors and solutions. ("Visualize that quarrel you had with your husband last night. What would happen
if you had said———instead of———?") These same techniques can
be and have been employed with patients in the conscious state. Hypnosis
only adds flexibility in their use.

Dissociative procedures

Individuals in conflict often dissociate themselves through amnesias
or multiple personalities, to keep apart cognitively dissonant components
of their self-structure. Since hypnosis is itself a dissociative procedure, it
may be used to resolve such dissociations, to create them for the purpose
of reducing anxiety, or to isolate significant parties to an inner conflict
for more intensive study.

Dissociative handwriting is one such procedure. The hypnotized patient is told that she can no longer move her hand and that it has no
sensation in it. It is "completely paralyzed." A hallucination is next induced, that it is no longer connected to the wrist but is simply floating
in air. The patient will have no control over it. Her eyes are opened
under hypnosis, so that she can see that it is no longer connected to
her. The hypnoanalyst then conducts an interview with the hand. It is
asked questions, and it writes the answers. Since it is no longer under
the patient's control, it is free to say anything it wants to. Sometimes, its
answers are most revealing, as both suppressed and repressed material
emerges.

Some people are more visual than motoric minded. The hand does
not write. It is possible then to hallucinate a school room, with a hand
writing on the blackboard. The hand is asked questions, and the patient
reads the answers which it writes on the blackboard. This constitutes
hallucinated dissociative handwriting.

If still further defenses are needed to elicit highly guarded or threatening material, the hand can be instructed to write its answers, with the
letters in the words scrambled—which then are gradually unscrambled.
In answer to a question as to who a certain woman symbolized, a patient
wrote O H T E R M—hence, mother.

HYPNOANALYTIC EGO-STATE THERAPY

Ego-state theory (Watkins & Watkins, 1979, 1981) holds that dissociation is on a continuum, with multiple personalities at the extreme end.
Normal and neurotic individuals have personality subsystems (or ego
states), which are organized patterns of behavior and experience. They

function like covert multiple personalities, and (like such entities) they can become maladaptive and develop conflicts with each other. These conflicts may be manifested in normal symptoms, like anxiety, headaches, fears, inability to study, etc. Ego states can be made manifest under hypnosis. They show consistency and identity and act like inner part-persons.

Ego-state therapy is the use of family and group techniques for the resolution of conflicts between the different ego states, which constitute a "family of self" within the individual. It is generally done under hypnosis. Care is taken to activate ego states which are present in the individual, not to create artifacts. Each state is interviewed separately, and a kind of internal diplomacy takes place. The therapist attempts to determine what is causing the conflict, to secure concessions and compromises between the states, and make constructive intervention in their conflicts.

Since ego states act like persons, they are treated as such. Accordingly, any of the therapeutic techniques (analytic, behavioral, cognitive, etc.) normally applied to complete persons can be applied to individual ego states. For example, we used a Wolpian desensitization technique to reduce the fear in a child ego state (Wolpe & Lazarus, 1966), which was acquired when the patient (at the age of three) was threatened by his mother with a knife. Through resolution of this transference, it was possible to shift him from a male to a female therapist.

Helen Watkins (1978) taught a male ego state (the Dark One) in a female patient to cease his opposition to her attempts at weight reduction and later to serve as a co-therapist in reducing the fear of an infantile ego state (the Little One). This had been apparently acquired when the patient (in her first year) had been placed in an oxygen tent. The Dark One was quite proud of his accomplishment in applying the desensitization techniques and eliminating the Little One's fear.

Ego states can also be activated by certain nonhypnotic methods, such as a projective-chair technique; but, in general, the hypnotic modality is much more effective in eliciting them. They seem to be developed in one or more of the following ways: (1) they are split off by a dissociative defense during traumatic experiences; (2) they are constructed around the introjects of significant figures, generally parents; or (3) they are developed as a normal differentiation of function in the individual's growth. We have found that, when multiple personalities are successfully integrated, and the separate entities are manifest no longer, they can be activated as normal ego states, much like those found in volunteer subjects for hypnotic experiments. In fact, they report, "We are just normal parts of her now; we don't come out any more as separate personalities."

Hypnoanalytic problems of transference and countertransference

No discussion of analytic therapy and hypnoanalytic therapy should omit some mention of the transference and countertransference reactions which arise in the course of such treatment. A true science of hypnotizing must be based on a deep and intimate knowledge of the transference needs and ego defenses of the patient. It further requires that the hypnotist be aware of his own countertransference needs, role abilities, and limitations (J. G. Watkins, 1963b).

Since hypnosis is a penetration—in some depth—of an individual's defenses and inner motivations, it is to be expected that transference reactions may be precipitated early and in considerable strength. The hypnotherapist is often endowed, by the patient, with the fears about parent figures, the angers originally felt toward them, or wishes for their benevolence and omnipotence. Such transferences will stir up counterreactions in the therapist. Hypnotists sometimes fall prey to a desire to play God. Because the modality does permit some rather potent and astounding interventions, it often stimulates adolescent power fantasies. The stage hypnotist exemplifies this reaction; but the clinical hypnotist can also be seduced into acting similarly. Passive receptive attitudes by patients may induce hypnotherapists to become dominating. Eroticized patients may become quite seductive, and the seeming power, which the hypnotic modality affords, can operate to stimulate acting-out desires in the therapist. Hypnotherapy is a rapid and potent technique, which demands of its practitioners considerable maturity. Changes in one's patient may come rather suddenly, sometimes dramatically, sometimes constructively—and even with increases in symptoms or acting out, to the dismay of the therapist who intervened too directly. Mistakes in conscious therapies are generally easier to correct. Reactions in such treatments occur over longer periods of time and, thus, permit more time for consideration of changes in tactics and therapy. The hypnotherapist should have been, first of all, a good psychotherapist with conscious patients.

HYPNOSIS RESEARCH

No space is available here for significant discussion of current research. The reader is referred to Fromm and Shor (1979), LeCron (1968), Frankel and Zamansky (1978), Sheehan and Perry (1976), Barber (1970), Kline (1963), Bowers (1976), and Hilgard (1965), as representative works in the field. Gardner (1980) has compiled the significant literature on hypnosis with children. The amount of hypnosis research has increased geometrically during the past few years, and many major universities now have active hypnosis laboratories.

Among the problems which have engaged the attention of experimenters is the reality of various hypnotic phenomena, such as regression, hypermnesia, dissociation, etc. The nature of hypnotic susceptibility and the factors which facilitate it have undergone considerable study. The ability of hypnotic intervention to influence physiologic processes and the relationship between hypnosis and brain function have been of much interest. Controversies over the possibilities of antisocial behavior being hypnotically induced have stimulated a number of studies and discussional seminars. The effect of hypnosis on fantasies and dreams has counted for other studies. Many different therapies (behavior, gestalt, existential, autogenic, etc.) have experimented with the integration of their approaches with hypnosis. Federal grants from the National Institute of Mental Health and the National Science Foundation have been awarded to many investigators. Annual meetings of hypnosis societies serve as a forum for the presentation of a wide variety of papers investigating the modality itself or using the modality for the investigation of other psychological and physiological phenomena. The days when hypnosis was not a respectable scientific field are gone—although remnants of the past remain, as many other scientists and practitioners are unaware of its development and present status.

SUMMARY

Hypnosis is a complex, psychological phenomena which, as yet, cannot be reduced to explanation by a single theory. These phenomena have been well charted but are under continuous scientific investigation aimed at validating or rejecting earlier conceptions. Hypnotherapy is not a treatment *by* hypnosis but *under* hypnosis. Many other therapies can be practiced within the hypnotic modality to their own benefit. These range from the directive and behavioral approaches, through the cognitive, the psychoanalytic, and the existential. Hypnosis has been applied in the treatment of a wide variety of disorders, psychological and organic. It is generally viewed as an altered state of consciousness; but some theorists emphasize its dissociative, its relationship, or its regressive aspects. In addition to its application by other forms of therapy, it has also developed a number of specific techniques, simple and complex, which are unique to the field called hypnotherapy. It is no cure-all, and it suffers equally from overardent exponents and from critics who are unfamiliar with it but castigate it with outworn cliches.

Hypnotherapy has established itself today as a legitimate discipline for research and therapy. As such, it is making a significant contribution toward the amelioration of human disabilities.

REFERENCES

Adler, G. *Studies in analytical psychology.* Boston: Routledge & Kegan Paul, 1948.

American Society of Clinical Hypnosis (ASCH). *A syllabus on hypnosis and a handbook of therapeutic suggestions.* Des Plaines, Ill.: Author, 1973.

Bandler, R., & Grinder, J. *Patterns of the hypnotic techniques of Milton H. Erickson, M.D.* (Vol. I). Cupertino, Calif.: Meta Publications, 1975.

Barber, T. X. *Hypnosis: A scientific approach.* New York: Van Nostrand Reinhold, 1969.

* Barber, T. X. *LSD, marihuana, yoga, and hypnosis.* Hawthorne, N.Y.: Aldine Publishing, 1970.

Bernheim, H. [*Hypnosis and suggestion in psychotherapy*] (C. A. Herter, trans.). New Hyde Park, N.Y.: University Books, 1964.

Blum, G. W., & Graef, J. R. The detection over time of subjects simulating hypnosis. *International Journal of Clinical and Experimental Hypnosis, 19*, 211–224.

*Bowers, K. S. *Hypnosis for the seriously curious.* Monterey, Calif.: Brooks/Cole Publishing, 1976.

Braid, J. *Neurohypnology, or the rationale of nervous sleep considered in relation with animal magnetism.* London: G. Redway, 1899.

Charcot, J. M. Complete works (in French): *Metalotherapie et hypnotisme* (Tome IX). Paris: Fourneville & Brissand, 1890.

Cheek, D. B., & LeCron, L. M. *Clinical hypnotherapy.* New York: Grune & Stratton, 1968.

Conn, J. H. Is hypnosis really dangerous? *International Journal of Clinical and Experimental Hypnosis, 1972, 20*, 118–131.

Crasilneck, H. G., & Hall, J. A. *Clinical hypnosis: Principles and applications.* New York: Grune & Stratton, 1975.

Dorcus, R. M., & Kirkner, F. J. The control of hiccoughs by hypnotic treatment. *Journal of Clinical and Experimental Hypnosis, 1955, 3*, 104–108.

Eiblmayr, K. *An examination of the phenomenon of trance logic using objective measurement and limiting the hypnotist/subject relationship.* Unpublished master's thesis, University of Montana, 1981. Presented at the meeting of the Society for Clinical and Experimental Hypnosis, Portland, Oregon, October 16, 1981.

Elliotson, J. *Numerous cases of surgical operations without pain in the mesmeric state.* Philadelphia: Lea & Blanchard, 1843.

Erickson, M. H. Deep hypnosis and its induction. In L. M. LeCron (Ed.), *Experimental hypnosis.* New York: Macmillan, 1952.

Erickson, M. H. Initial experiments investigating the nature of hypnosis. *The American Journal of Clinical Hypnosis, 1964, 7*, 152–162.

Erickson, M. H. Further experimental investigation of hypnosis: Hypnotic and nonhypnotic realities. *The American Journal of Clinical Hypnosis, 1967, 10*, 87–135.

Esdaile, J. *Hypnosis in medicine and surgery.* New York: Julian Press, 1957.

Ferenczi, S. *Further contributions to the theory and technique of psychoanalysis.* London: Hogarth Press, 1926.

*Frankel, F. H., & Zamansky, H. S. *Hypnosis at its bicentennial: Selected papers.* New York: Plenum Press, 1978.

Freud, A. *The ego and the mechanisms of defense.* New York: International Universities Press, 1946.

Freud, S., & Breuer, J. On the psychical mechanism of hysterical phenomena. In S. Freud, *Collected papers* (Vol. I). London: Hogarth Press and Institute of Psycho-Analysis, 1953.

*Fromm, E., & Shor, R. E. (Eds.). *Hypnosis: Developments in research and new perspectives* (2d ed). Hawthorne, N.Y.: Aldine Publishing, 1979.

---

* Note: Starred (*) items are general texts that are recommended to the reader who seeks a broad familiarization with the field.

Gardner, G. G. Hypnosis with children: Selected readings. *International Journal of Clinical and Experimental Hypnosis*, 1980, *28*, 289–293.

Gill, M. M., & Brenman, M. *Hypnosis and related states.* New York: International Universities Press, 1959.

Hibbard, W. S., & Worring, R. W. *Forensic hypnosis: The practical application of hypnosis in criminal investigation.* Springfield, Ill.: Charles C Thomas, 1981.

*Hilgard, E. R. *Hypnotic susceptibility.* New York: Harcourt Brace Jovanovich, 1965.

Hilgard, E. R. *Divided consciousness: Multiple controls in human thought and action.* New York: John Wiley & Sons, 1977.

Hilgard, E. R., & Hilgard, J. R. *Hypnosis in the relief of pain.* Los Altos, Calif.: William Kaufmann, 1975.

Hilgard, E. R., & Loftus, E. F. Effective interrogation of the eyewitness. *International Journal of Clinical and Experimental Hypnosis*, 1979, *27*, 342–357.

Hull, C. *Hypnosis and suggestibility.* New York: Appleton-Century-Crofts, 1933.

Ikemi, Y., & Nakagawa, S. A. A psychosomatic study of contagious dermatitis. *Kuyshu Journal of Medical Science*, 1962, *13*, 335–352.

Janet, P. *Psychological healing: A historical and clinical study* (2 vols.). New York: Macmillan, 1925.

Johnson, R. F. Q., Maher, B. A., & Barber, T. X. Artifact in the "essence of hypnosis": An evaluation of trance logic. *Journal of Abnormal Psychology*, 1972, *79*, 212–220.

Kline, M. V. Psoriasis and hypnotherapy. *Journal of Clinical and Experimental Hypnosis*, 1954, *2*, 318–322.

Kline, M. V. Theoretical and conceptual aspects of psychotherapy. In M. V. Kline (Ed.), *Hypnodynamic psychology.* New York: Julian Press, 1955.

Kline, M. V. *Freud and hypnosis.* New York: Julian Press and Institute for Research Publication Society, 1958.

*Kline, M. V. *Clinical correlations of experimental hypnosis.* Springfield, Ill.: Charles C Thomas, 1963.

Kline, M. V. The production of antisocial behavior through hypnosis: New clinical data. *International Journal of Clinical and Experimental Hypnosis*, 1972, *27*, 375–401.

Kroger, W. S. *Clinical and experimental hypnosis* (2d ed.). Philadelphia: J. B. Lippincott, 1977.

Kroger, W. S., & Fezler, W. D. *Hypnosis and behavior modification: Imagery conditioning.* Philadelphia: J. B. Lippincott, 1976.

Kubie, L. S., & Margolin, D. The process of hypnotism and the nature of the hypnotic state. *American Journal of Psychiatry*, 1944, *100*, 611–622.

*LeCron, L. M. (Ed.). *Experimental hypnosis.* New York: Citadel Press, 1968.

Liebeault, A. *Du sommeil et des états analogues, considérés surtout au point de vue de l'action du moral sur le physique.* Paris: Masson, 1866.

London, P. *The children's hypnotic susceptibility scale.* Palo Alto, Calif.: Consulting Psychologists Press, 1962.

McDonald, R. E., & Smith, J. R. Trance logic in tranceable and simulating subjects. *International Journal of Clinical and Experimental Psychology*, 1975, *23*, 80–89.

Marmer, M. J. *Hypnosis in anesthesiology.* Springfield, Ill.: Charles C Thomas, 1959.

Meares, A. *A system of medical hypnosis.* Philadelphia: W. B. Saunders, 1961.

Mesmer, F. A. *Mesmerism: A translation of the original medical and scientific writings of F. A. Mesmer, M.D.* (G. J. Bloch trans.). Los Altos, Calif.: William Kaufmann, 1981.

Moss, A. A. *Hypnodontics: Hypnosis in dentistry.* Brooklyn, N.Y.: Dental Items of Interest Publishing Company, 1952.

Naruse, G. Hypnosis as a state of meditative concentration and its relationship to the perceptual process. In M. V. Kline (Ed.), *The nature of hypnosis: Contemporary theoretical approaches.* New York: Institute for Research in Hypnosis and Postgraduate Center for Psychotherapy, 1962.

Orne, M. T. The nature of hypnosis: Artifact and essence. *Journal of Abnormal and Social Psychology,* 1959, *58,* 277–299.

Orne, M. T. Can a hypnotized subject be compelled to carry out otherwise unacceptable behavior? A discussion. *International Journal of Clinical and Experimental Hypnosis,* 1972, *20,* 101–117.

Orne, M. T. The use and misuse of hypnosis in court. *International Journal of Clinical and Experimental Hypnosis,* 1979, *27,* 311–341.

Pavlov, I. The identity of inhibition with sleep and hypnosis. *Scientific Monthly,* 1923, *17,* 603–608.

Rogers, C. R. *Client-centered therapy.* Boston: Houghton Mifflin, 1951.

Sarbin, T. R., & Coe, W. C. *Hypnosis: A social-psychological analysis of influence communication.* New York: Holt, Rinehart & Winston, 1972.

Schneck, J. M. A theory of hypnosis. *Journal of Clinical and Experimental Hypnosis,* 1953, *1,* 16–17.

*Schneck, J. M. *Hypnosis in modern medicine.* Springfield, Ill.: Charles C Thomas, 1963.

Schneck, J. M. *Principles and practice of hypnoanalysis.* Springfield, Ill.: Charles C Thomas, 1965.

*Sheehan, P. W., & Perry, C. W. *Methodologies of hypnosis: A critical appraisal of contemporary paradigms of hypnosis.* Hillsdale, N. J.: Lawrence Erlbaum Associates, 1976.

Shor, R. E. Three dimensions of hypnotic depth. *International Journal of Clinical and Experimental Hypnosis,* 1962, *10,* 23–28.

Shor, R. E., & Orne, E. C. *Harvard group scale of hypnotic susceptibility.* Palo Alto, Calif.: Consulting Psychologists Press, 1962.

Spector, R. S., & Foster, T. E. Admissability of hypnotic statements: Is the law of evidence susceptible? *Ohio State Law Journal,* 1977, *38,* 567–613.

Spiegel, H. A single-treatment method to stop smoking using ancillary self-hypnosis. *International Journal of Clinical and Experimental Hypnosis,* 1970, *18,* 235–250.

Spiegel, H. An eye-roll test for hypnotizability. *The American Journal of Clinical Hypnosis,* 1972, *15,* 25–28.

Watkins, H. H. Hypnosis and smoking: A five-session approach. *International Journal of Clinical and Experimental Hypnosis,* 1976, *24,* 381–390.

Watkins, J. G. Ego-state therapy. In J. G. Watkins (Ed.), *The therapeutic self.* New York: Human Sciences Press, 1978.

Watkins, H. H. The silent abreaction. *International Journal of Clinical and Experimental Hypnosis,* 1980, *28,* 101–113.

Watkins, J. G. Antisocial compulsions induced under hypnotic trance. *Journal of Social and Abnormal Psychology,* 1947, *42,* 256–259.

Watkins, J. G. *Hypnotherapy of war nueroses.* New York: Ronald Press, 1949.

Watkins, J. G. A case of hypnotic trance induced in a resistant subject in spite of active opposition. *British Journal of Medical Psychology,* 1951, *Summer,* 1–6.

Watkins, J. G. Psychodynamics of hypnotic induction and termination. In J. M. Schneck (Ed.), *Hypnosis in modern medicine.* Springfield, Ill.: Charles C Thomas, 1963. (a)

Watkins, J. G. Transference aspects of the hypnotic relationship. In M. V. Kline (Ed.), *Clinical correlations of experimental hypnosis.* Springfield, Ill.: Charles C Thomas, 1963. (b)

Watkins, J. G. Hypnosis and consciousness from the viewpoint of existentialism. In M. V. Kline (Ed.), *Psychodynamics and hypnosis.* Springfield, Ill.: Charles C Thomas, 1967.

Watkins, J. G. Projective hypnoanalysis. In L. M. LeCron (Ed.), *Experimental hypnosis.* New York: Citadel Press, 1968.

Watkins, J. G. The affect bridge: A hypnoanalytic technique. *International Journal of Clinical and Experimental Hypnosis,* 1971, *19,* 21–27.

Watkins, J. G. Antisocial behavior under hypnosis: Possible or impossible? *International Journal of Clinical and Experimental Hypnosis,* 1972, *20,* 95–100.

Watkins, J. G. *The therapeutic self.* New York: Human Sciences Press, 1978.

Watkins, J. G., & Watkins, H. H. *Abreactive technique* (audiotape). New York: Jason Aronson, Psychotherapy Tape Library, 1978.

Watkins, J. G., & Watkins, H. H. The theory and practice of ego-state therapy. In H. Grayson (Ed.), *Short-term approaches to psychotherapy.* New York: Human Sciences Press and National Institute for the Psychotherapies, 1979.

Watkins, J. G., & Watkins, H. H. Ego states and hidden observers. *Journal of Altered States of Consciousness,* 1979–1980, *5,* 3–18.

Watkins, J. G., & Watkins, H. H. Ego-state therapy. In R. Corsini (Ed.), *Handbook of innovative therapies.* New York: John Wiley & Sons, 1981.

Weitzenhoffer, A. M. *Hypnotism: An objective study of suggestibility.* New York: John Wiley & Sons, 1953.

Weitzenhoffer, A. M. *General techniques of hypnotism.* New York: John Wiley & Sons, 1957.

Weitzenhoffer, A. M., & Hilgard, E. R. *Stanford hypnotic susceptibility scale, forms A and B.* Palo Alto, Calif.: Consulting Psychologists Press, 1959.

Weitzenhoffer, A. M., & Hilgard, E. R. *Stanford profile scales of hypnotic susceptibility, forms I and II.* Palo Alto, Calif.: Consulting Psychologists Press, 1967.

White, R. W. A preface to the theory of hypnotism. *Journal of Abnormal and Social Psychology,* 1941, *36,* 477–505.

Wolberg, L. R. *Hypnoanalysis,* New York: Grune & Stratton, 1945.

Wolpe, J., & Lazarus, A. A. *Behavior-therapy techniques: A guide to the treatment of neuroses.* Elmsford, N.Y.: Pergamon Press, 1966.

31

Social and community interventions

Julian Rappaport*
and
Edward Seidman*

Why a chapter on social and community interventions in a handbook of clinical psychology? At first blush, the topic may seem outside the domain of the clinician, perhaps interesting, even worthwhile, but clearly of secondary import in the daily bump and grind of clinical work. Not so, we say in this chapter. Rather, we offer the thought that a clinician will be more useful than otherwise if his or her clinical work—diagnosis, treatment, client interactions and background conceptions—is informed by a social/community perspective. Not only may the clinician wish to become personally involved in community work, but he or she may wish to find out more about one's own locale and make appropriate referrals to a variety of nontraditional settings, or even help to create new ones. In a sense, it is a matter of increasing available options, for clinicians and for clients. Toward that aim, this chapter is intended as a beginning point for the clinician, hopefully moving one toward relevant ideas and choices by providing a conceptual framework.

Despite the tremendous advances in clinical treatment methods documented in this volume, many such treatments remain inaccessible to, or inappropriate for, a wide variety of people and problems. Like it or not, there remain a range of human problems for which standard clinical services are simply inadequate, inefficient, or inappropriate, and a large set of people who reject such services (cf. Sue, McKinney, Allen, & Hall, 1974). These difficulties are overrepresented among those who are in the lowest socioeconomic strata of society and include classical problems (such as official delinquency and chronic mental illness) as well as a variety of debilitating individual problems in living (such as poverty-re-

---

* University of Illinois, Urbana-Champaign.

lated apathy, withdrawal, and depression, poor educational experiences, unemployment, and undesirable living conditions).

Given the focus of this volume, this chapter is devoted to an explication of how clinical psychology has been expanded by the field of social and community intervention so as to be somewhat more applicable to such social problems. In order to stay within the limits of a single chapter, application of social and community intervention is demonstrated by confining examples to problems of serious psychological disturbance.

The onset of what came to be thought of as the community mental health movement in this century is generally agreed (despite the wealth of earlier roots) to have taken hold by the early 1960s, in the form of legislation (the Community Mental Health Centers Act of 1963) and in the development of formal settings, called community mental health centers (see Bloom, 1977, for an informative history of the development of community mental health centers). The movement was originally driven by a desire to de-institutionalize the mental hospital population and to extend the reach of services to underserved populations (Joint Commission, 1961); although, more recently, its leaders have taken a more preventive stance; i.e., to keep people out of hospitals altogether, by strengthening their social environment (President's Commission, 1978).

These changes have sometimes taken us far from the limits of psychiatry and the narrow definition of mental health. Comprehensive reviews of early developments—first stimulated by recognition that the amount of available psychiatric and psychological services, their reach to those most in need, and the efficacy of these services was, at best, limited—may be found in Cowen, Gardner, and Zax (1967). Many reviewers have since updated this field (Bloom, 1977, 1980; Cowen, 1973; Heller & Monahan, 1977; Kelly, Snowden, & Munoz, 1977; Munoz, Snowden, & Kelly, 1979; Price, Ketterer, Bader, & Monahan, 1980; Rappaport, 1977a; Zax & Specter, 1974); and this chapter is intended less as a review of the literature and more as a cognitive map by which the clinical psychologist may expand both the number and kind of questions asked and his or her options for intervention; i.e., "the universe of alternatives" (Sarason, 1971).

REFRAMING THE QUESTIONS

The social/community perspective assumes that individual and group treatments—held in the mode of weekly psychotherapy sessions with a professional, who delivers direct, clinical services—can never hope to handle the sort of difficulties mentioned above, either because the treatments are not well received by the potential clients, or because the treatments are simply too limited in scope. One may conclude that these difficulties are beyond the limits of the clinician; but, if one is to engage them at all, it will require a different way of thinking about problems in living than is typical for clinical psychology. To accomplish this, it is necessary to allow form (the roles and conceptions we adopt) to follow, rather than dictate, function. It is necessary to resist allowing the setting in which one works, its standard procedures, methodologies, questions and practices, to dictate how difficulties will be approached. It is perhaps this very insight—that organzational structure may limit the delivery of human services in unintended ways—which is most basic to what has been called first "community mental health," then "community psychology," and here "social and community intervention."

The insight has been most poetically expressed in what philosophers call the rule of the tool. Give a man or woman a hammer and he or she hammers, a wrench and he twists, a drug and she administers it, a test and he tests, a treatment technique and she uses it. Sometimes hammering may be appropriate, sometimes not. In every setting, including mental health settings, certain practices are sanctioned and others are prohibited. The rule of the tool is the tendency to do only what one already knows how to do, regardless of the task. It is a rule enforced by the setting or social niche in which one works. The social/community perspective often requres breaking this rule.

A primary value—which has sustained our ability to break the rules— is a belief that, in order to make progress toward solving serious social problems, it is necessary to reframe the very way in which we state the problem to ourselves (Watzlawick, Weakland, & Fisch, 1974). Rather than accepting the problem definition with which we are presented, reframing explicitly calls for a different way of thinking about the problem before one even looks for a solution. In the domain of mental health, for example, when those with a reframing ability found themselves presented with a problem (such as overcrowded mental hospitals) and saw that the problem was usually described as a function of intrapsychic inadequacies, or individual deficits, they began to ask questions such as: Why are there no appropriate niches in the world for these people? Why do we wait for people to become institutionalized? Why are people who have so many skills and abilities isolated from their communities?

Reframing the question requires stepping outside the usual role relationship between client and clinician. It allows one to ask questions like, "Why do clinical psychologists use psychotherapy, or some variant of it, for most people with problems in living?" Questions such as these are difficult to ask because they put established *role relationships* into question. Any change which puts role relationships in question is always more difficult to adopt than one that does not. For example, it has been difficult for physicians and surgeons to adopt the doctrine of informed consent, which requires them to tell their patients the variety of alternative treatment procedures available, as well as the estimated risk of each, so that the patient can choose his or her own treatment. On the other hand, it has been relatively easy for the same physicians to adopt an innovation, which is simply a change in technology, administered within their existing role relationships (i.e., prescribing a new drug).

Similarly, it is more difficult for a clinical psychologist to adopt a change (such as conducting treatment sessions in the client's home) than to introduce a new in-the-office technique (such as progressive relaxation). It is even more difficult to adopt a change such as encouraging self-help groups operated without any direct professional supervision. As the change in role relationships gets greater, so too will be the difficulty of adopting the change.

In order to see new possibilities, it is helpful to adopt a reframing attitude. Just as a clinician will encourage clients to reframe their difficulties in the search for new solutions, so too must a discipline encourage its practitioners. Reframing is a technique which necessarily increases the number and nature of potential solutions (see Rappaport, Lamiell, & Seidman, 1980; Seidman, 1978, for a variety of nonmental health examples).

The field of social and community intervention, by making explicit the value of reframing traditional, clinical problems, has had a three-step effect on clinical psychology. First, it has helped several central themes to emerge clearly among the ideas of psychologists. These themes have, in turn, led some clinical psychologists to try a wider variety of interventions. Experience with these new interventions has, in turn, led to an expansion of the data base, experience, and ideas available to clinical psychology.

CENTRAL THEMES PROMINENT IN THE SOCIAL/COMMUNITY PERSPECTIVE

Since the early 1960s, psychologists have been formally extending the borders of legitimacy for those trained as clinical psychologists to engage in social and community intervention by reframing, breaking the rules, and adding new tools and using them in new settings. These years have seen a vast growth in conception, knowledge, tools, and roles, enabling the clinical psychologist to adopt a perspective which is preventive and empowering rather than rehabilitative, competence and strength based as opposed to deficit oriented and policy concerned.

A good example of the result of reframing is the emergence of the theme of *prevention*. Central to this theme, is the idea that it may be possible to avoid some problems in living before they become so serious as to require clinical services, the very activity for which mental health settings are designed. This class of interventions involves a variety of social, educational, economic, political, and psychological strategies for change. Obviously, reframing the problem in this way necessarily requires change in the role relationships between client and clinician.

A second theme which has emerged from reframing is to pay a good deal of attention to the *competence* and *strengths* of people, rather than to their deficits. In clinical terms, diagnosis requires finding out what people are good at and and what they can do, rather than what they are failing to do. Reframing the problem this way influences the meta-communications and expectations offered by professionals to their clientele, as well as the substance of the interventions. This emphasis is applicable to a wide variety of interventions, both preventive and rehabilitative. It is not necessarily contradictory to clinical treatment, but it does tend to reverse the priority of behaviors to which one typically calls attention. Underlying the search for competence and strengths is the notion of diverse standards of adjustment. Once we begin to look for strengths in our clients, we are more likely to see a wider variety of ways in which people may find solutions to their problems in living.

A third central theme has emphasized *social* and *public policy*. This means that one is concerned with the well-being of entire populations, the effectiveness of systems for human well-being, public education, the social impact of formal law, informal rules, regulations, and procedures on individuals. It may involve program development, evaluation, implementation, and dissemination. It may involve even broader issues, such as how to influence public opinion, government officials, and the larger social milieu. An important challenge to those psychologists who assume a policy perspective is to add the psychological dimensions to a domain of interest traditionally dominated by law and economics and, to a lesser extent, political science and sociology (Bevan, 1980).

Because psychologists began to reframe clinical questions—so as to search for social programs which would prevent problems in living by discovery of competencies and strengths among people in distress—many new methods of problem solution, collectively called social and community intervention, have emerged in the last 25 years. Perhaps more important than any list of facts or tables of data, we have learned to stretch our ideas about the possible modes of psychological intervention. This experience has helped clinical psychology to expand its understanding and its techniques for intervention in at least six domains: conceptions of individuals, conceptions of society, styles of service delivery, levels of analysis, agents of transmission, and goals of intervention. Below, we first describe how each of these domains has been expanded and added to each other so as to increase the choices available to clinical psychologists. Then, as an example, we show how, taken together, they have created new possibilities for the delivery of mental health services to people experiencing serious psychological disturbances.

DOMAINS OF EXPANSION

Conceptions of individual behavior

The basic community mental health ideology is well summarized in Bloom's (1973) monograph (see Table 1), which contrasts community mental health to so-called traditional clinical services along nine dimensions. As can be seen from Table 1, community mental health has implied a critique of traditional services and has been largely based on practical (rather than theoretical) issues, i.e., location and level of intervention, type and form of service delivery, planning strategy, source of manpower, and decision making. The one theoretical stand taken has been an emphasis on the environmental (as opposed to intrapsychic) etiology of mental health problems. In this way, many community mental health advocates have followed the lead of, and have been compatible with, behavioral, environmental, ecological, and general systems theories (Bandura, 1969; Catalano, 1979; Mischel, 1968; Redd, Porterfield, & Andersen, 1979; Trickett, Kelly, & Todd, 1972) as well as with the notions of public health (Caplan, 1964; Maccoby & Alexander, 1979; Susser, 1968). These theories of individual behavior are widely accessible. Many (e.g., Fawcett, Mathews, & Fletcher, 1980; Nietzel, Winett, MacDonald, & Davidson, 1977; Rappaport, 1977b; Rappaport & Chinsky, 1974) have previously asserted the compatibility of these theories with community intervention methods, and here we simply note that an environmental conception of individual behavior is the first step toward community intervention.

Conceptions of society

While many community-oriented psychologists have explicitly stated their preferences for individual theories of behavior, few have done more than imply a conception of society. Nevertheless, those who are identified with social and community intervention usually implicitly take one of two views. When made explicit, these views expand the range of options for intervention.

To simplify a variety of differences, it is useful to term one view of society as *stability-oriented* and the other as *change-oriented*. For some, the major social issues confronting people with problems in living involve learning how to adjust, acquire new skills, and adapt to the current demands of society. This view suggests that society is, and should be, relatively stable. Psychologists in general, as well as many in the community mental health movement, have implicitly held such a stability-oriented perspective.

Many psychologists, concerned about issues such as where and how services might best be delivered, have been responsive to federal and state policies which put a great deal of money into community mental health centers. These professionals emphasize offering more, perhaps briefer, psychotherapy and other services (such as preschool education, parent training, and problem-solving skills) as means to promote adjustment to the demands of society (e.g., Allen, Chinsky, Larcen, Lochman, & Selinger, 1976; Spivak & Schure, 1974). Some of these programs and interventions are based on fairly traditional views of the dynamics of individual behavior; others have adopted one of the environmental

Table 1

Dimensions of community mental health versus clinically oriented services

Dimensions of comparison	Community mental health	Traditional clinical services.
1. Location of intervention	Practice in the community	Practice in institutional mental health settings
2. Level of intervention	Emphasis on a total or defined community (e.g., a catchment area, or population at risk)	Emphasis on individual clients
3. Type of services	Emphasis on preventive services	Emphasis on therapeutic services
4. How service is delivered	Emphasis on indirect services through consultation and education	Emphasis on direct clinical services to clients
5. Strategies of service	Strategies aimed at reaching large numbers of people, including brief psychotherapy and crisis intervention	Emphasis on extended psychotherapy
6. Kind of planning	Rational planning aimed at specification of unmet needs, high-risk populations, and coordinated services	Unplanned, individual services with no overall community coordination; a "free enterprise" system
7. Source of manpower	Mental health professionals together with new, including nonprofessional sources of manpower, such as college students and persons indigenous to the target group	Traditional mental health professionals (psychiatrists, psychologists, social workers)
8. Locus of decision making	Shared responsibility for control and decision making with regard to mental health programs between community and professionals	Professional control of all mental health services
9. Etiological assumptions	Environmental causes of mental disorder	Intrapsychic causes of mental disorder

Source: From Rappaport's (1977a) summary of Bloom's (1973) monograph.

approaches. Advocates of these positions have frequently engaged in debates on the relative merits of their theory of individual behavior. However, in the realm of social and community intervention, such conceptions of individual behavior, while important, pale in the face of one's conception of society.

An alternative to the stability-oriented viewpoint is that, despite the reality of individual problems in adjustment, social and community interventions should take place in a context which assumes change. First, it is assumed that society is not as stable as it appears to be in the time-bound present (consequently, the need for a historical perspective, which psychology usually lacks—cf. Gergin, 1973; Sarason, 1981). Second, it is assumed that the direction of social change can be influenced, so as to make it more likely that the people of concern to the interventionist will be more, rather than less, able to obtain necessary individual resources. The people of concern are most often a variety of marginal groups, ranging from chronic mental patients to those who find themselves in legal difficulties, the poor, the unemployed, and members of minority groups. This view presumes that changes in social policy are a necessary part of any comprehensive plan for mental health and human welfare and conceives of the mental health worker as an advocate as much as a therapist.

Given the wide range of conceptions, from stability- to change-oriented, and an infusion of both money and energy into the community mental health system during an initial period of growth and development (1963–1975), there has been considerable confusion and disagreement as to exactly what social and community intervention requires. As might be expected, early growth and optimism about bold new approaches gave way to pessimism about old wine in new bottles and, ultimately, to a more realistic set of expectations. The entire enterprise of community mental health is now being reevaluated, in light of the sociopolitical reality of the 1980s, the temper of the times, and the experiences of 20 years, such that, at present, there is a struggle to find the proper balance between these views of stability and change. Even though government-supported community mental health services are well past a growth period vis-à-vis resources, we are now in a position to select from among a wider variety of choices. Explicitly conceptualizing society as changing, rather than stable, is a second step toward increasing the number of choices available to clinical psychology.

Style of service delivery

One way to comprehend the variety of ways in which human services may be offered (i.e., the alternatives we have) is to view all human services as requiring a choice among the first two domains (conceptions of individuals and conceptions of society), combined with a third choice—the style of service delivery. Table 2 graphically presents a variety of examples based on eight combinations of these choices among: individual conceptions, societal conceptions, and styles or modes of intervention. As may be seen from the table, any intervention can be thought of in this way, although the particular examples are neither exhaustive of all possible choices nor mutually exclusive.

For convenience of illustration, only two of the many possible ways to conceptualize individual behavior are presented in Table 2—the disease/intrapsychic as opposed to the behavioral/environmental. In both cases, of course, these are rather simplified, catch phrases to capture

Table 2

Selected examples of interventions along the continuum of service delivery

Mode of intervention	Conceptions of individual behavior*	Conceptions of society	
		Stability-oriented	*Change-oriented*
Passive-waiting (clinical services)	Disease/intra-psychic	Traditional psychodynamic and/or relationship based psychotherapy	Radical psychotherapy and consciousness raising
	Behavioral/environmental	The various behavior therapies	In-house behavior modification programs aimed at value change, e.g., among teachers
Active-seeking (social/community interventions)	Disease/intra-psychic	Brief psychotherapy crisis intervention & competence training	Social psychiatry and epidemological public health approaches; creation of independent alternative settings; advocacy; reactive and proactive primary prevention
	Behavioral/environmental	Token economies applied in classrooms to maintain order; environmental design changes; crisis intervention; competence training of students or parents	Creation of new settings and alternative institutions; advocacy; reactive and proactive primary prevention

* The use of disease/intrapsychic as opposed to behavioral/environmental individual conceptions appears to be less salient within the seeking mode than the waiting. However, while the form of the intervention may appear to be similar (i.e., both might involve the creation of a new setting or advocacy), the specifics of how the program is systematically applied to individual people will differ, as might be expected.

the general outlines of a way to look at people with problems in living. There are a wide array of variants of each position, and as many additional cells might be added to Table 2 as there are theories of individual human behavior. Nevertheless, these two views are widely held and help to illustrate, by already well-known comparisons with one another, that how one conceives of individual behavior influences the kinds of services one offers.

A second issue depicted in Table 2 is labeled the style or mode of intervention. This determines how the service called for will be offered to the target population. In discussions of models for clinical psychology, this choice is frequently omitted. It is generally assumed that the proper mode of intervention is defined by the doctor-patient relationship. Even those who eschew a disease conception of human behavior tend to accept the medical style of intervention, in which the expert or authority, who holds some sort of advanced degree, is responsible for diagnosis and prescription. The diagnosis may be in behavioral terms, and the prescription may be a behavioral intervention, rather than a drug, but the essential *role relationship* remains. Diagnosis and treatment usually take place in the expert's office, hospital, or clinic. The expert passively waits for the client to find her or his office. This style is referred to, in Table 2, as the *waiting mode.*

An alternative style of intervention, described here as the *seeking mode,* is based on an attitude which allows the services or the intervention to be centered someplace other than in a mental health setting. It may be delivered by a variety of people, both professional and nonprofessional. The important point is that the seeking mode permits one to step out of traditional places, niches, and roles and to engage people in their own settings. It allows professionals to take on a variety of new roles: as consultants to others who deliver direct service, such as college students, volunteers, teachers, or policemen; as those who help to create new settings, such as neighborhood drop-in centers for adolescents or the elderly; as those who encourage the formation of self-help groups; as those who help to create alternative educational experiences, community betterment, economic development, and housing pograms.

Each of these choices among individual conceptions and styles of intervention are combined, implicitly or explicitly, with one's view of society as essentially stability- or change-oriented. For those who view society as stable, the range of intervention is from traditional mental health services (such as psychotherapy of various sorts, based on one's theory of individual behavior and personality) through community mental health adjustment-oriented interventions (such as brief psychotherapy, crisis intervention, competence training in social or educational skills, and designing of classroom environments). Each of these, delivered in a waiting or a seeking mode of delivery, assumes as its goal assisting people to cope with the demands of society. This is the classical view of mental health services.

A social change-oriented view may also be combined with the same variety of individual conceptions of behavior and personality and the waiting or seeking mode of delivery. Among those who hold a change-oriented view of society and use the waiting mode are psychologists who view themselves as "radical therapists," engaging in "consciousness raising" by intervention which stylistically looks like individual and group therapy, but which assumes that the client needs to question traditional social relationships. In the seeking mode, one may find behaviorists who seek to change the values of social institutions (Fawcett et al., 1980), or epidemiologically based public health oriented psychologists, who develop programs for enhancing physical health (Maccoby & Alexander, 1979) or the living conditions and quality of life in high-risk neighborhoods (Garbarino, 1980). Programs of advocacy and the creation of new settings (such as alternative schools) may also be developed (Weber & McCall, 1978). This view is responsive to the demands of a variety of people in powerless positions vis-à-vis the current social structure and explicitly attempts to create change.

As should be clear from this overview, the range of services and programs—which may be developed, encouraged, and created by those who are psychologists—need no longer be limited by the traditional rules, roles, and functions of the mental health professions. Expansion of the choices available is an important way in which community intervention has contributed to clinical psychology.

Levels of analysis

A fourth way in which the choices available to psychologists have been expanded has been to make explicit the notion of levels of analysis. Originally introduced into discussions of community psychology by Robert Reiff, these ideas have since been elaborated (Rappaport, 1977a, 1977b; Seidman & Rappaport, 1974). The basic point is a simple one; but, given that psychology is largely a study of individuals, it is quite easy to ignore.

Central to the idea is a rejection of reductionism. This means, in terms most familiar to clinical psychologists, that just as it would be an error to conceptualize all individual behavior vis-à-vis biological processes, so too would it be a mistake to conceptualize all group or social behavior in terms of individual decisions and motivations. For some questions, the biological level of analysis is most appropriate, for others, less so. For example, in the study of depression among post-menopausal women, one must take into account an understanding of hormonal changes; on the other hand, it is unlikely that much will be gained from the study of biological processes if one is asking questions about the mechanisms by which parents socialize their children. Similarly, in order to study how human service organizations may be improved, so as to accomplish their missions more effectively, we are more likely to benefit from the study of organizational processes, as opposed to the study of personality variables (cf. Campbell & Dunnette, 1976). It is not that biological factors are irrelevant to the behavior of family members, or that personality variables do not influence people in organizations, but simply that the kind of questions one asks make some levels of analysis less useful, or even misleading. Economists, aware of this same point, speak of the "Robinson Crusoe fallacy," which refers to the belief that, by understanding how a single person makes economic decisions, it is possible to understand the economic behavior of a nation. Similarly, the inability of principles of individual behavior and motivation to account for war, poverty, and other social dilemmas is well known.

Following this line of reasoning, a social/community perspective suggests that the social order may be thought of as a series of increasingly complex levels of organization. Each level serves as both a point for understanding and for intervention. Each level can be understood to operate according to variables and conceptions which are self-contained, although each level influences the other. However, principles and techniques for change at one level (i.e., the individual) are not necessarily operative at other levels (i.e., the organizational). In order to comprehend the social order, one would require conceptions and principles for understanding individuals, groups, organizations, institutions, communities, and societies, as well as the relationships within and between levels of analysis, and how they influence one another.

From this view of levels of analysis, a range of strategies and tactics for intervention naturally follows. From individual psychology flow clinical and community mental health interventions most consistent with the stability-oriented view of society. In the classical models of clinical intervention, variables or points of intervention beyond the individual and the small group are assumed to be both stable and outside the domain of interest. The values and goals which underlie this approach suggest that social problems are a function of the inability of people to fit into a relatively stable society or to be comfortable with their differences.

The classical model of clinical intervention has been extended in community mental health. People are usually viewed in terms of their deficits; and the aim of community mental health is to help individual people, as many as possible, by extending the reach of services to the undeserved, so as to enable them to adjust to the norms and expectations of the groups and organizations in which they participate. Person-centered strategies and tactics of intervention follow. Community mental health-oriented therapies such as brief treatment, crisis intervention, and pre-school programs which aim to prepare children for the demands of the public schools are examples. Each of these has a person-centered orientation. Although they may be aimed at prevention of problems in an individual life, they do not aim at structural changes (i.e., changing schools), which may influence large numbers of people without direct treatment.

The specific content of the intervention, with individuals, depends on how individual behavior is understood, such that one program for crisis intervention may be based on psychodynamic conceptions and another on principles of behavior modification. What they share is their person-centered focus, which derives from the individual level of analysis. This would be the case whether the intervention is intended to be preventive or rehabilitative. For example, if unemployment is viewed as a problem for mental health, then one might, as a clinical psychologist, be concerned about assisting individuals who seek help to develop personal strategies for increasing their employability. A community mental health worker interested in prevention may try to extend such strategies of individual counseling and training to an entire at-risk (high-unemployment) neighborhood. He or she would not be likely to develop programs for the creation of new jobs or to use tactics such as advocacy and/or attempts to influence social-policy legislation. Rather, one might set up more accessible centers for employment training, preparing people for tests and interviews.

A second source of intervention is derived from the small-group level of analysis. In this view, social problems are created by interpersonal difficulties within primary groups, such as family, peer, and work groups. Deficits in the group, rather than in the individual, are seen to account for problems ranging from a need for better communication (e.g., between police and members of a local neighborhood, or within a family) to problems of cooperation in the work place.

The small-group level of analysis leads one to use conceptions from the group dynamics and family treatment literature. Strategies of clinical intervention include family therapy, interpersonal communication training, sensitivity groups, and the group therapies—all variants of the classical, clinical model for service delivery.

A third source of intervention strategies follows from the organizational level of analysis. Attention to this level assumes that many social problems are created by the socialization, education, employment, and welfare organizations of society, which often fail to implement, as well as they might, and particularly for certain "out groups," their supposed social function.

Schein (1970) defines an organization as ". . . the rational coordination of the activities of a number of people for the achievement of some common or explicit purpose or goal, through division of responsibility, and through a hierarchy of authority and responsibility." The common purpose or goal often remains abstract or implicit; and an emphasis at this level of analysis is on how to accomplish the goal.

A useful distinction can be drawn here between organizations and institutions. An organization is a specific setting, usually (but not necessarily) contained within walls. These are the operational places by which a society attempts to actualize, in concrete form, its social intentions. For example, a public school is an organization designed to carry out the social values, goals, and abstract ideas behind the institution of public education. A mental health center is an organization designed to carry out the aims, values, goals, and sociocultural ideals of mental health, which have already been institutionalized.

Much of organizational-level intervention is an attempt to enhance the likelihood that organizations will assist individuals to fit into existing social roles. The deficits and weaknesses of people are usually implied, but the focus is on enhancing organizational ability to cope with them. Conceptions from public health, social-systems analysis, and ecological and environmental psychology are often involved (Rappaport, 1977b); systems-centered consultation and organization development are frequent strategies of intervention (Goodstein, 1978; Katz & Kahn, 1966).

A fourth level of analysis is based on broader social critique and may be thought of as the institutional, community, or social policy level. When applied to our field, this level has generally (but not necessarily) been consistent with a social change (as opposed to a social stability) orientation. It suggests that many social problems are created by our underlying institutions and policies per se, rather than by individual persons, groups, or specific organizations. Although there are many problems in an organization which may benefit from specific changes, the key to sensible, efficient improvement of problems in living for entire populations is viewed to require change at the level of social policy. Frequently used strategies are advocacy and the creation of new settings. This often involves cultural, value-based, political, and economic decisions. Power relationships, diversity of values, strengths of target populations, cultural relativity, and the need for resources are frequently confronted issues. The very intentions (implicit as well as explicit) of our social institutions, as well as the research questions asked (cf. Seidman, 1978) may come into question.

Although a consideration of the proper level of analysis for dealing with any given social problem is clearly an intellectual choice, it is also an intrinsically political one. It is not possible to know what form or direction any given intervention may take without knowing a good deal about the values and goals of the interventionist. The values and goals behind any social intervention tend to dictate the level of analysis, conception, strategy, and tactic used. To the extent that this is the case, an important contribution of the social and community perspective, which offers an expansion of our strategies and tactics by means of raising questions vis-à-vis the proper level of analysis, is to permit the clinician to examine his or her values and goals before applying an intervention strategy. It may very well turn out that the tools (strategies and tactics) one has been accustomed to using are actually contradictory to the values and goals one wishes to accomplish (Rappaport, 1977b). If so, the interventionist may need to learn new strategies and tactics more consistent with his or her values and goals.

In a discussion similar to this one, Goodstein and Sandler (1978) have attempted to understand intervention strategies, by an analysis of the target, the content, the process or style, and the knowledge base. Table 3 summarizes their "model for using psychology to promote human welfare." By *content*, Goodstein and Sandler mean the activity involved in bringing about change (e.g., psychotherapy, social action, and so on). By *process of intervention*, they refer to issues, such as those we have noted above, with regard to the waiting and the seeking modes of intervention. *Body of knowledge* refers to the theoretical and empirical underpinnings of any intervention. Finally, these authors speak of the *target* of the intervention. As they point out, "all interventions must affect the lives of individuals" (p. 883), but the immediate object of any intervention may range from troubled individuals, through social systems, to government administrators and legislators. It is this dimension (the target of the intervention) which they use to suggest that attention to level of analysis is important. They distinguish classical methods of clinical psychology from community mental health, community psychology, and public policy psychology, in this way. These latter two are the approaches which tend to involve social and community interventions (although community mental health will involve this to some extent). Table 3 provides another convenient way of summarizing many of the options open to psychologists who wish to explore the expansion of their tools, roles, problems of focus, and knowledge base.

The agent of transmission

In recent years, there have been two contradictory trends operative in the human service fields. One, the professionalization of clinical psychology, is marked by efforts to strengthen licensing laws and to impose more uniform controls or accreditation of training programs. The adoption, by the American Psychology Association, of the doctorate as the minimum standard for the practice of psychology represents protection of both the public and guild concerns. Issues such as third-party (government and private insurance) payments for health care are influential. Legitimate educational and professional issues are also at stake (Stern, 1981); but the trend toward professionalization has contributed little to our substantive understanding of the helping process. Rather, a trend in the opposite direction has been most important to the conceptual evolution of clinical psychology. This trend is one which has broadened our understanding and our choices as to who may be an appropriate and effective agent for the transmission of help to people experiencing problems in living.

Beginning with the pioneering work of people such as Rioch (1966),

Table 3

A conceptual model for using psychology to promote human welfare

		Conceptual elements		
Strategy	*Target*	*Content*	*Process or style*	*Knowledge*
Clinical psychology	Troubled individuals	Individual assessment and behavior change	Passive style; professional accountable to fulfill contract with individual clients	Individual differences; personality; psychopathology; individual assessment and behavior change
Community mental health	Catchment area	Planning, organizing, delivering, and evaluating relevant services	Accountability of residents of catchment area and funding sources	Program planning and development; administration and management; facilitating community involvement; evaluation research; program evaluation; specialized clinical services; selection and training of paraprofessionals; supervision
	Troubled individual within catchment area	Clinical services relevant to catchment area	Active marketing of service; accountability of consumer groups	
	Significant others in catchment area	Consultation; training; education; coordination of effort	Role definition and clarification; professional gatekeeper	Methods of consultation and training in helping relationships; understanding of other social agencies and community resources; organizational dynamics; psychopathology; cultural difference

Community psychology	Systems of deviance control	Analysis of system; technical advocacy; creation of settings; organizational development; evaluation research	Critic of system; advocate of change; facilitator of self-examination by system; developer of planned change strategies	Systems analysis; program design-evaluation research; consultation methods; advocacy strategies
	Systems of socialization and support	Restructuring organizations to facilitate healthy personal functioning	Organizational consultation outside of mental health; advocacy of social change; resolution of professional-client value discrepancies	Systems analysis; organizational theory; planned change strategies; social planning; environmental assessment; stress theory
Public policy psychology	Government policy makers, including administrators, legislators, and judges	Technical advice in formulation of public policy; social action on a broad front; program evaluation; expert witness	Adversary system; agent of control or countercontrol; participant in political process	Knowledge of policy formulation and implementation; broad knowledge of other relevant social sciences (e.g., economics); understanding of the political process and the law; evaluation research

Source: From Goodstein & Sandler, 1978.

Poser (1966), Reissman (Gartner & Reissman, 1977; Reiff & Reissman, 1965), Holzberg (1963), Bard (1970), and Cowen (Cowen, Trost, Lorion, Dorr, Izzo, & Isaacson, 1975), the 1960s saw a recognition of the value of nonprofessionals in the mental health delivery system (see reviews by Durlak, 1979; Gruver, 1971; Guerney, 1969; Karlsruher, 1974; Rappaport, 1977a; Sobey, 1970). Short of arguing that people other than those with formal degrees in a mental health profession are a panacea, there evolved in the 1970s a widespread acceptance of the reality that many people, who are earning their living in other than one of the mental health professions (such as students, housewives, or retired workers), can be helpful to others with problems in living.

There are several ways in which this development influenced clinical psychology to step outside the confines of the clinic. One is by allowing psychologists to supervise the work of nonprofessionals in the formal, mental health delivery system. Nonprofessionals have served as therapists, advocates, neighborhood outreach workers, and hospital or outpatient group leaders, for a variety of clients, ranging from children in public schools, through adolescents in legal difficulty (Seidman, Rappaport, & Davidson, 1980), and chronic mental patients (Rappaport, Chinsky, & Cowen, 1971). The use of this diverse, relatively more available, source of person power has extended the reach of human services to a variety of undeserved groups. Such services may be provided by paid nonprofessionals or by volunteers. In either case, their work has generally been under the training and supervision of professionals; and there are many examples in the literature as well as a variety of suggestions for evaluation (Seidman & Rappaport, 1974), training (Ehrlich, D'Augelli, & Conter, 1981), and selection (Kramer, Rappaport, & Seidman, 1979; Lindquist & Rappaport, 1973; Rappaport, Gross, & Lepper, 1973).

A second way in which other-than-professional mental health workers have been recognized as agents of human service is through the observation that certain occupations place people in role relationships which allow them to influence the course of coping with crisis for large numbers of people. For example, teachers, librarians, policemen, bartenders, divorce lawyers, ministers, nurses, hair dressers, and foremen in a plant, as a consequence of their occupational duties, are frequently placed in a position to listen to (and perhaps influence) people with problems in living (Cowen, 1982a; Haas & Weatherly, 1981). Such helpers are not hired by the mental health system, nor are they volunteering their services as mental health workers. In fact, they probably do not even think of themselves as having anything to do with mental health. An explicit acknowledgment of the fact that most people do not seek out professional mental health workers and that help is often wherever one finds it, provides the social/community interventionist with an almost endless set of possibilities for extending influence. Some may engage in consultation to people in key social roles, so as to help them to think more systematically about what they are already doing, or to enlist their aid as people to whom others in need might be referred for advice, friendship, and assistance. Others may conduct research to learn how such people are effective, in order to add to our own knowledge base.

A third way in which our understanding of the importance of other-than-professional helpers has expanded the continuum of potential agents of transmission is through the development of self-help groups (Lieberman & Borman, 1979; Lieberman & Glidewell, 1978). The ideology of the community mental health movement has been quite consistent with the rise in legitimacy of self-help groups. In many ways, people coming together out of mutual concern—not for pay, nor as volunteers, but rather as peers mutually sharing their lives, without professional intervention—is the ideal of a strength-based, preventively oriented, mental health system.

A further extension of the agent of transmission of help has come to be thought of as the vehicle of natural support systems (see reviews by Cobb, 1976; Collins & Pancoast, 1976; Dohrenwend & Dohrenwend, 1981; Gottlieb, 1979; Gottlieb & Todd, 1979; Hirsch, 1981; Mitchell & Trickett, 1980; Tolsdorf, 1976). These are the less-formal, less-intentional helping relationships which exist between significant others. The obvious (but heretofore, largely ignored) reality is that family, friends, church and neighborhood groups, clubs and organizations make up a human fabric in people's lives which is often the one through which problems in living are filtered, solved, made more complicated, or altered. It is important for those who take a public health-, preventive-, or policy-oriented view of mental health services to realize that most people never seek out professional or formal, nonprofessional mental health services. Most people work out their problems in living in their own natural support settings. Some of these settings will be effective, helpful ones, and others less so. Recognition of the phenomenon of natural support systems has lead to a realization that, by studying such settings, it may be possible for helping professionals to learn important information about how the process of help proceeds.

Comprehending that helping phenomena exist outside the rather narrowly defined therapeutic context enables us to study and influence it among a wider variety of populations and helpers. It enables clinical psychologists to enter the natural environment as observers, rather than manipulators and to learn from those settings and people the conditions under which helping is working well (Masterpasqua, 1981). It also enables the psychologist to appreciate the ways in which a diversity of people, such as members of minority groups, offer one another cultural strengths, even if those differ from mainstream, middle-class strengths (cf. Mitchell, Barbarin, & Hurley, 1981; Padilla, 1981; Rappaport, Davidson, Wilson,

& Mitchell, 1975). Given this perspective, the potential to learn the sorts of things we need to know for a genuinely preventive psychology that engages the richness of community life is considerably broadened.

To summarize, a fifth step toward expanding the choices available to clinical psychologists has been an expansion of our understanding of who can be an agent of transmission in the helping process. This has taken us from the study of professional mental health agents, to other professionals, nonprofessionals, self-help groups, and natural support people and settings, such as family, friends, clubs, churches, and neighbors. The social/community interventionist is interested in studying as well as in using all such agents of transmission. This perspective is particularly salient to those with an interest in prevention of problems in living, since learning how settings—which most people already have in their lives— work when they are helpful, and encouraging their use, may be a more realistic vehicle to the widespread reach of human helping than expecting everyone to seek out clinical services.

Goals of intervention

A sixth way in which the choices available to clinical psychologists have been expanded arises from the slow-but-sure development of ideas which were originally brought into the modern mental health movement from public health by Caplan's classic book, *The Principles of Preventive Psychiatry* (1964). Caplan described three different ways in which mental health professionals may help communities to reduce the probability of serious mental illness. Tertiary prevention, more properly called rehabilitation, involves providing community supports for those who have already experienced serious maladjustment. Here, the aim is to reduce the duration of an identified mental patient's career or need for continuous or revolving door custodial care in mental hospitals. Secondary prevention, on the other hand, by early diagnosis and treatment, attempts to reduce the length and severity of emotional problems, by providing services early in the course of the disorder. Secondary prevention entails both attempts to treat psychopathology at the early stages of its appearance and attempts to discover high-risk clients ontogenetically early (i.e., during childhood), so as to change the course of their psychological development.

Finally, Caplan introduced the notion of primary prevention. His definition remains the best available:

> Primary prevention is a community concept. It involves lowering the rate of new cases of mental disorder in a population over a certain period by counteracting harmful circumstances before they have had a chance to produce illness. It does not seek to prevent a specific person from becoming sick. Instead, it seeks to reduce the risk for a whole population, so that, although some may become ill, their number will be reduced. It thus con-

trasts with individual patient-oriented psychiatry, which focuses on a single person and deals with general influences only insofar as they are combined in his unique experience. (1964, p. 26)

Cowen (1980) has clearly articulated the "two key aspects of primary prevention's definition, i.e., its mass-orientation and before-the-fact qualities" (p. 262). Cowen (1980) and others (Bloom, 1979; Catalano & Dooley, 1980) have recently gone on to fine tune the meaning of primary prevention.

Bloom (1979) and Price, Bader, and Ketterer (1980) have noted the recent shift in attention from high-risk populations to high-risk situations and events. Thus, there has been a progression of interest, from predisposing factors, to stress-producing situations and life events (e.g., school transitions, alienating organizations, unemployment). Attempts to work with high-risk populations and attempts to alleviate high-risk situations and events are both aimed at preventing maladjustment. Recently, the definition of primary prevention has been expanded, even beyond the prevention of maladjustment, to include the promotion of health (Cowen, 1980). As Cowen depicts the prevention of maladjustment, its thrust is more reactive than proactive, and its mode is therapeutic with educational possibilities, while the promotion of health is fundamentally proactive with an educational or structural change mode. Catalano and Dooley (1980) describe two major subtypes of primary prevention as reactive and proactive; their definitions are reasonably congruent with those of Cowen (1980).

For those readers who may wish to concretize the wide variety of primary prevention programs current in the field, two recent collections are recommended. One, edited by Price, Ketterer, Bader, and Monahan (1980), reviews conceptual and empirical research as diverse as prevention of domestic violence, child maltreatment, problems among children of divorce, school maladjustment, delinquency, and problems in the workplace. The second is a series of empirical program evaluation studies assembled for a special issue of *The American Journal of Community Psychology,* under the editorship of Cowen (1982b). Targets of intervention in the special issue include: infants, young children, adolescents, young adults, middle-aged adults, and retired groups, all of whom are sociodemographically and ethnically diverse. Populations studied include predominantly healthy as well as at-risk groups.

The study of healthy people is long overdue for clinical psychology. It emerges quite logically, however, as an extension of the goals of prevention. For those who wish to prevent psychological dysfunction, understanding people who function well and the social conditions which make it possible is essential. Phrased otherwise, the goal of prevention must naturally lead psychology to the study of processes which foster "empowerment" (Kieffer, 1981; Rappaport, 1981). Psychologically, empowerment may be described as enhancing the sense of control over one's life. It is the opposite of alienation; yet, more than the study of individual people is implied. It also includes recognizing the broader potential of settings and environments in which people live their lives as places which can and do provide their members with a psychological sense of community and meaning. The study of such settings may provide us with clues about the kinds of social policies which we ought to be encouraging our society to adopt. In order to inform ourselves, we need to study well-functioning families, neighborhoods, churches, and voluntary groups, so as to discover what it is that enables a setting to provide well for its members. Armed with this knowledge and with the goal of making such settings accessible to more people, clinical psychologists may be able to help foster social policies which would make it more likely that larger numbers of people will benefit from our knowledge.

In the last section of this chapter, we trace the way in which the social and community perspective has been applied to one of society's most difficult and enduring social problems—serious emotional disturbance.

APPLICATION OF THE SOCIAL AND COMMUNITY PERSPECTIVE TO PROBLEMS OF SERIOUS EMOTIONAL DISTURBANCE

In the 1950s, mental hospitals were bursting at their seams with patients. The dominant view of the day was that these patients were diseased and suffering from various biological or intrapsychic maladies. Treatment was delivered almost exclusively in the passive waiting style of delivery. Hospital patients were most often treated by custodial or biological methods. Psychotherapy was reserved for the few who were better educated or financially better off. Problems were generally conceptualized from an individual level of analysis, and treatment required the individual to conform to the status quo. Patients were seen to have a variety of deficits or liabilities, with regard to a societally defined single standard of adjustment. Not surprisingly, the therapeutic agent was almost exclusively a mental health professional or someone acting under his or her instructions. As is evident from this description, treatment was rehabilitative in nature, in that it consisted of treating an already well-established chronic problem.

In the sociopolitical milieu of the 1960s, many psychologists became increasingly concerned with social issues; and, correspondingly, social and environmental explanations of human behavior became more prevalent (Levine & Levine, 1970). Concurrent with these changes, many began to develop new forms of treatment, with an emphasis on social and community intervention. The work of Fairweather and his colleagues is exemplary of the evolution of services for those with severe emotional disturbances (Fairweather, 1964; Fairweather, Sanders, Cressler, & Maynard, 1969; Fairweather, Sanders, & Tornatsky, 1974).

Fairweather's (1964) initial work began with an assessment of the comparative efficacy of individual and group treatment for seriously disturbed, Veterans Administration hospital patients. He eventually developed a program emphasizing an autonomous small group working together within a mental hospital and found that he was able to prepare patients for discharge. Here we can see expansion of the domains for understanding and intervention. The conception of individual behavior had become much more social environmental in nature. There was much less of an attempt to have the patient adapt to the prevailing mores of the hospital, as groups allowed patients greater freedom in developing their own treatment plans. The mode of service delivery was much more active than in traditional individual treatment. The level of analysis had moved more toward the small group and the individual patient's relationship to the small group setting. Each individual patient was expected to assume the role of agent of transmission of the services, while the professional's role was increasingly minimized; yet, the program remained one of rehabilitation.

Although successful in preparing patients to leave the hospital, Fairweather found that they were unable to remain in independent work and living arrangements for any significant length of time. They seemed to lack the necessary social supports to remain autonomous.

Eventually, Fairweather and his colleagues decided that the hospital-based work and living units needed to be placed as is in the community. What resulted has been referred to as the "community lodge" (Fairweather et al., 1969). Here, former mental patients worked and lived as an autonomous unit outside the hospital. Professionals helped to set up the initial arrangements and then gradually phased themselves out. Eventually, the patients received very minimal attention from mental health professionals, other than at their own request. Each lodge allowed its members the opportunity to be self-supporting, by being a part of a community and having a defined set of responsibilities in an autonomous, patient-run janitorial business. Consequently, patients no longer found themselves in the characteristic "one-down" relationship with the "doctor who knows best." They were empowered to make their own decisions vis-à-vis daily living and work, in an environment that was independent of the mental health system.

One of the key ingredients in the lodges was the fact that the peer group tolerated a much wider latitude of behavior than the typical community setting, so long as the behavior did not interfere with work. For example, at the lodge, a member might be permitted to hallucinate; but on the job, his peers expected him to control himself. Members of the lodge were demonstrably more successful in autonomous community living than patients randomly assigned to hospital treatment and eventual release without the lodge.

The success of the Fairweather lodge with people who were seriously and chronically disturbed has taught us several things: first, accepting the implicit assumption that severe emotional disturbance is best treated in the hospital may not lead to the most beneficial outcomes; second, questioning the implicit assumptions we make about individual behavior, style of delivery, and role of the professional is not only feasible, but can lead to more effective intervention than is typical; third, an expanding knowledge base is required of the mental health professional. It is no longer sufficient to be expert in individual diagnosis and treatment; one needs to understand the social psychology of small groups, the role of work in adjustment, the nature of community settings, and their differential receptivity to those who are different, and so on. Thus, it is incumbent upon the mental health professionals who deal with problems of serious psychopathology to increase their knowledge of fields such as social psychology, economics, and urban planning or to collaborate with others who are knowledgeable.

Fairweather and his colleagues provide us with an excellent illustration of the care and attention necessary to make de-institutionalization a reality. Unfortunately, while others began to favor reduction of the size of mental hospitals, many de-institutionalization efforts have been little more than dumping the unwanted into a hostile and ill-prepared community. Nevertheless, the success of a few, carefully done de-institutionalization efforts leads to the conclusion that the negative course of institutionalization can be arrested and reversed, if well conceived and executed. Others have suggested that it may be better to intervene at the point of psychiatric admission or even earlier, rather than to wait for people to become institutionalized.

The Stein, Test, and Marx group (in Madison, Wisconsin) have systematically worked at taking the patient at the point of hospital admission and sending him or her back into the community (Marx, Test, & Stein, 1973; Stein & Test, 1980; Stein, Test, & Marx, 1975). These patients have all had severe psychiatric problems and had spent about 50 percent of their time in the psychiatric hospital during the recent past. Nevertheless, within one week of hospital admission, they were placed in various independent-living situations, depending on their individual resources and needs. The goal was for them to make it in the natural environment, despite the fact that hospital officials deemed them not ready. Rather than working as hospital attendants, staff took on the roles of advocate, resource finder, and teacher. At first, staff were available on a 24-hour basis; but, gradually, they phased themselves out. Staff helped individual clients to find jobs, aided them in daily living and grooming skills, prodded and supported recreational and social activity, and encouraged others to view patients as responsible citizens, including allowing them to experience the natural consequences of their actions (e.g., spending a day or two in jail for breaking the law). In general, the staff endeavored to keep the patients independent of the usual mental health system and to help them obtain resources for daily living.

While there were few differences in psychiatric symptomatology between the community treatment group and those who were randomly assigned to the usual hospital regime, the community treatment group was far more successful at maintaining themselves in independent living arrangements. This is particularly remarkable for a group considered "unreleasable" by many mental health professionals.

Unlike traditional psychiatric services, the Madison project attributes increased importance to a socioenvironmental conception of individual psychopathology. The project endeavors to help the larger society to accept the patient, as much as it endeavors to get the patient to adapt to the norms of society. It discourages adaptation to the artificial and iatrogenic hospital setting. The style of delivering services is far more active than usual. The focus of change is not simply on the individual patient, but on the relationships between patient and family, employer, landlord, and mental health professionals. The initial primary agent of service delivery is the paraprofessional, who is phased out over time. The project focus is on development of social support networks and personal responsibility. Finally, this program has taken a small but significant step, by attempting to intervene earlier in the career of the potential chronic mental patient.

Both the Madison and the Lodge programs were part of the larger effort to de-institutionalize the mental health system. Of course, as experimental projects, they were carried out and observed with considerably greater diligence, care, and systematic research than the modal de-institutionalization effort, which has not been quite so successful. There are many reasons for the lack of success experienced by others. A useful way to understand the failures is to consider how they have tended not to take advantage of the new alternatives available to the field. This can be done systematically by returning to each of the six domains described above.

Most de-institutionalization programs never seriously question whether the antecedents to a patient's maladies are anything other than biochemical, genetic, or intrapsychic. It is usually held that the patient needs to adapt to society; society is seen as stable, rather than changing. The person continues to be viewed as the only legitimate object of change and is not provided with a clear niche into which he or she may fit, idiosyncrasies included. In many of these programs, the professional mental health worker or his agent continues to be viewed as the first line of defense. Few programs systematically pursue the individual or collective empowerment of former patients by structuring an environment and providing the necessary material resources. The strategy continues to be one of rehabilitation, but now in a community setting, which only tends to mean not in a hospital, but often does not have a systematic approach.

The failure to confront these difficulties makes it impossible to create novel and/or substantively different solutions. Nevertheless, this is not the only set of problems faced by those who would seriously work to keep as many people as possible out of mental hospitals.

Even for many of the more successful programs, recidivism seems to go up dramatically after two years (see, for example, reviews by Dellario & Anthony, 1981; Fenton, Tessier, & Struening, 1979; Test, 1981; Test & Stein, 1978). There is nothing magical about two years; but after two years, the experimental nature of the program has usually ended and, unless a sufficiently stable, ongoing social support network has been built-in, most patients can not make it on their own. In some sense, too little collective and individual empowerment has been established for this population to survive. This even appears to be true of the Madison project (Test, 1981).

Ironically, those programs that have been successful tend to remain experimental and temporary, rather than to become integrated into the ongoing network of community life. That problem is one which requires solution if we are to progress toward the goal of maintenance of more people living with a reasonable quality of life outside of the mental hospital. One way to solve the problem is to capitalize on naturally evolving community groups available to patients when they are released from professional care.

Ultimately, the success or failure in community adjustment will depend less on our ability as professionals to create supportive environments, or to teach specific skills, and more on our ability to find and encourage naturally occurring niches. These niches are where people find meaning in life, mutual (rather than unidirectional) relationships, and consistent, ongoing structures to depend on (Maton & Rappaport, 1983). These are the kinds of settings which those who experience serious psychopathology are often unable to find. Indeed, there has been very little research which has studied well-established, naturally occurring (that is, not professionally developed) settings, which are available to people who are left to maintain themselves in the world when the professionals, the aftercare workers, and the volunteers have gone home. This is one place to which future research must attend. We need to discover how to increase the likelihood that people with serious emotional disturbance can have access to such community settings. At this point, we can simply say that previous research clearly points us in that direction.

While most self-help groups have very little in common with these kinds of settings, self-help organizations which are more than simply groups (i.e., those that are entire social networks) may be one kind of answer. Such organizations, where the agents of transmission become the patients themselves, are of increasing interest to social and community interventionists (Seidman & Rappaport, 1981).

In addition to work with people who are already chronic patients, social and community interventions in the mental health system have attempted to prevent any hospital contact at all. Delaney, Seidman, and Willis (1978) report the development and evaluation of a novel and successful crisis-intervention project aimed at the prevention of institutionalization. Many people are institutionalized at the time of a crisis, because alternative solutions are neither thought about nor explored. Institutionalization frequently appears to family, friends, and legal and mental health personnel as the only available option. That is, the problem is traditionally framed as one of individual psychological deviance requiring institutional treatment. In the Delaney et al. (1978) project, a relationship was developed with the state attorney's office where all "mental petitions" for hospitalization were filed. Before acting on a petition, the crisis intervention team was notified and went out within 24 hours to see the client in his or her natural context. The team also established positive working relationships with other formal and informal helpers in the community (e.g., physicians, ministers). These helpers called upon the crisis team when they were presented with appropriate situations.

The first assessment issue for the crisis team was to determine if the crisis was in need of assistance from a mental health agency. In many cases, it was definitely not; although, in most of these cases, the people involved needed some type of assistance. The assistance may have taken any of a variety of forms including: education and help in the decision-making process; clarification of the lines of communication at the interfaces of individual and family, employer, school, or other social agency; referral to the appropriate resources in order to connect the person with the services he or she was in need of; or serving the not uncommon, "powerless" client in the role of advocate, enabling him or her to negotiate his or her needs with the bureaucratic organizational structure of some social agency.

If the need for additional evaluation and treatment by a mental health agency beyond the scope of the brief crisis-related activity was indicated, referral was made to a mental health agency. Referral was based on a hierarchy of desirable mental health alternatives. The hierarchy was developed as a function of the settings, consistent with the principles of the community mental health movement (i.e., local control, brevity, outpatient services).

The crisis team only accepted the problem as presented after exploring a variety of alternative problem definitions and resolutions. The locus of the problem and resolution was often found to be the relationships between the client and his or her significant others or social service agencies. Consequently, hospitalization or any form of mental health treatment was often unnecessary or inappropriate; other social and community resources were frequently mobilized for problem resolution.

Thus, once again, we see conceptions of individual behavior in community intervention to be socioenvironmental in nature; changes in organizational procedures are targeted, as opposed to individual adaptation to prevailing standards; delivery of services is quite active; the level of analysis crosses between different units of social organization; the agents of transmission are paraprofessionals and indigenous actors, not simply mental health professionals; and this project obviously illustrates expansion of the goals of intervention toward preventing (rather than coping) with institutionalization.

Social and community interventionists are also interested in preventing emotional distress even before it gets to the point of a crisis. A very robust relationship has been demonstrated between the state of the economy and psychological well-being or mental illness at the national, state, and regional levels (Brenner, 1973, 1976; Dooley & Catalano, 1980; Seidman & Rapkin, in press). This linkage leads directly to implications for primary prevention. Yet little, if any, primary prevention has been carried out on the basis of the economics-psychosocial dysfunction linkage. Thus, we must ask what types of primary prevention programs might be conducted on the basis of this linkage.

We might begin by developing and evaluating programs aimed at preventing maladjustment (i.e., reactive primary prevention). Dooley and Catalano (1980) review a variety of studies that demonstrate the negative impact of unemployment on psychological well-being. Counseling and educational programs to inform those about to become unemployed may serve to inoculate these potential victims against many of the untoward effects. Clinical psychologists already have the skills to create such an intervention program. A reactive primary prevention program of this nature must use an expanded knowledge base, an environmental conception of human dysfunction, an active style of delivering services, and multiple levels of intervention.

When we turn to health promotion (or proactive primary prevention), we need to expand the boundaries of our current modes of thinking and acting even further. Catalano and Dooley (1980) discuss the public management of economic change as a means of promoting psychological health. This involves, not only behavioral cost-benefit analyses, but involvement in the arena of economic policy, preferably at the local and regional levels. For a fuller understanding of their suggestions, the reader is referred to their chapter. Here, we point out that individual conceptions of human behavior play little role in such programs, and changing society is a prime focus. The program is not only active, but it is also aimed at an institutional level of analysis and intervention. Nevertheless, despite the obvious differences from a more traditional clinical psychology, the aim of such a program is legitimately within the domain of the clinical psychologist. What it requires is professionals who are willing to take advantage of the expanded number of alternative ways in which clinical psychologists may now approach the mental health field. For those who are dissatisfied with our limited progress to date, social and community intervention is a viable choice.

SUMMARY

In this chapter, we have endeavored to demonstrate an expanding universe of alternative solutions available to the clinical psychologist. The key element to this expanding universe is willingness and ability to reframe the very way in which one states or thinks about the initial problem. It requires both stepping outside the usual role relationship between client and clinician and a commitment to learning and adopting new and diverse methods for intervention.

Reframing is enhanced in two major ways. The first is by keeping the three central themes of the social/community perspective foremost in one's mind. These themes are prevention and empowerment, attention to competence and strengths, and an emphasis on social and public policy. The second is by questioning the implicit assumptions underlying traditional ways of thinking and modes of acting. This implies questioning the assumptions that: (a) psychological dysfunction is exclusively a consequence of biological or intrapsychic processes; (b) individuals need to adapt to static social norms and mores; (c) services can only be delivered in a passive-waiting style; (d) individuals or small groups are the appropriate unit of analysis/intervention; (e) only experts can deliver psychological services; and (f) problems should await the need for rehabilitation.

Application of the technique of reframing to problems of serious emotional disturbance illustrates the expansion of ways of conceptualizing and intervening in an area of historical and contemporary interest to clinical psychology. Hopefully, that example may serve as a model to facilitate continued expansion of the universe of alternatives in this and other areas of concern, with the ultimate goal being not only the improved psychosocial well-being of individuals, but of communities as well.

REFERENCES

Allen, G. J., Chinsky, J. M., Larcen, S. W., Lochman, J. E., & Selinger, H. E. *Community psychology and the schools: A behaviorally oriented, multilevel preventive approach.* Hillsdale, N.J.: Lawrence Erlbaum Associates, 1976.

Bandura, A. *Principles of behavior modification.* New York: Holt, Rinehart & Winston, 1969.

Bard, M. *Training police as specialists in family crisis intervention.* National Institute of Law Enforcement and Criminal Justice, Washington, D.C.: U.S. Government Printing Office, 1970.

Bevan, W. On getting in bed with a lion. *American Psychologist,* 1980, *35,* 779–789.

Bloom, B. L. *Community mental health: A historical and critical analysis.* Morristown, N.J.: General Learning Press, 1973.

Bloom, B. L. *Community mental health.* Monterey, Calif.: Brooks/Cole Publishing, 1977.

Bloom, B. L. The prevention of mental disorders: Recent advances in theory and practice. *Community Mental Health Journal,* 1979, *15,* 179–191.

Bloom, B. L. Social and community interventions. *Annual Review of Psychology,* 1980, *31,* 111–142.

Brenner, M. H. *Mental illness and the economy.* Cambridge, Mass.: Harvard University Press, 1973.

Brenner, M. H. *Estimating the social costs of economic policy: Implications for mental and physical health, and criminal aggression.* Report to the Congressional Research Service of the Library of Congress and Joint Economic Committee of Congress. Washington, D.C.: U.S. Government Printing Office, 1976.

Campbell, J. P., & Dunnette, M. D. (Eds.). *Handbook of industrial and organizational psychology.* Skokie, Ill.: Rand McNally, 1976.

Caplan, G. *Principles of preventive psychiatry.* New York: Basic Books, 1964.

Catalano, R. *Health, behavior, and the community.* Elmsford, N.Y.: Pergamon Press, 1979.

Catalano, R., & Dooley, D. Economic change in primary prevention. In R. H. Price, R. F. Ketterer, B. C. Bader, & J. Monahan (Eds.), *Prevention in mental health.* Beverly Hills, Calif.: Sage Publications, 1980.

Cobb, S. Social support as a moderator of life stress. *Psychosomatic Medicine,* 1976, *3,* 300–314.

Collins, A. H., & Pancoast, D. L. *Natural helping networks: A strategy for prevention.* Washington, D.C.: National Association of Social Workers, 1976.

Cowen, E. L. Social and community interventions. *Annual Review of Psychology,* 1973, *24,* 423–472.

Cowen, E. L. The wooing of primary prevention. *American Journal of Community Psychology,* 1980, *8,* 258–284.

Cowen, E. L. Help is where you find it: Four informal helping groups. *American Psychologist,* 1982a, *37,* 385–395.

Cowen, E. L. (Ed.). Research in primary prevention in mental health. *American Journal of Community Psychology,* 1982b, *10*(3-special issue).

Cowen, E. L., Gardner, E. A., & Zax, M. (Eds.). *Emergent approaches to mental health problems.* New York: Appleton-Century-Crofts, 1967.

Cowen, E. L., Trost, M. A., Lorion, R. P., Dorr, D., Izzo, L. D., & Isaacson, R. V. *New ways in school mental health: Early detection and prevention of school maladaption.* New York: Human Sciences Press, 1975.

Delaney, J. A., Seidman, E., & Willis, G. Crisis intervention and the prevention of institutionalization: An interrupted time-series analysis. *American Journal of Community Psychology,* 1978, *6,* 33–45.

Dellario, D. J., & Anthony, W. A. On the relative effectiveness of institutional and alternative placement for the psychiatrically disabled. *Journal of Social Issues,* 1981, *37,* 21–33.

Dohrenwend, B. S., & Dohrenwend, B. P. Socioenvironmental factors, stress, and psychopathology. *American Journal of Community Psychology,* 1981, *9,* 128–159.

Dooley, D., & Catalano, R. Economic change as a cause of behavioral disorder. *Psychological Bulletin,* 1980, *87,* 450–468.

Durlak, J. A. Comparative effectiveness of paraprofessional and professional helpers. *Psychological Bulletin,* 1979, *86,* 80–92.

Ehrlich, R. P., D'Augelli, A. R., & Conter, K. R. Evaluation of a community-based system for training natural helpers. I: Effects on verbal helping skills. *American Journal of Community Psychology*, 1981, *9*(3), 321–337.

Fairweather, G. W. (Ed.). *Social psychology in treating mental illness: An experimental approach.* New York: John Wiley & Sons, 1964.

Fairweather, G. W., Sanders, D. H., Cressler, D. L., & Maynard, H. *Community life for the mentally ill: An alternative to institutional care.* Hawthorne, N.Y.: Aldine Publishing, 1969.

Fairweather, G. W., Sanders, D. H., & Tornatzky, L. G. *Creating change in mental health organizations.* Elmsford, N.Y.: Pergamon Press, 1974.

Fawcett, S. B., Mathews, R. M., & Fletcher, R. K. Some promising dimensions for behavioral community technology. *Journal of Applied Behavior Analysis* 1980, *13*, 505–518.

Fenton, F. R., Tessier, L., & Struening, E. L. A comparative trial of home and hospital psychiatric care: One-year follow-up. *Archives of General Psychiatry*, 1979, *36*, 1073–1079.

Garbarino, J. Preventing child maltreatment. In R. H. Price, R. F. Ketterer, B. C. Bader, & J. Monahan (Eds.), *Prevention in mental health.* Beverly Hills, Calif.: Sage Publications, 1980.

Gartner, A., & Reissman, F. *Self-help in the human services.* San Francisco: Jossey-Bass, 1977.

Gergin, K. J. Social psychology as history. *Journal of Personality and Social Psychology*, 1973, *26*, 309–320.

Goodstein, L. D. (Ed.). *Consulting with human service systems.* Reading, Mass.: Addison-Wesley Publishing, 1978.

Goodstein, L. D., & Sandler, I. Using psychology to promote human welfare: A conceptual analysis of the role of community psychology. *American Psychologist*, 1978, *33*, 882–892.

Gottlieb, B. H. The primary groups as supportive milieu: Application to community psychology. *American Journal of Community Psychology*, 1979, *7*, 469–480.

Gottlieb, B. H., & Todd, D. M. Characterizing and promoting social support in natural settings. In R. F. Munoz, L. R. Snowden, J. G. Kelly, & Associates (Eds.), *Social and psychological research in community settings.* San Francisco: Jossey-Bass, 1979.

Gruver, G. G. College students as therapeutic agents. *Psychological Bulletin*, 1971, *76*, 111–127.

Guerney, B. G. (Ed.). *Psychotherapeutic agents: New roles for nonprofessionals, parents, and teachers.* New York: Holt, Rinehart & Winston, 1969.

Haas, L., & Weatherly, D. Community psychology in the library: Potentials for consultation. *American Journal of Community Psychology*, 1981, *9*, 109–122.

Heller, K., & Monahan, J. *Psychology and community change.* Homewood, Ill.: Dorsey Press, 1977.

Hirsch, B. J. Social networks and the coping process: Creating personal communities. In B. H. Gottlieb (Ed.), *Social networks and social support.* Beverly Hills, Calif.: Sage Publications, 1981.

Holzberg, J. D. The companion program: Implementing the manpower recommendations of the Joint Commission on Mental Illness and Health. *American Psychologist*, 1963, *18*, 224–226.

Joint Commission on Mental Health and Illness. *Action for mental health.* New York: John Wiley & Sons, 1961.

Karlsruher, A. E. The nonprofessional as a psychotherapeutic agent: A review of the empirical evidence pertaining to his effectiveness. *American Journal of Community Psychology,* 1974, *2,* 61–77.

Katz, D., & Kahn, R. L. *The social psychology of organizations.* New York: John Wiley & Sons, 1966.

Kelly, J. G., Snowden, L. R., & Munoz, R. F. Social and community interventions. *Annual Review of Psychology,* 1977, *28,* in press.

Kieffer, C. *The emergence of citizen empowerment: Research findings and developmental implications.* Paper presented at the National Conference on Lifelong Learning, University of Maryland, 1981.

Kramer J., Rappaport, J., & Seidman, E. Contribution of personal characteristics and interview training to the effectiveness of college student mental health workers. *Journal of Counseling Psychology,* 1979, *26,* 344–351.

Levine, M. & Levine, A. *A social history of helping services: Clinic, court, school, and community.* New York: Appleton-Century-Crofts, 1970.

Lieberman, M. A., & Borman, L. D. *Self-help groups for coping with crisis: Origins, members, processes, and impact.* San Francisco: Jossey-Bass, 1979.

Lieberman, M. A., & Glidewell, J. C. (Eds.). The helping process. *American Journal of Community Psychology,* 1978, *6* (5-special issue).

Lindquist, C. U., & Rappaport, J. Selection of college student therapeutic agents: Further analysis of the GAIT technique. *Journal of Consulting and Clinical Psychology,* 1973, *41,* 316.

Maccoby, N., & Alexander, J. Reducing heart disease risk using the mass media: Comparing the effects on three communities. In R. F. Munoz, L. R. Snowden, J. G. Kelly, & Associates (Eds.), *Social and psychological research in community settings.* San Francisco: Jossey-Bass, 1979.

Marx, A. J., Test, M. A., & Stein, L. I. Extrohospital management of severe mental illness. *Archives of General Psychiatry,* 1973, *29,* 505–511.

Masterpasqua, F. Toward a synergism of developmental and community psychology. *American Psychologist,* 1981, *36*(7), 782–786.

Maton, K. & Rappaport, J. Empowerment in a religious organization. *Prevention in Human Services* (special issue), 1983.

Mischel, W. *Personality and assessment.* New York: John Wiley & Sons, 1968.

Mitchell, R. E., Barbarin, O. A., & Hurley, D. J. Problem-solving resource utilization and community involvement in a black or white community. *American Journal of Community Psychology,* 1981, *9,* 233–246.

Mitchell, R. E., & Trickett, E. J. Social networks as mediators of social support: An analysis of the effects and determinants of social networks. *Community Mental Health Journal,* 1980, *16,* 27–44.

Munoz, R. F., Snowden, L. R., & Kelly, J. G. The process of implementing community-based research. In R. F. Munoz, L. R. Snowden, J. G. Kelly, & Associates (Eds.), *Social and psychological research in community settings.* San Francisco: Jossey-Bass, 1979.

Neitzel, M. T., Winett, R. A., MacDonald, M. S., & Davidson, W. S. *Behavioral approaches to community psychology.* Elmsford, N.Y.: Pergamon Press, 1977.

Padilla, A. Competent communities: A critical analyses of theories and public policy. In

O. Barbarin, P. Good, M. Pharr, & J. Suskind (Eds.), *Institutional racism and community competency. Rockville, Md.: Department of Health & Human Services, 1981.*

Poser, E. G. The effect of therapist training on group therapeutic outcome. *Journal of Consulting Psychology,* 1966, *30,* 283–289.

President's Commission on Mental Health. *Report to the President from the President's Commission on Mental Health* (Vols. 1–4). Washington, D.C.: U.S. Government Printing Office, 1978.

Price, R. H., Bader, B. C., & Ketterer, R. F. The state of the art. In R. H. Price, R. F. Ketterer, B. C. Bader, J. Monahan, & Associates (Eds.), *Prevention in mental health.* Beverly Hills, Calif.: Sage Publications, 1980.

Price, R. H., Ketterer, R. F., Bader, B. C., Monahan, J., & Associates (Eds.). *Prevention in mental health.* Beverly Hills, Calif.: Sage Publications, 1980.

Rappaport, J. *Community psychology: Values, research, and action.* New York: Holt, Rinehart & Winston, 1977. (a)

Rappaport, J. From Noah to Babel: Relationships between conceptions, values, analysis levels, and social intervention strategies. In I. Iscoe, B. Bloom, & C. D. Spielberger (Eds.), *Community psychology in transition.* New York: Hemisphere, 1977. (b)

Rappaport, J. In praise of paradox: A social policy of empowerment over prevention. *American Journal of Community Psychology,* 1981, *9,* 1–25.

Rappaport, J., & Chinsky, J. M. Models for delivery of service from a historical and conceptual perspective. *Professional Psychology,* 1974, *5,* 42–50.

Rappaport, J., Chinsky, J. M., & Cowen, E. L. *Innovations in helping chronic patients: College students in a mental institution.* New York: Academic Press, 1971.

Rappaport, J., Davidson, W., Mitchell, A., & Wilson, M. N. Alternatives to blaming the victim or the environment: Our places to stand have not moved the earth. *American Psychologist,* 1975, *30,* 525–528.

Rappaport, J., Gross, T., & Lepper, C. Modeling, sensitivity training, and instruction: Implications for the training of college student volunteers and for outcome research. *Journal of Consulting and Clinical Psychology,* 1973, *40,* 99–107.

Rappaport, J., Lamiell, J., & Seidman, E. Know and tell: Conceptual constraints, ethical issues, and alternatives for psychologists in (and out of) the juvenile justice system. In J. Monahan (Ed.), *Who is the client? The ethics of psychological intervention in the criminal justice system.* Washington, D.C.: American Psychological Association, 1980.

Redd, W. H., Porterfield, A. L., & Andersen, B. L. *Behavior modification: Behavioral approaches to human problems.* New York: Random House, 1979.

Reiff, R. R., & Reissman, F. The indigenous nonprofessional: A strategy of change in community action and community mental health programs. *Community Mental Health Journal Monograph,* 1965, (1).

Rioch, M. J. Changing concepts in the training of therapists. *Journal of Consulting Psychology,* 1966, *30,* 290–292.

Sarason, S. B. *The culture of the school and the problem of change.* Boston: Allyn & Bacon, 1971.

Sarason, S. B. *Psychology misdirected.* New York: Free Press, 1981.

Schein, E. H. *Organizational psychology.* Englewood Cliffs, N.J.: Prentice-Hall, 1970.

Seidman, E. Justice, values, and social science: Unexamined premises. In J. R. Simon (Ed.), *Research in law and sociology* (Vol. 1). Greenwich, Conn.: JAI Press, 1978.

Seidman, E., & Rapkin, B. Economics and psychosocial dysfunction: Toward a conceptual framework and prevention strategies. In R. D. Felner, et. al. (Eds.) *Preventive Psychology,* Elmsford, N.Y.: Pergamon Press, in press.

Seidman, E., & Rappaport, J. The educational pyramid: A paradigm for training, research, and manpower utilization in community psychology. *American Journal of Community Psychology,* 1974, *2,* 119–130.

Seidman, E., & Rappaport, J. *Serious mental illness and self-help treatment.* Grant proposal submitted to NIMH, October 1981.

Seidman, E., Rappaport, J., & Davidson, W. S. In P. R. Ross & P. Gendreau (Eds.), *Effective correctional treatment.* Toronto: Butterworth, 1980.

Sobey, F. *The nonprofessional revolution in mental health.* New York: Columbia University Press, 1970.

Spivack, G., & Schure, M. B. *Social adjustment of young children.* San Francisco: Jossey-Bass, 1974.

Stein, C. *Social networks and informal helping.* Book in preparation, 1981.

Stein, L. I., & Test, M. A. Alternative to mental hospital treatment. I: Conceptual model, treatment program, and clinical evaluation. *Archives of General Psychiatry,* 1980, *37,* 392–397.

Stein, L. I., Test, M. A., & Marx, A. J. Alternative to the hospital: A controlled study. *American Journal of Psychiatry,* 1975, *132,* 517–522.

Stern, S. *Critique of the professional training model in psychology: A study in educational volumes.* Psy. D. thesis, University of Illinois at Urbana-Champaign, 1981.

Sue, S., McKinney, H., Allen, D., & Hall, J. Delivery of community mental health services to black and white clients. *Journal of Consulting and Clinical Psychology,* 1974, *42,* 794–801.

Susser, M. *Community psychiatry: Epidemiologic and social themes.* New York: Random House, 1968.

Test, M. A. Effective community treatment of the chronically mentally ill: What is necessary? *Journal of Social Issues,* 1981, *37,* 71–86.

Test, M. A., & Stein, L. I. Community treatment of the chronic patient: Research overview. *Schizophrenia Bulletin,* 1978, *4,* 350–364.

Tolsdorf, C. Social networks, support, and coping: An exploratory study. *Family Process,* 1976, *15,* 407–417.

Trickett, E. J., Kelly, J. G., & Todd, D. M. The social environment of the high school: Guidelines for individual change and organizational redevelopment. In S. E. Golann & C. Eisdorfer (Eds.), *Handbook of community mental health.* New York: Appleton-Century-Crofts, 1972.

Watzlawick, P., Weakland, J. H., & Fisch, R. *Change: Principles of problem formation and problem resolution.* New York: W. W. Norton, 1974.

Weber, G. H., & McCall, G. J. *Social scientists as advocates.* Beverly Hills, Calif.: Sage Publications, 1978.

Zax, M., & Specter, G. A. *An introduction to community psychology.* New York: John Wiley & Sons, 1974.

32

Applications of biofeedback to therapy*

Frank Andrasik†
and
Edward B. Blanchard†

In the short time since its inception, biofeedback has emerged as one of the most popular and useful treatment approaches within the area of behavioral medicine, with applications ranging from anxiety to writer's cramp. The field is far too vast for us to review all important developments in the biofeedback-research literature, so we must, of necessity, limit our focus to certain aspects of this research. To this end, the chapter begins with a brief description of biofeedback, followed by a more in-depth discussion of the physiological bases of responses used in biofeedback, methods of instrumentation, and procedural concerns in the conduct of biofeedback. The chapter ends with a selective review of clinical applications of biofeedback, pointing out avenues that might be pursued most profitably in future research and application.

BIOFEEDBACK DEFINED

Biofeedback has been defined as:

> . . . a process in which a person learns to reliably influence physiological responses of two kinds: either responses which are not ordinarily under voluntary control or responses which ordinarily are easily regulated but for which regulation has broken down due to trauma or disease. (Blanchard & Epstein, 1978, p. 2)

The process of biofeedback involves three operations, which are depicted in Figure 1. In the first operation, a biological response is detected

---

* This chapter was supported, in part, by grants from the National Institute of Neurological and Communicative Disorders and Stroke (NS–15235) and the National Institute of Heart, Lung, and Blood (HL–27622).

† Department of psychology, State University of New York, Albany.

and amplified by using certain measurement devices (or transducers) and electronic amplifiers. The bioelectrical potentials detected at this stage are in a form that is difficult to utilize in biofeedback. For example, muscle-tension potentials detected at this stage resemble static one might hear between channels of a radio, and few individuals would be capable of detecting even gross changes in electrical activity. The second operation of biofeedback converts bioelectrical signals to a form that can be easily understood and easily processed by the subject. Averaging the electronic signal over a specified timeperiod and filtering out unwanted aspects of the signal are examples of ways in which this is accomplished. The third operation involves the relatively immediate feedback of the signal to the subject. This feedback is most often presented in auditory and visual modalities and in either binary (signal on, signal off) or continuous proportional fashion. Researchers have debated which of two models best accounts for biofeedback—reinforcement (or instrumental) model versus feedback (or information) model. Shapiro and Surwit (1976) offer a reconciliation, by proposing a two-stage, integrative model of biofeedback, which incorporates both learning paradigms: feedback for response development (stage 1) and reinforcement for response strengthening (stage 2).

Figure 1

The three operations of biofeedback

1. *Detection and amplification of BIOelectric potentials.*
2. *Convert bioelectric signals to easy-to-process information.*
3. *FEED this information BACK to the patient.*
4. *With immediate feedback, patient learns voluntary control of response.*

Source: From E. B. Blanchard & L. H. Epstein, *A biofeedback primer.* Copyright © 1978, by Addison-Wesley, Reading, MA. Reprinted by permission.

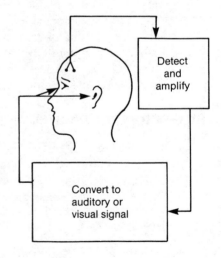

RESPONSE SYSTEMS IN BIOFEEDBACK

Since biological responses underlie all of biofeedback, it will be helpful to review the responses which have been used in biofeedback research and treatment. In establishing ways to measure the response, researchers have sought to use the most direct measures of the target responses whenever possible but, at the same time, have had to balance this preference against convenience and comfort to the subject. With all responses, care must be taken to ensure that areas of sensor placement are prepared adequately and that measurement devices are placed on the proper location. These factors are especially crucial in electromyography and electroencephalography, because of the weak electrical signals which must be detected. Here, electrode sites must be cleaned thoroughly with acetone or alcohol and lightly abraded. With most types of recordings, a conductive gel or electrolyte is placed between the electrodes and the subject's skin, to facilitate conductance and reduce measurement artifact. Discussion here is intended to provide only a basic understanding of physiology. Readers desiring additional information may wish to consult basic tests on psychophysiology, such as Brown (1967), Greenfield and Sternbach (1972), Hassett (1978), Martin and Venables (1980), Sternbach (1966), and Venables and Martin (1967).

Blood pressure

Blood pressure (BP) is the force created within the arteries as the blood meets resistance in the periphery. Blood pressure varies from moment to moment between two extreme values. The maximum value, termed *systolic* pressure (SBP), is associated with contraction of the left ventricle of the heart, as it pumps oxygenated blood to body parts. The minimum value, termed *diastolic* pressure (DBP), is associated with the heart relaxing between beats. Blood pressure is typically expressed as SBP over DBP in millimeters of mercury (mmHg).

Direct measurement of BP involves insertion of a cannula into an artery and linking this to a pressure-sensitive measuring device. However, this procedure is too noxious for routine use in research and long-term treatment. At present, two alternative, indirect procedures have been used in biofeedback. The first, and most widespread, involves the use of an inflatable cuff (which is usually placed around the subject's upper arm) and a speaker (which is placed beneath the cuff). The measurement involves listening for the absence or presence of Korotkoff sounds—those sounds made when blood flow is partially occluded. The cuff is first inflated to a level at which all blood flow under it ceases and Korotkoff sounds are no longer heard. By slowly deflating the cuff, Korotkoff sounds will again be heard, and the pressure at which the first sound is detected is termed *SBP*. The pressure at which the Korotkoff sounds cease to be heard is termed *DBP*. In early work, BP was measured by manual inflation and deflation of the cuff, a process which was slow and tedious (it required about 30 to 60 seconds for each measurement). In order to make feedback more immediately available, researchers varied this procedure somewhat. One such variation, which is commonly used, is the automated, constant cuff-pressure method of Tursky, Shapiro, and Schwartz (1972).

Use of the automated, constant cuff-pressure method to provide bio-feedback of SBP occurs as follows: after establishing a baseline level for SBP, the researcher inflates the cuff to a value just below that obtained for the subject during baseline; the presence of a Korotkoff sound follow-ing a pulse beat signals that the subject's SBP is above the criterion level; the absence of a Korotkoff sound indicates that the subject lowered his/her SBP to criterion. With this procedure, feedback is available on a beat-by-beat basis. As the subject becomes more proficient at achieving the criterion level, the experimenter gradually lowers the criterion level, to shape successively lower SBP. Treatment continues in this fashion, until the desired level of SBP is reached.

The second method uses pulse-wave velocity, which is assumed to be highly (but inversely) correlated to SBP (Obrist, Light, McCubbin, Hutcheson, & Hoffer, 1979; Steptoe, Smulylan, & Gribbin, 1976). In this procedure, the time between the initiation of a pulse (usually from the heart) to the detection of the pulse at another arterial site is determined. After obtaining the baseline level of transit time, a feedback device can be set to signal increases or decreases in transit times during biofeedback training. However, Lane, Greenstadt, and Shapiro (1979) have more recently questioned the relationship of pulse-wave velocity to arterial BP. Both methods for providing feedback of BP are complex, and their use can still be considered experimental.

Blood volume

In certain areas of application, volume of blood flow to a peripheral site is of major interest. Assessments of blood flow are possible by three different procedures: plethysmography, temperature sensing, and me-chanical transduction. As with BP, all measurement procedures are indi-rect, rather than direct.

In the plethysmography method, changes in blood flow are detected by use of a light (which is shined into a tissue) and a light-detecting source (or photocell). Two kinds of plethysmographs are used, and they are distinguished by the way the light and photocell are positioned. In transmission plethysmography, the photocell is placed on the opposite side of the tissue and measures the amount of light transmitted through the tissue (Figure 2). In reflectance plethysmography, the light and photo-cell are placed side by side, so the signal detected is the amount of light reflected back from the skin. In either case, blood flow is determined from the amount of light detected by the photocell, as these two measures are proportional. Even though this procedure is easy to implement, this method is infrequently used, because there is no easy way to quantify the measure in absolute terms (i.e., it provides only measures of relative blood flow). Hence, determining change across sessions and individuals is problematic.

Figure 2

The two ways in which a photoplethysmograph functions

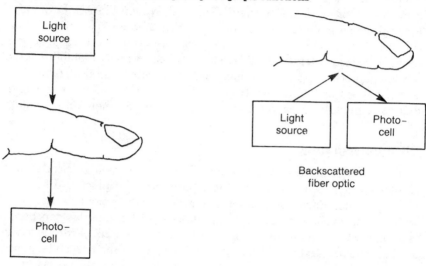

Transilluminated

Backscattered
fiber optic

In all cases, light produced by the light source is measured by a photocell. As the volume of the finger changes, the amount of light reaching the photocell changes which, in turn, is reflected in a difference in voltage. The positions of the light source and the photocell may vary, as indicated in the figure.

Source: From D. S. Olton & A. R. Noonberg, *Biofeedback: Clinical applications in behavioral medicine,* © 1980, p. 82. Reprinted by permission of Prentice-Hall, Inc., Englewood Cliffs, N.J.

The high degree of correspondence between peripheral blood flow and skin-surface temperature has led to temperature monitoring as an indirect measure of blood flow. Monitoring is accomplished by temperature-sensitive probes, whose resistance changes as a function of temperature change. Thermistors, composed of a semiconductor, are generally used; although thermocouples, composed of two different metals in juxtaposition, are used occasionally. It is important to remember that laboratory and outdoor temperatures (as well as heat) build up in the sensors, and conductive leads can influence accuracy of skin-temperature measurement (King & Montgomery, 1980; Taub & School, 1978). When measuring blood flow by the third method, mechanical transduction, the sensor—mounted over the artery—is directed to an electric crystal, which produces a small voltage proportional to the strain exerted upon it by movement of the sensor. This form of measurement is complex to implement, and it remains experimental at present.

A serendipitous finding by staff of the Menninger Clinic—that abatement of migraine headache was accompanied by a rapid rise in hand temperature—led to the development of hand-warming biofeedback as a treatment for migraine (Sargent, Green, & Walters, 1972). In practice, thermal biofeedback is usually augmented by autogenic training (Schultz & Luthe, 1969), which is termed *autogenic feedback*. Available evidence (Sovack, Kunzel, Sternbach, & Dalessio, 1978) suggests that thermal biofeedback produces general reductions in sympathetic arousal, rather than specific effects on blood flow. These findings have led clinicians to employ thermal biofeedback as yet another way to facilitate general relaxation.

Electromyography

The basis of the electromyogram (EMG) is the small electrochemical changes which occur when a muscle contracts. By placing a series of electrodes along the muscle fiber, the muscle-action potentials associated with the ion exchange across the membrane of the muscles can be detected. Most research involves use of fairly large-size electrode disks, so that electrical activity of many muscles and organs is simultaneously detected. When single motor units are the focus of research, as in the case of muscle rehabilitation, electrodes which penetrate the skin surface are used. The precise feedback provided by these indwelling electrodes is often necessary for subjects to learn muscle control in the initial stages of rehabilitation.

Electromyographic monitoring from surface sites is accomplished by the use of two active electrodes, separated by one ground electrode. When using a three-electrode placement, the resultant signal is a summation of the muscle activity occurring under each active electrode, minus the activity occurring under the ground electrode (considered to be noise). Electromyographic biofeedback is used for treatment of problems due both to excessive muscle tension (tension headache, chronic anxiety, and spastic movement or torticollis) and to decreased muscle activity (occurring because of muscle damage or disuse). The most widespread use of EMG biofeedback is to facilitate general relaxation. When used for this purpose, large-cup electrodes are placed over the patient's forehead, because this placement is sensitive to movements from several areas (head, neck, and, possibly, shoulders) (Basmajian, 1976). Originally, it was believed that reductions in forehead muscle tension (and immediately adjacent muscles) would generalize to most other untrained muscles. Research has shown that this does not occur often (Surwit & Keefe, 1978), so most clinicians train patients from several sites in the course of relaxation treatment.

Electromyographic activity can be displayed in three ways (see Figure 3). The easiest way to display EMG is by the raw signal. EMG is an alternating response with a very high frequency. These characteristics

Figure 3

Ways to display electromyographic activity

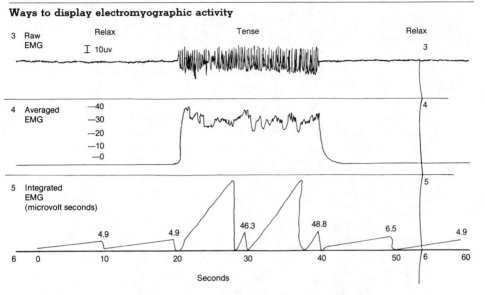

make it difficult, to nearly impossible, for subjects to discriminate the small changes in muscle activity that must be detected for learning to occur during biofeedback. Consequently, the raw signal is infrequently used. More frequently used displays are average and cumulative integrations. The average (or leaky) integrator (Shaw, 1967) takes into account frequency and amplitude of the response, as does the raw signal; but, it does so in a manner which provides a much smoother signal with less variation. By rectifying the signal and varying the interval over which the signal is averaged, the experimenter can control how much of a variation in muscle activity is needed before changes are provided in the average signal. Most EMG biofeedback is delivered from the averaged-EMG signal, with the time constant set at a moderate length (0.1 to 1.0 second).

The third way of displaying EMG signals uses cumulative integration, which involves the summation of all muscle activity within a specified period. In Figure 3, the cumulative integrator has been programmed to reset every 10 seconds. The distance or height the pen travels during the 10-second period corresponds to the level of muscle activity; i.e., higher pen excursions during the 10-second interval indicate increased muscle activity. Cumulative recordings can be converted to microvolt-seconds (the amount of electrical activity required to produce a certain amount of cumulative activity). This technique is felt to provide the best estimate of EMG level over time and is widely used in research.

Electroencephalography

For the most part, the electroencephalogram (EEG) represents the electrical activity of the cerebral cortex. The EEG signal results from the firing of many cortical neurons (hundreds of thousands) and not from the firing of specific neurons. The four major frequency bands of the EEG investigated in biofeedback research are presented in Figure 4, along with a representation of their wave form and their associated psychological states. Amplitude and frequency are needed to categorize brain waves. Amplitude (or magnitude of electrical change) is measured in microvolts, while frequency is measured in cycles per second (or Hz.). In biofeedback research, complex electronic circuitry is employed to eliminate unwanted brain frequencies. The resultant EEG activity can then be displayed directly or integrated in a manner similar to that described in the section on EMG.

Much of the early work in biofeedback concerned the EEG (Kamiya, 1968; Brown, 1970, 1971), with a special interest placed on enhancement of the alpha rhythm, which was felt to produce a special, attentional state. These claims have been challenged subsequently (Plotkin, 1976; Walsh, 1974), leaving alpha biofeedback a controversial area. Treatments of epilepsy have used other components of the EEG spectrum, such as the sensorimotor rhythm (12 to 16 Hz).

Electrocardiology

The electrocardiogram (EKG) is a recording of the electrical impulses associated with the beating of the heart. Figure 5 shows a recording of

Figure 4

Brain waves classified by frequency

Delta less than 4 cps	Thea 4-8 cps	Alpha 8-13 cps	Beta more than 13 cps
Asleep	Drowsy	Relaxed	Alert

The behavioral labels for each frequency band represent the very gross distinctions typically discussed in arousal theory.

Source: From J. Hassett, *A primer of psychophysiology.* W. H. Freeman and Company. Copyright © 1978.

Figure 5

A diagram of an electrocardiogram (EKG) showing two typical heart beats

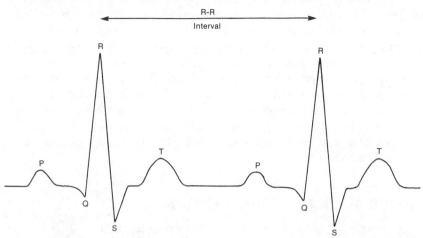

The QRS complex is associated with the contraction of the ventricles, the R peak is the largest potential, and the interbeat interval is usually calculated between successive R waves. Heart rate in beats per minute can be calculated by dividing 60 by the interbeat interval.

Source: From D. S. Olton & A. R. Noonberg, *Biofeedback: Clinical applications in behavioral medicine.* © 1980, p. 85. Reprinted by permission of Prentice-Hall, Inc., Englewood Cliffs, N.J.

two successive heart beats. The most striking feature of the EKG is the sharp voltage spike, labeled the *R-wave*, which is associated with contraction of the left ventricle.

In biofeedback, direct counts of heart rate over a timeperiod are rarely employed, as this does not provide immediate-enough feedback. Heart rate is arrived at in an indirect fashion, by taking the reciprocal of the interbeat interval. Interbeat interval is determined by calculating the elapsed time between two *R*-waves, by the use of a device (called a Schmitt trigger) capable of determining certain voltage levels. By using this procedure, measures of heart rate are available on a beat-by-beat basis. This operation can be performed automatically by electronic devices called cardiotachometers.

Two measurement electrodes, placed on opposite sides of the body in diagonal fashion (such as the left ankle and right arm), and one reference electrode are required for monitoring EKG. Recorded in this manner, the amplitude of the typical R-wave is about two millivolts (Brener, 1967), so surface preparation and electrode contact are not as critical as with EMG and EEG. Most clinical applications of heart rate (HR) biofeedback involve cardiac arrhythmias and anxiety disorders.

Other

A number of other measurement procedures have been utilized in biofeedback but, because of their infrequency and/or their complexity of use, they will be presented briefly. Palmar sweat-gland activity (or the galvanic skin response) has been extensively studied in basic research, yet little has been done with this response in the clinical realm (one exception being hypertension). Stomach pH of ulcer patients and resistance of airway passage of asthmatics are other responses being investigated in biofeedback. Strain gauges constitute yet another form of measurement, which has most success in the treatment of fecal incontinence (which is later reviewed) and is speculated to be of value in sexual dysfunction and deviation.

BIOFEEDBACK INSTRUMENTATION

In order to provide biofeedback, the therapist must be able to: (1) detect, transduce (when necessary), process, and amplify the physiological response of interest; (2) quantify moment-to-moment changes in physiological responding; and (3) provide feedback about changes in responding, in a manner that is comprehensible to the patient. There exist three basic instrumentation procedures for accomplishing the above functions: self-contained units, polygraph with solid-state logic, and individual solid-state modules.

Self-contained units accomplish all necessary steps of biofeedback for a particular response in a single, integrated unit. They are portable, easy to operate, and, hence, are used most frequently in clinical practice. Their operation is made easy, by factory presetting of response-processing characteristics in a manner likely to satisfy most clinical uses, and by narrowing the range of choices for feedback delivery and data acquisition. The locking-in of most features requires, however, that most troubleshooting be done by company or factory personnel.

The second basic approach uses a polygraph (for detecting and amplifying the response) and a series of solid-state programming modules (for providing feedback and quantifying data). This method is most popular with researchers because: it permits simultaneous recordings of multiple physiological responses; allows considerable flexibility in response processing, feedback delivery, and data quantification; and makes available a permanent tracing (or recording) of the response(s). Among the disadvantages of this approach are the complexity of operation, increased expenses, and lack of portability.

The third procedure involves interfacing individual modules which are designed to accomplish the separate steps in biofeedback (similar to a component, home stereo system). This approach shares many of the advantages of the polygraph approach, but with less expense. Despite this, the modular approach has not caught on with clinicians or researchers. The chief disadvantages of this approach are the lack of a permanent record and reduced portability.

In Table 1, we list the advantages and disadvantages associated with each of the three instrumentation procedures. The last item in the table presents expense ratios for each procedure. To arrive at this ratio, the average cost of purchasing equipment—which would enable the user to provide both EMG and thermal biofeedback—was first determined for each method. Expense ratios were then calculated, by dividing the cost of each procedure by the cost of the least-expensive procedure; since the self-contained units were the least expensive, they received an expense ratio of 1.0. In choosing a method, an individual needs to consider the intended use (clinical versus research), his/her technical-skill level, and available financial resources.

Table 1

Advantages and disadvantages of the three methods of biofeedback instrumentation

	Biofeedback method		
	Self-contained units	*Polygraph with solid-state logic*	*Individual solid-state modules*
Degree of control of response detection, transduction, and amplification	Low	High	High
Degree of control of data acquisition	Low	High	High
Degree of control of feedback delivery	Low	High	High
Skill level required for operation	Low	High	Moderate
Degree to which troubleshooting can be done in laboratory	Low	High	High
Degree of portability	High	Low	Low
Physiological trace available?	No	Yes	No
Expense ratio*	1.0	4.2	1.6

* Determined from figures reported in Andrasik, Coleman, & Epstein, 1982.

Source: Andrasik, F., Coleman, D., & Epstein, L. H., Biofeedback: Clinical and research considerations. In D. M. Doleys, R. L. Meredith, & A. R. Cirinero (Eds.), *Behavioral psychology in medicine: Assessment and treatment strategies* (New York: Plenum, 1982).

PROCEDURAL CONCERNS IN ADMINISTERING BIOFEEDBACK

A number of important decisions must be made in planning and conducting biofeedback for any patient. Many of these important procedural concerns are only now beginning to be addressed in the research literature; so, few guidelines are available at present. In this section, we review some of the procedural concerns when conducting biofeedback, based on our experience and supplemented by available data.

The therapeutic context

Biofeedback, as all therapies, should be administered in the appropriate therapeutic context. Therapist, relationship, and situational variables mentioned elsewhere in this text as being important during psychotherapy (Chapter 7, Lambert & Bergin; Chapter 9, Korchin & Sands) need consideration during biofeedback as well. Some direct evidence indicates that certain experimenter behaviors and instructional sets have a particular bearing on a patient's performance during biofeedback.

In his earliest research, Taub (see Taub, 1977; Taub & Emurian, 1976) employed an experimenter who was found to treat subjects impersonally and to possess what may be described as an unhealthy level of skepticism. This experimenter was able to train successfully only 2 of 22 subjects. A second experimenter, who behaved in an informal and friendly manner, produced dramatically different results and was able to train successfully 19 of 21 subjects—using experimental procedures identical to those of the first experimenter. These findings led Taub to conduct a more formal investigation of experimenter behavior which produced similar results. Taub investigated a number of experimental variables in thermal biofeedback and reported that no other single variable produced a greater effect.

Leeb, Fahrion, and French (1976) have found similar effects when researching effects of attitude set during autogenic training. In their investigation, subjects received either a positive instructional set ("Hand temperature training is quite easy and I have a lot of faith that you will do quite well at it."), a negative instructional set ("I am really skeptical as to some of the results reported in hand temperature-training work. I don't think it is as easy as they say it is, and frankly I don't think that you will do very well at it. But, give it a try."), or a neutral instructional set (instructions were automated and of the form: "Please, do what you can on the following task.") Efforts were made to equate the three experimental groups in all other respects. Subjects given the positive instructional set demonstrated the most pronounced abilities to regulate hand temperature, on all measures studied. It seems most plausible that experimenter and instructional variables play equally important roles in other types of biofeedback.

One cautionary note is in order. Borgeat, Hade, Larouche, & Bedwani (1980) found that too much therapist involvement, even though of a helping and encouraging nature, can interfere with biofeedback training. Such overinvolvement may prevent subjects from concentrating on the task with the intensity needed. The importance of experimenter and instructional variables cannot be denied, although the optimal mix and type of therapist/subject interaction needs further clarification by research.

Evaluation for biofeedback

The evaluation focuses on history taking, obtaining baseline levels of symptom complaints and physiological responding, and discussion of treatment options and their rationales. In cases with uncomplicated histories, all steps may be accomplished in a single session; other cases will require additional time.

History taking. The history is important for determining a subject's readiness and appropriateness for treatment and focuses on: current symptoms, their time of initiation, past treatments required, and suspected precipitating and maintaining factors; medical history, treatments, and evaluations; and current and past psychological functioning. Cautela (1981) has prepared a variety of self-report forms (for organic dysfunctions) that the beginning therapist may find useful in conducting the history.

The importance of a detailed history cannot be overstressed, as many of the problems encountered by clients seeking biofeedback are intricately related to life stress and/or are intertwined with other problems of a psychological nature. For instance, a patient's presenting problem may be associated with depression, assertion deficits, marital disharmony, and, in rare cases, secondary gain (in the form of sympathy from significant others or as a means of legitimizing the avoidance of undesirable activities). Ignoring these attendant problems, while focusing on modifying physiological activity alone, may limit the therapist's impact. For example, when pronounced depression accompanies headache, clients have been found to be fairly unresponsive to biofeedback alone (Blanchard, Andrasik, Neff, Teders, Pallmeyer, Arena, Jurish, Saunders, Ahles, & Rodichok, 1982; Diamond & Franklin, 1975). In cases where physiological complaints are secondary to other forms of psychopathology, or where multiple problems are evident, the clinician may decide to delay biofeedback until the other problems are resolved. Turk, Meichenbaum, and Berman (1979) stress that patients must be capable of effectively managing their environment, in addition to controlling their physiology for maximum therapeutic benefits; consequently, they urge therapists to routinely apply biofeedback with other physiological and psychological approaches.

Another aspect of the history deserves special mention. Organic pathology can be solely responsible for (or serve as a significant contributor to) many of the types of problems seen for biofeedback. Medical evaluation is needed to assess this possibility and to identify when a medical intervention may be the more appropriate form of treatment (Miller, 1978). Once treatment has begun, therapists are urged to maintain a consultative relationship with medical personnel: most important, when a client being maintained on medication decides to alter his/her regimen because of improvement obtained during biofeedback.

Establishing baseline levels of symptoms and physiology.   It is critical that therapists obtain accurate baselines of presenting symptoms and physiological responding so that treatment can be appropriately designed and evaluated. Pocket-sized diaries are most often used by patients to rate various parameters of their problems (e.g., intensity, frequency, and duration), medication taken, suspected precipitants, and, later, amount of practice completed at home and compliance with other homework assignments.

In order to establish an adequate physiological baseline, considerable time is needed to ensure that patients have adapted to the therapist and setting. Meeting the therapist for the first time, coming into a novel environment, and being attached to unfamiliar equipment may result in temporary increases in arousal for the subject. Without a proper baseline, the experimenter may mistake a habituation effect for a training effect. Adaptation time for forehead EMG and hand temperature has been studied most actively, and results indicate some individuals need 15 minutes or more to achieve a stable baseline (Lichstein, Sallis, Hill, & Young, 1981; Taub, 1977; Taub & Emurian, 1976; Van Boxtel & Van der Ven, 1978). The biofeedback practitioner is unlikely to employ this level of rigor in baseline assessment, but he/she should be mindful of this point.

Some researchers (Budzynski, 1981; Olton & Noonberg, 1980) suggest therapists obtain baseline physiological profiles from clients during simulated stressors as well, in order to identify those response systems most reactive to stress, so that they may be targeted for treatment. Stress profiles may be obtained by having patients imagine personal stressors or complete difficult mental or physical tasks.

Biofeedback training

Patient education.   Individuals presenting for biofeedback treatment may be confused about the nature of their disorder, discouraged, and uncertain about their chances for improvement. Brief instruction about factors underlying the patient's disorder, which points out those variables which may be controllable by the patient, is often helpful in counteracting the patient's initial feelings of helplessness and in mobilizing his/her interest in treatment. This is followed by a description of biofeedback (and any ancillary treatments that may be given). The explanation of biofeedback is best understood when accompanied by a live demonstration, which points out the steps involved in measurement and provision of feedback. Written materials and diagrams can be helpful with some clients. Verbatim examples of ways to explain biofeedback treatment to patients may be found in Olton and Noonberg (1980); and discussion of other factors to consider when preparing a patient for biofeedback treatment may be found in Lynn and Freedman (1979) and Meichenbaum (1976). Patel's (1977) approach to patient education, which devotes several sessions to film presentations and discussions about the relationship between emotion and physiology and the causes and treatments of hypertension, serves as an exemplary model.

Treatment parameters. The choice of a biofeedback approach is based on the pathology assumed to underlie the disorder and the results obtained from the baseline assessment. Once a particular type of biofeedback is chosen, the therapist must select from a wide array of options those parameters which will optimize performance for a given client. Some of these parameters are: rate, type, and modality of feedback; spacing of feedback trials; and length and number of training sessions (Miller & Dworkin, 1977).

A number of studies have been conducted to test these important parameters. Unfortunately, most of these investigations have been concerned with college students and other normal, nonpatient groups, or else have studied subject abilities to regulate physiologic responses in a direction for which there is minimal clinical utility—e.g., ways to optimize heart rate increases and temperature decreases (for a review of these findings, see Andrasik, Blanchard, & Edlund, in press; Williamson & Blanchard, 1979). Whether the present body of research findings will have applicability to clinical populations is uncertain. For example, nonpatients have been found to perform best when thermal biofeedback is given in short trials (about one minute), separated by brief rest periods (about 10 seconds). We recently attempted to replicate this procedure with vascular-headache patients and found it yielded quite poor results (Andrasik, Blanchard, & Pallmeyer, 1982). Patients commented that the frequent breaks served only to disrupt their concentration and performance and to produce frustration. Patients suggested that some mix of rest-and workperiods was preferred, but that feedback periods should be at much greater length than one minute (e.g., four to six minutes). Until more definitive research is conducted with patient populations, therapists may be best advised to allow patients to sample various levels of each parameter of concern and to select the level most suited to them.

Generalization and maintenance.   As pointed out by Epstein and Blanchard (1977), the ultimate goal of biofeedback therapy is for the patient to be able to discriminate when the target response is in need of control and then to effect the necessary change in the absence of feedback (or to exert self-control). Since biofeedback is most often used on an attack-contingent basis, the goal of discrimination is to enable the individual to begin self-regulation at the first perceptible sign of attack. Once the symptom cycle begins, it may be too difficult to gain a sufficient level of control of the target physiology. The important role that discrimination plays in self-regulation of physiology has been virtually overlooked by biofeedback researchers. Its importance is highlighted by a case-study report of the treatment of migraine headache.

Gainer (1978) describes the treatment of a 26-year-old patient, who had suffered from migraine headache since the age of 16, and who had been unsuccessfully treated on two prior occasions by assertion training and systematic desensitization. It was important that the patient reported no clear warning signs of her migraine attacks. The patient was provided 10 sessions of thermal biofeedback and, by the end of training, she could reliably produce exceptionally large-scale increases in her hand temperature, both with and without feedback. Despite this, her migraines continued unabated. Comparisons between the patient's perceived changes in hand temperature and her actual changes revealed poor correspondence. In subsequent sessions, training was instituted to rectify this situation.

At each of three discrimination-training sessions, the patient was presented 60 training trials of either 15- or 30-second duration, separated by a 5-second intertrial interval (ITI). The patient was instructed to increase her hand temperature during each discrimination-training trial while, most importantly, focusing on the sensations in her hand. During the ITI, the patient was informed of the magnitude and direction of change relative to the preceding trial. Following training, the patient revealed markedly improved abilities to discriminate hand-temperature changes. By having the patient implement hand warming when changes were first detected, migraine attacks disappeared completely, and medication was no longer needed. An eight-month follow-up revealed a high level of maintenance of treatment gains.

Gainer's findings raise some important concerns about the role of discrimination in self-regulation of physiology. Gainer asks, ". . . can a proportion of biofeedback 'failures' be accounted for in terms of an inability to discriminate temperature changes? . . . is the observation of those migraine patients who report no peripheral changes as warning signs . . . a function of their nonoccurrence or their occurrence having gone unnoticed?" (p. 187). We advise clinicians to test for discrimination and self-control abilities repeatedly during teatment. Successful demonstrations of discrimination and self-control in the relaxed, treatment environment do not ensure that a patient will be able to demonstrate these abilities with similar success in stressful, real-life encounters, although they do seem to be prerequisite.

Therapists need to be concerned with maintenance of self-regulation abilities, as well. Lynn and Freedman (1979) reviewed the literature and identified a number of ways by which biofeedback-training effects could be made more durable. Among those which may be easily implemented by the clinician are: (1) overlearning of the target response, (2) provision of booster treatments, (3) fading or gradual removal of feedback during treatment, (4) training under stimulating or stressful conditions (during noise and distractions, while engaged in a physical or mental task, etc.), (5) providing subjects portable-biofeedback equipment for use in real-life situations, and (6) augmenting biofeedback with other physiological interventions and with cognitive and behavioral procedures.

Maintaining the patient's involvement in treatment. Gaining control of a physiological response is difficult and often generates a high level of frustration in patients. Early failure experiences may cause patients to avoid or ignore the feedback display and to engage in negative or counterproductive self-statements. To minimize these occurrences, we inform patients of the difficulty of the task and of tendencies we have observed for patients to self-derogate after failure experiences. This permits patients to attribute failure experiences to the difficulty of the task, rather than to personal inadequacies (Lynn & Freedman, 1979). Judicious control of the feedback display, such as arranging feedback so that small changes in the therapeutic direction are presented to the patient as large-magnitude changes, is helpful in the initial sessions.

Most patients report that control is best gained by adopting a passive attitude and that initial failures are accounted for by trying too hard. Failures occasioned by trying too hard are used to illustrate to patients the effects that emotional processes can have upon their physiological functioning. Gaarder and Montgomery (1977) discuss other problems that can occur in biofeedback treatment and ways to manage them most effectively.

Progress review. Patients need to practice (at home) skills learned during treatment and, when sufficiently skilled, need to begin to use their skills to manage their problematic behaviors. It is helpful, at the beginning of each session, to review the patient's compliance with home practice and any other homework assignments and progress at applying the therapeutic skills. Regularity of practice needs to be emphasized, and attempts should be made to increase its frequency for patients who are lax in this practice, because home practice has been shown to be highly correlated with maintenance of treatment gains (Blanchard, 1977). Before terminating a session, it is helpful to have a second progress review, which focuses on changes made during the session.

A SELECTIVE REVIEW AND EVALUATION OF THE BIOFEEDBACK-TREATMENT LITERATURE

There is a vast array of clinical conditions to which biofeedback has been applied, and to summarize and critique that literature could easily take a book the size of this volume. Instead of undertaking such a task (which is obviously beyond the scope of this chapter), we have chosen to review a selected number of clinical applications of biofeedback. Our guidelines for including a particular application were as follows: (1) there were three or more published reports of this application of biofeedback training, and (2) there were at least two single group-outcome or controlled group-outcome evaluations of a selected application. As Blanchard and Young (1974), in an earlier comprehensive review of this literature, noted, one can have more confidence in the results of such studies than in less-controlled reports.

Three points need to be mentioned before we embark upon the body of this review: (1) this is a selective rather than exhaustive review of the applications we have included; (2) much of the information on the actual studies is summarized in tabular form; (3) there are four questions which we believe should be asked of every study: (*a*) is there evidence for physiological change, or did the response for which the biofeedback training was given show a training effect? (*b*) did the group receiving biofeedback training show more physiological change than control or comparison conditions? (*c*) is there evidence for symptomatic or clinical change? and (*d*) did the group receiving biofeedback training show more clinical change than control or comparison conditions? Affirmative answers to these four questions provide strong evidence, in our opinion, for the efficacy and utility of biofeedback training in that particular application.

Table 2 lists the applications to be reviewed and the sections in which they are discussed. In our opinion, these applications divide roughly into two groups (or clusters) which share certain common features. To explain this division, we need to introduce the idea of the general practice biofeedback clinician. This individual is most likely to be a clinical psychologist who has added biofeedback training to his/her armamentarium of therapeutic procedures. This individual will probably have equipment to conduct biofeedback training for EMG, peripheral temperature (thermal), and, probably, EEG alpha. The general practice biofeedback clinician may also have equipment to train GSR and, possibly, blood pressure. There are a relatively large number of such biofeedback GPs in the country, probably at least 2,000 to 4,000.

Table 2

Division of biofeedback clinical applications

Cluster 1	Cluster 2
1. Widely available	1. Available only at few specialized centers
2. Symptoms related to sympathetic arousal	2. Not much evidence for sympathetic arousal involvement
3. Relaxation training also usually effective	3. Relaxation training has not yet been effective
Anxiety disorders	Neuromuscular disorders
Recurrent headaches	Torticollis
Raynaud's disease	Stroke rehabilitation
Hypertension	Fecal incontinence
	Epilepsy

The applications in cluster 1 are much more likely to be available from the biofeedback GP, which means that these applications are in fairly widespread use throughout the country. The applications in this cluster also share three other characteristics: (1) the symptoms are generally related to arousal (or excessive sympathetic nervous system activity), and they are loosely characterized as stress-related disorders; (2) for most of these applications, as will be shown below, some form of nonbiofeedback-relaxation training has been shown to be effective; and (3) it is difficult, as Silver and Blanchard (1978) noted in a review of this topic, to show a systematic advantage of biofeedback training over relaxation training.

By way of contrast, the availability of biofeedback treatment for the disorders in the second cluster is fairly limited. A possible exception to this is the use of EMG biofeedback in neuromuscular rehabilitation. A growing number of rehabilitation centers are using EMG biofeedback as an adjunct to standard physical therapy techniques. The equipment used for cluster 2 applications is highly specialized; and finally, there is little evidence that relaxation or psychological relationship (nonspecific) factors play a large role in the clinical gains obtained.

Widely available applications of biofeedback

Anxiety disorders. It is fairly well recognized that patients with anxiety disorders (by which we mean the group of disorders so characterized by *DSM-III:* namely, fear and phobias, generalized anxiety disorder, panic disorder, and obsessive-compulsive disorder) manifest problems in at least two different response domains: physiological arousal and cognitive (or self-report of worry, concern, or sense of impending disaster). Given the pronounced physiological-arousal component, it is not surprising that various biofeedback training procedures have been applied in an effort to reduce the physiological arousal. At this point in time, there have been evaluations of three kinds of biofeedback training: biofeedback of heart rate (HR), EEG alpha, and frontal EMG. Results for each of these will be summarized below.

Heart rate. Biofeedback training to reduce HR has been used as an adjunct to the exposure-based treatment of simple phobics in two studies by Nunes and Marks (1975, 1976). In both instances, while patients showed significant control of HR lowering, the biofeedback training added nothing to the exposure-based treatment. In two case reports in which the biofeedback training was the principle therapy, both Blanchard and Abel (1976) and Gatchel (1977) reported clinical success and significant control of HR.

Gatchel and his colleagues have conducted most of the controlled research in this area (Gatchel, Hatch, Maynard, Turns, & Taunton-Blackwood, 1979; Gatchel, Hatch, Watson, Smith, & Gaas, 1977; Gatchel & Proctor, 1976). All of the studies have been done on college volunteers high in public speaking fear. In the first study (Gatchel & Proctor, 1976), veridical feedback of HR led both to more HR lowering and more reduction in anxiety than nonfeedback-control conditions. However, when HR biofeedback was compared to simple relaxation training (Gatchel et al., 1977), both conditions led to HR lowering and anxiety reduction. In the final study, a combination of HR biofeedback plus relaxation training led to more HR reduction than did systematic desensitization; however, both treatment conditions and the controls all reported equivalent degrees of anxiety reduction.

At this point, we conclude that HR biofeedback is no more effective than simpler relaxation techniques for anxiety reduction.

EEG alpha. Glueck and Stroebel (1975) reported on a large-scale (n=225), controlled comparison of alpha biofeedback to autogenic training and to transcendental meditation (TM) in mixed psychiatric inpatients with anxiety problems. Although there was some evidence for increased alpha in the EEGs of feedback recipients, only the patients receiving TM reported any clinical improvement.

Plotkin and Rice (1981) have recently reported that a comparison of feedback for alpha enhancement and feedback for alpha suppression, using anxious college volunteers, yielded equivalent clinical improvement. Patients in the alpha-suppression group did not show significant physiological change but had been led to believe they were succeeding at the task. The authors interpret the results as supporting the hypothesis that the experience of success in controlling the physiological response is the key factor, rather than actual physiological change.

In general, there seems little empirical support for the use of alpha-biofeedback training in anxiety disorders.

Frontal EMG. By far, the most widely researched aspect of this area is the application of frontal-EMG biofeedback training to generalized anxiety, with at least eight single-group or controlled comparisons having been reported. These studies are summarized in Table 3.

As reference to Table 3 will show, all groups of subjects who received frontal-EMG biofeedback did show a significant decrease in the targeted physiological response. Moreover, in four of six instances, the patients receiving the feedback training showed a greater reduction in frontal EMG than comparison conditions. In two of four studies, for which the comparison was some form of relaxation training, the biofeedback training led to greater physiological change; in two it did not. With regard to clinical improvement, the patients receiving the biofeedback training all showed some degree of improvement. In two studies, Le Bouef and Lodge (1980) and Raskin and Rondestvedt (1973), the overall clinical improvement was not very great.

The last item of Table 3 reveals a major problem in this area: in only one instance (Townsend, House, & Addario, 1975) does the biofeedback training lead to greater clinical improvement than comparison conditions. In all four of the comparisons to relaxation training, *there is no advantage for biofeedback training over relaxation training*. (We might note that this is a conclusion which will appear many times in this section of this chapter.)

Recurrent headaches. One of the most widespread uses of biofeedback is in the treatment of headaches. The pioneering work of Budzynski, Stoyva, and their associates (Budzynski, Stoyva, & Adler, 1970; Budzynski, Stoyva, Adler, & Mullaney, 1973) showed that frontal-EMG biofeedback training, combined with regular practice of relaxation, led to significant reduction in tension headaches. A subsequent study showed EMG biofeedback to be superior to an attention-placebo treatment rated by participants to be highly credible (Holroyd, Andrasik, & Noble, 1980). The major professional, biofeedback organization (Biofeedback Society of America—BSA) had proclaimed that tension headache is one disorder for which there is demonstrated efficacy.

To date, there have been six direct comparisons of frontal-EMG biofeedback to some form of relaxation training in the treatment of tension headaches. These studies are summarized in Table 4.

As one can note from Table 4, four of the direct comparisons find no advantage for frontal-EMG biofeedback over relaxation training. In one study (Chesney & Shelton, 1976), relaxation alone is superior to biofeedback alone; in another (Hutchings & Reinking, 1976), biofeedback training alone is superior to relaxation training alone. We conclude that the two procedures are equally efficacious, with no systematic advantage for one over the other.

In a recent, further analysis of the tension headache treatment-outcome data (Blanchard, Andrasik, Ahles, Teders, & O'Keefe, 1980), we com-

Table 3

Frontal-EMG biofeedback in the treatment of anxiety disorders

Authors	Subject population	Control or comparison conditions	Physiological response		Clinical response	
			Did FB group change	Did FB group change more than controls	Did FB group improve	Did FB group improve more than controls
Raskin, Johnson, & Rondestvedt, 1973	10 chronic-anxiety neurotics	None—all patients had failed to respond to tranquilizers and/or psychotherapy for 2 years	Yes	Not reported	4 out of 10 report improvement	Not reported
Townsend, House, & Addario, 1975	21 psychiatric patients with chronic anxiety	(1) 16 hours group psychotherapy ($n = 8$)	Yes	Yes	Yes	Yes
Canter, Kondo, & Knott, 1975	28 patients with anxiety neurosis	(1) Modified progressive relaxation ($n = 14$)	Yes	Yes	Yes 85% of sample	No
Kappes & Michaud, 1978	12 undergrad volunteers with high test anxiety	(1) Crossover design true FB versus noncontinuous FB	Yes	Not reported	Yes	No
Miller, Murphy, & Miller, 1978	21 patients with high dental anxiety	(1) Progressive relaxation (PR) ($n = 7$) (2) Attention control ($n = 7$)	Yes	FB = Pr > (2)	Yes	FB = PR > (2)

Gatchel et al., 1978	12 undergrads with high anxiety	(1) False FB (n = 6)	Yes	Yes	Yes	No
Raskin, Bali, & Peake, 1980	31 patients with anxiety neurosis	(1) Progressive relaxation (n = 10) (2) Transcendental meditation (n = 10)	Yes	No	Yes	No
LeBoeuf & Lodge, 1980	26 patients with chronic anxiety neurosis	(1) Progressive relaxation (n = 13)	Yes	Yes	Yes, on self-report, 2 out of 13 moderate improved	No—Same degree of improvement

Table 4

Direct comparisons of frontal-EMG biofeedback and relaxation training in the treatment of tension headaches

Authors	Sample size	Other control conditions	Length of training	Physiological responses			Clinical response	
				Did FB group change	*Did relax group change*	*Did FB group change more than others*	*Comparisons of FB, relax, & control*	*Percent improvement FB–Relax*
Cox, Freundlich, & Meyer, 1975	9 per group	Medication placebo	8 sessions over 4 weeks	Yes	Yes	FB = R > Control	FB = R > Control	FB −65 R −57
Haynes, Griffin, Mooney, & Parise, 1975	8 per group	HA monitoring ($n = 5$)	6 sessions over 3 weeks	No response	No response	No response	FB = R > Control	FB −75 R −82
Hutchings & Reinking, 1976	6 per group	FB = R	10 sessions	Yes	Yes	FB = R = FB + R	FB = FB + R > R	FB −66 FB + R −66 R −27
Chesney & Shelton, 1976	6 per group	FB + R, HA monitoring	9 sessions over 3 weeks	No response	No response	No response	R = FB + R > Control FB = Control	FB −42 FB + R −78 R −75
Martin & Mathews, 1978	12 per group	None	14 sessions over 14 weeks	No	No	No	FB = R	FB −12 R −22
Gray, Lyle, McGuire, & Peck, 1980	5 per group	None	9 sessions over 9 weeks	Yes	Yes	No	FB = R	No response

pared the average percent improvement for six different conditions across 27 studies and found these results:

Condition	Percent improvement
Frontal-EMG biofeedback alone	60.9
Relaxation training alone	59.2
Frontal-EMG biofeedback combined with relaxation training	58.8
Psychological placebo	35.3
Medication placebo	34.8
Headache monitoring	4.5

Thus, treatment is clearly better than no treatment or than placebo treatment. In the one comparison of biofeedback training to medication, Bruhn, Oleson, and Melgaard, (1979), frontal-EMG biofeedback was superior to medication in headache relief among chronic sufferers.

While the biofeedback treatment for tension (or muscle-contraction) headache makes intuitive sense (i.e., the feedback training is designed to teach headache sufferers to relax the muscles of the face and head, as sustained contractions of these muscles are ostensibly the etiology of tension headache), the accepted biofeedback training regimen for migraine does not. However, it has been repeatedly demonstrated that teaching patients to warm their hands (that is, to dilate the tiny blood vessels in the hands) has a therapeutic effect on migraine headaches.

Thermal biofeedback, combined with training in autogenic phrases (a meditative, self-instructed form of relaxation), was first reported to be beneficial in the treatment of migraine headache by Sargent et al. (1972). Although the field is not as advanced as the biofeedback treatment of tension headache, several controlled evaluations have been reported. Moreover, at least three comparisons of thermal-biofeedback training with some form of relaxation training have been reported: Andreychuk and Skriver (1975); Blanchard, Theobald, Williamson, Silver, and Brown (1978); and Lake, Raney, and Papsdorf (1979). In all three of these reports, there was no significant advantage for biofeedback training over relaxation training.

The present authors (Blanchard, Andrasik, Ahles, Teders, & O'Keefe, 1980) also compared several treatment conditions (for migraine headache) to each other and to medication placebo, with regard to percent improvement:

Condition	Percent improvement
Thermal biofeedback and autogenic training	65.1
Thermal biofeedback alone	51.8
Relaxation alone	52.7
Medication placebo	16.5

Again, the three treatments exceed the placebo condition but do not differ among themselves. For both forms of headache, available data suggest no differences in outcome between biofeedback and relaxation.

Despite the apparent equivalence in the treatment of headache with biofeedback training and relaxation training on a group-comparison basis, some recent data from our own laboratory casts a different light on this matter. We have completed what we have termed *sequential comparisons*. A group of headache sufferers have all been given a thorough course of relaxation training (10 sessions, spread over eight weeks, modeled after the procedures of Bernstein & Borkovec, 1973). Those patients who did not show substantial (at least 60 percent) reduction in headache activity after the relaxation training were then offered biofeedback: 12 sessions of frontal-EMG biofeedback (for the tension-headache sufferers) and 12 sessions of thermal biofeedback (for those suffering from pure migraine or a combination of migraine and tension headaches). Among the relaxation nonresponders, the following percentages of each group were now much improved, following biofeedback training, according to Blanchard, Andrasik, Neff, Teders, Pallmeyer, Arena, Jurish, Saunders, Ahles, and Rodichok (1982):

Tension	36%
Migraine	12
Combined migraine and tension	75

Thus, while there appears to be no empirical basis to select biofeedback over relaxation (or vice versa) for any variety of headache, the wisest course would probably be to treat any given patient with both in order to maximize that individual's chances of improvement. This situation also highlights the need for studies of individual differences so that a basis for matching patient to treatment can be found.

Factors mediating outcome in biofeedback treatment of headache are not fully understood at present. Recent studies (Andrasik & Holroyd, 1980; Kewman & Roberts, 1980) suggest that learned control of physiology may play only a minor role in treatment for certain individuals, but these studies provide no clear indications of what the mediating factors may be. Investigations of mechanisms of biofeedback are needed to illuminate the treatment process for headache and other disorders as well.

Peripheral vascular disease. A condition which was little known to psychologists prior to the advent of biofeedback is Raynaud's disease. This is a functional disorder of the peripheral vascular system in which the patient experiences painful vasoconstrictive episodes either when in contact with cold stimuli or when there is emotional stress.

After several case reports (e.g., Blanchard & Haynes, 1975), Surwit,

Pilon, and Fenton (1978) compared self-regulation of peripheral temperature through either autogenic training or the combination of autogenic training and thermal biofeedback. Also included were a group of patients who served on a waiting-list and assessment control. Half the patients were treated primarily at home. Results showed that all treated subjects, regardless of condition, showed more ability to cope with a cold-stress test and reduced frequency of vasospastic episodes than untreated subjects. Treatment later brought the latter group to the same improved state. Thermal biofeedback added little to the autogenic training; moreover, treatment at home was as successful as lab-based treatment. A one-year follow-up (Keefe, Surwit, & Pilon, 1979) on approximately two thirds of the patients revealed maintenance of the reduced level of vasospastic attacks but a deterioration to baseline levels of ability to withstand the cold-stress test.

In a second study, Keefe, Surwit, and Pilon (1980) compared autogenic training with and without thermal biofeedback to progressive relaxation. All three treatments led to decreases in frequency of vasospastic attacks, with no differential advantage of one form of treatment over the other.

In a somewhat similar study, Jacobson, Manschreck, and Silverberg (1979) compared thermal biofeedback combined with progressive relaxation to progressive relaxation alone in a controlled, group-outcome study. Again, both groups were improved by one month after treatment and maintained this degree of improvement at two years. Again, biofeedback added no significant degree of clinical improvement (or significant degree of temperature self-regulation) to relaxation training. Finally, Stroebel, Strong, Ford, and Szarek (1981), in an uncontrolled trial of a treatment combining EMG and thermal biofeedback with various relaxation and self-instructional procedures, report 52 percent of a sample of 23 primary Raynaud's disease patients to be much improved or cured.

As with the other conditions reviewed in this section, there seems to be no systematic advantage in outcome for biofeedback training over nonmachine-based, relaxation-training regimens.

Hypertension. In the early 1970s, a series of reports appeared describing the successful treatment of essential hypertension using direct feedback of blood pressure, either on a beat-by-beat basis (Benson, Shapiro, Tursky, & Schwartz, 1971; Miller, 1972) or on an intermittent basis (Elder, Ruiz, Deabler, & Dillenkoffer, 1974; Blanchard, Young, & Haynes, 1975). In each instance, clinically meaningful reductions in blood pressure (BP) were reported for a large portion of the sample studied. An impressive aspect of this work was that the results emanated from four different laboratories working independently.

Next, there appeared a second wave of reports from these laboratories. In each instance, there was a decided failure to replicate the initial, successful results. As noted in Table 5, in each of the second round of

Table 5

Biofeedback and hypertension: The failure to replicate

Initial report		Later report	
Authors	*Results*	*Authors*	*Results*
Benson et al.	ΔBP = −17mm	Schwartz & Shapiro	ΔBP = 0
(1971)	5 out of 7 improved	(1973)	1 out of 7 improved
Miller	ΔBP = −21mm	Miller	Failure in
(1972)	One patient	(1975)	27 cases
Elder et al.	ΔBP = −20%	Elder & Eustis	ΔBP = 8mm
(1973)	of baseline	(1975)	9 out of 22 improved
Blanchard et al.	ΔBP = −26mm	Blanchard et al.	ΔBP = −7mm
(1975)	4 out of 4 improved	(1977)	

studies, either much smaller changes in BP were observed or much smaller portions of the sample responded positively.

There have continued to appear studies of the successful treatment of hypertension using direct feedback of BP (Kristt & Engel, 1975; Goldman, Kleinman, Snow, & Korol, 1977); however, these studies have generally not been controlled evaluations. Furthermore, Steptoe (1978) has reported initial successful treatment of BP, using feedback of pulse-wave velocity.

Our own conclusion, at this point, is that the treatment of essential hypertension, through direct feedback of BP, has not been convincingly shown to be a viable treatment of hypertension.

An alternative biofeedback approach to the treatment of hypertension has been to teach patients to relax, using frontal-EMG biofeedback. However, controlled evaluations of this procedure (Surwit, Shapiro, & Good, 1978; Blanchard, Miller, Abel, Haynes, & Wicker, 1979), have failed to confirm the efficacy of this procedure.

Yet another alternative biofeedback procedure, thermal biofeedback, has been touted as very successful in the treatment of hypertension (Green, Green, & Norris, 1980). It has yet to be subjected to controlled evaluations, as of the time of this writing (Fall 1981).

Despite the somewhat pessimistic view portrayed in the paragraphs above, there is one area of the biofeedback treatment of hypertension which has shown consistently good results: the work of Patel. In an impressive series of studies, Patel and her colleagues (Patel, 1973, 1975, 1977; Patel & Datey, 1976; Patel & North, 1975) have shown that the combination of relaxation training (emphasizing meditation, breathing exercises, and regular practice) and biofeedback (of skin-resistence level, and/or frontal EMG, or peripheral temperature) leads to large-scale changes in BP, with a majority of treated patients showing clinically meaningful decreases. It is unclear, however, what role the biofeedback, per se, plays in this treatment package.

Specialized applications of biofeedback

Neuromuscular rehabilitation. Although we have categorized the use of EMG biofeedback for neuromuscular rehabilitation as a specialized application, one authority on the field of rehabilitation estimates that EMG biofeedback is being used in as many as 40 percent of the rehabilitation centers in North America. Despite this apparent widespread use of EMG biofeedback, there is a decided lack of controlled studies in the area. In fact, we could locate only one controlled, group-outcome study and one other series of single-subject experiments. However, a saving feature of most of this research, which consists primarily of single group-outcome studies, is that the patients generally have had the disorder for a considerable length of time, thus ruling out spontaneous remission to some extent, and most patients also have failed to respond to one or more trials of standard physical therapy.

There have been three major clinical neuromuscular problems to which EMG biofeedback has been applied: lower-extremity dysfunction (primarily foot drop), as a result of cerebrovascular accident (CVA); upper-extremity dysfunction, as a result of CVA; and spasmodic torticollis and other dystonias. For a comprehensive critical review of this literature, see Keefe and Surwit (1978).

Smooth, normal, body movement usually requires the coordinated action of at least two muscles: an agonist and its antagonist. Neuromuscular disorders can thus result from spasticity (or excessive activity) in one of the pairs of muscles controlling a movement and/or from faccidity (or deficit activity) in one of the pair. Biofeedback training, then, will usually require training to decrease EMG activity in one muscle, while increasing EMG activity in the other muscle of the pair.

Lower-extremity dysfunction. In this disorder, the primary goal is to enable the patient to regain voluntary dorsiflexion of the ankle, so that gait and mobility are improved and so the use of a short leg brace can be eliminated on the affected side of the hemiplegic.

Johnson and Garton (1973) reported on 10 cases, all of whom had failed to respond to standard physical therapy and who were at least one year post-injury. There was improvement in motor function in all 10 cases. In five of these cases, the need for the short leg brace was eliminated. Brudny, Korein, Gruynbaum, Friedmann, Weinstein, Sachs-Frankel, and Belandres (1976) reported success in three out of six patients, to whom EMG-biofeedback training for lower-extremity dysfunction was given.

In the most ambitious study in this area, Basmajian, Kukulka, Naragan, and Takebe (1975) compared, in a controlled, group-outcome study involving 20 hemiplegic patients with foot drop, standard physical rehabilitation for 40 minutes, three times per week, for five weeks to a regimen consisting of 20 minutes of standard physical rehabilitation and 20 minutes of EMG-biofeedback training. Results showed an advantage for the group receiving biofeedback, in terms of increased strength of dorsiflexion and increased range of motion. Furthermore, 4 of the 10 biofeedback-treated patients were able to discard the short leg brace, compared to none in the standard group. A later report (Takebe, Kukulka, Naragan, & Basmajian, 1976) on part of this sample revealed that, despite functional improvements, there were no reliable changes in physiological parameters (such as nerve-conduction velocity) or amount of spasticity in the EMG.

Finally, Fish, Mayer, and Herman (1976), in a critique of the study, noted that there were confounds in subject assignment which favored the biofeedback group and that most of the differences were not statistically different. We are left to conclude that EMG biofeedback appears to be a useful adjunct to physical therapy in lower-extremity dysfunctions, but that conclusive data are lacking at this time.

Upper-extremity dysfunction. Brudny and his colleagues have made several reports on the use of EMG biofeedback with upper-extremity dysfunction in hemiparetics. All of these reports are uncontrolled, single group-outcome studies of progressively larger samples of patients (Brudny et al., 1976; Brudny, Korein, Grynbaum, & Sachs-Frankel, 1977; Brudny, Korein, Grynbaum, Belandres, & Gianutsor, 1979). In the latest report (Brudny et al., 1979), the results with 70 patients showed that 37 (52.8 percent) made substantial functional improvements, in an initial eight-week phase. Thirty-six patients continued for a second 24-week phase. In this latter subset, 20 patients showed additional functional improvement.

It thus appears that EMG biofeedback can help with this neuromuscular problem also; however, as with lower-extremity dysfunctions, the field awaits a controlled evaluation of the role of biofeedback.

Spasmodic torticollis. As with upper-extremity dysfunction, the principle work with spasmodic torticollis and other dystonias has been reported by Brudny and his associates. In an initial report on nine cases (Brudny, Grynbaum, & Korein, 1974), the procedures are described. In seven of the nine cases, marked improvement was noted, including ability to keep the head in a neutral position for hours without feedback; the gains were maintained over periods of several months.

In the second report from this group (Brudny et al., 1976), 26 of 48 patients had initial, significant, functional improvement. On long-term follow-up, 19 of 48 (40 percent) maintained marked functional improvement. In a somewhat expanded series, containing (as best we can determine) all of the previously treated patients, 37 of 69 (54 percent) torticollis patients had shown good maintenance of these gains. All of these reports are, of course, uncontrolled.

Martin (1981) has reported on a series of six single-subject experiments, involving patients with torticollis. He compared, in an *ABAB* design, the regular practice of corrective exercises (some performed before a mirror for the visual feedback) with and without the addition of EMG biofeedback. Although his results confirm the role of biofeedback in altering sternocleidomastoid activity, there was an absence of a pronounced biofeedback effect on clinical status (such as, ability to maintain neutral head position).

Thus, in this area, as in other aspects of neuromuscular rehabilitation, the results are encouraging but still await definitive, controlled studies.

Fecal incontinence. As one can easily imagine, chronic fecal incontinence in an older child, adolescent, or adult is a severe, socially debilitating disorder. For those patients for whom the innervation of the internal and external anal sphincters is intact, a biofeedback procedure developed by Engel, Nikomanesh, and Schuster (1974) shows great promise. In this application, a three-part pressure transducer is inserted in the anus. One part acts to stimulate the lower colon; the second part measures response of the internal anal sphincters, a smooth muscle normally under reflex control; and the third part measures response of the external anal sphincter. Treatment is aimed at coordinating the response of these muscles. Typically treatment has been fairly brief, two to four 1½ hour sessions.

In the first report (Engel et al., 1974), six of seven patients showed marked clinical improvement: that is, they were cured, for all practical purposes. In a later, larger study (Cerulli, Nikoomanesh, & Schuster, 1976), 36 out of 50 consecutive patients showed marked clinical improvement. Finally, Wald (1981) reported 12 of 17 patients showed marked improvement. The importance of this latter report stems from its being completed at a center different from where the initial developmental work took place by an independent investigator. At this point, this form of treatment is available at the University of Pittsburgh Medical School, Johns Hopkins Medical Center, and in New York City (Dr. Cerulli). It may be available at other centers but it remains fairly specialized.

As with the neuromuscular work, this application has not been subjected to a controlled evaluation. However, given the long baselines and lack of response to other treatment (in fact, there is practically no other reasonable treatment), it certainly seems very promising.

Epilepsy. The last, major specialized problem to which biofeedback has been somewhat widely applied is epilepsy. Sterman and his colleagues (Sterman, 1973; Sterman & Friar, 1972; Sterman, MacDonald, & Stone, 1974) reported on four seizure patients who had been treated with sensorimotor-rhythm (SMR) feedback. These patients were subjected to informal or unplanned single-subject experiments of the *ABAB* type, due to the discontinuation of feedback training for some interval. In this form of treatment, patients are taught to produce increasing amounts of SMR. The SMR is a 12 to 16 Hz. rhythm recorded over the motor cortex. It is normally present in very small amounts in the normal or nonseizure patient EEG. In the patients in the initial series, it was virtually absent during baseline.

The equipment to conduct this type of training consists of very specialized electronic filters and amplifiers. Moreover, elaborate electronic logic or a small, on-line computer are also used to detect and record the occurrence of SMR and to provide appropriate feedback to the patient. Finally, most patients who have been treated by this procedure are evaluated by means of a power-spectral analysis of the EEG, that is, measurement of the relative amounts of energy present in different frequency bands of the EEG. The training regimens are fairly intensive: 3 to 5 sessions per week, for periods of 3 months to 2 years!

In Sterman's initial series, there was a good clinical response (in terms of reduced seizure frequency) for all four patients, after an initial period of SMR training; more important, from a causal analysis point of view, in the three patients for whom the biofeedback training was discontinued, there was a return of seizure rates to almost pre-treatment (or baseline) levels and later reductions of seizures, once treatment was reinstated.

Sterman's results were replicated, for the most part, by Lubar and his colleagues (Seifert & Lubar, 1975; Lubar & Bahler, 1976). In a series of eight patients with long-standing, relatively intractable seizure disorders, all patients showed some improvement following SMR biofeedback training (in terms of reduced seizure frequency or reduced severity of experienced seizures); three patients showed almost complete suppression of seizures. Again, reduction in seizure activity seemed closely related to continuation of biofeedback training and to the relative production of the SMR in the EEG.

Kaplan (1975) reported on a failure to replicate the results obtained by Sterman and by Lubar in a series of two patients given SMR training. One of these patients (and two others, later) experienced seizure-rate reduction when given training in another EEG-band width. Kuhlman (1978), in a carefully designed experimental analysis of the effects of biofeedback on a series of five patients, showed significant reduction (about 60 percent) in seizure rate in three of the five patients. He included control phases, during which random feedback was provided to the patient, both at the beginning of the treatment and during a withdrawal phase. His procedure varied somewhat, in that the band width was 9 to 14 Hz., rather than 12 to 14. As with Kaplan, Kuhlman (1978) found no evidence of increased SMR in the EEG in the improved patients; rather, there was an association between increased alpha (9 to 12 Hz. activity in the power-spectral analysis) and seizure reduction.

Gradually, in this field, there has evolved a new hypothesis of the mechanism of action of the EEG-biofeedback training and seizure reduction: it could best be described as the normalization hypothesis. By this is meant that the crucial, physiological changes in the EEG are not only production of the SMR but rather an overall shift in the power-spectral analysis in the direction of normalcy. For example, this shift might mean a reduction in slower (theta) activity in one patient, or an increase in alpha (8 to 12 Hz.) in another patient, with a concomitant reduction in 20+ Hz. activity. The key feature is, thus, the assessment of the power spectrum of the EEG for the individual patient and subsequent training directed at shifting the power spectrum in a direction of normalcy.

This hypothesis was partially tested in a single-blind, *ABA* study of eight patients by Sterman and Shouse (1979). Patients were given training to increase one frequency band while suppressing another. These conditions were reversed after three months, without the patients' knowledge, and then changed back again to the original regimen, after three more months. In general, power spectra, sleep EEGs, and seizure rates confirmed the value of normalizing the power spectrum of the EEG.

In by far the most ambitious study in this area, Lubar (in press) has tested the normalization hypothesis in a double-blind, *ABA* design, using three small ($n = 2$ or 3) groups of epileptics, whose training regimens differed according to frequency bands targeted. The technicians who conducted the training, as well as the patients, were blind to shifts in conditions, in this study. Although precise, functional relations between EEG-training condition and seizure rate did not occur in all cases, in general, the normalization hypothesis was supported.

The work in this area is impressive from two points of view: first, the general idea has been replicated by at least six different laboratories in this country and in Canada; second, although the numbers of patients in most studies have been small, the use of reversal and withdrawal designs and the use of single- and double-blind studies add great credibility to the conclusions. Moreover, a consensus has been approached, which states that the power spectrum of the individual patient's EEG must be taken into account in the particular training program, with the emphasis on normalizing the individual EEG. Finally, there is often repeated evidence that seizure reduction is significantly associated with changes in the EEG, or that the clinical, symptomatic change is closely tied to the change in the physiological substrate.

Available research supports the clinical utility of biofeedback and indicates it is a viable treatment for a large number of disorders. As is obvious from this brief review, for most of the general-practice applications of biofeedback in which the symptoms are linked to excessive physiological arousal, there is a lack of evidence from controlled studies showing an advantage for biofeedback training over relaxation training. Although biofeedback and relaxation training show no differences on a group basis, some recently collected data suggests both procedures may be needed for certain patients to obtain meaningful, clinical improvement. Perhaps the major research question facing biofeedback investigators is how to best match treatment approach to patient, so as to maximize therapeutic gains. To paraphrase an age-old quotation, researchers need to provide answers to what type of biofeedback, in combination with what other cognitive and behavioral procedures, is of most benefit to what type of person, with what symptoms and what life circumstances. Biofeedback treatments have suffered too long from patient and treatment uniformity myths (Kiesler, 1966). Qualls and Sheehan (1981) review data pertinent to this point in the area of EMG biofeedback, and we encourage the continuation of this type of research. One other research avenue is relatively untravelled: that concerning mechanisms underlying biofeedback. Many investigators have found sizable, durable treatment effects in clients who have been unable to reliably influence their physiology during biofeedback training. These findings have led some individuals (Lazarus, 1977; Meichenbaum, 1977) to posit that cognitive and behavioral processes may be more responsible for clinical effects. These interpretations remain speculative, for they are post hoc. Prospective analyses of changes in physiological, behavioral, and cognitive response systems that occur during biofeedback training will be helpful in achieving this goal of treatment-patient matching.

SUMMARY

Biofeedback is a process wherein a person learns to reliably influence responses not ordinarily under voluntary control or responses for which regulation has broken down. Biofeedback involves three operations: (1) detection and amplification of biological responses; (2) conversion of the bioelectrical signals into easy-to-process information; and (3) feedback of this information to the patient, so that he or she can learn to voluntarily control the response. A number of response systems have been utilized in biofeedback applications and research, chief among these being blood pressure, blood volume, electromyography, electroencephalography, and electrocardiology. The various ways for measuring the preceding responses are discussed, and examples are given. Three methods are presently available for providing biofeedback: self-contained units, polygraph with solid-state logic, and individual solid-state modules. Advantages and disadvantages associated with each are reviewed.

When administering biofeedback, the therapist must address a number of procedural matters. These are categorized and discussed in terms of the therapeutic context, the evaluation for biofeedback, and the biofeedback training itself. Available data suggest that clinical effects are optimized when biofeedback is administered in a positive, supportive environment. The evaluation for biofeedback concerns the collection of a thorough history and the establishment of baseline levels of symptoms and physiology. Biofeedback training is preceded by patient education. In planning and delivering biofeedback, clinicians need to decide which of several approaches and parameters to use, to plan and test for generalization and maintenance, to work to maintain the patient's involvement in treatment, and to perform periodic, progress reviews.

The chapter closes with a selective review of the biofeedback treatment literature, divided into widely available applications and specialized applications. Applications termed widely available consist of anxiety disorders, recurrent headaches, peripheral vascular disorders, and hypertension. A feature common to these disorders is the presence of excessive sympathetic nervous system activity. For these disorders, multiple types of biofeedback appear effective, but no form of biofeedback appears to be systematically superior to nonbiofeedback procedures designed to produce relaxation. For the specialized applications—neuromuscular rehabilitation, fecal incontinence, and epilepsy—biofeedback appears to offer a specific, nonrelaxation effect. Two main suggestions are offered for future research: the first concerns matching of treatment to patient, while the second consists of identifying mechanisms underlying biofeedback.

REFERENCES

Andrasik, F., Blanchard, E. B., & Edlund, S. R. Physiological responding during biofeedback. In S. R. Burchfield (Ed.), *Psychological and physiological interactions in the response to stress.* New York: Hemisphere, in press.

Andrasik, F., Blanchard, E. B., & Pallmeyer, T. P. *Massed versus distributed schedules in thermal biofeedback training of patients with vascular headaches.* Paper presented at the meeting of the Biofeedback Society of America, Chicago, March 1982.

Andrasik, F., Coleman, D., & Epstein, L. H. Biofeedback: Clinical and research considerations. In D. M. Doleys, R. L. Meredith, & A. R. Ciminero (Eds.), *Behavioral psychology in medicine: Assessment and treatment strategies.* New York: Plenum Press, 1982.

Andrasik, F., & Holroyd, K. A. A test of specific and nonspecific effects in the biofeedback treatment of tension headache. *Journal of Consulting and Clinical Psychology,* 1980, *48,* 575–586.

Andreychuk, T., & Skriver, C. Hypnosis and biofeedback in the treatment of migraine headache. *The International Journal of Clinical and Experimental Hypnosis,* 1975, *23,* 172–183.

Basmajian, J. V. Facts versus myths in EMG biofeedback. *Biofeedback and Self-Regulation,* 1976, *1,* 369–371.

Basmajian, J. V., Kukulka, C. G., Naragan, M. G., & Takebe, K. Biofeedback treatment of foot drop after stroke compared with standard rehabilitation technique: Effects on voluntary control and strength. *Archives of Physical Medicine and Rehabilitation,* 1975, *56,* 231–236.

Benson, H., Shapiro, D., Tursky, B., & Schwarta, G. E. Decreased systolic blood pressure through operant-conditioning techniques in patients with essential hypertension. *Science,* 1971, *173,* 740–742.

Bernstein, D. A., & Borkovec, T. D. *Progressive relaxation training: A manual for the helping professions.* Champaign, Ill.: Research Press, 1973.

Blanchard, E. B. Biofeedback: Basic research and clinical applications. Paper presented at the meeting of the Association for Advancement of Behavior Therapy, Atlanta, December 1977.

Blanchard, E. B., & Abel, G. G. An experimental case study of the biofeedback treatment of a rape-induced, psychophysiological cardiovascular disorder. *Behavior Therapy,* 1976, *7,* 113–119.

Blanchard, E. B., Andrasik, F., Ahles, T. A., Teders, S. J., & O'Keefe, D. Migraine and tension headache: A meta-analytic review. *Behavior Therapy,* 1980, *11,* 613–631.

Blanchard, E. B., Andrasik, F., Neff, D., Teders, S. J., Pallmeyer, T. P., Arena, J. G., Jurish, S. E., Saunders, N. L., Ahles, T. A., & Rodichok, L. D. Sequential comparisons of relaxation training and biofeedback in the treatment of three kinds of chronic headache or, the machines may be necessary some of the time. *Behaviour Research and Therapy,* 1982, *2,* 469–481.

Blanchard, E. B., & Epstein, L. H. *A biofeedback primer.* Reading, Mass.: Addison-Wesley, Publishing, 1978.

Blanchard, E. B., & Haynes, M. R. Biofeedback treatment of a case of Raynaud's disease. *Journal of Behavior Therapy and Experimental Psychiatry,* 1975, *6,* 230–234.

Blanchard, E. B., Miller, S. T., Abel, G. G., Haynes, M. R., & Wicker, R. Evaluation of Biofeedback in the treatment of borderline essential hypertension. *Journal of Applied Behavior Analysis,* 1979, *12,* 99–109.

Blanchard, E. B., Theobald, D. E., Williamson, D. A., Silver, B. V., & Brown, D. A. Temperature biofeedback in the treatment of migraine headaches. *Archives of General Psychiatry,* 1978, *35,* 581–588.

Blanchard, E. B., & Young, L. Clinical applications of biofeedback training: A review of evidence. *Archives of General Psychiatry,* 1974, *30,* 530–589.

Blanchard, E. B., Young, L. D., & Haynes, M. R. A simple feedback system for the treatment of elevated blood pressure. *Behavior Therapy,* 1975, *6,* 241–245.

Borgeat, F., Hade, B., Larouche, L. M., & Bedwani, C. N. Effect of therapist's active presence on EMG biofeedback training of headache patients. *Biofeedback and Self-Regulation,* 1980, *5,* 275–282.

Brener, J. Heart rate. In P. H. Venables & I. Martin (Eds.), *A manual of psychophysiological methods.* Amsterdam: North Holland, 1967.

Brown, B. B. Recognition aspects of consciousness through association with EEG-alpha activity represented by a light signal. *Psychophysiology,* 1970, *6,* 442–452.

Brown, B. B. Awareness of EEG-subjective activity relationships detected within a closed feedback system. *Psychophysiology,* 1971, *7,* 451–464.

Brown, C. C. (Ed.), *Methods in psychophysiology.* Baltimore: Williams & Wilkins, 1967.

Brudny, J., Grynbaum, B. B., & Korein, J. Spasmodic torticollis: Treatment by feedback display of EMG. *Archives of Physical Medicine and Rehabilitation,* 1974, *55,* 403–408.

Brudny, J., Korein, J., Grynbaum, B. B., Belandres, P. V., & Gianutsor, J. G. Helping hemiparetics to help themselves: Sensory-feedback therapy. *Journal of American Medical Association,* 1979, *241,* 814–818.

Brudny, J., Korein, J., Grynbaum, B. B., Friedmann, L. W., Weinstein, S., Sachs-Frankel,

G., & Belandres, P. V. EMG-feedback therapy: Review of treatment of 114 patients. *Archives of Physical Medicine and Rehabilitation,* 1976, *57,* 55–61.

Brudny, J., Korein, J., Grynbaum, B. B., & Sachs-Frankel, G. Sensory-feedback therapy in patients with brain insult. *Scandinavian Journal of Rehabilitation Medicine,* 1977, *9,* 155–163.

Bruhn, P., Oleson, J., & Melgaard, B. Controlled trial of EMG feedback in muscle-contraction headache. *Annals of Neurology,* 1979, *6,* 34–36.

Budzynski, T. (Chair). *Individual-response specificity in stress reactions.* Symposium presented at the meeting of the Biofeedback Society of America, Louisville, March 1981.

Budzynski, T. H., Stoyva, J., & Adler, C. S. Feedback-influenced muscle relaxation: Application to tension headache. *Journal of Behavior Therapy and Experimental Psychiatry,* 1970, *1,* 205–211.

Budzynski, T. H., Stoyva, J. M., Adler, C. S., & Mullaney, D. J. EMG biofeedback and tension headache: A controlled outcome study. *Psychosomatic Medicine,* 1973, *35,* 484–496.

Cautela, J. R. *Organic-dysfunction survey schedules.* Champaign, Ill.: Research Press, 1981.

Cerulli, M. A., Nikoomanesh, P., & Schuster, M. M. Progress in biofeedback treatment of fecal incontinence. *Gastroenterology,* 1976, *70,* part Z, A–11/869.

Chesney, M. A., & Shelton, J. L. A comparison of muscle-relaxation and electromyogram biofeedback treatment for muscle-contraction headache. *Journal of Behavior Therapy and Experimental Psychiatry,* 1976, *7,* 221–225.

Diamond, S., & Franklin, M. *Indications and contraindications for the use of biofeedback therapy in headache patients.* Paper presented at the meeting of the Biofeedback Research Society, Colorado Springs, February 1975.

Elder, S. T., Ruiz, Z. B., Deabler, H. L., & Dillenkoffer, R. L. Instrumental conditioning of diastolic blood pressure in essential-hypertensive patients. *Journal of Applied Behavior Analysis,* 1973, *6,* 377–382.

Engel, B. T., Nikoomanesh, P., & Schuster, M. M. Operant conditioning of rectosphincteric responses in the treatment of fecal incontinence. *New England Journal of Medicine,* 1974, *290,* 646–649.

Epstein, L. H., & Blanchard, E. B. Biofeedback, self-control, and self-management. *Biofeedback and Self-Regulation,* 1977, *2,* 201–211.

Fish, D., Mayer, N., & Herman, R. Biofeedback. *Archives of Physical Medicine and Rehabilitation,* 1976, *57,* 152.

Gaarder, K. R., & Montgomery, P. S. *Clinical biofeedback: A procedural manual.* Baltimore: Williams & Wilkins, 1977.

Gainer, J. C. Temperature-discrimination training in the biofeedback treatment of migraine headache. *Journal of Behavior Therapy and Experimental Psychiatry,* 1978, *9,* 185–188.

Gatchel, R. J. Therapeutic effectiveness of voluntary heart rate control in reducing anxiety. *Journal of Consulting and Clinical Psychology,* 1977, *45,* 689–691.

Gatchel, R. J., Hatch, J. P., Maynard, A., Turns, R., & Taunton-Blackwood, A. A. A comparison of heart rate feedback, false biofeedback, and systematic desensitization in reducing speech anxiety: Short- and long-term effectiveness. *Journal of Consulting and Clinical Psychology,* 1979, *47,* 620–622.

Gatchel, R. J., Hatch, J. P., Watson, P. J., Smith, D., & Gaas, E. Comparative effectiveness of voluntary heart rate control and muscular relaxation as active coping skills for reducing speech anxiety. *Journal of Consulting and Clinical Psychology,* 1977, *45,* 1093–1100.

Gatchel, R. J., & Proctor, J. D. Effectiveness of voluntary heart rate control in reducing speech anxiety. *Journal of Counseling and Clinical Psychology,* 1976, *44,* 381–389.

Gleuck, B. C., & Stroebel, C. F. Biofeedback and meditation in the treatment of psychiatric illnesses. *Comprehensive Psychiatry,* 1975, *16,* 303–321.

Goldman, H., Kleinman, K. N., Snow, M. Y., Bidus, D. R., & Korol, B. Relationship between essential hypertension and cognitive functioning: The effects of biofeedback. *Psychophysiology,* 1975, *12,* 569–573.

Green, E. E., Green, A. M., & Norris, P. A. Self-regulation training for control of hypertension. *Primary Cardiology,* 1980, *6,* 126–137.

Greenfield, N. S., & Sternbach, R. A. *Handbook of psychophysiology.* New York: Holt, Rinehart & Winston, 1972.

Hassett, J. *A primer of psychophysiology.* San Francisco: W. H. Freeman, 1978.

Holroyd, K., Andrasik, F., & Noble, J. A comparison of EMG biofeedback and a credible pseudotherapy in treating tension headache. *Journal of Behavioral Medicine,* 1980, *3,* 29–39.

Hutchings, D. F., & Reinking, R. H. Tension headache: What form of therapy is most effective? *Biofeedback and Self-Regulation,* 1976, *1,* 183–190.

Jacobson, A. N., Manschreck, T. C., & Silverberg, E. Behavioral treatment for Raynaud's disease: A comparative study with long-term follow-up. *American Journal of Psychiatry,* 1979, *136,* 844–846.

Johnson, H. E., & Garton, W. H. Muscle reeducation in hemiplegia by use of an electromyographic device. *Archives of Physical Medicine and Rehabilitation,* 1973, *54,* 320–322; 325.

Kamiya, J. Conscious control of brain waves. *Psychology Today,* 1968, *1,* 57–60.

Kaplan, B. J. Biofeedback in epileptics: Equivocal relationship of reinforced EEG frequency to seizure reduction. *Epilepsia,* 1975, *16,* 477–485.

Keefe, F. J., & Surwit, R. S. Electromyographic biofeedback: Behavioral treatment of neuromuscular disorders. *Journal of Behavioral Medicine,* 1978, *1,* 13–24.

Keefe, F. J., Surwit, R. S., & Pilon, R. N. A one-year follow-up of Raynaud's patients treated with behavioral-therapy techniques. *Journal of Behavioral Medicine,* 1979, *2,* 385–391.

Keefe, F. J., Surwit, R. S., & Pilon, R. N. Biofeedback, autogenic training, and progressive relaxation in the treatment of Raynaud's disease: A comparative study. *Journal of Applied Behavior Analysis,* 1980, *13,* 3–11.

Kewman, D., & Roberts, A. H. Skin-temperature biofeedback and migraine headaches: A double-blind study. *Biofeedback and Self-Regulation,* 1980, *5,* 327–345.

Kiesler, D. Some myths of psychotherapy research and the search for a paradigm. *Psychological Bulletin,* 1966, *65,* 110–136.

King, N. J., & Montgomery, R. B. Biofeedback-induced control of human peripheral temperature: A critical review of the literature. *Psychological Bulletin,* 1980, *88,* 738–752.

Kristt, D. A., & Engel, B. T. Learned control of blood pressure in patients with high blood pressure. *Circulation,* 1975, *51,* 370–378.

Kuhlman, W. N. EEG-feedback training of epileptic patients: Clinical and electroencephalographic analysis. *Electroencephalography in Clinical Neurophysiology*, 1978, *45*, 699–710.

Lake, A., Raney, J., & Papsdorf, J. D. Biofeedback and rational-emotive therapy in the management of migraine headache. *Journal of Applied Behavior Analysis*, 1979, *12*, 127–140.

Lane, J. D., Greenstadt, L., & Shapiro, D. Pulse transit time and blood pressure: An intensive analysis. In *Proceedings of the Biofeedback Society of America 10th Annual Meeting*. Denver: Biofeedback Society of America, 1979.

Lazarus, R. S. A cognitive analysis of biofeedback control. In G. E. Schwartz & J. Beatty (Eds.), *Biofeedback: Theory and research*. New York: Academic Press, 1977.

Le Bouef, A., & Lodge, J. Comparison of frontalis EMG-feedback training and progressive relaxation in the treatment of chronic anxiety. *British Journal of Psychiatry*, 1980, *137*, 279–284.

Leeb, C., Fahrion, S., & French, D. Instructional set, deep relaxation, and growth enhancement: A pilot study. *Journal of Humanistic Psychology*, 1976, *16*, 71–78.

Lichstein, K. L., Sallis, J. F., Hill, D., & Young, M. C. Psychophysiological adaptation: An investigation of multiple parameters. *Journal of Behavioral Assessment*, 1981, *3*, 111–121.

Lubar, J. F. EEG operant conditioning in intractable epileptics: Controlled, multidimensional studies. In L. White & B. Tursky (Eds.), *Clinical biofeedback: Efficacy in mechanisms*. New York: Guilford Press, 1982.

Lubar, J. F., & Bahler, W. W. Behavioral management of epileptic seizures following EEG-biofeedback training of the sensorimotor rhythm. *Biofeedback and Self-Regulation*, 1976, *1*, 77–104.

Lynn, S. J., & Freedman, R. R. Transfer and evaluation of biofeedback treatment. In A. P. Goldstein & F. Kanfer (Eds.), *Maximizing treatment gains: Transfer enhancement in psychotherapy*. New York: Academic Press, 1979.

Martin, I., & Venables, P. H. (Eds.). *Techniques in psychophysiology*. New York: John Wiley & Sons, 1980.

Martin, P. R. Spasmodic torticollis: Investigation and treatment using EMG-feedback training. *Behavior Therapy*, 1981, *12*, 247–262.

Meichenbaum, D. H. Toward a cognitive theory of self-control. In G. E. Schwartz & D. Shapiro (Eds.), *Consciousness and self-regulation* (Vol. 1). New York: Plenum Press, 1976.

Meichenbaum, D. H. *Cognitive-behavior modification: An integrative approach*. New York: Plenum Press, 1977.

Miller, N. E. Postscript. In D. Singh & C. T. Morgan (Eds.), *Current status of physiological psychology: Readings*. Monterey, Calif.: Brooks/Cole, 1972.

Miller, N. E. Biofeedback and visceral learning. *Annual Review of Psychology*, 1978, *29*, 373–404.

Miller, N. E., & Dworkin, B. R. Critical issues in therapeutic applications of biofeedback. In G. E. Schwartz & J. Beatty (Eds.), *Biofeedback: Theory and research*. New York: Academic Press, 1977.

Nunes, J. S., & Marks, I. M. Feedback of true heart rate during exposure in vivo. *Archives of General Psychiatry*, 1975, *32*, 933–936.

Nunes, J. S., & Marks, I. M. Feedback of true heart rate during exposure in vivo: Partial replication with methodological improvement. *Archives of General Psychiatry*, 1976, *33*, 1346–1350.

Obrist, P. A., Light, K. C., McCubbin, J. A., Hutcheson, J. S., & Hoffer, J. L. Pulse transit time: Relationship to blood pressure and myocardial performance. *Psychophysiology*, 1979, *16*, 292–301.

Olton, D. S., & Noonberg, A. R. *Biofeedback: Clinical applications in behavioral medicine.* Englewood Cliffs, N.J.: Prentice-Hall, 1980.

Patel, C. H. Yoga and biofeedback in the management of hypertension. *Lancet*, 1973, *2*, 1053–1055.

Patel, C. H. 12-month follow-up of yoga and biofeedback in the management of hypertension. *Lancet*, 1975, *1*, 62–67.

Patel, C. H. Biofeedback-aided relaxation and meditation in the management of hypertension. *Biofeedback and Self-Regulation*, 1977, *2*, 1–42.

Patel, C. H., & Datey, K. K. Relaxation and biofeedback techniques in the management of hypertension. *Angiology*, 1976, *27*, 106–113.

Patel, C. H., & North, W. R. S. Randomised, controlled trial of yoga and biofeedback in management of hypertension. *Lancet*, 1975, *2*, 93–95.

Plotkin, W. B. On the self-regulation of the occipital-alpha rhythm: Control strategies, states of consciousness, and the role of physiological feedback. *Journal of Experimental Psychology: General*, 1976, *105*, 66–99.

Plotkin, W. B., & Rice, K. M. Biofeedback as a placebo: Anxiety reduction facilitated by training in either suppression or enhancement of alpha brain waves. *Journal of Consulting and Clinical Psychology*, 1981, *49*, 590–596.

Qualls, P. J., & Sheehan, P. W. Electromyograph biofeedback as a relaxation technique: A critical appraisal and reassessment. *Psychological Bulletin*, 1981, *90*, 21–42.

Raskin, M., Johnson, M. G., & Rondestvedt, J. W. Chronic anxiety treated by feedback-induced muscle relaxation. *Archives of General Psychiatry*, 1973, *28*, 263–267.

Sargent, J. D., Green, E. E., & Walters, E. D. The use of autogenic-feedback training in a pilot study of migraine and tension headaches. *Headache*, 1972, *12*, 120–125.

Schultz, J. H., & Luthe, W. *Autogenic training* (Vol. 1). New York: Grune & Stratton, 1969.

Seifert, A. R., & Lubar, J. F. Reduction of epileptic seizures through EEG-biofeedback training. *Biological Psychology*, 1975, *3*, 157–184.

Shapiro, D., & Surwit, R. S. Learned control of physiological function and disease. In H. Leitenberg (Ed.), *Handbook of behavior modification and behavior therapy.* Englewood Cliffs, N.J.: Prentice-Hall, 1976.

Shaw, J. C. Quantification of biological signals using integration techniques. In P. H. Venables & I. Martin (Eds.), *Manual of psychophysiological methods.* New York: John Wiley & Sons, 1967.

Sovack, M., Kunzel, M., Sternbach, R. A., & Dalessio, P. J. Is volitional manipulation of hemodynamics a valid rationale for biofeedback therapy of migraine? *Headache*, 1978, *18*, 197–202.

Steptoe, A. The regulation of blood pressure reactions to taxing conditions using pulse transit-time feedback and relaxation. *Psychophysiology*, 1978, *15*, 429–438.

Steptoe, A., Smulylan, H., & Gribbin, B. Pulse-wave velocity and blood pressure change: Calibration and applications. *Psychophysiology*, 1976, *13*, 488–493.

Sterman, M. B. Neurophysiologic and clinical studies of sensorimotor EEG-biofeedback training: Some effects on epilepsy. In L. Birk (Ed.), *Biofeedback: Behavioral medicine.* New York: Grune & Stratton, 1973.

Sterman, M. B. & Friar, L. Suppression of seizures in an epileptic following sensorimotor EEG-feedback training. *Electroencephalography and Clinical Neurophysiology,* 1972, *33,* 89–95.

Sterman, M. B., MacDonald, L. R., & Stone, R. K. Biofeedback training of the sensorimotor-EEG rhythm in man: Effects on epilepsy. *Epilepsia,* 1974, *15,* 395–416.

Sterman, M. .B., & Shouse, M. N. Sleep electroencephalographic of reduced seizure in epileptics following operant conditioning. *Science,* 1979.

Sternbach, R. A. *Principles of psychophysiology: An introductory text and readings.* New York: Academic Press, 1966.

Stroebel, C. F., Strong, P., Ford, M. R., & Szarek, B. L. Quieting-response training: Five-year evaluation of a clinical-biofeedback practice. In *Proceedings of the Biofeedback Society of America 12th Annual Meeting.* Wheat Ridge, Colorado: Biofeedback Society of America, 1981.

Surwit, R. S., & Keefe, F. J. Frontalis EMG-feedback training: An electronic panacea? *Behavior Therapy,* 1978, *9,* 779—792.

Surwit, R. S., Pilon, R. N., & Fenton, C. H. Behavioral treatment of Raynaud's disease. *Journal of Behavioral Medicine,* 1978, *1,* 323–336.

Surwit, R. S., Shapiro, D., Good, M. I. Comparison of cardiovascular biofeedback, neuromuscular biofeedback, and meditation in the treatment of borderline essential hypertension. *Journal of Consulting an Clinical Psychology.* 1978, *46,* 252–263.

Takebe, K., Kukulka, C. G., Narayan, M. G., & Basmajian, J. V. Biofeedback treatment of foot drop after stroke compared with standard rehabilitation technique (Part 2): Effects on nerve conduction velocity and spasticity. *Archives of Physical Medicine and Rehabilitation,* 1976, *5,* 9–11.

Taub, E. Self-regulation of human tissue temperature. In G. E. Schwartz & J. Beatty (Eds.), *Biofeedback theory and research.* New York: Academic Press, 1977.

Taub, E., & Emurian, C. S. Feedback-aided self-regulation of skin temperature with a single-feedback locus. *Biofeedback and Self-Regulation,* 1976, *1,* 147–168.

Taub, E., & School, P. J. Some methodological considerations in thermal-biofeedback training. *Behavior Research Methods and Instrumentation.* 1978, *10,* 617–622.

Townsend, R. E., House, J. F., & Addario, D. A. Comparison of biofeedback-mediated relaxation and group therapy in the treatment of chronic anxiety. *American Journal of Psychiatry,* 1975, *132,* 598–601.

Turk, D. C., Meichenbaum, D. H., & Berman, W. H. Application of biofeedback for the regulation of pain: A critical review. *Psychological Bulletin,* 1979, *86,* 1322–1338.

Tursky, B., Shapiro, B. D., & Schwartz, G. E. Automated constant cuff-pressure system to measure average systolic and diastolic blood pressure in man. *Bio-Medical Engineering,* 1972, *19,* 217–276.

Van Boxtel, A., & van der Ven, J. R. Differential EMG activity in subjects with muscle-contraction headaches related to mental effort. *Headache,* 1978, *17,* 233–237.

Venables, P. H., & Martin, I. (Eds.) *A manual of psychophysical methods.* Amsterdam: North-Holland, 1967.

Wald, A. Biofeedback therapy for fecal incontinence. *Annals of Internal Medicine,* 1981, *95,* 146–149.

Walsh, D. H. Interactive effects of alpha feedback and instructional set on subjective state. *Psychophysiology,* 1974, *11,* 428–435.

Williamson, D. A. & Blanchard, E. B. Heart rate and blood pressure biofeedback. I: A review of the recent experimental literature. *Biofeedback and Self-Regulation,* 1979, *4,* 1–34.

33

Current status of psychopharmacology and organic treatments

Fernando Tapia, M.D. *

This chapter discusses those treatments for mental illness which physicians uniquely carry out. Within the medical model of etiology, pathology, diagnosis, and treatment, drugs have had an increasingly significant role, in view of greater apparent effectivity of drugs developed since the early 1950s. Not that drugs have not been used all along since Rush, the father of American psychiatry, but a revolution in psychopharmacology has been waxing since chlorpromazine found its way into the psychiatrists' armamentarium. At the same time, other organic treatments have lost favor for lack of genuine effectiveness, and only a few remain with active supporters, who insist that these treatments have stood the test of time and are, at this moment, the best that is available. Thus, this chapter discusses:

I. Psychopharmacology.
    A. Antipsychotics.
        1. Phenothiazines.
        2. Thioxanthenes.
        3. Butyrophenones.
    B. Antidepressants.
        1. Monoamine oxidase inhibitors.
        2. Tricyclic antidepressants.
        3. Stimulants.
    C. Sedatives.
    D. Lithium.

---

* Professor of Psychiatry and Behavioral Sciences, University of Oklahoma College of Medicine, Oklahoma City.

II.   Organic treatments.
    A.   Electroconvulsive therapy.
    B.   Insulin coma treatment.
    C.   The amytal interview.
    D.   Psychosurgery.

PSYCHOPHARMACOLOGY

ANTIPSYCHOTICS

The antipsychotic agents were formerly called tranquilizers. Even now, they are sometimes referred to as ataractics and neuroleptics. However, it is their ability to modify the symptoms of acute and chronic psychoses that makes them unique, and the term *antipsychotics* seems to be prevailing. The term *tranquilizer* gained its justification from the calming effect produced by the drug without overly sedating as would, for instance, a barbituate. Presently, the term *neuroleptic* has some favor, as it apparently implies the mode of action.

The history of chlorpromazine has been detailed by Swazey (1974). It is interesting that a drug developed as an antiallergenic was first tried on humans by an anesthetist and found to sooth the patient post-surgically. In 1952, it was presented to the Société Médico Psychologique in Paris, as a therapeutic agent with selective, central action. Along with Kline's (1954) recommendation of Rauwolfia serpentina in neuropsychiatric conditions, this began a new era—one which has reduced the population of mental hospitals and radically changed the treatment approach to schizophrenia and other psychotic conditions. After a flurry of use, Rauwolfia gave way to phenothiazine which, in spite of the frequent and severe jaundice attacks seen early on, was proving to be most effective.

Presently, the mode of action for its antipsychotic property is considered to arise from the drug's ability to block dopamine-mediated synaptic transmissions (Matthysse, 1973). Recent studies by Perontka and Snyder (1980), in which sophisticated, binding procedures were used to label neurotransmitter receptors in the brain, confirm this hypothesis. They found that the average antipsychotic chemical potency correlates with the drug's affinity for dopamine receptors. This, however, needs to be taken with caution, since they also found that—at chemically effective doses—there was also substantial occupancy of serotonin, alpha-adrenergic, and histamine receptors. Furthermore, the role of dopamine in schizophrenia is yet to be precisely established.

At present, there are three main classes of antipsychotic drugs: (1) Phenothiazines, the original, are further divided into three subclasses: (a) aliphatic compounds, (b) piperidine compounds, and (c) piperazine compounds; (2) Thioxanthenes; and (3) Butyrophenones (see Table 1).

Table 1

The antipsychotics

Generic name	Trade name	Daily oral dose range (mg)
Phenothiazines:		
Aliphatic compounds		
Chlorpromazine	Thorazine	75–1,000
Promazine	Sparine	150–800
Triflupromazine	Vesprin	30–150
Piperidine compounds		
Mesoridazine	Serentil	100–400
Piperacetazine	Quide	20–160
Thioridazine	Mellaril	300–800
Piperazine compounds		
Fluphenazine	Prolixin	5–30
Perphenazine	Trilafon	16–64
Prochlorperazine	Compazine	50–150
Trifluoperazine	Stelazine	4–30
Thioxanthenes:		
Chlorprothixene	Taractan	75–600
Thiothixene	Navane	6–60
Butyrophenones:		
Haloperidol	Haldol	3–15
Indoles:		
Molindone HCl	Moban	60–225

The history detailing the discoveries and developments associated with antipsychotic drugs has been mostly a search for a more-effective drug. A quarter of a century later, it has yet to be established that an antipsychotic more effective than chlorpromazine exists. However, drugs with much smaller effective doses have, indeed, appeared. At the same time, these very drugs have shown themselves more likely to cause such extrapyramidal side effects as parkinsonism. Such a dyad of low dose and extrapyramidal side effects nurtures the neuroleptic theory which postulates that drug effectiveness against psychoses correlates with their propensity to cause extrapyramidal side effects. Some of the drugs (fluphenazine, for instance) have been popularized by the mere low-dosage factor making them practical for combining with slowly absorbing vehicles and facilitating injectables that remain effective for up to four weeks at a time. Other antipsychotics have found favor because they are sedating: thioridazine, for instance, can prove helpful in an excited patient. Some antipsychotics find themselves preferred in certain cases, because of their low probability to affect the electrocardiogram: haloperidol, for instance, can be used when heart conditions are a complication of a psychotic crisis. Thus, the development of different compounds, though not increasing effectivity, has presented an opportunity to capitalize on the variations in other properties that exist among them.

Some general statements about the different classes and subclasses of antipsychotics are in order.

Phenothiazines

Aliphatic compounds. These drugs are usually high-dose drugs. They are known generally for their sedating ability (desirable with disruptive and sleepless patients) and for their low probability of extrapyramidal side effects. Doses in treatment-resistant patients with chlorpromazine have been raised above 1,500 mg per day. The probability of hypotension problems is high with chlorpromazine, especially when injected. Photosensitivity (which subjects patients to severe sunburns even with modest exposure) is attributed as most likely with chlorpromazine.

Piperidine compounds. Perhaps the best known and most frequently prescribed is thioridazine. This one drug has a specific, maximum (800 mg per day) recommended dosage, because of the development of retinal pigmentary degeneration leading to blindness. Impotency and ejaculatory difficulties have most frequently been reported by users of this drug.

Piperazine compounds. These are the low-dose, high-potency phenothiazines. They, of course, are more likely to cause the extrapyramidal side effects. The use of antiparkinson medication frequently accompanies these drugs, but such medications are never recommended prophylactically. The preferred, preventive approach is to reduce the dosage to just below the threshold of side effects. This may not be practical with the long-term injectable because of the variations in blood level, and thus, an antiparkinson drug is required.

Thioxanthenes

The two thioxanthenes currently on the market have not achieved a high frequency of use. Chlorprothixene is a high-dose drug, and its side-effect profile is much like chlorpromazine. Thiothixine, on the other hand, is a low-dose drug, and its actions are much like trifluoperazine.

Butyrophenones

Haloperidol is one of two butyrophenones marketed in America. The other is droperidol, sold under the trade name of Inapsine® and only in injectable form. Haloperidol has established itself as an antipsychotic frequently preferred in manics, geriatric cases, and organic brain syndromes. In Gilles de la Tourette's disease, it is the absolute drug of choice.

Clinical aspects of antipsychotics

The principal use of antipsychotics is in the treatment and management of schizophrenia. These drugs suppress psychotic ideation. Such an effect is not explained by the depressant quality of the drug. Not only does the antipsychotic effect last far beyond the time when the short-lived sedating effect has passed but, in fact, it is also effective even when they stimulate. Whether the stimulating effect is from true activation or merely the restlessness of side-effect akathisia is moot here. Along with bringing about changes in psychotic ideation, the antipsychotics have proven effective in controlling combative, aggressive, and other difficult behaviors of psychotic patients. This combination of effects has been responsible for the revolutionary changes in the overall treatment and management of acute and chronic schizophrenia. It has allowed for shorter hospital stays and for such easier management of chronic patients that state institutions have practically emptied out and have reduced the need for restraints and seclusion rooms.

The "right" antipsychotic for the "right" psychosis has yet to be found; i.e., for paranoid delusions versus catatonic symptoms. All the drugs accepted as effective are clearly superior to placebo, in controlling primary and secondary symptoms of schizophrenia. Their effectivity is noted within a week, with the bulk of the improvement seen during the first six weeks. After three months of sustained medication, not much further improvement can be anticipated. In acutely difficult cases, a rapid neuroleptization is used, and this may involve repeated injections of the drug until control is achieved. In these cases, the butyrophenones (Slotnick, 1971) or mesoridazine are preferred because their low autonomic-blocking activity makes them more tolerable.

Other psychotic episodes as well as problematic behaviors outside of schizophrenia are treated by the antipsychotics. Aged patients with chronic brain syndrome, who exhibit odd, psychoticlike behavior, are managed with these drugs. Acute brain syndromes are also managed with these drugs, but there is question of aggravating a toxic psychosis with added anticholinergic insult. However, if a sufficient dose can tranquilize and sedate, while not depressing respirations, then the drug's use may be justified.

With geriatric cases, thioridazine has been a favorite drug—mostly because of its sedating quality and the unlikelihood of causing parkinsonian side effects. Often relatively low doses are sufficient to reduce the elderly person's anxiety, agitation, and management difficulties.

Side effects.   The concern with side effects is now divided in two parts—immediate and long-term. The immediate side effects are those which appear as untoward symptoms during the acute administration of the drug to control the psychotic symptoms. Long-term side effects are those which seem to appear in cases maintained on antipsychotic medications over a prolonged period of time.

Immediate.   Sedation is the most frequently seen side effect of the high-dose antipsychotics—chlorpromazine and thioridazine. Subjects seem to overcome this after a few days. The drug may have been chosen precisely for this side effect; and increasingly higher doses may then be required. At the other end of the spectrum, extrapyramidal symptoms are the most commonly seen side effects of the low-dose antipsychotics. These include pseudoparkinsonism, dystonia, and akathisia. The parkinsonlike symptoms are the expressionless faces, the shuffling gait with a stiff body posture, and the lack of arm swinging on locomotion. The dystonias are seen as muscle spasm around the neck, which distort the position of the head. Often, the eyes are pulled upward into a fixed position (an oculo-gyric crisis), which requires quick intervention. Finally, akathisia is seen as a restlessness, of which the patient sometimes complains, but is often noted only by ward personnel experienced in these matters. A tragic series of events is set up when patients are given more drugs to quiet down that which the drug is already producing.

All these extrapyramidal symptoms (EPS) are amenable to antiparkinson drugs. In older patients, more likely to suffer such symptoms, the high-dose antipsychotics are preferred. However, when such symptoms appear in younger patients, the antiparkinson drugs may be added. The prophylactic use of antiparkinson drugs is not recommended. It is often not needed, as EPS do not invariably appear and, even then, a judicious reduction of the dose of antipsychotic medications is all it takes to clear the problem.

Blurred vision, constipation, and dry mouth are other complaints—frequently heard but of lesser consequence. Patients on antipsychotics, especially high-dose ones, must be advised to avoid sunburn and to use sunscreen protection.

Long-term.   Only several years after the introduction of the antipsychotics did tardive dyskinesia appear as a very significant problem. Patients began to have abnormal movements of the tongue, mouth, jaw, and lips. These are constant, repetitive movements, over which the individual has only brief, voluntary control. The bizarre grimacing, frequent tongue protrusions, and smackings make this a most serious problem. Patients with dentures tend to find themselves constantly moving them and sometimes protruding them in socially embarrassing situations, to say nothing of their own personal discomfiture. To date, no treatment has been found (though many have been tried) to relieve this problem. The younger the patient, the greater the hope of reversibility once the offending drug is discontinued. Unfortunately, the very discontinuation of the long-term drug precipitates the unmasking of the condition; and many patients have had to resume their medications, if only to conceal the problem. All that is left now is to try to prevent such an occurrence. Drugs should be at the lowest dosage which is effective and for the shortest length of time that is required. Special care must be entertained when used with older patients and with those who are EPS-prone and who need antiparkinson drugs.

Summary

It has now been over 25 years since the antipsychotic drugs appeared. They have had a profound effect in the treatment and management of schizophrenia and other psychotic problems. Perhaps they have been the single most significant features in the dramatic decline of state hospital populations. While no more effective antipsychotic has been developed as yet, a variety of features in the newer drugs has allowed for greater versatility in their use. Unfortunately, tardive dyskinesia, a serious side effect from prolonged use, has surfaced; and no treatment is yet available for it. Furthermore, the drug's mode of action has yet to be definitely determined; and a parsimonious interpretation of its usefulness cannot consider it a curative but, as Cole says, "It stabilizes the patient in a state of limited psychosis in which other ambulatory and psychosocial treatment procedures may be applied."

ANTIDEPRESSANTS

A group of drugs has emerged which are attributed valuable for depressive illnesses. There is, however, lingering cloudiness to the issue regarding their true effectivity and, if indeed effective, to their mode of action. Other clinical concerns which serve to make the total subject of antidepressant drugs an unclear one are, for instance, diagnostic variables in the spectrum of depressive illnesses. Whether the illness is bipolar (classical manic-depressive) or unipolar (possibly a variant of manic-depressives) or another unique, endogenous depression creates one issue. Another variable that needs to be addressed is precisely whether a depression called endogenous differs (from a drug-treatment point of view) from a neurotic and/or reactive depression. Genetic differences—which give rise to variations in the metabolism of the drugs and thus to extreme differences in plasma levels—have naturally complicated the issue.

The antidepressant drugs fall under three major categories at this time. They are: (1) Tricyclics, (2) Monoamine oxidase inhibitors (MOAI), and (3) Stimulant-energizers. The earliest of the known tricyclics was imipramine, reported in 1958 by Kuhn to have good effect in some depressive states. Interestingly, the drug was noted effective in depression, while being studied for schizophrenia. On the other hand, the monoamine oxidase inhibitors were an offshoot of an antitubercular drug (iproniazide), which has been noted to elevate the mood of patients while under treatment for their tuberculosis. What followed after this apparent effect was verified as a series of variations of MOAIs specifically for the treatment of depression. Finally, the stimulants may have their own predecessors in cocaine (long recognized as an euphoriant).

The mode of action of antidepressants is continuously being studied; to date, there is no certainty regarding the specific, biochemical changes responsible for the actions of the drugs. The biogenic amines have been the focus of present-day theories and explanations for the mode of action, while being studied for greater understanding of their effect on affective changes. The principle biogenic amines have been catecholamines (dopamine and norepinephrine) and indolamine (serotonin).

Great impetus for research of the biogenic amines was derived from a clearly observed clinical event among patients receiving reserpine for hypertension. A fairly high percentage of these individuals became significantly depressed on this drug meant to reduce blood pressure. Thus, while reducing norepinephrine and blood pressure, the drug was later suspected to deplete serotonin, with the consequence of a concomitant depression—a depression that readily lifted on discontinuation of the reserpine. Soon after, still in the 1950's, monoamine oxidase inhibitors, which raise the biogenic amines, were found to help some individuals with depression. Perhaps it is unfortunate that such an obvious and simple hypothesis has yet to be confirmed.

The tricyclic antidepressants are inhibitors of the normal process of re-uptake of amines by the presynaptic neuron from the site of the physiologic activity (the synapse). By this re-uptake process, the activity is concluded or decreased. Thus, by inhibiting the re-uptake, the effects of the amine neurotransmitters (serotonin and norepinephrine) are prolonged. Later studies, which show drugs with less ability to inhibit amine uptake but possessing equal antidepressant effectiveness (Fann, Davis, Janowsky, Kaufman, Griffith, & Qates, 1972; Carlsson, Fuxe, Hamberger, & Malmpors, 1969), have brought some question to what seemed an accepted fact. To complicate matters further, lithium also has antidepressant qualities in given cases, and lithium is known to enhance amine uptake.

The action by which monoamine oxidase inhibitors increase the concentration of the amines in the central nervous system is by slowing down their destruction, i.e., inhibiting their usual degradation by the oxidation process. The ongoing process of synthesizing norepinephrine and storing it in granules within the presynaptic neuron is accompanied by its continuous deactivation by monoamine oxidase. It is by inhibiting this process that MAOIs exert their influence, as when the increased levels of norepinephrine diffuse out of the cells onto receptors.

Monoamine oxidase inhibitors

Although still popular elsewhere (such as in England), the MAOIs lost favor in the United States when several serious, hypertensive crises were reported. These serious side effects were noted when the drug was taken with excesses of dietary amines, such as tyramine in ripe cheeses (Bethune, Burrell, Culpan, & Ogg, 1964; Blackwell, Marley, Price, & Taylor, 1967), or in conjunction with drugs such as ephedrine (Cuthbert, Greenberg, & Morley, 1969). The advent of tricyclics also accounted for the loss of interest in the MAOIs. However, they have always remained in the armamentarium against depressions and have even found ascendency in the treatment of depressions associated with phobias and anxiety.

Table 2 shows the most commonly prescribed MAOIs. With all of them, a judicious course is to slowly increase the dosage until arriving at the maximum, then sustaining three to four weeks of adequate dosage before disallowing the drug as noneffective. Always, the patient is instructed to avoid certain foods—cheese (particularly strong or aged varieties), sour cream, Chianti wine, sherry, beer, pickled herring, liver, canned figs, raisins, bananas, avocados, chocolate, soy sauce, the pods of broad beans (fava beans), yeast extracts, or meat prepared with tenderizers. Furthermore, MAOIs should not be administered in combination with sympathomimetics, including amphetamines, weight-reducing preparations that contain vasoconstrictors, cold and hay fever medications with nasal decongestants (such as ephedrine), and even dental analgesics that contain adrenaline.

At present, the MAOIs are not the drugs of choice in depression. However, in cases where previous, good results are reported, then the clinical choice is with the known, successful drug. More commonly, however, the MAOIs are tried when tricyclics have proven ineffective after appropriate efforts. There is no washout period indicated when discontinuing a tricyclic and instituting a MAOI. The opposite change of medication, from a MAOI to a tricyclic, is recommended only after 7 to 10 days of a drug-free period. This is to obviate a hypertensive crisis (created by

Table 2

Monoamine oxidase inhibitors

Generic drug (trade name)	Therapeutic dose (mg)	Maintenance dose (mg)
Isocarboxazid (Marplan)	20–30	10–20
Pargyline (Eutonyl)	25–50	10–50
Phenelzine (Nardil)	30–90	15–30
Tranylcypromine (Parnate)	20–30	10–20

the prolonged inhibition of amine degradation) which must await the synthesizing of new enzymes by the body. Such caution is not universally followed, and studies now show the concomitant use of tricyclics and MAOI (White, Pistole, & Boyd, 1980) with but a slight increase in side effects.

Investigators—with carefully designed, double-blind studies—have reported good response to phenelzine (Nardil®) by patients with atypical depression (Robinson, Nies, Ravaris, Ives, & Bartlett, 1978). These are depressions characterized by dysphoric mood, accompanied by anxiety, irritability, initial insomnia, and phobic and hypochondrical symptoms. These depressions appear to be more neurotic. However, in the main, MAOIs have been superseded by the tricyclic antidepressant.

Tricyclic antidepressants

The first tricyclic studied was imipramine. However, as a structural variant of the phenothiazine molecule, it was meant for schizophrenia. In 1958, it was reported to be effective in endogenous depressions. Its imputed mode of action—inhibiting the re-uptake of amines and thus increasing the available amines—was concordant with the observed depression caused by the depletion of amines induced by reserpine. Over the years, various controlled studies of psychopharmacology in depression have shown a consistently greater effectiveness of imipramine over placebo. The more accepted figures are 40 percent improvement with placebo and 70 percent improvement with imipramine. All tricyclics listed in Table 3 have been used in studies which show them consistently more effective than placebo.

The tricyclic antidepressants have been subjected to frequent inadequate use. Their effectivity requires an adequate dosage to reach therapeutic blood levels and, in turn, this blood level must be sustained for

Table 3

Tricyclic antidepressants

Generic name	Trade name	Therapeutic dose (mg per day)	Maintenance dose (mg per day)	Therapeutic blood level (ng/ml)
Amitriptalyine	Elavil, Endep	150–300	100–150	125–250
Desipramine	Norpramine, Pertofrane	150–300	100–150	150–300
Doxepin	Adapin, Sinequan	150–300	100–150	75–200
Imipramine	Tofranil	150–300	100–150	150–300
Nortriptyline	Aventyl	50–100	50–75	50–150
Protriptyline	Vivactyl	40–60	20–40	50–150
Maprotiline*	Ludiomil	150–300	75–150	

* A tetracyclic.

a period of between three to four weeks, before the drug can be considered ineffective. The effects of successful treatment may be noted as early as 5 to 10 days but also as late as four weeks of sustained medication at appropriate-dose level. The many side effects common to this drug frequently cause its discontinuation and therapeutic levels not to be reached. Clinical familiarity with the drug and a good working relationship with the patient are necessary to obtain a compliance that enhances the drug's opportunity to be effective.

The side effects of the tricyclics stem from their anticholinergic properties. These autonomic effects include most commonly a dry mouth, which many patients find difficult to tolerate. Perhaps, complaints of the sedating effects are the most commonly heard. To obviate or reduce this complaint, the drug is often recommended to be taken all at bedtime, thus capitalizing on the side effect as a hypnotic. By morning, the sedation is less. Amitriptyline is considered more sedating than protriptyline and, if sedation is a problem, the latter drug may be preferred. Perhaps, postural hypotension with dizziness and fainting, particularly troublesome when getting up from a bed or chair, is the next most common complaint. This complaint usually appears at the higher doses and, if the individual cannot adjust to it, then the dosage may have to be reduced. Also noted as side-effect complaints are constipation and urinary difficulties. The danger of aggravating a mild glaucoma needs to be kept in mind. The tricyclics are contraindicated when known glaucoma problems exist. A rare but interesting side effect of tricyclics is a memory problem called anomic aphasia, i.e., difficulty finding words for conversation.

In older patients, lower doses appear to be effective. This is fortunate, in view of a greater sensitivity to cardiovascular effects noted in that population group. A preexisting heart block can be tipped over into failure by the quinidinelike effect of tricyclics. Caution in the older age group must also be exercised in view of episodes of confusion and even hallucinations which anticholinergic drugs are wont to engender. Drug interaction, especially with other drugs having anticholinergic properties (like antiparkinson drugs), aggravates the side-effect problems. Some antihypertensive drugs (like guanethidine) have their effect annuled by tricyclics. Aspirin potentiates tricyclics; consequently, the fact that many elderly persons take aspirin for chronic, arthritic conditions must be taken into account.

The effectiveness of tricyclic drugs has been noted as more specific when the depression has more of the usual endogenous characteristics, instead of the hypochondriacal and hysterical ones. These characteristics include severe retardation, early morning awakening, weight loss, exaggerated guilt feelings, and overpowering hopelessness. Depressions with genetic taints are more likely to respond, as well. Delusional patients and those demonstrating other psychotic features tend to do better with a combined antipsychotic-antidepressant. One tricyclic (nortriptyline) has been reported to have a "therapeutic window," being ineffective at plasma levels below 50 ng/ml or above 150 ng/ml.

Perhaps of equal importance to the treatment of a depression is the prophylactic use of tricyclics in the prevention of relapses. Almost 50 percent of patients who suffer from acute depression will relapse. Studies of untreated relapse rates range from 30 percent to 90 percent. By using tricyclics on a maintenance level, the relapse rate can be greatly reduced. Kessler (1978) has compiled a series of studies showing the benefits of maintenance use of tricyclics and lithium in depressions, including bipolar depression. There seems to be no question that the drugs are indeed effective in reducing the relapse rates. Lithium appears more effective than tricyclics, in bipolar depressions. However, the length of time that the maintenance dose is given may be a prolonged one. This is specifically dictated in a person with a long history of frequent relapses. Where the drug is not planned for use as a prophylactic, there seems to be only rule-of-thumb indications for how long to continue the drugs after the depression has lifted. However, at least three months of maintenance medications should follow a treated episode.

Stimulants

Stimulants have never won real favor in the treatment of depressive illness, although they can quickly induce a mood change to reduce dysphoria. This improvement is short-lived, and ongoing treatment of depression with stimulants has seldom proven sustainable. At the same time, some researchers (Fawcett & Siomopoulos, 1971) have reported that a good response to amphetamines (after a short-lived trial) predicted the probability of a good response to tricyclic treatment.

Another use of a stimulant in the treatment of depression has been in combination with a tricyclic. Wharton, Perel, Dayton, and Malitz (1971) reported the potentiation of a tricyclic antidepressant by methylphenidate. The combination of a stimulant (such as amphetamine) with a MAOI is, however, potentially lethal. With the degradation of norepinephrine inhibited, and the amphetamines simultaneously promoting the release of norepinephrine, the accumulation can be so excessive as to produce a hypertensive crisis.

Perhaps the most judicious use of a stimulant in a depressive illness is for a few days while a tricyclic is being administered. Thus, an immediate boost to the mood and, at the same time, an antidote for the sedating effect of the tricyclic can serve to bring some relief, while the slower-acting antidepressant becomes effective.

Antidepressant/anxiolytic combinations

Several drug companies have marketed amitriptyline hydrochloride (Elavil®) in combination with another drug with the avowed purpose of reducing anxiety and agitation in the depressed patient receiving the antidepressant drug. Depressive symptoms in schizophrenic patients are another indication for these drug combinations. The most notable combination is perphenazine and amitriptyline. The combinations are variable, with 2 or 4 mg of perphenizine combined with 10 or 25 mg of amitriptyline. They are marketed, for instance, as Etrafon 4–25—with 25 signifying the milligrams of amitriptyline.

Limbitrol® is a combination of chlordiazepoxide and amitriptyline. Again, it purports to help especially when there is moderate-to-severe anxiety associated with depression. Experience has shown it to be very sedating, in spite of the relatively low levels of the drugs involved (i.e., 5 or 10 mg of chlordiazepoxide with 12.5 or 25 mg of amitriptyline). Hence, it has acquired some popularity. The fixed proportions of the drugs combined in one pill or capsule represent obvious disadvantages, while the use of one rather than two pills has an advantage for compliance.

SEDATIVES

Within the sedative category of pharmacological agents are found antianxiety agents and the hypnotics used for induction of sleep. Another term often used for some of these drugs is *minor tranquilizers.* An obfuscation of terms arises, because the designation for these drugs has been dictated by euphemistic (and sometimes, by commercial) expediencies. Even within a single class of sedatives (such as the barbiturates), we find that the short-acting ones, like secobarbital, tend to be used as and called *hypnotics,* while the long-acting ones, like phenobarbital, are used as antianxiety agents.

One can readily trace the confusion growing with the introduction of chlorapromazine in the early 1950s and with the sudden popularity of tranquilizers such as Miltown®, a meprobamate. Drugs like chlorpromazine and others (now more specifically called antipsychotic agents) were then labeled the major tranquilizers. Another group, more appropriately labeled antianxiety agents, were for a time called the minor tranquilizers. The term *minor tranquilizer* is slowly phasing out, in favor of antianxiety drugs. Over the years, new antipsychotic drugs have been developed specifically to avert the side effect of sedation. This has been shown by the appearance of such drugs as the piperazines (for example, Stelazine®) and the butyrophenones (for example, Haldol®)—drugs which are effective in much smaller doses and do not have the sedating quality of chlorapromazine (Thorazine®), or thioridazine (Mellaril®). As the specificity of antipsychotic medications improved, their use in minor emotional conditions began to disappear and new groups of drugs have emerged, of which the benzodiazepines are an example.

Sedatives in proper doses lead to sedation, and enough sedation diminishes anxiety. Unfortunately, further dosage leads to anesthesia, respiratory depression, and death. Hence, the use of certain sedatives, primarily the barbiturates, in suicide attempts. Sedatives have other qualities that enhance their reputation as a two-edged sword: they are anitconvulsants. Phenobarbital is one of the most widely used drugs in epilepsy, while diazepam is the drug of choice in status epilepticus. On the other hand, they are habituating and can create a dependency which brings on significant withdrawal symptoms. They are muscle relaxants but also spinal cord depressants. Although sedation is their usual effect, they can cause disinhibition, leading to excitement and loss of self-control. Consequently, research efforts in the past years have been toward the development of a more specific, antianxiety agent, which would obviate the addicting tendency, minimize side effects, and reduce their lethal quality. The physiological thrust has been the development and selection of drugs that act more on the limbic system (particularly the hippocampus) and less on the reticular activating system and the cortex.

The judicious use of hypnotic drugs is probably one of the most effective interventions in psychopharmacology. The therapeutic uses of sedatives tend to be symptom-specific, but this targeting of symptoms must be prudent. An example of this is in the use of a hypnotic for induction of sleep in a person who is complaining of insomnia. The causes of the sleeplessness may be quite variable and should be understood. Depression often shows sleep disturbances, and the mere prescribing of a hypnotic could prove to be an ill-advised palliative. On the other hand, the use of a hypnotic for someone needing to get a night's rest on a long airline flight seems quite indicated. Ideally, the proper drug should be prescribed for a relatively short span of time, while corrective measures to remove the causes of the insomnia are instituted. One to three weeks of the drug during stressful periods (such as acute grief, serious illness in the immediate family, a social crisis such as a divorce, a legal or fiscal complication, etc.) can be most useful. There is no evidence, for example, that grief work is delayed by adequate, drug-induced sleep during the acute phases of grief. The Council on Scientific Affairs of the American Medical Association (*JAMA,* February 20, 1981) considered that the importance of hypnotics in short-term management of insomnia precluded curbs be placed on them because of their potential for abuse. Their idea of short-term was two to six weeks. For chronic insomnia, they recommended physicians try nondrug therapy.

The anxious person may have sleep disturbances beginning with difficulty falling asleep to frequent awakening. Often, the very antianxiety drug prescribed for all-day sedation is recommended at bedtime as a hypnotic. For instance, Rickels, Clark, Ewing, Klingensmith, and Morris (1959) found meprobamate consistently and significantly more effective in psychoneurotic patients with sleep difficulties, and the best results were achieved when meprobamate was taken throughout the day. Some hypnotics have earned distinct popularity for certain conditions. Chloral hydrate is often prescribed for persons such as alcoholics and drug addicts, in view of its very low addicting quality. The same may be said of paraldehyde, a foul-tasting and -smelling liquid. Bromides, on the other hand, have lost their popularity, because of subtle but serious intoxication through their prolonged use. Short-acting barbituates are prescribed for persons having trouble falling asleep. The drug will have been eliminated by morning and no hangover effect persists. When short-acting barbiturates are used as sedatives or antianxiety agents throughout the day, too-direct drug-relief association is made, which may strengthen the patient's dependency on the drug. Thus a long-acting, more constant drug is preferable.

Table 4 lists the more commonly prescribed sedatives and divides them as they are used for sleep or as antianxiety agents. Dosage must be viewed as a range, because of the variability of response. A geriatric

Table 4

Sedatives (hypnotics and antianxiety agents)

Generic name	Brand name	Dose for sleep (mg)	Daily dose (mg) 3–4 times daily
Barbituates			
Long-acting			
Phenobarbital	Phenobarbital	—	15–60
Mephobarbital	Mebaral	—	50
Intermediate-acting			
Amobarbital	Amytal	100–200	30–50
Butabarbital	Butisol	100	15–30
Aprobital	Alurate	80–160	—
Short-acting			
Pentobarbital	Nembutal	100	—
Secobarbital	Seconal	100	—
Benzodiazepines			
Flurazepam	Dalmane	15–30	—
Chlorodiazepoxide	Librium	—	5–25
Diazepam	Valium	—	2–10
Oxazepam	Serax	—	10–20
Lorazepam	Ativan	—	1–2
Propanediols			
Meprobamate	Equanil, Miltown	—	200–400
Carisoprodol	Soma	—	350
Piperidinediones			
Glutethimide	Doriden	250–500	—
Methyprylon	Noludar	200–300	—
Dimethylmethane Derivitives			
Hydroxyaine	Atarax	—	50–100
Alcohols			
Chloral Hydrate	Chloral hydrate	500–1,000	—
Ethchlorvynol	Placidyl	500–1,000	—

case may require a lower dose; whereas another, younger patient may require a ten-fold amount, as pointed out by Katz (1972).

Benzodiazepines

A special word is in order about the benzodiazepines, since they are probably the most frequently prescribed drugs for anxiety. With minimal side effects, they have proven effective in controlling anxiety and the other symptoms of neurosis, such as nervousness and tension. Part of their wide usage is also based on their greater safety when compared to other sedatives commonly implicated in overdosing. For a one-year period (1976–1977), Valium® accounted for 0.3 reports of drug-related deaths per million pills, compared to 11.6 drug-related deaths per million secobarbital pills. The dosages of milligrams of Valium ingested by adults who recovered is extremely high (1,500–2,000 mgs) and sometimes even with alcohol and other CNS suppressants (Greenblatt, Woo, Allen, Orsulak, & Shader, 1978; Carrol, 1970). Hollister (1973) has called them "virtually suicide-proof" (page 90).

The use of antianxiety agents is recommended for symptomatic, concomitant usage. Their use is limited, then, to that period of treatment when the symptoms are severe and disabling. The drug is to be reduced and discontinued when the primary treatment has begun to show results. Consequently, a one- to three-week period of an antianxiety drug is generally acceptable as appropriate use. There are persons who suffer a permanent level of anxiety and discomfort who could profit from continuous use of a low level of a benzodiazepine. A low, maintenance dose would not be contraindicated, provided that there is no progressive-dose increase. However, there has been great concern over the misuse and abuse of the benzodiazepines. The issue is far from settled. An interesting booklet by Marks (1978), *The Benzodiazepines: Use, Overuse, Misuse, Abuse,* attempts to lay to rest many of the unwarranted apprehensions about that family of drugs.

The ethical use of the benzodiazepines continues unabated. Short-term use in pre-operative situations which arouse great anxiety in patients during hospitalization and during alcohol withdrawal is mostly unquestioned. Flurazepam (Dalmane®) is a well-accepted hypnotic in the alleviation of insomnia. Its effectivity in shortening the time for sleep onset, lengthening the time of total sleep, reducing awakenings, and yet not suppressing REM sleep makes it a desirable drug (Dement, Zarcone, Hodden, Smythe, & Carshadon, 1973; Kales & Scharf, 1973). Furthermore, flurazepam is viewed as a safer drug, as the risks from overdose have not been comparable to that of barbituates (Koch-Weser & Greenblatt, 1974). Diazepam has been used for the alleviation of night terrors, which apparently occur during stage-four sleep, a level of sleep suppressed by it (Fisher, Kahn, Edwards, & Davis, 1973).

As to the concerns with drug dependency on the benzodiazepines, these have reputedly been exaggerated—much to the disadvantage of patients who could benefit from them. Bookman and Randall (1976) state:

> The consensus appears to be that dependency on the benzodiazepines is unlikely within the recommended, therapeutic doses; the risks seem to be associated with excessive doses given for extended periods of time. Actual addiction to them appears to be a rare possibility, despite the large number of patients taking benzodiazepines throughout the world. (page 87)

LITHIUM

Lithium is one of the more specifically useful psychopharmacological drugs. Its success in manic-depressive psychosis is unquestioned. Not only is it established as an effective antimanic agent that can subdue a manic attack, but its ability to prevent recurrences of all aspects of this bipolar (and sometimes unipolar) condition makes it the drug of choice. The specific-target results make this drug diagnostically significant both to establish manic-depressive disease when effective, and, to a slightly lesser degree, exclude it when not effective.

For a salt that has been known for over 150 years and used medically for over 100 years (to treat gout, rheumatism, uremia, and renal calculi), it was a long time coming to its psychopharmacological place. In the early years of the 20th century, it was used as a sedative and anticonvulsant. In the early 1940s, it unfortunately gained a notorious reputation when its chloride salt was used as a table-salt substitute for hypertension patients. Deaths from severe poisoning occurred, and it quickly lost favor. In 1949, Cade reported in the *Medical Journal of Australia* the use of lithium salts in the treatment of psychotic excitement. It was five years later that a Danish group reported on the use of lithium salts in the treatment of manic psychosis. Their reports showed that 32 of 38 manic patients had a possible-to-definite improvement with lithium. Several studies followed through the 1960s; and, by the early 1970s, lithium was finally established as the drug of choice for manic illness, superior to both placebo and to available, antipsychotic drugs. In controlled studies, lithium had emerged more effective and free of the dampening, sedating mode of action obtained through high doses of such drugs as chlorpromazine.

The question has now been presented regarding lithium's effectivity in the depression phase of manic-depressive psychosis. Several studies on precisely this question have not provided definite answers. Apparently, tricyclics or ECT have better results than lithium in depressed patients with recognized bipolar conditions. However, as a prophylactic, lithium is considered effective against recurrences of either manic or depressive episodes. Generally, studies have shown half the number of relapses with lithium as with placebo and about equal effectiveness between lithium and the tricyclic, imipramine. Thus, lithium emerges as a truly effective drug, even more indicated in genetically identified cases of manic-depressive illness.

Lithium is usually administered as the carbonate salt, and many patients prefer capsules (they cause less gastric discomfort). Because lithium is potentially toxic, the blood levels are monitored; and therapeutic blood levels are, hopefully, sustained with maintenance doses. Therapeutic blood levels are at the 1.0 to 1.5 mEq/L level, with the upper limits pushed if the severity of the illness requires it and the patient tolerates it. Maintenance blood levels may be as low as .5mEq/L and seldom above 1.0 mEq/L. However, variations in patients can be expected to alter these figures, and one must be alert to such a contingency and not rigidly adhere to standard figures in the face of obvious contraindications.

Quite often, the maintenance dose is 300 mg of lithium carbonate taken three times a day with meals. Blood monitoring with relative frequency when patients are first placed on the drug will advise the physician whether the dose needs raising or lowering. Many patients have chosen to take their three capsules together with their supper, to avoid public consumption of a medication that may bring prejudices on them. Such practice is not recommended; and, with data on rare kidney problems appearing more often with the one-dose takers, spreading out the intake schedule seems preferable. Incidentally, to reach a therapeutic blood level, the usual maintenance dose is doubled or even tripled for a few days. Any suspicion of altered kidney function dictates a special care with the use of lithium.

As it was mentioned above, the usual maintenance dose is 900 mg of lithium carbonate each day. However, side effects may appear if the blood level rises. The most common symptoms of drug intoxication are queasiness, nausea and, sometimes, vomiting and diarrhea. A tremor of the hand is also frequently seen. All side effects should be viewed seriously, and the blood level assayed. As with psychotropics, patients often have discomforting side effects when new to the drug. These dissipate within a matter of days. Anyone taking lithium should be advised of its relationship with sodium chloride, the common table salt. For instance, heavy-handed "food salters" tend to suppress the lithium blood level and, in turn, require a higher maintenance dose. On the other hand, when profuse sweating (such as on hot days or with extended physical activity) causes a body loss of sodium chloride, a physiological shift ensues, which then allows the lithium blood level to rise dangerously in its replacement. Serious complications attributed to lithium-haldol therapeutic combinations are now considered to have been caused by a rise in lithium blood level induced by a loss of normal body salts through sweating.

A persistent hand tremor, in spite of well-managed therapeutic blood levels, may be treated with a drug such as Inderal® (propranolol hydrochloride). Many patients on lithium report a feeling of sluggishness—being slowed down—although, to the practiced eye, they appear quite normal. This sense of suppression and absence of the old high is interpreted as depression and judged by the patient as very undesirable. Unfortunately, it leads to reduced compliance and the consequent appearance of mania. It is for this reason that reassurances and explanations are essential to ensure success in long-term prophylactic compliance. Finally, with the population of long-term lithium users steadily rising, concerns are constantly expressed regarding the effect of the drug on the kidneys and on the blood-forming mechanisms of the body. The verdict is not in yet so that, for the time being, judicious monitoring of these body activities—hemotopoiesis and renal function—is warranted. When used in the aged population, special considerations to their lowered renal clearance and their reduced tolerance to common therapeutic levels should be given.

ORGANIC TREATMENTS

Electroconvulsive Therapy

Without a doubt, shock therapy (as it was called) or clonotherapy (as it is called euphemistically) is one of the more controversial therapies administered to mental patients. The essence of this form of therapy is to provoke a grand mal seizure by using an electrical stimulus applied to the cranial area. The use of chemical stimuli, intravenous Metrazol® (pentylenetetrezol), or inhaled Indoklon® (flurothyl) is all but discontinued now, except for an occasional use of the latter chemical agent. There are those (like Dr. Max Fink, professor of psychiatry and the Health Sciences Center of the State University of New York at Stony Brook) who consider ECT the single most successful treatment for depressive psychosis. Data is available to substantiate this position. On the other hand, there are psychiatrists who consider ECT an unnecessary and inhumane form of therapy.

The American Psychiatric Association (Task Force Report #14 on Electroconvulsive Therapy) showed that, in a survey of 3,000 randomly selected psychiatrists, 86 percent considered the use of ECT appropriate in treating major depressions, even though only 22 percent of the sample were users of ECT. Many of the criticisms leveled at ECT are not wholly relevant to the procedure, as it is used today. Today's techniques include putting the patient to sleep with a short, fast-acting barbituate and then using succinylcholine (a rapid and short-acting muscle paralyzer) to diminish the muscular contractions of the seizure. Furthermore, the recommended uses for ECT are now significantly limited to depressions in which all other treatment modalities have failed and there is a high risk of suicide, or where the use of available drugs entails high risks. ECT is also reccommended in severe psychosis (catatonic or mania), where usual methods are not effective or are contraindicated.

ECT is not administered without informed consent. Where the psychiatric illness modifies the patient's capacity to give informed consent, reasonable consideration is given to balance the patient's needs with his civil rights.

The consistent assessment of the patient's pre-treatment physical status has eliminated mortality and reduced morbidity to a point below the risk of not treating. The number of treatments in a series are limited to figures which have proven sufficient for patient improvement when the indications are correct. Long-treatment series are proscribed. For most depressions, 10 to 12 treatments are considered the maximum to be given, should no significant improvement be noted. Maintenance ECT is occasionally given on a regular basis, such as once a month.

The most common untoward effects of a treatment series are memory loss and confusion. Patients often forget such details as how many treatments they have had so far; and the more confused patients have difficulty remembering, for instance, which is their room on the ward or nurses' and doctors' names. Within a year after treatments are concluded, there are no vestiges of memory loss, except for events that occurred during the ECT regimen.

The use of unilaterally placed electrodes for inducing the convulsion has been shown to be nearly as effective as bilaterally induced seizures while, at the same time, reducing confusion and memory loss. The unilateral electrical stimulus is given to the nondominant cerebral hemisphere. In practice, there has been some increase in the use of unilateral electrodes, but many psychiatrists have not accepted the ostensible benefits of the quid pro quo—effectivity versus memory effects.

ECT's mode of action is still unknown, although various theories exist. The most parsimonious speculation is that the seizure has effects on neurotransmitters, and its mode of action may parallel that of active, antidepressant drugs.

INSULIN COMA TREATMENT

History has it that Dr. Manfred Sakel, in a sanitorium near Berlin, while using insulin in subcoma amounts on psychiatric patients (it sedated them and improved their appetites), made a distinct observation. He noted that some psychotics who entered the coma state from insulin overdose seemed to emerge in an improved mental state. From there to the early 1950s, when tranquilizers began to dominate therapy, insulin coma therapy had a rather popular appeal and application. Hardly a comprehensive treatment center did not offer insulin coma treatment.

The therapeutic technique consists of administering enough insulin

(100–400 units, subcutaneously) to assure a desirable level of coma and to sustain that level for 15 minutes to an hour. For some clinicians, the desirable level of coma was reached when the subject no longer responded to painful stimuli and lost corneal and tendon reflexes. The coma would then be discontinued by administering glucose (either tube fed or intravenously). The course of the treatment was often up to 25 comas but frequently carried much longer. Although insulin coma is a safe treatment, it requires close medical supervision. However, complications, irreversible comas, and even fatalities are not unknown. Statistical confirmation of its effectiveness has never been irrefutably presented, even when combined with electroconvulsive therapy. Insulin coma therapy's nearly complete abandonment at present probably speaks most poignantly of its perceived value.

THE AMYTAL INTERVIEW

A strategy in psychiatric therapy is not infrequently an interview under the influence of an intravenous barbituate. Sodium amytal or sodium pentothal are the most commonly employed drugs. The technique calls for the slow injection of the agent, while the patient lies comfortably in the privacy of a secluded, quiet room. The patient is constantly asked questions, asked to count, or other verbal productions are solicited, to determine the level of sedation. Essentially, just before falling asleep, the patient is considered relaxed enough and, hopefully, free of psychological defenses. The injection is stopped, but the needle is retained in the vein in case further amounts of the agent are needed.

Under this relaxed/sedated condition, the interview may garner material which the patient has been suppressing, because of its painful content. The interview may also alter behavior (such as hysterical behavior—dissociative or conversion), so that a quick diagnosis can be made. For instance, a paralyzed patient may move or walk. Stuporous patients, when injected, often come out of it, and this may serve to confirm the diagnosis of catatonic schizophrenia, in contrast to the depressed patients who will not lighten up, but rather go off to sleep. Abreactions, otherwise repressed, may occur through this technique.

The use of these chemical interviews has been considered potent truth serums. There may, in fact, be times when confessions are made. However, this is an inconsistent result, and the lack of confession cannot establish absence of crime, no more than a confession establishes the presence of crime. Certainly some individuals can overcome the disinhibiting effects of the drug, as may others be made so suggestible that they confess a crime of which they are innocent.

The amytal interview is certainly not a definitive treatment. It is only a tool that can help in the evaluation of patients and, perhaps, from there develop strategies for therapy. Oftentimes, a course of several interviews, while under the influence of amytal, serves to explore extended areas of painful psychic content.

PSYCHOSURGERY

Needless to say, psychosurgery is even more a controversial subject than ECT. Over the years, psychosurgery has accumulated an aura of being an invasive, destructive procedure which, in its wake, leaves victims rather than treated patients. The negative sequelae of such surgery include seizures, significant undesirable personality changes, and even deaths. Consequently, in the shadows of such stigma, many improvements in surgical techniques (as well as refinements in the indications for surgery) which have evolved over the course of years have been overlooked or discounted.

Today, the techniques for interfering with brain pathways or ablating a particular area are much more precise. Apparently, with more selective techniques, normal emotional responsiveness is preserved. There seems to be a return to the treatment of chronic neurosis and emotional overresponsiveness. At the same time, efforts to control behavior in cases of chronic schizophrenia are being abandoned. With the advent of effective, antipsychotic medications, the giant pool of schizophrenics posing insurmountable nursing problems no longer vegetates in back wards. It was frequently the pressure of this hopeless group that withered caution in the bright sunshine of overoptimistic enthusiasm for psychosurgery.

The refinements of the surgical procedures, interestingly enough, have continued in the face of the negative aura in which psychosurgery has remained. More precise techniques, though yielding better results, still leave 5 to 10 percent disabling personality defects. Birley (1964) had good results with 50 percent of depressives and up to 75 percent with obsessional neurosis. The same, more restricted operation (called bimedial leucotomy) has been reported to have had success (compared to controls) with agoraphobia. Depression has also been treated by this method, with 69 percent doing well (Sykes & Tredgold, 1964).

To enhance the siting of the surgical lesion and, thus, further control its size, stereotactic means are used to insert very small rods (7 mm long and 1 mm in diameter) containing a radioactive material. This new approach is called bifrontal stereotactic subcaudate tractotomy. In over 800 cases reported by 1975, there had been 40 percent to 60 percent improvements in depressions, anxiety, and obsessional neurosis. Only one death had been reported, along with the hoped-for decrease of ontoward, post-operative personality changes. Considering the indications for employing surgery, chronic or recurrent depression, and states of anxiety or phobias not responding to other treatments, the risks and trade-offs appear to approach an attractive alternative. Deaths, for instance, are less than the suicide expectancy for this group.

Other target sites for psychosurgery as well as other indications have been advocated from time to time: the corpus collosum (for anxiety and tension), the hypothalamus (for abnormal sexuality and obesity), the thalamus (for the "hyperresponsive syndrome"), and amygdalotomy (for abnormal aggressiveness or self-mutilating behavior). The overall offerings invariably find ethical concerns and questions regarding their values. But the tendency has been to lump all psychosurgery into a controversy that impugns even those procedures which have helped in very difficult cases, have produced minimal negative effects, and have been done under the aegis of informed consent. Hopefully, calm deliberation will continue. In 1976, the National Commission reported favorably on psychosurgery (Culliton, 1976). Presently, it appears that—with the indications limited to chronic and/or frequently recurring depression; incapacitating anxiety or obsessional neurosis; and stereotactically sited placement for the lesions in a proven area, while using means to localize the lesion in a controlled way—psychosurgery is a legitimate alternative to prolonged suffering, incapacity, and even suicide.

SUMMARY

Since the early 1950s, an entirely new pharmacopoeia for mental illnesses has emerged. This psychopharmacological revolution has been based on drugs which continue to show effectiveness in the treatment of mental illness. Even while this chapter was being written, it was becoming dated, such being the pressing surge of developments in this field. Nevertheless, the chapter reviews the bulk of what is known to date.

The present chapter is divided along lines which imply specificity in psychopharmacology—antipsychotics, antidepressants, and antianxiety. It also brings to bear many of the commonsense approaches and techniques which have evolved over the years in the administration of these drugs. Unfortunately, these drugs have proven to be less than innocuous, and their contraindications as well as complications are detailed herein. Comprehensive tables are presented, so the reader can consult at a glance for doses, both therapeutic and maintenance. Also, drugs which can be used at one dose for sedation and at another dose for promoting sleep have been specified.

The organic treatments which remain effective to date are described. Insulin coma treatment, although seldom used now, is described for historical purposes. Although electroconvulsive therapy and psychosurgery are very controversial subjects, the state of the art and the clinical thinking which goes into their present use are discussed.

REFERENCES

American Psychiatric Association. Electroconvulsive therapy. *Task Force Report # 14*, September 1978.

Bethune, H. C., Burrell, R. H., Culpan, R. H., & Ogg, G. J. Vascular crises associated with monoamine oxidase inhibitors. *American Journal of Psychiatry*, 1964, *121*, 245–248.

Birley, J. T. L. Modified frontal leucotomy: A review of 106 cases. *British Journal of Psychiatry*, 1964, *110*, 211–221.

Blackwell, B., Marley, E., Price, J., & Taylor, D. Hypertensive interactions between monoamine oxidase inhibitors and foodstuffs. *British Journal of Psychiatry*, 1967, *113*, 349–365.

Bookman, P. H., & Randall, L. O. The therapeutic uses of the benzodiazepines. In L. L. Simpson (Ed.), *Drug treatment of mental disorders*. New York: Raven Press, 1976.

Cade, J. F. J. Lithium in the treatment of psychotic excitement. *Medical Journal of Australia*, 1949, *2*, 349–352.

Carlsson, A., Fuxe, K., Hamberger, B., & Malmpors, T. Effect of a new series of (on) bicyclic compounds with potential thymoleptic properties on the reserpine-resistant uptake mechanism of central and peripheral monoamine neurons in vivo and in vitro. *British Journal of Pharmacology*, 1969, *36*, 18–28.

Carrol, B. J. Correspondence. *Medical Journal of Australia*, 1970, *2*, 806.

Cole, J. O. Phenothiazines. In L. L. Simpson (Ed.), *Drug Treatment of Mental Disorders*, New York: Raven Press, 1976, 28.

Council on Scientific Affairs of the American Medical Association. Hypnotic drugs and treatment of insomnia. *Journal of the American Medical Association*, 1981, *7*, 749–750.

Culliton, G. J. Psychosurgery: National Commission issues surprisingly favorable report. *Science*, 1976, *194*, 299–301.

Cuthbert, M. F., Greenberg, M. P., & Morley, S. W. Cough and cold remedies: A potential danger to patients on monoamine oxidase inhibitors. *British Medical Journal of Psychiatry*, 1969, *1*, 404–406.

Dement, W. C., Zarcone, V. P., Hodden, E., Smythe, H., & Carshadon, M. Sleep laboratory and clinical studies with flurazepam. In S. Garattini (Ed.), *The benzodiazepines*, 1973.

Fann, W. E., Davis, J. M., Janowsky, D. S., Kaufman, J. S., Griffith, J. D., & Qates, J. A. Effect of iprindole on amine uptake in man. *Archives of General Psychiatry*, 1972, *26*, 158–162.

Fawcett, J., & Siomopoulos, V. Dextroamphetamine response as a possible predictor of improvement with tricyclic therapy in depression. *Archives of General Psychiatry*, 1971, *25*, 247–255.

Fink, M. Myths of "shock therapy." *American Journal of Psychiatry*, 1977, *134*, 991–996.

Fisher, C., Kahn, E., Edwards, A., & Davis, D. A psychophysiological study of nightmares and night terrors. *Archives of General Psychiatry*, 1973, *28*, 252–259.

Greenblatt, D. J., Woo, E., Allen, M. D., Orsulak, P. J., & Shader, R. I. Rapid recovery from massive diazepam overdose. *Journal of the American Medical Association*, 1978, *240*, 1872–1874.

Hollister, L. E. Uses of psychotherapeutic drugs. *Annals of Internal Medicine*, 1973, *79*, 88–98.

Kales, A., & Scharf, M. B. Sleep laboratory and clinical studies of the effects of benzodiazepines on sleep: Flurazepam, diazepam, chloradiazepoxide, and RO 54200. In S. Garattini, E. Mussini, & L. O. Randall (Eds.), *The benzodiazepines*. New York: Raven Press, 1973.

Katz, R. L. Drug therapy: Sedatives and tranquilizers. *New England Journal of Medicine,* 1972, *286,* 757–760.

Kessler, K. A. Tricyclic antidepressants: Mode of action and clinical use. In M. A. Lipton, A. D. Mascio, & K. F. Killiam (Eds.), *Pharmacology: A generation of progress.* New York: Raven Press, 1978.

Kline, N. S. Use of rauwolfia serpentina in neuropsychiatric conditions. *Annals of New York Academy of Science,* 1954, *59,* 107.

Kock-Weser, J. R., & Greenblatt, D. J. The archaic barbiturate hypnotics. *New England Journal of Medicine,* 1974, *291,* 790–791.

Kuhn, R. The treatment of depressive states with G22355 (imipramine hydrochloride). *American Journal of Psychiatry,* 1958, *115,* 459–464.

Marks, J. *The benzodiazepines: Use, overuse, misuse, abuse.* Lancaster, England: MTP Press, 1978.

Matthysse, S. Antipsychotic drug actions: A clue to the neuropathology of schizophrenia? *Federal Proceedings,* 1973, *32,* 200–205.

Perontka, S. J., & Snyder, S. H. Relationship of neuroleptic-drug effects at brain dopamine, serotonin, a-adrenergic, and histamine receptors to clinical potency. *American Journal of Psychiatry,* 1980, *137,* 1518–1522.

Rickels, K. Clark, T. W., Ewing, J. H., Klingensmith, W. C., & Morris, H. M. Evolution of tranquilizing drugs in medical outpatients. *Journal of the American Medical Association,* 1959, *171,* 1649–1656.

Robinson, D. S., Nies, A., Ravaris, C. L., Ives, J. O., & Bartlett, D. Clinical pharmacology of phenelzine. *Archives of General Psychiatry,* 1978, *35,* 629–635.

Slotnick, V. B. *Management of acute agitated psychiatric patients with parenteral neuroleptics: A comparative symptom-effectiveness profile of haloperidol and chlorpromazine.* Paper presented at the fifth World Congress of Psychiatry, Mexico, 1971.

Swazey, M. *Chlorpromazine: The history of the psychiatric discovery.* Cambridge, Mass.: MIT Press, 1974.

Sykes, N. K., & Tredgold, R. F. Restricted orbital undercutting. *British Journal of Psychiatry,* 1964, *110,* 609–640.

Wharton, R. N., Perel, J. M., Dayton, P. G., & Malitz, S. A potential clinical use for methylphenidate with tricyclic antidepressants. *American Journal of Psychiatry,* 1971, *127,* 1619–1625.

White, K., Pistole, T., & Boyd, J. L. Combined monoamine oxidase inhibitor-tricyclic antidepressant treatment: A pilot study. *American Journal of Psychiatry,* 1980, *137,* 1422–1425.

34

Behavioral treatment of children's disorders

Paul W. Clement*
and
John W. Fantuzzo*

Behavioral treatment emphasizes the empirical events which are most relevant to child case management. The modifier *behavioral* refers both to the therapeutic agent and to the client. As applied to treatment input, *behavioral* indicates the observable actions, gestures, and statements of the therapist. As applied to treatment output, *behavioral* connotes the observable actions, gestures, and statements of the child. Although behavioral therapists emphasize observable events, they do not deny the existence of covert processes. Instead, they try to maintain a clear distinction between descriptions of what a therapist or child does in contrast to giving theoretical accounts of how or why the observable behaviors occurred. Presumably, observable treatment input has multiple impacts on internal psychological processes of the child; however, the behavior therapist minimizes hypotheses about such assumed, covert events and focuses instead on observable outcomes.

The article "Specialty Guidelines for the Delivery of Services by Clinical Psychologists" (APA, 1981) places emphasis on developing innovative procedures for helping clients, providing empirical evidence for the effects of those procedures, responding to the specific needs of the persons served, developing written treatment plans for each case, maintaining documentation of services provided, and evaluating the effects of those services. Although these guidelines apply to all clinical psychologists, regardless of their theoretical orientation, contemporary, behavioral case-management practices seem more consistent with these requirements than is true for any alternative approach.

---

* Graduate School of Psychology, Fuller Theological Seminary.

For present purposes, *childhood* is defined as the preteen years; therefore, *children* are persons from birth through 12 years of age. *Disorder* identifies an irregularity in behavior. The irregularity may involve the dimensions of frequency, intensity, setting, timing, or topography. In general, the problem is that too much or too little of the target behavior occurs along one or more of the preceding dimensions. These dimensions form the basis for formal, clinical diagnoses. Although no diagnostic system is fully adequate, the system presented in *DSM-III* (American Psychiatric Association, 1980) is the one currently used most commonly. The present chapter uses the diagnostic categories of *DSM-III*.

The primary objectives of the chapter are as follows: (*a*) to identify the basic steps in conducting any behavioral treatment with a child; (*b*) to illustrate the use of these steps in targeting several of the more common referral problems appearing in child outpatient clinics; (*c*) to list the major behavioral treatments under the broad categories of setting events, cues and prods, primary behaviors, and consequences and feedback; (*d*) to specify procedures which may promote generalization of treatment effects; and (*e*) to present efficient ways of determining published information on behavioral treatments for a given disorder and on the range of disorders which have been treated with a given behavioral intervention.

Because of limitations on allowable length, the following sections can only provide a small sample of the conceptual models and clinical procedures which constitute behavioral-treatment approaches. Although our intent was not to represent any particular brand of behavioral treatment, some readers may feel that some behavioral approaches have been overly emphasized, while others have been neglected. To help provide balanced coverage, Benson (1979) should prove an excellent resource for anyone who wants to achieve a comprehensive grasp of behavioral approaches to child case management.

BASIC STEPS TO EFFECTIVE BEHAVIORAL TREATMENT WITH CHILDREN

The purpose of this section is to identify the basic steps that are common to all behavioral treatment approaches. These basic steps are designed to provide the clinician with a guide to implementing effective treatment.

There are five major steps to effective behavioral treatment with children. These steps involve: (*a*) a general review of the presenting problem and establishing a working contract for treatment, (*b*) a thorough behavioral assessment, (*c*) implementation of proven behavioral techniques and procedures designed to modify maladaptive behaviors, shape new, desirable behaviors, and maximize existing assets, (*d*) efforts to maximize therapeutic effectiveness by programming for generalization of treatment effects to desired, nontargeted settings, behaviors, times, and children, and (*e*) follow-up.

General review of the problem and contracting

Prior to initiating an in-depth analysis of the problem areas, the following general points need to be addressed:

1. The parents and child's view of the problem (i.e., definition, duration, intensity, motivation for change, and prognosis for change).
2. Careful review of the child's medical history, to eliminate the possibility that there are significant medical factors involved in this problem that would necessitate referring the problem to another specialist.
3. A description and evaluation of previously sought interventions.
4. The parent's and child's views of treatment (i.e., what will need to happen for treatment to occur, who will be involved, and how long will it take).
5. Determination of the best treatment agent (i.e., parent, teacher, peer, or self; cf. Clement, 1974).

After these points have been clarified, the process of establishing a working treatment contract needs to be initiated. This process entails making the respective expectations of the parents, child, and clinician explicit, thereby minimizing misunderstanding. The contract should include the clinician's credentials, a general statement of the steps that will be followed in the treatment process (e.g., assessment, treatment, follow-up, and issues of informed consent), fees for services, the clinician's view of the parents' and child's responsibilities (e.g., keeping scheduled appointments, paying fees, collecting data, cooperating with the treatment plan), and specified review dates for evaluation. Stuart's *Treatment Contract* (1975) may help facilitate the process.

Behavioral assessment

The first component of a behavioral assessment is a careful description of the problematic behaviors and the environmental influences maintaining these behaviors. There are three categories of problematic behaviors: (1) behavioral excesses, (2) behavioral deficits, and (3) inappropriate behaviors. Assignment to a category is a function of the behavior occurring too frequently (excess), too infrequently (deficit), or at the wrong time or place or with deviant topography (inappropriate).

The next essential step is to establish a clear operational definition of the behaviors, to maximize accurate data collection. Once a workable definition has been obtained, a recording system (e.g., event, interval, or outcome—see Sulzer-Azaroff & Mayer, 1977) is chosen, and a data-collection procedure is designed. This procedure consists of a specific description of how, when, and by whom the data will be collected (cf. Chapter 12). After these procedures have been finalized, the second major component is to obtain a clear, graphic representation of the daily occurrence of the targeted, problematic behaviors, prior to treatment. Preferably, data are also collected across predetermined, nontargeted settings, times, behaviors, and other children, to provide an ongoing assessment of generalization.

A third important factor is a careful survey of existing resources that potentially may be incorporated into the treatment plan. This includes the child's behavioral assets (i.e., skills and other desirable behaviors which the child exhibits) and a thorough inventory of potential reinforcers in the child's environment. This inventory includes a list of positive events in the following categories: activities, foods, desirable objects (e.g., toys, records), enjoyable places (e.g., amusement parks, movies), and special time with significant others.

The final component of behavioral assessment is the selection and prioritization of goals for treatment. These goals should outline the direction of change, the evaluation criteria for successful change (e.g., percent of reduction/improvement), and the desired areas of generalization of treatment effects.

Systematic intervention

Selection of intervention techniques and procedures should be preceded by a review of the relevant behavioral literature. The purpose of this review is to derive a rank-ordered list of interventions documented as yielding the most effective treatment for specified problem behaviors. The intervention determined to be most efficacious is then selected and tailored to fit the unique characteristics of the child and the treatment setting. Prior to implementation, the potential cost of the intervention must be reviewed, in terms of time, energy, and materials required to institute the treatment as planned. The plan must then be introduced to parents and child, and their comprehension and willingness to carry out the intervention are assessed. Providing that the parent and child are willing and the intervention is cost effective, the last step in the process is to implement the intervention, eliciting as much support as possible from the significant individuals in the treatment setting.

Each intervention should be carefully evaluated. This evaluation consists of comparing the results with the specified goals and criteria for success. If satisfactory behavioral control has been achieved, it should be determined if the therapeutic effects have generalized across the desired dimensions. If generalization is not present, specific plans would be implemented to program for the desired generalization (see section on promoting generalization). If behavioral control has not been achieved, another intervention would then be chosen from the previously generated list of treatment options, and the cycle would be repeated until the desired changes have been obtained.

Follow-up

After the case has been formally terminated as a result of achieving therapeutic goals, arrangements should be made with parents and child to contact them at specified times, to monitor maintenance of treatment gains (e.g., a month, six months, a year) and to assess the need for booster sessions to fortify waning treatment effects.

ILLUSTRATIONS USING THE MORE COMMON REFERRAL PROBLEMS

The illustrations which appear below are examples of behavioral techniques applied to major referral problems. These problems fall under the following *DSM-III* (APA, 1980) diagnostic categories: (a) Attention Deficit Disorders, (b) Conduct Disorders, (c) Anxiety Disorders, and (d) Specific Developmental Disorders.

Attention deficit disorders

Attentional deficits and hyperactivity are often identified as central problems for children who are referred to clinical psychologists. These psychological processes seem to lie at the center of diagnoses such as minimal brain dysfunction and the hyperkinetic syndrome. *Attention* is a construct, rather than a set of observable behaviors. Some other psychological constructs which also relate to a child's behavior are comprehending, impulse, learning, memory, motivation, and perceiving. Such processes are inferred from observable aspects of a child's behavior and setting; therefore, the clinician does not measure attention directly. Instead, the child psychologist records events such as following instructions, establishing discriminations, imitating a model, acquiring incidental learning, performing academic tasks, or responding to a psychological test.

In contrast to attention, *hyperactivity* is observable. Restlessness, excitability, disruptive actions, failure to stick with and finish tasks, constant fidgeting, making demands on others, quick and drastic mood changes, frequent temper outbursts, and explosive and unpredictable behavior contribute to the definition of hyperactivity. Although such behaviors are easily monitored, the clinician is wise to focus on socially positive behaviors, which are incompatible with hyperactivity. Examples of such behaviors are playing appropriately with peers, sitting in one's assigned seat, completing the elements of an academic assignment, helping another child with a class project, and waiting to be called on by the teacher before speaking.

Directly observing and recording such behaviors—via event recording, time sampling, interval recording, tracking behavioral byproducts, and listing response latencies or durations—are the preferred methods for measuring how well the child does before, during, and after treatment. Parent or teacher rating forms are often used, but ratings are less-sensitive measures of change than are direct observations.

Although attentional deficits may occur with or without hyperactivity, the more efficient methods of treatment focus on target behaviors which relate to both problems. For example, Noland (1981) had six learning-disabled boys between the ages of 9 and 12 use self-reinforcement to target their academic performance on reading assignments. Self-reinforcement included the child's negotiating a written contract with the psychologist, setting a goal for his performance, defining the target behavior, self-monitoring and self-recording the number of reading questions answered, comparing the observed performance with his goals, and providing token reinforcers (points) to himself. The child exchanged these self-administered points for backup reinforcers, which were provided by the psychologist. All six boys chose to exchange their points for a fishing trip, which came at the end of the nine-week research project.

During the self-reinforcement phases, the boys also self-administered a pill (placebo) each morning. This pill was identical in size, shape, color, and markings to the pills the child self-administered in the other treatment phases: (a) Ritalin, and (b) Ritalin plus self-reinforcement. Each subject used each treatment for at least two, one-week phases, the order of treatments being counterbalanced across the six subjects. Within-subject analyses showed that five of six children worsened their academic performance during Ritalin phases, as compared to the two-week baseline phase. Averaging across the six boys, they were 55 percent worse under Ritalin. During the self-reinforcement, five of six boys significantly increased the amount of academic work completed. Their average improvement was 394 percent above baseline. Under Ritalin and self-reinforcement combined, five of six boys also improved significantly. The average improvement was 498 percent.

The experimental design allowed for directly comparing the effects of any two treatment conditions by examining the data of four subjects for adjacent phases. Self-reinforcement was statistically superior to Ritalin in all four cases. Likewise, self-reinforcement and Ritalin combined were superior to Ritalin alone in all four relevant cases. When self-reinforcement and the combined treatment were compared via adjacent phases, two of four children did reliably better under self-reinforcement plus Ritalin.

In addition to self-reinforcement, other interventions which have demonstrated some usefulness in treating attentional deficits and hyperactivity are self-instructional training (Bornstein & Quevillon, 1976), teacher-administered reinforcement of individual students (Ayllon, Layman, & Kandel, 1975), and group contingencies (Patterson, Jones, Whittier, & Wright, 1965).

Conduct disorders

Socialized, nonagressive. Conduct Disorder, Socialized, Non-agressive is "a repetitive and persistent pattern of nonaggresive conduct in which either the basic rights of others or major age-appropriate societal norms or rules are violated" (APA, 1980, p. 49). *Defiant* and *disobedient* are terms which parents and teahers often use to describe children who fit this diagnostic category. Defiance is a behavioral excess consisting of active refusals to comply with rules or requests, sassiness, negativistic, or rebellious responses, misconduct, and other oppositional actions which lead to conflicts with responsible adults. Disobedience is a behavioral deficit which is defined as the failure to comply with instructions, standing rules, or discrete requests.

In order to assess pre-treatment behavior and the effects of the intervention(s), at least one measure should be used for recording defiant behaviors and one for disobedient behaviors. For example, the clinical psychologist can ask the parent or teacher to record defiance by making a check mark on a sheet for each occasion defiant behavior occurs. Systematic observations should occur at the same time of day and for the same duration each day. If doing so is not possible, the observer should at least record the duration of each observation period, so that the rate of the behavior can be determined by dividing the number of daily episodes by the duration of the observation period. Trial scoring may be used to record obedience. A *trial* is defined by the statement of an instruction or request. When the request is made, the parent or teacher marks a small circle on a sheet of paper. If the child complies, the observer places a plus sign in the middle of the circle. Dividing the number of pluses by the total circles for a day produces a percent-obedience score. A disobedience score can be obtained by subtracting the percent-obedience score from 100. In order to obtain an accurate estimate of the target behaviors before treatment, at least seven days of recording should take place under baseline conditions. Recording should continue throughout intervention as well, in order to assess the effects of the treatment(s).

After baseline data have been gathered for at least seven days, treatment may begin. The intervention is designed to remove the cues and consequences for defiant acts and to present cues and consequences for obedient responses. Negotiating an intervention contract between the parent and child facilitates the treatment: by identifying the participants' choices, emphasizing cooperative planning for the immediate future, defining the target behavior in terms of observables, setting a goal for behavioral change, and listing the specific operations of the intervention package.

One possible treatment package for defiance would be the following: Initially, only the mother would carry out the interventions. Each time her child acted defiantly, she would immediately turn her back, say nothing, walk away from the child, and place a check mark on the sheet used to record defiant acts. During treatment, each such check mark would carry a response cost of one point. These fines for misbehavior would be levied at a parent/child conference just before bedtime each evening. The child would pay the fines from a "bank book" which contained points earned for good behavior. One way of earning points for good behavior would be through a differential reinforcement of other behavior (DRO) schedule. For the DRO procedure, the mother would set a kitchen timer for 15-minute intervals throughout the day, whenever the child was present. For each such interval in which he did not show any defiant behavior, his mother would give him a point on a prominently displayed chart and praise him for his good performance.

Her method for strengthening obedient responses would be to praise him each time that he complied with one of her requests. During the bedtime conference, the mother would enter all of the points he had earned that day into his bank book. Then she would subtract any fines.

The mother and the child would negotiate a list of activities and items which could be purchased by the child with his points. The list could include such things as going to a movie, purchasing a model, and staying up an extra half hour beyond normal bedtime.

Once mother and child reached the original goals for reducing defiance and increasing obedience, the treatment plan would be modified to promote maintenance and generalization of the improvements. First, the father would begin taking turns with the mother in carrying out the interventions described above. Once the child's performance became stable under parent-administered interventions, the parents transfer control of the interventions to the child. The self-regulation phase would be intended to promote maintenance and generalization of the gains achieved while the parents were carrying out the interventions. After three months of self-regulation conditions, formal programming would be terminated. The parents would conduct follow-up checks for temporal generalization at 4, 12, 20, 36, and 52 weeks after all planned interventions stopped.

Socialized and undersocialized, aggressive. Due to acute increases in aggression and violence in recent years, the detection and control of aggressive behavior in children has become a major challenge to clinicians. Aggressive behavior was a primary factor found in each of the 37 multivariate studies of deviant child behaviors surveyed by Quay and Werry (1979). Not only is aggressive behavior a prevalent factor in childhood psychopathology, it is also the best predictor of adolescent delinquency (Glick, 1972) and adult sociopathy (Cowen, Pederson, Babigian, Izzo, & Trost, 1973).

Various behavioral intervention strategies have proven effective in reducing the rate of aggressive behaviors. Notable among these strategies are: (a) differential reinforcement of nonaggressive behavior (Repp & Deitz, 1974), (b) behaviorally based parent training (Patterson & Fleischman, 1979), (c) response cost (Forman, 1980), (d) time-out from positive reinforcement (Wilson, Robertson, Herlong, & Haynes, 1979), and (e) cognitive-restructuring techniques (Camp, Zimet, van Doorninck, & Dahlem, 1977).

The following two studies provide illustrations of how response-cost, time-out, and cognitive restructuring techniques are employed to modify aggressive behavior.

Wilson, et al. (1979) successfully applied a time-out procedure to decrease the frequency of a child's aggressive behavior in a classroom setting. One highly aggressive male was selected from a class of 13 kindergarten children. During baseline, the percent of daily aggressive behavior was determined for both this target child and his classmates. Following baseline, the teacher utilized a time-out intervention contingent on aggressive behavior. Each time the child emitted aggressive behavior, the teacher placed him behind a small, open booth for five minutes. The booth blocked his visual contact with the rest of the class. This time-out procedure not only resulted in a sharp decline in the rate of the target child's aggressiveness, it also resulted in a reduction of the overall rate of deviant behavior in his untreated classmates.

In another study, Forman (1980) compared cognitive restructuring and response-cost techniques as means of modifying aggressive behavior in elementary-school children. Eighteen students were referred by the school psychologist for their aggressive behavior. These students were randomly assigned to one of three conditions: cognitive restructuring, response cost, and placebo. The cognitive restructuring consisted of 12 one-hour group meetings, spread over a six-week period. Each session involved: (a) having the children describe common, aggression-provoking situations specifically focusing on the self-statements that caused them to get mad, (b) having group members help them develop a new script of thoughts so they would not get mad, and (c) having them close their eyes, imagine the provocative situations, and practice their new script. The response-cost procedure involved giving the child a fine, consisting of subtracting two minutes from their free-fun time each time they exhibited aggressive behavior. The results revealed that both cognitive restructuring and response-cost interventions were equally successful in decreasing aggressive behavior and were significantly more effective that a placebo condition.

Anxiety disorders

Fears and phobias are common problems in children. A phobia normally consists of at least three elements—cognitive, emotional, and behavioral. Focusing on the behavioral element, fears and phobias are defined as inappropriate or excessive *avoidance behaviors*. In the case of fears, the avoidance behavior occurs in situations which have some reality-based threat to the child (e.g., fear of seeing physician or dentist). In contrast, phobias have little basis in reality; they involve situations which present very slight or no objective threat to the child (e.g., acrophobia).

Although many rating scales exist for the identification of fears and phobias in children, the clinical interview and direct observation of the child in the avoided situation is the most efficient means of assessment. The approach-avoidance dimensions which may be evaluated include frequency with which the feared situation is approached, distance maintained between the child and situation, time spent in contact with the feared situation (e.g., crying, using "fear" talk, tense posturing), and contact at a certain level along a graded series (e.g., reaching level 7 in a 20-item desensitization hierarchy relating to dogs, with level 1 describing a small puppy in a basket and level 20 a large dog running down the street toward the child). Regardless of which dimension is used, optimal assessment involves daily recording of the child's behavior.

Hatzenbuehler and Schroeder (1978) developed a set of hypotheses based on their review of the literature on desensitization of children's fears. Their hypotheses can be restated as a set of treatment recommendations: (a) When treating severe childhood fears/phobias, use passive-association techniques (such as systematic desensitization) at the beginning of the course of therapy. Vicarious and symbolic modeling are other types of passive procedures. (b) When treating severe childhood fears, do not use active-participation procedures in the early stages of treatment. Participant modeling, guided (prompted) participation, and reinforced practice are examples. (c) When treating severe childhood fears, the early phases of passive-association techniques should be followed by active participation. (d) When the child is only moderately fearful (i.e., will engage in some approach behaviors toward the feared situation), begin treatment with active-participation procedures and do not bother using passive-participation procedures.

Self-administered interventions may also be used to reduce fears and to promote approach behaviors. Not only may self-control strategies be used to produce initial treatment effects, they may also promote generalization and maintenance effects. For example, Dowrick and Dove (1980) used self-modeling videotapes to reduce fears and to increase skills and approach behaviors toward swimming and being in the water. The three children who participated in the study suffered from spina bifida. All three improved when exposed to videotapes of themselves performing appropriately, and the gains were maintained across a 10-week follow-up phase. Using a treatment package (which combined parent-administered and self-administered interventions), Graziano, Mooney, Huber, and Ignasiak (1979) had parents supervise, monitor, and reinforce their children's self-controlling responses. The self-control procedures included muscle relaxation, imagining a pleasant scene, and reciting self-statements for coping with nighttime fears. All seven children improved on all outcome measures, and the gains were maintained across a 12-month follow-up period. Graziano and Mooney (1980) replicated the preceding findings, using a between-groups design employing 33 families. The treated subjects did significantly better than the controls at post-treatment, on 16 measures of outcome. These gains increased across a 12-month follow-up phase.

Developmental reading and arithmetic disorders

One of the most frequent and pressing reasons for children being referred for psychological and psychiatric services is difficulty in school. According to recent estimates, 15 percent to 20 percent of the school population exhibits poor academic achievement (Abrams, 1980). This retardation of academic performance may be a function of: (a) specific learning disabilities, due to constitutional limitations, (b) disruptive behaviors, caused by emotional problems interfering with skill acquisition, or (c) some combination of the two. Whatever the etiology, the net result is the same—deficient academic skills.

Within the last two decades, the application of behavioral principles to modify academic performance in classroom settings has mushroomed (O'Leary & O'Leary, 1977). A wide variety of behavioral techniques and procedures have been successful in (a) controlling behavioral correlates of learning disabilities, such as overactivity and attentional deficits and (b) modifying academic performance (Klein, 1979). Recent research has demonstrated that only improving on-task behaviors has no clear effect on academic performance (Hay, Hay, & Nelson, 1977; Routh, 1979); however, the increased efforts to modify academic performance directly have revealed that doing so produces improvements in both achievement and deportment (Ayllon & Roberts, 1974).

The applied behavioral literature is replete with illustrations of effective modification of academic performance across a broad range of academic skills, including: reading/word recognition, reading comprehension, mathematics, vocabulary, spelling, and creative writing (e.g., Brent & Routh, 1978; Lahey & Drabman, 1974; Vasta & Stirpe, 1979).

Two treatment techniques that have particularly wide appeal in classroom settings to modify academic performance are token economy and teacher praise (Kazdin, 1977; Drabman, 1976). The following two studies demonstrate effective utilization of these techniques.

Ayllon and Roberts (1974) documented the effectiveness of using a token economy with five fifth-grade students. These students were identified as being both deficient in reading achievement and disruptive, with mean reading accuracy on daily reading assignments of 50 percent and mean levels of disruptiveness of 34 percent. A systematic token economy was employed with each child, consisting of a point system, in which each child was given points contingent on the percentage of correct responses in their daily reading workbook assignment. The children were allowed to exchange the points they earned for specially selected, backup reinforcers readily available in the classroom (e.g., daily reinforcers such as extra recess time, and weekly reinforcers such as seeing a movie). Introduction of the token system was followed by clear increases in targeted-reading accuracy to mean levels ranging from 70 percent to 85 percent and simultaneous decreases in disruptiveness to a 5 percent to 15 percent range across all five children.

Hay et al. (1977), in a study designed to compare the relative efficacy of on-task and academic-performance contingencies, selected 10 disruptive elementary school children and collected baseline data across: (a) on-task behavior, (b) number of academic problems completed, and (c) accuracy of work completed. To counterbalance for sequencing effects, five children received the following sequence: teacher praise for on-task behavior, baseline II, and teacher praise for academic performance; while the other five received teacher praise for academic performance, baseline II, and teacher praise for on-task behavior. During the on-task contingency, the teacher gave each subject praise and a star at least five times during the 30-minute session, contingent on on-task behavior; whereas, during the academic contingency, praise and stars were issued contingent on the presence of correctly completed problems at the time the teacher checked the student. The results revealed not only significant increases in the accuracy and rate of academic performance, but also improved on-task behavior. On the other hand, on-task contingencies only produced improvements in on-task behaviors.

Other promising techniques being utilized to improve academic performance are self-management (Rosenbaum & Drabman, 1979) and employing peers as behavior modifiers (McGee, Kaufman, & Nussen, 1977).

THE MAJOR BEHAVIORAL TREATMENTS

The preceding section illustrated the use of the basic steps to follow in conducting behavioral treatments with children. The following paragraphs provide a more systematic listing of the major behavioral treatments.

Setting events

Setting events are operations which change the general state of the child. They may alter thresholds for responding to antecedent stimuli or reinforcers; they may change various dimensions of behavior without first manipulating an immediate antecedent stimulus or consequence. The more common setting events are: (a) administration of a deprivation schedule, (b) administration of a satiation schedule, (c) administration of drugs, (d) application of physical restraints, (e) providing choices, (f) application of pleasant stimulation, (g) application of aversive stimulation, and (h) providing a relationship or rooting section. Whereas these setting events presumably affect performance without directly producing new learning, the better-known behavioral strategies are aimed at learning. Behaviorally oriented clinicians have tended to ignore setting events as treatment procedures. Those who do recommend the deliberate management of setting events suggest their use in conjunction with other clinical interventions (cf. Wahler & Fox, 1981).

Deprivation schedules. Child behavior therapists do not typically use deprivation schedules as a part of their treatment programming, except to take advantage of naturally occurring events. For example, in conducting a training session with developmentally disabled children, the therapist would hold the session the maximum number of hours following the last meal, in order to maximize the power of the food reinforcers during the training session. Although countless demonstrations of the effects of deprivation schedules have been published in the literature on animal behavior, published studies on the use of deprivation schedules in treating children are rare (cf. Frankel, Simmons, & Olson, 1977; Kazdin, 1977, pp. 263–264).

Satiation schedules. Satiation schedules are not as rare in the child clinical literature. For example, Holland (1969) used a satiation procedure as part of a treatment package for a seven-year-old boy who set fires in the home. The father had his son repeatedly strike matches, as the father watched. Since the satiation procedure was only one element out of several, its specific contribution to the cessation of fire setting could not be determined.

Administration of drugs. Although behavior therapists do not typically conceive of psychopharmacology as one of their modes of effecting change, the administration of drugs to children who are being seen by clinical child psychologists is commonplace. Particularly prevalent is the administration of stimulants to learning-disabled/hyperactive children (Barkley, 1979). In cases such as learning-disabled/hyperactive children, the combination of an appropriate medication and a psychological intervention may be more potent than either used alone (cf. Noland, 1981).

Application of physical restraints. This is another category of intervention not typically endorsed by behavior therapists, but there is no question that physical restraints modify behavior. In their review of methods of treating seriously disruptive behavior, Harris and Ersner-Hershfield (1978) describe some of the uses of restraint.

Providing choices. Providing a child with choices (or limited choices) is another method for changing the general state of the child. Many behavioral approaches to child case management emphasize presenting the child with options from which to choose, but the published clinical studies have not extensively explored the effects of providing choices to children as a major, independent variable. Perlmuter and Monty (1979), however, edited a volume which presents many contemporary studies on the behavioral effects of choice.

Application of pleasant stimulation. Any noncontingent administration of positive reinforcers may be classified as a setting event. Since the early work of Wolpe (1958), behavior therapists have included relaxation training as a normal part of their repertoire. The induction of deep-muscle relaxation is best conceived as a setting event, achieving some of the effects of certain drugs, without resorting to medication (cf. Walker, Hedberg, Clement, & Wright, 1981, p. 65).

Application of aversive stimulation. Because of the ethical problems which would be involved, child-behavior therapists do not apply aversive stimuli to their patients noncontingently. In contrast, the natural environments of children who come to clinical psychologists are often sources of extensive, aversive stimulation which is not contingent on what the children do. Examples include being exposed to an alcoholic parent who engages in spouse abuse, being called cruel names by peers because of birth defect, or suffering from a chronic illness. Comprehensive-behavioral treatments should engineer the reduction or elimination of such events.

Providing a relationship or rooting section. Behavior therapists have not spent much time researching the effects of providing a relationship for a child. The therapeutic relationship is normally treated as a constant, rather than as an independent variable. In the natural environment, the number and quality of active, interpersonal relationships form an important part of the child's behavioral setting. Social isolation (i.e., the lack of a peer rooting section) is a particularly common, childhood problem (Oden, 1980).

Cues, prods, and models

Setting events involve antecedents that have a broad impact across many behaviors by altering the general state of the child. In contrast, cues, prods, and models have a much narrower impact. Any particular cue, prod, or modeling stimulus typically impacts a relatively specific and narrow band of behavior.

Choosing and defining a target behavior. Before treatment begins, someone must decide what will be treated. The identification of specific, therapeutic targets may facilitate behavioral changes. Also, who determined the target behavior may also make a difference. Although experimental data which speak to these possible treatment effects are not available for children, the growing literature on goal setting suggests that researching these possibilities is justified.

Goal setting. The powerful effects of goal setting have been demonstrated in many investigations (e.g., Gagne, 1975). An explicit, therapeutic goal appears to be a special kind of discriminative stimulus. Children and the adults who care for them make a variety of mistakes in managing goals: (a) the goals are unstated; (b) the goals are stated, but they are not clear; (c) the goals are clear, but they are unrealistic or unreachable; (d) the goals are set too low; (e) too many goals are stated simultaneously.

One procedural accomplishment of effective contracting (as outlined earlier) is the articulation of realistic, reachable goals, which are accepted by the child and the adults participating in the treatment program.

Immediate cues and prods. If the therapist wished to strengthen a behavior, the therapist may present to the child a stimulus which has usually been followed by the target behavior in the past. If the therapist wants to weaken a behavior, presenting a stimulus which is rarely followed by the undesired behavior, removing cues which are usually followed by the undesirable behavior, or presenting a stimulus which is usually followed by a response that is incompatible with the undesired behavior may be employed. Stimulus-control procedures have been applied to a wide range of childhood problems (cf. "Cumulative Index," 1977, p. 806).

Simple requests and commands are the most common forms of child-management techniques. They are so ordinary that they may be overlooked as treatment operations. More difficult to miss as treatments would be procedures such as the stimulus control of eating behavior (Ferster, Nurnberger, & Levitt, 1962), stimulus control of insomnia (Coates & Thoresen, 1977, pp. 143–155), flooding (Baum, 1970), conditioning treatment of enuresis (Doleys, 1977), systematic desensitization (Graziano, De Giovanni, & Garcia, 1979; Hatzenbuehler & Schroeder, 1978), self-instructional training (Hobbs, Moguin, Tyroler, & Lahey, 1980; Ledwidge, 1978; O'Leary & Dubey, 1979), and stress-inoculation training (Meichenbaum, 1977, pp. 143–182).

Setting performance standards and writing contracts. Before any consequences are delivered in contingency-management programs, the therapist may clearly specify the performance standards for consequating the target behavior. The mere specification of future consequences may effect change in the target behavior without the consequences being applied. A common procedure is to spell out all of the elements in the planned-treatment program by preparing a written contract (DeRisi & Butz, 1975; Stuart, 1975). Such contracts are best viewed as complex, discriminative stimuli.

Choosing reinforcers. Other antecedent conditions which may affect the target behavior are selecting reinforcers before a contingency program is implemented or deciding before a treatment session or phase begins who will choose the reinforcers at the end of the session or phase. The available data suggest that treatment effects are enhanced by allowing the target child to decide these issues before the contingency program is implemented (Brigham, 1979).

Social models. The most complex (and perhaps, the most focused) antecedents for producing changes in children's behavior are modeling stimuli. Much evidence exists to support the proposition that behavior may be learned or modified without the learner engaging in the target behavior and without the learner receiving any consequences for engaging in the target behavior (Bandura, 1969, pp. 118–216). The modeling stimuli may be presented via live models, filmed models, imaginary characters (puppets, dolls, marionettes, and cartoons), and verbal behavior (cognitive restructuring, directions to instigate a particular action, or descriptions of behavioral topography as in covert modeling).

Modeling stimuli may be used as setting events (cf. *reinforcer exposure,* Ayllon & Azrin, 1968; Kazdin, 1977, pp. 160–161); sources of specific emotional conditioning (cf. *testimonials,* Goldstein, Heller, & Sechrest, 1966, pp. 112–123; *vicarious inhibitory conditioning,* Rosenthal, Rosenthal, & Chang, 1977); modifiers of response sets (cf. *time projection,* Lazarus, 1971, pp. 227–229; *emotive imagery,* Tasto & Chesney, 1977); examples of new behavior patterns (cf. *social skills,* O'Connor, 1969); social facilitators and sources of cognitive restructuring (Meichenbaum, 1977); vicarious reinforcers (Walker et al., 1981, pp. 331–332); and disinhibitors (cf. *contact desensitization/participant modeling,* Bandura, Blanchard, & Ritter, 1969).

Primary behaviors

Although behaviorists have allegedly emphasized the role of behavior in describing an empirically defined psychology, this emphasis has been tilted in a particular direction. Traditional, behavioral clinicians have emphasized the role of overt behaviors as dependent variables (i.e., *controlled responses*), but they have neglected the role of the child's own behaviors as independent variables (i.e., *controlling responses*). The development of self-administered child treatments has helped to identify the fact that children may directly modify their own behavior. They may deliberately practice a desired behavior, engage in a response which competes with an undesired behavior, or withhold a particular behavior. Performing any one of these three actions has the potential of altering the subsequent probability of the target behavior. Obviously, such direct-behavior modification is only available to the child when serving as a self-change agent. We have chosen to identify these self-controlling responses as ''primary behaviors.''

Deliberately practicing desired behaviors is commonplace in the child's general environment, but many therapeutic systems have failed to identify *practice* as a specific, therapeutic intervention in its own right. *Positive practice* is a typical component in assertiveness-training packages (e.g., Patterson, 1972), and in participant modeling (e.g., Bandura et al., 1969), and it is also known as *behavioral rehearsal.* Engaging in competing responses is an important part of *habit-reversal training* (Nunn & Azrin, 1976) and *overcorrection* (Foxx, 1977). Because of the difficulties in discriminating between when a child is deliberately withholding a response versus times when he/she is simply doing something other than the target behavior, treatments based on the third type of primary behavior do not appear to have been published.

Consequences and feedback

The clinical psychologist who is not familiar with the contemporary behavioral literature probably equates the systematic management of consequences as the hallmark of child behavior therapy. Although administering and removing reinforcers is certainly an important component of behavioral-treatment procedures, hopefully the present overview has illustrated that behavioral treatment is as broad as empirically based, general psychology. One important development which helps illustrate this point is biofeedback.

Biofeedback.   As a special area of research and practice, biofeedback draws heavily on physiological psychology, the psychology of learning, and electrical engineering. Biofeedback is a subcategory of a broader source of behavioral control—feedback. Theorists may argue whether there are any important differences between information, feedback, and reinforcers, but, in the present chapter, such issues will be ignored.

In his opening editorial for the first issue of the new journal, *Biofeedback and Self-Regulation,* Stoyva (1976) asserted, ''Biofeedback is a technology.'' This developing technology has been applied primarily to adults, but there are exceptions in which children have been treated (e.g., Finley, Smith, & Etherton, 1975). More extensive information may be obtained on biofeedback by referring to Chapter 32.

Other feedback procedures.   Children have been much more involved in clinical studies of other forms of feedback. The most extensively
explored procedures have been forms of self-observation or self-monitoring (Nelson, 1977; O'Leary & Dubey, 1979; Rosenbaum & Drabman,
1979; Workman & Hector, 1978). Children may observe, record, and
graph a target behavior or a behavioral by-product, such as the number
of academic problems completed within a class period. Such self-monitoring tends to strengthen desirable behaviors and to weaken undesirable
behaviors, but the mere provision of feedback may not be as powerful
as providing explicit self-reinforcers (Clement, Anderson, Arnold, Butman,
Fantuzzo, & Mays, 1978).

Administering and removing reinforcers.   There are four basic
types of consequences that significantly alter the response strength of a
behavior. They involve the contingent presentation or removal of positive
or aversive stimulus events. Consequent procedures which result in *increases* in response strength (either by the contingent presentation of
positive stimulus events or the removal of aversive events) are called
positive reinforcement and negative reinforcement, respectively. Procedures which affect *decreases* in response strength (either by the application of aversive stimulation or the removal of positive events) are referred
to as positive punishment and negative punishment, respectively.

Positive reinforcement.   Procedures based on positive reinforcement
involve presentation of special stimuli (positive reinforcers), contingent
on the occurrence of desired behavior. Two basic categories of positive
reinforcers are unconditioned and conditioned. Unconditioned positive
reinforcers are also termed *primary reinforcers*, because they independently yield reinforcing effects which do not have to be learned. Utilization
of unconditioned positive reinforcers to increase deficient behavior in
children may involve consequating this behavior with edible (Tramontana,
1972), tangible (Ward & Ward, 1974), activity (Lovitt, Guppy, & Blattner,
1969), or social reinforcers (Strain & Pierce, 1977).

Conditioned positive reinforcers, unlike unconditioned, are initially
neutral stimuli which come to acquire reinforcing properties as a result
of their contingent relationship with primary reinforcers. The most widely
used behavioral technique which utilizes conditioned reinforcers with children is the token economy (Kazdin, 1977). A token economy basically
involves providing conditioned reinforcers in the form of tokens (e.g.,
points, stars, poker chips), contingent on desirable behavior. These tokens
are exchanged for primary, backup reinforcers, that are readily available
in the child's environment.

In addition to providing stimuli as positive reinforcers, Premack (1959)
introduced the notion of using responses as positive reinforcers. This
concept, known as the Premack principle, involves making high-probabil-

ity behavior contingent on the occurrence of low-probability behavior. In other words, the high-probability behavior serves to consequate the occurrence of the low-probability behavior. Hopkins, Schutte, and Garton (1971) illustrated the use of the Premack principle to increase the rate and quality of academic responses in first- and second-grade students, by making play behaviors contingent on prompt and accurate completion of daily copying assignments.

Negative reinforcement. Negative reinforcement procedures result in increases in the response strength of behaviors that either terminate or prevent aversive events. Presenting an aversive event until the child makes the desired response to terminate it is referred to as an *escape* procedure; whereas, if a desired response is emitted to prevent an aversive event from occurring, the procedures is called *avoidance*. Renne and Creer (1976) illustrated these procedures in a pediatric setting.

Negative punishment. Negative punishment procedures are employed to reduce the rate of excessive behaviors by contingently removing positive events when the unwanted behaviors are emitted. The two most commonly used of these procedures are *response-cost* and *time-out*. With a response-cost procedure, each time the undesirable response occurs, the child is fined some prescribed quantity of a reinforcer (e.g., half of dessert or 10 minutes subtracted from recess).

Time-out is a procedure similar to response-cost, in that unwanted behaviors result in removal of positive events; however, in a time-out procedure, the consequence is not just the removal of a limited quantity of a reinforcer but the complete removal of all sources of positive reinforcement for a short period of time. This is accomplished by excluding the child from reinforcing events by separating him or her—usually behind some type of physical barrier—for a fixed period of time (e.g., five minutes), contingent upon the specified inappropriate behavior. The previously discussed study by Wilson et al. (1979) provides an excellent illustration of the application of this procedure with children.

Another procedure for reducing disruptive behavior in children which combines elements of time-out and modeling procedures is contingent observation (Porterfield, Herbert-Jackson, & Risley, 1976). Contingent observation is the removal of a child from participation in an ongoing activity (for a short period of time) as a result of an inappropriate behavior. This removal is different from time-out, in that the child is not taken away from the activity; he/she is only asked to sit back and is not allowed to participate. This procedure enables the child to watch other children model appropriate behaviors that lead to positive reinforcers.

Positive punishment. Probably the most common and most controversial category of consequences used to modify deviant child behavior is positive punishment. Although consequating unwanted child behavior with contingent-aversive events has historically been a dominant method of child control, it is important here to make the distinction between contingent-aversive events and positive punishment. Scientific study of contingent-aversive events by behavior analysts (Azrin & Holz, 1966) has revealed that contingent-aversive events are not necessarily effective punishers. Even when contingent-aversive events are effective punishers, they may be associated with undesirable side effects (Skinner, 1968). For these reasons, the following basic guidelines should be followed when using any positive punishment technique with children: (a) employ these techniques only when the above-mentioned categories of consequent procedures have proven unsuccessful; (b) utilize the least aversive events before proceeding up the hierarchy of aversives; (c) carefully monitor the application of contingent-aversive events to document their efficacy as punishers; and (d) design procedures to minimize negative reactions (e.g., aggression, withdrawal, negative modeling).

Within these procedures, a hierarchy of punishers has been successfully employed to reduce behaviors in children, ranging from the use of mild, verbal reprimands to reduce disruptive classroom behavior (O'Leary, Kaufman, Kass, & Drabman, 1970) to the use of electric shock to eliminate dangerous, self-injurious behavior (Tate & Baroff, 1966).

PROMOTING GENERALIZATION

One vital step beyond the successful utilization of behavioral techniques to treat deviant child behavior is the need to program for the spread and durability of treatment effects to areas outside the treatment context. In recent years, behavior analysts have emphasized the importance of developing a technology of generalization that would specify both the dimensions of generalization and methods for promoting generalization across these dimensions (Forehand & Atkeson, 1977; McLaughlin, 1979; Stokes & Baer, 1977). Building on the conceptual advances of such writers, Drabman, Hammer, and Rosenbaum (1979) identified 16 categories of generalization, which consist of combinations of the following dimensions: (a) subjects, (b) responses, (c) settings, and (d) time. Other writers, such as Wildman and Wildman (1975) and Marholin (1978), have summarized findings from the behavioral literature and have outlined basic strategies functionally related to the generalization of treatment effects with children. Marholin (1978) proposed the following ten strategies for promoting generalization:

1. Contingencies of reinforcement in the extra-treatment setting should be consistent with contingencies present in the treatment environment.
2. Efforts should be made to teach significant others (e.g., parents, siblings, peers) to provide appropriate contingencies in the natural environment.
3. Social stimuli need to be established in the natural environment, to serve as additional, functional reinforcers to the child.

4. Vary the stimulus conditions of the training environment, such that discriminative stimuli in the treatment setting will have a high probability of occurring in the post-treatment environment.
5. Fade reinforcement gradually during training, to an intermittent schedule that is consistent with the schedules in the post-treatment environment.
6. Train the child on a schedule of reinforcement that approximates the delays found in the natural environment.
7. Teach behaviors that are compatible with competing, undesirable behaviors.
8. Teach behaviors that permit the child to enter an environment that naturally reinforces and maintains responses associated with the target behaviors.
9. Teach the child to control the contingencies and antecedent conditions of his own behavior, by utilizing self-control strategies.
10. Provide treatment conditions that permit the child to attribute both success and failure to his/her own behavior.

Once desired dimensions of generalization have been selected, these strategies will assist in designing treatment programs that will maximize desired generalization effects.

EFFICIENT WAYS TO IDENTIFY TREATMENTS FOR A GIVEN PROBLEM AND PROBLEMS FOR A GIVEN TREATMENT

Behavioral treatments have tended to be more clearly defined and highly specific than their nonbehavioral predecessors. The desire to match specific treatment packages with particular childhood problems dates back to the early beginnings of child behavior therapy (e.g., Jones, 1924; Mowrer & Mowrer, 1938). This emphasis on specificity seems to have stimulated the development of bibliographies on behavior modification. In her own published bibliography, *Behavior Modification and the Child,* Benson (1979) listed 20 earlier bibliographies. Benson's volume covered the literature published in English through 1977. She included over 2,300 entries, most of which were annotated. Her format facilitates identifying articles on the treatment of complex syndromes, applications in different settings, use by different professions, training, research, audiovisual materials, and treatment techniques. Benson's book provides efficient means to survey much of the relevant literature. What she provides can easily be supplemented, for more recent years, by consulting *Child Development Abstracts, Dissertation Abstracts International, Index Medicus,* and *Psychological Abstracts.*

For persons seeking a comprehensive introduction to child behavior therapy, a number of books are available (e.g., Bandura, 1969; Browning

& Stover, 1971; Gelfand & Hartmann, 1975; Krumboltz & Krumboltz, 1972; Morris, 1976; Ross, 1980, 1981; Sulzer-Azaroff & Mayer, 1977; Tharp & Wetzel, 1969; Walker et al., 1981).

Critical reviews are also available across a wide range of topics: anorexia nervosa (Bemis, 1978), asthma (Knapp & Wells, 1978), behavior therapy with children (Phillips & Ray, 1980), cognitive-behavior therapy (Hobbs et al., 1980; Ledwidge, 1978; Urbain & Kendall, 1980), covert sensitization (Little & Curran, 1978), elective mutism (Sanok & Ascione, 1979), enuresis (Doleys, 1977; Morgan, 1978), fears and phobias (Graziano et al., 1979; Hatzenbuehler & Schroeder, 1978; Mathews, 1978), flooding (Baum, 1970), home-based reinforcement programs aimed at school performance (Atkeson & Forehand, 1978), juvenile delinquency (Davidson & Seidman, 1974), overcorrection (Ollendick, 1978), parents as therapists (Forehand & Atkeson, 1977), behavioral parent-training manuals (Bernal & North, 1978), punishment (Harris & Ersner-Hershfield, 1978), self-help manuals (Glasgow & Rosen, 1978), self-injurious behavior (Carr, 1977), self-regulation (Nelson, 1977; O'Leary & Dubey, 1979; Rosenbaum & Drabman, 1979; Workman & Hector, 1978), social withdrawal (Gelfand, 1978), and time-out (Leitenberg, 1965).

Perhaps the simplest way to stay current with developments in the behavioral treatment of children is to read the journal, *Child Behavior Therapy*, which began publication in 1979. *Education and Treatment of Children* is another journal which carries articles on the clinical management of children via behavioral techniques; it began publication in 1977. *Behavior Modification, Behaviour Research and Therapy, Behavior Therapy, Behavioral Counseling Quarterly, Journal of Applied Behavior Analysis*, and *Journal of Behavior Therapy and Experimental Psychiatry* are some additional behavioral journals which carry many articles relating to children.

SUMMARY

Empirically defined interventions and outcome measures for children through age 12 constitute the focus of this chapter. The first section covers basic steps to effective behavioral treatment with children. These basic steps include a general review of the referral problems and sketching a tentative treatment contract, performing a behavioral assessment, implementing and evaluating the effects of an intervention package, and follow-up.

The second section provides some illustrations of these steps in dealing with the common referral problems of attention deficit disorders, conduct disorders, anxiety disorders, and developmental reading and arithmetic disorders.

The third section outlines the major behavioral treatments: setting events (deprivation and satiation schedules, drugs, physical restraints, providing choices, pleasant and aversive stimulation, and providing a relationship), cues, prods, and models (choosing a target behavior, goal setting, immediate cuing, setting performance standards, contracting, choosing reinforcers, and social models), primary behaviors (positive practice, competing responses, and withholding), and consequences and feedback (biofeedback and managing reinforcers).

The last two sections present ways of promoting generalization and of obtaining an optimum match between problems and treatments.

REFERENCES

Abrams, J. C. Learning disabilities. In G. Sholevar, R. Benson, & B. Blinder (Eds.), *Emotional disorders in children and adolescents.* New York: Spectrum, 1980.

American Psychiatric Association. *Diagnostic and statistical manual of mental disorders* (3d ed.). Washington, D.C.: Author, 1980.

American Psychological Association. Specialty guidelines for the delivery of services by clinical psychologists. *American Psychologist,* 1981, *36,* 640–651.

Atkeson, B. M., & Forehand, R. Parent behavioral training for problem children: An examination of studies using multiple-outcome measures. *Journal of Abnormal Child Psychology,* 1978, *6,* 449–460.

Ayllon, T., & Azrin, N. *The token economy: A motivational system for therapy and rehabilitation.* Englewood Cliffs, N.J.: Prentice-Hall, 1968.

Ayllon, T., Layman, D., & Kandel, H. J. A behavioral-educational alternative to drug control of hyperactive children. *Journal of Applied Behavior Analysis,* 1975, *8,* 137–146.

Ayllon, T., & Roberts, M. D. Eliminating discipline problems by strengthening academic performance. *Journal of Applied Behavior Analysis,* 1974, *7,* 71–76.

Azrin, N. H., & Holz, W. C. Punishment. In W. K. Honig (Ed.), *Operant behavior: Areas of research and application.* New York: Appleton-Century-Crofts, 1966.

Bandura, A. *Principles of behavior modification.* New York: Holt, Rinehart & Winston, 1969.

Bandura, A., Blanchard, E. B., & Ritter, B. Relative efficacy of desensitization and modeling approaches for inducing behavioral, affective, and attitudinal changes. *Journal of Personality and Social Psychology,* 1969, *13,* 173–199.

Barkley, R. A. Predicting the response of hyperkinetic children to stimulant drugs: A review. In B. B. Lahey (Ed.), *Behavior therapy with hyperactive and learning disabled children.* New York: Oxford University Press, 1979.

Baum, M. Extinction of avoidance responding through response prevention (flooding). *Psychological Bulletin,* 1970, *74,* 276–284.

Bemis, K. M. Current approaches to the etiology and treatment of anorexia nervosa. *Psychological Bulletin,* 1978, *85,* 593–617.

Benson, H. B. *Behavior modification and the child: An annotated bibliography.* Westport, Conn.: Greenwood Press, 1979.

Bernal, M. E., & North, J. A. A survey of parent-training manuals. *Journal of Applied Behavior Analysis,* 1978, *11,* 533–544.

Bornstein, P. H., & Quevillon, R. P. The effects of a self-instructional package on overactive preschool boys. *Journal of Applied Behavior Analysis,* 1976, *9,* 179–188.

Brent, D. E., & Routh, D. K. Response cost and impulsive work-recognition errors in reading-disabled children. *Journal of Abnormal Child Psychology,* 1978, *6,* 211–219.

Brigham, T. A. Some effects of choice on academic performance. In L. C. Perlmuter & R. A. Monty (Eds.), *Choice and perceived control.* Hillsdale, N.J.: Lawrence Erlbaum Associates, 1979.

Browning, R. M., & Stover, D. O. *Behavior modification in child treatment: An experimental and clinical approach.* New York: Aldine-Atherton, 1971.

Camp, B. W., Zimet, S. G., van Doorninck, W. J., & Dahlem, N. W. Verbal abilities in young aggressive boys. *Journal of Educational Psychology,* 1977, *69,* 129–135.

Carr, E. G. The motivation of self-injurious behavior: A review of some hypotheses. *Psychological Bulletin,* 1977, *84,* 800–816.

Clement, P. W. Parents, peers, and child patients make the best therapists. In G. J. Williams & S. Gordon (Eds.), *Clinical child psychology: Current practices and future perspectives.* New York: Behavioral Publications, 1974.

Clement, P. W., Anderson, E., Arnold, J., Butman, R., Fantuzzo, J., & Mays, R. Self-observation and self-reinforcement as sources of self-control in children. *Biofeedback and Self-Regulation,* 1978, *3,* 247–267.

Coates, T. J., & Thoresen, C. E. *How to sleep better: A drug-free program for overcoming insomnia.* Englewood Cliffs, N.J.: Prentice-Hall, 1977.

Cowen, E. L., Pederson, A., Babigian, H., Izzo, L. D., & Trost, M. A. Long-term follow-up of early detected vulnerable children. *Journal of Consulting and Clinical Psychology,* 1973, *41,* 438–446.

Cumulative Index: Volumes 1–10 (1968–1977). *Journal of Applied Behavior Analysis,* 1977, *10,* 761–832.

Davidson, W. S., II., & Seidman, E. Studies of behavior modification and juvenile delinquency: A review, methodological critique, and social perspective. *Psychological Bulletin,* 1974, *81,* 998–1011.

DeRisi, W. J., & Butz, G. *Writing behavioral contracts: A case-simulation practice manual.* Champaign, Ill.: Research Press, 1975.

Doleys, D. M. Behavioral treatments for nocturnal enuresis in children: A review of the recent literature. *Psychological Bulletin,* 1977, *84,* 30–54.

Dowrick, P. W., & Dove, C. The use of self-modeling to improve the swimming performance of spina bifida children. *Journal of Applied Behavior Analysis,* 1980, *13,* 51–56.

Drabman, R. S. Behavior modification in the classroom. In E. Craighead, A. Kazdin, & M. Mahoney (Eds.), *Behavior modification: Principles, issues, and application.* Boston: Houghton Mifflin, 1976.

Drabman, R. S., Hammer, D., & Rosenbaum, M. S. Assessing generalization in behavior modification with children: The generalization map. *Behavioral Assessment,* 1979, *1,* 203–209.

Ferster, C. B., Nurnberger, J. I., & Levitt, E. B. The control of eating. *Journal of Mathematics,* 1962, *1,* 87–109.

Finley, W. W., Smith, H. A., & Etherton, M. D. Reduction of seizures and normalization of the EEG in a severe epileptic following sensorimotor-biofeedback training: Preliminary study. *Biological Psychology,* 1975, *2,* 189–203.

Forehand, R., & Atkeson, B. M. Generality of treatment effects with parents as therapists: A review of assessment and implementation procedures. *Behavior Therapy,* 1977, *8,* 575–593.

Forman, S. G. A comparison of cognitive-training and response-cost procedures in modifying aggressive behavior of elementary-school children. *Behavior Therapy,* 1980, *11,* 594–600.

Foxx, R. M. Attention training: The use of overcorrection avoidance to increase the eye contact of autistic and retarded children. *Journal of Applied Behavior Analysis,* 1977, *10,* 489–499.

Frankel, F., Simmons, J. Q., III, & Olson, S. Effects of social deprivation upon operant behavior in mentally retarded and autistic children. *Journal of Pediatric Psychology,* 1977, *2,* 172–175.

Gagne, E. E. Motivating the disabled learner. *Academic Therapy,* 1975, *10,* 361–362.

Gelfand, D. M. Social-withdrawal and negative-emotional states: Behavior therapy. In B. B. Wolman, J. Egan, & A. O. Ross (Eds.), *Handbook of treatment of mental disorders in childhood and adolescence.* Englewood Cliffs, N.J.: Prentice-Hall, 1978.

Gelfand, D. M., & Hartmann, D. P. *Child-behavior analysis and therapy.* Elmsford, N.Y.: Pergamon Press, 1975.

Glasgow, R. E., & Rosen, G. M. Behavioral bibliotherapy: A review of self-help behavior-therapy manuals. *Psychological Bulletin,* 1978, *85,* 1–23.

Glick, S. J. First follow-up study of Glueck table to identify predelinquents at school entrance. In S. Glueck & E. Glueck (Eds.), *Identification of predelinquents.* New York: Medical Book, 1972.

Goldstein, A. P., Heller, K., & Sechrest, L. B. *Psychotherapy and the psychology of behavior change.* New York: John Wiley & Sons, 1966.

Graziano, A. M., De Giovanni, I. S., & Garcia, K. A. Behavioral treatment of children's fears: A review. *Psychological Bulletin,* 1979, *86,* 804–830.

Graziano, A. M., & Mooney, K. C. Family self-control instruction for children's nighttime-fear reduction. *Journal of Consulting and Clinical Psychology,* 1980, *48,* 206–213.

Graziano, A. M., Mooney, K. A., Huber, C., & Ignasiak, D. Self-control instruction for children's fear reduction. *Journal of Behavior Therapy and Experimental Psychiatry,* 1979, *10,* 221–227.

Harris, S. L., & Ersner-Hershfield, R. Behavioral suppression of seriously disruptive behavior in psychotic and retarded patients: A review of punishment and its alternatives. *Psychological Bulletin,* 1978, *85,* 1352–1375.

Hatzenbuehler, L. C., & Schroeder, H. E. Desensitization procedures in the treatment of childhood disorders. *Psychological Bulletin,* 1978, *85,* 831–844.

Hay, W. M., Hay, L., & Nelson, R. O. Direct and collateral changes in on-task and academic behavior resulting from on-task versus academic contingencies. *Behavior Therapy,* 1977, *8,* 431–441.

Hobbs, A. S., Moguin, L. E., Tyroler, M., & Lahey, B. B. Cognitive-behavior therapy with children: Has clinical utility been demonstrated? *Psychological Bulletin,* 1980, *87,* 147–165.

Holland, C. J. Elimination by the parents of fire-setting behavior in a seven-year-old boy. *Behaviour Research and Therapy,* 1969, *7,* 135–137.

Hopkins, B. L., Schutte, R. C., & Garton, K. L. The effects of access to a playroom on the rate and quality of printing and writing of first- and second-grade students, *Journal of Applied Behavioral Analysis,* 1971, *4,* 77–87.

Jones, M. C. The elimination of children's fears. *Journal of Experimental Psychology,* 1924, *7,* 383–390.

Kazdin, A. E. *The token economy: A review and evaluation.* New York: Plenum Press, 1977.

Klein, R. D. Modifying academic performance in the grade-school classroom. In M. Hersen, R. Eisler, & P. Miller (Eds.), *Progress in behavior modification.* New York: Academic Press, 1979.

Knapp, T. J., & Wells, L. A. Behavior therapy for asthma: A review. *Behaviour Research and Therapy,* 1978, *16,* 103–115.

Krumboltz, J. D., & Krumboltz, H. B. *Changing children's behavior.* Englewood Cliffs, N.J.: Prentice-Hall, 1972.

Lahey, D., & Drabman, R. S. Facilitation of the acquisition and retention of sight-word vocabulary through token reinforcement. *Journal of Applied Behavior Analysis,* 1974, *7,* 307–312.

Lazarus, A. A. *Behavior therapy and beyond.* New York: McGraw-Hill, 1971.

Ledwidge, B. Cognitive-behavior modification: A step in the wrong direction? *Psychological Bulletin,* 1978, *85,* 353–375.

Leitenberg, H. Is time-out from positive reinforcement an aversive event? *Psychological Bulletin,* 1965, *64,* 428–511.

Little, L. M., & Curran, J. P. Covert sensitization: A clinical procedure in need of some explanations. *Psychological Bulletin,* 1978, *85,* 513–531.

Lovitt, T. C., Guppy, T. E., & Blattner, J. D. The use of a free-time contingency with fourth graders to increase spelling accuracy. *Behaviour Research and Therapy,* 1969, *7,* 151–156.

Marholin, D., II, & Siegel, L. J. Beyond the law of effect: Programming for the maintenance of behavioral change. In D. Marholin (Ed.), *Child behavior therapy.* New York: Gardner Press, 1978.

Mathews, A. Fear-reduction research and clinical phobias. *Psychological Bulletin,* 1978, *85,* 390–404.

McGee, C. S., Kauffman, J. M., & Nussen, J. L. Children as therapeutic-change agents: Reinforcement-intervention paradigms. *Review of Educational Research,* 1977, *47,* 451–478.

McLaughlin, T. F. Generalization of treatment effects: An analysis of procedures and outcomes. *Corrective and Social Psychiatry,* 1979, *25,* 33–38.

McLaughlin, T. F., & Scott, J. W. The use of response cost to reduce inappropriate behavior in educational settings. *Corrective and Social Psychiatry and Journal of Applied Behavior Therapy,* 1976, *22,* 32–34.

Meichenbaum, D. *Cognitive-behavior modification: An integrative approach.* New York: Plenum Press, 1977.

Morgan, R. T. T. Relapse and therapeutic response in the conditioning treatment of enuresis: A review of recent findings on intermittent reinforcement, overlearning, and stimulus intensity. *Behaviour Research and Therapy,* 1978, *16,* 273–279.

Morris, R. J. *Behavior modification with children: A systematic guide.* Cambridge, Mass.: Winthrop, 1976.

Mowrer, O. H., & Mowrer, W. M. Enuresis: A method for its study and treatment. *American Journal of Orthopsychiatry,* 1938, *8,* 436–459.

Nelson, R. O. Assessment and therapeutic functions of self-monitoring. In M. Hersen, R.

M. Eisler, & P. M. Miller (Eds.), *Progress in behavior modification* (Vol. 5). New York: Academic Press, 1977.

Noland, S. A. W. *The effects of Ritalin and self-reinforcement upon the academic performance of hyperactive boys.* Unpublished doctoral dissertation, Graduate School of Psychology, Fuller Theological Seminary, 1981.

Nunn, R. G., & Azrin, N. H. Eliminating nail biting by the Habit-Reversal Procedure. *Behaviour Research and Therapy,* 1976, *14,* 65–67.

O'Connor, R. D. Modification of social withdrawal through symbolic modeling. *Journal of Applied Behavior Analysis,* 1969, *2,* 15–22.

Oden, S. A child's social isolation: Origins, prevention, intervention. In G. Cartledge & J. F. Milburn (Eds.), *Teaching social skills to children: Innovative approaches.* Elmsford, N.Y.: Pergamon Press, 1980.

O'Leary, K. D., Kaufman, K. F., Kass, R. E., & Drabman, R. The effects of loud and soft reprimands on the behavior of disruptive children. *Exceptional Children,* 1970, *37,* 145–155.

O'Leary, K. D., & O'Leary, S. G. *Classroom management: The successful use of behavior modification* (2d ed.). Elmsford, N.Y.: Pergamon Press, 1977.

O'Leary, S. B., & Dubey, D. R. Applications of self-control procedures by children: A review. *Journal of Applied Behavior Analysis,* 1979, *12,* 449–465.

Ollendick, T. H., & Matson, J. L. Overcorrection: An overview: *Behavior Therapy,* 1978, *9,* 830–842.

Patterson, G. & Fleischman, M. J. Maintenance of treatment effects: Some considerations concerning family systems and follow-up data. *Behavior Therapy,* 1979, *10,* 168–185.

Patterson, G. R., Jones, R., Whittier, J., & Wright, M. A. A behavior-modification technique for the hyperactive child. *Behaviour Research and Therapy,* 1965, *2,* 217–226.

Patterson, R. L. Time-out and assertive training for a dependent child. *Behavior Therapy,* 1972, *3,* 466–468.

Perlmuter, L. C., & Monty, R. A. (Eds.), *Choice and perceived control.* Hillsdale, N.J.: Lawrence Earlbaum Associates, 1979.

Phillips, J. S., & Ray, R. S. Behavioral approaches to childhood disorders: Review and critique. *Behavior Modification,* 1980, *4,* 3–34.

Porterfield, J. K., Herbert-Jackson, E. & Risley, T. R. Contingent observation: An effective and acceptable procedure for reducing disruptive behavior of young children in a group setting. *Journal of Applied Behavior Analysis,* 1976, *9,* 55–64.

Premack, D. Toward empirical behavior laws. I: Positive reinforcement. *Psychological Review,* 1959, *66,* 219–233.

Quay, H. O., & Werry, J. S. *Psychopathological disorders of childhood.* New York: John Wiley & Sons, 1979.

Renne, C. M., & Creer, T. L. Training children with asthma to use inhalation-therapy equipment. *Journal of Applied Behavior Analysis,* 1976, *9,* 1–11.

Repp, A. C., & Deitz, S. M. Reducing aggressive and self-injurious behavior of institutionalized retarded children through reinforcement of other behaviors. *Journal of Applied Behavior Analysis,* 1974, *7,* 313–325.

Rosenbaum, M. S., & Drabman, R. S. Self-control training in the classroom: A review and critique. *Journal of Applied Behavior Analysis,* 1979, *12,* 467–485.

Rosenthal, T. L., Rosenthal, R. H., & Chang, A. F. Vicarious, direct, and imaginal aversion in habit control: Outcomes, heart rates, and subjective perceptions. *Cognitive Therapy and Research*, 1977, *1*, 143–159.

Ross, A. O. *Psychological disorders of children: A behavioral approach to theory, research, and therapy* (2d ed.). New York: McGraw-Hill, 1980.

Ross, A. O. *Child-behavior therapy: Principles, procedures, and empirical basis.* New York: John Wiley & Sons, 1981.

Routh, D. K. Activity, attention, and aggression in learning-disabled children. *Journal of Clinical Child Psychology*, 1979, *8*, 183–187.

Sanok, R. L., & Ascione, F. R. Behavioral interventions for childhood elective mutism: An evaluative review. *Child Behavior Therapy*, 1979, *1*, 49–68.

Skinner, B. F. *The technology of teaching.* New York: Appleton-Century-Crofts, 1968.

Stokes, T. F., & Baer, D. M. An implicit technology of generalization. *Journal of Applied Behavior Analysis*, 1977, *10*, 349–367.

Stoyva, J. Self-regulation: A context for biofeedback. *Biofeedback and Self-Regulation*, 1976, *1*, 1–6.

Strain, P. S., & Pierce, J. E. Direct and vicarious effects of social praise on mentally retarded preschool children's attentive behavior. *Psychology in the Schools*, 1977, *14*, 348–353.

Stuart, R. B. *Client-therapist treatment contract.* Champaign, Ill.: Research Press, 1975.

Sulzer-Azaroff, B., & Mayer, R. *Applying behavior-analysis procedures with children and youth.* New York: Holt, Rhinehart & Winston, 1977.

Tasto, D., & Chesney, M. A. The deconditioning of nausea and of crying by emotive imagery: A report of two cases. *Journal of Behavior Therapy and Experimental Psychiatry*, 1977, *8*, 139–142.

Tate, B. G., & Baroff, G. S. Aversive control of self-injurious behavior in a psychotic boy. *Behaviour Research and Therapy*, 1966, *4*, 281–287.

Tharp, R. G., & Wetzel, R. J. *Behavior modification in the natural environment.* New York: Academic Press, 1969.

Tramontana, J. Social versus edible rewards as a function of intellectual level and socioeconomic class. *American Journal of Mental Deficiency*, 1972, *77*, 33–38.

Urbain, E. S., & Kendall, P. C. Review of social-cognitive problem-solving interventions with children. *Psychological Bulletin*, 1980, *88*, 109–143.

Vasta, R., & Stirpe, L. A. Reinforcement effects on three measures of children's interest in math. *Behavior Modification*, 1979, *3*, 223–244.

Wahler, R. G., & Fox, J. J. Setting events in applied behavior analysis: Toward a conceptual and methodological expansion. *Journal of Applied Behavior Analysis*, 1981, *14*, 327–338.

Walker, C. E., Hedberg, A., Clement, P. W., & Wright, L. *Clinical procedures for behavior therapy.* Englewood Cliffs, N.J.: Prentice-Hall, 1981.

Ward, W. D., & Ward, W. L. In vivo transfer of behavioral control from tangible to conditioned social reinforcers. *Psychological Reports*, 1974, *35*, 747–751.

Wildman, R. W., II, & Wildman, R. U. The generalization of behavior-modification procedures: A review with special emphasis on classroom applications. *Psychology in the Schools*, 1975, *12*, 432–448.

Wilson, C. C., Robertson, S. J., Herlong, L. H., & Haynes, S. N. Vicarious effects of time-out in the modification of aggression in the classroom. *Behavior Modification,* 1979, *3,* 97–111.

Wolpe, J. *Psychotherapy by reciprocal inhibition.* Stanford, Calif.: Stanford University Press, 1958.

Workman, E. A., & Hector, M. A. Behavioral self-control in classroom settings: A review of the literature. *Journal of School Psychology,* 1978, *16,* 227–236.

35

Cultural issues in psychotherapy

Lynnda M. Dahlquist*
and
Anitra S. Fay†

Since the 1960s, there has been a growing concern that the health care professions, particularly counseling and clinical psychology, have not adequately met the needs of ethnic minorities. There are a number of bases for this concern, including increased political and social interest in the civil rights movement, which have prompted reevaluation of the quality of mental health services provided for minorities. Two aspects of mental health care have received particular scrutiny: the frequency with which minorities utilize mental health services and the quality of mental health treatment they subsequently receive.

Utilization of mental health services

In a review of mental health care for the Spanish-speaking/surnamed population in the United States, Padilla, Ruiz, and Alvarez (1975) note that, "Demographers consistently agree that ethnic group members, and particularly the poor, receive less health care than the rest of the population . . ." (p. 892). They argue that the problem may be even more serious in the area of mental health care, citing studies in California, Texas, Connecticut, and New York, which showed a disproportionately small number of Mexican Americans, Puerto Ricans, and other minority groups using existing mental health services. More recent studies have reported similar findings. Significantly fewer Asian Americans and Cubans have been found to utilize mental health facilities than one would expect on the basis of population statistics (Sue, 1981; Szapocznik, Scopetta, Arnalde, & Kurtines, 1978).

* West Virginia University School of Medicine.
† Psychological Consultants, Fort Smith, Arkansas.

Quality of mental health care

When minorities do seek mental health treatment, there appears to be some evidence that their therapy experience differs from that of Anglo clients. For example, Sue and his associates (Sue & Sue, 1977) report a series of studies in which they found that Asian Americans, blacks, Chicanos, and Native Americans terminated counseling at a rate of about 50 percent (compared with a dropout rate of 30 percent for Anglos). Hollingshead and Redlich (1958) report that blacks were more likely to be offered custodial care and medication rather than psychotherapy. Similarly, Spanish patients have been reported to be referred for individual or group therapy less often and receive less lengthy and less intensive treatment than Anglo patients (Karno, 1966; Yamamoto, James, & Palley, 1968).

Explanations for this phenomenon

It would be extremely naive to assume that minorities do not seek treatment or drop out of therapy simply because they are well adjusted and therefore do not need these services. It is common knowledge that minorities are overrepresented in the lower socioeconomic classes. Census figures indicate that 30 percent of all black families, 34 percent of all Native-American families, and 21 percent of all Spanish families fall into the lower socioeconomic strata, in contrast to only 8.7 percent of all white families (Korchin, 1980). The high rate of health problems, unemployment, substance abuse, juvenile delinquency, suicide, and related psychological problems associated with lower-income populations has been well documented (Dohrenwend & Dohrenwend, 1969; Hollingshead & Redlich, 1958; Srole, Langner, Michael, Opler, & Rennie, 1962; Sue, 1978; Wong, 1978).

Padilla et al. (1975) propose that minorities actually may have a greater need for psychological treatment than the majority population because of the following "high-stress indicators" associated with their environment: (a) poor English communication skills, (b) poverty (limited education, low income, poor housing, and limited social or political power), (c) the ineffectiveness of agrarian survival skills in urban technological society, (d) seasonal migration, and (e) the stress of acculturation. Thus, the underutilization of psyhchological services may be even more severe than the demographic data would indicate (Padilla et al., 1975; Wong, 1978).

Several alternative hypotheses have been suggested to account for the status of minorities in the mental health system. It has been argued that the ethnic subculture protects members from psychological stress and provides continued, familial support in the event of a psychological crisis, thus eliminating the need for contact with outside agencies. There appears to be some validity to this position. The important role of the extended family in ethnic subcultures has been emphasized by psychologists and sociologists. For example, Lin and Lin (1978) describe the typical coping style of Asian-American psychiatric patients' families as one of intensive attempts by individual family members to solve the individual's problem, eventual consultation with faith healers, community leaders, and the family physician, and, if all else fails, referral to a mental health facility. This coping style was characteristic of the majority of the Asian families of psychiatric patients they studied, while this response style was evident in only one non-Asian family in the study. Fernandez-Pol (1980) reports an "inverse relationship" between adherence to Latin American family beliefs and the development of psychopathology.

Thus, the significance of the extended family support system in ethnic subcultures need not be disputed. However, Padilla et al. (1975) emphasize that the effectiveness of the family support system is diminished considerably by the weakening of traditional social structure which accompanies acculturation into the majority society. The extended family, therefore, may provide some of the same support and treatment offered by mental health services, but it does not seem likely that the ethnic family system is an adequate explanation for the degree of underutilization reported in the literature.

Along similar lines, it has been suggested that religious organizations, folk medicine, and faith healers fill the role that might otherwise be played by mental health professionals (Hankins-McNary, 1979; Padilla et al., 1975). The accuracy of this hypothesis is difficult to assess, however, since precise data regarding the actual use of folk medicine or religious healers by minorities are not available. Padilla et al. (1975) argue that the use of folk medicine among Spanish populations in the United States is not extensive enough to account for the extent of overall underutilization of mental health services by this population.

Neither the family-system hypothesis nor the folk-medicine/faith-healer hypothesis addresses the issues of minority attrition in therapy and the differential therapy experiences of minorities. Thus, there must be something about the therapy process itself that is inadequate and/or inappropriate for minorities. In order to understand where such deficiencies or conflicts might emerge in therapy, it is important, first, to provide a basic framework for conceptualizing the implicit assumptions and basic characterisitics of traditional psychotherapy.

Women as a minority group

Women have been described as a minority group (Hacker, 1951; 1975). While the term *minority* seems contradictory with regard to the large proportion of women in the population and in psychotherapy, the term is appropriate with regard to their acceptance of society's view of them and their tendency to maintain a separate subculture. In the discussion that follows, potential conflicts in the therapy process will be examined with regard to sex as well as cultural or ethnic factors.

BASIC ASSUMPTIONS OF TRADITIONAL PSYCHOTHERAPY

Communication in psychotherapy

According to Sue (1981), therapists make a number of assumptions about how they will interact with their clients. The most obvious expectation of therapists is that communication will be monolingual. That is, it is expected that both the therapist and client will converse in good, standard English.

In addition, Sue argues, "Most theories of counseling place a high premium on verbal, emotional, and behavioral expressiveness and the obtaining of insight" (p. 29). Therapists, therefore, expect clients to exhibit some degree of openness and psychological sophistication and assume that the client will openly reveal intimate, personal information in a one-to-one interaction with the therapist.

The client also is expected to be an active participant in the communication process, discussing his/her problems while the therapist listens, questions, or clarifies. According to Sue, this is an ambiguous, relatively unstructured interaction when compared with normal social transactions.

On a much more subtle level, Sue proposes the additional assumption that a nonverbal-communication rule system exists in the therapy interaction which applies both to the therapist and client. In other words, it is anticipated that the client's gestures, posturing, eye contact, and silence can be interpreted on the basis of psychological theory and the therapist's experince. Similarly, it is assumed that the therapist's nonverbal behavior will be interpreted by the client within this same framework.

Goals and values in psychotherapy

Additional implicit assumptions which pertain to goals and values also are inherent in the therapy process, according to Sue (1981). One assumption is that therapy is "future-time oriented." The typical 50-minute, weekly scheduling of therapy, he argues, necessitates an emphasis on long-term goals. Sue also identifies the following philosophical assumptions which are incorporated into traditional psychotherapy: (a) the assumption that a clear distinction can be made between physical and mental health/illness, and (b) an emphasis on linear, cause-effect relationships. Finally, Szapocznik et al. (1978) suggest that many traditional therapy approaches are based on the model or value of the "growth-oriented, self-actualizing individual who is ready to take control over his or her identity" (p.968).

The preceding discussion of assumptions regarding interpersonal inter-actions and goals and values in therapy is admittedly global and not intended to be comprehensive. It must also be noted that some of the variables presented are more applicable to some systems of therapy than to others. However, these factors have been selected because of their significance to the issue of psychotherapy for minorities. As will be out-lined in the sections to follow, many of the basic assumptions underlying the traditional practice of psychotherapy are strongly rooted in the white, middle-class, Anglo culture of the majority of psychologists and well may be inappropriate for, or in direct conflict with, the value system of members of the lower social classes or ethnic minority groups.

CLASS-BASED ISSUES IN PSYCHOTHERAPY

Social class and type of therapy

There is substantial evidence that social class is related to clients' accep-tance of psychotherapy. Lower-class patients tend to be assigned to thera-pies which focus on their psychosomatic complaints, rather than to psy-chotherapy, according to Garfield (1971). It has also been noted that therapists use less-intensive therapy with lower-class patients (Hollings-head & Redlich, 1958) and that lower-class patients tend to receive fewer therapy sessions than middle-class patients (Garfield, 1971; Ryan & Gaier, 1968; Winder & Hersko, 1955). Differential treatment also is evident in the area of guidance and personnel. Sue (1981) cites a study in which doctoral-degree candidates in guidance and counseling more frequently placed low-SES students in a noncollege-bound track than into a college-preparatory track.

Garfield (1971) notes that differential treatment on the basis of social class is especially apparent in higher-status mental health agencies, in which senior staff members tend to see the higher-class patients, while social workers are assigned the lower-class patients. Garfield, Weiss, and Pollock (1976) describe a study in which ascribed socioeconomic status was systematically manipulated, while ego involvement of counselors was assessed. Counslors indicated more willingness to become more ego involved when clients were assigned the higher socioeconomic label.

Client expectations

The overall pattern of therapy utilization by low socioeconomic-status clients seems to be due to two factors: client expectations regarding ther-apy and therapist interpretations of client behavior. There is considerable evidence that lower-class patients have expectations regarding therapy that conflict with the usual nature of therapy. In general, lower-class pa-tients are concerned with day-to-day problems and survival (Lorion,

1974). As a consequence, they expect advice and suggestions from the therapist in a concrete format. Garfield (1971) cites evidence that they expect a therapist who is active and supportive in the initial interview. These expectations for concrete advice and an active therapist are contrary to the format of most interview and therapy sessions, which tend to be relatively nondirective, insight-oriented, and focus on taking a complete history, reflecting feelings, and examining intrapsychic dynamics. In fact, lower-class clients may see traditional therapy as pointless and inappropriate for meeting their needs (Sue, 1981; Sue & Sue, 1977).

Since lower-class patients see themselves as having immediate problems needing concrete solutions, they tend to expect to obtain immediate assistance and to experience quick improvement in symptoms. Garfield has indicated that lower-class patients expect improvement by the fifth session and that total treatment will be 10 sessions or less. Again, client expectations are contrary to the usual procedure in which appointments for treatment are made weeks in advance and are limited to 50-minute sessions. The traditional therapy process generally is considered to require several sessions before treatment termination would be recommended, probably at least 10 sessions. In one study, treatment terminators were individuals who had expected advice on problems in the first session (Garfield, 1971).

More practical issues also may interfere with lower-class patients obtaining mental health services. Mental health facilities serving the lower class frequently are associated with universities or medical schools and are located outside the barrio (Padilla et al., 1975). Obtaining services may require arranging for child-care facilities and transportation to an area where they normally might not travel.

Misinterpretation of client behavior

In addition to unmet expectations of clients, a deterrent to therapy with lower-class clients is the therapists' misinterpretations of clients' behavior. Therapists dealing with clients tend to interpret behavior in a manner consistent with their own theoretical orientations and therapeutic and personal experiences. There is evidence that many of these interpretations are incorrect when applied to lower-class patients. Often therapists unintentionally attribute attitudes resulting from physical and environmental adversity to individual traits of the client (Pollock & Menacker, 1971). For example, it may be reported that an adolescent boy has been sluggish and occasionally absent from school. While the therapist may interpret the behavior as laziness or delinquency, it may later be discovered that the boy was working long hours regularly to help his family financially. His sluggishness and absence resulted from fatigue.

Therapist misinterpretations also may focus on perceived attitudes toward therapy. There is some evidence that clients differentially self-disclose to therapists similar to themselves. Schindler-Rainman (1965) notes that lower-class patients also may have a different sense of time from that of middle-class clients. For example, lower-class clients typically have to wait several hours for their appointments in facilities such as medical clinics and police stations. Consequently, when such a client has an appointment at a mental health facility for a specific time, the client may assume that the session will not occur at the specified time and may come later. In the above examples involivng self-disclosure and time, therapists may interpret the client's behavior in terms of resistence (Sue, 1981; Sue & Sue, 1977), indifference, or hostility (Schindler-Rainman, 1965). By misinterpreting the client's behavior, the therapist has placed the client at a disadvantage by inaccurately conceptualizing the client's behavior and proceeding with therapy as usual.

CULTURAL FACTORS IN PSYCHOTHERAPY

While social-class differences are a significant source of bias in the practice of psychology with minorities, cultural and ethnic differences also are a major source of bias requiring investigation. Therapists make judgments on the basis of race in terms of acceptance for psychotherapy and type of therapy administered (Korchin, 1980). A clear example of therapist bias is a study which discovered that staff in a psychiatric hospital differentially ordered more occupational and recreational therapy for white patients than for blacks, although independent raters found no overt differences between the groups in disturbance severity (Flaherty & Meager, 1980). The staff, totally unaware of the bias in their actions, were appreciative of the feedback and made efforts to rectify the situation. Patient's sex also has been noted as a basis for decisions in psychotherapy. It has been reported that the degree of pathology in a patient's passivity is assessed differently in men and women when other factors remain equal (Miller, 1974). Also, children are rated as more disturbed when they do not display conformity to expected sex roles (Feinblatt & Gold, 1976).

Minority groups usually are thought of in terms of racial differences, such as Asian Americans, blacks, Chicanos, and Native Americans. It is useful also to think of ethnic variations within races. This would emphasize variations among groups, such as the Irish, Polish, Italian, Czech, and Jewish ethnic groups (Giordano, 1974). In the following discussion, cultural and ethnic variations and client's sex are emphasized with regard to their potential effect upon the practice of psychology. Specifically, various aspects and presuppositions of psychological practice are examined in order to shed light upon the sources of bias which are most evident during the client/therapist interaction.

Communication issues

Language. A major and obvious source of difficulty in working with the culturally different is the expectation that the client and therapist are able to communicate verbally in the same language, usually standard English (Sue & Sue, 1977). When the client and therapist do not speak the same language, therapy is hampered in a variety of ways. Attempts to communicate may involve the use of a translator. While using a translator is certainly better than nothing, the involvement of the third party can pose some problems. The therapist must be sure that the translator understands the therapist's general direction in the therapy process and will not undermine the therapist's efforts. Also, it is important to be aware that the translator is likely to be a major factor in the transference process (Kline, Acosta, Austin, & Johnson, 1976). In essence, the third party adds a great deal to the potential complexity of the therapeutic process.

Minority clients who are bilingual and can speak the same language as the therapist still may use different grammatical structures, which can lead to misunderstanding and misinterpretation on the part of the therapist. For example, blacks have been noted to use shorter sentences and less grammatical elaboration than occurs in standard English (Smith, 1973). Therapists may infer inaccurate characteristics on the basis of the client's verbal presentation. The client may be seen as uncooperative, sullen, negative, or nonverbal. Furthermore, because verbal ability is so highly valued in Western society, the client may be seen as inferior, lacking in awareness, and lacking in conceptual thinking powers (Sue & Sue, 1977).

Linguistic discrepancies are seen as a major problem in psychological testing. Individuals from lower socioeconomic backgrounds or from certain minority groups may evidence unclear enunciation or use phrases or jargon that are unfamiliar to the examiner. This can lead to particular problems in intelligence testing, where questionable responses tend to be scored zero. Thus, language-based misunderstanding may result in artificially lowered scores.

Language difficulties are even more significant when the client speaks a different language or is bilingual. Chavez and Gonzales-Singh (1980) described the case of a monolingual, Spanish-speaking woman who had been tested, determined mentally retarded, and placed in an inpatient ward with mentally retarded adolescents. She was retested at a later time and found to have progressive neurological damage. The discrepancy between the two testings was attributed to incompetence and blatant disregard for the patient's inability to communicate in English.

It is obviously inappropriate to evaluate someone with an instrument that is not in his/her native language. However, there is a paucity of testing instruments in different languages. Even for tests which have been translated into different languages, a number of problems remain. As

Chavez and Gonzales-Singh (1980) illustrate with Hispanics, the Spanish-speaking population in the United States is not a homogenous group. A test normed on Mexican Americans may not be appropriate for Puerto Ricans. Therefore, specific subgroup norms are needed.

Secondly, translation of an English test into another language does not necessarily ensure that the test is appropriate. For example, bilingual, Mexican-American children scored lower on a translation of the Stanford-Binet than on the English version (Keston Jiminez, 1954). Simple translation does not allow for geographic differences in idioms and does not take into account the "archaisms, contaminations, and Anglicisms" of bilingual individuals (Sattler, 1974, p. 37). Chavez and Gonzales-Singh (1980) argue that new tests, specifically designed for Hispanic populations, are necessary. Until such tests are available, however, they recommend using corrective formulas, such as the System of Multicultural Pluralistic Assessment (SOMPA) (Mercer, 1977). This system incorporates an IQ score into a regression equation with weighted, sociocultural modalities (including socioeconomic status, family size, urban acculturation, and family structure) and provides an average score for the individual's sociocultural group. For example, Mishra (1980) reports, in a well-controlled study that Mexican-American children scored higher on the WISC vocabulary subscale when the examiner was Mexican American than when the examiner was Anglo.

Expression of emotion. A second assumption regarding the client/therapist interaction is that therapy involves open communication and expresion of feelings (Sue & Sue, 1977). Such an assuumption is directly contrary to some minority groups' orientations. For example, Asian-American cultures value restraining of strong feelings and subtleness in approaching problems. Their orientation, seen as shy and passive, has been misinterpreted in terms of repressiveness. Such an interpretation is seen as ethnocentric—evaluating others' behaviors in terms of Western cultural values.

Another aspect of the open communication style is that traditional psychotherapy tends to emphasize a certain amount of passive attention on the part of the therapist. Berman (1979) compared videotapes of black, Anglo, and Spanish-speaking clients in an interview regarding obtaining a job. Black therapists tended to use more active-expressive skills, while white therapists tended to use more attending skills during the interview. It was suggested that high active-expression skills used intuitively by black therapists may reflect a more appropriate therapy style for black clients.

Therapists' interpretation of and reaction to women clients' emotional expressiveness may be biased or reflect sex-role stereotyping. Chesler (1971a, 1971b) described psychotherapy as thriving on the woman's dependence, emotionality, and hysterical symptomatology, rather than on her productivity. The woman's emotional style, she hypothesized, is fostered largely as a result of therapists' attitudes and expectations that women are dependent, emotional beings.

Learned helplessness has been seen as a response pattern which many women, as opposed to men, have learned and displayed in therapy (Van Hook, 1979). Although learned helplessness has a significant cognitive component (Seligman, 1975), an element of hopeless, depressive emotionality is often displayed in the therapy session. Van Hook stated that it is important to help the woman recognize that she has more control than she is aware and that she has the capacity for change.

Therapy structure. Another generally assumed aspect of psychotherapy is that the sessions are basically unstructured and ambiguous in nature and that the direction of the interaction is movement of information from client to therapist. The ambiguity of a therapy session conflicts with expectations of some cultures, such as the Chinese, whose environment, social relationships, and patterns of interaction are actively structured. When placed in an ambiguous situation, the Chinese client may feel anxious or confused (Sue & Sue, 1977).

In addition, some clients may become uncomfortable when asked to initiate conversation, possibly responding with short sentences. The therapist may misinterpret this response negatively. In reality, the client may be showing respect for the therapist, who is perceived as an authority figure. Several cultures (Asian, Chicano, and Native American) have been acculturated to show respect to elders and authority figures and not to speak unless spoken to by the authority (Sue & Sue, 1977). In other cultures, small talk may be viewed as inappropriate and interpreted by the client as disrespect or an effort to avoid talking about the client's problem (Vontress, 1971).

Nonverbal communication. Nonverbal rules are an aspect of psychotherapy which are subtle and often overlooked in the extent to which they affect therapy participants. Too often, it is assumed that nonverbal communication is universal and that nonverbal cues have the same meanings cross-culturally. In reality, there is a great deal of difference among cultures in the meanings ascribed to nonverbal cues.

Regarding personal space (appropriate distance by two interacting people), Latin Americans, Africans, and Indonesians utilize a much closer interpersonal distance than does Anglo culture. During a therapy session, a Latin American may be at a culturally appropriate distance, and the therapist may back away. As a consequence, the client may feel rejected or interpret the therapist as being cold and aloof. The therapist may have interpreted the client's behavior as overly intimate and pushy (Sue & Sue, 1977).

Eye contact is another aspect of nonverbal behavior which may be misinterpreted. Anglos value eye contact as a means of indicating attentiveness and interest. In black culture. proximity is enough to indicate attentiveness, and eye contact is not stressed (Hall, 1974). Mexican Americans and Japanese avoid eye contact as a means of showing respect (Knapp, 1972). Navajo Indians interpret sustained eye contact as sexual interest or aggressive assault; therefore, they may feel intruded upon by direct eye contact (Proskauer, 1980). Sue and Sue (1977) emphasize the importance of caution in therapists' interpretation of minorities' eye contact because it is used so frequently by therapists as a diagnostic indicator. Physical contact, gesturing, and animation are other nonverbal elements which have been identified as varying cross-culturally (Brown, 1979).

Cultural similarity. Client/therapist similarity is another aspect of the client/therapist interaction which has received much discussion. Specifically, is the therapy process more effective when the client and therapist are of a culturally similar background? Many of the studies which have focused on this issue have examined clients' preference for racially similar or different therapists, usually using hypothetical situations rather than actual treatment. In general, it has been shown that clients prefer therapists who are racially similar to themselves (Harrison, 1975; Thompson & Cimbolic, 1978). Proctor and Rosen (1981) polled subjects entering actual treatment and found that, of those subjects who stated a preference, a racially similar therapist was preferred. Interestingly, client race was not significantly associated with clients' expectations for a therapist; that is, most clients expected that they would receive a white therapist.

The relevance of therapist preference to therapy effectiveness has not been established. It is possible that therapist preference is an important element in a client's likelihood to seek therapy (Harrison, 1975). However, it is not clear that preference is related to successful therapy. Proctor and Rosen (1981) found no association between therapist preference and client dropout or satisfaction with treatment after two sessions. It is important to emphasize that, in many ways, the preference research is examining relative status or social desirability of therapists as perceived by potential clients. Other authors (Harrison, 1975; Sattler, 1977) have noted that competence and empathic understanding, regardless of race, are the foremost elements desired by minorities. Future study must examine not only the effects of therapist preference upon client's utilization of therapy services and clients' participation in therapy, it also must examine other aspects of client/therapist similarity as they interact with elements of the therapeutic process.

Whether or not client/therapist similarity is related to successful treatment outcome has not been established. Carkhuff and Pierce (1967) reported greater self-exploration in hospitalized mental patients with therapists of a similar race; however, length of treatment (Vail, 1978) and satisfaction with counselor (Cimbolic, 1972) have been shown to be unrelated to racial similarity. Another study (Yamamoto, James, Bloombaum, & Hattem, 1967) noted that therapists who were more socially distant from minorities saw their black patients for six sessions or less, while therapists who were less socially distant saw their black patients six or more sessions, which was equal to the mean number of sessions spent with white patients. The Yamamoto study, while not studying similarity directly, indicates that attitudes or biases of specific clients and therapists are the important issues to be examined when studying client/therapist similarity.

It now is necessary to examine how particular attitudes and biases are important in the client/therapist interaction. Some attitudinal aspects of client/therapist similarity are helpful to the therapeutic process, while other aspects are deterrents to successful therapy.

A positive aspect of client/therapist similarity is the therapist's knowledge and understanding of the client's background and experiences, particularly when the information can be utilized to accurately conceptualize the therapeutic process. Boyer and Boyer (1977) reported being able to use knowledge of Apache folklore in interpreting the dreams of a disturbed Apache woman. Dreams which the woman presented in therapy were based upon folklore; however, she presented idiosyncratic variations, which the therapist was able to identify by virtue of understanding the culture's folklore. Personality characteristics also can be more accurately assessed when the therapist has an understanding of a client's cultural values. For example, Navajo Indians value group interdependence and prohibit competing for property (Proskauer, 1980). Therefore, if a male Navajo client displays dependence upon family members and little motivation to maintain employment in a high-salaried position, a therapist unfamiliar with Navajo culture might see the client as being unassertive and value his behavior in terms of the therapist's achievement- and independence-oriented culture. Knowledge of the Navajo culture makes the client's behavior much more understandable.

Negative aspects of client/therapist similarity include issues which may be thought of as countertransference. That is, minority therapists may have biases regarding their own backgrounds which can interfere with the therapeutic process. Giordano (1974) reported a case in which she was treating an Italian woman whose ethnic background was very similar to her own. As a result of the similarity, Giordano was less objective in her handling of the therapeutic process. She later discovered that she had not asked questions when the client resisted answering—a cultural value of privacy in which she had unknowingly participated with her patient. Giordano noted that countertransference can occur when ethnic therapists are caught up in their own movement into middle-class professionalism and ignore their own ethnicity.

When the client and therapist are culturally different, there are negative effects which can occur, many of which are the negative counterparts to the advantages of cultural similarity described previously. Vontress (1971) noted that blacks often have negative transference to white therapists in response to habitual ways of relating to whites. Cavenar and Spaulding (1978) presented a case report of a white patient with a black therapist in which the patient displayed a transference reaction to the therapist's race at the very outset of therapy. Specifically, the patient had a dream in which the therapist's actual skin color was denied. It was noted that the reaction to the therapist's race may have interfered with the development of a normal, patient/therapist relationship. Vontress noted a type of bias which is common in white, female therapists. The bias occurs in a phobogenic reaction to black males; that is, a cautiousness regarding sexuality and possible advances by the black male clients.

Cultural differences need not result in negative evaluations of the client or the therapist. Merluzzi and Merluzzi (1978) examined therapists' evaluations of black and white clients' intake evaluations. The therapists were evaluated in terms of experience, contact with minorities, and physical-social distance from minorities. Overall, black cases were assessed more positively than white cases, and therapists with greater minority contact did not rate blacks as positively as therapists with less contact. This is evidence for overcompensation or responding to social desirability on the part on the less experienced therapists. Similarly, Vontress (1971) has noted tendencies for some therapists to be overzealous or overmotivated to prove that they are not biased against minorities or for therapists to see themselves as detached and scientific, assuming that they have no bias. Either stance is potentially dangerous.

The importance of sex similarity between client and therapist has not been established. Chesler (1971a, 1971b) has described the therapeutic relationship of male therapist and female client as paternalistic and similar to the marital relationship. Traditional psychotherapy with a male therapist, she feels, has a strong potential for reinforcement stereotypes. In particular, traditional therapy delegates a submissive, powerless role to the female client and thrives on the woman's dependence on a male authority.

Van Hook (1979) described learned helplessness as a characteristic in female patients which could be dealt with most effectively by a female therapist. A female therapist, it was reasoned, would be more effective as a role model for the patient in learning appropriate cognitive and emotional responses.

Bryson and Cody (1973) presented evidence that clients are not as affected by client/therapist differences as are therapists. While black and white therapists each indicated that they understood same-race clients better than different-race clients, Cimbolic (1972) also found that the black clients' satisfaction with their counselors was unrelated to the counselor's race.

In summarizing the available data, client/therapist similarity has not been established as being asssociated with successful treatment outcome. Other research has examined the effects of clients' and therapists' attitudes and biases upon the therapeutic process. The attitudinal research has shown that attitudes and biases can influence psychotherapy, whether clients and therapists have similar or different cultural backgrounds. It appears that attitudes and biases are more important than racial similarity in the therapeutic process (Parloff, Waskow, & Wolfe, 1978).

The assessment research regarding racial similarity between examiner and examinee also has been inconclusive. Sattler (1974) reports conflicting findings, with examiner race playing a significant role with some groups in some studies but not in others. He notes that the existing studies are flawed by design problems (such as too few examiners), which prevent conclusive generalization regarding the effects of examiner race on test performance.

Conflicts in goals and values

It is clear from the preceding discussion that cultural factors can significantly affect the therapeutic communication process. The impact of cultural issues, however, is not limited to the confines of the therapy room. Cultural values dictate the long-term goals and objectives of treatment, the means by which therapeutic change is instigated, and even the most basic assumptions about normal behavior.

Definitions of mental health. Sue (1981) argues that the criteria currently used by psychologists to define normal versus abnormal behavior are intricately tied to white Anglo-Saxon Protestant (WASP) middle-class culture. To illustrate, consider the three approaches to conceptualizing normality outlined by Buss (1966): (a) statistical, (b) research criteria, and (c) ideal.

Statistical definitions of mental health are based on phenomena which occur most frequently in the population. Behaviors which are uncommon, in this definitional system, are considered abnormal. Since minorities are, by definiton, fewer in number than members of the majority culture, it is inevitable that their unique characteristics are likely to be defined statistically as abnormal.

It is doubtful that anyone would argue that any unusual or unique behavior should necessarily be considered unhealthy. Certainly, very few people are truly gifted painters, musicians, or athletes, yet no one would venture, on the basis of mere statistical infrequency, to label artistic creativity or athletic prowess unhealthy. However, such errors in judgment are not as easily escaped in the mental health arena.

Part of the problem has to do with the heavy reliance placed on psychometric measures in psychology. Current tests of intellectual functioning, achievement, and personality are based, to a large degree, on the normal probability curve. Most commonly, these measures are standardized on white, middle-class populations, thus placing minorities at a disadvantage.

The normal-curve concept of mental health poses additional problems, in that it does not allow for the possibility that certain traits or behaviors may be very adaptive (or healthy) in one culture and very inappropriate in another culture. Although it is not within the scope of this chapter to address the wealth of data available regarding culture fairness in testing, the literature is replete with examples of test items which sample WASP values, which may be antagonistic to the values of other ethnic groups.

A classic example is the question in the WISC-R comprehension sub-test, "What is the thing to do if a boy (girl) much smaller than yourself starts to fight you?" The general criteria for a correct response is given as "Do not fight." Fighting back is scored as a failure. In many ghetto areas, however, fighting back is taught as a necessary, adaptive survival skill. The Association of Black Psychologists has used this and other examples to illustrate the inappropriateness of standardized tests for minorities (Williams, 1970). They argue that standardized test results may lead to inaccurate assessments and unfair decisions for minorities. They also propose that standardized tests do not tap the unique skills of minorities (Williams, 1970). Similar arguments have been raised in the realm of personality assessment. It has been suggested that a certain amount of paranoia, for example, may be adaptive in minorities and may reflect accurate, reality-based perceptions of oppression by a racist society, rather than pathology (Sue, 1981).

Research-based definitions of mental health are fraught with the same potential cultural biases as statistical definitions. Research criteria used to evaluate mental health among minorities often include variables such as psychiatric diagnosis or presence in mental hospitals. However, diagnoses and hospitalization decisions frequently are based on scores on objective measures and therefore are potentially culturally biased. In addition, psychiatric diagnosis is not a totally objective process. As was discussed previously, identical case reports can be diagnosed differently simply as a function of the assigned racial or ethnic label (Merluzzi & Merluzzi, 1978). Similarly, decisions regarding assignment to outpatient or inpatient treatments are not free from preconceptions based on race or ethnicity.

An alternative to statistical or research-based concepts of normality is the notion of ideal mental health. This approach proposes the achievement of certain psychological goals (such as insight, self-actualization, or autonomy) as indicative of mental health. Sue (1981) argues that these goals are not universal to all cultures but rather are based on the theoretical orientation and values of the therapist.

This issue also applies to women. According to surveys of clinician's judgments, being a woman or a healthy adult are mutually exclusive options. Broverman, Broverman, Clarkson, Rosenkrantz, and Vogel (1970) asked a cross section of mental health clinicians to describe the healthy adult, the healthy adult male, and the healthy adult female. Description of the healthy female was significantly different from that of the healthy adult. Healthy females were described as less independent, competitive, and objective and more submissive and emotional than healthy males. Fabricant (1974) replicated the study. Voss and Gannon (1978) summarized the findings as evidence that both men and women therapists characterize healthy males and females differently and according to sex-role stereotypes. This is an example of ideal mental health being based upon the values of the therapist.

In the following section, an attempt will be made to highlight potential areas of cultural conflict in the overall therapy process. It must be noted, however, that there is considerable variability within minority groups and that the concepts presented may or may not apply to the individual client. Practical considerations necessitate some degree of generalization in presentation, but the following format of discussion should not be viewed as justification for stereotyping. The degree to which values typical of an ethnic culture apply to an individual case is a function of a multitude of factors, including personality characteristics, learning history, environment, and the degree of acculturation of the individual into the majority culture (Vontress, 1971).

Potential conflicts. The cultural bias of traditional psychological concepts of ideal mental health becomes strikingly apparent when contrasted with the views of mental illness typical of Asian cultures. Lin and Lin (1978) describe three major Asian views of mental illness: (a) moralistic, (b) mystic/cosmic, and (c) physiological. The moralistic orientation views mental illness as punishment for violating Confucian moral ethics or filial piety. Thus, one's problems are seen as the result of deviation from socially acceptable behavior or neglecting to honor an ancestor. The mystic/cosmic viewpoint holds that mental illness is evidence of the wrath of the gods or ancestors brought on by family members in their present or former lives.

Both of these viewpoints strongly emphasize guilt and family shame. Admitting to mental illness, within this framework, necessitates admitting to misconduct and therefore subjects both the identified patient and the family to social disgrace.

The implications of these cultural values for therapy are significant. Because of potential social censure, the family can be expected to be reluctant to reveal psychological problems to anyone other than family members. The therapist must be careful not to misconstrue this reluctance as indicative of hostility or lack of motivation. Issues regarding the trustworthiness of the therapist and the confidentiality of treatment may be crucial to successful therapy and should be addressed in the intitial therapeutic contact. Several sessions may be necessary to establish an adequate trusting relationship.

Second, the traditional concept of individual growth- or insight-oriented therapy may well be inappropriate for Asians who ascribe to this viewpoint. Since all family members are implicated in this concept of mental illness, some sort of therapeutic contact with the family is likely to be necessary. Lin and Lin (1978) point out that psychological stresses are acknowledged as etiological factors within this conceptualization, but much heavier emphasis is placed on problems in family relationships. Traditional individual emphasis on insight and coping with stress is likely to be viewed as an inadequate treatment of the problem.

The third Asian view of mental illness outlined by Lin and Lin (1978) is physiological. Psychological problems are seen as due to an imbalance of yin and yang, caused by excesses or deficiencies in physiological functions. Sexuality, climate, diet, and exercise can be contributing factors. A similar orientation toward mental health has been attributed to Spanish subcultures. Padilla et al. (1975) cite several Spanish idioms—such as, *estar saludable* (to be healthy), *ser feliz* (to be happy), or *estar sano y fuerta* (to be healthy and strong)—which are used interchangeably to convey a state of well-being. They propose that these idioms reflect the cultural notion that physical and psychological health are inseparable. Native American, black, and European ethnic groups also have been reported to have similar orientations toward the relationship between physical and mental health (Giordano, 1974; Hibbs, Kobos, & Gonzales, 1979; Kinzie, Tran, Breckenridge, & Bloom, 1980; Proskauer, 1980).

This physiological concept of mental health obviously conflicts with the assumption traditionally made in therapy that a clear distinction can be made between physical and mental states. The danger of this culturally based bias is evident in the tendency of therapists to judge the minority client who complains of physical symptomatology as naive or repressive. It would seem unfair and unjustified to label such a person as hypochondriacal or lacking in insight, merely on the basis of physiological complaints. This suggests that the hysteria and hyponchondriasis subscales of the MMPI may need to be interpreted in a drastically different context for the ethnic-minority client.

It has also been suggested—on the basis of the physiological concept of mental health—that many minority-group members will expect a medical-model approach to diagnosis and treatment. In other words, a cursory history and specific treatment recommendations are expected in the initial interview. While such an approach may not be the therapeutic strategy of choice, therapists may need to be aware of and address this expectation in the initial interview.

Szapocznik et al. (1978) present one of the few empirical studies of cultural differences in value orientation, which has particular relevance to therapy. They developed a value-orientation scale, which they used to compare Cuban immigrants' and Anglo-American adolescents' values. Socioeconomic levels were controlled in their study, suggesting that their findings could not be attributed solely to class variables. Their findings will be presented in some detail, because of their similarity to the viewpoints expressed by other writers in nonempirical reports.

One significant value difference between Cuban and American values (identified by Szapocznik et al.) involves the concept of time. They report an Anglo preference for future planning, in contrast to a Cuban present-time orientation. Sue (1981) proposes a similar conflict between the long-range planning emphasis in Anglo culture (and therefore inherent in psychotherapy) and the more immediate, short-range planning, present-time orientation of Asian-American, black, and Hispanic populations. Smith (1981) suggests that Native-American culture stresses reliance on tradition and history and values looking backward into legends as a basis for learning.

Therapy oriented toward goals of personality restructuring in the course of a year or even six months of treatment may well be perceived as totally irrelevant by minority groups with different time orientations. Szapocznik et al. (1978) argue that therapy must be present-time oriented with these ethnic groups. They recommend that therapists focus on problem-oriented solutions to the crises that led to soliciting treatment. This does not necessarily imply that long-term personality development, self-actualization, and the like must be abandoned as therapeutic goals. However, Szapocznik et al. recommend that crises and day-to-day experiences be capitalized upon (or even manipulated) in order to promote growth. This process necessitates consideration of environmental factors in addition to intrapsychic variables.

Szapocznik et al,. (1978) also identify a discrepancy between Cuban and Anglo views of the relationship between the individual and nature. They report that Anglo adolescents tend to value mastery over nature, while Cuban adolescents endorse an orientation involving subjugation to nature. Reviews of locus-of-control and attribution-theory research substantiate this finding for other minority groups as well (Rotter, 1975; Sue, 1978). Minorities tend to be more likely to view external (rather than internal) factors as responsible for events. Thus, they may perceive themselves as unable to impact their environment (which may well be a fairly accurate perception, given the realistic constraints of poverty and social systems).

The philosophical and religious value systems of many minority cultures also differ significantly from Anglo values with respect to the person-nature relationship. Sue (1981) proposes that Eastern philosphy values harmony and oneness with nature, rather than control of the environment. A similar attitude has been attributed to Native-American cultures (Smith, 1981).

The traditional therapy emphasis on the individual taking control of his/her life, destiny, or environment obviously poses potential areas of conflict with the values of some minority cultures. Clients may see the therapist's recommendations as impossible to achieve or immoral in light of their religious orientation. It has also been suggested that adherence to a personal-responsibility viewpoint unfairly blames the victim, i.e., holds minorities responsible for social conditions and their environmental circumstances (Sue, 1981).

Szapocznik et al. (1978) suggest that environmental pressures are most likely to be perceived by minorities as the source of their problems. Rather than attempt to encourage minority clients to alter or control their environment, they recommend that therapists work directly on restructuring the client's interactions with the environment. This may require considerably more contact with community members and agencies and less time in individual psychotherapy.

The final issue addressed by Szapocznik et al. involved cultural variations in interpersonal relationships. They report that Anglos value individuality, whereas Cubans adhere to a more hierarchical structure in relationships. Highly structured, hierarchical, social-interaction patterns also have been attributed to Asian cultures (Sue, 1981). The Anglo value of individuality also contrasts sharply with the more linear, group-membership orientation of other ethnic groups. For example, Native-American cultures have been described in terms of group interdependence, family and tribal loyalty, and communal ownership of property (Proskauer, 1980; Smith, 1981). A similar value of ethnic-group and/or family membership has been attributed to Hispanic, black, and Asian cultures (Padilla et al., 1975; Richardson, 1981; Ruiz, 1981; Sue, 1981).

These value conflicts pose significant problems in psychotherapy. Many schools of therapy stress individuation from parents and the family of origin as a sign of psychological maturity and, therefore, as a goal of treatment. Obviously, this is a culturally based goal that may be very inappropriate for some minority groups.

Furthermore, many of the skills emphasized in psychotherapy involve assertion and negotiating skills, which can be conceptualized as means by which one can achieve one's personal objectives. In the strict, hierarchical structure of some ethnic social systems, such skills may be received very negatively by peers or family and may actually increase, rather than ameliorate, the client's problems.

Szapocznik et al. (1978) propose that therapists need to function within the interpersonal relationship system of the client's culture. Thus, if hierarchical structure is valued in the client's culture, the therapist should assume a position in this hierarchy, recognizing the client's perception of the therapist as an authority figure. They argue that the therapist must therefore assume responsibility for the therapy process (rather than expect the individual to self-direct his/her treatment).

Second, they propose that in linear (i.e., tribal- or family-based) interactional systems, dysfunction is likely to result from breakdowns in lineal patterns. They see the primary, initial role of the therapist as one of restoring the culturally based, hierarchical patterns. For example, in dealing with a Hispanic behavior-problem child, they would recommend first restoring the parents to a position of authority and then working with the parents in ways to handle possible moves toward independence on the part of the child. Clearly, such an approach requires family, rather than individual, treatment.

Goals and value conflicts also can be sex based. Voss and Gannon (1978) discuss how a therapist can introduce bias into therapy even though the therapist adheres to a nonsexist theory of psychotherapy. Specifically, sexist bias may appear in the therapeutic process of problem definition and goal setting. Some therapists may limit the potential goals they encourage patients to meet by imposition of sex-role stereotypes upon the patient. For a female patient presenting with a lack of meaning in her life, the therapist may encourage her either to strengthen her social relationships or develop skills and achieve vocationally. The former goal may be an instance of assuming a lower potential in the patient on the basis of sex.

It should be noted, however, that the issue of sex bias in therapy has not been researched extensively. Smith (1980) reviewed the sex-bias literature and offered the criticism that claims of psychotherapy being sexist are unfounded.

Cultural bias in testing.   Some of the potential sources of bias in clinical assessment already have been addressed, such as the unfamiliarity or inappropriateness of some test items for minorities or bilingual clients. Cultural bias in testing is a complex, widely debated issue, which has received a great deal of attention in the literature. Since it is not within the scope of this chapter to comprehensively review this topic, only a few, illustrative points will be presented. The interested reader is referred to Cleary, Humphreys, Kendrick, and Weisman (1975) and Sattler (1974), for a more extensive discussion of the topic.

Intelligence and aptitude tests have received the harshest criticism as culturally biased. Arguments against the use of these standardized measures have stressed that minorities may not have been exposed to the test material or to testing situations, which puts them at a disadvantage. Motivation to do well may not be strong, because the testing situation may not be perceived as an achievement situation. Children, especially, may be overly concerned with establishing a relationship with the examiner, which may detract from their performance. Limited educational experiences and/or poor reading skills also can hamper performance. It has also been argued that standardized intelligence tests are more related to the problem-solving skills of the white, middle class than the lower class.

Culture-fair or nonverbal tests have been employed in an attempt to avoid the biases inherent in standardized tests. However, Sattler (1974) argues that it is virtually impossible to design a test that predicts socially relevant criteria and that is not influenced by skills valued in the majority culture. He suggests that even nonverbal tests are dependent upon analytic-cognitive style, which is bound to white, middle-class culture, citing several studies illustrating that nonverbal tests are equally difficult for black children as for white children.

Cultural bias also has been identified in personality tests, with the MMPI receiving primary attention. Basically, cultural bias is assessed either by examining cultural-group differences on mean subscale scores or by testing the accuracy of predictions or inferences made within cultural groups on the basis of MMPI scores. (See Adebimpe, Gigandet, & Harris, 1979; Cleary et al., 1975; Hunter & Schmidt, 1976; Pritchard & Rosenblatt, 1980, for a more detailed discussion of various definitions of cultural bias.) While there appears to be substantial evidence that cultural subgroups vary in their personality profiles, there is considerable controversy as to whether this implies that the tests are inappropriate for minorities or that different means of interpretation need to be employed with different cultural groups.

THE INSTITUTIONALIZATION OF CULTURAL BIASES

If traditional psychotherapeutic practice is as inappropriate for minorities as the literature would suggest, one wonders how the current assumptions in therapy and testing are maintained. The primary modes of maintenance are through the training of psychology professionals and the basic structure of most established mental health centers. It is important to examine the elements involved in the self-maintaining systems of training and service providing.

The primary and most basic problems are that psychologists receive very little training in minority testing and therapy issues. In the general sense, psychologists receive very little training in conceptual framworks for considering minority and sex differences and little exposure to social problems and basic research relevant to psychotherapy with minorities (Proshansky, 1972). For example, some theoretical approaches presented to psychologists in training are quite sexist in their assumptions and orientation (Voss & Gannon, 1978). Although the therapist may be aware of minority issues in a general sense, lack of in-depth training may result in subtle biases being manifested in therapy without the therapist's awareness.

Flores (1979) noted the difficulty in obtaining adequate training in psychological testing of minorities, specifically Chicanos. In addition to general theoretical training, few graduate students have adequate therapy and testing experiences with minority clients (Flores, 1979), and there are few minority faculty members to supervise students with minority clients. Flores has illustrated his dilemma of being a Chicano graduate student, who felt that he had limited minority-patient contact during his training. An even greater problem was being unable to find a qualified supervisor who could bilingually supervise therapy-session audiotapes of Spanish-speaking clients.

The lack of qualified, minority mental health professionals is a major issue which deserves attention. Korchin (1980) reviewed relatively recent surveys which indicate that minority psychologists are greatly underrepresented. Smith, Burkes, Mosley, and Whitney (1978) noted that the American Psychological Association has over 46,000 members, while the Association of Black Psychologists has 500 members. Ruiz (1971) stated that there are 58 American psychologists with Spanish surnames, and 30 of these psychologists are European Spanish. The President's Commission on Mental Health (1978) cited an APA survey that delineated percentages of doctoral level psychological health service providers of various cultural groups: .9 percent black, .7 percent Asian, .4 percent Hispanic, .1 percent native American. Flores (1979) noted the more practical issue of numbers of Spanish-speaking people in the Los Angeles area and the existence of very few licensed, Spanish-speaking, mental health service providers. Soon, one fourth of the population in the Los Angeles area will be Hispanic, including approximately 1 million monolingual, Spanish-speaking people, many of whom are bound to need mental health services.

When bilingual therapists are available, their existence typically is not readily recognizable by examining the rosters of licensed professionals or professional organizations. The rosters of therapists generally do not contain information regarding bilingual abilities or minority status of professionals (Flores, 1979). While the rosters have successfully avoided discriminating against people on the basis of race, they are not helpful to people who need to find a minority or bilingual therapist or examiner. Flores describes episodes in which he searched for available, Spanish-speaking therapists. Spanish surnames were the only indications that a therapist might be bilingual. Minority professionals are invaluable as: therapy supervisors in graduate programs, role models for minority graduate students, and service providers to minority communities. It has been indicated that the employment situation for minority psychologists differs little from majority psychologists (Gottfredson & Swatko, 1979); therefore, once trained, the minority psychologist is fairly readily hired. The difficulty appears to be in the number of minority students being trained in graduate psychology programs.

Kennedy and Wagner (1979) examined trends in graduate programs, by comparing surveys of clinical psychology programs published during 1970, 1973, and 1977. Overall, there was a 400 percent increase in minority enrollment across the seven years, with blacks and Hispanics showing the greatest increases. Other minority groups did not increase as significantly. These data actually may be overestimates, because of nonrandom responding by the graduate programs surveyed. It was hypothesized that those programs which did respond to the survey were those that were making the most progress in the area of minority admissions. Attrition was noted as a possible reason for there being more minority first-year students than advanced students.

While substantial increases have been made in minority admissions, there are still very few minority psychologists and students (Korchin, 1980). Fisher and Stricker (1979) have noted that minority students are usually considered for graduate admission on the same criteria as and in competition with white students. The admission procedure typically requires excellence in three areas: undergraduate grade point, letters of recommendation, and Graduate Record Examination scores. In addition, graduate schools may require personal interviews, which are usually conducted by majority-group faculty members. Even excellent minority candidates may have difficulty competing with majority candidates in these areas. As a consequence, if graduate programs admit excellent minority candidates who have done less well on some admission criteria than other white candidates, reverse discrimination may be accused. Claims of reverse discrimination are seen as a potential barrier to continued increases in minority graduate students and minority psychologists.

The structure of the mental health system has been seen as a deterrent to involvement of minority patients in psychological services (Padilla et al., 1975). If the mental health center is not located near the community of the minority-group member, close, trusting relationships are not readily established (Lin & Lin, 1978). Padilla et al. also saw geographic isolation as a practical constraint. Two elements of that practicality are transportation to the center and availability of day care services, both of which are frequent deterrents to lower-class patients' involvement in mental health centers. As was mentioned earlier, the expectations of some minority patients to receive immediate advice or solutions to problems are not consistent with many centers' policies of long-waiting, staffing procedures.

The systems of graduate training and mental health-service providing are frequently not conducive to optimal involvement of minority groups. It is important to examine how these systems can be modified, to allow more integration of minority needs into the general framework of the overall therapy process.

RECOMMENDATIONS

Model for culturally sensitive psychotherapy

One of the things that needs to occur in order to meet the needs of minorities is the delineation of a conceptual model which would take cultural variance into account. Several models, formal and informal, have been in use by psychologists and other professionals. Korchin (1980) has pointed out three major views of cultural variance. One is a psychology or race differences, which compares individuals with measures standardized on white, middle-class populations. This model has been attacked as being motivated by a hypothesis that individuals who are not white or middle class are deficient in qualities necessary for mental health. Another model is a cross-cultural approach, which stresses the importance of understanding people's behavior in the context of their cultural background. A third model, sometimes confused with cross-culturalism, is cultural relativism, which acknowledges that what is considered pathological in one culture may be normal in another. Cultural relativism indicates that psychopathology should be viewed only in the context of the individual's cultural membership. In essence, cultural relativism implies the need for a separate psychology for each culture.

The model which seems more realistic is the one forwarded by Korchin which emphasizes cross-culturalism, yet views psychopathology in terms of general, panhuman criteria, which are applicable across cultures. Panhuman elements of adaptive functioning which have been suggested by Korchin include: capacity for voluntary control, ego strength, flexibility, adaptability, sense of personal identity, and stability of perception, learning, and memory. Rather than many psychologies for many cultures, the cross-cultural model maintains a general psychology, which would take into account specific variations as related to cultural differences. The present authors would like to expand the model to include variations according to culture, ethnicity, social class, and sex.

This expanded, cross-cultural model is offered as an ideal or guiding strategy for the practice of clinical psychology. Admittedly, the application of this model is a difficult and complex process, and in many areas, we lack the knowledge base necessary for actual implementation of this sort of approach. However, it seems useful to employ the expanded, cross-cultural model as a framework for identifying aspects of mental health care which need to be changed.

Therapist skills.   The application of the expanded, cross-cultural model to the therapy process requires, to some degree, broader skills on the part of the therapist, as well as more flexible approaches to therapy. On the basis of the areas of potential conflict outlined in previous sections of this chapter, the following generalizations and recommendations regarding effective therapy with ethnic minorities can be generated.

According to Sue (1981), the "culturally skilled counselor must be able to send and receive both verbal and nonverbal messages accurately and 'appropriately' " (p. 108). To do this, one must be a sensitive observer of one's own behavior, understand the communication nuances of the client's culture, and adapt the pattern of communication to the client.

Several factors need to be considered in this process. First, the therapist should be familiar with the client's language background. Ideally, the therapist and client should speak the same language, although this is not always possible. At the very least, the therapist must consider the client's language background in interpreting his/her behavior, both in the therapy session and in the context of diagnostic assessment.

Second, basic communication skills (such as eye contact, body language, tone of voice, rate of speech, and the like) may need to be adjusted. The therapist must be aware of the communication "rules" of the client's culture, in order to accurately interpret the client's behavior. In addition, the therapist must evaluate his/her own style of verbal and nonverbal communication and make the alterations necessary to minimize misinterpretation on the part of the client. This requires a wide range of skills and flexibility in exercising these skills.

The third area which needs to be considered involves the structure of the therapy interaction. As has already been mentioned, culture and social class play a significant role in client expectations regarding content of discussion, role of the therapist, and duration of treatment. It has been suggested that one deal with these potential areas of conflict when preparing clients for therapy by explaining the process or even showing videotapes of therapy interactions (Garfield, 1971; Korchin, 1980). The more frequent recommendation in the literature, however, is for the therapist to adapt the structure of the therapy session to fit the cultural background of the client.

For example, Brown (1979) suggests that therapists may need to be more informal with Chicanos, exhibit more warmth, answer personal questions, and use more physical contact and animation. Padilla et al. (1975) also report more informal structure (with the use of first names among professionals) as facilitating rapport with Spanish clients. Kinzie et al. (1980) suggest that a medically oriented intervention style is seen as congruent with Indochinese patient's expectations for a psychiatric clinic. With Native Americans, Smith (1981) recommends minimizing the authoritarian role of the therapist and utilizing an unpretentious, humble style in therapy.

Obviously, the key issue here is the importance of establishing a productive, therapeutic relationship. With individuals of different sex and cultural or social background, the steps toward developing the therapeutic relationship may need to be adjusted. It is the present authors' opinion, however, that once a basic trusting relationship is established, the general principles of positive therapeutic interaction apply to almost all clients. A good, therapeutic relationship, in the long run, can compensate for cultural differences or conflicts which might emerge.

Assessment. The expanded, cross-cultural model also has implications for psychological assessment. When a client is referred for psychological or educational testing, the referral question may indicate avenues of investigation and suggest testing instruments which have been shown to be relevant to the presenting problem. The model suggests that, when the client is referred, it is important for the examiner to know the client's social and ethnic background and language usage. Knowledge of the client's background may give the examiner information regarding potential areas of conflict with standard administration procedures, relationship variables during testing, or difficulties in test interpretation.

Test selection.   Two courses of action are open to the examiner, both of which may be appropriate in selecting a test battery. First, the examiner may need to research and/or review information regarding the client's particular cultural or ethnic background, taking into account the client's sex. Obtaining information is particularly appropriate when the examiner is not readily familiar with the client's culture. Here, it is important to emphasize that becoming familiar with research regarding a client's culture introduces potential areas of deviation from expected test behavior. While this cultural information is valuable, one must remember that there are large variations, subcultural and individual, within cultures. Therefore, stereotyping is a real danger which should be avoided.

The second course of action to explore in selecting the battery is the array of tests which could be utilized, given the client's background and referral question. Based on the given information and subsequently researched information, the examiner may delete, add, or cautiously modify tests, until a satisfactory battery is obtained. This second investigatory phase may require becoming aware of new tests, reviewing validity, reliability, and standardization samples of existing tests, and consulting the literature and/or other professionals regarding inventive testing techniques for particularly unusual or difficult testing situations.

Test administration.   Once a test battery has been selected, it is important to establish rapport and cooperation with the client. Chavez and Gonzales-Singh (1980) suggest that more time may be needed in this process when cultural differences are involved. They suggest using nonverbal tests with simple, easily translated instructions (such as drawing a person) initially, to create a less threatening atmosphere and to allow the client to relax.

A more creative, flexible approach to assessment also has been recommended for minorities. The results of standardized tests should not be taken at face value. It is crucial to sample from multiple areas, in order to obtain more accurate data. For example, the client's behavior during testing may provide very useful information to help in understanding the final test results. Behavioral assessment of daily living skills is another important area to evaluate and may act as corroboration or contradiction to scores on standard measures. This requires more extensive interviewing of the client and family members, as well as direct observation. Sattler

(1974) suggests placing less emphasis on normative testing and instead developing more goal-oriented or objective-based means of assessment.

Test interpretation. The final and most important factor to consider is the interpretation of the test data. Ideally, one would examine the test results in reference both to standard norms as well as to norms based on the individual's social or cultural group. Standard norms would suggest where the individual stands relative to members of the majority culture; while the subculture norms might provide an indication of the individual's potential level of functioning.

If such norms are not available, the examiner must be willing to examine cultural variables which might account for the client's performance. Any extra-test information which might refute the test results should be taken into account. The *Ethical Principles of Psychologists* (APA, 1981) address this issue very directly: "In reporting assessment results, psychologists, indicate any reservations that exist regarding validity or reliability because of the circumstances of the assessment or the inappropriateness of the norms for the person tested. Psychologists strive to ensure that the results of assessments and their interpretations are not misused by others" (p. 637).

In summary, one cannot assume that tests chosen, administered, and interpreted in the typical manner appropriately predict or reflect minority clients' current level of skills or future performance. One must be cognizant of potential errors, especially in test selection and interpretation, and be flexible in making changes that will maximize one's ability to make accurate assessments and dispositions of minority clients.

Type of treatment

In general, effective therapy with minorities requires (a) knowledge of minority-group cultures and experiences. (b) explicit awareness of the cultural and value biases of different therapy approaches, (c) evaluation of the degree of conflict or consistency between the cultural values of the client and the values inherent in therapy approaches, and finally, (d) selection of the most compatible approach for the particular client (Sue, 1981). Thus, primary recommendations offered in the literature are that different ethnic and cultural groups require different approaches in therapy (Brown, 1979; Herrera & Sanches, 1980; Sue, 1981) and that nonsexist theoretical approaches should be utilized (Voss & Gannon, 1978).

Although opinions regarding which approaches work best with different cultural groups are many and varied, the following common theme runs through the most of the literature: ". . . more attention will have to be paid to social or environmental variables as contrasted with essentially intrapsychic ones, and . . . psyhotherapy or counseling will have to go hand in hand with other attempts to alleviate the individual's distress instead of being relied upon almost exlusively to modify or remake the individual" (Garfield, 1971, p. 293). Therapists cannot ignore the pressing social problems of immediate concern to their minority clients.

However, attempting to deal with day-to-day, practical problems requires a broadening of the concept of therapy. Sue (1981) recommends that therapists become involved in teaching clients basic survival skills related to getting job interviews, study skills, social skills, filling out welfare forms, taking tests, etc. Home visits and crisis intervention also have been suggested (Garfield, 1971). A number of researchers have proposed that the more behavioral, problem-solving approaches to therapy and/ or family therapy are most appropriate with minorities because they deal directly with the immediate environmental context (Brown, 1979; Herrera & Sanches, 1980; Szapocznik et al., 1978). Brown (1979) argues that intrapsychic processes need not be ignored when working with minorities, but they can be dealt with in the process of meeting the patient's immediate needs.

It also may be useful to broaden the concept of who is involved in the therapy process. Several researchers (i.e., Padilla et al., 1975) have recommended employing paraprofessionals—of the same cultural background or similar experience as the client—in the treatment process. Therapists also may find valuable allies in community members who already have gained the trust and confidence of clients. By establishing a network of community contacts, the therapist may be able to broaden his/her referral base. In addition, initial rapport may be greatly facilitated by including a community member in the initial interview or incorporating the individual into some part of the treatment.

Finally, therapists must be flexible and sensitive to their own limitations. If a minority therapist or person specially trained in working with a particular client population is available, therapists should be willing to refer appropriate clients. Similarly, referral should be considered if the therapist cannot be tolerant or accepting of a culturally alien client.

Research implications

The reader, at this point, may find him/herself somewhat disappointed by the absence of many specific, empirically validated, "how to do therapy with minorities" recommendations. As a matter of fact, the present authors experienced the same disappointment in the process of researching this topic. Despite the long-standing tacit acknowledgement in the profession that "psychotherapy outcome research should be directed toward ascertaining which treatment by whom is most effective for a person with specific characteristics and problems in a particular set of circumstances" (Szapocznik et al., 1978, p. 961), there is very little controlled research on the differential effectiveness of therapy approaches with individuals from different cultural backgrounds. Most of the literature is anecdotal and philosophical, rather than scientific, and this accounts for the paucity of specific, direct recommendations in this chapter.

Before the mental health profession will be able to effectively meet the needs of minorities, much more research in this area is needed. Proshansky (1972) recommends changing the focus of graduate programs, from basic research within highly specialized disciplines, to multidisciplinary specialization, as one way to address this need. This would facilitate psychologists obtaining access to other fields, such as anthropology and sociology, which tend to be more involved in the study of cultural issues.

Clinical training

Despite the current limitations in our understanding of the optimal way to work with minorities, the model or philiosophy for conceptualizing minority issues in therapy presented thus far requires considerable familiarity with ethnic cultures and a high level of skill on the part of the therapist. However, very few clinical psychology graduate programs appear to adequately address cultural issues in their training programs. A number of writers have recognized this deficiency and suggested changes in training procedures to facilitate the development of culturally skilled therapists.

Content of curriculum. The first and most basic recommendation presented in the literature is the need for courses pertaining to the culture and unique needs of the ethnic-minority populations in our society (Bradshaw, 1978; Giordano, 1974; Vontress, 1971). Similarly, courses in psychotherapy and men's and women's issues need to be offered (Fleming, 1977; Voss & Gannon, 1978; APA, 1975). Students should be exposed to the history, family structure, group and family characteristics, religion, and social issues of the ethnic groups (Bradshaw, 1978). A major effort should be directed toward dispelling myths (Bradshaw, 1978) and facilitating understand of the psychological, physical, and social implications of being a minority in contemporary society (Vontress, 1971). Wong (1978) recommends that international or specialty training programs (which include training in ethnic languages) be established to accomplish these goals, while others have suggested the incorporation of new curriculum materials into existing training programs.

Practical experiences. Exposure to minority clientele also has been recommended as an integral part of training. Trainees should have direct contact with the social structures and minority agencies of the community, through training in outpatient lower-class community mental health centers

(Bradshaw, 1978), chronic aftercare services, and community-outreach consultation (Bradwshaw, 1978; Wong, 1978).

Vontress (1971) proposes that would-be therapists live and work in the ghetto in order to experience the minority culture and personally understand cultural alienation. Less drastic experiences—such as sensitivity training (Vontress, 1971) or group experiences involving role-playing minority clients—also have been suggested (Bradshaw, 1978). Group experiences have been employed to facilitate sex-fair counseling (Gilbert & Waldroop, 1978), with some success. They used structured role-plays and exercises designed to illustrate areas of perceived sex bias and sex-role stereotyping, in a course on counseling techniques. Participants in this program demonstrated more "liberal attitudes toward women's roles, greater sensitivity to sex bias in two videotaped counseling vignettes of female clients, and more positive evaluation of the two clients who appeared in the vignettes" than did control subjects (p. 410). Their findings suggest that it may be possible to use similar procedures to incorporate discussion of cultural issues into ongoing psychotherapy graduate courses.

Minority professionals.   Finally, considerable emphasis has been placed on the need for more clinical psychologists who are members of ethnic minority groups. It has been noted that minority psychologists may be better able to serve the mental health needs of minority clients because of: (*a*) their ability to understand cultural and linguistic issues, (*b*) their greater motivation to work with and study minorities, (*c*) their potential as role models and identification figures for clients, and (*d*) the possibility for increasing the knowledge and understanding of their white colleagues (Korchin, 1980). The importance of minority faculty in didactic and clinical teaching roles also has been stressed (Korchin, 1980; Wong, 1978).

Obviously, in order to increase the number of minority professionals, it is necessary to increase the number of minority students in clinical psychology graduate programs. Fisher and Striker (1979) describe a policy for encouraging minority candidacy in graduate school, which creates options for minorities, without reverse discrimination against majority candidates. In brief, their approach involves three components: (1) increased class size, (2) separate review of minority candidates, and (3) active recruitment. They advocate evaluating minority candidates on the basis of criteria which reflect potential (such as interviews) and minimizing criteria (such as quantitative scores) which can be confounded by distortions in educational and language experiences. Flexibility in course load and allocation of financial aid strictly on the basis of need also is recommended. By increasing class size, the majority candidates can continue to be evaluated in the traditional manner, without being hindered by eliminating potential positions to make special room for minorities. Fisher and Striker (1979) also stress the need for vigorous recruitment, involving speeches to undergraduates,contact with minority psychological associations, and informal contacts initiated by minority students. It seems reasonable that widespread application of this type of selection process would significantly facilitate an increase in the number of minority professionals in mental health.

Mental health facilities

There also are specific changes which could be made in mental health services, which would result in greater utilization by minorities. Padilla et al. (1975) describe several mental health facilities which have effectively served Spanish-speaking communities. Several characteristics of the successful facilities are reported here as recommendations for establishment of new, or modification of existing, facilities.

Accessibility is seen as important in getting the minority population to utilize services. Specifically, it is recommended that the facility be located near the neighborhood it is serving and be conveniently accessible. The physical plant should be clean and attractively furnished. It has been suggested that the waiting room resemble a living room in appearance and atmosphere (Padilla et al., 1975). The receptionist should be able to converse in the language of the client, and signs inside and outside the building should be in a language understandable to the client.

It is important that the mental health facility be sensitive to many minority groups' expectations of immediate treatment. This can be accomplished through providing immediate referral to a service provider or establishing an open-door clinic policy. Another possibility is providing home visits. In addition to arrangements which can reduce the time required to see a therapist, the clinic should be organized to provide short-term assistance to clients with immediate situational problems. Situational problems included pressing financial problems, lost paychecks, legal problems, and unwanted houseguests. It would be desirable to have available staff with whom the client could communicate regarding these problems.

Another set of recommendations pertains to encouraging the patient to maintain regular therapy contact throughout the treatment process. Continued convenience and accessibility of therapy can be maintained through implementation of a sliding-fee schedule, utilization of longer clinic hours, and provision of services such as transportation and child-care facilities. Transportation services may consist of a busing service or a share-a-ride service.

Continued use of the facility can be ensured by announcing available services on minority or ethnic radio stations. Also, encouraging community members to provide input regarding desired services can be valuable. Services suggested, such as youth activities or reading-improvement programs, can provide opportunities for other minority-group members to become involved in the mental health facility, and the facility may become more widely accepted in the community.

Overall, it would be beneficial for the facility to encourage a policy of flexibility within its structure and among its staff members in dealing with patients and in instituting and/or changing policies as different patient needs are identified. The current recommendations are by no means conclusive. They are provided as examples of changes that could be made in the present system and that allow the needs of minority groups to meet more effectively.

SUMMARY

Surveys demonstrating significant underutilization of mental health facilities by minorities as well as differential treatment of minorities in therapy have prompted considerable attention to the appropriateness of current mental health practices for minority clients. Although there is some evidence that minority subcultures offer support through family and social structure and may provide alternative sources of treatment through faith healers and folk medicine, these factors do not seem adequate to account for the pervasiveness of the underutilization problem.

Examination of the basic characteristics and value assumptions implicit in traditional psychotherapy reveals several areas of potential class, culture, and sex bias, which may conflict with the values of minority clients. For example, in the therapeutic communication process, potential areas of conflict include language usage, expression of emotions, structure of therapy, nonverbal styles of communication, client's expectations regarding therapy, and degree of similarity between client and therapist.

Cultural, social-class, and sex bias also can influence the goals of psychotherapy, the means by which therapeutic change is brought about, and the assumptions made about normal behavior. In addition, the structure of mental health services often are incompatible with the needs and lifestyles of lower-class or minority clients.

To minimize these biases in therapy and provide treatment that is appropriate for minorities, it is recommended that therapists strive to conceptualize treatment in light of an expanded, cross-cultural model, which posits general, panhuman elements of adaptive functioning, yet takes into account individual differences based on sex, social class, or cultural background. The application of this model to the practice of psychotherapy, however, requires a number of alterations in the traditional delivery of mental health care. First, therapists must possess a broader range of verbal and nonverbal communication skills and be willing to adapt their style of communication to the client's background. The assessment tools employed must be carefully selected for appropriateness for the individual client, and any test results must be considered in light of the idividual's cultural environment.

Greater flexibility in treatment approaches is also needed. Therapists must be familiar with their client's culture and must be able to choose treatment goals and treatment techniques which are consistent with the client's cultural values. It also may be necessary to place greater emphasis on day-to-day practical problems and to incorporate community members into phases of the treatment process, in order to more adequately serve special populations. Such changes in treatment approach may necessitate changes in the location, hours, atmosphere, and range of potential, practical services offered by mental health facilities, as well.

Finally, graduate programs need to address sex, social-class, and cultural issues more directly. A great deal of psychotherapy outcome research with special populations is needed. In addition, students must be familiar with the values of cultural groups and have practical training experience with clients of different social-class and ethnic-group membership. There also is a tremendous need for more minority professionals to teach as well as provide mental health services.

On the basis of the review conducted in this chapter, it seems that the challenge posed by Garfield in 1971 is one which clinical psychologists still need to heed. "Not only must we devise more effective techniques for dealing with serious problems of personality adjustment, but we must not find ourselves in the position of devoting most of our professional resources to working with those who may be in least need of our help. In the past we have been overly concerned with the client who fits our modes of psychotherapy. It appears that now we are beginning to think of devising therapeutic procedures to fit the client" (p. 294). This remains an important challenge facing those who work in the area of psychotherapy.

REFERENCES

Adebimpe, V., Gigandet, J., & Harris, E. MMPI diagnosis of black psychiatric patients. *American Journal of Psychiatry*, 1979, *136*, 85–87.

American Psychological Association. Ethical principles of psychologists. *American Psychologist*, 1981, *36*, 633–638.

American Psychological Association. Report of the Task Force on Sex Bias and Sex-Role Stereotyping in Psychotherapeutic Practice. *American Psychologist*, 1975, *30*, 1169–1175.

Berman, J. Individual versus societal focus: Problem diagnoses of black and white male and female counselors. *Journal of Cross-Cultural Psychology*, 1979, *10*, 497–507.

Boyer, L., & Boyer, R. Understanding the individual through folklore. *Contemporary Psychoanalysis*, 1977, *13*, 30–51.

Bradshaw, W. Training psychiatrists for working with blacks in basic residency programs. *American Journal of Psychiatry*, 1978, *135*, 1520–1524.

Broverman, I., Broverman, D., Clarkson, F., Rosenkrantz, P., & Vogel, S. Sex-role stereotypes and clinical judgments of mental health. *Journal of Consulting and Clinical Psychology,* 1970, *34,* 1–7.

Brown, J. Clinical social work with Chicanos: Some unwarranted assumptions. *Clinical Social Work Journal,* 1979, *7,* 256–266.

Bryson, S., & Cody, J. Relationship of race and level of understanding between counselor and client. *Journal of Counseling Psychology,* 1973, *20,* 495–498.

Buss, A. *Psychopathology.* New York: John Wiley & Sons, 1966.

Carkuff, R., & Pierce, R. Differential effects of therapist race and social class upon patient depth of self-exploration in the initial clinical interview. *Journal of Consulting Psychology,* 1967, *31,* 632–634.

Cavenar, J., & Spaulding, J. When the psychotherapist is black. *American Journal of Psychiatry,* 1978, *135,* 1084–1087.

Chavez, E., & Gonzales-Singh, E. Hispanic assessment: A case study. *Professional Psychology,* 1980, *11,* 163–168.

Chesler, P. Patient and patriarch: Women in the psychotherapeutic relationship. In V. Gornik & B. Moran (Eds.), *Women in sexist society.* N.Y.: New American Library, 1971. (a)

Chesler, P. Women as psychiatric and psychotherapy patients. *Journal of Marriage and the Family,* 1971, *4,* 746–759. (b)

Cimbolic, P. Counselor race and experience effects on black clients. *Journal of Consulting and Clinical Psychology,* 1972, *39,* 328–332.

Cleary, T., Humphreys, L., Kendrick, S., & Weisman, A. Educational uses of tests with disadvantaged students. *American Psychologist,* 1975, *30,* 15–41.

Dohrenwend, B., & Dohrenwend, B. *Social status and psychological disorder.* New York: John Wiley & Sons, 1974.

Fabricant, B. The psychotherapist and the female patient: Perception, misconceptions, and change. In V. Franks & V. Burthe (Eds.), *Women in therapy: New psychotherapies.* New York: Brunner & Mazel, 1974.

Feinblatt, J., & Gold, A. Sex roles and the psychiatric-referral process. *Sex Roles,* 1976, *2,* 109–122.

Fernandez-Pol, B. Culture and psychopathology: A study of Puerto Ricans. *American Journal of Psychiatry,* 1980, *137,* 724–726.

Fisher, M., & Stricker, G. Minority candidacy in professional psychology. *Professional Psychology,* 1979, *10,* 740–743.

Flaherty, J., & Meager, R. Measuring racial bias in inpatient treatment. *American Journal of Psychiatry,* 1980, *137,* 679–682.

Fleming, S. Developing a course on women in the residency curriculum. *Psychiatric Annals,* 1977, *7,* 197–202.

Flores, J. Becoming a marriage, family, and child counselor: Notes from a Chicano. *Journal of Marital and Family Therapy,* 1979, *5,* 17–22.

Garfield, J., Weiss, S., & Pollock, E. Effects of a child's social class on a school counselor's decision making. *Journal of Counseling Psychology,* 1976, *23,* 333–338.

Garfield, S. Research on client variables in psychotherapy. In A. Bergin & S. Garfield (Eds.), *Handbook of psychotherapy and behavior change.* New York: John Wiley & Sons, 1971.

Gilbert, L., & Waldroop, J. Evaluation of a procedure for increasing sex-fair counseling. *Journal of Counseling Psychology,* 1978, *25,* 410–415.

Giordano, J. Ethnics and minorities: A review of the literature. *Clinical Social Work Journal,* 1974, *2,* 207–220.

Gottfredson, G., & Swatko, M. Employment, unemployment, and the job search in psychology. *American Psychologist,* 1979, *34,* 1047–1060.

Hacker, H. Women as a minority group. *Social Forces,* 1951, *30,* 60–69.

Hacker, H. Women as a minority group 20 years later. In R. Unger & F. Denmark (Eds.), *Woman: Dependent or independent variable.* New York: Psychological Dimensions, 1975.

Hall, E. *Handbook for proxemic research.* Washington, D.C.: Society for the Antology of Visual Communications, 1974.

Harrison, D. Race as a counselor-client variable in counseling and psychotherapy: A review of the research. *Counseling Psychologist,* 1975, *4,* 124–133.

Herrera, A., & Sanches, B. Prescriptive group psychotherapy: A successful application in the treatment of low-income Spanish-speaking clients. *Psychotherapy: Theory, Research, and Practice,* 1980, *17,* 169–174.

Hibbs, B. J., Kobos, J. C., & Gonzales, J. Effectiveness of ethnicity, sex, and age on MMPI profiles. *Psychological Reports,* 1979, *45,* 591–597.

Hollingshead, A., & Redlich, F. *Social class and mental health.* New York: John Wiley & Sons, 1958.

Hunter, J., & Schmidt, F. Critical analysis of the statistical and ethical implications of various definitions of test bias. *Psychological Bulletin,* 1976, *83,* 1053–1071.

Karno, M. The enigma of ethnicity in a psychiatric clinic. *Archives of General Psychiatry,* 1966, *14,* 516–520.

Kennedy, C., & Wagner, N. Psychology and affirmative action: 1977. *Professional Psychology,* 1979, *10,* 234–243.

Keston, M., & Jiminez, C. A study of the performance on English and Spanish editions of the Stanford-Binet Intelligence Test by Spanish-American children. *Journal of Genetic Psychology,* 1954, *85,* 263–269.

Kinzie, J., Tran, K., Breckenridge, A., & Bloom, J. An Indochinese-refugee psychiatric clinic: Culturally accepted treatment approaches. *American Journal of Psychiatry,* 1980, *137,* 1429–1432.

Kline, L., Acosta, F., Austin, W., & Johnson, R. *Subtle bias in the treatment of Spanish-speaking clients via interpreters.* Paper presented at the meeting of the American Psychiatric Association, Puerto Rico, May 1976.

Knapp, M. *Nonverbal communication in human interaction.* New York: Holt, Rhinehart & Winston, 1972.

Korchin, S. Clinical psychology and minority problems. *American Psychologist,* 1980, *35,* 262–269.

Lin, T., & Lin, M. Service-delivery issues in Asian North American communities. *American Journal of Psychiatry,* 1978, *135,* 454–456.

Lorion, R. Patient and therapist variables in the treatment of low-income patients. *Psychological Bulletin,* 1974, *81,* 344–354.

Mercer, J. Identifying the gifted Chicano child. In J. Martinez (Ed.), *Chicano psychology.* New York: Academic Press, 1977.

Merluzzi, B., & Merluzzi, T. Influence of client race on counselor's assessment of case materials. *Journal of Counseling Psychology,* 1978, *25,* 399–404.

Miller, D. The influence of the patient's sex on clinical judgement. *Smith College Studies in Social Work,* 1974, *44,* 89–100.

Mishra, S. The influence of examiner's ethnic attributes on intelligence-test scores. *Psychology in the Schools,* 1980, *17,* 117–122.

Padilla, A., Ruiz, R., & Alvarez, R. Community mental health services for the Spanish-speaking/surnamed population. *American Psychologist,* 1975, *30,* 892–905.

Parloff, M., Waskow, I., & Wolfe, B. Research on therapist variables in relation to process and outcome. In S. Garfield & A. Bergin (Eds.), *Handbook of psychotherapy and behavior change: An empiral analysis,* (2d ed.). New York: John Wiley & Sons, 1978.

Pollock, E., & Menacker, J. *Spanish-speaking students and guidance.* Boston: Houghton Mifflin, 1971.

President's Commission on Mental Health. *Report to the President from the President's Commission on Mental Health.* Washington, D.C.: U.S. Government Printing Office, 1978.

Pritchard, D., & Rosenblatt, A. Racial bias in the MMPI: A methodological review. *Journal of Consulting and Clinical Psychology,* 1980, *48,* 263–267.

Proctor, E., & Rosen, A. Expectations and preferences for counselor race and their relation to intermediate-treatment outcomes. *Journal of Counseling Psychology,* 1981, *28,* 40–46.

Proshansky, H. For what are we training our graduate students? *American Psychologist,* 1972, *27,* 205–212.

Proskauer, S. Oedipal equivalents in a clan culture: Reflections on Navajo ways. *Psychiatry,* 1980, *43,* 43–50.

Richardson, E. Cultural and historical perspectives in counseling blacks. In D. Sue (Ed.), *Counseling the culturally different: Theory, research, and practice.* New York: John Wiley & Sons, 1981.

Rotter, J. Some problems and misconceptions related to the construct of internal versus external locus of control of reinforcement. *Journal of Consulting and Clinical Psychology,* 1975, *43,* 56–67.

Ruiz, R. Relative frequency of Americans with Spanish surnames in associations of psychology, psychiatry, and sociology. *American Psychologist,* 1971, *26,* 1022–1024.

Ruiz, R. Cultural and historical perspectives in counseling Hispanics. In D. Sue (Ed.), *Counseling the culturally different: Theory, research, and practice.* New York: John Wiley & Sons, 1981.

Ryan, D., & Gaier, E. Student socioeconomic status and counselor contact in junior high school. *Personnel and Guidance Journal,* 1968, *46,* 466–472.

Sattler, J. *Assessment of children's intelligence.* Philadelphia: W. B. Saunders, 1974.

Sattler, J. The effects of therapist-client racial similarity. In A. Gurman & A. Razin (Eds.), *Effective psychotherapy: A handbook of research.* Elmsford, N.Y.: Pergamon Press, 1977.

Schindler-Rainman, E. The poor and the PTA. *PTA Magazine,* 1965, *61,* 4–5.

Schneider, L., Laury, P., & Hughes, H. Ethnic-group perceptions of mental health-service providers. *Journal of Counseling Psychology,* 1980, *27,* 589–596.

Seligman, M. *Helplessness: On depression, development, and death.* San Francisco: W. H. Freeman, 1975.

Smith, E. *Counseling the culturally different youth.* Columbus, Ohio: Charles E. Merrill Publishing, 1973.

Smith, E. Cultural and historical perspectives in counseling American Indians. In D. Sue (Ed.), *Counseling the culturally different: Theory, research, and practice.* New York: John Wiley & Sons, 1981.

Smith, M. Sex bias in counseling and psychotherapy. *Psychological Bulletin,* 1980, *87,* 392–407.

Smith, W., Burkes, A., Mosley, M., & Whitney, W. *Minority issues in mental health.* Reading, Mass.: Addison-Wesley Publishing, 1978.

Srole, L., Langner, T., Michael, S., Opler, M., & Rennie, T. *Mental health in the metropolis* (Vol. 1). New York: McGraw-Hill, 1962.

Sue, D. Eliminating cultural oppression in counseling: Toward a general theory. *Journal of Counseling Psychology,* 1978, *25,* 419–428.

Sue, D. *Counseling the culturally different: Theory, research, and practice.* New York: John Wiley & Sons, 1981.

Sue, D. W., & Sue, D. Barriers to effective cross-cultural counseling. *Journal of Counseling Psychology,* 1977, *5,* 420–429.

Szapocznik, J., Scopetta, M., de los Angeles Arnalde, M., & Kurtines, W. Cuban value structure: Treatment implications. *Journal of Consulting and Clinical Psychology,* 1978, *46,* 961–970.

Thompson, R., & Cimbolic, P. Black students' counselor preference and attitudes toward counseling center use. *Journal of Counseling Psychology,* 1978, *25,* 570–575.

Vail, A. Factors influencing lower-class black patients remaining in treatment. *Journal of Consulting and Clinical Psychology,* 1978, *46,* 341.

Van Hook, M. Female clients, female counselors: Combating learned helplessness. *Social Work,* 1979, *24,* 63–65.

Vontress, D. E. Racial differences: Impediments to rapport. *Journal of Counseling Psychology,* 1981, *18,* 7–13.

Voss, J., & Gannon, L. Sexism in the theory and practice of clinical psychology. *Professional Psychology,* 1978, *9,* 623–632.

Williams, R. Danger: Testing and dehumanizing black children. *Clinical Child Psychology Newsletter,* 1970, *9,* 5–6.

Winder, A., & Hersko, M. The effects of social class on the length and type of psychotherapy in a Veterans Administration mental hygiene clinic. *Journal of Clinical Psychology,* 1955, *11,* 77–79.

Wong, N. Psychiatric education and training of Asian and Asian-American psychiatrists. *American Journal of Psychiatry,* 1978, *135,* 1525–1529.

Yamamoto, J., James, Q., Bloombaum, M., & Hattem, J. Racial factors in patient selection. *American Journal of Psychiatry,* 1967, *124,* 630–636.

Yamamoto, J., James, Q., & Palley, N. Cultural problems in psychiatric therapy. *Archives of General Psychiatry,* 1968, *19,* 45–49.

PART V

The practice of psychology

36

Starting and managing a practice

Mark H. Lewin, Ph.D.*

"It can't be done!"

That's what I was told in 1968 when I proposed to start a private practice of psychology in Rochester, New York. "The psychiatrists have the city locked up," a senior psychologist reported, "and they've thrown away the key."

That was the folklore. It wasn't so, but we, as a profession, were not yet sufficiently assertive or entrepreneurially inclined to test the assumption. That, I believe, was in large part due to our training. Until recently, we were reared in the academic and scientist-practitioner models; theory, training, and research were more highly valued than was direct service. Furthermore, making money through independent practice was denigrated by a large majority of our clinical-psychology role models. As late as 1974, Posluns (1974, p. 36), amplifying on Shakespeare ("The fault, dear Brutus, is not in our stars, but in ourselves, that we are underlings." *Julius Caesar*, Act I, Scene II), wrote, "I want to say things which may provoke anger. They are hard to say and I suspect they are also hard to hear. I think, as psychologists, we suffer from a collective feeling of group inferiority and I believe this feeling prevents us from getting what we want. Lots of individuals are symptom free but, en masse, I think we manifest some pretty self-retarding attitudes and behavior, which I attribute mostly to funny feelings we have about our collective self." A host of societal pressures (including, a shrinking market for academicians and researchers in psychology, and the antiestablishment bias that swept the country in the 1960s and 1970s) have dramatically changed the direction of our profession. Indeed, the delegates at the 1973 APA-NIMH-sponsored Vail conference (Korman, 1976) recognized, supported, and legitimized organized psychology's move toward the training of practitioners. The movement has grown rapidly; Watson, Caddy, Johnson,

---

* Upstate Psychological Service Center, P.C., Rochester, N.Y.

and Rimm (1981) detailed the growth of psychology's professional schools from 1 in 1951 and 6 by the end of 1969 to 36 (only 8 of which were accredited by the APA) in 1979. They also noted that their "data suggest that (practitioner-oriented rather than the scientist-practitioner model clinical programs) may well be producing a majority of the professional psychologists in the near future." (p. 514.) Many of these psychologists will seek to enter the private practice of psychology. Many of them will fail to develop a thriving, personally and financially rewarding practice. Why? Because, although psychology is a science and the practice of psychology is a profession, *the private practice of psychology is a business.* Our training prepares us to understand, predict, and attempt to control human behavior, but it gives us little or no appreciation of how to set fees, schedule appointments, select office equipment, rent or purchase an office, select a pension plan, or manage additional, essential business and administrative aspects of our work.

There is no magic to business planning. Indeed, it is very similar to treatment planning. It involves a careful assessment of the needs, strengths, and limitations of the practitioner and of the community in which the practice will be established. Quality-of-life variables should be a key to the process of determining if we should initiate a practice and to evaluating the business after we have established it. Indeed, only after we determine what we wish to do with our lives can we measure the success of our efforts to achieve our goals. Money, freedom to innovate, freedom to select the type of client seen, the ability to set one's hours, and the ability to avoid unwanted chores are all considerations to be assessed prior to launching an independent practice.

Lewin (1978), in the first of the recent rush of books on the theme of establishing and maintaining a successful, professional practice, included a Pre-Private Practice Personality Profile to help those considering entering independent practice determine whether or not they are suited for that means of expressing their skills. His questionnaire (pp. 2–11), worthy of serious deliberation, includes 10 items:

1. *Motivation.* Why do you want to start a practice?
2. *Need for close professional contacts.* How much social and professional stimulation do you need? How much consensual validation of your ideas?
3. *Administrative interest and ability.* Have you had any training in business or administration? Do you have an interest in it? A talent for it? A willingness to keep records and maintain controls over client case load and administrative matters?
4. *Are you a self-starter?* Have you started projects in the past or have you generally waited for the advice, guidance, and direction of others?
5. *Follow through.* Do you generally take responsibility for projects?

If you do, do you follow through or do you need prodding to complete assignments?

6. *Planning ability.* Planning and organizing one's workload are essential to keep a private practice viable.

7. *Decisiveness.* Can you make decisions? Do you vacillate, become tense and anxious, and look to others to take risks?

8. *Energy and drive.* How energetic are you? Are you able to maintain a high activity level over an extended period of time?

9. *Personal impact.* What is your initial impact on others? Are you able to quickly establish yourself as a forceful, competent, and respected professional? Do you speak clearly and well? Are your written reports clear, concise, and well formulated? Can you organize and present your ideas with good "selling" and influencing skills? Do you get along with other professionals, or are you seen as abrasive?

10. *Stress tolerance.* What is your tolerance for ambiguity, uncertainty, and stress? How many projects can you monitor simultaneously?

Quirk (1974) approached the basic requirements of the private practitioner from his experiential vantage point. In his words,

> the main things that a psychologist seems to need in order to succeed in business are a great deal of energy to permit him to work 12 to 16 hours a day; a great deal of patience to permit him to wait months and even years for a bill to be paid; a great deal of tenacity to permit him to keep working and billing regularly; a great sense of responsibility for the well-being of his fellow man and for the community in which he works; a willingness to be self-critical about everything he thinks he does; a clear and firm decisiveness at every instant in his work; a fair degree of compulsiveness in accurately keeping up all sorts of records; a fair range of skills which he can sell and in which he has developed a fair degree of confidence; a keen awareness of the ethical guidelines in which he must work for his own and his client's protection; and a bloody good sense of humor. With these and the patience to live through a few lean years, he may eventually become not rich, but able to live at least as well as his institutionally employed colleagues, and with the added advantage of knowing that he is providing value for each dollar he earns, since fees are collected only for service actually provided and since the costs of his services per unit of work are lower by far than those for the work of his institutionally employed colleagues. (pp. 47–48.)

Self-analysis can help would-be business persons determine the extent of their personal readiness to manage a professional practice and whether or not to proceed within the context of uncertainties of the flow of money, clients, competitors, and unforeseen events. Changes in local and national governmental policies, local political events, pressures on (and from) third-party payers, community economic patterns, and changes in the delivery of human services can all wreak havoc on well-laid plans.

ESTABLISHING A BUSINESS PLAN

Assuming that the decision to proceed is made, and assuming that each practitioner has sufficient professional knowledge, skill, and maturity to deal with the pressures and ethical choices that will appear daily, the next step is to establish a specific business plan. This involves the following three concepts.

Defining your motivation for establishing the practice

What it is that you wish to achieve through your professional efforts? Specifying the quality of career and personal-life variables important for you is essential, if you are to find fulfillment via your professional life.

Defining your practice

Perhaps a rose is a rose is a rose, but not all clinical psychologists are the same. Lack of careful definition of one's practice can have two negative effects. It can blur the image of the practitioner and lead to a weak referral base, and it can result in a referral flow that is inconsistent with the quality of work life which the psychologist sought. Figure 1 lists a wide range of services that psychologists often offer; it can aid us in analyzing and specifying the types of things we enjoy doing and do well.

Defining the practice is not an abstract concept. It is a key to fulfilling one's personal-professional needs as well as the financial realities of life. Lack of clarity about one's services can lead to a catastrophic lack of referrals. A *Psychotherapy Finance* (1979) section on practice building reported on one psychologist, who "told referral sources I did therapy. I soon found out that *wasn't the best approach in a highly competitive area."* Behaviorally oriented practitioners have highlighted the benefits of clearly defining goals for behavior change. The same techniques apply to psychologists building a practice as to parents trying to encourage their children to clean their rooms or cooperate with their siblings. General and vaguely defined practices are unlikely to grow. Specific specialties or subspecialties can act as magnets to increase the practitioner's visibility and lead to referrals from other professionals who might otherwise feel competitive and protect themselves from a potential loss of work. Narrow specialization, of course, also has its dangers; it may lead to such a narrow image that, even though everyone in the community refers all obese, diabetic, schizophrenic, men with right hemisphere brain damage to the same psychologist, the frequency of such referrals is unlikely to be suffi-cient to maintain a practice.

An example of a successful-practice definition may help. One clinical psychologist of my acquaintance spends a significant portion of her pro-

Figure 1

Psychological businesses and services potentially offerable by independent practitioners

1. Consultation to community organizations.
   a. General program evaluation.
   b. Organization analysis and organization development.
   c. Establishment of specific programs such as evaluation of clients prior and subsequent to treatment or rehabilitation.
2. Consultation to industrial organizations.
   a. Manager development.
   b. Training programs.
   c. Organization analysis and organization development.
   d. Reduction of communication blockages among key people.
   e. Conflict resolution.
   f. Appraisals of employees and candidates for hire.
   g. Consultation regarding specific problems, such as alcohol and drug abuse, absenteeism, and poor morale.
   h. General employee counseling.
   i. Stress-management training.
   j. Establishment of an assessment center.
3. Traditional clinical services.
   a. Child and family evaluation and treatment.
   b. Marital counseling.
   c. Group therapy.
   d. Individual diagnosis and treatment.
   e. Special programs for clients with phobias, anorexia, obesity, sustance abuse, or other identifiable symptoms.
   f. Supervision of subdoctoral-level practitioners.
4. Vocational and career-guidance services.
   a. Career planning.
   b. Outplacement counseling.
   c. Counseling regarding returning to the world of work.
   d. Interview-skill training.
5. Other services.
   a. Assessment and remediation of general-education and specific-learning disabilities.
   b. Summer-camp programs for "special" children.
   c. Supervised encounter-group programs.
   d. Adult psychological educational needs.
   e. Forensic psychology.
   f. Retirement and preretirement planning.
   g. In-service training for professional and paraprofessional workers.
   h. Provision of adequate housing for mentally retarded and emotionally handicapped citizens.
   i. Provision of supervised halfway houses to meet a wide variety of recognized needs.
   j. Day-care, respite, and training programs for many citizens currently unable to find adequate "mental health" facilities.
   k. Consultation to nursing homes.

fessional time outside of her office. She has developed an image as a community-based practitioner. Recently, while riding with an ambulance crew prior to developing a crisis-management and stress-management workshop series for the ambulance company drivers and emergency medical technicians, she received a call from a local bank that was undergoing a post-robbery, hostage-holding seige. She sped to the bank, worked with police and bank personnel, and counseled with the hostages and their families after the crisis had ended. She later developed a follow-up program with the victims as well as a proactive, stress-crisis inoculation service for personnel in all of the bank's branches. These assignments came about as a direct result of the psychologist's business plan. She was seen as an expert in group conflict management and team building. A significant part of her practice deals with marital and family counseling, which she considers similar to her community endeavors. She does minimal individual psychotherapy. She, therefore, is not seen as a threat by the local psychotherapists, who often refer family problems to her. Her definition of her practice and her image enhance the quality and quantity of her worklife.

Determining how to "sell" the services offered

This requires developing a marketing plan:

1. Selection of a location for an office, and the size, comfort, and decor should all be related to the type of clientele you expect to serve.
2. In identifying and evaluating the competition, it is important to define the competition broadly. We must recognize that our clientele may well seek services we perceive as psychological in nature from psychiatrists, social workers, internists, pediatricians, gynecologists, other physicians, marriage and family counselors, clergy people, lawyers, astrologers, hypnotists, self-help groups, community agencies, TM groups, TA groups, faith healers, self-help courses in churches and colleges, and many others.
3. Developing a plan to attract clients involves four variables: (a) establishing, sharpening, modifying, or making good use of your *image;* (b) deciding upon a *pricing* structure; (c) determining what *type* of client services you will offer, e.g., at what times will you see clients, how quickly can you meet a request for service, how quickly will your reports get to the referrer, will you testify in court, are you willing to travel to a client's home, school, or work establishment, will you communicate with referring professionals, etc.; and (d) developing a *plan* to communicate everything you have decided to the community.

A business-plan worksheet and six different psychological-practice plans are presented by Lewin (1978), along with a discussion of the practical utility of this means of preparing for an independent practice. Siegel and Rydman (1980), two experienced practitioners, presented an open and honest dialogue about how they started and built their very different practices; the need to avoid rigid "how to" rules becomes clear, as they discuss the differences (as well as the similarities) in their professional lives. Long-term practitioners (Kissel, in press; Pressman, 1979; Quirk, 1974; Shimberg, 1979) offer further insights into the lure and lore of independent practice. In addition, a fascinating historical contrast between today's world of psychology and that of 20 years ago can be found by comparing the approaches of the recent books on private practice with that of Harrower (1961), who "was among those attempting to define and develop the role of the independent clinical practitioner." Her book clearly illustrates the power of the medical model in the 1950s; it also demonstrates her commitment to the scientist-practitioner model, as well as her confidence in the ability of clinical psychologists to make significant contributions to the community, despite their self-accepted ancillary role in the mental health arena of the 1950s and early 1960s.

BUSINESS (PRACTICE) OPERATION

Managing

Most psychologists avoid looking at the business side of their practices. They look at themselves as professionals, not managers. Each independent practitioner is, indeed, primarily a service provider; it is this aspect of the practice that generates income. Independent practitioners must deliver psychological services in order to exist, but they must also manage. Managing can be conceptualized abstractly into the following areas: (1) planning and budgeting, priority setting, establishing objectives; (2) monitoring and controlling; (3) organizing; (4) staffing, specifying support needs (secretarial, accounting, legal, management, additional psychological services, etc.), recruiting personnel, selecting them, and training them; and (5) directing, guiding, motivating, and supervising the staff to achieve the practice's goals. Is this process really an essential part of establishing and maintaining a practice of clinical psychology? The following case history can illustrate the practical value of such a systematic approach. Indeed, the psychologist in question discovered that the quality of his work (and personal) life was directly related to the care taken to managing his practice:

> Dr. Arthur Brown's practice grew nicely. He enjoyed his mix of psychotherapy and psychodiagnostic work and derived much pleasure from the supervision and consulting he did at a rural community mental health center, about 30 miles south of his city. He decided that he could now afford a

secretary, and he asked some friends if they knew anyone who was available. He interviewed a few women and learned that he had given no thought to the specifics of what he expected her to do. He hired an attractive young woman, who was a pleasant receptionist and a fair typist. She, however, had a strong need for affiliation. She soon became lonely and unhappy in the solitary job setting of her office. She left. He then hired another woman, who spoke well and appeared to be well organized. She had previously worked for a law firm. She understood the concept of confidentiality, and she reported that she preferred working in a one-person office. At first he was pleased with her; then he began to note some paranoid ideation. He mentioned the change to a lawyer friend, who laughed and said, "And you're the psychologist!" His secretary had a long history of idiosyncratic and oftentimes bizarre behavior; she was well known and persona non grata in the legal community, where she had held several jobs. Why hadn't he checked references? Why indeed! Art Brown was a good learner. He had learned a little more about himself and about the employee selection procedure. The next time around, he took the hiring task more seriously. He defined the types of responsibilities he expected the secretary to assume, he developed a series of selection interview questions, and he called previous employers to verify the basic data and obtain references. He discovered that new governmental regulations severely restrict the sharing of specific judgments about a previous employee's performance, but he also discovered that his systematic search enabled him to select a winner.

Little by little, Art's secretary took over more and more responsibilities. She handled his banking, organized his records, and established a tickler file to insure his follow-up on numerous matters. She also began to schedule appointments for him. He had previously spent much time talking with referrers or potential clients before setting a time to meet with them. He was thrilled with the time savings that accrued. His practice was growing very profitable, but he was spending more time report writing than he had previously, and he was enjoying his work less. After a year went by, he began to realize what had happened. He had lost control of his practice. He was very busy, but he had never given any conscious thought to specifying plans and directions that he wanted to go. His professional life was being directed by others. Several community gatekeepers valued his diagnostic work. They kept a steady flow of clients coming his way. His secretary booked them as she had been instructed to do. As a result, so much time was filled in with diagnostic work that it began to crowd out opportunities for therapy and for "marketing" visits to people and settings that could broaden his work opportunities. Recognizing this, he decided to define the type of practice he wanted, specify specific action plans to achieve it, and develop a means of monitoring his practice on a monthly, quarterly, and annual basis, to insure that results conformed to his plans. For example, he decided to limit himself to four diagnostic evaluations per week. He scheduled appointments further ahead than he had ever done before, and he established a system whereby he could fill in canceled appointments from those on his waiting list.

The practical nuts-and-bolts aspects of establishing a practice

Few psychologists plunge into private practice immediately after obtaining their doctorates. State or provincial licensing (the minimum level of accreditation in our field) generally requires one to two years of post-doctoral experience, and the ABPP diploma, our profession's highest quality-control measure, requires a minimum of four years of post-doctoral training in order to become board eligible or board certified. In addition to the legal requirements, however, recognition of the level of professional and personal maturity required in private practice often leads us to seek a few years of seasoning in a supervised setting. This can be a helpful interlude, both professionally and from a business point of view. It enables the would-be private practitioner to slowly and systematically develop a business plan—and begin to test its practicality. The psychologist can determine the ideal mix of clientele desired in the practice and can identify the key community gatekeepers for those services. A systematic plan can be established to ease the transition from employee to part-time and then to a full-time private practice.

One practical approach involves starting a small, independent practice, while maintaining full-time employment. This forces the psychologist to put in longer hours than usual, and it will impact on family relationships, but it significantly lowers the risk of establishing a new professional identity. It also permits the implementation of a carefully planned, market research effort. Indeed, this transition time can enable the psychologist to identify and approach the key community gatekeepers of human services. This can lead to a fuller and more accurate appreciation of gaps in needed psychological services and to the development of a specific business plan. This method also permits a leisurely exploration of office space needs, costs, and availability; and it almost always opens up new and previously unconsidered options, which may include joining a group of colleagues who feel ready to expand, accepting a position in or consulting with a police force, an industrial organization, or a social agency that is expanding.

Budgeting

Although private practice is often seen as the golden yellow brick road to fortune, few nonentrepreneurs recognize the high costs of establishing and maintaining such an enterprise. Lewin (1978, p. 74) concluded by noting that "starting a business is exciting but scary. Starting one without doing one's homework is foolhardy. Those who rush into private practice fast often repent at leisure. So start slowly and increase the probability of enjoying your professional practice." Hendrickson, Janney, and Fraze (1980, p. 205) report,

Initially, many individuals who considered opening a private practice *under-estimated start-up costs*. They think in terms of renting office space, hanging out a shingle, and commencing practice. Upon second glance . . . there is a little more to it. The waiting room, office, and therapy rooms must be furnished. Lease, utility, and telephone deposits must be made. File cabinets, business and therapy forms, and supplies must be purchased. Insurance premiums must be paid in advance. . . . These can add up to a staggering sum.

But that's not all. The practitioner must also possess enough money to live until receipts start coming in. The financial worksheets in Figures 2 and 3 enable estimation of both one-time start-up costs and the ongoing monthly costs of doing business as a private practitioner.

The office

Several private-practice manuals (Hendrickson et al., 1980; Kissel, in press; Lewin, 1978; Pressman, 1979; *Psychotherapy Finances,* 1980; Shimberg, 1979; Siegel, 1980) discuss the variables involved in selecting and furnishing an office. Pressman (1979) includes an appendix with

Figure 2

Financial worksheet

Start-up one-time costs	Estimated cost
Rental security deposit	$_____
Initial professional supplies	_____
Office furniture (including typewriter, phone-answering device, desks, chairs, file cabinets, etc.)	_____
Office supplies—Expendables	_____
Signs for door and building	_____
Announcement promotional expenses	_____
Telephone installation	_____
Legal and accounting start-up costs	_____
Cash for first month's salary (or living expenses) (since there is likely to be a time lag between starting the practice and receiving initial payments of billings)	_____
Total	$_____

Figure 3

Estimated fixed and variable monthly payments

Item	Estimated expenses
Salary or draw of practitioner	$_____
FICA (Social Security)	_____
Secretarial and other wages	_____
Secretarial FICA	_____
State and federal taxes	_____
Unemployment insurance	_____
Office rent	_____
Office cleaning and maintenance	_____
Office supplies (pens, paper, stationary, type-writer ribbons, photocopying, etc.)	_____
Professional supplies	_____
Professional memberships, books, and journals	_____
Continuing-education and convention expenses	_____
Postage	_____
Telephone	_____
Utilities	_____
Travel expenses	_____
Professional liability insurance	_____
Medical insurance	_____
Income protection insurance	_____
Comprehensive: Fire, theft, office, liability insurance	_____
Life insurance	_____
Professional services (legal and accounting)	_____
Pension payments	_____
Depreciation on furniture and office equipment	_____
Miscellaneous (gifts, business lunches, charity, allowance for uncollectable bills, etc.)	_____
Total	$_____

examples of office layout and traffic flow; Hendrickson et al. (1980) detail the furniture and equipment likely to be required; and others discuss other aspects of office design, office soundproofing, and office supplies. Many helpful ideas can be obtained through these readings, but the final decision is a personal one. Practitioners spend many hours in their offices; they should select the setting in which they will feel most comfortable. The reception area, too, is important. It gives clients their initial impression of the psychologist.

Its impact is great. It should reflect what you want it to reflect. Neatness, security of files, manner of the secretary-receptionist, availability of books and magazines to read, and privacy during waiting periods should all be considered. It is as important as the psychologist's office, and as much care should be taken with it as with the inner sanctum. Books and magazines may seem like unimportant details, but they do play a role in how the professional is seen. Are they current and clean or old and torn? Do they deal with psychological issues and/or other matters relevant to the clientele? Is there a variety of materials for differing clientele?

A well-designed and cared-for office is easier for staff to live in and clients to visit. It can also have a major impact on the practioner's image in the eyes of all those who come in contact with it. It is an important variable in one's practice. (Lewin, 1978, p. 83)

Generating referrals

Announcement of services. Indirect contacts with potential clients of referrals are the easiest to arrange and the least expensive, in terms of cost per contact. Mailed announcements of the initiation of the practice and the services offered are in the category of indirect contacts, as are paid announcements in local newspapers and brief, local newspaper articles reporting on the practice opening. A listing in the telephone yellow pages is another indirect contact method. These methods, in my experience, are unlikely to generate many referrals; they may, however, have a cumulative effect by increasing the visibility and recognition level of the practitioner.

Psychological services are very personal and reasonably high priced. Few professionals will refer anyone to an unknown psychologist. The way to generate referrals, therefore, is by the time-intensive method of personal contact. Personal letters and a follow-up phone call can be used to set up face-to-face meetings with key gatekeepers. Breakfast or luncheon meetings are desirable; they give an opportunity to "break bread" and socialize briefly, as well as to inform the contact of your professional skills and interests. More important, of course, is to be an active listener who discovers the felt needs. A brief, follow-up letter can then focus on the personal aspects of the contact's psychological-service needs. This personal approach is likely to produce a much more satisfying referral base than the indirect method.

Referred leads. Every successful visit with key centers of referral influence can lead to new potential sources of referral. How? Simply and openly: just say, "Thanks so much for your time. I've enjoyed meeting you and learning about the way you deal with psychological issues that arise. You've had a change to learn about my interest, too. I wonder which of your colleagues you judge might also be interested in learning of my services." You will be pleasantly surprised at the number of physicians, attorneys, clergy people, and community-agency workers who gladly suggest names of people to visit.

Follow-up on contacts with gatekeepers. It is necessary to meet potential referrers, but it is also essential to convince them that you are both competent and available. When they judge that you can help them enhance their reputations with their clientele (by doing a good job and demonstrating that the referrer has access to good community resources), they are likely to continue to recommend that their clients seek out your services. The care and feeding of gatekeepers is an active process. It starts immediately after the first visit, when a personalized letter is sent, thanking the person for spending time with you and noting the special concerns or interests that were discussed. Enclosing an article, referral form, or some other sign of personal attention can also increase the likelihood of receiving a referral. And, when clients agree, sharing information on an as-needed basis can also enhance the quality of the relationship. Last, keeping a systematic record of all contacts with referring parties can help in monitoring and improving the quality of the relationship that evolves.

An overview of the referral-generating process. (From a prepublication draft of a monograph on professional marketing by Lewin.)

1. Clearly define the services you wish to offer.
2. Determine who are the key gatekeepers of these services in the community you wish to serve.
3. Set realistic goals for meeting them.
4. Call on the gatekeepers, listen to them, and learn their perceptions of community needs. Explain your services and your approach.
5. Obtain referral leads from each of your contacts.
6. Send each person you meet a personalized thank-you letter, in which you note their concerns and your willingness to meet them. Include a referral form, an article in which they expressed interest, or some other sign of personal attention to them.
7. Record the fact and the nature of the visit, so that a personalized follow-up can be made in the future.

Additional strategies. (1) Many psychologists have found that presenting full-day, half-day, or two-hour mini seminars geared to the needs of special categories of key gatekeepers (school counselors, pediatricians, internists, attorneys, industrial human-resources personnel, etc.) can highlight their skills and give them good visibility. A low-cost breakfast or luncheon meeting on "What's new in . . ." a particular field can give the presenter an opportunity to impart information, while also demonstrating specialized knowledge and skill. One caution: much follow-up is required to insure that people actually come to the workshop; merely sending out announcements is likely to result in a disappointing response. This process is not easy, but, when well managed, it does work. (2) Volunteering services, in addition to its intrinsic rewards, can also increase the psychologist's visibility and can lead to referrals. (3) Speaking before PTA groups, various Bar Association groups, medical-specialty groups, and other special-interest group organizations can also generate contacts and referrals. (4) Developing and distributing referral forms that can be easily completed by gatekeepers can encourage referrals to you while also helping to ensure that proper background information is received prior to the client's first visit. (5) Maintaining contacts with referral sources in a way that they find helpful can further strengthen their loyalties to you, while simultaneously improving the quality of care received by each client. Attention to the etiquette of managing relationships with other professionals, therefore, is a helpful tool in improving the quality of client care while enhancing the strength and breadth of your referral base. In addition, periodic requests for feedback from each referrer (Lewin, 1973, 1978) can also enhance your understanding of that gatekeeper's needs and interests. This, too, can lead to better treatment and to a more secure, mutually satisfying bonding between the referrer and the provider of psychological services.

Establishing fees

How much are psychological services worth? How much is it appropriate to charge? What does money mean to the psychologist, the client, and the community at large? How comfortable are you charging for your time? Each psychologist must grapple with these questions on a personal basis. There are, fortunately, some guidelines that can be used to establish a fee structure. State and local psychological associations often have data about rates charged in various locals; community mental health centers often have maximum rates that are close to the going rate in the community; and Blue Shield programs also usually set a maximum reimbursible rate for psychotherapy, which is close to the community standards. Asking local private practitioners their rates can also give you a good idea of the range of fees charged in your immediate locale. In general, it is good business practice to set a standard fee rather than a sliding scale; third-party payers (insurance companies) may well claim that your usual fee is your average fee when a sliding-fee schedule is used. It is therefore better to quote and use a single-fee structure, except in cases in which you elect to make an exception for any of a number of reasons.

Collecting fees

Not all clients pay their bills. This is a sad bit of reality that becomes apparent to all private practitioners. Proactive steps can be taken. They include informing referral sources and clients of the billing policies and procedures before the service is rendered. This fair approach permits people to determine their readiness to afford the bill when it comes. Many practitioners now expect payment on the day of service, and acceptance of credit-card payments is becoming more and more common. There is a small fee to the bank servicing the account, but this process lowers billing costs and results in quicker receipt of money owed. Close attention needs to be given to accounts receivable as they age, since long-overdue bills are hard to collect. Several of the practice manuals (Hendrickson et al., 1980; Kissel, in press; Lewin, 1978; Pressman, 1979; *Psychotherapy Finances,* 1980; Shimberg, 1979) detail the various, alternative approaches used to increase the speed of payments and decrease the bad-debt problems that are faced in most private practices. The ultimate step, of course, is to use a collection agency or a lawyer to sue the client in order to obtain the money due.

"How to File an Insurance Form" (Puffer, 1980) is a helpful cassette tape, that details ways to meet the needs of insurance companies. The quicker the practitioner learns to do this, the fewer "returned for correction or additional information" forms will be received from the third-party payers and the more quickly will payments be received.

Use of accountants

Fraze, of Hendrickson et al. (1980), is an accountant. Their book, therefore, emphasizes many aspects of finance and accounting. Even though psychologists tend to be bright and highly verbal, we are often unable to decipher many IRS regulations or jargon-filled financial guidelines. It is, therefore, helpful to find an accountant who speaks your language and who is familiar with the needs of other professionals in private practice. Indeed, asking your psychologist, lawyer, dentist, and physician friends to identify the accountant with whom they are pleased can help you develop a pool of potential financial consultants from which you will choose your accountant. What can accountants do for you? Basically, they can serve as financial and tax advisors. They can:

1. Help you budget and monitor your expense patterns and set up books, so that you can simply and accurately account for what comes in and what goes out of your practice.
2. Keep you aware of laws, rules, and regulations, so that you can most effectively use your money in ways consistent with IRS policies.
3. Advise on the tax implications of remaining an independent practitioner, forming a partnership, incorporating or "going Subchapter S," a means of incorporating while permitting income to be taxed as if it were purely personal income.
4. Help you establish depreciation schedules on your capital goods (typewriters, dictating machines, telephone-answering devices, furniture, photocopying machines, office building, car, etc.).

5. Give you guidelines regarding legal tax shelters, such as Keogh plans and pension and profit sharing plans.
6. Determine whether or not income averaging can help you save on taxes in peak-income years. Indeed, many individual practitioners may find that they can save on taxes if their income in any one year is more than $3,000 greater than 120 percent of their average net income of the previous four years.

Use of a secretary, receptionist, office manager, or administrative assistant

Many practitioners start out by being a one-person business. They are their own chief of professional services, secretary, receptionist, typist, bookkeeper, appointment scheduler, financial manager, janitor, and, like Pooh Bah in Gilbert and Sullivan's *Mikado,* "Lord High Everything Else." Once the business grows, especially if report writing becomes an important part of the workload, this is a penny-wise, pound-foolish choice. Not only does an office manager/administrative assistant enhance one's image and give the office a more organized and professional appearance, but it also saves professional time—the only billable commodity a private practitioner has. The specific duties of this employee often include typing reports and letters, answering the phone, scheduling appointments, sorting the mail, paying bills, posting the ledger, banking, maintaining a tickler file to ensure proper follow-up of all details, checking office and professional supplies, preparing a list of the practitioner's daily and weekly schedules, tidying up rooms, overseeing clients in the reception area, noting and reporting on the reception area idiosyncracies of clients and of those who accompany them, giving clients whatever forms are required for them, maintaining client and business files in a well-organized way, collecting monies received, and generally representing the practitioner to clients, referral sources, and all others who come in contact with the office.

Use of lawyers

Lewin (1978) devoted an entire chapter to the use of lawyers. It is an important theme that is often overlooked by psychologists. Much of what we do professionally involves informal (and sometimes formal) contracts of one form or another. All that means is that when people make promises to each other, as is the case between psychologists and their clients, their employees, and their colleagues, these agreements may well be binding even if they are not written and signed. Whenever we do this, or whenever we sign a purchase order or an insurance form without fully understanding it, or without fully understanding the consequences of what we have done, we may find ourselves in legal difficulties. Signing a lease; subletting an office; entering into a partnership; incorporating the practice; hiring an employee, either full- or part-time, either professional or a support person; and making a major purchase are all examples of actions that are likely to have implications of which a psychologist may be unaware. Legal advice should be sought before the action is taken; it is cheaper and more efficient when problems are avoided rather than resolved. The same principles involved in selecting an accountant apply to selecting a lawyer. After the lawyer is retained, he or she can be sought for advice about the legal structure of the practice (proprietorship, the easiest and least complicated type of business; a general or limited partnership; or a corporation). The lawyer will also be able to answer questions about confidentiality, collection procedures, and other little matters that arise regularly in the course of a practice.

Concluding thoughts

There are myriad, additional details that could be discussed under the rubric of establishing and maintaining a private practice in clinical psychology. The many manuals listed in the bibliography give guidelines for the nuts and bolts of the everyday worklife of the practitioner. Record keeping, insurance needs, part-time practice variables, time-management principles, and money-management principles are all covered in one or another of the publications listed. Advances in technology (word-processing machines, improved telephone systems, programming of computers to help us analyze personal history and test data, etc.) are going to change the nature of clinical practice; this will require flexibility and readiness to adapt to new aids and new conditions not yet dreamed of by most of us. This type of future shock will change our lives, but more important to the theme of this chapter, it will modify community needs. It is my firm belief that psychology has the capacity to greatly enhance its influence on our society. We know much more about understanding, predicting, and modifying human behavior than we credit ourselves. It is essential that we recognize our limitations, but this ought not to make us timid. Experiencing our doubts is wholesome, as long as our fear leads to the careful planning of professional actions, rather than to withdrawal from important societal areas.

Psychologists as businesspeople can find many undertapped markets to serve. Each of us can increase our service to society and our professional satisfactions by expanding our horizons and changing our model of clinical practice. Lewin (1978, pp. 136–40) wrote, "What are some areas to which we can contribute? They are almost infinite. Every stage of human and of group change involves individual and interpersonal stress. Our psychological and behavioral science skills can be used to help solve these problems. We are already somewhat active in early childhood development in preschool and school adjustment, in premarital and marital counseling, and in counseling of the aged in nursing homes, but we have had only minimal impact in areas such as:

1. Pre-college counseling

Helping college-bound students determine their interests and values so that they can make better choices of colleges to which they should apply, of major fields of study, and of transitional experiences they may need to improve their probability of enjoying and benefiting from training.

2. Pre-work counseling

Introducing high school or college graduates to the psychological aspects of the world of work. Introducing them to the wide varieties of jobs available on the outside. Offering an introduction to the behavioral and lifestyle differences between work and school. Teaching career-planning methodologies and job-survival skills, resume writing, interviewing skills, budgeting and money-management techniques to help ease this transition.

3. Pre-promotion counseling

Promotions often entail assuming new social and work roles and may lead to internal conflict as well as conflict with former peers. We have skills to help people function more smoothly and effectively in the circumstances.

4. Pre-job change

Change usually leads to stress and anxiety. Stress and anxiety reduce efficiency in complex tasks. People change jobs regularly. We know this effects individuals, spouses, and families. We can harness our knowledge to good advantage in these situations.

5. Pre-firings/layoffs

One of my industrial clients euphemistically speaks of helping unwanted employees 'redirect their careers.' These efforts are rarely wholehearted or guilt free. Don't we have the skills to help individuals and organizations see themselves and their unique configurations of assets and liabilities more accurately, so that they can use them most beneficially for themselves and for the community?

6. Pre-divorce counseling

When our society's divorce rate is soaring, ought we not consider ways of helping spouses leave a marriage with a sense of dignity and with sufficient knowledge to make a better choice of spouse the next time around?

7. *Career planning*

The average American appears to spend more time and effort selecting a car than either a spouse or a career. There are principles of career planning and career development that can be taught. They can help individuals and society make better use of human resources. Psychologists can contribute more than we have in this area.

8. *Pre-retirement planning*

A horrendous number of our citizens reach retirement age with nary a thought about what life will offer them. They dream of staying home and relaxing, of fishing, of gardening, or of enjoying time with their spouses. They are rarely introduced to life-planning skills. They too often discover that their dreams have no substance in reality. All their former social supports have been taken away and they lack substitutes.

9. *Retirement planning*

'Grow old along with me, the best is yet to be,' wrote Robert Browning (in the poem *Rabbi Ben Ezra*). 'Tain't so,' say hundreds of thousands of goal-less aged, living a marginal existence in our cities and countryside. They unknowingly await the services of social scientists with interests in developing life-planning methodologies for the over-60 age group.

10. *Pre-admission to nursing home counseling*

Many senile nursing home residents are more depressed than organically impaired. They see placement in the home as a last resort, an admission that they are either unmanageable or dying. Can we keep these thoughts from being self-fulfilling prophesies?

11. *Health counseling*

Alcohol, tobacco, and other drug abuse; reckless driving; poor attention to diet and nutrition; and unrealistic perception of one's physical condition and capabilities are all serious and major causes of human injuries and suffering. They also have a major impact on the country's economic functioning. Why don't people do what is in their best interest? Psychologists don't know, but we have the research skills to discover why.

12. *Illness of a loved one*

This often has dramatic and negative effects on the functioning of all concerned. Psychological preparation could help all concerned handle their feelings and actions more appropriately.

13. Environmental impact

Hospital—school—town planning: the quality of life is directly effected by environmental factors. Can't we learn and use our skills to help establish structures that are more likely to lead to social enhancement?

14. Vacation planning

Slowly, we are moving to a four-day week. It sounds great, but too few of us know how to use recreational time effectively. Computer dating programs appear to help some of their clientele. Why not computer vacation programs, in which we analyze the interests of a client and those of the client's intimates, spouse and/or family in order to suggest appropriate prevacation planning activities and vacation settings. Is the "psychoanalysis vacation service" a potentially profitable one for both clients and practitioners?

15. International relations

Can psychological and sociological principles help us interpret and control our actions and those of others more effectively? Should psychologists be placed in high positions in many government departments? Could we make contributions there? As consultants? As policy makers?

16. General policymaking

Psychologists tend to function as consultants in most large organizations. We can advise, guide, and counsel the chief executive officer using our knowledge, but we rarely are in positions to implement our ideas. We have accepted this ancillary staff role for many years. Clinicians have done so in large part because we (in George Albee's terms), like the cuckoo, are the only ones to lay our eggs in other bird's nests. One of the consequences of moving into hospitals has been our placement in a secondary role. Other professional psychologists have not been hampered in this way. Despite that, few of us have achieved major policymaking places. John Gardner has the distinction of having held the highest governmental position of any psychologist. He was a cabinet member who served as secretary of the Department of Health, Education, and Welfare. Warren Bennis is another professional psychologist to hold a top-level managerial job as a university president; Timothy Costello was vice mayor of New York City before returning to academia; Frank Stanton was president of CBS for many years; Alfred J. Marrow was president and chairman of the board of Harwood Manufacturing Companies; and others have achieved positions in which their psychological skills were integrated into overall management and policymaking positions. In general, however, we are underutilized; we have much more to offer as psychologists, planners, administrators, and organization developers.

These 16 areas are among the fertile grounds that psychologists have not yet tilled to any major degree. Some of these services would be easy to 'sell,' some would prove more difficult. In general, it is easier to sell psychological services to people who are in crisis. When they hurt, they seek help and are willing to pay for it. When things are comfortable, proactive preventive programs often seem too expensive."

It is my hope that an increasingly assertive group of sensitive, creative, clinical psychologists will emerge and play a major role in the betterment of society. We are a distinguished group of professionals who will, I have no doubt, generate new and socially valuable concepts, principles, tools, and techniques. Psychology is a vibrant science, but the practice of psychology is a business. We will need to learn the management sciences, in order to best implement our potential contributions to our community.

SUMMARY

This chapter provides a systematic method of assessing one's motivations for and readiness to enter into the independent practice of clinical psychology. It also presents a practical approach to the business-planning aspects of establishing and maintaining a successful practice that is both professionally and financially satisfying to the practitioner. Additional areas covered include: budgeting, generating referrals, establishing fees, collecting monies owed for services, use of accountants, use of lawyers, use of administrative-support staff, and nontraditional areas of service in which psychological skills remain underutilized.

REFERENCES

Harrower, M. *The practice of clinical psychology.* Springfield, Ill.: Charles C Thomas, 1961.

Hendrickson, D. E., Janney, S. P., & Fraze, J. E. *How to establish your own private practice.* Muncie, Ind.: Professional Consultants Associates, 1980.

Kissel, S. A. *A clinician's guide to private practice.* Kensington, Md.: Aspern Press, in press.

Korman, M. (Ed.). *Levels and patterns of professional training in psychology.* Washington, D.C.: American Psychological Association, 1976.

Lewin, M. H. Consumerism in the private office. *Professional Psychology,* 1973, *4,* 1.

Lewin, M. H. *Establishing and maintaining a successful professional practice.* Rochester, N.Y.: Professional Development Institute, 1978.

Posluns, D. Not in our stars. *Ontario Psychologist,* 1974, *6,* 36–41.

Practice building: How to make specialization pay. *Psychotherapy Finances.* 1979, *6,* 1–3.

Pressman, R. M. *Private practice: A handbook for the independent mental health practitioner.* New York: Gardner Press, 1979.

Psychotherapy Finances. Guide to private practice. Ridgewood, N.J.: Ridgewood Financial Institute, 1980.

Puffer, L. *How to file an insurance form.* Dallas: Wilmington Press, 1980.

Quirk, D. A. Personal reflections on private practice as business. *Ontario Psychologist,* 1974, *6,* 42–48.

Shimberg, E. *The handbook of private practice in psychology.* New York: Bruner & Mazel, 1979.

Siegel, J., & Rydman, E. *How to start and conduct a private practice.* Dallas: Wilmington Press, 1980.

Watson, N., Caddy, G. R., Johnson, J. H., & Rimm, D. C. Standards in the education of professional psychologists: The resolutions of the conference at Virginia Beach. *American Psychologist,* 1981, *36,* 514–519.

37

The psychologist
as administrator

*Rodney R. Baker, Ph.D.**

This chapter outlines the demands made on a psychologist serving in the role of administrator of service programs in such settings as community mental health centers and hospitals. Administrative demands are highlighted and clinical service demands are de-emphasized. This focus is not due to the lack of importance of clinical service demands, but rather is chosen because of the unfamiliarity and discomfort with administrative demands that lead to frustrations for psychologists serving in these roles. References to readings in management science texts are suggested to familiarize psychologists with management concepts and techniques. To include a variety of roles and settings in which the psychologist might function as administrator, the term *administrator* will be used interchangeably with such terms as *project director, program manager,* or *supervisor.* References to higher-level management will similarly include any designated superior to whom the psychologist administrator must report.

The chapter outlines an imposing array of demands on administrators. The purpose is not to discourage psychologists from assuming such roles but rather to prepare them to respond effectively to those demands. Psychologists have much to offer organizations in the management of people and programs. Those outside of the psychology profession are beginning to recognize and appreciate these contributions, and psychologists themselves are responding to the rewards and challenges of administrative roles.

THE EXPANDING ROLE OF THE
PSYCHOLOGIST AS ADMINISTRATOR

During the last 15 years, psychologists increasingly have been called upon to serve in administrative positions. In addition to traditional adminis-

* Chief of Psychology Service, VA Medical Center, San Antonio.

trative positions (such as, chief of a psychology department in a clinical or academic setting), psychologists occupy positions as directors of community mental health centers, directors of hospital treatment units, and project directors of federal, state, and community service programs. In a 1966 survey of chief psychologists, 23 percent reported that their staff were serving in a management position in their clinical setting (Stewart & Harsch, 1966). A replication of this survey 10 years later, by Wildman and Wildman (1976), indicated that this figure had risen to 60 percent. In these same surveys, the attitude of psychologists toward those administrative roles were also noted to change. In 1966, over half the respondents engaged in treatment-program administration had mixed feelings or reservations about their role. In 1976, two thirds reported a positive feeling about their role as administrator.

Even without a defined administrative position, psychologists in institutional settings spend from 20 to 40 percent of their time in such administrative functions as treatment program planning, program evaluation, preparation of management reports, and participation in administrative staff meetings and committees (Baker, 1978). Psychologists in community mental health centers spend an average of 15 hours a week of their on-duty time in administrative activities (Bloom & Parad, 1977).

This increasing administrative role for psychologists has not been without its problems. In many programs, psychologists are functioning as high-level administrators without formal training for their role (Bloom, 1969). According to Bloom and Parad (1977), almost half the psychologists working in community mental health centers have expressed a need for further training in administration, program planning, and program development. Even though psychologists may spend a smaller percentage of their time in administrative functions, when compared to time spent in clinical functions, most of the reported frustrations and job dissatisfactions of psychologists emerge from their administrative duties (Baker, 1978). Personal and professional rewards are usually associated with research and clinical activities involving direct patient care. The psychologist who assumes an administrative position must integrate professional and administrative roles. This integration is made difficult by the different demands and skills required in these roles (Felzer, 1970; Levenson & Klerman, 1967; Rubenstein, 1968). Management theory, in fact, suggests that the professional as administrator requires more management skills than professional skills to be effective, and yet professionals are often promoted or hired for administrative positions because of the recognition they have received in their professional field. In practice, especially in large programs, the clinical and academic skills of the psychologist may suffer from disuse, as administrative matters require more and more attention. The conflict between administrative and professional roles may finally take the form of competing demands which might arise in a managerial position. The psychologist administrator must sometimes choose between being an advocate for the program and being a member of management seeking to accomplish larger organizational goals. If the administrator assumes a systems view of the organization and the community in which that organization functions, what is best for the program is not always best for the organization and that community. The effectiveness of the psychologist as administrator is thus based on the appreciation of and responsiveness to organizational and system demands and the acquisition or refinement of skills to meet those demands.

DEMANDS MADE ON AN ADMINISTRATOR

Accountability demands

The primary demands made on an administrator in managing a program can be grouped under the general heading of accountability. From a systems viewpoint, the organizations in which psychologists may serve as administrators exist in a health care or service system, which is, in turn, embedded in a society with people who are concerned about the ability to use limited resources in meeting unlimited demands. Accountability systems have been established in the health care field to ensure that programs are needed, that quality services are provided, and that limited resources are being used effectively and efficiently. These accountability systems range from accrediting bodies (such as JCAH for hospital accreditation and APA for accreditation of graduate programs and internship sites) to review and audit processes (such as certificate-of-need programs, peer review, performance appraisal, and sunset legislation). These accountability systems have emerged from the concerns of an enlightened consumer population, professional groups, congressmen, and taxpayers. These systems may be criticized as imperfect and not accomplishing what they are supposed to accomplish, but they represent a concern for accountability that cannot be ignored by institutions and their program managers.

Accountability comprises two elements: an assessment of effectiveness and an assessment of efficiency. An assessment of effectiveness requires the institution to be clear about its objectives and to demonstrate that it is meeting those objectives. Administrators are asked to define program objectives in specific terms that can be observed or measured. General or vague objectives are no longer satisfactory. Performance is the key word in assessing effectiveness, and performance must be measured. Management by objectives and managing for results are management science concepts which have been developed to assist administrators in developing and evaluating program objectives (Drucker, 1965).

Program evaluation skills are also required of the administrator to complete the process of assessing program effectiveness. The establishment of specific program objectives is insufficient for accountability purposes, unless data is obtained which demonstrates the accomplishment of those objectives. Because of their research training, psychologists have an advantage over others serving as administrators. The advantage results from the psychologist's familiarity with the problems and strategies of collecting relevant data. The problem for the psychologist is the tendency to equate the methodology of research and that of program evaluation. This promotes attempts to use the statistical-inference and hypothesis-testing models of research in program evaluation. This is inappropriate for most program evaluation required of organizations. The process of program evaluation is more like that of performance appraisal. If it is important to note whether or not a program is achieving an established objective, and if that objective is clearly defined in terms of desired performance, no statistical tests are required to infer if the objective has been met—the objective either has or has not been met, as determined by the performance data. The process of program evaluation for accountability purposes is outlined in Baker, 1977; Skrovan, Donnell, Grimes, Hennes, and Tinnin, 1970; and Van Maanen, 1973.

The second element of accountability is the task of assessing efficiency. This demand requires the organization or program to demonstrate that the way it is using its resources in accomplishing its objectives is the best way to use them, i.e., at lowest cost or with most benefit to program clients. In practice, for example, if one alcohol treatment program has a 40 percent success rate and another has a 60 percent success rate (assuming similar objectives, resources, and success criteria), support ought to be given to the program with the higher success rate. If resources are limited, support ought to be withdrawn from the lower success rate program, or that program ought to be expected to make the changes necessary to increase its success rate.

The accountability demand to assess effectiveness has grown in importance over the last 10 years. The accountability demand to assess efficiency will have increased prominence during the next decade. Effectiveness and efficiency demands have a common sense base, hence their popularity with consumer advocates and public officials. However, converting the common sense logic of these concepts to operationally defined methods of assessment is difficult, especially in the health care field and other service programs. As noted above, appropriate methodology currently exists for assessing effectiveness, once objectives are appropriately defined; and these methods will be continually refined. The methodology for assessing efficiency, however, is complicated because of the focus on the best way to use resources. In economic terms, efficiency is assessed by cost analysis. A competent accountant or fiscal officer can determine financial costs of a program, including salary costs for service and support personnel and operating costs for space and supplies. These costs can further be described in terms of how much money it costs to provide a service to a single client. However, the accountant cannot adequately assess what the economists refer to as opportunity costs—those programs or services that are not being provided because the money is being spent on something else. The accountant similarly cannot fully assess the benefits of service programs—a determination which requires professional judgment, the establishment of organizational and system priorities, and philosophical and value considerations. Cost analysis stops at the point where a statement is made of how much it costs to provide a service, given an assessed performance level. A more complete assessment of efficiency requires answers to such questions as, "Could we produce the same results with fewer costs?" or "Could we produce quantitatively or qualitatively superior results without increasing costs?" The responsibility of the administrator is to manage programs in such a way that the answer to these questions is no, when the program is periodically reviewed by higher-level management. The accountability demand for assessing efficiency further requires a data base for the administrator's answer to these questions.

Obtaining data to answer such questions requires methodology that is, for the most part, in an early stage of development. Conceptually, the process of assessing efficiency can take many approaches. One approach can be described as the rational-dialogue decision method. This method is essentially a discussion between the program administrator and higher-level management in which the administrator outlines the rational basis for program decisions, including the deployment of staff and operating-cost resources. This method may be strengthened by a description of alternatives and why they are less desirable than current program operations. Cost and program-evaluation data may be part of this dialogue, as may be questions by higher-level management of the feasibility of other alternatives of program operation.

The rational-dialogue method of assessing efficiency has a weak data base and one that is often subjective, which is its major disadvantage. It is also a common method used, partly because of the lack of other agreed-upon methods and partly because of its simplicity. Its major advantage is that it allows for consideration of observations and values that cannot yet be easily quantified. It further encourages a discussion of programs that promotes clearer understanding, involvement, and commitment to those programs on the part of the total organization. Other methods of assessing efficiency may add a more extensive data base to the assessment, but they should not supplant this type of dialogue between the administrator and higher-level management.

More extensive, data-base strategies for assessing efficiency are developed from what have been called program evaluation research models (Struening & Guttentag, 1975). These models are designed to evaluate and compare program options using research strategies, which emphasize pragmatic differences in addition to statistically significant differences. Program evaluation research strategies can also emphasize the efficiency of a program by reporting improvements in program evaluation data over time as a result of program changes (Baker & Lewis, 1977). In the case of specialized treatment programs, benefit-prediction equations can be developed to exclude from programs clients who are unlikely to benefit from the program, thus increasing the number of clients receiving maximum benefits from specialized and expensive resource programs (Baker, 1973).

Accountability issues cannot be completely described in economic or even professional terms. Inherent in accountability demands is a determination of whether or not programs and organizations are responsive to their clients and to consumers and society at large. The values of society will ultimately affect and often override economic considerations, especially in the health care field, as our society struggles with the issue of whether or not health care is a right of its people and determines what programs and services ought to be funded (Fuchs, 1974).

Organizational and program demands

Organizational and program demands made on the administrator range from providing leadership in developing programs to maintaining effective work relationships among program staff. The administrator is also expected to maintain academic and professional skills and, especially in smaller programs, provide direct services to clients. The psychologist who seeks an administrative position often is drawn to these positions because of the opportunity to try out ideas and develop innovative programs. The challenge of developing programs must be considered in context, however. The development and maintenance of programs requires that the administrator initiate and justify requests for resources, manage program staff, inform management of program results and, in short, do all the things necessary to establish a support system for the program. The administrator initially may be given this support system or may inherit it but, if not nurtured and maintained, it may dissipate. Even the most creative and innovative program cannot survive without a support system based on an appropriate response to professional and administrative requirements.

The demands on an administrator require a response to the needs of a client population, the needs of a specific program and its staff, and the needs of the organization. A response to the needs of the client population requires a synthesis of administrative and professional skills. Clinical knowledge and skills are needed to identify client needs and to choose professional services that respond to those needs. Administrative skills in such areas as program planning and personnel management are needed to organize the delivery of professional services into a program consistent with organizational policies and procedures.

The primary need of the program is to justify and maintain its function in the organization. In responding to this need, the administrator must demonstrate the relevance of program objectives to client needs, keep staff informed of the program's role in meeting organizational objectives, and obtain resources to maintain program services. The primary needs of the organization are to justify and maintain its function in meeting client needs. The administrator is thus asked to assist the organization in the development of organizational objectives and the coordination and implementation of a set of programs which, taken together, most efficiently meet the collective needs of the client population. The administrator's primary responsibility in responding to this task is similar to the responsibility in responding to the program's needs. The administrator must keep management informed of the program's contribution to organizational objectives and must inform management of the resource needs of the program.

An incomplete or inadequate response by the administrator to these multiple and interdependent demands may result in a variety of problems for the program and the administrator. For example, a basic concern of the administrator is whether or not sufficient resources will be obtained for program functioning. The competition for resources within an organization is between programs; i.e., determining which programs make the greatest contribution (most unique or efficient) to the organization's objectives. If the administrator does not keep staff aware of the objectives of the organization and the role of the program in those objectives, it will be difficult for program staff to set goals and develop program elements which relate clearly to organizational objectives. The failure to relate program goals to organizational objectives will result in minimal support of the program by higher-level management. The same result will occur if higher-level management is not kept informed by the administrator of the program's value to the organization in accomplishing its objectives. The integration of program objectives with organizational objectives in meeting client needs is a crucial task for the manager and a significant source of satisfaction to the manager when successfully accomplished.

Consumer and labor-force demands

In addition to the demands of consumers and public officials for general accountability, demands are also being made to improve the quality of products and services. Post-World War II organizations operated from a philosophy that more was better, and management planning was directed toward increasing the quantity of goods and services. As resources have become more scarce relative to competing demands, maintaining quantity can only be accomplished by less of an emphasis on quality or by other methods to increase efficiency; i.e., using fewer resources per unit of product or service. Today's consumers complain that the quality of products and services is not sufficient.

A parallel change has occurred in relation to the work force. Whereas the interests of the post-World War II work force were dominated by needs for minimum pay and basic security, today's work force is demanding that organizations and managers pay attention to the quality of the work environment. This involves a variety of issues, ranging from concerns for doing interesting and useful work and being appreciated for work accomplishments to having some involvement in decisions that affect the employee's worklife. It can be noted parenthetically that these latter demands are those which have been ascribed traditionally only to higher-level managers.

In summary, the demands made on the administrator involve several complex tasks: competing for limited resources; responding to accountability demands; producing quality services that meet the needs of a client; and meeting the social and self-esteem needs of a work force. The psychologist administrator is faced with these tasks and must develop and refine skills to assume these responsibilities.

SKILLS REQUIRED OF THE ADMINISTRATOR

Certain skills required of the administrator have already been noted in the discussion of organizational and program demands. These include specific management skills, such as those for program evaluation, and general management skills involved in providing program leadership and in integrating program goals with the goals of the organization and higher-level management. In this section, these general skills are more closely examined under the general headings of planning, managing people, managing restricted resources, and managing within an organization.

Planning, planning, and more planning

Planning for health care on a national level took on new dimensions with the enactment of the National Health Planning and Resource Development Act of 1974 (P.L. 93–641). This represented, at a national level, the first attempt to define in legislation the health care needs in this country and to establish goals or priorities to be followed in meeting those needs (Klarman, 1978; Shonick, 1976). Health care institutions requesting federal funds were to have received approval for major program expansion based on demonstrated needs in the community in which the institution functions. Planning for the interface of programs within an institution within a community is a level of planning activity that may directly or indirectly involve the psychologist administrator. Regardless of the level of involvement, however, these activities underscored the importance of planning for the administrator involved in meeting accountability demands for managing programs.

The purpose of planning is to accomplish program and organizational objectives, and the success of planning is determined by whether or not the planning produces the desired results (Bergwall, 1974). The larger and more complicated the program, the more time the administrator must spend in planning. Some administrators will spend 50 percent or more of their time in planning. To an administrator beset with numerous, time-consuming demands, this seems like an impossibility. It is only when the administrator recognizes that planning is the foundation for effective program leadership that the administrator gives planning the time priority it needs. Planning is a method for dealing with change. For the manager who believes change will not occur or who resists thinking in such terms, planning is not too important. For the manager who recognizes the impact of change on programs, planning becomes an essential tool in dealing with change. Planning skills are needed to acquire and utilize available resources (always limited) to produce a service that accomplishes program objectives in an effective and efficient manner. Effective planning minimizes time spent in solving problems, particularly when problem solving is integrated with planning and considered a part of the planning process.

Managers and organizations traditionally have approached planning as a process of predicting the future and then preparing for it. Predicting the future is a tenuous activity at best, however, and system theorists like Ackoff have challenged this traditional approach. Ackoff (1969, 1974) has offered other planning methodology based on the proactive concept that planning should be based on what managers believe the future ought to be and then inventing ways to bring that future about.

Planning for effective team and program functioning can be summarized into a four-step process. The first step consists of a diagnosis of how the program and staff are currently functioning. This diagnosis is completed by determining both the positive and negative consequences of that functioning to the program, the organization, the client, and the community. The second step is establishing objectives of how the program staff would like to see the program function, setting objectives that will reduce the negative consequences of program functioning, while at the same time maintaining or increasing positive consequences. The third step involves an identification of action plans (who is going to do what and when) to accomplish the new objectives; and the fourth step is the establishment of an evaluation or feedback system to determine if the action plans are accomplishing their objectives (Baker, 1980). The third step involving action planning may be further facilitated by using a problem-solving model, such as force-field analysis (Baker & Paris, 1975).

Planning of the type described above gives direction and creates a focus of work energy for program staff. It also assists in the establishment of clear program objectives and in the evaluation of those objectives, which is required by the accountability demands made on the administrator. Planning of this type can be applied to any aspect of program or administrative functioning by: describing how the program currently functions in the areas being examined; identifying the consequences of that functioning; determining how program staff would like to function in that area; deciding how that functioning can be best accomplished; and determining how that functioning can be evaluated in order to modify plans, if necessary. For example, the program staff can examine how it provides services, makes decisions, solves problems, or resolves disagreement among staff by this planning model. The administrator can also apply this planning to personal behaviors, including how the administrator currently interacts with higher-level management, how resources and program support are maintained, and how program staff are managed. Whether a particular planning model is used or not, a structured approach to planning assists the administrator in providing effective program leadership. The development of planning skills might, in fact, start with a personal examination of how the administrator currently plans for the program and the consequences of those methods—or lack thereof.

Managing people

A major task of the administrator relevant to the success of a program is the selection, development, and utilization of program staff. Accomplishing program objectives through the work of others requires setting work standards, evaluating and correcting work behaviors, and motivating workers. The administrator must develop skills to manage the unproductive employee as well as the creative and highly productive employee. Felzer (1970) notes that the psychologist administrator in a mental health center is often faced with the problem of managing other professionals who may be inexperienced with or unappreciative of administrative procedures, who want to do their work without interference, and who expect to have everything in the way of space, equipment, supplies, and freedom of movement. The psychologist's training and knowledge about group process and human motivation may give them an edge over other administrators in knowing how to manage people, but this advantage is not likely to be sufficient when dealing with the management of people in a work environment helping an organization to accomplish work objectives more efficiently and effectively. The use of clinical techniques in interacting with employees (or higher-level management) may even be counterproductive or create suspicion and antagonism (Bindman, 1972).

Motivating employees and providing leadership for program staff is more than a matter of establishing a reward and punishment system. This carrot-and-stick approach of managing people is limited at best; and yet, many of today's managers are unwilling or unable to give up this philosophy in managing a work force. For example, if a manager believes that money is the only motivating factor in the work force, opportunities will be lost to tap into other motivational factors in accomplishing work objectives. In spite of the complexity of motivational theory as described in both psychological and management texts and journals, managers will often hold to a simplistic view of motivating employees and attempt only to refine strategies for reward and punishment (Herzberg, 1967).

The key to effective management of workers to direct and motivate their efforts for the attainment of program objectives can often be found in the beliefs that the manager has about workers. McGregor (1960) has pointed out that the reward and punishment approach to managing people is based on a belief that the worker is indifferent to organizational needs, prefers to be led, and will work as little as possible to get by. Operating from these beliefs, the manager can, indeed, reinforce behaviors that support these beliefs and, in turn, strengthen the notion that rewards and punishments are required to motivate workers. An alternative set of beliefs that can be assumed by managers in motivating workers is that the worker has the resources and potential to accomplish program objectives and is not inherently passive or indifferent to those objectives. McGregor argues that the passivity or indifference of workers is a result of their previous experiences in the work environment. Maximum productivity is achieved when the manager arranges organizational conditions and methods of operation so that workers can achieve their own goals by directing their efforts toward organizational objectives.

Establishing an environment and method of operation in which workers can achieve both personal and organizational objectives requires a sensitivity to what produces satisfaction in workers. In addition to economic considerations, worker satisfaction generally emerges from doing interesting and useful work, being appreciated for work accomplishments, and being involved in decisions that affect the employee's worklife. These general considerations must be refined further, however, so that the unique needs of workers and the organization can be incorporated into program operations. Specific data to assess worker-satisfaction factors can be obtained through interviews with workers or through formal or informal surveys. Lake, Miles, and Earle (1973) have described and reviewed a variety of instruments which have been used by managers to monitor and evaluate worker satisfaction and other factors affecting productivity and program effectiveness. When the productivity or performance of an individual does not meet established standards, managers must analyze work-environment or procedure factors as well as skill-deficiency factors and avoid labeling such individuals as unmotivated. Such labels are virtually useless for diagnostic purposes or for planning for corrective action. Mager and Pipe (1970) have presented a comprehensive model of analyzing performance problems and corrective options, with a quick-reference checklist of key issues to examine (pp. 101–105).

Crucial to the manager's success in accomplishing work objectives through others is the development and maintenance of effective work teams. The work potential of a group is more than the sum of the individual skills, resources, and contributions of its members. The administrator's task is to ensure that the potential of group effort is realized. Managing a group process requires group planning, group problem solving, communication, giving and receiving feedback, resolving conflict and disagreement, and making decisions that can be supported and implemented by team members. Managing work groups additionally requires the establishment of clear work objectives, work assignments, and expectations of performance. The manager must also establish written and verbal communication systems, including staff meetings with the structure and function needed to facilitate program objectives.

One problem in developing effective work groups in an organization is that there is no clear, universally applicable model for effective group functioning. Even in the same organization, work groups differ in their resources and in the personalities and skills of individuals in the group. Work groups also differ in their assigned work tasks, and they experience different pressures and influences external to the work group. Behaviors or procedures that work well at one point in time may not work well at another point. The manager can examine theory and research conducted over the past several years to identify some general characteristics of effective work groups (Dyer, 1977; Likert, 1961; McGregor, 1960), but these characteristics and models of functioning can only serve as a starting point for the development of effective work teams. The task for the manager interested in maximizing work-group effectiveness in accomplishing program goals is to develop a model of functioning that accomplishes program objectives and is compatible with organizational policy and the unique tasks and resources of program staff (Baker, 1980).

The management style of the administrator significantly affects productivity and morale and the ability of the administrator to effectively manage a work force. The concept of a "managerial grid" was proposed by Blake and Mouton (1968) and used by others to describe a variety of management styles which could be assessed on two dimensions: concern for task (getting the job done) and concern for people (their feelings and needs). Four management styles which emerge from this grid concept are the authoritarian or autocratic style (high concern for task and low concern for people), the permissive or peace-maker management style (low concern for task and high concern for people), the recessive or laissez-faire management style (low concern for task and low concern for people), and the democratic or participative management style (high concern for task and high concern for people). The personality of the administrator and the demands of the organization will determine, to some extent, which management style is adopted by the administrator. Each management style will have a different impact on the work attitude and productivity of workers (Bradford & Lippitt, 1961). With few exceptions, the laissez-faire management style is least effective in promoting work objectives because of the lack of sufficient concern or leadership in meeting the needs of either the organization or its workers. The permissive management style is similarly restricted in accomplishing work objectives, even with the emphasis on concern for people's feelings and needs. If this concern is not integrated with a concern for organizational or program objectives, the work will not be accomplished efficiently or effectively.

The autocratic or authoritarian management style traditionally has been viewed as the most effective by organizations because of its emphasis on tasks and getting the work done. Even when there are no clear, objective measurements indicating this style results in superior performance when compared to other styles, higher-level management will consistently rate the authoritarian manager as more effective (Mullen, 1966). The limitations of this style come from the failure of the authoritarian manager to utilize all of the resources of a work force, including the motivational resources of people to meet their needs for self-esteem. The low concern for people attributed to the authoritarian manager does not necessarily result from an intentional rejection of people's feelings and needs but, rather, comes from a belief that such concerns are relatively unimportant in determining how to best accomplish a work task.

The value of a democratic or participative management style emerges from a high concern for getting the job done while, at the same time, considering how the needs of people can be addressed in order to maximize work effort. Studies of organizational effectiveness will typically report that efficiency is greatest when there exists a good rapport between managers and their subordinates, when there is a congenial work atmosphere, and when there is a group unity or the tendency to work for a common purpose (Cartwright & Zandler, 1953). These factors are more often present in a work group led by a democratic or participative manager. Although the general leadership skills of a manager are crucial in determining the productivity of any work group, a participative management style is more likely to lead to a higher-quality work product (Hare, 1962).

The participative management style assumes an increased importance for the psychologist administrator managing a human-service program utilizing professional personnel. A manager cannot delegate the responsibility for program performance to others. The authoritarian manager generally responds to this responsibility by dictating to program staff both the objectives of the program and the methods to reach these objectives. The participative manager is more likely to establish program objectives with input from program staff and then allow them to devise their own methods of operation to accomplish program objectives. The participative manager thus makes more use of the training and professional expertise of program staff. The use of program staff in this manner not only meets the self-esteem needs of staff but, further, results in a work climate supportive of creative contributions and increased efficiency and effectiveness.

A final skill expected of an administrator in managing people is that of conflict management. Conflict among work-team members can be disruptive and disorganizing. An administrator cannot allow conflict to block work efforts or affect productivity. The effective management of conflict requires an appreciation of the fact that disagreement is often a byproduct of the sharing of ideas by people who have strong beliefs about an issue and who have different life experiences, training, interests, and values. Effective strategies for resolving or reducing conflict will almost invariably require a clarification and exploration of the issues in conflict and the affect generated. The administrator's ability to manage conflict is thus based on an ability to promote the clarification and exploration required. In mediating conflict between two or more team members, for example, the administrator must summarize, clarify, and define issues, with the goal of having team members test out perceptions and assumptions, appreciate consequences of proposed actions or decisions, or determine whether or not disagreement concerns goals or the methods to reach those goals. Walton (1969) points out the importance of such confrontation in diagnosing the sources of conflict, developing coping techniques, and finding ways to resolve or manage the conflict. Walton further describes additional roles, diagnostic issues, and interventions that can be used by administrators.

Managing restricted resources

Economic realities dictate that every program operate within certain budget restraints. Budgets have to be prepared and choices have to be made among competing demands for people, space, and equipment resources. Administrators who cannot or will not think in these terms will experience considerable frustrations in their management roles.

Budget planning or even thinking in cost terms is a skill area unfamiliar to many psychologists who become administrators. Program administrators should have program cost estimates readily available for use in planning, and yet, many managers might have difficulty in even identifying some of the basic cost elements which are used in determining total program costs. For example, in addition to salary costs for professional, paraprofessional, and secretarial staff, there are costs for equipment and supplies (including equipment maintenance or service contracts); insurance, retirement, and other fringe-benefit costs to the organization for employees working in the program; costs for utilities and housekeeping services (estimated on costs per square foot of space assigned to the program); and salary costs for personnel not assigned to the program but who provide program support services (fiscal, supply, personnel, and management support time). Space assigned to the program can also be added in, whether this is in terms of costs for leasing or an estimate of the value per square foot of occupied space. Higher-level management must include all of these cost figures in the budgeting process.

Managing restricted resources thus requires some familiarity with financial management, budgeting, and accounting techniques and concepts. Although choices made in planning are frequently based on value considerations in addition to economic considerations, economic considerations cannot be ignored. An understanding of cost analysis is needed, for example, if for no other reason than to prepare, compare, and defend budgets in the same terms as those used by financial planners at higher levels of management (Bindman, 1972). In developing these skills, the psychologist administrator is encouraged to review some general finance, budgeting, and accounting texts as well as reports of specific examples of cost analysis (Cleverly, 1978; Conley, 1969; Fein, 1958; Fuchs, 1974; Ruchlin & Rogers, 1973).

Managing within an organization

Managing a program in any organization requires an appreciation of how that organization functions. Every organization has both a formal system of operation as well as an informal system of operation. The formal system can be understood initially by examining organizational charts and lines of authority and by reviewing organizational policies and procedures. The formal system also requires an understanding of the interdependence between the elements of the organization as well as the organization's interdependence with the community and other organizations. In short, the formal system describes how the organization was designed to function.

The informal functioning system of any organization describes how things actually get accomplished in that organization. Control and influence factors are depicted inadequately in an organizational chart, for example, when a supply clerk, personnel specialist, or a secretary in the fiscal department can have more impact on the smooth functioning of a program than many designated, higher-level management personnel. Getting things accomplished in an organization is frequently dependent on the skills and ability of a manager to interact effectively with a variety of people and personalities.

The politics of the organization are similarly a part of the informal functioning system and a significant factor in the support and operation of any program. A frequently occurring political factor for psychologists managing health care programs is the fact that the health care field is generally controlled by physicians. This medical domination is a source of frustration for chief psychologists and staff in clinical settings (Baker, 1978; Wildman & Wildman, 1974). The psychologist administrator may believe that this domination is inappropriate but, as with other concerns between what is and what ought to be, must develop skills and expend efforts to function within the system while, at the same time, trying to change that system.

Aside from the political and professional issues involved in physician control of health care programs, the psychologist administrator must face the fact that there still remains a general lack of understanding of the value of psychological services in particular and the value of mental health services in general. The purpose and effectiveness of mental health programs are often viewed with some suspicion by nonpsychiatric physicians and higher-level management personnel. In marketing terms, one can have a good product but, if it is not advertised properly, it will not sell. The psychology profession in general has to do much more in selling its contributions. The selling process for mental health programs requires the development and presentation of an articulate statement of what can be expected or accomplished in a program and the benefits to the organization and its clients. The results must likewise be presented regularly to higher-level management and other influential contacts with the program.

In reviewing the skills required of an administrator, it can be questioned whether or not an individual of any professional discipline has the skills to handle the many administrative and professional demands made. Felzer (1970) notes that, in addition to flexibility and the ability to tolerate frustration,

> One must be comfortable in the nonstructured world and able to live with the uncertainties of budget and program support. Further, one must be authoritative, but accepting; strong, but compassionate; secure, but not dogmatic; tolerant, but not accepting of poor performance or mediocrity; decisive, but able to retract or change positions; and visionary and missionary, but yet concrete and practical enough to satisfy the traditionalists. (p. 449)

The demands can be met if the administrator has the intention of understanding and integrating these demands and seeks to learn the skills required for program leadership and performance.

PREPARATION AND TRAINING FOR ADMINISTRATIVE POSITIONS

In the past, psychologist administrators acquired managerial skills predominately by modeling others and using a trial-and-error approach to see what worked best in handling administrative demands. It was also helpful to the new administrator to have a knowledgable and competent secretary or administrative assistant who could outline and explain what needed to be done and when. Not only is this not the most efficient way to acquire administrative skills, but the increasing complexity of organizations and demands for accountability require a more structured and systematic approach to the preparation and training of administrators.

The current administrator interested in developing and refining management skills can seek out continuing education courses in such areas as budgeting and financial management, performance appraisal, planning, management by objectives, and the medical-legal aspects of health care. Personal skills can also be further developed in courses or seminars on time management, delegation of authority, and counseling employees to improve work performance. Graduate departments of health care administration additionally provide structured programs of administrative training that may interest some psychologists aspiring to higher-level management careers in the health care field. There is a body of knowledge in these areas that can be used to improve the ability of the administrator to respond to organizational and program demands. The administrator can also review general texts on management theory and practice to assist in understanding and responding to management tasks (Likert, 1967; Longest, 1976; Webber, 1979).

In spite of the need expressed by psychologists for administrative training, graduate psychology departments and psychology internship programs have generally not provided this training on a regular basis. In part, the lack of response stems from the increasing curriculum demands made on graduate psychology departments as the psychology profession expands in many specialized areas. Many who support administrative training for graduate school programs and internship programs are indeed uncertain what to delete in order to make room for this training (Bloom, 1969). Adequately preparing psychologists to work in institutional settings, however, requires some exposure to the administrative demands they will encounter and some guidance in how to respond to these demands.

Graduate programs in community psychology and counseling psychology have provided some leadership in identifying the importance of administrative training for psychologists (Golann, Wurm, & Magoon, 1964; Spielberger & Iscoe, 1972). A example of one such program is the University of Maryland Counseling Psychology Program. In a major reorganization of the program in 1972-73, procedures were established for insuring at least minimal involvement in program administration activities for all students. Both practicum- and internship-level training in administration was arranged by having graduate students serve as apprentices with managers involved in federal, state, and local agencies (Fretz, 1978). Programs of this nature in graduate schools and internship sites perform a valuable training function.

A final factor to be addressed in the training and preparation of the psychologist as administrator is the necessity of developing and maintaining clinical and academic skills. The development of appropriate mental health service programs to meet the needs of clients must be based on current theories, principles, practices, and techniques of the profession of psychology and those of related health care disciplines. Although the good clinician is not always a good administrator, the good administrator is almost always a good clinician. Maintaining clinical skills may be difficult because of time pressures and demands, but the competent clinician commands a respect of program staff as well as higher-level management that contributes to effective program leadership.

SUMMARY

Psychologist administrators must respond to demands for accountability, including the assessment of program effectiveness and efficiency. The role of program evaluation in this assessment process is described, as are other approaches to meeting these demands. Also reviewed are the demands made on an administrator to respond to the needs of clients, program staff, and the organization. The chapter further reviews skills required of the psychologist administrator, which include planning, managing people and work teams, managing restricted resources, and functioning within the formal and informal systems of an organization. Special focus is given to models of planning and management styles that promote productivity. Also addressed are issues of conflict management and resource budgeting. The chapter concludes with a description of needs for administrative training of psychologists in graduate schools, internship sites, and post-graduate, continuing-education activities.

REFERENCES

Ackoff, R. L. *Concept of corporate planning.* New York: John Wiley & Sons, 1969.

Ackoff, R. L. *Redesigning the future: A systems approach to societal problems.* New York: John Wiley & Sons, 1974.

Baker, R. R. *Treatment-program evaluation: Beyond program comparison.* Houston: Human Interaction Training Laboratory, Veterans Administration Medical Center, 1973.

Baker, R. R. Planning for program evaluation. In P. G. Hanson, R. R. Baker, J. Paris, R. L. Brown-Burke, R. Ermalinski, & Q. E. Dinardo (Eds.), *Training for individual and group effectiveness and resourcefulness: A handbook for trainers.* Washington, D.C.: Department of Medicine and Surgery, IB 11–41, Veterans Administration, 1977.

Baker, R. R. *Administrative demands and frustrations of psychologists in health care systems.* American Psychological Association, Division 18 Symposium, Toronto, 1978.

Baker, R. R. *Manual: Planning for effective team functioning.* Houston: Training & Measurement Systems, 1980.

Baker, R. R., & Lewis, F. *Ongoing program feedback/evaluation as an aid to program planning and modification.* Paper presented at the sixth annual Southwestern Partial Hospitalization Conference, Houston, 1977.

Baker, R. R., & Paris, N. M. *Manual for force-field analysis: A problem-solving system.* Houston: Training & Measurement Systems, 1975.

Bergwall, D. *Introduction to health planning.* Washington, D.C.: Information Resources Press, 1974.

Bindman, A. J. Psychologists as MR administrators. *Mental Retardation,* 1972, *10,* 12–13.

Blake, R., & Mouton, J. S. *Corporate excellence through grid organization development.* Houston: Gulf Publishing, 1968.

Bloom, B. L. Training the psychologist for a role in community change. *APA Division of Community Psychology Newsletter,* November 1969, *3,* (Special Issue)

Bloom, B. L., & Parad, H. J. Professional activities and training needs of community mental health center staff. In I. Iscoe, B. L. Bloom, & C. D. Spielberger, (Eds.), *Community psychology in transition.* New York: Hemisphere, 1977.

Bradford, L. P., & Lippitt, R. Building a democratic work group. In G. L. Lippitt (Ed.), *Leadership in action.* Washington, D.C.: National Training Laboratories, 1961.

Cartwright, D., & Zander, A. (Eds.). *Group dynamics: Research and theory.* Evanston, Ill.: Row/Peterson, 1953.

Cleverly, W. O. *Essentials of hospital finance.* Germantown, Md.: Aspen, 1978.

Conley, R. W. A benefit-cost analysis of the vocational rehabilitation program. *Journal of Human Resources,* 1969, *4,* 226.

Drucker, P. *Managing for results.* New York: Harper & Row, 1965.

Dyer, W. G. *Team building: Issues and alternatives.* Reading, Mass.: Addison-Wesley Publishing, 1977.

Fein, R. *Economics of mental illness.* New York: Basic Books, 1958.

Felzer, S. B. The psychologist as an administrator in a local community mental health facility. *Professional Psychology,* 1970, *1,* 448–452.

Fretz, B. *Graduate training for preparing psychologists for administrative and interdisciplinary roles.* American Psychological Association, Division 18 Symposium, Toronto, 1978.

Fuchs, V. R. *Who shall live?: Health, economics, and social change.* New York: Basic Books, 1974.

Golann, S. E., Wurm, C. A., & Magoon, T. M. Community mental health content of graduate programs in departments of psychology. *Journal of Clinical Psychology,* 1964, *20,* 518–522.

Hare, A. P. *Handbook of small-group research.* New York: Free Press, 1962.

Herzberg, F. One more time: How do you motivate employees? *Harvard Business Review,* 1967, *46,* 1.

Lake, D. G., Miles, M. B., & Earle, R. B. *Measuring human behavior.* New York: Teachers College Press, 1973.

Levinson, D. J., & Klerman, G. L. The clinician-executive. *Psychiatry,* 1967, *30,* 3–15.

Likert, R. *New patterns of management.* New York: McGraw-Hill, 1961.

Likert, R. *The human organization: Its management and value.* New York: McGraw-Hill, 1967.

Longest, B. *Management practices for the health professional.* Englewood Cliffs, N.J.: Prentice-Hall, 1976.

Klarman, H. Health planning: Progress, prospects, and issues. *Milbank Memorial Fund Quarterly,* 1978, *56,* 78–79.

Mager, R. F., & Pipe, P. *Analyzing performance problems.* Belmont, Calif.: Fearon Publishers, 1970.

McGregor, D. M. *The human side of enterprise.* New York: McGraw-Hill, 1960.

Mullen, J. H. *Personality and productivity in management.* New York: Columbia University Press, 1966.

Rubenstein, E. A. The federal health scientist-administrator: An opportunity for role integration. *American Psychologist,* 1968, *23,* 558–564.

Ruchlin, H. S., & Rogers, D. C. *Economics and health care.* Springfield, Ill.: Charles C Thomas, 1973.

Shonick, W. *Elements of planning for areawide personal health services.* St. Louis: C. V. Mosby, 1976.

Skrovan, C. C., Donnell, H. D., Grimes, R. M., Hennes, J. D., & Tinnin, H. L. *Fundamentals of evaluation in health programs.* Columbia: University of Missouri, Department of Community Health and Medical Practice, 1970.

Spielberger, C. D., & Iscoe, I. Graduate education in community psychology. In S. E. Golann & Eisdorfer (Eds.), *Handbook of community mental health.* New York: Appleton-Century-Crofts, 1972.

Stewart, H., & Harsch, H. The psychologist as a ward administrator: Current status. *Journal of Clinical Psychology,* 1966, *22,* 108–111.

Struening, E. L., & Guttentag, M. (Eds.). *Handbook of evaluation research* (Vols. 1 & 2). Beverly Hills, Calif.: Sage Publications, 1975.

Walton, R. E. *Interpersonal peacemaking: Confrontation and third-party consultation.* Reading, Mass.: Addison-Wesley Publishing, 1969.

Webber, R. A. *Management: Basic elements of managing organizations.* Homewood, Ill.: Richard D. Irwin, 1979.

Wildman, R. W., & Wildman, R. W., II. Administrative problems and patterns of agency clinical-psychology departments. *Journal of Community Psychology,* 1974, *2,* 336–344.

Wildman, R. W., & Wildman, R. W., II. The psychologist as a ward administrator: 1975. *Professional Psychology,* 1976, *7,* 371–376.

Van Maanen, J. *The process of program evaluation: A guide for managers.* Washington, D.C.: National Training & Development Service Press, 1973.

38

Relations with other professions

Nicholas A. Cummings*
and
Gary R. VandenBos†

The phrase *relations with other professions* suggests a broad examination of the professional relationships between psychologists and other recognized professionals, such as lawyers, judges, physicians, nurses, dentists, veterinarians, optometrists, social workers, educators, engineers, and psychiatrists. However, when professional psychologists mention relations with other professions, the topic generally focuses exclusively on the relationship between psychology and psychiatry. The reason for this is clear. With most other professions, we engage in collaborative efforts, with each profession bringing unique skills and perspectives to bear on a common concern. With psychiatry, however, psychologists are truly competitors.

Clinical psychology, as a professional activity, grew out of a context that included the overall field of psychology and a larger, partially overlapping, arena of psychiatric care. Simultaneous to the evolution and growth of clinical psychology, psychiatry was expanding, as was the broader arena of mental health (VandenBos, 1980). For the last 35 years, a tense and ambivalent relationship has existed between psychology and psychiatry. This has been reflected in an ever-changing pattern of collaboration and competition between individuals and organized groups in each profession.

To better understand the nature of the relationship between psychology

The authors would like to express our appreciation for the contributions of Joan Heffernan, Mary Uyeda, and Carla Waltz to the preparation of this manuscript, and we wish to express our appreciation for the comments and editorial suggestions of Jane Hildreth, Mary Uyeda, Rogers Wright, and C. Eugene Walker.

* Clinical director, Biodyne Institute, San Francisco and Honolulu; President, National Academies of Practice, Washington, D.C.

† Director, Office of National Policy Studies, American Psychological Association, Washington, D.C.

and psychiatry, it will be useful to review a few of the highlights in the evolution of modern clinical psychology—including the establishment of a training model and a system for accrediting standardized training, achieving legal recognition of professional practice through licensure or certification, and working toward economic recognition by third-party insurance carriers and governmental agencies. Each step in the process of this evolution has strained relationships between psychologists and psychiatrists, at times leading to a break in formal relationships between the national associations of the two professions.

THE PRE-1950 ERA

Before World War II, there were relatively few psychologists engaged in the applied usage of psychological knowledge. In 1917, the American Association of Clinical Psychologists had been established by a small group of professional psychologists displeased with APA's ambiguous interest in practice issues (Hilgard, 1978, p. 10); however, this group soon joined APA as a section on clinical psychology. In the late 30s, a few professional psychologists again became dissatisfied with APA and formed the American Association for Applied Psychology (AAAP), which would merge with the APA during the reorganization in the mid-40s.

A simplistic estimate of numbers of psychologists is membership in the American Psychological Association (APA). In 1939, this totaled 2,427. However, relatively few of these psychologists were professional psychologists. During this era, psychology was primarily an academically based discipline, engaging in research and university-level teaching, and most psychologists sought to understand human behavior, function, and experience through scientific research.

Psychiatry was also a relatively small profession. Membership in the American Psychiatric Association, in 1939, was 2,235. The modal psychiatric service was hospitalization in a large state or county mental hospital. Being a hospital, mental facilities were under the direction of a psychiatrist, the medical practitioner. In general, these facilities were primarily custodial in nature and had relatively few therapeutic services beyond attempts to control the most blatant psychopathology.

Obviously, these characterizations of the two professions are oversimplified. Within both, there were various pioneering psychotherapeutic efforts being developed, and particularly in urbanized areas, outpatient private practices existed.

Modern clinical psychology, however, was born in the military during World War II, not in the university (Cummings, 1979). Faced with a need to provide quick, decisive, short-term psychotherapeutic intervention as close to the military situation as possible, and faced with a shortage of psychiatrists and military staff trained in psychological intervention, the military was forced to resort to transforming young physicians and clinically naive psychologists into "90-day wonders,"—in this case, psychiatrists and clinical psychologists, rather than infantry officers. Psychologists' expertise in assessment, individual differences, psychological testing, and personal and social adjustment problems made them ideally suited to assist the military in matters of personnel selection and maintaining the mental health of armed forces personnel (Miller, 1946). Max Hutt, M.A., was the first psychologist to be commissioned by the U.S. Army as a clinical psychologist.

The majority of the training of these military mental health specialists took place at the School for Military Neuropsychiatry, Mason General Hospital, Long Island, New York. A rather remarkable faculty was assembled there. It was the unequivocal view that the clinical psychologists functioned as an adjunct to the psychiatrists and, for the most part, administered psychological tests; they had little real authority or independent responsibility. Nonetheless, because of the national emergency, many of these clinical psychologists found themselves in the role of "practitioner-by-the-seat-of-their-pants," and, through the contributions they made, they carved out for themselves responsibilities and respect far in excess of the original intention.

With the cessation of military hostility, however, psychologists reverted to their earlier, auxiliary role. The military—specifically, the Veterans Administration (VA)—continued to provide support and encouragement of clinical practice by psychologists after the war. The VA recognized the continuing need for mental health services by returning veterans and the shortage of medical professionals to provide such care (Miller, 1946). The VA undertook a massive effort to train service providers in psychiatry, psychology, social work, and psychiatric nursing. In 1946, a cooperative program for training clinical psychologists at the doctoral level was established between the VA and 22 universities (Ash, 1968b). The VA offered traineeships to students in university programs, and internship centers were established in VA hospitals. The program allowed for a four-year course, including one year of internship. It integrated clinical practice, research, and training. The program grew rapidly, from 200 trainees in 1946 to 650 by 1950. By 1968, there were an average of 700 trainees each year, and the program collaborated with 71 graduate schools and departments of psychology accredited by the APA in clinical psychology (Ash, 1968a). The control of mental health services was under medical domination; nonetheless, the VA provided early recognition of clinical psychology and provided many clinical psychologists with their first home.

With the establishment of the National Institute of Mental Health (NIMH) in 1948, the support of clinical training in psychology expanded. In the first year, total funding of the clinical training of mental health professionals was $1.1 million. This was distributed on approximately a 40 percent: 20 percent: 20 percent: 20 percent basis, between psychiatry, psychology, psychiatric social work, and psychiatric nursing. This initial pattern of the distribution of clinical training funds was not to last long, and for most of the years between 1950 and 1975, psychiatry was to receive between 47 and 48 percent of the NIMH clinical training dollars. By 1950, NIMH clinical training support increased to $3.1 million, of which psychology received $.5 million. (This support would grow to $4.6 million by 1955 and $22.9 million by 1960, with psychology receiving $.75 million in 1955 and $3.3 million in 1960). These funds were used to support university-based clinical faculty as well as to provide trainee-ships for individuals.

Thus, in the late 40s, the university—the logical home of clinical psychology—became, for the first time, heavily involved in the clinical training of psychologists through encouragement by and support of the federal government—especially the VA and the NIMH. To this point in time, there had been little conscious definition of professional activities (Miller, 1946) and appropriate academic preparation for such functioning. No examination of training appropriate for clinical practice had occurred, and there was no recognized standard or comprehensive curriculum in existence. Internships and practicums were not tied to academic course-work, although some institutions provided training programs. Without an earlier, applied orientation toward their work, clinical psychologists as a group had experienced little pressure to examine these issues.

The American Psychological Association (APA), as the national organization of psychologists in the United States, was asked after World War II to assist in identifying those universities with recognized clinical training programs which would be eligible for federal support. The APA was thus forced into a position to examine the standards of clinical training to recognize professional practice as a legitimate field of study and preparation. The APA established a Committee on Training and Clinical Psychology that began to look at the then-existing programs. Evaluations of existing programs were made in 1947, 1948, and 1949. Parts of the 1947 results were published as "Recommended Graduate Training Program in Clinical Psychology" (APA, 1947), which became known as the Shakow Report after the committee chair. Findings indicated that programs that passed as clinical training were, indeed, diverse. Without a standardized model for clinical training, it was difficult if not impossible to envision the standards for accrediting training programs. The stage was thus set for the convening of the Boulder Conference.

In August 1949, the Boulder Conference on Graduate Training and Clinical Psychology was held (Raimy, 1950) with funding from the NIMH. The Boulder Conference was psychology's first attempt to look at the social value of applied psychology. It represented an encouraging development for those within APA whose interests were in the applied use of psychology, but it was not appealing to those more satisfied with the traditional pursuit of scientific psychology—wherein applications were only incidental to research itself.

The outcome of the Boulder Conference was the establishment of a scientist-practitioner model for professional training. The model was a strongly academic one, and both didactic preparation and practical internship training became the responsibility of university-based departments of psychology. The dual-training model adopted by the Boulder Conference was to provide clinical psychology with unique skills and perspectives among mental health professionals. However, this dual-training model also set the stage for ongoing debates for the next quarter of a century about the appropriate balance between research training and professional training within clinical psychology. For the next 25 years, academic-based training in clinical psychology was essentially to be scientific with a relatively skimpy serving of applied techniques, leaving professional psychologists, upon the awarding of their doctoral degree, only partially prepared to fill the roles that society expected of clinical psychologists.

Some of the early, practicing professional psychologists were disappointed, though not surprised, that the conference call to clarify issues of professional training in clinical psychology concluded that the science of psychology had not progressed sufficiently to enable an explicit, independent professional practice. The conference reflected the profession's fledgling self-concept by, on the one hand, recommending that applied services take place only within medical settings, but then suggesting that medical settings were not the only place where such activities could occur. Ultimate decisions regarding accreditation were referred back to the committee. Supervision by psychiatrists was accepted, acknowledging the reality of psychiatry's position within the service setting as an extension of the medical profession. The implication, however, was strong that only out of necessity was supervision by psychiatrists accepted. The Boulder Conference recognized the doctoral degree as the minimal standard for the practicing professional psychologist and recommended that the APA and the state associations act to further legislation for the licensing and/or certification of psychologists (Pottharst, 1976). The move toward the recognition of clinical psychology as an independent profession was apparent. The stage was thus set for continuing conflict between the two professions.

Prior to the Boulder Conference, the APA had established an American Board of Examiners in Professional Psychology in 1946 as a step toward certification (APA, 1946). This board had no direct relationship to any accreditation program for training universities, and certification by ABEPP did not necessarily depend upon the awarding of the Ph.D. by one of the recently accredited universities (Raimy, 1950). ABEPP thus provided the mechanism for recognizing those professional psychologists who had received their training and gained professional experience and expertise prior to the establishment of standardized training programs and the minimal degree standards necessary for professional practice.

In the late 40s, however, psychology still lacked an official code of ethics. Efforts had been started in 1939 when the APA formed a special committee to study the issue of an ethical code for psychologists. These efforts were disrupted by the war. Work on a formal code of ethics was begun again in 1948. Over a period of four years, APA members were asked to generate and examine ethical problems. From this work, a code of ethics was finally adopted in 1953. Later, a distilled version appeared in 1959, and after further examination, these were adopted in 1963 (Golann, 1970). There have been several revisions of the APA ethical code since that time.

The APA had established a Committee on Clinical Psychology, in 1945, whose purpose was to clarify the relationship between clinical psychology and psychiatry, and the American Psychiatric Association had appointed a parallel committee (APA, 1945, p. 701). Interprofessional collaboration was stressed; not explicitly stated, however, was what kinds of collaboration were being proposed. For psychologists, it was consultation; for psychiatrists, it was supervision (Hildreth, 1967). The 1946 report of the APA Committee on Clinical Psychology contained numerous principles which were agreed upon by the committees of both associations (APA, 1946). Among these was one which gave unqualified endorsement to the APA taking steps toward the certification of clinical psychologists and the establishment of the American Board of Examiners in Professional Psychology. The American Medical Association, however, complicated the picture by being opposed to legislation for psychologists in any form; so psychiatrists were torn between the AMA position and the American Psychiatric Association position (which officially, at least, supported certification).

THE DECADE OF THE 50s

Armed with increasingly specific (although not universally agreed upon) standards for training content and a professional code of ethics, professional psychologists, primarily through state associations, took on the issue of statutory regulation and recognition. The relatively new entry of psychology into the health and human service field meant that initially it had to conform to existing patterns of similar practice, while simultaneously determining its own definitions and scope of activities. Concern with their standing as independent health providers had both legal and structural aspects that proceeded parallel to the intraprofessional debates regarding training content and professional role. State associations took the leadership in obtaining recognition for the rights of psychologists to practice in applied settings. Early standards were limited to defining academic and experience requirements for independent psychologists and made a distinction between those in private practice and those in institutional settings, which later provided additional focal points of dissension within professional groups (Dörken, 1976).

Nonetheless, the professional trappings developed by psychology were recognized by state authorities, and state associations fought with increasing success for individual licensing laws that would provide them autonomy as health care providers. In 1945, Connecticut had become the first state to *certify* psychologists, and in 1946, Virginia passed the first law that *licensed* individuals to practice psychology (Dörken, 1976). There is a distinction between licensing and certification. A licensing law is intended to define the practice of psychology and to restrict such functions to qualified individuals; a certification law permits the use of the title *psychology* to qualified individuals, and it may or may not include the definition of practice.

As psychology turned its attention to the achievement of legal recognition as a profession, psychology and psychiatry were soon to find themselves in considerable conflict. Psychiatrists often related to the pioneering professional psychologists as technicians. They sought to refer for psychological testing in the same manner they would order an Xray or a laboratory test, and they resented any attempt by the reporting psychologist to go beyond merely describing a patient's test performance into diagnosis or even personality description. Needless to say, this was met with fierce hostility from practicing psychologists, and eventually psychiatry decided to promote psychology to an ancillary role. Firmly believing this to be granting psychology more than its due, psychiatrists were bewildered that psychologists greeted the term *ancillary* with the hostility previously reserved for the word *technician*. The ancillary role included, of course, medical (psychiatric) referral and supervision.

At the local level, in individual agencies and training institutions, the relationship between psychologists and psychiatrists covered a full spectrum of relationships, from outright quarrelsomeness to collegial relationships. In fact, on an individual level, there was a surprising number of collegial relationships. However, at the national level, the relationship between organized psychology and organized psychiatry was becoming one of all-out war. Organized psychiatry began opposing the licensure of psychology. In the mid-50s, the joint APA/ApA[1] Committee on Clinical Psychology, concerned about the strain between psychology and psychiatry, agreed to a joint resolution that would have placed a moratorium on pursuing legislative action on the licensure of psychologists (Sanford, 1955, pp. 93–96). The proposal was never agreed to by the larger APA membership, and the joint APA/ApA committee broke off formal relation-

---

[1] The American Psychiatric Association, being half the size of the American Psychological Association, is often referred to as the "little APA," or the ApA, while the American Psychological Association is called the "big APA," or just APA.

ships (Hildreth, 1967). Relations between the two national associations were reestablished in 1959 (Darley, 1960). Failing to stem the tide of licensure, organized psychiatry, through its state and local chapters, fought hard to limit the definition of the practice of psychology, trying to define it as an adjunct to psychiatry. In many instances, state certification or licensure had to be rewritten and refought to correct previous mistakes which had limited the autonomy of professional psychology. By the end of 1959, 14 states would enact either psychology licensing or certification laws.

Simultaneous to this licensure effort, professional psychologists had concerns which were internal to organized psychology. These matters centered on the model of training for professional practice and the availability of intensive, high-quality, pre-doctoral and post-doctoral clinical training. In many ways, in the early 50s, many professional psychologists felt discouraged by their own national association. The Boulder Conference had appeared to relegate them to an auxiliary status in relationship to psychiatry and had adopted a training model which they felt left them less than fully trained at graduation to assume the expectant duties. The latter dissatisfaction would lead to two more national conferences on training in psychology—the 1955 Stanford conference on psychology and mental health and the 1958 Miami Beach conference on graduate training in psychology. Both conferences addressed themselves to models of training, and both conferences reaffirmed the earlier Boulder recommendations for training as a scientist-practitioner. Thus, during the 50s, while professional psychologists were able to continue to raise questions about the appropriate balance between research training and clinical training, they were unsuccessful in changing the basic training model endorsed by the APA.

This meant that many early clinical psychologists had to bootleg their significant professional training outside of the university. During the 50s, clinical psychologists throughout the United States made alliances with sympathetic psychiatrists who were, first, eager to provide dynamic training in psychotherapy, and, later, made referrals of clients. The psychiatrists who were helpful to psychologists during this era literally had to defy their own American Psychiatric Association, which had taken a strong stance declaring that clincial psychology must remain under the strict supervision of psychiatry. A similar stance had been taken by the American Psychoanalytic Association. Psychologists were barred from training as pychoanalysts in their training institutes. Those few orthodox psychoanalytic institutes that occasionally admitted a psychologist for training required a loyalty oath, whereby a psychologist agreed never to call himself or herself a psychoanalyst and to use the training only for the purposes of research. It was paradoxical that the American Psychoanalytic Society took such a stance in view of Sigmund Freud's strong stance in favor of "lay analysts" (a genre of the Jung medical psychoanalytic practitioner), and in fact, this stance was not taken until after his death. However, neither the American Psychiatric Association nor the American Psychoanalytic Society was able to prevent clinical psychologists from receiving the post-doctoral clinical training they sought. Off-shoot or rival psychoanalytic societies and institutes began to spring up, especially in New York, Washington, Chicago, and Los Angeles. Calling themselves neo-Freudians, Rankian, Reichian, Jungian, and so forth, most of these psychoanalytic institutes accepted psychologists for training. Consequently, clinical psychologists who were trained as psychoanalysts were trained in nonorthodox settings—a quirk of fate that suited the less rigid attitude that has characterized professional psychology.

In the late 50s, some clinical psychologists, particularly in New York and California, began to brave the plunge into private practice. These clinical psychologists were among the most extensively trained clinicians in the country, possessing not only Ph.D.s but often three to five years of post-doctoral clinical training. Increasingly, they found demeaning employment conditions within agencies and low salaries frustrating and intolerable. With the successful passage of licensure in their own states, it seemed economically feasible for them to enter private practice. Although their numbers were initially small and they were geographically confined to several highly urbanized areas, this cadre of early clinical psychologists in private practice provided the leaders who coordinated the effort, first, of the state psychological association, and, later, of the American Psychological Association on behalf of professional psychologists, including those in private practice. For the fledgling, independent practitioners in psychology, third-party reimbursement would soon emerge as a central issue.

THE DECADE OF THE 60s

For a profession to survive and flourish, it must not only have statutory recognition, but it must also have economic viability. Third-party reimbursement emerged as a critical issue for professional psychologists in the 60s. Whereas psychologists employed in the VA and other institutional settings had fought internal struggles for recognition within their systems, the private practitioner (and the general credibility of the profession as a whole) hinged upon recognition by third-party insurance carriers. Psychologists employed by the government, while not being accorded the recognition of an autonomous profession, still had employment, albeit not exactly as desired. On the other hand, under a national health care system (as Medicare/Medicaid purported to be), any profession not recognized as a provider would soon vanish into economic extinction. Professional psychologists would soon implore the APA to enter into these battles.

On these matters, however, professional psychologists would first have to do battle within organized psychology. The APA Board of Professional Affairs, in 1960, recommended working toward coverage of psychological services by the federal government when deemed necessary by those having medical responsibility for the treatment of the claimant. Professional psychologists, particularly those in independent practice in New York, New Jersey, and California, were outraged. Activities internal to organized psychology ensued, and in 1962, the APA Council of Representatives adopted as official policy the recognition of properly qualified professional psychologists as independent practitioners eligible for reimbursement from third-party reimbursers.

With this battle behind them, professional psychologists next sought recognition from individual insurance carriers. These efforts would again inflame the conflicts between organized psychology and organized psychiatry. Health insurance was originally devised to meet physical health needs, and the medical influence within the insurance industry was pervasive. The APA established several ad hoc committees on insurance during the early and mid-60s, and in 1968, a standing committee on health insurance (COHI) was established. These committees initially focused attention on individual carriers in an attempt to secure recognition for psychologists as qualified mental health providers. This strategy met with slow and limited success. Frustrated with the progress being made, the professional psychologists involved in these efforts conceptualized freedom-of-choice legislation within mental health care (Cummings, 1979). Such legislation required that, if a health insurance carrier covered mental health services, particularly those of psychiatrists, they must also recognize and reimburse similar health care provided by psychologists. COHI, working closely with state associations, worked toward amending insurance codes so that psychologists were reimbursable, on parity with psychiatrists, if the treatment covered was within the authorized scope of practice of qualified psychologists. Consumers thus had the freedom to choose between a psychologist or a psychiatrist in the delivery of mental health services. In the late 60s, Michigan and New Jersey were among the first states to enact such laws. (By 1980, 30 states—covering approximately 80 percent of the U.S. population—would be covered by mental health freedom-of-choice laws.)

The struggle for statutory recognition of psychology made its greatest progress during the 60s. On a state-by-state basis, psychologists would work for the enactment of licensure or certification laws. This process would be aided by the development and formal recognition by the APA of a model state licensing law, which adopted the doctoral degree as the standard for the independent practice of psychology (APA, 1967). By the end of the 60s, 39 states had passed psychology licensing/certification laws (and by 1978 all 50 states and the District of Columbia would achieve statutory recognition).

Professional psychologists remained concerned during the 60s about the quality and nature of professional preparation. Organized efforts to document, publicize, and (it was hoped) remedy the problems in professional training took many forms. The Corresponding Committee of Fifty, consisting of recently graduated clinical psychologists, sought to maintain a dialogue among concerned psychologists to make recommendations for change through the APA, particularly through the Division of Clinical Psychology (Pottharst, 1976). The various state and local groups of professional psychologists worked for broader representation of professionals within the organization of the APA. The APA Committee on the Scientific and Professional Aims of Psychology, in 1964, criticized existing professional training programs and made a number of recommendations designed to expand the extent and nature of professional training within academic training programs, including the establishment of psychology training programs under administrative auspices outside of university departments of psychology—such as medical schools or schools of applied behavioral science.

These efforts would lead to the Chicago Conference on Professional Preparation of Clinical Psychologists in the mid-60s (Hoch, Ross, & Winder, 1966). While the Chicago conference, like earlier training conferences, reaffirmed the scientist-practitioner model, it did call for diversification of training opportunities within programs and encouraged experimental programs within university departments of psychology. In many ways, the Chicago Conference clarified the issues surrounding a professional model of training in psychology, and while the conference did not legitimize the professional-role model, neither did it foreclose the possibilities for such a model. Forces were set in motion for the establishment of professional schools as well as the convening of the Vail Conference. A sizable majority of the Chicago conference participants, dissatisfied with the speed with which the APA acted upon the Chicago recommendations, organized a National Council in Graduate Education in Psychology (NCGEP), which, among other things, advocated the formation of professional schools of psychology. The Ad hoc Committee on Professional Training was created in 1969 to address the many still-unresolved issues in the preparation of practicing psychologists and to focus on expanding the glimmer of hope that had emerged from the Chicago Conference regarding the legitimacy of professional practice as an independent pursuit.

Plans for the first state-chartered, doctoral degree-granting, free-standing Professional School of Psychology were announced in 1969 by the California State Psychological Association. The California School of Professional Psychology (shepherded in its establishment by Nicholas Cummings) opened its doors in 1970 with voluntary facilities in both Los Angeles and San Francisco. However, this was not a totally isolated event. Adelphi University granted its clinical psychology training autonomous status as a professional school, and the University of Illinois established a Psy.D. program. In addition, an informal group began to organize in New Jersey to establish a professional school of psychology, which would ultimately be housed within Rutgers University. A new model of professional training was, de facto, coming to be accepted (Dörken & Cummings, 1977).

The 20-year campaign for professional training in psychology was nearing completion and would soon result in the Vail Conference. The campaign for statutory recognition of psychology, through state licensure/certification, was nearing completion. And the campaign for third-party recognition, through state freedom-of-choice laws, was achieving considerable success. The sustained progress by psychology toward legal recognition of its position as an independent and autonomous health profession set the stage for even more intense battles, legislative and legal, between psychology and psychiatry in the 70s.

THE DECADE OF THE 70s

The efforts of the Ad hoc Committee on Professional Training came to fruition in 1973, when the National Conference on Levels and Patterns of Professional Training in Psychology was held in Vail, Colorado. From the outset, the preparation was more optimistic and more volatile. Various social concerns that had emerged in the 60s—women's rights and minority rights—were judged appropriate as issues of concern, in addition to the preparation of professionals. The participants in the conference reflected the divergence from previous training meetings. Efforts were made to include significant numbers of minorities, women, and trainees, as well as individuals representing a range of specialties and roles.

The Vail Conference explicitly endorsed the professional model of training for health-service psychologists. This action was taken without abandoning comprehensive, psychological science as the substantive and methodological base of such training and without depreciating the value of the scientist training model and the scientist-professional training model for achieving other objectives. After 25 years of debate, professional psychologists had finally achieved recognition within psychology of the need for and acceptability of a practice-oriented training model. Organized psychology had officially recognized and accepted the de facto two-model system of professional preparation, although the detailed recommendations of the conference were never formally voted on by the APA Council of Representatives. The Vail Conference and its outcome was only one sign of the growing involvement and leadership of professional psychologists within the APA governing structure (Hersch, 1969).

In 1972, an informal political structure was launched within the APA governing structure, the Committee of Concerned Psychologists (CCP), composed largely of professional psychologists currently serving on the APA Council of Representatives and others who were concerned and interested in being active in such a movement. The avowed aim was to elect a professionally oriented APA president and to increase the representation of professional psychologists on the APA Board of Directors. In 1975, Ted Blau was elected as the president (for 1977) of the APA, becoming the first private practice clinical psychologist to achieve the office. Nick Cummings was elected in 1977 to become the APA president in 1979, and Max Siegel was elected in 1981 to become president in 1983. Blau and Cummings were not officially endorsed candidates of the CCP in the years they were elected; but they received much support from professional psychologists. By the time Cummings was elected, other segments of the APA had followed the lead of the CCP, and the scientist, the social-public interest, and the scientist-practitioner coalitions had been formed. Cummings was to become the last APA president to be elected without any official coalition endorsement. The CCP was instrumental in electing professionally oriented members to the Board of Directors in relative proportion to the number of professional psychologists within the APA. A balanced APA Board of Directors addressed the needs and issues of professional psychologists in a more appropriate manner.

Professional psychologists, however, knew that they also needed an active, national-level, lobbying effort. Activities by professional psychologists had been stirred when psychologists had been omitted as providers under Medicare and Medicaid in 1964. But many psychologists were uncomfortable with such an active legislative role for APA. Legislative advocacy was, however, regarded as essential if practicing psychologists were ever to achieve legitimate standing in the marketplace of health care delivery systems. In 1972, the Council for the Advancement of the Psychological Professions and Sciences (CAPPS) was created as an independent lobbying organization in Washington, D.C., separate from the APA.

The CAPPS had several early legislative successes. It also embarrassed psychiatry, by borrowing a concept from the railroad industry and labeling psychiatry's efforts to maintain supervisory control over psychologists as "medical featherbedding." The CAPPS, however, did not long exist. This advocacy organization unfortunately became embroiled in internal APA politics, for it was still the goal of the clinical activists to move the APA into the arena of advocacy. This goal was realized with the creation by the APA of the CAPPS' successor, the Association for the Advancement of Psychology (AAP) in 1974, and the two organizations merged in 1976. The AAP represented not only professional psychology, but also scientific and academic psychology.

Thus, by the middle of the 70s, professional psychologists could not devote a greater proportion of their time to issues outside of organized psychology per se because they had achieved recognition of a professional training model, were actively involved in the leadership of the APA, and an independent advocacy organization had been formed. With growing coherence in the field of professional psychology and the increase in statutory and public recognition, it is no surprise that psychology and psychiatry were intermittently at odds, both as organizations and as individuals.

One of the most colorful and challenging terms created by psychiatry was *medical psychotherapy*. This concept was intended as a concession to the insurance industry and government, both concerned about the cost of reimbursing for psychotherapy. The restriction to medical psychotherapy would accomplish two things: first, since only the functional neuroses and psychoses and the organic brain conditions would be covered, it would greatly limit the benefit by eliminating all personality or behavior disorders; and second, since the treatment of these would be medical, this would remove psychologists and social workers from the ranks of providers, essentially leaving psychiatry to perform all of the reimbursable services. Wisconsin was the state chosen to introduce the new medical-psychotherapy legislation in 1977, but the eventual targets were the nation's private insurance sector as well as all federal programs. The APA and the AAP had no alternative but to render technical assistance to the Wisconsin Psychological Association's successful effort that defeated the bill. The term still appears and remains a point of contention between the two professional groups.

Numerous states had passed freedom-of-choice legislation by the end of 1974. In addition, this same approach was applied successfully to the Federal Employee Health Benefits Plans in 1974. The consequence was that, as of 1975, over half the eligible psychologists were authorized for independent practice to over half the U.S. population in 23 states, and as noted, by 1980, such legislation would cover 80 percent of the population and 30 states. With this additional recognition, psychologists were in a position to insist on parity in reimbursement with psychiatrists and to seek legal recourse should this not be forthcoming.

An opportunity to do just that quickly presented itself. In 1973, shortly after the Virginia General Assembly adopted its freedom-of-choice law, Blue Shield of Richmond, which operated the master medical services contract in the state, announced it would not reimburse licensed psychologists unless both physician supervision and referral were documented. A court test of the case did not immediately materialize. Soon, however, a psychologist's client filed suit against Blue Shield (in 1974). The Virginia Psychological Association (VPA) joined the suit and, when it was referred for jury trial, sought the assistance of APA. The APA Board of Directors at the time expressed mixed feelings regarding either joining the suit or supporting it financially. VPA had equal difficulty mastering coherent support from its membership. A group of clinical psychologists within VPA formed the Virginia Academy of Clinical Psychologists (VACP) in 1975 to focus on issues of special concern to them (such as reimbursement). But for the next several years, the case floundered for lack of a systematic strategy and support. The turning point came in 1977, when the Commonwealth Attorney General's Office was asked to investigate the Blues' noncompliance with the freedom-of-choice law. The state board of psychology invited all licensed psychologists to submit evidence, and in the spring, the State Corporation Commission (SCC) served a "show cause" on Blue Shield asking them to demonstrate why they had not complied with the law. The commission's jurisdiction in the matter, challenged by Blue Shield, was nevertheless upheld by the State Supreme Court that fall, which denied a motion the following spring by Blue Shield to dismiss the case. Because of crowded court dockets for appeals of SCC decisions, the VACP then proceeded, in 1978, to file suit in the Eastern Virginia Federal District Court, charging Blue Shield with antitrust violations. The VACP President Robert Resnick turned to the APA Board of Professional Affairs in 1978, and that group recommended to the APA Board of Directors that the APA provide technical assistance to the VACP. The AAP, and particularly Anne Marie O'Keefe, also contributed technical and documentary support.

District Court hearings before Judge Warriner began in January 1979, and two American Psychiatric Association presidents (Jules Masserman and Donald Langsley) testified regarding psychiatrists' attention to the physical conditions of their patients (before and during psychotherapy) in an attempt to argue that psychiatrists are in a better position to diagnose physical disease and that the patients of psychologists are in danger of being debilitated by an undetected physical condition while being treated for a psychological problem. The psychotherapy training of psychologists—and psychiatrists—of course, has long held the proscription that the laying on of hands (necessary to conduct a physical examination, for example) would be deleterious to the psychotherapeutic process; and the lawyers for the VACP (Warwick "Bud" Furr and Tim Bloomfield) presented research evidence that showed that even recently graduated psychiatrists rarely performed physical examinations on their patients. Moreover, the testifying psychiatric association presidents were unable to produce a single case where a patient suffered harm because a psychologist had misdiagnosed a physical illness as psychological. However, the VACP lawyers were able to identify the unfortunate case of songwriter George Gershwin, who died of a brain tumor after months of intensive psychotherapy with a psychiatrist.

The District Court, however, cleared two Blue Shield organizations of antitrust violations. The VACP voted to appeal the decision to the Fourth Virginia District Federal Court of Appeals. The Federal Appeals Court concurred with the lower court on only one aspect of the suit—that no conspiracy had occurred between Blue Shield and the Neuropsychiatric Society of Virginia. The Appeals Court overruled other parts of the earlier findings, and the court declared that conspiracy against psychologists had taken place, that Blue Shield was not exempt from antitrust law, and that, in fact, competition did exist between psychiatrists and psychologists. (Indeed it is susceptible to judicial notice. Both provide psychotherapy, and are licensed to do so by state law.) Blue Shield appealed the ruling to the U.S. Supreme Court, which declined to hear the case. Thus, the U.S. Supreme Court left the lower Federal Appeals Court ruling in effect—and set a national precedent.

Cummings, who was the APA president-elect at the time the VACP was planning its suit against the Blues, cautioned that Virginia psychologists were being goaded into a showdown in a conservative and medically dominated state. The original decision of Judge Warriner went far beyond the initial matters of the litigation. It would probably have been a different initial decision had the case been tried in California or Ohio. In retrospect, however, the determination of the VACP and its president, Resnick, to proceed was fortunate for psychology. The final outcome of the *Virginia Blues* litigation was to secure the freedom-of-choice litigation passed in 30 states and the District of Columbia. Although technicalities can always be found to challenge any legislation, it is unlikely that the case will be retried in another jurisdiction. Furthermore, the reversal of the original decision by the appellate court seemed to demonstrate an attempt to eliminate the lower court's overstepping of the issues. The ruling (upheld by the Supreme Court in its refusal to rehear the case) that Blue Cross/Blue Shield are not exempt from antitrust laws and the further acknowledgement that psychologists and psychiatrists are in competition with each other place psychologists in an excellent position to challenge restrictive measures that may be promulgated by medicine in the future.

The struggle, including the *Virginia Blues* case, between organized psychiatry and organized psychology during the past 30 years has produced much colorful dialogue and outrageous comment—from members of both professions. The delight with which psychologists often refer to the American Psychiatric Association as "the little ApA" has already been noted. A regular reading of *Psychiatric News* reveals recurring expressions of fears of the encroachment of psychologists and demeaning portrayals of the inadequate, incomplete, and irrelevant training of psychologists. The language can become even more outlandish and extreme during a heated court battle. Most of the colorful quotes have been all but forgotten; and it is probably best to leave it that way.

But, psychology was not to suffer its ultimate embarrassment at the hands of psychiatry, but from one of its own APA presidents. George Albee's 1970 APA presidential address was touted in a cover story by *Psychology Today* under the banner, "The Short, Unhappy Life of Clinical Psychology—R.I.P." This infuriated Cummings, who was not to become the APA president for another nine years. The Albee-Cummings debate took place at the 1972 midwinter meeting of the APA Division of Psychotherapy. At that event, Albee conceded that he had not foreseen the birth of professional schools which would breathe new life into professional psychology. This resulted in Albee and Cummings being dubbed the mortician and the obstetrician, respectively, of professional psychology. In spite of this retraction, however, Albee has remained steadfast in his more important assertion that psychology is the only major profession that does not practice in its own house. By practicing in the house of medicine, professional psychology is subject to the vicissitudes imposed upon it by the exigencies of medicine.

It is the same Albee who has long contended that professional associations, by their necessary, self-serving nature, are incapable of self-policing or acting purely in the public interest. In this fox-guarding-the-henhouse view of professional guilds, Albee is at least neutral in that he does not regard one society more guilty than another, except for the possible exception of the AMA. He goes further to state that every profession must keep secret its bag of tricks. History will undoubtedly show that there never has been a profession more determined to give itself away than professional psychology. The popular literature is replete with examples of psychologists who have turned psychotherapeutic techniques into self-help procedures. If other sciences and professions were as determined to give knowledge away, society would not need a legion of technical writers to translate scientific jargon into everyday language so that the public can, indeed, avail itself of that knowledge.

The growth of professional psychology has been more thoroughly documented in the 70s than for any previous period. Early studies and surveys (Black, 1949; Clark, 1957; Jones, 1966) showed that applied psychology (and clinical psychology, in particular) was a rapidly growing field, but none of these focused on professional practice. After the National Science Foundation stopped producing the National Register of Scientific and Technical Personnel in 1970, the APA decided to expand its own personnel-survey activities. APA surveys (Boneau & Cuca, 1974; Gottfredson & Dyer, 1978; VandenBos, Stapp, & Kilburg, 1981) and numerous studies by Dörken (1976, 1977; Dörken & Webb, 1979a, 1981) also provide a comprehensive view of professional growth and practice in the 70s.

Professional psychologists in private practice have been a significant aspect of the overall increase in professional activities. Comparisons between the 1972 and 1978 APA surveys, especially in the area of full-time private practice, indicate the real growth in the field. In 1971, 7.3 percent of all doctoral psychologists were engaged in full-time private practice (Boneau & Cuca, 1974). By 1978, this figure increased to 15.6 percent of the total, doctoral-level APA membership (VandenBos et al., 1981)—26 percent of the APA members who are health-service providers. An important, additional feature about the private-practice activities of psychologists is that the distribution of hours per week in independent, fee-for-service practice is bimodal—one is either in private practice on a fairly limited, part-time basis (e.g., five to eight hours per week) or on a full-time basis. More than half the clinical hours of health services delivered in 1976 by doctoral-level psychologists were done in private settings (Gottfredson & Dyer, 1978).

The expansion of psychologists in private practice is a close corollary to the growth of licensure. Some of this increase in licensed psychologists is due to a simple increase in the numbers of doctoral candidates completing programs of study. Greater numbers are specializing in clinical psychology, and these individuals are most apt to seek licensure. Licensure and expanded reimbursement opportunities under freedom-of-choice legislation have also contributed to the growth of private practice. As psychologists have achieved more recognition and stature in the mental health field, however, they have also been more subject to criticism from other groups within the mental health field. In addition, not all psychologists are entirely satisfied with licensing requirements and procedures, which differ state by state and often make reciprocity impossible. One recourse is for the disagreeing groups to promote laws that would change current regulatory practices. One manner of doing this was the result of sunset legislation. This refers to the legislative review of existing regulatory programs in the states. It may assume several different forms: a periodic review of the need for regulation; express reauthorization of regulatory legislation and automatic termination without such reauthorization; or the termination of a statute because of a negative fitness finding. The irony in the achievement of universal licensure for psychologists (1978) was that in the next year (1979), sunset legislation resulted in the termination of licensing statutes in South Dakota and Florida. Universal licensure was reachieved in 1981. Numerous other states contemplate such measures as of this writing, but the initial momentum in this direction has slowed, as states realize the complexity of regulatory review and are reluctant to lock themselves into a required process. The APA's role in these cases has been to sustain licensing laws and, at the very least, to eliminate the possibility of automatic termination (APA, 1979).

Because of the increasing recognition of psychologists as providers of health care reimbursable under third-party payment systems, the need for review and quality-control mechanisms grew. In 1970, the APA started its first systematic approach to self-regulation (Claiborn & Zaro, 1979). Individuals were appointed to serve as coordinators for each of the 10 regional offices of the Department of Health, Education, and Welfare (now HHS) to setup psychology peer-review committees. The committees were concerned with issues of cost and utilization and customary and usual procedures for psychological treatment. Later, the Committee on Professional Standards Review was a national-level group set up to provide guidance and monitoring for state systems. These PSRCs now operate in all states and the District of Columbia, but they are not thoroughly effective, partly because payers often have their own review mechanisms and partly because of low public visibility of the PSRCs.

Development of a model peer-review system for the provision of psychological services was given a tremendous boost by the agreement (1977) between the APA and the Department of Defense Office of CHAMPUS (Civilian Health and Medical Program of the Uniformed Services). This provided for the development by the APA of a peer-review and quality-assurance system for outpatient psychological services offered through CHAMPUS. CHAMPUS had been one of the first health programs in the country to recognize psychologists as independent providers and eligible for direct reimbursement (in 1966). Since that time, it had developed quality-care standards for inpatient treatment through cooperation with the National Institute of Mental Health. When it signed the agreement with the APA, it negotiated a parallel one with the American Psychiatric Association.

The major tasks included the creation of a national advisory panel, development of criteria for "psychologically necessary" services, identification and education of peer reviewers, and implementation and monitoring of the system (Claiborn & Zaro, 1979). The central element in the peer-review system that was developed is a document-based system that centers on an explicit treatment plan and can include patient involvement and agreement with the plan. The treatment plan is supposed to contain a statement of the problem, treatment goals and strategies, and progress assessment. It is supposed to be reviewed periodically. The attempt was to develop a mechanism for the review of claims that was flexible but explicit and insisted on documented progress (but allowed for appeals beyond what are defined as normal limits in terms of time and treatment sessions).

Some problems recently have been identified with the system. The claim-review procedures are being reexamined, and modifications will need to be made.

The terminology of diagnosis and treatment is another area where differences between psychology and psychiatry emerge. The development of the third edition of the American Psychiatric Association *Diagnostic and Statistical Manual* (*DSM-III*), which replaced the *DSM-II*, took nearly a decade of labor, controversy, negotiation, and compromise. The work involved literally scores of psychiatrists and a few psychologists who functioned as consultants. It sought to meet the criticism that *DSM-II* was too medical by including behavioral and social variables, yet it concluded by making these nondisease dimensions essentially medical factors.

Psychologists are understandably troubled by the inherent medical bias built into *DSM-III*, but a significant segment of psychiatry is dissatisfied because a diagnosis based principally on symptoms may have little to do with the formulation of an effective treatment plan. Consequently, there are currently two groups with the American Psychiatric Association who see as their charge the development of the first *Psychiatric Treatment*

Manual (*PTM-I*). The originally charged Commission on Psychiatric Therapies (which includes psychologists Strupp and Cummings as permanent consultants and over 40 other psychologists as contributors) finds itself in a jurisdictional dispute with a more militant group that sees *PTM-I* as potentially the vehicle that could lock out nonmedical practitioners.

Unfortunately, both *DSM-III* and the proposed *PTM-I* have become part of the struggle for ownership and preeminence. In other words, following the classical Greek phrase, "who owns it controls it." There is considerable value in standardizing a nomenclature that would become acceptable to all third-party payers as well as to practitioners and in augmenting this by a treatment manual which would stress treatment planning and goals to be achieved. But for these efforts to be effective, they must be interdisciplinary and serve the political expediency of no one group. The development of *PTM-I* by other than the original Psychiatric Association Commission (which was interdisciplinary) could be more ominous for psychology than *DSM-III* because *PTM-I* speaks directly to what treatment is and by whom it is conducted.

Competition between psychiatrists and psychologists during the 1950s and 1960s primarily centered on outpatient treatment of mental health problems. Psychological and behavioral problems, however, are not treated exclusively on such a basis. In recent years, psycologists' privileges in relation to hospital-based care have become a focus of attention. Although a case can be made for discriminating in the kinds of treatment modalities provided by different professional groups, limiting the settings in which they are carried out does not necessarily follow. Policies and regulations which deny status to professional groups in selected settings deny that group full legitimacy and, in a very real sense, inhibit their professional practice. The concept of *continuity of care* also strongly supports the right of a professional to have responsibility for a patient throughout the course of his or her treatment. For this reason, hospital admitting privileges for psychologists are generally supported even by psychologists whose practice is primarily of an outpatient nature.

Dörken (1977), in a 10-state survey of licensed psychologists, found that 77 percent did not provide any direct services within hospital settings, either on a salary or a fee-for-service basis. Furthermore, there was considerable misunderstanding of the exact nature of their status within the hospital's organization (e.g., whether they were on the medical staff, professional staff, and clinical-privileges list). It appears that less than 20 percent of health service psychologists may actually hold any type of membership on hospital staffs; however, the most common status is to have clinical privileges provided on an informal basis (Dörken & Webb, 1979a).

Twenty-two states have no prohibitions in law or regulations against psychologists holding membership on professional staffs of hospitals (and with clinical authority), while 28 states have some type of restriction (generally regulatory, not legislative); the absence of clear state statutes in this area leaves a vacuum in which restrictive, extralegal-accreditation criteria can exercise a limiting effect (Dörken & Webb, 1979a). California was the first state to pass legislation (in 1978) specifically permitting psychologists to have hospital-admitting privileges (Faltz, 1978).

The most powerful influence on hospital operating procedures is the standards of the Joint Commission for the Accreditation of Hospitals (JCAH), a quasi-governmental agency whose standards have become accepted as "the hospital standards" by the majority of government licensing and funding authorities. The standards developed by this group are based almost exclusively on a medical model of health and illness, and they place sole responsibility for patient care on physicians. Nonphysician mental health providers must thus work under the supervision of or referral from a physician within such settings—regardless of their independence from such procedures, as detailed in the state licensing law for their profession. JCAH standards have been used not only to deny qualified psychologists admission and discharge authority, but also to prevent them from making notations on patient charts, directing hospital-based research projects, and participating in hospital-management councils. The 1977 JCAH standards for outpatient facilities did allow the possibility for psychologists having professional responsibility in JCAH-accredited settings. However, in January 1980, under the rubric of organizational streamlining, the JCAH attempted to merge their standards for several types of facilities into a single standard (and to mandate physicians as responsible for all medical treatment and as having responsibility for all clinical care). The JCAH Board of Commissioners did withdraw the objectionable language at their April 1980 meeting after vigorous opposition was voiced by many individual, nonphysician providers (in response to active publicity by Joan Zaro, the APA's representative to the JCAH PTAC, about the proposed JCAH action).

There is growing awareness that current standards regarding "medical" practice are designed primarily to serve the economic interests of physicians rather than the interests of consumers (Copeland, 1980). The pressure of this public awareness is beginning to have some effect, and in December 1979, the attorney general of the State of Ohio filed an antitrust complaint in Federal District Court against the Joint Commission on the Accreditation of Hospitals, charging that JCAH, the Ohio State Medical Association, the Ohio Psychiatric Association, and the physician member organizations of JCAH with violations of federal and state antitrust laws. Specifically, the complaint alleges that: defendant JCAH and its co-conspirators have continuously engaged in an unlawful combination and conspiracy to suppress and eliminate psychologists from competing as fully as their licenses permit with physician providers of psychological care in JCAH-accredited facilities and programs. This litigation is in its early stages, and a final outcome is still several years away (Foltz, 1980).

Despite the intensity with which differences among professional groups dominate relations among them, there is more agreement between the four core mental health professions than disagreement. The areas of disagreement concern central questions, such as the nature of supervision and responsibility, which lead directly to questions of eligibility for reimbursement. Public awareness of such disagreement, particularly when public debate on policy matters or legislative questions is involved, frequently renders them destructive to all mental health professionals and to the availability of mental health care. The serious impact of certain criticism was apparent when a representative of organized psychiatry, appearing before the U.S. Congress during the same hearing that a psychologist was testifying, denounced psychologists and claimed they were unqualified to provide psychotherapy.

As a result, the four core professions—psychology, psychiatry, psychiatic social work, and psychiatric nursing—recognized the importance of creating a joint and consistent effort to work together to emphasize common understandings and clarify disagreements. Each organization appointed three persons to form the Joint Commission on Interprofessional Affairs (initially known as the Interdisciplinary Role Relations Group), which would meet three times a year to discuss such issues. These meetings provided a forum in which to discuss issues of common concern— such as, interdisciplinary training, malpractice, ethics enforcement, reimbursement policies, and confidentiality. The commission quickly agreed that the organizations should adopt common guidelines on interprofessional ethics to eliminate inaccurate statements and decrease animosities. The guidelines developed and formally adopted by each of the national professional associations are:

1. Seek to achieve interprofessional unity and cooperation.
2. Recognize and respect the autonomy and specialized competency of each profession.
3. Know the facts before speaking or issuing public positions about interprofessional issues and utilize the facts in a responsible and appropriate fashion.
4. Attempt to resolve issues through direct discussion, debate, and negotiation.
5. Pursue joint actions toward mutually acceptable goals.

THE DECADE OF THE 80s

Since most of the discord among the four mental health professions (psychiatry, psychology, social work, psychiatric nursing) pertains to the issue of autonomy and third-party reimbursement, the future of psychotherapy and its possible effects on these professions is important. Those who would convince the insurance industry and the Congress that no comprehensive health delivery system is complete without a mental health provision are clearly on the defensive. There has been a great deal of evidence that the cost of providing psychotherapy is more than offset by the savings in medical costs (Jones & Vischi, 1979); yet, third-party reimbursers and potential reimbursers fear abuse of the benefit with subsequent runaway mental health costs (DeLeon & VandenBos, 1980). There are efforts on the part of the private insurance sector to retrench behind reduced benefits, increased deductibles, and larger coinsurance rates. For example, the CHAMPUS program has taken definite steps to limit the mental health benefit offered. The Health Maintenance Organization (HMO) legislation was scheduled for renewal in 1981, and the HMO industry itself lobbied the Congress to be relieved of the requirement to provide a modest mental health package of 20 outpatient sessions and 30 days of inpatient care per calendar year. Advocacy of adequate mental health coverage will need to be a continuing effort during the 1980s.

Faced with a highly competitive market as well as an alarming shrinkage in the number of medical school graduates entering psychiatric residencies, psychiatry may well find itself seeking even closer ties with medicine, reinstating to a greater degree the illness model, and relying on those services that only a physician can provide (such as prescribing psychotropic drugs and other organic treatments). Such interventions would render psychiatry impervious to assault from psychology, social work, and psychiatric nursing, but would, over time, leave most of the field of psychotherapy as we now know it to the nonmedical practitioners. This would seem a logical scenario were psychotherapy to become nonreimbursable, thus relegating it to the list of treatments for which the client would have to pay, such as acupuncture. This is not likely to happen. Medicine is not known for giving up anything, and a more plausible scenario would be that psychiatry will continue to press for expansion of mental health benefits while fighting a rearguard action against the continued encroachment of nonmedical practitioners.

There are those who advocate that psychology join with psychiatry, so that the two major mental health professions can prevent the seemingly inevitable third-party reimbursement of psychiatric social workers and psychiatric nurses. In a diametrically opposed view are those who believe psychology, social work, and nursing should form a united front against psychiatry. And still a third view holds that all four of the major mental health professions should band together to stop marriage counselors and other emerging professions that are looking for their share of the mental health market. In all of this is the clear recognition that competition in the future will be fierce. As in all competitive markets, the outcome will be determined by the profession that does the best job. As of now, psychology has the clear edge.

The phenomenal growth of professional schools has altered clinical training so that it is more responsive to consumer needs. By not being able to rely on the prescription pad, psychology had innovated an impressive array of new therapies, among which are operant conditioning and desensitization methods, biofeedback, and brief therapy techniques. In addition, these new techniques have been amalgamated into a variety of specialized treatment approaches with targeted populations, such as alcohol and drug abusers, geriatric populations, agoraphobics, persons suffering from intractible pain, and so forth. And finally, psychology has the research training to evaluate and modify new techniques that are founded on the rich, experimental basis upon which the entire profession rests.

Health psychology, the broad arena of promotion and maintenance of health as well as prevention and treatment of physical illness, has been an area of rapid expansion in research and practice during the 70s. Increasingly, psychologists are publishing articles describing behavioral interventions with general health conditions and presenting empirical data on their efficiency. These have included coronary artery disease, stress disorders, essential hypertension, migraine headaches, enuresis, sexual dysfunction, obesity, pre-surgery apprehension, and post-surgery recovery. For example, the number of psychologists on the faculties of medical schools has increased by over 650 percent during the 20-year period from 1955 to 1975. These trends will undoubtedly continue during the 80s (Matarazzo, 1980), and many of the developments in this area are described elsewhere in this volume. This expansion of clinical/professional practice in health psychology will cause another round of internal tension and conflict within psychology; the focus of this conflict will be different than earlier ones, however. This time, the struggle will be within the ranks of professional psychologists. Training in health psychology is different than training for clinical practice in mental health. Different training models are appropriate, and this will require modification of program-accrediting standards and state licensing laws. Health psychologists will soon be desirous of changes in health-reimbursement standards as well, and psychology will be facing organized medicine (not just organized psychiatry).

SUMMARY

For psychologists, the phrase *relations with other professions* most often translates into *relations with psychiatry*. The present chapter examines the struggle of professional psychologists within organized psychology, in relationship to psychiatry,and in the broad context of health care (including licensure, reimbursement, hospital practice, etc.). During the 1940s, the military (both the armed services and the Veterans Administration) played a significant role in the growth of professional psychology. During the 1950s, the professional training in psychology became increasingly standardized, and the university began to play an increasing role in such training; during this period, much of the beginning legal recognition of professional psychologists was undertaken—which brought psychology and psychiatry into increasing competition and conflict. During the 1960s, professional psychologists began to work forcefully across a range of health insurance-reimbursement issues, most particularly, freedom-of-choice legislation; and again, various crises between psychologists and psychiatrists developed. During the 1970s, professional psychologists consolidated many of their initiatives: universal, state-level licensure/certification of psychologists, large-scale adoption of freedom-of-choice legislation, and extensive federal recognition. These achievements brought psychology and psychiatry into direct conflict, including legal action, as in the *Virginia Blues* case. Nonetheless, attempts at interprofessional cooperation continue, as reflected in the guidelines of interprofessional conduct developed by the Joint Commission on Interprofessional Affairs and approved by each of the four core mental health professional associations. Nonetheless, competition and conflict between psychology and psychiatry (and possibly general medicine) will not decrease during the 1980s. In fact, general economic trends (including fewer federal dollars for health care and restrictions of health benefits and other limitations by insurance carriers), along with expansions in the nature and extent of practices by professional psychologists, will increase competition and conflict between the two professions during the 80s.

REFERENCES

American Psychological Association. Psychology as a profession. *American Psychologist,* 1968, *23,* 195–200.

American Psychological Association. Report of the Committee on Clinical Psychology. *Psychological Bulletin,* 1945, *42,* 724–725.

American Psychological Association. Report of the Committee on Clinical Psychology. *American Psychologist,* 1946, *1,* 520–522.

American Psychological Association. State Association Bulletin No. 2: A memo from the APA State Asociation Office, Washington, D.C.: American Psychological Association, 1979.

American Psychological Association Committee on Legislation. A model for state legislation affecting the practice of psychology. *American Psychologist,* 1967, *22,* 1095–1103.

American Psychological Association Committee on Scientific and Professional Responsibility. Social influences on the standards of psychologists. *American Psychologist,* 1964, *19,* 167–173.

American Psychological Association Committee on Training in Clinical Psychology. Recommended graduate training in clinical psycholoty. *American Psychologist,* 1947, *2,* 539–558.

Ash, E. Issues faced by the VA psychology training program in its early development. *Clinical Psychologist,* 1968, *21,* 121–123. (a)

Ash, E. The Veterans Administration psychology training program. *Clinical Psychologist,* 1968, *21,* 67–69. (b)

Black, J. D. A survey of employment in psychology and the place of personnel without the Ph.D. *American Psychologist,* 1949, *4,* 38–42.

Boneau, C. A., & Cuca, J. M. An overview of psychology's human resources: Characteristics and salaries from the 1972 APA survey. *American Psychologist,* 1974, *29,* 821–840.

Claiborn, W. L., & Zaro, J. S. The development of a peer-review system: The APA/CHAMPUS contract. In C. A. Kiesler, N. A. Cummings, & G. R. VandenBos (Eds.), *Psychology and national health insurance: A sourcebook.* Washington, D.C.: American Psychological Association, 1979.

Clark, K. E. *America's psychologists: A survey of a growing profession.* Washington, D.C.: American Psychological Association, 1957.

Copeland, B. A. Hospital privileges and staff membership for psychologists. *Professional Psychology,* 1980, *11,* 676–683.

Cummings, N. A. Mental health and national health insurance: A case history of the struggle for professional autonomy. In C. A. Kiesler, N. A. Cummings, & G. R. VandenBos (Eds.), *Psychology and national health insurance: A sourcebook.* Washington, D.C.: American Psychological Association, 1979.

Darley, J. Report of the executive secretary: 1959–60. *American Psychologist,* 1960, *15,* 746–749.

DeLeon, P. H., & VandenBos, G. R. Psychotherapy reimbursement in federal programs: Political factors. In G. R. VandenBos (Ed.), *Psychotherapy: Practice, research, policy.* Beverly Hills, Calif.: Sage Publications, 1980.

Dörken, H. *The professional psychologist today.* San Francisco: Jossey-Bass, 1976.

Dörken, H. The practicing psychologist: A growing force in private-sector health care delivery. *Professional Psychology,* 1977, *8,* 269–274.

Dörken, H., & Cummings, N. A. A school of psychology as innovation in professional education: The California school of psychology. *Professional Psychology,* 1977, *8,* 129–148.

Dörken, H., & Webb, J. T. The hospital practice of psychology: An interstate comparison. *Professional Psychology,* 1979, *10,* 619–630. (a)

Dörken, H., & Webb, J. T. Licensed psychologists in health care. In C. A. Kiesler, N. A. Cummings, & G. R. VandenBos (Eds.), *Psychology and national health insurance: A sourcebook.* Washington, D.C.: American Psychological Association, 1979. (b)

Dörken, H., & Webb, J. T. Licensed psychologists on the increase: 1974–1979. *American Psychologist,* 1981, *36,* 1419–1426.

Faltz, C. The history of S.B. 259: Psychologists' hospital-admitting privileges. *Professional Psychologist,* 1978, *9,* 433–437.

Foltz, D. SCAH held for restraining psychologists in hospitals. *APA Monitor,* 1980, *11,* 1.

Golann, S. E. Ethical standards for psychology: Development and revision, 1938–1968. *Annals of the New York Academy of Sciences,* 1970, *169,* 398–405.

Gottfredson, G. D., & Dyer, S. E. Health-service providers in psychology. *American Psychologist,* 1978, *33,* 314–338.

Hersch, C. From mental health to social action: Clinical psychology in historical perspective. *American Psychologist,* 1969, *24,* 909–916.

Hildreth, J. D. Psychology's relations with psychiatry: A summary report. In B. Lubin &

E. E. Levitt (Eds.), *The clinical psychologist: Background, roles, and functions.* Hawthorne, N.Y.: Aldine Publishing, 1967.

Hilgard, E. R. (Ed.). *American psychology in historical perspective.* Washington, D.C.: American Psychological Association, 1978.

Hoch, E. L., Ross, A. D., & Winder, C. L. *Professional preparation of clinical psychologists.* Washington, D.C.: American Psychological Association, 1966.

Joint report of the APA and CSPA committees on legislation. *American Psychologist,* 1955, *10,* 727–756.

Jones, D. R. *Psychologists in mental health based on the 1964 national register of the National Science Foundation* (U.S. Public Health Service Publication No. 1557). Washington, D.C.: U.S. Government Printing Office, 1966.

Jones, K. R., & Vischi, T. R. Impact of alcohol, drug abuse, and mental health treatment on medical care utilization. *Medical Care,* 1979, *17,* 1–82. (Supplement)

Korman, M. (Ed.). *Levels and patterns of professional training in psychology.* Washington, D.C.: American Psychological Association, 1976.

Matarazzo, J. D. Behavioral health and behavioral medicine. *American Psychologist,* 1980, *35,* 807–817.

Miller, J. G. Clinical psychology in the Veterans Administration. *American Psychologist,* 1946, *1,* 181–189.

Pottharst, K. E. A brief history of the professional model of training. In M. Korman (Ed.), *Levels and patterns of professional training in psychology.* Washington, D.C.: American Psychological Association, 1976.

Raimy, V. C. *Training in clinical psychology.* New York: Prentice-Hall, 1950.

Sanford, F. H. Across the secretary's desk: Relations with psychiatry. *American Psychologist,* 1953, *8,* 169–173.

Sanford, F. H. Across the secretary's desk: Relations with psychiatry. *American Psychologist,* 1955, *10,* 93–96.

VandenBos, G. R. (Ed.). *Psychotherapy: Practice, research, policy.* Beverly Hills, Calif.: Sage Publications, 1980.

VandenBos, G. R., Stapp, J., & Kilberg, R. R. Health-service providers in psychology: Results of the 1978 APA human-resources survey. *American Psychologist,* 1981, *36,* 1395–1418.

Values and ethics in clinical psychology

*Joseph R. Sanders**

ON BEING AN ETHICAL CLINICAL PSYCHOLOGIST

Until 1981, persons reading the American Psychological Association Code of Ethics had no way of knowing if that Association's members were required to abide by the code or simply use it, along with the APA *Standards for Providers of Psychological Services* (APA, 1974), as a set of standards toward which members should aspire. However, in that year, the APA Council of Representatives voted to change the title of the code from *Ethical Standards of Psychologists* to *Ethical Principles of Psychologists* and added the following statement to the preamble of the code: "Acceptance of membership in the American Psychological Association commits the member to adherence to these principles" (APA, 1981b).

In addition to a preamble, the 1981 *Ethical Principles of Psychologists* contains 10 principles which together consist of a total of 65 lettered subdivisions. These changes make it clear to all who read the code that it represents a body of principles to which all members of the APA *must adhere* rather than simply *aspire toward*. What is not clear is how APA members and those with whom they interact professionally are to interpret this new code of ethics. To help enlighten future psychologists concerning ethics, all APA-approved doctoral programs in psychology must now include coursework in ethics. However, there are as yet no texts available which attempt to clarify the meaning of the grammatical and substantive changes contained in the 1981 *Ethical Principles of Psychologists;* and, the only available ethics case summaries in print are based upon the wording of previous versions of the APA code of ethics for psychologists (APA, 1974; Sanders 1979; Sanders and Keith-Spiegel, 1980).

---

*American Board of Professional Psychology.

In 1981, the APA Committee on Scientific and Professional Ethics and Conduct (CSPEC), the group charged by the Association's Bylaws with responsibility for implementing the code of ethics, revised its *Rules and Procedures* (CSPEC, 1981), so as to eliminate loopholes and shorten the whole process of acting on complaints against psychologists. Hare-Mustin and Hall (1981) have written the first journal article attempting to relate the 1981 CSPEC *Rules and Procedures* to actual ethics cases handled by that committee.

This chapter includes some ideas on how clinical psychologists may lessen the risk of being accused of unethical conduct, either by their clients or colleagues. It also explains what clinicians can expect if they receive notification from CSPEC that a complaint of unethical professional conduct has been filed against them. The chapter quotes those elements of the 1981 *Ethical Principles of Psychologists* which are most open to multiple interpretation. After discussing possible ways of interpreting the various elements of the *Ethical Principles of Psychologists* and citing references which might help in such interpretations, the chapter closes with some proposed changes in the practice of clinical psychology growing out of enforcement of codes of ethics by not only APA but also state psychological associations and state boards of examiners of psychologists.

ON LOWERING THE RISKS OF AN ETHICS COMPLAINT

The search for a simple golden rule of ethical conduct has a long history. Religions such as Buddhism, Christianity, Islam, and Judaism have stressed essentially the same golden rule (Morain & Morain, 1954). According to Brahmanism, the sum of duty is: "Do nought unto others which would cause you pain if done to you" (Mahabharata, 5, 1517). According to Judaism: "What is hateful to you, do not to your fellow man. That is the entire Law; all the rest is commentary" (Talmud, Shabbat 31d). And, in Christianity, Matthew 7:12 tells us: "All things whatsoever ye would that man should do to you, do ye even so to them: For this is the Law and the Prophets." For Martin Buber, a student of both the Old and New Testaments, a study of scriptural law led to his becoming a mystic. According to Buber's biographer (Cohen, 1957), becoming a mystic means becoming essentially "preoccupied with the Self and the sacrifice of the world and others." Presumably, Buber saw such a preoccupation as consistent with the Talmud's interpretation of the golden rule. However, it was during this period of mystical preoccupation that Buber had an experience which converted him from a mystic to a humanist. As Buber himself described the experience,

> One afternoon, after a morning of "religious enthusiasm," I had a visit from an unknown young man, without being there in spirit. I certainly did not fail to let the meeting be friendly, I did not treat him anymore remissly

than all his contemporaries who were in the habit of seeking me out about this time of day as an oracle that is ready to listen to reason. I conversed attentively and openly with him—only I omitted to guess the questions which he did not put. Later, not long after, I learned from one of his friends— he himself was no longer alive—the essential content of these questions: I learned that he had come to me not casually, but borne by destiny, not for a chat but for a decision. He had come to me, he had come in this hour. What do we expect when we are in despair and yet go to a man? Surely a presence by means of which we are told that nevertheless there is meaning (Cohen, 1957, p. 42).

Cohen (1957) concludes that this experience was apparently decisive for Buber. He feels it led Buber to repudiate the mystical way and affirm, instead, "immersion in the stream of life." This conversion was articulated in Buber's publishing of the now-famous book entitled *I And Thou* (1958). Buber gives an example of the I And Thou type of relationship which might well serve as a sort of golden rule for clinical psychologists. Speaking of the relationship between a "genuine psychotherapist and his patient," Buber says,

> If he is satisfied to analyze him, i.e. to bring to light unknown factors from his microcosm, and to set to some conscious work in life the energies which have been transformed by such an emergence, then he may be successful in some repair work. At best he may help a soul which is diffused and poor in structure to collect and order itself to some extent. But the real matter, the regeneration of an atrophied personal centre, will not be achieved. This can only be done by one who grasps the buried latent unity of the suffering soul with the great glance of the doctor: and this can only be attained in the person-to-person attitude of a partner, not by the consideration and examination of an object. In order that he may coherently further the liberation and actualization of that unity in a new accord of the person with the world, the psychotherapist, like the educator, must stand again and again not merely at his own pole in the bipolar relation, but also with the strength of present realization at the other pole, and experience the effect of his own action. But again, the specific "healing" relation would come to an end the moment the patient thought of, and succeeded in, practicing "inclusion" and experiencing the event from the doctor's pole as well. Healing, like educating, is only possible to the one who lives over against the other, and yet is detached. (p. 132)

Here, Buber seems to be saying that it is not enough for genuine psychotherapists to treat their clients as they, the therapists, would like to be treated. It is not enough for psychotherapists to rely on the ethics of the golden rule. In addition, they must treat their clients as their clients would want to be treated if they were fully aware of their own needs. This suggests a new, more complex, golden rule: As a psychotherapist, I must:

1. Become one with my clients.
2. Discern their innermost, unrealized needs.

3. Act toward them in ways designed to help them realize these needs.
4. Note the degree to which my actions accomplish their goals; and
5. Reshape my actions accordingly.

Acceptance of such a revised golden rule would mean committing oneself to become increasingly accurate in evaluating the needs of one's clients and utilizing increasingly effective means of psychological intervention for helping clients meet their needs.

While learning how better to meet the legitimate needs of one's clients may decrease the risk of charges of unethical conduct being filed by clients, the reverse may be true for their relatives and even for colleagues, who may come to see their own needs as threatened by the process. Which experienced clinician has not had an angry call from a relative of a client moving away from either conformity or nonconformity and toward personal autonomy? And who has not wondered about the ethics of a colleague who claims a relatively high success rate with clients?

The search for a single, overall golden rule or simple modus operandi as a clinical psychologist may be worthwhile, but it is no panacea. There remains the need to study the details of the code of ethics to which one is committed and the set of rules and procedures to which the organization administering such a code is committed. For members of the APA, that means studying the 1981 revision of the *Ethical Principles of Psychologists* and CSPEC 1981 revision of its *Rules and Procedures*. For members of a state or provincial psychological association, it probably means the same, because most such associations have adopted the APA code and CSPEC's *Rules and Procedures* as their own. And some state boards of examiners of psychologists have even incorporated the APA Code of Ethics into the regulations for implementing their psychology statute. Thus, the focus of the remainder of this chapter will be on the APA *Ethical Principles of Psychologists* and the CSPEC *Rules and Procedures* for administering it.

THE POWER OF ETHICS COMMITTEES

The Bylaws of the American Psychological Association (APA, 1981a) grant considerable power to that Association's Committee on Scientific and Professional Ethics and Conduct (CSPEC). And the CSPEC, in turn, has become a model for state psychological associations and state psychology licensing board's ethics committees. Most state psychological associations and some state boards of examiners of psychologists have adopted the APA code of ethics and rules for enforcing it as their own. Thus, the focus of this section will be on those provisions of the APA Bylaws, *Ethical Principles of Psychologists*, and the CSPEC *Rules and Procedures* which are most relevant to the activities of clinical psychologists.

What the APA bylaws say about ethics

According to Article II, Section 18 of the APA Bylaws (APA, 1981a),

A member may be dropped from membership or otherwise disciplined for conduct which tends to injure the Association, or to affect adversely its reputation, or which is contrary to or destructive of its object. Allegations of injurious conduct shall be submitted to the Committee on Scientific and Professional Ethics and Conduct (hereinafter "Ethics Committee"). The Ethics Committee shall investigate the conduct of any member which raises a question of a violation of the Ethical Standards of the Association, whether or not specific allegations are submitted, and determine whether the matter shall be dropped or disposed of informally (such as by the establishment of a period of probation under fixed terms agreed to by the member), or whether formal charges shall be filed. (p. xxiii)

Article X, Section 5 goes on to say that it shall be the duty of the APA Ethics Committee "to formulate rules or principles of ethics for adoption by the Association." Given this provision of the APA Bylaws, the Association's Ethics Committee adopted its first set of rules and procedures in 1974 (CSPEC, 1974). A revision of the 1974 version of the CSPEC *Rules and Procedures* was adopted by the Committee in 1981 (CSPEC, 1981). Thus, what follows are the details of the revised CSPEC *Rules and Procedures* which are most relevant to the activities of clinical psychologists.

The CSPEC Rules and Procedures

The CSPEC *Rules and Procedures* (*R&P*) spell out in detail that Committee's three basic powers: namely, the power to suspend a member of the Association, to dispose of an ethics complaint against a member informally, or to vote formal charges of unethical conduct against a member.

Suspension of an APA member. When the CSPEC finds that a member has been convicted of a felony and has exhausted all rights of appeal of such a felony conviction, the CSPEC must review the record leading to the member's conviction and may then suspend the felon's membership without further proceedings. Similarly, the CSPEC may suspend a member who has been expelled for unethical conduct from an affiliated state or regional association or has had a license or certificate refused, suspended, or revoked on ethical grounds by a state board of examiners. The CSPEC *Rules and Procedures* require that its power of suspension be limited to those cases "where it appears necessary for the protection of the public."

Informal disposition of ethics complaints. Until it revised its *Rules and Procedures* in 1981, the CSPEC was forced to deal informally with over 90 percent of ethics complaints against APA members because the then-existing *Rules and Procedures* made it extremely difficult for the CSPEC to vote formal charges against a member. While the change in its *Rules and Procedures* has already resulted in a significant increase in the number of formal charges voted by the CSPEC, the Committee will probably continue to handle the majority of its ethics cases informally. Below is the sequence of steps that the CSPEC must take when it receives a signed complaint of unethical conduct against a member of the Association:

1. The CSPEC must first determine whether or not a complaint filed against a member has been received within the prescribed period. Members of the association must file complaints against another member within one year from the time the alleged unethical conduct either occurred or was discovered. This time limit is extended to five years when the complaint is brought by a nonmember of the Association. According to the *Rules and Procedures:* "Any complaint not received within these time limits shall not be considered and the parties involved so notified." However, these time limits do not apply to cases where a member has been convicted of a felony, malpractice, has been expelled from a state psychological association, or has had a license refused, suspended, or revoked by a state board of examiners. In such cases, the time limit for bringing complaints against a member "shall not begin until such actions have come to the attention, or reasonably should have come to the attention, of CSPEC."

2. Upon filing of a signed ethics complaint by a member or nonmember in the prescribed period, the complainant (the person filing the complaint) is sent a copy of the APA *Ethical Principles of Psychologists* and the CSPEC *Rules and Procedures*.

3. The comlainant is then asked: "to inform CSPEC of previous steps, if any, that have been taken to remedy the situation."

4. If the Administration Officer for Ethics and the Chairperson of the CSPEC determine that the conduct alleged, if proven, "would not constitute a violation of the Association's Ethical Principles, the Administrative Officer shall so inform the complainant and he/she shall be allowed to renew the complaint if additional information can be provided. If no new information is provided within 60 days from receipt of the request, the matter shall be closed."

5. However, if the Administrative Officer and the chairperson decide that there is not enough information to make a fair determination "of whether the alleged conduct would be cause for action by CSPEC, the Administrative Officer may request further information from the complainant or others."

6. If either the Administrative Officer or the CSPEC Chairperson de-

cides that there is sufficient information initially, or after additional information has been provided, to indicate the alleged conduct may violate ethical principles, "the Administrative Officer shall notify the complainant and request written permission to identify him/her to the complainee should CSPEC elect to take action."

7. If such permission is granted or if the CSPEC decides to proceed on its own initiative without a signed complaint, then the Administrative Officer writes the complainee (the person against whom the complaint is filed) a letter which contains the following:

    a. A precise description of the nature of the complaint, including the specific section(s) of the Ethical Principles which the complainee is alleged to have violated.

    b. A request for a reply within 30 days of receipt, containing information concerning facts surrounding the complaint.

    c. A copy of the *Ethical Principles of the Association* and CSPEC *Rules and Procedures*.

    d. The name of the complainant, unless CSPEC has for good cause decided to withhold the name or information that CSPEC has proceeded on its own initiative.

    e. A statement that information submitted by the complainee shall become part of the record in the case which could be used if further proceedings ensue.

8. The complainee in the case is then asked to "provide information that is relevant to the complaint." However, the rules provide that if the complainee believes there was a conflict between his/her responsibility to clients and the Administrative Officer's request for information, "the complainee may seek advice from CSPEC to resolve the conflict." At this point, *Rules and Procedures* note that: "Failure or unwarranted delay in responding or lack of cooperation in the investigation shall not prevent continuation of any proceedings and itself constitutes a violation of the Ethical Principles."

9. Within 30 days of the receipt of response from the complainee, both the Administrative Officer and the Chairperson must decide if the complaint "has no basis in fact, is insignificant, or is likely to be corrected." If they so decide, they "may close the matter without further action." If they close a complaint, this fact is made known to the complainant, the complainee, and "all other persons or groups that may have been involved or provided information concerning the complaint."

10. If the matter is not closed by the Administrative Officer and Chairperson, "CSPEC shall determine whether to":

    a. Close the case.

    b. Further investigate the complaint by means authorized by the Committee.

    c. Request the complainee to appear before the Committee.

  d. Pursue such dispositions within CSPEC as are available and appropriate.

  e. Permit the member to resign under stipulated conditions.

  f. Bring formal charges against the complainee with the President of the Association and the Board of Directors."

In making these determinations, "CSPEC shall receive all available information from the Administrative Officer."

11. If CSPEC decides that "the nature of the complainee's conduct is such that it would be resolved most appropriately within the Committee and without formal charges," it may decide to use "informal means to dispose of the case." If CSPEC decides on an informal disposition of a case, it has the option of adopting one or more of the following methods or any other action it deems necessary:

  a. Request the complainee to cease and desist the challenged conduct.

  b. Censure or reprimand the complainee.

  c. Request that the complainee accept supervision.

  d. Request that the complainee seek rehabilitative or educational training or psychotherapy.

  e. Place the complainee on probation.

  f. Refer the matter to a relevant state or regional psychological association, state board of examiners.

The complainee receiving notification of these proposed actions by CSPEC has 30 days to respond. If the complainee accepts CSPEC recommendations within the 30-day period, "the Administrative Officer shall notify the complainant that the matter has been resolved through an informal disposition within the Committee after the complainee agreed to a set of conditions outlined by CSPEC." However, if the complainee rejects CSPEC recommendations or fails to respond within 30 days after being notified of the CSPEC recommendations, the Committee must then decide whether to:

1. close the case;
2. ask the member to appear before the Committee or a Fact Finding Panel appointed by it;
3. bring formal charges against the complainee with the President of the Association and the Board of Directors;
4. take any other action it deems necessary.

Formal disposition of an ethics complaint. If a complainee rejects attempts to dispose of a matter within the Committee informally or when the complainee rejects CSPEC recommendation that the member resign under stipulated conditions, CSPEC may submit to the Board of Directors a formal charge, stating that "the Committee has concluded that it has probable cause to believe that the complainee has violated one or more of the Ethical Principles of the Association." If CSPEC elects to present a formal charge to APA board of directors:

1. It so informs the complainant. It also writes a letter to the complainee which contains, at a minimum, the following:
    a.   A description of the nature of the complaint, the conduct in question, and citation of the specific section(s) of the Ethical Principles which the complainee is alleged to have violated.
    b.   The disciplinary sanction CSPEC recommends.
    c.   A copy of the *Ethical Principles of the Association* and CSPEC *Rules and Procedures.*
2. Within 30 days after the complainee receives a copy of the formal charges against him/her, the member has the right to request a hearing. If the complainee fails to request such a hearing or does not respond within 30 days, the right to have such a hearing is considered waived. CSPEC must then consider "all available evidence and may make final recommendations based on the preponderance of relevant evidence at its disposal. The matter shall then be referred to the Board of Directors with CSPEC's recommendation for disciplinary sanction. CSPEC's recommendation shall then be treated as that of the Hearing Committee."
3. If the complainee in the case asks for a hearing within 30 days after being notified of formal charges, the complainee can select a "Hearing Committee of three members selected from the Association's Standing Hearing Panel." If the complainee does not make such a selection, the President of the Association chooses the members of the Hearing Committee and their names are then made known to the complainee. The President must then set a date for the hearing within 180 days from the time of the complainee's request for such a hearing. In the ensuing hearing, "CSPEC shall bear the burden to prove the charges by a preponderance of the evidence." Formal rules of evidence do not apply. And at the end of the hearing, the Hearing Committee has 30 days in which to "recommend whether the complainee shall be cleared of the charges, disciplined, allowed to resign, or be expelled." Finally, the Board of Directors must adopt the recommendation of the Hearing Committee, or of CSPEC if no hearing was held, unless it determines that:
    a.   The Ethical Principles of the Association were incorrectly applied.
    b.   The procedures used by the Hearing Committee or CSPEC were in serious and substantial violation of the Bylaws of the Association and CSPEC *Rules and Procedures.*
    c.   The findings of fact by the Hearing Committee were clearly erroneous. If the Board of Directors finds such a flaw in the proceedings, "it shall order a rehearing before a new Hearing Committee appointed from the Standing Hearing Panel."

Reporting the final outcome. According to the 1981 version of CSPEC *Rules and Procedures*, the Board of Directors must inform the complainant in an ethics case (as well as the complainee) of its final action, "including the principles violated, should there be any, and the rationale of the Association's actions." The Board must then report annually and in confidence to the membership "the names of members who have been expelled and the Ethical Principles involved." And "when the Board deems it necessary for the protection of the public or to maintain the standards of the Association, it may also notify affiliated state and regional associations, The American Board of Professional Psychology, and state examining boards."

THE APA CODE OF ETHICS

The code of ethics to which the over 57,000 members of the APA are committed is the *Ethical Principles of Psychologists* (APA, 1981b). This is also the code of most state psychological associations and some psychology licensing and certification statutes. It is the code to which the courts and the media turn most frequently when questions arise concerning the scientific and professional conduct of psychologists. Also, adherence to the APA code of ethics is required to become and remain a Diplomate of the American Board of Professional Psychology.

Those provisions of the *Ethical Principles of Psychologists* which pertain to clinical psychologists and which allow for multiple interpretations by them are the focus of the following section. Each such provision will first be quoted. The problems of interpreting it will then be discussed and references will be made to any publications which throw light upon the provision.

Preamble to the Ethical Principles of Psychologists

The one provision of the Preamble to the *Ethical Principles of Psychologists* which is of significant interest to clinicians and which allows for multiple interpretations is the statement: "They [psychologists] use their skills only for purposes consistent with these values and do not knowingly permit their misuse by others." While this provision in no way defines "others," it seems clear that a professional clinical psychologist is, according to this provision, responsible for those persons working under his or her supervision. In an effort to clarify the responsibility of psychologists for their assistants, the APA Committee on Professional Practice (COPP) prepared a document entitled "Appropriate Uses of Psychological Assistants in Health Care" (COPP, 1981). While this document is not yet official APA policy, it provides the best available guidelines for clinical psychologists wishing to employ assistants. It includes the requirement that the psychologist maintain "legal and professional responsibility for the direction and oversight of all services rendered by the assistant which shall be responsible for diagnosis and for the development and implementation of a treatment plan." It goes on to say that, "In order to protect the consumer, the assistant shall have at least two years of graduate study in psychology in a regionally accredited university or professional school or a master's or doctoral degree based upon a course of study which is psychological in nature and the licensed psychologist shall be responsibile for determining that assistants have appropriate and necessary education and, further, that they receive adequate training and supervision to competently discharge their duties." Among the other provisions of this set of guidelines is the one which says that, "All written reports and communications written by psychological assistants shall be countersigned as 'reviewed and approved by the employer psychologist.' "

Principle 1—Responsibility

Principle 1—Responsibility—of the *Ethical Principles of Psychologists* contains three provisions which are relevant to the work of clinical psychologists. The first of these is the entire Preamble to Principle 1, which reads as follows:

> In providing services, psychologists maintain the highest standards of their profession. They accept responsibility for the consequences of their acts and make every effort to ensure that their services are used appropriately.

The best guide for the interpretation of the first sentence of the above Preamble may be found in the "Specialty Guidelines For The Delivery Of Services By Clinical Psychologists," which was made official policy of APA in January 1980 (Committee of Professional Standards, 1981). The guidelines indicate that they "are intended to improve the quality and delivery of clinical psychological services by specifying criteria for key aspects of the practive setting." They then go on to define a professional clinical psychologist as well as "clinical psychological services." The rest of the document provides a set of guidelines for providers of clinical psychological services. The second section of the Preamble to Principle 1 is simply a restatement of the aforementioned statement in the Preamble to the entire *Ethical Principles of Psychologists*, with the difference that the words "by others" does not appear.

Principle 1*d* states: "As members of governmental or other organizational bodies, psychologists remain accountable as individuals to the highest standards of their profession." The use of the phrase *highest standards of their profession* is simply a restatement from the Preamble to Principle 1. Thus, the aforementioned "Specialty Guidelines" would seem to apply regardless of where a clinical psychologist works.

Perhaps one of the most difficult provisions of the *Ethical Principles of Psychologists* to interpret in individual situations is Principle 1*f*. According to this provision,

As practitioners, psychologists know that they bear a heavy social responsibility because their recommendations and professional actions may alter the lives of others. They are alert to personal, social, organizational, financial, or political situations and pressures that might lead to misuse of their influence.

Some light is cast on this provision by Case 80-1-1, in an article summarizing ethics cases handled by the APA Committee on Scientific and Professional Ethics and Conduct (Sanders & Keith-Spiegel, 1980). This case summary tells of how CSPEC censored an APA member "for misleading a colleague by distorting the true nature of the interactions between the member and the Ethics Committee." Specifically, the censored APA member had led a colleague to believe that CSPEC had rendered a decision on a question of who deserves to be given credit for contributions to a professional publication. Actually, a CSPEC member had simply referred the APA member to the Ethical Standards principle which deals with publication credit. Principle 1f is also relevant to the activities of clinical psychologists serving as expert witnesses in criminal or civil cases. This is particularly true where a clinical psychologist is subpoenaed by the courts to testify concerning a client who becomes involved in a child-custody case. Using a box in the *APA Monitor*, CSPEC invited psychologists to "provide critical incidents" concerning the giving of expert testimony in child-custody cases. However, the 1981 *Ethical Principles of Psychologists* does not yet reflect the CSPEC determination on how such testimony may ethically be given.

Principle 2—Competence

The entire Preamble to Principle 2—Competence—is relevant to the work of clinical psychologists. It reads as follows:

> The maintenance of high standards of competence is a responsibility shared by all psychologists in the interest of the public and the profession as a whole. Psychologists recognize the boundaries of their competence and the limitations of their techniques. They only provide services and only use techniques for which they are qualified by training and experience. In those areas in which recognized standards do not yet exist, psychologists take whatever precautions are necessary to protect the welfare of their clients. They maintain knowledge of current scientific and professional information related to the services they render.

Here again, the "Specialty Guidelines" offers psychologists guidance as to what constitutes the "high standards of competence" called for in the Preamble to Principle 2. Those "Specialty Guidelines" help psychologists to interpret the sentence of the Preamble which reads, "They only provide services and only use techniques for which they are qualified by training and experience." According to those guidelines, "In addition to a doctoral education, clinical psychologists acquire doctoral and post-doctoral training. Patterns of education and training in clinical psychology are consistent with the function to be performed and the services to be provided, in accordance with the ages, populations, and problems encountered in various settings." Clearly then, a clinical psychologist must be able to show a relationship between his or her education and training and services currently being offered to clients. And, as the last sentence of the Preamble to Principle 2 indicates, they must continue to keep abreast of the literature relevant to the services they are rendering.

While many post-doctoral training programs for clinical psychologists include the requirement that participants engage in ongoing personal psychotherapy or professional supervision, there is no such requirement in the APA Code of Ethics for psychologists. However, the code does state, in Principle 2, that:

> Psychologists recognize that personal problems and conflicts may interfere with professional effectiveness. Accordingly, they refrain from undertaking any activity in which their personal problems are likely to lead to inadequate performance or harm to a client, colleague, student, or research participant. If engaged in such activity when they become aware of their personal problems, they seek competent professional assistance to determine whether they should suspend, terminate, or limit the scope of their professional and/ or scientific activities.

Case 79–6–2 in an article on "Complaints Against Psychologists Adjudicated Informally By APA's Committee on Scientific and Professional Ethics And Conduct" provides an example of how this provision of the code of ethics can be violated (Sanders, 1979). CSPEC saw this as "a case of psychologist becoming emotionally involved with and eventually marrying an ex-client." CSPEC concluded that the psychologist involved "should have sought peer consultation when she saw herself becoming involved with a client, either during or soon after an ongoing therapy relationship." The CSPEC conclusions in this case suggest that clinical psychologists might seriously consider consultation with a colleague before either converting any personal relationship into a professional one or converting a psychologist-client relationship into some other type of relationship. But it leaves unanswered the question of how psychologists can reasonably be sure that they will " recognize that personal problems and conflicts may interfere with professional effectiveness." This problem of recognition seems most acute for those clinical psychologists engaged in "solo practice." It seems least acute for those clinical psychologists working in organizations which require periodic group discussion of those clients currently being seen by members of the organization's staff.

Principle 3—Moral and Legal Standards

Once again, the entire Preamble to a Principle is relevant to the work of clinical psychologists. The Preamble to Principle 3 reads as follows:

Psychologists' moral and ethical standards of behavior are a personal matter to the same degree as they are for any other citizen, except as these may compromise the fulfillment of their professional responsibilities or reduce the public trust in psychology and psychologists. Regarding their own behavior, psychologists are sensitive to prevailing community standards and to the possible impact that conformity to or deviation from these standards may have upon the quality of their performance as psychologists. Psychologists are also aware of the possible impact of their public behavior upon the ability of colleagues to perform their professional duties.

There are two cases handled by CSPEC which are relevant to this Preamble. They are Case 79–3–1 (Sanders, 1979) and Case 80–3–2 (Sanders & Keith-Spiegel, 1980). The first case involved a psychologist indicted in Medicaid fraud. The psychologist had been placed on probation by the courts until "the entire amount of money involved was repaid." The case had come to CSPEC's attention via a newspaper clipping. While the psychologist's activities did not directly pertain to the APA Code of Ethics, CSPEC got involved because there was a possibility that the publicity surrounding those activities might have the effect of compromising or reducing "the trust in psychology or psychologists held by the general public." The second case, 80–3–2, involved a psychologist who was found to be impersonating a physician after obtaining a bonafide Ph.D. in psychology. Here again, the case came to CSPEC's attention via a clipping from a news publication. In addition to impersonating a physician, the APA member had been "convicted of armed robbery and had no right to appeal, having pleaded guilty to this offense." The CSPEC voted to suspend the member and asked why suspension should not be followed by expulsion from the association. The member was unable, in CSPEC's and APA's Board of Trustees opinion, to "show good cause" why the member should not be expelled. Subsequently, the member was expelled for violating Principle 3—Moral and Legal Standards. The foregoing two examples suggest that any behavior of clinical psychologists outside of their professional practice may become grounds for investigation by CSPEC if that committee feels that their behavior may "reduce the trust in psychology or psychologists held by the general public."

Principle 4—Public Statements

While this Principle applies to all psychologists who make public statements, it has two provisions which are of particular concern to clinical psychologists.

Principle 4b states, in part, that public statements made by psychologists do not contain:

1. A false, fraudulent, misleading, deceptive, or unfair statement.
2. A misinterpretation of fact or a statement likely to mislead or deceive because in context it makes only a partial disclosure of relevant facts.

3. A testimonial from a patient regarding the quality of psychologist's services or products.
4. A statement intended or likely to create false or unjustified expectations of favorable results.
5. A statement implying unusual, unique, or one-of-a-kind abilities.
6. A statement intended or likely to appeal to a client's fears, anxieties, or emotions concerning the possible results of failure to obtain the offered services.
7. A statement concerning the comparative desirability of offered services.
8. A statement of direct solicitation of individual clients.

Three published ethics-case summaries are relevant to the foregoing provisions of Principle 4*b*. They are Cases 79–4–1, 79–4–2, and 79–4–4 (Sanders, 1979). The first case involved a public statement which was criticized by CSPEC because it said, in part, that the psychologist "would teach a form of psychotherapy that works." The second case's public statement was criticized because it was an advertizement for a book which "promised to eliminate abnormal habitual behaviors in 24 hours." The third public statement was criticized because it was a form letter, signed by an APA member, which invited the recipient "to join a weight-control program and quoted enthusiastic statements about the program made by former clients." While purported violations of Principle 4 are probably the most common type of case handled by CSPEC, they are usually considered what Principle 7 of *Ethical Principles of Psychologists* calls misconduct of "a minor nature." Thus, they are usually dealt with by simply asking the psychologist involved to cease and desist in the use of a particular type of public statement.

Perhaps the most controversial provision of the *Ethical Principles of Psychologists* is Principle 4*k*. It was revised several times and finally passed—after considerable discussion by the Council of Representatives—on January 24, 1981. Since then, it has been discussed in several articles, including two articles in the December 1981 issue of the *APA Monitor*. Principle 4*k* reads as follows:

> Individual diagnostic and therapeutic services are provided only in the context of a professional psychological relationship. When personal advice is given by means of public lectures or demonstration, newspaper or magazine articles, radio or television programs, mail, or similar media, the psychologist utilizes the most current relevant data and exercises the highest level of professional judgment.

In his December 1981 *APA Monitor* article entitled "Media Ethics," Portuges compares the work of "media therapists" with those of persons engaged in "crisis intervention." He sees similarities between the two but then adds, "However, the important difference is that crisis intervention's procedures assure its responsible conduct whereas media therapies do not. Media therapy is not simply a brief encounter with the therapist, it is typically the only interaction with the psychologist that the media client gets. There is no psychologist to assess the dynamics of the media client's problem before treatment begins, no *professional* consideration of whether the person's problem is appropriate for media treatment, and no structured opportunity for the post-intervention evaluation of the therapy's effects." In another article on the same subject in the December 1981 *APA Monitor*, Larson reports a meeting of the APA in October 1981, to which psychologists, television performers, newspaper columnists, radio talk-show hosts, and consultants to films were invited. According to Larson, those present had several suggestions for avoiding sensationalism in statements by "media psychologists." The group suggested the following guidelines:

1. Media psychologists should confine themselves to their areas of expertise and training and should resist requests to comment about issues beyond their professional competence.
2. Media psychologists should refrain from criticizing the competence of other professionals, based only on the reports of callers-in.
3. Media psychologists should avoid offering dogmatic advice recommending drastic changes.
4. Media psychologists should make every effort to understand a caller's specific issues, while relating these issues to a general understanding about underlying difficulties.

Neither of the aforementioned articles give a clear line of demarcation between "diagnostic and therapeutic services" and "personal advice." It seems likely that such a demarcation will come out of future, published ethics-case summaries dealing with complaints involving Principle 4*k* and, possibly, malpractice suits brought by recipients of personal advice offered by media psychologists.

Principle 5—Confidentiality

While all other Principles of the APA code of ethics were changed significantly in 1977 and 1979, Principle 5 remained the same from 1963 until 1981 (APA, 1979). The 1981 version of Principle 5 is a shorter version of the old Principle 5. It contains two new elements quoted below, which are very relevant to the work of clinical psychologists. According to the Preamble to Principle 5:

> Psychologists have a primary obligation to respect the confidentiality of information obtained from persons in the course of their work as psychologists. They reveal such information to others only with the consent of the person or the person's legal representative, except in those unusual circumstances in which not to do so would result in clear danger to the person or to others. Where appropriate, psychologists inform their clients of the legal limits of confidentiality.

While both the old and the new Preamble to Principle 5 state that psychologists do not reveal information obtained in the course of their work
except where there is a "clear and present danger" to the person with
whom they are working or to others, the old code limited such revelations
to "appropriate professional workers or public authorities." There is no
such restriction in the present version of Principle 5. And Principle 5
adds the admonition that "where appropriate, psychologists inform their
clients of the legal limits of confidentiality." This last statement is an outgrowth of the now well-known *Tarasoff* decision of the California Supreme
Court (Wilson, 1981; Wise, 1978). Even though the defendants in the
Tarasoff case, a university-based psychiatrist and psychologist, warned
the university and local police officials that their client was potentially
homicidal, these two professionals were taken to task by the court. According to the court, they should have also warned the potential victim of
their client. Thus, at least in California, clinical psychologists working
with a client whom they see as likely to commit either suicide or homicide
have an obligation to inform such a client that they may have to break
the traditional confidential relationship between psychologist and client.
And it alerts psychologists to be aware of other legal decisions limiting
confidentiality.

In spite of the changes made in Principle 5 in 1981, two case summaries
based on the old Principle 5 are still relevant. They are Case 79–5–1
(Sanders, 1979) and Case 80–5–1 (Sanders & Keith-Spiegel, 1980). In
the first case, a student claimed that "the confidentiality of the student-
counselor relationship was violated when the counselor's supervisor informed the student's mother of the student's attempt to commit suicide."
In a statement prepared for CSPEC, the supervisor (who was also a member of APA) said that, "Given the choice between sacrificing the student's
privacy and sacrificing the student's life, the supervisor was prepared
to do the former." The supervisor then "pointed to the student's being
alive and well for six months after the initial suicide attempt as evidence
of the rightness of the supervisor's decision." CSPEC agreed with the
supervisor and concluded that the supervisor had not violated any of
the Principles of the APA code of ethics. In the second case, an employee
of a large agency "complained that a psychologist [a colleague at the
same agency, who the employee was consulting as a private client] was
discussing aspects of the complainant's life as revealed during the outside-
therapy session, with other employees of the agency. The complainant
alleged that the information the psychologist was sharing with co-workers
was of a strictly personal nature and not job related." The case was
resolved when the psychologist against whom the complaint was filed
apologized in a way found acceptable to the complainant.

Deciding whether or not there is a "clear and present danger" that
one's client will commit suicide or homicide is bound to prove difficult
for most clinical psychologists. If they decide no such danger exists and

the client commits homicide or suicide, the psychologist may be accused to unethical conduct by a surviving relative of the deceased. If they decide that such a danger does exist, and no suicide or homicide takes place, the client may file an ethics complaint against his or her psyhcotherapist. In either case, the psychologist complained against would have to demonsrate to an ethics committee that good professional judgment was used. Thus, it seems prudent for a clinical psychologist working with potentially suicidial or homicidal clients to: (1) keep a detailed, written record of the psychologist-client interactions and (2) consult with at least one disinterested colleague before deciding whether or not there is a clear and present danger of either suicide or homicide.

Principle 6—Welfare of the Consumer

This Principle is only second to Principle 4 in the number of ethics complaints against psychologists generated by it. But unlike Principle 4's typically minor-nature complaints, most of the complaints concerning principle 6 have been "of a more serious nature." This is particularly true of complaints involving Principle 6a, which reads as follows:

> Psychologists are continually cognizant of their own needs and of their potentially influential position vis-à-vis persons such as clients, students, and subordinates. They avoid exploiting the trust and dependency of such persons. Psychologists make every effort to avoid dual relationships that could impair their professional judgment or increase the risk of exploitation. Examples of such dual relationships include, but are not limited to, research with and treatment of employees, students, supervisees, close friends, or relatives. Sexual intimacies with clients are unethical.

Six of the 33 cases summarized in the two articles on complaints against psychologists (Sanders, 1979; Sanders & Keith-Spiegel, 1980) concern Principle 6a. In five of these cases, the psychologist was accused of sexual intimacy with a client. In the sixth, the psychologist was accused of marrying a client's spouse soon after face-to-face contact with the client was ended by the psychologist. The conclusion reached by CSPEC in this sixth case seems relevant to the other five. CSPEC concluded that the psychologist "should have sought peer consultation" at the first signs of becoming emotionally involved with the client. However, this admonition to seek consultation at the first signs of a loss of objectivity in one's psychological work presents the same problems as those alluded to in the foregoing discussion of Principle 2f. Here again, the problem of recognition of a personal problem seems most acute for those clinical psychologists engaged in solo practice. It seems less acute for those clinical psychologists working in organizations which require periodic group discussions of those clients currently being seen by members of the organization's staff.

Principle 6e presents still another problem of recognition to clinical psychologists in solo practice. It states that:

> Psychologists terminate a clinical consulting relationship when it is reasonably clear that the consumer is not benefiting from it. They offer to help the consumer locate alternative sources of assistance.

Given the positive reinforcement inherent in the regular receipt of a fee for professional services and the dogged willingness of some clients to continue to consult with a psychologist even when they are not being helped, adherence to this Principle can pose difficulties for many clinical psychologists; and the degree of difficulty seems related to the degree of a psychologist's financial dependence on client fees.

Principle 8—Assessment Techniques

The one subdivision of Principle 8 which is likely to cause difficulty in interpretation for clinical psychologists is Principle 8f. It says:

> Psychologists do not encourage or promote the use of psychological assessment techniques by inappropriately trained or otherwise unqualified persons through teaching, sponsorships, or supervision.

The inclusion of this provision in the 1981 version of the APA Code of Ethics was sought by a group of APA members who cited specific instances of some psychologists teaching nonpsychologists to administer and interpret tests which the group felt require a professional level of sophistication concerning their reliability and validity as well as a sophisticated knowledge of intellectual abilities and personality.

Those seeking inclusion of this provision principally had in mind traditional, psychological assessment techniques. However, hypnosis may be considered an assessment technique, when used for eliciting otherwise unavailable information from a person. Such use of hypnosis is increasing among law enforcement agencies seeking evidence in criminal cases; and psychologists have been employed to teach police officers how to elicit information under hypnosis from witnesses to a crime. The question of the ethics of such teaching has been raised in various divisions of the APA. However, to date, no official policy statement has been issued concerning it.

Principle 9—Research with Human Participants

While there are may elements of Principle 9 which allow for multiple interpretation, the one subdivision which seems to pose particular problems for clinical psychologists is Principle 9e, which reads as follows:

> Methodological requirements of a study may make the use of concealment or deception necessary. Before conducting such a study, the investigator

has a special responsibility to: (1) determine whether the use of such techniques is justified by the study's prospective scientific, educational, or applied value; (2) determine whether alternative procedures are available that do not use concealment or deception; and (3) ensure that the participants are provided with sufficient explanation as soon as possible.

According to Sanders (1981), "the use of concealment or deception in research poses a particular dilemma to clinical psychologists." Sanders argues that "as long as research that includes deception is conducted in a setting primarily devoted to the advancement of science, it seems sufficient to present would-be participants in such research with a written or spoken statement that succeeds in communicating": that the research has been reviewed by the institution's review board; involves "no more than a minimal risk of harm"; and that each participant in the experiment will, at the completion of it, be "given a full and honest explanation of the true nature of the experiment." However, Sanders cites the dual-relationship clause of Principle 6a as the basis for arguing that research involving deception should not be given in a setting which provides some form of human services. His rationale for taking this position is that the use of deception in a human services setting would "permit participants to develop the false impression, from the incomplete or false explanation of the experiment given to them initially, that they would be helped personally by their participation in it."

Principle 10—Care and Use of Animals

This entirely new Principle was included in *Ethical Principles of Psychologists* without the usual accumulation of "critical incidents" of unethical behavior by psychologists. And, in the absence of any evidence that clinical psychologists are engaged in professional work with animals, no element of this Principle seems relevant to the work of clinical psychologists.

PROPOSED CHANGES IN THE PRACTICE OF CLINICAL PSYCHOLOGY

This chapter first considered the appropriateness of a single golden rule for guiding the professional conduct of clinical psychologists. It then outlined those rules and procedures which would have to be followed if a psychologist committed to the APA Code of Ethics was accused of unethical conduct. There followed a discussion of those elements of *Ethical Principles of Psychologists* which are most relevant to the scientific and professional activities of clinical psychologists and are most open to multiple interpretations. Given all of this material, it seems reasonable to conclude that there is no single, general principle which, if followed, would reasonably ensure clinical psychologists of a professional life free of ethics complaints against them.

Perennial sharpening of one's tools for understanding and changing one's self as well as one's clients should significantly diminish the risks of ethics complaints. But they alone will be of little help to those against whom a formal complaint of unethical scientific or professional conduct is filed. To deal with such an event, the Ad hoc Committee on Contracting and Informed Consent of the APA Division of Psychotherapy suggests two types of actions (Kovacs, 1981). The Committee suggests that psychologists share two documents with their clients. One of these would be "a generic document about the nature of the psychotherapeutic interprise, one usable by any practitioner." The document would outline the nature of psychotherapy, the probability of favorable outcome from such psychotherapy, other intervention modalities available for emotional problems, the possible deleterious effects of psychotherapy, and the limitations which will be placed on the confidential relationship between the psychologist and client. In addition, the Committee recommends that a contract be "executed between the parties at the beginning or soon after the beginning of treatment." Such a specific contract should include: the training, qualifications, and orientation of the practitioner; treatment goals and objectives; other places to secure psychotherapy in the practitioner's community; other forms of psychotherapy; fee and billing arrangements; appointment arrangements; understandings about the use of patient material in any teaching or publication activities of the practitioner; the rules which will govern confidentiality and privilege should the patient be engaged in conjoint, family, or group therapy; and any special arrangements which may be unique to individual practitioners.

The foregoing documents were developed as a result of Kovacs' survey (1981) of the literature on malpractice suits brought against physicians. But, in spite of apparent similarities, there is a basic difference between physicians—including psychiatrists—and clinical psychologists. By tradition and statute, people usually turn to physicians when they want something done *to* them—be it medication or surgery. They turn to clincial psychologists when they want something done *with* them—typically, help at self-understanding and self-improvement. As Buber (1958) put it, the relationship between a "genuine psychotherapist" and a client is "a partnership." However, to the extent that resistance to treatment and transference of feelings are also typical components of the relationship between clinical psychologists and their clients, one can expect fireworks in such a therapeutic partnership. Indeed, the more successful the mutual efforts at understanding and change, the more likely is it that there will be resistance to further understanding and change; and it is also more likely that clients will attribute to their therapist attitudes and actual behaviors of other significant persons in their lives.

To help clinical psychologists engaged in psychotherapy deal with such resistance and transferences and to protect them from their possible deleterious consequences, regular, uncensored interactions with a group of colleagues seem essential. Ideally, such interactions can take the form of weekly conferences, at which each participant agrees to answer any and all questions raised about any of his or her ongoing professional relationships with clients and colleagues. The goal of such conferences is two-fold: first and foremost, to help the participants do a better job as therapists; and second, to provide a documented record of their work as therapists in the event of a challenge by clients and/or an ethics committee.

The use of collegial consultation seems particularly important in dealing with at least four subdivisions of the APA *Ethical Principles of Psychologists*. These are: Principle 2*f*, which requires that psychologists recognize their personal problems and conflicts; Principle 4*k*, which admonishes psychologists to distinguish between individual diagnostic and therapeutic services and personal advice; Principle 6*a*, which states that "psychologists make every effort to avoid dual relationships that could impair their professional judgment or increase the risk of exploitation"; and Principle 9*e*, which spells out rules for conducting research which involves "the use of concealment or deception." For dealing with these and the other elements of *Ethical Principles of Psychologists* quoted in this chapter, the use of collegial input seems to be the best way for clinical psychologists to anticipate how an APA ethics committee would interpret the same ethical principles.

SUMMARY

This chapter first considers the appropriateness of a single golden rule for guiding the professional conduct of clinical psychologists. It then explains those rules and procedures which would have to be followed if a psychologist committed to the American Psychological Association Code of Ethics were formally accused of unethical conduct. This is followed by a discussion of those elements of the APA *Ethical Principles of Psychologists* which are both relevant to the scientific and professional activities of clinical psychologists and open to multiple interpretation. It closes with several proposals for changes in the practice of clinical psychology designed to make it both more ethical and less vulnerable to ethics complaints.

REFERENCES

American Psychological Association. *Standards for providers of psychological services*. Washington, D.C.: Author, 1974.

American Psychological Association. *Ethical standards of psychologists*. Washington, D.C.: Author, 1979.

American Psychological Association. Bylaws. In *Directory of the American Psychological Association (1981 Edition)*. Washington, D.C.: Author, 1981. (a)

American Psychological Association. Ethical principles of psychologists. *American Psychologist*, 1981, *36*, 633–639. (b)

Buber, M. *I and thou*. (2d ed.). New York: Charles Scribner's Sons, 1958.

Cohen, A. *Martin Buber*. New York: Hillary House, 1957.

Committee on Professional Practice. *Appropriate uses of psychological assistants in health care*. Washington, D.C.: American Psychological Association, 1981.

Committee on Professional Standards. Specialty guidelines for the delivery of services by clinical psychologists. *American Psychologist*, 1981, *36*, 640–651.

Committee on Scientific and Professional Ethics and Conduct. Rules and procedures. *American Psychologist*, 1974, *29*, 703–710.

Committee on Scientific and Professional Ethics and Conduct. *Rules and procdedures (1981 revision)*. Washington, D.C.: American Psychological Association, 1981.

Hare-Mustin, R. T., & Hall, J. E. Procedures for responding to ethics complaints against psychologists. *American Psychologist*, 1981, *36*, 1494–1505.

Kovacs, A. L. Report from the Ad hoc Committee on Contracting and Informed Consent. *The Psychotherapy Bulletin*, 1981, *16*, 14–16.

Morain, L., & Morain, M. *Humanism as the next step*. Boston: Beacon Press, 1954.

Sanders, J. R. Complaints against psychologists adjudicated informally by APA's Committee on Scientific and Professional Ethics and Conduct. *American Psychologist*, 1979, *34*, 1139–1144.

Sanders, J. R. Ethical dilemmas in covert and deceptive psychological research. In M. D. Hiller (Ed.), *Medical ethics and the law: Implications for public policy*. Cambridge, Mass: Ballinger Publishing, 1981.

Sanders, J. R., & Keith-Spiegel, P. Formal and informal adjudication of ethics complaints against psychologists. *American Psychologist*, 1980, *35*, 1095–1105.

Wilson, L. Thoughts on *Tarasoff*. *Clinical Psychologist*, 1981, *34*, 37.

Wise, T. P. Where public perial begins: A survey a psychotherapists to determine the effects of *Tarasoff*. *Standard Law Review, 1978, 31*, 165–190.

40

Continuing professional development

John W. Baker II, Ph.D.

The status of professional clinical psychology has been significantly enhanced during recent decades, as noted by such developments as licensure and/or certification of psychologists in all states, increased recognition of the profession by governmental and commercial insurance carriers, and utilization of the profession's resources and services in health care facilities such as hospitals, Health Maintenance Organizations (HMOs), industrial and business environments, and in the courts and law enforcement agencies of this country. These activities are part and parcel of the continuing professional development of the profession of clinical psychology as well as the continuing professional development of the individual clinical psychologist.

CONTINUING PROFESSIONAL DEVELOPMENT OF THE PROFESSION

Patterson (1979) makes the distinction of measuring continuing professional development not only in terms of the vocational growth of the individual psychologist but also in terms of those events which affect the continuing development of the profession. This duality of approach is an effective model by which to pursue and conceptualize continuing professional development for clinical psychology. The continuing professional development of the profession may well serve as the primary marketing cornerstone for the entry and maintenance of services to the consumer of professional psychological services. *Marketing* is a term borrowed from the business world that has impact upon psychology, particularly the professional practice of psychology. Continuing professional development is proposed as a marketing tool in the competitive marketplace of mental health services. Marketing is a concept of business

* Private independent clinical practice, New Windsor, N.Y.

which involves planning efforts and an implementation of concepts to meet business conditions and needs of the consumer. The key to effective marketing is a systematic approach by business or a profession to match its resources and activities to the needs of the consumer. Continuing professional development of clinical psychology is a way to match its personnel, services and contributions to the needs of the consumer of mental health practices in this country. Continuing professional development of the profession must minimally include a system of long-range planning that allows the needs of the consumer marketplace to determine the goals of the profession. This professional development model suggests, as does Jensen (1979), that the purposes, goals, resource requirements, and consequences for the maintenance of professional capabilities be favored to alternate models such as continuing education. A continuing professional development model could well encompass continuing education as a significant, but not sufficient, aspect of enhancing professional capabilities and competence. The application of marketing further enhances the model and places the practice of clinical psychology in a competitive as well as scientific and artistic mode for the consumer of services.

Continuing professional development as a marketing strategy provides a means of overcoming the common pitfalls associated with the historical perspective of the profession. Promoters of professional services, particularly in the mental health field, have consciously or otherwise adopted a product-oriented approach that suggests having a service (product) that is needed where the consumer public will find that service, if it is needed in sufficient degree of quantity and quality. This is a simplified application of supply-and-demand economic principles and historically would hold true; but in today's mental health world, there are many persons and professions offering a service. This provides the consumer with numerous choices in supply to meet the demand. With the entry of more providers from various disciplines, all suppliers must reassess their offerings.

The services or product application is countered by the selling approach that says, "We know what you need," and asserts an aggressive, promotional stance. This promotional approach has been intensified in some professions by lifting the ban on advertising. This sale of services has not always been heartily accepted by the consumer and has led to ethical controversy. Service-oriented professionals have difficulty promoting themselves in an aggressive fashion and may continue to resist because of ethical issues and a definitive lack of knowledge and training regarding sales approaches.

If continuing professional development of the profession is to meet marketing criteria, then the profession must continue to match its resources with the needs of the mental health consumer. This calls for creativity and planning to anticipate those needs in the short- and long-range future.

The marketing effort of the profession must also be effectively managed by all of the profession, from the local to the national level. Managing the effort is no small assignment, and the future development of the profession will call for effective management as well as timely marketing efforts. Professional clinical psychology must know its business, which is not just diagnosis, treatment, and consultation, but more broadly includes the delivery of mental health care under the umbrella of health care in general. Inflation, cost containment, care for the poor, national health systems, and insurance issues are but a few of the economic pressures involved in knowing our business beyond the boundaries of traditional textbook and internship-level training. Our business mission is the same as other professions in that our goals are the same, i.e., mental health care, but our methods may differ. It is clearly mandated that development of knowledge and skills must be diffused throughout the concept of mental health care delivery—and this is *our* business.

Psychology and the clinical practice of that profession is a technology in the mental health field that must be applied to its markets in an orderly and timely fashion to maintain its posture in care delivery. The profession has a definitive history that demonstrates its responsiveness to the consumer market by its entry into medical institutions, the provider side of the insurance business, and a growing application of its skills into the industrial world, the justice system, and social movements. The profession's continuing development is contingent upon the marriage of its skills with effective and continuing marketing efforts in the coming decades. The elected and appointed leaders of clinical psychology carry a major responsibility for effective and timely implementation of the profession into the mainstream of mental health care delivery.

Managing the growth of the profession may well be contingent upon not only developing new horizons, but also upon recognizing the boundaries of the clinical psychologist. Too often, an overzealous, idealistic approach can have catastrophic effects when a profession branches into areas for which it is inadequately prepared or where competence has not been demonstrated. To reach into another profession's arena must be done with caution and careful research. It is not only an issue of technology, service, or skills, but a question of what the market can tolerate. Clinical psychology has for years generalized its skills into many areas where other specialties already existed or are presently being developed. Because of differing standards, state examining boards, political pressures, and professional self-images, there is little of the consistency of purpose necessary to serve as an adequate watchdog over the sporadic adventure into unexplored or already saturated areas of development. The blind entry into unresearched professional enterprise can be a managerial blunder from which the profession could seriously suffer in the eyes of the consumer. This notion is most clearly noted as the boundary of the profession merges with the medical profession. The most significant boundary conflict regarding the independence of the profession rests in the health care facilities of this country. Hospitals, private or public, general or psychiatric, have been the facilities in which professional psychology has sought recognition and autonomy while being resisted by the established medical community.

The Joint Commission for the Accreditation of Hospitals (JCAH) and its Board of Commissions have set the standards for hospitals in this country, and the JCAH and its physician-dominated members have been charged by elements of organized psychology with the use of "arbitrary standards to suppress competition between psychologists and physicians in violation of the Sherman Act" (O'Keefe, 1981). During the 1970s, charges and countercharges, investigations and studies have involved the state of Ohio, the Federal Trade Commission, the Association for the Advancement of Psychology (AAP), the National Register of Health Service Providers in Psychology, the APA, and numerous physician groups to try to clarify the issues of hospital privileges for psychologists and membership on the professional, clinical, and/or medical staffs. Psychology has taken its stand with JCAH on issues of consumer rights, restraint of trade, freedom-of-provider choice, continuity of care, and on the economic principle of cost containment in the utilization of mental health care personnel and facilities.

Unfortunately for psychology, the most recent version of the JCAH Consolidated Standards for Child, Adolescent, and Adult Psychiatric, Alcoholism, and Drug Abuse Facilities enacted in June 1981 included the following wording in the professional staff organization chapter: "The Professional Staff bylaws, rules, and regulations, and the rules and regulations of the governing authority shall require, unless otherwise provided by law, that a licensed physician be responsible for diagnosis and all medical care and treatment" (JCAH Standards Final, 1981). While this statement is presently in effect (at press), many psychologists are neither discouraged nor surprised at this ruling since numerous professional psychologists are neither interested in nor restricted by the ruling. Further, there may be more flexibility than is apparent in that the "Joint Commission is claiming the *facility* itself will be responsible for the interpretation of the standard which holds considerable ambiguity for psychology. If the facility interprets state laws as permitting psychologists to independently engage in diagnosis, the JCAH claims it will not consider this a point of noncompliance" (JCAH Standards Final, 1981).

Litigation and controversy continue on this interface of psychology and JCAH, and while the final determination may not be made for some time, these issues become the cornerstones for future activity of professional psychology and serve well as benchmarks for psychology's evolvement from the laboratory and office to the social, legal, and economic arenas of this country.

A key to effective professional development is the recognition that quality is an ingredient to consumer loyalty. Voluntary continuing education has an important place within professional growth and this may be the major ingredient to an effective quality system (Jensen, 1979). Further discussion of continuing education as an aspect of continuing professional development will be elaborated later in this chapter.

A threat to the quality development of the profession is the growing number of psychology majors and the proliferation of both Ph.D. and Psy.D. programs. There are two current factors affecting the human-resource issues in professional clinical psychology. First is the requirement to have a doctoral degree to be identified as a professional clinical psychologist (APA, 1981). The second factor recognizes that over one third of the doctorates granted in psychology annually are in the subfield of clinical psychology ("Doctorate production," 1981).

Anyone wishing to enter the field of professional clinical psychology should be minimally familiar with the "Specialty Guidelines for the Delivery of Services by Clinical Psychologists" adopted by the American Psychological Association. These guidelines define providers, programs, accountability, and environments in which the professional clinical psychologist functions. These guidelines further define the parameters of human-resource entry and functioning and reflect the standards necessary to operate in the field.

Those people entering the field of psychology with doctorate degrees range between 3,000 and 3,200 per year. Of that number, a little over 1,000 are in the clinical subfield, and in 1980, 94 Psy.D.s were granted throughout the United States. Doctoral levels of psychology tend to be leveling off in general, and the Ph.D. clinicians now represent 35.7 percent, not including the 94 Psy.D.s. Data support the fact that women and minorities receiving the doctorate degree in psychology continue to increase in number. The trend is such that, as compensation increases for the professional clinical psychologist, there will be more competition for the mental health dollar, thus an increased emphasis on continuing professional development activities to maintain a share of the mental health dollar.

An increase in the number of professional psychologists must be done with a concern for quality and effective personnel development strategies. As a service profession, the psychologist must recognize that the consumer/patient utilizes our services one at a time, and flooding the market with increased numbers will never dilute the use of service on a singular basis at a singular time. All professions suffer the dilemma of growth versus quality, and professional clinical psychology is no exception. Economic considerations, political climate, and consumerism may well set the standards for quantity if the profession does not monitor its own growth.

This point of quality of the profession suggests the next critical professional management issue—strategy before structure. Intrinsic to this point is the recognition that planning the profession's development effectively will give the clues necessary for the type of structure. American psychology at the national level continues to debate centralized versus decentralized organizational structure. The debate seems fostered by questions of managing large numbers of psychologists or areas of specialization rather than developing a strategy for psychology in the future as a prerequisite to its appropriate structure. Professional clinical psychology has the same dilemma and may profitably spend more time talking of future strategy rather than proliferating special-interest groups as is evidenced by the sectional structure of the Clinical Division of the American Psychological Association. Based on the earlier premise that continuing professional development is the profession's marketing force, the need for effective strategy formation is self-evident.

The people who constitute the profession must be considered if the profession's development is to serve their needs. This does not refer to the professionals' skills and talents but, rather, to what the professional members think and feel about themselves and their profession. Too frequently, the tools of the people take priority over their needs and values. The factors that lead the constituency of psychologists to identify themselves as clinicians may be the real ingredients necessary to develop a strategy of professional growth for the profession.

Another aspect of managing the profession is to provide a sense of purpose. There must be meaning and justification for the profession's existence that also provides an identity. Professional clinical psychology is increasingly subject to review and monitoring not only from within but also from without the profession. A major obstacle to voluntary development activities has been discovering sufficient motivational ingredients to keep the development concept both voluntary and desirable. There is an inherent difficulty in having psychologists apply much of what they know about self-motivation to their own professional development. There exists an inertia in the field that precludes the profession from changing appropriately to the conditions in the field of the consumer. Clinical psychology's inertia results from the profession's own rigidity, which tends to promote a value on the way things were done as opposed to how they must now be done. Too often, this inertia results from our profession's past successes and its tendency to rest on those laurels. Further, our inertia may result from attempting to react to other mental health professions' behaviors rather than making an effort to develop our own.

Professional inertia may further result from experiencing setbacks in the profession's development. First-aid approaches rarely satisfy the problem. However, more long-range, creative strategies often provide the momentum necessary to overcome the reaction to setbacks in the profession's development. The purpose of the profession's development must stay focused on competence. Members of state licensing boards propose some development activities that are geared to provide competence, and these include continuing education, practice audits, specialty licensing exams, self-assessment exams, reexamination, and patient reports (Fish, 1981). These same techniques may well provide the activities necessary to overcome the inertia that frequently haunts the profession.

Another sign of inertia in professional circles is the extensive period of time between adjustments regarding policy, strategy, personnel distribution, and pricing. Continuing professional development activities properly managed and sent to market can go a long way in overcoming the inertia of untimely adjustments. The practice of professional clinical psychology is highly sensitive to policy matters both within the field as well as responsive to policy issues outside the profession that affect its practice. Internal policy statements regarding licensure, training facilities, credentialing matters, graduate education directives, and the like are all vital sources of data to the practicing of psychology. Policies outside the profession, but affecting the practice of such, are situations such as the previously discussed JCAH policy regarding nonmedical hospital personnel, HMO structure, commercial and governmental insurance underwriter postures on direct versus indirect reimbursement of psychological services, and state and national fiscal priorities. These and many other related matters must be distributed and remarked upon by professional psychologists if they are to remain current and competitive in the marketplace.

Fees, salary schedules, and the pricing of services must continually be monitored and distributed to the professional. Salaries for professional clinical psychologists reflect growth both with regard to absolute income and in comparison with other subfields of psychology and are further accentuated by place and circumstance of employment.

Doctoral-level APA members in faculty positions in both university and four-year college psychology departments have median salaries (9–10 month) at the entry level (assistant professor) of $17,000–$18,000 to an experienced level (full professor) of $28,000–$33,000. Median salaries of clinical psychologists providing direct, human-service delivery in community mental health care centers (CMHC) at entry level (2–4 years experience) are $21,000 to experienced levels (over 30 years) of $29,-000+. Public mental or psychiatric hospitals employ clinical psychologists in direct human service at median salaries ranging from entry level (2–4 years experience) of $23,000+ to experienced levels (30+ years) of $30,000 ("Salary Survey," 1981).

Professional clinical psychologists in private practice reveal a median income for those at a full-time level to be $27,777. The median hours seeing private patients for full-time is 26 per week. The median individual fee for psychologists is $50 per session. Almost half the psychologists in full-time private practice have salaried supplementary income and almost all part-timers (median hours = 10 per week) have salaried supplementary income. The median income for psychologists combining private practice and salaried positions is in the $30,000 to $40,000 range. Other fee and practice trends for professional clinical psychologists in some form of private practice reveal: a move to higher fees with inflationary pressures, a stability of income levels, collections holding well under recessionary influences, more providers moving to immediate payment, and the majority of patients having some insurance coverage (Ridgewood, 1980). The American Psychological Association and *Psychotherapy Finances,* a privately financed periodical, are major and significant sources of income data for psychologists on an annual basis.

New technologies, service-delivery patterns, administrative responsibilities, provider geographical concentration, credential clout, and various other issues must be known elements in the equation regarding financial compensation. Other fiscal matters—such as inflation, budgets, socioeconomic levels of the clientele, and what the market will bear—are vital to the pricing of services. It is neither unethical nor unprofessional to be aware of, discuss, and implement sound pricing practices for services rendered. Health-service providers are frequently referred to as poor business persons, and that can no longer be an acceptable accusation— if clinical psychology is to seek its proper place in the mental health marketplace.

Decisions regarding where to start or transfer one's professional practice or skills can only be accomplished through thorough research of the personnel distribution of our own profession and the awareness of distribution of other professional disciplines. Our counterparts in the business world are aware of the personnel and practices of their competition, and the effective penetration of our own professional resources will likewise be contingent upon good research and distribution of personnel. Many professional psychologists could well overcome the movement inertia if they were prone to do some personnel planning research and surrender the notion of how hard it is to start again in a new area. Too often, professional service personnel are resistant to seeking out new and creative markets into which they could apply their skills.

Professional clinical psychology, by its very success and growth during recent decades, may be confronted by a definitive paradox. Success— all too frequently—can lead to a sense of contentment, a legitimization of practices, and tunnel vision in values, activities, and strategy. Not being aware of consumer changes and demands for care, competitive conditions among related professionals, and changing environmental and economic conditions could lead to the profession's fixation and/or demise.

Continuing professional development activities for the profession of clinical psychology are seen as the necessary and sufficient ingredients to market our profession among the providers and the consumers of the services offered. A sense of urgency must be responded to by timely and appropriate reactions to environmental and professional conditions. Managing that marketing effort and overcoming poor planning, inertia, and tunnel vision are the responsibilities of the professional community and its chosen leaders. Patterson's (1979) perspective on the development of the profession is vital and is the umbrella under which other activities such as continuing education must be incorporated so that the needed vehicle is provided from which the optimal potential of every individual clinical psychologist can be developed.

CONTINUING PROFESSIONAL DEVELOPMENT OF THE INDIVIDUAL PSYCHOLOGIST

Guarantees for the competence of the individual, professional clinical psychologist are the basic quality-assurance activities of continuing professional development, when applied to practitioners in their delivery of services. Quality service by competent personnel is the cornerstone upon which professional practice must be built (Harvey, 1980). Empowering the patient with adaptive outcomes may be the basic variable of satisfaction for the provider-consumer, but competency as a professional must be looked upon in perspective to entry levels, credentialing, and measurement of alleged competence. For many years, the entry level of competence to practice has been the state certification and/or licensure. While this still stands as the entry level with its education and training review, plus examination procedures, there are many professionals who are frustrated and disappointed because they are ill-prepared for local jurisdictional requirements or have not made proper preparation for the national exam now being sponsored by the American Association of State Psychology Boards (Hess, 1977). This encounter with the boards is the professionals' first step in preparation for competence assessment. Strupp's (1976) concern for the "erosion of excellence" is testimony to the concern for reasserting standards, and this cannot begin too early in the professional's career.

Competence in its broadest sense for the professional must be designated by levels and degrees. Gale and Pol (1975) assert that *levels* are the extent to which a given set of skills have been acquired and reflect an increased capacity for, and functioning in, these skills. *Degree* indicates a stage of expertness and skillfulness in a position. *Entry competence through licensure* is a basic level of skill acquisition with a minimal degree of skillfulness. Preparing oneself for competence assessment as an individual practitioner must also include other readiness factors considered to be vital to helping professions. Menges (1975) discusses personality characteristics, knowledge and application of subject matter, and performance in the job as critical readiness factors.

There are frequent challenges to the entry-level competence assumption through licensure due to the lack of correlation between education/training programs and licensing requirements and the effectiveness of practitioners (Pottinger, 1979). Koocher (1979) further states that all existing credentials present problems if used as measures of competence per se. This myth of licensing is key to having all individual practitioners pursue their own competence assessment beyond the licensure level. Gross (1978) suggests that evidence of licensure does not protect the public but rather institutionalizes a lack of accountability to the public.

The fallout from this licensure concept is that the state protects a body of people with special knowledge, but the profession remains autonomous. Public representation on those boards may be a move of action to disband the internal breeding grounds (Cohen, 1973). Some research attests to licensing procedures governed by professional peer groups (Hoffman, 1976). At best, these are questionable measures to assure and/ or measure professional competence. This system raises many questions, including the need to establish minimal competency levels which can optimally describe competent performance. There is also the issue of practical ways to measure competency not assessed adequately by current credentialing procedures. The very question of dimensions of competence must be assessed before one can rely on peer-oriented credentialing bodies. The composition of state psychology licensing boards continues to show an increase of clinical psychologists on those boards (Hays & Smith, 1978). While this fact is encouraging to clinicians as a group, it nonetheless does not guarantee competence, and that is a major quality-assurance issue which must be addressed by our own profession.

McNamara (1975) recommended that professional competency could best be assessed by evaluating the facts, skills, and concepts used by the professional psychologist to provide effective consumer-oriented services. Objective examinations would continue to be used to assess factual information. This is the current model under state boards and seemingly would continue as a basic measurement approach. Skill development and adequacy could be determined by various forms of peer review. This is not unlike current peer-review procedures of CHAMPUS and various commercial insurance carriers to assess the skills required to provide psychotherapeutic intervention. McNamara (1975) further contends that the use of facts and skills to solve problems could be ascertained by means of simulation exercises much like the assessment centers that are used in larger business and government agencies. The success of this or any other competency-based model would call for statutory changes mandating assessment and support from all levels of psychological associations. Further, it would call for financial underwriting and an agreed-upon governing board to maintain standards.

It is estimated that 81 percent of doctoral-level providers are licensed. Ninety percent of those who serve in private practice are licensed (Gott-fredson & Dyer, 1978). These figures attest to the credentialing process and assumed minimal competence, but the data just mentioned regarding competency must lead to questions of validity not only by professionals but also by consumers—who are becoming more sophisticated and demanding of their service providers. Walker (1977) addressed the issue of professional obsolescence and the utilization of information in the field.

Competency is a construct not only of content but of timeliness; and, in a field of rapid change, the demands become acute and require an ongoing process of competency assessment and development, rather than some time-limited, project-oriented approach.

Competency must be considered not only as a consumer-oriented issue of continuing professional development, but also as a means of preventing professional and job burnout. The opposite pole of competent service is not only inadequate quality care to the consumer, but also a definitive lack of skill-related development for the professional provider. Care providers subject to burnout lose their respect for patients and develop cynical and, at times, dehumanizing perceptions of the recipients of their care (Kahn, 1978; Maslach, 1978).

Continuing individual professional development must meet the needs not only of quality care to the consumer, but also the internal need to prevent burnout and exhaustion too often related to human service providers. Individual professional development activities can be thought of in terms of programs developed from a perspective of internal stimulation and growth to a program that is externally responsive to the global, public policy to which the provider is responsive.

The most internally oriented process is that model based on self-assessment. This calls for minimal accountability to others but calls for a significant amount of internal discipline and responsibility. The second step in the process is a model of continuing education, wherein the provider would attend to information provided by others, presumably peers, where there is moderate accountability to others and a lessening of discipline and responsibility. The third step would be a peer-review process, where accountability is significantly increased toward professional peers. The fourth and final step would be a program of public policy, wherein the professional is accountable not only to his peers and the consumer, but also to the entire public sector to include economic, social, and governmental standards. This four-step process calls for a broadening accountability to others as the professionals expand on the succeeding steps to their own continuing individual professional development. As one broadens the realm of accountability from self to the public sector, there is an increasing responsiveness to competency as seen by others and a resultant professional service to include optimal quality care to the consumer. Following is a descriptive portrayal of the four-step process. These procedures do not require temporal sequence or prerequisite but serve as a broadly based concept for development that is to be used in one's professional-career development.

Self-assessment

The concept of self-assessment is the most novel and least explored of the individual development approaches by the profession of psychology. Several other professions, particularly medicine, have used the approach for several years, and the process has practical as well as professional significance as a competency-assessment technique. The technique clearly offers a cost-conscious, objective, and private means of assessment. Geographically and professionally isolated providers could have ready access and up-to-date availability of material. Privacy and minimal intrusiveness are features of this technique that are appealing to the professional (Fish, 1981). The APA is beginning to pursue this competency technique, and a Task Force on Self-Assessment met at the APA in 1980 to discuss the relevancy of self-assessment for psychology and how it might be used in an overall, continuing professional-development context. This task force was charged to report to the APA Continuing Education Committee. The task force is in its second year, and reports continue to be forthcoming on its progress. Efforts to set up self-assessment must be considered in the context of which competencies are to be assessed, at what validity and reliability, for how much cost, and with what benefits, usage, practicality, and satisfaction to all concerned.

The task force (APA, 1980b) identified the purposes of self-assessment in relative importance as follows:

1.   To demonstrate professional competence: to oneself, to the profession, to the public.
2.   To improve the quality of practice.
3.   To permit professionwide and specialty assessment.
4.   To serve as a basis for developing continuing-education curricula in psychology.
5.   To motivate psychologists to engage in continuing education.
6.   To make learning more accessible.
7.   To serve as an educational activity in and of itself.
8.   To enhance the image of the field.

Whether the above purposes succeed or not, self-assessment, in addition to privacy and cost efficiency, also provides for immediate feedback assuming the instructional materials are so designed. This has motivational appeal based on learning principles. Additionally, other motivational concepts help the providers with their self-assessments. Questions and situations would be intrinsically appealing and provide a wide range of clinical and management problems that are part of everyday practice. The system would be simple to use and easily understood. Credits for continuing education may serve as valuable external motivation for participation in a self-assessment program.

Self-assessment assumes that people benefit from the process of assessing their own knowledge and skill levels so remedial action may take place. It is in itself a self-diagnostic and remedial program that is a first step for the most inexperienced as well as the most senior-level professional as they pursue their own development in what is seen as the least-threatening, competency-based program.

A major ingredient of one's development is broadening one's base of stimulation, and various specialty self-assessment programs may provide not only feedback in practicing areas, but may also provide additional areas of consideration for the provider. Having explored new arenas of interest, the provider can then engage in some remedial reading and research toward developing the new skills. A reassessment may then confirm a basic knowledge and stimulate the provider to move into the other programs of individual-professional development.

Continuing education

Probably the most widespread and popular form of individual-professional development comes through continuing-education systems. Continuing education has been used in many disciplines and is mandated in several professions as a criterion for recertification and/or licensure. The goals of continuing education are defined by acquisition of knowledge and skill through basic instruction in a course which may be part of an overall training program (Jensen, 1979). It is defined in the present context as the second step because it now involves some external resources, usually a faculty or training staff, to teach the participants. Continuing-education programs are formally designed and scheduled and require some proir planning by the participants.

Jones (1975) called for central governance of continuing-education programs by the APA. Jones asserted that pressures for professional competence were coming from sources outside psychology as well as from within the system. There was a call for central resources, registration, and calendars for all psychologists. At about the same time, Ross (1974) declared that professional education, since it affected client welfare, became an issue of professional ethics. The National Academy of Professional Psychologists, sponsored by the American Board of Professional Psychologists (ABPP), was set up to address this need and was formed to provide post-doctoral opportunities for practitioners in four specialty areas.

The academy has lost some of its prominence but certainly served as a forerunner to the present-day APA-sponsored programs, which have gained increasing significance in the last several years. Most early, continuing-educational efforts were defined by attendance at state, regional, and national conventions, reading journals and books, and listening to tapes (McNamara, 1977). The major problems with these approaches were poor monitoring systems, quality control, and questionable validity of presentation to practice. These early efforts raised numerous issues that included: (1) need for increased participation, (2) lack of stable funding, (3) evaluation of consequences of programs, (4) continuing education and recertification, (5) responsiveness to change in human-service delivery, (6) questions of multidisciplinary continuing education, and (7) broadening the base of an expanding constituency (Bloom, 1977). McQuire (1979) states further that continuing education may be valuable only in the context of job performance sampled in natural situations or carefully structured simulations. Efforts to reduce the confusion or questionable relationship of capability and performance on continuing education versus competent professional service still remain the critical issues in all continuing-education efforts (Jensen, 1979). To date, these issues still plague the continuing-education movement, but continuing education still retains its popularity as a development technique.

State licensing boards claim continuing education is first in effectiveness and the most easily developed of all competency-based measures. Additionally, continuing education is seen as inexpensive, highly flexible, easily varied to fill knowledge gaps, and minimally intrusive (Fish, 1981). A major issue now revolves around the use of entrepreneurs to develop continuing education as opposed to sponsorship by nonprofit and/or educational institutions. The APA sponsor-approval program includes both profit and nonprofit programs, and the evaluation of their relative effectiveness is yet to be determined.

The American Psychological Association has responded to the call for developing continuing-education guidelines by establishing the APA Continuing Education Sponsor-Approval System (Stetson, 1980–81). There are three parts to the system: review and approval of sponsors of providers of continuing-education activities for psychologists, a national computerized registry, and a calendar and information clearinghouse. The APA has clearly stated that continuing education is all those activities that contribute to the scientific, scholarly, or professional development of psychologists. Several constituencies are responded to by the APA continuing-education program including: the public, which needs assurance of continued competence from professionals; the individual psychologist, who needs to know which continuing-education programs have the profession's stamp of approval; and continuing-education sponsors, who look to guidelines to help conduct continuing-education programs. In addition, state examining boards are requiring continuing education for relicensure and recertification (Stetson, 1980–81).

The APA (1979) has set the goals of continuing education to facilitate the highest quality of professional work. To meet this goal, the APA has approved over 50 programs for continuing-education recognition; and the sponsor program is seemingly flourishing and stands to show steady growth during the 1980s. The states of this country are continuing to examine continuing education for psychologists; and, as of October 1980, there were 10 states (Georgia, Iowa, Maryland, Oregon, Washington, Utah, Colorado, New Mexico, Texas, and West Virginia) where continuing education was required for relicensure or recertification. Nine states (Alaska, Arkansas, Kansas, Louisiana, Michigan, Minnesota, North Carolina, Vermont, and Wyoming) had enabling legislation only, and eight states (California, Mississippi, Rhode Island, Alabama, Delaware, Massachusetts, Nevada, and New Hampshire) had continuing-education requirements under consideration. These numbers are constantly changing; but they did reveal, in late 1980, that better than half the states had procedures in place to facilitate the continuing-education movement as a requirement for continuing competence through relicensure or recertification (APA, 1980a).

Continuing-education programs clearly have strong support from the public, the profession, and the government as viable, practical, and cost-conscious methods of facilitating competence. The rush of voluntary and mandated continuing-education programs is further testimony to its grip on recipients and providers, and careful monitoring must be a vital force to ensure quality programs for professional participants. As the second step in one's individual professional development program, continuing education has the momentum and potential to be the most widely accepted means of competency assessment. Professional clinical psychologists must maintain an awareness of action by their state examining boards regarding requirements for continuing education and relicensure. Proper, long-range planning by the professional psychologist must include timing, cost, intent, and application if the psychologist in practice is to maintain a contemporary stance with colleagues and their professional growth patterns.

Peer review

The third step in the individual development series relates to the professionals making themselves visible to their peers for review and assessment. At this level of development, privacy must be sacrificed, and the participants must be willing to expose their professional styles. Also, they now become vulnerable to the preferences and orientations of the reviewers. Peer review may generate levels of concern beyond competence and may actually be a method to promote excellence and prevent mediocrity (Reiss, 1977). The forerunner of peer review is the diplomating process that is part of the American Board of Professional Psychology. Presentation of one's credentials, preparation of a work sample, and open review by one's peers are unique opportunities for the professional, which have rarely occurred to most since the defense of their dissertations in graduate school. Peer review has broadened its application since the inception of the ABPP process and now includes the CHAMPUS project of both the American Psychological and Psychiatric Associations. The stimulus behind the CHAMPUS project is not just excellence or competence but now focuses on cost and treatment factors.

As cost containment becomes a more critical issue in the delivery of care for the insurance carriers, mental health personnel find themselves increasingly called upon to provide review services for the appropriateness of care rather than calling on insurance-carrier clerks to provide that same task (Gibson, 1977). The assumption is clearly that peers reviewing services will improve the quality of care to the patient and, at the same time, reduce the cost to the carrier and ultimately to the premuim payers. Mental health training sites are now including instruction in the rationale and methods of peer review not only as an educational process but also on the quality of patient care (Kass, Charles, & Buckley, 1980).

As all professionals, and certainly psychologists, move into independent practice, there will be additional demands for competence, and peer review will become an increasingly relevant method for individual deliverers. Professional standards review organizations are part of the peer-review process (Albee, 1977). The momentum for this internal movement by psychology to review itself is done, in part, to prevent outside influences taking over this role, particularly with the rationale for cost containment. The insurance carriers, both commercial and governmental, think peer review has an impact in that voluntary peer review for the diplomate is more of an ego or status need for some, but under the insurance-carrier requirements, psychologists must now look at the profit-and-loss motive in their practices. Having a professional practitioner focus on patient problems, goals, and treatment plans cannot but help the provider as well as the consumer have a more focused perspective on the treatment process. Both the reviewer and the provider are now drawn into the competence forum, in that both parties would want to have a positive impact upon one another. Although the peer review by carriers is still voluntary and has an appeal process, the motive of financial gain serves as a significant motivator for improved planning of care. The entire process of peer review needs further support from the profession and could ultimately become mandated as a part of competency-based and excellence-based assessment.

The major problem areas for peer-review mechanics include: cost; invasion of privacy, both for the patient and the provider; and difficulties surrounding who will review whom, regarding such issues as seniority, theoretical orientation, and finances. The cost factors are potentially monumental in that most peer reviews require some layered effect where more than one review opinion is offered. The time requirements are also significant in that reviewers are faced with trying to understand an overall treatment process on paper of segmented observations that are well known to the provider and the consumer. The asset of objectivity may be the real balancing factor in the equation that offsets the time and familiarity issues.

The selection factors of reviewers becomes a critical variable in the process. Selection of reviewers must be made in the context of the peer-rating method to be used, applicability of peer assessments, and the effectiveness of peer nomination and peer ratings (Brief, 1980; Kane, & Lawler, 1980). In the diplomating process of ABPP, reviewers take the role of mentors, evaluators, and critics, toward the end of increasing competence and excellence of the candidates. The reviewers in ABPP volunteer their time and may have little concern for cost containment or analysis. Insurance-carrier reviewers are concerned not only with competence and excellence, but also must be concerned with third-party cost issues and perhaps motivated by the reviewer's financial remuneration for time and services provided. The state board of examiners sees practice audits as the second most effective techniques for assessing competence, but most difficult in terms of the ease with which they might be accomplished (Fish, 1981).

Peer review, peer-standard review organizations, and practice audits, in spite of their present problematical issues, may stand to be the most promising quality assurance individual development methods for future application. As psychologists become more sophisticated regarding business as well as professional matters, they will be able to take a more responsible perspective and will not be motivated by self-protective survival support of their less-competent colleagues. Psychologists have needed to ban together to both collaborate and compete with other professions in the economic struggle for a share of the mental health dollars. Now, as psychology acquires greater parity, the professional must take a responsibility to self-monitor not only for intrinsic reasons, but also with the realization that if we do not monitor ourselves, we will certainly be monitored by others.

Public issues and policy

The individual psychologists' development is becoming contingent upon their perceptions, knowledge, and actions regarding their involvement in the public domain. Assessing themselves, attending continuing-education efforts, and exposing themselves to peer review are critical and vital internal efforts to the profession, but the fourth step calls for a broader responsiveness to public issues. Psychologists in clinical practice are in a clear posture to give effective testimony to Congress, to seek reimbursement through national health insurance, to assist the public welfare, to support public advocacy, and to influence the formation of public policy (Sobel, 1979; VandenBos, 1979).

One of the most critical areas of concern to the professional clinical psychologist in the public domain is the consumer movement and its subsequent effects on accountability and cost factors. Mental health professions are noted to be deficient in their knowledge and concern about economic assumptions and consequences. Free-market pricing of services and advertising are elements of little consequence to providers; but with increasing government and insurance subsidy of providers, clinical psychologists must educate themselves in these areas (Buck & Hirschman, 1980). There are also increasing demands for consumer-protection boards and client involvement in problem definition and resolution as means of protecting clients' rights (Morrison, 1979). Dörken (1980), in his comments regarding Blue Cross-Blue Shield policies, discusses matters of market pressure on provider competition and consumer choice. There are definitive requirements to not only evaluate cost effectiveness, but also to improve the equation (Yates, 1979).

These fiscally related issues are contemporary arenas of concern for the remainder of the 20th century, and individual psychologists would be wise to call upon their skills in measurement and research to play a vital role in cost effectiveness of human services (Stewart, 1977). The growing reliance on third-party influence and economics has affected and will continue to affect issues such as supply and demand, payment schedules that differentiate the professions, and the growing competition between professions for the mental health dollar (Chodoff, 1978; McGuire, 1980). Control of costs will remain the vital issue in the viability of insurance for mental health because of professional inconsistency on types and duration of treatment for various psychological conditions (Guillette, 1977). Since psychotherapy is a major instrument in the profession's arsenal, it must be carefully scrutinized and studied in context of increased utilization, third-party payment, and questionable inclusion in pending, national health-insurance deliberations.

There are increasing suggestions in research to enhance and support the notion of the effectiveness of short-term psychotherapy (Albin, 1980; Aldrich, 1975; Bennett & Wisneski, 1979; Cummings, 1977b). Needless to say, the aspects of a tighter economy in the 1970s have influenced the need to study cost benefits of psychotherapy. Cost benefits and effectiveness of shorter forms of psychotherapy are noted in terms of prevention of medical care and hospitalization (Albin, 1980; Cummings, 1977a, 1977b). With the rash of new therapies and techniques, there is an increased need for scrutiny and control of these therapies plus the utilization of peer review in making providers more conscious of and focused on their methods of treatment (Albin, 1980; Claiborn & Stricker, 1979; Kisch & Kroll, 1980; Stricker, 1979).

DeMuth and Kamis (1980) have written about fees, utilization, duration, and measurement of psychotherapy effectiveness. They have demonstrated that third-party reimbursement does not lead to excessive utilization. They further dispel the notion of a direct relationship between effectiveness of outcome and cost. Cost can be reduced, without significant changes in effectiveness, by using less expensive therapists, less frequent sessions, and outpatient rather than inpatient therapy (Karon & Vanden-Bos, 1976; Washburn, Vannicelli, Lonabaugh, & Scheff, 1976; Yates, 1978).

DeMuth and Yates (1981) further explore the cost-benefit issue by suggesting three directions of how to optimize outcomes and minimize costs. First, a revised training model would call for a concept of scientist-practitioner-manager. Operation research and management science would be new educational directions for professional psychology. Second, expanded methodologies in policymaking and administrative skills could enhance the psychologists' grasp of the relationship between clinical and economic variables. Third, institutionalizing new incentives to reward cost saving could be used to overcome the ineffectiveness of supply-and-demand principles in health care services.

Significant sources of data suggest that the well-enlightened, professional clinical psychologist may well expand his/her continuing development and education beyond theory and practice into areas of economics, management, and quality control, in a society of increased consumer knowledge and sophistication.

HMOs are already being proposed as alternatives to fee-for-service payment schedules as prices escalate and the less wealthy are out of reach of private care (Ridgewood, 1981). The HMO may become the center for application of psychological services unless there is a more responsible professional approach to the cost-control issue.

Cost of care and economic responsibility have become critical public issues to which the practicing psychologist must be ever mindful and responsive, if one is to survive the next several decades.

In addition to cost and fiscal accountability, other public-domain issues (such as patient rights and the law, ethics, training, and standards) must be of critical concern to the practicing psychologist. The treatment-rights movement and treatment suits have been demonstrated as change agents in the quality of care; and they subsequently will affect the practice of all providers, whether they are mindful of the issues or remain unconcerned (Simon, 1975; Kaufman, 1979). These rights issues will significantly impact on liability and malpractice. Psychologists are seen to possess only the most rudimentary understanding of legal concepts surrounding professional malpractice suits (DeLeon, 1978). Due process concepts likewise have become common jargon in all elements of consumer rights and even in the arena of professional-provider identification and licensure (Smith, 1978). These concepts in legal arenas impinge on all professions, and psychologists must be aware of their impacts. Ignorance of the law is rarely a viable defense when it comes to liability and consumer rights. There is little doubt that the practicing clinician must maintain not only a psychological frame of reference, but also a legal-economic point of view.

Closely related to the legal arena is the spillover into ethical matters. The minimal training in the legal-ethical domain leads to conflicts regarding clients rights, institutional needs, and ethical obligations (Roston, 1975). Matters of privacy and confidentiality are often ignored but, in perspective, should be made clear to the client during the initial contact

(Siegel, 1979). Practitioners need be aware of these issues and to seek consultation in such. Matters of ignorance and poor judgment versus willful disregard of ethics too often appear before legal bodies and lead to problems for both clients and providers (Keith-Spiegel, 1977). The APA attempts to keep psychologists informed on these matters, and each professional has a responsibility to follow these cases (Sanders, 1979). Matters such as advertising affect ethics as well as fiscal issues, and individual psychologists entering the free-market competition must be responsive to the spirit as well as the letter of the law regarding the advertisement of services (Koocher, 1977). In a human service profession, psychologists' regard for social change is a hidden ethic that may be a more overt force in the decades ahead (Arthur, 1976). This focus on ethics resulted from the consumer movement and was further influenced by a rather pervasive "therapeutic ideology" of the 1960s and 1970s (Silber, 1976). Silber (1976) further reflects on the expert status of applied psychologists and how this position now leads to further potential abuse of the profession unless there is a heightened sense of ethical ideology and behavior.

The psychologists' continuing professional development in the public domain may most concretely be summarized as an issue of accountability and ethics. Both of these elements contribute to quality assurance and competence. Ethics are seen as a value system of the provider, and accountability is the mechanism through which the ideals of the value system are realized (McMillan, 1976). These components of quality require more professional time and responsiveness and certainly provide a proper umbrella under which many development activities could be realized.

SUMMARY

Continuing professional development (CPD) is a marketing method for the profession of clinical psychology and a quality-assurance device for the individual clinical psychologist. Effective marketing techniques for the profession call for organizational management that is goal-oriented to what the consumer needs and to what the profession has to offer. CPD is the effective and timely interface of professional resources in psychology to meet a growing consumer public that is more sophisticated, demanding, and intelligent.

The individual clinical psychologist's continuing professional development is the quality-assurance method that provides both competence and excellence to the consumer. A four-step concurrent system of CPD includes self-assessment, continuing education, peer review, and public responsiveness as the critical elements of continued professionalism.

The combined effects of a well-managed and marketed profession with a quality-conscious, competent professional will provide the benchmarks for satisfaction, sophistication, and survival of clinical psychology well into the next century.

REFERENCES

Albee, G. W., & Kessler, M. Evaluating individual deliverers: Private practice and professional-standards review organizations. *Professional psychology,* 1977, *8,* 502–515.

Albin, R. Psychotherapy: Keeping it short. *APA Monitor,* 1980, *II,* 6–7.

Aldrich, C. K. The long and short of psychotherapy. *Psychiatric Annals,* 1975, *5,* 507–512.

American Psychological Association. *Approval of sponsors of continuing education for psychologists: Criteria, standards, and procedures.* Washington, D.C.: Author, 1979.

American Psychological Association. *Status of continuing-education requirements among states.* Washington, D.C.: Author, 1980. (a)

American Psychological Association. *Task Force on Self-Assessment: Interim report.* Washington, D.C.: Author, 1980. (b)

American Psychological Association. Specialty guidelines for the delivery of services by clinical psychologists. *American Psychologist,* 1981, *36,* 640–651.

Arthur, A. Z. Hidden ethics in clinical psychology: Success is not enough. *Ontario Psychologist,* 1976, *8,* 6–13.

Bennett, M. J., & Wisneski, M. J. Continuous psychotherapy within an HMO. *American Journal of Psychiatry,* 1979, *136,* 1283–1287.

Bloom, B. L. Current issues in mental health continuing education. *American Journal of Community Psychology,* 1977, *5,* 121–130.

Brief, A. P. Peer assessment revisited: A brief comment on Kane and Lawler. *Psychological Bulletin,* 1980, *88,* 78–79.

Buck, J. A., & Hirschman, R. Economic and mental health services: Enhancing the power of the consumer. *American Psychologist,* 1980, *35,* 653–661.

Chodoff, P. Psychiatry and the fiscal third party. *American Journal of Psychiatry,* 1978, *135,* 1141–1147.

Claiborn, W. L., & Stricker, G. Professional-standards review organization, peer review, and CHAMPUS. *Professional Psychology,* 1979, *10,* 631–639.

Cohen, H. S. Professional licensure, organizational behavior, and the public interest. *Milbank Memorial Fund Quarterly: Health and Society,* 1973, *51,* 73–88.

Cummings, N. A. The anatomy of psychotherapy under national health insurance. *American Psychologist,* 1977, *32,* 711–718. (a)

Cummings, N. A. Prolonged (ideal) versus short-term (realistic) psychotherapy. *Professional Psychology,* 1977, *8,* 491–501. (b)

DeLeon, P. H., & Borreliz, M. Malpractice: Professional liability and the law. *Professional Psychology,* 1978, *9,* 467–477.

DeMuth, N. M., & Kamis, E. Fees and therapy: Clarification of the relationship of payment source to service utilization. *Journal of Consulting and Clinical psychology,* 1980, *48,* 793–795.

DeMuth, N. M., & Yates, B. T. Improving psychotherapy: Old beliefs, new research, and future directions. *Professional Psychology,* 1981, *12,* 587–595.

Doctorate production levels off. *APA Briefly,* September 1981, S1; S3.

Dörken, H. 1976 third-party reimbursement experience: An interstate comparison by insurance carrier. *American Psychologist,* 1980, *35,* 355–363.

Fish, J. E. Continuing education and alternative forms of competence assurance. *Newsletter: Section II of the Division of Clinical Psychology of the American Pychological Association,* 1981, *17,* 11–16.

Gale, L. E., & Pol, G. Competence: A definition and conceptual scheme. *Educational Technology,* 1975, *15,* 19–25.

Gibson, R. W. Claims review for psychiatric services: Survival of the most reimbursable. *Journal: National Association of Private Psychiatric Hospitals,* 1977, *9,* 33–35.

Gottfredson, G. D., & Dyer, S. E. Health-service providers in psychology. *American Psychologist,* 1978, *33,* 314–338.

Gross, S. J. The myth of professional licensing. *American Psychologist,* 1978, *33,* 1009–1016.

Guillette, W. Is psychotherapy insurable? *Journal: National Association of Private Psychiatric Hospitals,* 1977, *9,* 30–32.

Harvey, M. R. *Competence-based mental health service: A synthesis for social planning* (Publication No. 80–09–05.). Washington, D.C.: National Center for the Study of Professions, March 1980.

Hays, J. R., & Smith, A. L. Composition of state psychology licensing boards. *Psychological Reports,* 1978, *43,* 39–43.

Hess, H. F. Entry requirements for professional practice of psychology. *American Psychologist,* 1977, *32,* 365–368.

Hoffman, P. J. *Continuing competency assurance: Some research and measurement considerations.* Paper presented at the Conference on Evaluating Competence in Health Professions, New York, 1976.

Jensen, R. E. Professional development or continuing education: A choice point. *Clinical Psychologist,* 1979, *33,* 20–22.

Joint Commission for the Accreditation of Hospitals. Standards Final: Physician role upheld. *APA Monitor,* 1981, *12,* S3.

Jones, N. F. Continuing education: A new challenge for psychology. *American Psychologist,* 1975, *30,* 842–847.

Kahn, R. Job burnout: Prevention and remedies. *Public Welfare,* 1978, *Spring,* 61–63.

Kane, J. S., & Lawler, E. E. In defense of peer assessment: A rebuttal to Brief's critique. *Psychological Bulletin,* 1980, *88,* 80–81.

Karon, B. P., & VandenBos, G. R. Cost/benefit analysis: Psychologist versus psychiatrist for schizophrenics. *Professional Psychology,* 1976, *7,* 107–111.

Kass, F., Charles, E., & Buckley, P. Two-year follow-up of a peer-review training program for residents. *American Journal of Psychiatry,* 1980, *137,* 244–245.

Kaufman, E. The right to treatment suit as an agent of change. *American Journal of Psychiatry,* 1979, *136,* 1428–1432.

Keith-Spiegel, P. Violation of ethical principles due to ignorance or poor professional judgement versus willful disregard. *Professional Psychology,* 1977, *8,* 288–296.

Kisch, J., & Kroll, J. Meaningfulness versus effectiveness: Paradoxical implications in the evaluation of psychotherapy. *Psychotherapy: Theory, Research, and Practice,* 1980, *17,* 401–413.

Koocher, G. P. Advertising for psychologists: Pride and prejudice or sense and sensibility? *Professional Psychology,* 1977, *8,* 149–160.

Koocher, G. P. Credentialing in psychology: Close encounters with competence? *American Psychologist,* 1979, *34,* 696–702.

Maslach, C. Job burnout: How people cope. *Public Welfare,* 1978, *Spring,* 56–58.

McGuire, T. Markets for psychotherapy. In G. VandenBos (Ed.), *Psychotherapy: From practice to research to policy.* Beverly Hills, Calif.: Sage Publications, 1980.

McMillan, J. J. Accountability among providers of psychological services. *Clinical Psychologist,* 1976, *29,* 7–13.

McNamara, J. R. An assessment proposal for determining the competence of professional psychologists. *Professional Psychology,* 1975, *6,* 135–139.

McNamara, J. R. Patterns of continuing education for Ohio psychologists: A survey of interests and activities (1972–1974). *Professional Psychology,* 1977, *8,* 368–376.

McQuire, C. *Issues in the assessment of continuing professional competence.* Paper presented at the annual meeting of the American Educational Research Association, San Francisco, April 1979.

Menges, R. J. Assessing readiness for professional practice. *Review of Educational Research,* 1975, *45,* 173–207.

Morrison, J. K. A consumer-oriented approach to psychotherapy. *Psychotherapy: Theory, Research, and Practice,* 1979, *16,* 381–384.

O'Keefe, A. M. Congress, federal courts ponder applying antitrust to health care. *Association for the Advancement of Psychology Advance,* 1981, *4,* 1–3.

Patterson, T. W. The status of continuing professional development. *Clinical Psychologist,* 1979, *33,* 22–23.

Pottinger, P. S. *Defining competence in the mental health professions.* Paper presented at the annual meeting of the American Psychological Association, New York, September 1979.

Reiss, B. F. The presence of excellence in professional psychology. *Transnational Mental Health Research Newsletter,* 1977, *19,* 10–11.

Ridgewood Financial Institute. 1980 survey report. *Psychotherapy Finances,* 1980 *7,* 1–8.

Ridgewood Financial Institute. Expanding practice: Is there still an HMO in your future? *Psychotherapy Finances,* 1981, *8,* 3–6.

Ross, A. D. Continuing professional development in psychology. *Professional Psychology,* 1974, *5,* 122–128.

Roston, R. A. Ethical uncertainties and "technical" validities. *Professional Psychology,* 1975, *6,* 50–54.

Salary survey results available. *APA Briefly,* September 1981, S3.

Sanders, J. R. Complaints against psychologists adjudicated informally by APA's Committee on Scientific and Professional Ethics and Conduct. *American Psychologist,* 1979, *34,* 1139–1144.

Siegel, M. Privacy, ethics, and confidentiality. *Professional Psychology,* 1979, *10,* 249–258.

Silber, D. E. Ethical relativity and professional psychology. *Clinical Psychologist,* 1976, *29,* 3–5.

Simon, G. C. Psychology and the "treatment-rights movement." *Professional Psychology,* 1975, *6,* 243–251.

Smith, R. C. Psychology and the courts: Some implications of recent judicial decisions for state licensing boards. *Professional Psychology,* 1978, *9,* 489–497.

Sobel, S. B. Nick Cummings reflects on psychology's future in public policy. *Clinical Psychologist,* 1979, *33,* 13–15.

Stetson, E. Continuing education: A primer. In P. M. Cunningham (Ed.), *Yearbook of adult and continuing education* (6th ed.). Chicago: Marquis Academic Media, 1980–81.

Stewart, D. W. Psychology and accounting: An interface or a red face. *Professional Psychology,* 1977, *8,* 178–184.

Stricker, G. Criteria for insurance review of psychological services. *Professional Psychology,* 1979, *10,* 118–122.

Strupp, H. H. Clinical psychology, irrationalism, and the erosion of excellence. *American Psychologist,* 1976, *31,* 561–571.

VandenBos, G. Psychology and national policy: An interview with Charles A. Kiesler. *Clinical Psychologist,* 1979, *33,* 15.

Walker, C. E. Continuing professional development: The future for clinical psychology. *Clinical Psychologist,* 1977, *30,* 6–7.

Washburn, S., Vannicelli, M., Lonabaugh, R., & Scheff, B. T. A controlled comparison of psychiatric day treatment and inpatient hospitalization. *Journal of Consulting and Clinical Psychology,* 1976, *44,* 665–675.

Yates, B. T. Improving the cost effectiveness of obesity programs. *International Journal of Obesity,* 1978, *2,* 249–266.

Yates, B. T. How to improve, rather than evaluate, cost effectiveness. *Counseling Psychologist,* 1979, *8,* 72–75.

41

Professional issues

Alan Barclay*

INTRODUCTION AND OVERVIEW

Let it be understood at the outset that this is a selective overview of some current professional issues—issues that confront the practicing clinician as well as those involved with administration, with clinical training, with clinical research; in point of fact, the whole enterprise of clinical psychology.

The selectivity is not that of choice but that of necessity, for clinical psychology has expanded its compass geometrically and hence has concerns that are far-ranging and much too broad to be accommodated in the brief scope of this essay on professional issues.

It will be helpful, perhaps, to afford an overview of some of the issues which will affect clinical psychology in both the near-term and the longer-term future. This overview is principally concerned with the impact of current and pending legislation, since it is in the legislative arena that policy decisions are enacted into laws that affect education, training, practice, reimbursement for services, and other aspects of the practice of clinical psychology, the education and training of future clinicians, and the research base of the field of clinical psychology.

Of particular concern is the recent shift in the attitude of the federal government relative to the behavioral and social sciences. The present administration is committed to a reduction in support of the behavioral and social sciences for both research and training, as witnessed by statements such as the following made by David Stockman; (personal communication, 1981) from the Office of Management and Budget (OMB):

> The supply of mental health professionals is now generally adequate, mental health professionals generally have a good income potential, and thus federal subsidies for such training are no longer necessary.

On the research and training side of the enterprise, the research budget of the National Institutes of Mental Health, the major source of federal

---

*School of Professional Psychology, Wright State University.

funding for mental health research, has declined for more than a decade, and the present administration proposes to slash research funding even further. For example, fiscal year (FY) 1981 funding was at a level of $141.7 million, but it was reduced in FY 1982 to $130.9. And research training funds were reduced from $19.5 million in FY 1981 to $15.4 million in FY 1982. Witness also the proposed exclusionary language offered by the Alcohol, Drug Abuse, and Mental Health Administration relative to social research;

> Unless explicitly focused on mental illness or mental health, NIMH does not support studies of large scale social conditions or problems (poverty, unemployment, inadequate housing and slums, divorce, day care arrangements, accidents, and criminal behavior), social class and groups and their interrelations. . . .

Circumstances are no better with the National Science Foundation, which has funded basic psychological research in the past and has provided significant underpinnings for the basic science aspects of professional psychology. The present administration proposes, among other things, drastic reductions for the Division of Behavioral and Neural Sciences, amounting to a reduction of 50 percent, together with a proposal to eliminate science education support and the Women and Minorities in Science program. Such reductions would seriously compromise the ability of the science and profession of psychology to gain new knowledge that would assist in the education and training of future generations of psychologists.

A brief listing of some of the issues facing clinical psychology, indeed the whole enterprise of psychology in all its facets, is instructive. These issues are:

1. Research training funding from NIMH or NIH.
2. National Science Foundation fund reductions.
3. National Institute of Mental Health research funding.
4. National Institute of Alcohol Abuse fund reductions.
5. National Institute on Drug Abuse research funding.
6. Administration for Children, Youth, and Families funding.
7. National Institute of Mental Health clinical training funds.
8. U.S. Criminal Code revisions affecting psychologists.
9. Employee Retirement Income Security Act concerns.
10. Federal Employees Health Benefits Act problems.
11. Federal Trade Commission continuance.
12. Medicare/Medicaid use of psychologists.

As can be readily observed, the magnitude of these issues is immense. Some, such as the revisions to the Criminal Code to permit psychiatric examinations by either a psychiatrist or a clinical psychologist, have been in process for as much as six years.

Coupled with the magnitude of these issues, is the major reorganization of the federal government proposed by the present administration. The effects of this will be felt in federal, state, and local contexts and particularly in the behavioral and social sciences. This present overview attempts to delineate some of the major areas of concern, and subsequent discussion will touch upon their impact on the field.

As a last and grim coda to this litany of woes regarding prospects for the behavioral sciences, including clinical psychology, a quote from the associate director of the Office of Science and Technology Policy, Executive Office of the President, dated July 1981, (Prager, 1981) reflects the attitude of the administration:

> as a result of (federal) budget imperatives, important social and behavioral sciences research will not receive adequate support. One of the problems is, of course, that it is often difficult to demonstrate the claim . . . for "the significance of the contributions which these disciplines have offered in the vital areas of health, human relations, education . . . and more." It is my personal belief that social and behavioral scientists . . . have done a particularly poor job of demonstrating the significance of these putative contributions.

It should be clear from the forgoing comment, and, indeed, from the actions of the federal government, that future support for clinical psychological education, training, and research will be won but grudgingly from the present and possibly future, administrations. Hence, the importance of the continuing development of advocacy efforts at the federal level, notably through the Association for the Advancement of Psychology, the legislative advocacy group representing American psychology, and working in close conjunction with the legislative and advocacy efforts of the American Psychological Association. In the presentations to follow, selected areas of professional issues are discussed with respect to their impact on the field and their implications and ramifications. And a prognosis is offered for the future of these efforts to obtain and maintain recognition of the science and profession of psychology at local, state, regional, and federal levels. While psychology is a diverse enterprise, comprising both theoretical and applied interests, research and application, the discipline of psychology *qua* psychology must unite in an organized advocacy effort. As Patrick Henry observed in the face of determined British opposition: "Gentlemen, we must hang together, or we shall surely hang singly."

EDUCATION, TRAINING, AND RESEARCH ISSUES

In this section, an effort will be made to delineate issues related to the education, training, and research activities of the field of clinical psychology since it is obvious that without education, training, and research efforts, clinical psychology would quickly become moribund.

In order to fully appreciate the scope of what is being proposed for federal support for education as of this writing, consider that the administration proposes a cut of 5.5 percent for student financial assistance programs in higher education in general. This translates into a possible reduction of some 800,000 students who could attend college. It would have a significant impact at both the undergraduate and graduate level in the field of psychology, as well as other fields, since many students are partially or fully dependent on such loans for their education. Further, such reductions may well have the effect of a restructuring of education along social class lines; i.e., families and students most in need of support will not be able to afford the costs of higher education, and only families and students with greater financial resources will be able to support students from their own resources. Thus, since greater financial resources are highly correlated with social class, it is obvious as to the probable pernicious effect of these reductions.

With respect to clinical training in psychology, funding for such training is the responsibility of the National Institute of Mental Health and is almost the only source of such funds within the Department of Health and Human Services. Historically, these funds first became available in 1948 at a level of approximately $1 million. The high point was 1969 with funding at $93 million, but funding later declined to a level of about $70 million annually. Of this amount, the field of psychology obtains somewhere between 15–20 percent, supporting approximately 1,000 trainees yearly. As noted previously, the present administration proposes abolition of such training support with obvious disastrous consequences for clinical training programs. Congress, on the other hand, has recognized that while there has been an absolute increase in mental health professionals, there remain documented needs for these professionals with such special populations as the elderly, children, minorities, and so on. Successful efforts have been made by various advocacy groups, such as the American Psychological Association, (1981) and the Association for the Advancement of Psychology (1982), to call attention to these problems, but the threat remains as to the continued funding of clinical training programs.

On the research training side of the enterprise of clinical psychology, there are current proposals for major cuts in such funds. For example, from a FY 1980 base of about $18 million, current proposals involve reduction to $11.8 million in FY 1982. In addition, as noted previously, all new funding for "social researchers" would be eliminated. For general research support, while so-called stable funding was proposed, there would be both a relative as well as an absolute decrease in research support, from FY 1981 support of $109 million to FY 1982 support of $102 million, with support of investigators external to NIMH being decreased and reallocated within the institute. Additionally, so-called social research would be phased out, including research on families, children, divorce, mass media effects, and general social policy research.

Taken together, these proposed and actual reductions would result in decreased opportunity for access to education in the field of psychology at both graduate and undergraduate levels, decreased opportunity for clinical training support, decreased opportunity for research training support, and lack of funds for fundamental research in clinical psychological processes.

This is, perhaps, the most critical issue that most clinical psychologists will face during the rest of the present century. If these proposed reductions are not thwarted, then the viability of clinical psychology as a field of study and as an applied discipline may very well wither and vanish.

HEALTH PSYCHOLOGY AND RELATED ISSUES

Recent observations noted in *The Health Psychologist* (Ferguson & Wellons, 1981) are of considerable import, since the health and illness industry is the largest in the United States. It has been estimated that approximately 3.5 million persons are employed in this industry, with something like 7,000 hospitals, 40 million hospital admissions per year, and an average daily hospital census of over 1 million persons. Given the size of this industry, the market penetration of clinical psychologists into it has been miniscule. However, there is some hope, since Secretary of Health and Human Services Richard S. Schweiker has stated publicly that it is his intent to direct the programs of the National Institutes of Health to develop a focus on health research on "wellness." To afford an idea of the potential of participation in these programs, note that the budget for Health and Human Services is $274.2 billion, which comprises 36 percent of the federal budget, more than that of all 50 states and more than the budget of any other nation except the United States and the Soviet Union, and $56 billion more than the Department of Defense budget. This budget will include, *inter alia*, $1 million for health risk reduction and health education, $117 million for the training of health professionals, $4 million for curricular projects related to health education, health promotion, and related activities, and $2 million designated for research related to smoking and smoking reduction programs (an obvious area for clinical psychology intervention). Finally, and perhaps most important, an allocation of $2 million is requested for the Office of Health Promotion, whose activities are viewed as the most promising area for future improvement in the health status of the nation. Unfortunately, clinical psychologists are notable for their absence in effective participation in health policy matters, and the majority of Congress and congressional staff simply do not understand the important role that clinical psychologists have played in the development of such areas as biofeedback, weight reduction, smoking control, and other preventive health activities. While this gap is being narrowed through a variety of legislative advocacy efforts, there is much to be done if the field of clinical psychology is to become significantly involved in such health activities. As a final note worth reflecting on, the surgeon general notes that of the 10 leading causes of death in this nation, at least 7 are largely behaviorally determined and could be substantially reduced by behavioral interventions.

FEDERAL HEALTH INSURANCE PROGRAMS

There are currently two federal health insurance programs that affect clinical psychologists. The first of these is the Federal Employees Health Benefits Plan, the largest organized health insurance program in the nation. Among other coverages, the FEHBP provides for mental health benefits, and current actions are being initiated to mandate a standard benefit level for alcoholism, drug abuse, and mental benefits. It has been demonstrated that such benefits result in increased productivity—an $8 return for each $1 invested in such benefits under employee assistance programs. This return comes from reduced absenteeism, reduced accidents and disability claims, and reduced use of medical services. The median reduction is about 20 percent for mental health benefits and 40 percent for alcoholism benefits. Obviously, clinical psychologists can and do serve as providers in such programs. However, the insurance carriers have consistently attempted to restrict reimbursements to psychologists unless treatment was done under medical supervision. While this has been successfully fought, notably in the so-called Virginia Blues suit (624 F. 2d 476, 4th Circuit, 1980) in which psychologists sought relief from Blue Cross and Blue Shield restrictions on direct reimbursement to psychologists, there are still efforts to reduce the pool of providers, and psychologists need to be alert to such efforts.

The second program is the Employees Retirement Income Security Act, which is a complex program relating to ensuring that employees receive appropriate benefits during their employment and on retirement. Of interest to clinical psychologists is the fact that, as it now stands, ERISA permits the preemption of state laws mandating minimum mental health benefits coverage and guaranteeing recognition of nonmedical health care practitioners. The specific concern relates to the possible preemption of the Freedom of Choice statutes obtained through lengthy efforts by state psychological associations. If the ERISA reform legislation currently under consideration is not passed, it would permit the insurance carrier to ignore the Freedom of Choice statute and to mandate only medical coverage for the mental health benefit.

Of less interest because of current neglect is national health insurance. At the present time, little is being considered, but it is certain that there will be future congressional consideration of such legislation. Efforts need to be made to ensure appropriate recognition of clinical psychologists as independent health care providers.

FEDERAL TRADE COMMISSION

The Federal Trade Commission is empowered to enforce antitrust laws based upon traditional judicial restraints against price-fixing, boycotts, and conspiracies in restraint of trade. Such activities in the health care field can be dated to the 1943 decision of the Supreme Court, which found that the American Medical Association was in violation of the Sherman Antitrust Act. Antitrust laws should continue to apply to all professions who benefit from the American free enterprise system. However, recent efforts have been made, and are continuing to be made, to strip the Federal Trade Commission of its power to enforce antitrust laws against the professions, notably medicine and dentistry. Of particular note is the federal antitrust case of the *Virginia Academy of Clinical Psychologists* v. *Blue Shield of Virginia.* In that case, it was found that Blue Shield organizations in Virginia were being used by physicians to restrict competition in the delivery of mental health care services in violation of the Sherman Act, and *inter alia,* the court noted that:

> it is not the function of a group of professionals to decide that competition is not beneficial in their line of work, [*and*] we are not inclined to condone anticompetitive conduct upon an incantation of "good medical practice. Moreover, we fail to see how the policy in question fulfills that goal. . . . It defies logic to assume that the average family practitioner can supervise a licensed psychologist in psychotherapy, and there is no basis in the record for such an assumption." (624 F. 2d 476, 4th Circuit, 1980)

The major effect of efforts to strip the Federal Trade Commission of its jurisdiction would be to increase the danger of anticompetitive practices that would adversely affect the practice of clinical psychologists, as illustrated by the attempts of Virginia Blue Shield to restrict the practice of clinical psychology. It seems likely that the mood of the current Congress may be such as to defend against such efforts to restrict the jurisdiction; however, the issue remains to be resolved.

MEDICARE AND MEDICAID

Title XVIII of the Social Security Act provides for mental health benefits under the Medicare Supplemental Benefits program, but it does not provide for direct recognition of psychologists as eligible providers. The Health Care Financing Administration is proposing changes in Title XVIII to create more flexibility at the state level in the administration of the Medicare programs, but there continues to be opposition to the inclusion of clinical psychologists as eligible providers of mental health services. Such exclusionary practices are consistent with other manifestations of the effort to exclude clinical psychologists from full staff privileges in hospital settings, notably the actions of the Joint Commission on the Accreditation of Hospitals whose requirements for accreditation exclude clinical psychologists from full recognition on the medical staffs of hospitals. In 1980, the attorney general of Ohio brought suit against the JCAH for antitrust restraint of trade in the practice of psychology, and this suit is still in process. In response, the Ohio Medical Association attempted to enact new legislation to limit membership on hospital medical staffs, and these problems continue. The implications are clear—the profession of clinical psychology must remain vigilant to preserve its right to the independent practice of clinical psychology and must be alert to the encroachments of other professions that would attempt to suppress the full and free practice of clinical psychology.

CRIMINAL CODE REFORM AND THE NOT GUILTY BY REASON OF INSANITY PLEA

For the past six years, the Congress has made attempts at reform of the Criminal Code without success. However, with respect to clinical psychology, pieces of legislation both in the House and in the Senate include recognition that psychologists are competent to determine mental status:

> (b) Psychiatric Examination. A psychiatric examination ordered pursuant to this subchapter or section 2002 (c) shall be conducted by a licensed or certified psychiatrist or clinical psychologist, or, if the court finds it appropriate, by more than one such examiner. . . .

While this legislative effort is still in limbo, its eventual enactment will permit the clinical psychologist parity with psychiatrists relative to psychiatric examinations. In addition, it is probable that the term "psychiatric examination" may be amended to that of "psychological examination" to reflect the broader approach of the psychologist who may use multiple assessments to provide for such examinations (Senate Bill 1630).

With respect to the Not Guilty by Reason of Insanity plea, the assassination attempt on President Reagan has sparked numerous efforts to deal with the problem of crimes committed by mentally disordered individuals and the resultant insanity defense. Morse (1982), in testimony presented to the House Committee on the Judiciary, notes that:

> As a society, we must decide if the insanity defense is morally necessary. If it is, we should insure that trials are conducted rationally, that questionable verdicts are minimized, and that the disposition of those acquitted by reason of insanity protects society and the person acquitted . . . The basic moral issue is whether it is just to punish a person who was terribly crazy at the time of the offense. I use the word "crazy" advisedly, with no lack of respect for disordered persons or professionals who try to help them.

The relevant question in this situation is to establish whether the crime was committed by a mentally disordered individual and who is to provide testimony to that effect. The aforementioned legislative efforts direct themselves to this question and do recognize psychologists as qualified experts to determine this question as well as the competency of the individual to be held accountable for his or her actions. This recognition is yet another step forward in the legislative acknowledgement of the independent practice of clinical psychology.

TRAINING IN PROFESSIONAL PSYCHOLOGY

Yet another issue that confronts the clinical psychologist is the nature of education and training to prepare the individual for practice. Recent developments in the field have suggested that there is a need for rethinking the proper approach to what is increasingly being termed professional psychology (McNamara & Barclay, 1982). The professional psychologist is not the hybrid envisioned by the traditional program; i.e., a scientist and a practitioner. Rather, it is the view of professional psychology training programs that the individual must primarily be an applied practitioner, mindful of the science base, but not expected to embody all of the attitudes of the scientist and researcher. The growth of the professional school movement (Fox, Barclay, & Rodgers, 1982) is clear evidence of the viability of such ideas, but the lack of clarity regarding the definition of the professional psychologist, and the lack of a generally agreed upon educational process, have been significant impediments to future growth and development of the professional psychology movement. As noted in *Science* (Walsh, 1979):

> Emergence of the schools of professional psychology is a significant step in the professionalization process, but the schools are very much in the formative stage and face a number of thorny fundamental issues. There is concern, for example, that the new schools set a proper balance between research and practice, so that their graduates are well prepared as practitioners but are also receptive to new knowledge and thus able to avoid early professional obsolence, the proverbial pitfall when "training" is stressed over "education."

The field of professional psychology, it should be noted, is broader than simply clinical psychology. There is merit in the notion that individuals should be trained as generalists in professional psychology, with broad knowledge in the various fields of applied psychology but without extensive depth, the in-depth experience coming in the postdoctoral years either through formal study or guided experience or a combination of both. In any event, the practitioner of the future will be a considerably different product than that of the past.

CONCLUDING OBSERVATIONS

As can be noted from the foregoing review of some salient issues in the field of clinical psychology, there is an urgent need for psychologists to become much more involved with the political and legislative process (Martin, 1981, 1982). Although there is an emerging good track record for psychology, principally for the professional sector of psychology, the cadre of activists is woefully small and pitifully funded. Perhaps this is due to something in the training of psychologists or in the culturally transmitted ethic; but in any event, in the legislative arena the profession of psychology is, as Hamlet was; "sicklied o'er with the pale cast of thought, they lose the name of action; and thus enterprises of great pith and moment are lost."

SUMMARY

Professional issues pertaining to the field of psychology both in the near and long-term future are examined. The focus on current and pending legislation in the federal government suggests potential repercussions in a broad spectrum of areas in the field of psychology. The actions and attitudes of the federal government and the current administration suggest further reductions in funds related to education, training, practice, and research.

However, the federal budget for Health and Human Services reflects the current emphasis on the health and illness industry in the United States. Unfortunately, the potential role of the clinical psychologist in this industry is not being realized. Psychologists must become advocates for their field to ensure proportionate penetration into this growing industry.

Several examples are cited to demonstrate attempts to liberate or suppress the full and free practice of clinical psychology by various groups. Federal legislation on Criminal Code reform and the Not Guilty by Reason of Insanity Plea represent the legislative acknowledgement of clinical psychology as an independent practice.

REFERENCES

American Psychological Association. *Task force report on psychologist's use of physical interventions.* Washington, D.C., 1981

American Psychological Association, Association for the Advancement of Psychology. *Proceedings of the Joint Executive Committee,* Washington, D.C., 1982

Ferguson, D., & Wellons, R. Hospitals, health care, and health psychology. *The Health Psychologist,* 1981, *3,* 1

Fox, R., Barclay, A., & Rodgers, D. The foundations of professional psychology. *American Psychologist,* 1982, *37*(3), 306–312

Martin, C. J., Association for the Advancement of Psychology. Personal communication, July 29, 1981

Martin, C. J., Association for the Advancement of Psychology. Personal communication, February 8, 1982

McNamara, J. R., & Barclay, A. (Eds.). *Critical issues, trends, and developments in professional psychology.* New York: Praeger Publishers, 1982

Morse, S. J. *Testimony on the insanity defense legislation.* The United States House of Representatives Committee on the Judiciary, 1982

Prager, D. J., Executive Office of the President. Personal communication to C. J. Martin, Association for the Advancement of Psychology, July 29, 1981

Senate Bill 1630, 97th Congress, 1st Session, September 17, 1981

Stockman, D. Additional details on budget savings, Fiscal Year 1982, April 1982. Cited in personal communication to M. Pallak, Executive Officer, American Psychological Association, April 24, 1981

Virginia Academy of Clinical Psychologists et al. v. *Blue Shield of Virginia* et al., 624 F. 2d 476, 4th Circuit, 1980

Walsh, J., Professional psychologists seek to change roles and rules in the field. *Science,* 1979, *203,* 338–340

PART VI

Forensic psychology

42

Law and the practice of clinical psychology

*Jenny Boyer**

Clinical psychologists traditionally provide services in three arenas: diagnosis, treatment, and consultation. Clinicians who function primarily in one or more of these traditional arenas are sometimes faced with the need for legal expertise. This chapter will focus on providing legal information and practical suggestions for clinicians who function as diagnosticians, therapists, and expert witnesses. The consultation role will be limited to that of expert witness, although it is recognized that expert testimony is a very limited conception of the consultation role. In addition, a brief discussion of general malpractice issues will be included.

THE DIAGNOSTIC ARENA

Referrals to clinical psychologists in the diagnostic arena fall into five categories: state civil commitment for the mentally ill, state criminal commitment for the mentally ill, state commitment of juveniles, family law, and adult guardianship. The first section of this chapter will focus on issues relating to these five categories.

State civil commitment for the mentally ill

In the United States, all the states and the District of Columbia have a duty to protect their citizens from harm to themselves or others. The restraint of such persons may be accomplished under criminal statutes if a felony or misdemeanor has been committed or under civil statutes if the behavior is related to mental illness and not prosecuted as a felony or misdemeanor. Incarceration is involuntary in either situation, but the type of institution varies, i.e., a mental hospital, prison, or a mental hospital for the criminally insane.

---

* University of Oklahoma Health Services Center, Oklahoma City, Oklahoma.

Civil commitment law has its sources in state statutes and in case law. Case law is exemplary of how statutes may be interpreted but may also apply when there is no statute pertaining to a specific issue. Thus, it is important to be aware of state statutes, which vary in specific provisions from jurisdiction to jurisdiction, as well as case law which provides examples of what actually has been required for implementation of a general statutory standard. Obviously, clinicians would be well advised to read a copy of a pertinent state's civil commitment statute and familiarize themselves with examples of behavior from case law which were previously judged commitable by local courts. One practical way to obtain such information is to call the local district attorney's office, ask who handles civil commitment in the state, and request the reference for the commitment statute. In a law library, a state statute should be available in an annotated volume, with references to pertinent state cases that have already been litigated. Another practical way to obtain such information is to ask for assistance from private attorneys who handle mental health cases.

General procedures. It is important to understand that a mentally ill person may be involuntarily detained without court order in most states under statutory emergency-detention procedures, although a few states require minimal judicial approval prior to emergency detention (see Ennis & Siegal, 1973). Formal commitment procedures are only by court order and require that stringent criteria be met. An analogy may be made between an arrest for an alleged crime, with involuntary detention until a court hearing, and detention for alleged mental illness and dangerousness, with involuntary detention until a court hearing. Clinicians should not attempt to use emergency-detention procedures unless the commitment standard is likely to be met. To do so is a violation of the patient's civil rights. Of course, mentally ill persons may no longer meet criteria for formal commitment after emergency detention. Clinicians should also be aware that little or no treatment occurs during the emergency-detention period. Thus, from a legal viewpoint, the initial phase of civil commitment is much like an arrest.

The most recent state statutory standard for civil commitment or emergency detention is twofold: first, a person is judged dangerous to self or others or unable to adequately care for self; and second, that person is judged mentally ill by a physician or possibly by a director of a mental health facility (e.g., Oklahoma Stat. Ann.). Some states use a likelihood-of-serious-harm standard rather than the dangerous standard (e.g., Alaska Stat.). Other states still employ the older standard of needing psychological treatment, although this standard is probably too vague to withstand a federal constitutional challenge and is therefore likely to be replaced by the dangerous or likelihood-of-serious-harm standards (e.g., Missouri Ann. Stat.).

Although statutes do vary from state to state, civil commitment procedures may be summarized as follows:

A mental health professional, a police officer, a family member, or in some states, a citizen, may initiate involuntary detention by alleging that a person has threatened his own life or the life of another person or is unable to provide for basic personal needs such as food or shelter. The person is examined by a physician (or the director of a mental health facility, in some states), and if the examining person agrees that the person is mentally ill, an affidavit is signed by the examiner. The person is subsequently detained on an emergency basis for a widely variable duration, depending on the state statute. For example, Texas allows 24 hours for emergency detention, while the District of Columbia allows 72 hours (Texas Rev. Civil Statutes Ann.; District of Columbia Code, Ann.). Because the affidavit is typically signed by a *physician* rather than by a clinical psychologist, the physician is likely to testify in court as to whether the person is mentally ill. However, clinical psychologists may be involved in testimony about observed behavior, especially if the person is referred for psychological testing or if the clinical psychologist initially referred the patient for civil commitment. Perhaps clinical psychologists, as a professional group, should consider whether emergency detention is a legal privilege which they should pursue in order to better serve patients' needs.

The process of formal commitment, as opposed to emergency detention, usually begins when a concerned person (for example, a family member or a mental health professional) petitions the court for an examination of the person who has been detained. In some states, the district attorney's office may proceed as the formal petitioner, if the case appears legally meritorious. Legal merit minimally requires that the evidence is not hearsay and that the witnesses are reliable. The allegedly mentally ill person receives a copy of the petition and an order for examination, which the concerned person filed. The allegedly mentally ill person is entitled to legal representation, and if an attorney is unaffordable, one may be appointed by the court, depending on the particular state's statutes.

On the day of the formal hearing, the petitioner must prove that the standard for commitment in that state has been met. For example, under the dangerousness standard, the person who heard the allegedly mentally ill person threaten to kill himself must so testify. The legal rules of evidence require that the evidence not be hearsay; that is, the facts must be testified to by the person who observed the allegedly dangerous behavior. But if the allegedly dangerous person is not represented by an attorney, there may not be an objection to hearsay evidence, and it may be allowed. It is critical to understand that the rules of evidence protect only those persons who object to violations of them.

If the examining commission appointed by the court (usually composed of physicians, but sometimes clinical psychologists depending on the state) finds the person mentally ill *and* the judge or jury also believe the person is dangerous or harmful to self or others, then the person may be committed. Clinicians should be aware that a mentally ill person is not the only type of person who may be involuntarily committed to a civil court. There may be committment statutes for alcoholics, drug addicts, mentally retarded persons, etc., depending on the individual state. Clinicians using the *Diagnostic and Statistical Manual of Mental Disorders* (*DSM-III*) may diagnose substance abuse or mental retardation as mental disorders, but drug abusers or alcoholics are usually not regarded by lay persons as mentally ill.

The length of the involuntary commitment varies, usually depending on the individual patient's adjustment. A clinician's judgment of a patient's adjustment is subject to periodic legal review. Individual state statutes should specify the time periods for review. Unconditional release and conditional release are the two primary ways a patient leaves an institution. Unconditional release is typically a decision of the hospital, although the court usually reviews the decision prior to release. Conditional release, a decision of the court, often requires that a patient continue in outpatient care and make a satisfactory adjustment to the community. The Writ of Habeas Corpus is another method of leaving the hospital, used when the patient believes his constitutional rights are being violated by involuntary incarceration. The patient or his attorney may file the Writ of Habeas Corpus, and clinicians are then required to justify the incarceration. The Writ is considered a last resort by attorneys.

Least restrictive alternative.   Civil commitment may be to an inpatient ward, or in some states, to a group home or to outpatient services. Within an inpatient setting, a particular placement may be required by court order. The legal doctrine of "least restrictive alternative," which originally evolved from case law, is now statutory in some states (e.g., North Carolina Gen. Stat.). It is responsible for the consideration by courts of alternatives to inpatient commitment. The doctrine is based on the premise that police power, which allows the restraining of an individual's activity for the protection of society, must be restricted in order to prevent unnecessary incarceration.

Clinicians often recommend treatment alternatives in diagnostic reports. Thus, they may be required to defend in court the alternatives they have recommended in the reports. One immediate obstacle in recommending placement for treatment is that many states lack appropriate treatment alternatives. Further, treatment outcome research has not clearly delineated which treatment alternatives are most effective for specifically dangerous or harmful behaviors. In addition, some judges and attorneys, as a result of clinical naivete, anticipate results from treatment that are unlikely. It is, therefore, advisable for clinicians to offer conservative prognoses for individual patients assigned to specific settings.

Finally, clinicians are not responsible for the final commitment decision and would do well to remind themselves of that fact. Rather, clinicians are primarily responsible for communicating sincere concern about the allegedly mentally ill person to the involved parties and to the court. They are also responsible for presenting an opinion of the allegedly mentally ill person's mental status of the court, along with any personally observed behaviors indicating imminent harm to self or others.

State criminal commitment for the mentally ill who have allegedly committed a crime

Criminal commitment differs from civil commitment in that a criminal statute has been violated. Further, criminal commitment follows harmful behavior rather than anticipating it. There are some areas where mental disorders and criminal behaviors overlap to such an extent that courts have formally recognized the overlap. Examples include offenders found not guilty by reason of insanity and sexual exhibitionists who are referred for outpatient treatment.

Competency to stand trial. Clinicians are often asked to help determine whether an alleged offender is competent to stand trial. Competency to stand trial refers to *present* mental status. Clinicians must present an opinion as to whether the person is minimally capable of understanding the nature of the charge against him and of aiding his lawyer in his defense. If difficulty in rational understanding is found, clinicians must also indicate whether they believe mental illness to be the reason for the difficulty. A recommended instrument for assessing competency may be found in a NIMH publication by McGarry, Curran, Lipsitt, Lelos, Schwitzgebel, and Rosenberg (1973). The publication provides brief definitions of 13 assessment items and includes a form for rating the degree of incapacity on each of the items. Examples of items are "unmanagable behavior" and "quality of relating to attorney."

Clinicians should begin any evaluation by explaining the ramifications of the evaluation to defendants, preferably with attorneys present. Criminal defendants are typically involuntary clients because they are required by the court to undergo evaluation. Thus, clinicians should inform defendants that everything they say or do as involuntary clients may be reported to the court. Courts may choose not to question clinicians about the details of the interview, but they can do so. Clinicians working with involuntary clients may not keep their clients' confidences due to the conflict of interest between court and criminal defendants. An excellent discussion of ethics with involuntary clients may be found in Monahan (1980).

A list of questions (clearly not exhaustive) which might be asked of defendants in assessing competency are as follows:

1. Do you know that you have a right to remain silent?
2. What are you here for?
3. If you are willing to tell me, what happened that you ended up in jail?
4. What are the consequences of pleading guilty or not guilty?
5. What does the prosecuting attorney do? What does your attorney do? What does the judge do?
6. What is a plea bargain? Who bargains? What might you gain or lose in a plea bargain?
7. What is direct and cross-examination? Who cross-examines you?

Clinicians not only will be able to assess whether defendants have a minimal understanding of the situation by asking the above questions, but will also be able to teach them about the court process. With some defendants, the teaching function is mandatory if they are ever to be competent to stand trial.

Clinicians are sometimes not aware that competency to stand trial is an absolute legal standard, regardless of charge. It can be argued that it takes more competency to defend for some crimes, but the legal standard is typically absolute. Clinicians may call a court's attention to this issue in their reports by mentioning specific abilities for a specific defense. A court will then accept or reject the clinician's opinion of competency.

Two situations clinicians may face are defendant patients who refuse to use insanity as a defense because they believe they are sane, and defendant patients who refuse to defend themselves. Clinicians may include in their reports observations of self-defeating behaviors or absence of understanding the right to remain silent. Clinicians should remember, however, that a defense of insanity may be imposed on defendants only if they meet civil commitment requirements. Further, it may be difficult to show recent dangerous acts to meet the civil commitment standard if defendants have been in the hospital.

Defendant patients may also be malingerers. Examinations of criminal defendants are preferably completed in an inpatient setting for 60 days because it is difficult for malingerers to pretend at all times for 60 days. It is almost always a good idea to ask guards, hospital staff, and family members about the defendant's behavior. Team meetings tend to help clinicians assess malingering. It is also advisable, when clinicians suspect malingering, to give a Minnesota Multiphasic Personality Inventory (MMPI) in an individual evaluation session and check the subscales, which may indicate malingering.

Clinicians also will encounter defendant patients who will predictably deteriorate during trial but who are competent and marginally fit when examined. It is a good idea for clinicians to indicate that continued competency is dependent upon supportive therapy or medication or absence of prolonged incarceration.

A frequently encountered situation is a claim of amnesia. Clinicians may interview to assess whether memory has faded in areas other than the one where defendants claim absence of memory. Neuropsychological testing may also be used to determine inconsistencies in memory capabilities. In addition, relaxation procedures may be used to aid defendants' recall. Clinicians should note that amnesia does not necessarily mean that defendants are incompetent to stand trial. Incompetency depends on whether lost memory is critical to the case and whether evidence can be extraneously reconstructed. Incompetency also depends on whether amnesia affects consultation with legal counsel and the ability to testify. Clinicians should also be aware of the issue of temporary versus permanent amnesia. If amnesia is judged permanent, defendants usually remain incompetent to stand trial. Therefore, the underlying issue is whether the amnesia is treatable. Thus, clinicians might want to use sodium amytol to assess whether amnesia is functional (presumably treatable) or organic (presumably not treatable). Clinicians should secure permission from defendant patients in the presence of their attorneys if they use sodium amytol. Hypnosis is not a reliable technique to assess functionality since some defendants convincingly lie under hypnosis. In addition, information gleaned under hypnosis is subject to arguments by the opposing side that the information was suggested by clinicians to defendants under hypnosis. Because of such arguments and resultant damage to a case, hypnosis is not recommended as a routine procedure. If hypnosis is used, the attorneys from both sides should be present so that clinicians are not so vulnerable to a suggestibility argument. Finally, since amnesia is a difficult assessment question which requires considerable experience, consultation with colleagues is always advisable.

Clinicians typically prepare two reports in criminal assessment: a summary for the court and a full report to be kept in the hospital files. The court can subpoena the hospital file but usually does not do so except in highly contested cases. Clinicians should inform their staff that a court order is required for raw data as well as for the hospital file. Clinicians should be careful that unaware staff employees do not give permission to view files to anyone without a verified court order. Thus, education of employees may be crucial in protecting files from unauthorized persons.

Criminal responsibility and the insanity defense.   Clinicians are also sometimes requested to help determine criminal responsibility. A court or party requesting the evaluation is gathering evidence (e.g., the clinician's expert opinion) to help determine whether the accused person was legally insane at the time the crime was committed. Thus, criminal responsibility refers to the mental status of the person at the time the crime was committed. The insanity defense is said to be successful if the person is found by the court not to be criminally responsible for his actions. Further, the successful insanity defense results in a verdict of innocence and criminal commitment for treatment rather than in incarceration in a penal institution.

There are three primary standards for the determination of criminal responsibility (see Perkins, 1969, pp. 858, 868, 877). The oldest is the M'Naghten rule, which states that the person is not criminally responsible if the crime was committed while the person was unaware of what occurred or if the person was aware of what occurred but did not realize that it was wrong. Under the irresistible-impulse standard, the person may recognize the wrongfulness of behavior, but because the person was overwhelmed by an impulse, that person was not responsible or was less responsible for the behavior. The third standard proposes that a person is not responsible for criminal behavior if there was an absence of substantial capacity either to appreciate the criminality of conduct or to conform conduct to the requirements of the law. This third standard is typically used in federal courts and is part of the Model Penal Code.

Another standard of criminal responsibility, with which most clinicians are familiar, is the Durham rule (see *Durham* v. *United States,* 1954). This standard was formulated in the District of Columbia in 1954 but has not received support from courts in other states. The rule is that a person is not criminally responsible if his unlawful act was the product of mental disease or defect. Under this rule, many more persons may qualify for the insanity defense since *mental defect* is a broad term. Because of the possibility of abuse of the insanity defense, the Durham standard was not adopted as part of the Model Penal Code.

There are a couple of other standards for criminal responsibility that are substantially different from the three primary standards and the Durham standard but which do not enjoy wide acceptance in legal circles. They are of importance to clinicians because they represent some appreciation of the idea that the question of mental disorder does not perfectly overlap with the question of guilt. Rather, the presence of a mental disorder indicates a need for treatment in order to reduce the likelihood of subsequent crimes. The two additional standards are diminished capacity (partial insanity) and guilty but insane (see Perkins, 1969, pp. 878, 883). Under diminished capacity, there is a consideration of the degree of guilt without establishing total innocence. The diminished-capacity standard would likely result in a greater number of persons receiving treatment than would the three traditional standards since more persons would likely be judged partially responsible rather than totally responsible. The guilty-but-insane standard completely eliminates the question of guilt from the question of mental disorder. After a determination of guilty, persons would be sentenced to penal incarceration or referred for appropriate treatment. The critical element in the adoption of this standard is showing that treatment is preferable to penal incarceration from a societal viewpoint. Punishment as a goal of penal incarceration would necessarily be sacrificed if guilty persons were treated rather than punished. It is the opinion of the author that society will gradually move toward a guilty-but-insane standard as the societal goal of punishment decreases in acceptability.

A person may be referred for the determination of both competency to stand trial and criminal responsibility. Since competency to stand trial and criminal responsibility refer to mental status at different points in time, it is possible for a person to be presently competent but not criminally responsible at the time of the crime; or a person might be criminally responsible at the time of the crime but not presently competent to stand trial.

Clinicians are sometimes faced with evaluating mentally retarded persons. Mild mental retardation will not result in a finding of incompetency to stand trial or an absence of criminal responsibility. From a legal viewpoint, "criminal incapacity is not established by a mere showing of weakness of intellect" (Perkins, 1969, p. 878). However, if a person is so mentally retarded as to not be able to understand what is happening to him, that person might be incompetent to stand trial and remain so indefinitely. Thus, there may be a problem with long-term incarceration of severely mentally retarded persons who have allegedly committed crimes. What if those persons are innocent and never come to trial? In 1972, the Supreme Court held that persons may be confined only for reasonable periods of time in order to determine whether competency to stand trial will be likely in the near future (*Jackson* v. *Indiana,* 1972). If persons are not likely to become competent, then civil commitment procedures should be instigated. Most civil commitment procedures include in their standard for commitment not being able to care for self. If a mentally retarded person did not meet the standard of not being able to care for self, then statutes specifically for the commitment of the mentally retarded might apply, depending upon the state.

Insanity is a purely legal construct and does not necessarily mean psychosis as clinicians understand psychosis. However, a psychotic diagnosis is more likely to meet one of the three traditional standards of criminal responsibility than any other clinical diagnosis. That is not to say that a severely suicidal patient who is not psychotic is necessarily capable of appreciating the criminality of conduct. A judgment about the defendant's level of functioning is made by clinicians in writing reports and by courts and juries after hearing evidence. Clinicians' reports reflect their understanding of the person's functioning at the time of the crime and the standard for insanity should not affect what is written in the reports. However, a standard of criminal responsibility will make a difference as to the judge's instructions to the jury so that a defendant is more likely to be found guilty under the M'Naghten rule as compared to the irresistible-impulse standard or the ability-to-appreciate-the-criminality-of-conduct standard.

Clinicians will prepare their reports or testimony more effectively if they remember that the key issue is whether the defendant could form criminal intent at the time of the crime. A defendant is criminally responsible only if criminal intent was present at the time the crime was committed. The three primary standards of criminal responsibility previously discussed pertain to the formations of legal intent. Most clinicians agree that defendants may be diagnosed under *DSM-III* criteria, may be in need of treatment, and may still be able to form criminal intent. Clinicians also need to be aware that the relationship between criminal intent and the crime is critical. The mental disorder must be related to the crime in order for there to be an absence of criminal responsibility. For example, if a delusional person robs a grocery store, the issue is whether that person's delusional system caused the robbery. In order to be aware of such legal issues in a particular case, clinicians should require a commitment of time from attorneys to help them prepare for court and to write a detailed report. The referral questions and issues in the case should be clear to clinicians. Attorneys who claim they are too busy to spend time with clinicians should not receive reports or testimony from clinicians until they are ready to spend time providing necessary assistance.

Clinicians' evaluations of criminal responsibility should include information gleaned from police, government witnesses, family members, jailors, and transporters. It is a good idea to use dated, written forms to record information from these sources. Clinicians should be aware that such persons will likely be required to testify personally about the information.

The family history may be the most important source of information for clinicians to investigate before writing reports. For example, the crime may be so bizarre that almost complete remission of manic-depressive illness might be postulated based on episodal history. Occasionally, physical evidence is important to clinicians. For example, bitemarks may be lovebites rather than aggressive bites, according to a forensic dentist, or the pattern of blood stains might be inconsistent with a temporal lobe seizure. Clinicians are advised to seek other experts' opinions if allowed to do so.

Clinicians may be asked to recommend treatment for persons who are judged to have committed crimes where mental illness is a factor. Criminal trials are usually bifurcated; that is, judgment of guilt or innocence is a separate proceeding from the disposition of determination of treatment or sentence. Some comments about treatment that clinicians wish to include will clearly be more appropriate for the dispositional phase than for the initial or adjudication phase.

State commitment of juveniles

For adults, the term *commitment* usually refers to incarceration, whether it be in a penal or a mental institution. For juveniles, commitment may mean incarceration in reform schools or may mean being in the custody of the state. Juveniles committed to the custody of the state can be in foster homes, mental institutions, orphan's homes, or on parole from homes for delinquent children, to enumerate some of the situations. Thus, the juvenile commitment process may be viewed as analogous in a procedural sense to the adult civil and criminal commitment process.

Dependent, deprived, neglected, and abused children. Broadly speaking, a dependent child is one who requires support other than that given by his natural parents or guardians. Such a child is said to be dependent on the public for support. *Dependent* is a broader term than *deprived, neglected,* or *abused.* Deprived refers to situations where the parent is presently incapable of providing proper care for the child, even though the child may not have yet experienced legal deprivation. In some states, statutes referring to a deprived child are used by judges to involuntarily commit a suicidal child or adolescent for treatment when the parents are not available or are unwilling to consent for commitment. A court order declaring the child deprived is required for involuntary psychiatric hospitalization. Clinicians often contact judges directly in emergency situations in order to procure such a court order.

Neglect refers to inadequate child care over a substantial period of time. The care referred to in neglect cases usually means physical care, but it has also meant psychological care. Abuse in a physical sense refers to intentional force resulting in significant injury to the child. Abuse in an emotional sense is best understood by looking at case law. Parent behaviors which have been held in whole or in conjunction with others to show neglect or abuse in various state courts are: failure to provide food and clothing (e.g., *Franzel* v. *Michigan,* 1971), failure to work regularly or financially provide for children (e.g., *In Interest of Norwood,* 1976), failure to maintain contact with children (e.g., *Evan* v. *Moore,* 1972), physical or sexual abuse of children (e.g., *Franzel* v. *Michigan,* 1971), and failure to provide necessary medical care (e.g., *In re Corneliusen,* 1972). Intermittent confinement of parents to a hospital due to mental illness is not sufficient in itself to show neglect or abuse (e.g., *In re Daniel C.,* 1975).

In legal circles, evidence of emotional abuse or neglect is often considered supportive and does not carry the same weight in courts as physical abuse or neglect. For example, where children were not undernourished, received ample food, had minimal clothing, were in reasonably good health, and were not physically abused, termination of parental rights was not justified—even if the emotional atmosphere of the home was submarginal (*In re Geiger,* 1975). The reasoning of some courts is that emotional abuse or neglect is a value judgment made by middle-class mental health professionals about lower-class parents. Further, the use of emotional criteria solely in lower-class homes would be subject to the constitutional issue of equal protection. Still, evidence of emotional abuse or neglect can be crucial in the presentation of the total environment in which children live. Further, extreme emotional abuse or neglect can be enough to terminate parental rights. For example, a child living alone with a chronic paranoid and severely psychotic schizophrenic mother was judged neglected due to imminent danger of becoming impaired (*In re Millar*, 1972).

In neglect or abuse cases, the state attempts to gain legal custody of the child, either temporarily or permanently, and to place the neglected or abused child in a better environment. The environment is often a series of foster homes or institutions or, if permanent custody has been acquired by the state, an adoptive home. Parents may seek to regain custody of a child when the state has temporary custody. Clinicians experienced in giving testimony in custody cases realize that judges have considerable discretion in terminating parental custody—that is, in granting permanent custody to the state. Therefore, clinicians may experience more consistency with individual judges than with the system itself. The best interests of a child are an important consideration where termination of parental rights is sought on the basis of neglect or abuse; but best interests are not completely determinable. A court cannot remove a child from its parents merely because a child would be better off in another person's custody. Rather, the parents must be shown to be unfit—that is, guilty of abuse or neglect of a child.

Ethical considerations in doing evaluations in neglect and abuse cases include informing parents of the clinician's stance before any evaluation. The clinician's stance may be for the welfare of the child, and parents should be aware the clinician is not necessarily on their side. Clinicians' evaluations of a child and/or a parent in a neglect or abuse case should include all evidence of emotional harm, but clinicians must be aware of the difficulty of removing children from their parents on the sole basis of emotional harm. Clinicians should also note the often limited resources of alternative environments for a child. For example, is it better to be in a series of foster homes and possibly form no long-term relationships or to be in one marginal home with natural parents? Further, clinicians may find themselves recommending to judges that some decision be made immediately, whatever it may be, so that consistency and permanency will be possible for the child.

Dependent, neglect, or abuse cases are usually presented to the court in two phases, just as criminal cases are. The first phase is the hearing for the determination of dependency, neglect, or abuse. The second phase is the dispositional phase where placement of the child is determined. Clinicians should be aware of the second phase and should make realistic, appropriate treatment recommendations wherever possible.

Delinquent children.   Children who allegedly have commited acts which, if committed by an adult, would be violations of criminal statutes, are subject to state delinquency laws. Whether offenders are under or over the age below which they are to be treated as delinquent and not as criminal is determined, in some jurisdictions, by the age at the time the acts were committed. In other jurisdictions, the age may be that age at the time of adjudication. Delinquency proceedings are civil rather than criminal in nature and are designed to encourage rehabilitation of children. However, there is case law that a juvenile charged with violation of criminal law does not have an absolute right to be treated as a delinquent child just because of age (*Johnson* v. *State,* 1975).

A juvenile is entitled to representation by an attorney, so clinicians may be asked by the juvenile's attorney or by the judge to evaluate the juvenile (*In re Gault,* 1966). The evaluation situation is much like that of a criminal defendant if the evaluation is to be used in the initial, adjudicatory phase of the prosecution. The adjudication is the phase in which the determination of guilt or innocence of the juvenile is made. The rules of evidence apply in the adjudication phase. The rules of evidence provide guidelines as to what testimony may be heard by the judge or jury. A confession secured by the police without advising the juvenile of his rights or a seizure by the police of drugs without probable cause to search are examples of inadmissible evidence.

The second phase, or disposition phase, is considerably different from the adjudication phase in that the purpose is to determine how best to rehabilitate the guilty juvenile who has already been adjudicated delinquent. The rules of evidence typically do not apply in the disposition phase. Thus, all information, whether legally admissible or not, is available to a court in the disposition phase. Clinicians' reports or testimony may be especially valuable in the disposition phase because there is an opportunity to suggest a treatment plan to the court. Thus, in preparing a report on a juvenile who is involved in delinquency proceedings, clinicians should make a concerted effort to elaborate on various treatment alternatives. Alternatives may include residential as well as outpatient treatment (e.g., *In re L. L.,* 1974).

Minors adjudicated delinquent may be placed on probation at the discretion of a court or committed for custodial care and rehabilitation. Committed juvenile delinquents may be paroled from commitment, but parole may be revoked if they violate its conditions. Clinicians should be aware that the recommendations they make may influence a court in its determination of probation versus institutionalization. Further, if a condition of parole was mandatory treatment, clinicians' reports of attendance and progress in treatment will influence parole decisions.

Occasionally, clinicians may be asked to determine whether juveniles are competent to stand trial, and the issues are the same as with criminal defendants. Clinicians would not be asked to determine criminal responsibility at the time of the crime for juveniles in delinquency proceedings since they are not subject to criminal proceedings. However, if juveniles have been certified as adults, they are subject to criminal statutes rather than delinquency statutes, and a determination of both competency to stand trial and criminal responsibility could be requested.

Children in need of supervision.   In some jurisdictions, provision is made for the control or commitment of children in need of supervision. Examples of behavior judged as in need of supervision include habitual truancy (e.g., *In re Napier,* 1975) and threats to injure self or others (e.g., *In Interest of Dalhbert,* 1969). While there is a similarity between children in need of supervision and delinquent children, there is the difference that an adjudication of in need of supervision does not require commission of acts which would be criminal if committed by adults.

It is possible that an in-need-of-supervision statute might be used by a court or a court may involuntarily commit suicidal or homicidal children for inpatient psychiatric treatment (e.g., *Lavette M.* v. *Corp. Counsel of City of New York,* 1975). Clinicians are advised to seek information in their particular states as to how involuntary commitment of a suicidal child may be accomplished. Clinicians also need to be aware that parents or guardians cannot involuntarily commit children to a mental hospital without some potential review by the courts (e.g., *Bartley* v. *Kremens,* 1975).

Juveniles' right to treatment.   Minors found to be delinquent have the right to rehabilitative treatment (e.g., *Morales* v. *Turman,* 1973). Under applicable statutory authority, a court may be empowered to charge an agency with the responsibility of finding or creating treatment for an adjudicated minor (e.g., *In re Leopolodo Z.,* 1974). So before making a commitment to a particular facility, a court may be required to find that the juvenile will benefit from available treatment (e.g., *In re Arnold,* 1971). Clinicians may recommend in reports or in testimony specific examples of appropriate inpatient or outpatient care.

Family law

Child custody.   In child custody disputes between parents or between other relatives of the child, the standard is the best interests of the child. The Uniform Marriage and Divorce Act's best-interests test recommends consideration of such topics as the nature of the emotional ties between the competing parties and the child, the length of time the child has lived in a satisfactory environment, and the capacity of the competing parties to provide the child with emotional and physical needs. Courts in the various states may take into account all relevant factors; thus, in practice, morality often plays a significant role in the determination of child custody. The Uniform Act does specifically forbid consideration of parties' behavior which does not affect the relationship to the child. However, the Uniform Act is merely a model rather than statutory law for most states. Clinicians will generally address issues such as capacity to parent and psychological parenthood under the best-interests standard.

Parties, independently of a court, may request clinicians to evaluate parents and children. In this situation, clinicians will be paid by one side, typically one of the parents. Alternatively, a court—under the Federal Rules of Civil Procedure—may order parents in a custody suit to submit to a mental examination by a qualified physician. A physician may delegate part of the examination to a clinical psychologist or other mental health professional. State procedures vary as to which mental health professional group may be court-ordered to conduct a child custody evaluation. Watson (1969), in a classic law review article, has suggested that the following steps be taken in preparing a child custody evaluation:

1. Receive permission from the parent-client to use confidential information. If you believe that revealing certain information such as test scores would be detrimental to the client, the client and his/her lawyer should be told.
2. If the youngster is in a treatment center or there is reason to believe that his/her best interests are likely to be overlooked, raise the matter with the client or both attorneys about appointing a guardian *ad litem* or counsel for the child.
3. Inform the parties as to how information in the diagnostic or therapeutic process might be used so they can be selective in their revelations if they so chose. The individual may have to choose between protecting privacy and appearing evasive to the court.
4. Carefully conduct the examination. As a general guideline, an adequate clinical examination of the parent may last between one and three hours, supplemented by psychological tests. Examination of a child may last between two and five hours, and one or two hours may be spent going over background information such as school records, home observations, and so forth.
5. Organize observations and conclusions in a manner to withstand the validating procedure of cross-examination. Cross-examination is the means used by an opposing attorney to bring relevant information to the attention of the court.

Under the second step recommended by Watson (1969), the term guardian *ad litem* is mentioned. The guardian *ad litem* is an independent representative of the best interests of the child and may be an attorney (attorney *ad litem*) or a lay person. Recall that the other attorneys represent the state or the parents rather than the child.

Child custody issues between divorced parents may be relitigated, if there has been substantial and material change of circumstances (e.g., remarriage). Relitigation may occur also if retention of the present custody arrangements would be injurious to the child and a change of custody would be beneficial to the child. Clinicians are wise to keep a file of past evaluations in case they are requested to reevaluate under a motion to modify child custody.

Regardless of whether clinicians are requested by a court to conduct a child custody evaluation or by attorneys of one or both parents, they are expected to offer independent, unbiased opinions to the court. The attorney's role differs greatly from the clinician's role in that the attorney is bound by a legal code of ethics to present the client's case in as favorable a light as possible. Thus, there may be conflict between the clinician's role to provide an independent, unbiased opinion and the attorney's role to present the client in the most favorable light. Clinicians, if they are to remain unbiased, must make it clear to attorneys who request evaluations that their opinions may or may not be favorable to the clients whom the attorneys represent. The attorney is ethically bound to exclude unfavorable evidence, so the clinician's opinion will likely not be used if it is unfavorable to the client whom the requesting attorney represents. On the other hand, a court-appointed clinician (called a "friend of the court"), is protected from adversarial issues in that the judge has requested the opinion. Additional practical suggestions for working with attorneys are included in the expert-witness section of this chapter.

Adult guardianship

Recent statutes define adult incompetency or the need for adult guardianship as mental incapability to care for oneself or one's property (e.g., Oregon Rev. Stat.). An incompetent person might have an adult guardian appointed for a variety of reasons (for example, because he is senile, habitually drunk, or mentally ill). Thus, competency and commitment are separate legal issues and have considerably different legal standards. The reader is referred to the previous discussion in this chapter on standards in the adult commitment area. Incompetency hearings are usually held because the family of the allegedly incompetent person wants to avoid a contract or a will. Clinicians may be asked by the family or by the allegedly incompetent person's attorney to evaluate competency in such situations.

The standard for voiding a contract on competency grounds is very high. Generally, incompetent persons must not be cognizant of what they are doing. Mere poor judgment is not enough. For example, a person in a manic psychosis was not allowed to void a contract that was obviously poor judgment (*Fingerhut* v. *Kralyn Enterprises, Inc.*, 1971). Further, involuntary commitment of a person to a hospital is not necessarily enough to show that the person is incompetent to contract or make a will (*Willis* v. *James*, 1961). For a checklist of evidence for and against incapacity, the reader is referred to the *Psychiatry for Lawyers Handbook* (Shapiro & Needhaus, 1967). This checklist includes the following main categories: (1) physical appearance, demeanor, and communication skill; (2) age; (3) physical condition; (4) mental capacity; (5) history of mental illness in the family; (6) person's own mental health history; and (7) opinion of family and acquaintances.

THE TREATMENT ARENA

There are several legal topics which are potentially of interest to clinicians who are performing a treatment function. The discussion in this section of the chapter will be limited to three such topics: contractual treatment agreements, consent for treatment, and privileged communication.

Contractual agreements for treatment

In practice, voluntary patients usually do not select the form of their treatment, and clinicians do not obtain written consent for treatment. Attempts made by clinicians to obtain full consent for treatment can be time-consuming or impossible. Nevertheless, there are definite legal and therapeutic advantages in keeping records of treatment options presented to patients and in obtaining contractual agreement for treatment when feasible.

The treatment contract is a legal document specifying what the therapist and patient agree to do over a period of time. The contract may be verbal or written, although verbal contracts for services lasting over a year are not legally enforceable. It is better to write agreements than to verbally state them because of the record-keeping function served by written agreements. Contractual agreements could be utilized by clinicians to formally communicate to patients the limits of confidentiality. More specifically, clinicians could indicate in treatment contracts a legal obligation to report to appropriate authorities probable suicidal or homicidal behavior. Then if malpractice issues arise, clinicians will be better able to specify the intent and boundary conditions of therapy to an ethics committee or a court. (See Figure 1 for an example of a treatment contract.) Last, written treatment contracts may always be voided by mutual agreement of the parties so that renegotiation is possible.

One therapeutic benefit of written contracts is a more explicit understanding by patients and clinicians of what they may expect from each other over a specific period of time. For example, termination issues are explicitly a part of therapy from the point of initial contact when contractual agreements are used. The total financial investment by patients in therapy may be projected and payment plans may be agreed upon initially if contractual agreements are used. Finally, goals of therapy may be included in contractual agreements if patients and clinicians have a clear idea of what problem areas might be reasonable to include. It is recognized that specific goals are likely to change as therapy progresses; however, it may be possible to initially include general goals, such as feeling less depressed or anxious. The inclusion of general goals is not to specifi-

Figure 1

Contract for Psychotherapeutic Services

I _____ (client) (clients) agree to meet with _____ (therapist) on a _____ (weekly, biweekly, monthly) basis beginning on _____ (date).
Thus, I, _____ (client) agree to meet with _____ (therapist) _____ times. I understand that the contract may be renegotiated on _____ (date).

I _____ (client) agree to pay _____ (therapist) $_____ per meeting for psychotherapeutic services. I _____ (client) agree to pay in the following manner: (Please check one in each column)

_____	Cash or check	_____	Monthly
_____	Insurance	_____	Weekly
_____	Supplement to insurance by cash or check	_____	Biweekly
_____	Other		

I _____ (client) understand that _____ (therapist) and I will formulate specific goals together in the psychotherapy sessions but that the general goal at the time of signing this contract is _____. I _____ (client) understand that there are no guarantees as to the attainment of goals since success is dependent upon me as well as upon _____ (therapist).

I _____ (client) may cancel the meetings described above if I _____ (client) give _____ days of notice of cancellation. Notice may be _____ (written or oral).

OR

I _____ (client) understand that I may *not* cancel any of the meetings so agreed to in this agreement and that I am responsible for paying for all meetings whether or not I attend them.

Figure 1 (concluded)

I _____ (client) (clients) understand that I will receive _____ days of notice of cancellation should _____ (therapist) be unable to attend a meeting. If I do not receive such notice and come for the meeting, I _____ (client) (clients) will be paid the sum of ___ for the inconvenience.

I _____ (client) (clients) further understand that _____ (therapist) will respect the confidentiality of what I disclose to _____ (therapist) and will not disclose or publish, without my written consent, any information which would injure me.

I _____ (client) (clients) further understand that _____ (therapist) is obligated to report to a potential victim any serious homicidal threats made by me _____ (client) (clients) to _____ (therapist).

I _____ (client) (clients) further understand that _____ (therapist) is also obligated to report imminent suicidal behavior on my part to appropriate authorities for my own protection.

I _____ (client) (clients) further understand that _____ (therapist) is also obligated to report child abuse to the appropriate authorities.

I _____ (client) (clients) further understand that _____ (therapist) is obligated to immediately refer for appropriate treatment should a situation arise where the agreed upon treatment is clinically inappropriate.

_____　　　　　_____
Signature of Client　　　　　　　　　　Signature of Therapist

_____　　　　　_____
Signature of Client　　　　　　　　　　Date

_____
Witness

_____
Witness

cally guarantee results but to indicate the intent of the contracting parties.

Arguably, contractual approaches can be especially helpful to patients for whom short-term intervention is likely or for whom limit setting or long-term dependency are major issues. Koss (1979) reported that the median length spent by patients in private psychotherapy was eight weeks. Possibly, clinicians could foresee short-term intervention as especially likely with individual patients or in certain settings and utilize contractual agreements. It would be interesting to know to what extent the use of contractual or time-limited approaches on the actual time spent in psychotherapy for what types of individuals or settings such approaches were effective. Examples of therapy contracts exist in the literature and could be readily adapted by clinicians to fit their own needs (Adams & Argel, 1975; Ayllon & Skiban, 1973; Stuart, 1975).

Consent for treatment

Consent for treatment is a qualitatively different concept than contractual agreement in that it implies permission to do treatment rather than agreement as to the terms of treatment. Consent for treatment or informed consent requires competence, voluntariness, and knowledge to be valid. However, patients who do not possess the capacity to make an informed, voluntary decision about treatment may be treated anyway if certain procedural requirements are followed. Patients' representatives (typically attorneys) must have access to records. Attorneys should be notified if hazardous treatment is planned. Routine review by a human rights committee is a good idea and must be allowed upon the patient's request. Treatment should be planned with patients as much as patients are able to do so (see the American Bar Association's Commission on the Mentally Disabled, 1977). Valid consent for treatment may be implied for some treatment areas such as outpatient services, but it is usually not implied in inpatient settings. Consent from an inpatient is always suspect due to the restrictive nature of the environment in which consent is secured. Consent from the patient's legal guardian may be the only viable alternative for some patients. Consent forms granting permission for treatment are likely to have to be tailored to treatment programs. Therefore, clinicians may find themselves constructing their own consent-for-treatment forms. An article that is helpful in constructing such forms is one by Marvin (1976). For example, Marvin suggests that patients be given 48 hours to think over a treatment program to show the absence of coercion and that patients be given the name of someone who has experienced the program and be encouraged to discuss the advantages and disadvantages of the program.

Involuntary patients include all patients who have not given valid consent or who have been involuntarily committed by the state. The use of time-out, punishment, or deprivation procedures is legally inadvisable without valid consent because such treatment may be construed as a violation of patients' constitutionally guaranteed rights. A widely cited federal case (*Wyatt* v. *Stickney,* 1971) has specified such minimal constitutional rights. For example, patients must be allowed to visit and make telephone calls, send sealed mail, wear their own clothes, attend religious services, interact with the opposite sex (with supervision), avoid forced labor, take a shower and use the toilet in privacy, have meals in the dining rooms, and have individualized treatment plans. While it is legally acceptable to withdraw privileges, as compared to basic rights, the clinician's dilemma lies in deciding what constitutes privileges. The basic legal guideline is that privileges are not enumerated in case law as basic rights.

Privileged communication and duty to warn third parties

Confidentiality is an ethical practice followed by clinicians. Privileged communication is a legal right protecting clients from disclosures by clinicians during legal procedures. The right of privileged communication belongs to clients, not therapists. Thus, clients could waive the right to legal proceedings, and clinicians would then be legally required to testify. The right of privileged communication is statutory and varies from state to state. Typically, licensed physicians are granted the privilege, but many states also extend the privilege to licensed clinical psychologists. Other mental health professionals are generally less protected by the right of privileged communication than are physicians and psychologists.

Ethical guidelines established by the American Psychological Association (1977) require that confidentiality be broken when there is a clear and imminent danger to an individual or society. Further, case law supports the ethical stance of the American Psychological Association. In *Tarasoff* v. *Regents of the University of California* (1974), the State Supreme Court of California held that therapists have a duty to warn potential victims of serious danger from patients. For example, therapists would be ethically and legally expected to warn persons whom patients have threatened to seriously harm or kill. This legal duty to warn a potential victim of a homicidal threat probably does not extend to the relatives of suicidal patients (see *Bellah* v. *Greenspan,* 1977). There is a duty to attempt to civilly commit suicidal patients themselves but not to warn those patients' relatives. The duty to attempt to commit seriously suicidal patients is based on the legal requirement of reasonable care during the course of treatment (see Schwartz, 1971). There is probably a duty to warn parents of suicidal danger to their children who have not yet reached age 18 as an exercise of reasonable care during the course of treatment.

The difference between warning parents of imminently suicidal children and warning relatives of imminently suicidal adults lies in the fact that parents are the legal custodians of their children who are under age 18. Relatives of adults are not legal custodians unless the relative is a guardian of a legally incompetent adult. In the case of a legally incompetent adult, clinicians would probably treat the guardian much like a parent. In short, there is some legal precedent in the area of suicide, but the area remains fuzzy. Clinicians can best protect themselves and their patients by attempting to civilly commit patients, hopefully with the consent of parents if patients are under age 18.

Privilege is lost when the patient introduces his mental condition as part of his defense of claim in a civil suit or in child custody suits where either parent (party) raises the mental condition of the other parent as part of claim or defense. The privilege will also be lost if the therapist has reasonable knowledge of child abuse in a child custody suit. Another situation where privilege is not maintained is where the patient has been told by the court that his communications will not be privileged. Examples of situations where privilege may be lost are in workers' compensation suits, malpractice actions, will contests, and criminal homicide cases.

Perhaps the most common area where privilege is lost is when the clinician determines that the patient is suicidal. Usually, clinicians determine the likelihood of suicide by considering predictive demographic variables, the history and nature of suicidal gestures, and the availability of supportive persons in the environment to which patients may return. Should clinicians decide that danger of suicide is very likely, they are ethically bound to attempt to treat the patient. There is no clear legal duty to prevent patients from committing suicide, although reasonable care is legally required when patients' suicide attempts are foreseeable. An example of a suicide judged as legally foreseeable was leaving a teenaged training-school resident alone after physical punishment (see *McBride* v. *State,* 1968).

THE EXPERT WITNESS

Clinicians who function as expert witnesses need to understand and respect the adversary system in order to perform adequately in a courtroom setting. They must be informed about the qualifications for expert witnesses. They also need information about subpoenas, depositions, and the preparation and giving of testimony. This segment of the chapter will address these topics from a pragmatic standpoint.

The adversary system

Most attorneys in the United States agree that vigorous legal representation must be guaranteed to all persons. Thus, the likely guilty criminal defendant or abusing parent is entitled to a legal presentation of a point of view in the most favorable light possible. The rationale for every individual's entitlement to vigorous legal representation is that the advocacy on one side will balance the advocacy on the other side. Justice is presumed to be most likely when representation is equally vigorous on both sides.

There are minimal limits to vigorous representation, such as bribing the judge or jury or presenting testimony known to be false or perjured. Attorneys disagree on the point to which further limits should be enforced. Clinicians sometimes view attorneys' vigorous representation as unethical because of the absence of limits on how cases may be presented. No way exists to force attorneys to recognize limits in favor of clinicians' interests in the treatment of a mentally ill person or in the placement of an abused child. Private attorneys may overwhelm the state's overworked attorneys with vigorous representation of abusing parents because it is not illegal to do so. Further, attorneys are encouraged to vigorously represent whomever they agree to represent, although they may refuse initially to take cases for personal reasons, as distinguished from a community attitude against potential clients. Attorneys are especially encouraged to represent persons who a community has shunned under their ethical considerations (see American Bar Association's Code of Professional Responsibility, 1971). They also may not ethically discontinue representation once it has begun just because they wish to do so. They must present a reason to the court for withdrawal from representation, such as nonpayment, absence of cooperation, or illegality. Attorneys may find they have taken a case in which the evidence is overwhelmingly against them and in which they are ethically bound to continue representation.

There is tremendous conflict between clinicians' interests in an abused child's welfare or in a mentally ill person's welfare and vigorous representation of a very likely guilty criminal defendant or of an abusing parent. Thus, the roles of clinicians and attorneys are vastly different in the courtroom. Clinicians should never expect cooperation from attorneys who represent clients with interests opposed to that of the clinicians. Such is the nature of a legal system that has survived for hundreds of years.

Qualifications

A legal definition of expert witness includes any person who has special knowledge or experience not generally familiar to the public (Black, 1968). In the determination of competency to stand trial and criminal responsibility, physicians are typically the experts, although other mental health professionals may also testify. In *Jenkins* v. *United States* (1962), a federal court held that clinical psychologists may testify on the issue of mental defect. However, commitment certificates typically must be signed by physicians, so clinical psychologists are not usually the experts in adult civil or criminal commitment suits.

Clinical psychologists are more likely to testify in competency hearings where the issue is whether the person is mentally capable of disposing of his property as he chooses. Psychologists are also heavily utilized in child custody hearings and in juvenile commitment hearings. For personal injury suits where the issue is the nature of the mental stress or anxiety a person has suffered, psychologists are often requested to do diagnostic interviewing and psychological testing. Clinicians are qualified as experts in court before any testimony is given. Licensure and experience are desirable qualifications, as are publications distinguishing clinicians in specialty areas. Especially desirable are publications in an area relevant to the testimony to be offered. However, clinicians who are not licensed may testify if they are persons whom the court has qualified as experts for whatever reasons.

The time of referral

Most cases never go to trial but are settled out of court. Thus, clinicians will be expected to prepare for court many more times than they will actually go. In every case, it is crucial to prepare from the beginning on the assumption that the case will be litigated rather than to risk being unable to reasonably defend opinions in court. It is almost impossible to reliably predict which cases will go to trial at the time of referral. Before accepting cases, clinicians should inform attorneys that they will offer their honest opinions regardless of who pays them. Clinicians should explain their role to attorneys as that of presenting unbiased, independent opinions. Clinicians will lose respect from attorneys if they succumb to pressure from attorneys to slant testimony. Clinicians should never commit themselves to a position prior to extended contact with clients because it is often the case that the clinicians will discover something negative about clients. Clinicians should understand that attorneys will refuse to utilize their opinions if they are unfavorable to their side of the case. Clinicians who prefer to have their opinions utilized regardless of the side their opinions support should request that attorneys seek court-appointed experts. Court appointment is more likely in juvenile areas.

The moment a referral which potentially involves court testimony is accepted, prompt scrutiny and recording of health care and evaluation issues are advisable. Credibility of clinicians' reports or testimony will be greater when the details of evaluation or treatment are competently handled from the beginning. Clinicians are advised to initially seek understanding of the legal issues in a particular case so they will be able to determine the consequences of their opinions. It is important to remember that clinicians themselves may be biased for or against clients as a result of opinions offered from various sources. To guard against such bias, both normal and abnormal behavior should be anticipated by clinicians in all clients referred to them.

Subpoenas and depositions

Clinicians should be certain subpoenas are valid before responding to them. Attorneys are good sources to learn about such matters. It is also important to be certain that the rules of protocol for professional witnesses are followed for both subpoenas and depositions. Depositions involve testimony under oath just like courtroom testimony. The difference is that the deposition situation may appear friendly and informal rather than adversary. Clinicians should always remember that the enemy deposes, so the purpose is to use testimony for impeachment of clinicians at trial. It is wise to testify at depositions just as if in a formal courtroom situation. Testimony should consist only of brief answers with no volunteering of information.

The preparation and giving of testimony

Before taking referrals, clinicians are advised to request from attorneys a minimum number of hours of paid preparation for trial. If attorneys refuse to prepare with clinicians for court, clinicians should refuse to testify. Clinicians will lose credibility if they go to court ill-prepared. Clinicians cannot prepare adequately for court without attorneys' cooperation.

The first part of direct examination includes qualification of the expert. Clinicians should submit an extensive list of qualifications to attorneys and request that the qualifications be enumerated in court. It is important not to be modest. Further, clinicians are advised to review articles they have written because the other side may ask specific questions about the articles when challenging professional qualifications.

Attorneys vary in experience, so clinicians are well advised to request a list of questions to be asked on direct examination. If questions are inadequate to address crucial issues, clinicians should request more appropriate questions. The questions for direct examination must be open ended so as not to lead the witness. An example of an open-ended question would be, "Where do you work, doctor?" Whereas, an example of a leading question would be, "You work at the Health Sciences Center, don't you doctor?" Leading questions are only allowed on cross-examination. After spending some preparation time with clinicians, attorneys should know the answer to every question that might be asked on direct examination. Attorneys should also inform clinicians of what is likely to be asked on cross-examination. Clinicians should disclose all weaknesses in their opinions or qualifications to the attorneys with whom they are working. Such weaknesses should be incorporated into the direct examination so that cross-examination will not be so deadly. For example, weaknesses might be the absence of publications or the small number of hours of contact with clients.

Clinicians are responsible for clearly stated opinions that are understandable in court. Clinicians should especially try to refrain from overqualifying opinions. Clinicians will be vulnerable enough in a courtroom situation without discrediting their own statements. They should base their opinions as much as possible on what clients have told them, personal observations of the client's behavior, or personal history taking. The federal rules of evidence, which have been adopted by many states, permit an expert to rely on sources of information which are relied upon in standard practice. For example, a psychiatrist might base his testimony on reports from a lab technician, a psychologist, a social worker, and a neurologist, even though the reports are technically hearsay. Before the adoption of this exception to the hearsay rule in the federal rules, an expert witness was not permitted to testify to anything which was not personally observed. Nevertheless, it is wise for an expert to do as much direct observation as possible, because testimony will then be more likely to withstand cross-examination. The judge will rule on whether extrinsic sources are admissible under the previously discussed exception to the hearsay rule. In a situation where an expert evaluated a child, statements made by parents about the child might or might not be admissible. Arguably, the parents' statements are a source relied upon in standard practice. However, the exception to the hearsay rule is based on the necessity for use of and the reliability of the source. The parents' statements could be ruled inadmissible because they are unreliable. Clinicians understand that parents' explanations of children's behavior can be exaggerated and unreliable. The best way to handle extrinsic sources of information that are not absolutely reliable is to avoid using them as the basis of expert opinion.

The use of technical words should be avoided at all costs. For example, instead of using the word *depressed*, explain that the person is really down in the dumps. Instead of using the term *obsessive-compulsive*, explain that the person is upset and out of sorts if he does not get his cream of wheat at exactly 7:00 A.M. If at all possible, clinicians should refrain from giving a diagnosis such as paranoid schizophrenia because the other side will challenge the concept of schizophrenia. Instead, enumerate examples of schizophrenic behavior.

The amount of time spent with clients is critical to the clinician's credibility in court. It is advisable to see clients several times over a prolonged period of time. It is important to see clients just before going to court in order to defend against arguments that clients were seen six months previously and have since that time improved. There is no such thing as economy in cases that require court testimony. Clinicians should require payment for all hours they spend working on a case, just as the attorneys require payment for the hours they work. A clinician may preserve credibility when asked how much was received in payment for his opinion by replying that the charges were based on the usual hourly rate for clinical services.

Tests should be used to supplement opinions and should not constitute the primary basis of opinion. Psychologists seem to make the mistake of relying too heavily on tests—more than other professional clinicians do. Tests are especially difficult for jury members to understand because their level of education is usually that of high school or less; however, tests may be successfully used with judges who are likely to understand their significance. Clinicians should be prepared to discuss the reliability and validity of any tests they have used.

Clinicians are sometimes asked to respond to hypothetical questions. The hypothetical questions are of two kinds. The first is a question based on things testified to. Clinicians will typically not have heard testimony by all the witnesses, so an answer to this type of hypothetical question would be based only on what has been personally heard in court. The second type of hypothetical question is based on facts framed by the questioner and can include facts only favorable to his side. Clinicians have to rely on their attorneys to point out the biased nature of the hypothetical facts during redirect examination.

It is much different to testify before a jury than before a judge. The jury is typically very conservative, so young experts or fashionably dressed experts will be handicapped. The Ten Commandments are the value system of most jury members, despite the fact that, as individuals, they may behave otherwise. Clinicians probably will be disliked by jury members from the moment they enter the courtroom. Clinicians can be subsequently liked by the jury if they relate to the jury as ordinary human beings and if they express sincere concern for clients. Looking at and speaking directly to jury members in language they can understand is a good way to communicate respect for them as human beings.

Finally, there is one rule that must be followed in a courtroom: *Never* appear irritated or angry. Since the primary goal of the opposing attorney can be to irritate a witness, a degree of self restraint by clinicians is required.

MALPRACTICE

Malpractice is defined in *Black's Law Dictionary* (Black, 1968, p. 1,111) as "any professional misconduct, unreasonable lack of skill or fidelity in professional or fiduciary duties, evil practice, or illegal or immoral conduct." Clinicians are subject to civil malpractice suits if they behave negligently within a professional relationship. The critical aspects in malpractice are the definition of behavior as professionally negligent and the determination of whether a professional relationship exists. Negligence legally requires that four elements be proven: a *duty* on the part of the practitioner, a *breach* of that duty, actual *loss* or injury, and a *causal relationship* between the breach of duty and the resultant injury (see Prosser, 1971).

Clinicians should conform generally to professional ethics and statutory law in order to meet the duty owed to persons with whom they have a professional relationship. Legally speaking, technical violations of professional ethics may be viewed by courts as reasonable deviations and therefore not constitute malpractice. However, violations of professional ethics are used as a general guideline in malpractice suits. Some areas in which malpractice suits might be filed against clinical psychologists are as follows: negligent performance of diagnostic or psychotherapeutic services, slander or libel, negligence leading to suicide, birth control or abortion counseling, sex therapy or nude encounter groups, illegal search or violation of privacy, and failure to adequately supervise a disturbed client (adapted from Van Hoose & Kottler, 1977). Physicians would be more likely than clinical psychologists to be sued in areas like wrongful commitment or electroshock or drug therapy.

To protect against malpractice claims, clinicians should familiarize themselves with their professional codes of ethics. Clinical psychologists are referred to the *Standards for Educational and Psychological Tests* (1974), the *Standards for Providers of Psychological Services* (1977), the *Guidelines for Psychologists Conducting Growth Groups* (1973), and the *Ethical Standards of Psychologists* (1977). Clinicians should also consult with licensed colleagues when they are uncertain about interpretation of ethical questions. They should document in writing all consultations. Further, clinicians should refer patients who are not improving with treatment within a reasonable time period or who require consultation with specialists to be certain of diagnoses or to provide adequate treatment. The reader is referred to the treatment segment of this chapter under privileged communication for a discussion of liability for suicidal or homicidal behavior.

SUMMARY

This chapter is a general information source for clinicians who practice in the area of clinical psychology and law. Information for the diagnostician is provided in the areas of: (1) state civil commitment for the mentally ill; (2) state criminal commitment for the mentally ill; (3) state commitment for juveniles; and (4) family law. Information for the therapist is provided in the areas of: (1) contractual agreements for treatment; (2) consent for treatment; and (3) privileged communication. Practical suggestions for the expert witness are also offered. Finally, there is an overview of malpractice issues.

No attempt has been made to be exhaustive in the coverage of any topics. Readers interested in more comprehensive information about the topics are referred to the list of suggested readings in the Appendix.

APPENDIX: SUGGESTED READINGS

Allen, R. C., Forster, E. Z., & Rubin, J. G. (Eds.). *Readings in law and psychiatry* (2nd ed.). Baltimore: The Johns Hopkins University Press, 1975, 165–180.

Brodsky, S. L. The mental health professional on the witness stand: A survival guide. In B. D. Sales (Ed.), *Psychology in the legal process.* New York: Spectrum, 1977, 269–276.

Brodsky, S., & Smitherman, N. (Eds.). *Research scales in crime and delinquency.* New York: Plenum, in press (Vol. 5 in the Perspectives in Law and Psychology series).

Grisso, T. *Juveniles' waiver of rights: Legal and psychological competence.* New York: Plenum, 1981 (Vol. 3 in the Perspectives in Law and Psychology series).

Liebenson, A. A., & Wepman, J. M. *The psychologist as a witness.* Mundelein, Ill.: Callaghan, 1964.

Rada, Richard T. The psychiatrist as an expert witness. In Charles K. Hofling (Ed.), *Law and ethics in the practice of psychiatry.* New York: Brunner/Mazel, 1981.

Sadoff, R. L. *Forensic psychiatry: A practical guide.* Springfield, Ill.: Charles C Thomas, 1975.

Sales, B. D. (Ed.). *The criminal justice system.* New York: Plenum, 1977 (Vol. 1 in the Perspectives in Law and Psychology series).

Sales, B. D. (Ed.). *The trial process.* New York: Plenum, 1981 (Vol. 2 in the Perspectives in Law and Psychology series).

Schwitzgebel, R. L., & Schwitzgebel, R. K. The expert witness. In *Law and psychological practice.* New York: John Wiley & Sons, 1980.

Slovenko, R. Psychological testimony and presumptions in child custody cases. In Charles K. Hofling (Ed.), *Law and ethics in the practice of psychiatry.* New York: Brunner/Mazel, 1981.

Wexler, D. *Mental health law: Major issues.* New York, Plenum, 1981 (Vol. 4 in the Perspectives in Law and Psychology series).

Woody, R. H. *Getting custody/Winning the last battle of marital war.* New York: Macmillan, 1978.

Ziskin, J. *Coping with psychological and psychiatric testimony.* Los Angeles: Behavior and Science Books, 1973.

REFERENCES

Adams, S., & Argel, M. Through the mental health maze: A consumers guide to finding a psychotherapist, including a sample consumer/therapist contract. Washington D.C.: Public Citizens Health Research Group, 1975.

Alaska Stat. gg 47.30.070 (1977).

American Bar Association Code of Professional Responsibility, Canon 7, 1971.

American Bar Association, Commission on the Mentally Disabled; Suggested Statute on Civil Commitment, *Legal issues in state mental health care:* Proposals for change. (As reported in 2 *Mental Disability Law Reporter,* 1977, *127.*)

American Law Institute, Model Penal Code, Tentative Draft No. 4, 1956.

American Psychological Association. *Guidelines for psychologists conducting growth groups.* Washington, D.C.: Author, 1973.

American Psychological Association. *Standards for educational and psychological tests.* Washington, D.C.: Author, 1974.

American Psychological Association. *Ethical standards for psychologists.* Washington, D.C.: Author, 1977.

American Psychological Association. *Standards for providers of psychological services.* Washington, D.C.: Author, 1977.

In re Arnold, 278 A. 2d 658 (Md., 1971).

Ayllon, T., & Skiban, W. Accountability in psychotherapy: A test case. *Journal of Behavior Therapy and Experimental Psychiatry,* 1973, *4,* 19–29.

Bartley v. *Kremens,* 402 F. Supp. 1039 (1975).

Bellah v. *Greenspan,* 1 Civ. No. 39770 (Cal., Oct. 5, 1977). As reported in *Mental Disability Law Reporter,* September/December 1977, *176,* 19.

Black, H. C. *Black's law dictionary* (4th ed. rev.). St. Paul: West Publishing, 1968.

In re Corneliusen, 494 P. 2d 908 (Mont., 1972).

In Interest of Dahlbert, 167 N.W. 2d 190 (Neb., 1969).

In re Daniel C., 365 N.Y.S. 2d 535, 47 A.D. 2d 160 (1975).

District of Columbia Code, Ann. 21–523 (1973).

Durham v. *United States,* 94 U.S. App. D.C. 228, 214 F. 2d 862 (1954).

Ennis, B., & Siegal, L. *The rights of mental patients.* New York: Avon Books, 1973.

Evan v. *Moore* 472 S.W. 2d 540 (Tex., 1972).

Fingerhut v. *Kralyn Enterprises, Inc.,* 337 N.Y.S. 2d 394 (Sup. Ct. N.Y., 1971).

Franzel v. *Michigan State Dept. of Social Welfare,* 180 N.W. 2d 375 (Mich., 1971).

In re Gault, 87 S Ct. 1428 (Ariz., 1966).

In re Geiger, 331 A. 2d 172 (Pa., 1975).

Jackson v. *Indiana,* 406 U.S. 715 (1972).

Jenkins v. *United States,* 307 F. 2d (D.C. Cir. 1962).

Johnson v. *State,* 314 So. 2d 573 (Fla., 1975).

Koss, M. P. Length of psychotherapy for clients seen in private practice. *Journal of Counseling and Clinical Psychology,* 1979, *47,* 210–212.

Lavette M. v. *Corp. Counsel of City of New York,* 316 N.E. 2d, 314 35 N.Y.S. 2d 136 (1975).

In re Leopolodo Z., 358 N.Y.S. 2d 811 (1974).

In re L. L., 39 C.A. 3d 205 (1974).

Marvin, R. Consent—A negotiation for services. *Law and Behavior,* 1976, *Fall,* 4–7.

McBride v. *State,* 294, N.Y.S. 2d 265 (1968).

McGarry, A. L., Curran, W. J., Lipsitt, P. D., Lelos, D., Schwitzgebel, R. K., & Rosenberg, A. H. *Competency to stand trial and mental illness.* Rockville, Md.: National Institute of Mental Health, Center for Studies of Crime and Delinquency, 1973.

In re Millar, 336 N.Y.S. 2d 144, 40 A.D. 2d 637 (1972).

Missouri Ann. Stat. gg 202.807 (1977).

Monahan, J. *Who is the client?* Washington, D.C.: American Psychological Association, 1980.

Morales v. *Turman,* 364 F. Supp. 166 (1973).

In re Napier, 532 P. 2d 423 (Okla., 1975).

National Conference of Commissioners on Uniform State Laws, Uniform Marriage and Divorce Act of 1970 (Ammended 1971, 1973). Sec. 402.

North Carolina Gen. Stat., Sec. 122–51.1. (1976).

In Interest of Norwood, 234 N.W. 2d 601 (Neb., 1976).

Oklahoma Stat. Ann. tit. 43A gg3, 54.1 (Supp. 1977).

Ore. Rev. Stat., Sec. 126.006(3), Supp. (1968).

Perkins, R. M. *Criminal law.* Brooklyn: Foundation Press, 1969.

Prosser, W. L. *The law of the torts* (4th ed.). St. Paul: West Publishing, 1971.

Schwartz, V. E. Civil liability for causing suicide. *Vanderbilt Law Review,* 1971, *24,* 217.

Schwitzgebel, R. L., & Schwitzgebel, R. K. *Law and psychological practice.* New York: John Wiley & Sons, 1980.

Selzer, M. L. Outline checklist of evidence for and against incapacity. In E. D. Shapiro & R. H. Needham (Eds.), *Psychiatry for lawyers handbook.* Ann Arbor: Institution of Continuing Legal Education, 1967.

Shapiro, E. D., & Needhaus, R. H. (Eds.) *Psychiatry for Lawyers Handbook.* Ann Arbor: Michigan Institution of Continuing Legal Education, 1967, 143.

Stuart, R. B. *Behavior change systems.* Champaign, Ill.: Research Press, 1975.

Tarasoff v. *Regents of the University of California,* 529 P. 2d 533 (Cal., 1974).

Texas Rev. Civil Statutes Ann., Article 547–27 (Supp. 1973).

Van Hoose, W. H., & Kottler, J. A. *Ethical and legal issues in counseling and psychotherapy.* San Francisco: Jossey-Bass, 1977.

Watson, A. S. The children of Armageddon: Problems of custody following divorce. *Syracuse Law Review,* 1969, *55,* 75.

Willis v. *James,* 227 So. 2d 573 (Ala., 1969).

Wyatt v. *Stickney,* 325 F. Supp. 781 (Ala., 1971).

43

Techniques for handling psycholegal cases

*Robert Henley Woody**

For the past 50 years, scientific knowledge of human behavior has expanded, become more sophisticated, and gained credibility among the professions. Accordingly, social and behavioral scientists are increasingly contributing their professional expertise to the improvement of legal operations. More specifically, psychologists are called upon for analyses, assessments, consultation, and expert testimony vis-à-vis legal cases. As might be anticipated with any relatively new area of professional practice, the social theory may be complete and adequate for a broad structure, but sorely lacking for the technical definitions necessary to assure that the practitioner's input is, in fact, beneficial to: (1) the society; (2) the legal system; (3) the parties in the legal case; and (4) last, but certainly not to be forgotten, the professional status of the practitioner and his/her discipline.

In this chapter, the focus will be on the technical considerations for blending clinical psychology and law into efficacious services. This interdisciplinary union can be termed *psycholegal*. That is, the legal matter requires analyses and decisions that consider the psychological components while still honoring the legal parameters.

FORENSIC PSYCHOLOGY

From the onset, it should be acknowledged that, in psycholegal cases, the psychologist is not afforded a traditional, well-defined role. The specialties of clinical, counseling, and school psychology (among others) have been reasonably articulated—at least to the point that delineated services can be aligned with the specialty. With psycholegal services (also known as forensic psychology), there has yet to be a succinct delineation of services.

---

* University of Nebraska at Omaha.

Historically, forensic psychology was viewed as a secondary service provided by psychologists with other specialties. Most notably, forensic psychology was seen as what took place when the clinical psychologist entered the courtroom and gave expert testimony, typically about criminal cases. But psychological practices have yielded to the expectations of society, and this simple view of forensic psychology is no longer adequate.

Instead, the contemporary definition of forensic psychology is broad, with the divergent services being somewhat loosely connected by the single objective: to apply psychology to legal matters. To capture the breadth of the modern practice of forensic psychology, the information booklet published by the American Board of Forensic Psychology (American Board of Forensic Psychology, 1981) states that the functions include (but are not limited to): (1) consultation and training to attorneys, law students, criminal justice and correctional personnel, law enforcement officers, and mental health workers who deal with legal cases; (2) diagnosis, treatment, and recommendations for criminal and juvenile justice populations, children's interests, test-validity litigation, testamentary capacity, and tort-related incapacities (all of which could lead to serving as an expert witness in civil, criminal, and administrative law cases); and (3) miscellaneous, other services that translate psychological knowledge into usable information for legally related research questions, policy and program development, and decision making.

This more comprehensive role and increased societal reliance on psychological services in the legal system have spawned a distinct forensic psychology specialization. That is, while the forensic psychology practitioner is still one who has been trained in a traditional specialty (usually clinical psychology), the profession has endorsed a distinct specialty status. This endorsement was first witnessed with the formation of the American Psychology-Law Society. In turn, the American Board of Forensic Psychology was established to examine candidates for the status of diplomate in forensic psychology. Most recently, the American Psychological Association (APA) has accepted the Division of Psychology and Law (Division 41).

All of these efforts underscore the needs for psychological services in the legal arena and the ever-increasing demand for high-level practitioner skills. The fundamental message is twofold: (1) the application of psychology in the legal system is different from other service contexts; and (2) the psychologist must make a special effort to tailor his/her competencies and skills to the idiosyncrasies of legal cases.

THE PSYCHOLOGIST-ATTORNEY RELATIONSHIP

Success in forensic psychology depends upon establishing and maintaining effective relationships with attorneys. Attorneys are the sources for invitations into legal cases (or stated pragmatically, attorneys are the employers). Even when the psychologist's involvement comes from being employed by a public agency that is designated to serve the needs of the courts, the attorneys representing the parties must be willing to accept the psychologist on an individual basis.

The relationship between the psychologist and the attorney is influenced by the type of training each has received. Let us contrast the two disciplines.

Clinical psychologists, of course, are brought through a training program that emphasizes research-based knowledge, behavioral science methods, and practices that (usually) stem from the so-called scientist-practitioner model. An objective stance is promoted in clinical psychology training. The professionalization of the psychologist, with all of its inherent political considerations, urges an allegiance to the scientific method and independent, scientist-practitioner status (that is, there must be no subservience to another profession, such as medicine).

Law school training, on the other hand, can be described as a method of legal analysis and reasoning. A commitment to objectivity is secondary to a commitment to advocacy. That is, every client, be he/she right or wrong or guilty or innocent, is entitled to the best legal representation possible. Unless the attorney enters law school with training in another discipline (such as an engineer who studies the law), the legal practitioner may not possess an understanding of the scientific method.

Given the preceding preparatory qualities, it is easy to recognize how the clinical psychologist and the attorney are of different academic and professional ilks: (1) their knowledge bases differ; (2) their professional goals foster a subjectivity versus objectivity conflict; and (3) communications may be discrepant (i.e., in different languages).

There are, however, similarities, and these must be capitalized upon in order to minimize the differences. Foremost, the clinical psychologist and attorney are both concerned with individualization (Brieland & Lemmon, 1977). They have the shared purpose of helping the client receive individualized consideration in the legal processes. No doubt, social policy shapes this individualization (such as, creating axioms of what the person can or cannot expect in justice), but overall there is a mutual effort by the clinical psychologist and attorney to implement social control (through the legal systems) for the person and society.

Another commonality between clinical psychologists and attorneys comes from the fact that professional participation cannot be self-determined. There is a duty to serve. In a sense, once there is a call for service, professional responsibility (unless there is reason to the contrary) requires that both the psychologist and attorney follow through with unreserved commitment. In fact, an attorney cannot ethically withdraw from a case (e.g., for the reason he/she has not been paid by the client) unless the court approves. While this ethical restriction has not yet been imposed on forensic psychologists, there is reason to believe that it could be appropriately extended to all professionals who begin work on a legal case.

Self-determination is further limited by the statutory-based rules of evidence that apply to legal proceedings. To ensure that all parties in a legal case have equal protection in judicial practices, federal and state legislation prescribes what and how information can be entered into the legal controversy.

For the clinical psychologist, this means that he/she typically does not have the breadth for opinion giving that would be present in, say, a clinical treatment situation. In the courtroom, the testimony cannot be conjecture as such (which would, of course, be part of prognosticating about treatment alternatives in a clinical context). The psychologist will be restricted to opinions based on a reasonable degree of psychological certainty.

Perhaps even more taxing on the value of self-determination, the testimony commonly consists of responses to specific questions presented by the attorneys in the examination and cross-examination. That is, the psychologist is usually not allowed an open license to say anything that he/she thinks should be said. The psychologist's input is limited to questions posed by the attorneys, and if they fail to cover an area deemed critical by the psychologist, so be it!

Psychologists and attorneys alike are influenced by the considerable amount of discretion allowed to the trial judge (this is particularly true in the lower courts and for domestic cases, e.g., child custody). While it is popular to talk about appealing to the Supreme Court, this in actuality is a highly restricted option. Generally, what the trial judge wants to hear (such as how much weight should be given to psychological testimony or what sentencing options should be imposed) will have to be accepted.

The nature of legal proceedings deserve special emphasis. As opposed to clinical practices where the framework emphasizes scientific objectivity for diagnosis, planning, and treatment, legal practices are to be placed within an adversarial framework. It is not uncommon for a clinical psychologist to sense that a legal proceeding was wrong because objective evidence was not accorded greater weight than subjective evidence.

The adversarial nature of the proceedings creates other strains on the clinical psychologist. Unless appointed (and paid) by the court, the psychologist will be brought into the legal case by the attorney for only one of the parties. This fosters viewing the other party as the opposition and that party's attorney as the enemy. As might be expected, the consequence is that, when the psychologist is in the courtroom giving testimony (or when his/her psychological report is submitted for admission as evidence), the other party will object and attempt to impeach the qualifications and credibility of the psychologist. More will be said about this later; but for now, it should be noted that there is no reason to expect that the other party should give automatic endorsement to a psychologist for the other side. In fact, the attorney who does not attempt to impeach the testimony of the psychologist brought in by the other party is, it would seem, failing to fulfill his/her responsibility.

Even when the involvement results from a court appointment (i.e., the psychologist is not hired per se by one of the parties), there may be a tendency to side with one party more than the other party. This might come about because the attorney for one party has patronized the psychologist (or the attorney on the other side has alienated the psychologist); or it could come from the psychologist's becoming convinced that one party is right and the other is wrong (e.g., one parent is better suited for custody of a child than the other parent). Here again, the adversarial nature of the proceedings often result in the psychologist being subjected to less than friendly cross-examination and a tone that may seem threatening, disrespectful, and hostile.

In establishing effective psychologist-attorney relations, it is important to orient the attorney to the scientist-practitioner framework in which the psychologist operates. For example, the attorney should be helped to appreciate that the testimony cannot be preordained, it must evolve from the formal assessment procedures. Therefore, the attorney cannot be allowed to create an expectation of specific statements from the psychologist on behalf of his/her client. There must be acceptance for the approach that would involve: (1) the psychologist conducts the assessment; (2) the psychologist tells the attorney what can and cannot be said; and (3) if the attorney believes it is not in the best interest of the client to have the testimony, the psychologist should bow out of the case with no hard feelings.

A common question at this point is: "What if I, as a psychologist, learn something about the client that should be in evidence, but the attorney decides not to call me as a witness?" The answer is complex.

Most basically, there is no automatic recourse when the attorney decides not to submit the psychologist to the court as an expert. This means that, in many instances, it would be unethical for the psychologist to contact the attorney for the other party and say something like, "Hey, I know something about the other side that could really help your case!"

There can, however, be an exception. Usually, the exception is one of two alternatives: (1) if the psychologist legitimately assesses that the party in question poses a significant threat of violence and dangerousness to self or others, it could be appropriate to warn the relevant persons (thereby opening the door to being called into court regardless of an attorney's preferences); and (2) if the psychologist senses that the best interests and welfare of a child will be endangered unless he/she offers professional information (such as about admitted child abuse), it could be appropriate to notify the authorities (again making it likely that his/ her testimony would be solicited despite objections from one of the attorneys). More will be said about the duty to warn later.

In view of the somewhat nebulous involvement of the clinical psychologist in legal cases (such as possibly not being used fully in the case), there are several pragmatic actions that seem advisable, especially in private practice. First, a clear orientation to what can and cannot be done in psychology should be given to the attorney and client (a printed information sheet or a letter detailing these matters is helpful and avoids later misperceptions). Second, the initial involvement with the case should be circumspect. That is, it is best to agree only to the diagnostic/assessment phase of a possible involvement. This safeguards against undue pressure to stay in the case and to say something that is not honestly derived from the appraisal methods or that is dictated by the attorney's preferences. Third, forensic services should be contractual. There should be a reasonable estimate of time made at the onset and a payment arrangement formalized. The nature of legal decisions often means dissatisfaction by the loser, and even though the psychologist gave high-quality service, there may be less willingness to pay after the legal proceedings than there was before they got underway. As attorneys routinely do, the psychologist would be well advised to require an up-front retainer for the majority or total amount of time estimated for the case. Fourth, when a case is over, the psychologist should follow up with both the client and the attorney. This is especially helpful for the client (e.g., counseling with the client to resolve any remaining mental conflicts about the case); and with the attorney, follow-up contacts promote continued communications and future involvement with other legal cases.

UNDERSTANDING THE LAW

To provide effective psychological services in legal cases, it is necessary to be able to comprehend the legal dimensions of the case. It is impractical to expect all psychologists to study the law to the point of having a comprehensive legal knowledge. It does seem reasonable, however, to require at least one graduate course in any doctoral clinical psychology program that would expose the trainee to the fundamentals of legal analysis and reasoning, the structure and operations of the legal system, and legal research methods. In addition, there are several practical actions that the clinical psychologist can take to assure that legal considerations enter into his/her psychological formulations.

It would be inappropriate here to explain the referencing system for legal materials. Suffice it to say, legal research relies upon analysis of statutory materials, critical position statements (e.g., law review articles), and precedent cases. There are dictionaries that define legal terms, and there are sources for understanding the reference system (which is quite different from the APA style). All of these matters and primary legal sources can be well explained by a law librarian.

The cogent message is that the clinical psychologist should be able to locate and understand some of the legal cases or materials relevant to the case on which he/she is working. A practical approach is to ask one of the attorneys for citations for a few of the cases that would be relevant to the legal issues to be dealt with in the proceedings. With a list of statutes and several cases, the psychologist can enter a library and do his/her homework in preparation for psycholegal testimony or consultation. Note that a specialized law library need not be readily available. Most university libraries and many public (city) libraries have a legal section that includes primary sources. Most law firms, especially the larger ones, have extensive legal libraries and are potentially open to a visiting scholar's using their materials. Finally, the state and local bar associations usually maintain a law library and would be accessible to a psychologist.

In reading a legal case, there is no checklist of informational items that must be fulfilled. Generally, it is wise to notice: (1) where the case was decided (if it is in the same locale and/or state, it usually carries more weight than if it is from somewhere else in the country); (2) what the main issues and relevant facts were; and (3) what the court's decision was.

It is important to remember that most cases can be distinguished. That is, there is always something that makes a case unique from other cases. Unless this distinction is evaluated by a legalist, it is difficult to know exactly how relevant a given case is to a case at hand.

With a layperson's knowledge of a case, the clinical psychologist should talk about the case(s) and/or statutory materials with one of the attorneys to ensure that his/her psychological interpretation is not misguided from the point of view of a legalist. The old adage, "a little knowledge is a dangerous thing," should be heeded, but an appreciation of the legal considerations can enhance the psycholegal services.

PSYCHOLOGICAL INFORMATION

As surprising as it may seem, there is no definite legal requirement that the clinical psychologist base his/her testimony on psychological methods with an established validity for the specific question. The use of psychological tests in employment-related cases requires, by law, that there be established validity (American Psychological Association, 1980). The tests used to determine an employment decision must have a proven relationship to the work. This validity requirement is the exception in legal cases. Of course, the tests or assessment methods used must fulfill the standards propagated by the American Psychological Association, but they need not be researched for their applicability for a given legal question.

This leaves the clinical psychologist with a crucial responsibility: to select an evaluation scheme that is both professionally respectable and suitable for the legal issues in the particular case at hand. As might be anticipated, this is a decision which the attorney for the opposing side will carefully scrutinize; and to avoid impeachment of professional credibility, the clinical psychologist must formulate a reasonable rationale supporting that the tests selected and procedures used will yield information that deserves evidence status in the legal proceedings.

Given the subjectivity that is an inevitable part of expert opinion, it behooves the clinical psychologist to rigorously adhere to standardized usages of tests. For example, one well-credentialed clinical psychologist had his testimony greatly reduced in value to his client when the other party introduced a clinical psychologist to testify that the first psychologist's failure to score the Rorschach Inkblots Method, to administer all of the subtests on the Wechsler Adult Intelligence Scale (WAIS), and to follow the sequence of Thematic Apperception Test (TAT) cards left his clinical judgments highly suspect. In this instance, the psychologist had not done an inquiry on the Rorschach, had given only six of the WAIS subtests, and had selected TAT cards admittedly to "get the kind of information I was looking for." All of this suggested that his opinions were vulnerable to personal bias.

Technically, the clinical psychologist should: (1) select an assessment approach that is as objective as possible and that uses tests that have at least face validity for the legal questions; (2) religiously follow the standardized administration and scoring; and (3) carefully calculate interpretations to honor theoretical foundations.

When giving testimony that requires placing a diagnostic label on the person, it is essential that the clinical psychologist be academically prepared for the task. In one case, a psychologist described a client as being a kleptomaniac. In the cross-examination, the attorney for the other side started questioning him for the depth of his knowledge of kleptomania. The psychologist had not done his homework—he could not offer a seemingly knowledgeable definition. When an attorney is able to talk more knowledgeably about a psychological condition than a psychologist, the end result is sure to be impeachment of the psychologist's testimony. And in this case, the proverbial grapevine carried the story to other attorneys, and the psychologist experienced a significant decrease in subsequent referrals. In another case (only three days after the *DSM-III* had been delivered in that city), attorneys for both sides showed up in the courtroom with copies of the *DSM-III* and based their questions to the psychologists on specific points therein. The psychologists' views were evaluated, in part, on how well-versed they were on the new *DSM-III*.

Part of the dilemma can be resolved by unabashedly taking reference sources to the courtroom. There is no reason why an expert cannot cite from a scientific reference, such as an encyclopedia-like source on the Minnesota Multiphasic Personality Inventory (MMPI). Of course, the degree of familiarity with the source will be evident, and the demand is still there for the psychologist to do formal preparation of an academic nature before appearing to give testimony. Incidentally, the clinical psychologist should let the client and attorney know ahead of time that there will be a charge for reasonable preparation for the testimony (note that attorneys routinely charge for background research).

PRIVILEGED COMMUNICATION

Clinical psychologists are trained to believe that their communications with clients are confidential and need not be released to anyone else. This may or may not be true.

In psycholegal cases, the psychologist may have a testimonial privilege through a shield law. Theoretically, society decides that there are certain relationships (such as physician-patient, psychologist-client, or attorney-client) that deserve special legal protection.

Privileged communication is narrowly interpreted (as opposed to receiving broad application). At the discretion of the court and upon motion by one of the parties, even privileged communication defined by state statute (which is, incidentally, the only way privileged communication can exist), can be rejected, and a subpoena can be issued that requires the professional to testify and/or produce official records (e.g., therapy notes or copies of the test protocols) even against the wishes of the client.

In addition, if a client brings up a psychologically related issue, he/she has opened the door on an area that might otherwise be legally protected by the privileged-communication statute. When this happens, the other party can receive court support for requiring a total release of all relevant information. This kind of revelation is exactly why an attorney should be orchestrating what information is or is not introduced into the legal proceedings. In other words, there are certain things that might help the case in one way but that should not be said because they would open the door to information that would hurt the case in another way.

Much like the previously discussed question about what to do if the clinical psychologist knows something that should be said but the attorney does not want him/her to testify, the psychologist may encounter a situation where he/she believes that the information should be made available to the court, but the client wants to invoke privileged communication. After all, privileged communication does, in fact, belong to the client and not to the professional.

In most instances, the right to invoke privileged communication by the client will preclude the psychologist's releasing information—and to do so against the client's wishes will raise the possibility of a malpractice charge by the client. On the contrary, there are some states that have statutory prescriptions holding that there is a denial of privileged communication in certain types of cases, such as child custody. In one case, the clinical psychologist had been treating the mother, and when she decided to divorce and seek custody, she forbade him to testify because she was aware that he viewed her as being emotionally unstable. The father, however, sought his testimony. Since the father and mother had once been seen together by the psychologist, this justified testimony on the issues raised when they had both been present. These joint contacts alone would probably have been enough to get the psychologist's assessment of the mother into the proceedings, but the case occurred in a state that is strongly committed to children's rights; so the court quickly ordered the psychologist to testify in an unfettered fashion for the best interests of the children.

A word of caution is in order. The clinical psychologist must not let either an attorney or a judge lead him/her to make statements that cannot be justly made under the ethics of the American Psychological Association. For example, a psychologist giving testimony about a father and children (all of whom he had evaluated) was asked by a judge what was needed to help the father, mother, and children. The psychologist innocently responded, "they all need counseling." The mother lost custody. Promptly thereafter, she initiated an ethics charge against the psychologist, claiming that he had issued a professional opinion about her without having ever examined her. This led to a somewhat inept series of exchanges between the state board of psychologist examiners, the state psychological association's ethics committee, and the psychologist. While the charge was eventually dismissed, the psychologist had spent much mental energy and considerable time and money for legal representation for what seemed to be a frivolous, hostility-based allegation.

The message is simple: whenever a clinical psychologist speaks, it must be in a manner compatible with professional standards and ethics. If a situation arises, such as being asked a question by a judge that perhaps should not be answered for ethical reasons, the psychologist should respectfully request that he/she not be required to answer. If the judge orders a response, an answer should be given, but at least the psychologist has shifted the burden for any possible fault from his/her own shoulders to the judicial process.

Another frequent source of discussion among psychologists is about records. Some professionals (from medicine, psychology, and social work) have made comments about keeping two sets of records, or "taking my real therapy notes home so nobody can get them, even by subpoena." This sort of scheming is foolish.

In deciding upon a record-keeping system, there are three basic questions. First and foremost, what information needs to be recorded to facilitate the intervention in the best interests of the client? Second, what information is needed to safeguard the psychologist (i.e., establish proof of the standard of care that was maintained in the intervention)? Third, what should be available for any potential legal action? Let us consider each of these separately.

Information is recorded to help the client. Through having a clear and comprehensive record, the psychologist can process intervention alternatives. Even with legal concerns, this objective should remain paramount, and it should not be diluted by, say, caution about legal consequences.

As for safeguarding the psychologist, there is often a professional tendency to neglect to document what did or did not occur in an intervention. One's office can easily seem far removed from the scrutiny of others; but in the event that a legal action is instituted, this seeming isolation is quickly penetrated by the courts. It is only prudent to use a record-keeping system that documents that professional standards were, in fact, honored.

The final matter of what information should be available to a potential legal action blends social philosophy, public policy, and client welfare. While the psychologist has a specific commitment to the individual client, there is an all-pervasive governance from the society that has endorsed professional functioning. Thus, there should be a recording of information that will allow the courts to fulfill the societal axiom of "justice for all." Client welfare may have to be secondary to the welfare of others.

As a record-keeping system is developed, it should be remembered that the court, such as through its subpoena power, can have access to virtually *every bit of information.* Numerous situations have arisen where a psychologist has been told by an employing agency that an administrative policy precludes anyone from getting certain types of information. These kinds of policies are not shields from lawful requests for access. For example, one large mental health agency had a policy that only summary reports would be issued to attorneys and other professionals involved with child custody cases; the actual test protocols, such as the psychologist's recording of Rorschach responses and scoring, would not be released under any circumstances. This policy was short lived. In fact, it was not even necessary to obtain a subpoena. When the agency director sought legal counsel when the policy was challenged, he quickly learned that it was not going to be accommodated by the rules of evidence in that state. Consequently, even when client welfare is the rationale, agency or professional policies to withhold certain types of information (such as, for certain kinds of services or for special types of clients) are no guarantee. Hopefully, the court will evaluate the client-welfare rationale; but in the long run, the decision to allow access to any and all professional information rests with the court, not with the psychologist.

Society has vested the legal system with the authority to regulate privileged communication, including the contents of professional records. For a clinical psychologist (or any type of professional) to assert personal superiority over this societal mandate is presumptuous, ill-advised, and possibly even paranoid—not to mention downright foolish from a legal point of view. To fail to produce any and all relevant materials required by the court is to risk liability for concealment and contempt of court. It would take a nonprofessional, unethical, illegal rationale to oppose such a legal order.

At the same time, a self-determined breach of confidentiality cannot be condoned either. A breach of the psychologist-client confidential relationship can be viewed as: (1) slander; (2) a tort-based invasion of privacy; or (3) a contract-based breach of confidence. If proven, any of these charges can lead to disciplinary action by both the court and professional associations (e.g., a license to practice could be revoked, especially if the breach were for willful or malicious purposes).

What if the client wants information that the psychologist believes should not be released? The psychologist does have a so-called limited property right to the materials. For example, one client wanted her folder, especially an MMPI profile, totally destroyed. The clinical psychologist justly refused.

It is well accepted that a psychologist (or other professional as well) has a right to self-protection. To destroy a record in total could leave the psychologist vulnerable to subsequent allegations that could otherwise be refuted with a complete record.

Further, the professional judgment by the psychologist that the release of certain psychological information will do more harm than good cannot, without evidence to the contrary, be contradicted by the client. For example, one clinical psychologist refused to give testimony about the mother's and father's mental status in front of the children. The mother wanted the children to hear the father's presumably negative personality profile. The psychologist believed that the children would be harmed in their later relationship with the father, and probably with the mother as well, if they heard a description of his pathology. The court agreed and heard the testimony with the children excluded from the courtroom.

When considering privileged communication, it must be acknowledged that societal interests transcend individual rights. Whether this is ideal or not remains for conjecture, but that is the legal stance—as will become more pronounced in the later discussion of duty to warn. Therefore, the clinical psychologist must be prepared to balance the social versus individual considerations. For example, one psychiatrist was deemed to have been in error for failing to write into the hospital records that a patient had told him of a self-inflicted gunshot wound—society has prescribed legally that incidents involving gunshot wounds, contagious diseases, drug dependence, and child abuse must be recorded and reported (note that states vary in how extensive the statutory requirements will be).

The rules of evidence, as applied to the federal and state courts, recognize (although there may be some difference among the states) that privileged communication does not exist: (1) when the information is relevant to an issue to hospitalize the patient for mental illness; (2) when the judge orders an examination of the mental or emotional condition of the patient; or (3) if the patient in a legal proceeding relies on his/her mental or emotional condition as an element of the claim or defense (or after the patient's death in a proceeding where the mental or emotional condition is an element of the claim or defense).

The best guideline, aside from being well informed about any state statutory grant of privileged communication and the applicability of professional ethics, is for the clinical psychologist to unhesitatingly seek legal counsel when there is a question about maintaining or breaching confidentiality. Note that if advice by legal counsel proves to be wrong, that will not be a defense per se; but it will be supportive of an unwillful, nonmalicious breach.

An action of choice would seem to be to urge an attorney in the legal case to subpoena the testimony. Many courts require only a minimal showing to issue a subpoena. This rather low requirement is due to the belief that justice requires having all relevant information available and that the court (be it judge or jury) should have the responsibility of deciding whether information should be weighted significantly in the case (as opposed to allowing one of the parties singularly to determine the availability of evidence). When operating under a subpoena, the clinical psychologist is afforded much-needed protection.

Whenever an ethical dilemma arises, the prudent psychologist would be well advised to seek advisement from seasoned colleagues or, better yet, official sources (e.g., the ethics committee for the state psychological association or the state board of examiners of psychologists). As with legal counsel, ethical views from colleagues or official sources will not insulate the psychologist from liability, but they will serve as a defense for the course of action that was pursued. Obviously, the more thorough and reputable the views collected, the more weight they will be accorded by the court. Therefore, it is best to maintain a preventive outlook: instead of waiting for a legal challenge, readily seek opinions (preferably in formal fashion) from professionals or official sources that could buttress decisions to honor or breach privileged communication.

DUTY TO WARN

In 1976, the supreme court of California handed down a decision that created great controversy among the health professions. The case of *Tarasoff* v. *Regents of the University of California* (1976) involved a psychologist having been told by a patient that he had an intended victim. When the patient killed his girlfriend, the victim's parents charged that the psychologist should have warned authorities—despite the presumed privileged communication of the psychotherapy relationship. The judicial rule was:

> When a therapist determines, or pursuant to the standards of his profession should determine, that his patient presents a serious danger of violence to another, he incurs an obligation to use reasonable care to protect the intended victim against such danger. The discharge of this duty may require the therapist to take one or more of various steps, depending upon the nature of the case. Thus it may call for him to warn the intended victim or others likely to apprise the victim of the danger, to notify the police, or to take whatever other steps are reasonably necessary under the circumstances. (pp. 431–432)

The court indicated that the most important consideration in establishing a duty to warn was foreseeability. The connotation was that the therapist must implement diagnostic measures to appraise the possibility of harm. The therapist could not find exemption from this duty:

> By entering into a doctor-patient relationship, the therapist becomes sufficiently involved to assume some responsibility for the safety, not only of the patient himself, but also of any third persons whom the doctor knows to be threatened by the patient. (p. 437)

Various defenses (e.g., the difficulty of making predictions of violence, and the jeopardy in which the tenets of psychotherapy would be put by a duty to warn) were uniformly rejected by the court. The decision seemed to support incontrovertibly that societal interests supercede individual rights.

As might be expected, this led to long and hard debates in the pages of professional literature. The sacrosanct psychotherapeutic relationship had, according to many wags, been put asunder by judicial fiat. But the legal world did not heed these doomsayers.

A similar case, *McIntosh* v. *Milano* (1979), held that a psychiatrist had a duty to take reasonable steps to protect the potential victim of one of his patients. In that case, a 15-year-old male, who had told the psychiatrist of his fantasies to use a knife to threaten people, killed his girlfriend (a woman 5 years his senior). The court accepted that therapists could not be 100 percent accurate in their predictions but stated that the duty to warn remained and involved the weighing of the relationship of the parties, the nature of the risk involved, and the public interest in imposing the duty under the circumstances. The court acknowledged confidentiality, but asserted that the welfare of the individual (victim) and the community must come first—the considerations of confidentiality were given "no overriding influence."

Actually, cases supporting a duty to warn are not as new and unique as the *Tarasoff* and *McIntosh* cases might suggest. *The Merchants National Bank and Trust Company of Fargo* v. *United States of America*

(1967) involved the estate administrator (the bank) suing the veterans hospital for ignoring indications of a mental patient's illness, not predicting dangerousness, and failing to prevent his returning to fulfill a threat to kill his wife. The court held that there was negligence in releasing the patient on a leave of absence without taking sufficient precautions.

This line of legal cases leads to the conclusion that: a clinical psychologist should include in his/her regular service system a method for assessing the potential dangerousness of every client. It should be noted that while, heretofore, cases have focused on predicting dangerousness to others, there seems to be reason to believe that the duty to warn could readily be extended by the courts to predicting dangerousness to self and, consequently, notifying others responsible for the client of his/her potential for suicide.

It should be kept in mind that it is not a viable defense to claim that prediction is often spurious at best or that there is no objective method. The courts seem emphatic in requiring that predictions err on the side of overprediction of dangerousness.

As for the dilemma posed by the *Tarasoff* decision, the APA Task Force on the Role of Psychology in the Criminal Justice System (Monahan, 1980) adopts the position that an absolutist view of confidentiality (i.e., that confidentiality should never be breached) must undergo modification. A set of considerations, which can be translated into guidelines, suggests that assessment should encompass past behavior, risk to others, probable consequences for the client, prognosis of response to treatment, obtaining informed consent, and consequences for the therapy relationship.

The duty to warn is, of course, prospective. *Dangerousness* is a concept that refers to behavior that will occur in the future. Consideration of past behavior can reveal the occurrence of violence in the past, but there is dubious validity for an assumption that the violent history preordains future behavior.

Inspection of past violence should not be limited to observable, physical assaults. Violence includes more subtle cues, such as verbal threats and even a behavioral attitude that is ominous in the eyes of beholders. Of course, the subjectivity inherent to the perception of threatening behavior must be carefully evaluated.

In a review of the research on dangerousness, Walters (1980) points out that an error in prediction "may be of literally life-and-death significance to potential victims" (p.1109). He surveys existing psychological tests and notes that projective instruments (e.g., the Rorschach Inkblots Method, the Holtzman Inkblot Technique, the Thematic Apperception Test, and the Hand Test) may be useful for estimating hostility and acting-out behavior. Also, the MMPI Psychopathic Deviate-Hysteria (4–3) profile code has support as a predictor of acting out of impulses. Walters concludes that: (1) "an actual history of overt, violent behavior provides the single best predictor of future violence" (p. 1108); and (2) a small proportion of multiple offenders account for a disproportionately large amount of violence, i.e., "those individuals with a history of more than a single violent act may be viewed as likely to commit future acts of the same nature" (p. 1108). His analysis of statistical compilations of demographic data supports that "the criminally violent individual is most likely young (under 25), male, of minority background and low socioeconomic status, and lives in the inner city of a large urban center" (p. 1109)—but obviously, these are generalities that do not include individual criteria (such as personal stress, drug and alcohol abuse, and intense provocations) that could allow some surety of prediction.

This leaves the clinical psychologist with a potent, but ill-defined, requirement in psycholegal cases. While pledging allegiance to professional ethics and standards (e.g., knowing there is no valid and reliable means for prediction and wanting to maintain confidentiality and/or privileged communication), the clinical psychologist is mandated by society to make assessments of dangerousness (to self and others) and, when necessary, take steps to ward off the violence (i.e., warning other responsible persons, law enforcement officers, and victims). If the clinical psychologist fails to fulfill this duty in a reasonable fashion, the legal system stands prepared to impose liability for malpractice (e.g., liability for a wrongful death).

MALPRACTICE

This is an era of increased public concern about the quality of professional services, as witnessed by the plethora of legal suits alleging malpractice. While these have been directed primarily at medical physicians, clinical psychologists are in no way immune.

There is reason to believe that suits against mental health professionals, particularly psychiatrists, are increasing in number. Twardy (1978) states, "Today, the fear of malpractice litigation or civil rights hangs like the proverbial sword of Damocles over the heads of many psychiatrists" (p. 161).

Although it is tempting to find comfort in the belief that clinical psychologists are not to be matched legally with psychiatrists, this would be false assurance. King (1977) believes that many of the legal principles that govern medical malpractice claims apply to other health care providers, including psychologists.

The quality of professional care is required legally to meet the standard of the minimum knowledge, skill, and intelligence common to the members of the profession. While it is possible to draw up a contract that is an express waiver of liability, this is not a guarantee against liability (not to mention that there might be ethical questions posed by an overt attempt to avoid liability for one's professional practices).

A client must give informed consent for any professional practice; this may be implied or expressed. But informed consent is not precise. There can be effects that were not fully comprehended by the client; and therefore, the consent would not constitute a waiver of liability for the professional.

The fact that an entire profession endorses certain practices does not constitute legal justification for the practices. As Prosser (1971) states, "Even an entire industry, by adopting such careless methods to save time, effort, or money, cannot be permitted to set its own uncontrolled standard" (p. 167). Custom is not enough; as Prosser points out, an established professional practice "must meet the challenge of 'learned reason,' and be given only the evidentiary weight which the situation deserves" (p. 168). For example, it is feasible that a failure to take formal appraisal steps during an initial counseling session and the client's leaving to commit violence to self or others could not be defended by the assertion that "psychologists don't administer the MMPI or any other test all the time." A court might be prone to evaluate whether a psychologist who serves potentially disturbed persons should, regardless of custom, consistently apply some sort of appraisal method for the prediction of dangerousness from the onset of professional contact.

In the past, the standard of care was predicated on the locale in which the professional practiced. Thus, a clinical psychologist in New York would be compared to the minimum standards maintained by New York clinical psychologists with comparable educational, experiential, and service characteristics; while a clinical psychologist in Omaha would be compared with his/her counterparts in that locale. This is no longer the frame of reference—a national perspective is now applied when determining a standard of care.

Not only are national standards used, any sort of specialization elevates the standard (Shrallow, 1977). Consequently, a psychologist who has earned the status of diplomate in clinical psychology from the American Board of Professional Psychology would be compared to other diplomates, not to clinical psychologists of a lesser level of certification. Further, any special skills, such as advanced training in psychotherapy, could be the basis for applying a higher standard of care than that appropriate to psychologists in general.

Clinical psychologists who practice nontraditional psychotherapy will not find solace in claiming that their special school does not intervene in the same way as other therapists. For example, encounter-group leaders could not exempt themselves from liability simply because most encounterists do not screen group participants (i.e., "we take them in the here and now"). Glenn (1974), from a legal analysis, concludes that, "Since traditional psychotherapy is the closest accepted professional school, it can be argued that its more settled standard should be applied, in the absence of a specially tailored 'encounter' standard" (p. 62). While courts customarily strain to give the benefit of the doubt to practitioners cloaked in professionalism, this protection is stripped away by practices that deviate from the traditional. A definitive court ruling is lacking, but it seems likely that nontraditional psychotherapy would have to live up to the standard of care applied in more traditional forms of psychotherapy.

In psycholegal cases, this means that the clinical psychologist should use methods of assessment and treatment that can be linked to a solid, behavioral-science basis. To do otherwise is to risk legal sanctions.

APOSTOLIC ZEAL

In the past, the involvement of psychiatrists and clinical psychologists in legal cases has met with significant resistance from legalists and, to some extent, from the public. Contrary to popular belief, the resistance is not due to wanting to exclude other professionals from the legal arena. Rather, it can be attributed to the many professionals who attempt to use their professional status as a license to pursue a personal value or social belief with an apostolic zeal.

When the psycholegal testimony expounds on a concept of personality theory, such as a lack of conscious motivation eliminating the *mens rea* (i.e., the criminal intent) and thus negating responsibility, the court is prone to reject the psychodynamic ideas. For example, the court—in *State* v. *Sikora* (1965)—interpreted the psychiatrist's thesis as being that the defendant was a helpless victim of his genetic endowment and lifelong environmental influences and that unconscious forces dictated his behavior without his being able to alter it; this thesis—actions motivated by subconscious influences of which the defendant was not aware—was rejected as a basis for the insanity defense. This sort of court interpretation of psychodynamic testimony led to rejection of the previously accepted irresistible-impulse test (which was highly dependent upon psycholegal testimony to establish) and to the adoption of insanity-defense tests that give psycholegal testimony probative consideration but not conclusive weight and that leave the sanity-versus-insanity decision to legalists and juries (Loewy, 1975; Fingarette & Hasse, 1979).

Apostolic zeal has given the prosecution ample ammunition to shoot down psycholegal testimony. In this framework, however, Zagel (1977) states about psychologists, "Their tests are much more objective than psychiatric examinations and especially valuable in determining mental competence to stand trial" (p. 609). Authoritative materials designed for the prosecution viewpoint can be found in Healy and Manak (1977).

In the final analysis, as Zagel suggests, clinical psychologists have the potential of fulfilling a critical role in legal proceedings. The scientific bases for psychological methods stand to enhance psychological testimony. This is the era of behavioral science in the law. Clinical psychologists have the overall training and skills necessary to offer invaluable assistance to legal cases. The technical handling requires simply an awareness of the distinctions of psychology and the law, knowledge of legal rudiments and courtroom protocol, and a personal willingness to set aside the safety of traditional functioning in favor of assertive pursuit of a relatively uncharted professional course.

SUMMARY

Clinical psychology has earned a prominent place in the American legal system. This chapter defines the nature of forensic psychology, pointing out that the application of psychology in the legal system is necessarily different from other service contexts and that the psychologist must tailor his/her competencies and skills to the uniqueness of legal cases. An effective relationship between the attorney and psychologist is critical. Likewise, the psychologist must understand the law, both conceptually and procedurally; this may involve being able to locate and use legal materials. Due to the rigors of the rules of evidence maintained in legal proceedings, the psychologist must establish systematic technical practices (such as with psychological assessment), reformulate notions about privileged communications (such as what information should be recorded), and be prepared to deviate from traditional, professional practices (such as violating the therapeutic relationship in favor of the duty to warn). Avoidance of malpractice will require a well-delineated standard of care.

REFERENCES

American Board of Forensic Psychology. Summary brochure. Ann Arbor, Mich.: American Board of Forensic Psychology, 1981.

American Psychological Association, Division of Industrial-Organizational Psychology. *Principles for the validation and use of personnel-selection procedures* (2d ed.). Washington, D.C.: Author, 1980.

Brieland, D., & Lemmon, J. *Social work and the law.* St. Paul: West Publishing, 1977.

Fingarette, H., & Hasse, A. F. *Mental disabilities and criminal responsibility.* Berkeley: University of California Press, 1979.

Glenn, R. D. Standard of care in administering nontraditional psychotherapy. In University of California, Davis Law Review (Eds.), *Problems in law and medicine* (Vol. 7). Davis, Calif.: University of California, Davis Law Review, 1974.

Healy, P. F., & Manak, J. P. (Eds.). *The prosecutor's deskbook* (2d ed.). Chicago: National District Attorneys Association, 1977.

King, J. H., Jr. *The law of medical malpractice.* St. Paul: West Publishing, 1977.

Loewy, A. H. *Criminal law.* St. Paul: West Publishing, 1975.

McIntosh v. *Milano,* 403 A.2d 500, N.J. Super. Ct., 1979.

Merchants National Bank and Trust Company of Fargo v. *United States of America,* 272 F.Supp. 409, 1967.

Monahan, J. (Ed.). *Who is the client?* Washington, D.C.: American Psychological Association, 1980.

Prosser, W. L. *Handbook of the law of torts* (4th ed.). St. Paul: West Publishing, 1971.

Shrallow, D. P. The standard of care for the medical specialist in Ohio: *Bruni* v. *Tatsumi. Ohio State Law Journal,* 1977, *38,* 203–218.

State v. *Sikora,* 44 N.J. 453, 210 A.2d 193, 1965.

Tarasoff v. *Regents of the University of California,* 17 Cal.3d 359, 551 P.2d 334, 1976.

Twardy, S. The issue of malpractice in psychiatry. *Medical Trial Technique Quarterly,* 1978, *25,* 161–176.

Walters, H. A. Dangerousness. In R. H. Woody (Ed.), *Encyclopedia of clinical assessment.* San Francisco: Jossey-Bass, 1980.

Zagel, J. B. Psychiatric issues and the criminal law—The prosecution viewpoint. In P. F. Healy & J. P. Manak (Eds.), *The prosecutor's deskbook* (2d ed.). Chicago: National District Attorneys Association, 1977.

Index

Note: Lightface page numbers are in Volume I; boldface page numbers are in Volume II.

Note: Lightface page numbers are in Volume I; boldface page numbers are in Volume II.

Note: Lightface page numbers are in Volume I; boldface page numbers are in Volume II.

Note: Lightface page numbers are in Volume I; boldface page numbers are in Volume II.

Note: Lightface page numbers are in Volume I; boldface page numbers are in Volume II.

Note: Lightface page numbers are in Volume I; boldface page numbers are in Volume II.

Note: Lightface page numbers are in Volume I; boldface page numbers are in Volume II.

This book has been set CAP/VideoComp, in 10 and 9 point Stymie Light, leaded 2 points. Part numbers and titles and chapter titles are 36 point Stymie Light. Chapter titles are 20 point Stymie Light. The size of the type page is 27 by 47 picas.

Note: Lightface page numbers are in Volume I; boldface page numbers are in Volume II.